Swing

Ben Wong 2001

Swing

Matthew Robinson
Pavel Vorobiev

UI Guidelines by David Anderson
Code Notes by David Karr

MANNING

Greenwich
(74° w. long.)

For electronic browsing and ordering of this and other Manning books,
visit http://www.manning.com. The publisher offers discounts on this book
when ordered in quantity. For more information, please contact:

Special Sales Department
Manning Publications Co.
32 Lafayette Place   Fax: (203) 661-9018
Greenwich, CT 06830   email: orders@manning.com

Library of Congress Cataloging-in-Publication Data
Robinson, Matthew, 1974-
    Swing / Matthew Robinson, Pavel Vorobiev
        p.   cm.
    Includes bibliographical references.
    ISBN 1-884777-84-8 (alk. paper)
    1. Java (Computer program language)   2. Swing (Computer file)
I. Vorobiev, Pavel A., 1959-   . II. Title.
QA76.73.J38R62   1999
055.13'3—dc21   99-27792
                                                        CIP

Manning Publications Co.   Copyeditor: Kristen Black
32 Lafayette Place   Typesetter: Denis Dalinnik
Greenwich, CT 06830   Cover designer: Leslie Haimes

Second, corrected printing May 2000
Printed in the United States of America
2 3 4 5 6 7 8 9 10 – CM – 02 01 00

To my parents, Joan M. Robinson and Kenneth B. Robinson, D.M.D.
—Matthew Robinson

To my wife, Marina Vorobiev
—Pavel Vorobiev

brief contents

contents

Part IV   Special topics   811

foreword

It was late in the spring of 1996 when I first heard that James Gosling had pulled a team together to begin work on a new set of GUI components called Swing. This was the best news possible for those of us who were using early AWT to implement user interfaces that would be consistent across multiple platforms. The painful and meticulous work we performed to complete given tasks made complex projects almost impossible to implement at the time. Knowing that future GUI development with Swing would now be accelerated and made more efficient than AWT was a great relief to developers everywhere.

Many Java applications these days require cross-platform interoperability, or an application that works well on a single platform. So what GUI tools should we select? If the application runs on a Mac, shouldn't Mac users be familiar with the interface controls? If we're programming an interactive Java web game, shouldn't the interface be tailored to match the game's theme? Say our application isn't platform-specific and we want to distribute it across multiple platforms. Wouldn't it be great to have a generic GUI we could use that is already designed?

The Java Foundation Classes (JFC) answer all these questions. They include the components from the original Swing project, and they are an official part of the Java 2 core that includes AWT, Swing, Java 2D, Drag and Drop, and Accessibility for users with disabilities. You can now choose well-known appearances and behaviors of windowing components, and you can also invent your own custom look and feel or use one that is included.

During a recent technical Java presentation at a very large company (with an army of programmers representing a number of senior backgrounds), the engineers complained of the numerous shortcomings they saw in Java. Many had implemented several large Java applications over the last ten months. The griping grew and grew, one comment dovetailing another with, "Yeah, I found the way Java handles exceptions impossible to deal with in my situation," and "I agree—we've been able to get it to work on a Mac, PC, and Unix, but…?," and so on. After the groundswell of comments died down, I looked out across the talented group of gurus and offered, "Well, you can always go back and try to do this in C++." All at once, they cringed, their faces looking as if they all had bitten into a sour lemon at the same time. Some grabbed their heads in agony. A few applauded and laughed with Java-biased glee. Let's face it, Java makes our programming lives easier, and Swing makes it even better.

After completing a few projects using the Swing components and infrastructure discussed in this book, you will probably never want to return to VB, MFC, or C++ either. This book is a superb programmer's guide that provides exhaustive coverage of Swing. Each component is excellently presented with solid and detailed explanations. Add to that the numerous light-shedding examples, and you're holding the best comprehensive Swing book available today.

Kirk Brown
Senior Engineer
Sun Microsystems Advanced Internet Practice

preface

This book is best described as a programmer's guide, serving both as a reference and a tutorial. Emphasis is placed on using Swing to solve a broad selection of realistic and creative problems. We assume an intermediate knowledge of Java, including the basics of putting together an AWT-based GUI, how the 1.1 event model works, and familiarity with anonymous and explicit inner classes. Those who do not have this background can pick it up in any beginner book on AWT or Swing. We recommend Manning's own *Up to Speed with Swing*, second edition, by Steven Gutz.

Our goal was to write a book that contains enough explanation and examples to satisfy the most demanding Swing developer, while still catering to the motivated newcomer. We feel that we have accomplished this goal in a unique and generous way. From day one, our manuscript has been freely available on the publisher's web site. By responding and reacting to all feedback and suggestions we received, this book has taken on many diverse perspectives. Together with our efforts, the Swing developer community has helped shape this book into its current form.

Organization

In general, each chapter starts with class and interface explanations occasionally interspersed with small examples to demonstrate key features. The bulk of each chapter is then devoted to the construction of several larger examples, often building on top of previous examples, illustrating more complex aspects of the components under investigation.

Part I contains two chapters that introduce Swing and discuss the most significant mechanisms underlying it. The first chapter is a brief overview that we suggest for all Swing newcomers. More experienced developers will want to read straight through most of chapter 2, as it provides an understanding of Swing's most significant underlying behavior. This chapter is referenced throughout the book, and we expect all readers to refer to it often. We recommend that Swing beginners skim this chapter to at least get a rough idea of what is covered.

Part II consists of twelve chapters covering all the basic Swing components with detailed descriptions and helpful examples of each. These chapters discuss the bread and butter of Swing-based GUIs, and each includes usage guidelines written by a usability and interface design expert.

Part III contains seven chapters dealing with the more advanced components. These chapters are significantly more complex than those in part II, and they require a thorough understanding of Swing's architecture, as well as the basic Swing components.

Part IV consists of two chapters on special topics with a focus on Swing, including printing and Java2D.

Four other chapters are available on the Manning web site at www.manning.com/robinson. They cover Accessibility, JavaHelp, CORBA, and contributions from several experienced Swing developers. These chapters vary in complexity. Unfortunately, due to space limitations, we were unable to include these chapters in part IV, but you'll find them in their entirety on the web site.

Most examples are presented in three distinct parts:

The code: After a general introduction to the example, including one or more screenshots, the underlying code is listed. Annotations appear to the right of significant blocks of code to provide a brief summary of its purpose. Each annotation has a number which links it to the explanation of that code in the *Understanding the code* section.

Understanding the code: This section contains a detailed explanation of the code. Most paragraphs are accompanied by a number which links that text with the associated annotated code listed in the code section.

Running the code: After the code is explained, this brief section provides suggestions for testing the program. This section may also include references and suggestions for taking the example further.

Conventions

NOTE Throughout the book we point out specific behaviors or functionality that either differ from what is expected or that can be achieved through alternate techniques. We also use this icon to denote various other types of notes, such as a reference or suggested background knowledge for the material being discussed.

BUG ALERT Occasionally, incorrect or unexpected behavior is caused by known Swing bugs. We do not attempt to hide or gloss over these; rather, we explicitly discuss these bugs and explain possible workarounds or fixes where applicable.

UI GUIDELINE David Anderson, a usability and interface design expert, has provided detailed usage guidelines throughout the book. These guidelines do not represent hard-and-fast rules, but they are highly recommended for the development of consistent, user-friendly interfaces (see the bibliography for David's references and recommended UI design readings).

All source code appears in Courier font. For example:

```
public void main( String args[] ) {
   Example myExample = new Example();
}
```

We prefix all instance variables with "m_," and capitalize all static variables with underscores separating compound words. For example:

```
protected int m_index;
protected static int INSTANCE_COUNT;
```

Many examples are built from examples presented earlier in the book. In these cases we have minimized the amount of repeated code by replacing all unchanged code with references to the sections that contain that code. All new and modified code of any class is highlighted in bold. When a completely new class is added, we do not highlight that class in bold (the only exceptions to this rule are anonymous inner classes).

author online

Purchase of *Swing* includes free access to a private Internet forum where you can make comments about the book, ask technical questions, and receive help from the authors and from other Swing users. To access the forum, point your web browser to www.manning.com/robinson. There you will be able to subscribe to the forum. This site also provides information on how to access the forum once you are registered, what kind of help is available, and the rules of conduct on the forum.

Matt can be contacted directly at matt@mattrobinson.com, and through his web site at www.mattrobinson.com.

Pavel can be contacted directly at pavelv@netfish.com.

David Anderson, author of the UI Guidelines, can be contacted through www.uidesign.net.

Obtaining the source code

All source code for the examples presented in *Swing* is available from www.manning.com/robinson.

acknowledgments

We would like to thank David Anderson for his professional and unique UI guidelines. Thanks to David Karr for his contribution, code annotations throughout the book, and his extensive manuscript feedback. Thanks to Kirk Brown for writing our foreword, and thanks to James Tan, Albert Ting, and Ron Widitz for their contributions.

Thanks to Deirdre O'Brien for her corrections and suggestions, and John Sullivan for his valuable investigations into several performance issues.

Special thanks to our publisher, Marjan Bace, for his consistent reality checks, innovations, and friendly phone calls. Also thanks to everyone else at Manning for making this happen: Lee Fitzpatrick, Ted Kennedy, Mary Piergies, Bruce Murray, Leslie Haimes, Helen Trimes, Syd Brown, Maureen Newmeyer, Kristen Black, Denis Dalinnik, and Ben Kovitz, author of *Practical Software Requirements*.

Thanks to the reviewers of the manuscript for taking the time to provide insight and comments which have accounted for numerous improvements: Albert Ting, Ben Kovitz, Brill Pappin, Claes Tolleback, David Karr, Douglas Nehring, Filipo Morrelli, Jaideep Baphna, Joel Goldberg, Jorgen Erik Assentoft, Mark Newman, Matthew Schmidt, Paul Pazandak, Prakash Palani, Ron Widitz, Steve Wilson, Wong Kok Wai, and the dozens of unofficial reviewers we have been in contact with over the course of this book's development.

MATT ROBINSON:

I owe everything to my parents for their patience, direction, support, and insurmountable love. I must specifically thank my mother for keeping my stomach full of delicious food, and for keeping the entire family strong, healthy, and organized. I also owe a lot to my sisters, Melissa and Mara, and my animal friends, Magnolia and Moose.

Working with Pavel has been a pleasure and a great privilege. I look forward to working with him on future projects.

PAVEL VOROBIEV:

I thank my wife Marina for all of the encouragement, love, and support that she gave me throughout the process of writing this book. I would also like to thank my co-author Matt for his dedication to this project.

about the cover illustration

The cover illustration of this book is from the 1805 edition of Sylvain Maréchal's four-volume compendium of regional dress customs. This book was first published in Paris in 1788, one year before the French Revolution. Its title alone required no fewer than 30 words.

> *"Costumes Civils actuels de tous les peuples connus dessinés d'après nature gravés et coloriés, accompagnés d'une notice historique sur leurs coutumes, moeurs, religions, etc., etc., redigés par M. Sylvain Maréchal"*

The four volumes include an annotation on the illustrations: "gravé à la manière noire par Mixelle d'après Desrais et colorié." Clearly, the engraver and illustrator deserved no more than to be listed by their last names—after all they were mere technicians. The workers who colored each illustration by hand remain nameless.

The remarkable diversity of this collection reminds us vividly of how distant and isolated the world's towns and regions were just 200 years ago. Dress codes have changed everywhere and the diversity by region, so rich at the time, has melted away. It is now hard to tell the inhabitant of one continent from another. Perhaps we have traded cultural diversity for a more varied personal life—certainly a more varied and interesting technology environment.

At a time when it is hard to tell one computer book from another, Manning celebrates the inventiveness and initiative of the computer business with book covers based on the rich diversity of regional life of two centuries ago, brought back to life by Maréchal's pictures. Just think, Maréchal's was a world so different from ours people would take the time to read a book title 30 words long.

PART I

Foundations

Part I consists of two chapters that lay the foundation for a successful and productive journey through the JFC Swing class library. The first chapter begins with a brief overview of what Swing is and an introduction to its architecture. The second chapter contains a detailed discussion of the key mechanisms underlying Swing, and it shows you how to interact with them. There are several sections on topics that are fairly advanced, such as multithreading and painting. This material is central to many areas of Swing and by introducing it in chapter 2, your understanding of what is to come will be significantly enhanced. We expect that you will want to refer back to this chapter quite often, and we explicitly refer you to it throughout the text. At the very least, we recommend that you know what chapter 2 contains before moving on.

C H A P T E R   1

Swing overview

1.1   AWT

The Abstract Window Toolkit (AWT) is the part of Java designed for creating user interfaces and painting graphics and images. It is a set of classes intended to provide everything a developer needs to create a graphical interface for any Java applet or application. Most AWT components are derived from the `java.awt.Component` class, as figure 1.1 illustrates. (Note that AWT menu bars and menu bar items do not fit within the `Component` hierarchy.)

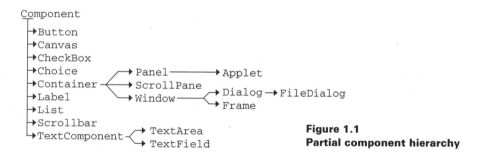

Figure 1.1
Partial component hierarchy

The Java Foundation Classes (JFC) consist of five major parts: AWT, Swing, Accessibility, Java 2D, and Drag and Drop. Java 2D has become an integral part of AWT, Swing is built on top of AWT, and Accessibility support is built into Swing. The five parts of JFC are certainly

3

not mutually exclusive, and Swing is expected to merge more deeply with AWT in future versions of Java. (The Drag and Drop API was far from mature at the time of this writing, but we expect this technology to integrate further with Swing and AWT in the near future.) Thus, AWT is at the core of JFC, which in turn makes it one of the most important libraries in Java 2.

1.2   SWING

Swing is a large set of components ranging from the very simple, such as labels, to the very complex, such as tables, trees, and styled text documents. Almost all Swing components are derived from a single parent called JComponent which extends the AWT Container class. For this reason, Swing is best described as a layer on top of AWT rather than a replacement for it. Figure 1.2 shows a partial JComponent hierarchy. If you compare this with the AWT Component hierarchy of figure 1.1, you will notice that each AWT component has a Swing equivalent that begins with the prefix "J". The only exception to this is the AWT Canvas class, for which JComponent, JLabel, or JPanel can be used as a replacement (we discuss this in detail in section 2.8). You will also notice many Swing classes that don't have AWT counterparts.

Figure 1.2 represents only a small fraction of the Swing library, but this fraction contains the classes you will be dealing with the most. The rest of Swing exists to provide extensive support and customization capabilities for the components these classes define.

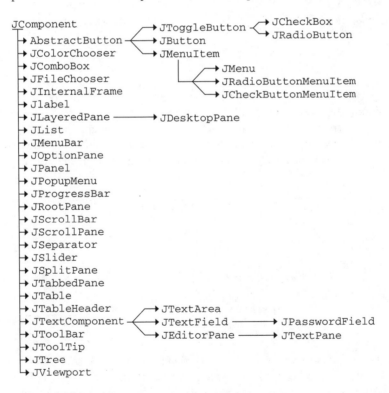

Figure 1.2   Partial JComponent **hierarchy**

1.2.1 Z-order

Swing components are referred to as *lightweight*s while AWT components are referred to as *heavyweight*s. The difference between lightweight and heavyweight components is *z-order*: the notion of depth or layering. Each heavyweight component occupies its own z-order layer. All lightweight components are contained inside heavyweight components, and they maintain their own layering scheme as defined by Swing. When you place a heavyweight inside another heavyweight container, it will, by definition, overlap all lightweights in that container.

What this ultimately means is that you should avoid using both heavyweight and lightweight components in the same container whenever possible. This does not mean that you can *never* mix AWT and Swing components successfully. It just means you have to be careful and know which situations are safe and which are not. Since you probably won't be able to completely eliminate the use of heavyweight components anytime soon, you have to find ways to make the two technologies work together in an acceptable way.

The most important rule to follow is that you should never place heavyweight components inside lightweight containers that commonly support overlapping children. Some examples of these containers are JInternalFrame, JScrollPane, JLayeredPane, and JDesktopPane. Secondly, if you use a pop-up menu in a container holding a heavyweight component, you need to force that pop-up to be heavyweight. To control this for a specific JPopupMenu instance, you can use its setLightWeightPopupEnabled() method.

> **NOTE** For JMenus (which use JPopupMenus to display their contents) you first have to use the getPopupMenu() method to retrieve the associated pop-up menu. Once it is retrieved, you can then call setLightWeightPopupEnabled(false) on that pop-up to enforce heavyweight functionality. This needs to be done with each JMenu in your application, including menus contained within menus.

Alternatively, you can call JPopupMenu's static setDefaultLightWeightPopupEnabled() method, and pass it a value of false to force all popups in a Java session to be heavyweight. Note that this will only affect pop-up menus created *after* this call is made. It is therefore a good idea to call this method early within initialization.

1.2.2 Platform independence

The most remarkable thing about Swing components is that they are written in 100% Java and they do not directly rely on peer components, as most AWT components do. This means that a Swing button or text area will look and function identically on Macintosh, Solaris, Linux, and Windows platforms. This design reduces the need to test and debug applications on each target platform.

> **NOTE** The only exceptions to this are four heavyweight Swing components that are direct subclasses of AWT classes that rely on platform-dependent peers: JApplet, JDialog, JFrame, and JWindow. See chapter 3 for more information.

1.2.3 Swing package overview

javax.swing

Contains the most basic Swing components, default component models and interfaces. (Most of the classes shown in figure 1.2 are contained in this package.)

`javax.swing.border`

Contains the classes and interfaces used to define specific border styles. Note that borders can be shared by any number of Swing components, as they are not components themselves.

`javax.swing.colorchooser`

Contains classes and interfaces that support the `JColorChooser` component, which is used for color selection. (This package also contains some interesting undocumented private classes.)

`javax.swing.event`

Contains all Swing-specific event types and listeners. Swing components also support events and listeners defined in `java.awt.event` and `java.beans`.

`javax.swing.filechooser`

Contains classes and interfaces supporting the `JFileChooser` component used for file selection.

`javax.swing.plaf`

Contains the pluggable look and feel API used to define custom UI delegates. Most of the classes in this package are abstract. They are subclassed and implemented by look and feel implementations such as metal, motif, and basic. The classes in this package are intended for use only by developers who, for one reason or another, cannot build on top of an existing look and feel.

`javax.swing.plaf.basic`

This package is the Basic look and feel implementation upon which all look and feels provided with Swing are built on top of. We are normally expected to subclass the classes in this package if we want to create our own customized look and feel.

`javax.swing.plaf.metal`

Metal is the default look and feel of Swing components; it is also known as the Java look and feel. It is the only look and feel that ships with Swing which is not designed to be consistent with a specific platform.

`javax.swing.plaf.multi`

This package is the Multiplexing look and feel. This is not a regular look and feel implementation in that it does not define the actual look or feel of any components. Instead, it provides the ability to combine several look and feels for simultaneous use. A typical example might be using an audio-based look and feel in combination with metal or motif.

`javax.swing.table`

Contains classes and interfaces that support the `JTable` control. This component is used to manage tabular data in spreadsheet form. It supports a high degree of customization without requiring look and feel enhancements.

`javax.swing.text`

Contains classes and interfaces used by the text components, including support for plain and styled documents, the views of those documents, highlighting, caret control and customization, editor actions, and keyboard customization.

`javax.swing.text.html`

Contains support for HTML documents. (HTML support was being completely rewritten and expanded upon while we were writing this book. Because of this, our coverage of it is regrettably limited.)

```
javax.swing.text.html.parser
```
Contains support for parsing HTML.
```
javax.swing.text.rtf
```
Contains support for RTF (rich text format) documents.
```
javax.swing.tree
```
Contains classes and interfaces that support the JTree component. This component is used for the display and management of hierarchical data. It supports a high degree of customization without requiring look and feel enhancements.
```
javax.swing.undo
```
Contains support for implementing and managing undo/redo functionality.

1.3   *MVC* ARCHITECTURE

The Model-View-Controller architecture (MVC) is a well known object-oriented user interface design decomposition that dates back to the late 1970s. Components are broken down into three parts: a model, a view, and a controller. Each Swing component is based on a more modern version of this design. Before we discuss how MVC works in Swing, we need to understand how it was originally designed to work.

NOTE   The three-way separation described here, and illustrated in figure 1.3, is only used today by a small number of user interface frameworks, VisualWorks being the most notable.

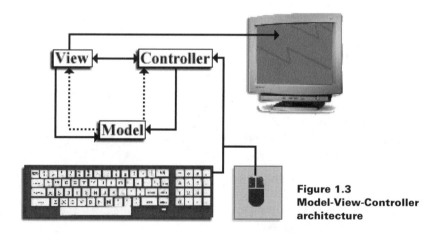

**Figure 1.3
Model-View-Controller
architecture**

1.3.1   Model

The model is responsible for maintaining all aspects of the component state. This includes, for example, such values as the pressed/unpressed state of a push button, and a text component's character data and information about how it is structured. A model may be responsible for *indirect* communication with the view and the controller. By indirect, we mean that the model does not "know" its view and controller—it does not maintain or retrieve references to them. Instead, the model will send out notifications or *broadcasts* (what we know as events). In figure 1.3 this indirect communication is represented by dashed lines.

1.3.2 View

The view determines the visual representation of the component's model. This is a component's "look." For example, the view displays the correct color of a component, whether the component appears raised or lowered (in the case of a button), and the rendering of a desired font. The view is responsible for keeping its on-screen representation updated, which it may do upon receiving indirect messages from the model or direct messages from the controller.

1.3.3 Controller

The controller is responsible for determining whether the component should react to any input events from input devices such as the keyboard or mouse. The controller is the "feel" of the component, and it determines what actions are performed when the component is used. The controller can receive direct messages from the view, and indirect messages from the model.

For example, suppose we have a checked (selected) check box in our interface. If the controller determines that the user has performed a mouse click, it may send a message to the view. If the view determines that the click occurred on the check box, it sends a message to the model. The model then updates itself and broadcasts a message, which will be received by the view(s), to tell it that it should update itself based on the new state of the model. In this way, a model is not bound to a specific view or controller; this allows us to have several views and controllers manipulating a single model.

1.3.4 Custom view and controller

One of the major advantages Swing's MVC architecture provides is the ability to customize the "look" and "feel" of a component without modifying the model. Figure 1.4 shows a group of components using two different user interfaces. The important point to know about this figure is that the components shown are actually the same, but they are shown using two different *look and feel* implementations (different views and controllers as discussed below).

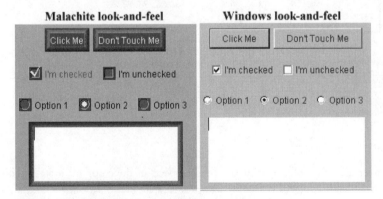

Figure 1.4 Malachite and Windows look and feels of the same components

Some Swing components also provide the ability to customize specific parts of a component without affecting the model. More specifically, these components allow us to define custom cell renderers and editors used to display and accept specific data, respectively. Figure 1.5 shows the columns of a table containing stock market data rendered with custom icons and colors. We will examine how to take advantage of this functionality in our study of Swing combo boxes, lists, tables, and trees.

Sun Microsystems	140 5/8	10.625	⇑ SUNW	130 15/16	10	17,734,600
Lucent Technology	64 5/8	9.65	⇑ LU	59 15/16	4 11/16	29,856,300
Dell Computers	46 3/16	6.24	⇑ DELL	44 1/2	1 11/16	47,310,000
Sony Corp.	96 3/16	1.18	⇑ SNE	95 5/8	1 1/8	330,600
Hitachi, Ltd.	78 1/2	1.12	⇑ HIT	77 5/8	7/8	49,400
Enamelon Inc.	4 7/8	0.0	⇓ ENML	5	-1/8	35,900
AT&T	65 3/16	-0.1	⇓ T	66	-13/16	554,000
Intl. Bus. Machines	183	-0.51	⇓ IBM	183 1/8	-1/8	4,371,400
Microsoft Corp.	94 1/16	-0.92	⇓ MSFT	95 3/16	-1 1/8	19,836,900
Egghead.com	17 1/4	-1.43	⇓ EGGS	17 7/16	-3/16	2,146,400
Sprint	104 9/16	-1.82	⇓ FON	106 3/8	-1 13/16	1,135,100
Hewlett-Packard	70	-2.01	⇓ HWP	71 1/16	-1 7/16	2,410,700
Compaq Computers	30 7/8	-2.18	⇓ CPQ	31 1/4	-3/8	11,853,900

Figure 1.5 Custom rendering

1.3.5 Custom models

Another major advantage of Swing's MVC architecture is the ability to customize and replace a component's data model. For example, we can construct our own text document model that enforces the entry of a date or phone number in a very specific form. We can also associate the same data model with more than one component. For instance, two JTextAreas can store their textual content in the same document model, while maintaining two different views of that information.

We will design and implement our own data models for JComboBox, JList, JTree, JTable, and throughout our coverage of text components. We've listed some of Swing's model interface definitions below, along with a brief description of what data their implementations are designed to store and what components they are used with:

BoundedRangeModel
> *Used by*: JProgressBar, JScrollBar, JSlider.
> *Stores*: 4 integers: value, extent, min, max.
> The value and the extent must be between specified min and max values. The extent is always <= max and >=value.

ButtonModel
> *Used by*: All AbstractButton subclasses.
> *Stores*: A boolean representing whether the button is selected (armed) or unselected (disarmed).

ListModel
> *Used by*: JList.
> *Stores*: A collection of objects.

ComboBoxModel
> *Used by*: JComboBox.
> *Stores*: A collection of objects and a selected object.

`MutableComboBoxModel`

> *Used by*: `JComboBox`.
>
> *Stores*: A `Vector` (or another mutable collection) of objects and a selected object.

`ListSelectionModel`

> *Used by*: `JList, TableColumnModel`.
>
> *Stores*: One or more indices of selected list or table items. Allows single, single-interval, or multiple-interval selections.

`SingleSelectionModel`

> *Used by*: `JMenuBar, JPopupMenu, JMenuItem, JTabbedPane`.
>
> *Stores*: The index of the selected element in a collection of objects owned by the implementor.

`ColorSelectionModel`

> *Used by*: `JColorChooser`.
>
> *Stores*: A `Color`.

`TableModel`

> *Used by*: `JTable`.
>
> *Stores*: A two-dimensional array of objects.

`TableColumnModel`

> *Used by*: `JTable`.
>
> *Stores*: A collection of `TableColumn` objects, a set of listeners for table column model events, the width between columns, the total width of all columns, a selection model, and a column selection flag.

`TreeModel`

> *Used by*: `JTree`.
>
> *Stores*: Objects that can be displayed in a tree. Implementations must be able to distinguish between branch and leaf objects, and the objects must be organized hierarchically.

`TreeSelectionModel`

> *Used by*: `JTree`.
>
> *Stores*: Selected rows. Allows single, contiguous, and discontiguous selection.

`Document`

> *Used by*: All text components.
>
> *Stores*: Content. Normally this is text (character data). More complex implementations support styled text, images, and other forms of content (such as embedded components).

Not all Swing components have models. Those that act as containers, such as `JApplet`, `JFrame, JLayeredPane, JDesktopPane`, and `JInternalFrame`, do not have models. However, interactive components such as `JButton, JTextField`, and `JTable` *do* have models. In fact, some Swing components have more than one model (for example, `JList` uses one model to hold selection information and another model to store its data). The point is that MVC is not a hard-and-fast rule in Swing. Simple components, or complex components that don't store lots of information (such as `JDesktopPane`), do not need separate models. The view and controller of each component is, however, almost always separate for each component, as we will see in the next section.

So how does the component itself fit into the MVC picture? The component acts as a mediator between the model(s), the view, and the controller. It is neither the M, the V, nor the C, although it can take the place of any or all of these parts if we so design it. This will become more clear as we progress through this chapter, and throughout the rest of the book.

1.4   UI DELEGATES AND PLAF

Almost all modern user interface frameworks coalesce the view and the controller, whether they are based on SmallTalk, C++, or Java. Examples include MacApp, Smalltalk/V, Interviews, and the X/Motif widgets used in IBM Smalltalk. Swing is the newest addition to this crowd. Swing packages each component's view and controller into an object called a UI delegate. For this reason Swing's underlying architecture is more accurately referred to as model-delegate rather than model-view-controller. Ideally, communication between both the model and the UI delegate is indirect, allowing more than one model to be associated with one UI delegate, and vice versa. Figure 1.6 illustrates this principle.

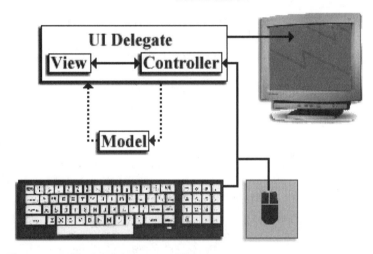

Figure 1.6   Model-delegate architecture

1.4.1   The ComponentUI class

Each UI delegate is derived from an abstract class called ComponentUI. ComponentUI methods describe the fundamentals of how a UI delegate and a component using it will communicate. Note that each method takes a JComponent as a parameter.

Here are the ComponentUI methods:

```
static ComponentUI createUI(JComponent c)
```
        Returns an instance of the UI delegate defined by the defining ComponentUI subclass itself, in its normal implementation. This instance is often used for sharing among components of the same type (for example, all JButtons using the Metal look and feel share the same static UI delegate instance defined in javax.swing. plaf.metal.MetalButtonUI by default).

```
installUI(JComponent c)
```
Installs this `ComponentUI` on the specified component. This normally adds listeners to the component and/or its model(s), to notify the UI delegate when changes in state occur that require a view update.

```
uninstallUI(JComponent c)
```
Removes this `ComponentUI` and any listeners added in `installUI()` from the specified component and/or its model(s).

```
update(Graphics g, JComponent c)
```
If the component is opaque, this method paints its background and then calls `paint(Graphics g, JComponent c)`.

```
paint(Graphics g, JComponent c)
```
Gets all information it needs from the component and possibly its model(s) to render it correctly.

```
getPreferredSize(JComponent c)
```
Returns the preferred size for the specified component based on this `ComponentUI`.

```
getMinimumSize(JComponent c)
```
Returns the minimum size for the specified component based on this `ComponentUI`.

```
getMaximumSize(JComponent c)
```
Returns the maximum size for the specified component based on this `ComponentUI`.

To enforce the use of a specific UI delegate, we can call a component's `setUI()` method:

```
JButton m_button = new JButton();
m_button.setUI((MalachiteButtonUI)
  MalachiteButtonUI.createUI(m_button));
```

Most UI delegates are constructed so that they know about a component and its models only while performing painting and other view-controller tasks. Swing normally avoids associating UI delegates on a per-component basis by using a shared instance.

NOTE   The `JComponent` class defines methods for assigning UI delegates because the method declarations required do not involve component-specific code. However, this is not possible with data models because there is no base interface that all models can be traced back to (for example, there is no base class such as `ComponentUI` for Swing models). For this reason, methods to assign models are defined in subclasses of `JComponent` where necessary.

1.4.2   Pluggable look and feel

Swing includes several sets of UI delegates. Each set contains `ComponentUI` implementations for most Swing components; we call each of these sets a *look and feel* or a *pluggable look and feel* (PLAF) implementation. The `javax.swing.plaf` package consists of abstract classes derived from `ComponentUI`, and the classes in the `javax.swing.plaf.basic` package extend these abstract classes to implement the Basic look and feel. This is the set of UI delegates that all other look and feel classes are expected to use as a base for building from. (Note that the Basic look and feel cannot be used on its own, as `BasicLookAndFeel` is an abstract class.) There are three main pluggable look and feel implementations derived from the Basic look and feel:

Windows: `com.sun.java.swing.plaf.windows.WindowsLookAndFeel`
CDE\Motif: `com.sun.java.swing.plaf.motif.MotifLookAndFeel`
Metal (default): `javax.swing.plaf.metal.MetalLookAndFeel`

There is also a `MacLookAndFeel` for simulating Macintosh user interfaces, but this does not ship with Java 2—it must be downloaded separately. The Windows and Macintosh pluggable look and feel libraries are only supported on the corresponding platform.

The Multiplexing look and feel, `javax.swing.plaf.multi.MultiLookAndFeel`, extends all the abstract classes in `javax.swing.plaf`. It is designed to allow combinations of look and feels to be used simultaneously, and it is intended for, but not limited to, use with Accessibility look and feels. The job of each Multiplexing UI delegate is to manage each of its child UI delegates.

Each look and feel package contains a class derived from the abstract class `javax.swing.LookAndFeel`; these include `BasicLookAndFeel`, `MetalLookAndFeel`, and `WindowsLookAndFeel`. These are the central points of access to each look and feel package. We use them when changing the current look and feel, and the `UIManager` class (used to manage installed look and feels) uses them to access the current look and feel's `UIDefaults` table (which contains, among other things, UI delegate class names for that look and feel corresponding to each Swing component). To change the current look and feel of an application we can simply call the `UIManager`'s `setLookAndFeel()` method, passing it the fully qualified name of the `LookAndFeel` to use. The following code can be used to accomplish this at run-time:

```
try {
  UIManager.setLookAndFeel(
    "com.sun.java.swing.plaf.motif.MotifLookAndFeel");
  SwingUtilities.updateComponentTreeUI(myJFrame);
}
catch (Exception e) {
  System.err.println("Could not load LookAndFeel");
}
```

`SwingUtilities.updateComponentTreeUI()` informs all children of the specified component that the look and feel has changed and they need to discard their UI delegate in exchange for a different one of the new look and feel.

1.4.3 Where are the UI delegates?

We've discussed `ComponentUI` and the packages that `LookAndFeel` implementations reside in, but we haven't really mentioned anything about the specific UI delegate classes derived from `ComponentUI`. Each abstract class in the `javax.swing.plaf` package extends `ComponentUI` and corresponds to a specific Swing component. The name of each class follows the general scheme of class name (without the "J" prefix) plus a "UI" suffix. For instance, `LabelUI` extends `ComponentUI` and is the base delegate used for `JLabels`.

These classes are extended by concrete implementations such as those in the `basic` and `multi` packages. The names of these subclasses follow the general scheme of the look and feel name prefix added to the superclass name. For instance, `BasicLabelUI` and `MultiLabelUI` both extend `LabelUI` and reside in the `basic` and `multi` packages respectively. Figure 1.7 illustrates the `LabelUI` hierarchy.

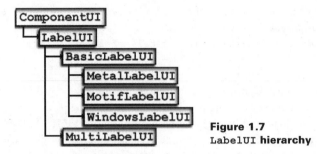

Figure 1.7
LabelUI **hierarchy**

Most look and feel implementations are expected to either extend the concrete classes defined in the basic package, or use them directly. The Metal, Motif, and Windows UI delegates are built on top of Basic versions. The Multi look and feel, however, is unique in that each implementation does not extend from Basic; each is merely a shell allowing an arbitrary number of UI delegates to be installed on a given component.

Figure 1.7 should emphasize the fact that Swing supplies a very large number of UI delegate classes. If we were to create an entire pluggable look and feel implementation, it would be evident that some serious time and effort would be involved. In chapter 21 we will learn all about this process, as well as how to modify and work with the existing look and feels.

NOTE   We do not detail the complete functionality and construction of any of the provided UI delegate classes in this book. The only reference available at the time of this writing with coverage of the Basic UI delegates is Manning's *Java Foundation Classes: Swing Reference* by Stephen C. Drye and William C. Wake.

CHAPTER 2

Swing mechanics

2.1   JCOMPONENT PROPERTIES, SIZING, AND POSITIONING

2.1.1   Properties

All Swing components conform to the JavaBeans specification, which we'll discuss in detail in section 2.7. Among the five features a JavaBean is expected to support is a set of properties and associated accessor methods. A *property* is a global variable, and its accessor methods, if any, are normally of the form set*Propertyname*(), get*Propertyname*(), or is*Propertyname*() (in which the terms in italics would be replaced by real terms).

A property that has no event firing associated with a change in its value is called a *simple* property. A *bound* property is one for which PropertyChangeEvents are fired after it changes state. We can register PropertyChangeListeners to listen for PropertyChangeEvents through JComponent's addPropertyChangeListener() method. A *constrained* property is one for which PropertyChangeEvents are fired *before* a change in state occurs. We can register

15

`VetoableChangeListeners` to listen for `PropertyChangeEvents` through `JComponent`'s `addVetoableChangeListener()` method. A change can be vetoed in the event handling code of a `VetoableChangeListener` by throwing a `PropertyVetoException`. (There is only one Swing class with constrained properties: `JInternalFrame`.)

NOTE   Each of these event and listener classes is defined in the `java.awt.beans` package.

`PropertyChangeEvents` carry three pieces of information with them: the name of the property, the old value, and the new value. Beans can use an instance of `PropertyChangeSupport` to manage the dispatching, to each registered listener, of the `PropertyChangeEvents` corresponding to each bound property. Similarly, an instance of `VetoableChangeSupport` can be used to manage the dispatching of all `PropertyChangeEvents` corresponding to each constrained property.

Swing introduces a new class called `SwingPropertyChangeSupport` (defined in `javax.swing.event`) which is a subclass of, and almost identical to, `PropertyChangeSupport`. The difference is that `SwingPropertyChangeSupport` has been built to be more efficient. It does this by sacrificing thread safety, which, as we will see later in this chapter, is not an issue in Swing if the multithreading guidelines are followed consistently (because all event processing should occur on only one thread—the event-dispatching thread). So if we are confident that our code has been constructed in a thread-safe manner, we are encouraged to use this more efficient version, rather than `PropertyChangeSupport`.

NOTE   There is no Swing equivalent of `VetoableChangeSupport` because there are currently only four constrained properties in Swing; all are defined in `JInternalFrame`.

Swing also introduces a new type of property which we will call a *change* property, for lack of a given name. We use `ChangeListeners` to listen for `ChangeEvents` that get fired when these properties change state. A `ChangeEvent` only carries one piece of information with it: the source of the event. For this reason, change properties are less powerful than bound or constrained properties, but they are more widespread. A `JButton`, for instance, sends change events whenever it is armed (pressed for the first time), pressed, and released (see chapter 5).

NOTE   You can always find out which properties have change events associated with them, as well as any other type of event, by referencing the Swing source code. Unless you are using Swing for simple interfaces, we strongly suggest getting used to this concept.

Another new property-like feature Swing introduces is the notion of *client properties*. These are basically key/value pairs stored in a `Hashtable` provided by each Swing component. This feature allows properties to be added and removed at run-time.

WARNING   Client properties may seem like a great way to add property change support for custom components, but we are explicitly advised against this according to the API documentation: "The `clientProperty` dictionary is not intended to support large scale extensions to `JComponent` nor should it be considered an alternative to subclassing when designing a new component."

Client properties are bound properties: when a client property changes, a `PropertyChangeEvent` is dispatched to all registered `PropertyChangeListeners`. To add a property to a component's client properties `Hashtable`, we can do something like the following:

```
myComponent.putClientProperty("myname", myValue);
```

To retrieve a client property:

```
myObject = myComponent.getClientProperty("myname");
```

To remove a client property we can provide a `null` value:

```
myComponent.putClientProperty("myname", null);
```

For example, `JDesktopPane` uses a client property to control the outline dragging mode for `JInternalFrames` (this will work no matter which look and feel is in use):

```
myDesktop.putClientProperty("JDesktopPane.dragMode", "outline");
```

Five Swing components have special client properties that only the Metal look and feel pays attention to. Briefly, these are:

`JTree.lineStyle`

A `String` used to specify whether node relationships are displayed as angular connecting lines ("Angled"), horizontal lines defining cell boundaries ("Horizontal" (default)), or no lines at all ("None").

`JScrollBar.isFreeStanding`

A `Boolean` value used to specify whether all sides of a `JScrollbar` will have an etched border (`Boolean.FALSE` (default)) or only the top and left edges (`Boolean.TRUE`).

`JSlider.isFilled`

A `Boolean` value used to specify whether the lower portion of a slider should be filled (`Boolean.TRUE`) or not (`Boolean.FALSE` (default)).

`JToolBar.isRollover`

A `Boolean` value used to specify whether a toolbar button displays an etched border only when the mouse is within its bounds and no border if it is not (`Boolean.TRUE`), or whether to always use an etched border (`Boolean.FALSE` (default)).

`JInternalFrame.isPalette`

A `Boolean` value used to specify whether a very thin border is used (`Boolean.TRUE`) or the regular border is used (`Boolean.FALSE` (default)). As of Java 2 First Customer Shipment (FCS), this property is not used.

2.1.2   Size and positioning

Because `JComponent` extends `java.awt.Container`, it inherits all the sizing and positioning functionality we are used to. We suggest you manage a component's preferred, minimum, and maximum sizes using the following methods:

`setPreferredSize(), getPreferredSize()`

The most comfortable size of a component. Used by most layout managers to size each component.

`setMinimumSize(), getMinimumSize()`

Used during layout to act as a lower boundary for a component's dimensions.

`setMaximumSize(), getMaximumSize()`

Used during layout to act as an upper boundary for a component's dimensions.

Each `setXX()`/`getXX()` method accepts/returns a `Dimension` instance. We will learn more about what these sizes mean in terms of each layout manager in chapter 4. Whether a layout manager pays attention to these sizes is solely based on that layout manager's implementation. It is perfectly feasible to construct a layout manager that simply ignores all of them, or pays attention to only one. The sizing of components in a container is layout-manager specific.

JComponent's setBounds() method can be used to assign a component both a size and a position within its parent container. This overloaded method can take either a Rectangle parameter (java.awt.Rectangle) or four int parameters representing the x-coordinate, y-coordinate, width, and height. For example, the following two code segments are equivalent:

```
myComponent.setBounds(120,120,300,300);

Rectangle rec = new Rectangle(120,120,300,300);
myComponent.setBounds(rec);
```

Note that setBounds() will not override any layout policies in effect due to a parent container's layout manager. For this reason, a call to setBounds() may appear to have been ignored in some situations because it tried to do its job and was forced back to its original size by the layout manager (layout managers always have the first crack at setting the size of a component).

setBounds() is commonly used to manage child components in containers with no layout manager (such as JLayeredPane, JDesktopPane, and JComponent itself). For instance, we normally use setBounds() when adding a JInternalFrame to a JDesktopPane.

A component's size can safely be queried in typical AWT style, such as this:

```
int h = myComponent.getHeight();
int w = myComponent.getWidth();
```

Size can also be retrieved as a Rectangle or a Dimension instance:

```
Rectangle rec2 = myComponent.getBounds();
Dimension dim = myComponent.getSize();
```

Rectangle contains four publicly accessible properties describing its location and size:

```
int recX = rec2.x;
int recY = rec2.y;
int recWidth = rec2.width;
int recHeight = rec2.height;
```

Dimension contains two publicly accessible properties describing size:

```
int dimWidth = dim.width;
int dimHeight = dim.height;
```

The coordinates returned in the Rectangle instance using getBounds() represent a component's location within its parent. These coordinates can also be obtained using the getX() and getY() methods. Additionally, we can set a component's position within its container using the setLocation(int x, int y) method.

JComponent also maintains an alignment. Horizontal and vertical alignments can be specified by float values between 0.0 and 1.0: 0.5 means center, closer to 0.0 means left or top, and closer to 1.0 means right or bottom. The corresponding JComponent methods are:

```
setAlignmentX(float f)
setAlignmentY(float f)
```

These values are used only in containers managed by BoxLayout and OverlayLayout.

2.2   *EVENT HANDLING AND DISPATCHING*

Events occur any time a key or mouse button is pressed. The way components receive and process events has not changed from JDK1.1. Swing components can generate many different types of events, including those in `java.awt.event` and even more in `javax.swing.event`. Many of the new Swing event types are component-specific. Each event type is represented by an object that, at the very least, identifies the source of the event (and often carries additional information about what specific kind of event it is) and information about the state of the source before and after the event was generated. Sources of events are most commonly components or models, but different kinds of objects can also generate events.

In order to receive notification of events, we need to register listeners with the source object. A listener is an implementation of any of the `XXListener` interfaces (where XX is an event type) defined in the `java.awt.event`, `java.beans` and `javax.swing.event` packages. There is always at least one method defined in each interface that takes a corresponding `XXEvent` as a parameter. Classes that support notification of `XXEvents` generally implement the `XXListener` interface, and have support for registering and unregistering those listeners through the use of the `addXXListener()` and `removeXXListener()` methods, respectively. Most event sources allow any number of listeners to be registered with them. Similarly, any listener instance can be registered to receive events from any number of event sources. Usually classes that support `XXEvents` provide protected `fireXX()` methods used for constructing event objects and sending them to the event handlers for processing.

2.2.1   EventListenerList

class javax.swing.event.EventListenerList

`EventListenerList` is an array of `XXEvent`/`XXListener` pairs. `JComponent` and each of its descendants use an `EventListenerList` to maintain their listeners. All default models also maintain listeners and an `EventListenerList`. When a listener is added to a Swing component or model, the associated event's `Class` instance (used to identify event type) is added to its `EventListenerList` array, followed by the listener itself. Since these pairs are stored in an array rather than a mutable collection (for efficiency purposes), a new array is created on each addition or removal using the `System.arrayCopy()` method. When events are received, the list is gone through and events are sent to each listener with a matching type. Because the array is ordered in an `XXEvent`, `XXListener`, `YYEvent`, `YYListener` fashion, a listener corresponding to a given event type is always next in the array. This approach allows very efficient event-dispatching routines (see section 2.7.7). For thread safety the methods for adding and removing listeners from an `EventListenerList` synchronize access to the array when it is manipulated.

`JComponent` defines its `EventListenerList` as a protected field called `listenerList` so that all subclasses inherit it. Swing components manage most of their listeners directly through `listenerList`.

2.2.2   Event-dispatching thread

All events are processed by the listeners that receive them within the event-dispatching thread (an instance of `java.awt.EventDispatchThread`). All painting and component layout is expected to occur within this thread as well. The event-dispatching thread is of primary importance to Swing and AWT, and it plays a key role in keeping updates to component state and display in an application under control.

Associated with this thread is a FIFO queue of events—the system event queue (an instance of java.awt.EventQueue). This gets filled up, as does any FIFO queue, in a serial fashion. Each request takes its turn executing event-handling code, whether it is updating component properties, layout, or repainting. All events are processed serially to avoid such situations as a component's state being modified in the middle of a repaint. Knowing this, we must be careful not to dispatch events *outside* of the event-dispatching thread. For instance, calling a fireXX() method directly from a separate thread of execution is unsafe. We must also be sure that event-handling code and painting code can be executed quickly. Otherwise, the whole system event queue will be blocked waiting for one event process, repaint, or layout to occur, and our application will appear to be frozen or locked up.

2.3 MULTITHREADING

To help ensure that all our event-handling code gets executed only from within the event-dispatching thread, Swing provides a very helpful class that, among other things, allows us to add Runnable objects to the system event queue. This class is called SwingUtilities and it contains two methods that we are interested in: invokeLater() and invokeAndWait(). The first method adds a Runnable to the system event queue and returns immediately. The second method adds a Runnable and waits for it to be dispatched, then returns after it finishes. The basic syntax of each follows:

```
Runnable trivialRunnable = new Runnable() {
 public void run() {
  doWork(); // do some work
 }
};
SwingUtilities.invokeLater(trivialRunnable);

try {
 Runnable trivialRunnable2 = new Runnable() {
  public void run() {
   doWork(); // do some work
  }
 };
 SwingUtilities.invokeAndWait(trivialRunnable2);
}
catch (InterruptedException ie) {
 System.out.println("...waiting thread interrupted!");
}
catch (InvocationTargetException ite) {
 System.out.println(
  "...uncaught exception within Runnable's run()");
}
```

Because these Runnables are placed into the system event queue for execution within the event-dispatching thread, we should be just as careful that they execute quickly, as we are with any other event-handling code. In the above two examples, if the doWork() method did something that took a long time (like loading a large file), we would find that the application would freeze up until the load finishes. In time-intensive cases such as this, we should use our own separate thread to maintain responsiveness.

The following code shows a typical way to build our own thread to do some time-intensive work. In order to safely update the state of any components from inside this thread, we must use invokeLater() or invokeAndWait():

```
Thread workHard = new Thread() {
 public void run() {
  doToughWork(); // do some really time-intensive work
  SwingUtilities.invokeLater( new Runnable () {
   public void run() {
    updateComponents(); // update the state of component(s)
   }
  });
 }
};
workHard.start();
```

NOTE   invokeLater() should be used instead of invokeAndWait() whenever possible. If we do have to use invokeAndWait(), we should make sure that there are no locks held by the calling thread that another thread might need during the operation.

Our use of a separate thread solves the problem of responsiveness, and it does dispatch component-related code to the event-dispatching thread, but it still cannot be considered completely user friendly. Normally, the user should be able to interrupt a time-intensive procedure. If we are waiting to establish a network connection, we certainly don't want to continue waiting indefinitely if the destination is not responding. In most circumstances the user should have the option to interrupt our thread. The following pseudocode shows a typical way to accomplish this, where stopButton causes the thread to be interrupted, updating component state accordingly:

```
Thread workHarder = new Thread() {
 public void run() {
  doTougherWork();
  SwingUtilities.invokeLater( new Runnable () {
   public void run() {
    updateMyComponents(); // update the state of component(s)
   }
  });
 }
};
workHarder.start();

public void doTougherWork() {
 try {
 // [some sort of loop]
 // ...If, at any point, this involves changing
 // component state, we'll have to use invokeLater
 // here because this is executed in a separate thread.
 //
```

```
// We must do at least one of the following:
// 1. Periodically check Thread.interrupted()
// 2. Periodically sleep or wait
if (Thread.interrupted()) {
  throw new InterruptedException();
}
Thread.wait(1000);
}
catch (InterruptedException e) {
  // Let somebody know we've been interrupted
  // ...if this involves changing component state
  // we'll have to use invokeLater here.
}
}

JButton stopButton = new JButton("Stop");
ActionListener stopListener = new ActionListener() {
 public void actionPerformed(ActionEvent event) {
  // Interrupt the thread and let the user know the
  // thread has been interrupted by disabling the
  // Stop button.
  // ...This will occur on the regular event dispatch thread.
  workHarder.interrupt();
  stopButton.setEnabled(false);
 }
};
stopButton.addActionListener(stopListener);
```

Our `stopButton` interrupts the `workHarder` thread when it is pressed. There are two ways that `doTougherWork()` will know whether `workHarder` (the thread it is executed in) has been interrupted. If it is currently `sleeping` or `waiting`, an `InterruptedException` will be thrown which we can catch and process accordingly. The only other way to detect interruption is to periodically check the interrupted state by calling `Thread.interrupted()`.

This approach is commonly used for constructing and displaying complex dialogs, I/O processes that result in component state changes (such as loading a document into a text component), intensive class loading or calculations, waiting for messages, and to establish a network connection, among other tasks.

> **REFERENCE**   Members of the Swing team have written a few articles about using threads with Swing, and have provided a class called `SwingWorker` that makes managing the type of multithreading described here more convenient. See http://java.sun.com/products/jfc/tsc/archive/tech_topics_arch/threads/threads.html

2.3.1   Special cases

There are some special cases in which we do not *need* to delegate code affecting the state of components to the event-dispatching thread:

1 Some methods in Swing, although few and far between, are marked as thread-safe in the API documentation and do not need special consideration. Some methods are thread-safe but are not marked as such: `repaint()`, `revalidate()`, and `invalidate()`.

2 A component can be constructed and manipulated in any fashion we like, without regard for threads, as long as it has not yet been *realized* (meaning it has been displayed or a repaint request has been queued). Top-level containers (JFrame, JDialog, JApplet) are realized after any of setVisible(true), show(), or pack() have been called on them. Also note that a component is considered realized as soon as it is added to a realized container.

3 When dealing with Swing applets (JApplets), all components can be constructed and manipulated without regard for threads until the start() method has been called; this occurs after the init() method.

2.3.2 How do we build our own thread-safe methods?

Building our own thread-safe cases is quite easy. Here is a thread-safe method template we can use to guarantee that a method's code only executes in the event-dispatching thread:

```
public void doThreadSafeWork() {
  if (SwingUtilities.isEventDispatchThread()) {
  //
  // do all work here...
  //
  }
  else {
  Runnable callDoThreadSafeWork = new Runnable() {
   public void run() {
    doThreadSafeWork();
   }
  };
  SwingUtilities.invokeLater(callDoThreadSafeWork);
  }
}
```

2.3.3 How do invokeLater() and invokeAndWait() work?

class javax.swing.SystemEventQueueUtilities [package private]

This section is only of interest to those seeking a low-level understanding of how Runnables are dispatched and processed. When SwingUtilities receives a Runnable object through invokeLater(), it immediately passes the object to the postRunnable() method of a class called SystemEventQueueUtilities. If a Runnable is received through invokeAndWait(), the current thread is first checked to make sure that it is not the event-dispatching thread. (It would be fatal to allow invokeAndWait() to be invoked from the event-dispatch thread itself!) An error is thrown if invokeAndWait() is run in the event-dispatching thread. Otherwise, we construct an Object to use as the lock on a critical section (a synchronized block). This block contains two statements. The first sends the Runnable to SystemEvent- QueueUtilities' postRunnable() method, along with a reference to the lock object. The second waits on the lock object so the calling thread won't proceed until this object is notified—hence "invoke and wait."

The postRunnable() method first communicates with the private SystemEventQueue, an inner class of SystemEventQueueUtilities, to return a reference to the system event queue. The `Runnable` is then wrapped in an instance of `RunnableEvent`, another private inner class. The `RunnableEvent` constructor takes a `Runnable` and an `Object` representing the lock object (`null` if `invokeLater()` was called) as parameters.

The `RunnableEvent` class is a subclass of `AWTEvent`, and it defines its own static `int` event ID—`EVENT_ID`. (Note that whenever we define our own event, we are expected to use an event ID greater than the value of `AWTEvent.RESERVED_ID_MAX`.) `RunnableEvent`'s `EVENT_ID` is `AWTEvent.RESERVED_ID_MAX + 1000`. `RunnableEvent` also contains a static instance of `RunnableTarget`, yet another private inner class. `RunnableTarget` is a subclass of `Component`; its only purpose is to act as the source and target of `RunnableEvent`s.

How does `RunnableTarget` do this? Its constructor enables events with an event ID matching `RunnableEvent`'s ID:

```
enableEvents(RunnableEvent.EVENT_ID);
```

It also overrides `Component`'s protected `processEvent()` method to receive `RunnableEvent`s. Inside this method, `RunnableTarget` first checks to see if the event passed as a parameter is in fact an instance of `RunnableEvent`. If it is, it is passed to `SystemEventQueueUtilities`' `processRunnableEvent()` method (this occurs after the `RunnableEvent` has been dispatched from the system event queue).

Now back to `RunnableEvent`. The `RunnableEvent` constructor calls its superclass (`AWTEvent`) constructor, passing its static instance of `RunnableTarget` as the event source and `EVENT_ID` as the event ID. It also keeps references to the given `Runnable` and lock object.

So, in short, when `invokeLater()` or `invokeAndWait()` are called, the `Runnable` passed to them is then passed to the `SystemEventQueueUtilities.postRunnable()` method along with a lock object that the calling thread (if it was `invokeAndWait()`) is waiting on. This method first tries to gain access to the system event queue, then it wraps the `Runnable` and the lock object in an instance of `RunnableEvent`.

Once the `RunnableEvent` instance has been created, the `postRunnable()` method (which we have been in this whole time) checks to see if it did successfully gain access to the system event queue. This will only occur if we are not running as an applet, because applets do not have direct access to the system event queue. At this point, there are two possible paths, depending on whether we are running an applet or an application.

Applications

Since applications have direct access to the system event queue, we just post the `RunnableEvent` and return. The event gets dispatched at some point in the event-dispatching thread by being sent to `RunnableTarget`'s `processEvent()` method, which then sends it to the `processRunnableEvent()` method. If there was no lock used (for example, if `invokeLater()` was called) the `Runnable` is just executed and we are done. If there was a lock used (for example, if `invokeAndWait()` was called), we enter a synchronized block on the lock object so that nothing else can access that object when we execute the `Runnable`. Remember that this is the same lock object that the calling thread is waiting on from within `SwingUtilities.invokeAndWait()`. Once the `Runnable` finishes, we call `notify()` on this object, which then wakes up the calling thread. Then we are done.

Applets

`SystemEventQueueUtilities` does some very interesting things to get around the fact that applets do not have direct access to the system event queue. To summarize a quite involved workaround procedure, an invisible `RunnableCanvas` (a private inner class that extends `java.awt.Canvas`) is maintained for each applet and stored in a static `Hashtable` using the calling thread as its key. A `Vector` of `RunnableEvents` is also maintained. Instead of manually posting an event to the system event queue, a `RunnableCanvas` posts a `repaint()` request. Then, when the repaint request is dispatched in the event-dispatching thread, the appropriate `RunnableCanvas`'s `paint()` method is called as expected. This method has been overridden to locate any `RunnableEvents` (stored in the `Vector`) associated with a given `RunnableCanvas`, and to execute them (this is somewhat of a hack, but it works).

2.4   TIMERS

class javax.swing.Timer

You can think of the `Timer` as a unique thread conveniently provided by Swing to fire `ActionEvents` at specified intervals (although this is not exactly how a `Timer` works internally, as we will see in section 2.6). `ActionListeners` can be registered to receive these events just as we register them on buttons and other components. To create a simple `Timer` that fires `ActionEvents` every second, we can do something like the following:

```
import java.awt.event.*;
import javax.swing.*;

class TimerTest
{
 public TimerTest() {
  ActionListener act = new ActionListener() {
   public void actionPerformed(ActionEvent e) {
    System.out.println("Swing is powerful!!");
   }
  };
  Timer tim = new Timer(1000, act);
  tim.start();

  while(true) {};
 }

 public static void main( String args[] ) {
  new TimerTest();
 }
}
```

First we set up an `ActionListener` to receive `ActionEvents`. Then we build a new `Timer` by passing the following parameters to the constructor: the time in milliseconds between events, (the delay time), and an `ActionListener` to send `Timer` events to. Finally, we call the `Timer`'s `start()` method to turn it on. Since a GUI isn't running for us, the program will immediately exit; therefore, we set up a loop to let the `Timer` continue to do its job indefinitely (we will explain why this is necessary in section 2.6).

When you run this code, you will see "Swing is powerful!!" sent to standard output every second. Note that the Timer does not fire an event right when it is started. This is because its *initial delay* time defaults to the delay time passed to the constructor. If we want the Timer to fire an event right when it is started, we need to set the initial delay time to 0 using the setInitialDelay() method.

At any point, we can call stop() to stop the Timer and start() to start it (start() does nothing if the Timer is already running). We can call restart() on a Timer to start the whole process over. The restart() method is just a shortcut way to call stop() and start() sequentially.

We can set a Timer's delay using the setDelay() method and tell it whether to repeat using the setRepeats() method. Once a Timer has been set to non-repeating, it will fire only one action when started (or if it is currently running), and then it will stop.

The setCoalesce() method allows several Timer event postings to be combined (coalesced) into one. This can be useful under heavy loads when the TimerQueue thread (see 2.6) doesn't have enough processing time to handle all its Timers.

Timers are easy to use and can often be used as convenient replacements for building our own threads. However, there is a lot more going on behind the scenes that deserves to be revealed. Before we are ready to look at how Timers work under the hood, we'll take a look at Swing's SecurityContext-to-AppContext service class mapping for applets, as well as how applications manage their service classes (also using AppContext). If you are *not* curious about how Swing manages the sharing of service classes behind the scenes, you will want to skip the next section. Although we will refer to AppContext from time to time, it is by no means necessary for you to understand the details.

2.5   APPCONTEXT SERVICES

class sun.awt.AppContext [platform specific]

This section is only of interest to those seeking a low-level understanding of how service classes are shared throughout a Java session. Be aware that AppContext is not meant to be used by *any* developer, as it is not part of the Java 2 core API. We are discussing it here only to facilitate a more thorough understanding of how Swing service classes work behind the scenes.

AppContext is an application/applet (we'll say "app" for short) *service* table that is unique to each Java session. For applets, a separate AppContext exists for each SecurityContext which corresponds to an applet's codebase. For instance, if we have two applets on the same page, each using code from a different directory, both of those applets would have distinct SecurityContexts associated with them. If, however, they each were loaded from the same codebase, they would necessarily share a SecurityContext. Java applications do not have SecurityContexts. Rather, they run in namespaces which are distinguished by ClassLoaders. We will not go into the details of SecurityContexts or ClassLoaders here, but suffice it to say that they can be used by SecurityManagers to indicate security domains. The App-Context class is designed to take advantage of this by allowing only one instance of itself to exist per security domain. In this way, applets from different codebases cannot access each other's AppContext. So why is this significant? We're getting there!

A *shared instance* is an instance of a class that can normally be retrieved using a static method defined in that class. Each AppContext maintains a Hashtable of shared instances available to the associated security domain, and each instance is referred to as a *service*. When a service is requested for the first time, it registers its shared instance with the associated AppContext, meaning it creates a new instance of itself and adds it to the AppContext key/value mapping.

One reason these shared instances are registered with an AppContext, instead of being implemented as normal static instances directly retreivable by the service class, is for security purposes. Services registered with an AppContext can only be accessed by trusted apps, whereas classes directly providing static instances of themselves allow these instances to be used on a global basis (therefore requiring us to implement our own security mechanism if we want to limit access to them). Another reason is robustness. According to Tom Ball of Sun Microsystems, the less applets interact with each other in undocumented ways, the more robust they can be.

For example, suppose an app tries to access all of the key events on the system EventQueue (where all events get queued for processing in the event-dispatching thread) to try to steal passwords. By using distinct EventQueues in each AppContext, the only key events that the app would have access to are its own. (There is, in fact, only one EventQueue per AppContext.)

So how do we access our AppContext to add, remove, and retrieve services? AppContext is not meant to be accessed by developers. But we *can* if we really need to, though it would guarantee that our code would never be certified as 100% pure, because AppContext is not part of the core API. Nevertheless, here's what is involved: The static AppContext.getAppContext() method determines the correct AppContext to use, depending on whether we are running an applet or an application. We can then use the returned AppletContext's put(), get(), and remove() methods to manage shared instances. In order to do this, we would need to implement our own methods, such as the following:

```
private static Object appContextGet(Object key) {
  return sun.awt.AppContext.getAppContext().get(key);
}

private static void appContextPut(Object key, Object value) {
  sun.awt.AppContext.getAppContext().put(key, value);
}

private static void appContextRemove(Object key) {
  sun.awt.AppContext.getAppContext().remove(key);
}
```

In Swing, this functionality is implemented as three SwingUtilities static methods (refer to SwingUtilities.java source code):

```
static void appContextPut(Object key, Object value)
static void appContextRemove(Object key, Object value)
static Object appContextGet(Object key)
```

However, we cannot access these methods because they are package private. They are used by Swing's service classes. Some of the Swing service classes that register shared instances with AppContext include EventQueue, TimerQueue, ToolTipManager, RepaintManager, FocusManager, and UIManager.LAFState (all of which we will discuss at some point in this book). Interestingly, SwingUtilities secretly provides an invisible Frame instance registered with AppContext to act as the parent to all JDialogs and JWindows with null owners.

2.6 INSIDE TIMERS AND THE TIMERQUEUE

class javax.swing.TimerQueue [package private]

A `Timer` is an object containing a small `Runnable` capable of dispatching `ActionEvents` to a list of `ActionListeners` (which are stored in an `EventListenerList`). Each `Timer` instance is managed by the shared `TimerQueue` instance (which is registered with `AppContext`).

A `TimerQueue` is a service class whose job it is to manage all `Timer` instances in a Java session. The `TimerQueue` class provides the static `sharedInstance()` method to retrieve the `TimerQueue` service from `AppContext`. Whenever a new `Timer` is created and started it is added to the shared `TimerQueue`, which maintains a singly linked list of `Timers` sorted by the order in which they will expire (which is equal to the amount of time before a `Timer` will fire the next event).

The `TimerQueue` is a *daemon* thread which is started immediately upon instantiation. This occurs when `TimerQueue.sharedInstance()` is called for the first time (such as when the first `Timer` in a Java session is started). It continuously waits for the `Timer` with the nearest expiration time to expire. Once this occurs, it signals that `Timer` to post `ActionEvents` to all its listeners, it assigns a new `Timer` as the head of the list, and finally, it removes the expired `Timer`. If the expired `Timer`'s repeat mode is set to `true`, it is added back into the list at the appropriate place based on its delay time.

> **NOTE**   The real reason why the `Timer` example from section 2.4 would exit immediately if we didn't build a loop is because the `TimerQueue` is a *daemon* thread. Daemon threads are service threads. When the Java virtual machine has only daemon threads running, it will exit because it assumes that no real work is being done. Normally, this behavior is desirable.

A `Timer`'s events are always posted in a thread-safe manner to the event-dispatching thread by sending its `Runnable` object to `SwingUtilities.invokeLater()`.

2.7 JAVABEANS ARCHITECTURE

Since we are concerned with creating Swing applications in this book, we need to understand and appreciate the fact that every component in Swing is a JavaBean.

If you are familiar with the JavaBeans component model, you may want to skip to section 2.8.

2.7.1 The JavaBeans component model

The JavaBeans specification identifies five features that each bean is expected to provide. We will review these features here, along with the classes and mechanisms that make them possible. We'll construct a simple component such as a label, and apply what we discuss in this section to that component. We will also assume that you have a basic knowledge of the Java reflection API (the following list comes directly from the API documentation):

- Instances of `Class` represent classes and interfaces in a running Java application.
- A `Method` provides information about, and access to, a single method of a class or an interface.
- A `Field` provides information about, and dynamic access to, a single field of a class or an interface.

2.7.2 Introspection

Introspection is the ability to discover the methods, properties, and events information of a bean. This is accomplished through use of the `java.beans.Introspector` class. `Introspector` provides static methods to generate a `BeanInfo` object containing all discoverable information about a specific bean. This includes information from each of a bean's superclasses, unless we specify at which superclass introspection should stop (for example, we can specify the "depth" of an introspection). The following code retrieves all discoverable information of a bean:

```
BeanInfo myJavaBeanInfo =
    Introspector.getBeanInfo(myJavaBean);
```

A `BeanInfo` object partitions all of a bean's information into several groups. Here are a few:

- A `BeanDescriptor`: Provides general descriptive information such as a display name.
- An array of `EventSetDescriptors`: Provides information about a set of events a bean fires. These can be used to retrieve that bean's event-listener-related methods as `Method` instances, among other things.
- An array of `MethodDescriptors`: Provides information about the methods of a bean that are externally accessible (this would include, for instance, all public methods). This information is used to construct a `Method` instance for each method.
- An array of `PropertyDescriptors`: Provides information about each property that a bean maintains which can be accessed through `get`, `set`, and/or `is` methods. These objects can be used to construct `Method` and `Class` instances corresponding to that property's accessor methods and class type respectively.

2.7.3 Properties

As we discussed in section 2.1.1, beans support different types of properties. *Simple* properties are variables that, when modified, mean a bean will do nothing. *Bound* and *constrained* properties are variables that, when modified, instruct a bean to send notification events to any listeners. This notification takes the form of an event object which contains the property name, the old property value, and the new property value. Whenever a bound property changes, the bean should send out a `PropertyChangeEvent`. Whenever a constrained property is about to change, the bean should send out a `PropertyChangeEvent` *before* the change occurs, allowing the change to possibly be vetoed. Other objects can listen for these events and process them accordingly; this leads to *communication* (see 2.7.5).

Associated with properties are a bean's `setXX()`, `getXX()`, and `isXX()` methods. If a `setXX()` method is available, the associated property is said to be *writeable*. If a `getXX()` or `isXX()` method is available, the associated property is said to be *readable*. An `isXX()` method normally corresponds to retrieval of a boolean property (occasionally, `getXX()` methods are used for this as well).

2.7.4 Customization

A bean's properties are exposed through its `setXX()`, `getXX()`, and `isXX()` methods, and they can be modified at run-time (or design-time). JavaBeans are commonly used in interface development environments where property sheets can be displayed for each bean, thereby allowing read/write (depending on the available accessors) property functionality.

2.7.5 Communication

Beans are designed to send events that notify all event listeners registered with that bean whenever a bound or constrained property changes value. Apps are constructed by registering listeners from bean to bean. Since we can use introspection to determine event listener information about any bean, design tools can take advantage of this knowledge to allow more powerful, design-time customization. Communication is the basic glue that holds an interactive GUI together.

2.7.6 Persistency

All JavaBeans must implement the `Serializable` interface, either directly or indirectly, to allow serialization of their state into persistent storage (storage that exists beyond program termination). All objects are saved except those declared `transient`. (Note that `JComponent` directly implements this interface.)

Classes which need special processing during serialization need to implement the following private methods:

```
private void writeObject(java.io.ObjectOutputStreamout)
private void readObject(java.io.ObjectInputStream in )
```

These methods are called to write or read an instance of this class to a stream. The default serialization mechanism will be invoked to serialize all subclasses because these are private methods. (Refer to the API documentation or Java tutorial for more information about serialization.)

> **NOTE** As of the first release of Java 2, long-term persistence of Swing-based classes is not recommended, and it is subject to change in future releases. However, there is nothing wrong with implementing short-term persistence for things such as RMI or miscellaneous data transfer.

Classes that intend to take complete control of their serialization and deserialization should, instead, implement the `Externalizable` interface.

Two methods are defined in the `Externalizable` interface:

```
public void writeExternal(ObjectOutput out)
public void readExternal(ObjectInput in)
```

These methods will be invoked when `writeObject()` and `readObject()` (discussed above) are invoked to handle any serialization/deserialization.

2.7.7 A simple Swing-based JavaBean

Example 2.1 demonstrates how to build a serializable Swing-based JavaBean with simple, bound, constrained, and change properties.

Example 2.1

see \Chapter1\1

```java
import javax.swing.*;
import javax.swing.event.*;
import java.beans.*;
import java.awt.*;
import java.io.*;

public class BakedBean extends JComponent implements Externalizable
{
 // Property names (only needed for bound or constrained properties)
 public static final String BEAN_VALUE = "Value";
 public static final String BEAN_COLOR = "Color";

 // Properties
 private Font m_beanFont;        // simple
 private Dimension m_beanDimension; // simple
 private int m_beanValue;        // bound
 private Color m_beanColor;       // constrained
 private String m_beanString;     // change

 // Manages all PropertyChangeListeners
 protected SwingPropertyChangeSupport m_supporter =
  new SwingPropertyChangeSupport(this);

 // Manages all VetoableChangeListeners
 protected VetoableChangeSupport m_vetoer =
  new VetoableChangeSupport(this);

 // Only one ChangeEvent is needed since the event's only
 // state is the source property. The source of events generated
 // is always "this". You'll see this in lots of Swing source.
 protected transient ChangeEvent m_changeEvent = null;

 // This can manage all types of listeners, as long as we set
 // up the fireXX methods to correctly look through this list.
 // This makes you appreciate the XXSupport classes.
 protected EventListenerList m_listenerList =
  new EventListenerList();

 public BakedBean() {
  m_beanFont = new Font("SanSerif", Font.BOLD | Font.ITALIC, 12);
  m_beanDimension = new Dimension(150,100);
  m_beanValue = 0;
  m_beanColor = Color.black;
  m_beanString = "BakedBean #";
 }

 public void paintComponent(Graphics g) {
  super.paintComponent(g);
  g.setColor(m_beanColor);
  g.setFont(m_beanFont);
```

```java
    g.drawString(m_beanString + m_beanValue,30,30);
  }

  public void setBeanFont(Font font) {
    m_beanFont = font;
  }

  public Font getBeanFont() {
    return m_beanFont;
  }

  public void setBeanValue(int newValue) {
    int oldValue = m_beanValue;
    m_beanValue = newValue;

    // Notify all PropertyChangeListeners
    m_supporter.firePropertyChange(BEAN_VALUE,
      new Integer(oldValue), new Integer(newValue));
  }

  public int getBeanValue() {
    return m_beanValue;
  }

  public void setBeanColor(Color newColor)
    throws PropertyVetoException {
    Color oldColor = m_beanColor;

    // Notify all VetoableChangeListeners before making change
    // ...an exception will be thrown here if there is a veto
    // ...if not, we continue on and make the change
    m_vetoer.fireVetoableChange(BEAN_COLOR, oldColor, newColor);

    m_beanColor = newColor;
    m_supporter.firePropertyChange(BEAN_COLOR, oldColor, newColor);
  }

  public Color getBeanColor() {
    return m_beanColor;
  }

  public void setBeanString(String newString) {
    m_beanString = newString;

    // Notify all ChangeListeners
    fireStateChanged();
  }

  public String getBeanString() {
    return m_beanString;
  }

  public void setPreferredSize(Dimension dim) {
    m_beanDimension = dim;
  }

  public Dimension getPreferredSize() {
    return m_beanDimension;
  }
```

```java
    public void setMinimumSize(Dimension dim) {
     m_beanDimension = dim;
    }

    public Dimension getMinimumSize() {
     return m_beanDimension;
    }

    public void addPropertyChangeListener(
     PropertyChangeListener l) {
     m_supporter.addPropertyChangeListener(l);
    }

    public void removePropertyChangeListener(
     PropertyChangeListener l) {
     m_supporter.removePropertyChangeListener(l);
    }

    public void addVetoableChangeListener(
     VetoableChangeListener l) {
     m_vetoer.addVetoableChangeListener(l);
    }

    public void removeVetoableChangeListener(
     VetoableChangeListener l) {
     m_vetoer.removeVetoableChangeListener(l);
    }

    // Remember that EventListenerList is an array of
    // key/value pairs:
    //  key = XXListener class reference
    //  value = XXListener instance
    public void addChangeListener(ChangeListener l) {
     m_listenerList.add(ChangeListener.class, l);
    }

    public void removeChangeListener(ChangeListener l) {
     m_listenerList.remove(ChangeListener.class, l);
    }

    // This is typical EventListenerList dispatching code.
    // You'll see this in lots of Swing source.
    protected void fireStateChanged() {
     Object[] listeners = m_listenerList.getListenerList();
     // Process the listeners last to first, notifying
     // those that are interested in this event
     for (int i = listeners.length-2; i>=0; i-=2) {
      if (listeners[i]==ChangeListener.class) {
       if (m_changeEvent == null)
        m_changeEvent = new ChangeEvent(this);
        ((ChangeListener)listeners[i+1]).stateChanged(m_changeEvent);
      }
     }
    }

    public void writeExternal(ObjectOutput out) throws IOException {
     out.writeObject(m_beanFont);
```

```
    out.writeObject(m_beanDimension);
    out.writeInt(m_beanValue);
    out.writeObject(m_beanColor);
    out.writeObject(m_beanString);
  }

 public void readExternal(ObjectInput in)
  throws IOException, ClassNotFoundException {
  setBeanFont((Font)in.readObject());
  setPreferredSize((Dimension)in.readObject());
  // Use preferred size for minimum size
  setMinimumSize(getPreferredSize());
  setBeanValue(in.readInt());
  try {
   setBeanColor((Color)in.readObject());
  }
  catch (PropertyVetoException pve) {
   System.out.println("Color change vetoed.");
  }
  setBeanString((String)in.readObject());
 }

 public static void main(String[] args) {
  JFrame frame = new JFrame("BakedBean");
  frame.getContentPane().add(new BakedBean());
  frame.setVisible(true);
  frame.pack();
 }
}
```

BakedBean has a visual representation (this is not a requirement for a bean). It has *properties*: m_beanValue, m_beanColor, m_beanFont, m_beanDimension, and m_beanString. It supports *persistency* by implementing the Externalizable interface and implementing the writeExternal() and readExternal() methods to control its own serialization (note that the orders in which data is written and read match). BakedBean supports *customization* through its setXX() and getXX() methods, and it supports *communication* by allowing the registration of PropertyChangeListeners, VetoableChangeListeners, and ChangeListeners. And, without having to do anything special, it supports *introspection*.

Attaching a main method to display BakedBean in a frame does not get in the way of any JavaBeans functionality. Figure 2.1 shows BakedBean when it is executed as an application.

Figure 2.1
BakedBean in our custom Java-
Beans property editor

In chapter 18, section 18.9, we will construct a full-featured JavaBeans property editing environment. Figure 2.2 shows a BakedBean instance in this environment. The BakedBean shown has had its m_beanDimension, m_beanColor, and m_beanValue properties modified with our property editor, and it was then serialized to disk. What figure 2.2 really shows is an instance of that BakedBean after it had been deserialized (loaded from disk). Any Swing component can be created, modified, serialized, and deserialized using this environment because every component is JavaBeans compliant.

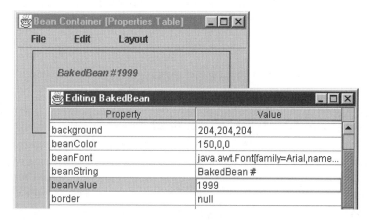

Figure 2.2   BakedBean in our custom JavaBeans property editor

2.8   *FONTS, COLORS, GRAPHICS, AND TEXT*

2.8.1   Fonts

class java.awt.Font, abstract class java.awt.GraphicsEnvironment

As we saw in the BakedBean example above, fonts are quite easy to create:

```
m_beanFont = new Font("SanSerif", Font.BOLD | Font.ITALIC, 12);
```

In this code, SanSerif is the font *name*, Font.BOLD | Font.ITALIC is the font *style* (which in this case is both bold and italic), and 12 is the font *size*. The Font class defines three static int constants to denote font style: Font.BOLD, Font.ITALIC, and Font.PLAIN. We can specify font size as any int in the Font constructor, as shown above. Using Java 2, we ask the local GraphicsEnvironment for a list of available font names at run-time.

```
GraphicsEnvironment ge = GraphicsEnvironment.
 getLocalGraphicsEnvironment();
String[] fontNames = ge.getAvailableFontFamilyNames();
```

NOTE   Java 2 introduces a new, powerful mechanism for communicating with devices that can render graphics, such as screens, printers, or image buffers. These devices are represented as instances of the GraphicsDevice class. Interestingly, a GraphicsDevice might reside on the local machine, or it might reside on a remote machine. Each GraphicsDevice has a set of GraphicsConfiguration objects associated with it. A GraphicsConfiguration describes specific characteristics of the associated device. Usually each GraphicsConfiguration of a GraphicsDevice represents a different mode of operation (for instance, resolution and the number of colors).

In JDK1.1 code, getting a list of font *name*s often looked like this:

```
String[] fontnames = Toolkit.getDefaultToolkit().getFontList();
```

The `getFontList()` method has been deprecated in Java 2, and this code should be updated.

`GraphicsEnvironment` is an abstract class that describes a collection of `GraphicsDevices`. Subclasses of `GraphicsEnvironment` must provide three methods for retrieving arrays of `Fonts` and `Font` information:

`Font[] getAllFonts()`: Retrieves all available `Fonts` in one-point size.

`String[] getAvailableFontFamilyNames()`: Retrieves the names of all available font families.

`String[] getAvailableFontFamilyNames(Locale l)`: Retrieves the names of all available font families using the specific `Locale` (internationalization support).

`GraphicsEnvironment` also provides static methods for retrieving `GraphicsDevices` and the local `GraphicsEnvironment` instance. In order to find out what `Fonts` are available to the system on which our program is running, we must refer to this local `GraphicsEnvironment` instance, as shown above. It is much more efficient and convenient to retrieve the available names and use them to construct `Fonts` than it is to retrieve an actual array of `Font` objects (no less, in one-point size).

We might think that, given a `Font` object, we can use typical `getXX()`/`setXX()` accessors to alter its name, style, and size. Well, we would be half right. We *can* use `getXX()` methods to retrieve this information from a `Font`:

```
String getName()
int getSize()
float getSize2D()
int getStyle()
```

However, we *cannot* use typical `setXX()` methods. Instead, we must use one of the following `Font` instance methods to derive a new `Font`:

```
deriveFont(float size)
deriveFont(int style)
deriveFont(int style, float size)
deriveFont(Map attributes)
deriveFont(AffineTransform trans)
deriveFont(int style, AffineTransform trans)
```

Normally, we will only be interested in the first three methods.

`AffineTransforms` are used in the world of Java 2D to perform things such as translations, scales, flips, rotations, and shears. A `Map` is an object that maps keys to values (it does not contain the objects involved), and the *attributes* referred to here are key/value pairs as described in the API documents for `java.text.TextAttribute` (this class is defined in the `java.awt.font` package that is new to Java 2, and is considered part of Java 2D—see chapter 23).

2.8.2 Colors

class java.awt.Color

The Color class provides several static Color instances to be used for convenience (Color.blue, Color.yellow, etc.). We can also construct a Color using the following constructors, among others:

```
Color(float r, float g, float b)
Color(int r, int g, int b)
Color(float r, float g, float b, float a)
Color(int r, int g, int b, int a)
```

Normally we use the first two methods, and if you are familiar with JDK1.1, you will probably recognize them. The first method allows red, green, and blue values to be specified as floats from 0.0 to 1.0. The second method takes these values as ints from 0 to 255.

The second two methods are new to Java 2. They each contain a fourth parameter which represents the Color's *alpha* value. The alpha value directly controls transparency. It defaults to 1.0 or 255, which means completely opaque. 0.0 or 0 means completely transparent.

As with Fonts, there are plenty of getXX() accessors but no setXX() accessors. Instead of modifying a Color object, we are normally expected to create a new one.

NOTE The Color class does have static brighter() and darker() methods that return a Color brighter or darker than the Color specified, but their behavior is unpredictable due to internal rounding errors. We suggest staying away from these methods for most practical purposes.

By specifying an alpha value, we can use the resulting Color as a component's background to make it transparent. This will work for any lightweight component provided by Swing such as labels, text components, and internal frames. (Of course, there will be component-specific issues involved, such as making the borders and title bar of an internal frame transparent.) The next section demonstrates a simple Swing canvas example that uses the alpha value to paint some transparent shapes.

NOTE A Swing component's opaque property, controlled using setOpaque(), is not directly related to Color transparency. For instance, if we have an opaque JLabel whose background has been set to a transparent green (Color(0,255,0,150)) the label's bounds will be completely filled with this color only because it is opaque. We will be able to see through it only because the color is transparent. If we then turned off opacity, the background of the label would not be rendered. Both need to be used together to create transparent components, but they are not directly related.

2.8.3 Graphics and text

abstract class java.awt.Graphics, abstract class java.awt.FontMetrics

Painting is different in Swing than it is in AWT. In AWT we typically override Component's paint() method to do rendering, and we override the update() method for things like implementing our own double-buffering or filling the background before paint() is called.

With Swing, component rendering is much more complex. Though JComponent is a subclass of Component, it uses the update() and paint() methods for different reasons. In fact, the update() method is never invoked at all. There are also five additional stages of painting that normally occur from within the paint() method. We will discuss this process in section 2.11, but suffice it to say here that any JComponent subclass that wants to take control of its own rendering should override the paintComponent() method and not the paint() method. Additionally, it should always begin its paintComponent() method with a call to super.paintComponent().

Knowing this, it is quite easy to build a JComponent that acts as our own *lightweight canvas*. All we have to do is subclass it and override the paintComponent() method. We can do all of our painting inside this method. This is how to take control of the rendering of simple custom components. However, do not attempt this with normal Swing components because UI delegates are in charge of their rendering (we will show you how to customize UI delegate rendering at the end of chapter 6 and throughout chapter 21).

NOTE   The AWT Canvas class can be replaced by a simplified version of the JCanvas class we define in the following example.

Inside the paintComponent() method, we have access to that component's Graphics object (often referred to as a component's *graphics context*) which we can use to paint shapes and draw lines and text. The Graphics class defines many methods used for these purposes; refer to the API docs for more information on these methods. Example 2.2 shows how to construct a JComponent subclass that paints an ImageIcon and some shapes and text using various Fonts and Colors, some completely opaque and some partially transparent (we saw similar but less interesting functionality in BakedBean). Figure 2.3 illustrates the output of example 2.2.

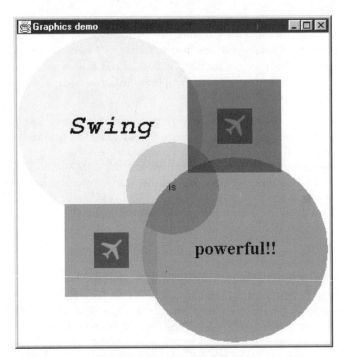

Figure 2.3 A Graphics demo in a lightweight canvas

Example 2.2

see \Chapter1\2

```java
import java.awt.*;
import javax.swing.*;
class TestFrame extends JFrame
{
 public TestFrame() {
  super( "Graphics demo" );
  getContentPane().add(new JCanvas());
 }

 public static void main( String args[] ) {
  TestFrame mainFrame = new TestFrame();
  mainFrame.pack();
  mainFrame.setVisible( true );
 }
}

class JCanvas extends JComponent {
 private static Color m_tRed = new Color(255,0,0,150);
 private static Color m_tGreen = new Color(0,255,0,150);
 private static Color m_tBlue = new Color(0,0,255,150);

 private static Font m_biFont =
  new Font("Monospaced", Font.BOLD | Font.ITALIC, 36);
 private static Font m_pFont =
  new Font("SanSerif", Font.PLAIN, 12);
 private static Font m_bFont = new Font("Serif", Font.BOLD, 24);

 private static ImageIcon m_flight = new ImageIcon("flight.gif");

 public JCanvas() {
  setDoubleBuffered(true);
  setOpaque(true);
 }

 public void paintComponent(Graphics g) {
  super.paintComponent(g);

  // Fill the entire component with white
  g.setColor(Color.white);
  g.fillRect(0,0,getWidth(),getHeight());

  // Filled yellow circle
  g.setColor(Color.yellow);
  g.fillOval(0,0,240,240);

  // Filled magenta circle
  g.setColor(Color.magenta);
  g.fillOval(160,160,240,240);

  // Paint the icon below the blue square
  int w = m_flight.getIconWidth();
```

```
    int h = m_flight.getIconHeight();
    m_flight.paintIcon(this,g,280-(w/2),120-(h/2));

    // Paint the icon below the red square
    m_flight.paintIcon(this,g,120-(w/2),280-(h/2));

    // Filled transparent red square
    g.setColor(m_tRed);
    g.fillRect(60,220,120,120);

    // Filled transparent green circle
    g.setColor(m_tGreen);
    g.fillOval(140,140,120,120);

    // Filled transparent blue square
    g.setColor(m_tBlue);
    g.fillRect(220,60,120,120);

    g.setColor(Color.black);

    // Bold, Italic, 36-point "Swing"
    g.setFont(m_biFont);
    FontMetrics fm = g.getFontMetrics();
    w = fm.stringWidth("Swing");
    h = fm.getAscent();
    g.drawString("Swing",120-(w/2),120+(h/4));

    // Plain, 12-point "is"
    g.setFont(m_pFont);
    fm = g.getFontMetrics();
    w = fm.stringWidth("is");
    h = fm.getAscent();
    g.drawString("is",200-(w/2),200+(h/4));

    // Bold, 24-point "powerful!!"
    g.setFont(m_bFont);
    fm = g.getFontMetrics();
    w = fm.stringWidth("powerful!!");
    h = fm.getAscent();
    g.drawString("powerful!!",280-(w/2),280+(h/4));
  }

  // Most layout managers need this information
  public Dimension getPreferredSize() {
   return new Dimension(400,400);
  }

  public Dimension getMinimumSize() {
   return getPreferredSize();
  }

  public Dimension getMaximumSize() {
   return getPreferredSize();
  }
}
```

Note that we override JComponent's getPreferredSize(), getMinimumSize(), and getMaximumSize() methods so most layout managers can intelligently size this component (otherwise, some layout managers will set its size to 0×0). It is always a good practice to override these methods when implementing custom components.

The Graphics class uses what is called the *clipping area*. Inside a component's paint() method, this is the region of that component's view that is being repainted (we often say that the clipping area represents the *damaged* or *dirtied* region of the component's view). Only painting done within the clipping area's bounds will actually be rendered. We can get the size and position of these bounds by calling getClipBounds(), which will give us back a Rectangle instance describing it. A clipping area is used for efficiency purposes: there is no reason to paint undamaged or invisible regions when we don't have to. We will show you how to extend this example to work with the clipping area for maximum efficiency in the next section.

NOTE All Swing components are double buffered by default. If we are building our own lightweight canvas, we do not have to worry about double-buffering. This is not the case with an AWT Canvas.

As we mentioned earlier, Fonts and Font manipulation are very complex under the hood. We are certainly glossing over their structure, but one thing we should discuss is how to obtain useful information about fonts and the text rendered using them. This involves the use of the FontMetrics class. In the example above, FontMetrics allowed us to determine the width and height of three Strings, rendered in the current Font associated with the Graphics object, so that we could draw them centered in the circles.

Figure 2.4 illustrates some of the most common information that can be retrieved from a FontMetrics object. The meaning of *baseline, ascent, descent,* and *height* should be clear from the diagram. The ascent is supposed to be the distance from the baseline to the top of most characters in that font. Notice that when we use g.drawString() to render text, the coordinates specified represent the position in which to place the baseline of the first character.

FontMetrics provides several methods for retrieving this and more detailed information, such as the width of a String rendered in the associated Font.

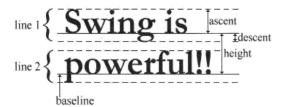

Figure 2.4
Using FontMetrics

In order to get a FontMetrics instance, we first tell our Graphics object to use the Font we are interested in examining using the setFont() method. Then we create the FontMetrics instance by calling getFontMetrics() on our Graphics object:

```
g.setFont(m_biFont);
FontMetrics fm = g.getFontMetrics();
```

A typical operation when rendering text is to center it on a given point. Suppose we want to center the text "Swing" on 200,200. Here is the code we would use (assuming we have retrieved the FontMetrics object, fm, as shown above):

```
int w = fm.stringWidth("Swing");
int h = fm.getAscent();
g.drawString("Swing",200-(w/2),200+(h/4));
```

We get the width of "Swing" in the current font, divide it by two, and subtract it from 200 to center the text horizontally. To center it vertically, we get the ascent of the current font, divide it by four, and add 200. The reason we divide the ascent by four is probably NOT so clear but we'll explain it in the following example.

It is now time to address a common mistake that has arisen with Java 2. Figure 2.4 is not an accurate way to document FontMetrics. This is the way we have seen things documented in the Java tutorial and just about everywhere else that we have referenced. However, there appear to be a few problems with FontMetrics as of Java 2 FCS. Example 2.3 is a simple program that demonstrates these problems. Our program will draw the text "Swing" in a 36-point bold, monospaced font. We'll draw lines where its ascent, ascent/2, ascent/4, baseline, and descent lie. Figure 2.5 illustrates this.

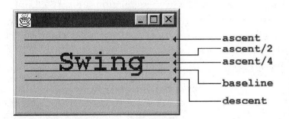

Figure 2.5
The real deal with
FontMetrics **in Java 2**

Example 2.3

TestFrame.java

See \Chapter1\2\fontmetrics

```java
import java.awt.*;
import javax.swing.*;

class TestFrame extends JFrame
{
 public TestFrame() {
  super( "Let's get it straight!" );
  getContentPane().add(new JCanvas());
 }
 public static void main( String args[] ) {
  TestFrame mainFrame = new TestFrame();
  mainFrame.pack();
  mainFrame.setVisible( true );
 }
}

class JCanvas extends JComponent
{
 private static Font m_biFont = new Font("Monospaced", Font.BOLD, 36);

 public void paintComponent(Graphics g) {
  g.setColor(Color.black);
```

CHAPTER 2 SWING MECHANICS

```
    // Bold, 36-point "Swing"
    g.setFont(m_biFont);
    FontMetrics fm = g.getFontMetrics();
    int h = fm.getAscent();

    g.drawString("Swing",50,50); // Try these as well: Ñ Ö Ü ^

    // Draw ascent line
    g.drawLine(10,50-h,190,50-h);

    // Draw ascent/2 line
    g.drawLine(10,50-(h/2),190,50-(h/2));

    // Draw ascent/4 line
    g.drawLine(10,50-(h/4),190,50-(h/4));

    // Draw baseline line
    g.drawLine(10,50,190,50);

    // Draw descent line
    g.drawLine(10,50+fm.getDescent(),190,50+fm.getDescent());
  }

 public Dimension getPreferredSize() {
  return new Dimension(200,100);
  }
}
```

We encourage you to try this demo program with various fonts, font sizes, and even characters with diacritical marks such as Ñ, Ö, or Ü. You may find that the ascent is always much higher than it is typically documented to be, and the descent is always lower. The most reliable means of vertically centering text we found turned out to be baseline + ascent/4. However, baseline + descent might also be used, and, depending on the font being used, it may provide more accurate centering.

The point is that there is no correct way to perform this task because of the current state of FontMetrics in Java 2. You may experience very different results if you're not using the first release of Java 2. It is a good idea to run the sample program we just gave you and verify whether results similar to those shown in figure 2.5 are produced on your system. If they're not, you may want to use a different centering mechanism for your text; it should be fairly simple to determine through experimentation with this application.

NOTE   In JDK1.1 code, getting a FontMetrics instance often looked like this:

FontMetrics fm = Toolkit.getDefaultToolkit().getFontMetrics(myfont);

The getFontMetrics() method has been deprecated in Java 2 and this code should be updated.

2.9   *USING THE GRAPHICS CLIPPING AREA*

We can use the clipping area to optimize component rendering. This may not noticeably improve rendering speed for simple components such as JCanvas above, but it is important to understand how to implement such functionality, as Swing's whole painting system is based on this concept (you will find out more about this in the next section).

In example 2.4, we'll modify JCanvas so that each of our shapes, strings, and images is only painted if the clipping area intersects its bounding rectangular region. (These intersections are fairly simple to compute, and it may be helpful for you to work through and verify each one.) Additionally, we'll maintain a local counter that is incremented each time one of our items is painted. At the end of the paintComponent() method, we'll display the total number of items that were painted. Our optimized JCanvas paintComponent() method (with counter) follows.

Example 2.4

JCanvas.java

see \Chapter1\3

```
public void paintComponent(Graphics g) {
 super.paintComponent(g);

 // Counter
 int c = 0;

 // For use below
 int w = 0;
 int h = 0;
 int d = 0;

 // Get damaged region
 Rectangle r = g.getClipBounds();
 int clipx = r.x;
 int clipy = r.y;
 int clipw = r.width;
 int cliph = r.height;

 // Fill damaged region only
 g.setColor(Color.white);
 g.fillRect(clipx,clipy,clipw,cliph);

 // Draw filled yellow circle if bounding region has been damaged
 if (clipx <= 240 && clipy <= 240) {
  g.setColor(Color.yellow);
  g.fillOval(0,0,240,240); c++;
 }

 // Draw filled magenta circle if bounding region has been damaged
 if (clipx + clipw >= 160 && clipx <= 400
   && clipy + cliph >= 160 && clipy <= 400) {
  g.setColor(Color.magenta);
  g.fillOval(160,160,240,240); c++;
 }

 w = m_flight.getIconWidth();
 h = m_flight.getIconHeight();
 // Paint the icon below blue square if bounding region is damaged
 if (clipx + clipw >= 280-(w/2) && clipx <= (280+(w/2))
   && clipy + cliph >= 120-(h/2) && clipy <= (120+(h/2))) {
  m_flight.paintIcon(this,g,280-(w/2),120-(h/2)); c++;
 }

 // Paint the icon below red square if bounding region is damaged
```

```
if (clipx + clipw >= 120-(w/2) && clipx <= (120+(w/2))
  && clipy + cliph >= 280-(h/2) && clipy <= (280+(h/2))) {
 m_flight.paintIcon(this,g,120-(w/2),280-(h/2)); c++;
}

// Draw filled transparent red square if bounding region is damaged
if (clipx + clipw >= 60 && clipx <= 180
  && clipy + cliph >= 220 && clipy <= 340) {
 g.setColor(m_tRed);
 g.fillRect(60,220,120,120); c++;
}

// Draw filled transparent green circle if bounding region is damaged
if (clipx + clipw > 140 && clipx < 260
  && clipy + cliph > 140 && clipy < 260) {
 g.setColor(m_tGreen);
 g.fillOval(140,140,120,120); c++;
}

// Draw filled transparent blue square if bounding region is damaged
if (clipx + clipw > 220 && clipx < 380
  && clipy + cliph > 60 && clipy < 180) {
 g.setColor(m_tBlue);
 g.fillRect(220,60,120,120); c++;
}

g.setColor(Color.black);

g.setFont(m_biFont);
FontMetrics fm = g.getFontMetrics();
w = fm.stringWidth("Swing");
h = fm.getAscent();
d = fm.getDescent();
// Bold, Italic, 36-point "Swing" if bounding region is damaged
if (clipx + clipw > 120-(w/2) && clipx < (120+(w/2))
  && clipy + cliph > (120+(h/4))-h && clipy < (120+(h/4))+d)
{
 g.drawString("Swing",120-(w/2),120+(h/4)); c++;
}

g.setFont(m_pFont);
fm = g.getFontMetrics();
w = fm.stringWidth("is");
h = fm.getAscent();
d = fm.getDescent();
// Plain, 12-point "is" if bounding region is damaged
if (clipx + clipw > 200-(w/2) && clipx < (200+(w/2))
  && clipy + cliph > (200+(h/4))-h && clipy < (200+(h/4))+d)
{
 g.drawString("is",200-(w/2),200+(h/4)); c++;
}

g.setFont(m_bFont);
fm = g.getFontMetrics();
w = fm.stringWidth("powerful!!");
h = fm.getAscent();
```

```
   d = fm.getDescent();
   // Bold, 24-point "powerful!!" if bounding region is damaged
   if (clipx + clipw > 280-(w/2) && clipx < (280+(w/2))
     && clipy + cliph > (280+(h/4))-h && clipy < (280+(h/4))+d)
   {
    g.drawString("powerful!!",280-(w/2),280+(h/4)); c++;
   }

   System.out.println("# items repainted = " + c + "/10");
 }
```

Try running this example and dragging another window in your desktop over parts of the JCanvas. Keep your console in view so that you can monitor how many items are painted during each repaint. Your output should be displayed something like the following (of course, you'll probably see different numbers):

```
# items repainted = 4/10
# items repainted = 0/10
# items repainted = 2/10
# items repainted = 2/10
# items repainted = 1/10
# items repainted = 2/10
# items repainted = 10/10
# items repainted = 10/10
# items repainted = 8/10
# items repainted = 4/10
```

Optimizing this canvas wasn't that bad, but imagine how tough it would be to optimize a container with a variable number of children, possibly overlapping, with double-buffering options and transparency. This is what JComponent does, and it does it quite efficiently. We will learn a little more about how this is done in section 2.11. But first we'll finish our high-level overview of graphics by introducing a very powerful and well-met feature new to Swing: graphics debugging.

2.10 GRAPHICS DEBUGGING

Graphics debugging provides the ability to observe each painting operation that occurs during the rendering of a component and all of its children. This is done in slow motion, using distinct flashes to indicate the region being painted. It is intended to help find problems with rendering, layouts, and container hierarchies—just about any display-related problems. If graphics debugging is enabled, the Graphics object used in painting is actually an instance of DebugGraphics (a subclass of Graphics). JComponent, and thus all Swing components, supports graphics debugging and it can be turned on or off with JComponent's setDebug-GraphicsOptions() method. This method takes an int parameter which is normally one of four static values defined in DebugGraphics (or it's a bitmask combination using the bitwise | operator).

2.10.1 Graphics debugging options

There are four graphics debugging options: DebugGraphics.FLASH_OPTION, DebugGraphics.LOG_OPTION, DebugGraphics.BUFFERED_OPTION, and DebugGraphics.NONE_OPTION. They will all be discussed in this section.

With the `DebugGraphics.FLASH_OPTION`, each paint operation flashes a specified number of times, in a specified flash color, with a specified flash interval. The default flash interval is 250ms, the default flash number is 4, and the default flash color is red. These values can be sct with the following `DebugGraphics` static methods:

```
setFlashTime(int flashTime)
setFlashCount(int flashCount)
setFlashColor(Color flashColor)
```

If we don't disable double-buffering in the `RepaintManager` (which is discussed in the next section), we will not see the painting as it occurs:

```
RepaintManager.currentManager(null).
 setDoubleBufferingEnabled(false);
```

NOTE   Turning off buffering in the `RepaintManager` has the effect of ignoring *every* component's `doubleBuffered` property.

The `DebugGraphics.LOG_OPTION` sends messages describing each paint operation as it occurs. By default, these messages are directed to standard output (the console: `System.out`). However, we can change the log destination with `DebugGraphics`' static `setLogStream()` method. This method takes a `PrintStream` parameter. To send output to a file, we would do something like the following:

```
PrintStream debugStream = null;
try {
 debugStream = new PrintStream(
  new FileOutputStream("JCDebug.txt"));
}
catch (Exception e) {
 System.out.println("can't open JCDebug.txt..");
}
DebugGraphics.setLogStream(debugStream);
```

If at some point we need to change the log stream back to standard output, we can do this:

```
DebugGraphics.setLogStream(System.out);
```

We can insert any string into the log by retrieving it with `DebugGraphics`' static `logStream()` method, and then printing into it:

```
PrintStream ps = DebugGraphics.logStream();
ps.println("\n===> paintComponent ENTERED <===");
```

WARNING   Writing a log to a file will overwrite that file each time we reset the stream.

Each operation is printed with the following syntax:

```
"Graphics" + (isDrawingBuffer() ? "<B>" : "") +
 "(" + graphicsID + "-" + debugOptions + ")"
```

Each line starts with "Graphics." The `isDrawingBuffer()` method tells us whether buffering is enabled. If it is, a "<B>" is appended. The `graphicsID` and `debugOptions` values are then placed in parentheses, and separated by a "-." The `graphicsID` value represents the number of DebugGraphics instances that have been created during the application's lifetime (it's a static int counter). The debugOptions value represents the current debugging mode:

```
LOG_OPTION = 1
LOG_OPTION and FLASH_OPTION = 3
LOG_OPTION and BUFFERED_OPTION = 5
LOG_OPTION, FLASH_OPTION, and BUFFERED_OPTION = 7
```

For example, with logging and flashing enabled, we see output similar to the following for each operation:

```
Graphics(1-3) Setting color: java.awt.Color[r=0,g=255,b=0]
```

Calls to each Graphics method will get logged when this option is enabled. The above line was generated when a call to setColor() was made.

The DebugGraphics.BUFFERED_OPTION is supposed to pop up a frame showing rendering as it occurs in the offscreen buffer if double-buffering is enabled. As of the Java 2 FCS, this option is not functional.

The DebugGraphics.NONE_OPTION nullifies graphics debugging settings and shuts off graphics debugging altogether.

2.10.2 Graphics debugging caveats

There are two issues to be aware of when using graphics debugging. First, graphics debugging will not work for any component whose UI is null. Thus, if you have created a direct JComponent subclass without a UI delegate, as we did with JCanvas above, graphics debugging will simply do nothing. The simplest way to work around this is to define a trivial (empty) UI delegate. We'll show you how to do this in the example below.

Second, DebugGraphics does not properly clean up after itself. By default, a solid red flash color is used. When a region is flashed, that region is filled in with the red flash color and it does not get erased—it just gets painted over. This presents a problem because transparent rendering will not show up as transparent. Instead, it will be alpha-blended with the red below (or whatever the flash color happens to be set to). This is not necessarily a design flaw, because there is nothing stopping us from using a completely transparent flash color. With an alpha value of 0, the flash color will never be seen. The only downside is that we don't see any flashing. However, in most cases it is easy to follow what is being drawn if we set the flashTime and flashCount to wait long enough between operations.

2.10.3 Using Graphics debugging

We'll now enable graphics debugging in our JCanvas example from the last two sections. Because we must have a non-null UI delegate, we define a trivial extension of ComponentUI and implement its createUI() method to return a static instance of itself:

```
class EmptyUI extends ComponentUI
{
 private static final EmptyUI sharedInstance = new EmptyUI();

 public static ComponentUI createUI(JComponent c) {
  return sharedInstance;
 }
}
```

In order to properly associate this UI delegate with JCanvas, we simply call `super.setUI(EmptyUI.createUI(this))` from the JCanvas constructor. We also set up a `PrintStream` variable in JCanvas and use it to add a few of our own lines to the log stream during the `paintComponent()` method in order to log when the method starts and finishes. Other than this, no changes have been made to the JCanvas's `paintComponent()` code.

In our test application, `TestFrame` (example 2.5), we create an instance of JCanvas and enable graphics debugging with the LOG_OPTION and FLASH_OPTION options. We disable buffering in the `RepaintManager`, set the flash time to 100ms, set the flash count to 2, and use a completely transparent flash color.

Example 2.5

TestFrame.java

see \Chapter1\4

```java
import java.awt.*;
import javax.swing.*;
import javax.swing.plaf.*;
import java.io.*;

class TestFrame extends JFrame
{
 public TestFrame() {
  super( "Graphics demo" );
  JCanvas jc = new JCanvas();
  RepaintManager.currentManager(jc).
   setDoubleBufferingEnabled(false);
  jc.setDebugGraphicsOptions(DebugGraphics.LOG_OPTION |
   DebugGraphics.FLASH_OPTION);
  DebugGraphics.setFlashTime( 100 );
  DebugGraphics.setFlashCount( 2 );
  DebugGraphics.setFlashColor(new Color(0,0,0,0));
  getContentPane().add(jc);
 }

 public static void main( String args[] ) {
  TestFrame mainFrame = new TestFrame();
  mainFrame.pack();
  mainFrame.setVisible( true );
 }
}

class JCanvas extends JComponent
{
 // Unchanged code from example 2.4

 private PrintStream ps;

 public JCanvas() {
  super.setUI(EmptyUI.createUI(this));
 }
```

```
public void paintComponent(Graphics g) {
  super.paintComponent(g);

  ps = DebugGraphics.logStream();
  ps.println("\n===> paintComponent ENTERED <===");

  // All painting code unchanged

  ps.println("\n# items repainted = " + c + "/10");
  ps.println("===> paintComponent FINISHED <===\n");
}

  // Unchanged code from example 2.4
}

class EmptyUI extends ComponentUI
{
 private static final EmptyUI sharedInstance = new EmptyUI();
 public static ComponentUI createUI(JComponent c) {
  return sharedInstance;
 }
}
```

By setting the LOG_OPTION, graphics debugging provides us with a more informative way of checking how well our clipping area optimization we discussed in the last section works. When this example is run, you should see the following output in your console, assuming you don't obscure JCanvas's visible region as it is painted for the first time:

```
Graphics(0-3) Enabling debug
Graphics(0-3) Setting color:
  javax.swing.plaf.ColorUIResource[r=0,g=0,b=0]
Graphics(0-3) Setting font:
  javax.swing.plaf.FontUIResource[family=dialog,name=Dialog,
  style=plain,size=12]

===> paintComponent ENTERED <===
Graphics(1-3) Setting color: java.awt.Color[r=255,g=255,b=255]
Graphics(1-3) Filling rect: java.awt.Rectangle[x=0,y=0,
  width=400,height=400]
Graphics(1-3) Setting color: java.awt.Color[r=255,g=255,b=0]
Graphics(1-3) Filling oval: java.awt.Rectangle[x=0,y=0,
  width=240,height=240]
Graphics(1-3) Setting color: java.awt.Color[r=255,g=0,b=255]
Graphics(1-3) Filling oval:
  java.awt.Rectangle[x=160,y=160,width=240,height=240]
Graphics(1-3) Drawing image: sun.awt.windows.WImage@32a5625a at:
  java.awt.Point[x=258,y=97]
Graphics(1-3) Drawing image: sun.awt.windows.WImage@32a5625a at:
  java.awt.Point[x=98,y=257]
Graphics(1-3) Setting color: java.awt.Color[r=255,g=0,b=0]
Graphics(1-3) Filling rect:
  java.awt.Rectangle[x=60,y=220,width=120,height=120]
Graphics(1-3) Setting color: java.awt.Color[r=0,g=255,b=0]
Graphics(1-3) Filling oval:
  java.awt.Rectangle[x=140,y=140,width=120,height=120]
```

```
Graphics(1-3) Setting color: java.awt.Color[r=0,g=0,b=255]
Graphics(1-3) Filling rect:
  java.awt.Rectangle[x=220,y=60,width=120,height=120]
Graphics(1-3) Setting color: java.awt.Color[r=0,g=0,b=0]
Graphics(1-3) Setting font:
  java.awt.Font[family=monospaced.bolditalic,name=Mono
  spaced,style=bolditalic,size=36]
Graphics(1-3) Drawing string: "Swing" at:
  java.awt.Point[x=65,y=129]
Graphics(1-3) Setting font:
  java.awt.Font[family=Arial,name=SanSerif,style=plain,size=12]
Graphics(1-3) Drawing string: "is" at:
  java.awt.Point[x=195,y=203]
Graphics(1-3) Setting font:
  java.awt.Font[family=serif.bold,name=Serif,style=bold,size=24]
Graphics(1-3) Drawing string: "powerful!!" at:
  java.awt.Point[x=228,y=286]
# items repainted = 10/10
===> paintComponent FINISHED <===
```

2.11   PAINTING AND VALIDATION

At the heart of JComponent's painting and validation mechanism lies a service class called
RepaintManager. The RepaintManager is responsible for sending painting and validation
requests to the system event queue for dispatching. To summarize, it does this by intercepting
repaint() and revalidate() requests, coalescing any requests where possible, wrapping
them in Runnable objects, and sending them to invokeLater(). A few issues we have
encountered in this chapter deserve more attention here before we actually discuss details of
the painting and validation processes.

NOTE   This section contains a relatively exhaustive explanation of the most complex
mechanism underlying Swing. If you are relatively new to Java or Swing, we encourage you to skim this section now and come back at a later time for a more complete reading. If you are just looking for information on how to override and use
your own painting methods, see section 2.8. For customizing UI delegate rendering, see chapter 21.

REFERENCE   For a higher-level summary of the painting process, see the Swing Connection article "Painting in AWT and Swing" at http://java.sun.com/products/jfc/tsc/special_
report/Painting/painting.html.

2.11.1   Double-buffering

We've mentioned double-buffering, but you may be wondering how to disable it in the
RepaintManager and how to specify the double-buffering of individual components with
JComponent's setDoubleBuffered() method. In this section, we'll explain how it works.

Double-buffering is the technique of painting into an off-screen image rather than painting directly to a visible component. In the end, the resulting image is painted to the screen relatively quickly. Using AWT components, developers were required to implement their own

double-buffering to reduce flashing. It was clear that double-buffering should be a built-in feature because of its widespread use. Thus, it is not much of a surprise to find this feature in Swing.

Behind the scenes, double-buffering consists of creating an `Image` and retrieving its `Graphics` object for use in all painting methods. If the component being repainted has children, this `Graphics` object will be passed down to them to use for painting, and so on. So if we are using double-buffering for a component, all its children will also be using double-buffering (regardless of whether they have double-buffering enabled) because they will be rendering into the same `Graphics` object. There is only one off-screen image per `RepaintManager`, and there is normally only one `RepaintManager` instance per applet or application (`RepaintManager` is a service class that registers a shared instance of itself with `AppContext`; see section 2.5 for details).

As we will discuss in chapter 3, `JRootPane` is the top-level Swing component in any window, including `JInternalFrame` (which isn't really a window). By enabling double-buffering on `JRootPane`, all of its children will also be painted using double-buffering. As we saw in the last section, `RepaintManager` also provides global control over all component double-buffering. So another way to guarantee that all components will use double-buffering is to call

```
RepaintManager.currentManager(null).setDoubleBufferingEnabled(true);
```

2.11.2   Optimized drawing

We haven't yet really discussed the fact that components can overlap each other in Swing, but they can. `JLayeredPane`, for example, is a container that allows any number of components to overlap each other. Repainting such a container is much more complex than repainting a container we know does not allow overlapping, mainly because of the ability for components to be transparent.

What does it mean for a component to be transparent? Technically, this means its `isOpaque()` method returns `false`. We can set this property by calling `setOpaque()`. Opacity means, in this context, that a component will paint every pixel within its bounds. If the opaque property is set to `false`, we are not guaranteed that this will happen. We will see that when it is set to `false`, it increases the workload of the whole painting mechanism.

`JComponent`'s `isOptimizedDrawingEnabled()` method is overriden to return `true` for almost all `JComponent` subclasses except `JLayeredPane`, `JViewport`, and `JDesktopPane` (which is a subclass of `JLayeredPane`). Basically, calling this method is equivalent to asking a component whether it is possible that any of its child components can overlap each other. If it is possible, then much more repainting work must be done to take into account the fact that any number of components, from virtually anywhere in our container hierarchy, can overlap each other. Since components can be transparent, components layered completely behind others may still show through. Such components are not necessarily siblings (meaning in the same container) because we could conceivably have several non-opaque containers layered one on top of another. In situations like this, we must do a whole lot of "tree walking" to figure out which components need to be refreshed. If `isOptimizedDrawingEnabled()` is overridden to return `true`, then we assume we do not have to consider any situations like this. Thus, painting becomes more efficient, or optimized.

2.11.3 Root validation

A `revalidate()` request is generated when a component needs to be laid out again. When a request is received from a certain component, there must be some way of determining whether laying that component out will affect anything else. `JComponent`'s `isValidateRoot()` method returns `false` for most components. Calling this method is equivalent to asking it the question: If I lay your contents out again, can you guarantee that none of your parents or siblings will be adversely affected—meaning will they need to be laid out again? By default, only `JRootPane`, `JScrollPane`, and `JTextField` return `true`. This seems surprising at first, but it is true that these components are the only Swing components whose contents can be successfully laid out in any situation without affecting parents or siblings. No matter how big we make anything *inside* a `JRootPane`, `JScrollPane`, or `JTextField`, the container will not change size or location unless some *outside* influence comes into play, such as a sibling or parent. To help convince you of this, try adding a multi-line text component to a container *without* placing it in a scroll pane. You may notice that creating new lines will change its size, depending on the layout. The point is not that it rarely happens or that it can be prevented, but that it *can* happen. This is the type of incident that `isValidateRoot()` is supposed to warn us about. So where is this method used?

A component or its parent is normally revalidated when a property value changes and that component's size, location, or internal layout has been affected. By recursively calling `isValidateRoot()` on a Swing component's parent until we obtain `true`, we will end with the closest ancestor of that component that guarantees us its validation will not affect its siblings or parents. We will see that `RepaintManager` relies on this method for dispatching validation requests.

NOTE   When we say siblings, we mean components in the same container. When we say parents, we mean parent containers.

NOTE   Cell renderers used in components such as `JList`, `JTree`, and `JTable` are special in that they are wrapped in instances of `CellRendererPane` and all validation and repainting requests do not propogate up through containment hierarchy. See chapter 17 for more information about `CellRendererPane` and why this behavior exists. We'll simply say here that cell renderers do not follow the painting and validation scheme discussed in this section.

2.11.4 RepaintManager

class javax.swing.RepaintManager

There is usually only one instance of a service class in use per applet or application. So unless we specifically create our own instance of `RepaintManager`, which we will almost never need to do, all repainting is managed by the shared instance which is registered with `AppContext`. We normally retrieve it using `RepaintManager`'s static `currentManager()` method:

```
myRepaintManager = RepaintManager.currentManager(null);
```

This method takes a `Component` as its parameter. However, it doesn't matter what we pass it. In fact, the component passed to this method is not used anywhere inside the method at all (see the RepaintManager.java source code), so a value of `null` can safely be used here. (This definition exists for subclasses to use if they want to work with more than one `RepaintManager`, possibly on a per-component basis.)

`RepaintManager` exists for two purposes: to provide efficient revalidation and repainting. It intercepts all `repaint()` and `revalidate()` requests. This class also handles all double-buffering in Swing and maintains a single `Image` used for this purpose. This `Image`'s maximum size is, by default, the size of the screen. However, we can set its size manually using `RepaintManager`'s `setDoubleBufferMaximumSize()` method. (All other `RepaintManager` functionality will be discussed throughout this section where applicable.)

2.11.5 Revalidation

`RepaintManager` maintains a `Vector` of components that need to be validated. Whenever a `revalidate()` request is intercepted, the source component is sent to the `addInvalidComponent()` method and its `validateRoot` property is checked using `isValidateRoot()`. This occurs recursively on that component's parent until `isValidateRoot()` returns `true`. The resulting component, if any, is then checked for visibility. If any one of its parent containers is not visible, there is no reason to validate it. Otherwise, if no parent container returns true for `isValidateRoot()`, `RepaintManager` "walks down the component's tree" until it reaches the root component, which will be a `Window` or an `Applet`. `RepaintManager` then checks the invalid components `Vector`, and if the component isn't already there, it is added. After being successfully added, `RepaintManager` then passes the root container to the `SystemEventQueueUtilities`' `queueComponentWorkRequest()` method (we saw this class in section 2.3). This method checks to see if there is a `ComponentWorkRequest` (this is a private static class in `SystemEventQueueUtilities` that implements `Runnable`) corresponding to that root already stored in the work requests table. If there isn't one, a new one is created. If one already exists, we just grab a reference to it. Then we synchronize access to that `ComponentWorkRequest`, place it in the work requests table if it is a new one, and check if it is pending (meaning it has been added to the system event queue). If it isn't pending, we send it to `SwingUtilities.invokeLater()`. It is then marked as pending and we leave the synchronized block. When it is finally run from the event-dispatching thread, it notifies `RepaintManager` to execute `validateInvalidComponents()`, followed by `paintDirtyRegions()`.

The `validateInvalidComponents()` method checks `RepaintManager`'s `Vector` that contains the components which are in need of validation, and it calls `validate()` on each one. (This method is actually a bit more careful than we describe here, as it synchronizes access to prevent the addition of invalid components while executing).

NOTE   Remember that `validateInvalidComponents()` should only be called from within the event-dispatching thread. Never call this method from any other thread. The same rules apply for `paintDirtyRegions()`.

The `paintDirtyRegions()` method is much more complicated, and we'll discuss *some* of its details below. For now, all you need to know is that this method paints all the damaged regions of each component maintained by `RepaintManager`.

2.11.6 Repainting

`JComponent` defines two `repaint()` methods, and the no-argument version of `repaint()` is inherited from `java.awt.Container`:

```
public void repaint(long tm, int x, int y, int width, int height)
```

```
public void repaint(Rectangle r)
public repaint() // Inherited from java.awt.Container
```

If you call the no-argument version, the whole component is repainted. For small, simple components, this is fine. But for larger, more complex components, this is often not efficient. The other two methods take the bounding region to be repainted (the *dirtied* region) as parameters. The first method's int parameters correspond to the x-coordinate, y-coordinate, width, and height of that region. The second method takes the same information encapsulated in a Rectange instance. The second repaint() method shown above just sends its traffic to the first. The first method sends the dirtied region's parameters to RepaintManager's addDirty-Region() method.

NOTE   The long parameter in the first repaint() method represents absolutely nothing and is not used at all. It does not matter what value you use for this. The only reason it is here is to override the correct repaint() method from java.awt.Component.

RepaintManager maintains a Hashtable of dirty regions. Each component will have, at most, one dirty region in this table at any time. When a dirty region is added using addDirtyRegion(), the size of the region and the component are checked. If either item has a width or height <= 0, the method returns and nothing happens. If a measurement is bigger than 0×0, the source component's visibility is then tested, along with each of its ancestors. If they are all visible, its root component, a Window or Applet, is located by "walking down its tree," similar to what occurs in addInvalidateComponent(). The dirty regions Hashtable is then asked if it already has a dirty region of our component stored. If it does, it returns its value (a Rectangle) and the handy SwingUtilities.computeUnion() method is used to combine the new dirty region with the old one. Finally, RepaintManager passes the root to the SystemEventQueueUtilities' queueComponentWorkRequest() method. What happens from here on is identical to what we saw earlier for revalidation.

Now we can talk a bit about the paintDirtyRegions() method we summarized earlier. (Remember that this should only be called from within the event-dispatching thread.) This method starts out by creating a local reference to RepaintManger's dirty regions Hashtable and redirecting RepaintManager's dirty regions Hashtable reference to a different, empty one. This is all done in a critical section so that no dirty regions can be added while the swap occurs. The remainder of this method is fairly long and complicated, so we'll conclude with a summary of the most significant code (see the RepaintManager.java source code for details).

The paintDirtyRegions() method continues by iterating through an Enumeration of the dirty components, calling RepaintManager's collectDirtyComponents() method for each one. This method looks at all the ancestors of the specified dirty component and checks each one for any overlap with its dirty region using the SwingUtilities.computeInter-section() method. In this way, each dirty region's bounds are minimized so that only its visible region remains. (Note that collectDirtyComponents() *does* take transparency into account.) Once this has been done for each dirty component, the paintDirtyRegions() method enters a loop which computes the final intersection of each dirty component and its dirty region. At the end of each iteration, paintImmediately() is called on the associated dirty component, which actually paints each minimized dirty region in its correct location (we'll discuss this later). This completes the paintDirtyRegions() method, but we still have the most significant feature of the whole process left to discuss: painting.

2.11.7   Painting

JComponent includes an update() method which simply calls paint(). The update() method is never actually used by any Swing components; it is provided only for backward compatibility. The JComponent paint() method, unlike typical AWT paint() implementations, does not handle all of a component's painting. In fact, it very rarely handles *any* of it directly. The only rendering work JComponent's paint() method is really responsible for is working with clipping areas, translations, and painting pieces of the Image used by RepaintManager for double-buffering. The rest of the work is delegated to several other methods. We will briefly discuss each of these methods and the order in which painting operations occur. But first we need to discuss how paint() is actually invoked.

As you know from our discussion of the repainting process above, RepaintManager is responsible for invoking a method called paintImmediately() on each component to paint its dirty region (remember, there is always just one dirty region per component because they are intelligently coalesced by RepaintManager). This method, together with the private ones it calls, makes an intelligently crafted repainting process even more impressive. It first checks to see if the target component is visible, as it could have been moved, hidden, or disposed since the original request was made. Then it recursively searches the component's non-opaque parents (using isOpaque()) and it increases the bounds of the region to repaint accordingly until it reaches an opaque parent. It then has two options.

1   If the parent reached is a JComponent subclass, the private _paintImmediately() method is called and the newly computed region is passed to it. This method queries the isOptimizedDrawing() method, checks whether double-buffering is enabled (if so, it uses the off-screen Graphics object associated with RepaintManager's buffered Image), and continues working with isOpaque() to determine the final parent component and bounds to invoke paint() on.

   A   If double-buffering is *not* enabled, a single call to paint() is made on the parent.

   B   If double-buffering *is* enabled, it calls paintWithBuffer(), which is another private method. This method works with the off-screen Graphics object and its clipping area to generate many calls to the parent's paint() method, passing it the off-screen Graphics object using a specific clipping area each time. After each call to paint(), it uses the off-screen Graphics object to draw directly to the visible component.

2   If the parent is not a JComponent subclass, the region's bounds are sent to that parent's repaint() method, which will normally invoke the java.awt.Component paint() method. This method will then forward traffic to each of its lightweight children's paint() methods. However, before doing this, it makes sure that each lightweight child it notifies is not completely covered by the current clipping area of the Graphics object that was passed in.

In all cases, we have *finally* reached JComponent's paint() method!

Inside JComponent's paint() method, if graphics debugging is enabled, a Debug-Graphics instance will be used for all rendering.

NOTE   Interestingly, a quick look at `JComponent`'s painting code shows heavy use of a class called `SwingGraphics`. (This isn't in the API docs because it's package private). It appears to be a very slick class for handling custom translations, clipping area management, and a `Stack` of `Graphics` objects used for caching, recyclability, and undo-type operations. `SwingGraphics` actually acts as a wrapper for all `Graphics` instances used during the painting process. It can only be instantiated by passing it an existing `Graphics` object. This functionality is made even more explicit by the fact that it implements an interface called `GraphicsWrapper`, which is also package private.

The `paint()` method checks whether double-buffering is enabled and whether it was called by `paintWithBuffer()` (see above). There are two possible scenarios.

1 If `paint()` was called from `paintWithBuffer()` or if double-buffering is not enabled, `paint()` checks whether the clipping area of the current `Graphics` object is completely obscured by any child components. If it isn't, `paintComponent()`, `paintBorder()`, and `paintChildren()` are called in that order. If it is completely obscured, then only `paintChildren()` needs to be called. (We will see what these three methods do shortly.)

2 If double-buffering is enabled and this method was not called from `paintWith-Buffer()`, it will use the off-screen `Graphics` object associated with `RepaintMan-ager`'s buffered `Image` throughout the remainder of this method. Then it will check whether the clipping area of the current `Graphics` object is completely obscured by any child components. If it isn't, `paintComponent()`, `paintBorder()`, and `paintChildren()` will be called in that order. If it is completely obscured, only `paintChildren()` needs to be called.

   A The `paintComponent()` method checks to see if the component has a UI delegate installed. If it doesn't, the method just exits. If it does, it simply calls `update()` on that UI delegate and then exits. The `update()` method of a UI delegate is normally responsible for painting a component's background if it is opaque, and then calling `paint()`. A UI delegate's `paint()` method is what actually paints the corresponding component's content. (We will see how to customize UI delegates throughout this text.)

   B The `paintBorder()` method simply paints the component's border, if it has one.

   C The `paintChildren()` method is a bit more involved. To summarize, it searches through all child components and determines whether `paint()` should be invoked on them using the current `Graphics` clipping area, the `isOpaque()` method, and the `isOptimizedDrawingEnabled()` method. The `paint()` method called on each child will essentially start that child's painting process from part 2 above, and this process will repeat until either no more children exist or none need to be painted.

In summary, here is the bottom line to custom painting: When building or extending lightweight Swing components, it is normally expected that if we want to do any painting within the component itself (instead of in the UI delegate where it normally should be done), we will override the `paintComponent()` method and immediately call `super.paintComponent()`. In this way, the UI delegate will be given a chance to render the component first. Overriding the `paint()` method, or any of the other methods mentioned above, should rarely be necessary, and it is always good practice to avoid doing so.

2.12   FOCUS MANAGEMENT

When Swing components are placed in a Swing container, the route of keyboard focus is, by default, left to right and top to bottom. This route is referred to as a *focus cycle*, and moving focus from one component to the next in a cycle is accomplished using the TAB key or CTRL-TAB. To move in the reverse direction through a cycle, use SHIFT-TAB or CTRL-SHIFT-TAB. This cycle is controlled by an instance of the abstract FocusManager class.

FocusManager relies on five JComponent properties of each component to tell it how to treat each component when the current focus reaches or leaves it:

- focusCycleRoot: Specifies whether the component contains a focus cycle of its own. If it contains a focus cycle, focus will enter that component and loop through its focus cycle until it is manually or programatically moved out of that component. By default, this property is false (for most components), and it cannot be assigned with a typical setXX() accessor. It can only be changed by overriding the isFocusCycleRoot() method and returning the appropriate boolean value.
- managingFocus: Specifies whether KeyEvents corresponding to a focus change will be sent to the component itself or intercepted and devoured by the FocusManager. By default, this property is false (for most components), and it cannot be assigned with a typical setXX() accessor. It can only be changed by overriding the isManagingFocus() method and returning the appropriate boolean value.
- focusTraversable: Specifies whether focus can be transferred to the component by the FocusManager due to a focus shift in the focus cycle. By default, this property is true (for most components), and it cannot be assigned with a typical setXX() accessor. It can only be changed by overriding the isFocusTraversable() method and returning the appropriate boolean value. (Note that when focus reaches a component through a mouse click, its requestFocus() method is called. By overriding requestFocus(), we can respond to focus requests on a component-specific basis.)
- requestFocusEnabled: Specifies whether a mouse click will give focus to that component. This does not affect how the FocusManager works; it will continue to transfer focus to the component as part of the focus cycle. By default, this property is true (for most components), and it can be assigned with JComponent's setRequestFocusEnabled() method.
- nextFocusableComponent: Specifies the component to transfer focus to when the TAB key is pressed. By default, this is set to null, as focus traversal is handled by a default FocusManager service. Assigning a component as the nextFocusableComponent will overpower FocusManager's focus traversal mechanism. This is done by passing the component to JComponent's setNextFocusableComponent() method.

2.12.1   FocusManager

abstract class javax.swing.FocusManager

This abstract class defines the responsibility of determining how focus moves from one component to another. FocusManager is a service class whose shared instance is stored in AppContext's service table (see section 2.5). To access the FocusManager, we use its static getCurrentManager() method. To assign a new FocusManager, we use the static setCurrentManager() method. We can disable the current FocusManager service using the static `disableFocusManager()` method, and we can check whether it is enabled at any given point using the static `isFocusManagerEnabled()` method.

The following three abstract methods must be defined by subclasses:

- `focusNextComponent(Component aComponent)`: Called to shift focus to the next component in the focus cycle whose `focusTraversable` property is `true`.
- `focusPreviousComponent(Component aComponent)`: Called to shift focus to the previous focusable component in the focus cycle whose `focusTraversable` property is `true`.
- `processKeyEvent(Component focusedComponent, KeyEvent anEvent)`: Called to either consume a `KeyEvent` sent to the given component, or allow it to pass through and be processed by that component itself. This method is normally used to determine whether a key press corresponds to a shift in focus. If this is determined to be the case, the `KeyEvent` is normally consumed and focus is moved forward or backward using the `focusNextComponent()` or `focusPreviousComponent()` methods respectively.

> **NOTE** "FocusManager will receive KEY_PRESSED, KEY_RELEASED, and KEY_TYPED key events. If one event is consumed, all other events should be consumed" (API documentation).

2.12.2 DefaultFocusManager

class javax.swing.DefaultFocusManager

`DefaultFocusManager` extends `FocusManager` and defines the three required methods as well as several additional methods. The most significant method in this class is `compareTabOrder()`, which takes two `Component`s as parameters and determines first which component is located closer to the top of the container that is acting as their focus cycle root. If they are both located at the same height, this method will determine which is left-most. A value of `true` will be returned if the first component passed in should be given focus before the second. Otherwise, `false` will be returned.

The `focusNextComponent()` and `focusPreviousComponent()` methods shift focus as expected, and the `getComponentBefore()` and `getComponentAfter()` methods are defined to return the previous or next component, respectively, that will receive the focus after a given component in the focus cycle. The `getFirstComponent()` and `getLastComponent()` methods return the first and last component to receive focus in a given container's focus cycle.

The `processKeyEvent()` method intercepts `KeyEvent`s sent to the currently focused component. If these events correspond to a shift in focus (such as TAB, CTRL-TAB, SHIFT-TAB, and SHIFT-CTRL-TAB), they are consumed and the focus is changed accordingly. Otherwise, these events are sent to the component for processing (see section 2.13). Note that the `FocusManager` always has the first crack at keyboard events.

> **NOTE** By default, CTRL-TAB and SHIFT-CTRL-TAB can be used to shift focus out of text components. TAB and SHIFT-TAB will move the caret instead (see chapters 11 and 19).

2.12.3 Listening for focus changes

As with AWT components, we can listen for focus changes on a component by attaching an instance of the `java.awt.FocusListener` interface. `FocusListener` defines two methods, each of which take a `java.awt.FocusEvent` instance as a parameter:

- `focusGained(FocusEvent e)`: This method receives a `FocusEvent` when focus is given to a component this listener is attached to.
- `focusLost(FocusEvent e)`: This method receives a `FocusEvent` when focus is removed from a component this listener is attached to.

`FocusEvent` extends `java.awt.ComponentEvent` and defines, among others, the `FOCUS_LOST` and `FOCUS_GAINED` IDs to distinguish between its two event types. A `FOCUS_LOST` event will occur corresponding to the *temporary* or *permanent* loss of focus. Temporary loss occurs when another application or window is given focus. When focus returns to this window, the component that originally lost the focus will once again gain the current focus, and a `FOCUS_GAINED` event will be dispatched at that time. Permanent focus loss occurs when the focus is moved by either clicking on another component in the same window, programmatically invoking `requestFocus()` on another component, or dispatching any `KeyEvents` that cause a focus change when they are sent to the current `FocusManager`'s `processKeyEvent()` method. As expected, we can attach and remove `FocusListener` implementations to any Swing component using `Component`'s `addFocusListener()` and `removeFocusListener()` methods.

2.13 KEYBOARD INPUT, KEYSTROKES, AND ACTIONS

2.13.1 Listening for keyboard input

`KeyEvents` are fired by a component whenever that component has the current focus and the user presses a key. To listen for these events on a particular component, we can attach `KeyListeners` using the `addKeyListener()` method. We can devour these events using the `consume()` method before they are handled further by key bindings or other listeners. We'll discuss in this section exactly who gets notification of keyboard input, and in what order this occurs.

There are three `KeyEvent` event types, each of which normally occurs at least once per keyboard activation (such as a press and release of a single keyboard key):

- `KEY_PRESSED`: This type of key event is generated whenever a keyboard key is pressed. The key that is pressed is specified by the `keyCode` property and a *virtual key code* representing it can be retrieved with `KeyEvent`'s `getKeyCode()` method. A virtual key code is used to report the exact keyboard key that caused the event, such as `KeyEvent.VK_ENTER`. `KeyEvent` defines numerous static `int` constants that each start with the prefix "VK," meaning *Virtual Key* (see the `KeyEvent` API docs for a complete list). For example, if CTRL-C is typed, two `KEY_PRESSED` events will be fired. The `int` returned by `getKeyCode()` corresponding to pressing CTRL will be a value matching `KeyEvent.VK_CTRL`. Similarly, the `int` returned by `getKeyCode()` corresponding to pressing the C key will be a value matching `KeyEvent.VK_C`. (Note that the order in which these are fired depends on the order in which they are pressed.) `KeyEvent` also maintains a `keyChar` property which specifies the Unicode representation of the character that was pressed (if there is no Unicode representation, `KeyEvent.CHAR_UNDEFINED` is used—for example, the function keys on a typical PC keyboard). We can retrieve the `keyChar` character corresponding to any `KeyEvent` using the `getKeyChar()` method. For example, the character returned by `getKeyChar()` corresponding to pressing the C key will be c. If SHIFT was pressed and held while the C key was pressed, the character returned by `getKeyChar()` corresponding to the C key press would be C. (Note that distinct `keyChars` are returned for upper- and lower-case characters, wheras the same `keyCode` is used in both situations—for example, the value of VK_C will be returned by `getKeyCode()` regardless of whether SHIFT is held down when the C key is pressed. Also note that there is no `keyChar` associated with keys such as CTRL, and `getKeyChar()` will simply return an empty `char` in this case.)

- KEY_RELEASED: This type of key event is generated whenever a keyboard key is released. Other than this difference, KEY_RELEASED events are identical to KEY_PRESSED events; however, as we will discuss below, they occur much less frequently.
- KEY_TYPED: This type of event is fired somewhere between a KEY_PRESSED and KEY_ RELEASED event. It never carries a `keyCode` property corresponding to the actual key pressed, and 0 will be returned whenever `getKeyCode()` is called on an event of this type. For keys with no Unicode representation (such as PAGE UP and PRINT SCREEN), no KEY_ TYPED event will be generated at all.

Most keys with Unicode representations, when held down for longer than a few moments, repeatedly generate KEY_PRESSED and KEY_TYPED events, in this order. The set of keys that exhibit this behavior, and the rate at which they do so, cannot be controlled and is platform-specific.

Each `KeyEvent` maintains a set of modifiers which specifies the state of the SHIFT, CTRL, ALT, and META keys. This is an `int` value that is the result of the bitwise OR of `InputEvent.SHIFT_MASK`, `InputEvent.CTRL_MASK`, `InputEvent.ALT_MASK`, and `InputEvent.META_MASK`, depending on which keys are pressed at the time of the event. We can retrieve this value with `getModifiers()`, and we can query specifically whether any of these keys was pressed at the time the event was fired using `isShiftDown()`, `isControlDown()`, `isAltDown()`, and `isMetaDown()`.

`KeyEvent` also maintains the boolean `actionKey` property which specifies whether the invoking keyboard key corresponds to an action that should be performed by that app (`true`) versus data that is normally used for such things as addition to a text component's document content (`false`). We can use `KeyEvent`'s `isActionKey()` method to retrieve the value of this property.

2.13.2 KeyStrokes

Using `KeyListeners` to handle all keyboard input on a component-by-component basis was required prior to Java 2. Because of this, a significant and often tedious amount of time was spent planning and debugging keyboard operations. The Swing team recognized this, and thankfully included functionality for key event interception regardless of which component currently has the focus. This functionality is implemented by binding instances of the `javax.swing.KeyStroke` class with `ActionListeners` (normally instances of `javax.swing.Action`).

NOTE   Registered keyboard actions are also commonly referred to as keyboard accelerators.

Each `KeyStroke` instance encapsulates a `KeyEvent` `keyCode`, a `modifiers` value (identical to that of `KeyEvent`), and a boolean property specifying whether it should be activated on a key press (`false`, which is the default) or on a key release (`true`). The `KeyStroke` class provides five static methods for creating `KeyStroke` objects. Note that all `KeyStrokes` are cached, and it is not necessarily the case that these methods will not always necessarily return a brand-new instance. (Actually `KeyStroke` provides six static methods for creating `Key-Strokes`, but `getKeyStroke(char keyChar, boolean onKeyRelease)` has been deprecated.)

- `getKeyStroke(char keyChar)`
- `getKeyStroke(int keyCode, int modifiers)`
- `getKeyStroke(int keyCode, int modifiers, boolean onKeyRelease)`
- `getKeyStroke(String representation)` `// This method is not implemented as of Java 2 FCS, and it will always return null.`
- `getKeyStroke(KeyEvent anEvent)`

The last method will return a `KeyStroke` with properties corresponding to the given `KeyEvent`'s attributes. The `keyCode`, `keyChar`, and `modifiers` properties are taken from the `KeyEvent` and the `onKeyRelease` property is set to `true` if the event is of type `KEY_RELEASED`; otherwise, it returns `false`.

To register a `KeyStroke`/`ActionListener` combination with any `JComponent`, we can use its `registerKeyBoardAction(ActionListener action, KeyStroke stroke, int condition)` method. The `ActionListener` parameter is expected to be defined such that its `actionPerformed()` method performs the necessary operations when keyboard input corresponding to the `KeyStroke` parameter is intercepted. The `int` parameter specifies under what conditions the given `KeyStroke` is considered to be valid:

- `JComponent.WHEN_FOCUSED`: The corresponding `ActionListener` will only be invoked if the component this `KeyStroke` is registered with has the current focus.
- `JComponent.WHEN_ANCESTOR_OF_FOCUSED_COMPONENT`: The corresponding `Action-Listener` will only be invoked if the component this `KeyStroke` is registered with is the ancestor of (meaning, it contains) the component with the current focus.
- `JComponent.WHEN_IN_FOCUSED_WINDOW`: The corresponding `ActionListener` will be invoked if the component this `KeyStroke` is registered with is anywhere within the peer-level window (such as `JFrame`, `JDialog`, `JWindow`, `JApplet`, or any other heavyweight component) that has the current focus. Keyboard actions registered with this condition are handled in an instance of the private `KeyBoardManager` service class (see section 2.13.4) rather than the component itself.

For example, to associate the invocation of an `ActionListener` corresponding to ALT-H, no matter what component has the focus in a given `JFrame`, we can do the following:

```
KeyStroke myKeyStroke =
  KeyStroke.getKeyStroke(KeyEvent.VK_H,
    InputEvent.ALT_MASK, false);

myJFrame.getRootPane().registerKeyBoardAction(
  myActionListener, myKeyStroke,
  JComponent.WHEN_ANCESTOR_OF_FOCUSED_COMPONENT);
```

Each `JComponent` maintains a `Hashtable` client property containing all bound `Key-Strokes`. Whenever a `KeyStroke` is registered using the `registerKeyboardAction()` method, it is added to this structure. Only one `ActionListener` can be registered corresponding to each `KeyStroke`, and if there is already an `ActionListener` mapped to a particular `KeyStroke`, the new one will effectively overwrite the previous one. We can retrieve an array of `KeyStrokes` corresponding to the current bindings stored in this `Hashtable` using

JComponent's `getRegisteredKeyStrokes()` method, and we can wipe out all bindings with the `resetKeyboardActions()` method. Given a `KeyStroke` object, we can retrieve the corresponding `ActionListener` with JComponent's `getActionForKeyStroke()` method, and we can retrieve the corresponding condition property with the `getConditionForKey-Stroke()` method.

2.13.3 Actions

An `Action` instance is basically a convenient `ActionListener` implementation that encapsulates a `Hashtable` of bound properties similar to `JComponent`'s client properties (see chapter 12 for details about working with `Action` implementations and their properties). We often use `Action` instances when registering keyboard actions.

NOTE   Text components are special in that they use hierarchically resolving `KeyMaps`. A `KeyMap` is a list of `Action`/`KeyStroke` bindings and `JTextComponent` supports multiple levels of such mappings. See chapters 11 and 19 for more information.

2.13.4 The flow of keyboard input

Each `KeyEvent` is first dispatched to the focused component and the `FocusManager` gets first crack at processing it. If the `FocusManager` doesn't want it, then the focused `JComponent` it is sent to calls `super.processKeyEvent()`, which gives any `KeyListeners` a chance to process the event. If the listeners don't consume it and the focused component is a `JTextComponent`, the `KeyMap` hierarchy is traversed (see chapters 11 and 19 for more about `KeyMaps`). If the event is not consumed by this time, the key bindings registered with the focused component get a shot.

First, `KeyStrokes` defined with the `WHEN_FOCUSED` condition get a chance. If none of these handle the event, then the component walks through its parent containers (until a `JRootPane` is reached) looking for `KeyStrokes` defined with the `WHEN_ANCESTOR_OF_FOCUSED_COMPONENT` condition. If the event hasn't been handled after the top-most container is reached, it is sent to `KeyboardManager`, a package-private service class (unlike most service classes in Swing, `KeyboardManager` does not register its shared instance with `AppContext`—see section 2.5). `KeyboardManager` looks for components with registered `KeyStrokes` with the `WHEN_IN_FOCUSED_WINDOW` condition and sends the event to them. If none of these are found, then `KeyboardManager` passes the event to any `JMenuBars` in the current window and lets their accelerators have a crack at it. If the event is still not handled, we check to see if the current focus resides in a `JInternalFrame`, because it is the only `RootPaneContainer` that can be contained inside another Swing component. If this is the case, we move up to the `JInternalFrame`'s parent. This process continues until either the event is consumed or the top-level window is reached.

2.14   *SwingUtilities*

class javax.swing.SwingUtilities

In section 2.3 we discussed two methods in the `SwingUtilities` class used for executing code in the event-dispatching thread. These are just two of the 36 generic utility methods defined in `SwingUtilities`, which break down logically into seven groups: computational methods, conversion methods, accessibility methods, retrieval methods, multithreading/ event-related methods, mouse button methods, and layout/rendering/UI methods. Each of these methods is static, and they are described very briefly in this section (for a more thorough understanding, see the SwingUtilities.java source code).

2.14.1   Computational methods

- `Rectangle[] computeDifference(Rectangle rectA, Rectangle rectB)`: Returns those rectangular regions representing the portion of `rectA` that do not intersect with `rectB`.
- `Rectangle computeIntersection(int x, int y, int width, int height, Rectangle dest)`: Returns the intersection of two rectangular areas. The first region is defined by the `int` parameters and the second by the `Rectangle` parameter. The `Rectangle` parameter is altered and returned as the result of the computation so that a new `Rectangle` does not have to be instantiated.
- `Rectangle computeUnion(int x, inty, int width, int height, Rectangle dest)`: Returns the union of two rectangular areas. The first region is defined by the `int` parameters and the second by the `Rectangle` parameter. The `Rectangle` parameter is altered and returned as the result of the computation so that a new `Rectangle` does not have to be instantiated.
- `isRectangleContainingRectangle(Rectangle a, Rectangle b)`: Returns `true` if `Rectangle b` is completely contained in `Rectangle a`.
- `computeStringWidth(FontMetrics fm, String str)`: Returns the width of the given `String` according to the given `FontMetrics` object (see section 2.8.3).

2.14.2   Conversion methods

- `MouseEvent convertMouseEvent(Component source, MouseEvent sourceEvent, Component destination)`: Returns a new `MouseEvent` with `destination` as its source and x,y coordinates converted to the coordinate system of `destination` (both assuming `destination` is not `null`). If `destination` is `null`, the coordinates are converted to the coordinate system of `source`, and `source` is set as the source of the event. If both are `null`, the `MouseEvent` returned is identical to the event passed in.
- `Point convertPoint(Component source, Point aPoint, Component destination)`: Returns a `Point` representing `aPoint` converted to the coordinate system of the `destination` component as if it were originating in the `source` component. If either component is `null`, the coordinate system of the other is used, and if both are `null`, the `Point` returned is identical to the `Point` passed in.
- `Point convertPoint(Component source, int x, int y, Component destination)`: This method acts the same as the `convertPoint()` method except that it takes `int` parameters representing the `Point` to convert rather than a `Point` instance.
- `Rectangle convertRectangle(Component source, Rectangle aRectangle, Component destination)`: Returns a `Rectangle` converted from the source component's coordinate system to the `destination` component's coordinate system. This method behaves similarly to `convertPoint()`.
- `void convertPointFromScreen(Point p, Component c)`: Converts a given `Point` in screen coordinates to the coordinate system of the given `Component`.

- void convertPointToScreen(Point p, Component c): Converts a given Point in the given Component's coordinate system to the coordinate system of the screen.

2.14.3 Accessibility methods

- Accessible getAccessibleAt(Component c, Point p): Returns the Accessible component at the given Point in the coordinate system of the given Component (null will be returned if none is found). An Accessible component is one that implements the javax.accessibility.Accessible interface.
- Accessible getAccessibleChild(Component c, int i): Returns the ith Accessible child of the given Component.
- int getAccessibleChildrenCount(Component c): Returns the number of Accessible children contained in the given Component.
- int getAccessibleIndexInParent(Component c): Returns the index of the given Component in its parent, disregarding all contained components that do not implement the Accessible interface. -1 will be returned if the parent is null or does not implement Accessible, or if the given Component does not implement Accessible.
- AccessibleStateSet getAccessibleStateSet(Component c): Returns the set of AccessibleStates that are active for the given Component.

2.14.4 Retrieval methods

- Component findFocusOwner(Component c): Returns the component contained within the given Component (or the given Component itself) that has the current focus. If there is no such component, null is returned.
- Container getAncestorNamed(String name, Component comp): Returns the closest ancestor of the given Component with the given name. Otherwise, null is returned. (Note that each Component has a name property which can be assigned and retrieved using the setName() and getName() methods respectively.)
- Container getAncestorOfClass(Class c, Component comp): Returns the closest ancestor of the given Component that is an instance of c. Otherwise, null is returned.
- Component getDeepestComponentAt(Component parent, int x, int y): Returns the most "contained" child of the given Component containing the point (x,y) in terms of the coordinate system of the given Component. If the given Component is not a Container, this method simply returns it immediately.
- Rectangle getLocalBounds(Component c): Returns a Rectangle representing the bounds of a given Component in terms of its own coordinate system (thus it always starts at 0,0).
- Component getRoot(Component c): Returns the first ancestor of c that is a Window. Otherwise, this method returns the last ancestor that is an Applet.
- JRootPane getRootPane(Component c): Returns the first JRootPane parent of c, or c itself if it is a JRootPane.
- Window windowForComponent(Component c): Returns the first ancestor of c that is a Window. Otherwise, this method returns null.
- boolean isDescendingFrom(Component allegedDescendant, Component allegedAncestor): Returns true if allegedDescendant is contained in allegedAncestor.

2.14.5   Multithreading/event-related methods

Refer to section 2.3 for more information about these methods.

- `void invokeAndWait(Runnable obj)`: Sends the given `Runnable` to the event-dispatching queue and blocks on the current thread.
- `void invokeLater(Runnable obj)`: Sends the given `Runnable` to the event-dispatching queue and continues.
- `boolean isEventDispatchThread()`: Returns `true` if the current thread is the event-dispatching thread.

2.14.6   Mouse button methods

- `boolean isLeftMouseButton(MouseEvent)`: Returns `true` if the given `MouseEvent` corresponds to left mouse button activation.
- `boolean isMiddleMouseButton(MouseEvent)`: Returns `true` if the given `MouseEvent` corresponds to middle mouse button activation.
- `boolean isRightMouseButton(MouseEvent)`: Returns `true` if the given `MouseEvent` corresponds to right mouse button activation.

2.14.7   Layout/rendering/UI methods

- `String layoutCompoundLabel(FontMetrics fm, String text, icon icon, int verticalAlignment, int horizontalAlignment, int verticalTextPosition, int horizontalTextPosition, Rectangle viewR, Rectangle iconR, Rectangle textR, int textIconGap)`: This method is normally used by `JLabel`'s UI delegate to lay out text and/or an icon using the given `FontMetrics` object, alignment settings, and text positions within the `viewR` `Rectangle`. If it is determined that the label text will not fit within this `Rectangle`, an elipsis ("...") is used in place of the text that will not fit. The `textR` and `iconR` `Rectangles` are modified to reflect the new layout, and the `String` that results from this layout is returned.
- `String layoutCompoundLabel(JComponent c, FontMetrics fm, String text, icon icon, int verticalAlignment, int horizontalAlignment, int verticalTextPosition, int horizontalTextPosition, Rectangle viewR, Rectangle iconR, Rectangle textR, int textIconGap)`: This method is identical to the above method, but it takes a target component to see whether text orientation should play a role. See the article *Component Orientation in Swing: How JFC Components Support BIDI Text* at the Swing Connection (http://java.sun.com/products/jfc/tsc/tech_topics/bidi/bidi.html) for more information about orientation.
- `void paintComponent(Graphics g, Component c, Container p, int x, int y, int w, int h)`: Paints the given `Component` in the given graphical context, using the rectangle defined by the four `int` parameters as the clipping area. The given `Container` is used to act as the `Component`'s parent so that any validation and repaint requests that occur on that component do not fill up the ancestry tree of the component owning the given graphical context. This is the same methodology used by component renderers of `JList`, `JTree`, and `JTable` to properly exhibit "rubber stamp" behavior. This behavior is accomplished through the use of a `CellRendererPane` (see chapter 17 for more about this class and why it is used to wrap renderers).

- void paintComponent(Graphics g, Component c, Container p, Rectangle r): Functions the same way as the above method, but it takes a Rectangle parameter rather than four ints.
- void updateComponentTreeUI(Component c): Notifies all components contained in c, and c itself, to update their UI delegates to match the current UIManager and UIDefaults settings (see chapter 21).

PART II

The basics

Part II consists of twelve chapters containing discussion and examples of the basic Swing components.

Chapter 3 introduces frames, panels, and borders, including an example showing how to create a custom rounded-edge border.

Chapter 4 is devoted to layout managers with a comparison of the most commonly used layouts, a contributed section on the use of `GridBagLayout`, the construction of several custom layouts, and the beginnings of a JavaBeans property editing environment with the ability to change the layout manager dynamically.

Chapter 5 covers labels and buttons, and presents the construction of a custom transparent polygonal button designed for use in applets, as well as a custom tooltip manager to provide proper tooltip functionality for these polygonal buttons.

Chapter 6 is about using and customizing tabbed panes, including an example showing how to customize `JTabbedPane` and its UI delegate to build a tabbed pane which uses background images.

Chapter 7 discusses scroll panes and how to customize scrolling functionality. Examples show how to use the row and column headers for tracking scroll position, how to change the speed of scrolling through implementation of the `Scrollable` interface, how to implement grab-and-drag scrolling, and how to programmatically invoke scrolling.

Chapter 8 takes a brief look at split panes with an example showing how to base programmatic actions on the position of the divider (a gas model simulation).

Chapter 9 covers combo boxes with examples showing how to build custom combo box models and cell renderers, add functionlity to the default combo box editor, and serialize a combo box model for later use.

Chapter 10 is about list boxes with examples of building a custom tab-based cell renderer, adding keyboard search functionality for quick item selection, and constructing a custom check box cell renderer.

Chapter 11 introduces the text components and undo/redo functionality with basic examples and discussions of each (text package coverage continues in chapters 19 and 20).

Chapter 12 is devoted to menu bars, menus, menu items, toolbars and actions. Examples include the construction of a basic text editor with floatable toolbar, custom toolbar buttons, and a custom color chooser menu item.

Chapter 13 discusses progress bars, sliders and scroll bars, including a custom scroll pane, a slider-based date chooser, a JPEG image quality editor, and an FTP client application.

Chapter 14 covers dialogs, option panes, and file and color choosers. Examples demonstrate the basics of custom dialog creation and the use of `JOptionPane`, as well as how to add a custom component to `JColorChooser`, and how to customize `JFileChooser` to allow multiple file selection and the addition of a custom component (a ZIP/JAR archive creation, extraction and preview tool).

CHAPTER 3

Frames, panels, and borders

3.1 FRAMES AND PANELS OVERVIEW

3.1.1 JFrame

class javax.swing.JFrame

The main container for a Swing-based application is JFrame. All objects associated with a JFrame are managed by its only child, an instance of JRootPane. JRootPane is a simple container for several child panes. When we add components to a JFrame, we don't directly add them to the JFrame as we did with an AWT Frame. Instead we have to specify into exactly which pane of the JFrame's JRootPane we want the component to be placed. In most cases components are added to the contentPane by calling:

```
getContentPane().add(myComponent);
```

Similarly, when setting a layout for a JFrame's contents, we usually just want to set the layout for the contentPane:

```
getContentPane().setLayout(new FlowLayout());
```

Each JFrame contains a JRootPane as protected field rootPane. Figure 3.1 illustrates the hierarchy of a JFrame and its JRootPane. The lines in this diagram extend downward representing the "has a" relationship of each container.

71

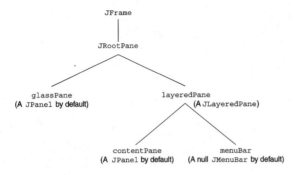

Figure 3.1 The default JFrame and JRootPane "has a" relationship

3.1.2   JRootPane

class javax.swing.JRootPane

Each JRootPane contains several components referred to here by variable name: glassPane (a JPanel by default), layeredPane (a JLayeredPane), contentPane (a JPanel by default), and menuBar (a JMenuBar).

NOTE   glassPane and contentPane are just variable names used by JRootPane. They are not unique Swing classes, as some explanations might lead you to believe.

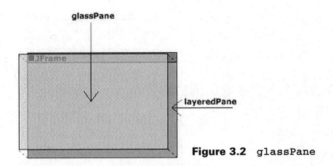

Figure 3.2 glassPane

The glassPane is initialized as a non-opaque JPanel that sits on top of the JLayered-Pane as illustrated in figure 3.2. This component is very useful in situations where we need to intercept mouse events to display a certain cursor over the whole frame or to redirect the current application focus. The glassPane can be any component, but it is a JPanel by default. To change the glassPane from a JPanel to another component, a call to the set-GlassPane() method must be made:

```
setGlassPane(myComponent);
```

Though the glassPane does sit on top of the layeredPane, it is, by default, not visible. It can be set visible (show itself) by calling:

```
getGlassPane().setVisible(true);
```

The glassPane allows you to display components in front of an existing JFrame's contents. (In chapter 15 we will find that it can be useful as an invisible panel for detecting internal frame focus changes.)

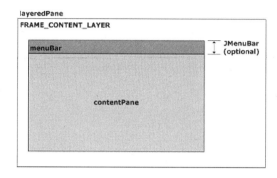

Figure 3.3   Default `JFrame`
contents of the `JLayeredPane`
`FRAME_CONTENT_LAYER`

The `contentPane` and optional `menuBar` are contained within `JRootPane`'s `layered-Pane` at the `FRAME_CONTENT_LAYER` (this is layer –30000; see chapter 15). The `menuBar` does not exist by default, but it can be set by calling the `setJMenuBar()` method:

```
JMenuBar menu = new JMenuBar();
setJMenuBar(menu);
```

When the `JMenuBar` is set, it is automatically positioned at the top of the `FRAME_CONTENT_LAYER`. The rest of the layer is occupied by the `contentPane` as illustrated in figure 3.3.

The `contentPane` is, by default, an opaque `JPanel`. It can be set to any other component by calling:

```
setContentPane(myComponent);
```

NOTE   The default layout for the `contentPane` is `BorderLayout`. The default layout for any other `JPanel` is `FlowLayout`. Be careful not to set the layout of a `JFrame` directly. This will generate an exception. You should also avoid setting the layout of the `rootPane`, because every `JRootPane` uses its own custom layout manager called `RootLayout`. We will discuss layout managers further in chapter 4.

3.1.3   RootLayout

class javax.swing.JRootPane.RootLayout

`RootLayout` is a layout manager built specifically to manage `JRootPane`'s `layeredPane`, `glassPane`, and `menuBar`. If it is replaced by another layout manager, that manager must be able to handle the positioning of these components. `RootLayout` is an inner class defined within `JRootPane` and as such, it is not intended to have any use outside of this class. Thus it is not discussed in this text.

3.1.4   The RootPaneContainer interface

abstract interface javax.swing.RootPaneContainer

The purpose of the `RootPaneContainer` interface is to organize a group of methods that should be used to access a container's `JRootPane` and its different panes (refer to the API docs for more information). Because `JFrame`'s main container is a `JRootPane`, it implements this interface (as does `JFrame` and `JDialog`). If we were to build a new component which uses a `JRootPane` as its main container, we would most likely implement the `RootPaneContainer` interface.

(Note that this interface exists for convenience, consistency, and organizational purposes. We are encouraged, but certainly not required, to use it in our own container implementations.)

3.1.5 The WindowConstants interface

abstract interface javax.swing.WindowConstants

We can specify how a JFrame, JInternalFrame, or JDialog act in response to a close using the setDefaultCloseOperation() method. There are three possible settings, as defined by WindowConstants interface fields:

```
WindowConstants.DISPOSE_ON_CLOSE
WindowConstants.DO_NOTHING_ON_CLOSE
WindowConstants.HIDE_ON_CLOSE
```

The names are self-explanatory. DISPOSE_ON_CLOSE disposes of the container and its contents, DO_NOTHING_ON_CLOSE renders the Close button useless, and HIDE_ON_CLOSE removes the container from view. HIDE_ON_CLOSE may be useful if we need the container, or something it contains, at a later time but do not want it to be visible until then. DO_NOTHING_ ON_CLOSE is very useful, as you will see below.

3.1.6 The WindowListener interface

abstract interface java.awt.event.WindowListener

Classes that want explicit notification of window events (such as window closing or iconification) need to implement this interface. Normally, the WindowAdapter class is extended instead. "When the window's status changes by virtue of being opened, closed, activated or deactivated, iconified or deiconified, the relevant method in the listener object is invoked, and the WindowEvent is passed to it." (API documentation)

The methods any implementation of this interface must define are these:

```
void windowActivated(WindowEvent e)
void windowClosed(WindowEvent e)
void windowClosing(WindowEvent e)
void windowDeactivated(WindowEvent e)
void windowDeiconified(WindowEvent e)
void windowIconified(WindowEvent e)
void windowOpened(WindowEvent e)
```

3.1.7 WindowEvent

class java.awt.event.WindowEvent

This is the type of event used to indicate that a window has changed state. This event is passed to every WindowListener or WindowAdapter object which is registered on the source window to receive such events. The method getWindow() returns the window that generated the event. The method paramString() retrieves a String describing the event type and its source, among other things.

Six types of WindowEvents can be generated; each is represented by the following static WindowEvent fields: WINDOW_ACTIVATED, WINDOW_CLOSED, WINDOW_CLOSING, WINDOW_ DEACTIVATED, WINDOW_DEICONIFIED, WINDOW_ICONIFIED, and WINDOW_OPENED.

3.1.8   WindowAdapter

abstract class java.awt.event.WindowAdapter

This is an abstract implementation of the `WindowListener` interface. It is normally more convenient to extend this class than to implement `WindowListener` directly.

Notice that none of the `WindowConstants` close operations actually terminate program execution. This can be accomplished by extending `WindowAdapter` and overriding the methods we are interested in handling (in this case, it's just the `windowClosing()` method). We can create an instance of this extended class, cast it to a `WindowListener` object, and register this listener with a `JFrame` using the `addWindowListener()` method. This can easily be added to any application as follows:

```
WindowListener l = new WindowAdapter() {
  public void windowClosing(WindowEvent e) {
    System.exit(0);
  }
};
myJFrame.addWindowListener(l);
```

A useful idea for real-world applications is to combine `WindowAdapter`, values from the `WindowConstants` interface, and `JOptionPane`, to present the user with an exit confirmation dialog as follows:

```
myJFrame.setDefaultCloseOperation(
  WindowConstants.DO_NOTHING_ON_CLOSE);
WindowListener l = new WindowAdapter() {
  public void windowClosing(WindowEvent e) {
    int confirm = JOptionPane.showOptionDialog(myJFrame,
      "Really Exit?", "Exit Confirmation",
      JOptionPane.YES_NO_OPTION,
      JOptionPane.QUESTION_MESSAGE,
      null, null, null);
    if (confirm == 0) {
      myJFrame.dispose();
      System.exit(0);
    }
  }
};
myJFrame.addWindowListener(l);
```

NOTE   This can also be done for `JDialog`. However, to do the same thing for a `JInternal-Frame`, we must build a custom `JInternalFrame` subclass and implement the `PropertyChangeListener` interface. See chapter 16 for details.

Inserting this code into your application will always display the dialog shown in figure 3.4 when the `JFrame` Close button is clicked.

REFERENCE   Dialogs and `JOptionPane` are discussed in chapter 14.

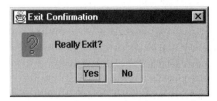

Figure 3.4 **An application exit confirmation dialog**

3.1.9 Custom frame icons

We might often want to use a custom icon to replace the default coffee cup icon. Because JFrame is a subclass of `java.awt.Frame`, we can set its icon using the `setIconImage()` method.

GUIDELINE

Brand identity   Use the frame icon to establish and reinforce your brand identity. Pick a simple image which can be both effective in the small space and reused throughout the application and any accompanying material. Figure 3.4 shows the Sun Coffee Cup which was used as a brand mark for Java.

```
ImageIcon image = new ImageIcon("spiral.gif");
myFrame.setIconImage(image.getImage());
```

There is no limit to the size of the icon that can be used. A JFrame will resize any image passed to `setIconImage()` to fit the bound it needs. Figure 3.5 shows the top of a JFrame with a custom icon.

Figure 3.5 JFrame **custom icon**

3.1.10 Centering a frame on the screen

By default, a JFrame displays itself in the upper left-hand corner of the screen, but we often want to place it in the center of the screen. Using the `getToolkit()` method of the Window class (of which JFrame is a second-level subclass), we can communicate with the operating system and query the size of the screen. (The Toolkit methods make up the bridge between Java components and their native, operating-system-specific, peer components.)

The `getScreenSize()` method gives us the information we need:

```
Dimension dim = getToolkit().getScreenSize();
```

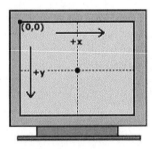

Figure 3.6
Screen coordinates

CHAPTER 3   FRAMES, PANELS, AND BORDERS

When setting the location of the JFrame, the upper left-hand corner of the frame is the relevant coordinate. So to center a JFrame on the screen, we need to subtract half its width and half its height from the center-of-screen coordinate:

```
myJFrame.setLocation(dim.width/2 - myJFrame.getWidth()/2,
  dim.height/2 - myJFrame.getHeight()/2);
```

Figure 3.6 illustrates how the screen coordinates work.

3.1.11 JApplet

class javax.swing.JApplet

JApplet is the Swing equivalent of the AWT Applet class. Like JFrame, JApplet's main child component is a JRootPane and its structure is the same. JApplet acts just like Applet, so we won't go into detail about how applets work.

REFERENCE We suggest that readers unfamiliar with applets refer to the Java tutorial to learn more: http://java.sun.com/docs/books/tutorial/.

Several examples in later chapters are constructed as Swing applets, so we will see JApplet in action soon enough.

3.1.12 JWindow

class javax.swing.JWindow

JWindow is very similar to JFrame except that it has no title bar and it is not resizable, minimizable, maximizable, or closable. Thus it cannot be dragged without writing custom code to do so in the same way that JToolBar's UI delegate provides this functionality for docking and undocking (see chapter 12). We normally use JWindow to display a temporary message or splash screen logo. Since JWindow is a RootPaneContainer, we can treat it just like JFrame or JApplet when manipulating its contents.

3.1.13 JPanel

class javax.swing.JPanel

This is the simple container component commonly used to organize a group or groups of child components. JPanel is an integral part of JRootPane, as we discussed above, and it is used in each example throughout this book. Each JPanel's child components are managed by a layout manager. A layout manager controls the size and location of each child in a container. JPanel's default layout manager is FlowLayout (we will discuss this further in chapter 4). The only exception to this is JRootPane's contentPane, which is managed by a Border-Layout by default.

3.2 BORDERS

package javax.swing.border

The border package provides us with the following border classes; they can be applied to any Swing component.

`BevelBorder`

A 3-D border with a raised or lowered appearance.

`CompoundBorder`

A combination of two borders: an inside border and an outside border.

`EmptyBorder`

A transparent border used to define empty space (often referred to as *white space*) around a component.

`EtchedBorder`

A border with an etched line appearance.

`LineBorder`

A flat border with a specified thickness and color.

`MatteBorder`

A border consisting of either a flat color or a tiled image.

`SoftBevelBorder`

A 3-D border with a raised or lowered appearance, and slightly rounded edges.

`TitledBorder`

A border which allows a `String` title in a specific location and position. We can set the title font, color, and justification, and the position of the title text using `Title-Border` methods and constants where necessary (refer to the API docs).

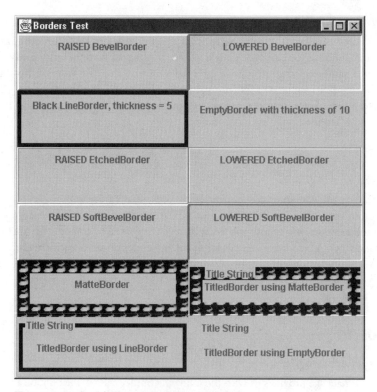

Figure 3.7   A simple borders demonstration

To set the border of a Swing component, we simply call JComponent's setBorder() method. There is also a convenience class called BorderFactory, contained in the javax.swing package (not the javax.swing.border package as you might think), which contains a group of static methods used for constructing borders quickly. For example, to create an EtchedBorder, we can use BorderFactory as follows:

```
myComponent.setBorder(BorderFactory.createEtchedBorder());
```

The border classes do not provide methods for setting preferences such as dimensions and colors. Instead of modifying an existing border, we are normally expected to create a new instance to replace the old one.

Example 3.1 creates a JFrame containing twelve JPanels using borders of all types. The output is shown in figure 3.7.

Example 3.1

BorderTest.java

see \Chapter3\1

```
import java.awt.*;
import javax.swing.*;
import javax.swing.border.*;

class BorderTest extends JFrame
{
  public BorderTest() {
    setTitle("Border Test");
    setSize(450, 450);

    JPanel content = (JPanel) getContentPane();
    content.setLayout(new GridLayout(6,2));

    JPanel p = new JPanel();
    p.setBorder(new BevelBorder (BevelBorder.RAISED));
    p.add(new JLabel("RAISED BevelBorder"));
    content.add(p);

    p = new JPanel();
    p.setBorder(new BevelBorder (BevelBorder.LOWERED));
    p.add(new JLabel("LOWERED BevelBorder"));
    content.add(p);

    p = new JPanel();
    p.setBorder(new LineBorder (Color.black, 5));
    p.add(new JLabel("Black LineBorder, thickness = 5"));
    content.add(p);

    p = new JPanel();
    p.setBorder(new EmptyBorder (10,10,10,10));
    p.add(new JLabel("EmptyBorder with thickness of 10"));
    content.add(p);

    p = new JPanel();
    p.setBorder(new EtchedBorder (EtchedBorder.RAISED));
```

```
        p.add(new JLabel("RAISED EtchedBorder"));
        content.add(p);

        p = new JPanel();
        p.setBorder(new EtchedBorder (EtchedBorder.LOWERED));
        p.add(new JLabel("LOWERED EtchedBorder"));
        content.add(p);

        p = new JPanel();
        p.setBorder(new SoftBevelBorder (SoftBevelBorder.RAISED));
        p.add(new JLabel("RAISED SoftBevelBorder"));
        content.add(p);

        p = new JPanel();
        p.setBorder(new SoftBevelBorder (SoftBevelBorder.LOWERED));
        p.add(new JLabel("LOWERED SoftBevelBorder"));
        content.add(p);

        p = new JPanel();
        p.setBorder(new MatteBorder (new ImageIcon("spiral.gif")));
        p.add(new JLabel("MatteBorder"));
        content.add(p);

        p = new JPanel();
        p.setBorder(new TitledBorder (
          new MatteBorder (new ImageIcon("spiral.gif")),
          "Title String"));
        p.add(new JLabel("TitledBorder using MatteBorder"));
        content.add(p);

        p = new JPanel();
        p.setBorder(new TitledBorder (
          new LineBorder (Color.black, 5),
          "Title String"));
        p.add(new JLabel("TitledBorder using LineBorder"));
        content.add(p);

        p = new JPanel();
        p.setBorder(new TitledBorder (
          new EmptyBorder (10,10,10,10),
          "Title String"));
        p.add(new JLabel("TitledBorder using EmptyBorder"));
        content.add(p);

        setVisible(true);
    }

    public static void main(String args[]) {
      new BorderTest();
    }
}
```

Borders for visual layering   Use borders to create a visual association between components in a view. Beveled borders are graphically very striking and can be used to strongly associate items. The Windows look and feel does this. For example, buttons use a raised `BevelBorder` and data fields use a lowered `Bevel-Border`. If you want to visually associate components or draw attention to a component, then you can create a *visual layer* by careful use of `BevelBorder`. If you want to draw attention to a particular button or group of buttons, you might consider thickening the RAISED bevel using `BorderInsets` as discussed in section 3.2.1

Borders for visual grouping   Use borders to create group boxes. `EtchedBorder` and `LineBorder` are particularly effective for this, as they are graphically weaker then `BevelBorder`. `EmptyBorder` is also very useful for grouping. It uses the power of negative (white) space to visually associate the contained components and draw the viewer's eye to the group.

You may wish to create a visual grouping of attributes or simply signify the bounds of a set of choices. Grouping related radio buttons and check boxes is particularly useful.

Achieving visual integration and balance using negative space   Use a compound border including an `EmptyBorder` to increase the negative (white) space around a component or panel. Visually, a border sets what is known as a ground (or area) for a figure. The figure is what is contained within the border. It is important to keep the figure and the ground in balance by providing adequate white space around the figure. The stronger the border, the more white space will be required; for example, a `BevelBorder` will require more white space than an `EtchedBorder`.

Border for visual grouping with layering   Doubly compounded borders can be used to group information and communicate hierarchy using visual layering. Consider the following implementation which is shown in figure 3.8. Here we are indicating a common container for the attributes within the border. They are both attributes of Customer. Because we have indicated the label Customer (top left-hand side of the box) in the border title, we do not need to repeat the label for each field. We are further communicating the type of the Customer with the VIP label (bottom right-hand side of the box).

Visual layering of the hierachy involved is achieved by position and font.

• Position: In western cultures, the eye is trained to scan from top left to bottom right. Thus, something located top left has a visual higher rank than something located bottom right.

• Font: By bolding the term Customer, we are clearly communicating it as the highest ranking detail.

What we are displaying is a Customer of type VIP, not a VIP of type Customer. The positioning and heavier font reinforcement clearly communicate this message.

Figure 3.8
Visual grouping
with layering

3.2.1 Inside borders

It is important to understand that borders are not components. In fact, AbstractBorder, the abstract class all border classes are derived from, directly extends Object. Therefore, we cannot attach action and mouse listeners to borders, set tooltips, etc.

> **NOTE** The fact that borders are not components has certain side effects, one of which is that borders are much less efficient in painting themselves. There is no optimization support like there is in JComponent. We *can* do interesting things like using a very thick MatteBorder to tile a panel with an image, but this is an inefficient and unreliable solution. In general, don't use really large borders for anything. If you need an extremely large border, consider simulating one using JLabels and a container managed by BorderLayout.

One major benefit of Borders not being components is that we can use a single Border instance with an arbitrary number of components. In large-scale applications, this can reduce a significant amount of overhead.

When a Swing component is assigned a border, its Insets are defined by that border's width and height settings. When layout managers lay out JComponents, as we will see in the next chapter, they take into account their Insets; they normally use JComponent's getInsets() method to obtain this information. Inside the getInsets() method, the current border is asked to provide its Insets using the getBorderInsets() method.

The Insets class consists of four publicly accessible int values: bottom, left, right, and top. TitleBorder must compute its Insets based on its current font and text position since these variables could potentially affect the size of any of the Insets values. In the case of CompoundBorder, both its outer and inner Insets are retrieved through calls to getBorderInsets(), and then they are added up. A MatteBorder's Insets are determined by the width and height of its image. BevelBorder and EtchedBorder have Insets values: 2, 2, 2, 2. SoftBevelBorder has Insets values: 3, 3, 3, 3. EmptyBorder's Insets are simply the values that were passed in to the constructor. Each of LineBorder's Insets values equal the thickness that was specified in the constructor (or 1 as the default).

Borders get painted late in the JComponent rendering pipeline to ensure that they always appear on top of each associated component. AbstractBorder defines several getInteriorRectangle() methods to get a Rectangle representing the interior region of the component a border is attached to: getInteriorRectangle(). Any JComponent subclass implementing its own painting methods may be interested in this area. Combined with the Graphics clipping area, components may use this information to minimize their rendering work (refer back to chapter 2 for more information).

3.3 CREATING A CUSTOM BORDER

To create a custom border, we can implement the `javax.swing.Border` interface and define the following three methods:

- `void paintBorder(Component c, Graphics g)`: Performs the border rendering; only paint within the `Insets` region.
- `Insets getBorderInsets(Component c)`: Returns an `Insets` instance representing the top, bottom, left, and right thicknesses.
- `boolean isBorderOpaque()`: Returns whether or not the border is opaque or transparent.

The following class, shown in example 3.2, is a simple implementation of a custom rounded-rectangle border which we call `OvalBorder`.

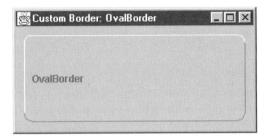

Figure 3.9   A custom rounded-corner border implementation

Example 3.2

OvalBorder.java

see \Chapter3\2

```
import java.awt.*;

import javax.swing.*;
import javax.swing.border.*;

public class OvalBorder implements Border
{
  protected int m_w=6;
  protected int m_h=6;
  protected Color m_topColor = Color.white;
  protected Color m_bottomColor = Color.gray;

  public OvalBorder() {
    m_w=6;
    m_h=6;
  }

  public OvalBorder(int w, int h) {
    m_w=w;
    m_h=h;
  }

  public OvalBorder(int w, int h, Color topColor,
    Color bottomColor) {
```

```
    m_w=w;
    m_h=h;
    m_topColor = topColor;
    m_bottomColor = bottomColor;
  }

  public Insets getBorderInsets(Component c) {
    return new Insets(m_h, m_w, m_h, m_w);
  }

  public  boolean isBorderOpaque() { return true; }

  public void paintBorder(Component c, Graphics g,
   int x, int y, int w, int h) {
    w--;
    h--;
    g.setColor(m_topColor);
    g.drawLine(x, y+h-m_h, x, y+m_h);
    g.drawArc(x, y, 2*m_w, 2*m_h, 180, -90);
    g.drawLine(x+m_w, y, x+w-m_w, y);
    g.drawArc(x+w-2*m_w, y, 2*m_w, 2*m_h, 90, -90);

    g.setColor(m_bottomColor);
    g.drawLine(x+w, y+m_h, x+w, y+h-m_h);
    g.drawArc(x+w-2*m_w, y+h-2*m_h, 2*m_w, 2*m_h, 0, -90);
    g.drawLine(x+m_w, y+h, x+w-m_w, y+h);
    g.drawArc(x, y+h-2*m_h, 2*m_w, 2*m_h, -90, -90);
  }

  public static void main(String[] args) {
    JFrame frame = new JFrame("Custom Border: OvalBorder");
    JLabel label = new JLabel("OvalBorder");
    ((JPanel) frame.getContentPane()).setBorder(new CompoundBorder(
      new EmptyBorder(10,10,10,10), new OvalBorder(10,10)));
    frame.getContentPane().add(label);
    frame.setBounds(0,0,300,150);
    frame.setVisible(true);
  }
}
```

3.3.1   Understanding the code

This border consists of a raised shadowed rectangle with rounded corners. Instance variables:

Table 3.1   OvalBorder.java instance variables

Variables	Description
int m_w	Left and right inset value.
int m_h	Top and bottom inset value.
Color m_topColor	Non-shadow color.
Color m_bottomColor	Shadow color.

Three constructors are provided to allow optional specification of the width and height of the left/right and top/bottom inset values respectively. We can also specify the shadow color (bottom color) and non-shadow color (top color). The inset values default to 6, the top color defaults to white, and the shadow color defaults to gray.

The `isBorderOpaque()` method always returns `true` to signify that this border's region will be completely filled. `getBorderInsets()` simply returns an `Insets` instance made up of the left/right and top/bottom inset values.

The `paintBorder()` method is responsible for rendering our border, and it simply paints a sequence of four lines and arcs in the appropriate colors. By reversing the use of `bottomColor` and `topColor`, we can switch from a raised look to a lowered look (a more flexible implementation might include a raised/lowered flag and an additional constructor parameter used to specify this).

The `main()` method creates a `JFrame` with a content pane surrounded by a `CompoundBorder`. The outer border is an `EmptyBorder` to provide white space, and the inner border is an instance of our `OvalBorder` class with width and height values of 10.

3.3.2   Running the code

Figure 3.9 illustrates the output of example 3.2. Try running this class and resizing the parent frame. Notice that with a very small width or height, the border does not render itself perfectly. A more professional implementation will take this into account in the `paintBorder()` routine.

CHAPTER 4

Layout managers

4.1 LAYOUTS OVERVIEW

In this chapter, we'll present several examples that show how to use various layouts to satisfy specific goals, and we'll also show how to create two custom layout managers that simplify the construction of many common interfaces. You'll also learn how to construct a basic container for JavaBeans which must be able to manage a dynamic number of components. But before we present these examples, it will help you to understand the big picture of layouts, which classes use their own custom layouts, and exactly what it means to be a layout manager.

All layout managers implement one of two interfaces defined in the `java.awt` package: `LayoutManager` or its subclass, `LayoutManager2`. `LayoutManager` declares a set of methods that are intended to provide a straightforward, organized means of managing component positions and sizes in a container. Each implementation of `LayoutManager` defines these methods in different ways according to its specific needs. `LayoutManager2` enhances this by adding methods intended to aid in managing component postions and sizes using *constraints-based* objects. Constraints-based objects usually store position and sizing information about one component, and implementations of `LayoutManager2` normally store one constraints-based object per component. For instance, `GridBagLayout` uses a `Hashtable` to map each `Component` it manages to its own `GridBagConstraints` object.

Figure 4.1 shows all the classes that implement LayoutManager and LayoutManager2. Notice that there are several UI classes that implement these interfaces to provide custom layout functionality for themselves. The other classes—the classes with which we are most familar and concerned—are built solely to provide help in laying out the containers they are assigned to.

Each container should be assigned one layout manager, and no layout manager should be used to manage more than one container.

```
LayoutManager
 ┬
 ├→ GridLayout
 ├→ FlowLayout
 ├→ ViewportLayout
 ├→ ScrollPaneLayout
 ├→ BasicOptionPaneUI.ButtonAreaLayout
 ├→ BasicTabbedPaneUI.TabbedPaneLayout
 ├→ BasicSplitPaneDivider.DividerLayout
 ├→ BasicInternalFrameTitlePane.TitlePaneLayout
 ├→ BasicScrollBarUI
 ├→ BasicComboBoxUI.ComboBoxLayoutManager
 └→ BasicInternalFrameUI.InternalFrameLayout
 └→ LayoutManager2
     ┬
     ├→ CardLayout
     ├→ GridBagLayout
     ├→ BorderLayout
     ├→ BoxLayout
     ├→ JRootPane.RootLayout
     ├→ OverlayLayout
     └→ BasicSplitPaneUI.BasicHorizontalLayoutManager
```

┌─────────────────────┐
│ — Extended by   │
│ ··· Implemented by │
└─────────────────────┘

Figure 4.1 LayoutManager
and LayoutManager2
implementations

NOTE   We have purposely omitted the discussion of several layout managers in this chapter (such as ViewportLayout, ScrollPaneLayout, and JRootPane.RootPaneLayout) because they are rarely used by developers and are more appropriately discussed in terms of the components that rely on them. For instance, we discuss ViewportLayout and ScrollPaneLayout in chapter 7.

4.1.1   LayoutManager

abstract interface java.awt.LayoutManager

This interface must be implemented by any layout manager. Two methods are especially noteworthy:

- layoutContainer(Container parent): Calculates and sets the bounds for all components in the given container.
- preferredLayoutSize(Container parent): Calculates the preferred size requirements to lay out components in the given container and returns a Dimension instance representing this size.

4.1.2   LayoutManager2

abstract interface java.awt.LayoutManager2

This interface extends LayoutManager to provide a framework for those layout managers that use constraints-based layouts. The method addLayoutComponent(Component comp, Object constraints) adds a new component associated with a constraints-based object which carries information about how to lay out this component.

A typical implementation is BorderLayout, which requires a direction (such as north or east) to position a component. In this case, the constraint objects used are static Strings such as BorderLayout.NORTH and BorderLayout.EAST. We are normally blind to the fact that BorderLayout is constraints-based because we are never required to manipulate the constraint objects at all. This is not the case with layouts such as GridBagLayout, where we must work directly with the constraint objects (which are instances of GridBagConstraints).

4.1.3   BoxLayout

class javax.swing.BoxLayout

BoxLayout organizes the components it manages along either the x-axis or y-axis of the owner panel. The only constructor, BoxLayout(Container target, int axis), takes a reference to the Container component it will manage and a direction (BoxLayout.X_AXIS or BoxLayout.Y_AXIS). Components are laid out according to their preferred sizes and they are not wrapped, even if the container does not provide enough space.

4.1.4   Box

class javax.swing.Box

To make using the BoxLayout manager easier, Swing also provides a class named Box which is a container with an automatically assigned BoxLayout manager. To create an instance of this container, we simply pass the desired alignment to its constructor. The Box class also supports the insertion of invisible blocks (instances of Box.Filler—see below) which allow regions of unused space to be specified. These blocks are basically lightweight components with bounds (position and size) but no view.

4.1.5   Filler

static class javax.swing.Box.Filler

This static inner class defines invisible components that affect a container's layout. The Box class provides convenient static methods for the creation of three different variations: glue, struts, and rigid areas.

- createHorizontalGlue(), createVerticalGlue(): Returns a component which fills the space between its neighboring components, pushing them aside to occupy all available space (this functionality is more analagous to a spring than it is to glue).
- createHorizontalStrut(int width), createVerticalStrut(int height): Returns a fixed-width (height) component which provides a fixed gap between its neighbors.
- createRigidArea(Dimension d): Returns an invisible component of fixed width and height.

  NOTE   All relevant Box methods are static and, as such, they can be applied to any container managed by a BoxLayout, not just instances of Box. Box should be thought of as a utilities class as much as it is a container.

4.1.6 FlowLayout

class java.awt.FlowLayout

This is a simple layout which places components from left to right in a row using the preferred component sizes (the size returned by `getPreferredSize()`), until no space in the container is available. When no space is available a new row is started. Because this placement depends on the current size of the container, we cannot always guarantee in advance in which row a component will be placed.

`FlowLayout` is too simple to rely on in serious applications where we want to be sure, for instance, that a set of buttons will reside at the bottom of a dialog and not on its right side. However, it can be useful as a pad for a single component to ensure that this component will be placed in the center of a container. Note that `FlowLayout` is the default layout for all `JPanels` (the only exception is the content pane of a `JRootPane` which is always initialized with a `BorderLayout`).

4.1.7 GridLayout

class java.awt.GridLayout

This layout places components in a rectangular grid. There are three constructors:

- `GridLayout()`: Creates a layout with one column per component. Only one row is used.
- `GridLayout(int rows, int cols)`: Creates a layout with the given number of rows and columns.
- `GridLayout(int rows, int cols, int hgap, int vgap)`: Creates a layout with the given number of rows and columns, and the given size of horizontal and vertical gaps between each row and column.

`GridLayout` places components from left to right and from top to bottom, assigning the same size to each. It forces the occupation of all available container space and it shares this space evenly between components. When it is not used carefully, this can lead to undesirable component sizing, such as text boxes three times higher than expected.

4.1.8 GridBagLayout

class java.awt.GridBagLayout, class java.awt.GridBagConstraints

This layout extends the capabilities of `GridLayout` to become constraints-based. It breaks the container's space into equal rectangular pieces (like bricks in a wall) and places each component in one or more of these pieces. You need to create and fill a `GridBagConstraints` object for each component to inform `GridBagLayout` how to place and size that component.

`GridBagLayout` can be effectively used for placement of components if no special behavior is required on resizing. However, due to its complexity, it usually requires some helper methods or classes to handle all the necessary constraints information. James Tan, a usability expert and `GridBagLayout` extraordinaire, gives a comprehensive overview of this manager in section 4.3. He also presents a helper class to ease the burden of dealing with `GridBagConstraints`.

4.1.9   BorderLayout

class java.awt.BorderLayout

This layout divides a container into five regions: center, north, south, east, and west. To specify the region in which to place a component, we use Strings of the form "Center," "North," and so on, or the static String fields defined in BorderLayout, which include BorderLayout.CENTER, BorderLayout.NORTH, etc. During the layout process, components in the north and south regions will first be allotted their preferred height (if possible) and the width of the container. Once north and south components have been assigned sizes, components in the east and west regions will attempt to occupy their preferred width as well as any remaining height between the north and south components. A component in the center region will occupy all remaining available space. BorderLayout is very useful, especially in conjunction with other layouts, as we will see in this and future chapters.

4.1.10   CardLayout

class java.awt.CardLayout

CardLayout treats all components as similar to cards of equal size overlapping one another. Only one card component is visible at any given time (see figure 4.2). The methods first(), last(), next(), previous(), and show() can be called to switch between components in the parent Container.

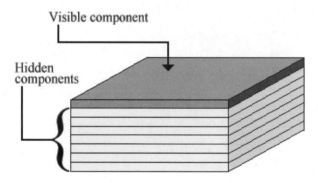

Figure 4.2 CardLayout

In a stack of several cards, only the top-most card is visible.

4.1.11   JPanel

class javax.swing.JPanel

This class represents a generic lightweight container. It works in close cooperation with layout managers. The default constructor creates a JPanel with a FlowLayout, but different layouts can be specified in a constructor or assigned using the setLayout() method.

> **NOTE**   The content pane of a JRootPane container is a JPanel, which, by default, is assigned a BorderLayout, not a FlowLayout.

4.2 COMPARING COMMON LAYOUT MANAGERS

Example 4.1 demonstrates the most commonly used AWT and Swing layout managers. It shows a set of JInternalFrames that contain identical sets of components, each using a different layout. The purpose of this example is to allow direct simultaneous layout manager comparisons using resizable containers.

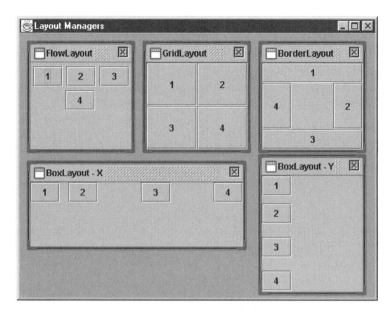

Figure 4.3   Comparing common layouts

Example 4.1

CommonLayouts.java

see \Chapter4\1

```java
import java.awt.*;
import java.awt.event.*;
import java.util.*;

import javax.swing.*;
import javax.swing.border.*;
import javax.swing.event.*;

public class CommonLayouts extends JFrame
{
  public CommonLayouts() {
    super("Common Layout Managers");
    setSize(500, 380);

    JDesktopPane desktop = new JDesktopPane();
    getContentPane().add(desktop);
```

```
JInternalFrame fr1 =
  new JInternalFrame("FlowLayout", true, true);
fr1.setBounds(10, 10, 150, 150);
Container c = fr1.getContentPane();
c.setLayout(new FlowLayout());
c.add(new JButton("1"));
c.add(new JButton("2"));
c.add(new JButton("3"));
c.add(new JButton("4"));
desktop.add(fr1, 0);

JInternalFrame fr2 =
  new JInternalFrame("GridLayout", true, true);
fr2.setBounds(170, 10, 150, 150);
c = fr2.getContentPane();
c.setLayout(new GridLayout(2, 2));
c.add(new JButton("1"));
c.add(new JButton("2"));
c.add(new JButton("3"));
c.add(new JButton("4"));
desktop.add(fr2, 0);

JInternalFrame fr3 =
  new JInternalFrame("BorderLayout", true, true);
fr3.setBounds(330, 10, 150, 150);
c = fr3.getContentPane();
c.add(new JButton("1"), BorderLayout.NORTH);
c.add(new JButton("2"), BorderLayout.EAST);
c.add(new JButton("3"), BorderLayout.SOUTH);
c.add(new JButton("4"), BorderLayout.WEST);
desktop.add(fr3, 0);

JInternalFrame fr4 = new JInternalFrame("BoxLayout - X",
  true, true);
fr4.setBounds(10, 170, 250, 120);
c = fr4.getContentPane();
c.setLayout(new BoxLayout(c, BoxLayout.X_AXIS));
c.add(new JButton("1"));
c.add(Box.createHorizontalStrut(12));
c.add(new JButton("2"));
c.add(Box.createGlue());
c.add(new JButton("3"));
c.add(Box.createHorizontalGlue());
c.add(new JButton("4"));
desktop.add(fr4, 0);

JInternalFrame fr5 = new JInternalFrame("BoxLayout - Y",
  true, true);
fr5.setBounds(330, 170, 150, 180);
c = fr5.getContentPane();
c.setLayout(new BoxLayout(c, BoxLayout.Y_AXIS));
c.add(new JButton("1"));
c.add(Box.createVerticalStrut(10));
c.add(new JButton("2"));
```

```
    c.add(Box.createGlue());
    c.add(new JButton("3"));
    c.add(Box.createVerticalGlue());
    c.add(new JButton("4"));
    desktop.add(fr5, 0);

    try {
      fr1.setSelected(true);
    }
    catch (java.beans.PropertyVetoException ex) {}

    WindowListener wndCloser = new WindowAdapter() {
      public void windowClosing(WindowEvent e) {
        System.exit(0);
      }
    };
    addWindowListener(wndCloser);

    setVisible(true);
  }

  public static void main(String argv[]) {
    new CommonLayouts();
  }
}
```

4.2.1 Understanding the code

Class CommonLayouts

The CommonLayouts constructor creates five JInternalFrames and places them in a JDesktopPane. Each of these frames contains four JButtons labeled "1," "2," "3," and "4." Each frame is assigned a unique layout manager: a FlowLayout, a 2×2 GridLayout, a Border-Layout, an x-oriented BoxLayout, and a y-oriented BoxLayout. Notice that the internal frames using BoxLayout also use strut and glue filler components to demonstrate their behavior.

4.2.2 Running the code

Figure 4.3 shows CommonLayouts in action. Notice the differences in each frame's content as it changes size.

- FlowLayout places components in one or more rows depending on the width of the container.
- GridLayout assigns an equal size to all components and fills all container space.
- BorderLayout places components along the sides of the container.
- x-oriented BoxLayout always places components in a row. The distance between the first and second components is 12 pixels (determined by the horizontal strut component). Distances between the second, third, and fourth components are equalized and take up all remaining width (determined by the two glue filler components).
- y-oriented BoxLayout always places components in a column. The distance between the first and second components is 10 pixels (determined by the vertical strut component). Distances between the second, third, and fourth components are equalized and take up all available height (determined by the two glue filler components).

4.3   USING GRIDBAGLAYOUT

This section was written by James Tan, a systems analyst with
United Overseas Bank Singapore (jamestan@earthling.net).

Of all the layouts included with Swing and AWT, `GridBagLayout` is by far the most complex. In this section, we will walk through the various constraints attributes it relies on, along with several short examples showing how to use them. We'll follow up this discussion with a comprehensive input dialog example which puts all these attributes together. We'll then conclude this section with the construction and demonstration of a helper class designed to make using `GridBagLayout` more convenient.

4.3.1   Default behavior of GridBagLayout

By simply setting a container's layout to a `GridBagLayout` and adding `Component`s to it, the result will be a row of components, each set to their preferred size, tightly packed and placed in the center of the container. Unlike `FlowLayout`, `GridBagLayout` will allow components to be clipped by the edge of the managing container, and it will not move child components down into a new row. The following code demonstrates this, and figure 4.4 shows the result:

```
JInternalFrame fr1 = new JInternalFrame(
   "Example 1", true, true );
fr1.setBounds( 5, 5, 270, 100 );
cn = fr1.getContentPane();
cn.setLayout( new GridBagLayout() );
cn.add( new JButton( "Wonderful" ) );
cn.add( new JButton( "World" ) );
cn.add( new JButton( "Of" ) );
cn.add( new JButton( "Swing !!!" ) );
desktop.add( fr1, 0 );
```

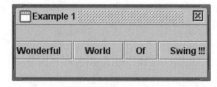

Figure 4.4   Default
`GridBagLayout` **behavior**

4.3.2   Introducing GridBagConstraints

When a component is added to a container which has been assigned a `GridBagLayout`, the layout manager uses a default `GridBagConstraints` object to place the component accordingly, as shown in the above example. By creating and setting the attributes of a `GridBag-Constraints`' object and passing it in as an additional parameter in the `add()` method, we can flexibly manage the placement of our components.

Listed below are the various attributes we can set in a `GridBagConstraints` object along with their default values. The behavior of these attributes will be explained in the examples that follow.

```
public int gridx = GridBagConstraints.RELATIVE;
public int gridy = GridBagConstraints.RELATIVE;
```

```
public int gridwidth = 1;
public int gridheight = 1;
public double weightx = 0.0;
public double weighty = 0.0;
public int anchor = GridBagConstraints.CENTER;
public int fill = GridBagConstraints.NONE;
public Insets insets = new Insets( 0, 0, 0, 0 );
public int ipadx = 0;
public int ipady = 0;
```

4.3.3 Using the gridx, gridy, insets, ipadx, and ipady constraints

The gridx and gridy constraints (or column and row constraints) are used to specify the exact grid cell location where we want our component to be placed. Component placement starts from the upper left-hand corner of the container, and gridx and gridy begin with values of 0. Specifying negative values for either of these attributes is equivalent to setting them to GridBagConstraints.RELATIVE, which means that the next component added will be placed directly after the previous gridx or gridy location.

The insets constraint adds an invisible exterior padding around the associated component. Negative values can be used which will force the component to be sized larger than the cell it is contained in.

The ipadx and ipady constraints add an interior padding which increases the preferred size of the associated component. Specifically, the padding adds ipadx * 2 pixels to the preferred width and ipady * 2 pixels to the preferred height (* 2 because this padding applies to both sides of the component).

In this example, we place the "Wonderful" and "World" buttons in the first row and the other two buttons in the second row. We also associate insets with each button so that they don't look too cluttered, and they vary in both height and width.

```
JInternalFrame fr2 = new JInternalFrame("Example 2", true, true );
fr2.setBounds( 5, 110, 270, 140 );
cn = fr2.getContentPane();
cn.setLayout( new GridBagLayout() );

c = new GridBagConstraints();
c.insets = new Insets( 2, 2, 2, 2 );
c.gridx = 0;    // Column 0
c.gridy = 0;    // Row 0
c.ipadx = 5;    // Increases component width by 10 pixels
c.ipady = 5;    // Increases component height by 10 pixels
cn.add( new JButton( "Wonderful" ), c );

c.gridx = 1;    // Column 1
c.ipadx = 0;    // Reset the padding to 0
c.ipady = 0;
cn.add( new JButton( "World" ), c );

c.gridx = 0;    // Column 0
c.gridy = 1;    // Row 1
cn.add( new JButton( "Of" ), c );

c.gridx = 1;    // Column 1
```

```
cn.add( new JButton( "Swing !!!" ), c );

desktop.add( fr2, 0 );
```

We begin by creating a `GridBagConstraints` object to set the constraints for the first button component. We pass it in together with the button in the `add()` method. We reuse this same constraints object by changing the relevant attributes and passing in again for each remaining component. This conserves memory, and it also relieves us of having to reassign a whole new group of attributes. Figure 4.5 shows the result.

Figure 4.5 Using the `gridx`, `gridy`, `insets`, `ipadx`, **and** `ipady` **constraints**

4.3.4   Using the weightx and weighty constraints

When the container in the example above is resized, the components respect the constraints we have assigned, but the whole group remains in the center of the container. Why don't the buttons grow to occupy a proportional amount of the increased space surrounding them? The answer lies in the use of the `weightx` and `weighty` constraints, which both default to zero when `GridBagConstraints` is instantiated.

These two constraints specify how any extra space in a container should be distributed among each component's cells. The `weightx` attribute specifies the fraction of extra horizontal space to occupy. Similarly, `weighty` specifies the fraction of extra vertical space to occupy. Both constraints can be assigned values ranging from `0.0` to `1.0`.

For example, let's say we have two buttons, A and B, placed in columns 0 and 1 of row 0 respectively. If we specify `weightx = 1.0` for the first button and `weightx = 0` for the second button, when we resize the container, all extra space will be distributed to the first button's cell—50% on the left of the button and 50% on the right. The other button will be pushed to the right of the container as far as possible. Figure 4.6 illustrates this concept.

Figure 4.6 Using `weightx`
and `weighty` **constraints**

Getting back to our "Wonderful World Of Swing !!!" example, we now modify all button cells to share any extra container space equally as the container is resized. Specifying `weightx = 1.0` and `weighty = 1.0`, and keeping these attributes constant as each component is added, will tell `GridBagLayout` to use all available space for each cell. Figure 4.7 illustrates these changes.

```
JInternalFrame fr3 = new JInternalFrame("Example 3", true, true );
fr3.setBounds( 5, 255, 270, 140 );
cn = fr3.getContentPane();
cn.setLayout( new GridBagLayout() );
```

```
c = new GridBagConstraints();
c.insets = new Insets( 2, 2, 2, 2 );
c.weighty = 1.0;
c.weightx = 1.0;
c.gridx = 0;
c.gridy = 0;
cn.add( new JButton( "Wonderful" ), c );

c.gridx = 1;
cn.add( new JButton( "World" ), c );

c.gridx = 0;
c.gridy = 1;
cn.add( new JButton( "Of" ), c );

c.gridx = 1;
cn.add( new JButton( "Swing !!!" ), c );

desktop.add( fr3, 0 );
```

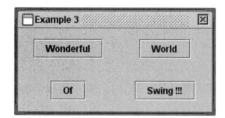

Figure 4.7 Using `weightx`
and `weighty` **constraints**

4.3.5   Using the gridwidth and gridheight constraints

GridBagLayout also allows us to span components across multiple cells using the `gridwidth` and `gridheight` constraints. To demonstrate, we'll modify our example to force the "Wonderful" button to occupy two rows and the "World" button to occupy two columns. Figure 4.8 illustrates this. Notice that occupying more cells forces more rows and/or columns to be created based on the current container size.

```
JInternalFrame fr4 = new JInternalFrame("Example 4", true, true );
fr4.setBounds( 280, 5, 270, 140 );
cn = fr4.getContentPane();
cn.setLayout( new GridBagLayout() );

c = new GridBagConstraints();
c.insets = new Insets( 2, 2, 2, 2 );
c.weighty = 1.0;
c.weightx = 1.0;
c.gridx = 0;
c.gridy = 0;
c.gridheight = 2; // Span across 2 rows
cn.add( new JButton( "Wonderful" ), c );

c.gridx = 1;
c.gridheight = 1; // Remember to set back to 1 row
c.gridwidth = 2; // Span across 2 columns
cn.add( new JButton( "World" ), c );
```

```
c.gridy = 1;
c.gridwidth = 1; // Remember to set back to 1 column
cn.add( new JButton( "Of" ), c );

c.gridx = 2;
cn.add( new JButton( "Swing !!!" ), c );

desktop.add( fr4, 0 );
```

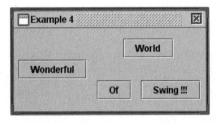

Figure 4.8 Using `gridwidth`
and `gridheight` **constraints**

4.3.6 Using anchor constraints

We can control how a component is aligned within its cell(s) by setting the `anchor` constraint. By default this is set to `GridBagConstraints.CENTER`, which forces the component to be centered within its occupied cell(s). We can choose from the following `anchor` settings:

```
GridBagConstraints.NORTH
GridBagConstraints.SOUTH
GridBagConstraints.EAST
GridBagConstraints.WEST
GridBagConstraints.NORTHEAST
GridBagConstraints.NORTHWEST
GridBagConstraints.SOUTHEAST
GridBagConstraints.SOUTHWEST
GridBagConstraints.CENTER
```

In the code below, we've modified our example to anchor the "Wonderful" button NORTH and the "World" button SOUTHWEST. The "Of" and "Swing !!!" buttons are achored in the CENTER of their cells. Figure 4.9 illustrates.

```
JInternalFrame fr5 = new JInternalFrame("Example 5", true, true );
fr5.setBounds( 280, 150, 270, 140 );
cn = fr5.getContentPane();
cn.setLayout( new GridBagLayout() );

c = new GridBagConstraints();
c.insets = new Insets( 2, 2, 2, 2 );
c.weighty = 1.0;
c.weightx = 1.0;
c.gridx = 0;
c.gridy = 0;
c.gridheight = 2;
c.anchor = GridBagConstraints.NORTH;
cn.add( new JButton( "Wonderful" ), c );

c.gridx = 1;
c.gridheight = 1;
```

```
c.gridwidth = 2;
c.anchor = GridBagConstraints.SOUTHWEST;
cn.add( new JButton( "World" ), c );

c.gridy = 1;
c.gridwidth = 1;
c.anchor = GridBagConstraints.CENTER;
cn.add( new JButton( "Of" ), c );

c.gridx = 2;
cn.add( new JButton( "Swing !!!" ), c );

desktop.add( fr5, 0 );
```

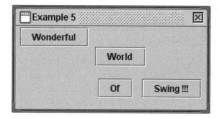

Figure 4.9 Using `gridwidth`
and `gridheight` **constraints**

4.3.7   Using fill constraints

The most common reason for spanning multiple cells is that we want the component contained in that cell to occupy the enlarged space. To do this we use the `gridheight/gridwidth` constraints as described above, as well as the `fill` constraint. The `fill` constraint can be assigned any of the following values:

```
GridBagConstraints.NONE
GridBagConstraints.HORIZONTAL
GridBagConstraints.VERTICAL
GridBagConstraints.BOTH
```

In the code below, we modify our example to force the "Wonderful" button to occupy all available cell space, both vertically and horizontally. The "World" button now occupies all available horizontal cell space, but it continues to use its preferred vertical size. The "Of" button does not make use of the fill constraint; it simply uses its preferred size. The "Swing !!!" button occupies all available vertical cell space, but it uses its preferred horizontal size. Figure 4.10 illustrates.

```
JInternalFrame fr6 = new JInternalFrame("Example 6", true, true );
fr6.setBounds( 280, 295, 270, 140 );
cn = fr6.getContentPane();
cn.setLayout( new GridBagLayout() );

c = new GridBagConstraints();
c.insets = new Insets( 2, 2, 2, 2 );
c.weighty = 1.0;
c.weightx = 1.0;
c.gridx = 0;
c.gridy = 0;
c.gridheight = 2;
```

```
c.fill = GridBagConstraints.BOTH;
cn.add( new JButton( "Wonderful" ), c );

c.gridx = 1;
c.gridheight = 1;
c.gridwidth = 2;
c.fill = GridBagConstraints.HORIZONTAL;
cn.add( new JButton( "World" ), c );

c.gridy = 1;
c.gridwidth = 1;
c.fill = GridBagConstraints.NONE;
cn.add( new JButton( "Of" ), c );

c.gridx = 2;
c.fill = GridBagConstraints.VERTICAL;
cn.add( new JButton( "Swing !!!" ), c );

desktop.add( fr6, 0 );
```

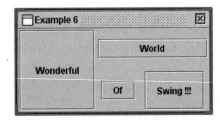

**Figure 4.10 Using
fill constraints**

4.3.8   Putting it all together: constructing a complaints dialog

Figure 4.11 shows a sketch of a generic complaints dialog that can be used for various forms of user feedback. This sketch clearly shows how we plan to lay out the various components, and the columns and rows in which they will be placed. In order to set the constraints correctly so that the components will be laid out as shown, we must do the following:

- For the "Short Description" text field, we set the `gridwidth` constraint to 3 and the `fill` constraint to `GridBagConstraints.HORIZONTAL`. In order to make this field occupy all the horizontal space available, we also need to set the `weightx` constraints to `1.0`.
- For the "Description" text area, we set the `gridwidth` constraint to 3, the `gridheight` to 2, and the `fill` constraint to `GridBagConstraint.BOTH`. In order to make this field occupy all the available horizontal and vertical space, we set the `weightx` and `weighty` constraints to `1.0`.
- For the "Severity," "Priority," "Name," "Telephone," "Sex," and "ID Number" input fields, we want each to use their preferred width. Since the widths each exceed the width of one cell, we set `gridwidth` to 3, and we set `weightx` to `0.0` so that they have enough space to fit, but they will not use any additional available horizontal space.
- For the Help button, we set the `anchor` constraint to `GridBagConstraint.NORTH` so that it will stick together with the upper two buttons, "Submit" and "Cancel." The `fill` constraint is set to `HORIZONTAL` to force each of these buttons to occupy all available horizontal cell space.
- All labels use their preferred sizes, and each component in this dialog is anchored `WEST`.

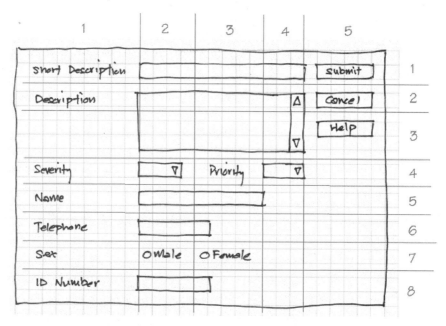

Figure 4.11 A sketch of a generic complaints dialog

Our implementation follows in example 4.2, and figure 4.12 shows the resulting dialog.

Example 4.2

ComplaintsDialog.java

see \Chapter4\Tan

```java
import javax.swing.*;
import javax.swing.border.*;
import java.awt.*;
import java.awt.event.*;

public class ComplaintsDialog extends JDialog
{
  public ComplaintsDialog( JFrame frame ) {
    super( frame, true );
    setTitle( "Simple Complaints Dialog" );
    setSize( 500, 300 );

    // Creates a panel to hold all components
    JPanel panel = new JPanel( new BorderLayout() );
    panel.setLayout( new GridBagLayout() );

    // Give the panel a border gap of 5 pixels
    panel.setBorder( new EmptyBorder( new Insets( 5, 5, 5, 5 ) ) );
    getContentPane().add( BorderLayout.CENTER, panel );

    GridBagConstraints c = new GridBagConstraints();
```

```
// Define preferred sizes for input fields
Dimension shortField = new Dimension( 40, 20 );
Dimension mediumField = new Dimension( 120, 20 );
Dimension longField = new Dimension( 240, 20 );
Dimension hugeField = new Dimension( 240, 80 );

// Spacing between label and field
EmptyBorder border = new EmptyBorder( new Insets( 0, 0, 0, 10 ) );
EmptyBorder border1 = new EmptyBorder( new Insets( 0, 20, 0, 10 ) );

// Add space around all components to avoid clutter
c.insets = new Insets( 2, 2, 2, 2 );

// Anchor all components WEST
c.anchor = GridBagConstraints.WEST;

JLabel lbl1 = new JLabel( "Short Description" );
lbl1.setBorder( border ); // Add some space to the right
panel.add( lbl1, c );
JTextField txt1 = new JTextField();
txt1.setPreferredSize( longField );
c.gridx = 1;
c.weightx = 1.0; // Use all available horizontal space
c.gridwidth = 3; // Spans across 3 columns
c.fill = GridBagConstraints.HORIZONTAL; // Fills the 3 columns
panel.add( txt1, c );

JLabel lbl2 = new JLabel( "Description" );
lbl2.setBorder( border );
c.gridwidth = 1;
c.gridx = 0;
c.gridy = 1;;
c.weightx = 0.0; // Do not use any extra horizontal space
panel.add( lbl2, c );
JTextArea area1 = new JTextArea();
JScrollPane scroll = new JScrollPane( area1 );
scroll.setPreferredSize( hugeField );
c.gridx = 1;
c.weightx = 1.0; // Use all available horizontal space
c.weighty = 1.0; // Use all available vertical space
c.gridwidth = 3; // Span across 3 columns
c.gridheight = 2; // Span across 2 rows
c.fill = GridBagConstraints.BOTH; // Fills the columns and rows
panel.add( scroll, c );

JLabel lbl3 = new JLabel( "Severity" );
lbl3.setBorder( border );
c.gridx = 0;
c.gridy = 3;
c.gridwidth = 1;
c.gridheight = 1;
c.weightx = 0.0;
c.weighty = 0.0;
c.fill = GridBagConstraints.NONE;
panel.add( lbl3, c );
```

```
JComboBox combo3 = new JComboBox();
combo3.addItem( "A" );
combo3.addItem( "B" );
combo3.addItem( "C" );
combo3.addItem( "D" );
combo3.addItem( "E" );
combo3.setPreferredSize( shortField );
c.gridx = 1;
panel.add( combo3, c );

JLabel lbl4 = new JLabel( "Priority" );
lbl4.setBorder( border1 );
c.gridx = 2;
panel.add( lbl4, c );
JComboBox combo4 = new JComboBox();
combo4.addItem( "1" );
combo4.addItem( "2" );
combo4.addItem( "3" );
combo4.addItem( "4" );
combo4.addItem( "5" );
combo4.setPreferredSize( shortField );
c.gridx = 3;
panel.add( combo4, c );

JLabel lbl5 = new JLabel( "Name" );
lbl5.setBorder( border );
c.gridx = 0;
c.gridy = 4;
panel.add( lbl5, c );
JTextField txt5 = new JTextField();
txt5.setPreferredSize( longField );
c.gridx = 1;
c.gridwidth = 3;
panel.add( txt5, c );

JLabel lbl6 = new JLabel( "Telephone" );
lbl6.setBorder( border );
c.gridx = 0;
c.gridy = 5;
panel.add( lbl6, c );
JTextField txt6 = new JTextField();
txt6.setPreferredSize( mediumField );
c.gridx = 1;
c.gridwidth = 3;
panel.add( txt6, c );

JLabel lbl7 = new JLabel( "Sex" );
lbl7.setBorder( border );
c.gridx = 0;
c.gridy = 6;
panel.add( lbl7, c );
JPanel radioPanel = new JPanel();

// Create a FlowLayout JPanel with 5 pixel horizontal gaps
// and no vertical gaps
```

```java
        radioPanel.setLayout( new FlowLayout( FlowLayout.LEFT, 5, 0 ) );
        ButtonGroup group = new ButtonGroup();
        JRadioButton radio1 = new JRadioButton( "Male" );
        radio1.setSelected( true );
        group.add( radio1 );
        JRadioButton radio2 = new JRadioButton( "Female" );
        group.add( radio2 );
        radioPanel.add( radio1 );
        radioPanel.add( radio2 );
        c.gridx = 1;
        c.gridwidth = 3;
        panel.add( radioPanel, c);

        JLabel lbl8 = new JLabel( "ID Number" );
        lbl8.setBorder( border );
        c.gridx = 0;
        c.gridy = 7;
        c.gridwidth = 1;
        panel.add( lbl8, c );
        JTextField txt8 = new JTextField();
        txt8.setPreferredSize( mediumField );
        c.gridx = 1;
        c.gridwidth = 3;
        panel.add( txt8, c );

        JButton submitBtn = new JButton( "Submit" );
        c.gridx = 4;
        c.gridy = 0;
        c.gridwidth = 1;
        c.fill = GridBagConstraints.HORIZONTAL;
        panel.add( submitBtn, c );

        JButton cancelBtn = new JButton( "Cancel" );
        c.gridy = 1;
        panel.add( cancelBtn, c );

        JButton helpBtn = new JButton( "Help" );
        c.gridy = 2;
        c.anchor = GridBagConstraints.NORTH; // Anchor north
        panel.add( helpBtn, c );

        WindowListener wndCloser = new WindowAdapter() {
          public void windowClosing(WindowEvent e) {
            System.exit(0);
          }
        };
        addWindowListener( wndCloser );

        setVisible( true );
    }
    public static void main( String[] args ) {
      new ComplaintsDialog( new JFrame() );
    }
}
```

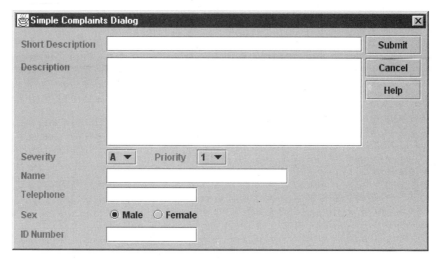

Figure 4.12   The Complaints Dialog

4.3.9   A simple helper class example

As we can see from example 4.2, constructing dialogs with more than a few components becomes a very tedious task and reduces source code legibility as well as organization. One way to make the use of `GridBagLayout` cleaner and easier is to create a helper class that manages all the constraints for us, and provides self-explanatory method names and pre-defined parameters.

The source code of a simple helper class we have constructed for this purpose is shown below in example 4.3. The method names used are easier to understand and laying out our components using row and column parameters is more intuitive than `gridx` and `gridy`. The methods implemented in this class are each a variation of one of the following:

- `addComponent`: Used to add a component that needs to adhere to its preferred size.
- `addAnchoredComponent`: Used to add a component that needs to be anchored.
- `addFilledComponent`: Used to add a component that will fill the entire cell space allocated to it.

Example 4.3

GriddedPanel.java

see \Chapter4\Tan

```java
import javax.swing.*;
import java.awt.*;

public class GriddedPanel extends JPanel
{
  private GridBagConstraints constraints;

  // Default constraints value definitions
  private static final int C_HORZ = GridBagConstraints.HORIZONTAL;
  private static final int C_NONE = GridBagConstraints.NONE;
```

```java
private static final int C_WEST = GridBagConstraints.WEST;
private static final int C_WIDTH = 1;
private static final int C_HEIGHT = 1;

// Create a GridBagLayout panel using a default insets constraint
public GriddedPanel() {
  this(new Insets(2, 2, 2, 2));
}

// Create a GridBagLayout panel using the specified insets
// constraint
public GriddedPanel(Insets insets) {
  super(new GridBagLayout());
  constraints = new GridBagConstraints();
  constraints.anchor = GridBagConstraints.WEST;
  constraints.insets = insets;
}

// Add a component to the specified row and column
public void addComponent(JComponent component, int row, int col) {
  addComponent(component, row, col, C_WIDTH,
    C_HEIGHT, C_WEST, C_NONE);
}

// Add a component to the specified row and column, spanning across
// a specified number of columns and rows
public void addComponent(JComponent component, int row, int col,
 int width, int height ) {
  addComponent(component, row, col, width,
    height, C_WEST, C_NONE);
}

// Add a component to the specified row and column, using a specified
// anchor constraint
public void addAnchoredComponent(JComponent component, int row,
 int col, int anchor ) {
  addComponent(component, row, col, C_WIDTH,
    C_HEIGHT, anchor, C_NONE);
}

// Add a component to the specified row and column, spanning across
// a specified number of columns and rows, using a specified
// anchor constraint
public void addAnchoredComponent(JComponent component,
 int row, int col, int width, int height, int anchor) {
  addComponent(component, row, col, width,
    height, anchor, C_NONE);
}

// Add a component to the specified row and column,
// filling the column horizontally
public void addFilledComponent(JComponent component,
 int row, int col) {
  addComponent(component, row, col, C_WIDTH,
    C_HEIGHT, C_WEST, C_HORZ);
}
```

```java
// Add a component to the specified row and column
// with the specified fill constraint
public void addFilledComponent(JComponent component,
 int row, int col, int fill) {
  addComponent(component, row, col, C_WIDTH,
   C_HEIGHT, C_WEST, fill);
}

// Add a component to the specified row and column,
// spanning a specified number of columns and rows,
// with the specified fill constraint
public void addFilledComponent(JComponent component,
 int row, int col, int width, int height, int fill) {
  addComponent(component, row, col, width, height, C_WEST, fill);
}

// Add a component to the specified row and column,
// spanning the specified number of columns and rows, with
// the specified fill and anchor constraints
public void addComponent(JComponent component,
 int row, int col, int width, int height, int anchor, int fill) {
  constraints.gridx = col;
  constraints.gridy = row;
  constraints.gridwidth = width;
  constraints.gridheight = height;
  constraints.anchor = anchor;
  double weightx = 0.0;
  double weighty = 0.0;

  // Only use extra horizontal or vertical space if a component
  // spans more than one column and/or row
  if(width > 1)
    weightx = 1.0;
  if(height > 1)
    weighty = 1.0;

  switch(fill)
  {
    case GridBagConstraints.HORIZONTAL:
      constraints.weightx = weightx;
      constraints.weighty = 0.0;
      break;
    case GridBagConstraints.VERTICAL:
      constraints.weighty = weighty;
      constraints.weightx = 0.0;
      break;
    case GridBagConstraints.BOTH:
      constraints.weightx = weightx;
      constraints.weighty = weighty;
      break;
    case GridBagConstraints.NONE:
      constraints.weightx = 0.0;
      constraints.weighty = 0.0;
      break;
```

```
      default:
      break;
  }
  constraints.fill = fill;
  add(component, constraints);
  }
}
```

Example 4.4 is the source code used to construct the same complaints dialog as in example 4.2, using our helper class methods instead of manipulating the constraints directly. Notice that the length of the code has been reduced and the readability has been improved. Also note that we add components starting at row 1 and column 1, rather than row 0 and column 0 (see figure 4.11).

Example 4.4

ComplaintsDialog2.java

see \Chapter4\Tan

```java
import javax.swing.*;
import javax.swing.border.*;
import java.awt.*;
import java.awt.event.*;

public class ComplaintsDialog2 extends JDialog
{
  public ComplaintsDialog2( JFrame frame ) {
    super( frame, true );
    setTitle( "Simple Complaints Dialog" );
    setSize( 500, 300 );

    GriddedPanel panel = new GriddedPanel();
    panel.setBorder(new EmptyBorder(new Insets(5, 5, 5, 5)));
    getContentPane().add(BorderLayout.CENTER, panel);

    // Input field dimensions
    Dimension shortField = new Dimension( 40, 20 );
    Dimension mediumField = new Dimension( 120, 20 );
    Dimension longField = new Dimension( 240, 20 );
    Dimension hugeField = new Dimension( 240, 80 );

    // Spacing between labels and fields
    EmptyBorder border = new EmptyBorder(
      new Insets( 0, 0, 0, 10 ));
    EmptyBorder border1 = new EmptyBorder(
      new Insets( 0, 20, 0, 10 ));

    JLabel lbl1 = new JLabel( "Short Description" );
    lbl1.setBorder( border );
    panel.addComponent( lbl1, 1, 1 );
    JTextField txt1 = new JTextField();
    txt1.setPreferredSize( longField );
    panel.addFilledComponent( txt1, 1, 2, 3, 1,
      GridBagConstraints.HORIZONTAL );
```

```
JLabel lbl2 = new JLabel( "Description" );
lbl2.setBorder( border );
panel.addComponent( lbl2, 2, 1 );
JTextArea area1 = new JTextArea();
JScrollPane scroll = new JScrollPane( area1 );
scroll.setPreferredSize( hugeField );
panel.addFilledComponent( scroll, 2, 2, 3, 2,
  GridBagConstraints.BOTH );

JLabel lbl3 = new JLabel( "Severity" );
lbl3.setBorder( border );
panel.addComponent( lbl3, 4, 1 );
JComboBox combo3 = new JComboBox();
combo3.addItem( "A" );
combo3.addItem( "B" );
combo3.addItem( "C" );
combo3.addItem( "D" );
combo3.addItem( "E" );
combo3.setPreferredSize( shortField );
panel.addComponent( combo3, 4, 2 );

JLabel lbl4 = new JLabel( "Priority" );
lbl4.setBorder( border1 );
panel.addComponent( lbl4, 4, 3 );
JComboBox combo4 = new JComboBox();
combo4.addItem( "1" );
combo4.addItem( "2" );
combo4.addItem( "3" );
combo4.addItem( "4" );
combo4.addItem( "5" );
combo4.setPreferredSize( shortField );
panel.addComponent( combo4, 4, 4 );

JLabel lbl5 = new JLabel( "Name" );
lbl5.setBorder( border );
panel.addComponent( lbl5, 5, 1 );
JTextField txt5 = new JTextField();
txt5.setPreferredSize( longField );
panel.addComponent( txt5, 5, 2, 3, 1 );

JLabel lbl6 = new JLabel( "Telephone" );
lbl6.setBorder( border );
panel.addComponent( lbl6, 6, 1 );
JTextField txt6 = new JTextField();
txt6.setPreferredSize( mediumField );
panel.addComponent( txt6, 6, 2, 3, 1 );

JLabel lbl7 = new JLabel( "Sex" );
lbl7.setBorder( border );
panel.addComponent( lbl7, 7, 1 );
JPanel radioPanel = new JPanel();
radioPanel.setLayout(new FlowLayout(FlowLayout.LEFT, 5, 0));
ButtonGroup group = new ButtonGroup();
JRadioButton radio1 = new JRadioButton( "Male" );
radio1.setSelected( true );
```

```
        group.add( radio1 );
        JRadioButton radio2 = new JRadioButton( "Female" );
        group.add( radio2 );
        radioPanel.add( radio1 );
        radioPanel.add( radio2 );
        panel.addComponent( radioPanel, 7, 2, 3, 1 );

        JLabel lbl8 = new JLabel( "ID Number" );
        lbl8.setBorder( border );
        panel.addComponent( lbl8, 8, 1 );
        JTextField txt8 = new JTextField();
        txt8.setPreferredSize( mediumField );
        panel.addComponent( txt8, 8, 2, 3, 1 );

        JButton submitBtn = new JButton( "Submit" );
        panel.addFilledComponent( submitBtn, 1, 5 );

        JButton cancelBtn = new JButton( "Cancel" );
        panel.addFilledComponent( cancelBtn, 2, 5 );

        JButton helpBtn = new JButton( "Help" );
        panel.addComponent(helpBtn, 3, 5, 1, 1,
          GridBagConstraints.NORTH, GridBagConstraints.HORIZONTAL);

        WindowListener wndCloser = new WindowAdapter() {
          public void windowClosing(WindowEvent e) {
            System.exit(0);
          }
        };
        addWindowListener( wndCloser );

        setVisible( true );
    }

  public static void main( String[] args ) {
    new ComplaintsDialog2( new JFrame() );
  }
}
```

4.4   CHOOSING THE RIGHT LAYOUT

In this section we'll show how to choose the right combination of layouts and intermediate containers to satisfy a predefined program specification. Consider a sample application which makes airplane ticket reservations. The following specification describes which components should be included and how they should be placed in the application frame:

1   A text field labeled "Date:", a combo box labeled "From:", and a combo box labeled "To:" must reside at the top of the frame. Labels must be placed to the left side of their corresponding component. The text fields and combo boxes must be of equal size, reside in a column, and occupy all available width.

2   A group of radio buttons entitled "Options" must reside in the top right corner of the frame. This group must include "First class," "Business," and "Coach" radio buttons.

3 A list component entitled "Available Flights" must occupy the central part of the frame and it should grow or shrink when the size of the frame changes.

4 Three buttons entitled "Search," "Purchase," and "Exit" must reside at the bottom of the frame. They must form a row, have equal sizes, and be center-aligned.

Our `FlightReservation` example demonstrates how to fulfill these requirements. We do not process any input from these controls and we do not attempt to put them to work; we just display them on the screen in the correct position and.size. (Three variants are shown to accomplish the layout of the text fields, combo boxes, and their associated labels. Two are commented out, and a discussion of each is given below.)

NOTE   A similar control placement assignment is part of Sun's Java Developer certification exam.

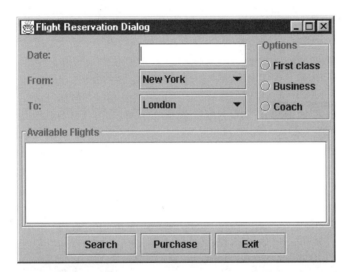

Figure 4.13
`FlightReservation`
layout: variant 1

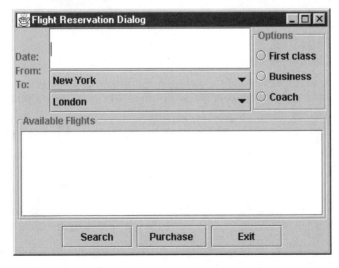

Figure 4.14
`FlightReservation`
layout: variant 2

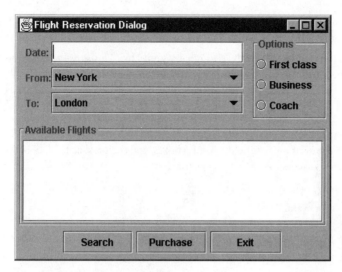

Figure 4.15
FlightReservation
layout: variant 3

Example 4.5

FlightReservation.java

see \Chapter4\3

```java
import java.awt.*;
import java.awt.event.*;

import javax.swing.*;
import javax.swing.border.*;
import javax.swing.event.*;

public class FlightReservation extends JFrame
{
  public FlightReservation() {
    super("Flight Reservation Dialog");
    setSize(400, 300);

    JPanel p1 = new JPanel();
    p1.setLayout(new BoxLayout(p1, BoxLayout.X_AXIS));

    JPanel p1r = new JPanel();
    p1r.setBorder(new EmptyBorder(10, 10, 10, 10));

    // Variant 1
    p1r.setLayout(new GridLayout(3, 2, 5, 5));

    p1r.add(new JLabel("Date:"));
    p1r.add(new JTextField());

    p1r.add(new JLabel("From:"));
    JComboBox cb1 = new JComboBox();
    cb1.addItem("New York");
    p1r.add(cb1);

    p1r.add(new JLabel("To:"));
```

❶ Constructor positions all necessary GUI components

❺ North panel with EmptyBorder for spacing

❻ 3 by 2 grid

❷ Put 3 labeled components in grid (labels too wide)

```
JComboBox cb2 = new JComboBox();
cb2.addItem("London");
p1r.add(cb2);

p1.add(p1r);

///////////////
// Variant 2 //
///////////////
// p11.setLayout(new BoxLayout(p11, BoxLayout.Y_AXIS));
//
// JPanel p12 = new JPanel();
// p12.setLayout(new BoxLayout(p12, BoxLayout.Y_AXIS));
//
// p11.add(new JLabel("Date:"));
// p12.add(new JTextField());
//
// p11.add(new JLabel("From:"));
// JComboBox cb1 = new JComboBox();
// cb1.addItem("New York");
// p12.add(cb1);
//
// p11.add(new JLabel("To:"));
// JComboBox cb2 = new JComboBox();
// cb2.addItem("London");
// p12.add(cb2);
//
// p1.add(p11);
// p1.add(Box.createHorizontalStrut(10));
// p1.add(p12);

///////////////
// Variant 3 //
///////////////
// JPanel p11 = new JPanel();
// p11.setLayout(new GridLayout(3, 1, 5, 5));
//
// JPanel p12 = new JPanel();
// p12.setLayout(new GridLayout(3, 1, 5, 5));
//
// p11.add(new JLabel("Date:"));
// p12.add(new JTextField());
//
// p11.add(new JLabel("From:"));
// JComboBox cb1 = new JComboBox();
// cb1.addItem("New York");
// p12.add(cb1);
//
// p11.add(new JLabel("To:"));
// JComboBox cb2 = new JComboBox();
// cb2.addItem("London");
// p12.add(cb2);
//
```

2 Put 3 labeled components in grid (labels too wide)

7 Second variant, using two vertical BoxLayouts (labels and components not aligned)

8 Third variant, using two 3 by 1 grids (arranged correctly, but complex)

```
// p1r.setLayout(new BorderLayout());
// p1r.add(p11, BorderLayout.WEST);
// p1r.add(p12, BorderLayout.CENTER);
// p1.add(p1r);

JPanel p3 = new JPanel();
p3.setLayout(new BoxLayout(p3, BoxLayout.Y_AXIS));
p3.setBorder(new TitledBorder(new EtchedBorder(),
  "Options"));

ButtonGroup group = new ButtonGroup();
JRadioButton r1 = new JRadioButton("First class");
group.add(r1);
p3.add(r1);

JRadioButton r2 = new JRadioButton("Business");
group.add(r2);
p3.add(r2);

JRadioButton r3 = new JRadioButton("Coach");
group.add(r3);
p3.add(r3);

p1.add(p3);

getContentPane().add(p1, BorderLayout.NORTH);

JPanel p2 = new JPanel(new BorderLayout());
p2.setBorder(new TitledBorder(new EtchedBorder(),
  "Available Flights"));
JList list = new JList();
JScrollPane ps = new JScrollPane(list);
p2.add(ps, BorderLayout.CENTER);
getContentPane().add(p2, BorderLayout.CENTER);

JPanel p4 = new JPanel();
JPanel p4c = new JPanel();
p4c.setLayout(new GridLayout(1, 3, 5, 5));

JButton b1 = new JButton("Search");
p4c.add(b1);

JButton b2 = new JButton("Purchase");
p4c.add(b2);

JButton b3 = new JButton("Exit");
p4c.add(b3);

p4.add(p4c);
getContentPane().add(p4, BorderLayout.SOUTH);

WindowListener wndCloser = new WindowAdapter() {
  public void windowClosing(WindowEvent e) {
    System.exit(0);
  }
};
addWindowListener(wndCloser);

setVisible(true);
```

⑨ Vertical BoxLayout for radio buttons, on East side of frame

② Place grid with labeled components in North side of frame

⑩ Scrollable list in titled panel

④ Place list in center of frame

⑪ Implicitly FlowLayout

③ Place row of push buttons in South of frame

```
    }
  public static void main(String argv[]) {
    new FlightReservation();
  }
}
```

4.4.1 Understanding the code

Class FlightReservation

1 The constructor of the `FlightReservation` class creates and positions all necessary GUI components. We will explain step by step how we've chosen intermediate containers and their layouts to fulfill the requirements listed at the beginning of this section.

2 The frame (more specifically, its `contentPane`) is managed by a `BorderLayout` by default. A text field, the combo boxes, and associated labels are added in a separate container to the **3** north along with the radio buttons; push buttons are placed in the south; and the list compo-**4** nent is placed in the center. This guarantees that the top and bottom (north and south) containers will receive their natural height, and that the central component (the list) will occupy all the remaining space.

5 The intermediate container, `JPanel p1r`, holds the text field, combo boxes, and their associated labels; it is placed in panel `p1` which is managed by a horizontally aligned `BoxLayout`. The `p1r` panel is surrounded by an `EmptyBorder` to provide typical surrounding white space.

6 This example offers three variants of managing `p1r` and its six child components. The first variant uses a 3×2 `GridLayout`. This places labels and boxes in two columns opposite one another. Since this panel resides in the north region of the `BorderLayout`, it receives its natural (preferable) height. In the horizontal direction this layout works satisfactorily: it resizes boxes and labels to occupy all available space. The only remaining problem is that `GridLayout` assigns too much space to the labels (see figure 4.13). We do not need to make labels equal in size to their corresponding input boxes—we need only allow them to occupy their preferred width.

7 The second variant uses two vertical `BoxLayouts` so that one can hold labels and the other can hold the corresponding text field and combo boxes. If you try recompiling and running the code with this variant, you'll find that the labels now occupy only their necessary width, and the boxes occupy all the remaining space. This is good, but another problem arises: now the labels are not aligned exactly opposite with their corresponding components. Instead, they are shifted in the vertical direction (see figure 4.14).

8 The third variant offers the best solution. It places the labels and their corresponding components in two columns, but it uses 3×1 `GridLayouts` instead of `BoxLayouts`. This places all components evenly in the vertical direction. To provide only the minimum width to the labels (the first column) and assign all remaining space to the boxes (the second column), we place these two containers into another intermediate container managed by a `BorderLayout`: labels in the west, and corresponding components in the center. This solves our problem (see figure 4.15). The only downside to this solution is that it requires the construction of three intermediate containers with different layouts. In the next section we'll show how to build a custom layout manager that simplifies this relatively common layout task.

9 Now let's return to the remaining components. A group of JRadioButtons seems to be the simplest part of our design. They're placed into an intermediate container, JPanel p3, with a TitledBorder containing the required title: "Options". A vertical BoxLayout is used to place these components in a column and a ButtonGroup is used to coordinate their selection. This container is then added to panel p1 (managed by a horizontal BoxLayout) to sit on the eastern side of panel p1r.

10 The JList component is added to a JScrollPane to provide scrolling capabilities. It is then placed in an intermediate container, JPanel p2, with a TitledBorder containing the required title "Available Flights."

> **NOTE** We do not want to assign a TitledBorder to the JScrollPane itself because this would substitute its natural border, resulting in quite an awkward scroll pane view. So we nest the JScrollPane in its own JPanel with a TitledBorder.

Since the list should grow and shrink when the frame is resized and the group of radio buttons (residing to the right of the list) must occupy only the necessary width, it only makes sense to place the list in the center of the BorderLayout. We can then use the south region for the three remaining buttons.

8 Since all three buttons must be equal in size, they're added to a JPanel, p4c, with a 1×3 GridLayout. However, this GridLayout will occupy all available width (fortunately, it's limited in the vertical direction by the parent container's BorderLayout). This is not exactly the

11 behavior we are looking for. To resolve this problem, we use another intermediate container, JPanel p4, with a FlowLayout. This sizes the only added component, p4c, based on its preferred size, and centers it both vertically and horizontally.

4.4.2 Running the code

Figures 4.13, 4.14, and 4.15 show the resulting placement of our components in the parent frame using the first and the third variants described above. Note that the placement of variant 3 satisfies our specification—components are resized as expected when the frame container is resized.

When the frame is stretched in the horizontal direction, the text field, combo boxes, and list component consume additional space, and the buttons at the bottom are shifted to the center. When the frame is stretched in the vertical direction, the list component and the panel containing the radio buttons consume all additional space and all other components remain unchanged.

GUIDELINE

Harnessing the power of java layouts Layout managers are powerful but awkward to use. In order to maximize the effectiveness of the visual communication, we must make extra effort with the code. Making a bad choice of layout or making sloppy use of default settings may lead to designs which look poorly or communicate badly.

In this example, we have shown three alternative designs for the same basic specification. Each exhibits pros and cons and highlights the design trade-offs which can be made.

A sense of balance This occurs when sufficient white space is used to balance the size of the components. An unbalanced panel can be fixed by bordering the components with a compound border that includes an empty border.

A sense of scale   Balance can be further affected by the extraordinary size of some components such as the combo boxes shown in figure 4.14. The combo boxes are bit too big for the intended purpose. This affects the sense of scale as well as the balance of the design. It's important to size combo boxes appropriately. Layout managers have a tendency to stretch components to be larger than might be desirable.

4.5   CUSTOM LAYOUT MANAGER, PART I: LABEL/FIELD PAIRS

This section and its accompanying example are intended to familiarize you with developing custom layouts. You may find this information useful in cases where the traditional layouts are not satisfactory or are too complex. In developing large-scale applications, it is often more convenient to build custom layouts, such as the one we develop here, to help with specific tasks. This often provides increased consistency, and may save a significant amount of coding in the long run.

Example 4.5 in the previous section highlighted a problem: what is the best way to lay out input field components (such as text fields and combo boxes) and their corresponding labels? We have seen that it can be done using a combination of several intermediate containers and layouts. This section shows how we can simplify the process using a custom-built layout manager. The goal is to construct a layout manager that knows how to lay out labels and their associated input fields in two columns, allocating the minimum required space to the column containing the labels, and using the remainder for the column containing the input fields.

We first need to clearly state our design goals for this layout manager, which we will appropriately call `DialogLayout`. It is always a good idea to reserve plenty of time for thinking about your design. Well-defined design specifications can save you tremendous amounts of time in the long run, and can help pinpoint flaws and oversights before they arise in the code. (We strongly recommend that a design-specification stage becomes part of your development regimen.)

`DialogLayout` specification:

1 This layout manager will be applied to a container that has all the necessary components added to it in the following order: `label1`, `field1`, `label2`, `field2`, etc. (Note that when components are added to a container, they are tracked in a list. If no index is specified when a component is added to a container, it will be added to the end of the list using the next available index. As usual, this indexing starts from 0. A component can be retrieved by index using the `getComponent(int index)` method.) If the labels and fields are added correctly, all even-numbered components in the container will correspond to labels, and all odd-numbered components will correspond to input fields.

2 The components must be placed in pairs that form two vertical columns.

3 Components that make up each pair must be placed opposite one another, for example, `label1` and `field1`. Each pair's label and field must receive the same preferable height, which should be the preferred height of the field.

4 Each left component (labels) must receive the same width. This width should be the maximum preferable width of all left components.

5 Each right component (input fields) must also receive the same width. This width should occupy all the remaining space left over from that taken by the left component's column.

Example 4.6, found below, introduces our custom `DialogLayout` class which satisfies the above design specification. This class is placed in its own package named `dl`. The code used to construct the GUI is almost identical to that of the previous example. However, we will now revert back to variant 1 and use an instance of `DialogLayout` instead of a `GridLayout` to manage the `p1r JPanel`.

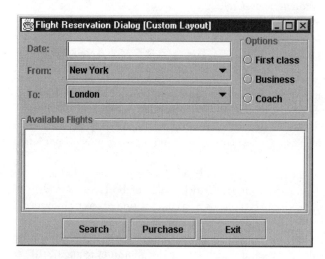

Figure 4.16 Using `DialogLayout`: **custom layout manager part I**

Example 4.6

FlightReservation.java

see \Chapter4\4

```
import java.awt.*;
import java.awt.event.*;

import javax.swing.*;
import javax.swing.border.*;
import javax.swing.event.*;

import dl.*;                                          ❶  Import for
                                                          DialogLayout class
public class FlightReservation extends JFrame
{
  public FlightReservation() {
    super("Flight Reservation Dialog [Custom Layout]");

    // Unchanged code from example 4.5

    // Variant 1
    JPanel p1r = new JPanel();
    p1r.setBorder(new EmptyBorder(10, 10, 10, 10));
    p1r.setLayout(new DialogLayout(20, 5));            ❶  Import
                                                          class
    p1r.add(new JLabel("Date:"));
    p1r.add(new JTextField());
```

```
plr.add(new JLabel("From:"));
JComboBox cb1 = new JComboBox();
cb1.addItem("New York");
plr.add(cb1);

plr.add(new JLabel("To:"));
JComboBox cb2 = new JComboBox();
cb2.addItem("London");
plr.add(cb2);

p1.add(plr);
getContentPane().add(p1, BorderLayout.NORTH);
// End Variant 1
```

// All remaining code is unchanged from example 4.5

DialogLayout.java

see \Chapter4\4\dl

```
package dl;

import java.awt.*;
import java.util.*;

public class DialogLayout implements LayoutManager
{
  protected int m_divider = -1;
  protected int m_hGap = 10;
  protected int m_vGap = 5;

  public DialogLayout() {}

  public DialogLayout(int hGap, int vGap) {
    m_hGap = hGap;
    m_vGap = vGap;
  }

  public void addLayoutComponent(String name, Component comp) {}

  public void removeLayoutComponent(Component comp) {}

  public Dimension preferredLayoutSize(Container parent) {
    int divider = getDivider(parent);

    int w = 0;
    int h = 0;
    for (int k=1 ; k<parent.getComponentCount(); k+=2) {
      Component comp = parent.getComponent(k);
      Dimension d = comp.getPreferredSize();
      w = Math.max(w, d.width);
      h += d.height + m_vGap;
    }
    h -= m_vGap;

    Insets insets = parent.getInsets();
    return new Dimension(divider+w+insets.left+insets.right,
      h+insets.top+insets.bottom);
```

Means DialogLayout ❷ can be used anywhere a LayoutManager is used

❷ Width and gap values

❸ Constructor which uses default gaps

Constructor to ❸ set gap values

From base interface, ❹ not managing internal components list

Returns preferred size ❺ to lay out all managed components

Determine width ❻ of labels column

❽ Determine maximum input field width and accumulate height

❾ Calculate total preferred size

```
        }
        public Dimension minimumLayoutSize(Container parent) {
          return preferredLayoutSize(parent);
        }
        public void layoutContainer(Container parent) {
          int divider = getDivider(parent);

          Insets insets = parent.getInsets();
          int w = parent.getWidth() - insets.left
            - insets.right - divider;
          int x = insets.left;
          int y = insets.top;

          for (int k=1 ; k<parent.getComponentCount(); k+=2) {
            Component comp1 = parent.getComponent(k-1);
            Component comp2 = parent.getComponent(k);
            Dimension d = comp2.getPreferredSize();

            comp1.setBounds(x, y, divider-m_hGap, d.height);
            comp2.setBounds(x+divider, y, w, d.height);
            y += d.height + m_vGap;
          }
        }
        public int getHGap() { return m_hGap; }

        public int getVGap() { return m_vGap; }

        public void setDivider(int divider) {
          if (divider > 0)
            m_divider = divider;
        }

        public int getDivider() { return m_divider; }

        protected int getDivider(Container parent) {
          if (m_divider > 0)
            return m_divider;

          int divider = 0;
          for (int k=0 ; k<parent.getComponentCount(); k+=2) {
            Component comp = parent.getComponent(k);
            Dimension d = comp.getPreferredSize();
            divider = Math.max(divider, d.width);
          }
          divider += m_hGap;
          return divider;
        }
        public String toString() {
          return getClass().getName() + "[hgap=" + m_hGap + ",vgap="
            + m_vGap + ",divider=" + m_divider + "]";
        }
      }
```

(10) Minimum size will be the same as the preferred size

(11) Most important method, calculates position and size of each managed component

(12) Determine divider size and width of all input fields

(13) Set each label and input field to calculated bounds

(14) Minimum size will be the same as the preferred size

(7) If no divider set yet

(7) Determine maximum label size plus gap

(15) Useful debugging information

4.5.1 Understanding the code

Class FlightReservation

1 This class now imports the `dl` package and uses the `DialogLayout` layout manager for `JPanel` `p1r`, which contains the labels and input fields. The `dl` package contains our custom layout, `DialogLayout`.

Class DialogLayout

2 This class implements the `LayoutManager` interface to serve as our custom layout manager. Three instance variables are needed:

- `int m_divider`: Width of the left components. This can be calculated or set to some mandatory value.
- `int m_hGap`: Horizontal gap between components.
- `int m_vGap`: Vertical gap between components.

3 Two constructors are available to create a `DialogLayout`: a no-argument default constructor and a constructor which takes horizontal and vertical gap sizes as parameters. The rest of the code implements methods from the `LayoutManager` interface.

4 The `addLayoutComponent()` and `removeLayoutComponent()` methods are not used in this class, and they receive empty implementations. We do not support an internal collection of the components to be managed. Rather, we refer to these components directly from the container which is being managed.

5 The purpose of the `preferredLayoutSize()` method is to return the preferable container size required to lay out the components in the given container according to the rules used in

6 this layout. In our implementation, we first determine the `divider` size (the width of the first column plus the horizontal gap, `m_hGap`) by calling our `getDivider()` method.

```
int divider = getDivider(parent);
```

7 If no positive divider size has been specified using our `setDivider()` method (see below), the `getDivider()` method looks at each even-indexed component in the container (this should be all the labels if the components were added to the container in the correct order) and returns the largest preferred width found plus the horizontal gap value, `m_hGap` (which defaults to 10 if the default constructor is used):

```
if (m_divider > 0)
  return m_divider;

int divider = 0;
for (int k=0 ; k<parent.getComponentCount(); k+=2) {
  Component comp = parent.getComponent(k);
  Dimension d = comp.getPreferredSize();
  divider = Math.max(divider, d.width);
}
divider += m_hGap;
return divider;
```

8 Now, let's go back to the `preferredLayoutSize()` method. Once `getDivider()` returns, we then examine all the components in the container with odd indices (this should be all the input fields) and determine the maximum width, w. This is found by checking the preferred width of each input field. While we are determining this maximum width, we are also continuing to accumulate the height, h, of the whole input fields column by summing each field's preferred height (not forgetting to add the vertical gap size, m_vGap, each time; notice that m_vGap is subtracted from the height at the end because there is no vertical gap for the last field. Also remember that m_vGap defaults to 5 if the the default constructor is used.)

```
int w = 0;
int h = 0;
for (int k=1 ; k<parent.getComponentCount(); k+=2) {
  Component comp = parent.getComponent(k);
  Dimension d = comp.getPreferredSize();
  w = Math.max(w, d.width);
  h += d.height + m_vGap;
}
h -= m_vGap;
```

9 So at this point we have determined the width of the labels column (including the space between columns), divider, and the preferred height, h, and width, w, of the input fields column. So divider+w gives us the preferred width of the container, and h gives us the total preferred height. Not forgetting to take into account any Insets that might have been applied to the container, we can now return the correct preferred size:

```
Insets insets = parent.getInsets();
return new Dimension(divider+w+insets.left+insets.right,
  h+insets.top+insets.bottom);
```

10 The purpose of the minimumLayoutSize() method is to return the minimum size required to lay out the components in the given container according to the rules used in this layout. We return preferredLayoutSize() in this method, because we choose not to make a distinction between minimum and preferred sizes (to avoid over-complication).

11 **12** layoutContainer() is the most important method in any layout manager. This method is responsible for actually assigning the bounds (position and size) for the components in the container being managed. First it determines the size of the divider (as discussed above), which represents the width of the labels column plus an additional m_hGap. From this, it determines the width, w, of the fields column by subtracting the container's left and right insets and divider from the width of the whole container:

```
int divider = getDivider(parent);

Insets insets = parent.getInsets();
int w = parent.getWidth() - insets.left
  - insets.right - divider;
int x = insets.left;
int y = insets.top;
```

13 Then all pairs of components are examined in turn. Each left component receives a width equal to divider-m_hGap, and all right components receive a width of w. Both left and right components receive the preferred height of the right component (which should be an input field).

Coordinates of the left components are assigned starting with the container's Insets, x and y. Notice that y is continually incremented based on the preferred height of each right component plus the vertical gap, m_vGap. The right components are assigned a y-coordinate identical to their left component counterpart, and an x-coordinate of x+divider (remember that divider includes the horizontal gap, m_hGap):

```
for (int k=1 ; k<parent.getComponentCount(); k+=2) {
  Component comp1 = parent.getComponent(k-1);
  Component comp2 = parent.getComponent(k);
  Dimension d = comp2.getPreferredSize();

  comp1.setBounds(x, y, divider-m_hGap, d.height);
  comp2.setBounds(x+divider, y, w, d.height);
  y += d.height + m_vGap;
}
```

14 The setDivider() method allows us to manually set the size of the left column. The int value, which is passed as a parameter, gets stored in the m_divider instance variable. Whenever m_divider is greater than 0, the calculations of divider size are overridden in the get-Divider() method and this value is returned instead.

15 The toString() method provides typical class name and instance variable information. (It is always a good idea to implement informative toString() methods for each class. Although we don't consistently do so throughout this text, we feel that production code should often include this functionality.)

4.5.2   Running the code

Figure 4.16 shows the sample interface introduced in the previous section now using Dia-logLayout to manage the layout of the input fields (the text field and two combo boxes) and their corresponding labels. Note that the labels occupy only their preferred space and they do not resize when the frame resizes. The width of the left column can be managed easily by manually setting the divider size with the setDivider() method, as discussed above. The input fields form the right column and occupy all the remaining space.

Using DialogLayout, all that is required is to add the labels and input fields in the correct order. We can now use this layout manager each time we encounter label/input field pairs without worrying about intermediate containers. In the next section, we will build upon DialogLayout to create an even more general layout manager that can be used to create complete dialog GUIs very easily.

GUIDELINE

Alignment across controls as well as within   It is a common mistake in UI design to achieve good alignment with a control or component but fail to achieve this across a whole screen, panel, or dialog. Unfortunately, the architecture of Swing lends itself to this problem. For example, say you have four custom components which inherit from a JPanel, each has its own layout manager and each is functional in its own right. You might want to build a composite component which requires all four. So you create a new component with a Grid-Layout, for example, then add each of your four components in turn.

The result can be very messy. The fields within each component will align—three radio buttons, for example—but those radio buttons will not align with the three text fields in the next component. Why not? The answer is simple.

With Swing, there is no way for the layout manager within each component to negotiate with the others, so alignment cannot be achieved across the components. The answer to this problem is that you must flatten out the design into a single panel, as DialogLayout achieves.

4.6 CUSTOM LAYOUT MANAGER, PART II: COMMON INTERFACES

In section 4.4 we saw how to choose both intermediate containers and appropriate layouts for placing components according to a given specification. This required the use of several intermediate containers, and several variants were developed in a search for the best solution. This raises a question: can we somehow just add components one after another to a container which is intelligent enough to lay them out as we would typically expect? The answer is yes, to a certain extent.

In practice, the contents of many Java frames and dialogs are constructed using a scheme similar to the following (we realize that this is a big generalization, but you will see these situations arise in other examples later in this text):

1 Groups (or panels) of controls are laid out in the vertical direction.

2 Labels and their corresponding input fields form two-column structures as described in the previous section.

3 Large components (such as lists, tables, text areas, and trees) are usually placed in scroll panes and they occupy all space in the horizontal direction.

4 Groups of buttons, including check boxes and radio buttons, are centered in an intermediate container and laid out in the horizontal direction. (In this example we purposefully avoid the vertical placement of buttons for simplicity.)

Example 4.7, found below, shows how to build a layout manager that places components according to this specification. Its purpose is to further demonstrate that layout managers can be built to define template-like pluggable containers. By adhering to intelligently designed specifications, such templates can be developed to help maximize code reuse and increase productivity. Additionally, in the case of large-scale applications, several different interface designers may consider sharing customized layout managers to enforce consistency.

Example 4.7 introduces our new custom layout manager, DialogLayout2, which builds upon DialogLayout. To provide boundaries between control groupings, we construct a new component, DialogSeparator, which is simply a label containing text and a horizontal bar that is drawn across the container. Both DialogLayout2 and DialogSeparator are added to our dl package. The FlightReservation class now shows how to construct the sample airline ticket reservation interface we have been working with since section 4.4 using Dialog-Layout2 and DialogSeparator. In order to comply with our new layout scheme, we are forced to place the radio buttons in a row above the list component. The main things to note are that the code involved to build this interface is done with little regard for the existence of a layout manager, and that absolutely no intermediate containers need to be created.

NOTE Constructing custom layout managers for use in a single application is not recommended. Only build them when you know that they will be reused again and again to perform common layout tasks. In general, custom layout manager classes belong within custom packages or they should be embedded as inner classes in custom components.

Figure 4.17 Using the `DialogLayout2` **custom layout manager**

Example 4.7

FlightReservation.java

see \Chapter4\5

```java
import java.awt.*;
import java.awt.event.*;

import javax.swing.*;
import javax.swing.border.*;
import javax.swing.event.*;

import dl.*;

public class FlightReservation extends JFrame
{
  public FlightReservation() {
    super("Flight Reservation Dialog [Custom Layout - 2]");

    Container c = getContentPane();
    c.setLayout(new DialogLayout2(20, 5));

    c.add(new JLabel("Date:"));
    c.add(new JTextField());

    c.add(new JLabel("From:"));
```

1 All components added directly to the content pane and managed by the new layout

```
                JComboBox cb1 = new JComboBox();
                cb1.addItem("New York");
                c.add(cb1);

                c.add(new JLabel("To:"));
                JComboBox cb2 = new JComboBox();
                cb2.addItem("London");
                c.add(cb2);

                c.add(new DialogSeparator("Available Flights"));
                JList list = new JList();
                JScrollPane ps = new JScrollPane(list);
                c.add(ps);

                c.add(new DialogSeparator("Options"));

                ButtonGroup group = new ButtonGroup();
                JRadioButton r1 = new JRadioButton("First class");
                group.add(r1);
                c.add(r1);

                JRadioButton r2 = new JRadioButton("Business");
                group.add(r2);
                c.add(r2);

                JRadioButton r3 = new JRadioButton("Coach");
                group.add(r3);
                c.add(r3);

                c.add(new DialogSeparator());

                JButton b1 = new JButton("Search");
                c.add(b1);

                JButton b2 = new JButton("Purchase");
                c.add(b2);

                JButton b3 = new JButton("Exit");
                c.add(b3);

                WindowListener wndCloser = new WindowAdapter() {
                  public void windowClosing(WindowEvent e) {
                    System.exit(0);
                  }
                };
                addWindowListener(wndCloser);

                setVisible(true);
              }
            public static void main(String argv[]) {
              new FlightReservation();
            }
          }
```

② Separates groups
of components

② Separates groups
of components

① All components
added directly to
the content pane
and managed by
the new layout

DialogLayout2.java

see \Chapter4\5\dl

```
package dl;
```

```java
import java.awt.*;
import java.util.*;

import javax.swing.*;

public class DialogLayout2 implements LayoutManager
{
  protected static final int COMP_TWO_COL = 0;
  protected static final int COMP_BIG = 1;
  protected static final int COMP_BUTTON = 2;

  protected int m_divider = -1;
  protected int m_hGap = 10;
  protected int m_vGap = 5;
  protected Vector m_v = new Vector();

  public DialogLayout2() {}

  public DialogLayout2(int hGap, int vGap) {
    m_hGap = hGap;
    m_vGap = vGap;
  }

  public void addLayoutComponent(String name, Component comp) {}

  public void removeLayoutComponent(Component comp) {}

  public Dimension preferredLayoutSize(Container parent) {
    m_v.removeAllElements();
    int w = 0;
    int h = 0;

    int type = -1;
    for (int k=0 ; k<parent.getComponentCount(); k++) {
      Component comp = parent.getComponent(k);
      int newType = getLayoutType(comp);
      if (k == 0)
        type = newType;

      if (type != newType) {
        Dimension d = preferredLayoutSize(m_v, type);
        w = Math.max(w, d.width);
        h += d.height + m_vGap;
        m_v.removeAllElements();
        type = newType;
      }

      m_v.addElement(comp);
    }
    Dimension d = preferredLayoutSize(m_v, type);
    w = Math.max(w, d.width);
    h += d.height + m_vGap;

    h -= m_vGap;

    Insets insets = parent.getInsets();
    return new Dimension(w+insets.left+insets.right,
      h+insets.top+insets.bottom);
```

3 Implements LayoutManager to be a custom LayoutManager

4 Constants to specify how to manage specific component types

5 Width and gap values and components list

6 Steps through parent's components totalling preferred layout size

7 Found break in sequence of component types

8 Process last block of same-typed components

9 Compute final preferred size

```
    }
    protected Dimension preferredLayoutSize(Vector v, int type) {
        int w = 0;
        int h = 0;
        switch (type)
        {
            case COMP_TWO_COL:
                int divider = getDivider(v);
                for (int k=1 ; k<v.size(); k+=2) {
                    Component comp = (Component)v.elementAt(k);
                    Dimension d = comp.getPreferredSize();
                    w = Math.max(w, d.width);
                    h += d.height + m_vGap;
                }
                h -= m_vGap;
                return new Dimension(divider+w, h);
            case COMP_BIG:
                for (int k=0 ; k<v.size(); k++) {
                    Component comp = (Component)v.elementAt(k);
                    Dimension d = comp.getPreferredSize();
                    w = Math.max(w, d.width);
                    h += d.height + m_vGap;
                }
                h -= m_vGap;
                return new Dimension(w, h);
            case COMP_BUTTON:
                Dimension d = getMaxDimension(v);
                w = d.width + m_hGap;
                h = d.height;
                return new Dimension(w*v.size()-m_hGap, h);
        }
        throw new IllegalArgumentException("Illegal type "+type);
    }

    public Dimension minimumLayoutSize(Container parent) {
        return preferredLayoutSize(parent);
    }

    public void layoutContainer(Container parent) {
        m_v.removeAllElements();
        int type = -1;
        Insets insets = parent.getInsets();
        int w = parent.getWidth() - insets.left - insets.right;
        int x = insets.left;
        int y = insets.top;
        for (int k=0 ; k<parent.getComponentCount(); k++) {
            Component comp = parent.getComponent(k);
            int newType = getLayoutType(comp);
            if (k == 0)
                type = newType;
            if (type != newType) {
                y = layoutComponents(m_v, type, x, y, w);
```

10 — Steps through a components list of a specific type, totalling preferred layout size

11 — Assumes two-column arrangement, computes preferred size

12 — Assumes components take up entire width, computes preferred size

13 — Assumes centered row of equal width components, computes preferred size

14 — Lays out container, treating blocks of same-typed components in the same way

```
        m_v.removeAllElements();
        type = newType;
      }
    m_v.addElement(comp);
  }
  y = layoutComponents(m_v, type, x, y, w);
  m_v.removeAllElements();
}

protected int layoutComponents(Vector v, int type,
 int x, int y, int w)
{
  switch (type)
  {
    case COMP_TWO_COL:
      int divider = getDivider(v);
      for (int k=1 ; k<v.size(); k+=2) {
        Component comp1 = (Component)v.elementAt(k-1);
        Component comp2 = (Component)v.elementAt(k);
        Dimension d = comp2.getPreferredSize();
        comp1.setBounds(x, y, divider-m_hGap, d.height);
        comp2.setBounds(x+divider, y, w-divider, d.height);
        y += d.height + m_vGap;
      }
      return y;
    case COMP_BIG:
      for (int k=0 ; k<v.size(); k++) {
        Component comp = (Component)v.elementAt(k);
        Dimension d = comp.getPreferredSize();
        comp.setBounds(x, y, w, d.height);
        y += d.height + m_vGap;
      }
      return y;
    case COMP_BUTTON:
      Dimension d = getMaxDimension(v);
      int ww = d.width*v.size() + m_hGap*(v.size()-1);
      int xx = x + Math.max(0, (w - ww)/2);
      for (int k=0 ; k<v.size(); k++) {
        Component comp = (Component)v.elementAt(k);
        comp.setBounds(xx, y, d.width, d.height);
        xx += d.width + m_hGap;
      }
      return y + d.height;
  }
  throw new IllegalArgumentException("Illegal type "+type);
}

public int getHGap() { return m_hGap; }

public int getVGap() { return m_vGap; }

public void setDivider(int divider) {
  if (divider > 0)
```

15 Lays out block of same-typed components, checking for component type

16 Assumes two-column arrangement, lays out each pair in that fashion

17 Assumes components take up entire width, one component per row

18 Assumes centered row of equal width components, lays them out in that fashion

```java
        m_divider = divider;
    }

    public int getDivider() { return m_divider; }

    protected int getDivider(Vector v) {
        if (m_divider > 0)
            return m_divider;
        int divider = 0;
        for (int k=0 ; k<v.size(); k+=2) {
            Component comp = (Component)v.elementAt(k);
            Dimension d = comp.getPreferredSize();
            divider = Math.max(divider, d.width);
        }
        divider += m_hGap;
        return divider;
    }

    protected Dimension getMaxDimension(Vector v) {
        int w = 0;
        int h = 0;
        for (int k=0 ; k<v.size(); k++) {
            Component comp = (Component)v.elementAt(k);
            Dimension d = comp.getPreferredSize();
            w = Math.max(w, d.width);
            h = Math.max(h, d.height);
        }
        return new Dimension(w, h);
    }

    protected int getLayoutType(Component comp) {
        if (comp instanceof AbstractButton)
            return COMP_BUTTON;
        else if (comp instanceof JPanel ||
          comp instanceof JScrollPane ||
          comp instanceof DialogSeparator)
            return COMP_BIG;
        else
            return COMP_TWO_COL;
    }

    public String toString() {
        return getClass().getName() + "[hgap=" + m_hGap + ",vgap="
            + m_vGap + ",divider=" + m_divider + "]";
    }
}
```

DialogSeparator.java

see \Chapter4\5\dl

```java
package dl;

import java.awt.*;

import javax.swing.*;
```

```
public class DialogSeparator extends JLabel          ⑲  Implements horizontal
{                                                         separator between
  public static final int OFFSET = 15;                    vertically-spaced
                                                          components
  public DialogSeparator() {}

  public DialogSeparator(String text) { super(text); }          Returns shallow    ⑳
                                                                area with a small
  public Dimension getPreferredSize() {                         fixed height and
    return new Dimension(getParent().getWidth(), 20);           variable width
  }
  public Dimension getMinimumSize() { return getPreferredSize(); }
  public Dimension getMaximumSize() { return getPreferredSize(); }

  public void paintComponent(Graphics g) {            ㉑  Draws separating
    super.paintComponent(g);                               bar with raised
    g.setColor(getBackground());                           appearance
    g.fillRect(0, 0, getWidth(), getHeight());

    Dimension d = getSize();
    int y = (d.height-3)/2;
    g.setColor(Color.white);
    g.drawLine(1, y, d.width-1, y);
    y++;
    g.drawLine(0, y, 1, y);
    g.setColor(Color.gray);
    g.drawLine(d.width-1, y, d.width, y);
    y++;
    g.drawLine(1, y, d.width-1, y);

    String text = getText();
    if (text.length()==0)
      return;

    g.setFont(getFont());
    FontMetrics fm = g.getFontMetrics();
    y = (d.height + fm.getAscent())/2;
    int l = fm.stringWidth(text);

    g.setColor(getBackground());
    g.fillRect(OFFSET-5, 0, OFFSET+1, d.height);

    g.setColor(getForeground());
    g.drawString(text, OFFSET, y);
  }
}
```

4.6.1   Understanding the code

Class FlightReservation

① This variant of our airplane ticket reservation sample application uses an instance of DialogLayout2 as a layout for the whole content pane. No other JPanels are used, and no other layouts are involved. All components are added directly to the content pane and managed by the new layout. This incredibly simplifies the creation of the user interface. Note, however, that we still need to add the label/input field pairs in the correct order because `DialogLayout2` manages these pairs the same way that `DialogLayout` does.

② Instances of our `DialogSeparator` class are used to provide borders between groups of components.

Class DialogLayout2

③ This class implements the `LayoutManager` interface to serve as a custom layout manager. It builds on features from `DialogLayout` to manage all components in its associated container. Three constants declared at the top of the class correspond to the three types of components which are recognized by this layout:

④
- `int COMP_TWO_COL`: Text fields, combo boxes, and their associated labels which must be laid out in two columns using a `DialogLayout`.
- `int COMP_BIG`: Wide components (instances of `JPanel`, `JScrollPane`, or `Dialog-Separator`) which must occupy the maximum horizontal container space wherever they are placed.
- `int COMP_BUTTON`: Button components (instances of `AbstractButton`) which must all be given an equal size, laid out in a single row, and centered in the container.

⑤ The instance variables used in `DialogLayout2` are the same as those used in `DialogLayout` with one addition: we declare `Vector m_v` to be used as a temporary collection of components.

To lay out components in a given container we need to determine, for each component, which category it falls under with regard to our `DialogLayout2.COMP_XX` constants. All components of the same type which are added in a contiguous sequence must be processed according to the specific rules described above.

⑥ The `preferredLayoutSize()` method steps through the list of components in a given container, determines their type with our custom `getLayoutType()` method (see below), and stores it in the `newType` local variable. The local variable `type` holds the type of the *previous* component in the sequence. For the first component in the container, `type` receives the same value as `newType`.

```
public Dimension preferredLayoutSize(Container parent) {
  m_v.removeAllElements();
  int w = 0;
  int h = 0;

  int type = -1;
  for (int k=0 ; k<parent.getComponentCount(); k++) {
    Component comp = parent.getComponent(k);
    int newType = getLayoutType(comp);
    if (k == 0)
      type = newType;
```

⑦ A break in the sequence of types triggers a call to the overloaded `preferredLayoutSize(Vector v, int type)` method (discussed below) which determines the preferred size for a temporary collection of the components stored in the `Vector m_v`. Then `w` and `h` local variables, which are accumulating the total preferred width and height for this layout, are adjusted, and the temporary collection, `m_v`, is cleared. The newly processed component is then added to `m_v`.

```
if (type != newType) {
  Dimension d = preferredLayoutSize(m_v, type);
```

```
    w = Math.max(w, d.width);
    h += d.height + m_vGap;
    m_v.removeAllElements();
    type = newType;
}

m_v.addElement(comp);
}
```

8 Once our loop finishes, we make the unconditional call to `preferredLayoutSize()` to take into account the last (unprocessed) sequence of components and update h and w accordingly (just as we did in the loop). We then subtract the vertical gap value, m_vGap, from h because we know that we have just processed the last set of components and therefore no vertical gap

9 is necessary. Taking into account any `Insets` set on the container, we can now return the computed preferred size as a `Dimension` instance:

```
    Dimension d = preferredLayoutSize(m_v, type);
    w = Math.max(w, d.width);
    h += d.height + m_vGap;

    h -= m_vGap;

    Insets insets = parent.getInsets();
    return new Dimension(w+insets.left+insets.right,
       h+insets.top+insets.bottom);
}
```

10 The overloaded method `preferredLayoutSize(Vector v, int type)` computes the preferred size to lay out a collection of components of a given type. This size is accumulated in w

11 and h local variables. For a collection of type `COMP_TWO_COL`, this method invokes a mecha-

12 nism that should be familiar (see section 4.5). For a collection of type `COMP_BIG`, this method adjusts the preferable width and increments the height for each component, since these components will be placed in a column:

```
    case COMP_BIG:
      for (int k=0 ; k<v.size(); k++) {
        Component comp = (Component)v.elementAt(k);
        Dimension d = comp.getPreferredSize();
        w = Math.max(w, d.width);
        h += d.height + m_vGap;
      }
      h -= m_vGap;
      return new Dimension(w, h);
```

13 For a collection of type `COMP_BUTTON`, this method invokes our `getMaxDimension()` method (see below) to calculate the desired size of a single component. Since all components of this type will have an equal size and be contained in one single row, the resulting width for this collection is calculated through multiplication by the number of components, `v.size()`:

```
    case COMP_BUTTON:
      Dimension d = getMaxDimension(v);
      w = d.width + m_hGap;
      h = d.height;
      return new Dimension(w*v.size()-m_hGap, h);
```

14 The `layoutContainer(Container parent)` method assigns bounds to the components in the given container. (Remember that this is the method that actually performs the layout of its associated container.) It processes an array of components similar to the `preferredLayoutSize()` method. It steps through the components in the given container, forms a temporary collection from contiguous components of the same type, and calls our overloaded `layoutComponents(Vector v, int type, int x, int y, int w)` method to lay out that collection.

15 The `layoutContainer(Vector v, int type, int x, int y, int w)` method lays out components from the temporary collection of a given type, starting from the given coordinates `x` and `y`, and using the specified width, `w`, of the container. It returns an adjusted y-coordinate which may be used to lay out a new set of components.

16
17 For a collection of type `COMP_TWO_COL`, this method lays out components in two columns identical to the way `DialogLayout` did this (see section 4.5). For a collection of type `COMP_BIG`, the method assigns all available width to each component:

```
case COMP_BIG:
  for (int k=0 ; k<v.size(); k++) {
    Component comp = (Component)v.elementAt(k);
    Dimension d = comp.getPreferredSize();
    comp.setBounds(x, y, w, d.height);
    y += d.height + m_vGap;
  }
  return y;
```

18 For a collection of type `COMP_BUTTON`, this method assigns an equal size to each component and places the components in the center, arranged horizontally:

```
case COMP_BUTTON:
  Dimension d = getMaxDimension(v);
  int ww = d.width*v.size() + m_hGap*(v.size()-1);
  int xx = x + Math.max(0, (w - ww)/2);
  for (int k=0 ; k<v.size(); k++) {
    Component comp = (Component)v.elementAt(k);
    comp.setBounds(xx, y, d.width, d.height);
    xx += d.width + m_hGap;
  }
  return y + d.height;
```

NOTE A more sophisticated implementation might split a sequence of buttons into several rows if not enough space is available. To avoid over-complication, we do not do that here. This might be an interesting exercise to give you more practice at customizing layout managers.

The remainder of the `DialogLayout2` class contains methods which were either explained already, or which are simple enough to be considered self-explanatory.

Class DialogSeparator

19 This class implements a component that is used to separate two groups of components placed in a column. It extends `JLabel` to inherit all its default characteristics such as font and foreground. Two available constructors allow the creation of a `DialogSeparator` with or without a text label.

20 The `getPreferredSize()` method returns a fixed height, and a width equal to the width of the container. The methods `getMinimumSize()` and `getMaximumSize()` simply delegate calls to the `getPreferredSize()` method.

21 The `paintComponent()` method draws a separating bar with a raised appearance across the available component space, and it draws the title text (if any) at the left-most side, taking into account a pre-defined offset, 15.

4.6.2 Running the code

Figure 4.17 shows our sample application which now uses `DialogLayout2` to manage the layout of *all* components. You can see that we have the same set of components placed and sized in accordance with our general layout scheme presented in the beginning of this section. The most important thing to note is that we did not have to use any intermediate containers or layouts to achieve this: all components are added directly to the frame's content pane, which is intelligently managed by `DialogLayout2`.

GUIDELINE

Button placement consistency It is important to be consistent with the placement of buttons in dialogs and option panes. In the example shown here, a symmetrical approach to button placement has been adopted. This is a good safe choice and it ensures balance. With data entry dialogs, it is also common to use an asymmetrical layout such as the bottom right-hand side of the dialog.

In addition to achieving balance with the layout, by being consistent with your placement you allow the user to rely on directional memory to find a specific button location. Directional memory is strong. Once the user learns where you have placed buttons, he will quickly be able to locate the correct button in many dialog and option situations. It is therefore vital that you place buttons in a consistent order—for example, always use OK, Cancel, never Cancel, OK. As a general rule, always use a symmetrical layout with option dialogs and be consistent with whatever you decide to use for data entry dialogs.

It makes sense to develop custom components such as `JOKCancelButtons` and `JYesNoButtons`. You can then reuse these components every time you need such a set of buttons. This encapsulates the placement and ensures consistency.

4.7 DYNAMIC LAYOUT IN A JAVABEANS CONTAINER

In this section we will use different layouts to manage JavaBeans in a simple container application. This will help us to further understand the role of layouts in dynamically managing containers with a variable number of components. Example 4.8 also sets up the framework for a powerful bean editor environment that we will develop in chapter 18 using `JTables`. By allowing modification of component properties, we can use this environment to experiment with preferred, maximum, and minimum sizes, and we can observe the behavior that different layout managers exibit in various situations. This provides us with the ability to learn much more about each layout manager, and allows us to prototype simple interfaces without actually implementing them.

Example 4.8 consists of a frame container that allows the creation, loading, and saving of JavaBeans using serialization. Beans can be added and removed from this container, and we implement a focus mechanism to visually identify the currently selected bean. Most importantly, the layout manager of this container can be changed at run-time. (You may want to review the JavaBeans material in chapter 2 before attempting to work through this example.) Figures 4.18 through 4.23 show `BeanContainer` using five different layout managers to arrange four `Clock` beans. These figures and figure 4.24 are explained in more detail in section 4.7.2.

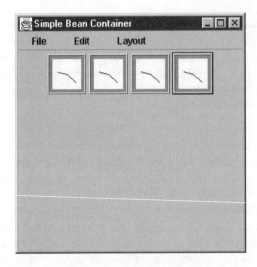

Figure 4.18 `BeanContainer` **displaying four clock components using a** `FlowLayout`

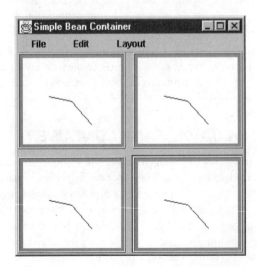

Figure 4.19 `BeanContainer` **displaying four clock components using a** `GridLayout`

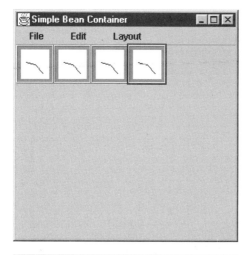

Figure 4.20 BeanContainer
displaying four clock components
using a horizontal BoxLayout

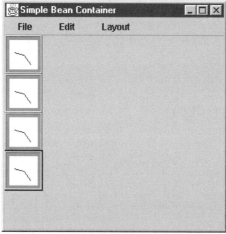

Figure 4.21 BeanContainer
displaying four clock components
using a vertical BoxLayout

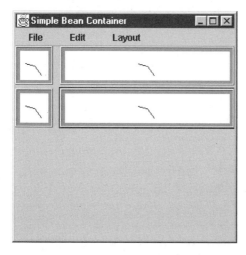

Figure 4.22 BeanContainer
displaying four clock components
using a DialogLayout

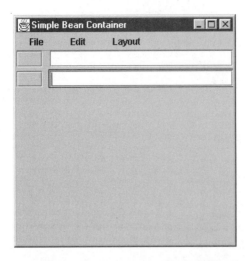

Figure 4.23 BeanContainer **displaying button/input field pairs using** DialogLayout

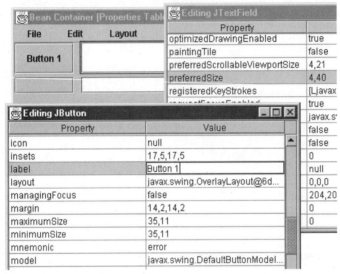

Figure 4.24 The BeanContainer **property editor environment as it is continued in chapter 18**

Example 4.8

BeanContainer.java

see \Chapter4\6

```
import java.awt.*;
import java.awt.event.*;
import java.io.*;
import java.beans.*;
import java.lang.reflect.*;
```

```java
import javax.swing.*;

import dl.*;

public class BeanContainer extends JFrame implements FocusListener
{
  protected File m_currentDir = new File(".");
  protected Component m_activeBean;
  protected String m_className = "clock.Clock";
  protected JFileChooser m_chooser = new JFileChooser();

  public BeanContainer() {
    super("Simple Bean Container");
    getContentPane().setLayout(new FlowLayout());

    setSize(300, 300);

    JPopupMenu.setDefaultLightWeightPopupEnabled(false);

    JMenuBar menuBar = createMenuBar();
    setJMenuBar(menuBar);

    WindowListener wndCloser = new WindowAdapter() {
      public void windowClosing(WindowEvent e) {
        System.exit(0);
      }
    };
    addWindowListener(wndCloser);

    setVisible(true);

  }

  protected JMenuBar createMenuBar() {
    JMenuBar menuBar = new JMenuBar();

    JMenu mFile = new JMenu("File");

    JMenuItem mItem = new JMenuItem("New...");
    ActionListener lst = new ActionListener() {
      public void actionPerformed(ActionEvent e) {
        Thread newthread = new Thread() {
          public void run() {
            String result = (String)JOptionPane.showInputDialog(
              BeanContainer.this,
              "Please enter class name to create a new bean",
              "Input", JOptionPane.INFORMATION_MESSAGE, null,
              null, m_className);
            repaint();
            if (result==null)
              return;
            try {
              m_className = result;
              Class cls = Class.forName(result);
              Object obj = cls.newInstance();
              if (obj instanceof Component) {
                m_activeBean = (Component)obj;
```

1 Provides frame for application and listens for focus transfer between beans in container

2 Creates menu bar, menu items, and action listeners

3 Load class, instantiate it, and add it to container

```
              m_activeBean.addFocusListener(
                 BeanContainer.this);
               m_activeBean.requestFocus();
               getContentPane().add(m_activeBean);
           }
           validate();
         }
         catch (Exception ex) {
           ex.printStackTrace();
           JOptionPane.showMessageDialog(
             BeanContainer.this, "Error: "+ex.toString(),
             "Warning", JOptionPane.WARNING_MESSAGE);
         }
       }
     };
     newthread.start();
  }
};
mItem.addActionListener(lst);
mFile.add(mItem);

mItem = new JMenuItem("Load...");
lst = new ActionListener() {
  public void actionPerformed(ActionEvent e) {
    Thread newthread = new Thread() {
      public void run() {
        m_chooser.setCurrentDirectory(m_currentDir);
        m_chooser.setDialogTitle(
          "Please select file with serialized bean");
        int result = m_chooser.showOpenDialog(
          BeanContainer.this);
        repaint();
        if (result != JFileChooser.APPROVE_OPTION)
          return;
        m_currentDir = m_chooser.getCurrentDirectory();
        File fChoosen = m_chooser.getSelectedFile();
        try {
          FileInputStream fStream =
            new FileInputStream(fChoosen);
          ObjectInput  stream  =
            new ObjectInputStream(fStream);
          Object obj = stream.readObject();
          if (obj instanceof Component) {
            m_activeBean = (Component)obj;
            m_activeBean.addFocusListener(
              BeanContainer.this);
            m_activeBean.requestFocus();
            getContentPane().add(m_activeBean);
          }
          stream.close();
          fStream.close();
          validate();
```

4 Request focus and set up FocusListener

3 Load class, instantiate it, and add it to container

5 Select a file containing a serialized bean

6 Open a stream, read the object, and add it to the container, if it is a Component

```
              }
            catch (Exception ex) {
              ex.printStackTrace();
              JOptionPane.showMessageDialog(
                BeanContainer.this, "Error: "+ex.toString(),
                "Warning", JOptionPane.WARNING_MESSAGE);
            }
            repaint();
          }
        };
        newthread.start();
      }
    };
    mItem.addActionListener(lst);
    mFile.add(mItem);

    mItem = new JMenuItem("Save...");
    lst = new ActionListener() {
      public void actionPerformed(ActionEvent e) {
        Thread newthread = new Thread() {
          public void run() {
            if (m_activeBean == null)
              return;
            m_chooser.setDialogTitle(
              "Please choose file to serialize bean");
            m_chooser.setCurrentDirectory(m_currentDir);
            int result = m_chooser.showSaveDialog(
              BeanContainer.this);
            repaint();
            if (result != JFileChooser.APPROVE_OPTION)
              return;
            m_currentDir = m_chooser.getCurrentDirectory();
            File fChoosen = m_chooser.getSelectedFile();
            try {
              FileOutputStream fStream =
                new FileOutputStream(fChoosen);
              ObjectOutput stream  =
                new ObjectOutputStream(fStream);
              stream.writeObject(m_activeBean);
              stream.close();
              fStream.close();
            }
            catch (Exception ex) {
              ex.printStackTrace();
            JOptionPane.showMessageDialog(
              BeanContainer.this, "Error: "+ex.toString(),
              "Warning", JOptionPane.WARNING_MESSAGE);
            }
          }
        };
        newthread.start();
      }
```

❼ Serialize component to stream and write it to file

```
    };
    mItem.addActionListener(lst);
    mFile.add(mItem);

    mFile.addSeparator();

    mItem = new JMenuItem("Exit");
    lst = new ActionListener() {
      public void actionPerformed(ActionEvent e) {
        System.exit(0);
      }
    };
    mItem.addActionListener(lst);
    mFile.add(mItem);
    menuBar.add(mFile);

    JMenu mEdit = new JMenu("Edit");

    mItem = new JMenuItem("Delete");
    lst = new ActionListener() {
      public void actionPerformed(ActionEvent e) {
        if (m_activeBean == null)
          return;
        getContentPane().remove(m_activeBean);
        m_activeBean = null;
        validate();
        repaint();
      }
    };
    mItem.addActionListener(lst);
    mEdit.add(mItem);
    menuBar.add(mEdit);

    JMenu mLayout = new JMenu("Layout");
    ButtonGroup group = new ButtonGroup();

    mItem = new JRadioButtonMenuItem("FlowLayout");
    mItem.setSelected(true);
    lst = new ActionListener() {
      public void actionPerformed(ActionEvent e){
        getContentPane().setLayout(new FlowLayout());
        validate();
        repaint();
      }
    };
    mItem.addActionListener(lst);
    group.add(mItem);
    mLayout.add(mItem);

    mItem = new JRadioButtonMenuItem("GridLayout");
    lst = new ActionListener() {
      public void actionPerformed(ActionEvent e){
        int col = 3;
        int row = (int)Math.ceil(getContentPane().
          getComponentCount()/(double)col);
```

8 Item and action to exit application

9 Delete will remove the currently active component from the container

10 Relayout with FlowLayout configuration

Relayout with GridLayout configuration **10**

```
        getContentPane().setLayout(new GridLayout(row, col, 10, 10));
        validate();
        repaint();
      }
    };
    mItem.addActionListener(lst);
    group.add(mItem);
    mLayout.add(mItem);

    mItem = new JRadioButtonMenuItem("BoxLayout - X");
    lst = new ActionListener() {
      public void actionPerformed(ActionEvent e) {
        getContentPane().setLayout(new BoxLayout(
         getContentPane(), BoxLayout.X_AXIS));
        validate();
        repaint();
      }
    };
    mItem.addActionListener(lst);
    group.add(mItem);
    mLayout.add(mItem);

    mItem = new JRadioButtonMenuItem("BoxLayout - Y");
    lst = new ActionListener() {
      public void actionPerformed(ActionEvent e) {
        getContentPane().setLayout(new BoxLayout(
          getContentPane(), BoxLayout.Y_AXIS));
        validate();
        repaint();
      }
    };
    mItem.addActionListener(lst);
    group.add(mItem);
    mLayout.add(mItem);

    mItem = new JRadioButtonMenuItem("DialogLayout");
    lst = new ActionListener() {
      public void actionPerformed(ActionEvent e) {
        getContentPane().setLayout(new DialogLayout());
        validate();
        repaint();
      }
    };
    mItem.addActionListener(lst);
    group.add(mItem);
    mLayout.add(mItem);

    menuBar.add(mLayout);

    return menuBar;
  }
  public void focusGained(FocusEvent e) {
    m_activeBean = e.getComponent();
    repaint();
  }
```

10 Relayout with GridLayout configuration

10 Relayout with vertical BoxLayout configuration

11 On focus change, stores currently active component and redisplays

```
    public void focusLost(FocusEvent e) {}

    // This is a heavyweight component so we override paint
    // instead of paintComponent. super.paint(g) will
    // paint all child components first, and then we
    // simply draw over top of them.
    public void paint(Graphics g) {
      super.paint(g);

      if (m_activeBean == null)
        return;

      Point pt = getLocationOnScreen();
      Point pt1 = m_activeBean.getLocationOnScreen();
      int x = pt1.x - pt.x - 2;
      int y = pt1.y - pt.y - 2;
      int w = m_activeBean.getWidth() + 2;
      int h = m_activeBean.getHeight() + 2;

      g.setColor(Color.black);
      g.drawRect(x, y, w, h);
    }

    public static void main(String argv[]) {
      new BeanContainer();
    }
  }
}
```

⑫ Redraw container with box around currently active component

Clock.java

see \Chapter4\6\clock

```
package clock;

import java.applet.*;
import java.awt.*;
import java.awt.event.*;
import java.beans.*;
import java.io.*;
import java.util.*;

import javax.swing.*;
import javax.swing.border.*;

public class Clock extends JButton
 implements Customizer, Externalizable, Runnable
{

 protected PropertyChangeSupport m_helper;
 protected boolean  m_digital = false;
 protected Calendar m_calendar;
 protected Dimension m_preffSize;

 public Clock() {
  m_calendar = Calendar.getInstance();
  m_helper = new PropertyChangeSupport(this);

  Border br1 = new EtchedBorder(EtchedBorder.RAISED,
```

⑬ Clock bean on button which can listen for property changes, manage its own serialization, and run on a separate thread

⑭ Constructor creates helper objects, puts "clock-like" border on, and starts a new thread to run on

```
    Color.white, new Color(128, 0, 0));
 Border br2 = new MatteBorder(4, 4, 4, 4, Color.red);
   setBorder(new CompoundBorder(br1, br2));

 setBackground(Color.white);
 setForeground(Color.black);

 (new Thread(this)).start();
}

public void writeExternal(ObjectOutput out)
 throws IOException {
  out.writeBoolean(m_digital);
  out.writeObject(getBackground());
  out.writeObject(getForeground());
  out.writeObject(getPreferredSize());
}

public void readExternal(ObjectInput in)
 throws IOException, ClassNotFoundException {
  setDigital(in.readBoolean());
  setBackground((Color)in.readObject());
  setForeground((Color)in.readObject());
  setPreferredSize((Dimension)in.readObject());
}

public Dimension getPreferredSize() {
   if (m_preffSize != null)
     return m_preffSize;
   else
     return new Dimension(50, 50);
}

public void setPreferredSize(Dimension preffSize) {
  m_preffSize = preffSize;
}

public Dimension getMinimumSize() {
  return getPreferredSize();
}

public Dimension getMaximumSize() {
  return getPreferredSize();
}

public void setDigital(boolean digital) {
  m_helper.firePropertyChange("digital",
    new Boolean(m_digital),
    new Boolean(digital));
  m_digital = digital;
  repaint();
}

public boolean getDigital() {
  return m_digital;
}
```

15 **Managed serialization, writing out each field and reading it back in the same order**

```java
public void addPropertyChangeListener(
  PropertyChangeListener lst) {
    if (m_helper != null)
      m_helper.addPropertyChangeListener(lst);
}

public void removePropertyChangeListener(
  PropertyChangeListener lst) {
    if (m_helper != null)
      m_helper.removePropertyChangeListener(lst);
}

public void setObject(Object bean) {}

public void paintComponent(Graphics g) {
    super.paintComponent(g);

    g.setColor(getBackground());
    g.fillRect(0, 0, getWidth(), getHeight());
    getBorder().paintBorder(this, g, 0, 0, getWidth(), getHeight());

    m_calendar.setTime(new Date()); // Get current time
    int hrs = m_calendar.get(Calendar.HOUR_OF_DAY);
    int min = m_calendar.get(Calendar.MINUTE);

    g.setColor(getForeground());
    if (m_digital) {
      String time = ""+hrs+":"+min;
      g.setFont(getFont());
      FontMetrics fm = g.getFontMetrics();
      int y = (getHeight() + fm.getAscent())/2;
      int x = (getWidth() - fm.stringWidth(time))/2;
      g.drawString(time, x, y);
    }
    else {
      int x = getWidth()/2;
      int y = getHeight()/2;
      int rh = getHeight()/4;
      int rm = getHeight()/3;

      double ah = ((double)hrs+min/60.0)/6.0*Math.PI;
      double am = min/30.0*Math.PI;

      g.drawLine(x, y, (int)(x+rh*Math.sin(ah)),
        (int)(y-rh*Math.cos(ah)));
      g.drawLine(x, y, (int)(x+rm*Math.sin(am)),
        (int)(y-rm*Math.cos(am)));
    }
}

public void run() {
    while (true) {
      repaint();
      try {
        Thread.sleep(30*1000);
      }
```

16 **Displays clock value in either digital or analog form**

```
        catch(InterruptedException ex) { break; }
    }
  }
}
```

4.7.1   Understanding the code

Class BeanContainer

1 This class extends `JFrame` to provide the frame for this application. It also implements the `FocusListener` interface to manage focus transfer between beans in the container. Four instance variables are declared:

- `File m_currentDir`: The most recent directory used to load and save beans.
- `Component m_activeBean`: A bean component which currently has the focus.
- `String m_className`: The fully qualified class name of our custom `Clock` bean.
- `JFileChooser m_chooser`: Used for saving and loading beans.

2 The only GUI provided by the container itself is the menu bar. The `createMenuBar()` method creates the menu bar, its items, and their corresponding action listeners. Three menus are added to the menu bar: File, Edit, and Layout.

> **NOTE**   All code corresponding to New, Load, and Save in the File menu is wrapped in a separate thread to avoid an unnecesary load on the event-dispatching thread. See chapter 2 for more information about multithreading.

3 The New... menu item in the File menu displays an input dialog (using the `JOption-Pane.showInputDialog()` method) to enter the class name of a new bean to be added to the container. Once a name has been entered, the program attempts to load that class, create a **4** new class instance using a default constructor, and add that new object to the container. The newly created component requests the focus and receives a `this` reference to `BeanContainer` as a `FocusListener`. Any exceptions caught will be displayed in a message box.

5 The Load... menu item from the File menu displays a `JFileChooser` dialog to select a file **6** containing a previously serialized bean component. If this succeeds, the program opens an input stream on this file and reads the first stored object. If this object is derived from the `java.awt.Component` class, it is added to the container. The loaded component requests the focus and receives a `this` reference to `BeanContainer` as a `FocusListener`. Any exceptions caught will be displayed in a message box.

7 The Save... menu item from the File menu displays a `JFileChooser` dialog to select a file destination for serializing the bean component which currently has the focus. If this succeeds, the program opens an output stream on that file and writes the currently active component to that stream. Any exceptions caught will be displayed in a message box.

8 The Exit menu item simply quits and closes the application with `System.exit(0)`.

9 The Edit menu contains a single item entitled Delete, which removes the currently active bean from the container:

```
getContentPane().remove(m_activeBean);
m_activeBean = null;
validate();
repaint();
```

(10) The Layout menu contains several `JRadioButtonMenuItems` managed by a `ButtonGroup` group. These items are entitled "FlowLayout," "GridLayout," "BoxLayout – X," "BoxLayout – Y," and "DialogLayout." Each item receives an `ActionListener` which sets the corresponding layout manager of the application frame's content pane, calls `validate()` to lay out the container again, and then `repaints` it. For example:

```
getContentPane().setLayout(new DialogLayout());
validate();
repaint();
```

(11)
(12) The `focusGained()` method stores a reference to the component which currently has the focus as instance variable `m_activebean`. The `paint()` method is implemented to draw a rectangle around the component which currently has the focus. It is important to note here the static `JPopupMenu` method called in the `BeanContainer` constructor:

```
JPopupMenu.setDefaultLightWeightPopupEnabled(false);
```

This method forces all pop-up menus (which menu bars use to display their contents) to use heavyweight popups rather than lightweight popups. (By default, pop-up menus are lightweight unless they cannot fit within their parent container's bounds.) The reason we disable this is because our `paint()` method will render the bean selection rectangle over the top of the lightweight popups otherwise.

Class Clock

(13) This class is a simple bean clock component which can be used in a container just as any other bean. This class extends the `JButton` component to inherit its focus-grabbing functionality. This class also implements three interfaces: `Customizer` to handle property listeners, `Externalizable` to completely manage its own serialization, and `Runnable` to be run by a thread. Four instance variables are declared:

- `PropertyChangeSupport m_helper`: An object to manage `PropertyChangeListeners`.
- `boolean m_digital`: A custom property for this component which manages the display state of the clock (digital or arrow-based).
- `Calendar m_calendar`: A helper object to handle Java's time objects (instances of `Date`).
- `Dimension m_preffSize`: A preferred size for this component which may be assigned using the `setPreferredSize()` method.

(14) The constructor of the `Clock` class creates the helper objects and sets the border for this component as a `CompoundBorder` that contains an `EtchedBorder` and a `MatteBorder`. It then sets the background and foreground colors and starts a new `Thread` to run the clock.

(15) The `writeExternal()` method writes the current state of a `Clock` object into an `ObjectOutput` stream. Four properties are written: `m_digital`, `background`, `foreground`, and `preferredSize`. The `readExternal()` method reads the previously saved state of a `Clock` object from an `ObjectInput` stream. It reads these four properties and applies them to the object previously created with the default constructor. These methods are called from the Save and Load menu bar action listener code in `BeanContainer`. Specifically, they are called when `writeObject()` and `readObject()` are invoked.

The serialization mechanism in Swing has not yet fully matured. You can readily discover that both lightweight and heavyweight components throw exceptions during the process of serialization. For this reason, we implement the `Externalizable` interface to take complete control over the serialization of the `Clock` bean. Another reason is that the default serialization mechanism tends to serialize a substantial amount of unnecessary information, whereas our custom implementation stores only the necessities.

16 The rest of this class need not be explained here, as it does not relate directly to the topic of this chapter and it represents a simple example of a bean component. If you're interested, take note of the `paintComponent()` method which, depending on whether the clock is in digital mode (determined by `m_digital`), either computes the current position of the clock's arrows and draws them, or renders the time as a digital `String`.

4.7.2   Running the code

This application provides a framework for experimenting with any available JavaBeans; both lightweight (Swing) and heavyweight (AWT) components: we can create, serialize, delete, and restore them.

We can apply several layouts to manage these components dynamically. Figures 4.18 through 4.22 show `BeanContainer` using five different layout managers to arrange four `Clock` beans. To create a bean, choose New from the File menu and type the fully qualified name of the class. For instance, to create a `Clock` you need to type "clock.Clock" in the input dialog.

Once you've experimented with `Clock` beans, try loading some Swing JavaBeans. Figure 4.23 shows `BeanDialog` with two `JButton`s and two `JTextField`s. They were created in the following order (and thus have corresponding container indices): `JButton`, `JText-Field`, `JButton`, and `JTextField`. Try doing this: remember that you need to specify fully qualified class names such as `javax.swing.JButton` when you add a new bean. This ordering adheres to our `DialogLayout` label/input field pairs scheme, except that here we are using buttons in place of labels. That way, when we set `BeanContainer`'s layout to `DialogLayout`, we know what to expect.

NOTE   You will notice selection problems with components such as `JComboBox`, `JSplit-Pane`, and `JLabel` (which has no selection mechanism). A more complete version of `BeanContainer` would take this into account and implement more robust focus-requesting behavior.

Later in this book, after a discussion of tables, we will add powerful functionality to this example to allow bean property manipulation. We highly suggest that you skip ahead for a moment and run example 18.8.

Start the chapter 18 example and create `JButton` and `JTextField` beans exactly as described above. Select `DialogLayout` from the Layout menu and then click on the top-most `JButton` to give it the focus. Now select Properties from the Edit menu. A separate frame will pop up with a `JTable` that contains all of the `JButton`'s properties. Navigate to the `label` property and change it to "Button 1" (by double-clicking on its Value field). Now select the corresponding top-most `JTextField` and change its `preferredSize` property to "4,40." Figure 4.24 illustrates what you should see.

By changing the preferred, maximum, and minimum sizes, as well as other component properties, we can directly examine the behavior that different layout managers impose on our container. Experimenting with this example is a very convenient way to learn more about how the layout managers behave. It also forms the foundation for an interface development environment (IDE), which many developers use to simplify interface design.

![Chapter illustration]

C H A P T E R　5

Labels and buttons

5.1　Labels and buttons overview　151
5.2　Custom buttons, part I: transparent buttons　160
5.3　Custom buttons, part II: polygonal buttons　167
5.4　Custom buttons, part III: tooltip management　176

5.1　LABELS AND BUTTONS OVERVIEW

5.1.1　JLabel

class javax.swing.JLabel

JLabel is one of the simplest Swing components, and it is most often used to identify other components. JLabel can display text, an icon, or both in any combination of positions (note that text will always overlap the icon). The code in example 5.1 creates four different JLabels and places them in a GridLayout as shown in figure 5.1.

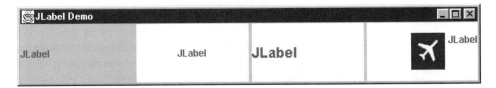

Figure 5.1　JLabel **demo**

151

Example 5.1

see \Chapter5\6

```java
import java.awt.*;
import javax.swing.*;

class LabelDemo extends JFrame
{
  public LabelDemo() {
    super("JLabel Demo");
    setSize(600, 100);

    JPanel content = (JPanel) getContentPane();
    content.setLayout(new GridLayout(1, 4, 4, 4));

    JLabel label = new JLabel();
    label.setText("JLabel");
    label.setBackground(Color.white);
    content.add(label);

    label = new JLabel("JLabel",
      SwingConstants.CENTER);
    label.setOpaque(true);
    label.setBackground(Color.white);
    content.add(label);

    label = new JLabel("JLabel");
    label.setFont(new Font("Helvetica", Font.BOLD, 18));
    label.setOpaque(true);
    label.setBackground(Color.white);
    content.add(label);

    ImageIcon image = new ImageIcon("flight.gif");
    label = new JLabel("JLabel", image,
      SwingConstants.RIGHT);
    label.setVerticalTextPosition(SwingConstants.TOP);
    label.setOpaque(true);
    label.setBackground(Color.white);
    content.add(label);

    setVisible(true);
  }
  public static void main(String args[]) {
    new LabelDemo();
  }
}
```

The first label is created with the default constructor and its text is set using the setText() method. We then set its background to white, but when we run this program the background of the label shows up as light gray. This happens because we didn't force the label to be opaque. In chapter 2 we learned that Swing components support transparency, which means that a component does not have to paint every pixel within its bounds. So when a component is not opaque, it will not fill its background. A JLabel (as with most components) is non-opaque by default.

We can also set the font and foreground color of a JLabel using JComponent's set-Font() and setForeground() methods. Refer back to chapter 2 for information about working with the Font and Color classes.

The default horizontal alignment of JLabel is LEFT if only text is used, and CENTER if an image or an image and text are used. An image will appear to the left of the text by default, and every JLabel is initialized with a centered vertical alignment. Each of these default behaviors can easily be adjusted, as we will see below.

5.1.2   Text alignment

To specify alignment or position in many Swing components, we use the javax.swing. SwingConstants interface. This defines several constant strings, five of which are applicable to JLabel's text alignment settings:

```
SwingConstants.LEFT
SwingConstants.CENTER
SwingConstants.RIGHT
SwingConstants.TOP
SwingConstants.BOTTOM
```

Alignment of both a label's text and icon can be specified either in the constructor or through the setHorizontalAlignment() and setVerticalAlignment() methods. The text can be aligned both vertically or horizontally, independent of the icon (text will overlap the icon when necessary) using the setHorizontalTextAlignment() and setVertical-TextAlignment() methods. Figure 5.2 shows where a JLabel's text will be placed, corresponding to each possible combination of vertical and horizontal text alignment settings.

Vertical = TOP Horizontal = LEFT	Vertical = TOP Horizontal = CENTER	Vertical = TOP Horizontal = RIGHT
Vertical = CENTER Horizontal = LEFT	Vertical = CENTER Horizontal = CENTER	Vertical = CENTER Horizontal = RIGHT
Vertical = BOTTOM Horizontal = LEFT	Vertical = BOTTOM Horizontal = CENTER	Vertical = BOTTOM Horizontal = RIGHT

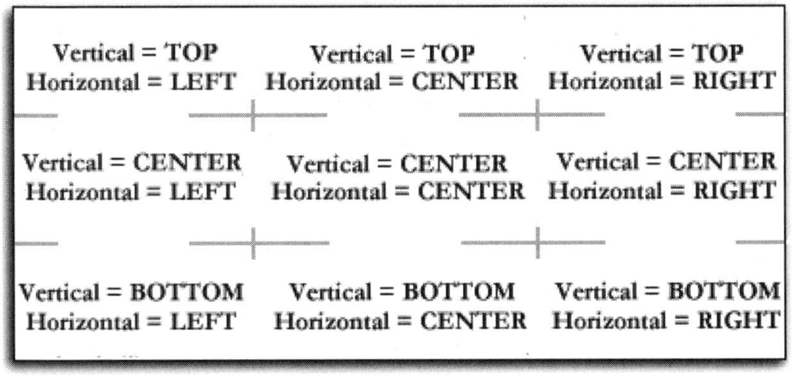

Figure 5.2 JLabel **text alignment**

5.1.3   Icons and icon alignment

The simple example in figure 5.1 included a label with an image of an airplane. This was done by reading a GIF file in as an ImageIcon and passing it to a JLabel constructor:

```
ImageIcon image = new ImageIcon("flight.gif");
```

```
label = new JLabel("JLabel", image,
  SwingConstants.RIGHT);
```

An image can also be set or replaced at any time using the `setIcon()` method (passing `null` will remove the current icon, if any). `JLabel` also supports a disabled icon to be used when a label is in the disabled state. To assign a disabled icon, we use the `setDisabled-Icon()` method.

NOTE   Animated GIFs can be used with `ImageIcon`s and labels just as any static GIF can be, and they don't require any additional code. `ImageIcon` also supports JPGs.

5.1.4 GrayFilter

class javax.swing.GrayFilter

The static `createDisabledImage()` method of the `GrayFilter` class can be used to create "disabled" images.

```
ImageIcon disabledImage = new ImageIcon(
  GrayFilter.createDisabledImage(image.getImage()));
```

Figure 5.3 shows the fourth label in `LabelDemo` now using a disabled icon generated by `GrayFilter`. `JLabel` only displays the disabled icon when it has been disabled using `JComponent`'s `setEnabled()` method.

Figure 5.3   Demonstrating a disabled icon using `GrayFilter`

5.1.5 The labelFor and the displayedMnemonic properties

`JLabel` maintains a `labelFor` property and a `displayedMnemonic` property. The displayed mnemonic is a character that, when pressed in synchronization with ALT (for example, ALT+R), will call `JComponent`'s `requestFocus()` method on the component referenced by the `labelFor` property. The first instance of the displayed mnemonic character (if any) in a label's text will be underlined. We can access these properties using typical get/set accessors.

5.1.6 AbstractButton

abstract class javax.swing.AbstractButton

`AbstractButton` is the template class from which all buttons are defined. This includes push buttons, toggle buttons, check boxes, radio buttons, menu items, and menus themselves. Its direct subclasses are `JButton`, `JToggleButton`, and `JMenuItem`. There are no subclasses of `JButton` in Swing. `JToggleButton` has two subclasses: `JCheckBox` and `JRadioButton`. `JMenuItem` has three subclasses: `JCheckBoxMenuItem`, `JRadioButtonMenuItem`, and `JMenu`. The remainder of this chapter will focus on `JButton` and the `JToggleButton` family. Refer to chapter 12 for more information about menus and menu items.

5.1.7 The ButtonModel interface

abstract interface javax.swing.ButtonModel

Each button class uses a model to store its state. We can access any button's model with `AbstractButton`'s `getModel()` and `setModel()` methods. The `ButtonModel` interface is the template interface from which all button models are defined. `JButton` uses the `DefaultButtonModel` implementation. `JToggleButton` defines an inner class extension of `DefaultButtonModel`; this extension is `JToggleButton.ToggleButtonModel`, which is used by `JToggleButton` and both `JToggleButton` subclasses.

The following boolean property values represent the state of a button, and they have associated `isXX()` and `setXX()` accessors in `DefaultButtonModel`:

- `selected`: Switches state on each click (only relevant for `JToggleButton`s).
- `pressed`: Returns `true` when the button is held down with the mouse.
- `rollover`: Returns `true` when the mouse is hovering over the button.
- `armed`: Stops events from being fired when we press a button with the mouse and then release the mouse when the cursor is outside that button's bounds.
- `enabled`: Returns `true` when the button is active. None of the other properties can normally be changed when this is `false`.

A button's keyboard mnemonic is also stored in its model, as is the `ButtonGroup` it belongs to, if any. (We'll discuss the `ButtonGroup` class when we discuss `JToggleButton`s, as it only applies to this family of buttons.)

5.1.8 JButton

class javax.swing.JButton

`JButton` is a basic push button, which is one of the simplest Swing components. Almost everything we know about `JLabel` also applies to `JButton`. We can add images, specify text and image alignment, set foreground and background colors (remember to call `setOpaque(true)`), and set fonts, among other tasks. Additionally, we can add `ActionListeners`, `ChangeListeners`, and `ItemListeners` to receive `ActionEvents`, `ChangeEvents`, and `ItemEvents` respectively when any properties in its model change value.

In most application dialogs, we might expect to find a button which initially has the focus and will capture an Enter key press, regardless of the current keyboard focus, unless focus is within a multi-line text component. This is referred to as the *default button*. Any `JRootPane` container can define a default button using `JRootPane`'s `setDefaultButton()` method (passing `null` will disable this feature). For instance, to make a button, the default button for a `JFrame`, we would do the following:

```
myJFrame.getRootPane().setDefaultButton(myButton);
```

The `isDefaultButton()` method returns a boolean value indicating whether the button instance it was called on is a default button for a `JRootPane`.

We most often register an `ActionListener` with a button to receive `ActionEvents` from that button whenever it is clicked (if a button has the focus, pressing the Space bar will also fire an `ActionEvent`). `ActionEvents` carry with them information about the event that occurred, including, most importantly, which component they came from.

To create an `ActionListener`, we need to create a class that implements the `Action-Listener` interface, which requires the definition of its `actionPerformed()` method. Once we have built an `ActionListener` we can register it with a button using `JCompo-nent`'s `addActionListener()` method. The following code segment is a typical inner class implementation. When an `ActionEvent` is intercepted, "Swing is powerful!!" is printed to standard output.

```
JButton myButton = new JButton();
ActionListener act = new ActionListener() {
  public void actionPerformed(ActionEvent e) {
    System.out.println("Swing is powerful!!");
  }
};
myButton.addActionListener(act);
```

We primarily use this method throughout this book to attach listeners to components. However, some developers prefer to implement the `ActionListener` interface in the class that owns the button instance. With classes that have several registered components, this is not as efficient as using a separate listener class, and it can require writing common code in several places.

An icon can be assigned to a `JButton` instance via the constructor or the `setIcon()` method. We can optionally assign individual icons for the normal, selected, pressed, rollover, and disabled states. See the API documentation for more detail on the following methods:

```
setDisabledSelectedIcon()
setPressedIcon()
setRolloverIcon()
setRolloverSelectedIcon()
setSelectedIcon()
```

A button can also be disabled and enabled the same way as a `JLabel`, using `setEnabled()`. As we would expect, a disabled button will not respond to any user actions.

A button's keyboard mnemonic provides an alternative means of activation. To add a keyboard mnemonic to a button, we use the `setMnemonic()` method:

```
button.setMnemonic('R');
```

We can then activate a button (equivalent to clicking it) by pressing ALT and its mnemonic key simultaneously (for example, ALT+R). The first appearance of the assigned mnemonic character, if any, in the button text will be underlined to indicate which key activates it. No distinction is made between upper- and lower-case characters. Avoid duplicating mnemonics for components that share a common ancestor.

5.1.9 JToggleButton

class javax.swing.JToggleButton

`JToggleButton` provides a selected state mechanism which extends to its children, `JCheckBox` and `JRadioButton`, and corresponds to the `selected` property we discussed in section 5.1.7. We can test whether a toggle button is selected using `AbstractButton`'s `isSelected()` method, and we can set this property with its `setSelected()` method.

5.1.10 ButtonGroup

class javax.swing.ButtonGroup

JToggleButtons are often used in ButtonGroups. A ButtonGroup manages a set of buttons by guaranteeing that only one button within that group can be selected at any given time. Thus, only JToggleButton and its subclasses are useful in a ButtonGroup because a JButton does not maintain a selected state. Example 5.2 constructs three JToggleButtons and places them in a single ButtonGroup.

Figure 5.4 JToggleButtons in a ButtonGroup

Example 5.2

ToggleButtonDemo.java

see \Chapter5\6

```
import java.awt.*;
import java.awt.event.*;
import javax.swing.*;

class ToggleButtonDemo extends JFrame
{
  public ToggleButtonDemo () {
    super("ToggleButton/ButtonGroup Demo");
    getContentPane().setLayout(new FlowLayout());

    JToggleButton button1 = new JToggleButton("Button 1",true);
    getContentPane().add(button1);
    JToggleButton button2 = new JToggleButton("Button 2",false);
    getContentPane().add(button2);
    JToggleButton button3 = new JToggleButton("Button 3",false);
    getContentPane().add(button3);

    ButtonGroup buttonGroup = new ButtonGroup();
    buttonGroup.add(button1);
    buttonGroup.add(button2);
    buttonGroup.add(button3);

    pack();
    setVisible(true);
  }
  public static void main(String args[]) {
    new ToggleButtonDemo();
  }
}
```

5.1.11 JCheckBox and JRadioButton

class javax.swing.JCheckBox, class javax.swing.JRadioButton

JCheckBox and JRadioButton both inherit all JToggleButton functionality. In fact, the only significant differences between all three components is their UI delegates (how they are rendered). Both button types are normally used to select the mode of a particular application function. Figures 5.5 and 5.6 show the previous example running with JCheckBoxes and JRadioButtons as replacements for the JToggleButtons.

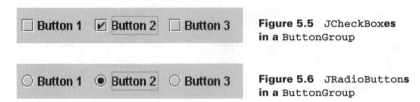

Figure 5.5 JCheckBoxes in a ButtonGroup

Figure 5.6 JRadioButtons in a ButtonGroup

5.1.12 JToolTip and ToolTipManager

class javax.swing.JToolTip, class javax.swing.ToolTipManager

A JToolTip is a small pop-up window designed to contain informative text about a component when the mouse moves over it. We don't generally create instances of these components ourselves. Rather, we call setToolTipText() on any JComponent subclass and pass it a descriptive String. This String is then stored as a client property within that component's client properties Hashtable, and that component is then registered with the ToolTipManager using ToolTipManager's registerComponent() method. The ToolTipManager adds a MouseListener to each component that registers with it.

To unregister a component, we can pass null to that component's setToolTipText() method. This invokes ToolTipManager's unregisterComponent() method, which removes its MouseListener from that component. Figure 5.7 shows a JToggleButton with simple tooltip text.

Figure 5.7 JToggleButton with tooltip text

The ToolTipManager is a service class that maintains a shared instance registered with AppContext (see chapter 2). We can access the ToolTipManager directly by calling its static sharedInstance() method:

```
ToolTipManager toolTipManager = ToolTipManager.sharedInstance();
```

Internally this class uses three non-repeating Timers with delay times defaulting to 750, 500, and 4000. ToolTipManager uses these Timers in coordination with mouse listeners to determine if and when to display a JToolTip with a component's specified tooltip text. When the mouse enters a component's bounds, ToolTipManager will detect this and wait 750ms before displaying a JToolTip for that component. This is referred to as the *initial delay time*. A JToolTip will stay visible for 4000ms or until we move the mouse outside of that component's bounds, whichever comes first. This is referred to as the *dismiss delay time*. The 500ms `Timer` represents the *reshow delay time*, which specifies how soon the `JToolTip` we have just seen will appear again when this component is re-entered. These delay times can be set using `ToolTip-Manager`'s `setDismissDelay()`, `setInitialDelay()`, and `setReshowDelay()` methods.

    `ToolTipManager` is a very nice service, but it does have significant limitations. When we construct our polygonal buttons in section 5.6 below, we will find that it is not robust enough to support non-rectangular components.

5.1.13   Labels and buttons with HTML text

JDK1.2.2 offers a particularly interesting new feature. Now we can use HTML text in `JButton` and `JLabel` components as well as for tooltip text. We don't have to learn any new methods to use this functionality, and the UI delegate handles the HTML rendering for us. If a button/label's text starts with `<HTML>`, Swing knows to render the text in HTML format. We can use normal paragraph tags (`<P>` and `</P>`), line break tags (`<BR>`), and other HTML tags. For instance, we can assign a multiple-line tooltip to any component like this:

```
myComponent.setToolTipText("<html>Multi-line tooltips<br>" +
  "are easy!");
```

The `<br>` tag specifies a line break. Example 5.3 demonstrates this functionality.

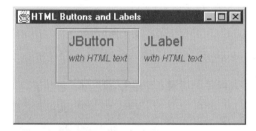

Figure 5.8   A `JButton` **and**
`JLabel` **with HTML text**

Example 5.3

HtmlButtons.java

see \Chapter5\3

```
import java.awt.*;
import java.awt.event.*;
import javax.swing.*;

public class HtmlButtons extends JFrame
{
  public HtmlButtons() {
    super("HTML Buttons and Labels");
    setSize(400, 300);

    getContentPane().setLayout(new FlowLayout());

    String htmlText =
      "<html><p><font color=\"#800080\" "+
      "size=\"4\" face=\"Verdana\">JButton</font> </p>"+
```

```
        "<address><font size=\"2\"><em>"+
        "with HTML text</em></font>"+
        "</address>";
      JButton btn = new JButton(htmlText);
      getContentPane().add(btn);

      htmlText =
        "<html><p><font color=\"#800080\" "+
        "size=\"4\" face=\"Verdana\">JLabel</font> </p>"+
        "<address><font size=\"2\"><em>"+
        "with HTML text</em></font>"+
        "</address>";
      JLabel lbl = new JLabel(htmlText);
      getContentPane().add(lbl);

      WindowListener wndCloser = new WindowAdapter() {
        public void windowClosing(WindowEvent e) {
          System.exit(0);
        }
      };
      addWindowListener(wndCloser);
      setVisible(true);
    }

    public static void main(String args[]) {
      new HtmlButtons();
    }
  }
}
```

5.2 *CUSTOM BUTTONS, PART I: TRANSPARENT BUTTONS*

Buttons in Swing can adopt almost any presentation we can think of. Of course, some presentations are tougher to implement than others. In the remainder of this chapter we will deal directly with these issues. Example 5.4 in this section shows how to construct invisible buttons which only appear when the user moves the mouse cursor over them. Specifically, a border will be painted, and tooltip text will be activated in the default manner.

Buttons such as these can be useful in applets for predefined hyperlink navigation, and we will design our invisible button class with this in mind. Thus, we will show how to create an applet that reads a set of parameters from the HTML page in which it is embedded and loads a corresponding set of invisible buttons. For each button, the designer of the HTML page must provide three parameters: the desired hyperlink URL, the button's bounds (positions and size), and the button's tooltip text. Additionally, our sample applet in example 5.4 will require a background image parameter. Our button's bounds are intended to directly correspond to an "active" region of this background image, much like the venerable HTML image mapping functionality.

Figure 5.9 Transparent rectangular buttons in an applet

Example 5.4

ButtonApplet.java

see \Chapter5\4

```java
import java.applet.*;
import java.awt.*;
import java.awt.event.*;
import java.net.*;
import java.util.*;

import javax.swing.*;
import javax.swing.border.*;
import javax.swing.event.*;

public class ButtonApplet extends JApplet
{
  public ButtonApplet() {}

  public synchronized void init() {
    String imageName = getParameter("image");
    if (imageName == null) {
      System.err.println("Need \"image\" parameter");
      return;
    }
    URL imageUrl = null;
    try {
      imageUrl = new URL(getDocumentBase(), imageName);
    }
```

❶ Applet instead of Frame, so it can run on a web page

❷ Reads "image" parameter to set background image on label

```
    catch (MalformedURLException ex) {
      ex.printStackTrace();
      return;
    }
    ImageIcon bigImage = new ImageIcon(imageUrl);
    JLabel bigLabel = new JLabel(bigImage);
    bigLabel.setLayout(null);

    int index = 1;
    int[] q = new int[4];
    while(true) {
      String paramSize = getParameter("button"+index);
      String paramName = getParameter("name"+index);
      String paramUrl = getParameter("url"+index);
      if (paramSize==null || paramName==null || paramUrl==null)
        break;

      try {
        StringTokenizer tokenizer = new StringTokenizer(
          paramSize, ",");
        for (int k=0; k<4; k++) {
          String str = tokenizer.nextToken().trim();
          q[k] = Integer.parseInt(str);
        }
      }
      catch (Exception ex) { break; }

      NavigateButton btn = new NavigateButton(this,
        paramName, paramUrl);
      bigLabel.add(btn);
      btn.setBounds(q[0], q[1], q[2], q[3]);

      index++;
    }

    getContentPane().setLayout(null);
    getContentPane().add(bigLabel);
    bigLabel.setBounds(0, 0, bigImage.getIconWidth(),
      bigImage.getIconHeight());
  }

  public String getAppletInfo() {
    return "Sample applet with NavigateButtons";
  }

  public String[][] getParameterInfo() {
    String pinfo[][] = {
      {"image",   "string",  "base image file name"},
      {"buttonX","x,y,w,h", "button's bounds"},
      {"nameX",   "string",  "tooltip text"},
      {"urlX",    "url",     "link URL"} };
    return pinfo;
  }
}

class NavigateButton extends JButton implements ActionListener
{
```

3 Sets up one transparent button for each iteration

4 Creates the button and adds it to the container

5 Useful information for applets, but not required

6 Implementation of invisible button

```java
protected Border m_activeBorder;
protected Border m_inactiveBorder;

protected Applet m_parent;
protected String m_text;
protected String m_sUrl;
protected URL    m_url;

public NavigateButton(Applet parent, String text, String sUrl) {
  m_parent = parent;
  setText(text);
  m_sUrl = sUrl;
  try {
    m_url = new URL(sUrl);
  }
  catch(Exception ex) { m_url = null; }

  setOpaque(false);
  enableEvents(AWTEvent.MOUSE_EVENT_MASK);

  m_activeBorder = new MatteBorder(1, 1, 1, 1, Color.yellow);
  m_inactiveBorder = new EmptyBorder(1, 1, 1, 1);
  setBorder(m_inactiveBorder);

  addActionListener(this);
}

public void setText(String text) {
  m_text = text;
  setToolTipText(text);
}

public String getText() {
  return m_text;
}

protected void processMouseEvent(MouseEvent evt) {
  switch (evt.getID()) {
    case MouseEvent.MOUSE_ENTERED:
      setBorder(m_activeBorder);
      setCursor(Cursor.getPredefinedCursor(
        Cursor.HAND_CURSOR));
      m_parent.showStatus(m_sUrl);
      break;
    case MouseEvent.MOUSE_EXITED:
      setBorder(m_inactiveBorder);
      setCursor(Cursor.getPredefinedCursor(
        Cursor.DEFAULT_CURSOR));
      m_parent.showStatus("");
      break;
  }
  super.processMouseEvent(evt);
}

public void actionPerformed(ActionEvent e) {
  if (m_url != null) {
```

7 Borders shown when button has and does not have focus

8 Sets URL for button

9 Sets up to process its own mouse events

10 Overrides methods from JButton, but to manage tooltip text, not label text

11 Gets all mouse events, but only handles mouse enter and exit events, to change the border and cursor

9 Called when user presses button with mouse or keyboard

```
      AppletContext context = m_parent.getAppletContext();
      if (context != null)
        context.showDocument(m_url);
    }
  }

  public void paintComponent(Graphics g) {
    paintBorder(g);
  }
}
```

5.2.1   Understanding the code

Class ButtonApplet

1 This class extends `JApplet` to provide web page functionality. The `init()` method creates
2 and initializes all GUI components. It starts by reading the applet's `image` parameter, which is
then used along with the applet's codebase to construct a URL:

```
      imageUrl = new URL(getDocumentBase(), imageName);
```

This URL points to the image file which is used to create our `bigLabel` label, which is
used as the applet's background image.

3 The applet can be configured to hold several invisible buttons for navigating to predefined
URLs. For each button, three applet parameters must be provided:

- `buttonN`: Holds four comma-delimited numbers for the x, y, width, and height of button N.
- `nameN`: Tooltip text for button N.
- `urlN`: URL to redirect the browser to when the user clicks the mouse over button N.

4 As soon as these parameters are parsed for a given N, a new button is created and added to
`bigLabel`:

```
      NavigateButton btn = new NavigateButton(this,
        paramName, paramUrl);
      bigLabel.add(btn);
      btn.setBounds(q[0], q[1], q[2], q[3]);
```

Finally, the `bigLabel` component is added to the applet's content pane. It receives a fixed
size to avoid any repositioning if the label's parent is somehow resized.

5 The `getAppletInfo()` method returns a `String` description of this applet. The `getPa-
rameterInfo()` method returns a two-dimensional `String` array that describes the parame-
ters accepted by this applet. Both are strongly recommended constituents of any applet, but
they are not required for raw functionality.

Class NavigateButton

6 This class extends `JButton` to provide our custom implementation of an invisible button. It
implements the `ActionListener` interface, eliminating the need to add an external listener, and
it shows how we can enable mouse events without implementing the `MouseListener` interface.

7 Several parameters are declared in this class:

- `Border m_activeBorder`: The border which will be used when the button is active
(when the mouse cursor is moved over the button).

- `Border m_inactiveBorder`: The border which will be used when the button is inactive (when no mouse cursor is over the button). This will not usually be visible.
- `Applet m_parent`: A reference to the parent applet.
- `String m_text`: The tooltip text for this button.
- `String m_sUrl`: A string representation of the URL (for display in the browser's status bar).
- `URL m_url`: The actual URL to redirect the browser to when a mouse click occurs.

(8) The constructor of the `NavigateButton` class takes three parameters: a reference to the parent applet, the tooltip text, and a `String` representation of a URL. It assigns all instance variables and creates a URL from the given `String`. If the URL address cannot be resolved, it is set to `null` (this will disable navigation). The `opaque` property is set to `false` because this component

(9) is supposed to be transparent. Notice that this component processes its own `MouseEvents`, which is enabled with the `enableEvents()` method. This button will also receive `Action-Events` by way of implementing `ActionListener` and adding itself as a listener.

(10) The `setText()` and `getText()` methods manage the `m_text` (tooltip text) property. They also override the corresponding methods inherited from the `JButton` class.

(11) The `processMouseEvent()` method will be called for notification about mouse events on this component. We want to process only two kinds of events: `MOUSE_ENTERED` and `MOUSE_EXITED`. When the mouse enters the button's bounds, we set the border to `m_activeBorder`, change the mouse cursor to the hand cursor, and display the `String` description of the URL in the browser's status bar. When the mouse exits the button's bounds, we perform the opposite actions: set the border to `m_inactiveBorder`, set the mouse cursor to the default cursor, and clear the browser's status bar.

(12) The `actionPerformed()` method will be called when the user presses this button (note that we use the inherited `JButton` processing for both mouse *clicks* and the keyboard mnemonic). If both the URL and `AppletContext` instances are not `null`, the `showDocument()` method is called to redirect the browser to the button's URL.

> **NOTE**   Do not confuse `AppletContext` with the `AppContext` class we discussed in section 2.5. `AppletContext` is an interface for describing an applet's environment, including information about the document in which it is contained, as well as information about other applets that might also be contained in that document.

The `paintComponent()` method used for this button has a very simple implementation. We just draw the button's border by calling `paintBorder()`. Since this component is not designed to have a UI delegate, we do not need to call `super.paintComponent()` from this method.

5.2.2   Running the code

To run example 5.4 in a web browser, we have constructed the following HTML file:

```
<html>

<head>
<title></title>
</head>

<body>
```

```
<OBJECT classid="clsid:8AD9C840-044E-11D1-B3E9-00805F499D93"
WIDTH = 563 HEIGHT = 275  codebase="http://java.sun.com/products/plugin/
1.2/jinstall-12-win32.cab#Version=1,2,0,0">
<PARAM NAME = "CODE" VALUE = "ButtonApplet.class" >
<PARAM NAME = "type" VALUE ="application/x-java-applet;version=1.2">
  <param name="button1" value="49, 134, 161, 22">
  <param name="button2" value="49, 156, 161, 22">
  <param name="button3" value="16, 178, 194, 22">
  <param name="button4" value="85, 200, 125, 22">
  <param name="button5" value="85, 222, 125, 22">
  <param name="image" value="nasa.gif">
  <param name="name1" value="What is Earth Science?">
  <param name="name2" value="Earth Science Missions">
  <param name="name3" value="Science of the Earth System">
  <param name="name4" value="Image Gallery">
  <param name="name5" value="For Kids Only">
  <param name="url1"
   value="http://www.earth.nasa.gov/whatis/index.html">
  <param name="url2"
   value="http://www.earth.nasa.gov/missions/index.html">
  <param name="url3"
   value="http://www.earth.nasa.gov/science/index.html">
  <param name="url4"
   value="http://www.earth.nasa.gov/gallery/index.html">
  <param name="url5"
   value="http://kids.mtpe.hq.nasa.gov/">

<COMMENT>
<EMBED type="application/x-java-applet;version=1.2" CODE = "ButtonAp-
plet.class"
  WIDTH = "563" HEIGHT = "275"
  codebase="./"
  button1="49, 134, 161, 22"
  button2="49, 156, 161, 22"
  button3="16, 178, 194, 22"
  button4="85, 200, 125, 22"
  button5="85, 222, 125, 22"
  image="nasa.gif"
  name1="What is Earth Science?"
  name2="Earth Science Missions"
  name3="Science of the Earth System"
  name4="Image Gallery"
  name5="For Kids Only"
  url1="http://www.earth.nasa.gov/whatis/index.html"
  url2="http://www.earth.nasa.gov/missions/index.html"
  url3="http://www.earth.nasa.gov/science/index.html"
  url4="http://www.earth.nasa.gov/gallery/index.html"
  url5="http://kids.mtpe.hq.nasa.gov/"
  pluginspage=
    "http://java.sun.com/products/plugin/1.2/plugin-install.html">
<NOEMBED>
</COMMENT>
```

```
alt="Your browser understands the &lt;APPLET&gt; tag but isn't
running the applet, for some reason."
Your browser is completely ignoring the &lt;APPLET&gt; tag!
</NOEMBED>
</EMBED>
</OBJECT>
</p>

<p> </p>
</body>
</html>
```

NOTE The HTML file above works with appletviewer, Netscape Navigator 4.0, and Micro-soft Internet Explorer 4.0. This compatibility is achieved thanks to Java plug-in technology. See http://www.javasoft.com/products/plugin/1.2/docs/tags.html for details on how to write plug-in-compatible HTML files. The downside to this file is that we need to include all applet parameters two times for each web browser.

REFERENCE For additional information about the Java plug-in and the plug-in HTML convert-er (a convenient utility to generate plug-in-compliant HTML), see Swing Connec-tion's "Swinging on the Web" article at: http://java.sun.com/products/jfc/tsc/java_plug-in/java_plug-in.html.

Figure 5.9 shows `ButtonApplet` running in Netscape Navigator 4.05 using the Java plug-in. Notice how invisible buttons react when the mouse cursor moves over them. Click a button and navigate to one of the NASA sites.

5.3 *CUSTOM BUTTONS, PART II: POLYGONAL BUTTONS*

The approach described in the previous section assumes that all navigational buttons have a rectangular shape. This can be too restrictive for the complex active regions that are needed in the navigation of images such as geographical maps. In example 5.5, we will show how to extend the idea of transparent buttons, developed in the previous example, to transparent non-rectangular buttons.

The `java.awt.Polygon` class is extremely helpful for this purpose, especially the two related methods which follow (see the API documentation for more information):

- `Polygon.contains(int x, int y)`: Returns `true` if a point with the given coordi-nates is contained inside the `Polygon`.
- `Graphics.drawPolygon(Polygon polygon)`: Draws an outline of a `Polygon` using the given `Graphics` object.

The first method is used in this example to verify that the mouse cursor is located inside a given polygon. The second method will be used to actually draw a polygon representing the bounds of a non-rectangular button.

This seems fairly basic, but there is one significant complication. All Swing components are encapsulated in rectangular bounds; nothing can be done about this. If some component receives a mouse event which occurs in its rectangular bounds, the overlapped underlying com-ponents do not have a chance to receive this event. Figure 5.10 illustrates two non-rectangular buttons. The part of Button B that lies under the rectangle of Button A will never receive mouse events and cannot be clicked.

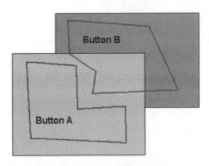

Figure 5.10 Illustration of two overlapping non-rectangular buttons

To resolve this situation, we can skip any mouse event processing in our non-rectangular components. Instead, all mouse events can be directed to the parent container. All buttons can then register themselves as `MouseListeners` and `MouseMotionListeners` with that container. In this way, mouse events can be received without worrying about overlapping and all buttons will receive notification of all events without any preliminary filtering. To minimize the resulting impact on the system's performance, we need to provide a quick discard of events lying outside a button's bounding rectangle.

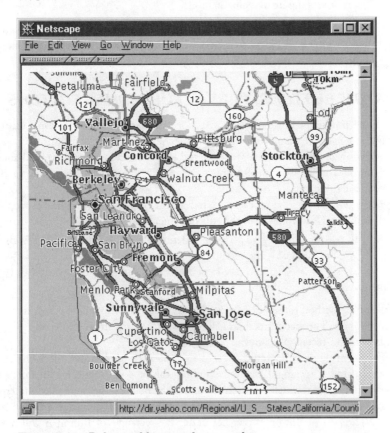

Figure 5.11 Polygonal buttons in an applet

Example 5.5

ButtonApplet2.java

see \Chapter5\5

```java
import java.applet.*;
import java.awt.*;
import java.awt.event.*;
import java.net.*;
import java.util.*;

import javax.swing.*;
import javax.swing.border.*;
import javax.swing.event.*;

public class ButtonApplet2 extends JApplet
{
  public ButtonApplet2() {}

  public synchronized void init() {
    // Unchanged code from example 5.4

    int index = 1;
    while(true) {
      String paramSize = getParameter("button"+index);
      String paramName = getParameter("name"+index);
      String paramUrl = getParameter("url"+index);
      if (paramSize==null || paramName==null || paramUrl==null)
        break;

      Polygon p = new Polygon();
      try {
        StringTokenizer tokenizer = new StringTokenizer(
          paramSize, ",");
        while (tokenizer.hasMoreTokens()) {
          String str = tokenizer.nextToken().trim();
          int x = Integer.parseInt(str);
          str = tokenizer.nextToken().trim();
          int y = Integer.parseInt(str);
          p.addPoint(x, y);
        }
      }
      catch (Exception ex) { break; }

      PolygonButton btn = new PolygonButton(this, p,
        paramName, paramUrl);
      bigLabel.add(btn);

      index++;
    }

    getContentPane().setLayout(null);
    getContentPane().add(bigLabel);
    bigLabel.setBounds(0, 0, bigImage.getIconWidth(),
    bigImage.getIconHeight());
  }
```

❶ Like ButtonApplet, but buttons are polygons, instead of just rectangles

❶ Form polygon from unspecified number of integer coordinates

```java
  public String getAppletInfo() {
    return "Sample applet with PolygonButtons";
  }

  public String[][] getParameterInfo() {
    String pinfo[][] = {
      {"image",   "string",  "base image file name"},
      {"buttonX","x1,y1, x2,y2, ...", "button's bounds"},
      {"nameX",   "string",  "tooltip text"},
      {"urlX",    "url",       "link URL"} };
    return pinfo;
  }
}

class PolygonButton extends JComponent
 implements MouseListener, MouseMotionListener
{
  static public Color ACTIVE_COLOR = Color.red;
  static public Color INACTIVE_COLOR = Color. darkGray;

  protected JApplet m_parent;
  protected String m_text;
  protected String m_sUrl;
  protected URL     m_url;

  protected Polygon m_polygon;
  protected Rectangle m_rc;
  protected boolean m_active;

  protected static PolygonButton m_currentButton;

  public PolygonButton(JApplet parent, Polygon p,
   String text, String sUrl)
  {
    m_parent = parent;
    m_polygon = p;
    setText(text);
    m_sUrl = sUrl;
    try {
      m_url = new URL(sUrl);
    }
    catch(Exception ex) { m_url = null; }

    setOpaque(false);

    m_parent.addMouseListener(this);
    m_parent.addMouseMotionListener(this);

    m_rc = new Rectangle(m_polygon.getBounds()); // Bug alert!
    m_rc.grow(1, 1);

    setBounds(m_rc);
    m_polygon.translate(-m_rc.x, -m_rc.y);
  }
  public void setText(String text) { m_text = text; }

  public String getText() { return m_text; }
```

❶ Format of polygon coordinates

❷ Replaces NavigateButton from previous example, but gets all mouse events from parent to check against polygon

❸ This component listens to parent's events

❹ Create bounding rectangle

```java
public void mouseMoved(MouseEvent e) {
    if (!m_rc.contains(e.getX(), e.getY()) || e.isConsumed()) {
        if (m_active)
            setState(false);
        return; // Quickly return, if outside our rectangle
    }
    int x = e.getX() - m_rc.x;
    int y = e.getY() - m_rc.y;
    boolean active = m_polygon.contains(x, y);

    if (m_active != active)
        setState(active);
    if (m_active)
        e.consume();
}

public void mouseDragged(MouseEvent e) {}

protected void setState(boolean active) {
    m_active = active;
    repaint();
    if (m_active) {
        if (m_currentButton != null)
            m_currentButton.setState(false);
        m_currentButton = this;
        m_parent.setCursor(Cursor.getPredefinedCursor(
            Cursor.HAND_CURSOR));
        m_parent.showStatus(m_sUrl);
    }
    else {
        m_currentButton = null;
        m_parent.setCursor(Cursor.getPredefinedCursor(
            Cursor.DEFAULT_CURSOR));
        m_parent.showStatus("");
    }
}

public void mouseClicked(MouseEvent e) {
    if (m_active && m_url != null && !e.isConsumed()) {
        AppletContext context = m_parent.getAppletContext();
        if (context != null)
            context.showDocument(m_url);
        e.consume();
    }
}
public void mousePressed(MouseEvent e) {}
public void mouseReleased(MouseEvent e) {}
public void mouseExited(MouseEvent e) { mouseMoved(e); }
public void mouseEntered(MouseEvent e) { mouseMoved(e); }

public void paintComponent(Graphics g) {
    g.setColor(m_active ? ACTIVE_COLOR : INACTIVE_COLOR);
    g.drawPolygon(m_polygon);
}
```

5 Compare against polygon; fix activation state

6 Translate event coordinates to button coordinates and set state accordingly

7 Resets active button; redraws component, cursor, and URL

8 If mouse click is for this button, then show the URL document

9 Draws Red if active, Grey if inactive

5.3.1 Understanding the code

Class ButtonApplet2

1 This class is a slightly modified version of the `ButtonApplet` class in the previous section; it accommodates polygonal button sizes rather than rectangles (the parser has been modified to read in an arbitrary number of points). Now it creates a `Polygon` instance and parses a data string, which is assumed to contain pairs of comma-separated coordinates, adding each coordinate to the `Polygon` using the the `addPoint()` method. The resulting `Polygon` instance is used to create a new `PolygonButton` component.

Class PolygonButton

2 This class serves as a replacement for the `NavigateButton` class in the previous example. Notice that it extends `JComponent` directly. This is necessary to disassociate any mouse handling inherent in buttons (the mouse handling is actually built into the button UI delegates). Remember, we want to handle mouse events ourselves, but we want them each to be sent from within the parent's bounds to each `PolygonButton`, not from each `PolygonButton` to the parent.

> **NOTE** This is the opposite way of working with mouse listeners than we are used to. The idea may take a few moments to sink in because directing events from child to parent is so much more common that we generally don't think of things the other way around.

So, to be notified of mouse events from the parent, we'll need to implement the `MouseListener` and `MouseMotionListener` interfaces.

Four new instance variables are declared:

- `Polygon m_polygon`: The polygonal region representing this button's bounds.
- `Rectangle m_rc`: This button's bounding rectangle as seen in the coordinate space of the *parent*.
- `boolean m_active`: The flag indicating that this button is active.
- `PolygonButton m_currentButton`: A static reference to the instance of this class which is currently active.

3 The constructor of the `PolygonButton` class takes four parameters: a reference to the parent applet, the `Polygon` instance representing this component's bounds, the tooltip text, and a `String` representation of a URL. It assigns all instance variables and instantiates a `URL` using the associated `String` parameter (similar to what we saw in the last example). This component adds itself to the parent applet as a `MouseListener` and a `MouseMotionListener`:

```
m_parent.addMouseListener(this);
m_parent.addMouseMotionListener(this);
```

4 The bounding rectangle `m_rc` is computed with the `Polygon.getBounds()` method. This method does not create a new instance of the `Rectangle` class, but it does return a reference to an internal `Polygon` instance variable which is subject to change. This is not safe, so we must explicitly create a new `Rectangle` instance from the supplied reference. This `Rectangle`'s bounds are expanded (using its `grow()` method) to take border width into account. Finally, the Rectangle `m_rc` is set as the button's bounding region, and the `Polygon` is translated into the component's local coordinates by shifting its origin using its `translate()` method.

❺ The `mouseMoved()` method is invoked when mouse events occur in the parent container. We first quickly check whether the event lies inside our bounding rectangle and if it has not yet been consumed by another component. If both conditions are met, we continue processing this event; otherwise, our method returns. Before we return, however, we first must check whether this button is still active for some reason—this can happen if the mouse cursor moves too fast out of this button's bounds, and the given component did not receive a `MOUSE_EXITED` MouseEvent to deactivate itself. If this is the case, we deactivate the button and then exit the `mouseMoved()` method.

❻ We next manually translate the coordinates of the event into our button's local system (remember that this is an event from the parent container) and check whether the point lies within our polygon. This gives us a boolean result which should indicate whether this component is currently active or inactive. If our button's current activation state (`m_active`) is not equal to this value, we call the `setState()` method to change it so that it is. Finally, if this component is active, we consume the given `MouseEvent` to avoid activation of two components simultaneously.

❼ The `setState()` method is called, as described above, to set a new activation state of this component. It takes a boolean value as a parameter and stores it in the `m_active` instance variable. Then it repaints the component to reflect a change in state, if any. Depending on the state of the `m_active` flag in the `setState()` method, one of the following will happen:
  - If the `m_active` flag is set to `true`, this method checks the static reference to the currently active button stored in the `m_currentButton` static variable. In the case where this reference still points to some other component (again, it potentially can happen if the mouse cursor moves too quickly out of a component's rectangular bounds), we force that component to be inactive. Then we store a `this` reference as the `m_currentButton` static variable, letting all the other buttons know that this button is now the currently active one. We then change the mouse cursor to the hand cursor (as in the previous example) and display our URL in the browser's status bar.
  - If the `m_active` flag is set to `false`, this method sets the `m_currentButton` static variable to `null`, changes the mouse cursor to the default cursor, and clears the browser's status bar.

❽ The `mouseClicked()` method checks whether this component is active (this implies that the mouse cursor is located within our polygon, and not just within the bounding rectangle), the URL is resolved, and the mouse event is not consumed. If all three checks are satisfied, this method redirects the browser to the component's associated URL and consumes the mouse event to avoid processing by any other components.

The rest of this class's methods, implemented due to the `MouseListener` and `MouseMotionListener` interfaces, receive empty bodies, except for `mouseExited()` and `mouseEntered()`. Both of these methods send all their traffic to the `mouseMoved()` method to notify the component that the cursor has left or has entered the container, respectively.

❾ The `paintComponent()` method simply draws the component's `Polygon` in gray if it's inactive, and in red if it's active.

NOTE We've purposefully avoided including tooltip text for these non-rectangular buttons because the underlying Swing `ToolTipManager` essentially relies on the rectangular shape of the components it manages. Somehow, invoking the Swing tooltip API destroys our model of processing mouse events. In order to allow tooltips, we have to develop our own version of a tooltip manager—this is the subject of the next example.

5.3.2 Running the code

To run this code in a web browser, we have constructed the following HTML file (see the Java plug-in and Java plug-in HTML converter notes in the previous example):

```
<html>
<head>
<title></title>
</head>
<body>

<OBJECT classid="clsid:8AD9C840-044E-11D1-B3E9-00805F499D93"
WIDTH = 400 HEIGHT = 380  codebase="http://java.sun.com/products/plugin/
1.2/jinstall-12-win32.cab#Version=1,2,0,0">
<PARAM NAME = "CODE" VALUE = "ButtonApplet2.class" >
<PARAM NAME = "type"
       VALUE ="application/x-java-applet;version=1.2">
<param name="image" value="bay_area.gif">

<param name="button1"
       value="112,122, 159,131, 184,177, 284,148, 288,248, 158,250,
100,152">
<param name="name1" value="Alameda County">
<param name="url1"
       value="http://dir.yahoo.com/Regional/U_S__States/
California/Counties_and_Regions/Alameda_County/">

<param name="button2"
       value="84,136, 107,177, 76,182, 52,181, 51,150">
<param name="name2" value="San Francisco County">
<param name="url2"
       value="http://dir.yahoo.com/Regional/U_S__States/
California/Counties_and_Regions/San_Francisco_County/">

<param name="button3"
       value="156,250, 129,267, 142,318, 235,374, 361,376, 360,347, 311,324,
291,250">
<param name="name3" value="Santa Clara County">
<param name="url3"
       value="http://dir.yahoo.com/Regional/U_S__States/
California/Counties_and_Regions/Santa_Clara_County/">

<param name="button4"
       value="54,187, 111,180, 150,246, 130,265, 143,318, 99,346, 63,314">
<param name="name4" value="San Mateo County">
<param name="url4"
       value="http://dir.yahoo.com/Regional/U_S__States/
```

```
California/Counties_and_Regions/San_Mateo_County/">

<param name="button5"
       value="91,71, 225,79, 275,62, 282,147, 185,174, 160,129, 95,116,
79,97">
<param name="name5" value="Contra Costa County">
<param name="url5"
       value="http://dir.yahoo.com/Regional/U_S__States/
California/Counties_and_Regions/Contra_Costa_County/">

<COMMENT>
<EMBED type="application/x-java-applet;version=1.2" CODE =
"ButtonApplet2.class"
  WIDTH = "400" HEIGHT = "380"
  codebase="./"
  image="bay_area.gif"
  button1="112,122, 159,131, 184,177, 284,148, 288,248, 158,250, 100,152"
  name1="Alameda County"
  url1="http://dir.yahoo.com/Regional/U_S__States/California/
Counties_and_Regions/Alameda_County/"
  button2="84,136, 107,177, 76,182, 52,181, 51,150"
  name2="San Francisco County"
  url2="http://dir.yahoo.com/Regional/U_S__States/California/
Counties_and_Regions/San_Francisco_County/"
  button3="156,250, 129,267, 142,318, 235,374, 361,376, 360,347, 311,324,
291,250"
  name3="Santa Clara County"
  url3="http://dir.yahoo.com/Regional/U_S__States/California/
Counties_and_Regions/Santa_Clara_County/"
  button4="54,187, 111,180, 150,246, 130,265, 143,318, 99,346, 63,314"
  name4="San Mateo County"
  url4="http://dir.yahoo.com/Regional/U_S__States/California/
Counties_and_Regions/San_Mateo_County/"
  button5="91,71, 225,79, 275,62, 282,147, 185,174, 160,129, 95,116, 79,97"
  name5="Contra Costa County"
  url5="http://dir.yahoo.com/Regional/U_S__States/California/
Counties_and_Regions/Contra_Costa_County/"
  pluginspage="http://java.sun.com/products/plugin/1.2/plugin-
install.html">
<NOEMBED></COMMENT>
alt="Your browser understands the &lt;APPLET&gt; tag but isn't running the
applet, for some reason."
        Your browser is completely ignoring the &lt;APPLET&gt; tag!
</NOEMBED>
</EMBED>
</OBJECT>
</p>

<p> </p>
</body>
</html>
```

Figure 5.10 shows the `ButtonApplet2` example running in Netscape 4.05 with the Java plug-in. Our HTML file has been constructed to display an active map of the San Francisco bay area. Five non-rectangular buttons correspond to this area's five counties. Watch how the non-rectangular buttons react when the mouse cursor moves in and out of their boundaries. Verify that they behave correctly even if a part of a given button lies under the bounding rectangle of another button (a good place to check is the sharp border between Alameda and Contra Costa counties). Click over the button and notice the navigation to one of the Yahoo sites containing information about the selected county.

It is clear that tooltip displays would help to dispel any confusion as to which county is which. The next example shows how to implement this feature.

5.4 CUSTOM BUTTONS, PART *III*: TOOLTIP MANAGEMENT

In this section we'll discuss how to implement custom management of tooltips in a Swing application. If you're completely satisfied with the default `ToolTipManager` provided with Swing, you can skip this section. But there may be situations when this default implementation is not satisfactory, as in our example above using non-rectangular components.

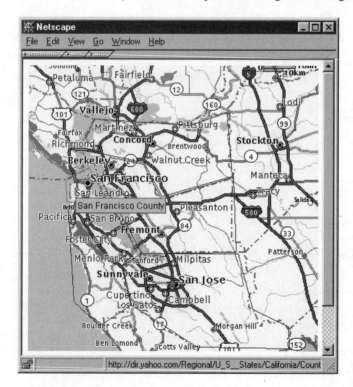

Figure 5.12 Polygonal buttons with a custom tooltip manager

In example 5.6, we will construct our own version of a tooltip manager to display a tooltip window if the mouse cursor rests over some point inside a button's polygonal area longer than a specified time interval. It will be displayed for a specified amount of time; then, to avoid annoying the user, we will hide the tooltip window until the mouse cursor moves to a new position.

In designing our tooltip manager, we will take a different approach than that taken by Swing's default ToolTipManager (see 5.1.12). Instead of using three different Timers, we will use just one. This involves tracking more information, but it is slightly more efficient because it avoids the handling of multiple ActionEvents.

Example 5.6

see \Chapter5\6

```java
import java.applet.*;
import java.awt.*;
import java.awt.event.*;
import java.net.*;
import java.util.*;

import javax.swing.*;
import javax.swing.border.*;
import javax.swing.event.*;

public class ButtonApplet3 extends JApplet
{
  protected ToolTipManager m_manager;

  public ButtonApplet3() {}

  public synchronized void init() {
    // Unchanged code from example 5.5

    m_manager = new ToolTipManager(this);
    PolygonButton.m_toolTip = m_manager.m_toolTip;

    getContentPane().setLayout(null);
    getContentPane().add(bigLabel);
    bigLabel.setBounds(0, 0, bigImage.getIconWidth(),
      bigImage.getIconHeight());
  }

  // Unchanged code from example 5.5
}

class PolygonButton extends JComponent
 implements MouseListener, MouseMotionListener
{
  // Unchanged code from example 5.5

  public static JToolTip m_toolTip;

  protected void setState(boolean active) {
    m_active = active;
    repaint();
    if (active) {
      if (m_currentButton != null)
        m_currentButton.setState(false);
      m_parent.setCursor(Cursor.getPredefinedCursor(
```

① Like ButtonApplet2, but manages tooltips

② Set sole tooltip instance for all buttons in applet

③ Same as in ButtonApplet2, but sets "global" tooltip to tooltip for this button

```
          Cursor.HAND_CURSOR));
        m_parent.showStatus(m_sUrl);
        if (m_toolTip != null)
          m_toolTip.setTipText(m_text);
      }
      else {
        m_currentButton = null;
        m_parent.setCursor(Cursor.getPredefinedCursor(
          Cursor.DEFAULT_CURSOR));
        m_parent.showStatus("");
        if (m_toolTip != null)
          m_toolTip.setTipText(null);
      }
    }
  }
}

class MyToolTipManager extends MouseMotionAdapter
  implements ActionListener
{
  protected Timer m_timer;
  protected int m_lastX = -1;
  protected int m_lastY = -1;
  protected boolean m_moved = false;
  protected int m_counter = 0;

  public JToolTip m_toolTip = new JToolTip();

  ToolTipManager(JApplet parent) {
    parent.addMouseMotionListener(this);
    m_toolTip.setTipText(null);
    parent.getContentPane().add(m_toolTip);
    m_toolTip.setVisible(false);
    m_timer = new Timer(1000, this);
    m_timer.start();
  }

  public void mouseMoved(MouseEvent e) {
    m_moved = true;
    m_counter = -1;
    m_lastX = e.getX();
    m_lastY = e.getY();
    if (m_toolTip.isVisible()) {
      m_toolTip.setVisible(false);
      m_toolTip.getParent().repaint();
    }
  }

  public void actionPerformed(ActionEvent e) {
    if (m_moved || m_counter==0 || m_toolTip.getTipText()==null) {
      if (m_toolTip.isVisible())
        m_toolTip.setVisible(false);
      m_moved = false;
      return;
    }
```

4 TooltipManager that doesn't assume rectangular components

5 Listens for mouse events on parent; installs tooltip in parent; installs timer to check and control tooltip state

6 Mouse has moved, so reset tooltip state

7 Called for Timer events; hides or displays tooltip

```
    if (m_counter < 0) {
      m_counter = 4;
      m_toolTip.setVisible(true);
      Dimension d = m_toolTip.getPreferredSize();
      m_toolTip.setBounds(m_lastX, m_lastY+20,
      d.width, d.height);
    }
    m_counter--;
  }
}
```

8 If ready to display tooltip, set it up to display for about 4 seconds, over the last mouse position

5.4.1 Understanding the code

Class ButtonApplet3

1 This class requires very few modifications from `ButtonApplet2` in the last section. It declares and creates `MyToolTipManager m_manager` and passes a `this` reference to it:

> **m_manager = new MyToolTipManager(this);**

2 As you will see below, our `MyToolTipManager` class manages a publicly accessible `JToolTip`, `m_toolTip`. `MyToolTipManager` itself is not intended to provide any meaningful content to this tooltip. Rather, this is to be done by other components—in our case, by `PolygonButtons`. Thus, our `PolygonButton` class declares a `static` reference to a `JToolTip` component. Whenever a button becomes active, this `JToolTip`'s text will be assigned to that of the active button. So, when we create our instance of `MyToolTipManager`, we assign its publicly accessible `JToolTip` as our `Polygon` class's static `JToolTip` (which is also publicly accessible):

> **PolygonButton.m_toolTip = m_manager.m_toolTip;**

Thus, only one `JToolTip` instance will exist for the lifetime of this applet, and both `MyToolTipManager` and our `PolygonButtons` have control over it.

Class PolygonButton

3 As we've mentioned earlier, this class now declares the static variable `JToolTip m_toolTip`. The `PolygonButton` class does not initialize this reference. However, this reference is checked during `PolygonButton` activation in the `setState()` method. If `m_toolTip` is not `null` (set to point to a valid tooltip window by some outer class, which, in our example, is done in the `ButtonApplet3 init()` method shown above), the `setTipText()` method is invoked to set the proper text while the mouse cursor hovers over the button.

Class MyToolTipManager

4 This class represents a custom tooltip manager which is free from assumption of the rectangularity of its child components. It extends the `MouseMotionAdapter` class and implements the `ActionListener` interface to work as both a `MouseMotionListener` and an `Action-Listener`. Six instance variables are declared:

- `Timer m_timer`: Our managing timer.
- `int m_lastX, m_lastY`: The last coordinates of the mouse cursor, these two variables are reassigned each time the mouse is moved.
- `boolean m_moved`: A flag indicating that the mouse cursor has moved.

- `int m_counter`: The time ticks counter that is used to manage the tooltip's time to live (see below).
- `JToolTip m_toolTip`: The tooltip component to be displayed.

5 The constructor of the `MyToolTipManager` class takes a reference to the parenting `JApplet` as a parameter and registers itself as a `MouseMotionListener` on this component. Then it creates the `JToolTip m_toolTip` component and adds it to the applet's content pane. `m_toolTip` is set invisible, using `setVisible(false)`; it can then be used by any interested class by repositioning it and calling `setVisible(true)`. Finally, a `Timer` with a 1000ms delay time is created and started.

6 The `mouseMoved()` method will be invoked when the mouse cursor moves over the applet. It sets the `m_moved` flag to `true`, `m_counter` to -1, and stores the coordinates of the mouse cursor. Then this method hides the tooltip component if it's visible.

7 The `actionPerformed()` method is called when the `Timer` fires events (see section 2.6 for details). It implements the logic of displaying/hiding the tooltip window based on two instance variables: `m_moved` and `m_counter`:

```
if (m_moved || m_counter==0 || m_toolTip.getTipText()==null) {
  if (m_toolTip.isVisible())
    m_toolTip.setVisible(false);
  m_moved = false;
  return;
}
```

The block of code above is invoked when any one of the following statements are true:

1 The mouse cursor has been moved since the last time tick.

2 The counter has reached zero.

3 No tooltip text is set.

In any of these cases, the tooltip component is hidden (if it was previously visible), and the `m_moved` flag is set to `false`. The `m_counter` variable remains unchanged.

```
if (m_counter < 0) {
  m_counter = 4;
  m_toolTip.setVisible(true);
  Dimension d = m_toolTip.getPreferredSize();
  m_toolTip.setBounds(m_lastX, m_lastY+20,
  d.width, d.height);
}
```

8 The above block of code is responsible for displaying the tooltip component. It will be executed only when `m_counter` is equal to -1 (set by `mouseMoved()`), and when the `m_moved` flag is `false` (cleared by the previous code fragment). `m_counter` is set to 4, which determines the amount of time the tooltip will be displayed (4000ms in this example). Then we make the tooltip component visible and place it at the current mouse location with a vertical offset approximately equal to the mouse cursor's height. This construction provides an arbitrary delay between the time when mouse motion stops and the tooltip is displayed.

The last line of code in the `actionPerformed()` method is `m_counter--`, which decrements the counter each time tick until it reaches 0. As we saw above, once it reaches 0 the tooltip will be hidden.

NOTE The actual delay time may vary from 1000ms to 2000ms since the mouse movements and time ticks are not synchronized. A more accurate and complex implementation could start a new timer after each mouse movement, as is done in Swing's `ToolTipManager`.

The following table illustrates how the `m_counter` and `m_moved` variables control this behavior.

Table 5.1 `m_counter` **and** `m_moved` **variables**

Timer tick	m_moved flag	m_counter before	m_counter after	Comment
0	false	0	0	
1	true	−1	−1	Mouse moved between 0th and 1st ticks.
2	false	−1	4	Tooltip is displayed.
3	false	4	3	
4	false	3	2	
5	false	2	1	
6	false	1	0	
7	false	0	0	Tooltip is hidden.
8	false	0	0	Waiting for the next mouse move.

5.4.2 Running the code

Figure 5.12 shows `ButtonApplet3` running in Netscape Navigator 4.05 with the Java plug-in. You can use the same HTML file that was presented in the previous section. Move the mouse cursor over some non-rectangular component and note how it displays the proper tooltip message. This tooltip disappears after a certain amount of time or when the mouse is moved to a new location.

C H A P T E R   6

Tabbed panes

6.1 *JTABBEDPANE*

class javax.swing.JTabbedPane

JTabbedPane is simply a stack of components in selectable layers. Each layer can contain one component which is normally a container. Tab extensions are used to move a given layer to the front of the tabbed pane view. These tab extensions are similar to labels in that they can have assigned text, an icon (as well as a disabled icon), background and foreground colors, and a tooltip.

To add a component to a tabbed pane, we use one of its overloaded add() methods. This creates a new selectable tab and reorganizes the other tab extensions, if necessary, so the new one will fit. We can also use the addTab() and insertTab() methods to create new selectable layers. The remove() method takes a component as a parameter and removes the tab associated with that component, if there is one.

Tab extensions can reside to the north, south, east, or west of the tabbed pane's content. The location is specified using its setTabPlacement() method and passing one of the corresponding SwingConstants fields as a parameter.

GUIDELINE

Vertical or horizontal tabs?   When is it best to choose between vertical or horizontal tabs?

Three possible rules of thumb help make the decision whether to place tabs horizontally or vertically. First, consider the nature of the data to be displayed.

Is vertical or horizontal space at a premium within the available display space? If, for example, you have a list with a single column but 200 entries, then clearly vertical space is at a premium. If you have a table with only 10 entries but 15 columns, then horizontal space is at a premium. Simply place the tabs where space is cheaper to obtain. In the first example with the long list, place the tabs vertically so they use horizontal space which is available. In the second example, place the tabs horizontally so you use vertical space which is available while horizontal space is completely taken by the table columns.

The second rule concerns the number and size of the tabs. If you need to display 12 tabs, for example, each with a long label, then it is unlikely that these will fit across the screen horizontally. In this case you are more likely to fit them by placing them vertically. Using space in these ways when introducing a tabbed pane should minimize the introduction of scroll panes and maximize ease of use. Finally, the third rule of thumb is to consider the layout and mouse movements required for operating the software. If, for example, your application uses a toolbar, then it may make sense to align the tabs close to the toolbar, thus minimizing mouse movements between the toolbar buttons and the tabs. If you have a horizontal toolbar across the top of the screen, then choose a horizontal set of tabs across the top (to the north).

We can get and set the selected tab index at any given time using its `getSelectedIndex()` and `setSelectedIndex()` methods respectively. We can get/set the component associated with the selected tab similarly, using the `getSelectedComponent()` and `setSelectedComponent()` methods.

One or more `ChangeListeners` can be added to a `JTabbedPane`, which gets registered with its model (an instance of `DefaultSingleSelectionModel` by default—see chapter 12 for more information about `SingleSelectionModel` and `DefaultSingleSelectionModel`). When a new tab is selected, the model will send out `ChangeEvents` to all registered `ChangeListeners`. The `stateChanged()` method of each listener is invoked, so we can capture and perform any desired actions when the user selects any tab. `JTabbedPane` also fires `PropertyChangeEvents` whenever its model or tab placement properties change state.

GUIDELINE

Transaction boundaries and tabbed panes   If you're using a tabbed pane within a dialog, the transaction boundary is normally clear—it will be an OK or Cancel button on the dialog. In this case, it is obvious that the OK and Cancel buttons would lie outside the tabbed pane and in the dialog itself. This is an important point. Place action buttons which terminate a transaction outside the tabbed panes. If, for example, you had a tabbed pane which contained a Save and Cancel button within the first tab, would it be clear that the Save and Cancel buttons work across all tabs or only on the first? Actually, it can be very ambiguous. To clearly define the transaction, define the buttons outside the tabbed pane so it is clear to the user that any changes made to any tab will be accepted or saved when OK or Save is pressed or discarded when Cancel is pressed. The action buttons will then apply across the complete set of tabs.

6.2   A DYNAMICALLY CHANGEABLE TABBED PANE

We will now turn to a JTabbedPane example applet that demonstrates a dynamically recon-figurable tab layout as well as the addition and removal of any number of tabs. A ChangeLis-tener is attached to the tabbed pane to listen for tab selection events and to display the currently selected tab index in a status bar. For enhanced feedback, audio clips are played when the tab layout changes and whenever a tab is added and removed. Example 6.1 contains the code.

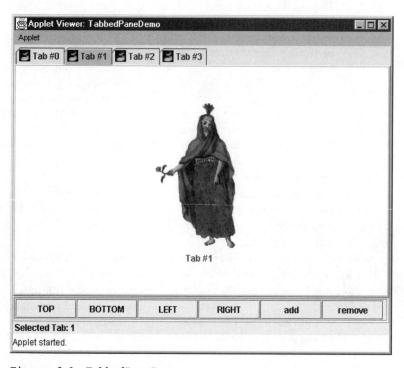

Figure 6.1   TabbedPaneDemo

Example 6.1

TabbedPaneDemo.java

see \Chapter6\1

```
import java.awt.*;
import java.applet.*;
import java.awt.event.*;
import javax.swing.*;
import javax.swing.event.*;
import javax.swing.border.*;

public class TabbedPaneDemo extends JApplet
  implements ActionListener
```

```
{
  protected ImageIcon m_tabimage;
  protected ImageIcon m_utsguy;
  protected ImageIcon m_jfcgirl;
  protected ImageIcon m_sbeguy;
  protected ImageIcon m_tiger;
  protected JTabbedPane m_tabbedPane;
  protected JButton m_topButton;
  protected JButton m_bottomButton;
  protected JButton m_leftButton;
  protected JButton m_rightButton;
  protected JButton m_addButton;
  protected JButton m_removeButton;
  protected JLabel m_status;
  protected JLabel m_loading;
  protected AudioClip m_layoutsound;
  protected AudioClip m_tabsound;

  public void init() {
    m_loading = new JLabel("Initializing applet...",
      SwingConstants.CENTER);
    getContentPane().add(m_loading);

    Thread initialize = new Thread() {
      public void run() {
        m_tabimage = new ImageIcon("tabimage.gif");
        m_utsguy = new ImageIcon("utsguy.gif");
        m_jfcgirl = new ImageIcon("jfcgirl.gif");
        m_sbeguy = new ImageIcon("sbeguy.gif");
        m_tiger = new ImageIcon("tiger.gif");
        m_tabbedPane = new JTabbedPane(SwingConstants.TOP);
        m_topButton = new JButton("TOP");
        m_bottomButton = new JButton("BOTTOM");
        m_leftButton = new JButton("LEFT");
        m_rightButton = new JButton("RIGHT");
        m_addButton = new JButton("add");
        m_removeButton = new JButton("remove");
        m_status = new JLabel();

        Color buttonColor = new Color(245,242,219);
        JPanel buttonPanel = new JPanel();
        buttonPanel.setLayout(new GridLayout(1,6));
        JPanel lowerPanel = new JPanel();
        lowerPanel.setLayout(new BorderLayout());

        m_topButton.setBackground(buttonColor);
        m_bottomButton.setBackground(buttonColor);
        m_leftButton.setBackground(buttonColor);
        m_rightButton.setBackground(buttonColor);
        m_addButton.setBackground(buttonColor);
        m_removeButton.setBackground(buttonColor);
        m_topButton.addActionListener(TabbedPaneDemo.this);
        m_bottomButton.addActionListener(TabbedPaneDemo.this);
        m_leftButton.addActionListener(TabbedPaneDemo.this);
```

❶ Images for tab extensions and tab container

❶ Buttons to control tab alignment

❷ Buttons in GridLayout

```
      m_rightButton.addActionListener(TabbedPaneDemo.this);
      m_addButton.addActionListener(TabbedPaneDemo.this);
      m_removeButton.addActionListener(TabbedPaneDemo.this);

      buttonPanel.add(m_topButton);
      buttonPanel.add(m_bottomButton);
      buttonPanel.add(m_leftButton);
      buttonPanel.add(m_rightButton);
      buttonPanel.add(m_addButton);
      buttonPanel.add(m_removeButton);
      buttonPanel.setBackground(buttonColor);
      buttonPanel.setOpaque(true);
      buttonPanel.setBorder(new CompoundBorder(
        new EtchedBorder(EtchedBorder.RAISED),
        new EtchedBorder(EtchedBorder.LOWERED)));

      lowerPanel.add("Center", buttonPanel);
      m_status.setHorizontalTextPosition(SwingConstants.LEFT);
      m_status.setOpaque(true);
      m_status.setBackground(buttonColor);
      m_status.setForeground(Color.black);
      lowerPanel.add("South", m_status);

      createTab();
      createTab();
      createTab();
      createTab();

      getContentPane().setLayout(new BorderLayout());
      m_tabbedPane.setBackground(new Color(245,232,219));
      m_tabbedPane.setOpaque(true);
      getContentPane().add("South", lowerPanel);
      getContentPane().add("Center", m_tabbedPane);
      m_tabbedPane.addChangeListener(new MyChangeListener());
      m_layoutsound = getAudioClip(getCodeBase(), "switch.wav");
      m_tabsound = getAudioClip(getCodeBase(), "tab.wav");

      getContentPane().remove(m_loading);
      getRootPane().revalidate();
      getRootPane().repaint();
    }
  };
  initialize.start();
}

public void createTab() {
  JLabel label = null;
  switch (m_tabbedPane.getTabCount()%4) {
    case 0:
      label = new JLabel("Tab #" + m_tabbedPane.getTabCount(),
        m_utsguy, SwingConstants.CENTER);
      break;
    case 1:
      label = new JLabel("Tab #" + m_tabbedPane.getTabCount(),
        m_jfcgirl, SwingConstants.CENTER);
```

2 Buttons in
GridLayout

3 Creates a tab with
image icon

```
        break;
      case 2:
        label = new JLabel("Tab #" + m_tabbedPane.getTabCount(),
          m_sbeguy, SwingConstants.CENTER);
        break;
      case 3:
        label = new JLabel("Tab #" + m_tabbedPane.getTabCount(),
          m_tiger, SwingConstants.CENTER);
        break;
    }
    label.setVerticalTextPosition(SwingConstants.BOTTOM);
    label.setHorizontalTextPosition(SwingConstants.CENTER);
    label.setOpaque(true);
    label.setBackground(Color.white);
    m_tabbedPane.addTab("Tab #" + m_tabbedPane.getTabCount(),
      m_tabimage, label);
    m_tabbedPane.setBackgroundAt(m_tabbedPane.getTabCount()-1,
      new Color(245,232,219));
    m_tabbedPane.setForegroundAt(m_tabbedPane.getTabCount()-1,
      new Color(7,58,141));
    m_tabbedPane.setSelectedIndex(m_tabbedPane.getTabCount()-1);
    setStatus(m_tabbedPane.getSelectedIndex());
}

public void killTab() {
    if (m_tabbedPane.getTabCount() > 0) {
      m_tabbedPane.removeTabAt(m_tabbedPane.getTabCount()-1);
      setStatus(m_tabbedPane.getSelectedIndex());
    }
    else
      setStatus(-1);
}

public void setStatus(int index) {
    if (index > -1)
      m_status.setText(" Selected Tab: " + index);
    else
      m_status.setText(" No Tab Selected");
}

public void actionPerformed(ActionEvent e) {
    if (e.getSource() == m_topButton) {
      m_tabbedPane.setTabPlacement(SwingConstants.TOP);
      m_layoutsound.play();
    }
    else if(e.getSource() == m_bottomButton) {
      m_tabbedPane.setTabPlacement(SwingConstants.BOTTOM);
      m_layoutsound.play();
    }
    else if(e.getSource() == m_leftButton) {
      m_tabbedPane.setTabPlacement(SwingConstants.LEFT);
      m_layoutsound.play();
    }
```

4 Removes the tab with the highest index

5 Changes display of selected tab when different tab is selected

6 Called when one of the buttons is clicked; changes tab orientation or adds/removes tab

```
      else if(e.getSource() == m_rightButton) {
        m_tabbedPane.setTabPlacement(SwingConstants.RIGHT);
        m_layoutsound.play();
      }
      else if(e.getSource() == m_addButton)
        createTab();
      else if(e.getSource() == m_removeButton)
        killTab();
      m_tabbedPane.revalidate();
      m_tabbedPane.repaint();
    }

    public static void main(String[] args) {
      new TabbedPaneDemo();
    }

    class MyChangeListener implements ChangeListener
    {
      public void stateChanged(ChangeEvent e) {
        setStatus(
          ((JTabbedPane) e.getSource()).getSelectedIndex());    ❼ Updates
        m_tabsound.play();                                          selected tab
      }
    }
  }
}
```

6.2.1 Understanding the code

Class TabbedPaneDemo

TabbedPaneDemo extends JApplet and implements ActionListener to listen for button events. Several instance variables are used:

❶
- ImageIcon m_tabimage: The image used in each tab extension.
- ImageIcon m_utsguy, m_jfcgirl, m_sbeguy, m_tiger: The images used in the tab containers.
- JTabbedPane m_tabbedPane: The main tabbed pane.
- JButton m_topButton: The top tab alignment button.
- JButton m_bottomButton: The bottom tab alignment button.
- JButton m_leftButton: The left tab alignment button.
- JButton m_rightButton: The right tab alignment button.
- JButton m_addButton: The add tab button.
- JButton m_removeButton: The remove tab button.
- JLabel m_status: The status bar label.

Our JTabbedPane, m_tabbedPane, is created with TOP tab alignment. (Note that TOP is actually the default, so this is really not necessary here. The default JTabbedPane constructor would do the same thing.)

❷ The init() method organizes the buttons inside a JPanel using GridLayout, and it associates ActionListeners with each one. We wrap all instantiation and GUI initialization processes in a separate thread and start the thread in this method. (Loading can take several seconds and it is best to allow the interface to be as responsive as possible during this time.)

We also provide an explicit visual cue to the user that the application is loading by placing an "Initializing applet..." label in the content pane where the tabbed pane will be placed once it is initialized. In this initialization, our createTab() method (discussed below) is called four times. We then add both the panel containing the tabbed pane controller buttons and our tabbed pane to the content pane. Finally, an instance of MyChangeListener (see below) is attached to our tabbed pane to listen for tab selection changes.

3 The createTab() method is called whenever m_addButton is clicked. Based on the current tab count, this method chooses between four ImageIcons, creates a JLabel containing the **4** chosen icon, and adds a new tab containing that label. The killTab() method is called whenever m_removeButton is clicked to remove the tab with the highest index.

5 The setStatus() method is called each time a different tab is selected. The m_status JLabel is updated to reflect which tab is selected at all times.

6 The actionPerformed() method is called whenever any of the buttons are clicked. Clicking m_topButton, m_bottomButton, m_leftButton, or m_rightButton causes the tab layout of the JTabbedPane to change accordingly, using the setTabPlacement() method. Each time one of these tab layout buttons is clicked, a WAV file is played. Similarly, when a tab selection change occurs, a different WAV file is invoked. These sounds, m_tabsound and m_layoutsound, are loaded at the end of the init() method:

```
m_layoutsound = getAudioClip(getCodeBase(), "switch.wav");
m_tabsound = getAudioClip(getCodeBase(), "tab.wav");
```

Before the actionPerformed() method exits, it revalidates the JTabbedPane. (If this revalidation were to be omitted, we would see that a layout change caused by clicking one of our tab layout buttons will result in incorrect tabbed pane rendering.)

Class TabbedPaneDemo.MyChangeListener

7 MyChangeListener implements the ChangeListener interface. Only one method must be defined when implementing this interface: stateChanged(). This method can process ChangeEvents corresponding to when a tabbed pane's selected state changes. In our state-Changed() method, we update the status bar in TabbedPaneDemo and play an appropriate tab switching sound:

```
public void stateChanged(ChangeEvent e) {
  setStatus(
    ((JTabbedPane) e.getSource()).getSelectedIndex());
  m_tabsound.play();
}
```

6.2.2 Running the code

Figure 6.1 shows TabbedPaneDemo in action. To deploy this applet, the following simple HTML file is used (this is not Java plug-in compliant):

```
<HTML> <BODY>
<applet code=TabbedPaneDemo width=570 height=400> </applet>
</BODY> </HTML>
```

A DYNAMICALLY CHANGEABLE TABBED PANE   *189*

Add and remove some tabs, and play with the tab layout to get a feel for how it works in different situations. You can use your arrow keys to move from tab to tab (if the focus is currently on a tab), and remember to turn your speakers on for the sound effects.

NOTE   You may have problems with this applet if your system does not support WAV files. If so, comment out the audio-specific code and recompile the applet.

6.2.3   Interesting JTabbedPane characteristics

In cases where there is more than one row or column of tabs, most of us are used to the situation where selecting a tab that is not already in the frontmost row or column moves that row or column to the front. This does not occur in a JTabbedPane using the default Metal look and feel, as you can see in the TabbedPaneDemo example above. However, this does occur when using the Windows, Motif, and Basic look and feel tabbed pane UI delegates. This feature was purposefully disabled in the Metal look and feel (as can be verified in the MetalTabbedPaneUI source code).

GUIDELINE

Avoid multiple rows of tabs   As a general rule, you should seek to design for no more than a single row or column of tabs.

There are three key reasons for this. The first is a cognitive reason: the user has trouble discerning what will happen with the multiple rows of tabs. With the Windows look and feel for example, the behavior somewhat mimics the behavior of a Rolodex filing card system. For some users this mental model is clear and the behavior is natural; for others it is simply confusing.

The second reason is a human factors/usability problem. When a rear set of tabs comes to the front, as with the Windows look and feel, the positions of all the other tabs change. Therefore the user has to discern the new position of a tab before visually selecting it and moving the mouse toward it. This makes it harder for the user to learn the positions of the tabs. Directional memory is a strong attribute and is highly productive for usability. Thus it is always better to keep the tabs in the same position. This was the reason why Sun and Apple designers chose to implement multiple tabs in this fashion.

The final reason is a design problem. When a second or subsequent row or column of tabs is introduced, the tabbed pane must be resized. Although the layout manager will cope with this, it may not look visually satisfactory when completed. The size of the tabbed pane becomes dependent on the ability to render the tabs in a given space. Those who remember the OS2 Warp UI will recall that the designers avoided this problem by allowing only a single row of tabs and the ability to scroll them if they didn't fit into the given space. So far, no one has implemented a Swing look and feel with this style of tabbed pane (at least not a freely available one).

6.3   *CUSTOMIZED JTABBEDPANE AND TABBEDPANEUI DELEGATES*

Although we intend to save most of our discussion of customizing UI delegates for chapter 21, building fancy-looking tabs is too tempting to pass up, and the example in this section may satisfy your UI customization appetite for now. You can use the techniques shown here to implement custom UI delegates for almost any Swing component. However, there will be major differences from delegate to delegate, so you will always need to reference the Swing source code.

In example 6.2, we will first build a customized `JTabbedPane` with two properties: a background image used for each tab, and a background image used for the tabbed pane itself. We will then build a subclass of `BasicTabbedPaneUI` to use with our customized `JTabbedPane`, and design it so that it paints the tab background image on each tab. This will require its `paint()` method to be modified. Our custom delegate will also be responsible for painting the tabbed pane background. As we learned in chapter 2 in our discussion of painting, a UI delegate's `update()` method is used for filling the background of opaque components and then it should pass control to the delegate's `paint()` method. Both images need to be accessible from our customized `JTabbedPane` using `set` and `get` accessors. (In keeping with the concept of UI delegates not being bound to specific component instances, it would not be a good idea to assign these images as UI delegate properties, unless we were building an image-specific look and feel.)

`BasicTabbedPaneUI` is one of the largest and most complex UI delegates. It contains, among other things, its own custom layout manager, `TabbedPaneLayout`, and a long rendering routine spread out over several different methods. As complex as it is, you do not need to understand its inner workings in order to build on top of it. Since we are concerned only with how it does its rendering, we can narrow our focus considerably. To start, its `paint()` method calls the `paintTab()` method, which is responsible for painting each tab. This method calls several other methods to perform various aspects of this process (see BasicTabbedPaneUI.java). Briefly, and in order, these methods are:

```
paintTabBackground()
paintTabBorder()
layoutLabel()
paintText()
paintIcon()
paintFocusIndicator()
```

By overriding any combination of these methods, we can control the tab rendering process however we like. Our customized `TabbedPaneUI`, which we'll call `ImageTabbedPaneUI`, overrides the `paintTabBackground()` method to construct tabs with background images.

Figure 6.2 `TabbedPaneDemo`
with custom tab rendering,
LEFT layout

Figure 6.3 `TabbedPaneDemo` **with custom tab rendering, BOTTOM layout**

Example 6.2

TabbedPaneDemo.java

see \Chapter6\2

```java
import java.awt.*;
import java.applet.*;
import java.awt.event.*;
import javax.swing.*;
import javax.swing.event.*;
import javax.swing.border.*;
import javax.swing.plaf.TabbedPaneUI;
import javax.swing.plaf.ComponentUI;
import javax.swing.plaf.basic.BasicTabbedPaneUI;

public class TabbedPaneDemo extends JApplet
implements ActionListener
{
  // Unchanged code from example 6.1

  public void init() {
    m_loading = new JLabel("Initializing applet...",
      SwingConstants.CENTER);
    getContentPane().add(m_loading);

    Thread initialize = new Thread() {
      public void run() {
        // Unchanged code from example 6.1

        m_tabbedPane = new ImageTabbedPane(
          new ImageIcon("bloo.gif"),
          new ImageIcon("bubbles.jpg"));

        // Unchanged code from example 6.1
      }
    };
    initialize.start();
  }
  public void createTab() {
    // Unchanged code from example 6.1

    label.setBackground(Color.white);
    m_tabbedPane.addTab("Tab #" + m_tabbedPane.getTabCount(),
      m_tabimage, label);
    m_tabbedPane.setForegroundAt(m_tabbedPane.getTabCount()-1,
      Color.white);
    m_tabbedPane.setSelectedIndex(m_tabbedPane.getTabCount()-1);
    setStatus(m_tabbedPane.getSelectedIndex());
  }
```

1 Uses special
ImageTabbedPane subclass,
instead of JTabbedPane

2 Make tab text
readable on black
background

```
    // Unchanged code from example 6.1
}

class ImageTabbedPane extends JTabbedPane
{
  // Display properties
  protected Image m_tabBackground;
  protected Image m_paneBackground;

  public ImageTabbedPane(ImageIcon tabBackground,
    ImageIcon paneBackground) {
    m_tabBackground = tabBackground.getImage();
    m_paneBackground = paneBackground.getImage();
    setUI((ImageTabbedPaneUI) ImageTabbedPaneUI.createUI(this));
  }

  public void setTabBackground(Image i) {
    m_tabBackground = i;
    repaint();
  }

  public void setPaneBackground(Image i) {
    m_paneBackground = i;
    repaint();
  }

  public Image getTabBackground() {
    return m_tabBackground;
  }

  public Image getPaneBackground() {
    return m_paneBackground;
  }
}

class ImageTabbedPaneUI extends BasicTabbedPaneUI
{
  protected Image m_image;

  public static ComponentUI createUI(JComponent c) {
    return new ImageTabbedPaneUI();
  }

  public void update(Graphics g, JComponent c) {
    if (c instanceof ImageTabbedPane) {
      Image paneImage = ((ImageTabbedPane) c).getPaneBackground();
      int w = c.getWidth();
      int h = c.getHeight();
      int iw = paneImage.getWidth(tabPane);
      int ih = paneImage.getHeight(tabPane);
      if (iw > 0 && ih > 0) {
        for (int j=0; j < h; j += ih) {
          for (int i=0; i < w; i += iw) {
            g.drawImage(paneImage,i,j, tabPane);
          }
        }
      }
```

③ JTabbedPane which manages tab and panel background images

④ Extends "look and feel" base class to manage the tab background image

⑤ Fills pane background and calls paint() method

⑤ Tiles image smaller than pane

⑥ tabpane is protected from BasicTabbedPaneUI

```
    }
    paint(g,c);
  }

  public void paint(Graphics g, JComponent c) {
    if (c instanceof ImageTabbedPane)
      m_image = ((ImageTabbedPane) c).getTabBackground();
    super.paint(g,c);
  }

  protected void paintTabBackground(Graphics g, int tabPlacement,
    int tabIndex, int x, int y, int w, int h, boolean isSelected )
  {
    Color tp = tabPane.getBackgroundAt(tabIndex);
    switch(tabPlacement) {
      case LEFT:
        g.drawImage(m_image, x+1, y+1, (w-2)+(x+1), (y+1)+(h-3),
          0, 0, w, h, tp, tabPane);
        break;
      case RIGHT:
        g.drawImage(m_image, x, y+1, (w-2)+(x), (y+1)+(h-3),
          0, 0, w, h, tp, tabPane);
        break;
      case BOTTOM:
        g.drawImage(m_image, x+1, y, (w-3)+(x+1), (y)+(h-1),
          0, 0, w, h, tp, tabPane);
        break;
      case TOP:
        g.drawImage(m_image, x+1, y+1, (w-3)+(x+1), (y+1)+(h-1),
          0, 0, w, h, tp, tabPane);
    }
  }
}
```

7 Sets m_image, which will be used in overridden paintTabBackground(), called from superclass paint() method

8 Overridden method; uses m_image to draw tab background

6.3.1   Understanding the code

Class TabbedPaneDemo

1 We have replaced the JTabbedPane instance with an instance of our custom ImageTabbedPane class. This class's constructor takes two ImageIcons as parameters. The first represents the tab background and the second represents the pane background:

```
m_tabbedPane = new ImageTabbedPane(
  new ImageIcon("bloo.gif"),
  new ImageIcon("bubbles.jpg"));
```

2 We've also modified the createTab() method to make the tab foreground text white because the tab background image we are using is dark.

Class ImageTabbedPane

3 This JTabbedPane subclass is responsible for keeping two Image variables that represent our custom tab background and pane background properties. The constructor takes two ImageIcons as parameters, extracts the Images, and assigns them to these variables. It calls setUI() to enforce the use of our custom `ImageTabbedPaneUI` delegate. `ImageTabbedPane` also defines `set()` and `get()` accessors for both `Image` properties.

Class ImageTabbedPaneUI

4 This class extends `BasicTabbedPaneUI` and maintains an `Image` variable to be used for painting tab backgrounds. The `createUI()` method is overridden to return an instance of itself (remember that this method was used in the `ImageTabbedPane` constructor):

```
public static ComponentUI createUI(JComponent c) {
  return new ImageTabbedPaneUI();
}
```

5 The `update()` method, as we discussed above, is responsible for filling the pane background and then calling `paint()`, so we override it to perform a tiling of the pane background image. We first grab a reference to that image and check its dimensions. If any dimensions are 0 or less, we do not go through with the painting procedure. Otherwise, we tile a region of the pane equal in size to the current size of the `ImageTabbedPane` itself. In order to get the width and height of the `Image`, we use the following code:

```
int iw = paneImage.getWidth(tabPane);
int ih = paneImage.getHeight(tabPane);
```

6 The `tabPane` reference is `protected` in `BasicTabbedPaneUI` and we use it for the `Image-Observer` here—it is a reference to the `JTabbedPane` component being rendered.

7 Once the tiling is done, we call `paint()`. The `paint()` method simply assigns this class's tab background `Image` variable to that of the `ImageTabbedPane` being painted. It then calls its superclass's `paint()` method, with which we do not concern ourselves, let alone fully understand. What we do know is that the superclass's `paint()` method calls its `paintTab()` method, which in turn calls its `paintTabBackground()` method, which is actually respon-

8 sible for filling the background of each tab. That's why we overrode this method—so we could use our tab background `Image` instead.

The `paintTabBackground()` method specifies four cases based on which layout mode the `JTabbedPane` is in: LEFT, RIGHT, BOTTOM, and TOP. These cases were obtained directly from the `BasicTabbedPaneUI` source code and we did not modify their semantics at all. What we did modify is what each case does.

We use the `drawImage()` method of the `awt.Graphics` class to fill a rectangular area defined by the first four `int` parameters (which represent two points). The second four `int` parameters specify an area of the `Image` (passed in as the first parameter) that will be scaled and mapped onto the rectangular area above. The last parameter represents an `ImageObserver` instance.

NOTE   A more professional implementation would tile the images used in painting each tab's background; this implementation assumes that a large enough image will be used to fill a tab's background of any size.

6.3.2   Running the code

Figures 6.2 and 6.3 show `TabbedPaneDemo` in action. To run this applet in appletviewer, you can use the same HTML file that was used in the previous example. Try out all the different tab positions.

Notice that the images used are only used within the `paint()` and `update()` methods of our UI delegate. In this way, we keep with Swing's UI delegate/component separation. One instance of `ImageTabbedPaneUI` could be assigned to multiple `ImageTabbedPane` instances using different `Image`s, and there would be no conflicts.

UI
GUIDELINE

Custom tabs look and feel   After reading chapter 21 on look and feel, you may want to think more about customizing tabbed pane styles. Many possibilities are worthy of your consideration. For example, the OS2 Warp style of scrolling tabs is particularly good in situations where you cannot afford to give away screen space for an additional row or column of tabs. Another possibility is to fix the size of a tab. Currently tab size is largely controlled by the length of text and font selected. This lends greater graphical weight to tabs with long labels. The size of the visual target is greater so tabs with long labels are easier to select than tabs with short labels. You may want to consider using a standard-size tab, which would equalize the size of the target and avoid biasing the usability toward the longer-labeled tabs. Further possibilities are tabs with color and tabs with icons to indicate useful information such as "updated" or "new" or "mandatory input required."

CHAPTER 7

Scrolling panes

7.1 *JSCROLLPANE*

class javax.swing.JScrollPane

Using JScrollPane is normally very simple. Any component or container can be placed in a JScrollPane and scrolled. You can easily create a JScrollPane by passing its constructor the component you'd like to scroll:

```
JScrollPane jsp = new JScrollPane(myLabel);
```

Normally, our use of JScrollPane will not need to be much more extensive than the one line of code shown above. Example 7.1 is a simple JScrollPane demo application. Figure 7.1 illustrates the output.

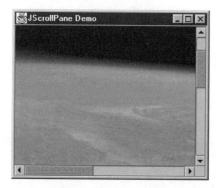

Figure 7.1 JScrollPane **demo**

Example 7.1

ScrollPaneDemo.java

see \Chapter7\1

```java
import java.awt.*;
import javax.swing.*;

public class ScrollPaneDemo extends JFrame
{
  public ScrollPaneDemo() {
    super("JScrollPane Demo");
    ImageIcon ii = new ImageIcon("earth.jpg");
    JScrollPane jsp = new JScrollPane(new JLabel(ii));
    getContentPane().add(jsp);
    setSize(300,250);
    setVisible(true);
  }

  public static void main(String[] args) {
    new ScrollPaneDemo();
  }
}
```

When you run this example, try scrolling by pressing or holding down any of the scroll bar buttons. You will find this unacceptably slow because the scrolling occurs one pixel at a time. We will see how to control this shortly.

Many components use a JScrollPane internally to display their contents, such as JComboBox and JList. On the other hand, we are normally expected to place all multi-line text components inside scroll panes, as this is not default behavior.

GUIDELINE

Using scroll panes For many applications, it is best to avoid introducing a scroll pane; instead, concentrate on placing the required data on the screen so that scrolling is unnecessary. As you have probably found, however, this is not always possible. When you do need to introduce scrolling, put some thought into the type of data and application you have. If possible, try to introduce scrolling in only one direction. For example, with text documents, western culture has been used to scrolling vertically since Egyptian times. Usability studies for world wide web pages have shown that readers can find data quickly when they are vertically scrolling. Scrolling horizontally, on the other hand, is laborious and difficult with text. Try to avoid it. With visual information, such as tables of information, horizontal scrolling may be more appropriate, but try to avoid both horizontal and vertical scrolling if at all possible.

We can access a JScrollPane's scroll bars directly with its getXXScrollBar() and setXXScrollBar() methods, where XX is either HORIZONTAL or VERTICAL.

REFERENCE In chapter 13 we'll talk more about JScrollBars.

7.1.1 The ScrollPaneConstants interface

abstract interface javax.swing.ScrollPaneConstants

We can specify policies for when and when not to display a `JScrollPane`'s horizontal and vertical scroll bars. We simply use its `setVerticalScrollBarPolicy()` and `setHorizontal-ScrollBarPolicy()` methods, providing one of three constants for each that are defined in the `ScrollPaneConstants` interface:

```
HORIZONTAL_SCROLLBAR_AS_NEEDED
HORIZONTAL_SCROLLBAR_NEVER
HORIZONTAL_SCROLLBAR_ALWAYS
VERTICAL_SCROLLBAR_AS_NEEDED
VERTICAL_SCROLLBAR_NEVER
VERTICAL_SCROLLBAR_ALWAYS
```

For example, to enforce the display of the vertical scroll bar at all times and always keep the horizontal scroll bar hidden, we could do the following where `jsp` is a `JScrollPane`:

```
jsp.setHorizontalScrollBarPolicy(
    ScrollPaneConstants.HORIZONTAL_SCROLLBAR_NEVER);

jsp.setVerticalScrollBarPolicy(
    ScrollPaneConstants.VERTICAL_SCROLLBAR_ALWAYS);
```

7.1.2 JViewport

class javax.swing.JViewport

The `JViewport` class is the container that is really responsible for displaying a specific visible region of the component in a `JScrollPane`. We can set/get a viewport's *view* (the component it contains) using its `setView()` and `getView()` methods. We can control how much of this component `JViewport` displays by setting its *extent* size to a specified `Dimension` using its `setExtentSize()` method. We can also specify where the origin (upper left corner) of a `JViewport` should begin displaying its contained component by providing specific coordinates (as a `Point`) of the contained component to the `setViewPosition()` method. In fact, when we scroll a component in a `JScrollPane`, this view position is constantly being changed by the scroll bars.

NOTE `JViewport` enforces a view position that lies within the view component only. We cannot set negative or extremely large view positions (as of JDK1.2.2 we can assign negative view positions). However, since the view position is the upper right hand corner of the viewport, we are still allowed to set the view position such that only part of the viewport is filled by the view component. We will show how to watch for this, and how to stop it from happening, in some of the examples below.

Whenever a change is made to the position or size of the visible portion of the view, `JViewport` fires `ChangeEvent`s. We can register `ChangeListener`s to capture these events using `JViewport`'s `addChangeListener()` method. These are the only events that are associated with `JScrollPane` by default. For instance, whenever we scroll using `JScroll-Pane`'s scroll bars, its main viewport, as well as its row and column header viewports (see below), will each fire `ChangeEvent`s.

The visible region of `JViewport`'s view can be retrieved as a `Rectangle` or `Dimension` instance using the `getViewRect()` and `getViewSize()` methods respectively. This will give us the current view position as well as the extent width and height. The view position alone can be retrieved with `getViewPosition()`, which returns a `Point` instance. To remove a component from `JViewport` we use its `remove()` method.

We can translate specific `JViewport` coordinates to the coordinates of its contained component by passing a `Point` instance to its `toViewCoordinates()` method. We can do the same for a region by passing a `Dimension` instance to `toViewCoordinates()`. We can also manually specify the visible region of the *view* component by passing a `Dimension` instance to `JViewport`'s `scrollRectToVisible()` method.

We can retrieve `JScrollPane`'s main `JViewport` by calling its `getViewport()` method, or assign it a new one using `setViewport()`. We can replace the component in this viewport through `JScrollPane`'s `setViewportView()` method, but there is no `getViewportView()` counterpart. Instead, we must first access its `JScrollPane`'s `JViewport` by calling `getViewport()`, and then call `getView()` on that (as discussed above). Typically, to access a `JScrollPane`'s main child component, we would do the following:

```
Component myComponent = jsp.getViewport().getView();
```

7.1.3 ScrollPaneLayout

class javax.swing.ScrollPaneLayout

By default, `JScrollPane`'s layout is managed by an instance of `ScrollPaneLayout`. `JScrollPane` can contain up to nine components and it is `ScrollPaneLayout`'s job to make sure that they are positioned correctly. These components are listed here:

- A `JViewport` that contains the main component to be scrolled.
- A `JViewport` that is used as the row header. This viewport's view position changes vertically in sync with the main viewport.
- A `JViewport` that is used as the column header. This viewport's view position changes horizontally in sync with the main viewport.
- Four components for placement in each corner of the scroll pane.
- Two `JScrollBars` for vertical and horizontal scrolling.

The corner components will only be visible if the scroll bars and headers surrounding them are also visible. To assign a component to a corner position, we call `JScrollPane`'s `setCorner()` method. This method takes both a `String` and a component as parameters. The `String` is used to identify in which corner this component is to be placed, and it is recognized by `ScrollPaneLayout`. In fact, `ScrollPaneLayout` identifies each `JScrollPane` component with a unique `String`. Figure 7.2 illustrates this concept.

To assign `JViewports` as the row and column headers, we use `JScrollPane`'s `setRowHeader()` and `setColumnHeader()` methods respectively. We can also avoid having to create a `JViewport` ourselves by passing the component to be placed in the row or column viewport to `JScrollPane`'s `setRowHeaderView()` or `setColumnHeaderView()` methods.

Because `JScrollPane` is often used to scroll images, an obvious use for the row and column headers is to function as some sort of ruler. In example 7.2, we present a basic example showing how to populate each corner with a label and create simple rulers for the row and column headers that display ticks every 30 pixels and render themselves based on their current viewport position. Figure 7.3 illustrates the result.

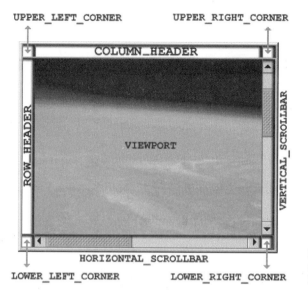

UPPER_LEFT_CORNER   UPPER_RIGHT_CORNER

COLUMN_HEADER

ROW_HEADER

VIEWPORT

VERTICAL_SCROLLBAR

HORIZONTAL_SCROLLBAR

LOWER_LEFT_CORNER   LOWER_RIGHT_CORNER

Figure 7.2 JScrollPane
**components as identified
by** ScrollPaneLayout

Figure 7.3
A JScrollPane **demo with
four corners, a row header,
and a column header**

Example 7.2

HeaderDemo.java

see \Chapter7\2

```
import java.awt.*;
import javax.swing.*;

public class HeaderDemo extends JFrame
{
  public HeaderDemo() {
    super("JScrollPane Demo");
```

```
ImageIcon ii = new ImageIcon("earth.jpg");
JScrollPane jsp = new JScrollPane(new JLabel(ii));

JLabel[] corners = new JLabel[4];
for(int i=0;i<4;i++) {
  corners[i] = new JLabel();
  corners[i].setBackground(Color.yellow);
  corners[i].setOpaque(true);
  corners[i].setBorder(BorderFactory.createCompoundBorder(
    BorderFactory.createEmptyBorder(2,2,2,2),
    BorderFactory.createLineBorder(Color.red, 1)));
}

JLabel rowheader = new JLabel() {
  Font f = new Font("Serif",Font.ITALIC | Font.BOLD,10);
  public void paintComponent(Graphics g) {
    super.paintComponent(g);
    Rectangle r = g.getClipBounds();
    g.setFont(f);
    g.setColor(Color.red);
    for (int i = 30-(r.y % 30);i<r.height;i+=30) {
      g.drawLine(0, r.y + i, 3, r.y + i);
      g.drawString("" + (r.y + i), 6, r.y + i + 3);
    }
  }
  public Dimension getPreferredSize() {
    return new Dimension(25,label.getPreferredSize().getHeight());
  }
};
rowheader.setBackground(Color.yellow);
rowheader.setOpaque(true);

JLabel columnheader = new JLabel() {
  Font f = new Font("Serif",Font.ITALIC | Font.BOLD,10);
  public void paintComponent(Graphics g) {
    super.paintComponent(g);
    Rectangle r = g.getClipBounds();
    g.setFont(f);
    g.setColor(Color.red);
    for (int i = 30-(r.x % 30);i<r.width;i+=30) {
      g.drawLine(r.x + i, 0, r.x + i, 3);
      g.drawString("" + (r.x + i), r.x + i - 10, 16);
    }
  }
  public Dimension getPreferredSize() {
    return new Dimension(label.getPreferredSize().getWidth(),25);
  }
};
columnheader.setBackground(Color.yellow);
columnheader.setOpaque(true);

jsp.setRowHeaderView(rowheader);
jsp.setColumnHeaderView(columnheader);
jsp.setCorner(JScrollPane.LOWER_LEFT_CORNER, corners[0]);
```

① Each row header uses clipping for speed

② Thin and very tall

① Clipping for speed

② Short and very wide

```
        jsp.setCorner(JScrollPane.LOWER_RIGHT_CORNER, corners[1]);
        jsp.setCorner(JScrollPane.UPPER_LEFT_CORNER, corners[2]);
        jsp.setCorner(JScrollPane.UPPER_RIGHT_CORNER, corners[3]);

        getContentPane().add(jsp);
        setSize(400,300);
        setVisible(true);
    }

    public static void main(String[] args) {
        new HeaderDemo();
    }
}
```

❶
❷ Notice that the row and column headers use the graphics clipping area in their `paintCompo-`
`nent()` routine for optimal efficiency. We also override the `getPreferredSize()` method
so that the proper width (for the row header) and height (for the column header) will be used
by `ScrollPaneLayout`. The other dimensions are obtained by simply grabbing the label's
preferred size, as they are completely controlled by `ScrollPaneLayout`.

Note that we are certainly not limited to labels for corners, row headers, or the main viewport itself. As we mentioned in the beginning of this chapter, any component can be placed in
a `JViewport`.

7.1.4 The Scrollable interface

abstract interface javax.swing.Scrollable

The `Scrollable` interface describes five methods that allow us to customize how `JScrollPane`
scrolls its contents. Specifically, by implementing this interface we can specify how many pixels are scrolled when a scroll bar button or scroll bar *paging area* (the empty region between
the scroll bar *thumb* and the buttons) is pressed. (The thumb is the part of the scroll bar that
you drag.) Two methods control this functionality: `getScrollableBlockIncrement()` and
`getScrollableUnitIncrement()`. The former is used to return the amount to scroll when
a scroll bar paging area is pressed, and the latter is used when the button is pressed.

> **NOTE**   In text components, these two methods are implemented so that scrolling will
> move one line of text at a time. (`JTextComponent` implements the `Scrollable`
> interface.)

The other three methods of this interface involve `JScrollPane`'s communication with
the main viewport. The `getScrollableTracksViewportWidth()` and `getScrollable-`
`TracksHeight()` methods can return `true` to disable scrolling in the horizontal or vertical
direction respectively. Normally these just return `false`. The `getPreferredSize()` method
is supposed to return the preferred size of the viewport that will contain this component (the
component implementing the `Scrollable` interface). Normally we just return the preferred
size of the component.

Example 7.3 shows how to implement the `Scrollable` interface to create a custom `JLabel`
whose *unit* and *block* increments will be 10 pixels. As we saw in example 7.1, scrolling one pixel
at a time is tedious at best. Increasing this to a 10-pixel increment provides a more natural feel.

Example 7.3

see \Chapter7\3

```java
import java.awt.*;
import javax.swing.*;

public class ScrollableDemo extends JFrame
{
  public ScrollableDemo() {
    super("JScrollPane Demo");
    ImageIcon ii = new ImageIcon("earth.jpg");
    JScrollPane jsp = new JScrollPane(new MyScrollableLabel(ii));
    getContentPane().add(jsp);
    setSize(300,250);
    setVisible(true);
  }

  public static void main(String[] args) {
    new ScrollableDemo();
  }
}

class MyScrollableLabel extends JLabel implements Scrollable
{
  public MyScrollableLabel(ImageIcon i){
    super(i);
  }

  public Dimension getPreferredScrollableViewportSize() {
    return getPreferredSize();
  }

  public int getScrollableBlockIncrement(Rectangle r,
    int orietation, int direction) {
      return 10;
  }

  public boolean getScrollableTracksViewportHeight() {
    return false;
  }

  public boolean getScrollableTracksViewportWidth() {
    return false;
  }

  public int getScrollableUnitIncrement(Rectangle r,

    int orientation, int direction) {
      return 10;
  }
}
```

7.2 GRAB-AND-DRAG SCROLLING

Many paint programs and document readers (such as Adobe Acrobat) support grab-and-drag scrolling, which is the ability to click on an image and drag it in any direction with the mouse. It is fairly simple to implement; however, we must take care to make the operation smooth without allowing users to scroll past the view's extremities. JViewport takes care of the negative direction for us, as it does not allow the view position coordinates to be less than 0. But it *will* allow us to change the view position to very large values, which can result in the viewport displaying a portion of the view smaller than the viewport itself.

NOTE   As of JDK1.2.2 we are allowed to specify negative view position coordinates.

Example 7.4 demonstrates how to support grab-and-drag scrolling.

Example 7.4

GrabAndDragDemo.java

see \Chapter7\4

```java
import java.awt.*;
import java.awt.event.*;
import javax.swing.*;
import javax.swing.event.*;

public class GrabAndDragDemo extends JFrame
{
  public GrabAndDragDemo() {
    super("Grab-and-drag Demo");
    ImageIcon ii = new ImageIcon("earth.jpg");
    JScrollPane jsp = new JScrollPane(new GrabAndScrollLabel(ii));
    getContentPane().add(jsp);
    setSize(300,250);
    setVisible(true);

    WindowListener l = new WindowAdapter() {
      public void windowClosing(WindowEvent e) {
        System.exit(0);
      }
    };
    addWindowListener(l);
  }

  public static void main(String[] args) {
    new GrabAndDragDemo();
  }
}

class GrabAndScrollLabel extends JLabel
{
  public GrabAndScrollLabel(ImageIcon i){
    super(i);
    MouseInputAdapter mia = new MouseInputAdapter() {
      int m_XDifference, m_YDifference;
```

❶ JLabel which can scroll by dragging the mouse

```
         Container c;

         public void mouseDragged(MouseEvent e) {
           c = GrabAndScrollLabel.this.getParent();
           if (c instanceof JViewport) {
             JViewport jv = (JViewport) c;
             Point p = jv.getViewPosition();
             int newX = p.x - (e.getX()-m_XDifference);
             int newY = p.y - (e.getY()-m_YDifference);

             int maxX = GrabAndScrollLabel.this.getWidth()
               - jv.getWidth();
             int maxY = GrabAndScrollLabel.this.getHeight()
               - jv.getHeight();
             if (newX < 0)
               newX = 0;
             if (newX > maxX)
               newX = maxY;
             if (newY < 0)
               newY = 0;
             if (newY > maxY)
               newY = maxY;

               jv.setViewPosition(new Point(maxX, maxY));
           }
         }

         public void mousePressed(MouseEvent e) {
           setCursor(Cursor.getPredefinedCursor(
           Cursor.MOVE_CURSOR));
           m_XDifference = e.getX();
           m_YDifference = e.getY();
         }

         public void mouseReleased(MouseEvent e) {
           setCursor(Cursor.getPredefinedCursor(
           Cursor.DEFAULT_CURSOR));
         }
       };
       addMouseMotionListener(mia);
       addMouseListener(mia);
     }
   }
```

❸ Scroll the Viewport the label is contained in

❹ Only scroll to maximum coordinates

❷ Start dragging, saving start location

7.2.1 Understanding the code

Class GrabAndScrollLabel

❶ This class extends JLabel and overrides the JLabel(Imageicon ii) constructor. The Grab-AndScrollLabel constructor starts by calling the superclass version and then it proceeds to set up a MouseInputAdapter. This adapter is the heart of the GrabAndScrollLabel class. The adapter uses three variables:

- int m_XDifference: The x-coordinate which has been saved on a mouse press event and used for dragging horizontally.

- `int m_YDifference`: The y-coordinate which has been saved on a mouse press event and used for dragging vertically.
- `Container c`: Used to hold a local reference to the parent container in the `mouse-Dragged()` method.

2 The `mousePressed()` method changes the cursor to `MOVE_CURSOR` and stores the event coordinates in the variables `m_XDifference` and `m_YDifference`, so they can be used in `mouseDragged()`.

3 The `mouseDragged()` method first grabs a reference to the parent, then it checks to see if it is a `JViewport`. If it isn't, we do nothing. If it is, we store the current view position and calculate the new view position the drag will bring us into:

```
Point p = jv.getViewPosition();
int newX = p.x - (e.getX()-m_XDifference);
int newY = p.y - (e.getY()-m_YDifference);
```

4 When dragging components, this would normally be enough (as we will see in future chapters); however, we must make sure that we do not move the label in such a way that it does not fill the viewport. So we calculate the maximum allowable x- and y-coordinates by subtracting the viewport dimensions from the size of this label (since the view position coordinates start from the upper-left hand corner):

```
int maxX = GrabAndScrollLabel.this.getWidth()
  - jv.getWidth();
int maxY = GrabAndScrollLabel.this.getHeight()
  - jv.getHeight();
```

The remainder of this method compares the `newX` and `newY` values with the `maxX` and `maxY` values, and adjusts the view position accordingly. If `newX` or `newY` is ever greater than the `maxX` or `maxY` values respectively, we use the max values instead. If `newX` or `newY` is ever less than `0` (which can happen only with JDK1.2.2), we use `0` instead. This is necessary to allow smooth scrolling in all situations.

7.3 SCROLLING PROGRAMMATICALLY

We are certainly not required to use a `JScrollPane` for scrolling. We can place a component in a `JViewport` and control the scrolling ourselves if we want to. This is what `JViewport` was designed for; it just happens to be used by `JScrollPane` as well. We've constructed this example to show how to implement our own scrolling in a `JViewport`. Four buttons are used for scrolling. We enable and disable these buttons based on whether the view component is at any of its extremities. These buttons are assigned keyboard mnemonics which we can use as an alternative to clicking.

This example also shows how to use a `ChangeListener` to capture `ChangeEvents` that are fired when the `JViewport` changes state. We need to capture these events so that when our viewport is resized to be bigger than its view component child, the scrolling buttons will become disabled. If these buttons are disabled and the viewport is then resized so that it is no longer bigger than its child view component, the buttons should then become enabled. It is quite simple to capture and process these events, as we will see in example 7.5. (As with most of the examples we have presented, it may help if you run this example before stepping through the code.)

Figure 7.4   Programmatic scrolling with `JViewport`

Example 7.5

ButtonScroll.java

see \Chapter7\5

```java
import java.awt.*;
import java.awt.event.*;

import javax.swing.*;
import javax.swing.event.*;

public class ButtonScroll extends JFrame
{
  protected JViewport m_viewport;
  protected JButton m_up;
  protected JButton m_down;
  protected JButton m_left;
  protected JButton m_right;

  protected int m_pgVert;
  protected int m_pgHorz;

  public ButtonScroll() {
    super("Scrolling Programmatically");
    setSize(400, 400);
    getContentPane().setLayout(new BorderLayout());
```

❶ Viewport, scroll buttons, and scrolling distances

❷ Constructor places label with image along with scroll buttons

```
ImageIcon shuttle = new ImageIcon("shuttle.gif");
m_pgVert = shuttle.getIconHeight()/5;
m_pgHorz = shuttle.getIconWidth()/5;
JLabel lbl = new JLabel(shuttle);
```
Listen for size changes on Viewport and reconfigure scroll buttons ❸
```
m_viewport = new JViewport();
m_viewport.setView(lbl);
m_viewport.addChangeListener(new ChangeListener() {
  public void stateChanged(ChangeEvent e) {
    enableButtons(
      ButtonScroll.this.m_viewport.getViewPosition());
  }
});
getContentPane().add(m_viewport, BorderLayout.CENTER);

JPanel pv = new JPanel(new BorderLayout());
m_up = createButton("up", 'u');
ActionListener lst = new ActionListener() {
  public void actionPerformed(ActionEvent e) {
    movePanel(0, -1);
  }
};
m_up.addActionListener(lst);
pv.add(m_up, BorderLayout.NORTH);
```
Create buttons to scroll image up and down ❹
```
m_down = createButton("down", 'd');
lst = new ActionListener() {
  public void actionPerformed(ActionEvent e) {
    movePanel(0, 1);
  }
};
m_down.addActionListener(lst);
pv.add(m_down, BorderLayout.SOUTH);
getContentPane().add(pv, BorderLayout.EAST);

JPanel ph = new JPanel(new BorderLayout());
m_left = createButton("left", 'l');
lst = new ActionListener() {
  public void actionPerformed(ActionEvent e) {
    movePanel(-1, 0);
  }
};
m_left.addActionListener(lst);
ph.add(m_left, BorderLayout.WEST);
```
Create buttons to scroll image left and right ❹
```
m_right = createButton("right", 'r');
lst = new ActionListener() {
  public void actionPerformed(ActionEvent e) {
    movePanel(1, 0);
  }
};
m_right.addActionListener(lst);
ph.add(m_right, BorderLayout.EAST);
getContentPane().add(ph, BorderLayout.SOUTH);
```

```
    WindowListener wndCloser = new WindowAdapter() {
      public void windowClosing(WindowEvent e) {
        System.exit(0);
      }
    };
    addWindowListener(wndCloser);

    setVisible(true);
    movePanel(0, 0);
  }
```

Create scroll button with direction string and mnemonic ⑤

```
  protected JButton createButton(String name, char mnemonics) {
    JButton btn = new JButton(new ImageIcon(name+"1.gif"));
    btn.setPressedIcon(new ImageIcon(name+"2.gif"));
    btn.setDisabledIcon(new ImageIcon(name+"3.gif"));
    btn.setToolTipText("Move "+name);
    btn.setBorderPainted(false);
    btn.setMargin(new Insets(0, 0, 0, 0));
    btn.setContentAreaFilled(false);
    btn.setMnemonic(mnemonics);
    return btn;
  }

  protected void movePanel(int xmove, int ymove) {
    Point pt = m_viewport.getViewPosition();
    pt.x += m_pgHorz*xmove;
    pt.y += m_pgVert*ymove;

    pt.x = Math.max(0, pt.x);
    pt.x = Math.min(getMaxXExtent(), pt.x);
    pt.y = Math.max(0, pt.y);
    pt.y = Math.min(getMaxYExtent(), pt.y);

    m_viewport.setViewPosition(pt);
    enableButtons(pt);
  }
```

⑥ **Move the image panel in the specified direction, from which scroll button was pressed**

```
  protected void enableButtons(Point pt) {
    if (pt.x == 0)
      enableComponent(m_left, false);

    else enableComponent(m_left, true);
    if (pt.x >= getMaxXExtent())
      enableComponent(m_right, false);
    else enableComponent(m_right, true);

    if (pt.y == 0)
      enableComponent(m_up, false);
    else enableComponent(m_up, true);

    if (pt.y >= getMaxYExtent())
      enableComponent(m_down, false);
    else enableComponent(m_down, true);
  }

  protected void enableComponent(JComponent c, boolean b) {
    if (c.isEnabled() != b)
```

⑦ **Enable or disable scroll buttons based on whether the image is already scrolled to edge of range**

```
        c.setEnabled(b);
    }
    protected int getMaxXExtent() {
      return m_viewport.getView().getWidth()-m_viewport.getWidth();
    }
    protected int getMaxYExtent() {
      return m_viewport.getView().getHeight()-m_viewport.getHeight();
    }
    public static void main(String argv[])  {
      new ButtonScroll();
    }
}
```

8 Get maximum scrolling dimensions

7.3.1   Understanding the code

Class ButtonScroll

1 Several instance variables are declared:

- JViewport m_viewport: The viewport used to display a large image.
- JButton m_up: The button to scroll up programmatically.
- JButton m_down: The button to scroll down programmatically.
- JButton m_left: The button to scroll left programmatically.
- JButton m_right: The button to scroll right programmatically.
- int m_pgVert: The number of pixels for a vertical scroll.
- int m_pgHorz: The number of pixels for a horizontal scroll.

2 The constructor of the ButtonScroll class creates and initializes the GUI components for this example. A BorderLayout is used to manage the components in this frame's content pane. JLabel lbl which stores a large image, is placed in the viewport, m_viewport, to provide programmatic viewing capabilities. This JViewport is added to the center of our frame.

3 As we mentioned above, we need to capture the ChangeEvents that are fired when our JViewport changes size so that we can enable and disable our buttons accordingly. We do this by attaching a ChangeListener to our viewport and calling our enableButtons() method (see below) from stateChanged():

```
m_viewport.addChangeListener(new ChangeListener() {
  public void stateChanged(ChangeEvent e) {
    enableButtons(
      ButtonScroll.this.m_viewport.getViewPosition());
  }
});
```

4 Two buttons, m_up and m_down, are created for scrolling in the vertical direction. The createButton() method is used to create a new JButton component and set a group of properties for it (see below). Each of the new buttons receives an ActionListener which calls the movePanel() method in response to a mouse click. These two buttons are added to the intermediate container, JPanel pv, which is added to the east side of our frame's content pane. Similarly, two buttons, m_left and m_right, are created for scrolling in the horizontal direction and are added to the south region of the content pane.

5 The `createButton()` method creates a new `JButton` component. It takes two parameters: the name of the scrolling direction as a `String` and the button's mnemonic as a `char`. This method assumes that three image files are prepared:

- name1.gif: The default icon.
- name2.gif: The pressed icon.
- name3.gif: The disabled icon.

These images are loaded as `ImageIcons` and attached to the button with the associated `setXX()` method:

```
JButton btn = new JButton(new ImageIcon(name+"1.gif"));
btn.setPressedIcon(new ImageIcon(name+"2.gif"));
btn.setDisabledIcon(new ImageIcon(name+"3.gif"));
btn.setToolTipText("Move "+name);
btn.setBorderPainted(false);
btn.setMargin(new Insets(0, 0, 0, 0));
btn.setContentAreaFilled(false);
btn.setMnemonic(mnemonic);
return btn;
```

Then we remove any border or content area rendering, so the presentation of our button is completely determined by our icons. Finally, we set the tooltip text and mnemonic and return that component instance.

6 The `movePanel()` method programmatically scrolls the image in the viewport in the direction determined by the `xmove` and `ymove` parameters. These parameters can have the value −1, 0, or 1. To determine the actual amount of scrolling, we multiply these parameters by `m_pgHorz` (`m_pgVert`). The local variable `Point pt` determines a new viewport position. It is limited so the resulting view will not display any empty space (space not belonging to the displayed image), similar to how we enforce the viewport view position in the grab-and-drag scrolling example above. Finally, the `setViewPosition()` method is called to scroll to the new position, and `enableButtons()` enables/disables buttons according to the new position:

```
Point pt = m_viewport.getViewPosition();
pt.x += m_pgHorz*xmove;
pt.y += m_pgVert*ymove;

pt.x = Math.max(0, pt.x);
pt.x = Math.min(getMaxXExtent(), pt.x);
pt.y = Math.max(0, pt.y);
pt.y = Math.min(getMaxYExtent(), pt.y);

m_viewport.setViewPosition(pt);
enableButtons(pt);
```

7 The `enableButtons()` method disables a button if scrolling in the corresponding direction is not possible; otherwise, it enables the button. For example, if the viewport position's x-coordinate is 0, we can disable the scroll left button (remember that the view position will never be negative, as enforced by `JViewport`):

```
if (pt.x <= 0)
  enableComponent(m_left, false);
else enableComponent(m_left, true);
```

Similarly, if the viewport position's x-coordinate is greater than or equal to our maximum allowable x-position (determined by `getMaxXExtent()`), we disable the scroll right button:

```
if (pt.x >= getMaxXExtent())
  enableComponent(m_right, false);
else enableComponent(m_right, true);
```

8 The methods `getMaxXExtent()` and `getMaxYExtent()` return the maximum coordinates available for scrolling in the horizontal and vertical directions, respectively, by subtracting the appropriate viewport dimension from the appropriate dimension of the child component.

7.3.2 Running the code

NOTE   The shuttle image for this example was found at http://shuttle.nasa.gov/sts-95/ images/esc/.

Press the buttons and watch how the image is scrolled programmatically. Use the keyboard mnemonic as an alternative way to pressing buttons, and notice how this mnemonic is displayed in the tooltip text. Also note how a button is disabled when scrolling in the corresponding direction is no longer available, and how it is enabled otherwise. Now try resizing the frame and see how the buttons will change state depending on whether the viewport is bigger or smaller than its child component.

CHAPTER 8

Split panes

8.1 JSPLITPANE

class javax.swing.JSplitPane

Split panes allow the user to dynamically change the size of two or more components that are displayed side by side (either within a window or another panel). A divider can be dragged with the mouse to increase space for one component and decrease the display space for another; however, the total display area does not change. A familiar example is the combination of a tree and a table separated by a horizontal divider (such as in file explorer-like applications). The Swing framework for split panes consists only of JSplitPane.

JSplitPane can hold two components that are separated by a horizontal or vertical divider. The components on either side of a JSplitPane can be added either in one of the constructors, or with the proper setXXComponent() methods (where XX is substituted by Left, Right, Top, or Bottom). We can also set the orientation to vertical split or horizontal split at run-time using its setOrientation() method.

The divider between the components is the only visible part of JSplitPane. Its size can be managed with the setDividerSize() method, and its position can be managed by the two overloaded setDividerLocation() methods (which take an absolute location in pixels or a proportional location as a double). The divider location methods have no effect until a JSplitPane is displayed. JSplitPane also maintains a oneTouchExpandable property which, when `true`, places two small arrows inside the divider that will move the divider to its extremities when clicked.

GUIDELINE

Resizable paneled display   Split panes are useful when your design has paneled the display for ease of use but you (as designer) have no control over the actual window size. The Netscape email reader is a good example of this; a split pane is introduced to let the user vary the size of the message header panel against the size of the message text panel.

An interesting feature of the `JSplitPane` component is that you can specify whether to repaint side components *during* the divider's motion using the `setContinuousLayout()` method. If you can repaint components fast enough, resizing will have a more natural view with this setting. Otherwise, this flag should be set to `false`, in which case side components will be repainted only when the divider's new location is chosen. In this latter case, a divider line will be shown as the divider location is dragged to illustrate the new position.

`JSplitPane` will not size any of its constituent components smaller than their minimum sizes. If the minimum size of each component is larger than the size of the split pane, the divider will be effectively disabled (unmovable). We can call its `resetToPreferredSize()` method to resize its children to their preferred sizes, if possible.

GUIDELINE

Using split panes in conjunction with scroll panes   It's important to use a scroll pane on the panels which are being split with the split pane. Scroll bars will then appear automatically as required when data is obscured as the split pane is dragged back and forth. With the introduction of the scroll pane, the viewer has a clear indication that there is hidden data. They can then choose to scroll with the scroll bar or uncover the data using the split pane.

8.2   BASIC SPLIT PANE EXAMPLE

Example 8.1 shows `JSplitPane` at work in a basic, introductory demo. We can manipulate the size of four custom panels placed in three `JSplitPanes`:

Example 8.1

SplitSample.java

see \Chapter8\1

```
import java.awt.*;
import java.awt.event.*;

import javax.swing.*;

public class SplitSample extends JFrame
{
  protected JSplitPane m_sp;
```

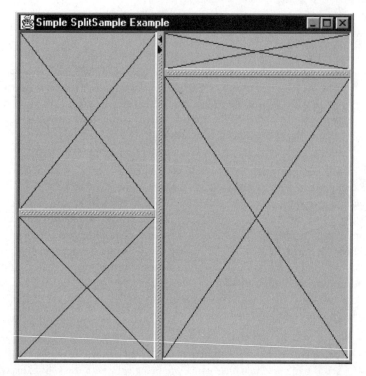

Figure 8.1   A split pane example displaying simple custom panels

```
.public SplitSample() {
  super("Simple SplitSample Example");
  setSize(400, 400);

  Component c11 = new SimplePanel();
  Component c12 = new SimplePanel();
  JSplitPane spLeft = new JSplitPane(
    JSplitPane.VERTICAL_SPLIT, c11, c12);
  spLeft.setDividerSize(8);
  spLeft.setContinuousLayout(true);

  Component c21 = new SimplePanel();
  Component c22 = new SimplePanel();
  JSplitPane spRight = new JSplitPane(
    JSplitPane.VERTICAL_SPLIT, c21, c22);
  spRight.setDividerSize(8);
  spRight.setContinuousLayout(true);

  m_sp = new JSplitPane(JSplitPane.HORIZONTAL_SPLIT,
    spLeft, spRight);
  m_sp.setContinuousLayout(false);
  m_sp.setOneTouchExpandable(true);

  getContentPane().add(m_sp, BorderLayout.CENTER);
```

1 Constructor composes
4 SimplePanels into
2 JSplitPanes, 2 panels
in each

1 Two SimplePanels
in left pane

1 Two SimplePanels
in right pane

1 One JSplitPane
to hold the
other two

```
        WindowListener wndCloser = new WindowAdapter() {
          public void windowClosing(WindowEvent e) {
            System.exit(0);
          }
        };
        addWindowListener(wndCloser);

        setVisible(true);
      }

      public static void main(String argv[]) {
        new SplitSample();
      }
    }

    class SimplePanel extends JPanel
    {
      public Dimension getPreferredSize() {
        return new Dimension(200, 200);
      }

      public Dimension getMinimumSize() {
        return new Dimension(40, 40);
      }

      public void paintComponent(Graphics g) {
        g.setColor(Color.black);
        Dimension sz = getSize();
        g.drawLine(0, 0, sz.width, sz.height);
        g.drawLine(sz.width, 0, 0, sz.height);
      }
    }
```

② Simple component to take up space in halves of JSplitPane

8.2.1   Understanding the code

Class SplitSample

❶ Four instances of SimplePanel (see below) are used to fill a 2x2 structure. The two left components (c11 and c12) are placed in the spLeft vertically split JSplitPane. The two right components (c21 and c22) are placed in the spRight vertically split JSplitPane. The spLeft and spRight panels are placed in the m_sp horizontally split JSplitPane. The continuousLayout property is set to true for spLeft and spRight, and false for m_sp. So as the divider moves inside the left and right panels, child components are repainted continuously, producing immediate results. However, as the vertical divider is moved, it is denoted by a black line until a new position is chosen (when the mouse is released). Only then are its child components validated and repainted. The first kind of behavior is recommended for simple components that can be rendered quickly, while the second is recomended for components whose repainting can take a significant amount of time.

The oneTouchExpandable property is set to true for the vertical JSplitPane m_sp. This places small arrow widgets on the divider. By pressing these arrows with the mouse, we can instantly move the divider to the left-most or right-most position. When the slider is in the left-most or right-most positions, pressing these arrows will then move the divider to its most recent location, which is maintained by the lastDividerLocation property.

Class SimplePanel

❷ SimplePanel represents a simple Swing component whose paintComponent() method draws two diagonal lines across it's area. The overridden getMinimumSize() method defines the minimum space required for this component. JSplitPane will prohibit the user from moving the divider if the resulting child size will become less than its minimum size.

NOTE The arrow widgets associated with the oneTouchExpandable property will move the divider to the extreme location without regard to minimum sizes of child components.

8.2.2 Running the code

Notice how child components can be resized with dividers. Also notice the difference between resizing with continuous layout (side panes) and without it (center pane). Play with the "one touch expandable" widgets for quick expansion and collapse.

8.3 GAS MODEL SIMULATION USING A SPLIT PANE

In this section we'll use JSplitPane for an interesting scientific experiment: a simulation of the gas model. In example 8.2, left and right components represent containers holding a two-dimensional "ideal gas." The JSplitPane component provides a moveable divider between them. By moving the divider, we can see how gas reacts when its volume is changed. Online educational software is ever-increasing as the Internet flourishes; here we show how Swing can be used to demonstrate one of the most basic laws of thermodynamics.

NOTE As you may remember from a physics or chemistry course, an ideal gas is a physical model in which gas atoms or molecules move in random directions bouncing elastically from a container's bounds (in this example we refer to all particles as atoms). Mutual collisions are negligible. The speed of the atoms depends on gas temperature. Several laws can be demonstrated with this model. Boyle's Law states that under the condition of constant temperature, multiplication of pressure P and volume V is constant: $PV = const$.

To model the motion of atoms, we'll use threads. So this example also gives a good demonstration of using several threads with Swing.

Example 8.2

Split.java

see\Chapter8\2

```
import java.awt.*;
import java.awt.event.*;
import java.util.*;

import javax.swing.*;
import javax.swing.border.*;
import javax.swing.event.*;

public class Split extends JFrame implements Runnable
{
```

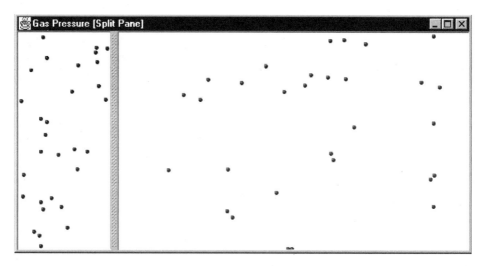

Figure 8.2 A gas model simulation showing moving atoms

```
protected GasPanel m_left;
protected GasPanel m_right;

public Split() {
  super("Gas Pressure [Split Pane]");
  setSize(600, 300);

  ImageIcon ball1 = new ImageIcon("ball1.gif");
  m_left = new GasPanel(30, ball1.getImage());
  ImageIcon ball2 = new ImageIcon("ball2.gif");
  m_right = new GasPanel(30, ball2.getImage());
  JSplitPane sp = new JSplitPane(
    JSplitPane.HORIZONTAL_SPLIT, m_left, m_right);
  sp.setDividerSize(10);
  sp.setContinuousLayout(true);
  getContentPane().add(sp, BorderLayout.CENTER);

  WindowListener wndCloser = new WindowAdapter() {
    public void windowClosing(WindowEvent e) {
      System.exit(0);
    }
  };
  addWindowListener(wndCloser);

  setVisible(true);

  new Thread(m_left).start();
  new Thread(m_right).start();
  new Thread(this).start();
}
public void run() {
  while (true) {
    int p1 = (int)m_left.m_px2;
```

❶ Constructor splits two GasPanel instances, with threads to work on the two GasPanels and one thread to manage the other two

❶ Threads to do work in background

❷ Split thread periodically reads pressure value of left and right containers

```java
      int pv1 = p1*m_left.getWidth();
      int p2 = (int)m_right.m_px1;
      int pv2 = p2*m_right.getWidth();
      System.out.println("Left: p="+p1+"\tpv="+pv1+
        "\tRight: p="+p2+"\tpv="+pv2);
      m_left.clearCounters();
      m_right.clearCounters();

      try {
        Thread.sleep(20000);
      }
      catch(InterruptedException e) {}
    }
  }

  public static void main(String argv[]) { new Split(); }
}

class GasPanel extends JPanel implements Runnable
{
  protected Atom[] m_atoms;
  protected Image   m_img;
  protected Rectangle m_rc;

  public double m_px1 = 0;
  public double m_px2 = 0;
  public double m_py1 = 0;
  public double m_py2 = 0;

  public GasPanel(int nAtoms, Image img) {
    setBackground(Color.white);
    enableEvents(ComponentEvent.COMPONENT_RESIZED);

    m_img = img;
    m_atoms = new Atom[nAtoms];
    m_rc = new Rectangle(getPreferredSize());
    for (int k=0; k<nAtoms; k++) {
      m_atoms[k] = new Atom(this);
    }
  }

  public Dimension getPreferredSize() {
    return new Dimension(300, 300);
  }

  public void run() {
    while (true) {
      for (int k=0; k<m_atoms.length; k++)
        m_atoms[k].move(m_rc);
      repaint();

      try {
        Thread.sleep(100);
      }
      catch(InterruptedException e) {}
    }
  }
```

3 Panel which simulates a two-dimensional gas container

4 Constructor sets number of atoms and image for atom display

5 Returns preferred size, which determines initial position of divider

6 Activates gas container, moves each atom and then sleeps for short period

```
public void paintComponent(Graphics g) {
  g.setColor(getBackground());
  g.fillRect(m_rc.x, m_rc.y, m_rc.width, m_rc.height);

  for (int k=0; k<m_atoms.length; k++)
    g.drawImage(m_img, m_atoms[k].getX(),
      m_atoms[k].getY(), this);
}

protected void processComponentEvent(ComponentEvent e) {
  if (e.getID() == ComponentEvent.COMPONENT_RESIZED) {
    m_rc.setSize(getSize());
    for (int k=0; k<m_atoms.length; k++)
      m_atoms[k].ensureInRect(m_rc);
  }
}

public void clearCounters() {
  m_px1 = 0;
  m_px2 = 0;
  m_py1 = 0;
  m_py2 = 0;
}
}

class Atom
{
  protected double m_x;
  protected double m_y;
  protected double m_vx;
  protected double m_vy;

  protected GasPanel m_parent;

  public Atom(GasPanel parent) {
    m_parent = parent;
    m_x = parent.m_rc.x + parent.m_rc.width*Math.random();
    m_y = parent.m_rc.y + parent.m_rc.height*Math.random();
    double angle = 2*Math.PI*Math.random();
    m_vx = 10*Math.cos(angle);
    m_vy = 10*Math.sin(angle);
  }

  public void move(Rectangle rc) {
    double x = m_x + m_vx;
    double y = m_y + m_vy;
    int x1 = rc.x;
    int x2 = rc.x + rc.width;
    int y1 = rc.y;
    int y2 = rc.y + rc.height;
    for (int bounce = 0; bounce<2; bounce++) {
      if (x < x1) {
        x += 2*(x1-x);
        m_vx = - m_vx;
        m_parent.m_px1 += 2*Math.abs(m_vx);
      }
```

7 Overridden to draw each child atom

8 Overridden to process component resize events

9 Represents single object moving within a rectangular region

10 Constructor sets Atom to move within bounds of supplied GasPanel

11 Moves the Atom; called each iteration of the GasPanel's run() loop

12 Bounces off left wall

```
        if (x > x2) {
            x -= 2*(x-x2);
            m_vx = - m_vx;
            m_parent.m_px2 += 2*Math.abs(m_vx);
        }
        if (y < y1) {
            y += 2*(y1-y);
            m_vy = - m_vy;
            m_parent.m_py1 += 2*Math.abs(m_vy);
        }
        if (y > y2) {
            y -= 2*(y-y2);
            m_vy = - m_vy;
            m_parent.m_py2 += 2*Math.abs(m_vy);
        }
    }
    m_x = x;
    m_y = y;
}

public void ensureInRect(Rectangle rc) {
    if (m_x < rc.x)
        m_x = rc.x;
    if (m_x > rc.x + rc.width)
        m_x = rc.x + rc.width;
    if (m_y < rc.y)
        m_y = rc.y;
    if (m_y > rc.y + rc.height)
        m_y = rc.y + rc.height;
}

public int getX() { return (int)m_x; }
public int getY() { return (int)m_y; }
}
```

12 Bounces off right wall

12 Bounces off ceiling

12 Bounces off floor

13 After GasPanel resize, pushes Atom into bounding rectangle if resize placed it outside

8.3.1   Understanding the code

Class Split

1 The Split constructor creates two instances of the GasPanel class (which models a gas container) and places them in a JSplitPane. Both the Split and GasPanel classes implement the Runnable interface, so threads are created and started to run all three instances.

> REMINDER   The Runnable interface should be implemented by classes which do not intend to use any Thread functionality other than the run() method. In such a case, we don't have to subclass the Thread class. Instead we can simply implement Runnable and define the run() method. In this method we can use the static Thread.sleep() method to yield control to other threads for a specified amount of time.

2 The run() method of our Split class periodically interrogates the pressure on the divider (which can be shown to be proportional to the cumulative sum of twice each colliding atom's velocity in the direction of collision) from the left and right containers, as well as each container's width (which is proportional to the container's volume).

> **NOTE** Because of the random nature of the gas model, all observations are statistical. Each time you run this simulation you're likely to observe slightly different results. The more atoms that constitute the gas, and the longer the measurement (time) interval, the more accurate the results will be. A real gas has about 10^{20} atoms/cm^3. In our model only a few dozen "atoms" (in reality these may be either atoms or molecules) are participating, so fluctuations are considerable, and we have to wait a bit before we can obtain meaningful measurements (through averaging several results).

Class GasPanel

3 The `GasPanel` class models a two-dimensional gas container. It implements the `Runnable` interface and simulates the random motion of its contained atoms. Seven instance variables have the following definitions:

- `Atom[] m_atoms`: An array of `Atom` instances hosted by this container.
- `Image m_img`: The image used to represent each atom.
- `Rectangle m_rc`: The container's rectangular bounds.
- `double m_px1`: The counter to measure pressure on the left wall.
- `double m_px2`: The counter to measure pressure on the right wall.
- `double m_py1`: The counter to measure pressure on the top wall.
- `double m_py2`: The counter to measure pressure on the bottom wall.

4 The `GasPanel` constructor takes the number of atoms to be created as a parameter as well as a reference to the image to represent them. The `enableEvents()` method is called to enable the processing of resize events on this component. Finally, an array of atoms is created (see the `Atom` class below).

5 The `getPreferredSize()` method returns the preferred size of this component (used by our split pane to determine the initial position of its divider).

6 The `run()` method activates the gas container. For each child atom, it invokes the `Atom` `move()` method (see below) which changes an `Atom`'s coordinates. The component is then repainted and the calling thread sleeps for 100ms to provide smooth continuous motion.

7 The `paintComponent()` method is overridden to draw each child atom. It clears the component's area and, for each atom, draws the specified image (typically a small ball) at the atom's current location.

8 The `processComponentEvent()` method is overridden to process resizing events. It updates the `m_rc` rectangle (which is used to limit atom motion) and calls the `ensureInRect()` method for all child atoms to force them to stay inside this component's bounds. A check for the `COMPONENT_RESIZED` ID is done to skip the processing of `COMPONENT_MOVED` events (which are also delivered to this component even though we've explicitly asked for only `COMPONENT_RESIZED` events (see the `enableEvents()` call in the constructor)).

The `clearCounters()` method clears the counters used to measure the pressure on each of the walls.

Class Atom

9 An `Atom` represents a single object moving within a specific rectangular region and bouncing elastically from its walls. Here are the instance variables:

- `double m_x`: The current x-coordinate.
- `double m_y`: The current y-coordinate.
- `double m_vx`: The current x-component of velocity.
- `double m_vy`: The current y-component of velocity.
- `GasPanel m_parent`: The reference to the parent container.

10 The `Atom` constructor takes a reference to a parent `GasPanel` as a parameter. It initializes its coordinates randomly within the parent's bounding rectangle using `Math.random()` as a random number generator. An atom's velocity vector is assigned a fixed absolute magnitude (10) and a random orientation in the x-y plane.

> **NOTE** In a more realistic model, velocity would be a normally distributed random value. However, this is not very significant for our purposes.

11 The `move()` method moves an atom to a new position, and this method is called each time the parent `GasPanel`'s `run()` loop is executed. When new coordinates x, y are calculated, this method checks for possible bounces from the container's walls:

```java
public void move(Rectangle rc) {
   double x = m_x + m_vx;
   double y = m_y + m_vy;
   int x1 = rc.x;
   int x2 = rc.x + rc.width;
   int y1 = rc.y;
   int y2 = rc.y + rc.height;
   for (int bounce = 0; bounce<2; bounce++) {
     // Pseudo-code

     if (x < x1) { // bounce off of left wall... }
     if (x > x2) { // bounce off of right wall... }
     if (y < y1) { // bounce off of top wall... }
     if (y > y2) { // bounce off of bottom wall... }
   }
   m_x = x;
   m_y = y;
}
```

12 If a new point lies behind one of the four walls, a bounce occurs, which changes the coordinate and velocity vector. This contributes to the pressure on the wall where the bounce occurred (as an absolute change in the velocity component in the direction of collision), which is accumulated in the parent `GasPanel`. Bouncing is checked twice to take into account the rare case in which two subsequent bounces occur in a single step. This can occur near the container's corners, when, after the first bounce, the moving particle is repositioned beyond the nearest perpendicular wall.

13 The final methods of our `Atom` class are fairly straightforward. The `ensureInRect()` method is called to ensure that an `Atom`'s coordinates lie within the given rectangle, and the `getX()` and `getY()` methods return the current coordinates as integers.

8.3.2   Running the code

Notice how the gas reacts to the change in the parent container's volume by adjusting the position of the split pane divider. Also try adjusting the size of the application frame.

The following are some *P* and *PV* measurements we obtained when experimenting with this example:

```
Left: p=749    pv=224700    Right: p=996    pv=276888
Left: p=701    pv=210300    Right: p=1006   pv=279668
Left: p=714    pv=214200    Right: p=1028   pv=285784
Left: p=770    pv=231000    Right: p=1018   pv=283004
Left: p=805    pv=241500    Right: p=1079   pv=299962
Left: p=1586   pv=190320    Right: p=680    pv=311440
Left: p=1757   pv=210840    Right: p=594    pv=272052
Left: p=1819   pv=218280    Right: p=590    pv=270220
Left: p=1863   pv=223560    Right: p=573    pv=262434
Left: p=1792   pv=215040    Right: p=621    pv=284418
```

We can see that somewhere between the fifth and sixth measurments the divider had been moved from right to left by the increase in pressure on the left side, and a decrease in pressure on the right side. However, each side's *PV* value (in arbitrary units) remains practically unchanged. The average *PV* value for the first 5 measurements on the left side is 1121700/5 = 224340, and the average *PV* value for the second 5 measurements on the left side is 1058040/5 = 211608. The average *PV* value for the first 5 measurements on the right side is 1425306/5 = 285061, and the average *PV* value for the second 5 measurements on the right side is 1400564/5 = 280112.

CHAPTER 9

Combo boxes

9.1 JCOMBOBOX

class javax.swing.JComboBox

This class represents a basic GUI component which consists of two parts:

- A pop-up menu (an implementation of `javax.swing.plaf.basic.ComboPopup`). By default, this is a `JPopupMenu` subclass (`javax.swing.plaf.basic.BasicCombo-Popup`) that contains a `JList` in a `JScrollPane`.

- A button that acts as a container for an editor or renderer component, and an arrow button that is used to display the pop-up menu.

The `JList` uses a `ListSelectionModel` (see chapter 10) that allows `SINGLE_SELEC-TION` only. Apart from this, `JComboBox` directly uses only one model, a `ComboBoxModel`, which manages data in its `JList`.

A number of constructors are available to build a `JComboBox`. The default constructor can be used to create a combo box with an empty list, or we can pass data to a constructor as a one-dimensional array, a `Vector`, or an implementation of the `ComboBoxModel` interface (this will be explained later). The last variant allows maximum control over the properties and appearance of a `JComboBox`, as we will see.

As do other complex Swing components, `JComboBox` allows a customizable renderer for displaying each item in its drop-down list (by default, this is a `JLabel` subclass implementation of `ListCellRenderer`), and it allows a customizable editor to be used as the combo box's data entry component (by default, this is an instance of `ComboBoxEditor` which uses a `JTextField`). We can use the existing default implementations of `ListCellRenderer` and `ComboBoxEditor`, or we can create our own according to our particular needs (as we will see later in this chapter). Unless we use a custom renderer, the default renderer will display each element as a `String` defined by that object's `toString()` method; the only exceptions to this are `Icon` implementations which will be renderered as they would be in any `JLabel`. Take note that a renderer returns a `Component`, but that component is not interactive and it is only used for display purposes (meaning it acts as a "rubber stamp," according to the API documentation). For instance, if a `JCheckBox` is used as a renderer, we will not be able to check and uncheck it. Editors, however, are fully interactive.

Similar to `JList`, which is discussed in the next chapter, this class uses `ListDataEvents` to deliver information about changes in the state of its drop-down list's model. `ItemEvents` and `ActionEvents` are fired from any source when the current selection changes—the source can be programmatic or input from the user. Correspondingly, we can attach `ItemListeners` and `ActionListeners` to receive these events.

The drop-down list of a `JComboBox` is a pop-up menu that contains a `JList` (this is actually defined in the UI delegate, not the component itself) and it can be programmatically displayed/hidden using the `showPopup()` and `hidePopup()` methods. As with any other Swing pop-up menu (which we will discuss in chapter 12), it can be displayed as either heavyweight or lightweight. `JComboBox` provides the `setLightWeightPopupEnabled()` method, which allows us to choose between these modes.

`JComboBox` also defines an inner interface called `KeySelectionManager` that declares one method, `selectionForKey(char aKey, ComboBoxModel aModel)`, which we can define to return the index of the list element that should be selected when the list is visible (meaning the pop-up is showing) and the given keyboard character is pressed.

The `JComboBox` UI delegate represents `JComboBox` graphically using a container with a button. This button contains both an arrow button and either a renderer displaying the currently selected item or an editor that allows changes to be made to the currently selected item. The arrow button is displayed on the right of the renderer/editor and it will show the pop-up menu that contains the drop-down list when it is clicked.

NOTE Because of the `JComboBox` UI delegate construction, setting the border of a `JComboBox` does not have the expected effect. Try this and you will see that the container containing the main `JComboBox` button gets the assigned border, when in fact we want that button to receive the border. There is no easy way to set the border of this button without customizing the UI delegate. We hope to see this limitation disappear in a future version.

When a `JComboBox` is editable (which it is not by default) the editor component will allow modification of the currently selected item. The default editor will appear as a `JTextField` that accepts input. This text field has an `ActionListener` attached that will accept an edit and change the selected item accordingly when/if the ENTER key is pressed. If the focus changes while editing, all editing will be cancelled and a change will not be made to the selected item.

`JComboBox` can be made editable with its `setEditable()` method, and we can specify a custom `ComboBoxEditor` with `JComboBox`'s `setEditor()` method. Setting the `editable` property to `true` causes the UI delegate to replace the renderer in the button with the assigned editor. Similarly, setting this property to `false` causes the editor in the button to be replaced by a renderer.

The cell renderer used for a `JComboBox` can be assigned and retrieved with the `setRenderer()` and `getRenderer()` methods, respectively. Calls to these methods actually get passed to the `JList` contained in the combo box's pop-up menu.

Advice on usage and design

Usage Combo boxes and list boxes are very similar to each other. In fact, a combo box is an entry field with a drop-down list box. Deciding when to use one or the other can be difficult. Our advice is to think about reader output rather than data input. When the reader only needs to see a single item, then a combo box is the best choice. Use a combo box where a single selection is made from a collection and users only need to see a single item, such as "Currency USD." You'll learn about using list boxes in the next chapter.

Design There are a number of things affect the usability of a combo box. If it contains more than a few items, it becomes unusable unless the data is sorted in some logical fashion, such as in alphabetical or numerical order. When a list gets longer, usability is affected in yet another way. Once a list gets beyond a couple of hundred items, even when sorted, locating a specific item in the list becomes a very slow process for the user. Some implementations have solved this by offering the ability to type in partial text, and the list "jumps" to the best match or a partial match item; for example, type in "ch" and the combo box will jump to "Chevrolet" in example 9.1. You may want to consider such an enhancement to a `JComboBox` to improve the usability of longer lists.

There are a number of graphical considerations, also. Like all other data entry fields, combo boxes should be aligned to fit attractively into a panel. However, this is not always easy. Avoid making a combo box which is simply too big for the list items it contains. For example, a combo box for a currency code only needs to be 3 characters long (USD is the code for U.S. dollars), so don't make it big enough to take 50 characters. It will look unbalanced. Another problem concerns the nature of the list items. If you have 50 items in a list where most items are around 20 characters long but one item is 50 characters long, should you make the combo box big enough to display the longer one? Possibly, but for most occasions your display will be unbalanced again. It is probably best to optimize for the more common length, providing the longer one still has meaning when read in its truncated form. One solution to display the whole length of a truncated item is to use the tooltip facility. When the user places the mouse over an item, a tooltip appears that contains the full text.

One thing you must never do is dynamically resize the combo box to fit a varying length item selection. This will incur alignment problems and it may also add a usability problem because the pull-down button may become a moving target, which then makes it harder for the user to learn its position through directional memory.

9.1.1 The ComboBoxModel interface

abstract interface javax.swing.ComboBoxModel

This interface extends the `ListModel` interface which handles the combo box drop-down list's data. This model separately handles its selected item with two methods, `setSelectedItem()` and `getSelectedItem()`.

9.1.2 The MutableComboBoxModel interface

abstract interface javax.swing.MutableComboBoxModel

This interface extends `ComboBoxModel` and adds four methods to modify the model's contents dynamically: `addElement()`, `insertElementAt()`, `removeElement()`, and `removeElementAt()`.

9.1.3 DefaultComboBoxModel

class javax.swing.DefaultComboBoxModel

This class represents the default model used by `JComboBox`, and it implements `MutableComboBoxModel`. To programmatically select an item, we can call its `setSelectedItem()` method. Calling this method, as well as any of the `MutableComboBoxModel` methods mentioned above, will cause a `ListDataEvent` to be fired. To capture these events we can attach `ListDataListeners` with `DefaultComboBoxModel`'s `addListDataListener()` method. We can also remove these listeners with its `removeListDataListener()` method.

9.1.4 The ListCellRenderer interface

abstract interface javax.swing.ListCellRenderer

This is a simple interface used to define the component to be used as a renderer for the `JComboBox` drop-down list. It declares one method, `getListCellRendererComponent(JList list, Object value, int Index, boolean isSelected, boolean cellHasFocus)`, which is called to return the component used to represent a given combo box element visually. The component returned by this method is not at all interactive, and it is used for display purposes only (it's referred to as a "rubber stamp" in the API documentations).

When a `JComboBox` is in noneditable mode, `-1` will be passed to this method to return the component used to represent the selected item in the main `JComboBox` button. Normally, this component is the same as the component used to display that same element in the drop-down list.

9.1.5 DefaultListCellRenderer

class javax.swing.DefaultListCellRenderer

This is the concrete implementation of the `ListCellRenderer` interface that is used by `JList` by default (and thus by `JComboBox`'s drop-down `JList`). This class extends `JLabel` and its `getListCellRenderer()` method returns a `this` reference. It also renders the given value by setting its text to the `String` returned by the value's `toString()` method (unless the value is an instance of `Icon`, in which case it will be rendered as it would be in any `JLabel`), and it uses `JList` foreground and background colors, depending on whether the given item is selected.

> **NOTE** Unfortunately, there is no easy way to access `JComboBox`'s drop-down `JList`, which prevents us from assigning new foreground and background colors. Ideally, `JComboBox` would provide this communication with its `JList`. We hope to see this functionality in a future version.

A single static `EmptyBorder` instance is used for all cells that do not have the current focus. This border has top, bottom, left, and right spacing of 1, and unfortunately, it cannot be reassigned.

9.1.6 The ComboBoxEditor interface

abstract interface javax.swing.ComboBoxEditor

This interface describes the `JComboBox` editor. The default editor is provided by the only implementing class, `javax.swing.plaf.basic.BasicComboBoxEditor`, but we are certainly not limited to this. The purpose of this interface is to allow us to implement our own custom editor. The `getEditorComponent()` method should be overridden to return the editor component to use. `BasicComboBoxEditor`'s `getEditorComponent()` method returns a `JTextField` that will be used for the currently selected combo box item. Unlike cell renderers, components returned by the `getEditorComponent()` method are fully interactive.

The `setItem()` method is intended to tell the editor which element to edit (this is called when an item is selected from the drop-down list). The `getItem()` method is used to return the object being edited (which is a `String` using the default editor).

`ComboBoxEditor` also declares functionality for attaching and removing `ActionListeners` which are notified when an edit is accepted. In the default editor this occurs when ENTER is pressed while the text field has the focus.

> **NOTE** Unfortunately, Swing does not provide an easily reusable `ComboBoxEditor` implementation, forcing custom implementations to manage all `ActionListener` and item selection/modification functionality from scratch. We hope to see this limitation accounted for in a future Swing release.

9.2 BASIC JCOMBOBOX EXAMPLE

Example 9.1 displays information about popular cars in two symmetrical panels to provide a natural means of comparison. To be realistic, we need to take into account the fact that any car model can come in several trim lines which actually determine the car's characteristics and price. Numerous characteristics of cars are available on the web. For this simple example, we've selected the following two-level data structure:

CAR

Name	Type	Description
Name	String	Model's name
Manufacturer	String	Company manufacturer
Image	Icon	Model's photograph
Trims	Vector	A collection of the model's trims

TRIM

Name	Type	Description
Name	String	Trim's name
MSRP	int	Manufacturer's suggested retail price
Invoice	int	Invoice price
Engine	String	Engine description

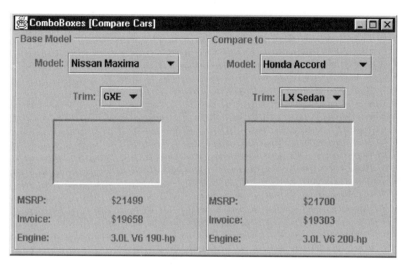

Figure 9.1 Dynamically changeable JComboBoxes **that allow comparison of car model and trim information**

Example 9.1

ComboBox1.java

see \Chapter9\1

```java
import java.awt.*;
import java.awt.event.*;
import java.util.*;

import javax.swing.*;
import javax.swing.border.*;
import javax.swing.event.*;

public class ComboBox1 extends JFrame
{
  public ComboBox1() {
    super("ComboBoxes [Compare Cars]");
    getContentPane().setLayout(new BorderLayout());

    Vector cars = new Vector();
    Car maxima = new Car("Maxima", "Nissan", new ImageIcon(
      "maxima.gif"));
    maxima.addTrim("GXE", 21499, 19658, "3.0L V6 190-hp");
```

One of several Cars with Trims in car list ❶

```
maxima.addTrim("SE",  23499, 21118, "3.0L V6 190-hp");
maxima.addTrim("GLE", 26899, 24174, "3.0L V6 190-hp");
cars.addElement(maxima);

Car accord = new Car("Accord", "Honda", new ImageIcon(
  "accord.gif"));
accord.addTrim("LX Sedan", 21700, 19303, "3.0L V6 200-hp");
accord.addTrim("EX Sedan", 24300, 21614, "3.0L V6 200-hp");
cars.addElement(accord);

Car camry = new Car("Camry", "Toyota", new ImageIcon(
  "camry.gif"));
camry.addTrim("LE V6", 21888, 19163, "3.0L V6 194-hp");
camry.addTrim("XLE V6", 24998, 21884, "3.0L V6 194-hp");
cars.addElement(camry);

Car lumina = new Car("Lumina", "Chevrolet", new ImageIcon(
  "lumina.gif"));
lumina.addTrim("LS", 19920, 18227, "3.1L V6 160-hp");
lumina.addTrim("LTZ", 20360, 18629, "3.8L V6 200-hp");
cars.addElement(lumina);

Car taurus = new Car("Taurus", "Ford", new ImageIcon(
  "taurus.gif"));
taurus.addTrim("LS", 17445, 16110, "3.0L V6 145-hp");
taurus.addTrim("SE", 18445, 16826, "3.0L V6 145-hp");
taurus.addTrim("SHO", 29000, 26220, "3.4L V8 235-hp");
cars.addElement(taurus);

Car passat = new Car("Passat", "Volkswagen", new ImageIcon(
  "passat.gif"));
passat.addTrim("GLS V6", 23190, 20855, "2.8L V6 190-hp");
passat.addTrim("GLX", 26250, 23589, "2.8L V6 190-hp");
cars.addElement(passat);

getContentPane().setLayout(new GridLayout(1, 2, 5, 3));
CarPanel pl = new CarPanel("Base Model", cars);
getContentPane().add(pl);
CarPanel pr = new CarPanel("Compare to", cars);
getContentPane().add(pr);

WindowListener wndCloser = new WindowAdapter() {
  public void windowClosing(WindowEvent e) {
    System.exit(0);
  }
};
addWindowListener(wndCloser);

pl.selectCar(maxima);
pr.selectCar(accord);
setResizable(false);
pack();
setVisible(true);
}

public static void main(String argv[]) {
```

One of several Cars with Trims in car list ❶

```
      new ComboBox1();
    }
  }

class Car
{
  protected String m_name;
  protected String m_manufacturer;
  protected Icon    m_img;
  protected Vector m_trims;

  public Car(String name, String manufacturer, Icon img) {
    m_name = name;
    m_manufacturer = manufacturer;
    m_img = img;
    m_trims = new Vector();
  }

  public void addTrim(String name, int MSRP, int invoice,
    String engine) {
    Trim trim = new Trim(this, name, MSRP, invoice, engine);
    m_trims.addElement(trim);
  }

  public String getName() { return m_name; }

  public String getManufacturer() { return m_manufacturer; }

  public Icon getIcon() { return m_img; }

  public Vector getTrims() { return m_trims; }

  public String toString() { return m_manufacturer+" "+m_name; }
}

class Trim
{
  protected Car     m_parent;
  protected String m_name;
  protected int     m_MSRP;
  protected int     m_invoice;
  protected String m_engine;

  public Trim(Car parent, String name, int MSRP, int invoice,
    String engine) {
    m_parent = parent;
    m_name = name;
    m_MSRP = MSRP;
    m_invoice = invoice;
    m_engine = engine;
  }

  public Car getCar() { return m_parent; }

  public String getName() { return m_name; }

  public int getMSRP() { return m_MSRP; }
```

2 Simple data object with basic car model information, including list of trims

3 Creates new Trim and adds it to Trims list

4 Simple data object with Trim information, including link to owning Car object

```
    public int getInvoice() { return m_invoice; }

    public String getEngine() { return m_engine; }

    public String toString() { return m_name; }
}

class CarPanel extends JPanel
{
    protected JComboBox m_cbCars;
    protected JComboBox m_cbTrims;
    protected JLabel m_lblImg;
    protected JLabel m_lblMSRP;
    protected JLabel m_lblInvoice;
    protected JLabel m_lblEngine;

    public CarPanel(String title, Vector cars) {
        super();
        setLayout(new BoxLayout(this, BoxLayout.Y_AXIS));
        setBorder(new TitledBorder(new EtchedBorder(), title));

        JPanel p = new JPanel();
        p.add(new JLabel("Model:"));
        m_cbCars = new JComboBox(cars);
        ActionListener lst = new ActionListener() {
            public void actionPerformed(ActionEvent e) {
                Car car = (Car)m_cbCars.getSelectedItem();
                if (car != null)
                    showCar(car);
            }
        };
        m_cbCars.addActionListener(lst);
        p.add(m_cbCars);
        add(p);

        p = new JPanel();
        p.add(new JLabel("Trim:"));
        m_cbTrims = new JComboBox();
        lst = new ActionListener() {
            public void actionPerformed(ActionEvent e) {
                Trim trim = (Trim)m_cbTrims.getSelectedItem();
                if (trim != null)
                    showTrim(trim);
            }
        };
        m_cbTrims.addActionListener(lst);
        p.add(m_cbTrims);
        add(p);
        p = new JPanel();
        m_lblImg = new JLabel();
        m_lblImg.setHorizontalAlignment(JLabel.CENTER);
        m_lblImg.setPreferredSize(new Dimension(140, 80));
        m_lblImg.setBorder(new BevelBorder(BevelBorder.LOWERED));
        p.add(m_lblImg);
        add(p);
```

5 GUI components to display Car information

7 Vertical BoxLayout for major components

7 FlowLayout for labels and input fields

6 Combo box to select Car models

7 FlowLayout for labels and input fields

6 Combo box to select Trims

```
      p = new JPanel();
      p.setLayout(new GridLayout(3, 2, 10, 5));
      p.add(new JLabel("MSRP:"));
      m_lblMSRP = new JLabel();
      p.add(m_lblMSRP);

      p.add(new JLabel("Invoice:"));
      m_lblInvoice = new JLabel();
      p.add(m_lblInvoice);

      p.add(new JLabel("Engine:"));
      m_lblEngine = new JLabel();
      p.add(m_lblEngine);
      add(p);
   }

   public void selectCar(Car car) { m_cbCars.setSelectedItem(car); }

   public void showCar(Car car) {
      m_lblImg.setIcon(car.getIcon());
      if (m_cbTrims.getItemCount() > 0)
         m_cbTrims.removeAllItems();
      Vector v = car.getTrims();
      for (int k=0; k<v.size(); k++)
         m_cbTrims.addItem(v.elementAt(k));
      m_cbTrims.grabFocus();
   }

   public void showTrim(Trim trim) {
      m_lblMSRP.setText("$"+trim.getMSRP());
      m_lblInvoice.setText("$"+trim.getInvoice());
      m_lblEngine.setText(trim.getEngine());
   }
}
```

⑧ Labels and values in GridLayout

⑩ For selected Car, updates image and available Trims

⑨ Used by client of this class to select a particular Car

⑪ Bad to remove items from empty combo box

⑫ Updates value labels for selected Car and Trim

9.2.1   Understanding the code

Class ComboBox1

❶ The ComboBox1 class extends JFrame to implement the frame container for this example. It has no instance variables. The constructor creates a data collection with the car information as listed above. A collection of cars is stored in Vector cars, and each car, in turn, receives one or more Trim instances. Other than this, the ComboBox1 constructor doesn't do much. It creates two instances of CarPanel (see below) and arranges them in a GridLayout. These panels are used to select and display car information. Finally, two cars are initially selected in both panels.

Class Car

❷ The Car class is a typical data object that encapsulates three data fields which are listed at the beginning of this section: car name, manufacturer, and image. In addition, it holds the m_trims vector that stores a collection of Trim instances.

❸ The addTrim() method creates a new Trim instance and adds it to the m_trims vector. The rest of this class implements typical getXX() methods to allow access to the protected data fields.

Class Trim

④ The `Trim` class encapsulates four data fields, which are listed at the beginning of this section: trim name, suggested retail price, invoice price, and engine type. In addition, it holds a reference to the parent `Car` instance. The rest of this class implements typical `getXX()` methods to allow access to the `protected` data fields.

Class CarPanel

The `CarPanel` class extends `JPanel` to provide the GUI framework for displaying car information. Six components are declared as instance variables:

⑤
- `JComboBox m_cbCars`: Used to select a car model.
- `JComboBox m_cbTrims`: Used to select a car trim of the selected model.
- `JLabel m_lblImg`: Used to display the model's image.
- `JLabel m_lblMSRP`: Used to display the MSRP.
- `JLabel m_lblInvoice`: Used to display the invoice price.
- `JLabel m_lblEngine`: Used to display the engine description.

⑥ Two combo boxes are used to select cars and trims respectively. Note that `Car` and `Trim` data objects are used to populate these combo boxes, so the actual displayed text is determined by their `toString()` methods. Both combo boxes receive `ActionListeners` to handle item selection. When a `Car` item is selected, this triggers a call to the `showCar()` method described below. Similarly, selecting a `Trim` item triggers a call to the `showTrim()` method.

⑦ The rest of the `CarPanel` constructor builds `JLabels` to display a car's image and trim data. Notice how layouts are used in this example. A y-oriented `BoxLayout` creates a vertical axis used to align and position all components. The combo boxes and supplementary labels are encapsulated in horizontal `JPanels`. `JLabel m_lblImg` receives a custom preferred size to **⑧** reserve enough space for the photo image. This label is encapsulated in a panel (with its default `FlowLayout`) to ensure that this component will be centered over the parent container's space. The rest of `CarPanel` is occupied by six labels, which are hosted by a 3x2 `GridLayout`.

⑨ The `selectCar()` method allows us to select a car programmatically from outside this class. It invokes the `setSelectedItem()` method on the `m_cbCars` combo box. This call will trigger an `ActionEvent` which will be captured by the proper listener, resulting in a `showCar()` call.

⑩
⑪ The `showCar()` method updates the car image, and it updates the `m_cbTrims` combo box to display the corresponding trims of the selected model. The `(getItemCount() > 0)` condition is necessary because Swing throws an exception if `removeAllItems()` is invoked on an empty `JComboBox`. Finally, focus is transferred to the `m_cbTrims` component.

⑫ The `showTrim()` method updates the contents of the labels that display trim information: MSRP, invoice price, and engine type.

9.2.2 Running the code

Figure 9.1 shows the `ComboBox1` application that displays two cars simultaneously for comparison. All the initial information is displayed correctly. Try experimenting with various selections and notice how the combo box contents change dynamically.

GUIDELINE

Symmetrical layout In example 9.1, the design avoids the problem of having to align the different length combo boxes by using a symmetrical layout. Overall, the window has a good balance and it uses white space well; so do each of the bordered panes used for individual car selections.

9.3 CUSTOM MODEL AND RENDERER

Ambitious Swing developers may want to provide custom rendering in combo boxes to display structured data in the drop-down list. Different levels of structure can be identified by differing left margins and icons; this is also how it's done in trees, which we will study in chapter 17. Such complex combo boxes can enhance functionality and provide a more sophisticated appearance.

In this section we will show how to merge the model and trim combo boxes from the previous section into a single combo box. To differentiate between model and trim items in the drop-down list, we can use different left margins and different icons for each. Our list should look something like this:

```
Nissan Maxima
    GXE
    SE
    GLE
```

We also need to prevent the user from selecting models (such as "Nissan Maxima" above), since they do not provide complete information about a specific car, and they only serve as separators between sets of trims.

NOTE The hierarchical list organization shown here can easily be extended for use in a JList, and it can handle an arbitrary number of levels. We only use two levels in example 9.2, but the design does not limit us to this.

Example 9.2

ComboBox2.java

see \Chapter9\2

```java
// Unchanged code from example 9.1

class CarPanel extends JPanel
{
  protected JComboBox m_cbCars;
  protected JLabel m_txtModel;
  protected JLabel m_lblImg;
  protected JLabel m_lblMSRP;
  protected JLabel m_lblInvoice;
  protected JLabel m_lblEngine;

  public CarPanel(String title, Vector cars) {
    super();
    setLayout(new BoxLayout(this, BoxLayout.Y_AXIS));
```

❶ Label to show Car model name

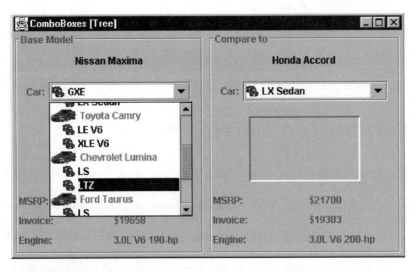

Figure 9.2 A `JComboBox` with a custom model and a custom hierarchical rendering scheme

```
setBorder(new TitledBorder(new EtchedBorder(), title));

JPanel p = new JPanel();
m_txtModel = new JLabel("");
m_txtModel.setForeground(Color.black);
p.add(m_txtModel);
add(p);

p = new JPanel();
p.add(new JLabel("Car:"));
CarComboBoxModel model = new CarComboBoxModel(cars);
m_cbCars = new JComboBox(model);
m_cbCars.setRenderer(new IconComboRenderer());
ActionListener lst = new ActionListener() {
  public void actionPerformed(ActionEvent e) {
    ListData data = (ListData)m_cbCars.getSelectedItem();
    Object obj = data.getObject();
    if (obj instanceof Trim)
      showTrim((Trim)obj);
  }
};
m_cbCars.addActionListener(lst);
p.add(m_cbCars);
add(p);

//Unchanged code from example 9.1
}
public synchronized void selectCar(Car car) {
  for (int k=0; k < m_cbCars.getItemCount(); k++) {
    ListData obj = (ListData)m_cbCars.getItemAt(k);
```

2 Variable length label will always be centered

3 m_cbCars will show model names along with icons

4 Both Car and Trim instances, although only Trims can be selected

5 Finds ListData object in combo box whose Car object is equal to the parameter, and selects that one

```
          if (obj.getObject() == car) {
            m_cbCars.setSelectedItem(obj);
            break;
          }
        }
    }

  public synchronized void showTrim(Trim trim) {
    Car car = trim.getCar();
    m_txtModel.setText(car.toString());
    m_lblImg.setIcon(car.getIcon());
    m_lblMSRP.setText("$" + trim.getMSRP());
    m_lblInvoice.setText("$" + trim.getInvoice());
    m_lblEngine.setText(trim.getEngine());
  }
}

class ListData
{
  protected Icon      m_icon;
  protected int       m_index;
  protected boolean   m_selectable;
  protected Object    m_data;

  public ListData(Icon icon, int index, boolean selectable,
   Object data) {
    m_icon = icon;
    m_index = index;
    m_selectable = selectable;
    m_data = data;
  }

  public Icon getIcon() { return m_icon; }

  public int getIndex() { return m_index; }

  public boolean isSelectable() { return m_selectable; }

  public Object getObject() { return m_data; }

  public String toString() { return m_data.toString(); }
}

class CarComboBoxModel extends DefaultComboBoxModel
{
  public static final ImageIcon ICON_CAR =
    new ImageIcon("car.gif");
  public static final ImageIcon ICON_TRIM =
    new ImageIcon("trim.gif");

  public CarComboBoxModel(Vector cars) {
    for (int k=0; k<cars.size(); k++) {
      Car car = (Car)cars.elementAt(k);
      addElement(new ListData(ICON_CAR, 0, false, car));

      Vector v = car.getTrims();
      for (int i=0; i < v.size(); i++) {
```

5 Finds ListData object in combo box whose Car object is equal to the parameter, and selects that one

6 Now displays Model name in addition to Trim name

7 Encapsulates combo box data and rendering information

8 Data model for combo box; holds icons for Car and Trim

8 Adds list element for Car; not selectable

```
        Trim trim = (Trim)v.elementAt(i);
        addElement(new ListData(ICON_TRIM, 1, true, trim));
      }
    }
  }
```

8 Adds list element for Trim; selectable

```
  // This method only allows trims to be selected
  public void setSelectedItem(Object item) {
    if (item instanceof ListData) {
      ListData ldata = (ListData)item;
      if (!ldata.isSelectable()) {
        Object newItem = null;
        int index = getIndexOf(item);
        for (int k = index + 1; k < getSize(); k++) {
          Object item1 = getElementAt(k);
          if (item1 instanceof ListData) {
            ListData ldata1 = (ListData)item1;
            if (!ldata1.isSelectable())
              continue;
          }
          newItem = item1;
          break;
        }
        if (newItem==null)
          return;          // Selection failed
        item = newItem;
      }
    }
    super.setSelectedItem(item);
  }
}
```

9 If not selectable, try to move selection to next selectable item (a Trim object)

```
class IconComboRenderer extends JLabel implements ListCellRenderer
{
  public static final int OFFSET = 16;

  protected Color m_textSelectionColor = Color.white;
  protected Color m_textNonSelectionColor = Color.black;
  protected Color m_textNonselectableColor = Color.gray;
  protected Color m_bkSelectionColor = new Color(0, 0, 128);
  protected Color m_bkNonSelectionColor = Color.white;
  protected Color m_borderSelectionColor = Color.yellow;

  protected Color  m_textColor;
  protected Color  m_bkColor;

  protected boolean m_hasFocus;
  protected Border[] m_borders;

  public IconComboRenderer() {
    super();
    m_textColor = m_textNonSelectionColor;
    m_bkColor = m_bkNonSelectionColor;
    m_borders = new Border[20];
    for (int k=0; k < m_borders.length; k++)
      m_borders[k] = new EmptyBorder(0, OFFSET * k, 0, 0);
```

10 Acts as custom combo box list item renderer; shows text with icon

11 Creates set of stepped EmptyBorders to provide "indents" for list items

```
    setOpaque(false);
}

public Component getListCellRendererComponent(JList list,
 Object obj, int row, boolean sel, boolean hasFocus) {
  if (obj == null)
    return this;
  setText(obj.toString());
  boolean selectable = true;
  if (obj instanceof ListData) {
    ListData ldata = (ListData)obj;
    selectable = ldata.isSelectable();
    setIcon(ldata.getIcon());
    int index = 0;
    if (row >= 0)     // No offset for editor (row=-1)
      index = ldata.getIndex();
    Border b = (index < m_borders.length ? m_borders[index] :
      new EmptyBorder(0, OFFSET * index, 0, 0));
    setBorder(b);
  }
  else
    setIcon(null);

  setFont(list.getFont());
  m_textColor = (sel ? m_textSelectionColor :
    (selectable ? m_textNonSelectionColor :
    m_textNonselectableColor));
  m_bkColor = (sel ? m_bkSelectionColor :
    m_bkNonSelectionColor);
  m_hasFocus = hasFocus;
  return this;
}

public void paint (Graphics g) {
  Icon icon = getIcon();
  Border b = getBorder();

  g.setColor(m_bkNonSelectionColor);
  g.fillRect(0, 0, getWidth(), getHeight());

  g.setColor(m_bkColor);
  int offset = 0;
  if(icon != null && getText() != null) {
    Insets ins = getInsets();
    offset = ins.left + icon.getIconWidth() + getIconTextGap();
  }
  g.fillRect(offset, 0, getWidth() - 1 - offset,
    getHeight() - 1);

  if (m_hasFocus) {
    g.setColor(m_borderSelectionColor);
    g.drawRect(offset, 0, getWidth()-1-offset, getHeight()-1);
  }

  setForeground(m_textColor);
```

12 Use matching EmptyBorder from list

13 Draws background excluding icon, and draws focus highlight

```
        setBackground(m_bkColor);
        super.paint(g);
    }
}
```

9.3.1 Understanding the code

Class CarPanel

1 The ComboBox2 (formerly ComboBox1), Car, and Trim classes remain unchanged in this example, so we'll start from the CarPanel class. Compared to example 9.1, we've removed combo box m_cbTrims and added JLabel m_txtModel, which is used to display the current model's name. When the combo box pop-up is hidden, the user can see only the selected trim, so we need to display the corresponding model name separately. Curiously, the constructor of the CarPanel class places this label component in its own JPanel (using its default FlowLayout) to ensure its location in the center of the base panel.

2   **NOTE**   The reason for this is that JLabel m_txtModel has a variable length, and the Box-Layout which manages CarPanel cannot dynamically center this component correctly. Placing this label in a FlowLayout panel will make sure it's always centered.

3 The single combo box, m_cbCars, has a bit in common with the component of the same name in example 9.1. First, it receives a custom model, an instance of the CarComboBoxModel class, which will be described below. It also receives a custom renderer, an instance of the IconCombo-Renderer class, which is also described below.

4 The combo box is populated by both Car and Trim instances encapsulated in ListData objects (see below). This requires some changes in the actionPerformed() method which handles combo box selection. We first extract the data object from the selected ListData instance by calling the getObject() method. If this call returns a Trim object (as it should, since Cars cannot be selected), we call the showTrim() method to display the selected data.

5 The selectCar() method has been modified. As we mentioned above, our combo box now holds ListData objects, so we cannot pass a Car object as a parameter to the setSelected-Item() method. Instead, we have to examine, in turn, all items in the combo box, cast them to ListData objects, and verify that the encapsulated data object is equal to the given Car instance.

6 The showTrim() method now displays the model data as well as the trim data. To do this we obtain a parent Car instance for a given Trim and display the model's name and icon.

Class ListData

7 The ListData class encapsulates the data object to be rendered in the combo box and adds new attributes for our rendering needs.

These are the instance variables:

- Icon m_icon: The icon associated with the data object.
- int m_index: The item's index which determines the left margin (the hierarchical level, for example).
- boolean m_selectable: The flag indicating that this item can be selected.
- Object m_data: The encapsulated data object.

All variables are assigned parameters that have been passed to the constructor. The rest of the `ListData` class contains four `getXX()` methods and a `toString()` method, which all delegate calls to the `m_data` object.

Class CarComboBoxModel

(8) This class extends `DefaultComboBoxModel` to serve as a data model for our combo box . It first creates two static `ImageIcons` to represent the model and the trim. The constructor takes a `Vector` of `Car` instances and converts them and their trims into a linear sequence of `ListData` objects. Each `Car` object is encapsulated in a `ListData` instance with an `ICON_CAR` icon, the index set to `0`, and the `m_selectable` flag set to `false`. Each `Trim` object is encapsulated in a `ListData` instance with an `ICON_TRIM` icon, the index set to `1`, and the `m_selectable` flag set to `true`.

(9) These manipulations could have been done without implementing a custom `ComboBoxModel`, of course. The real reason we implement a custom model here is to override the `setSelectedItem()` method to control item selection in the combo box. As we learned above, only `ListData` instances with the `m_selectable` flag set to `true` should be selectable. To achieve this goal, the overridden `setSelectedItem()` method casts the selected object to a `ListData` instance and examines its selection property using `isSelectable()`.

If `isSelectable()` returns `false`, a special action needs to be handled to move the selection to the first item following this item for which `isSelectable()` returns `true`. If no such item is found, our `setSelectedItem()` method returns and the selection in the combo box remains unchanged. Otherwise, the `item` variable receives a new value which is finally passed to the `setSelectedItem()` implementation of the superclass `DefaultComboBoxModel`.

> **NOTE** You may notice that the `selectCar()` method discussed above selects a `Car` instance which cannot be selected. This internally triggers a call to `setSelectedItem()` of the combo box model, which shifts the selection to the first available `Trim` item. You can verify this when running the example.

Class IconComboRenderer

(10) This class extends `JLabel` and implements the `ListCellRenderer` interface to serve as a custom combo box renderer.

Class variable:

- `int OFFSET`: The offset, in pixels, to use for the left trim margin.

Here are the instance variables:

- `Color m_textColor`: The current text color.
- `Color m_bkColor`: The current background color.
- `boolean m_hasFocus`: The flag that indicates whether this item has the focus.
- `Border[] m_borders`: An array of borders used for this component.

(11) The constructor of the `IconComboRenderer` class initializes these variables. `EmptyBorders` are used to provide left margins while rendering components of the drop-down list. To avoid generating numerous temporary objects, an array of 20 `Borders` is prepared with increasing left offsets corresponding to the array index (incremented by `OFFSET`). This provides us with a set of different borders to use for white space in representing data at 20 distinct hierarchical levels.

NOTE   Even though we only use two levels in this example, `IconComboRenderer` has been designed for maximum reusability. We've designed `getListCellRenderer-Component()` (see below) to create a new `EmptyBorder` in the event that more than 20 levels are used.

⓬ The `getListCellRendererComponent()` method is called prior to the painting of each cell in the drop-down list. We first set this component's text to that of the given object (which is passed as a parameter). Then, if the object is an instance of `ListData`, we set the icon and left margin by using the appropriate `EmptyBorder` from the previously prepared array (which is based on the given `ListData`'s `m_index` property). A call to this method with `row=-1` will be invoked prior to the rendering of the combo box button, which is the part of the combo box that is always visible (see section 9.1). In this case we don't need to use any border offset. Offset only makes sense when there are hierarchical differences between items in the list, not when an item is rendered alone.

The rest of the `getListCellRendererComponent()` method determines the background and foreground colors to use, based on whether an item is selected and selectable, and stores them in instance variables to be used within the `paint()` method. Non-selectable items receive their own foreground to distinguish them from selectable items.

⓭ The `paint()` method performs a bit of rendering before invoking the superclass implementation. It fills the background with the stored `m_bkColor`, excluding the icon's area (the left margin is already taken into account by the component's `Border`). It also draws a border-like rectangle if the component currently has the focus. This method then ends with a call to its superclass's `paint()` method, which takes responsibility for painting the label text and icon.

9.3.2   Running the code

Figure 9.2 shows our hierarchical drop-down list in action. Note that models and trim lines can be easily differentiated because of the varying icons and offsets. In addition, models have a gray foreground to imply that they cannot be selected.

This implementation is more user-friendly than example 9.1 because it displays all available data in a single drop-down list. Try selecting different trims and notice how this changes data for both the model and trim information labels. Try selecting a model and notice that it will result in the first trim of that model being selected instead.

GUIDELINE

Improved usability   From a usability perspective, the solution in figure 9.2 is an improvement over the one presented in figure 9.1. By using a combo box with a hierarchical data model, the designer has reduced the data entry to a single selection and has presented the information in an accessible and logical manner which also produces a visually cleaner result.

Further improvements could be made here by sorting the hierarchical data. In this example, it would seem appropriate to sort in a two-tiered fashion: alphabetically by manufacturer, and alphabetically by model. Thus Toyota would come after Ford and Toyota Corolla would come after Toyota Camry.

This is an excellent example of how a programmer can improve UI design and usability to make the program easier for the user to use.

9.4 COMBO BOXES WITH MEMORY

In some situations, you may want to use editable combo boxes which keep a historical list of choices for future reuse. This conveniently allows the user to select a previous choice rather than typing the same text over and over. A typical example of an editable combo box with memory is found in Find/Replace dialogs in many modern applications. Another example, familiar to almost every modern computer user, is provided in many Internet browsers which use an editable URL combo-box-with-history mechanism. These combo boxes accumulate typed addresses so the user can easily return to any previously visited site by selecting it from the drop-down list instead of manually typing it in again.

Example 9.3 shows how to create a simple browser application using an editable combo box with memory. It uses the serialization mechanism to save data between program sessions, and the `JEditorPane` component (which is described in more detail in chapters 11 and 19) to display non-editable HTML files.

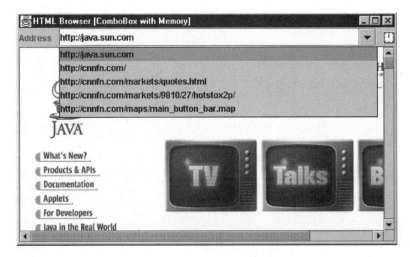

Figure 9.3   A `JComboBox` with memory of previously visited URLs

Example 9.3

Browser.java

see \Chapter9\3

```
import java.awt.*;
import java.awt.event.*;
import java.io.*;
import java.net.*;

import javax.swing.*;
import javax.swing.event.*;
import javax.swing.text.*;
import javax.swing.text.html.*;
```

```java
public class Browser extends JFrame
{
  protected JEditorPane m_browser;
  protected MemComboBox m_locator;
  protected AnimatedLabel m_runner;

  public Browser() {
    super("HTML Browser [ComboBox with Memory]");
    setSize(500, 300);

    JPanel p = new JPanel();
    p.setLayout(new BoxLayout(p, BoxLayout.X_AXIS));
    p.add(new JLabel("Address"));
    p.add(Box.createRigidArea(new Dimension(10, 1)));

    m_locator = new MemComboBox();
    m_locator.load("addresses.dat");
    BrowserListener lst = new BrowserListener();
    m_locator.addActionListener(lst);

    p.add(m_locator);
    p.add(Box.createRigidArea(new Dimension(10, 1)));

    m_runner = new AnimatedLabel("clock", 8);
    p.add(m_runner);
    getContentPane().add(p, BorderLayout.NORTH);

    m_browser = new JEditorPane();
    m_browser.setEditable(false);
    m_browser.addHyperlinkListener(lst);

    JScrollPane sp = new JScrollPane();
    sp.getViewport().add(m_browser);
    getContentPane().add(sp, BorderLayout.CENTER);

    WindowListener wndCloser = new WindowAdapter() {
      public void windowClosing(WindowEvent e) {
        m_locator.save("addresses.dat");
        System.exit(0);
      }
    };
    addWindowListener(wndCloser);

    setVisible(true);
    m_locator.grabFocus();
  }

  class BrowserListener implements ActionListener, HyperlinkListener
  {
    public void actionPerformed(ActionEvent evt) {
      String sUrl = (String)m_locator.getSelectedItem();
      if (sUrl == null || sUrl.length() == 0 ||
       m_runner.getRunning())
        return;
      BrowserLoader loader = new BrowserLoader(sUrl);
      loader.start();
    }
```

❶ Creates custom combo box and loads it with some history

❷ Saves history list

❸ Listens for selected URLs, either from the combo box or from a hyperlink

```
      public void hyperlinkUpdate(HyperlinkEvent e) {
        URL url = e.getURL();
        if (url == null || m_runner.getRunning())
          return;
        BrowserLoader loader = new BrowserLoader(url.toString());
        loader.start();
      }
    }
    class BrowserLoader extends Thread
    {
      protected String m_sUrl;

      public BrowserLoader(String sUrl) { m_sUrl = sUrl; }

      public void run() {
        setCursor(Cursor.getPredefinedCursor(Cursor.WAIT_CURSOR));
        m_runner.setRunning(true);

        try {
          URL source = new URL(m_sUrl);
          m_browser.setPage(source);
          m_locator.add(m_sUrl);
        }
        catch (Exception e) {
          JOptionPane.showMessageDialog(Browser.this,
            "Error: "+e.toString(),
            "Warning", JOptionPane.WARNING_MESSAGE);
        }
        m_runner.setRunning(false);
        setCursor(Cursor.getPredefinedCursor(Cursor.DEFAULT_CURSOR));
      }
    }
    public static void main(String argv[]) { new Browser(); }
  }
  class MemComboBox extends JComboBox
  {
    public static final int MAX_MEM_LEN = 30;

    public MemComboBox() {
      super();
      setEditable(true);
    }

    public void add(String item) {
      removeItem(item);
      insertItemAt(item, 0);
      setSelectedItem(item);
      if (getItemCount() > MAX_MEM_LEN)
        removeItemAt(getItemCount()-1);
    }

    public void load(String fName) {
      try {
        if (getItemCount() > 0)
          removeAllItems();
```

4 Background thread to load documents from URLs into the browser

5 Retrieves, parses, and renders web page

6 JComboBox subclass which provides history mechanism

7 Adds to history list

8 Loads history list from file, using object serialization

```
          File f = new File(fName);
          if (!f.exists())
            return;
          FileInputStream fStream =
            new FileInputStream(f);
          ObjectInput  stream  =
            new  ObjectInputStream(fStream);
          Object obj = stream.readObject();
          if (obj instanceof ComboBoxModel)
            setModel((ComboBoxModel)obj);
          stream.close();
          fStream.close();
        }
      catch (Exception e) {
        e.printStackTrace();
        System.err.println("Serialization error: "+e.toString());
      }
    }

    public void save(String fName) {
      try {
        FileOutputStream fStream =
          new FileOutputStream(fName);
        ObjectOutput  stream  =
          new  ObjectOutputStream(fStream);
        stream.writeObject(getModel());
        stream.flush();
        stream.close();
        fStream.close();
      }
      catch (Exception e) {
        e.printStackTrace();
        System.err.println("Serialization error: "+e.toString());
      }
    }
  }

class AnimatedLabel extends JLabel implements Runnable
{
  protected Icon[] m_icons;
  protected int m_index = 0;
  protected boolean m_isRunning;

  public AnimatedLabel(String gifName, int numGifs) {
    m_icons = new Icon[numGifs];
    for (int k=0; k<numGifs; k++)
      m_icons[k] = new ImageIcon(gifName+k+".gif");
    setIcon(m_icons[0]);

    Thread tr = new Thread(this);
    tr.setPriority(Thread.MAX_PRIORITY);
    tr.start();
  }

  public void setRunning(boolean isRunning) {
```

8 Stores history list to file, reverse of load() method

9 Implements label which presents a "slide show" of several icons in sequence

```
      m_isRunning = isRunning;
    }
    public boolean getRunning() { return m_isRunning; }
    public void run() {
      while(true) {
        if (m_isRunning) {
          m_index++;
          if (m_index >= m_icons.length)
            m_index = 0;
          setIcon(m_icons[m_index]);
          Graphics g = getGraphics();
          m_icons[m_index].paintIcon(this, g, 0, 0);
        }
        else {
          if (m_index > 0) {
            m_index = 0;
            setIcon(m_icons[0]);
          }
        }
        try { Thread.sleep(500); } catch(Exception ex) {}
      }
    }
  }
```

⑩ In background thread, displays each icon in sequence, sleeping between each one

9.4.1 Understanding the code

Class Browser

This class extends JFrame to implement the frame container for our browser. Here are the instance variables:

- JEditorPane m_browser: The text component to parse and render HTML files.
- MemComboBox m_locator: The combo box to enter/select a URL address.
- AnimatedLabel m_runner: The label that contains an icon which becomes animated when the browser requests a URL.

❶ The constructor creates the custom combo box, m_locator, and an associated label. Then it creates the m_runner icon and places all three components in the northern region of our frame's content pane. JEditorPane m_browser is created and placed in a JScrollPane to provide scrolling capabilities. This is then added to the center of the content pane.

❷ A WindowListener, which has been used in many previous examples to close the frame and terminate execution, receives an additional function: it invokes our custom save() method (see below) on our combo box component before destroying the frame. This saves the list of visited URLs that have been entered as a file called **addresses.dat** in the current running directory.

Class Browser.BrowserListener

❸ This inner class implements both the ActionListener and HyperlinkListener interfaces to manage navigation to HTML pages. The actionPerformed() method is invoked when the user selects a new item in the combo box. It verifies that the selection is valid and that the browser is not currently busy (requesting a URL, for example). If these checks are passed, it then creates and starts a new BrowserLoader instance (see below) for the specified address.

The hyperlinkUpdate() method is invoked when the user clicks a hyperlink in the currently loaded web page. This method also determines the selected URL address and starts a new BrowserLoader to load it.

Class Browser.BrowserLoader

4 This inner class extends Thread to load web pages into our JEditorPane component. It takes a URL address parameter in the constructor and stores it in an instance variable. The run() method sets the mouse cursor to an hourglass (Cursor.WAIT_CURSOR) and starts the animated icon to indicate that the browser is busy.

The core functionality of this thread is enclosed in its try/catch block. If an exception occurs during the processing of the requested URL, it is displayed in a simple JOptionPane dialog message box (we will discuss JOptionPane in chapter 14).

5 The actual job of retrieving, parsing, and rendering the web page is hidden in a single call to the setPage() method. So why do we need to create this separate thread instead of making that simple call in BrowserListener, for example? As we discussed in chapter 2, by creating separate threads to do potentially time-consuming operations, we avoid clogging up the event-dispatching thread.

Class MemComboBox

6 This class extends JComboBox to add a history mechanism. The constructor simply sets its editable property to true.

7 The add() method adds a new text string to the beginning of the list. If this item is already present in the list, it is removed from the old position. If the resulting list is longer than the predefined maximum length, the last item in the list is truncated.

8 The load() method loads a previously stored ComboBoxModel from the **addresses.dat** file using the serialization mechanism. The significant portion of this method reads an object from an ObjectInputStream and sets it as the ComboBoxModel. Any possible exceptions are printed to the standard output.

Similarly, the save() method serializes our combo box's ComboBoxModel. Any possible exceptions are, again, printed to standard output.

Class AnimatedLabel

9 Surprisingly, Swing does not provide any special support for animated components, so we have to create our own component for this purpose. This provides us with an interesting example of using threads in Java.

> **NOTE** Animated GIFs are fully supported by ImageIcon (see chapter 5) but we want complete control over each animated frame in this example.

AnimatedLabel extends JLabel and implements the Runnable interface. Here are the instance variables:

- Icon[] m_icons: An array of images to be used for animation.
- int m_index: The index of the current image.
- boolean m_isRunning: The flag that indicates whether the animation is running.

The constructor takes a common name of a series of GIF files that contain images for animation, and the number of those files. These images are loaded and stored in an array. When all images are loaded, a thread with maximum priority is created and started to run this Runnable instance.

The setRunning() and getRunning() methods simply manage the m_isRunning flag.

10 In the run() method, we cyclically increment the m_index variable and draw an image from the m_icons array with the corresponding index, exactly as one would expect from an animated image. This is done only when the m_isRunning flag is set to true. Otherwise, the image with index 0 is displayed. After an image is painted, AnimatedLabel yields control to other threads and sleeps for 500 ms.

The interesting thing about this component is that it runs parallel with other threads which do not necessarily yield control explicitly. In our case, the concurrent BrowserLoader thread spends the main part of its time inside the setPage() method, and our animated icon runs in a separate thread that signals to the user that something is going on. This is made possible because this animated component is running in the thread with the maximum priority. Of course, we should use such thread priority with caution. In our case it is appropriate since our thread consumes only a small amount of the processor's time and it *does* yield control to the lesser-priority threads when it sleeps.

NOTE   As a good exercise, try using threads with normal priority or Swing's Timer component in this example. You will find that this doesn't work as expected: the animated icon does not show any animation while the browser is running.

9.4.2   Running the code

Figure 9.3 shows the Browser application displaying a web page. The animated icon comes to life when the browser requests a URL. Notice how the combo box is populated with URL addresses as we navigate to different web pages. Now quit the application and restart it. Notice that our addresses have been saved and restored by serializing the combo box model, as we discussed above.

NOTE   HTML rendering functionality is not yet matured. Do not be surprised if your favorite web page looks significantly different in our Swing-based browser. As a matter of fact, even the JavaSoft home page throws several exceptions while being displayed in this Swing component. (These exceptions occur outside our code, during the JEditorPane rendering—this is why they are not caught and handled by our code.)

GUIDELINE

Memory combo box usage   The example given here is a good place to use a combo box with memory. However, a memory combo box will not always be appropriate. Remember the advice that the usability of an unsorted combo box tends to degrade rapidly as the number of items grows. Therefore, it is sensible to use this technique where the likelihood of more than 20 entries (to pick a good number) is very small.

If you have a domain problem which is likely to need a larger number of memory items, but you still want to use a memory combo box, consider adding a sorting algorithm. Rather than sorting the most recent item first, you sort into a more meaningful index, such as alphabetical order. Usability will improve and you could easily populate the list with up to 200 or 300 items.

9.5 CUSTOM EDITING

In this section, we will discuss a custom editing feature to make example 9.3 even more convenient and similar to modern browser applications. We will attach a key event listener to our combo box's editor and search for previously visited URLs with matching beginning strings. If a match occurs, the remainder of that URL is displayed in the editor, and we can accept the suggestion by pressing ENTER. Most modern browsers also provide this functionality.

In example 9.4, the caret position will remain unchanged, as will the text on the left side of the caret (this is the text the user typed). The text on the right side of the caret represents the browser's suggestion, which may or may not correspond to the user's intentions. To avoid distracting the user, this portion of the text is highlighted, so any newly typed character will replace that suggested text.

Figure 9.4 A `JComboBox` **with a custom editor that suggests previously visited URLs**

Example 9.4

Browser.java

see\Chapter9\4

```
public class Browser extends JFrame
{
  // Unchanged code from example 9.3

  public Browser() {
    super("HTML Browser [Advanced Editor]");

    // Unchanged code from example 9.3

    MemComboAgent agent = new MemComboAgent(m_locator);
```

1 **Creates KeyAdapter which attaches itself to combo box**

```
    // Unchanged code from example 9.3
  }
  // Unchanged code from example 9.3
}

class MemComboAgent extends KeyAdapter
{
  protected JComboBox   m_comboBox;
  protected JTextField  m_editor;

  public MemComboAgent(JComboBox comboBox) {
    m_comboBox = comboBox;
    m_editor = (JTextField)comboBox.getEditor().
      getEditorComponent();
    m_editor.addKeyListener(this);
  }

  public void keyReleased(KeyEvent e) {
    char ch = e.getKeyChar();
    if (ch == KeyEvent.CHAR_UNDEFINED || Character.isISOControl(ch))
      return;
    int pos = m_editor.getCaretPosition();
    String str = m_editor.getText();
    if (str.length() == 0)
      return;

    for (int k=0; k<m_comboBox.getItemCount(); k++) {
      String item = m_comboBox.getItemAt(k).toString();
      if (item.startsWith(str)) {
        m_editor.setText(item);
        m_editor.setCaretPosition(item.length());
        m_editor.moveCaretPosition(pos);
        break;
      }
    }
  }
}
```

2 Find list item that text begins with

9.5.1   Understanding the code

Class Browser

1 This class has only one change in comparison with the previous example: it creates an instance of our custom MemComboAgent class and passes it a reference to our m_locator combo box.

Class MemComboAgent

This class extends KeyAdapter to listen for keyboard activity. It takes a reference to a JComboBox component and stores it in an instance variable along with the JTextField component that is used as that combo box's editor. Finally, a MemComboAgent object adds itself to that editor as a KeyListener to be notified of all keyboard input that is passed to the editor component.

2 The keyReleased() method is the only method we implement. This method first retrieves the pressed characters and verifies that they are not control characters. We also retrieve the contents of the text field and check that it is not empty to avoid annoying the user with suggestions in an empty field. Note that when this method is invoked, the pressed key will already have been included in this text.

This method then walks through the list of combo box items and searches for an item starting with the combo box editor text. If such an item is found, it is set as the combo box editor's text. Then we place the caret at the end of that string using setCaretPosition(), and move it back to its initial position, going backward, using the moveCaretPosition() method. This method places the caret in its original position and highlights all the text to its right.

NOTE   A more sophisticated realization of this idea may include the separate processing of the URL protocol and host, as well as using threads for smooth execution.

9.5.2   Running the code

Figure 9.4 shows our custom combo box's editor displaying a portion of a URL address taken from its list. Try entering some new addresses and browsing to them. After some experimentation, try typing in an address that you have already visited with this application. Notice that the enhanced combo box suggests the remainder of this address from its pull-down list. Press ENTER as soon as an address matches your intended selection to avoid typing the complete URL.

C H A P T E R   1 0

List boxes

10.1   LIST API OVERVIEW

class javax.swing.JList

This class represents a basic GUI component that allows the selection of one or more items from a list of choices. JList has two models: ListModel, which handles data in the list, and ListSelectionModel, which handles item selection (three different selection modes are supported; we will discuss them below). JList also supports custom rendering, as we learned in the last chapter, through the implementation of the ListCellRenderer interface. We can use the existing default implementation of ListCellRenderer (DefaultListCellRenderer) or create our own according to our particular needs, as we will see later in this chapter. Unless we use a custom renderer, the default renderer will display each element as a String defined by that object's toString() method. The only exceptions to this are Icon implementations which will be rendered as they would be in any JLabel. Keep in mind that a ListCellRenderer returns a Component, but that component is not interactive and is only used for display purposes (it acts as a "rubber stamp"). For instance, if a JCheckBox is used as a renderer, we will not be able to check and uncheck it. Unlike JComboBox, however, JList does not support editing of any sort.

255

A number of constructors are available to create a `JList` component. We can use the default constructor or pass list data to a constructor as a one-dimensional array, as a `Vector`, or as an implementation of the `ListModel` interface. The last variant provides maximum control over a list's properties and appearance. We can also assign data to a `JList` using either the `setModel()` method or one of the overloaded `setListData()` methods.

`JList` does not provide direct access to its elements, and we must access its `ListModel` to gain access to this data. `JList` does, however, provide direct access to its selection data by implementing all `ListSelectionModel` methods and delegating their traffic to the actual `ListSelectionModel` instance. To avoid repetition, we will discuss selection functionality in our overview of `ListSelectionModel`.

`JList` maintains selection foreground and background colors (which are assigned by its UI delegate when installed), and the default cell renderer, `DefaultListCellRenderer`, will use these colors to render selected cells. These colors can be assigned with `setSelectedForeground()` and `setSelectedBackground()`. Nonselected cells will be rendered with the component foreground and background colors that are assigned to `JList` with `setForeground()` and `setBackground()`.

`JList` implements the `Scrollable` interface (see chapter 7) to provide vertical unit incremental scrolling corresponding to the list cell height, and vertical block incremental scrolling corresponding to the number of visible cells. Horizontal unit increment scrolling corresponds to the size of the list's font (1 if the font is `null`), and horizontal block unit increment scrolling corresponds to the current width of the list. Thus `JList` does not directly support scrolling, and it is intended to be placed in a `JScrollPane`.

The `visibleRowCount` property specifies how many cells should be visible when a `JList` is placed in a scroll pane. This defaults to 8, and it can be set with the `setVisibleRowCount()` method. Another interesting method provided by `JList` is `ensureIndexIsVisible()`, which forces the list to scroll itself so that the element corresponding to the given index becomes visible. `JList` also supports autoscrolling; for example, it will scroll element by element every 100ms if the mouse is dragged below or above its bounds.

By default, the width of each cell is the width of the widest item, and the height of each cell corresponds to the height of the tallest item. We can overpower this behavior and specify our own fixed cell width and height of each list cell using the `setFixedCellWidth()` and `setFixedCellHeight()` methods.

Another way to control the width and height of each cell is through the `setPrototypeCellValue()` method. This method takes an `Object` parameter and uses it to automatically determine the `fixedCellWidth` and `fixedCellHeight`. A typical use of this method would be to give it a `String`. This forces the list to use a fixed cell width and height equal to the width and height of that string when it is rendered in the `Font` currently assigned to the `JList`.

`JList` also provides a method called `locationToIndex()` which will return the index of a cell at the given `Point` (in coordinate space of the list). -1 will be returned if the given point does not fall on a list cell. Unfortunately, `JList` does not provide support for double-clicking, but this method comes in very handy in implementing our own support for notification of double clicks. The following pseudocode shows how we can use a `MouseAdapter`, a `MouseEvent`, and the `locationToIndex()` method to determine which `JList` cell a double-click occurs on:

```
myJist.addMouseListener(new MouseAdapter() {
  public void mouseClicked(MouseEvent e) {
    if (e.getClickCount() == 2) {
      int cellIndex = myJList.locationToIndex(e.getPoint());
      // We now have the index of the double-clicked cell.
    }
  }
});
```

UI
GUIDELINE

Advice on usage and design

Usage   Much of the UI Guideline advice for list boxes is similar to that given for combo boxes. Clearly the two components are different and they are intended for different purposes. Deciding when to use one or another can be difficult. Again, our advice is to think about reader output rather than data input. When the reader needs to see a collection of items, a list box is the correct choice. Use a list box where there is a collection of data which may grow dynamically, and when, for reading purposes, it is useful to see the whole collection or as much of the collection as can reasonably fit in the available space.

Design   Like combo boxes, a number of things affect the usability of a list box. Beyond more than a few items, it becomes unusable unless the data is sorted in some logical fashion, such as alphabetical or numerical. List boxes are designed to be used with scroll panes because lists are often too long to display each item in the available screen space at once. Using a sensible sorted order for the list allows the user to predict how much he needs to scroll to find what he is looking for.

When a list gets longer, usability is affected yet again. Once a list gets beyond a couple of hundred items, even when sorted, it becomes very slow for the user to locate a specific item in the list. When a list becomes that long, you may want to consider either providing a search facility or grouping the data inside the list using a tree-like organization.

Graphical considerations for list boxes are much like those for combo boxes. List boxes should be aligned to fit attractively into a panel. However, you must avoid making a list box which is simply too big for the list items contained. For example, a list box showing supported file formats such as ".gif" need only be a few characters long—don't make it big enough to handle 50 characters, as it will look unbalanced.

The nature of the list items must also be considered. If you have 50 items in a list where most items are around 20 characters but one item is 50 characters long, then should you make the list box big enough to display the longest item? Maybe, but for most occasions your display will be imbalanced again. It is probably best to optimize for the more common length, providing the longer one still has meaning when read in its truncated form. One solution to displaying the whole length of a truncated item is to use the tooltip facility. When the user places the mouse over an item, a tooltip appears with the full-length data text.

10.1.1 The ListModel interface

abstract interface javax.swing.ListModel

This interface describes a data model that holds a list of items. The getElementAt() method retrieves the item at the given position as an Object instance. The getSize() method returns the number of items in the list. ListModel also contains two methods that allow ListData-Listeners (see below) to be registered and notified of any additions, removals, and changes that occur to this model. This interface leaves the job of specifying how we store and structure the data, as well as how we add, remove, or change an item, completely up to its implementations.

10.1.2 AbstractListModel

abstract class javax.swing.AbstractListModel

This class represents a partial implementation of the ListModel interface. It defines the default event-handling functionality, and it implements the add/remove ListDataListener methods, as well as methods to fire ListDataEvents (see below) when additions, removals, and changes occur. The remainder of ListModel, the methods getElementAt() and get-Size(), must be implemented in any concrete subclass.

10.1.3 DefaultListModel

class javax.swing.DefaultListModel

This class represents the concrete default implementation of the ListModel interface. It extends AbstractListModel and uses a java.util.Vector to store its data. Almost all of the methods of this class correspond directly to Vector methods; we will not discuss them here. Familiarity with Vectors implies familiarity with how DefaultListModel works (refer to the API documentation if you need further information).

10.1.4 The ListSelectionModel interface

abstract interface javax.swing.ListSelectionModel

This interface describes the model used for selecting list items. It defines three modes of selection: single selection, single contiguous interval selection, and multiple contiguous interval selection. A selection is defined as an indexed range, or set of ranges, of list elements. The beginning of a selected range (where it originates) is referred to as the *anchor,* while the last item is referred to as the *lead* (the anchor can be greater than, less than, or equal to the lead). The lowest selected index is referred to as the *minimum,* and the highest selected index is referred to as the *maximum,* regardless of the order in which selection takes place. Each of these indices represents a ListSelectionModel property. The minimum and maximum properties should be –1 when no selection exists, and the anchor and lead maintain their most recent value until a new selection occurs.

To change the selection mode we use the setSelectionMode() method, passing it one of the following constants: MULTIPLE_INTERVAL_SELECTION, SINGLE_INTERVAL_SELEC-TION, or SINGLE_SELECTION. In SINGLE_SELECTION mode, only one item can be selected. In SINGLE_INTERVAL_SELECTION mode, a contiguous group of items can be selected by selecting an anchor item, holding down the SHIFT key, and choosing a lead item (which can be at a higher or lower index than the anchor). In MULTIPLE_INTERVAL_SELECTION mode, any number of items can be selected regardless of their location by holding down the CTRL key and clicking. Multiple selection mode also allows you to use SHIFT to select a contiguous interval; however, this clears the current selection.

ListSelectionModel provides several methods for adding, removing, and manipulating ranges of selections. Methods for registering/removing ListSelectionListeners are provided as well (see below). Each of these methods is explained clearly in the API documentation, so we will not describe them in detail here.

JList defines all the methods declared in this interface and it delegates all traffic to its ListSelectionModel instance, thereby allowing access to selection data without the need to explicitly communicate with the selection model.

10.1.5   DefaultListSelectionModel

class javax.swing.DefaultListSelectionModel

This class represents the concrete default implementation of the ListSelectionModel interface. It defines methods to fire ListSelectionEvents (see below) when a selection range changes.

10.1.6   The ListCellRenderer interface

abstract interface javax.swing.ListCellRenderer

This interface describes a component that is used for rendering a list item. We discussed this interface, as well as its default concrete implementation, DefaultListCellRenderer, in the last chapter (see sections 9.1.4 and 9.1.5). We will show how to construct several custom renderers in the examples that follow.

10.1.7   The ListDataListener interface

abstract interface javax.swing.event.ListDataListener

This interface defines three methods for dispatching ListDataEvents when list elements are added, removed, or changed in the ListModel: intervalAdded(), intervalRemoved(), and contentsChanged().

10.1.8   ListDataEvent

class javax.swing.event.ListDataEvent

This class represents the event that is delivered when changes occur in a list's ListModel. It includes the source of the event as well as the indexes of the lowest and highest indexed elements affected by the change. It also includes the type of event that occurred. Three ListDataEvent types are defined as static ints: CONTENTS_CHANGED, INTERVAL_ADDED, and INTERVAL_REMOVED. We can use the getType() method to discover the type of any ListDataEvent.

10.1.9   The ListSelectionListener interface

abstract interface javax.swing.event.ListSelectionListener

This interface describes a listener which listens for changes in a list's ListSelectionModel. It declares the valueChanged() method, which accepts a ListSelectionEvent.

10.1.10 ListSelectionEvent

class javax.swing.event.ListSelectionEvent

This class represents an event that is delivered by `ListSelectionModel` when changes occur in its selection. It is almost identical to `ListDataEvent`, except that the indices specified signify where there has been a change in the selection model, rather than in the data model.

10.2 BASIC JLIST EXAMPLE

Example 10.1 displays a list of the states in the United States using an array of `Strings` in the following format:

2-character abbreviation*<tab character>*full state name*<tab character>*state capital

The states are listed alphabetically by their 2-letter abbreviation.

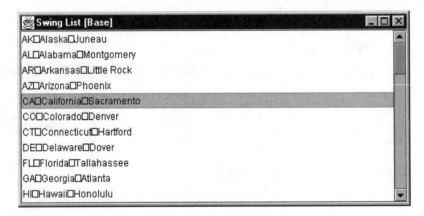

Figure 10.1   A `JList` **that displays a list of strings containing tab characters**

Example 10.1

StatesList.java

see \Chapter10\1

```java
import java.awt.*;
import java.awt.event.*;
import java.util.*;

import javax.swing.*;
import javax.swing.border.*;
import javax.swing.event.*;

public class StatesList extends JFrame
{
  protected JList m_statesList;

  public StatesList() {
```

```java
super("Swing List [Base]");
setSize(500, 240);

String [] states = {
  "AK\tAlaska\tJuneau",
  "AL\tAlabama\tMontgomery",
  "AR\tArkansas\tLittle Rock",
  "AZ\tArizona\tPhoenix",
  "CA\tCalifornia\tSacramento",
  "CO\tColorado\tDenver",
  "CT\tConnecticut\tHartford",
  "DE\tDelaware\tDover",
  "FL\tFlorida\tTallahassee",
  "GA\tGeorgia\tAtlanta",
  "HI\tHawaii\tHonolulu",
  "IA\tIowa\tDes Moines",
  "ID\tIdaho\tBoise",
  "IL\tIllinois\tSpringfield",
  "IN\tIndiana\tIndianapolis",
  "KS\tKansas\tTopeka",
  "KY\tKentucky\tFrankfort",
  "LA\tLouisiana\tBaton Rouge",
  "MA\tMassachusetts\tBoston",
  "MD\tMaryland\tAnnapolis",
  "ME\tMaine\tAugusta",
  "MI\tMichigan\tLansing",
  "MN\tMinnesota\tSt.Paul",
  "MO\tMissouri\tJefferson City",
  "MS\tMississippi\tJackson",
  "MT\tMontana\tHelena",
  "NC\tNorth Carolina\tRaleigh",
  "ND\tNorth Dakota\tBismarck",
  "NE\tNebraska\tLincoln",
  "NH\tNew Hampshire\tConcord",
  "NJ\tNew Jersey\tTrenton",
  "NM\tNew Mexico\tSantaFe",
  "NV\tNevada\tCarson City",
  "NY\tNew York\tAlbany",
  "OH\tOhio\tColumbus",
  "OK\tOklahoma\tOklahoma City",
  "OR\tOregon\tSalem",
  "PA\tPennsylvania\tHarrisburg",
  "RI\tRhode Island\tProvidence",
  "SC\tSouth Carolina\tColumbia",
  "SD\tSouth Dakota\tPierre",
  "TN\tTennessee\tNashville",
  "TX\tTexas\tAustin",
  "UT\tUtah\tSalt Lake City",
  "VA\tVirginia\tRichmond",
  "VT\tVermont\tMontpelier",
  "WA\tWashington\tOlympia",
  "WV\tWest Virginia\tCharleston",
```

```
      "WI\tWisconsin\tMadison",
      "WY\tWyoming\tCheyenne"
    };

    m_statesList = new JList(states);

    JScrollPane ps = new JScrollPane();
    ps.getViewport().add(m_statesList);
    getContentPane().add(ps, BorderLayout.CENTER);

    WindowListener wndCloser = new WindowAdapter() {
      public void windowClosing(WindowEvent e) {
        System.exit(0);
      }
    };
    addWindowListener(wndCloser);

    setVisible(true);
  }
  public static void main(String argv[]) {
    new StatesList();
  }
}
```

10.2.1　Understanding the code

Class StatesList

The StatesList class extends JFrame to implement the frame container for this example. One instance variable, JList m_statesList, is used to store an array of state Strings. This list is created by passing the states String array to the JList constructor. The list is then added to a JScrollPane instance to provide scrolling capabilities.

10.2.2　Running the code

Figure 10.1 shows StatesList in action displaying the list of states and their capitals. The separating tab character is displayed as an unpleasant square symbol, but we'll fix this in the next example.

GUIDELINE

Unbalanced layout　In this example, the design is unbalanced because the tab character is not displayed correctly. The box is ugly, and the spacing is also wrong. The large white space area to the right ought to be avoided. The next example corrects these problems.

10.3　CUSTOM RENDERING

In this section we'll add the ability to align Strings that contain tab separators into a table-like arrangement. We want each tab character to shift all text to its right, to a specified location instead of being rendered as the square symbol we saw above. These locations should be determined uniformly so that all elements of the list will form columns that line up correctly.

Example 10.2 works as well with proportional fonts as it does with fixed width fonts; it doesn't matter what font we use because alignment is not designed to be font-dependent. This makes JList a powerful but simple component which can be used in place of JTable. In simple cases such as the example presented here (where the involvement of JTable would create unnecessary overhead in this example).

To accomplish the desired rendering, we construct a custom renderer, TabListCell-Renderer, which exposes accessor methods to specify and retrieve tab positions based on the index of a tab character in a String that is being rendered. These are the accessor methods:

- getDefaultTab()/setDefaultTab(int): Manages the tab size (default is 50). In case a position is not specified for a given tab index, we use this default size to determine how far to offset a portion of text.
- getTabs()/setTabs(int[]): Manages an array of positions based on the index of a tab character in a String being rendered. These positions are used in rendering each element in the list to provide consistent alignment.

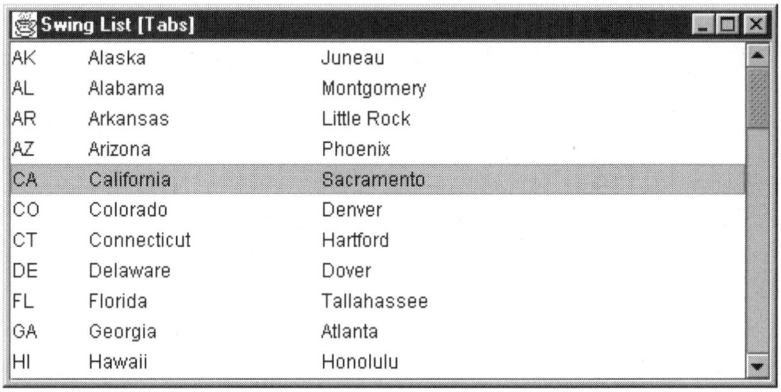

Figure 10.2 A custom `ListCellRenderer` that displays tab-separated strings in a table-like fashion

Example 10.2

StatesList.java

see \Chapter10\2

```java
import java.awt.*;
import java.awt.event.*;
import java.util.*;

import javax.swing.*;
import javax.swing.border.*;
import javax.swing.event.*;

public class StatesList extends JFrame
{
  protected JList m_statesList;

  public StatesList() {
```

```
      // Unchanged code from example 10.1

    m_statesList = new JList(states);
    TabListCellRenderer renderer = new TabListCellRenderer();
    renderer.setTabs(new int[] {50, 200, 300});
    m_statesList.setCellRenderer(renderer);

      // Unchanged code from example 10.1
  }
}

class TabListCellRenderer extends JLabel
 implements ListCellRenderer
{
  protected static Border m_noFocusBorder;
  protected FontMetrics m_fm = null;
  protected Insets m_insets = new Insets(0, 0, 0, 0);

  protected int m_defaultTab = 50;
  protected int[] m_tabs = null;

  public TabListCellRenderer() {
    super();
    m_noFocusBorder = new EmptyBorder(1, 1, 1, 1);
    setOpaque(true);
    setBorder(m_noFocusBorder);
  }

  public Component getListCellRendererComponent(JList list,
   Object value, int index, boolean isSelected, boolean cellHasFocus)
  {
    setText(value.toString());

    setBackground(isSelected ? list.getSelectionBackground() :
      list.getBackground());
    setForeground(isSelected ? list.getSelectionForeground() :
      list.getForeground());

    setFont(list.getFont());
    setBorder((cellHasFocus) ? UIManager.getBorder(
      "List.focusCellHighlightBorder") : m_noFocusBorder);

    return this;
  }

  public void setDefaultTab(int defaultTab) {
    m_defaultTab = defaultTab;
  }

  public int getDefaultTab() { return m_defaultTab; }

  public void setTabs(int[] tabs) { m_tabs = tabs; }

  public int[] getTabs() { return m_tabs; }

  public int getTab(int index) {
    if (m_tabs == null)
      return m_defaultTab*index;
    int len = m_tabs.length;
```

1 Create renderer component which will be used to draw each item

2 List cell renderer that aligns fields in tab columns

3 Returns component with text colors, font, and border all set

4 Accessors for default tab (tab column width used when no tab column list is present) and tab column list

5 Computes pixel offset for a specified tab number

```
        if (index>=0 && index<len)
          return m_tabs[index];
        return m_tabs[len-1] + m_defaultTab*(index-len+1);
      }

      public void paint(Graphics g) {
        m_fm = g.getFontMetrics();

        g.setColor(getBackground());
        g.fillRect(0, 0, getWidth(), getHeight());
        getBorder().paintBorder(this, g, 0, 0, getWidth(), getHeight());

        g.setColor(getForeground());
        g.setFont(getFont());
        m_insets = getInsets();
        int x = m_insets.left;
        int y = m_insets.top + m_fm.getAscent();

        StringTokenizer    st = new StringTokenizer(getText(), "\t");
        while (st.hasMoreTokens()) {
          String sNext = st.nextToken();
          g.drawString(sNext, x, y);
          x += m_fm.StringWidth(sNext);
          if (!st.hasMoreTokens())
            break;
          int index = 0;
          while (x >= getTab(index))
            index++;
          x = getTab(index);
        }
      }
    }
}
```

6 Draw background and border

7 Set foreground color, font, and text baseline

8 Parse each text piece, draw each one, and position to next tab position

10.3.1   Understanding the code

Class StatesList

1 Minor changes have been made to this class as compared to StatesList from example 10.1. We create an instance of our custom TabListCellRenderer, pass it an array of positions, and set it as the renderer for our JList component.

Class TabListCellRenderer

2 The TabListCellRenderer class extends JLabel and implements the ListCellRenderer interface for use as our custom renderer.
Class variable:

- Border m_noFocusBorder: The border to be used when a list item has no focus.

Instance variables:

- FontMetrics m_fm: Used in calculating text positioning when drawing.
- Insets m_insets: The insets of the cell being rendered.
- int m_defaultTab: The default tab size.
- int[] m_tabs: An array of positions based on the tab index in a String being rendered.

The constructor assigns text, sets its opaque property to true (to render the component's area with the specified background color), and sets the border to m_noFocusBorder.

The getListCellRendererComponent() method is required when implementing ListCellRenderer, and it is called each time a cell is about to be rendered. It takes five parameters:

- JList list: The reference to the list instance.
- Object value: The data object to be painted by the renderer.
- int index: The index of the item in the list.
- boolean isSelected: Returns true if the cell is currently selected.
- boolean cellHasFocus: Returns true if the cell currently has the focus.

③ Our implementation of this method assigns new text, sets the background and foreground (depending on whether or not the cell is selected), sets the font to the one taken from the parent list component, and sets the border according to whether the cell has input focus.

④
⑤ Four additional methods provide set/get support for the m_defaultTab and m_tabs variables, and they do not require detailed explanation beyond the code listing. Now let's take a close look at the getTab() method, which calculates and returns the position for a given tab index. If no tab array, m_tabs, is set, this method returns the m_defaultTab distance (it defaults to 50) multiplied by the given tab index. If the m_tabs array is not null and the tab index is less than its length, the proper value from that array is returned. Otherwise, if the tab index is greater than the array's length, we have no choice but to use the default tab size again.

Since the JLabel component does not render tab characters properly, we do not benefit much from its inheritance, so we implement the paint() method to draw tabbed Strings ourselves.

NOTE Because this is a very simple component that we do not plan to enhance with custom UI functionality, overriding paint() is acceptable.

⑥ First, our paint() method requests a reference to the FontMetrics instance for the given Graphics. Then we fill the component's bounds with the background color (which is set in the getListCellRendererComponent() method depending on whether the cell is selected), and paint the component's border.

NOTE Alternatively, we could use the drawTabbedText() method from the javax.swing.text.Utilities class to draw tabbed text. However, this requires us to implement the TabExpander interface. In our case it's easier to draw text directly without using that utility. As an interesting exercise you can modify the code from this example to use the drawTabbedText() method.

⑦ In the next step, we prepare to draw the tabbed String. We set the foreground color and font, and determine the initial x and y positions for drawing the text, taking into account the component's insets.

REMINDER To draw text in Java you need to use a baseline y-coordinate. This is why the getAscent() value is added to the y position. The getAscent() method returns the distance from the font's baseline to the top of most alphanumeric characters. See chapter 2 for more information on drawing text and Java 2 FontMetrics caveats.

8 We then use a `StringTokenizer` to parse the `String` and extract the portions separated by tabs. Each portion is drawn with the `drawString()` method, and the x-coordinate is adjusted to the length of the text. We cycle through this process, positioning each portion of text by calling the `getTab()` method, until no more tabs are found.

10.3.2 Running the code

Figure 10.2 shows `StatesList` displaying an array of tab-separated `Strings`. Notice that the tab symbols are not drawn directly, but they form consistently aligned columns inside the list.

GUIDELINE

Improved balance   With the tab character being displayed correctly, the list box has much better balance. The available area for the capital city is still very large, and as the designer you may want to consider reducing it, thus reducing the excessive white space on the right-hand side. Such a decision would normally be made after the list box is seen as it will appear and the necessary alignment and overall panel balance is taken into consideration.

10.4 PROCESSING KEYBOARD INPUT AND SEARCHING

In this section we will continue to enhance our `JList` states example by adding the ability to select an element whose text starts with a character corresponding to a key press. We will also show how to extend this functionality to search for an element whose text starts with a *sequence* of typed key characters.

To do this, we must use a `KeyListener` to listen for keyboard input, and we need to accumulate this input in a `String`. Each time a key is pressed, the listener must search through the list and select the first element whose text matches the `String` we have accumulated. If the time interval between two key presses exceeds a certain pre-defined value, the accumulated `String` must be cleared before appending a new character to avoid overflow.

Swing List [Selection]		
MS	Mississippi	Jackson
MT	Montana	Helena
NC	North Carolina	Raleigh
ND	North Dakota	Bismarck
NE	Nebraska	Lincoln
NH	New Hampshire	Concord
NJ	New Jersey	Trenton
NM	New Mexico	SantaFe
NV	Nevada	Carson City
NY	New York	Albany
OH	Ohio	Columbus

Figure 10.3   A `JList` that allows accumulated keyboard input to search for a matching item

Example 10.3

StatesList.java

see \Chapter10\3

```java
import java.awt.*;
import java.awt.event.*;
import java.util.*;

import javax.swing.*;
import javax.swing.border.*;
import javax.swing.event.*;

public class StatesList extends JFrame
{
  protected JList m_statesList;

  public StatesList() {
    // Unchanged code from example 10.2

    m_statesList = new JList(states);
    TabListCellRenderer renderer = new TabListCellRenderer();
    renderer.setTabs(new int[] {50, 200, 300});
    m_statesList.setCellRenderer(renderer);
    m_statesList.addKeyListener(new ListSearcher(m_statesList));

    // Unchanged code from example 10.2
  }
}

class ListSearcher extends KeyAdapter
{
  protected JList m_list;
  protected ListModel m_model;
  protected String m_key = "";
  protected long m_time = 0;

  public static int CHAR_DELTA = 1000;

  public ListSearcher(JList list) {
    m_list = list;
    m_model = m_list.getModel();
  }

  public void keyTyped(KeyEvent e) {
    char ch = e.getKeyChar();
    if (!Character.isLetterOrDigit(ch))
      return;

    if (m_time+CHAR_DELTA < System.currentTimeMillis())
      m_key = "";
    m_time = System.currentTimeMillis();

    m_key += Character.toLowerCase(ch);
    for (int k=0; k<m_model.getSize(); k++) {
      String str = ((String)m_model.getElementAt(k)).toLowerCase();
      if (str.startsWith(m_key)){
        m_list.setSelectedIndex(k);
```

① Add ListSearcher KeyListener to JList

② If key is letter/digit, and event occurred shortly after last key, append it to search string and look for list item with that prefix

```
            m_list.ensureIndexIsVisible(k);
            break;
          }
        }
      }
    }
```

10.4.1 Understanding the code

Class StatesList

❶ An instance of `ListSearcher` is added to the `m_statesList` component as a `KeyListener`. This is the only change made to this class with respect to example 10.2.

Class ListSearcher

The `ListSearcher` class extends the `KeyAdapter` class and defines one class variable:

- `int CHAR_DELTA`: A static variable to hold the maximum time interval in ms between two subsequent key presses before clearing the search key character `String`.

Instance variables:

- `JList m_list`: The list component to search and change the selection based on keyboard input.
- `ListModel m_model`: The list model of `m_list`.
- `String m_key`: The key character `String` that is used to search for a match.
- `long m_time`: The time in ms of the last key press.

The `ListSearcher` constructor simply takes a reference to a `JList` component and stores it in instance variable `m_list`; its model is stored in `m_model`.

❷ The `keyTyped()` method is called each time a new character is typed. Our implementation first obtains the typed character and returns if that character is not a letter or a digit. `keyTyped()` then checks the time interval between now and the time when the previous key type event occurred. If this interval exceeds `CHAR_DELTA`, the `m_key` `String` is cleared. Finally, this method walks through the list and performs a case-insensitive comparison of the list `Strings` and the searching `String` (`m_key`). If an element's text starts with `m_key`, this element is selected and it is forced to appear within our current `JList` view using the `ensureIndexIsVisible()` method.

10.4.2 Running the code

Try out the search functionality. Figure 10.3 shows our list's selection after pressing "n" immediately followed by "j." As expected, New Jersey is selected.

GUIDELINE

Extending usability and list size This technique of allowing accumulated keyboard input to sift and select a list item improves usability by making the task of searching and locating an item in the list easier. This extends the number of items you can put in a list and still have a usable design. A technique like this can easily improve the usefulness of the list for up to several thousand entries.

This is another good example of the improved usability that is possible when the developer takes extra time to provide additional code to make the user's task easier.

10.5   LIST OF CHECK BOXES

Lists can certainly be used for more than just Strings. We can easily imagine a list of Swing components. A list of check boxes is actually common in software packages when users are prompted to select optional constituents during installation. In Swing, such a list can be constructed by implementing a custom renderer that uses the JCheckBox component. The catch is that mouse and keyboard events must be handled manually to check/uncheck these boxes.

Example 10.4 shows how to create a list of check boxes that represent imaginary optional program constituents. Associated with each component is an instance of our custom Install-Data class with the following fields:

Field	Type	Description
m_name	String	Option name.
m_size	int	Size in KB.
m_selected	boolean	Returns true if the option is selected.

Figure 10.4   A JList with JCheckBox renderers

Example 10.4

CheckBoxList.java

see \Chapter 10\4

```java
import java.awt.*;
import java.awt.event.*;
import java.util.*;

import javax.swing.*;
import javax.swing.border.*;
import javax.swing.event.*;

public class CheckBoxList extends JFrame
{
  protected JList  m_list;
  protected JLabel m_total;

  public CheckBoxList() {
```

```
      super("Swing List [Check boxes]");
      setSize(280, 250);
      getContentPane().setLayout(new FlowLayout());
```
1 List items for JList

```
      InstallData[] options = {
        new InstallData("Program executable", 118),
        new InstallData("Help files", 52),
        new InstallData("Tools and converters", 83),
        new InstallData("Source code", 133)
      };

      m_list = new JList(options);
      CheckListCellRenderer renderer = new CheckListCellRenderer();
      m_list.setCellRenderer(renderer);
      m_list.setSelectionMode(ListSelectionModel.SINGLE_SELECTION);

      CheckListener lst = new CheckListener(this);
      m_list.addMouseListener(lst);
      m_list.addKeyListener(lst);

      JScrollPane ps = new JScrollPane();
      ps.getViewport().add(m_list);

      m_total = new JLabel("Space required: 0K");
```
2 "total" field below list, which is below the title label

```
      JPanel p = new JPanel();
      p.setLayout(new BorderLayout());
      p.add(ps, BorderLayout.CENTER);
      p.add(m_total, BorderLayout.SOUTH);
      p.setBorder(new TitledBorder(new EtchedBorder(),
        "Please select options:"));
      getContentPane().add(p);

      WindowListener wndCloser = new WindowAdapter() {
        public void windowClosing(WindowEvent e) {
          System.exit(0);
        }
      };
      addWindowListener(wndCloser);

      setVisible(true);

      recalcTotal();
    }
    public void recalcTotal() {
      ListModel model = m_list.getModel();
      int total = 0;
      for (int k=0; k<model.getSize(); k++) {
        InstallData data = (InstallData)model.getElementAt(k);
        if (data.isSelected())
          total += data.getSize();
      }
      m_total.setText("Space required: "+total+"K");
    }

    public static void main(String argv[]) {
```
3 Adds up "size" field of checked items and sets that in "total" field

```
        new CheckBoxList();
    }
}

class CheckListCellRenderer extends JCheckBox
 implements ListCellRenderer
{
  protected static Border m_noFocusBorder =
    new EmptyBorder(1, 1, 1, 1);

  public CheckListCellRenderer() {
    super();
    setOpaque(true);
    setBorder(m_noFocusBorder);
  }

  public Component getListCellRendererComponent(JList list,
   Object value, int index, boolean isSelected, boolean cellHasFocus)
  {
    setText(value.toString());

    setBackground(isSelected ? list.getSelectionBackground() :
      list.getBackground());
    setForeground(isSelected ? list.getSelectionForeground() :
      list.getForeground());

    InstallData data = (InstallData)value;
      setSelected(data.isSelected());

    setFont(list.getFont());
    setBorder((cellHasFocus) ?
    UIManager.getBorder("List.focusCellHighlightBorder")
      : m_noFocusBorder);

    return this;
  }
}

class CheckListener implements MouseListener, KeyListener
{
  protected CheckBoxList m_parent;
  protected JList m_list;

  public CheckListener(CheckBoxList parent) {
    m_parent = parent;
    m_list = parent.m_list;
  }

  public void mouseClicked(MouseEvent e) {
    if (e.getX() < 20)
    doCheck();
  }

  public void mousePressed(MouseEvent e) {}
  public void mouseReleased(MouseEvent e) {}
  public void mouseEntered(MouseEvent e) {}
  public void mouseExited(MouseEvent e) {}
```

4 Renderer shows a check box with label

5 Processes mouse and key input to change check box states

5 If mouse click is less than 20 pixels from left edge, consider it a click on check box

```
public void keyPressed(KeyEvent e) {
  if (e.getKeyChar() == ' ')
    doCheck();
}

public void keyTyped(KeyEvent e) {}
public void keyReleased(KeyEvent e) {}

protected void doCheck() {
  int index = m_list.getSelectedIndex();
  if (index < 0)
    return;
  InstallData data = (InstallData)m_list.getModel().
    getElementAt(index);
  data.invertSelected();
  m_list.repaint();
  m_parent.recalcTotal();
}
}
class InstallData
{
  protected String m_name;
  protected int m_size;
  protected boolean m_selected;

  public InstallData(String name, int size) {
    m_name = name;
    m_size = size;
    m_selected = false;
  }

  public String getName() { return m_name; }

  public int getSize() { return m_size; }

  public void setSelected(boolean selected) {
    m_selected = selected;
  }

  public void invertSelected() { m_selected = !m_selected; }

  public boolean isSelected() { return m_selected; }

  public String toString() { return m_name+" ("+m_size+" K)"; }
}
```

⑤ Space key does the same as the check box mouse click

⑥ Toggles InstallData "selected" flag and recalculates total

⑦ Data object to represent install item, including size and "selected" flag

10.5.1 Understanding the code

Class CheckBoxList

The CheckBoxList class extends JFrame to provide the basic frame for this example. Here are the instance variables:

- JList m_list: The list to display program constituents.
- JLabel m_total: The label to display the total space required for installation based on the selected constituents.

1 An array of four `InstallData` objects is passed to the constructor of our `JList` component (note that we use a `DefaultListModel`, which is sufficient for our purposes here). `SINGLE_SELECTION` is used as our list's selection mode. An instance of our custom `CheckListCellRenderer` is created and set as the cell renderer for our list. An instance of our custom `CheckListener` is then registered as both a mouse and a key listener to handle item checking and unchecking for each check box (see below).

The list component is added to a `JScrollPane` to provide scrolling capabilities. Then `JLabel m_total` is created to display the total amount of space required for installation based on the currently selected check boxes.

2 In previous examples, the `JList` component occupied all of our frame's available space. In this example, however, we are required to consider a different layout. `JPanel p` is now used to hold both the list and the label (`m_total`). To ensure that the label will always be placed below the list we use a `BorderLayout`. We also use a `TitledBorder` for this panel's border to provide visual grouping.

3 The `recalcTotal()` method steps through the sequence of `InstallData` instances contained in the list, and it calculates the sum of the sizes of the selected items. The result is then displayed in the `m_total` label.

Class CheckListCellRenderer

4 This class implements the `ListCellRenderer` interface, and it is similar to our `TabListCellRenderer` class from example 10.2. An important difference is that `CheckListCellRenderer` extends `JCheckBox` (not `JLabel`) and it uses that component to render each item in our list. The `getListCellRendererComponent()` method sets the check box text, determines whether the current list item is selected, and sets the check box's selection state accordingly (using its inherited `JCheckBox.setSelected()` method).

NOTE   We could alternatively use `JLabel`s with custom icons to imitate checked and unchecked boxes. However, the use of `JCheckBox` is preferred for graphical consistency with other parts of a GUI.

Class CheckListener

5 This class implements both `MouseListener` and `KeyListener` to process all user input which can change the state of check boxes in the list. Its constructor takes a `CheckBoxList` instance as parameter in order to gain access to the `CheckBoxList.recalcTotal()` method.

We've assumed in this example that an item's checked state should be changed if:

1   The user clicks the mouse close enough to the item's check box (for example, up to 20 pixels from the left edge).

2   The user transfers focus to the item (with the mouse or keyboard) and then presses the SPACE bar.

Bearing this in mind, two methods need to be implemented: `mouseClicked()` and `keyPressed()`. They both call the `protected` method `doCheck()` if either of the conditions described above are satisfied. All other methods from the `MouseListener` and `KeyListener` interfaces have empty implementations.

6 The `doCheck()` method determines the first selected index (the only selected index—recall that our list uses single-selection mode) in the list component and it retrieves the corresponding `InstallData` object. This method then calls `invertSelected()` to change the checked state of that object. It then repaints the list component and displays the new total by calling the `recalcTotal()` method.

Class InstallData

7 The `InstallData` class describes a data unit for this example. `InstallData` encapsulates three variables described at the beginning of this section: `m_name`, `m_size`, and `m_selected`. Its only constructor takes three parameters to fill these variables. Besides the obvious set/get methods, the `invertSelected()` method is defined to negate the value of `m_selected`. The `toString()` method determines the `String` representation of this object to be used by the list renderer.

10.5.2 Running the code

Figure 10.4 shows our list composed of check boxes in action. Select any item and click over the check box, or press the Space bar to change its checked state. Note that the total kilobytes required for these imaginary implementations is dynamically displayed in the label at the bottom.

GUIDELINE

When to use check boxes in a list Check boxes tend to be used inside bordered panes to show groupings of mutually related binary attributes. This technique is good for a fixed number of attributes; however, it becomes problematic when the number of items can vary.

The technique shown here is a good way to solve the problem when the collection of attributes or data is of an undetermined size. Use a check box list for binary (true/false) selection of items from a collection of a size which cannot be determined at design time.

For example, imagine the team selection for a football team. The coach has a pool of players and he needs to indicate who has been picked for the Saturday game. You could show the whole pool of players (sorted alphabetically or by number) in the list and allow the coach to check off each selected player.

CHAPTER 11

Text components and undo

11.1 TEXT COMPONENTS OVERVIEW

This chapter summarizes the most basic and commonly used text component features, and it introduces the undo package. In the next chapter we'll develop a basic JTextArea application to demonstrate the use of menus and toolbars. In chapter 19, we'll discuss the inner workings of text components in much more detail. In chapter 20, we'll develop an extensive JText-Pane word processor application with powerful font, style, paragraph, find and replace, and spell-checking dialogs.

11.1.1 JTextComponent

abstract class javax.swing.text.JTextComponent

The JTextComponent class serves as the superclass of each Swing text component. All text component functionality is defined by this class, along with the plethora of supporting classes and interfaces provided in the text package. The text components themselves are members of the javax.swing package: JTextField, JPasswordField, JTextArea, JEd-itorPane, and JTextPane.

> **NOTE** We have purposely left out most of the details behind text components in this chapter so we could provide only the information that you will most likely need on a regular basis. If, after reading this chapter, you would like a more thorough understanding of how text components work, and how to customize them or take advantage of some of the more advanced features, see chapters 19 and 20.

276

`JTextComponent` is an abstract subclass of `JComponent`, and it implements the `Scrollable` interface (see chapter 7). Each multi-line text component is designed to be placed in a `JScrollPane`.

Textual content is maintained in instances of the `javax.swing.text.Document` interface, which acts as the text component model. The text package includes two concrete `Document` implementations: `PlainDocument` and `StyledDocument`. `PlainDocument` allows one font and one color, and it is limited to character content. `StyledDocument` is much more complex, allowing multiple fonts, colors, embedded images and components, and various sets of hierarchically resolving textual attributes. `JTextField`, `JPasswordField`, and `JTextArea` each use a `PlainDocument` model. `JEditorPane` and `JTextPane` use a `StyledDocument` model. We can retrieve a text component's `Document` with `getDocument()`, and assign one with `setDocument()`. We can also attach `DocumentListener`s to a document to listen for changes in that document's content (this is much different than a key listener because all document events are dispatched *after* a change has been made).

We can assign and retrieve the color of a text component's `Caret` with `setCaretColor()` and `getCaretColor()`. We can also assign and retrieve the current `Caret` position in a text component with `setCaretPosition()` and `getCaretPosition()`.

The `disabledColor` property assigns a font color to be used in the disabled state. The `foreground` and `background` properties inherited from `JComponent` also apply; the foreground color is used as the font color when a text component is enabled, and the background color is used as the background for the whole text component. The `font` property specifies the font to render the text in. The font property and the foreground and background color properties do not overpower any attributes assigned to styled text components such as `JEditorPane` and `JTextPane`.

All text components maintain information about their current selection. We can retrieve the currently selected text as a `String` with `getSelectedText()`, and we can assign and retrieve specific background and foreground colors to use for selected text with `setSelectionBackground()`/`getSelectionBackground()` and `setSelectionForeground()`/`getSelectionForeground()` respectively.

`JTextComponent` also maintains a bound `focusAccelerator` property, which is a `char` that is used to transfer focus to a text component when the corresponding key is pressed simultaneously with the ALT key. This works internally by calling `requestFocus()` on the text component, and it will occur as long as the top-level window containing the given text component is currently active. We can assign/retrieve this character with `setFocusAccelerator()`/`getFocusAccelerator()`, and we can turn this functionality off by assigning '\0'.

The `read()` and `write()` methods provide convenient ways to read and write text documents. The `read()` method takes a `java.io.Reader` and an `Object` that describes the `Reader` stream, and it creates a new document model appropriate to the given text component containing the obtained character data. The `write()` method stores the content of the document model in a given `java.io.Writer` stream.

WARNING   We can customize any text component's document model. However, it is important to realize that whenever the `read()` method is invoked, a new document will be created. Unless this method is overriden, a custom document that had been previously assigned with `setDocument()` will be lost whenever `read()` is invoked, because the current document will be replaced by a default instance.

11.1.2 JTextField

class javax.swing.JTextField

JTextField is a single-line text component that uses a PlainDocument model. The horizontalAlignment property specifies text justification within the text field. We can assign/retrieve this property with setHorizontalAlignment()/getHorizontalAlignment. Acceptable values are JTextField.LEFT, JTextField.CENTER, and JTextField.RIGHT.

There are several JTextField constructors, two of which allow us to specify a number of columns. We can also assign/retrieve this number, the columns property, with setColumns()/getColumns(). Specifying a certain number of columns will set up a text field's preferred size to accommodate at least an equivalent number of characters. However, a text field might not receive its preferred size due to the current layout manager. Also, the width of a column is the width of the character 'm' in the current font. Unless a monospaced font is used, this width will be greater than most other characters.

The following example creates 14 JTextFields with a varying number of columns. Each field contains a number of ms equal to its number of columns.

Example 11.1

JTextFieldTest.java

see \Chapter11\1

```java
import javax.swing.*;
import java.awt.*;

public class JTextFieldTest extends JFrame
{
  public JTextFieldTest() {
    super("JTextField Test");

    getContentPane().setLayout(new FlowLayout());

    JTextField textField1 = new JTextField("m",1);
    JTextField textField2 = new JTextField("mm",2);
    JTextField textField3 = new JTextField("mmm",3);
    JTextField textField4 = new JTextField("mmmm",4);
    JTextField textField5 = new JTextField("mmmmm",5);
    JTextField textField6 = new JTextField("mmmmmm",6);
    JTextField textField7 = new JTextField("mmmmmmm",7);
    JTextField textField8 = new JTextField("mmmmmmmm",8);
    JTextField textField9 = new JTextField("mmmmmmmmm",9);
    JTextField textField10 = new JTextField("mmmmmmmmmm",10);
    JTextField textField11 = new JTextField("mmmmmmmmmmm",11);
    JTextField textField12 = new JTextField("mmmmmmmmmmmm",12);
    JTextField textField13 = new JTextField("mmmmmmmmmmmmm",13);
    JTextField textField14 = new JTextField("mmmmmmmmmmmmmm",14);

    getContentPane().add(textField1);
    getContentPane().add(textField2);
    getContentPane().add(textField3);
    getContentPane().add(textField4);
```

```
      getContentPane().add(textField5);
      getContentPane().add(textField6);
      getContentPane().add(textField7);
      getContentPane().add(textField8);
      getContentPane().add(textField9);
      getContentPane().add(textField10);
      getContentPane().add(textField11);
      getContentPane().add(textField12);
      getContentPane().add(textField13);
      getContentPane().add(textField14);

      setSize(300,170);
      setVisible(true);
   }

   public static void main(String argv[]) {
      new JTextFieldTest();
   }
}
```

Figure 11.1 illustrates the output. Notice that none of the text completely fits in its field. This happens because `JTextField` does not factor in the size of its border when calculating its preferred size, as we might expect. To work around this problem, though this is not an ideal solution, we can add one more column to each text field. The result is shown in figure 11.2. This solution is more appropriate when a fixed width font (monospaced) is being used. Figure 11.3 illustrates this last solution.

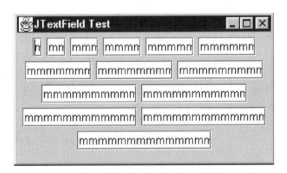

Figure 11.1 `JTextFields` using an equal number of columns and "m" characters

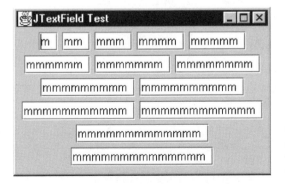

Figure 11.2 `JTextFields` using one more column than the number of "m" characters

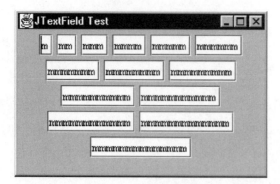

Figure 11.3 `JTextFields` using a monospaced font, and one more column than the number of "m" characters

NOTE   Using a monospaced font is always more appropriate when a fixed character limit is desired.

`JTextField` also maintains a `BoundedRangeModel` (see chapter 13) as its `horizontal-Visibility` property. This model is used to keep track of the amount of currently visible text. The `minimum` is 0 (the beginning of the document), and the `maximum` is equal to the width of the text field or the total length of the text in pixels (whichever is greater). The `value` is the current offset of the text displayed at the left edge of the field, and the `extent` is the width of the text field in pixels.

By default, a `KeyStroke` (see section 2.13.2) is established with the ENTER key that causes an `ActionEvent` to be fired. By simply adding an `ActionListener` to a `JTextField`, we will receive events whenever ENTER is pressed while that field has the current focus. This is very convenient functionality, but it may also get in the way of things. To remove this registered keystroke, do the following:

```
KeyStroke enter = KeyStroke.getKeyStroke(KeyEvent.VK_ENTER, 0);
Keymap map = myJTextField.getKeymap();
map.removeKeyStrokeBinding(enter);
```

`JTextField`'s document model can be customized to allow only certain forms of input; this is done by extending `PlainDocument` and overriding the `insertString()` method. The following code shows a class that will only allow six or fewer digits to be entered. We can assign this document to a `JTextField` with the `setDocument()` method (see chapter 19 for more about working with `Document`s).

```
class SixDigitDocument extends PlainDocument
{
  public void insertString(int offset,
    String str, AttributeSet a)
    throws BadLocationException {
      char[] insertChars = str.toCharArray();

      boolean valid = true;
      boolean fit = true;
      if (insertChars.length + getLength() <= 6) {
        for (int i = 0; i < insertChars.length; i++) {
          if (!Character.isDigit(insertChars[i])) {
            valid = false;
            break;
```

CHAPTER 11   TEXT COMPONENTS AND UNDO

```
              }
            }
          }
        else
          fit = false;

        if (fit && valid)
          super.insertString(offset, str, a);
        else if (!fit)
          getToolkit().beep();
    }
  }
```

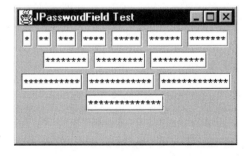
Don't overly restrict input   Filtering text fields during data entry is a powerful aid to usability. It helps prevent the user from making a mistake and it can speed operations by removing the need for validation and correction procedures. However, it is important not to overly restrict the allowable input. Make sure that all reasonable input is expected and accepted.

For example, with a phone number, allow "00 1 44 654 7777," "00+1 44 654 7777," and "00-1-1-654-7777," as well as "00144654777." Phone numbers can contain more than just numbers!

Another example involves dates. You should allow "04-06-99," "04/06/99," and "04:06:99," as well as "040699."

11.1.3   JPasswordField

class javax.swing.JPasswordField

JPasswordField is a fairly simple extension of JTextField that displays an echo character instead of the actual content that is placed in its model. This echo character defaults to *, and we can assign a different character with setEchoChar().

Unlike other text components, we cannot retrieve the actual content of a JPassword-Field with getText() (this method, along with setText(), has been deprecated in JPass-wordField). Instead we must use the getPassword() method, which returns an array of chars. JPasswordField overrides the JTextComponent copy() and cut() methods to do nothing but emit a beep, for security reasons.

Figure 11.4 shows the JTextFieldDemo example of section 11.1.2. It uses JPassword-Fields instead, and each is using a monospaced font.

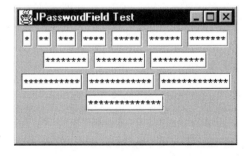

Figure 11.4 JPasswordFields using a monospaced font, and one more column than number of characters

11.1.4 JTextArea

class javax.swing.JTextArea

JTextArea allows multiple lines of text and, like JTextField, it uses a PlainDocument model. As we discussed earlier, JTextArea cannot display multiple fonts or font colors. JTextArea can perform line wrapping and, when line wrapping is enabled we can specify whether lines break on word boundaries. To enable/disable line wrapping we set the lineWrap property with setLineWrap(). To enable/disable wrapping on boundaries (which will only have an effect when lineWrap is set to true) we set the wrapStyleWord property using set-WrapStyleWord(). Both lineWrap and wrapStyleWord are bound properties.

JTextArea overrides isManagingFocus() (see section 2.12) to return true, indicating that the FocusManager will not transfer focus out of a JTextArea when the TAB key is pressed. Instead, a tab is inserted into the document (the number of spaces in the tab is equal to tabSize). We can assign/retrieve the tab size with setTabSize()/getTabSize() respectively. tabSize is also a bound property.

There are several ways to add text to a JTextArea's document. We can pass this text in to one of the constructors, append it to the end of the document using the append() method, insert a string at a given character offset using the insert() method, or replace a given range of text with the replaceRange() method. As with any text component, we can also set the text with the JTextComponent setText() method, and we can add and remove text directly from its Document (see chapter 19 for more details about the Document interface).

JTextArea maintains lineCount and rows properties which can easily be confused. The rows property specifies how many rows of text JTextArea is actually displaying. This may change whenever a text area is resized. The lineCount property specifies how many lines of text the document contains. Each line consists of a set of characters ending in a line break (\n). We can retrieve the character offset of the end of a given line with getLineEndOffset(), the character offset of the beginning of a given line with getLineStartOffset(), and the line number that contains a given offset with getLineOfOffset().

The rowHeight and columnWidth properties are determined by the height and width of the current font. The width of one column is equal to the width of the "m" character in the current font. We cannot assign new values to the properties, but we can override the getColumn-Width() and getRowHeight() methods in a subclass to return any value we like. We can explicitly set the number of rows and columns a text area contains with setRows() and set-Columns(), and the getRows() and getColumns() methods will only return these explicitly assigned values (not the current row and column count, as we might assume at first glance).

Unless JTextArea is placed in a JScrollPane or a container using a layout manager which enforces a certain size, it will resize itself dynamically depending on the amount of text that is entered. This behavior is rarely desired.

11.1.5 JEditorPane

class javax.swing.JEditorPane

JEditorPane is a multi-line text component capable of displaying and editing various different types of content. Swing provides support for HTML and RTF, but there is nothing stopping us from defining our own content type, or implementing support for an alternate format.

NOTE   Swing's support for HTML and RTF is located in the `javax.swing.text.html` and `javax.swing.text.rtf` packages. At the time of this writing, the `html` package was still going through major changes. The `rtf` package was also still under development, but it was closer to a finalized state than HTML support. For this reason, we devoted chapter 20 to the step-wise construction of an RTF word processor application. We expect to see stronger support for displaying and editing HTML in a future Java 2 release.

Support for different content is accomplished in part through the use of custom `EditorKit` objects. `JEditorPane`'s `contentType` property is a `String` that represents the type of document the editor pane is currently set up to display. The `EditorKit` maintains this value which, for `DefaultEditorKit`, defaults to "text/plain." `HTMLEditorKit` and `RTFEditorKit` have `contentType` values of "text/html" and "text/rtf", respectively (see chapter 19 for more about `EditorKit`s).

In chapter 9 we built a simple web browser using a non-editable `JEditorPane` by passing a URL to its constructor. When it's in non-editable mode, `JEditorPane` displays HTML pretty much as we might expect, although it has a long way to go to match Netscape. By allowing editing, `JEditorPane` will display an HTML document with many of its tags specially rendered, as shown in figure 11.5 (compare this to figure 9.4).

`JEditorPane` is smart enough to use an appropriate `EditorKit`, if one is available, to display a document passed to it. When it's displaying an HTML document, `JEditorPane` can fire `HyperlinkEvents` (which are defined in the `javax.swing.event package`). We can attach `HyperlinkListeners` to `JEditorPane` to listen for hyperlink invocations, as demonstrated by the examples at the end of chapter 9. The following code shows how simple it is to construct an HTML browser using an active `HyperlinkListener`.

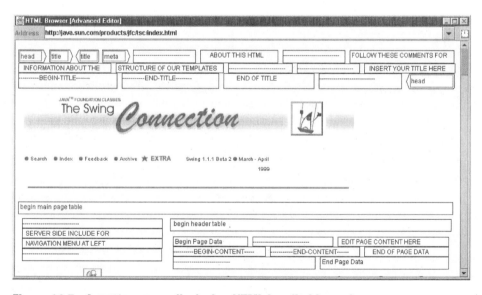

Figure 11.5   A `JEditorPane` displaying HTML in editable mode

```
m_browser = new JEditorPane(
  new URL("http://java.sun.com/products/jfc/tsc/index.html"));
m_browser.setEditable(false);
m_browser.addHyperlinkListener( new HyperlinkListener() {
  public void hyperlinkUpdate(HyperlinkEvent e) {
    if (e.getEventType() == HyperlinkEvent.EventType.ACTIVATED) {
      URL url = e.getURL();
      if (url == null)
        return;
      try { m_browser.setPage(e.getURL); }
      catch (IOException e) { e.printStackTrace(); }
    }
  }
}
```

JEditorPane uses a Hashtable to store its editor kit/content type pairs. We can query this table and retrieve the editor kit associated with a particular content type, if there is one, using the getEditorKitForContentType() method. We can get the current editor kit with getEditorKit(), and the current content type with getContentType(). We can set the current content type with setContentType(), and if there is already a corresponding editor kit in JEditorPane's hashtable, an appropriate editor kit will replace the current one. We can also assign an editor kit for a given content type using the setEditorKitForContentType() method (we will discuss EditorKits, and the ability to construct our own, in chapter 19).

JEditorPane uses a DefaultStyledDocument as its model. In HTML mode, an HTML-Document, which extends DefaultStyledDocument, is used. DefaultStyledDocument is quite powerful, as it allows us to associate attributes with characters and paragraphs, and to apply logical styles (see chapter 19).

11.1.6   JTextPane

class javax.swing.JTextPane

JTextPane extends JEditorPane and thus inherits its abilities to display various types of content. The most significant functionalities JTextPane offers are the abilities to programmatically assign attributes to regions of its content, embed components and images within its document, and work with named sets of attributes called Styles (we will discuss Styles in chapters 19 and 20).

To assign attributes to a region of document content, we use an AttributeSet implementation. We will describe AttributeSets in detail in chapter 19, but we will tell you here that they contain a group of attributes such as font type, font style, font color, and paragraph and character properties. These attributes are assigned through the use of various static methods which are defined in the StyleConstants class, which we will also discuss further in chapter 19.

Example 11.2 demonstrates embedded icons, components, and stylized text. Figure 11.6 illustrates the output.

Figure 11.6 A JTextPane with inserted ImageIcons, text with attributes, and an active JButton

Example 11.2

JTextPaneDemo.java

see \Chapter11\2

```
import java.awt.*;
import java.awt.event.*;
import java.io.*;
import javax.swing.*;
import javax.swing.text.*;

public class JTextPaneDemo extends JFrame
{
  // Best to reuse attribute sets as much as possible.

  static SimpleAttributeSet ITALIC_GRAY = new SimpleAttributeSet();
  static SimpleAttributeSet BOLD_BLACK = new SimpleAttributeSet();
  static SimpleAttributeSet BLACK = new SimpleAttributeSet();

  static {
    StyleConstants.setForeground(ITALIC_GRAY, Color.gray);
    StyleConstants.setItalic(ITALIC_GRAY, true);
    StyleConstants.setFontFamily(ITALIC_GRAY, "Helvetica");
```

```
        StyleConstants.setFontSize(ITALIC_GRAY, 14);

        StyleConstants.setForeground(BOLD_BLACK, Color.black);
        StyleConstants.setBold(BOLD_BLACK, true);
        StyleConstants.setFontFamily(BOLD_BLACK, "Helvetica");
        StyleConstants.setFontSize(BOLD_BLACK, 14);

        StyleConstants.setForeground(BLACK, Color.black);
        StyleConstants.setFontFamily(BLACK, "Helvetica");
        StyleConstants.setFontSize(BLACK, 14);
    }

    JTextPane m_editor = new JTextPane();

    public JTextPaneDemo() {
        super("JTextPane Demo");

        JScrollPane scrollPane = new JScrollPane(m_editor);
        getContentPane().add(scrollPane, BorderLayout.CENTER);

        setEndSelection();
        m_editor.insertIcon(new ImageIcon("manning.gif"));
        insertText("\nHistory: Distant\n\n", BOLD_BLACK);

        setEndSelection();
        m_editor.insertIcon(new ImageIcon("Lee_fade.jpg"));
        insertText("                              ", BLACK);
        setEndSelection();
        m_editor.insertIcon(new ImageIcon("Bace_fade.jpg"));

        insertText("\n      Lee Fitzpatrick              "
            + "                              "
            + "Marjan Bace\n\n", ITALIC_GRAY);

        insertText("When we started doing business under " +
            "the Manning name, about 10 years ago, we were a very " +
            "different company. What we are now is the end result of " +
            "an evolutionary process in which accidental " +
            "events played as big a role, or bigger, as planning and " +
            "foresight.\n", BLACK);

        setEndSelection();
        JButton manningButton = new JButton("Visit Manning");
        manningButton.addActionListener(new ActionListener() {
            public void actionPerformed(ActionEvent e) {
                m_editor.setEditable(false);
                try { m_editor.setPage("http://www.manning.com"); }
                catch (IOException ioe) { ioe.printStackTrace(); }
            }
        });
        m_editor.insertComponent(manningButton);

        setSize(500,450);
        setVisible(true);
    }

    protected void insertText(String text, AttributeSet set) {
        try {
            m_editor.getDocument().insertString(
```

```
          m_editor.getDocument().getLength(), text, set);
      }
      catch (BadLocationException e) {
        e.printStackTrace();
      }
    }

    protected void setEndSelection() {
      m_editor.setSelectionStart(m_editor.getDocument().getLength());
      m_editor.setSelectionEnd(m_editor.getDocument().getLength());
    }

    public static void main(String argv[]) {
      new JTextPaneDemo();
    }
}
```

As example 11.2 demonstrates, we can insert images and components with JTextPane's insertIcon() and insertComponent() methods. These methods insert the given object by replacing the current selection. If there is no current selection, they will be placed at the beginning of the document. This is why we defined the setEndSelection() method in our example above to point the selection to the end of the document where we want to do insertions.

When inserting text, we cannot simply append it to the text pane itself. Instead we retrieve its document and call insertString(). To give attributes to inserted text we can construct AttributeSet implementations, and we can assign attributes to that set using the StyleConstants class. In the example above we do this by constructing three SimpleAttributeSets as static instances (so that they may be reused as much as possible).

As an extension of JEditorPane, JTextPane uses a DefaultStyledDocument for its model. Text panes use a special editor kit, DefaultStyledEditorKit, to manage their Actions and Views. JTextPane also supports the use of Styles, which are named collections of attributes. We will discuss styles, actions, and views as well as many other advanced features of JTextPane in chapters 19 and 20.

11.2 UNDO/REDO

Undo/redo options are commonplace in applications such as paint programs and word processors, and they have been used extensively throughout the writing of this book. It is interesting that this functionality is provided as part of the Swing library, as it is completely Swing independent. In this section we will briefly introduce the javax.swing.undo constituents and, in the process of doing so, we will present an example showing how undo/redo functionality can be integrated into any type of application. The text components come with built-in undo/redo functionality, and we will also discuss how to take advantage of this.

11.2.1   The UndoableEdit interface

abstract interface javax.swing.undo.UndoableEdit

This interface acts as a template definition for anything that can be undone/redone. Implementations should normally be very lightweight, as undo/redo operations commonly occur quickly in succession.

`UndoableEdit`s are designed to have three states: undoable, redoable, and dead. When an `UndoableEdit` is in the undoable state, calling `undo()` will perform an undo operation. Similarly, when an `UndoableEdit` is in the redoable state, calling `redo()` will perform a redo operation. The `canUndo()` and `canRedo()` methods provide ways to see whether an `UndoableEdit` is in the undoable or redoable state. We can use the `die()` method to explicitly send an `UndoableEdit` to the dead state. In the dead state, an `UndoableEdit` cannot be undone or redone, and any attempt to do so will generate an exception.

`UndoableEdit`s maintain three `String` properties, which are normally used as menu item text: `presentationName`, `undoPresentationName`, and `redoPresentationName`. The `addEdit()` and `replaceEdit()` methods are meant to be used to merge two edits and replace an edit, respectively. `UndoableEdit` also defines the concept of significant and insignificant edits. An insignificant edit is one that `UndoManager` (see section 11.2.6) ignores when an undo/redo request is made. `CompoundEdit` (see section 11.2.3), however, will pay attention to both significant and insignificant edits. The `significant` property of an `UndoableEdit` can be queried with `isSignificant()`.

11.2.2   AbstractUndoableEdit

class javax.swing.undo.AbstractUndoableEdit

`AbstractUndoableEdit` implements `UndoableEdit` and defines two boolean properties that represent the three `UndoableEdit` states. The `alive` property is `true` when an edit is not dead. The `done` property is `true` when an undo can be performed, and `false` when a redo can be performed.

The default behavior provided by this class is good enough for most subclasses. All `AbstractUndoableEdit`s are *significant*, and the `undoPresentationName` and `redoPresentationName` properties are formed by simply appending "Undo" and "Redo" to `presentationName`.

The following example demonstrates a basic square painting program with undo/redo functionality. This application simply draws a square outline wherever a mouse press occurs. A `Vector` of `Points` is maintained which represents the upper left-hand corner of each square that is drawn on the canvas. We create an `AbstractUndoableEdit` subclass to maintain a reference to a `Point`, with `undo()` and `redo()` methods that remove and add that `Point` from the `Vector`. Figure 11.7 illustrates the output of example 11.3.

Example 11.3

UndoRedoPaintApp.java

see \Chapter11\3

```
import java.util.*;
import java.awt.*;
import java.awt.event.*;
import javax.swing.*;
import javax.swing.undo.*;

public class UndoRedoPaintApp extends JFrame
{
```

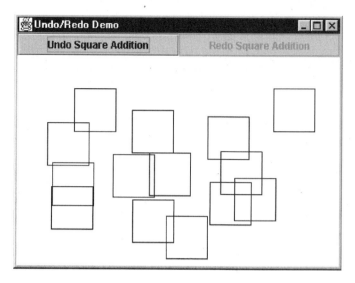

Figure 11.7 A square painting application with one level of undo/redo

```
protected Vector m_points = new Vector();
protected PaintCanvas m_canvas = new PaintCanvas(m_points);
protected UndoablePaintSquare m_edit;
protected JButton m_undoButton = new JButton("Undo");
protected JButton m_redoButton = new JButton("Redo");

public UndoRedoPaintApp() {
  super("Undo/Redo Demo");

  m_undoButton.setEnabled(false);
  m_redoButton.setEnabled(false);

  JPanel buttonPanel = new JPanel(new GridLayout());
  buttonPanel.add(m_undoButton);
  buttonPanel.add(m_redoButton);

  getContentPane().add(buttonPanel, BorderLayout.NORTH);
  getContentPane().add(m_canvas, BorderLayout.CENTER);

  m_canvas.addMouseListener(new MouseAdapter() {
    public void mousePressed(MouseEvent e) {
      Point point = new Point(e.getX(), e.getY());
      m_points.addElement(point);
      m_edit = new UndoablePaintSquare(point, m_points);
      m_undoButton.setText(m_edit.getUndoPresentationName());
      m_redoButton.setText(m_edit.getRedoPresentationName());
      m_undoButton.setEnabled(m_edit.canUndo());
      m_redoButton.setEnabled(m_edit.canRedo());
      m_canvas.repaint();
    }
  });

  m_undoButton.addActionListener(new ActionListener() {
```

```java
      public void actionPerformed(ActionEvent e) {
        try { m_edit.undo(); }
        catch (CannotRedoException cre) { cre.printStackTrace(); }
        m_canvas.repaint();
        m_undoButton.setEnabled(m_edit.canUndo());
        m_redoButton.setEnabled(m_edit.canRedo());
      }
    });

    m_redoButton.addActionListener(new ActionListener() {
      public void actionPerformed(ActionEvent e) {
        try { m_edit.redo(); }
        catch (CannotRedoException cre) { cre.printStackTrace(); }
        m_canvas.repaint();
        m_undoButton.setEnabled(m_edit.canUndo());
        m_redoButton.setEnabled(m_edit.canRedo());
      }
    });

    setSize(400,300);
    setVisible(true);
  }

  public static void main(String argv[]) {
    new UndoRedoPaintApp();
  }
}

class PaintCanvas extends JPanel
{
  Vector m_points;
  protected int width = 50;
  protected int height = 50;

  public PaintCanvas(Vector vect) {
    super();
    m_points = vect;
    setOpaque(true);
    setBackground(Color.white);
  }

  public void paintComponent(Graphics g) {
    super.paintComponent(g);
    g.setColor(Color.black);
    Enumeration enum = m_points.elements();
    while(enum.hasMoreElements()) {
      Point point = (Point) enum.nextElement();
      g.drawRect(point.x, point.y, width, height);
    }
  }
}

class UndoablePaintSquare extends AbstractUndoableEdit
{
  protected Vector m_points;
```

```
    protected Point m_point;

    public UndoablePaintSquare(Point point, Vector vect) {
      m_points = vect;
      m_point = point;
    }

    public String getPresentationName() {
      return "Square Addition";
    }

    public void undo() {
      super.undo();
      m_points.remove(m_point);
    }

    public void redo() {
      super.redo();
      m_points.add(m_point);
    }
  }
}
```

One thing to note about example 11.3 is that it is extremely limited. Because we are not maintaining an ordered collection of `UndoableEdit`s, we can only perform one undo/redo. `CompoundEdit` and `UndoManager` directly address this limitation.

11.2.3 CompoundEdit

class javax.swing.undo.CompoundEdit

This class extends `AbstractUndoableEdit` to support an ordered collection of `Undoable-Edits`, which are maintained as a protected `Vector` called `edits`. `UndoableEdits` can be added to this vector with `addEdit()`, but they cannot so easily be removed (for this, a subclass would be necessary).

Even though `CompoundEdit` is more powerful than `AbstractUndoableEdit`, it is far from the ideal solution. Edits cannot be undone until all edits have been added. Once all `UndoableEdits` are added, we are expected to call `end()`, at which point `CompoundEdit` will no longer accept any additional edits. Once `end()` is called, a call to `undo()` will undo all edits, whether they are *significant* or not. A `redo()` will then redo them all, and we can continue to cycle back and forth like this as long as the `CompoundEdit` itself remains alive. For this reason, `CompoundEdit` is useful for a predefined or intentionally limited set of states.

`CompoundEdit` introduces an additional state property called `inProgress`, which is `true` if `end()` has not been called. We can retrieve the value of `inProgess` with `isIn-Progress()`. The `significant` property, inherited from `UndoableEdit`, will be `true` if one or more of the contained `UndoableEdits` is significant, and it will be `false` otherwise.

11.2.4 UndoableEditEvent

class javax.swing.event.UndoableEditEvent

This event encapsulates a source `Object` and an `UndoableEdit`, and it is meant to be passed to implementations of the `UndoableEditListener` interface.

11.2.5 The UndoableEditListener interface

class javax.swing.event.UndoableEditListener

This listener is intended for use by any class wishing to listen for operations that can be undone/redone. When such an operation occurs, an `UndoableEditEvent` can be sent to an `UndoableEditListener` for processing. `UndoManager` implements this interface so we can simply add it to any class that defines undoable/redoable operations. It is important to emphasize that `UndoableEditEvents` are not fired when an undo or redo actually occurs, but when an operation occurs which has an `UndoableEdit` associated with it. This interface declares one method, `undoableEditHappened()`, which accepts an `UndoableEditEvent`. We are generally responsible for passing `UndoableEditEvents` to this method. Example 11.4 in the next section demonstrates this.

11.2.6 UndoManager

class javax.swing.undo.UndoManager

`UndoManager` extends `CompoundEdit` and relieves us of the limitation where undos and redos cannot be performed until `edit()` is called. It also relieves us of the limitation where all edits are undone or redone at once. Another major difference from `CompoundEdit` is that `UndoManager` simply skips over all insignificant edits when `undo()` or `redo()` is called, effectively not paying them any attention. Interestingly, `UndoManager` allows us to add edits while `inProgress` is `true`, but if `end()` is ever called, `UndoManager` immediately starts acting like a `CompoundEdit`.

UndoManager introduces a new state called `undoOrRedo` which, when `true`, signifies that calling `undo()` or `redo()` is valid. This property can only be `true` if there is more than one edit stored, and only if there is at least one edit in the undoable state and one in the redoable state. The value of this property can be retrieved with `canUndoOrRedo()`, and the `getUndoOrRedoPresentationName()` method will return an appropriate name for use in a menu item or elsewhere.

We can retrieve the next significant `UndoableEdit` that is scheduled to be undone or redone with `editToBeUndone()` or `editToBeRedone()`. We can kill all stored edits with `discardAllEdits()`. The `redoTo()` and `undoTo()` methods can be used to programmatically invoke `undo()` or `redo()` on all edits from the current edit to the edit that is provided as parameter.

We can set the maximum number of edits that can be stored with `setLimit()`. The value of the `limit` property (100 by default) can be retrieved with `getLimit()`, and if it is set to a value smaller than the current number of edits, the edits will be reduced using the protected `trimForLimit()` method. Based on the index of the current edit within the `edits` vector, this method will attempt to remove the most balanced number of edits, in undoable and redoable states, as it can in order to achieve the given limit. The further away an edit is (based on its vector index in the edits vector), the more of a candidate it is for removal when a trim occurs, as edits are taken from the extreme ends of the `edits` vector.

It is very important to note that when an edit is added to the `edits` vector, all edits in the redoable state (those appearing after the index of the current edit) do not simply get moved up one index. Rather, they are removed. So, for example, suppose in a word processor application you enter some text, change the style of ten different regions of that text, and then undo the five most recent style additions. Then a new style change is made. The first five style changes that were made remain in the undoable state, and the new edit is added, also in the undoable state. However, the five style changes that were undone (moved to the redoable state) are now completely lost.

NOTE All public UndoManager methods are synchronized to enable thread safety, and to make UndoManager a good candidate for use as a central undo/redo manager for any number of functionalities.

Example 11.4 shows how we can modify our UndoRedoPaintApp example to allow multiple undos and redos using an UndoManager. Because UndoManager implements UndoableEdit-Listener, we should normally add UndoableEditEvents to it using the undoableEdit-Happened() method rather than addEdit()—undoableEditHappened() calls addEdit() for us, and at the same time allows us to keep track of the source of the operation. This enables UndoManager to act as a central location for all undo/redo edits in an application.

Example 11.4

UndoRedoPaintApp.java

see \Chapter11\4

```
import java.util.*;
import java.awt.*;
import java.awt.event.*;
import javax.swing.*;
import javax.swing.undo.*;
import javax.swing.event.*;
public class UndoRedoPaintApp extends JFrame
{
  protected Vector m_points = new Vector();
  protected PaintCanvas m_canvas = new PaintCanvas(m_points);
  protected UndoManager m_undoManager = new UndoManager();
  protected JButton m_undoButton = new JButton("Undo");
  protected JButton m_redoButton = new JButton("Redo");

  public UndoRedoPaintApp() {
    super("Undo/Redo Demo");

    m_undoButton.setEnabled(false);
    m_redoButton.setEnabled(false);

    JPanel buttonPanel = new JPanel(new GridLayout());
    buttonPanel.add(m_undoButton);
    buttonPanel.add(m_redoButton);

    getContentPane().add(buttonPanel, BorderLayout.NORTH);
    getContentPane().add(m_canvas, BorderLayout.CENTER);

    m_canvas.addMouseListener(new MouseAdapter() {
      public void mousePressed(MouseEvent e) {
        Point point = new Point(e.getX(), e.getY());
        m_points.addElement(point);
```

```
    m_undoManager.undoableEditHappened(new UndoableEditEvent(m_canvas,
        new UndoablePaintSquare(point, m_points)));

    m_undoButton.setText(m_undoManager.getUndoPresentationName());
    m_redoButton.setText(m_undoManager.getRedoPresentationName());
    m_undoButton.setEnabled(m_undoManager.canUndo());
    m_redoButton.setEnabled(m_undoManager.canRedo());
    m_canvas.repaint();
      }
  });

  m_undoButton.addActionListener(new ActionListener() {
    public void actionPerformed(ActionEvent e) {
      try { m_undoManager.undo(); }
      catch (CannotRedoException cre) { cre.printStackTrace(); }
      m_canvas.repaint();
      m_undoButton.setEnabled(m_undoManager.canUndo());
      m_redoButton.setEnabled(m_undoManager.canRedo());
    }
  });

  m_redoButton.addActionListener(new ActionListener() {
    public void actionPerformed(ActionEvent e) {
      try { m_undoManager.redo(); }
      catch (CannotRedoException cre) { cre.printStackTrace(); }
      m_canvas.repaint();
      m_undoButton.setEnabled(m_undoManager.canUndo());
      m_redoButton.setEnabled(m_undoManager.canRedo());
    }
  });

  setSize(400,300);
  setVisible(true);
  }

 public static void main(String argv[]) {
    new UndoRedoPaintApp();
  }
}

// Classes PaintCanvas and UndoablePaintSquare are unchanged
// from example 11.3
```

Run this example and notice that we can have up to 100 squares in the undoable or redoable state at any given time. Also notice that when several squares are in the redoable state, adding a new square will eliminate them, and the redo button will become disabled, indicating that no redos can be performed.

11.2.7   The StateEditable interface

abstract interface javax.swing.undo.StateEditable

The StateEditable interface is intended to be used by objects that wish to maintain specific *before* (pre) and *after* (post) states. This provides an alternative to managing undos and redos in

UndoableEdits. Once a before and after state is defined, we can use a `StateEdit` object to switch between the two states. Two methods must be implemented by `StateEditable` implementations. `storeState()` is to be used by an object to store its state as a set of key/value pairs in a given `Hashtable`. Normally this entails storing the name of an object and a copy of that object (unless a primitive is stored). `restoreState()` is to be used by an object to restore its state according to the key/vaue pairs stored in a given `Hashtable`.

11.2.8   StateEdit

class javax.swing.undo.StateEdit

`StateEdit` extends `AbstractUndoableEdit`, and it is meant to store the before and after `Hashtable`s of a `StateEditable` instance. When a `StateEdit` is instantiated, it is passed a `StateEditable` object, and a protected `Hashtable` called `preState` is passed to that `StateEditable`'s `storeState()` method. Similarly, when `end()` is called on a `StateEdit`, a protected `Hashtable` called `postState` is passed to the corresponding `StateEditable`'s `storeState()` method. After `end()` is called, undos and redos toggle the state of the `StateEditable` between `postState` and `preState` by passing the appropriate `Hashtable` to that `StateEditable`'s `restoreState()` method.

11.2.9   UndoableEditSupport

class javax.swing.undo.UndoableEditSupport

This convenience class is used for managing `UndoableEditListeners`. We can add and remove an `UndoableEditListener` with `addUndoableEditListener()` and `removeUndoableEditListener()`.`UndoableEditSupport` maintains an `updateLevel` property which specifies how many times the `beginUpdate()` method has been called. As long as this value is above 0, `UndoableEdits` added with the `postEdit()` method will be stored in a temporary `CompoundEdit` object without being fired. The `endEdit()` method decrements the `updateLevel` property. When `updateLevel` is 0, any calls to `postEdit()` will fire the edit that is passed in, or the `CompoundEdit` that has been accumulating edits up to that point.

WARNING   The `endUpdate()` and `beginUpdate()` methods may call `undoableEditHappened()` in each `UndoableEditListener`, possibly resulting in deadlock if these methods are actually invoked from one of the listeners themselves.

11.2.10   CannotUndoException

class javax.swing.undo.CannotUndoException

This exception is thrown when `undo()` is invoked on an `UndoableEdit` that cannot be undone.

11.2.11   CannotRedoException

class javax.swing.undo.CannotRedoException

This exception is thrown when `redo()` is invoked on an `UndoableEdit` that cannot be redone.

11.2.12 Using built-in text component undo/redo functionality

All default text component `Document` models fire `UndoableEdit`s. For `PlainDocument`s, this involves keeping track of text insertions and removals, as well as any structural changes. For `StyledDocument`s, however, this involves keeping track of a much larger group of changes. Fortunately this work has been built into these document models for us. The following example, 11.5, shows how easy it is to add undo/redo support to text components. Figure 11.8 illustrates the output.

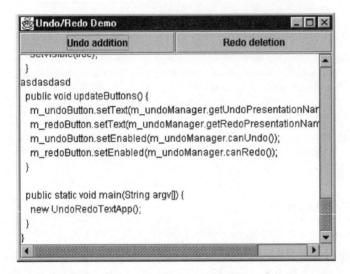

Figure 11.8 Undo/redo functionality added to a `JTextArea`

Example 11.5

UndoRedoTextApp.java

see \Chapter11\5

```
import java.awt.*;
import java.awt.*;
import java.awt.event.*;
import javax.swing.*;
import javax.swing.undo.*;
import javax.swing.event.*;

public class UndoRedoTextApp extends JFrame
{
  protected JTextArea m_editor = new JTextArea();
  protected UndoManager m_undoManager = new UndoManager();
  protected JButton m_undoButton = new JButton("Undo");
  protected JButton m_redoButton = new JButton("Redo");

  public UndoRedoTextApp() {
    super("Undo/Redo Demo");
```

CHAPTER 11   TEXT COMPONENTS AND UNDO

```
    m_undoButton.setEnabled(false);
    m_redoButton.setEnabled(false);

    JPanel buttonPanel = new JPanel(new GridLayout());
    buttonPanel.add(m_undoButton);
    buttonPanel.add(m_redoButton);

    JScrollPane scroller = new JScrollPane(m_editor);

    getContentPane().add(buttonPanel, BorderLayout.NORTH);
    getContentPane().add(scroller, BorderLayout.CENTER);

    m_editor.getDocument().addUndoableEditListener(
     new UndoableEditListener() {
      public void undoableEditHappened(UndoableEditEvent e) {
        m_undoManager.addEdit(e.getEdit());
        updateButtons();
      }
    });

    m_undoButton.addActionListener(new ActionListener() {
      public void actionPerformed(ActionEvent e) {
        try { m_undoManager.undo(); }
        catch (CannotRedoException cre) { cre.printStackTrace(); }
        updateButtons();
      }
    });

    m_redoButton.addActionListener(new ActionListener() {
      public void actionPerformed(ActionEvent e) {
        try { m_undoManager.redo(); }
        catch (CannotRedoException cre) { cre.printStackTrace(); }
        updateButtons();
      }
    });

    setSize(400,300);
    setVisible(true);
  }

  public void updateButtons() {
    m_undoButton.setText(m_undoManager.getUndoPresentationName());
    m_redoButton.setText(m_undoManager.getRedoPresentationName());
    m_undoButton.setEnabled(m_undoManager.canUndo());
    m_redoButton.setEnabled(m_undoManager.canRedo());
  }

  public static void main(String argv[]) {
    new UndoRedoTextApp();
  }
}
```

C H A P T E R   1 2

Menus, toolbars and actions

12.1   MENUS, TOOLBARS, AND ACTIONS OVERVIEW

Drop-down menu bars, context-sensitive popup menus, and draggable toolbars have become commonplace in many modern applications. It is no surprise that Swing offers these features, and in this section we will discuss the classes and interfaces that lie beneath them. The remainder of this chapter is then devoted to the step-wise construction of a basic text editor application which demonstrates each feature discussed here.

12.1.1   The SingleSelectionModel interface

abstract interface javax.swing.SingleSelectionModel

This simple interface describes a model which maintains a single selected element from a given collection. Methods to assign, retrieve, and clear a selected index are declared, as well as methods for attaching and removing `ChangeListener`s. Implementations are responsible for the storage and manipulation of the collection to be selected from, maintaining an `int` property representing the selected element, and maintaining a `boolean` property specifying whether an element is selected. They are expected to fire `ChangeEvent`s whenever the selected index changes.

12.1.2 DefaultSingleSelectionModel

class javax.swing.DefaultSelectionModel

This is the default implementation of `SingleSelectionModel` that is used by `JMenuBar` and `JMenuItem`. The `selectedIndex` property represents the selected index at any given time, and it is `-1` when nothing is selected. As expected, we can add and remove `ChangeListeners`, and the protected `fireStateChanged()` method is responsible for dispatching `ChangeEvents` whenever the `selectedIndex` property changes.

12.1.3 JMenuBar

class javax.swing.JMenuBar

`JMenuBar` is a container for `JMenus` that are laid out horizontally in a row; menu bars typically reside at the top of a frame or applet. We use the `add(JMenu menu)` method to add a new `JMenu` to a `JMenuBar`. We use the `setJMenuBar()` method in `JFrame`, `JDialog`, `JApplet`, `JRoot-Pane`, and `JInternalFrame` to set the menu bar for these containers (remember from chapter 3 that each of these containers implements `RootPaneContainer`, which enforces the definition of `setJMenuBar()`). `JMenuBar` uses a `DefaultSingleSelectionModel` to enforce the selection of only one child at any given time.

A `JMenuBar` is a `JComponent` subclass and, as such, it can be placed anywhere in a container just as with any other Swing component (this functionality is not available with AWT menu bars).

> **WARNING** `JMenuBar` defines the method `setHelpMenu(JMenu menu)`, which is intened to mark a single menu contained in a `JMenuBar` as the designated Help menu. The `JMenuBar` UI delegate may be responsible for positioning and somehow treating this menu differently than other menus. However, this is not implemented as of Java 2 FCS, and it generates an exception if it's used.

> **NOTE** One feature missing in the current `JMenuBar` implementation, or its UI delegate, is the ability to easily control the spacing between its `JMenu` children. As of Java 2 FCS, the easiest way to control this is by overriding `JMenuBar` and manually taking control of its layout. (JDK 1.2.2 addressed this problem by minimizing the amount of white space between menus.) By default, `JMenuBar` uses an x-oriented `BoxLayout`.

`JMenuBar` provides several methods to retrieve its child components, set/get the currently selected item, and register/unregister with the current `KeyBoardManager` (see section 2.13). It also provides the `isManagingFocus()` method which simply returns `true` to indicate that `JMenuBar` handles focus management internally. The public methods `processKeyEvent()` and `processMouseEvent()` are implemented only to satisfy the `MenuElement` interface requirements (see below), and they do nothing by default.

12.1.4 JMenuItem

class javax.swing.JMenuItem

This class extends `AbstractButton` (see section 4.1) and it represents a single menu item. We can assign icons and keyboard mnemonics just as we can with buttons. A mnemonic is represented graphically by underlining the first instance of the corresponding character, just as it is in buttons. Icon and text placement can be dealt with in the same way we deal with this functionality in buttons.

We can also attach keyboard accelerators to a JMenuItem (i.e. we can register keyboard actions with a JMenuItem (see section 2.13)). When an accelerator is assigned to a JMenuItem, it will appear as small text to the right of the menu item text. An accelerator is a combination of keys that can be used to activate a menu item. Contrary to a mnemonic, an accelerator will invoke a menu item even when the popup containing it is not visible. The only necessary condition for accelerator activation is that the window containing the target menu item must be currently active. To add an accelerator corresponding to CTRL+A we can do the following:

```
myJMenuItem.setAccelerator(KeyStroke.getKeyStroke(
    KeyEvent.VK_A, KeyEvent.CTRL_MASK, false);
```

NOTE   JMenuItem is the only Swing component that graphically displays an assigned keyboard accelerator.

We normally attach an ActionListener to a menu item. As with buttons, whenever the menu item is clicked the ActionListener is notified. Alternatively we can use Actions (discussed below and briefly in section 2.13), which provide a convenient means of creating a menu item as well as defining the corresponding action-handling code. A single Action instance can be used to create an arbitrary number of JMenuItems and JButtons with identical action-handling code. We will see how this is done soon enough. It's enough to say here that when an Action is disabled, all JMenuItems associated with that Action are disabled, and, as buttons always do in the disabled state, they appear grayed out.

Like any other AbstractButton descendant, JMenuItem fires ActionEvents and ChangeEvents and allows the attachment of ActionListeners and ChangeListeners accordingly. JMenuItem will also fire MenuDragMouseEvents (see below) when the mouse enters, exits, or is dragged, or when a mouse button is released inside its bounds. It will fire MenuKeyEvents when a key is pressed, typed, or released. Both of these Swing-specific events will only be fired when the popup containing the corresponding menu item is visible. As expected, we can add MenuDragMouseListeners and MenuKeyEventListeners for notification of these events. Several public processXXEvent() methods are also provided to receive and respond to events dispatched to a JMenuItem, some of which are forwarded from the current MenuSelectionManager (see below).

12.1.5   JMenu

class javax.swing.JMenu

This class extends JMenuItem and is usually added to a JMenuBar or to another JMenu. In the former case it will act as a menu item which pops up a JPopupMenu containing child menu items. If a JMenu is added to another JMenu, it will appear in that menu's corresponding popup as a menu item with an arrow on its right side. When that menu item is activated by mouse movement or keyboard selection, a popup will appear that displays its corresponding child menu items. Each JMenu maintains a topLevelMenu property which is false for submenus and true otherwise.

JMenu uses a DefaultButtonModel to manage its state, and it holds a private instance of JPopupMenu (see below) to display its associated menu items when it is activated with the mouse or a keyboard mnemonic.

Unlike its `JMenuItem` parent, `JMenu` specifically overrides `setAccelerator()` with an empty implementation to disallow keyboard accelerators. This happens because it assumes that we will only want to activate a menu when it is already visible; for this, we can use a mnemonic.

We can display/hide the associated popup programmatically by setting the `popupMenu-Visible` property, and we can access the popup using `getPopupMenu()`. We can set the coordinate location where the popup is displayed with `setMenuLocation()`. We can also assign a specific delay time in milliseconds using `setDelay()` to specify how long a `JMenu` should wait before displaying its popup when activated.

We use the overloaded `add()` method to add `JMenuItems`, `Components`, `Actions` (see below), or `Strings` to a `JMenu`. (Adding a `String` simply creates a `JMenuItem` child with the given text.) Similarly we can use several variations of the overloaded `insert()` and `remove()` methods to insert and remove child components. `JMenu` also directly supports the creation and insertion of separator components in its popup, using `addSeparator()`, which provides a convenient means of visually organizing child components into groups.

The protected `createActionChangeListener()` method is used when an `Action` is added to a `JMenu` to create a `PropertyChangeListener` for internal use in responding to bound property changes that occur in that `Action` (see below). The `createWinListener()` method is used to create an instance of the protected inner class `JMenu.WinListener`, which is used to deselect a menu when its corresponding popup closes. We are rarely concerned with these methods; only subclasses desiring a more complete customization will override them.

Along with the event dispatching/handling that is inherited from `JMenuItem`, `JMenu` adds functionality for firing and capturing `MenuEvents` that are used to notify attached `MenuListeners` when its selection changes (see below).

UI

GUIDELINE

Flat and wide design   Recent usability research has shown that menus with too many hierarchical levels don't work well. Features get buried under too many layers. Some operating systems restrict menus to three levels—for example, the main menu bar, a pull down menu, and a single walking popup menu.

A maximum of three levels appears to be a good rule of thumb. Don't let yourself be tempted to use popup menus to create a complex series of hierarchical choices. Instead, keep menus more flat.

For each menu, another good rule of thumb is to provide 7 ± 2 options. However, if you have too many choices that must be displayed, it is better to break this rule and go to 10 or more items than to introduce additional hierarchy.

12.1.6   JPopupMenu

class javax.swing.JPopupMenu

This class represents a small popup window that contains a collection of components laid out in a single column by default using, suprisingly, a `GridBagLayout` (there is nothing stopping us from changing `JPopupMenu`'s layout manager). `JPopupMenu` uses a `DefaultSingle-SelectionModel` to enforce the selection of only one child at any given time.

`JMenu` simply delegates all its calls such as `add()`, `remove()`, `insert()`, and `add-Separator()` to its internal `JPopupMenu`. As expected, `JPopupMenu` provides similar methods.

The addSeparator() method inserts an instance of the inner class JPopupMenu.Separator (a subclass of JSeparator, which is discussed below). The show() method displays a JPopup-Menu at a given position within the coordinate system of a given component. This component is referred to as the *invoker* component; JPopupMenu can be assigned an invoker by setting its invoker property. JComponent's setVisible() method is overridden to display a JPopup-Menu with respect to its current invoker (by passing the invoker component as a parameter to the show() method), and we can change the location in which it will appear using setLocation(). We can also control a JPopupMenu's size with the overloaded setPopupSize() methods, and we can use the pack() method (similar to the java.awt.Window method of the same name) to request that a popup change size to the minimum required for the correct display of its child components.

NOTE   JComboBox's UI delegate uses a JPopupMenu subclass to display its popup list.

When we need to display our own JPopupMenu, it is customary, but certainly not necessary, to do so in response to a platform-dependent mouse gesture (such as a right-click on Windows platforms). The java.awt.event.MouseEvent class provides a simple method we can use in a platform-independent manner to check whether a platform-dependent popup gesture has occurred. This method, isPopupTrigger(), will return true if the MouseEvent it is called on represents the current operating system's popup trigger gesture.

JPopupMenu has the unique ability to act as either a heavyweight or lighweight component. It is smart enough to detect when it will be displayed completely within a Swing container and adjust itself accordingly. However, the default behavior may not be acceptable in some cases. You might recall from chapter 2 that we must set JPopupMenu's lightWeight-PopupEnabled property to false to force it to be heavyweight and to allow the overlapping of other heavyweight components that might reside in the same container. Setting this property to true will force a JPopupMenu to remain lightweight. The static setDefaultLight-WeightPopupEnabled() method serves the same purpose, but it effects all JPopupMenus created from that point on (in the current implementation, all popups that exist *before* this method is called will retain their previous lightweight/heavyweight settings).

BUG ALERT   Due to an AWT bug, all popups are forced into lightweight mode when they are displayed in dialogs, regardless of the state of the lightWeightPopupEnabled property.

The protected createActionChangeListener() method is used when an Action is added to a JPopupMenu to create a PropertyChangeListener for internal use in responding to bound property changes that occur in that Action.

A JPopupMenu fires PopupMenuEvents (discussed below) whenever it is made visible, hidden, or cancelled. As expected, we can attatch PopupMenuListeners to capture these events.

12.1.7   JSeparator

class javax.swing.JSeparator

This class represents a simple separator component with a UI delegate responsible for displaying it as a horizontal or vertical line. We can specify which orientation a JSeparator should use by changing its orientation property. This class is most often used in menus and toolbars; but it is a JComponent subclass, and nothing stops us from using JSeparators anywhere we want.

We normally do not use JSeparator explicitly. Rather, we use the addSeparator() method of JMenu, JPopupMenu, and JToolBar. JMenu delegates this call to its JPopupMenu which, as we know, uses an instance of its own custom JSeparator subclass which is rendered as a horizontal line. JToolBar also uses its own custom JSeparator subclass which has no graphical representation, and it appears as just an empty region. Unlike menu separators, however, JToolBar's separator allows explicit instantiation and provides a method for assigning a new size in the form of a Dimension.

GUIDELINE

Use of a separator   Use a separator to group related menu choices and separate them from others. This provides better visual communication and better usability by providing a space between the target areas for groups of choices. It also reduces the chance of an error when making a selection with the mouse.

12.1.8   JCheckBoxMenuItem

class javax.swing.JCheckBoxMenuItem

This class extends JMenuItem and it can be selected, deselected, and rendered the same way as JCheckBox (see chapter 4). We use the isSelected()/setSelected() or getState()/setState() methods to determine/set the selection state. ActionListeners and ChangeListeners can be attached to a JCheckBoxMenuItem for notification about changes in its state (see the JMenuItem discussion for inherited functionality).

12.1.9   JRadioButtonMenuItem

class javax.swing.JRadioButtonMenuItem

This class extends JMenuItem and it can be selected, deselected, and rendered the same way as JRadioButton (see chapter 4). We use the isSelected()/setSelected() or getState()/setState() methods to determine/set the selection state. ActionListeners and ChangeListeners can be attached to a JRadioButtonMenuItem for notification about changes in its state (see the JMenuItem discussion for inherited functionality). We often use JRadioButtonMenuItems in ButtonGroups to enforce the selection of only one item in a group at any given time.

GUIDELINE

Component overloading   As a general UI design rule, it is not good to overload components by using them for two purposes. By adding check boxes or radio buttons to a menu, you are changing the purpose of a menu from one of navigation to one of selection. This is an important point to understand.

Making this change is an acceptable design technique when it will speed operation and enhance usability by removing the need for a cumbersome dialog or option pane. However, it is important to assess that it does not otherwise adversely affect usability.

Groups of radio button or check box menu items are probably best isolated using a JSeparator.

12.1.10 The MenuElement interface

abstract interface javax.swing.MenuElement

This interface must be implemented by all components that want to act as menu items. By implementing the methods of this interface, any components can act as menu items, making it quite easy to build our own custom menu items.

The `getSubElements()` method returns an array of `MenuElements` that contains the given item's sub-elements. The `processKeyEvent()` and `processMouseEvent()` methods are called to process keyboard and mouse events when the implementing component has the focus. Unlike methods with the same name in the `java.awt.Component` class, these two methods receive three parameters: the `KeyEvent` or `MouseEvent`, which should be processed; an array of `MenuElements` which forms the path to the implementing component; and the current `MenuSelectionManager` (see below). The `menuSelectionChanged()` method is called by the `MenuSelectionManager` when the implementing component is added or removed from its current selection state. The `getComponent()` method returns a reference to a component that is responsible for rendering the implementing component.

NOTE   The `getComponent()` method is interesting, as it allows classes that are not `Components` themselves to implement the `MenuElement` interface and *act* as menu elements when necessary. Such a class would contain a `Component` used for display in a menu, and this `Component` would be returned by `getComponent()`. This design has powerful implications, as it allows us to design robust JavaBeans that encapsulate an optional GUI representation. We can imagine a complex spell-checker or dictionary class implementing the `MenuElement` interface and providing a custom component for display in a menu; this would be a powerful and highly object-oriented bean, indeed.

`JMenuItem`, `JMenuBar`, `JPopupMenu`, and `JMenu` all implement this interface. Note that each of their `getComponent()` methods simply returns a `this` reference. By extending any of these implementing classes, we inherit `MenuElement` functionality and are not required to implement it. (We won't explicitly use this interface in any examples, as the custom component we will build at the end of this chapter is an extension of `JMenu`.)

12.1.11 MenuSelectionManager

class javax.swing.MenuSelectionManager

`MenuSelectionManager` is a service class that is responsible for managing menu selection throughout a single Java session. (Unlike most other service classes in Swing, `MenuSelectionManager` does not register its shared instance with `AppContext`—see chapter 2.) When `MenuElement` implementations receive `MouseEvents` or `KeyEvents`, these events should not be processed directly. Rather, they should be handed off to the `MenuSelectionManager` so that it may forward them to subcomponents automatically. For instance, whenever a `JMenuItem` is activated by the keyboard or mouse, or whenever a `JMenuItem` selection occurs, the menu item UI delegate is responsible for forwarding the corresponding event to the `MenuSelectionManager`, if necessary. The following code shows how `BasicMenuItemUI` deals with mouse releases:

```
public void mouseReleased(MouseEvent e) {
  MenuSelectionManager manager =
```

```
        MenuSelectionManager.defaultManager();
      Point p = e.getPoint();
      if(p.x >= 0 && p.x < menuItem.getWidth() &&
       p.y >= 0 && p.y < menuItem.getHeight()) {
        manager.clearSelectedPath();
        menuItem.doClick(0);
      }
      else {
        manager.processMouseEvent(e);
      }
    }
```

The static `defaultManager()` method returns the `MenuSelectionManager` shared instance, and the `clearSelectedPath()` method tells the currently active menu hierarchy to close and unselect all menu components. In the code shown above, `clearSelected-Path()` will only be called if the mouse release occurs within the corresponding `JMenuItem` (in which case there is no need for the event to propagate any further). If this is not the case, the event is sent to `MenuSelectionManager`'s `processMouseEvent()` method, which forwards it to other subcomponents. `JMenuItem` doesn't have any subcomponents by default, so nothing very interesting happens in this case. However, in the case of `JMenu`, which considers its popup menu a subcomponent, sending a mouse-released event to the `MenuSelection-Manager` is expected no matter what (the following code is from `BasicMenuUI`):

```
public void mouseReleased(MouseEvent e) {
  MenuSelectionManager manager =
    MenuSelectionManager.defaultManager();
  manager.processMouseEvent(e);
  if (!e.isConsumed())
    manager.clearSelectedPath();
}
```

`MenuSelectionManager` will fire `ChangeEvent`s whenever its `setSelectedPath()` method is called (for example, each time a menu selection changes). As expected, we can attach `ChangeListener`s to listen for these events.

12.1.12 The MenuDragMouseListener interface

abstract interface javax.swing.event.MenuDragMouseListener

This listener receives notification when the mouse cursor enters, exits, is released, or is moved over a menu item.

12.1.13 MenuDragMouseEvent

class javax.swing.event.MenuDragMouseEvent

This event class is used to deliver information to `MenuDragMouseListener`s. It encapsulates the following information:

- The component source.
- The event ID.
- The time of the event.

- A bitwise OR-masked `int` specifying which mouse button and/or keys (CTRL, SHIFT, ALT, or META) were pressed at the time of the event.
- The x and y mouse coordinates.
- The number of clicks immediately preceding the event.
- Whether the event represents the platform-dependent popup trigger.
- An array of `MenuElement`s leading to the source of the event.
- The current `MenuSelectionManager`.

This event inherits all `MouseEvent` functionality (see the API documentation) and it adds two methods for retrieving the array of `MenuElement`s and the `MenuSelectionManager`.

12.1.14 The MenuKeyListener interface

abstract interface javax.swing.event.MenuKeyListener

This listener is notified when a menu item receives a key event corresponding to a key press, release, or type. These events don't necessarily correspond to mnemonics or accelerators; they are received whenever a menu item is simply visible on the screen.

12.1.15 MenuKeyEvent

class javax.swing.event.MenuKeyEvent

This event class is used to deliver information to `MenuKeyListener`s. It encapsulates the following information:

- The component source.
- The event ID.
- The time of the event.
- A bitwise OR-masked `int` specifying which mouse button and/or keys (CTRL, SHIFT, or ALT) were pressed at the time of the event.
- An `int` and `char` identifying the source key that caused the event.
- An array of `MenuElement`s leading to the source of the event.
- The current `MenuSelectionManager`.

This event inherits all `KeyEvent` functionality (see the API documentation) and it adds two methods for retrieving the array of `MenuElement`s and the `MenuSelectionManager`.

12.1.16 The MenuListener interface

abstract interface javax.swing.event.MenuListener

This listener receives notification when a menu is selected, deselected, or canceled. Three methods must be implemented by `MenuListener`s, and each takes a `MouseEvent` parameter: `menuCanceled()`, `menuDeselected()`, and `menuSelected()`.

12.1.17 MenuEvent

class javax.swing.event.MenuEvent

This event class is used to deliver information to `MenuListener`s. It simply encapsulates a reference to its source `Object`.

12.1.18 The PopupMenuListener interface

abstract interface javax.swing.event.PopupMenuListener

This listener receives notification when a JPopupMenu is about to become visible or hidden, or when it is canceled. Canceling a JPopupMenu also causes it to be hidden, so two PopupMenu-Events are fired in this case. (A cancel occurs when the *invoker* component is resized or when the window containing the invoker changes size or location.) Three methods must be implemented by PopupMenuListeners, and each takes a PopupMenuEvent parameter: popupMenuCanceled(), popupMenuWillBecomeVisible(), and popupMenuWillBecomeInvisible().

12.1.19 PopupMenuEvent

class javax.swing.event.PopupMenuEvent

This event class is used to deliver information to PopupMenuListeners. It simply encapsulates a reference to its source Object.

12.1.20 JToolBar

class javax.swing.JToolBar

This class represents the Swing implementation of a toolbar. Toolbars are often placed directly below menu bars at the top of a frame or applet, and they act as a container for any component (buttons and combo boxes are most common). The most convenient way to add buttons to a JToolBar is to use Actions; this is discussed below.

> **NOTE** Components often need their alignment setting tweaked to provide uniform positioning within JToolBar. This can be accomplished using the setAlignmentY() and setAlignmentX() methods. The need to tweak the alignment of components in JToolBar has been alleviated for the most part, as of JDK 1.2.2.

JToolBar also allows the convenient addition of an inner JSeparator subclass, JTool-Bar.Separator, to provide an empty space for visually grouping components. These separators can be added with either of the overloaded addSeparator() methods, one of which takes a Dimension parameter that specifies the size of the separator.

Two orientations are supported, VERTICAL and HORIZONTAL, and the current orientation is maintained by JToolBar's orientation property. It uses a BoxLayout layout manager which is dynamically changed between Y_AXIS and X_AXIS when the orientation property changes.

JToolBar can be dragged in and out of its parent container if its floatable property is set to true. When it is dragged out of its parent, a JToolBar appears as a floating window (during a mouse drag) and its border changes color depending on whether it can re-dock in its parent at a given location. If a JToolBar is dragged outside of its parent and released, it will be placed in its own JFrame which will be fully maximizable, minimizable, and closable. When this frame is closed, JToolBar will jump back into its most recent dock position in its original parent, and the floating JFrame will disappear. We recommend that you place JToolBar in one of the four sides of a container using a BorderLayout and leave the other sides unused, to allow the JToolBar to be docked in any of that container's side regions.

The protected createActionChangeListener() method is used when an Action (see below) is added to a JToolBar to create a PropertyChangeListener for internal use in responding to bound property changes that occur in that Action.

Uses for a toolbar   Toolbars have become ubiquitous in modern software. They are often overused or misused, and therefore, they fail to achieve their objective of increased usability. The three key uses have subtle differences and implications.

Tool selection or mode selection   Perhaps the most effective use of a toolbar is, as the name suggests, for the selection of a tool or operational mode. This is most common in drawing or image manipulation packages. The user selects the toolbar button to change the mode from "paintbrush" to "filler" to "draw box" to "cut," for example. This is a highly effective use of toolbar, as the small icons are usually sufficient to render a suitable tool image. Many images for this purpose have been adopted as a defacto standard. If you are developing a tool selection toolbar, we advise you to stick closely to icons which have been used by similar existing products.

Functional selection   The earliest use of a toolbar was to replace the selection of a specific function from the menu. This led to them being called "speedbars" or "menubars". The idea was that the small icon button was faster and easier to acquire than the menu selection and that usability was enhanced as a result. This worked well for many common functions in file-oriented applications, such as Open File, New File, Save, Cut, Copy, and Paste. In fact, most of us would recognize the small icons for all of these functions. However, with other more application-specific functions, it has become more difficult for icon designers to come up with appropriate designs. This often leads to applications which have a confusing and intimidating array of icons across the top of the screen, which therefore detracts from usability. As a general rule of thumb, stick to common cross-application functions when you're overloading menu selections with toolbar buttons. If you do need to break the rule, consider selecting annotated buttons for the toolbar.

Navigational selection   The third use for toolbars has been for navigational selection. This often means replacing or overloading menu options. These menu options are used to select a specific screen to move to the front. The toolbar buttons replace or overload the menu option and allow the navigational selection to be made by supposedly faster means. However, this usage also suffers from the problem of appropriate icon design. It is usually too difficult to devise a suitable set of icons which have clear and unambiguous meaning. Therefore, as a rule of thumb, consider the use of annotated buttons on the toolbar.

12.1.21   Custom JToolBar separators

Unfortunately, Swing does not include a toolbar-specific separator component that will display a vertical or horizontal line depending on current toolbar orientation. The following psuedocode shows how we can build such a component under the assumption that it will always have a JToolBar as a direct parent:

```
public class MyToolBarSeparator extends JComponent
{
```

```
    public void paintComponent(Graphics g) {
      super.paintComponent(g);
      if (getParent() instanceof JToolBar) {
        if (((JToolBar) getParent()).getOrientation()
         == JToolBar.HORIZONTAL) {
          // Paint a vertical line
        }
        else {
          // Paint a horizontal line
        }
      }
    }

    public Dimension getPreferredSize() {
      if (getParent() instanceof JToolBar) {
        if (((JToolBar) getParent()).getOrientation()
         == JToolBar.HORIZONTAL) {
          // Return horizontal size
        }
        else {
          // Return vertical size
        }
      }
    }
  }
```

GUIDELINE

Use of a separator   The failure to include a graphical separator for toolbars really was an oversight on the part of the Swing designers. Again, the separator is used to group related functions or tools. For example, if the functions all belong on the same menu, then group them together, or if the tools (or modes) are related, such as Cut, Copy, and Paste, then group them together and separate them from others with a separator.

Grouping like this improves perceived separation by introducing a visual layer. The viewer can first acquire a group of buttons and then a specific button. He will also learn, using directional memory, the approximate position of each group. By separating the groups, you will improve the usability by helping the user to acquire the target better when using the mouse.

12.1.22   Changing JToolBar's floating frame behavior

The behavior of JToolBar's floating JFrame is certainly useful, but whether the maximization and resizability should be allowed is arguable. Though we cannot control whether a JFrame can be maximized, we can control whether it can be resized. To enforce non-resizability in JToolBar's floating JFrame (and to set its displayed title while we're at it), we need to override its UI delegate and customize the createFloatingFrame() method as follows:

```
public class MyToolBarUI
  extends javax.swing.plaf.metal.MetalToolBarUI {
    protected JFrame createFloatingFrame(JToolBar toolbar) {
```

```
JFrame frame = new JFrame(toolbar.getName());
frame.setTitle("My toolbar");
frame.setResizable(false);
WindowListener wl = createFrameListener();
frame.addWindowListener(wl);
return frame;
  }
}
```

To assign `MyToolBarUI` as a `JToolBar`'s UI delegate, we can do the following:

```
mytoolbar.setUI(new MyToolBarUI());
```

To force the use of this delegate on a global basis, we can do the following *before* any `JToolBar`s are instantiated:

```
UIManager.getDefaults().put(
  "ToolBarUI","com.mycompany.MyToolBarUI");
```

Note that we may also have to add an associated `Class` instance to the `UIDefaults` table for this to work (see chapter 21).

GUIDELINE

Use of a floating frame   It is probably best to restrict the use of a floating toolbar frame to toolbars being used for *tool or mode selection* (see the UI Guideline in section 12.1.20).

12.1.23   The Action interface

abstract interface javax.swing.Action

This interface describes a helper object which extends `ActionListener` and which supports a set of bound properties. We use appropriate `add()` methods in the `JMenu`, `JPopupMenu`, and `JToolBar` classes to add an `Action` which will use information from the given instance to create and return a component that is appropriate for that container (a `JMenuItem` in the case of the first two, a `JButton` in the case of the latter). The same `Action` instance can be used to create an arbitrary number of menu items or toolbar buttons.

Because `Action` extends `ActionListener`, the `actionPerformed()` method is inherited and it can be used to encapsulate appropriate `ActionEvent` handling code. When a menu item or toolbar button is created using an `Action`, the resulting component is registered as a `PropertyChangeListener` with the `Action`, and the `Action` is registered as an `ActionListener` with the component. Thus, whenever a change occurs to one of that `Action`'s bound properties, all components with registered `PropertyChangeListeners` will receive notification. This provides a convenient means for allowing identical functionality in menus, toolbars, and popup menus with minimum code repetition and object creation.

The `putValue()` and `getValue()` methods are intended to work with a `Hashtable`-like structure to maintain an `Action`'s bound properties. Whenever the value of a property changes, we are expected to fire `PropertyChangeEvents` to all registered listeners. As expected, methods to add and remove `PropertyChangeListeners` are provided.

The `Action` interface defines five static property keys that are intended to be used by `JMenuItems` and `JButtons` created with an `Action` instance:

- String DEFAULT: [Not used].
- String LONG_DESCRIPTION: Used for a lengthy description of an Action.
- String NAME: Used as the text displayed in JMenuItems and JButtons.
- String SHORT_DESCRIPTION: Used for the tooltip text of associated JMenuItems and JButtons.
- String SMALL_ICON: Used as the icon in associated JMenuItems and JButtons.

12.1.24 AbstractAction

class javax.swing.AbstractAction

This class is an abstract implementation of the Action interface. Along with the properties inherited from Action, AbstractAction defines the enabled property which provides a means of enabling/disabling all associated components registered as PropertyChangeListeners. A SwingPropertyChangeSupport instance is used to manage the firing of Property-ChangeEvents to all registered PropertyChangeListeners (see chapter 2 for more about SwingPropertyChangeSupport).

NOTE Many UI delegates define inner class subclasses of AbstractAction, and the TextAction subclass is used by DefaultEditorKit to define action-handling code corresponding to specific KeyStroke bindings (see chapter 19).

12.2 BASIC TEXT EDITOR, PART I: MENUS

In example 12.1 we begin the construction of a basic text editor application using a menu bar and several menu items. The menu bar contains two JMenus labeled "File" and "Font." The File menu contains JMenuItems for creating a new (empty) document, opening a text file, saving the current document as a text file, and exiting the application. The Font menu contains JCheckBoxMenuItems for making the document bold and/or italic, as well as JRadioButtonMenuItems organized into a ButtonGroup that allows the selection of a single font.

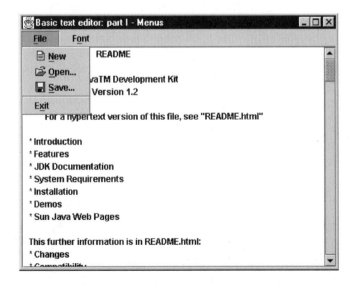

Figure 12.1
JMenu **containing**
JMenuItems **with**
mnemonics and icons

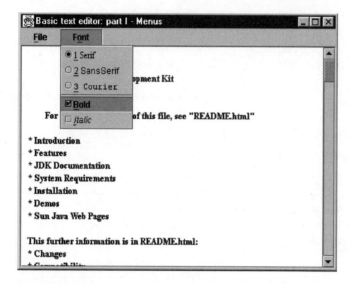

Figure 12.2 Menu containing JRadio-ButtonMenuItems **and** JCheckBoxMenuItems

Example 12.1

BasicTextEditor.java

see \Chapter12\1

```java
import java.awt.*;
import java.awt.event.*;
import java.io.*;
import java.util.*;

import javax.swing.*;
import javax.swing.event.*;

public class BasicTextEditor extends JFrame
{
  public static final String FONTS[] =
    { "Serif", "SansSerif", "Courier" };

  protected Font m_fonts[];

  protected JTextArea m_monitor;
  protected JMenuItem[] m_fontMenus;
  protected JCheckBoxMenuItem m_bold;
  protected JCheckBoxMenuItem m_italic;
  protected JFileChooser m_chooser;

  public BasicTextEditor(){
    super("Basic text editor: part I - Menus");
    setSize(450, 350);

    m_fonts = new Font[FONTS.length];
    for (int k=0; k<FONTS.length; k++)
      m_fonts[k] = new Font(FONTS[k], Font.PLAIN, 12);
```

 Creates list of real fonts from list of font names

```
      m_monitor = new JTextArea();
      JScrollPane ps = new JScrollPane(m_monitor);
      getContentPane().add(ps, BorderLayout.CENTER);

      m_monitor.append("Basic text editor");

      JMenuBar menuBar = createMenuBar();
      setJMenuBar(menuBar);

      m_chooser = new JFileChooser();
      m_chooser.setCurrentDirectory(new File("."));

      WindowListener wndCloser = new WindowAdapter() {
        public void windowClosing(WindowEvent e) {
          System.exit(0);
        }
      };
      addWindowListener(wndCloser);

      updateMonitor();
      setVisible(true);
    }

    protected JMenuBar createMenuBar() {
      final JMenuBar menuBar = new JMenuBar();

      JMenu mFile = new JMenu("File");
      mFile.setMnemonic('f');

      JMenuItem item = new JMenuItem("New");
      item.setIcon(new ImageIcon("file_new.gif"));
      item.setMnemonic('n');
      ActionListener lst = new ActionListener() {
        public void actionPerformed(ActionEvent e) {
          m_monitor.setText("");
        }
      };
      item.addActionListener(lst);
      mFile.add(item);

      item = new JMenuItem("Open...");
      item.setIcon(new ImageIcon("file_open.gif"));
      item.setMnemonic('o');
      lst = new ActionListener() {
        public void actionPerformed(ActionEvent e) {
          BasicTextEditor.this.repaint();
          if (m_chooser.showOpenDialog(BasicTextEditor.this) !=
           JFileChooser.APPROVE_OPTION)
            return;
          Thread runner = new Thread() {
            public void run() {
              File fChoosen = m_chooser.getSelectedFile();
              try {
                FileReader in = new FileReader(fChoosen);
                m_monitor.read(in, null);
```

1 Creates main text area

2 Creates menu items to manipulate files and fonts

3 Shows file chooser to get file to open and read

```java
        in.close();
      }
      catch (IOException ex) { ex.printStackTrace(); }
    }
  };
  runner.start();
}
};
item.addActionListener(lst);
mFile.add(item);

item = new JMenuItem("Save...");
item.setIcon(new ImageIcon("file_save.gif"));
item.setMnemonic('s');
lst = new ActionListener() {
  public void actionPerformed(ActionEvent e){
    BasicTextEditor.this.repaint();
    if (m_chooser.showSaveDialog(BasicTextEditor.this) !=
    JFileChooser.APPROVE_OPTION)
      return;
    Thread runner = new Thread() {
      public void run() {
        File fChoosen = m_chooser.getSelectedFile();
        try {
          FileWriter out = new FileWriter(fChoosen);
          m_monitor.write(out);
          out.close();
        }
        catch (IOException ex) { ex.printStackTrace(); }
      }
    };
    runner.start();
  }
};
item.addActionListener(lst);
mFile.add(item);

mFile.addSeparator();

item = new JMenuItem("Exit");
item.setMnemonic('x');
lst = new ActionListener() {
  public void actionPerformed(ActionEvent e) {
    System.exit(0);
  }
};
item.addActionListener(lst);
mFile.add(item);
menuBar.add(mFile);

ActionListener fontListener = new ActionListener() {
  public void actionPerformed(ActionEvent e) {
    updateMonitor();
```

```
        }
    };

    JMenu mFont = new JMenu("Font");
    mFont.setMnemonic('o');

    ButtonGroup group = new ButtonGroup();
    m_fontMenus = new JMenuItem[FONTS.length];
    for (int k = 0; k < FONTS.length; k++) {
      int m = k+1;
      m_fontMenus[k] = new JRadioButtonMenuItem(
        m + " " + FONTS[k]);
      boolean selected = (k == 0);
      m_fontMenus[k].setSelected(selected);
      m_fontMenus[k].setMnemonic('1' + k);
      m_fontMenus[k].setFont(m_fonts[k]);
      m_fontMenus[k].addActionListener(fontListener);
      group.add(m_fontMenus[k]);
      mFont.add(m_fontMenus[k]);
    }

    mFont.addSeparator();

    m_bold = new JCheckBoxMenuItem("Bold");
    m_bold.setMnemonic('b');
    Font fn = m_fonts[1].deriveFont(Font.BOLD);
    m_bold.setFont(fn);
    m_bold.setSelected(false);
    m_bold.addActionListener(fontListener);
    mFont.add(m_bold);

    m_italic = new JCheckBoxMenuItem("Italic");
    m_italic.setMnemonic('i');
    fn = m_fonts[1].deriveFont(Font.ITALIC);
    m_italic.setFont(fn);
    m_italic.setSelected(false);
    m_italic.addActionListener(fontListener);
    mFont.add(m_italic);

    menuBar.add(mFont);

    return menuBar;
  }

  protected void updateMonitor() {
    int index = -1;
    for (int k = 0; k < m_fontMenus.length; k++) {
      if (m_fontMenus[k].isSelected()) {
        index = k;
        break;
      }
    }
    if (index == -1)
      return;
```

❹ Creates menu to select fonts and font styles with which to display text

❺ Updates current font from menu selection and redisplays text area

```
    if (index == 2) {   // Courier
      m_bold.setSelected(false);
      m_bold.setEnabled(false);
      m_italic.setSelected(false);
      m_italic.setEnabled(false);
    }
    else {
      m_bold.setEnabled(true);
      m_italic.setEnabled(true);
    }

    int style = Font.PLAIN;
    if (m_bold.isSelected())
      style |= Font.BOLD;
    if (m_italic.isSelected())
      style |= Font.ITALIC;
    Font fn = m_fonts[index].deriveFont(style);
    m_monitor.setFont(fn);
    m_monitor.repaint();
  }

  public static void main(String argv[]) {
    new BasicTextEditor();
  }
}
```

12.2.1   Understanding the code

Class BasicTextEditor

This class extends JFrame and provides the parent frame for our example. One class variable is declared:

- String FONTS[]: An array of font family names.

Instance variables:

- Font[] m_fonts: An array of Font instances which can be used to render our JText-Area editor.
- JTextArea m_monitor: Used as our text editor.
- JMenuItem[] m_fontMenus: An array of menu items representing available fonts.
- JCheckBoxMenuItem m_bold: The menu item which sets/unsets the bold property of the current font.
- JCheckBoxMenuItem m_italic: The menu item which sets/unsets the italic property of the current font.
- JFileChooser m_chooser: Used to load and save simple text files.

❶ The BasicTextEditor constructor populates our m_fonts array with Font instances corresponding to the names provided in FONTS[]. The m_monitor JTextArea is then created and placed in a JScrollPane. This scroll pane is added to the center of our frame's content pane, and we then append some simple text to m_monitor for display at startup. Our createMenu-Bar() method is called to create the menu bar to manage this application, and this menu bar is then added to our frame using the setJMenuBar() method.

❷ The `createMenuBar()` method creates and returns a `JMenuBar`. Each menu item receives an `ActionListener` to handle its selection. Two menus are added; they are titled "File" and "Font." The New menu item in the File menu is responsible for creating a new (empty) document. It doesn't really replace `JTextArea`'s `Document`. Instead it simply clears the contents of our editor component. Note that an icon is used in this menu item. Also note that this menu item can be selected with the keyboard by pressing "n" when the File menu's popup is visible, because we assigned it "n" as a mnemonic. The File menu was also assigned a mnemonic character, "f," and if you press ALT-F while the application frame is active, the File popup will be displayed so you can navigate it with either the mouse or the keyboard (all other menus and menu items in this example also receive appropriate mnemonics).

> **BUG ALERT** Even though ALT-F will get processed by the corresponding menu in the menu bar, the key event that is generated is still received by `JTextArea`. Thus, you will see an "f" added to the text area even though ALT was held down when "f" was pressed. It is possible to work around this problem by extending `JTextArea` (or any other `JTextComponent`) as follows:

```
public class MyTextArea extends JTextArea
{
  protected synchronized void processComponentKeyEvent(
   KeyEvent anEvent) {
    super.processComponentKeyEvent(anEvent);
    ivLastKeyEventWasAlt = anEvent.isAltDown();
  }

  protected synchronized void processInputMethodEvent(
   InputMethodEvent e) {
    if (ivLastKeyEventWasAlt) {
      e.consume();
    }
    super.processInputMethodEvent(e);
  }
  private transient boolean ivLastKeyEventWasAlt = false;
}
```

Note that this workaround was orginally posted to the JDC Bug Parade and should only be considered a temporary solution until the problem is actually fixed.

❸ The Open menu item brings up our `m_chooser` `JFileChooser` component (which is discussed in chapter 14) to allow the selection of a text file to be opened. Once a text file is selected, we open a `FileReader` on it and invoke `read()` on our `JTextArea` component to read the file's content. This creates a new `PlainDocument` containing the selected file's content to replace the current `JTextArea` document; see chapter 11 for more information. The Save menu item brings up `m_chooser` to select a destination and file name to save the current text to. Once a text file is selected, we open a `FileWriter` on it and invoke `write()` on our `JTextArea` component to write its contents to the destination file. Both of these I/O operations are wrapped in separate threads to avoid clogging up the event-dispatching thread.

We have added code to repaint the whole application frame before the I/O operations occur. We have done this because when a Swing menu is hidden by a dialog (in this case a JFileChooser dialog) that pops up immediately in response to a menu selection, the menu will often not perform all the necessary repainting of itself and components that lie below its popup. To make sure that no remnants of menu rendering are left around, we force a repaint of the whole frame before moving on.

The Exit menu item terminates the program execution. It is set apart from the first three menu items with a menu separator to create a more logical display.

❹ The Font menu consists of several menu items that are used to select the font and font style used in our editor. All of these items receive the same ActionListener which invokes our updateMonitor() method (see below). To give the user an idea of how each font looks, each font is used to render the corresponding menu item text. Since only one font can be selected at any given time, we use JRadioButtonMenuItems for these menu items, and we add them all to a ButtonGroup instance which manages a single selection.

To create each menu item, we iterate through our FONTS array and create a JRadioButtonMenuItem corresponding to each entry. Each item is set to "unselected" (except for the first one), assigned a numerical mnemonic corresponding to the current FONTS array index, assigned the appropriate Font instance for rendering its text, assigned our multipurpose ActionListener, and added to our ButtonGroup along with the others.

The two other menu items in the Font menu manage the bold and italic font properties. They are implemented as JCheckBoxMenuItems since these properties can be selected or unselected independently. These items also are assigned the same ActionListener as the radio button items to process changes in their selected state.

❺ The updateMonitor() method updates the current font used to render the editing component by checking the state of each check box item and determining which radio button item is currently selected. (The m_bold and m_italic components are disabled and unselected if the Courier font is selected, and they are enabled otherwise.) The appropriate m_fonts array element is selected and a Font instance is derived from it that corresponds to the current state of the check box items using Font's deriveFont() method (see chapter 2).

NOTE Surprisingly, the ButtonGroup class does not provide a direct way to determine which component is currently selected. Therefore, we have to examine each m_fontMenus array element in turn to determine the selected font index. Alternatively, we could save the font index in an enhanced version of our ActionListener.

12.2.2 Running the code

Open a text file, make some changes, and save it as a new file. Change the font options and watch how the text area is updated. Select the Courier font and notice how it disables the bold and italic check box items (it also unchecks them if they were previously checked). Select another font and notice how this re-enables check box items. Figure 12.1 shows BasicTextEditor's File menu, and figure 12.2 shows the Font menu. Notice how the mnemonics are underlined and the images appear to the left of the text by default, just like buttons.

GUIDELINE

File-oriented applications   Example 12.1 is an example of a menu being used in a file-oriented application. Menus were first developed to be used in this fashion. Including a menu in such an application is essential, as users have come to expect one. There are clearly defined platform standards for menu layout and it is best that you adhere to these. For example, the File menu almost always comes first (from the left-hand side).

Also notice the use of the elipsis "..." on the Open... and Save... options. This is a standard technique which gives a visual confirmation that a dialog will open when the menu item is selected.

Correct use of separator and component overloading   This example shows clearly how adding selection controls to a menu in a simple application can speed operation and ease usability. The separator is used to group and separate the selection of the font type from the font style.

12.3   BASIC TEXT EDITOR, PART II: TOOLBARS AND ACTIONS

Swing provides the `Action` interface to simplify the creation of menu items. As we know, implementations of this interface encapsulate both the knowledge of what to do when a menu item or toolbar button is selected (by extending the `ActionListener` interface) and the knowledge of how to render the component itself (by holding a collection of bound properties such as `NAME` and `SMALL_ICON`). We can create both a menu item and a toolbar button from a single `Action` instance, conserving code and providing a reliable means of ensuring consistency between menus and toolbars.

Example 12.2 uses the `AbstractAction` class to add a toolbar to our `BasicTextEditor` application. By converting the `ActionListeners` used in the example above to `Abstract-Actions`, we can use these actions to create both toolbar buttons and menu items with very little additional work.

Example 12.2

BasicTextEditor.java

see \Chapter12\2

```
import java.awt.*;
import java.awt.event.*;
import java.io.*;
import java.util.*;

import javax.swing.*;
import javax.swing.event.*;

public class BasicTextEditor extends JFrame
{
   // Unchanged code from example 12.1
```

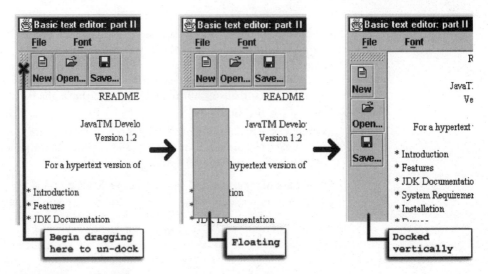

Figure 12.3 The process of undocking, dragging, and docking a floating JToolBar

Figure 12.4 A floating JToolBar
placed in a non-dockable region

```
protected JToolBar m_toolBar;
```

① Toolbar for shortcuts

```
protected JMenuBar createMenuBar() {
  final JMenuBar menuBar = new JMenuBar();
  JMenu mFile = new JMenu("File");
  mFile.setMnemonic('f');

  ImageIcon iconNew = new ImageIcon("file_new.gif");
  Action actionNew = new AbstractAction("New", iconNew) {
    public void actionPerformed(ActionEvent e) {
      m_monitor.setText("");
    }
  };

  JMenuItem item =  mFile.add(actionNew);
  item.setMnemonic('n');

  ImageIcon iconOpen = new ImageIcon("file_open.gif");
  Action actionOpen = new AbstractAction("Open...", iconOpen) {
    public void actionPerformed(ActionEvent e) {
      // Unchanged code from example 12.1
    }
  };
```

① Creates
AbstractAction
instead of
ActionListener

Creates **①**
AbstractAction
instead of
ActionListener

```
    item = mFile.add(actionOpen);
    item.setMnemonic('o');

    ImageIcon iconSave = new ImageIcon("file_save.gif");
    Action actionSave = new AbstractAction("Save...", iconSave) {
      public void actionPerformed(ActionEvent e) {
        // Unchanged code from example 12.1
      }
    };

    item = mFile.add(actionSave);
    item.setMnemonic('s');

    mFile.addSeparator();

    Action actionExit = new AbstractAction("Exit") {
      public void actionPerformed(ActionEvent e) {
        System.exit(0);
      }
    };

    item = mFile.add(actionExit);
    item.setMnemonic('x');
    menuBar.add(mFile);

    m_toolBar = new JToolBar();
    JButton btn1 = m_toolBar.add(actionNew);
    btn1.setToolTipText("New text");
    JButton btn2 = m_toolBar.add(actionOpen);
    btn2.setToolTipText("Open text file");
    JButton btn3 = m_toolBar.add(actionSave);
    btn3.setToolTipText("Save text file");

    // Unchanged code from example 12.1

    getContentPane().add(m_toolBar, BorderLayout.NORTH);

    return menuBar;
  }

  // Unchanged code from example 12.1
}
```

1 Creates
AbstractAction
instead of
ActionListener

1 Creates toolbar
buttons using the same
Actions used for the
menu items

12.3.1   Understanding the code

Class BasicTextEditor

1 This class now declares one more instance variable, JToolBar m_toolBar. The constructor
remains unchanged and it is not listed here. The createMenuBar() method now creates
AbstractAction instances instead of ActionListeners. These objects encapsulate the
same action handling code we defined in example 12.1, as well as the text and icon to display
in associated menu items and toolbar buttons. This allows us to create JMenuItems using
the JMenu.add(Action a) method, and JButtons using the JToolBar.add(Action a)
method. These methods return instances that we can treat like any other button component
and we can do things such as set the background color or assign a different text alignment.

Our `JToolBar` component is placed in the `NORTH` region of our content pane, and we make sure to leave the `EAST`, `WEST`, and `SOUTH` regions empty, thereby allowing it to dock on all sides.

12.3.2 Running the code

Verify that the toolbar buttons work as expected by opening and saving a text file. Try dragging the toolbar from its handle and notice how it is represented by an empty gray window as it is dragged. The border will change to a dark color when the window is in a location where it will dock if the mouse is released. If the border does not appear dark, releasing the mouse will result in the toolbar being placed in its own `JFrame`. Figure 12.3 illustrates the simple process of undocking, dragging, and docking our toolbar in a new location. Figure 12.4 shows our toolbar in its own `JFrame` when it is undocked and released outside of a dockable region (this is also referred to as a *hotspot*).

NOTE   The current `JToolBar` implementation does not easily allow the use of multiple floating toolbars as is common in many modern applications. We hope to see more of this functionality built into future versions of Swing.

GUIDELINE

Vertical or horizontal?   In some applications, you may prefer to leave the selection of a vertical or horizontal toolbar to the user. More often than not, you as the designer can make that choice for them. Consider whether vertical or horizontal space is more valuable for what you need to display. If, for example, you are displaying letter text then you probably need vertical space more than horizontal space. In PC applications, vertical space is usually at a premium.

When vertical space is at a premium, place the toolbar vertically to free up valuable vertical space. When horizontal space is at a premium, place the toolbar horizontally to free up valuable horizontal space.

Almost never use a floating toolbar, as it has a tendency to get lost under other windows. Floating toolbars are for advanced users who understand the full operation of the computer system, so consider the technical level of your user group before making the design choice for a floating toolbar.

12.4   BASIC TEXT EDITOR, PART III: CUSTOM TOOLBAR COMPONENTS

Using `Actions` to create toolbar buttons is easy, but it is not always desirable if we want to have complete control over our toolbar components. In this section's example 12.3, we build off of `BasicTextEditor` and place a `JComboBox` in the toolbar to allow `Font` selection. We also use instances of our own custom buttons, `SmallButton` and `SmallToggleButton`, in the toolbar. Both of these button classes use different borders to signify different states. `SmallButton` uses a raised border when the mouse passes over it, no border when the mouse is not within its bounds, and a lowered border when a mouse press occurs. `SmallToggleButton` uses a raised border when it is unselected and a lowered border when selected.

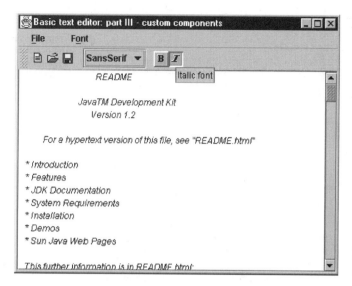

Figure 12.5 JToolBar with custom buttons and a JComboBox

Example 12.3

BasicTextEditor.java

see \Chapter12\3

```java
import java.awt.*;
import java.awt.event.*;
import java.io.*;
import java.util.*;

import javax.swing.*;
import javax.swing.event.*;

public class BasicTextEditor extends JFrame
{
  // Unchanged code from example 12.2

  protected JComboBox m_cbFonts;
  protected SmallToggleButton m_bBold;
  protected SmallToggleButton m_bItalic;

  // Unchanged code from example 12.2

  protected JMenuBar createMenuBar()
  {
    // Unchanged code from example 12.2

    m_toolBar = new JToolBar();
    JButton bNew = new SmallButton(actionNew,
      "New text");
    m_toolBar.add(bNew);
```

1 Custom buttons for toolbar

2 Creates instances of custom buttons and adds them to toolbar

```
JButton bOpen = new SmallButton(actionOpen,
  "Open text file");
m_toolBar.add(bOpen);

JButton bSave = new SmallButton(actionSave,
  "Save text file");
m_toolBar.add(bSave);

JMenu mFont = new JMenu("Font");
mFont.setMnemonic('o');

// Unchanged code from example 12.2

mFont.addSeparator();

m_toolBar.addSeparator();
m_cbFonts = new JComboBox(FONTS);
m_cbFonts.setMaximumSize(m_cbFonts.getPreferredSize());
m_cbFonts.setToolTipText("Available fonts");
ActionListener lst = new ActionListener() {
  public void actionPerformed(ActionEvent e) {
    int index = m_cbFonts.getSelectedIndex();
    if (index < 0)
      return;
    m_fontMenus[index].setSelected(true);
    updateMonitor();
  }
};
m_cbFonts.addActionListener(lst);
m_toolBar.add(m_cbFonts);

m_bold = new JCheckBoxMenuItem("Bold");
m_bold.setMnemonic('b');
Font fn = m_fonts[1].deriveFont(Font.BOLD);
m_bold.setFont(fn);
m_bold.setSelected(false);
m_bold.addActionListener(fontListener);
mFont.add(m_bold);

m_italic = new JCheckBoxMenuItem("Italic");
m_italic.setMnemonic('i');
fn = m_fonts[1].deriveFont(Font.ITALIC);
m_italic.setFont(fn);
m_italic.setSelected(false);
m_italic.addActionListener(fontListener);
mFont.add(m_italic);

menuBar.add(mFont);

m_toolBar.addSeparator();

ImageIcon img1 = new ImageIcon("font_bold1.gif");
ImageIcon img2 = new ImageIcon("font_bold2.gif");
m_bBold = new SmallToggleButton(false, img1, img2,
  "Bold font");
```

2 Creates instances of custom buttons and adds them to toolbar

3 Custom checks boxes for toolbar, to control bold and italic properties

```
        lst = new ActionListener() {
          public void actionPerformed(ActionEvent e) {
            m_bold.setSelected(m_bBold.isSelected());
            updateMonitor();
          }
        };
        m_bBold.addActionListener(lst);
        m_toolBar.add(m_bBold);

        img1 = new ImageIcon("font_italic1.gif");
        img2 = new ImageIcon("font_italic2.gif");
        m_bItalic = new SmallToggleButton(false, img1, img2,
          "Italic font");
        lst = new ActionListener() {
          public void actionPerformed(ActionEvent e) {
            m_italic.setSelected(m_bItalic.isSelected());
            updateMonitor();
          }
        };
        m_bItalic.addActionListener(lst);
        m_toolBar.add(m_bItalic);

        getContentPane().add(m_toolBar, BorderLayout.NORTH);
        return menuBar;
      }

    protected void updateMonitor() {
      int index = -1;
      for (int k=0; k<m_fontMenus.length; k++) {
        if (m_fontMenus[k].isSelected()) {
          index = k;
          break;
        }
      }
      if (index == -1)
        return;
      boolean isBold = m_bold.isSelected();
      boolean isItalic = m_italic.isSelected();

      m_cbFonts.setSelectedIndex(index);

      if (index==2) {    //Courier
        m_bold.setSelected(false);
        m_bold.setEnabled(false);
        m_italic.setSelected(false);
        m_italic.setEnabled(false);
        m_bBold.setSelected(false);
        m_bBold.setEnabled(false);
        m_bItalic.setSelected(false);
        m_bItalic.setEnabled(false);
      }
      else {
        m_bold.setEnabled(true);
        m_italic.setEnabled(true);
```

4 **Keeps toolbar and menu bar settings in sync**

```
        m_bBold.setEnabled(true);
        m_bItalic.setEnabled(true);
      }

    if (m_bBold.isSelected() != isBold)
      m_bBold.setSelected(isBold);
    if (m_bItalic.isSelected() != isItalic)
      m_bItalic.setSelected(isItalic);

    int style = Font.PLAIN;
    if (isBold)
      style |= Font.BOLD;
    if (isItalic)
      style |= Font.ITALIC;
    Font fn = m_fonts[index].deriveFont(style);
    m_monitor.setFont(fn);
    m_monitor.repaint();
  }

  public static void main(String argv[]) {
    new BasicTextEditor();
  }
}

class SmallButton extends JButton implements MouseListener
{
  protected Border m_raised;
  protected Border m_lowered;
  protected Border m_inactive;

  public SmallButton(Action act, String tip) {
    super((Icon)act.getValue(Action.SMALL_ICON));
    m_raised = new BevelBorder(BevelBorder.RAISED);
    m_lowered = new BevelBorder(BevelBorder.LOWERED);
    m_inactive = new EmptyBorder(2, 2, 2, 2);
    setBorder(m_inactive);
    setMargin(new Insets(1,1,1,1));
    setToolTipText(tip);
    addActionListener(act);
    addMouseListener(this);
    setRequestFocusEnabled(false);
  }

  public float getAlignmentY() { return 0.5f; }

  public void mousePressed(MouseEvent e) {
    setBorder(m_lowered);
  }
  public void mouseReleased(MouseEvent e) {
    setBorder(m_inactive);
  }
  public void mouseClicked(MouseEvent e) {}
  public void mouseEntered(MouseEvent e) {
    setBorder(m_raised);
  }
```

4 Keeps toolbar and menu bar settings in sync

5 Used for small buttons in toolbar

```
    public void mouseExited(MouseEvent e) {
      setBorder(m_inactive);
    }
}

class SmallToggleButton extends JToggleButton
    implements ItemListener
{
  protected Border m_raised;
  protected Border m_lowered;

  public SmallToggleButton(boolean selected,
    ImageIcon imgUnselected, ImageIcon imgSelected, String tip) {
    super(imgUnselected, selected);
    setHorizontalAlignment(CENTER);
    setBorderPainted(true);
    m_raised = new BevelBorder(BevelBorder.RAISED);
    m_lowered = new BevelBorder(BevelBorder.LOWERED);
    setBorder(selected ? m_lowered : m_raised);
    setMargin(new Insets(1,1,1,1));
    setToolTipText(tip);
    setRequestFocusEnabled(false);
    setSelectedIcon(imgSelected);
    addItemListener(this);
  }

  public float getAlignmentY() { return 0.5f; }

  public void itemStateChanged(ItemEvent e) {
    setBorder(isSelected() ? m_lowered : m_raised);
  }
}
```

⑥ Used for small toggle buttons in toolbar

12.4.1   Understanding the code

Class BasicTextEditor

❶ `BasicTextEditor` now declares three new instance variables:

- `JComboBox m_cbFonts`: A combo box containing available font names.
- `SmallToggleButton m_bBold`: A custom toggle button representing the bold font style.
- `SmallToggleButton m_bItalic`: A custom toggle button representing the italic font style.

❷ The `createMenuBar()` method now creates three instances of the `SmallButton` class (see below) corresponding to our pre-existing New, Open, and Save toolbar buttons. These are constructed by passing the appropriate `Action` (which we built in part II) as well as a tooltip `String` to the `SmallButton` constructor. Then we create a combo box with all the available font names and add it to the toolbar. The `setMaximumSize()` method is called on the combo box to reduce its size to a necessary maximum (otherwise, it will fill all the unoccupied space in our toolbar). An `ActionListener` is then added to monitor combo box selection. This listener selects the corresponding font menu item (containing the same font name) because the combo box and font radio button menu items must always be in synch. It then calls our `updateMonitor()` method.

❸ Two `SmallToggleButtons` are created and added to our toolbar to manage the bold and italic font properties. Each button receives an `ActionListener` which selects/deselects the corresponding menu item (because both the menu items and toolbar buttons must be in synch) and calls our `updateMonitor()` method.

❹ Our `updateMonitor()` method receives some additional code to provide consistency between our menu items and toolbar controls. This method relies on the state of the menu items, which is why the toolbar components first set the corresponding menu items when selected. The code added here is self-explanatory; it just involves enabling/disabling and selecting/deselecting components to preserve consistency.

Class SmallButton

❺ `SmallButton` represents a small push button intended for use in a toolbar. It implements the `MouseListener` interface to process mouse input. Three instance variables are declared:

- `Border m_raised`: The border to be used when the mouse cursor is located over the button.
- `Border m_lowered`: The border to be used when the button is pressed.
- `Border m_inactive`: The border to be used when the mouse cursor is located outside the button.

The `SmallButton` constructor takes an `Action` parameter (which is added as an `ActionListener` and performs an appropriate action when the button is pressed) and a `String` representing the tooltip text. Several familiar properties are assigned and the icon encapsulated within the `Action` is used for this button's icon. `SmallButton` also adds itself as a `MouseListener` and sets its tooltip text to the given `String` passed to the constructor. The `requestFocusEnabled` property is set to `false` so that when this button is clicked, focus will not be transferred out of our `JTextArea` editor component.

The `getAlignmentY()` method is overriden to return a constant value of `0.5f`, indicating that this button should always be placed in the middle of the toolbar in the vertical direction (Note that this is only necessary in JDK 1.2.1 and earlier.). The remainder of `SmallButton` represents an implementation of the `MouseListener` interface which sets the border based on mouse events. The border is set to `m_inactive` when the mouse is located outside its bounds, `m_active` when the mouse is located inside its bounds, and `m_lowered` when the button is pressed.

Class SmallToggleButton

❻ `SmallToggleButton` extends `JToggleButton` and implements the `ItemListener` interface to process changes in the button's selection state. Two instance variables are declared:

- `Border m_raised`: The border to be used when the button is unselected (unchecked).
- `Border m_lowered`: The border to be used when the button is selected (checked).

The `SmallToggleButton` constructor takes four arguments:

- `boolean selected`: The initial selection state.
- `ImageIcon imgUnselected`: The icon for use when unselected.
- `ImageIcon imgSelected`: The icon for use when selected.
- `String tip`: The tooltip message.

In the constructor, several familiar button properties are set, and a raised or lowered border is assigned depending on the initial selection state. Each instance is added to itself as an `ItemListener` to receive notification about changes in its selection. Thus the `itemState-Changed()` method is implemented; it simply sets the button's border accordingly based on the new selected state.

12.4.2 Running the code

Verify that the toolbar components (combo box and toggle buttons) change the editor's font as expected. Notice which menu and toolbar components work in synchronization (meaning the menu item selections result in changes in the toolbar controls, and vice versa). Figure 12.5 shows our new basic text editor toolbar with a `SmallToggleButton` in the pressed state displaying its tooltip text.

Tooltip help   Tooltip Help on mouse-over is a must-have technical addition for small toolbar buttons. The relatively recent innovation of tooltips has greatly improved the usability of toolbars. Don't get caught delivering a toolbar without one—make sure that your tooltip text is meaningful to the user!

12.5   *BASIC TEXT EDITOR, PART IV: CUSTOM MENU COMPONENTS*

In example 12.4 we will show how to build a custom menu component, `ColorMenu`, which allows the selection of a color from a grid of small colored panes (which are instances of the inner class `ColorMenu.ColorPane`). By extending `JMenu`, we inherit all `MenuElement` functionality (see section 12.1.10), making custom menu creation quite easy.

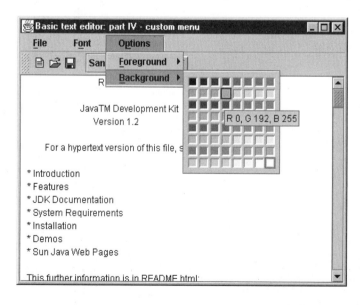

Figure 12.6 Custom menu component used for quick color selection

Example 12.4

BasicTextEditor.java

see \Chapter12\4

```java
import java.awt.*;
import java.awt.event.*;
import java.io.*;
import java.util.*;

import javax.swing.*;
import javax.swing.event.*;
import javax.swing.border.*;

public class BasicTextEditor extends JFrame
{
  // Unchanged code from example 12.3

  protected JMenuBar createMenuBar()
  {
    // Unchanged code from example 12.3

    JMenu mOpt = new JMenu("Options");
    mOpt.setMnemonic('p');

    ColorMenu cm = new ColorMenu("Foreground");
    cm.setColor(m_monitor.getForeground());
    cm.setMnemonic('f');
    lst = new ActionListener() {
      public void actionPerformed(ActionEvent e) {
        ColorMenu m = (ColorMenu)e.getSource();
        m_monitor.setForeground(m.getColor());
      }
    };
    cm.addActionListener(lst);
    mOpt.add(cm);

    cm = new ColorMenu("Background");
    cm.setColor(m_monitor.getBackground());
    cm.setMnemonic('b');
    lst = new ActionListener() {
      public void actionPerformed(ActionEvent e) {
        ColorMenu m = (ColorMenu)e.getSource();
        m_monitor.setBackground(m.getColor());
      }
    };
    cm.addActionListener(lst);
    mOpt.add(cm);
    menuBar.add(mOpt);

    getContentPane().add(m_toolBar, BorderLayout.NORTH);
    return menuBar;
  }
```

1 Presents color selector for foreground color

1 Presents color selector for background color

```
  // Unchanged code from example 12.3
}

class ColorMenu extends JMenu
{
  protected Border m_unselectedBorder;
  protected Border m_selectedBorder;
  protected Border m_activeBorder;

  protected Hashtable m_panes;
  protected ColorPane m_selected;

  public ColorMenu(String name) {
    super(name);
    m_unselectedBorder = new CompoundBorder(
      new MatteBorder(1, 1, 1, 1, getBackground()),
      new BevelBorder(BevelBorder.LOWERED,
      Color.white, Color.gray));
    m_selectedBorder = new CompoundBorder(
      new MatteBorder(2, 2, 2, 2, Color.red),
      new MatteBorder(1, 1, 1, 1, getBackground()));
    m_activeBorder = new CompoundBorder(
      new MatteBorder(2, 2, 2, 2, Color.blue),
      new MatteBorder(1, 1, 1, 1, getBackground()));

    JPanel p = new JPanel();
    p.setBorder(new EmptyBorder(5, 5, 5, 5));
    p.setLayout(new GridLayout(8, 8));
    m_panes = new Hashtable();

    int[] values = new int[] { 0, 128, 192, 255 };
    for (int r=0; r<values.length; r++) {
      for (int g=0; g<values.length; g++) {
        for (int b=0; b<values.length; b++) {
          Color c = new Color(values[r], values[g], values[b]);
          ColorPane pn = new ColorPane(c);
          p.add(pn);
          m_panes.put(c, pn);
        }
      }
    }
    add(p);
  }

  public void setColor(Color c) {
    Object obj = m_panes.get(c);
    if (obj == null)
      return;
    if (m_selected != null)
      m_selected.setSelected(false);
    m_selected = (ColorPane)obj;
    m_selected.setSelected(true);
  }

  public Color getColor() {
```

2 Custom menu which presents a grid of colors to select from

3 Creates one ColorPane for each of the 64 (4*4*4) colors

4 Finds a ColorPane of a given color and sets that as the selected color

```
      if (m_selected == null)
        return null;
      return m_selected.getColor();
  }

  public void doSelection() {
    fireActionPerformed(new ActionEvent(this,
      ActionEvent.ACTION_PERFORMED, getActionCommand()));
  }

  class ColorPane extends JPanel implements MouseListener
  {
    protected Color m_c;
    protected boolean m_selected;

    public ColorPane(Color c) {
      m_c = c;
      setBackground(c);
      setBorder(m_unselectedBorder);
      String msg = "R "+c.getRed()+", G "+c.getGreen()+
        ", B "+c.getBlue();
      setToolTipText(msg);
      addMouseListener(this);
    }

    public Color getColor() { return m_c; }

    public Dimension getPreferredSize() {
      return new Dimension(15, 15);
    }
    public Dimension getMaximumSize() { return getPreferredSize(); }
    public Dimension getMinimumSize() { return getPreferredSize(); }

    public void setSelected(boolean selected) {
      m_selected = selected;
      if (m_selected)
        setBorder(m_selectedBorder);
      else
        setBorder(m_unselectedBorder);
    }

    public boolean isSelected() { return m_selected; }

    public void mousePressed(MouseEvent e) {}

    public void mouseClicked(MouseEvent e) {}

    public void mouseReleased(MouseEvent e) {
      setColor(m_c);
      MenuSelectionManager.defaultManager().clearSelectedPath();
      doSelection();
    }

    public void mouseEntered(MouseEvent e) {
      setBorder(m_activeBorder);
    }
```

5 Notifies listeners that a color selection has occurred

6 Displays a single color for selection

7 Sets new color, closes all menus, and notifies listeners of color change

```
      public void mouseExited(MouseEvent e) {
        setBorder(m_selected ? m_selectedBorder :
          m_unselectedBorder);
      }
    }
  }
}
```

12.5.1   Understanding the code

Class BasicTextEditor

1 The `createMenuBar()` method now creates a new `JMenu` titled "Options" and populates it with two `ColorMenus`. The first of these menus receives an `ActionListener` which requests the selected color using `ColorMenu`'s `getColor()` method, and assigns it as the foreground color of our editor component. Similarly, the second `ColorMenu` receives an `ActionListener` which manages our editor's background color.

Class ColorMenu

2 This class extends `JMenu` and represents a custom menu component which serves as a quick color chooser. Here are the instance variables:

- `Border m_unselectedBorder`: The border to be used for a `ColorPane` (see below) when it is not selected and the mouse cursor is located outside of its bounds.
- `Border m_selectedBorder`: The border to be used for a `ColorPane` when it is selected and the mouse cursor is located outside of its bounds.
- `Border m_activeBorder`: The border to be used for a `ColorPane` when the mouse cursor is located inside its bounds.
- `Hashtable m_panes`: A collection of `ColorPanes`.
- `ColorPane m_selected`: A reference to the currently selected `ColorPane`.

3 The `ColorMenu` constructor takes a menu name as a parameter and creates the underlying `JMenu` component using that name. This creates a root menu item which can be added to another menu or to a menu bar. Selecting this menu item will display its `JPopupMenu` component, which normally contains several simple menu items. In our case, however, we add a `JPanel` to it using `JMenu`'s `add(Component c)` method. This `JPanel` serves as a container for 64 `ColorPanes` (see below) which are used to display the available selectable colors, as well as the current selection. A triple `for` cycle is used to generate the constituent `ColorPanes` in 3-dimensional color space. Each `ColorPane` takes a `Color` instance as a constructor parameter, and each `ColorPane` is placed in our `Hashtable` collection, `m_panes`, using its associated `Color` as the key.

4 The `setColor()` method finds a `ColorPane` which holds a given `Color`. If such a component is found, this method clears the previously selected `ColorPane` and selects the new one by calling its `setSelected()` method. The `getColor()` method simply returns the currently selected color.

5 The `doSelection()` method sends an `ActionEvent` to registered listeners notifying them that an action has been performed on this `ColorMenu`, which means a new color may have been selected.

Class ColorMenu. ColorPane

6 This inner class is used to display a single color available for selection in a `ColorMenu`. It extends `JPanel` and implements `MouseListener` to process its own mouse events. This class uses the three `Border` variables from the parent `ColorMenu` class to represent its state, whether it is selected, unselected, or active. These are the instance variables:

- `Color m_c`: The color instance represented by this pane.
- `boolean m_selected`: A flag indicating whether this pane is currently selected.

   The `ColorPane` constructor takes a `Color` instance as a parameter and stores it in our `m_c` instance variable. The only thing we need to do to display that color is to set it as the pane's background. We also add a tooltip indicating the red, green, and blue components of this color.

7 All `MouseListener`-related methods should be familiar by now. However, take note of the `mouseReleased()` method which plays the key role in color selection: If the mouse is released over a `ColorPane`, we first assign the associated `Color` to the parenting `ColorMenu` component using the `setColor()` method (so it can be retrieved later by any attached listeners). We then hide all opened menu components by calling the `MenuSelectionManager.clearSelected-Path()` method since menu selection is complete at this point. Finally, we invoke the `doSelection()` method on the parenting `ColorMenu` component to notify all attached listeners.

12.5.2 Running the code

Experiment with changing the editor's background and foreground colors using our custom menu component available in the Options menu. Notice that a color selection will not affect anything until the mouse is released, and a mouse release also triggers the collapse of all menu popups in the current path. Figure 12.6 shows `ColorMenu` in action.

GUIDELINE

Usability and design alternatives   A more traditional approach to this example would be to have an elipsis option in the Options menu that opens a color chooser dialog. Consider what an improvement the presented design makes to usability. Within a limited range of colors, this design allows for faster selection with the possible minor problem that there is a greater chance of a mistake being made in the selection. However, a mistake like that can be easily corrected. As you will see in the next chapter, knowing that you have a bounded range of input selections can be put to good use when you're improving a design and its usability.

CHAPTER 13

Progress bars, sliders, and scroll bars

13.1 BOUNDED-RANGE COMPONENTS OVERVIEW

JScrollBar, JSlider, and JProgressBar provide visualization and selection within a bounded interval, thereby allowing the user to conveniently select a value from that interval or to simply observe its current state. In this section we'll give a brief overview of these components and the significant classes and interfaces that support them.

13.1.1 The BoundedRangeModel interface

abstract interface javax.swing.BoundedRangeModel

The BoundedRangeModel interface describes a data model that is used to define an integer *value* between *minimum* and *maximum* values. This value can have a subrange called an *extent*, which can be used to define the size of, for instance, a scrollbar "thumb." The extent often changes dynamically corresponding to how much of the entire range of possible values is visible. The value can never be set larger than the maximum or minimum values, and the extent always starts at the current value and never extends past the maximum. Another property called valueIsAdjusting is declared and is expected to be true when the value is in the state of being adjusted (for example, when a slider thumb is being dragged).

Implementations are expected to fire ChangeEvents when any of the minimum, maximum, value, extent, or valueIsAdjusting properties change state. Thus, BoundedRangeModel includes method declarations for adding and removing ChangeListeners: addChangeListener() and removeChangeListener(). This model is used by JProgressBar, JSlider, and JScrollBar.

Why choose a bounded range component? The bounded range components are essentially analog devices in nature. They are good at providing relative, positional, approximate, or changing (in time) data. They are also excellent at visually communicating the bounds or limits of a data selection and at communicating a percentage of the whole through approximate visual means. Where you have several values which share the same bounds (such as RGB values for a color chooser), you can easily communicate relative values of the three choices through use of a bounded range component. The position of each component shows the relative value of one against another.

Therefore, use bounded range components when there is an advantage to communicating either a range of values and/or an approximate position or changing value to the user.

13.1.2   DefaultBoundedRangeModel

class javax.swing.DefaultBoundedRangeModel

DefaultBoundedRangeModel is the default concrete implementation of the BoundedRangeModel interface. The default constructor initializes a model with 0 for minimum, 100 for maximum, and 0 for the value and extent properties. Another constructor allows the specification of each of these initial values as int parameters. As expected, this implementation does fire ChangeEvents whenever one of its properties changes.

13.1.3   JScrollBar

class javax.swing.JScrollBar

Scroll bars can be used to choose a new value from a specified interval by sliding a *knob* (often referred to as the *thumb*) between the given maximum and minimum bounds, or by using small buttons at the ends of the component. The area not occupied by the thumb and buttons is known as the *paging area*; this can also be used to change the current scroll bar value. The thumb represents the extent of this bounded-range component, and its value is stored in the visibleAmount property.

JScrollBar can be oriented horizontally or vertically, and its value increases to the right or upward, respectively. To specify orientation, which is stored in the orientation property, we call the setOrientation() method and pass it one of the JScrollBar.HORIZONTAL or JScrollBar.VERTICAL constants.

Clicking on a button moves the thumb (and thus the value—recall that a bounded-range component's value lies at the beginning of the extent) by the value of JScrollBar's unitIncrement property. Similarly, clicking the paging area moves the thumb by the value of JScrollBar's blockIncrement property.

NOTE It is common to match the `visibleAmount` property with the `blockIncrement` property. This is a simple way to visually signify to the user how much of the available range of data is currently visible.

UI

GUIDELINE

Using a scroll bar

Background   The scroll bar is really a computer-enhanced development from an original analog mechanical idea. Scroll bars are, in some respects, more advanced than sliders (see section 13.1.4). The thumb of the scroll bar can very cleverly be used to show the current data as a percentage of a whole, as described in the note above. If the scroll bar is placed onto an image and the thumb is approximately 50% of the total size, then the user is given a clear indication that the viewing area is roughly half of the total size. The ability for the thumb in a scroll bar to change size to accurately reflect this is something which could not have been achieved with a mechanical device. Scroll bars are, in this respect, a very good example of taking a metaphor based on a mechanical device and enhancing it to improve usability.

Choosing position   By far, the best use of a scroll bar is position selection. They are, by nature, analog, so the viewer only sees an approximate position. Scroll bars are used by a `JScrollPane` to select the viewing position of the component the `JScrollPane` contains. Users have become accustomed to this method of using them. For most other occasions where you want to use a sliding control for selection, a `JSlider` is probably best.

As expected, `JScrollBar` uses a `DefaultBoundedRangeModel` by default. In addition to the `ChangeEvents` fired by this model, `JScrollBar` fires `PropertyChangeEvents` when its `orientation`, `unitIncrement`, or `blockIncrement` properties change state. `JScroll-Pane` also fires `AdjustmentEvents` whenever any of its bound properties change, or when any of its model's properties change (this is done solely for backward compatibility with the AWT scroll bar class). Accordingly, `JScrollBar` provides methods to add and remove `Adjust-mentListeners`; we don't need to provide methods for adding and removing `Property-ChangeListeners` because this functionality is inherited from `JComponent`.

NOTE   `AdjustmentListeners` receive `AdjustmentEvents`. Both are defined in `java.awt.event`; refer to the API documentation for more detail.

13.1.4   JSlider

class javax.swing.JSlider

Sliders can be used to choose a numerical value from a specified interval. To use a slider, slide a knob between the given borders using the mouse, arrow keys, or PageDown and PageUp. Sliders are very useful when we know in advance the range of input from which the user should be able to choose.

`JSlider` supports horizontal and vertical orientations, and its `orientation` property can be set to either `JSlider.HORIZONTAL` or `JSlider.VERTICAL`. The `extent` property specifies the number of values to skip forward/up or back/down when PageUp or PageDown is pressed, respectively. Tick marks can be used to denote value locations. *Minor* and *major* tick marks are supported; major ticks are usually longer and more spread apart than minor ticks. In the case where a major and minor tick fall on the same location, the major tick takes precedence and the minor tick will not be displayed. Spacing between minor tick marks is specified by the `minorTickSpacing` property, and spacing between major tick marks is specified by the `majorTickSpacing` property.

> **NOTE** The tick spacing properties specify the number of values to be skipped between successive ticks. Their names are somewhat misleading because they actually have nothing to do with the physical space (in pixels) between ticks. They would be more appropriately named "`minorTickDisplayInterval`" and "`majorTickDisplayInterval`."

Setting either spacing property to 0 has a disabling effect, and the `paintTicks` property also provides a way of turning ticks on and off.

> **NOTE** The `snapToTicks` property is intended to only allow the slider knob to lie on a tick-marked value; however, this feature does not work as expected as of Java 2 FCS.

Major ticks can be annotated by components and, by default, each of `JSlider`'s major ticks are adorned with `JLabel`s that denote the integer tick value. We can turn this functionality on and off by changing the `paintLabels` property, and we can customize which components are used to annotate, and at what values they are placed, by passing a `Dictionary` of `Integer`/`Component` pairs to the `setLabelTable()` method. The `createStandardLabels()` method is used by default to set up `JSlider` with its `JLabel`s at each major tick value. This method returns a `Hashtable` (a subclass of `Dictionary`) which can then be assigned to `JSlider` using `setLabelTable()`.

By default, `JSlider`'s values increment from left to right or bottom to top depending on whether horizontal or vertical orientation is used. To reverse the incrementation direction, we can set the `inverted` property to `true`.

UI GUIDELINE

Using a Slider   Sliders are really a close graphical and behavioral representation of a real world analog slider—a hi-fi system or an older TV volume control are good examples. As such, sliders are analog devices and they are designed to be used to determine an approximate or positional setting for something. They usually rely on direct user feedback to help select a position. With the TV volume control example, the volume would go up and down as the slider is moved and the user would stop moving it when the volume was at a comfortable level.

The Swing version of a slider is actually a digital device disguised as an analog one. Each tick of the slider is a digital increment. The slider can therefore be used to determine an accurate value, provided the user is given some additional digital feedback, such as a numeric display of the absolute value or a scale along the side of the slider. Where accurate values are important, such as with a color chooser, be sure to provide an absolute value as output alongside the slider.

Feedback   Immediate feedback is important with sliders because of their analog nature. Provide actual feedback, such as the brightness of a picture which increases or decreases as the slider is moved, or provide an absolute numeric value readout which the user can see change as the slider is moved. Judicious use of the change event with a `ChangeListener` is important so that the feedback mechanism can be updated—for example, to show brightness or contrast in an image.

Movement   The two default orientations of a slider are conventions which date back to the original analog electronic devices. When a slider is vertical, the down position is lower and you move it up to increase in value. When it is horizontal, the left position is lower and you move it right to increase in value. Users should be very familiar with this convention. If you wish to switch it, you should have a very very good reason for doing so. We wouldn't recommend it!

Slider vs. Scroll bar   On the whole, use a slider for choosing a value when the value needed is approximate and subjective (such as color, volume, and brightness) and when the user needs to make the subjective judgement. Conversely, use a scroll bar for positional choice, where the desired position is approximate and judged relative to the whole.

The `paintTrack` property specifies whether the whole slider track is filled in. The Metal look and feel UI delegate for `JSlider` pays attention to the client property with the key "JSlider.isFilled" and a `Boolean` value. Adding this property to a `JSlider`'s client properties hashtable (using `putClientProperty()`; see chapter 2) with a value of `Boolean.TRUE` will fill in only the lower half of the slider track from the position of the knob. This client property will have no effect if the `paintTrack` property is set to `true`, and it will work only if the slider is using the Metal look and feel UI delegate.

As expected, `JSlider` uses a `DefaultBoundedRangeModel` by default. In addition to the `ChangeEvent`s fired by this model, `JSlider` fires `PropertyChangeEvents` when any of its properties described above change state. Unlike `JScrollBar`, `JSlider` provides the ability to add and remove `ChangeListeners` directly.

13.1.5   JProgressBar

Class javax.swing.JProgressBar

Progress bars can be used to display how far or close a given numerical value is from the bounds of a specified interval. They are typically used to indicate progress during a certain lengthy job to show the user that the job being monitored is alive and active. As with `JScrollBar` and `JSlider`, `JProgressBar` can be oriented horizontally or vertically. Notice also that `JProgressBar` acts the same way as `JSlider` with respect to incrementing: left to right in horizontal orientation, bottom to top in vertical orientation.

A `JProgressBar` is painted and filled from the minimum value to its current value (with the exception of the Windows look and feel, which paints a series of small rectangles). A percentage representing how much of a job has been completed can optionally be displayed in the center of `JProgressBar`. The `string` property represents the `String` to be painted (it's usually of the form XX%, where X is a digit), `stringPainted` specifies whether `string` should be painted, and `percentComplete` is a `double` between 0 and 1 to specify how much of the job has been completed so far.

NOTE   We normally do not need to take control of this rendering functionality, because by setting the `string` property to `null`, and the `stringPainted` property to `true`, the `percentComplete` property is converted to the XX% form for us, and it is displayed in the progress bar.

JProgressBar's foreground and background can be assigned just like any JComponent; however, the color used to render its status text is not directly modifiable. Instead, this is handled by the UI delegate. The easiest way to assign specific colors is to replace the appropriate UI resources in the UIManager's defaults table (see chapter 21 for more about look and feel customization).

The borderPainted property (which defaults to true) specifies whether a border is rendered around JProgressBar. As expected, JProgressBar uses a DefaultBoundedRange-Model by default, and ChangeListeners can be added to receive ChangeEvents when any of JProgressBar's properties change state.

During a monitored operation, we simply call setValue() on a JProgressBar and all updating is taken care of for us. We must be careful to make this call in the event-dispatching thread. Consider the following basic example (13.1). Figure 13.1 illustrates the output.

Figure 13.1 A basic JProgressBar example showing custom colors and proper updating

Example 13.1

JProgressBarDemo.java

see \Chapter13\1

```
import java.awt.*;
import java.awt.event.*;

import javax.swing.*;
import javax.swing.event.*;

public class JProgressBarDemo
  extends JFrame
{
  protected int m_min = 0;
  protected int m_max = 100;
  protected int m_counter = 0;
  protected JProgressBar jpb;

  public JProgressBarDemo()
  {
    super("JProgressBar Demo");
    setSize(300,50);

    UIManager.put("ProgressBar.selectionBackground", Color.black);
    UIManager.put("ProgressBar.selectionForeground", Color.white);
    UIManager.put("ProgressBar.foreground", new Color(8,32,128));

    jpb = new JProgressBar();
    jpb.setMinimum(m_min);
```

```
jpb.setMaximum(m_max);
jpb.setStringPainted(true);

JButton start = new JButton("Start");
start.addActionListener(new ActionListener() {
  public void actionPerformed(ActionEvent c) {
    Thread runner = new Thread() {
      public void run() {
        m_counter = m_min;
        while (m_counter <= m_max) {
          Runnable runme = new Runnable() {
            public void run() {
              jpb.setValue(m_counter);
            }
          };
          SwingUtilities.invokeLater(runme);
          m_counter++;
          try {
            Thread.sleep(100);
          }
          catch (Exception ex) {}
        }
      }
    };
    runner.start();
  }
});

getContentPane().add(jpb, BorderLayout.CENTER);
getContentPane().add(start, BorderLayout.WEST);

WindowListener wndCloser = new WindowAdapter()
{
  public void windowClosing(WindowEvent e)
  {
    System.exit(0);
  }
};
addWindowListener(wndCloser);
setVisible(true);
}

public static void main(String[] args)
{
  new JProgressBarDemo();
}
}
```

NOTE　The JProgressBar UI delegate centers the progress text horizontally and vertically. However, its centering scheme enforces a certain amount of white space around the text and has undesirable effects when using thin progress bars. In order to fix this, we can override BasicProgressBarUI's getStringPlacement() method (refer to the API documentation and the BasicProgressBarUI.java source code) to return the desired Point location where the text should be rendered.

Using progress bar long operations Progress bars are commonly used as a filter for operations which take a long time. A long time in human interaction is often defined as one second or longer. The progress bar is usually rendered inside a JOptionPane.

You will need to pay special attention to the business logic code so that it is capable of notifying a progress bar of the progress of an operation.

Progress bars are inherently analog in nature. Analog data is particularly good for displaying change and for relative comparison. It is not good for exact measurement. In this situation, the analog nature of a progress bar means that it is good for showing that something is happening and that progress is taking place. However, it is not good for giving an exact measure of completeness. If you need to show the user exactly what percentage of the task is complete, you may need to supplement the progress bar with a digital progress reading. This is common with Internet download dialogs and option panes.

A digital readout is particularly useful when the task to be completed will take a very long time. The progress bar may give you a granularity of 3% or so for each graphic. If it takes a significantly long time to progress by such a jump, say greater than 5 seconds, the digital readout will give you a finer grained reading at 1%, and, it will change approximately three times faster than your progress bar. The combination of the two helps to pass the time for the user and it gives them the reassurance that something is happening; it also gives them a very accurate view of their progress. This is why the dual combination of digital and analog progress is popular with Internet download dialogs, as the task can be very long and its length cannot be determined by the application developer.

13.1.6   ProgressMonitor

class javax.swing.ProgressMonitor

The ProgressMonitor class is a convenient means of deploying a dynamic progress bar in an application that performs time-consuming operations. This class is a direct subclass of Object, so it does not exist in the component hierarchy.

ProgressMonitor displays a JDialog containing a JOptionPane-style component. The note property represents a String that can change during the course of an operation and it is displayed in a JLabel above the JProgressBar (if null is used, this label is not displayed).

Two buttons, OK and Cancel, are placed at the bottom of the dialog. They serve to dismiss the dialog and abort the operation, respectively. The OK button simply hides the dialog. The Cancel button hides the dialog, and it also sets the canceled property to true, providing us with a way to test whether the user has canceled the operation. Since most time-consuming operations occur in loops, we can test this property during each iteration, and abort if necessary.

The millisToDecideToPopup property is an int value that specifies the number of milliseconds to wait before ProgressMonitor should determine whether to pop up a dialog (it defaults to 500). This is used to allow a certain amount of time to pass before questioning whether the job is long enough to warrant a progress dialog. The millisToPopup property is an int value that specifies the minimum time a job must take in order to warrant popping up a dialog (it defaults to 2000). If `ProgressMonitor` determines that the job will take less than `millisToPopup` milliseconds, the dialog will not be shown.

The `progress` property is an `int` value that specifies the current value of the `JProgress-Bar`. During an operation, we are expected to update the `note` and `progress` in the event-dispatching thread.

WARNING In light of these properties, we should only use a `ProgressMonitor` for simple, predictable jobs. `ProgressMonitor` bases the estimated time to completion on the value of its `JProgressBar` from the start time to the current evaluation time, and it assumes that a constant rate of progression will exist throughout the whole job. For transferring a single file this may be a fairly valid assumption. However, the rate of progress is highly dependent on how the job is constructed.

NOTE `ProgressMonitor` does not currently give us access to its `JProgressBar` component. We hope that in future implementations it will be accounted for, as it currently makes customization more difficult.

13.1.7 ProgressMonitorInputStream

class javax.swing.ProgressMonitorInputStream

This class extends `java.io.FilterInputStream` and contains a `ProgressMonitor`. When it is used in place of an `InputStream`, this class provides a very simple means of displaying job progress. This `InputStream`'s overloaded `read()` methods read data and update the `ProgressMonitor` at the same time. We can access `ProgressMonitorInputStream`'s `ProgressMonitor` with `getProgressMonitor()`, but we cannot assign it a new one. (See the API documentation for more information about `InputStream`s.)

13.2 BASIC JSCROLLBAR EXAMPLE

The `JScrollBar` component is most often seen as part of a `JScrollPane`. We rarely use this component alone, unless customized scrolling is desired. In example 13.2 in this section, we'll show how to use `JScrollBar` to create a simple custom scrolling pane from scratch.

Example 13.2

ScrollDemo.java

see \Chapter13\2

```
import java.awt.*;
import java.awt.event.*;

import javax.swing.*;
import javax.swing.event.*;

public class ScrollDemo extends JFrame
{
  public ScrollDemo() {
    super("JScrollBar Demo");
```

❶ Presents a frame with a `CustomScrollPane` to scroll a large image

**Figure 13.2 The running
ScrollDemo example
showing an image in the
custom scroll pane**

```
    setSize(300,250);

    ImageIcon ii = new ImageIcon("earth.jpg");
    CustomScrollPane sp = new CustomScrollPane(new JLabel(ii));
    getContentPane().add(sp);

    WindowListener wndCloser = new WindowAdapter() {
      public void windowClosing(WindowEvent e) {
        System.exit(0);
      }
    };
    addWindowListener(wndCloser);
    setVisible(true);
  }

  public static void main(String[] args) {
    new ScrollDemo();
  }
}

class CustomScrollPane extends JPanel
{
  protected JScrollBar m_vertSB;
  protected JScrollBar m_horzSB;
  protected CustomViewport m_viewport;
  protected JComponent m_comp;

  public CustomScrollPane(JComponent comp) {
    setLayout(null);
    m_viewport = new CustomViewport();
    m_viewport.setLayout(null);
    add(m_viewport);
    m_comp = comp;
    m_viewport.add(m_comp);

    m_vertSB = new JScrollBar(
```

**❷ Constructor takes
component to be
scrolled; creates
viewport and
scroll bars**

```
      JScrollBar.VERTICAL, 0, 0, 0, 0);
    m_vertSB.setUnitIncrement(5);
    add(m_vertSB);

    m_horzSB = new JScrollBar(
      JScrollBar.HORIZONTAL, 0, 0, 0, 0);
    m_horzSB.setUnitIncrement(5);
    add(m_horzSB);

    AdjustmentListener lst = new AdjustmentListener() {
      public void adjustmentValueChanged(AdjustmentEvent e) {
        m_viewport.doLayout();
      }
    };
    m_vertSB.addAdjustmentListener(lst);
    m_horzSB.addAdjustmentListener(lst);
  }

  public void doLayout() {
    Dimension d = getSize();
    Dimension d0 = m_comp.getPreferredSize();
    Dimension d1 = m_vertSB.getPreferredSize();
    Dimension d2 = m_horzSB.getPreferredSize();

    int w = Math.max(d.width - d1.width-1, 0);
    int h = Math.max(d.height - d2.height-1, 0);
    m_viewport.setBounds(0, 0, w, h);
    m_vertSB.setBounds(w+1, 0, d1.width, h);
    m_horzSB.setBounds(0, h+1, w, d2.height);

    int xs = Math.max(d0.width - w, 0);
    m_horzSB.setMaximum(xs);
    m_horzSB.setBlockIncrement(xs/5);
    m_horzSB.setEnabled(xs > 0);

    int ys = Math.max(d0.height - h, 0);
    m_vertSB.setMaximum(ys);
    m_vertSB.setBlockIncrement(ys/5);
    m_vertSB.setEnabled(ys > 0);

    m_horzSB.setVisibleAmount(m_horzSB.getBlockIncrement());
    m_vertSB.setVisibleAmount(m_vertSB.getBlockIncrement());
  }

  public Dimension getPreferredSize() {
    Dimension d0 = m_comp.getPreferredSize();
    Dimension d1 = m_vertSB.getPreferredSize();
    Dimension d2 = m_horzSB.getPreferredSize();
    Dimension d = new Dimension(d0.width+d1.width,
      d0.height+d2.height);
    return d;
  }

  class CustomViewport extends JPanel
  {
```

3 Sets bounds
for viewport
and scroll bars

4 Viewport sets its
bounds from
scroll bar positions

```
public void doLayout() {
    Dimension d0 = m_comp.getPreferredSize();
    int x = m_horzSB.getValue();
    int y = m_vertSB.getValue();
    m_comp.setBounds(-x, -y, d0.width, d0.height);
  }
 }
}
```

13.2.1 Understanding the code

Class ScrollDemo

❶ This simple frame-based class creates a `CustomScrollPane` instance to scroll a large image. This class is very similar to the first example in chapter 7 and it does not require any additional explanation here.

Class CustomScrollPane

This class extends `JPanel` to represent a simple custom scroll pane. Four instance variables are declared:

- `JScrollBar m_vertSB`: The vertical scroll bar.
- `JScrollBar m_horzSB`: The horizontal scroll bar.
- `CustomViewport m_viewport`: The custom viewport component.
- `JComponent m_comp`: The component to be placed in our custom viewport.

❷ The `CustomScrollPane` constructor takes a component to be scrolled as a parameter. It instantiates the instance variables described above and adds them to itself using a `null` layout (because this component acts as its own layout manager). The `JScrollBars` are created with proper orientation and zero values across the board because these are meaningless if they're not based on the size of the component being scrolled.

An `AdjustmentListener` is created and added to both scroll bars. The `adjustment-ValueChanged()` method calls the `doLayout()` method on the `m_viewport` component to perform the actual component scrolling according to the new scroll bar values.

❸ The `doLayout()` method sets the bounds for the viewport (in the center), the vertical scroll bar (on the right), and the horizontal scroll bar (on the bottom). New maximum values and block increment values are set for the scroll bars based on the sizes of the scrolling pane and the component to be scrolled. If either dimension of the scroll pane is bigger (or the same size as) the corresponding scrolling component's dimension, the corresponding scroll bar is disabled. The `visibleAmount` property of each is set to the corresponding `blockIncrement` value to provide proportional thumb sizes.

The `getPreferredSize()` method simply calculates the preferred size of this component based on the preferred sizes of its children.

Class CustomViewport

❹ This class extends `JPanel` and represents a simple realization of a viewport for our custom scrolling pane. The only implemented method, `doLayout()`, reads the current scroll bar values and assigns bounds to the scrolling component accordingly.

13.2.2   Running the code

Figure 13.2 shows an image in the custom scroll pane. Use the horizontal and vertical scroll bars to verify that the scrolling works as expected. Resize the frame component to verify that the scroll bar values and thumbs are adjusted correctly as the container's size is changed.

13.3   *JSLIDER DATE CHOOSER*

In example 13.3, we'll show how three JSliders can be combined to allow date selection. We will also address some resizing issues and show how to dynamically change JSlider's annotation components and tick spacing based on size constraints.

NOTE   While month and day are limited values, year is not. We can use a JSlider to select year only if we define a finite, static range of years to choose from, because JSlider must have a minimum and maximum value at all times. In this example we bound the year slider value between 1990 and 2010.

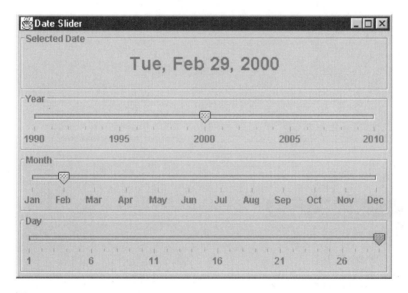

Figure 13.3 JSliders **with dynamically changable bound values, tick spacing, and annotation components**

GUIDELINE

Feedback in readable form   Using sliders to pick the values for a date may be an interesting method for data input, but it does not lend itself to easy and clear output communication. It can be visually tedious to determine the actual selected date; users may need to look at each slider and put the information together themselves. This problem is fixed by the use of the clearly human readable form (the label) at the top of the dialog. This label directly follows the advice that sliders should be used to provide immediate visual feedback.

Visual noise Visual noise or clutter is avoided by spacing annotations and avoiding the temptation to annotate each day and each year. The change in rendering as the device is made smaller is also a clear example of how extra coding and the adoption of an advanced technique can aid visual communication and usability.

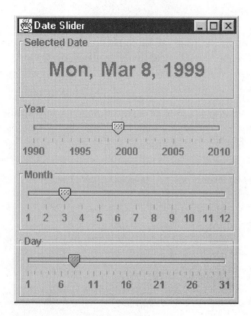

Figure 13.4 `JSliders` showing altered maximum bound and annotation labels

Example 13.3

DateSlider.java

see \Chapter13\3

```java
import java.awt.*;
import java.awt.event.*;
import java.util.*;
import java.text.*;

import javax.swing.*;
import javax.swing.border.*;
import javax.swing.event.*;

public class DateSlider extends JFrame
{
  public final static Dimension RIGID_DIMENSION =
    new Dimension(1,3);

  protected JLabel  m_lbDate;
  protected JSlider m_slYear;
  protected JSlider m_slMonth;
  protected JSlider m_slDay;
```

```java
protected Hashtable m_labels;
protected GregorianCalendar m_calendar;
protected SimpleDateFormat m_dateFormat;

public DateSlider() {
  super("Date Slider");
  setSize(500, 340);

  m_calendar = new GregorianCalendar();
  Date currDate = new Date();
  m_calendar.setTime(currDate);
  m_dateFormat = new SimpleDateFormat("EEE, MMM d, yyyyy");

  JPanel p1 = new JPanel();
  p1.setLayout(new GridLayout(4, 1));

  JPanel p = new JPanel();
  p.setBorder(new TitledBorder(new EtchedBorder(),
    "Selected Date"));
  m_lbDate = new JLabel(
    m_dateFormat.format(currDate) + "        ");
  m_lbDate.setFont(new Font("Arial",Font.BOLD,24));
  p.add(m_lbDate);
  p1.add(p);

  m_slYear = new JSlider(JSlider.HORIZONTAL, 1990, 2010,
    m_calendar.get(Calendar.YEAR));
  m_slYear.setPaintLabels(true);
  m_slYear.setMajorTickSpacing(5);
  m_slYear.setMinorTickSpacing(1);
  m_slYear.setPaintTicks(true);
  DateListener lst = new DateListener();
  m_slYear.addChangeListener(lst);

  p = new JPanel();
  p.setBorder(new TitledBorder(new EtchedBorder(), "Year"));
  p.setLayout(new BoxLayout(p, BoxLayout.Y_AXIS));
  p.add(Box.createRigidArea(RIGID_DIMENSION));
  p.add(m_slYear);
  p.add(Box.createRigidArea(RIGID_DIMENSION));
  p1.add(p);

  m_slMonth = new JSlider(JSlider.HORIZONTAL, 1, 12,
    m_calendar.get(Calendar.MONTH)+1);
  String[] months =
    (new DateFormatSymbols()).getShortMonths();
  m_labels = new Hashtable(12);
  for (int k=0; k<12; k++)
    m_labels.put(new Integer(k+1), new JLabel(
      months[k], JLabel.CENTER));
  m_slMonth.setLabelTable(m_labels);
  m_slMonth.setPaintLabels(true);
  m_slMonth.setMajorTickSpacing(1);
  m_slMonth.setPaintTicks(true);
  m_slMonth.addChangeListener(lst);
```

❶ Creates calendar and date information

❷ Slider to set year

❸ Slider to set month

```
p = new JPanel();
p.setBorder(new TitledBorder(new EtchedBorder(), "Month"));
p.setLayout(new BoxLayout(p, BoxLayout.Y_AXIS));
p.add(Box.createRigidArea(RIGID_DIMENSION));
p.add(m_slMonth);
p.add(Box.createRigidArea(RIGID_DIMENSION));
p1.add(p);

int maxDays = m_calendar.getActualMaximum(
  Calendar.DAY_OF_MONTH);
m_slDay = new JSlider(JSlider.HORIZONTAL, 1, maxDays,
  m_calendar.get(Calendar.DAY_OF_MONTH));
m_slDay.setPaintLabels(true);
m_slDay.setMajorTickSpacing(5);
m_slDay.setMinorTickSpacing(1);
m_slDay.setPaintTicks(true);
m_slDay.addChangeListener(lst);

p = new JPanel();
p.setBorder(new TitledBorder(new EtchedBorder(), "Day"));
p.setLayout(new BoxLayout(p, BoxLayout.Y_AXIS));
p.add(Box.createRigidArea(RIGID_DIMENSION));
p.add(m_slDay);
p.add(Box.createRigidArea(RIGID_DIMENSION));
p1.add(p);

getContentPane().add(p1, BorderLayout.CENTER);

WindowListener wndCloser = new WindowAdapter() {
  public void windowClosing(WindowEvent e) {
    System.exit(0);
  }
};
addWindowListener(wndCloser);

enableEvents(ComponentEvent.COMPONENT_RESIZED);
setVisible(true);
}

protected void processComponentEvent(ComponentEvent e) {
  if (e.getID() == ComponentEvent.COMPONENT_RESIZED) {
    int w = getSize().width;

    m_slYear.setLabelTable(null);
    if (w > 200)
      m_slYear.setMajorTickSpacing(5);
    else
      m_slYear.setMajorTickSpacing(10);
    m_slYear.setPaintLabels(w > 100);

    m_slMonth.setLabelTable(w > 300 ? m_labels : null);
    if (w <= 300 && w >=200)
      m_slMonth.setMajorTickSpacing(1);
    else
      m_slMonth.setMajorTickSpacing(2);
```

4 Slider to set day of month

5 Enables receipt of resize events

6 Reconfigures tick spacing depending on width of frame

```
      m_slMonth.setPaintLabels(w > 100);

      m_slDay.setLabelTable(null);
      if (w > 200)
        m_slDay.setMajorTickSpacing(5);
      else
        m_slDay.setMajorTickSpacing(10);
      m_slDay.setPaintLabels(w > 100);
    }
  }

  public void showDate() {
    m_calendar.set(m_slYear.getValue(),
    m_slMonth.getValue()-1, 1);
    int maxDays = m_calendar.getActualMaximum(
      Calendar.DAY_OF_MONTH);

    if (m_slDay.getMaximum() != maxDays) {
      m_slDay.setValue(
        Math.min(m_slDay.getValue(), maxDays));
      m_slDay.setMaximum(maxDays);
      m_slDay.repaint();
    }

    m_calendar.set(
      m_slYear.getValue(), m_slMonth.getValue()-1,
      m_slDay.getValue());
    Date date = m_calendar.getTime();
    m_lbDate.setText(m_dateFormat.format(date));
  }

  class DateListener implements ChangeListener
  {
    public void stateChanged(ChangeEvent e) {
      showDate();
    }
  }

  public static void main(String argv[]) {
    new DateSlider();
  }
}
```

❼ Retrieves values from sliders to format date string into m_cbDate

❽ Listens for slider changes, causing date display update

13.3.1   Understanding the code

Class DateSlider

DateSlider extends JFrame and declares seven instance variables and one class constant. This is the class constant:

  • Dimension RIGID_DIMENSION: Used to create rigid areas above and below each slider.

There are seven instance variables:

  • JLabel m_lbDate: The label to display the selected date.
  • JSlider m_slYear: The slider to select the year.
  • JSlider m_slMonth: The slider to select the month.

- `JSlider m_slDay`: The slider to select the day.
- `Hashtable m_labels`: A collection of labels to denote months by short names rather than numbers.
- `GregorianCalendar m_calendar`: A calendar that performs date manipulations.
- `SimpleDateFormat m_dateFormat`: The object to format the date as a string.

1 The `DateSlider` constructor initializes the `m_calendar` instance defined above, and the date format `m_dateFormat`. A `JPanel` with a `GridLayout` of one column and four rows is used as a base panel, `p1`. `JLabel m_lbDate` is created and embedded in a `JPanel` with a simple `TitledBorder`, and placed in the first row.

2 The `m_slYear` slider is created and placed in the second row. This slider is used to select the year from the interval 1990 to 2010. It takes its initial value from the current date. A number of settings are applied to `m_slYear`. The `paintLabels` and `paintTicks` properties are set to `true` to allow for drawing ticks and labels, `majorTickSpacing` is set to 5 to draw major ticks for every fifth value, and `minorTickSpacing` is set to 1 to draw minor ticks for every value. Finally, a new `DateListener` instance (see below) is added as a `ChangeListener` to monitor changes to this slider's properties. Notice that `m_slYear` is placed in a `JPanel` that is surrounded by a `TitledBorder`. Two rigid areas are added to ensure vertical spacing between our slider and this parent panel (see chapter 4 for more about `Box` and its invisible `Filler` components).

3 The `m_slMonth` slider is created and placed in the third row. This slider is used to select the month from the interval 1 to 12. This component is constructed similar to `m_slYear`, but it receives a `Hashtable` of `JLabels` to denote months by short names rather than numbers. These names are taken from an instance of the `DateFormatSymbols` class (see the API documentation) and they are used to create pairs in a local `m_labels Hashtable` in the form `Integer/JLabel`. The `Integer` represents slider value (from 1 to 12) as key, and the `JLabel` is used to display this value. Finally, the `setLabelTable()` method is invoked to assign these custom labels to the slider.

4 The `m_slDay` slider is created and placed in the fourth row. It is used to select the day of the month from an interval which dynamically changes depending on the current month and, for February, the year. Aside from this difference, `m_slDay` is constructed very similar to `m_slYear`.

5 A slider's tick annotation components may overlap each other and become unreadable if not enough space is provided, and it is up to us to account for this possibility. This becomes a more significant problem when (as in this example) slider components can be resized by simply resizing the parent frame. To work around this problem, we can simply enforce a certain size, but this may not be desirable in all situations. If we ever find ourselves in such a situation, we need to change our slider's properties dynamically depending on its size. For this reason, the `processComponentEvent()` method is overridden to process resizing events that occur on the parent frame. This event processing is enabled in the `DateSlider` constructor with the `enableEvents()` method.

6 The `processComponentEvent()` method only responds to `ComponentEvents` with the ID `COMPONENT_RESIZED`. For each of our three sliders, this method changes the `majorTickSpacing` property based on the container's width. `m_slDay` and `m_slYear` receive a spacing of 5 if the width is greater than 200; otherwise they receive a spacing of 10. `m_slMonth` receives a `majorTickSpacing` of 1 if the container's width is anywhere from 200 to 300, and it receives 2 otherwise. If this width is greater than 300, our custom set of labels is used to annotate m_slMonth's major ticks. The default numerical labels are used otherwise. For each slider, if the width is less than 100 the paintLabels property is set to false, which disables all annotations; otherwise, paintLabels is set to true.

7 Our custom showDate() method is used to retrieve values from our sliders and display them in m_lbDate as the new selected date. First, we determine the maximum number of days for the selected month by passing m_calendar a year, a month, and 1 as the day. Then, if necessary, we reset m_slDay's current and maximum values. Finally, we pass m_calendar a year, month, and the selected (possibly adjusted) day, retrieve a Date instance corresponding to these values, and invoke format() to retrieve a textual representation of the date.

> **NOTE** Java 2 does not really provide a direct way to convert a year, month, and day triplet into a Date instance (this functionality has been deprecated). We need to use Calendar.set() and Calendar.getTime() for this. Be aware that the day parameter is not checked against the maximum value for the selected month. If the day is set to 30 when the month is set to February, it will be silently treated as March 2.

Class DateSlider.DateListener

8 The DateListener inner class implements the ChangeListener interface, and it is used to listen for changes in each of our sliders' properties. Its stateChanged() method simply calls the showDate() method described above.

13.3.2   Running the code

Notice how the date is selected and displayed, and how the range of the Day slider is adjusted when a new month is selected. Figure 13.3 shows the selection of February 29, 2000, demonstrating that this is a leap year.

> **NOTE** A leap year is a year whose last two digits are evenly divisible by 4, except for centenary years not divisible by 400.

Now try resizing the application frame to see how the slider annotations and ticks change to their more compact variants as the available space shrinks. Figure 13.4 illustrates the changes.

UI GUIDELINE

Exact value selection   Although sliders are best used for selections where an exact value is not needed, this example gets around situations where an exact value is needed by providing an adequate gap between ticks, making an exact choice easy to achieve.

The use of a slider for the year selection is an unusual choice, as the year is not normally a bounded input. However, in certain domains it may be a more suitable choice such as this example. Once the year and the month have been displayed using sliders, it is visually attractive and consistent to use a slider for the day. There may be some debate about doing so, as the bound will change depending on the month that is selected. However, it is fair to argue that the changing bound on the day, as the month is selected, gives a clear, instant, visual feedback of how many days are in the month, which meets with the criteria of providing instant feedback when using a slider.

13.4 JSLIDERS IN A JPEG IMAGE EDITOR

Java 2 ships with a special package, `com.sun.image.codec.jpeg`, that provides a set of classes and interfaces for working with JPEG images (this package is created at least in part by Eastman Kodak Company). Although this package is not a part of Swing, it can be very useful in Swing-based applications. By reducing image quality (which is actually a result of compression), required storage space can be decreased. Using reduced quality JPEGs in web pages increases response time by decreasing download time, and the editor application we will develop here allows us to load an existing JPEG, modify its quality, and then save the result. `JSliders` are used for the main editing components.

NOTE   JPEG stands for Joint Photographic Experts Group. It is a popular graphical format that allows images to be compressed up to 10 or 20 times.

Before we decide to use functionality in this package, you should know that, even though this package is shipped with Java 2, according to the API documentation, "... the classes in the `com.sun.image.codec.jpeg` package are not part of the core Java APIs. They are a part of Sun's JDK and JRE distributions. Although other licensees may choose to distribute these classes, developers cannot depend on their availability in non-Sun implementations. We expect that equivalent functionality will eventually be available in a core API or standard extension."

13.4.1   The JPEGDecodeParam interface

abstract interface com.sun.image.codec.jpeg.JPEGDecodeParam

This interface encapsulates the parameters used to control the decoding of a JPEG image. It provides a rich set of `getXX()` and `isXX()` accessor methods. Instances contain information about how to decode a JPEG input stream, and they are created automatically by `JPEGImage-Decoder` (see below) if none is specified when an image is decoded. A `JPEGImageDecoder`'s associated `JPEGDecoderParam` can be obtained with its `getJPEGDecodeParam()` method.

13.4.2   The JPEGEncodeParam interface

abstract interface com.sun.image.codec.jpeg.JPEGEncodeParam

This interface encapsulates parameters that are used to control the encoding of a JPEG image stream. It provides a rich set of `getXX()` and `setXX()` accessor methods. Instances contain information about how to encode a JPEG to an output stream, and a default instance will be created atomically by `JPEGImageEncoder` (see below) if none is specified when an image is encoded. A `JPEGImageEncoder`'s associated `JPEGEncodeParam` can be obtained with its `getJPEGEncodeParam()` method, or with one of its overriden `getDefaultJPEGEncode-Param()` methods.

Particularly relevant to this example are `JPEGEncodeParam`'s `xDensity`, `yDensity`, and `quality` properties, all of which can be assigned using typical `setXX()` methods. `xDensity` and `yDensity` represent horizontal and vertical pixel density, which depends on `JPEGEncoder-Param`'s current pixel density setting. The pixel density setting is controlled with `JPEGEncode-Param`'s `setDensityUnit()` method. It can be, for instance, `DENSITY_UNIT_DOTS_INCH`, which means pixel density will be interpreted as pixels per inch. The quality property is specified as a float within the range 0.0 to 1.0, where 1.0 means perfect quality. In general, 0.75 means high quality, 0.5 means medium quality, and 0.25 means low quality.

13.4.3 The JPEGImageDecoder interface

abstract interface com.sun.image.codec.jpeg.JPEGImageDecoder

This interface describes an object used to decode a JPEG data stream into an image. We invoke the `decodeAsBufferedImage()` method to perform the actual decoding into a `Buffered-Image` instance, or we invoke `decodeAsRaster()` to perform the decoding into a `Raster` instance. An instance of this interface can be obtained with one of the `JPEGCodec.create-JPEGDecoder()` methods, which takes the delivering data `InputStream` as a parameter. `JPEGImageDecoder` decodes according to its associated `JPEGDecodeParam`, and a default instance will be provided if we do not specify one.

13.4.4 The JPEGImageEncoder interface

abstract interface com.sun.image.codec.jpeg.JPEGImageEncoder

This interface describes an object used to encode an image into a JPEG data stream. We invoke the overloaded `encode()` method to perform the actual encoding. Instances of this interface can be obtained with one of the `JPEGCodec.createJPEGEncoder()` methods, which takes the destination `OutputStream` as a parameter. `JPEGImageEncoder` encodes according to its associated `JPEGImageEncoder`, and a default instance will be provided if we do not specify one.

13.4.5 JPEGCodec

class com.sun.image.codec.jpeg.JPEGCodec

This class contains a collection of static methods used to create JPEG encoders and decoders. Particularly useful are the overloaded `createJPEGDecoder()` and `createJPEGEncoder()` methods which take an `InputStream` and `OutputStream`, respectively, as parameters (along with an optional `JPEGDecodeParam` or `JPEGEncodeParam` instance).

Example 13.4

JPEGEditor.java

see \Chapter13\4

```
import java.awt.*;
import java.awt.event.*;
import java.awt.image.*;
import java.util.*;
import java.io.*;

import javax.swing.*;
import javax.swing.border.*;
import javax.swing.event.*;
import javax.swing.filechooser.*;

import com.sun.image.codec.jpeg.*;

public class JPEGEditor extends JFrame
{
  public final static Dimension VERTICAL_RIGID_SIZE
    = new Dimension(1,3);
```

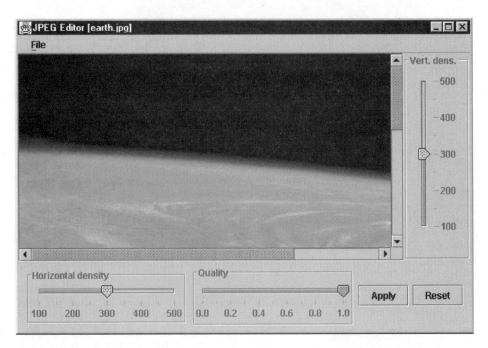

Figure 13.5 `JPEGEditor` **showing a high-quality image of Earth (using** `JSlider`**s with the "isFilled" client property)**

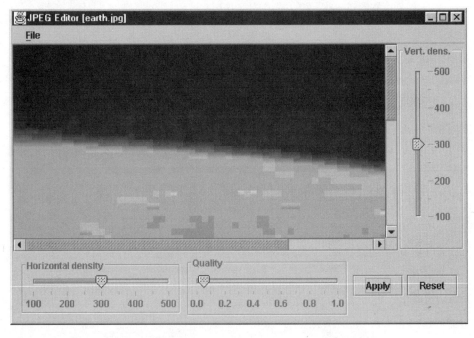

Figure 13.6 `JPEGEditor` **showing a reduced-quality image of Earth**

```
public final static Dimension HORIZONTAL_RIGID_SIZE
  = new Dimension(3,1);

protected File m_currentDir = new File(".");
protected File m_currentFile = null;

protected JFileChooser m_chooser;
protected JPEGPanel m_panel;
protected JSlider m_slHorzDensity;
protected JSlider m_slVertDensity;
protected JSlider m_slQuality;

protected BufferedImage m_bi1, m_bi2;

public JPEGEditor() {
  super("JPEG Editor");
  setSize(600, 400);

  m_chooser = new JFileChooser();
  SimpleFilter filter = new SimpleFilter("jpg",
    "JPEG Image Files");
  m_chooser.setFileFilter(filter);
  m_chooser.setCurrentDirectory(m_currentDir);

  m_panel = new JPEGPanel();
  JScrollPane ps = new JScrollPane(m_panel,
    JScrollPane.VERTICAL_SCROLLBAR_ALWAYS,
    JScrollPane.HORIZONTAL_SCROLLBAR_ALWAYS);
  getContentPane().add(ps, BorderLayout.CENTER);

  JPanel p, p1;

  m_slVertDensity = new JSlider(JSlider.VERTICAL,
    100, 500, 300);
  m_slVertDensity.setExtent(50);
  m_slVertDensity.setPaintLabels(true);
  m_slVertDensity.setMajorTickSpacing(100);
  m_slVertDensity.setMinorTickSpacing(50);
  m_slVertDensity.setPaintTicks(true);
  m_slVertDensity.putClientProperty(
    "JSlider.isFilled", Boolean.TRUE);

  p = new JPanel();
  p.setBorder(new TitledBorder(new EtchedBorder(),
    "Vert. dens."));
  p.add(Box.createRigidArea(HORIZONTAL_RIGID_SIZE));
  p.add(m_slVertDensity);
  p.add(Box.createRigidArea(HORIZONTAL_RIGID_SIZE));
  getContentPane().add(p, BorderLayout.EAST);

  m_slHorzDensity = new JSlider(JSlider.HORIZONTAL,
    100, 500, 300);
  m_slHorzDensity.setExtent(50);
  m_slHorzDensity.setPaintLabels(true);
  m_slHorzDensity.setMajorTickSpacing(100);
  m_slHorzDensity.setMinorTickSpacing(50);
  m_slHorzDensity.setPaintTicks(true);
```

① Creates file chooser which can select JPEG files

① Slider for JPEGEncodeParam "yDensity" property

① Slider for JPEGEncodeParam "xDensity" property

```
m_slHorzDensity.putClientProperty(
  "JSlider.isFilled", Boolean.TRUE);

p = new JPanel();
p.setBorder(new TitledBorder(new EtchedBorder(),
  "Horizontal density"));
p.setLayout(new BoxLayout(p, BoxLayout.Y_AXIS));
p.add(Box.createRigidArea(VERTICAL_RIGID_SIZE));
p.add(m_slHorzDensity);
p.add(Box.createRigidArea(VERTICAL_RIGID_SIZE));
p1 = new JPanel();
p.setLayout(new BoxLayout(p, BoxLayout.X_AXIS));
p1.add(p);

m_slQuality = new JSlider(JSlider.HORIZONTAL,
  0, 100, 100);
Hashtable labels = new Hashtable(6);
for (float q = 0; q <= 1.0; q += 0.2)
  labels.put(new Integer((int)(q*100)),
  new JLabel("" + q, JLabel.CENTER));
m_slQuality.setLabelTable(labels);
m_slQuality.setExtent(10);
m_slQuality.setPaintLabels(true);
m_slQuality.setMinorTickSpacing(10);
m_slQuality.setPaintTicks(true);
m_slQuality.putClientProperty(
  "JSlider.isFilled", Boolean.TRUE);

p = new JPanel();
p.setBorder(new TitledBorder(new EtchedBorder(),
  "Quality"));
p.setLayout(new BoxLayout(p, BoxLayout.Y_AXIS));
p.add(Box.createRigidArea(VERTICAL_RIGID_SIZE));
p.add(m_slQuality);
p.add(Box.createRigidArea(VERTICAL_RIGID_SIZE));
p1.add(p);

JButton btApply = new JButton("Apply");
ActionListener lst = new ActionListener() {
  public void actionPerformed(ActionEvent e) {
    apply();
  }
};
btApply.addActionListener(lst);
p1.add(btApply);

JButton btReset = new JButton("Reset");
lst = new ActionListener() {
  public void actionPerformed(ActionEvent e) {
    reset();
  }
};
btReset.addActionListener(lst);
p1.add(btReset);
getContentPane().add(p1, BorderLayout.SOUTH);
```

① Slider for JPEGEncodeParam "xDensity" property

① Slider for JPEGEncodeParam "quality" property

② Apply button calls apply() method to read slider values

```
  setJMenuBar(createMenuBar());

  WindowListener wndCloser = new WindowAdapter() {
    public void windowClosing(WindowEvent e) {
      System.exit(0);
    }
  };
  addWindowListener(wndCloser);

  setVisible(true);
}

protected JMenuBar createMenuBar() {
  JMenuBar menuBar = new JMenuBar();

  JMenu mFile = new JMenu("File");
  mFile.setMnemonic('f');

  JMenuItem mItem = new JMenuItem("Open...");
  mItem.setMnemonic('o');
  ActionListener lst = new ActionListener() {
    public void actionPerformed(ActionEvent e) {
      if (m_chooser.showOpenDialog(JPEGEditor.this) !=
        JFileChooser.APPROVE_OPTION)
          return;
      m_currentDir = m_chooser.getCurrentDirectory();
      File fChoosen = m_chooser.getSelectedFile();
      openFile(fChoosen);
    }
  };
  mItem.addActionListener(lst);
  mFile.add(mItem);

  mItem = new JMenuItem("Save");
  mItem.setMnemonic('s');
  lst = new ActionListener() {
    public void actionPerformed(ActionEvent e) {
      saveFile(m_currentFile);
    }
  };
  mItem.addActionListener(lst);
  mFile.add(mItem);

  mItem = new JMenuItem("Save As...");
  mItem.setMnemonic('a');
  lst = new ActionListener() {
    public void actionPerformed(ActionEvent e) {
      m_chooser.setSelectedFile(m_currentFile);
      if (m_chooser.showSaveDialog(JPEGEditor.this) !=
        JFileChooser.APPROVE_OPTION)
      return;
      m_currentDir = m_chooser.getCurrentDirectory();
      File fChoosen = m_chooser.getSelectedFile();
      if (fChoosen!=null && fChoosen.exists()) {
        String message = "File " + fChoosen.getName()+
```

3 Creates file operations menu items

4 Gets a JPEG file to open

4 Saves current JPEG file

4 Saves current file with newly specified file name

```
                    " already exists. Override?";
            int result = JOptionPane.showConfirmDialog(
              JPEGEditor.this, message, getTitle(),
              JOptionPane.YES_NO_OPTION);
            if (result != JOptionPane.YES_OPTION)
              return;
          }
          setCurrentFile(fChoosen);
          saveFile(fChoosen);
        }
      };
      mItem.addActionListener(lst);
      mFile.add(mItem);

      mFile.addSeparator();

      mItem = new JMenuItem("Exit");
      mItem.setMnemonic('x');
      lst = new ActionListener() {
        public void actionPerformed(ActionEvent e) {
          System.exit(0);
        }
      };
      mItem.addActionListener(lst);
      mFile.add(mItem);
      menuBar.add(mFile);
      return menuBar;
  }

  protected void setCurrentFile(File file) {
    if (file != null) {
      m_currentFile = file;
      setTitle("JPEG Editor ["+file.getName()+"]");
    }
  }

  protected void openFile(final File file) {
    if (file == null || !file.exists())
      return;
    setCurrentFile(file);

    setCursor(Cursor.getPredefinedCursor(Cursor.WAIT_CURSOR));
    Thread runner = new Thread() {
      public void run() {
        try {
          FileInputStream in = new FileInputStream(file);
          JPEGImageDecoder decoder =
            JPEGCodec.createJPEGDecoder(in);
          m_bi1 = decoder.decodeAsBufferedImage();
          m_bi2 = null;
          in.close();
          SwingUtilities.invokeLater(new Runnable() {
            public void run() { reset(); }
          });
        }
```

4 Saves current file with newly specified file name

4 Exits the application

5 Reads in and decodes a JPEG file, into a BufferedImage

5 The reset() method modifies a Swing component, so it runs on the event

```
      catch (Exception ex) {
        ex.printStackTrace();
        System.err.println("openFile: "+ex.toString());
      }
      setCursor(Cursor.getPredefinedCursor(
        Cursor.DEFAULT_CURSOR));
    }
  };
  runner.start();
}

protected void saveFile(final File file) {
  if (file == null || m_panel.getBufferedImage() == null)
    return;

  setCursor(Cursor.getPredefinedCursor(Cursor.WAIT_CURSOR));
  Thread runner = new Thread() {
    public void run() {
      try {
        FileOutputStream out = new FileOutputStream(file);
        JPEGImageEncoder encoder =
          JPEGCodec.createJPEGEncoder(out);
        encoder.encode(m_panel.getBufferedImage());
        out.close();
      }
      catch (Exception ex) {
        ex.printStackTrace();
        System.err.println("apply: "+ex.toString());
      }
      setCursor(Cursor.getPredefinedCursor(
        Cursor.DEFAULT_CURSOR));
    }
  };
  runner.start();
}

protected void apply() {
  if (m_bi1 == null)
    return;

  setCursor(Cursor.getPredefinedCursor(Cursor.WAIT_CURSOR));
  Thread runner = new Thread() {
    public void run() {
      try {
        ByteArrayOutputStream out = new ByteArrayOutputStream();
        JPEGImageEncoder encoder =
          JPEGCodec.createJPEGEncoder(out);
        JPEGEncodeParam param =
          encoder.getDefaultJPEGEncodeParam(m_bi1);

        float quality = m_slQuality.getValue()/100.0f;
        param.setQuality(quality, false);

        param.setDensityUnit(
          JPEGEncodeParam.DENSITY_UNIT_DOTS_INCH);
```

6 Encodes image into JPEG-format file

7 Processes BufferedImage with slider values into JPEG image, into OutputStream

```
              int xDensity = m_slHorzDensity.getValue();
              param.setXDensity(xDensity);
              int yDensity = m_slVertDensity.getValue();
              param.setYDensity(yDensity);

              encoder.setJPEGEncodeParam(param);
              encoder.encode(m_bi1);

              ByteArrayInputStream in = new ByteArrayInputStream(
                out.toByteArray());
              JPEGImageDecoder decoder =
                JPEGCodec.createJPEGDecoder(in);
              final BufferedImage bi2 = decoder.decodeAsBufferedImage();
              SwingUtilities.invokeLater(new Runnable() {
                public void run() {
                  m_panel.setBufferedImage(bi2);
                }
              });
            }
            catch (Exception ex) {
              ex.printStackTrace();
              System.err.println("apply: "+ex.toString());
            }
            setCursor(Cursor.getPredefinedCursor(
              Cursor.DEFAULT_CURSOR));
          }
        };
        runner.start();
      }

      protected void reset() {
        if (m_bi1 != null) {
          m_panel.setBufferedImage(m_bi1);
          m_slQuality.setValue(100);
          m_slHorzDensity.setValue(300);
          m_slVertDensity.setValue(300);
        }
      }

      public static void main(String argv[]) {
        new JPEGEditor();
      }
    }

    class JPEGPanel extends JPanel
    {
      protected BufferedImage m_bi = null;

      public JPEGPanel() {}

      public void setBufferedImage(BufferedImage bi) {
        if (bi == null)
          return;
        m_bi = bi;
        Dimension d = new Dimension(m_bi.getWidth(this),
```

⑦ Processes
BufferedImage
with slider values
into JPEG image,
into OutputStream

⑦ Reads input
from OutputStream
into a BufferedImage

⑧ Container for a
single JPEG image

```
        m_bi.getHeight(this));
      setPreferredSize(d);
      revalidate();
      repaint();
    }

    public void paintComponent(Graphics g) {
      super.paintComponent(g);
      Dimension d = getSize();
      g.setColor(getBackground());
      g.fillRect(0, 0, d.width, d.height);
      if (m_bi != null)
        g.drawImage(m_bi, 0, 0, this);
    }

    public BufferedImage getBufferedImage() {
      return m_bi;
    }
  }
}

//The SimpleFilter class is taken from chapter 14
```

⑨ Inside a JScrollPane, this will re-layout the panel

13.4.6   Understanding the code

Class JPEGEditor

Class variables:

- `Dimension VERTICAL_RIGID_SIZE`: The size of the rigid area used for vertical spacing.
- `Dimension HORIZONTAL_RIGID_SIZE`: The size of the rigid area used for horizontal spacing.

Instance variables:

- `File m_currentDir`: The current directory navigated to by our `JFileChooser`.
- `File m_currentFile`: The JPEG image file currently in our editing environment.
- `JFileChooser m_chooser`: The file chooser used for loading and saving JPEGs.
- `JPEGPanel m_panel`: The custom component used to display JPEGs.
- `JSlider m_slHorzDensity`: The slider to choose horizontal pixel density.
- `JSlider m_slVertDensity`: The slider to choose vertical pixel density.
- `JSlider m_slQuality`: The slider to choose image quality.
- `BufferedImage m_bi1`: The original image.
- `BufferedImage m_bi2`: The modified image.

① `JPEGEditor`'s constructor starts by instantiating our `JFileChooser` and applying a `Simple-Filter` (see chapter 14) file filter to it, in order to restrict file selection to JPEG images (files with a .jpg extension). The custom panel `m_panel` is used to display a JPEG image (see the `JPEG-Panel` class below) and it is added to a `JScrollPane` to provide scrolling capabilities. Three sliders are used to select `JPEGEncodeParam` properties as described above: `xDensity`, `yDensity`, and `quality`. Each is surrounded by a `TitledBorder` with an appropriate title. Similar to the previous example, `RigidAreas` are used to ensure proper spacing between the slider and the border. Each slider makes use of the Metal look and feel client property "JSlider.isFilled" with the value `Boolean.TRUE` to force the lower portion of each slider track to be filled.

The m_slQuality slider must represent values from 0 to 1.0. We scale this interval to [0, 100], but we display the annotation labels 0.0, 0.2, 0.4,…,1.0, which are stored in Hashtable labels. The selected image quality value is the slider's value divided by 100. Note the use of setExtent() for each slider in this example. The value of the extent property is used when the slider has focus and the user presses the PAGEUP or PAGEDN key to increment or decrement the slider's value, respectively.

2 An Apply button is created and assigned an ActionListener to retrieve the current slider settings and apply them to the current JPEG image by calling our custom apply() method. Because of the large amount of work the apply method performs, it does not make sense to do this on-the-fly by listening for slider change events. A Reset button undoes any changes and returns the image to its original state by calling our custom reset() method. Finally, a JMenuBar is created with our createMenuBar() method.

3 The createMenuBar() method creates and returns a JMenuBar that contains one menu entitled File, which, in turn, contains four menu items: Open..., Save, Save As..., and Exit. Each item receives its own ActionListener.

4 The Open menu item brings up our JFileChooser for selecting a JPEG image file. After a successful selection, the current directory is stored in our m_currentDir variable for future use, and our custom openFile() method is invoked to load the image into our environment. The Save menu item invokes our custom saveFile() method to save the image currently in our environment. The Save As... menu item instructs JFileChooser to prompt the user for a new name and possibly a location, to which to save the current image. This code is fairly similar to the code for the Open menu, except that showSaveDialog() is used instead of showOpenDialog(). If the selected file already exists, a request for confirmation is invoked using JOptionPane.showConfirmDialog(). (Interestingly, this is not a standard feature of JFileChooser—see chapter 14 for more about JFileChooser.) Finally, our saveFile() method is invoked to save the current image as the selected file. The Exit menu item calls System.exit(0) to quit this application.

The setCurrentFile() method stores a reference to the newly opened file in m_currentFile. This method also modifies the frame's title to display the file name. It is called whenever the Open and Save As menu items are activated.

5 The openFile() method opens a given File corresponding to a stored JPEG image. It first checks to see whether the selected file exists. If it does, a new thread is created to execute all remaining code in this method so as to avoid clogging up the event-dispatching thread. A FileInputStream is opened and a JPEGImageDecoder is created for the given file. Then a call to decodeAsBufferedImage() retrieves a BufferedImage from the JPEGImageDecoder and stores it in our m_bi1 variable. The file stream is closed and our image is passed to JPEGPanel by calling the reset() method (see below). Because our reset method directly modifies the state of Swing components, we place this call in a Runnable and send it to the event-dispatching queue with SwingUtilities.invokeLater() (see chapter 2 for more about invokeLater()).

6 The saveFile() method saves the current image in the given File. In a separate thread, a FileOutputStream is opened and a JPEGImageEncoder is created that correspond to this File. Then a call to the JPEGImageEncoder's encode() method saves the current image (retrieved by our JPEGPanel's getBufferedImage() method) to the opened stream.

7 The `apply()` method applies the current slider settings to the current image. In a separate thread, this method creates a `ByteArrayOutputStream` to stream the operations in memory. Then a `JPEGImageEncoder` is created for this stream, and a `JPEGEncodeParam` is retrieved that corresponds to the original image, `m_bi1` (which is assigned in `openFile()`). Three property values are retrieved from our sliders and sent to a `JPEGEncodeParam` object via `setXX()` methods: `quality`, `xDensity`, and `yDensity`. (Note that `quality` is converted to a `float` through division by `100.0f`). Then this `JPEGEncodeParam` object is assigned to our `JPEG-ImageEncoder`, and the `encode()` method is used to perform the actual encoding of the `m_bi1` image. Next, a new image is retrieved from this encoder by first retrieving a `Byte-ArrayInputStream` from our `ByteArrayOutputStream` using its `toByteArray()` method. A `JPEGImageDecoder` is created for this stream, and the `decodeAsBufferedImage()` method retrieves a `BufferedImage` instance. Finally, in a `Runnable` sent to `SwingUtilities.invokeLater()`, this image is assigned to our image panel for display with `JPEG-Panel`'s `setBufferedImage()` method.

The `reset()` method, as you might guess from its name, resets the current image to its original state (the state it was in when it was opened) and it resets the slider values.

Class JPEGPanel

8 `JPEGPanel` extends `JPanel` and provides a placeholder for JPEG images. It declares a single instance variable:

- `BufferedImage m_bi`: Holds the current JPEG.

The `setBufferedImage()` method assigns the given image to `m_bi`, and it changes this panel's preferred size to the size of that image. The panel is then revalidated and repainted to display the new image properly.

9 **NOTE**   We learned in chapter 2 that when a `revalidate()` request is invoked on a component, all ancestors below the first ancestor whose `validateRoot` property is true get validated. `JRootPane`, `JScrollPane`, and `JTextField` are the only Swing components with a `true` `validateRoot` property by default. Thus, calling `revalidate()` on our `JPEGPanel` will result in validation of the `JScrollPane` it is contained in within our `JPEGEditor` application. `JPEGPanel` is then properly laid out and displayed; this would not occur by simply calling `repaint()`.

The `paintComponent()` method clears the background and draws the current image (if there is one). The `getBufferedImage()` method simply returns the most recent image associated with this panel.

13.4.7   **Running the code**

Figure 13.6 shows `JPEGEditor` displaying a high-quality image of Earth. By applying our sliders to reduce the quality, and clicking the Apply button, we produce the image shown in figure 13.7. Saving this image as a new file gives us a representation that occupies much less disk space than the original. Making a decision on the balance between quality and size often needs to be done when space or latency issues are important.

GUIDELINE

Component selection This example provides some tricky problems for the designer. The nature of the calculation means that instant feedback is not possible. However, the user needs to see what the result of a choice would mean. The Apply button solves the problem. This is justifiable in a case such as this due to the complex and time-consuming nature of the effect of the selection. Otherwise, we don't recommend it.

The shaded area on the sliders gives a clear indication that an amount or quantity rather than an exact, discrete value is being selected and that the amount is a percentage of the bounded whole. This helps the viewer understand what is happening.

13.5   *JProgressBar in an FTP client application*

Example 13.5 uses a JProgressBar to display progress when downloading and uploading files using the File Transfer Protocol (FTP). Support for this protocol is provided in the sun.net and sun.net.ftp packages.

13.5.1   FtpClient

class sun.net.ftp.FtpClient

This class provides functionality for an FTP client. The methods particularly relevant to this example include the following:

- FTPClient(String host): The constructor to create a new instance and connect to the given host address.
- login(String user, String password): Login to an FTP host with the given username and password.
- cd(String directory): Change the directory.
- binary(): Set the mode to binary for proper file transferring.
- closeSever(): Disconnect from the host.
- list(): Returns an InputStream that supplies the printout of the ls -l command (the list contents of the directories, one per line).
- get(String filename): Returns an InputStream for retrieving the specified file from the host.
- put(String filename): Returns an OutputStream for writing the specified file to the host.

NOTE This application's GUI is laid out using our custom DialogLayout2 layout manager, which we developed in chapter 4. Refer to chapter 4 for more information about how this manager works.

Figure 13.7 FTP client application with a `JProgressBar`
to show the upload/download status

Example 13.5

FTPApp.java

see \Chapter13\5

```java
import java.awt.*;
import java.awt.event.*;
import java.util.*;
import java.io.*;
import java.net.*;
import java.lang.reflect.*;

import sun.net.ftp.*;
import sun.net.*;

import javax.swing.*;
import javax.swing.border.*;
import javax.swing.event.*;

import dl.*;

public class FTPApp extends JFrame
{
  public static int BUFFER_SIZE = 10240;

  protected JTextField m_txtUser;
  protected JPasswordField m_txtPassword;
```

```
protected JTextField m_txtURL;
protected JTextField m_txtFile;
protected JTextArea  m_monitor;
protected JProgressBar m_progress;
protected JButton m_btPut;
protected JButton m_btGet;
protected JButton m_btFile;
protected JButton m_btClose;
protected JFileChooser m_chooser;

protected FtpClient m_client;
protected String m_sLocalFile;
protected String m_sHostFile;

public FTPApp() {
  super("FTP Client");

  JPanel p = new JPanel();
  p.setLayout(new DialogLayout2(10, 5));
  p.setBorder(new EmptyBorder(5, 5, 5, 5));

  p.add(new JLabel("User name:"));
  m_txtUser = new JTextField("anonymous");
  p.add(m_txtUser);

  p.add(new JLabel("Password:"));
  m_txtPassword = new JPasswordField();
  p.add(m_txtPassword);

  p.add(new JLabel("URL:"));
  m_txtURL = new JTextField();
  p.add(m_txtURL);

  p.add(new JLabel("File:"));
  m_txtFile = new JTextField();
  p.add(m_txtFile);

  p.add(new DialogSeparator("Connection Monitor"));

  m_monitor = new JTextArea(5, 20);
  m_monitor.setEditable(false);
  JScrollPane ps = new JScrollPane(m_monitor);
  p.add(ps);

  m_progress = new JProgressBar();
  m_progress.setStringPainted(true);
  m_progress.setBorder(new BevelBorder(BevelBorder.LOWERED,
    Color.white, Color.gray));
  m_progress.setMinimum(0);
  JPanel p1 = new JPanel(new BorderLayout());
  p1.add(m_progress, BorderLayout.CENTER);
  p.add(p1);

  p.add(new DialogSeparator());
  m_btPut = new JButton("Put");
  ActionListener lst = new ActionListener() {
    public void actionPerformed(ActionEvent e) {
```

❶ Uses custom DialogLayout2 layout manager

❶ Labels and text fields are laid out opposite from each other, one pair per row

```
            if (connect()) {
              Thread uploader = new Thread() {
                public void run() {
                  putFile();
                  disconnect();
                }
              };
              uploader.start();
            }
          }
        };
        m_btPut.addActionListener(lst);
        m_btPut.setMnemonic('p');
        p.add(m_btPut);

        m_btGet = new JButton("Get");
        lst = new ActionListener() {
          public void actionPerformed(ActionEvent e) {
            if (connect()) {
              Thread downloader = new Thread() {
                public void run() {
                  getFile();
                  disconnect();
                }
              };
              downloader.start();
            }
          }
        };
        m_btGet.addActionListener(lst);
        m_btGet.setMnemonic('g');
        p.add(m_btGet);

        m_btFile = new JButton("File");
        lst = new ActionListener() {
          public void actionPerformed(ActionEvent e) {
            if (m_chooser.showSaveDialog(FTPApp.this) !=
              JFileChooser.APPROVE_OPTION)
                return;
            File f = m_chooser.getSelectedFile();
            m_txtFile.setText(f.getPath());
          }
        };
        m_btFile.addActionListener(lst);
        m_btFile.setMnemonic('f');
        p.add(m_btFile);

        m_btClose = new JButton("Close");
        lst = new ActionListener() {
          public void actionPerformed(ActionEvent e) {
            if (m_client != null)
              disconnect();
            else
              System.exit(0);
```

2 Action to upload a selected file

2 Action to download a selected file

2 Action to choose a local file name

2 Action to disconnect from the FTP host, or exit the application

```
        }
      };
      m_btClose.addActionListener(lst);
      m_btClose.setDefaultCapable(true);
      m_btClose.setMnemonic('g');
      p.add(m_btClose);

      getContentPane().add(p, BorderLayout.CENTER);

      m_chooser = new JFileChooser();
      m_chooser.setCurrentDirectory(new File("."));
      m_chooser.setApproveButtonToolTipText(
        "Select file for upload/download");

      WindowListener wndCloser = new WindowAdapter() {
        public void windowClosing(WindowEvent e) {
          disconnect();
          System.exit(0);
        }
      };
      addWindowListener(wndCloser);

      setSize(340,340);
      setResizable(false);
      setVisible(true);
    }

    public void setButtonStates(boolean state) {
      m_btPut.setEnabled(state);
      m_btGet.setEnabled(state);
      m_btFile.setEnabled(state);
    }

    protected boolean connect() {
      m_monitor.setText("");
      setButtonStates(false);
      m_btClose.setText("Cancel");
      setCursor(Cursor.getPredefinedCursor(
        Cursor.WAIT_CURSOR));

      String user = m_txtUser.getText();
      if (user.length()==0) {
        message("Please enter user name");
        setButtonStates(true);
        return false;
      }
      String password = new String(m_txtPassword.getPassword());
      String sUrl = m_txtURL.getText();
      if (sUrl.length()==0) {
        message("Please enter URL");
        setButtonStates(true);
        return false;
      }
      m_sLocalFile = m_txtFile.getText();
```

❸ Connects to specified host with name and password

```
// Parse URL
int index = sUrl.indexOf("//");
if (index >= 0)
sUrl = sUrl.substring(index+2);

index = sUrl.indexOf("/");
String host = sUrl.substring(0, index);
sUrl = sUrl.substring(index+1);

String sDir = "";
index = sUrl.lastIndexOf("/");
if (index >= 0) {
  sDir = sUrl.substring(0, index);
  sUrl = sUrl.substring(index+1);
}
m_sHostFile = sUrl;

try {
  message("Connecting to host "+host);
  m_client = new FtpClient(host);
  m_client.login(user, password);
  message("User "+user+" login OK");
  message(m_client.welcomeMsg);
  m_client.cd(sDir);
  message("Directory: "+sDir);
  m_client.binary();
  return true;
}
catch (Exception ex) {
  message("Error: "+ex.toString());
  setButtonStates(true);
  return false;
}
}

protected void disconnect() {
  if (m_client != null) {
    try { m_client.closeServer(); }
    catch (IOException ex) {}
    m_client = null;
  }
  Runnable runner = new Runnable() {
    public void run() {
      m_progress.setValue(0);
      setButtonStates(true);
      m_btClose.setText("Close");
      FTPApp.this.setCursor(Cursor.getPredefinedCursor(
        Cursor.DEFAULT_CURSOR));
    }
  };
  SwingUtilities.invokeLater(runner);
}
protected void getFile() {
  if (m_sLocalFile.length()==0) {
```

③ **Creates FtpClient object, logs in with name and password, and sets to "binary" transmission mode**

④ **Downloads a prespecified file name**

```
      m_sLocalFile = m_sHostFile;
      SwingUtilities.invokeLater(new Runnable() {
        public void run() {
          m_txtFile.setText(m_sLocalFile);
        }
      });
    }
    byte[] buffer = new byte[BUFFER_SIZE];
    try {
      int size = getFileSize(m_client, m_sHostFile);
      if (size > 0) {
        message("File " + m_sHostFile + ": " + size + " bytes");
        setProgressMaximum(size);
      }
      else
        message("File " + m_sHostFile + ": size unknown");
      FileOutputStream out = new
        FileOutputStream(m_sLocalFile);
      InputStream in = m_client.get(m_sHostFile);
      int counter = 0;
      while(true) {
        int bytes = in.read(buffer);
        if (bytes < 0)
          break;

        out.write(buffer, 0, bytes);
        counter += bytes;
        if (size > 0) {
          setProgressValue(counter);
          int proc = (int) Math.round(m_progress.
            getPercentComplete() * 100);
          setProgressString(proc + " %");
        }
        else {
          int kb = counter/1024;
          setProgressString(kb + " KB");
        }
      }
      out.close();
      in.close();
    }
    catch (Exception ex) {
      message("Error: "+ex.toString());
    }
  }
  protected void putFile() {
    if (m_sLocalFile.length()==0) {
      message("Please enter file name");
    }
    byte[] buffer = new byte[BUFFER_SIZE];
    try {
      File f = new File(m_sLocalFile);
```

④ Reads each file in 10240 byte blocks

❺ Uploads a specified file name

```
      int size = (int)f.length();
      message("File " + m_sLocalFile + ": " + size + " bytes");
      setProgressMaximum (size);
      FileInputStream in = new
        FileInputStream(m_sLocalFile);
      OutputStream out = m_client.put(m_sHostFile);

      int counter = 0;
      while(true) {
        int bytes = in.read(buffer);
        if (bytes < 0)
          break;
        out.write(buffer, 0, bytes);
        counter += bytes;
        setProgressValue(counter);
        int proc = (int) Math.round(m_progress.
          getPercentComplete() * 100);
        setProgressString(proc + " %");
      }

      out.close();
      in.close();
    }
    catch (Exception ex) {
      message("Error: " + ex.toString());
    }
  }

  protected void message(final String str) {
    if (str != null) {
      Runnable runner = new Runnable() {
        public void run() {
          m_monitor.append(str + '\n');
          m_monitor.repaint();
        }
      };
      SwingUtilities.invokeLater(runner);
    }
  }

  protected void setProgressValue(final int value) {
    Runnable runner = new Runnable() {
      public void run() {
        m_progress.setValue(value);
      }
    };
    SwingUtilities.invokeLater(runner);
  }

  protected void setProgressMaximum(final int value) {
    Runnable runner = new Runnable() {
      public void run() {
        m_progress.setMaximum(value);
      }
    };
```

❺ Writes each file in 10240 byte blocks

```
      SwingUtilities.invokeLater(runner);
    }

    protected void setProgressString(final String string) {
      Runnable runner = new Runnable() {
        public void run() {
          m_progress.setString(string);
        }
      };
      SwingUtilities.invokeLater(runner);
    }

    public static void main(String argv[]) {
      new FTPApp();
    }

    public static int getFileSize(FtpClient client, String fileName)
      throws IOException {
      TelnetInputStream lst = client.list();
      String str = "";
      fileName = fileName.toLowerCase();
      while(true) {
        int c = lst.read();
        char ch = (char) c;
        if (c < 0 || ch == '\n') {
          str = str.toLowerCase();
          if (str.indexOf(fileName) >= 0) {
            StringTokenizer tk = new StringTokenizer(str);
            int index = 0;
            while(tk.hasMoreTokens()) {
              String token = tk.nextToken();
              if (index == 4)
                try {
                  return Integer.parseInt(token);
                }
                catch (NumberFormatException ex) {
                  return -1;
                }
              index++;
            }
          }
          str = "";
        }
        if (c <= 0)
          break;
        str += ch;
      }
      return -1;
    }
  }
```

**Parses output of "ls –l"
on remote host, to get
size of remote file** — **6**

13.5.2 Understanding the code

Class FTPApp

Class variable:

- `int BUFFER_SIZE`: The size of the buffer used for input/ouput operations.

Instance variables:

- `JTextField m_txtUser`: The login username text field.
- `JPasswordField m_txtPassword`: The login password field.
- `JTextField m_txtURL`: The field for the URL of the file to be downloaded/uploaded on the remote site.
- `JTextField m_txtFile`: The field for the file name of the file to be uploaded/downloaded on the local machine.
- `JTextArea m_monitor`: Used as a log to display various status messages.
- `JProgressBar m_progress`: Indicates the progress of an upload/download operation.
- `JButton m_btPut`: Initiates uploading.
- `JButton m_btGet`: Initiates downloading.
- `JButton m_btFile`: Brings up a file chooser dialog to choose a local file or to specify a file name and location.
- `JButton m_btClose`: Closes the application.
- `JFileChooser m_chooser`: Used to choose a local file or specify a file name and location.
- `FtpClient m_client`: The client connection to the host which manages I/O operations.
- `String m_sLocalFile`: The name of the most recent local file involved in a data transfer.
- `String m_sHostFile`: The name of the most recent host file involved in a data transfer.

1 The `FTPApp` constructor first creates a panel using a `DialogLayout2` layout manager, then it instantiates and adds our four text fields with corresponding labels (recall that our `Dialog-Layout2` manager requires that label/input field pairs are added in the specific label1, field1, label2, field2, ... order). The `m_monitor` text area is created and placed in a `JScrollPane`, and it is separated from the label/field panel by an instance of our custom `DialogSeparator` class entitled "Connection Monitor." The `m_progress` `JProgressBar` is created and placed in a `JPanel` with a `BorderLayout` to ensure that `DialogLayout2` allows it to occupy the maximum width across the frame, as well as its preferred height.

2 A plain `DialogSeparator` is added below the progress bar, and our four buttons are created with attached `ActionListeners`. They are then added to the `DialogLayout2` panel, resulting in a horizontal row at the bottom of the frame. The button titled Put attempts to connect to a host using our `connect()` method. If it is successful, a new thread is started which calls `putFile()` to upload a selected file; it then calls `disconnect()` to terminate the connection to the host. Similarly, the button entitled Get attempts to connect to a host, and, if it is successful, it starts a thread which calls our `getFile()` method to download a file, then `disconnect()`. The button entitled File brings up our `JFileChooser` dialog to allow the user to select a local file or specify a new file name and location. The button entitled Close invokes `disconnect()` to terminate a connection to the host if an FTP transfer is in progress (if the `m_client` is not `null`). If a transfer is not in progress the application is terminated.

   The `setButtonStates()` method takes a boolean parameter and enables/disables the Put, Get, and File buttons accordingly.

3 The connect() method establishes a connection to the remote host and returns true in the case of success, or false otherwise. This method first disables our Put, Get, and File push buttons, and it sets the text of the last button to "Cancel." This method then reads the contents of the text fields to obtain the login name, password, URL, and local file name. The URL is parsed and split into the host name, remote directory, and host file name. A new FtpClient instance is created to connect to the remote host, and it is stored in our m_client instance variable. Then the login() method is invoked on m_client to log in to the server using the specified username and password. If the login is successful, we change the remote directory and set the connection type to binary (which is almost always required for file transfers). If no exceptions have been thrown during this process, connect() returns true. Otherwise, it shows an exception in our m_monitor text area, re-enables our buttons, and returns false.

> **NOTE** The connect() method code that connects to a host and changes the directory would be better off in a separate thread. We suggest this enhancement for more professional implementations. All other time-intensive code in this example is executed in separate threads.

The disconnect() method invokes closeServer() on the current m_client FTP-Client instance if it is in use. It then sets the m_client reference to null, allowing garbage collection of the FTPClient object. This method also clears the progress bar component, enables all push buttons which may have been disabled by the connect() method, and restores the text of the Close button. All component updates are wrapped in a Runnable and sent to the event-dispatching queue with SwingUtilities.invokeLater().

4 The getFile() method downloads a prespecified file from the current host. If the name of the destination local file is not specified, the name of the remote file is used. This method tries to determine the size of the remote file by calling our getFileSize() helper method (see below). If that succeeds, the file size is set as the maximum value of the progress bar (the minimum value is always 0) using our custom setProgressMaximum() method. Then a File-OutputStream is opened to write to the local file, and an InputStream is retrieved from the FTPClient to read from the remote file. A while loop is set up to perform typical read/write operations until all content of the remote file is written to the local file. During this process, the number of bytes read is accumulated in the counter local variable. If the size of the file is known, this number is assigned to the progress bar using our custom setProgressValue() method. We also calculate the percentage of downloading that is complete with our custom getPercentComplete() method, and we display it in the progress bar using our custom setProgressString() method. If the size of the file is unknown (meaning it is less than or equal to 0), we can only display the number of kilobytes currently downloaded at any given time. To obtain this value we simply divide the current byte count, which is stored in the local counter variable, by 1024.

5 The putFile() method uploads the content of a local file to a remote pre-specified URL. If the name of the local file is not specified, a "Please enter file name" message is printed using our custom message() method, and we simply return. Otherwise, the size of the local file is determined and used as the maximum value of our progress bar using our custom setMaximum() method (the minimum value is always 0). A FileInputStream is opened to read from the local file, and an OutputStream is retrieved from the FTPClient to write to the remote file. A while loop is set up to perform typical read/write operations until all the content of the local file is written to the remote host. During this process, the number of bytes written is accumulated in the `counter` local variable. This number is assigned to the progress bar using our custom `setProgressValue()` method. As in the `getFile()` method, we also calculate the percentage of downloading that is complete with our `getPercentComplete()` method, and we display it in the progress bar using our `setProgressString()` method. Since we can always determine the size of a local `File` object, there is no need to display the progress in terms of kilobytes as we did in `getFile()` above.

The `message()` method takes a `String` parameter to display in our `m_monitor` text area. The `setProgressValue()` and `setProgressMaximum()` methods assign selected and maximum values to our progress bar, respectively. Since each of these methods modifes the state of our progress bar component, and each is called from a custom thread, we wrap their bodies in `Runnables` and send them to the event-dispatching queue using `SwingUtilities.invokeLater()`.

6 Unfortunately, the `FtpClient` class does not provide a direct way to determine either the size of a remote file or any other available file specifics. The only way we can get any information about files on the remote host using this class is to call its `list()` method, which returns a `TelnetInputStream` that supplies the printout of the results of an `ls -l` command. Our `getFileSize()` method uses this method in an attempt to obtain the length of a remote file specified by a given file name and `FTPClient` instance. This method captures the printout from the remote server, splits it into lines separated by "\n" characters, and uses a `StringTokenizer` to parse them into tokens. According to the syntax of the `ls -l` command output, the length of the file in bytes appears as the fifth token, and the last token contains the file name. So we go character by character through each line until a line containing a matching file name is found; the length is then returned to the caller. If this does not succeed, we return -1 to indicate that the server either does not allow its content to browsed, or that an error has occurred.

13.5.3   Running the code

Figure 13.8 shows `FTPApp` in action. Try running this application and transferring a few files. Start by entering your username and password, a URL containing the host FTP server, and (optionally) a local file name and path to act as the source or destination of a transfer. Click the Get button to download a specified remote file, or click the Put button to upload a specified local file to the host. If the required connection is established successfully, you will see the transfer progress updated incrementally in the progress bar.

In figure 13.8 we specified "anonymous" as the user name and we used an email address as the password. In our URL text field we specified the remote **tutorial.zip** file (the most recent Java Tutorial) on the java.sun.com FTP server in its docs directory. In our File text field, we specified **tutorial.zip** as the destination file in the current running directory. Clicking on Get establishes a connection, changes the remote directory to **docs**, determines the size of the remote **tutorial.zip** file, and starts retrieving and storing it as a local file in the current running directory. Try performing this transfer and watch how smoothly the progress bar updates itself (it can't hurt to keep a local copy of the Java Tutorial, but be aware that this archive is close to 10 megabytes).

NOTE   In the next chapter we will customize `JFileChooser` to build a ZIP/JAR archive tool. This can be used to unpackage **tutorial.zip** if you do not have access to an appropriate tool.

C H A P T E R   1 4

Dialogs

14.1   DIALOGS AND CHOOSERS OVERVIEW

Swing's JDialog class allows the implementation of both modal and non-modal dialogs. In simple cases, when we need to post a short message or ask for a single value input, we can use standardized pre-built dialog boxes provided by the JOptionPane convenience class. Additionally, two special dialog classes provide powerful selection and navigation capabilities for choosing colors and files: JColorChooser and JFileChooser.

GUIDELINE

When to use a dialog   Dialogs are intended for the acquisition of a set of inter-related data; for example, selecting a group of files and the type of action to perform on them. This may be the set of attributes for a particular object or group of objects. A dialog is particularly useful when validation across those attributes must be performed before the data can be accepted. The validation code can be executed when an Accept button is pressed, and the dialog will only dismiss when the data is validated as good.

Dialogs are also useful for complex manipulations or selections. For example, a dialog with two lists, "Available Players" and "Team for Saturday's Game," might allow the selection, addition, and deletion of items to and/or from each list. When the team for the Saturday game is selected, the user can accept the selection by clicking OK.

Data entry and complex data manipulation which requires a clear boundary or definition of acceptance are good uses for a dialog.

When to use an option pane   Option panes are best used when the system needs to hold a conversation with the user, either for simple directed data entry such as "Enter your name and password" or for navigation choices such as View, Edit, or Print.

When to use a chooser   Choosers facilitate consistency for common selections across a whole operating environment. If you need to select files or colors, you should use the appropriate chooser. The user gets the benefit of only learning one component which appears again and again across applications. Using a chooser when appropriate should improve customer acceptance of your application.

14.1.1   JDialog

class javax.swing.JDialog

This class extends `java.awt.Dialog` and is used to create a new dialog box in a separate native platform window. We typically extend this class to create our own custom dialog, as it is a container almost identical to `JFrame`.

> **NOTE**   `JDialog` is a `JRootPane` container just like `JFrame`, and familiarity with chapter 3 is assumed here. All `WindowEvents`, default close operations, sizing and positioning, etc., can be controlled identically to `JFrame` and we will not repeat this material.

We can create a `JDialog` by specifying a dialog owner (`Frame` or `Dialog` instances), a dialog title, and a modal/non-modal state. We are not required to pass a valid parent, and we are free to use `null` as the parent reference. As we discussed in chapter 2, the `SwingUtilities` class maintains a non-visible `Frame` instance that is registered with the `AppContext` service mapping, which is used as the parent of all null-parent dialogs. If a valid parent is used, the dialog's icon will be that of the parent frame set with the `setIconImage()` method.

A modal dialog will not allow other windows to become active (respond to user input) at the same time that it is active. Modal dialogs also block the invoking thread of execution and do not allow it to continue until they are dismissed. Non-modal dialogs do allow other windows to be active and do not affect the invoking thread.

To populate a dialog we use the same layout techniques discussed for `JFrame`, and we are prohibited from changing the layout or adding components directly. Instead we are expected to deal with the dialog's content pane.

From the design perspective, it is very common to add push buttons to a dialog. Typical buttons are OK or Save to continue with an action or save data, and Cancel or Close to close the dialog and cancel an action or avoid saving data.

> **BUG ALERT**   Because of certain AWT problems, `JDialog` will allow lightweight pop-up menus only. `JPopupMenu` and the components that use it, such as `JComboBox` and `JMenu`, will always be lightweight in modal dialogs. For this reason we need to be especially careful when implementing a modal dialog containing heavyweight components.

As with `JFrame`, `JDialog` will appear in the upper left-hand corner of the screen unless another location is specified. It is usually more natural to center a dialog with respect to its owner, as follows:

```
Window owner = myDialog.getParent();
myDialog.setResizable(false);
Dimension d1 = myDialog.getSize();
Dimension d2 = owner.getSize();
int x = Math.max((d2.width-d1.width)/2, 0);
int y = Math.max((d2.height-d1.height)/2, 0);
myDialog.setBounds(x, y, d1.width, d1.height);
```

We can also use JDialog's `setLocationRelativeTo(Component c)` method to center a dialog relative to a given component. If the component is not visible, the dialog will be centered relative to the screen.

NOTE   It is common practice to show dialogs in response to menu selections. In such cases, a menu's pop-up may remain visible and the parent frame needs to be manually repainted. Therefore, we suggest calling `repaint()` on the parent before displaying dialogs invoked by menus.

To display a JDialog window we can use either the `show()` method inherited from `java.awt.Dialog` or the `setVisible()` method inherited from `java.awt.Component`.

NOTE   When building complex dialogs, it is normally preferable that one instance of that dialog be used throughout a given Java session. We suggest instantiating such dialogs when the application/applet is started, and storing them as variables for repetitive use. This avoids the often significantly long delay time required to instantiate a dialog each time it is needed. We also suggest wrapping dialog instantiation in a separate thread to avoid clogging up the event-dispatching thread.

14.1.2   JOptionPane

class javax.swing.JOptionPane

This class provides an easy and convenient way to display the standard dialogs used for posting a message, asking a question, or prompting for simple user input. Each JOptionPane dialog is modal and will block the invoking thread of execution, as described above (this does not apply to internal dialogs; we will discuss these soon enough).

It is important to understand that JOptionPane is not itself a dialog (note that it directly extends JComponent). Rather, it acts as a container that is normally placed in a JDialog or a JInternalFrame, and it provides several convenient methods for doing so. There is nothing stopping us from creating a JOptionPane and placing it in any container we choose, but this will rarely be useful. Figure 14.1 illustrates the general JOptionPane component arrangement:

The JOptionPane class supports four pre-defined types: Message, Confirm, Input, and Option. We will discuss how to create and work with each type, but first we need to understand the constituents. To create a JOptionPane that is automatically placed in either a JDialog or JInternalFrame, we need to supply some or all of the following parameters to one if its static `showXXDialog()` methods (discussed below):

- A parent Component. If the parent is a Frame, the option pane will be placed in a JDialog and centered with respect to the parent. If this parameter is null, it will instead be centered with respect to the screen. If the parent is a JDesktopPane, or is contained in one, the option pane will be contained in a JInternalFrame and placed in the parent

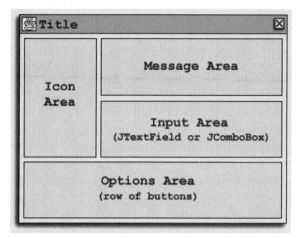

Figure 14.1 The components of a JOptionPane dialog

desktop's MODAL_LAYER (see chapter 15). For other types of parent components, a JDialog will be used and placed below that component on the screen.

- A message Object is a message to be displayed in the top right of the pane (in the Message area). Typically this is a String which may be broken into separate lines using "\n" characters. However this parameter has a generic Object type and JOptionPane deals with non-String objects in the following way:

  - Icon: This will be displayed in a JLabel.
  - Component: This will simply be placed in the message area.
  - Object[]: Dealt with as described here, these will be placed vertically in a column (this is done recursively).
  - Object: The toString() method will be called to convert this to a String for display in a JLabel.

- An int message type can be one of the following static constants defined in JOptionPane: ERROR_MESSAGE, INFORMATION_MESSAGE, WARNING_MESSAGE, QUESTION_MESSAGE, or PLAIN_MESSAGE. This is used by the current look and feel to customize the look of an option pane by displaying an appropriate icon (in the *Icon area*) corresponding to the message type's meaning.

- An int option type can be one of the following static constants defined in JOptionPane: DEFAULT_OPTION, YES_NO_OPTION, YES_NO_CANCEL_OPTION, or OK_CANCEL_OPTION. This parameter specifies a set of corresponding buttons to be displayed at the bottom of the pane (in the *Options area*). One of a set of similar parameters will be returned from JOptionPane's showXXDialog() methods (see below) specifying which button was pressed: CANCEL_OPTION, CLOSED_OPTION, NO_OPTION, OK_OPTION, and YES_OPTION. Note that CLOSED_OPTION is only returned when the pane is contained in a JDialog or JInternalFrame, and that container's close button (located in the title bar) is pressed.

- An Icon is displayed in the left side of the pane (in the *Icon area*). If it's not explicitly specified, the icon is determined by the current look and feel based on the message type (this does not apply to panes using the PLAIN_MESSAGE message type).

- An array of option `Objects`. We can directly specify an array of option `Objects` to be displayed at the bottom of the pane (in the *Options area*). This array can also be specified with the `setOptions()` method. It typically contains an array of `Strings` to be displayed on a set of `JButtons`, but `JOptionPane` also honors `Icons` (which are also displayed in `JButtons`) and `Components` (which are placed directly in a row). Similar to message `Objects`, the `toString()` method will be called to convert all objects that are not `Icons` or `Components` to a `String` for display in a `JButton`. If `null` is used, the option buttons are determined by the specified option type.
- An initial value `Object` specifies which button or component in the *Options area* has the focus when the pane is initially displayed.
- An array of selection value `Objects` specifies an array of allowed choices the user can make. If this array contains more than twenty items, a `JList` is used to display them using the default rendering behavior (see chapter 10). If the array contains twenty or less items, a `JComboBox` is used to display them (also using the default `JList` rendering behavior). If `null` is used, an empty `JTextField` is displayed. In any case, the component used for selection is placed in the *Input area*.
- A `String` title is used for display as the title bar title in the parent `JDialog` or `JInternalFrame`.

The following static methods are provided for the convenient creation of `JOptionPanes` placed in `JDialogs`:

- `showConfirmDialog()`: This method displays a dialog with several buttons and returns an `int` option type corresponding to the button pressed. Four overloaded methods are provided that allow the specification of, at most, a parent component, message, title, option type, message type, and icon.
- `showInputDialog()`: This method displays a dialog which is intended to receive user input, and it returns a `String` if the input component is a text field, or an `Object` if the input component is a list or a combo box. Four overloaded methods are provided that allow the specification of, at most, a parent component, message, title, option type, message type, icon, array of possible selections, and an initially selected item. Two buttons are always displayed in the Options area: OK and Cancel.
- `showMessageDialog()`: This method displays a dialog with an OK button, and it doesn't return anything. Three overloaded methods are provided that allow the specification of, at most, a parent component, message, title, message type, and icon.
- `showOptionDialog()`: This method displays a dialog which can be customized a bit more than the above dialogs, and it returns either the index into the array of option `Objects` specified, or an option type if no option `Objects` are specified. Only one method is provided that allows the specification of a parent component, message, title, option type, message type, icon, array of option `Objects`, and an option `Object` with the initial focus. The option `Objects` are laid out in a row in the Options area.

To create `JOptionPanes` contained in `JInternalFrames` rather than `JDialogs`, we can use the `showInternalConfirmDialog()`, `showInternalInputDialog()`, `showInternalMessageDialog()`, and `showInternalOptionDialog()` overloaded methods. These work the same as the methods described above, only they expect that a given parent is a `JDesktopPane` (or has a `JDesktopPane` ancestor).

Internal dialogs are not modal and, as such, do not block execution of the invoking thread.

Alternatively, we can directly create a `JOptionPane` as illustrated by the following pseudo-code:

```
JOptionPane pane = new JOptionPane(...); // Specify parameters

pane.setXX(...); // Set additional properties

JDialog dialog = pane.createDialog(parent, title);
dialog.show();

// Process result (may be null)
Object result = pane.getValue();
```

This code creates an instance of `JOptionPane` and specifies several parameters (see the API documentation). Additional settings are then provided with `setXX` accessor methods. The `createDialog()` method creates a `JDialog` instance that contains our `JOptionPane` which is then displayed (we could also have used the `createInternalFrame()` method to wrap our pane in a `JInternalFrame`). Finally, the `getValue()` method retrieves the option selected by the user, so the program may react accordingly. This value may be `null` (if the user closes the dialog window). Because program execution blocks until the dialog is dismissed, `getValue()` will not be called until a selection is made.

NOTE The advantage of `JOptionPane` is its simplicity and convenience. In general, you shouldn't need to customize it to any large extent. If you find yourself needing a different layout, we suggest writing your own container instead.

Figure 14.2 illustrates the use of `JOptionPane` where a custom dialog may be more suitable. Note the extremely long button, text field, and combo box. Such extreme sizes have detrimental effects on the overall usability and appearance of an application.

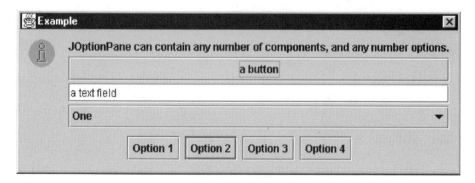

Figure 14.2 Awkward use of components in a `JOptionPane` (from the SwingSet demo)

GUIDELINE

JOptionPane JOptionPane is not designed as a general purpose input dialog. The primary restriction is the defined layout. JOptionPane is designed for use in conversations between the system and the user where the desired result is a navigation choice or a data selection, or where the user must be notified of an event.

Therefore, JOptionPane is best used with a single entry field or combo box selection, possibly with a set of buttons for selection or navigational choice.

For example, an Answer Phone application might require an option dialog displaying "You have 1 message," with options Play, Save, Record outgoing message, and Delete messages. Such a requirement can be met with a JOptionPane which provides a single label for the message and four buttons for each of the available choices.

14.1.3   JColorChooser

class javax.swing.JColorChooser

This class represents a powerful, pre-built component that is used for color selection. JColorChooser is normally used in a modal dialog. It consists of a tabbed pane containing three panels, each offering a different method of choosing a color: Swatches, HSB, and RGB. A color preview pane is displayed below this tabbed pane and it always displays the currently selected color. Figure 14.3 illustrates.

The static showDialog() method instantiates and displays a JColorChooser in a modal dialog, and returns the selected Color (or null if no selection is made):

```
Color color =  JColorChooser.showDialog(myComponent,
  "Color Chooser", Color.red);
if (color != null)
  myComponent.setBackground(c);
```

A more complex variant is the static createDialog() method which allows two ActionListeners to be invoked when a selection is made or canceled. We can also do the following:

- Retrieve color selection panels with the getChooserPanels() method.
- Add custom color selection panels using the addChooserPanel() method.
- Assign a new custom color preview pane using the setPreviewPanel() method.

Several classes and interfaces (discussed below) that support JColorChooser are grouped into the javax.swing.colorchooser package.

14.1.4   The ColorSelectionModel interface

abstract interface javax.swing.colorchooser.ColorSelectionModel

This is a simple interface describing the color selection model for JColorChooser. It declares methods for adding and removing ChangeListeners which are intended to be notified when the selected Color changes, and getSelectedColor()/setSelectedColor() accessors to retrieve and assign the currently selected Color, respectively.

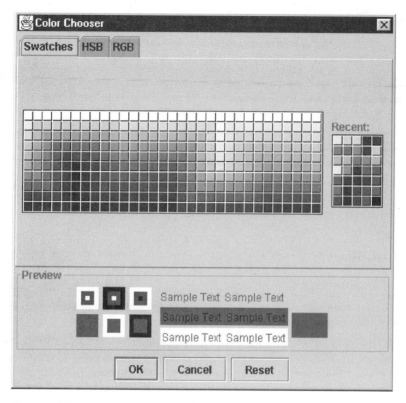

Figure 14.3 JColorChooser **in a** JDialog

14.1.5   DefaultColorSelectionModel

class javax.swing.colorchooser.DefaultColorSelectionModel

This is the default concrete implementation of the ColorSelectionModel interface. It simply implements the necessary methods as expected, stores registered ChangeListeners in an EventListenerList, and implements an additional method to perform the actual firing of ChangeEvents to all registered listeners.

14.1.6   AbstractColorChooserPanel

abstract class javax.swing.colorchooser.AbstractColorChooserPanel

This abstract class describes a color chooser panel which can be added to JColorChooser as a new tab. We can subclass AbstractColorChooserPanel to implement a custom color chooser panel of our own. The two most important methods that must be implemented are buildChooser() and updateChooser(). The former is normally called only once at instantiation time and is intended to perform all GUI initialization tasks. The latter is intended to update the panel to reflect a change in the associated JColorChooser's ColorSelectionModel. Other required methods include those allowing access to a display name and icon which are used to identify the panel when it is displayed in JColorChooser's tabbed pane.

14.1.7 ColorChooserComponentFactory

class javax.swing.colorchooser.ColorChooserComponentFactory

This is a very simple class that is responsible for creating and returning instances of the default color chooser panels and the preview pane used by JColorChooser. The three color chooser panels are instances of private classes: DefaultSwatchChooserPanel, DefaultRGBChooser-Panel, and DefaultHSBChooserPanel. The preview pane is an instance of DefaultPre-viewPane. Other private classes used in the colorchooser package include two custom layout managers, CenterLayout and SmartGridLayout; a class for convenient generation of synthetic images, SyntheticImage; and a custom text field that only allows integer input, JIntegerTextField. These undocumented classes are very interesting and we urge curious readers to spend some time with the source code. Because they are only used within the color-chooser package and are defined as a package private, we will not discuss them further here.

14.1.8 JFileChooser

class javax.swing.JFileChooser

This class represents the standard Swing directory navigation and file selection component which is normally used in a modal dialog. It consists of a JList and several button and input components all linked together to offer functionality similar to the file dialogs we are used to on our native platforms. The JList is used to display a list of files and subdirectories residing in the current directory being navigated. Figure 14.4 illustrates.

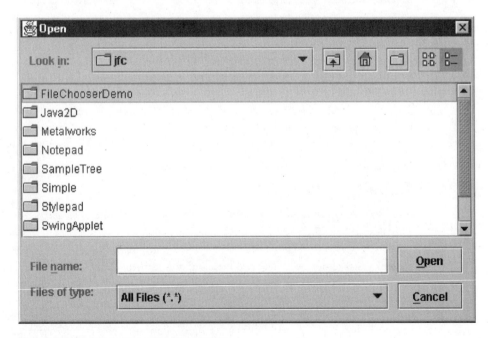

Figure 14.4 JFileChooser **in a** JDialog

Cross-application consistency   The key reason for promoting the use of a standard file chooser dialog is to promote the consistency of such an operation across the whole operating system or machine environment. The user's experience is improved because file selection is always the same no matter which application he is running. This is an important goal and is worthy of recognition. Thus, if you have a requirement to manipulate files, you ought to be using the JFileChooser component.

The fact that such a reusable component exists and that much of the complex coding is provided as part of the implementation is merely a bonus for the developer.

We can set the current directory by passing a String to its setCurrentDirectory() method. JFileChooser also has the ability to use special FileFilters (discussed below) to allow navigation of only certain types of files. Several properties control whether directories and/ or files can be navigated and selected, and how the typical Open (*approve*) and Cancel (*cancel*) buttons are represented (see the API documentation for more on these straightforward methods.)

To use this component, we normally create an instance of it, set the desired options, and call showDialog() to place it in an active modal dialog. This method takes the parent component and the text to display for its Approve button as parameters. Calling showOpenDialog() or showSaveDialog() will show a modal dialog with Open or Save for the Approve button text.

NOTE   JFileChooser can take a significant amount of time to instantiate. Consider storing an instance as a variable and performing instantiation in a separate thread at startup time.

The following code instantiates a JFileChooser in an Open file dialog, verifies that a valid file is selected, and retrieves that file as a File instance:

```
JFileChooser chooser = new JFileChooser();
chooser.setCurrentDirectory(".");
if (chooser.showOpenDialog(myComponent) !=
  JFileChooser.APPROVE_OPTION)
    return;
File file = chooser.getSelectedFile();
```

JFileChooser generates PropertyChangeEvents when any of its properties change state. The Approve and Cancel buttons generate ActionEvents when they are pressed. We can register PropertyChangeListeners and ActionListeners to receive these events respectively. As any well-defined JavaBean should, JFileChooser defines several static String constants corresponding to each property name; JFileChooser.FILE_FILTER_CHANGED_PROPERTY is one example (see the API documentation for a full listing). We can use these constants in determining which property a JFileChooser-generated PropertyChangeEvent corresponds to.

JFileChooser also supports the option of inserting an *accessory* component. This component can be any component we want and it will be placed to the right of the JList. In constructing such a component, we are normally expected to implement the Property-ChangeListener interface. This way the component can be registered with the associated JFileChooser to receive notification of property state changes. The component should use these events to update its state accordingly. We use the setAccessory() method to assign an accessory component to a `JFileChooser`, and `addPropertyChangeListener()` to register it for receiving property state change notification.

REFERENCE For a good example of an accessory component used to preview selected images, see the `FileChooserDemo` example that ships with Java 2. In the final example of this chapter, we will show how to customize `JFileChooser` in a more direct mannar.

Several classes and interfaces related to `JFileChooser` are grouped into the `javax.swing.filechooser` package.

NOTE `JFileChooser` is still somewhat incomplete. For example, multi-selection mode is specified, but it has not been implemented yet. Later in this chapter we will show how to work around this, as well as how to build our own accessory-like component in a location different from that of a normal accessory.

14.1.9   FileFilter

abstract class javax.swing.filechooser.FileFilter

This abstract class is used to implement a filter for displaying only certain file types in `JFileChooser`. Two methods must be implemented in concrete subclasses:

- `boolean accept(File f)`: Returns `true` if the given file should be displayed, `false` otherwise.
- `String getDescription()`: Returns a description of the filter used in the `JComboBox` at the bottom of `JFileChooser`.

To manage `FileFilters`, we can use several methods in `JFileChooser`, including these:

- `addChoosableFileFilter(FileFilter f)`: Adds a new filter.
- `removeChoosableFileFilter(FileFilter f)`: Removes an existing filter.
- `setFileFilter(FileFilter f)`: Sets a filter as currently active (and adds it, if necessary).

By default, `JFileChooser` receives a filter that accepts all files. Special effort must be made to remove this filter if we do not want our application to accept all files:

```
FileFilter ft = myChooser.getAcceptAllFileFilter();
myChooser.removeChoosableFileFilter(ft);
```

So how do we create a simple file filter instance to allow navigation and selection of only certain file types? The following class can be used as a template for defining most of our own filters, and we will see it used in this and future chapters:

```
class SimpleFilter extends FileFilter
{
  private String m_description = null;
  private String m_extension = null;

  public SimpleFilter(String extension, String description) {
    m_description = description;
    m_extension = "." + extension.toLowerCase();
  }

  public String getDescription() {
```

```
      return m_description;
  }
  public boolean accept(File f) {
    if (f == null)
      return false;
    if (f.isDirectory())
      return true;
    return f.getName().toLowerCase().endsWith(m_extension);
  }
}
```

This filter only shows files that match the given extension `String` that is passed into our constructor and stored as variable m_extension. In more robust, multipurpose filters we might store an array of legal extensions, and check for each in the `accept()` method.

NOTE The `SimpleFilter` accept() method always returns `true` for directories because we normally want to be able to navigate any directory.

Notice that the description `String` passed into the constructor, and stored as the variable m_description, is the `String` shown in the combo box at the bottom of `JFileChooser` representing the corresponding file type. `JFileChooser` can maintain multiple filters, all added using the addChoosableFileFilter() method, and removable with its removeChoosable-FileFilter() method.

14.1.10   FileSystemView

abstract class javax.swing.filechooser.FileSystemView

This class includes functionality which extracts information about files, directories, and partitions, and supplies this information to the `JFileChooser` component. This class is used to make `JFileChooser` independent from both platform-specific file system information, and the JDK/Java 2 release version (since the JDK1.1 File API doesn't allow access to more specific file information available in Java 2). We can provide our own `FileSystemView` subclass and assign it to a `JFileChooser` instance using the setFileSystemView(FileSystem-View fsv) method. Four abstract methods must be implemented:

- createNewFolder(File containingDir): Creates a new folder (directory) within the given folder.
- getRoots(): Returns all root partitions. The notion of a root differs significantly from platform to platform.
- isHiddenFile(File f): Returns whether the given `File` is hidden.
- isRoot(File f): Returns whether the given `File` is a partition or drive.

These methods are called by `JFileChooser` and `FileFilter` implementations. We will, in general, have no need to extend this class unless we need to tweak the way `JFile-Chooser` interacts with our operating system. The static getFileSystemView() method currently returns a Unix- or Windows-specific instance for use by `JFileChooser` in the most likely event that one of these platform types is detected. Otherwise, a generic instance is used. Support for Macintosh, OS2, and several other operating systems is expected to be provided in future releases.

14.1.11 FileView

abstract class javax.swing.filechooser.FileView

This abstract class is used to provide customized information about files and their types (typically determined by the file extension), including icons and a string description. Each look and feel provides its own subclass of FileView, and we can construct our own FileView subclass fairly easily. Each of the five methods in this class is abstract and must be implemented by subclasses. The following generalized template can be used when creating our own FileViews:

```
class MyExtView extends FileView
{
  // Store icons to use for list cell renderer.
  protected static ImageIcon MY_EXT_ICON =
    new ImageIcon("myexticon.gif");
  protected static ImageIcon MY_DEFAULT_ICON =
    new ImageIcon("mydefaulticon.gif");

  // Return the name of a given file. "" corresponds to
  // a partition, so in this case we must return the path.
  public String getName(File f) {
    String name = f.getName();
    return name.equals("") ? f.getPath() : name;
  }

  // Return the description of a given file.
  public String getDescription(File f) {
    return getTypeDescription(f);
  }

  // Return the String to use for representing each specific
  // file type.  (Not used by JFileChooser in Java 2 FCS.)
  public String getTypeDescription(File f) {
    String name = f.getName().toLowerCase();
    if (name.endsWith(".ext"))
      return "My custom file type";
    else
      return "Unrecognized file type";
  }

  // Return the icon to use for representing each specific
  // file type in JFileChooser's JList cell renderer.
  public Icon getIcon(File f) {
    String name = f.getName().toLowerCase();
    if (name.endsWith(".ext"))
      return MY_EXT_ICON;
    else
      return MY_DEFAULT_ICON;
  }

  // Normally we should return true for directories only.
  public Boolean isTraversable(File f) {
    return (f.isDirectory() ? Boolean.TRUE : Boolean.FALSE);
  }
}
```

We will see how to build a custom `FileView` for JAR and ZIP archive files in the final example of this chapter.

14.2 ADDING AN ABOUT DIALOG

Most GUI applications have at least one About dialog, usually modal, which often displays copyright, company, and other important information such as product name, version number, and authors. Example 14.1 illustrates how to add such a dialog to our text editor example we developed in chapter 12. We build a subclass of `JDialog`, populate it with some simple components, and store it as a variable which can be shown and hidden indefinitely without having to instantiate a new dialog each time it is requested. We also implement centering so that whenever the dialog is shown, it will appear in the center of our application's frame.

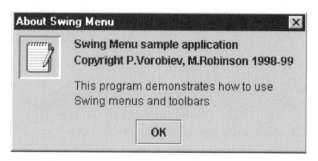

Figure 14.5   A typical About custom `JDialog` with dynamic centering

Example 14.1

BasicTextEditor.java

see \Chapter14\1

```java
import java.awt.*;
import java.awt.event.*;
import java.io.*;
import java.util.*;

import javax.swing.*;
import javax.swing.event.*;
import javax.swing.border.*;

public class BasicTextEditor extends JFrame
{
  // Unchanged code from example 12.4
  protected AboutBox m_dlg;

  public BasicTextEditor() {
    super("\"About\" BasicTextEditor");
    setSize(450, 350);
    ImageIcon icon = new ImageIcon("smallIcon.gif");      ❶ Assigns
    setIconImage(icon.getImage());                             frame icon
```

```
        // Unchanged code from example 12.4

        updateMonitor();
        m_dlg = new AboutBox(this);
        setVisible(true);
    }

    protected JMenuBar createMenuBar() {
        // Unchanged code from example 12.4

        JMenu mHelp = new JMenu("Help");
        mHelp.setMnemonic('h');
        Action actionAbout = new AbstractAction("About") {
            public void actionPerformed(ActionEvent e) {
                Dimension d1 = m_dlg.getSize();
                Dimension d2 = BasicTextEditor.this.getSize();
                int x = Math.max((d2.width-d1.width)/2, 0);
                int y = Math.max((d2.height-d1.height)/2, 0);
                m_dlg.setBounds(x+BasicTextEditor.this.getX(),
                    y+ BasicTextEditor.this.getY(),
                    d1.width, d1.height);
                m_dlg.show();
            }
        };
        item =  mHelp.add(actionAbout);
        item.setMnemonic('a');
        menuBar.add(mHelp);

        getContentPane().add(m_toolBar, BorderLayout.NORTH);
        return menuBar;
    }
    // Unchanged code from example 12.4
}

class AboutBox extends JDialog
{
    public AboutBox(Frame owner) {
        super(owner, "About Swing Menu", true);

        JLabel lbl = new JLabel(new ImageIcon("icon.gif"));
        JPanel p = new JPanel();
        Border b1 = new BevelBorder(BevelBorder.LOWERED);
        Border b2 = new EmptyBorder(5, 5, 5, 5);
        lbl.setBorder(new CompoundBorder(b1, b2));
        p.add(lbl);
        getContentPane().add(p, BorderLayout.WEST);

        String message = "Swing Menu sample application\n"+
            "Copyright P.Vorobiev, M.Robinson 1998-99";
        JTextArea txt = new JTextArea(message);
        txt.setBorder(new EmptyBorder(5, 10, 5, 10));
        txt.setFont(new Font("Helvetica", Font.BOLD, 12));
        txt.setEditable(false);
        txt.setBackground(getBackground());
        p = new JPanel();
```

❶ Connects frame to AboutBox

❷ About dialog centers itself on parent

❸ Creates modal dialog with icon, text, and OK button

```
p.setLayout(new BoxLayout(p, BoxLayout.Y_AXIS));
p.add(txt);

message = "This program demonstrates how to use\n"+
  "Swing menus and toolbars";
txt = new JTextArea(message);
txt.setBorder(new EmptyBorder(5, 10, 5, 10));
txt.setFont(new Font("Arial", Font.PLAIN, 12));
txt.setEditable(false);
txt.setBackground(getBackground());
p.add(txt);

getContentPane().add(p, BorderLayout.CENTER);

JButton btOK = new JButton("OK");
ActionListener lst = new ActionListener() {
  public void actionPerformed(ActionEvent e) {
    setVisible(false);
  }
};
btOK.addActionListener(lst);
p = new JPanel();
p.add(btOK);
getContentPane().add(p, BorderLayout.SOUTH);

pack();
setResizable(false);
  }
}
```

14.2.1   Understanding the code

Class BasicTextEditor

This class contains one new instance variable:

- AboutBox m_dlg: Used to reference an instance of our custom About dialog class.

1 The constructor now assigns a custom icon to the application frame, instantiates an AboutBox, and directs our m_dlg reference to the resulting instance. In this way we can simply show and hide the dialog as necessary, without having to build a new instance each time it is requested. Notice that we use a this reference for its parent because BasicTextEditor extends JFrame.

2 We also modify the createMenuBar() method by adding a new Help menu that contains an About menu item. This menu item is created as an Action implementation and its action-Performed() method determines the dimensions of our dialog, as well as where it should be placed on the screen so that it will appear centered relative to its parent.

Class AboutBox

3 This class extends JDialog to implement our custom About dialog. The constructor creates a modal JDialog instance entitled "About Swing Menu," and populates it with some simple components. A large icon is placed in the left side and two JTextAreas are placed in the center to display multiline text messages with different fonts. A push button entitled "OK" is placed at the bottom. Its ActionListener's actionPerformed() method invokes set-Visible(false) when pressed.

NOTE We could have constructed a similar About dialog using a JOptionPane message dialog. However, the point of this example is to demonstrate the basics of custom dialog creation, which we will be using later in chapter 20 to create several complex custom dialogs that could not be derived from JOptionPane.

14.2.2 Running the code

Select the About menu item to bring up the dialog shown in figure 14.5. This dialog serves only to display information, and it has no functionality other than the OK button which hides it. Notice that no matter where the parent frame lies on the screen, when the dialog is invoked, it appears centered. Also notice that the dialog displays very quickly, because we are working with the same instance throughout the application's lifetime. This is, in general, a common practice to which one should adhere.

14.3 *JOPTIONPANE MESSAGE DIALOGS*

Message dialogs provided by the JOptionPane class can be used for many purposes in Swing applications: to post a message, ask a question, or get simple user input. Example 14.2 brings up several message boxes of different types with a common Shakespeare theme. Both internal and regular dialogs are constructed, demonstrating how to use the convenient showXXDialog() methods (see section 14.1.2), as well as how to manually create a JOptionPane component and place it in a dialog or internal frame for display.

Each dialog is instantiated as needed and we perform no caching here (for purposes of demonstration). A more professional implementation might instantiate each dialog at startup and store them as variables for use throughout the application's lifetime.

Example 14.2

DialogBoxes.java

see \Chapter14\2

```
import java.awt.*;
import java.awt.event.*;

import javax.swing.*;

public class DialogBoxes extends JFrame
{
  static final String BOX_TITLE = "Shakespeare Boxes";

  public DialogBoxes() {
    super(BOX_TITLE);
    setSize(400,300);
    setLayeredPane(new JDesktopPane());

    JMenuBar menuBar = createMenuBar();
    setJMenuBar(menuBar);

    WindowListener wndCloser = new WindowAdapter() {
      public void windowClosing(WindowEvent e) {
```

① Constructor creates empty frame with menu bar

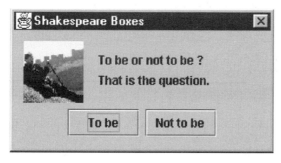

Figure 14.6 A `JOptionPane` with custom icon, message, and option button strings in a `JDialog`

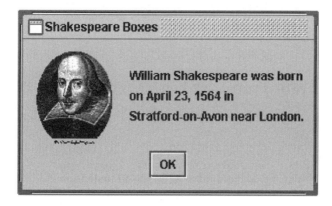

Figure 14.7 A `JOptionPane` with a custom icon and message in a `JInternalFrame`

```
        System.exit(0);
      }
    };
    addWindowListener(wndCloser);

    setVisible(true);
  }

  protected JMenuBar createMenuBar() {
    JMenuBar menuBar = new JMenuBar();

    JMenu mFile = new JMenu("File");
    mFile.setMnemonic('f');

    JMenuItem mItem = new JMenuItem("Ask Question");
    mItem.setMnemonic('q');
    ActionListener lst = new ActionListener() {
      public void actionPerformed(ActionEvent e) {
```

② Creates menus and actions which will create various dialogs

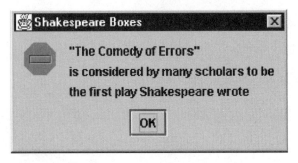

Figure 14.8 A JOptionPane ERROR_MESSAGE **message dialog with a multi-line message**

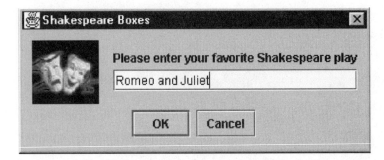

Figure 14.9 A JOptionPane INFORMATION_MESSAGE **input dialog with custom icon, message, text field input, and initial selection**

```
JOptionPane pane = new JOptionPane(
  "To be or not to be ?\nThat is the question.");
pane.setIcon(new ImageIcon("Hamlet.gif"));
Object[] options =
  new String[] {"To be", "Not to be"};
pane.setOptions(options);
JDialog dialog = pane.createDialog(
DialogBoxes.this, BOX_TITLE);
dialog.show();
Object obj = pane.getValue();
int result = -1;
for (int k=0; k<options.length; k++)
  if (options[k].equals(obj))
  result = k;
System.out.println("User's choice: "+result);
}
};
mItem.addActionListener(lst);
mFile.add(mItem);

mItem = new JMenuItem("Info Message");
```

2   Question dialog with custom buttons

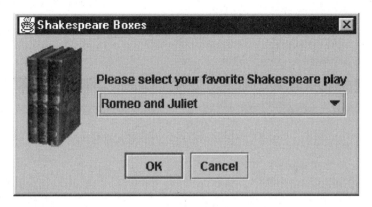

Figure 14.10 A `JOptionPane` `INFORMATION_MESSAGE` **input dialog with custom icon, message, combo box input, and initial selection**

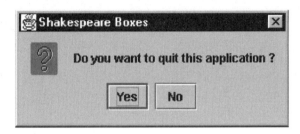

Figure 14.11 A `JOptionPane` `YES_NO_OPTION` confirm dialog

```
mItem.setMnemonic('i');
lst = new ActionListener() {
  public void actionPerformed(ActionEvent e) {
    String message = "William Shakespeare was born\n"+
      "on April 23, 1564 in\n"
      +"Stratford-on-Avon near London";
    JOptionPane pane = new JOptionPane(message);
    pane.setIcon(new ImageIcon("Shakespeare.gif"));
    JInternalFrame frame = pane.createInternalFrame(
      (DialogBoxes.this).getLayeredPane(), BOX_TITLE);
    getLayeredPane().add(frame);
  }
};
mItem.addActionListener(lst);
mFile.add(mItem);

mItem = new JMenuItem("Error Message");
mItem.setMnemonic('e');
lst = new ActionListener() {
  public void actionPerformed(ActionEvent e) {
```

Creates internal frame with information dialog ❸

```
        String message = "\"The Comedy of Errors\"\n"+
          "is considered by many scholars to be\n"+
          "the first play Shakespeare wrote";
        JOptionPane.showMessageDialog(
          DialogBoxes.this, message,
          BOX_TITLE, JOptionPane.ERROR_MESSAGE);
    }
};
mItem.addActionListener(lst);
mFile.add(mItem);

mFile.addSeparator();

mItem = new JMenuItem("Text Input");
mItem.setMnemonic('t');
lst = new ActionListener() {
  public void actionPerformed(ActionEvent e) {
    String input = (String) JOptionPane.showInputDialog(
      DialogBoxes.this,
      "Please enter your favorite Shakespeare play",
      BOX_TITLE, JOptionPane.INFORMATION_MESSAGE,
      new ImageIcon("Plays.jpg"), null,
      "Romeo and Juliet");
    System.out.println("User's input: "+input);
  }
};
mItem.addActionListener(lst);
mFile.add(mItem);

mItem = new JMenuItem("Combobox Input");
mItem.setMnemonic('c');
lst = new ActionListener() {
  public void actionPerformed(ActionEvent e) {
    String[] plays = new String[] {
      "Hamlet", "King Lear", "Othello", "Romeo and Juliet" };
    String input = (String) JOptionPane.showInputDialog(
      DialogBoxes.this,
      "Please select your favorite Shakespeare play",
      BOX_TITLE, JOptionPane.INFORMATION_MESSAGE,
      new ImageIcon("Books.gif"), plays,
      "Romeo and Juliet");
    System.out.println("User's input: "+input);
  }
};
mItem.addActionListener(lst);
mFile.add(mItem);

mFile.addSeparator();

mItem = new JMenuItem("Exit");
mItem.setMnemonic('x');
lst = new ActionListener() {
  public void actionPerformed(ActionEvent e) {
    if (JOptionPane.showConfirmDialog(
```

4 Shows error dialog

5 Shows input dialog with message, using text field

5 Shows input dialog with message, using combo box

6 Shows a confirm dialog

```
            DialogBoxes.this,
            "Do you want to quit this application ?",
            BOX_TITLE, JOptionPane.YES_NO_OPTION)
            == JOptionPane.YES_OPTION)
              System.exit(0);
        }
      };
      mItem.addActionListener(lst);
      mFile.add(mItem);
      menuBar.add(mFile);

      return menuBar;
    }
  public static void main(String argv[]) {
    new DialogBoxes();
  }
}
```

6 Shows a confirm dialog

14.3.1   Understanding the code

Class DialogBoxes

1 This class represents a simple frame which contains a menu bar created with our `create-MenuBar()` method, and a `JDesktopPane` (see chapter 16) which is used as the frame's layered pane. The menu bar contains a single menu, File, which holds several menu items.

2 The `createMenuBar()` method is responsible for populating our frame's menu bar with seven menu items, each with an `ActionListener` to invoke the display of a `JOptionPane` in either a `JDialog` or a `JInternalFrame`. The first menu item, Ask Question, creates an instance of `JOptionPane`, and assigns it a custom icon using its `setIcon()` method and custom option button `String`s using `setOptions()`. A `JDialog` is created to hold this message box, and the `show()` method displays this dialog on the screen and waits until it is dismissed. At that point the `getValue()` method retrieves the user's selection as an `Object`, which may be `null` or one of the option button `String`s assigned to this message box. The resulting dialog is shown in figure 14.6.

GUIDELINE

Affirmative text   The use of the affirmative and unambiguous text "To Be" and "Not to be" greatly enhances the usability of the option dialog. For example, if the text read "To be or not to be? That is the question," "Yes" or "No," would have been somewhat ambiguous and may have confused some users. The explicit text "To Be," "Not to be" is much clearer.

This is another example of how to improve usability with just a little extra coding effort.

3 The second menu item, Info Message, creates a `JOptionPane` with a multi-line message `String` and a custom icon. The `createInternalFrame()` method is used to create a `JInternalFrame` that holds the resulting `JOptionPane` message box. This internal frame is then added to the layered pane, which is now a `JDesktopPane` instance. The resulting internal frame is shown in figure 14.7.

❹ The third menu item, Error Message, produces a standard error message box using JOption-Pane's static `showMessageDialog()` method and the `ERROR_MESSAGE` message type. The resulting dialog is shown in figure 14.8. Recall that JOptionPane dialogs appear, by default, centered with respect to the parent if the parent is a frame. This is why we don't do any manual positioning here.

❺ The next two menu items, Text Input and Combobox Input, produce `INFORMATION_MESSAGE` JOptionPanes which take user input in a `JTextField` and `JComboBox`, respectively. The static `showInputDialog()` method is used to display these JOptionPanes in JDialogs. Figures 14.9 and 14.10 illustrate. The Text Input pane takes the initial text to display in its text field as a `String` parameter. The Combobox Input pane takes an array of `Strings` to display in the combo box as possible choices, as well as the initial `String` to be displayed by the combo box.

GUIDELINE

Added usability with constrained lists   Figures 14.9 and 14.10 clearly highlight how usability can be improved through effective component choice. The combo box with a constrained list of choices is clearly the better tool for the task at hand.

The options in this example consist of a fixed number of choices. Shakespeare is clearly dead and the plays attributed to him are widely known. Thus the combo box in figure 14.10 is a better choice. It should be populated with a list of all the known plays.

The option pane in figure 14.9 is better used for unknown data entry such as "Please enter your name."

❻ The final menu item, Exit, brings up a `YES_NO_OPTION` confirmation JOptionPane in a JDialog (shown in figure 14.11) by calling `showConfirmDialog()`. The application is terminated if the user answers "Yes."

14.4   CUSTOMIZING JCOLORCHOOSER

In chapter 12 we developed a custom menu item that allowed quick and easy selection of a color for the background and foreground of a JTextArea. In section 14.1 we built off this example to add a simple About dialog. In this section we'll build off it further, and construct a customized JColorChooser that allows a much wider range of color selection. Our implementation in example 14.3 includes a preview component, `PreviewPanel`, that illustrates how text will appear with chosen background and foreground colors. We have to return both background and foreground selection values when the user dismisses the color chooser in order to update the text component properly.

GUIDELINE

Previewing improves usability   In this example, the user's goal may be to select suitable colors for a banner headline. Allowing the user to view a WYSIWYG preview improves usability. The user doesn't have to experiment with his selection, which involves opening and closing the dialog several times. Instead, he can achieve his goal on a single visit to the color chooser dialog.

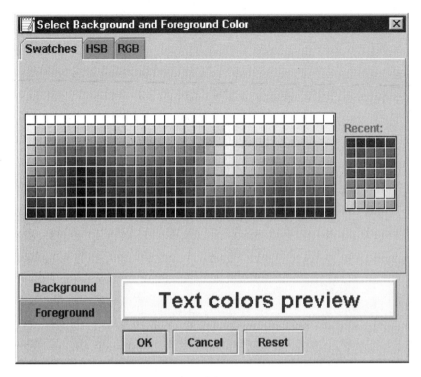

Figure 14.12 A JColorChooser **with a custom** PreviewPanel **component capable of returning two color selections**

Example 14.3

BasicTextEditor.java

see \Chapter14\3

```java
import java.awt.*;
import java.awt.event.*;

import javax.swing.*;

public class BasicTextEditor extends JFrame
{
  // Unchanged code from example 14.1

  protected JColorChooser m_colorChooser;
  protected PreviewPanel m_previewPanel;
  protected JDialog m_colorDialog;

  public BasicTextEditor() {
    super("BasicTextEditor with JColorChooser");
    setSize(450, 350);
    ImageIcon icon = new ImageIcon("smallIcon.gif");
    setIconImage(icon.getImage());

    m_colorChooser = new JColorChooser();
```

❶ **Constructor creates color chooser and PreviewPane and connects them**

```java
      m_previewPanel = new PreviewPanel(m_colorChooser);
      m_colorChooser.setPreviewPanel(m_previewPanel);

      // Unchanged code from example 14.1
   }

   protected JMenuBar createMenuBar() {
      // Unchanged code from example 14.1

      Action actionChooser = new AbstractAction("Color Chooser") {
         public void actionPerformed(ActionEvent e) {
            BasicTextEditor.this.repaint();
            if (m_colorDialog == null)
            m_colorDialog = JColorChooser.createDialog(
               BasicTextEditor.this,
               "Select Background and Foreground Color",
               true, m_colorChooser, m_previewPanel, null);
            m_previewPanel.setTextForeground(
               m_monitor.getForeground());
            m_previewPanel.setTextBackground(
               m_monitor.getBackground());
            m_colorDialog.show();

            if (m_previewPanel.isSelected()) {
               m_monitor.setBackground(
                  m_previewPanel.getTextBackground());
               m_monitor.setForeground(
                  m_previewPanel.getTextForeground());
            }
         }
      };
      mOpt.addSeparator();
      item = mOpt.add(actionChooser);
      item.setMnemonic('c');

      menuBar.add(mOpt);

      // Unchanged code from example 14.1
   }
}

// Unchanged code from example 14.1

class PreviewPanel extends JPanel
 implements ChangeListener, ActionListener
{
   protected JColorChooser m_chooser;
   protected JLabel m_preview;
   protected JToggleButton m_btBack;
   protected JToggleButton m_btFore;
   protected boolean m_isSelected = false;

   public PreviewPanel(JColorChooser chooser) {
      this(chooser, Color.white, Color.black);
   }

   public PreviewPanel(JColorChooser chooser,
```

2 Creates dialog for color chooser

3 Copies colors from text area

4 After dialog is dismissed, copies out new colors

5 Panel to preview selected colors

6 First constructor creates white background and black foreground; calls second constructor

```
      Color background, Color foreground) {
       m_chooser = chooser;
       chooser.getSelectionModel().addChangeListener(this);

       setLayout(new BorderLayout());
       JPanel p = new JPanel(new GridLayout(2, 1, 0, 0));
       ButtonGroup group = new ButtonGroup();
       m_btBack = new JToggleButton("Background");
       m_btBack.setSelected(true);
       m_btBack.addActionListener(this);
       group.add(m_btBack);
       p.add(m_btBack);
       m_btFore = new JToggleButton("Foreground");
       m_btFore.addActionListener(this);
       group.add(m_btFore);
       p.add(m_btFore);
       add(p, BorderLayout.WEST);

       p = new JPanel(new BorderLayout());
       Border b1 = new EmptyBorder(5, 10, 5, 10);
       Border b2 = new BevelBorder(BevelBorder.RAISED);
       Border b3 = new EmptyBorder(2, 2, 2, 2);
       Border cb1 = new CompoundBorder(b1, b2);
       Border cb2 = new CompoundBorder(cb1, b3);
       p.setBorder(cb2);

       m_preview = new JLabel("Text colors preview",
         JLabel.CENTER);
       m_preview.setBackground(background);
       m_preview.setForeground(foreground);
       m_preview.setFont(new Font("Arial",Font.BOLD, 24));
       m_preview.setOpaque(true);
       p.add(m_preview, BorderLayout.CENTER);
       add(p, BorderLayout.CENTER);

       m_chooser.setColor(background);
     }
    protected boolean isSelected() {
       return m_isSelected;
    }

    public void setTextBackground(Color c) {
       m_preview.setBackground(c);
    }

    public Color getTextBackground() {
       return m_preview.getBackground();
    }

    public void setTextForeground(Color c) {
       m_preview.setForeground(c);
    }

    public Color getTextForeground() {
       return m_preview.getForeground();
    }
```

7 Background and foreground buttons in vertical grid

7 Raised, button-like border for big label

7 Big label to show text colors

```
public void stateChanged(ChangeEvent evt) {
  Color c = m_chooser.getColor();
  if (c != null) {
    if (m_btBack.isSelected())
      m_preview.setBackground(c);
    else
      m_preview.setForeground(c);
  }
}

public void actionPerformed(ActionEvent evt) {
  if (evt.getSource() == m_btBack)
    m_chooser.setColor(getTextBackground());
  else if (evt.getSource() == m_btFore)
    m_chooser.setColor(getTextForeground());
  else
    m_isSelected = true;
}
```

8 Called for change
events on color
chooser

9 Called when either
the background or
foreground button
is pressed

14.4.1   Understanding the code

Class BasicTextEditor

This class includes three new instance variables:

- JColorChooser m_colorChooser: Used to store JColorChooser to avoid unnecessary instantiation.
- PreviewPanel m_previewPanel: An instance of our custom color previewing component.
- JDialog m_colorDialog: Used to store the JDialog that acts as the parent of m_colorChooser.

1 The constructor instantiates m_colorChooser and m_previewPanel, assigning m_previewPanel as m_colorChooser's preview component using the setPreviewPanel() method.

2 The menu bar receives a new menu item, Color Chooser, which is set up in the createMenuBar() method as an Action implementation. When selected, this item first repaints our application frame to ensure that the area covered by the pop-up menu is refreshed properly. Then it checks to see if our m_colorDialog has been instantiated yet. If it has not, we call JColorChooser's static createDialog() method to wrap m_colorChooser in a dialog, and we use m_previewPanel as an ActionListener for the OK button (see section 14.1.3). This instantiation only occurs once.

3 We then assign the current colors of m_monitor to m_previewPanel (recall that m_monitor is the JTextArea central to this application). We do this because the foreground and background can also be assigned by our custom menu color choosers. If this occurs, m_previewPanel is not notified, so we update the selected colors each time the dialog is invoked.

4 The dialog is then shown and the main application thread waits for it to be dismissed. When the dialog is dismissed, m_previewPanel is checked to see whether new colors have been selected using its isSelected() method. If new colors have been chosen, they are assigned to m_monitor.

NOTE We have purposely avoided updating the selected colors in our custom color menu components. The reason we did this is that in a more professional implementation we would most likely not offer both methods for choosing text component colors. If we did want to support both methods, we would need to determine the closest color in our custom color menus that matches the corresponding color selected with JColorChooser, because JColorChooser offers a much wider range of choices.

Class PreviewPanel

5 This class represents our custom color preview component which is designed to be used with JColorChooser. It extends JPanel and implements two listener interfaces, ChangeListener and ActionListener. It displays selected foreground and background colors in a label, and it includes two JToggleButtons that are used to switch between background color and foreground color selection modes. There are five instance variables:

- JColorChooser m_chooser: A reference to the hosting color chooser.
- JLabel m_preview: The label to preview background and foreground colors.
- JToggleButton m_btBack: The toggle button to switch to the background color selection.
- JToggleButton m_btFore: The toggle button to switch to the foreground color selection.
- boolean m_isSelected: The flag indicating a selection has taken place.

6 The first PreviewPanel constructor takes a JColorChooser as a parameter and delegates its work to the second constructor, passing it the JColorChooser as well as white and black Colors for the initial background and foreground colors, respectively. As we discussed in the beginning of this chapter, JColorChooser's ColorSelectionModel fires ChangeEvents when the selected Color changes. So we start by registering this component as a ChangeListener with the given color chooser's model.

7 A BorderLayout is used to manage this container and two toggle buttons are placed in a 2x1 GridLayout, which is added to the WEST region. Both buttons receive a this reference as an ActionListener. A label with a large font is then placed in the CENTER region. This label is surrounded by a decorative, doubly-compounded border consisting of an EmptyBorder, a BevelBorder, and another EmptyBorder. The foreground and background colors of this label are assigned the values passed to the constructor.

8 Several methods are used to set and get the selected colors; they do not require any special explanation. The stateChanged() method will be called when the color chooser model fires ChangeEvents. Depending on which toggle button is selected, this method updates the background or foreground color of the preview label.

9 The actionPerformed() method will be called when one of the toggle buttons is pressed. It assigns the stored background or foreground, depending which button is clicked, as the color of the hosting JColorChooser. This method is also called when the OK button is clicked, in which case the m_isSelected flag is set to true.

14.4.2   Running the code

Select the Color Chooser menu item to bring up our customized JColorChooser (shown in figure 14.12). Select a background and foreground color using any of the available color panes. Verify that the preview label is updated to reflect the current color selection and the currently selected toggle button. Click the OK button to dismiss the dialog and notice that both the selected foreground and background colors are assigned to our application's text area. Also notice that clicking the Cancel button dismisses the dialog without making any color changes.

14.5   CUSTOMIZING JFILECHOOSER

Examples that use `JFileChooser` to load and save files are scattered throughout this book. In this section we'll take a closer look at the more advanced features of this component as we build a powerful JAR and ZIP archive creation, viewing, and extraction tool. We will see how to implement a custom `FileView` and `FileFilter`, and how to access and manipulate the internals of `JFileChooser` to allow multiple file selection and add our own components. Since this example deals with Java 2 archive functionality, we will first briefly summarize the classes from the `java.util.zip` and `java.util.jar` packages we will be using.

NOTE   The GUI presented in this section is extremely basic, and professional implementations would surely construct a more elaborate counterpart. We have purposely avoided this construction here due to the complex nature of the example, and to avoid straying from the `JFileChooser` topics central to the GUI's construction.

14.5.1   ZipInputStream

class java.util.zip.ZipInputStream

This class represents a filtered input stream which uncompresses ZIP archive data. The constructor takes an instance of `InputStream` as a parameter. Before we can read data from this stream, we need to find a ZIP file entry using the `getNextEntry()` method. Each entry corresponds to an archived file. We can `read()` an array of `bytes` from an entry, and then close it using the `closeEntry()` method when reading is complete.

14.5.2   ZipOutputStream

class java.util.zip.ZipOutputStream

This class represents a filtered output stream which writes binary data into an archive in the compressed (default) or uncompressed (optional) form. The constructor of this class takes an instance of `OutputStream` as a parameter. Before writing data to this stream, we need to create a new `ZipEntry` using the `putNextEntry()` method. Each `ZipEntry` corresponds to an archived file. We can `write()` an array of bytes to a `ZipEntry`, and close it using the `closeEntry()` method when writing is complete. We can also specify the compression method for storing `ZipEntrys` using `ZipOutputStream`'s `setMethod()` method.

14.5.3   ZipFile

class java.util.zip.ZipFile

This class encapsulates a collection of `ZipEntrys` and represents a read-only ZIP archive. We can fetch an `Enumeration` of the contained `ZipEntrys` using the `entries()` method. The `size()` method tells us how many files are contained, and `getName()` returns the archive's full path name. We can retrieve an `InputStream` for reading the contents of a contained `ZipEntry` using the `getInputStream()` method. When we are finished reading, we are expected to call the `close()` method to close the archive.

14.5.4 ZipEntry

class java.util.zip.ZipEntry

This class represents a single archived file or directory within a ZIP archive. It allows retrieval of its name and it can be cloned using the `clone()` method. Using typical set/get accessors, we can access a `ZipEntry`'s compression method, CRC-32 checksum, size, modification time, and a comment attachment. We can also query whether a `ZipEntry` is a directory using its `isDirectory()` method.

14.5.5 The java.util.jar package

This package contains a set of classes for managing JAR files. The relevant classes that we will be dealing with (`JarEntry`, `JarFile`, `JarInputStream`, and `JarOutputStream`) are direct subclasses of the zip package counterparts (`ZipEntry`, `ZipFile`, `ZipInputStream`, and `ZipOutputStream`), and thus they inherit the functionality described above.

14.5.6 Manifest

class java.util.jar.Manifest

This class represents a JAR `Manifest` file. A `Manifest` contains a collection of names and their associated attributes specific both for the archive as a whole and for a particular `JarEntry`, such as a file or directory in the archive. We are not concerned with the details of JAR manifest files in this chapter; suffice it to say that the `JarOutputStream` constructor takes a `Manifest` instance as a parameter, along with an `OutputStream`.

In example 14.4, we create a simple, two-button GUI with a status bar (a label). One button corresponds to creating a ZIP or JAR archive, and the other corresponds to decompressing an archive. In each case, two `JFileChooser`s are used to perform the operation. The first chooser allows the user to either enter an archive name to use or select an archive to decompress. The second chooser allows the user to select files to compress or decompress. (As noted above, more professional implementations would most likely include a more elaborate GUI.) A custom `FileView` class represents ZIP and JAR archives using a custom icon, and a `FileFilter` class allows ZIP (.zip) and JAR (.jar) files only to be viewed. We also work with `JFileChooser` as a container by adding our own custom component, taking advantage of the fact that it uses a y-oriented `BoxLayout` to organize its children. Using similar tactics, we show how to gain access to its `JList` (which is used for the display and selection of files and directories) to allow multiple selection (an unimplemented feature in `JFileChooser` as of Java 2 FCS).

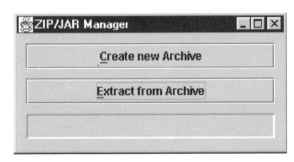

Figure 14.13
The ZIP/JAR Manager
`JFileChooser` **example**
at startup

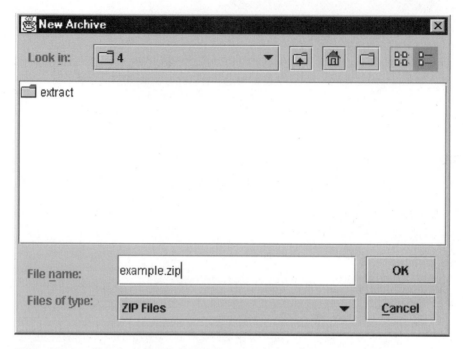

Figure 14.14 **The first step in creating an archive: using** `JFileChooser`
to select an archive location and name

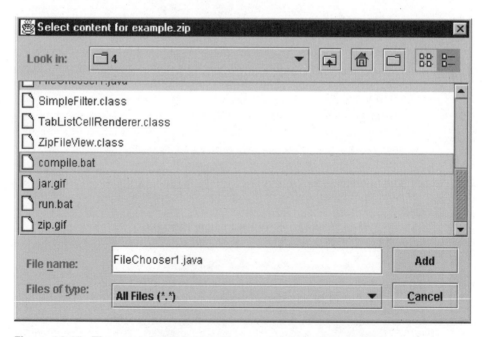

Figure 14.15 **The second step in creating an archive: using** `JFileChooser`
to select archive content

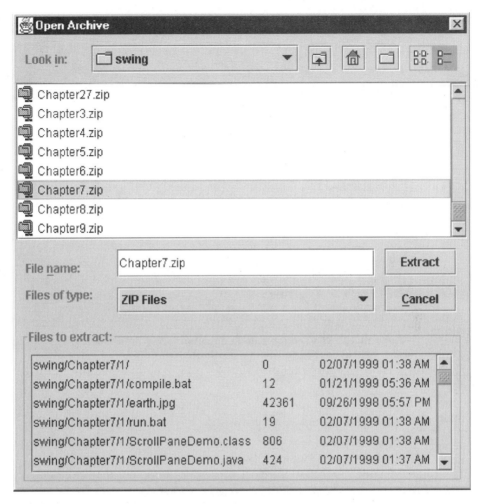

Figure 14.16 The first step in uncompressing an archive: using a custom component in `JFileChooser`

Example 14.4

ZipJarManager.java

see \Chapter14\4

```
import java.awt.*;
import java.awt.event.*;
import java.io.*;
import java.util.*;
import java.util.zip.*;
```

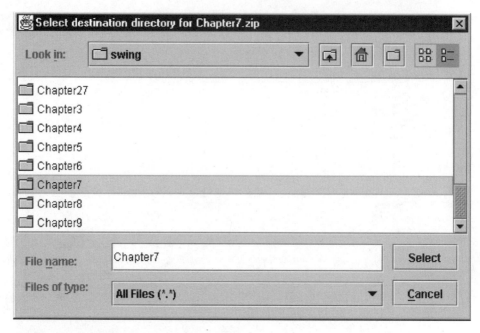

Figure 14.17 The second step in uncompressing an archive: using `JFileChooser` **to select a destination directory**

```
import java.util.jar.*;
import java.beans.*;
import java.text.SimpleDateFormat;

import javax.swing.*;
import javax.swing.event.*;
import javax.swing.border.*;

public class ZipJarManager extends JFrame
{
  public static int BUFFER_SIZE = 10240;

  protected JFileChooser chooser1;
  protected JFileChooser chooser2;

  protected File  m_currentDir = new File(".");
  protected SimpleFilter m_zipFilter;
  protected SimpleFilter m_jarFilter;
  protected ZipFileView  m_view;

  protected JButton m_btCreate;
  protected JButton m_btExtract;
  protected JLabel  m_status;

  protected JList m_zipEntries;
  protected File  m_selectedFile;

  public ZipJarManager()
  {
```

```
    super("ZIP/JAR Manager");

    JWindow jwin = new JWindow();
    jwin.getContentPane().add(new JLabel(
      "Loading ZIP/JAR Manager...", SwingConstants.CENTER));
    jwin.setBounds(200,200,200,100);
    jwin.setVisible(true);

    chooser1 = new JFileChooser();
    chooser2 = new JFileChooser();

    JPanel p = new JPanel(new GridLayout(3, 1, 10, 10));
    p.setBorder(new EmptyBorder(10, 10, 10, 10));

    m_btCreate = new JButton("Create new Archive");
    ActionListener lst = new ActionListener() {
      public void actionPerformed(ActionEvent e) {
        m_btCreate.setEnabled(false);
        m_btExtract.setEnabled(false);
        createArchive();
        m_btCreate.setEnabled(true);
        m_btExtract.setEnabled(true);
      }
    };
    m_btCreate.addActionListener(lst);
    m_btCreate.setMnemonic('c');
    p.add(m_btCreate);

    m_btExtract = new JButton("Extract from Archive");
    lst = new ActionListener() {
      public void actionPerformed(ActionEvent e) {
        m_btCreate.setEnabled(false);
        m_btExtract.setEnabled(false);
        extractArchive();
        m_btCreate.setEnabled(true);
        m_btExtract.setEnabled(true);
      }
    };
    m_btExtract.addActionListener(lst);
    m_btExtract.setMnemonic('e');
    p.add(m_btExtract);

    m_status = new JLabel();
    m_status.setBorder(new BevelBorder(BevelBorder.LOWERED,
      Color.white, Color.gray));
    p.add(m_status);

    m_zipFilter = new SimpleFilter("zip", "ZIP Files");
    m_jarFilter = new SimpleFilter("jar", "JAR Files");
    m_view = new ZipFileView();

    chooser1.addChoosableFileFilter(m_zipFilter);
    chooser1.addChoosableFileFilter(m_jarFilter);
    chooser1.setFileView(m_view);
    chooser1.setMultiSelectionEnabled(false);
```

1 One file chooser to choose the jar/zip archive, the other to select files to add or a directory to extract to

```
  chooser1.setFileFilter(m_jarFilter);

  javax.swing.filechooser.FileFilter ft =
    chooser1.getAcceptAllFileFilter();
  chooser1.removeChoosableFileFilter(ft);

  getContentPane().add(p, BorderLayout.CENTER);
  setBounds(0,0,300,150);
  WindowListener wndCloser = new WindowAdapter() {
    public void windowClosing(WindowEvent e) {
      System.exit(0);
    }
  };
  addWindowListener(wndCloser);

  jwin.setVisible(false);
  jwin.dispose();

  setVisible(true);
}

public void setStatus(String str) {
  m_status.setText(str);
  m_status.repaint();
}

protected void createArchive() {
  chooser1.setCurrentDirectory(m_currentDir);
  chooser1.setDialogType(JFileChooser.SAVE_DIALOG);
  chooser1.setDialogTitle("New Archive");
  chooser1.setPreferredSize(new Dimension(450,300));

  if (chooser1.showDialog(this, "OK") !=
    JFileChooser.APPROVE_OPTION)
      return;
  m_currentDir = chooser1.getCurrentDirectory();

  final File archiveFile = chooser1.getSelectedFile();
  if (!isArchiveFile(archiveFile))
    return;

  // Show chooser to select entries
  chooser2.setCurrentDirectory(m_currentDir);
  chooser2.setDialogType(JFileChooser.OPEN_DIALOG);
  chooser2.setDialogTitle("Select content for "
    + archiveFile.getName());
  chooser2.setMultiSelectionEnabled(true);
  chooser2.setFileSelectionMode(JFileChooser.FILES_ONLY);

  if (chooser2.showDialog(this, "Add") !=
    JFileChooser.APPROVE_OPTION)
      return;

  m_currentDir = chooser2.getCurrentDirectory();
  final File[] selected = getSelectedFiles(chooser2);

  String name = archiveFile.getName().toLowerCase();
  if (name.endsWith(".zip")) {
```

2 Shows dialog to get archive name

3 Verifies file name is ZIP or JAR file

4 Shows dialog to select files to add to archive

```java
      Thread runner = new Thread() {
        public void run() {
          createZipArchive(archiveFile, selected);
        }
      };
      runner.start();
    }
    else if (name.endsWith(".jar")) {
      Thread runner = new Thread() {
        public void run() {
          createJarArchive(archiveFile, selected);
        }
      };
      runner.start();
    }
  }

  protected void createZipArchive(File archiveFile,
  File[] selected) {
    try {
      byte buffer[] = new byte[BUFFER_SIZE];

      // Open archive file
      FileOutputStream stream =
        new FileOutputStream(archiveFile);
      ZipOutputStream out = new ZipOutputStream(stream);

      for (int k=0; k<selected.length; k++) {
        if (selected[k]==null || !selected[k].exists() ||
          selected[k].isDirectory())
            continue;  // Just in case...
        setStatus("Adding "+selected[k].getName());

        // Add archive entry
        ZipEntry zipAdd = new ZipEntry(selected[k].getName());
        zipAdd.setTime(selected[k].lastModified());
        out.putNextEntry(zipAdd);

        // Read input and write to output
        FileInputStream in = new FileInputStream(selected[k]);
        while (true) {
          int nRead = in.read(buffer, 0, buffer.length);
          if (nRead <= 0)
            break;
          out.write(buffer, 0, nRead);
        }
        in.close();
      }

      out.close();
      stream.close();
      setStatus("Adding completed OK");
    }
    catch (Exception e) {
```

5 **Creates ZIP archive and writes selected files to it**

```
      e.printStackTrace();
      setStatus("Error: "+e.getMessage());
      return;
    }
  }

  protected void createJarArchive(
   File archiveFile, File[] selected) {
    try {
      byte buffer[] = new byte[BUFFER_SIZE];

      // Open archive file
      FileOutputStream stream =
        new FileOutputStream(archiveFile);
      JarOutputStream out = new JarOutputStream(stream,
        new Manifest());

      for (int k=0; k<selected.length; k++) {
        if (selected[k]==null || !selected[k].exists() ||
          selected[k].isDirectory())
            continue;  // Just in case...
        setStatus("Adding "+selected[k].getName());

        // Add archive entry
        JarEntry jarAdd = new JarEntry(selected[k].getName());
        jarAdd.setTime(selected[k].lastModified());
        out.putNextEntry(jarAdd);

        // Write file to archive
        FileInputStream in = new FileInputStream(selected[k]);
        while (true) {
          int nRead = in.read(buffer, 0, buffer.length);
          if (nRead <= 0)
            break;
          out.write(buffer, 0, nRead);
        }
        in.close();
      }

      out.close();
      stream.close();
      setStatus("Adding completed OK");
    }
    catch (Exception ex) {
      ex.printStackTrace();
      setStatus("Error: "+ex.getMessage());
    }
  }
  protected void extractArchive() {
    chooser1.setCurrentDirectory(m_currentDir);
    chooser1.setDialogType(JFileChooser.OPEN_DIALOG);
    chooser1.setDialogTitle("Open Archive");
    chooser1.setPreferredSize(new Dimension(470,450));

    // Construct a JList to show archive entries
```

6 **Creates JAR archive and writes selected files to it**

7 **Gives first file chooser a little more screen space**

```
m_zipEntries = new JList();
m_zipEntries.setSelectionMode(
  ListSelectionModel.MULTIPLE_INTERVAL_SELECTION);
TabListCellRenderer renderer = new TabListCellRenderer();
renderer.setTabs(new int[] {240, 300, 360});
m_zipEntries.setCellRenderer(renderer);

// Place entries list in a scroll pane and add it to the chooser
JPanel p = new JPanel(new BorderLayout());
p.setBorder(new CompoundBorder(
  new CompoundBorder(
    new EmptyBorder(5, 5, 5, 5),
    new TitledBorder("Files to extract:")),
  new EmptyBorder(5,5,5,5)));
JScrollPane ps = new JScrollPane(m_zipEntries);
p.add(ps, BorderLayout.CENTER);
chooser1.add(p);

PropertyChangeListener lst = new PropertyChangeListener() {
  SimpleDateFormat m_sdf = new SimpleDateFormat(
    "MM/dd/yyyy hh:mm a");
  DefaultListModel m_emptyModel = new DefaultListModel();

  public void propertyChange(PropertyChangeEvent e) {
    if (e.getPropertyName() ==
    JFileChooser.FILE_FILTER_CHANGED_PROPERTY) {
      m_zipEntries.setModel(m_emptyModel);
      return;
    }
    else if (e.getPropertyName() ==
    JFileChooser.SELECTED_FILE_CHANGED_PROPERTY) {
      File f = chooser1.getSelectedFile();
      if (f != null) {
        if (m_selectedFile!=null && m_selectedFile.equals(f)
        && m_zipEntries.getModel().getSize() > 0) {
          return;
        }
        String name = f.getName().toLowerCase();
        if (!name.endsWith(".zip") && !name.endsWith(".jar")) {
          m_zipEntries.setModel(m_emptyModel);
          return;
        }
        try {
          ZipFile zipFile = new ZipFile(f.getPath());
          DefaultListModel model = new DefaultListModel();
          Enumeration en = zipFile.entries();
          while (en.hasMoreElements()) {
            ZipEntry zipEntr = (ZipEntry)en.nextElement();
            Date d = new Date(zipEntr.getTime());
            String str = zipEntr.getName()+'\t'+
              zipEntr.getSize()+'\t'+m_sdf.format(d);
            model.addElement(str);
          }
```

Embedded list component to select files to extract from archive ⑧

Sets up list model containing all the files from selected archive ⑨

```
          zipFile.close();
          m_zipEntries.setModel(model);
          m_zipEntries.setSelectionInterval(0,
            model.getSize()-1);
        }
        catch(Exception ex) {
          ex.printStackTrace();
          setStatus("Error: "+ex.getMessage());
        }
      }
    }
    else {
      m_zipEntries.setModel(m_emptyModel);
      return;
    }
  }
};
chooser1.addPropertyChangeListener(lst);
chooser1.cancelSelection();

if (chooser1.showDialog(this, "Extract") !=
 JFileChooser.APPROVE_OPTION) {
  chooser1.remove(p);
  chooser1.removePropertyChangeListener(lst);
  return;
}
m_currentDir = chooser1.getCurrentDirectory();
final File archiveFile = chooser1.getSelectedFile();

if (!archiveFile.exists() || !isArchiveFile(archiveFile)) {
  chooser1.remove(p);
  chooser1.removePropertyChangeListener(lst);
  return;
}

Object[] selObj = m_zipEntries.getSelectedValues();
if (selObj.length == 0) {
  setStatus("No entries have been selected for extraction");
  chooser1.removePropertyChangeListener(lst);
  chooser1.remove(p);
  return;
}
final String[] entries = new String[selObj.length];
for (int k=0; k<selObj.length; k++) {
  String str = selObj[k].toString();
  int index = str.indexOf('\t');
  entries[k] = str.substring(0, index);
}
// Show dialog to select output directory
chooser2.setCurrentDirectory(m_currentDir);
chooser2.setDialogType(JFileChooser.OPEN_DIALOG);
chooser2.setDialogTitle("Select destination directory for "
  + archiveFile.getName());
```

Sets up list model containing all the files from selected archive — **9**

On dismiss, removes panel with files to extract — **10**

Sets second file chooser to select directory to extract files into — **11**

```
chooser2.setMultiSelectionEnabled(false);
chooser2.setFileSelectionMode(JFileChooser.DIRECTORIES_ONLY);

if (chooser2.showDialog(this, "Select") !=
JFileChooser.APPROVE_OPTION) {
  chooser1.remove(p);
  chooser1.removePropertyChangeListener(lst);
  return;
}

m_currentDir = chooser2.getCurrentDirectory();
final File outputDir = chooser2.getSelectedFile();

Thread runner = new Thread() {
  public void run() {
    try {
      byte buffer[] = new byte[BUFFER_SIZE];

      // Open the archive file
      FileInputStream stream =
        new FileInputStream(archiveFile);
      ZipInputStream in = new ZipInputStream(stream);

      // Find archive entry
      while (true) {
        ZipEntry zipExtract = in.getNextEntry();
        if (zipExtract == null)
          break;
        boolean bFound = false;
        for (int k=0; k<entries.length; k++) {
          if (zipExtract.getName().equals(entries[k])) {
            bFound = true;
            break;
          }
        }
        if (!bFound) {
          in.closeEntry();
          continue;
        }
        setStatus("Extracting " + zipExtract.getName());

        // Create output file and check required directory
        File outFile = new File(outputDir,
          zipExtract.getName());
        File parent = outFile.getParentFile();
        if (parent != null && !parent.exists())
          parent.mkdirs();

        // Extract unzipped file
        FileOutputStream out = new FileOutputStream(outFile);
        while (true) {
          int nRead = in.read(buffer, 0, buffer.length);
          if (nRead <= 0)
            break;
          out.write(buffer, 0, nRead);
        }
```

⑪ Sets second file chooser to select directory to extract files into

⑫ Extraction process runs in background thread

⑫ ZipInputStream reads entire archive

⑫ ZipEntry represents one file in archive

⑫ Reads from archive and writes to normal file

```
                out.close();
                in.closeEntry();
              }

              in.close();
              stream.close();
              setStatus("Extracting completed OK");
            }
        catch (Exception ex) {
          ex.printStackTrace();
          setStatus("Error: "+ex.getMessage());
        }
      }
    };
    runner.start();
    chooser1.removePropertyChangeListener(lst);
    chooser1.remove(p);
  }
```

**Returns list of
selected files
from a file chooser** **13**

```
  public static File[] getSelectedFiles(JFileChooser chooser) {
    // Although JFileChooser won't give us this information,
    // we need it...
    Container c1 = (Container)chooser.getComponent(3);
    JList list = null;
    while (c1 != null) {
      Container c = (Container)c1.getComponent(0);
      if (c instanceof JList) {
        list = (JList)c;
        break;
      }
      c1 = c;
    }
    Object[] entries = list.getSelectedValues();
    File[] files = new File[entries.length];
    for (int k=0; k<entries.length; k++) {
      if (entries[k] instanceof File)
        files[k] = (File)entries[k];
    }
    return files;
  }
```

13 **Workaround
to find real JList
component**

```
  public static boolean isArchiveFile(File f) {
    String name = f.getName().toLowerCase();
    return (name.endsWith(".zip") || name.endsWith(".jar"));
  }

  public static void main(String argv[]) {
    new ZipJarManager();
  }
}

class SimpleFilter extends javax.swing.filechooser.FileFilter
{
  private String m_description = null;
```

**FileFilter which
lists files of
a given extension** **14**

```java
    private String m_extension = null;

    public SimpleFilter(String extension, String description) {
      m_description = description;
      m_extension = "."+extension.toLowerCase();
    }

    public String getDescription() {
      return m_description;
    }

    public boolean accept(File f) {
      if (f == null)
        return false;
      if (f.isDirectory())
        return true;
      return f.getName().toLowerCase().endsWith(m_extension);
    }
  }

class ZipFileView extends javax.swing.filechooser.FileView
{
    protected static ImageIcon ZIP_ICON = new ImageIcon("zip.gif");
    protected static ImageIcon JAR_ICON = new ImageIcon("jar.gif");

    public String getName(File f) {
      String name = f.getName();
      return name.equals("") ? f.getPath() : name;
    }

    public String getDescription(File f) {
      return getTypeDescription(f);
    }

    public String getTypeDescription(File f) {
      String name = f.getName().toLowerCase();
      if (name.endsWith(".zip"))
        return "ZIP Archive File";
      else if (name.endsWith(".jar"))
        return "Java Archive File";
      else
        return "File";
    }

    public Icon getIcon(File f) {
      String name = f.getName().toLowerCase();
      if (name.endsWith(".zip"))
        return ZIP_ICON;
      else if (name.endsWith(".jar"))
        return JAR_ICON;
      else
        return null;
    }

    public Boolean isTraversable(File f) {
```

FileView subclass which shows a ZIP or JAR icon 15

```
        return (f.isDirectory() ? Boolean.TRUE : Boolean.FALSE);
    }
}

// Class TabListCellRenderer is taken from Chapter 10,
// section 10.3, without modification.
```

14.5.7 Understanding the code

Class ZipJarManager

This class extends `JFrame` to provide a very simple GUI for our ZIP/JAR archive manager application. One class variable is defined:

- `int BUFFER_SIZE`: Defines the size of an array of bytes for reading and writing files.

There are eleven instance variables:

- `JFileChooser chooser1`: The file chooser used to select an archive for creation or extraction.
- `JFileChooser chooser2`: The file chooser used to select the files to include in an archive or the files to extract from an archive.
- `File m_currentDir`: The currently selected directory.
- `SimpleFilter m_zipFilter`: The filter for files with a .zip extension.
- `SimpleFilter m_jarFilter`: The filter for files with a .jar extension.
- `ZipFileView m_view`: A custom `FileView` implementation for JAR and ZIP files.
- `JButton m_btCreate`: Initiates the creation of an archive.
- `JButton m_btExtract`: Initiates extraction from an archive.
- `JLabel m_status`: The label to display status messages.
- `JList m_zipEntries`: The list component that displays an array of entries in an archive.
- `File m_selectedFile`: The currently selected archive file.

1 The `ZipJarManager` constructor first creates and displays a simple `JWindow` splash screen to let the user know that the application is loading (a progress bar might be more effective here, but we want to stick to the point). Our two `JFileChoosers` are then instantiated (which takes a significant amount of time) and then the buttons and label are created, encapsulated in a `JPanel` using a `GridLayout`, and added to the content pane. The first button, Create new Archive, is assigned an `ActionListener` which invokes `createArchive()`. The second button, Extract from Archive, is assigned an `ActionListener` which invokes `extractArchive()`. Our custom `SimpleFilters` and `FileView` are then instantiated and assigned to `chooser1`. We then set `chooser1`'s `multiSelectionEnabled` property to `false`, tell it to use the JAR filter initially, and remove the All Files filter. Finally, the splash window is disposed before the frame is made visible.

The `setStatus()` method simply assigns a given `String` to the `m_status` label.

2 The `createArchive()` method is used to create a new archive file using both `JFileChoosers`. First, we set `chooser1`'s title to New Archive and its type to `SAVE_DIALOG`, and we assign it a new preferred size (the reason we change its size will become clear below). Then we show `chooser1` in a dialog to prompt the user for a new archive name. If the dialog is dismissed by pressing Cancel or the Close button, we do nothing and return. Otherwise, we store the current directory in our m_currentDir instance variable and create a File instance that corresponds to the file specified in the chooser.

3 Interestingly, JFileChooser does not check whether the filename entered in its text field is valid with respect to its filters when the Approve button is pressed. So we are forced to manually check if our File's name has a .zip or .jar extension using our custom isArchiveFile() method. If this method returns false, we do nothing and return. Otherwise, we set up chooser2 to allow multiple selections to make up the content of the archive, and we only allow file selections (by setting the fileSelectionMode property to FILES_ONLY) to avoid overcomplicating our archive-processing scheme. We also set the dialog title to specify the name of the archive we are creating.

4 We use JFileChooser's showDialog() method to display chooser2 in a JDialog and assign "Add" as its approve button text. If the approve button is not pressed, we do nothing and return. Otherwise, we create an array of Files to be placed in the specified archive using our custom getSelectedFiles() method (see below). Finally, we invoke our createZip-Archive() method if the selected archive file has a .zip extension, or createJarArchive() if it has a .jar extension. These method calls are wrapped in separate threads to avoid clogging up the event-dispatching thread.

5 The createZipArchive() method takes two parameters: a ZIP archive file and an array of files to be added to the archive. It creates a ZipOutputStream to write the selected archive file. Then for each file in the given array, it creates a ZipEntry instance, places it in the ZipOutputStream, and performs standard read/write operations until all data has been written into the archive. The status label is updated, using our setStatus() method, each time a file is written and when the operation completes, to provide feedback during long operations.

6 The createJarArchive() method works almost identically to createZipArchive(), using the corresponding java.util.jar classes. Note that a default Manifest instance is supplied to the JarOutputStream constructor.

7 The extractArchive() method extracts data from an archive file using both JFile-Choosers. First we assign chooser1 a preferred size of 470x450 because we will be adding a custom component which requires a bit more space than JFileChooser normally offers (this is also why we set the preferred size of chooser1 in our createArchive() method discussed earlier). Since JFileChooser is derived from JComponent, we can add our own components to it just like any other container. A quick look at the source code shows that JFileChooser uses a y-oriented BoxLayout. This implies that new components added to a JFileChooser will be placed below all other existing components (see chapter 4 for more information about BoxLayout).

8 We take advantage of this knowledge and add a JList component, m_zipEntries, to allow the selection of compressed entries to be extracted from the selected archive. This JList component receives an instance of our custom TabListCellRenderer as its cell renderer to process Strings with tabs (see chapter 10, section 10.3). The location of the String segments between tabs are assigned using its setTabs() method. Finally, this list is placed in a JScroll-Pane to provide scrolling capabilities, and it is added to the bottom of the JFileChooser component.

A PropertyChangeListener is added to chooser1 to process the user's selection. This anonymous class maintains two instance variables:

- `SimpleDateFormat m_sdf`: Formats file time stamps.
- `DefaultListModel m_emptyModel`: Assigned to `m_zipEntries` when non-archive files are selected, or when the file filter is changed.

9 This listener's `propertyChange()` method will receive a `PropertyChangeEvent` when, among other things, `chooser1`'s selection changes. The selected file can then be retrieved using `PropertyChangeEvent`'s `getNewValue()` method. If this file represents a ZIP or JAR archive, our implementation creates a `ZipFile` instance to read its contents, and it retrieves an `Enumeration` of `ZipEntries` in this archive (recall that `JarFile` and `JarEntry` are subclasses of `ZipFile` and `ZipEntry`, allowing us to display the contents of a JAR or a ZIP archive identically). For each entry we form a `String` containing that entry's name, size, and time stamp. This `String` is added to a `DefaultListModel` instance. After each entry has been processed, this model is assigned to our `JList`, and all items are initially selected. The user can then modify the selection to specify the entries that need to be extracted from the archive.

10 Once the `PropertyChangeListener` is added, `chooser1` is displayed with "Extract" as its approve button text. If it is dismissed, we remove both the panel containing our list component and the `PropertyChangeListener`, as they are only temporary additions (remember that we use this same chooser to initiate the creation of an archive in the `createArchive()` method). Otherwise, if the Approve button is pressed, we check whether the selected file exists and represents an archive. We then create an array of `Objects` corresponding to each selected item in our list (which are `Strings`). If no items are selected, we report an error in our status label, remove our temporary component and listener, and return. Otherwise, we form an array of entry names corresponding to each selected item (which is the portion of each `String` before the appearance of the first tab character).

11 Now we need to select a directory to be used to extract the selected archive entries. We use `chooser2` for this purpose. We set its `fileSelectionMode` property to `DIRECTORIES_ONLY`, and we allow only single selection by setting its `multiSelectionEnabled` property to `false`. We then show `chooser2` using "Select" for its Approve button text. If it is dismissed, we remove our temporary component and listener, and return. Otherwise, we start the extraction process in a separate thread.

12 To begin the extraction process, we create a `ZipInputStream` to read from the selected archive file. Then we process each entry in the archive by retrieving a corresponding `ZipEntry` and verifying whether each `ZipEntry`'s name matches a `String` in our previously obtained array of selected file names (from our list component that was added to `chooser1`). If a match is found, we create a `File` instance to write that entry to. If a `ZipEntry` includes subdirectories, we create these subdirectories using `File`'s `mkdirs()` method. Finally, we perform standard read/write operations until all files have been extracted from the archive. Note that we update the status label each time a file is extracted and when the operation completes.

13 The `getSelectedFiles()` method takes a `JFileChooser` instance as a parameter and it returns an array of `Files` selected in the given chooser's list. Interestingly, `JFileChooser` provides the `getSelectedFiles()` method which does not work properly as of Java 2 FCS (it always returns `null`). In order to work around this problem, we use `java.awt.Container` functionality (which, as we know, all Swing components inherit) to gain access to `JFileChooser`'s components. With a little detective work we find that the component with index 3 represents the central part of the chooser. This component contains several children nested inside one another. One of these child components is the JList component we need access to in order to determine the current selection state. So we can simply loop through these nested containers until we find the JList. As soon as we have gained access to this component, we can retrieve an array of the selected objects using JList's getSelectedValues() method. As expected, these objects are instances of the File class, so we need only upcast each and return them in a File[] array.

NOTE This solution should be considered a temporary bug workaround. We expect the getSelectedFiles() method to be implemented correctly in future releases, and we suggest that you try substituting this method here to determine whether it has been fixed in the release with which you are working.

Class SimpleFilter

14 This class represents a basic FileFilter that accepts files with a given String extension, and it displays a given String description in JFileChooser's Files of Type combo box. We have already seen and discussed this filter in section 14.1.9. It is used here to create our JAR and ZIP filters in the ZipJarManager constructor.

Class ZipFileView

15 This class extends FileView to provide a more user-friendly graphical representation of ZIP and JAR files in JFileChooser. Two instance variables, ImageIcon ZIP_ICON and Image-Icon JAR_ICON, represent small images corresponding to each archive type: 🗒 (jar.gif) and 💻 (zip.gif). This class is a straightforward adaptation of the sample FileView class presented in section 14.1.11.

14.5.8   Running the code

Note that a JWindow is displayed as a simple splash screen because instantiating of JFile-Chooser takes a significant amount of time. Press the Create new Archive button and select a name and location for the new archive file in the first file chooser that appears. Press the OK button and then select the files you want to add to that archive in the second chooser. Figure 14.13 shows ZipJarManager in action, and figures 14.14 and 14.15 show the first and second choosers that appear during the archive creation process.

Try uncompressing an existing archive. Press the Extract from Archive button and select an existing archive file in the first chooser that appears. Notice the custom list component that is displayed in the bottom of this chooser (see figure 14.16). Each time an archive is selected, its contents are displayed in this list. Select the entries to extract and press the Extract button. A second chooser will appear, as shown in figure 14.17, allowing selection of a destination directory.

BUG ALERT As of Java 2 FCS, PropertyChangeEvents are not always fired as expected when JFileChooser's selection changes. This causes the updating of our custom list component to fail occasionally. We expect this to be fixed in a future release.

PART **III**

Advanced topics

In chapters 15 through 21 we discuss the most advanced Swing components and the classes and interfaces that support them. We start with `JLayeredPane` in chapter 15, and implement our own MDI internal frame component from scratch.

Chapter 16 is about `JDesktopPane` and `JInternalFrame`, the MDI components that ship with Swing. This chapter culminates with the implementation of a multi-user networked desktop environment.

Chapters 17 and 18 discuss the powerful and intricate tree and table components. Among other examples, we show how to build a directory browser using the tree component, and a sortable, JDBC-aware stocks application using the table component.

Chapter 19 continues the text component coverage where chapter 11 left off, and it discusses them at a much lower level.

Chapter 20 presents a complete RTF word processor application using `JTextPane`; several powerful custom dialogs are used to manage fonts, paragraph formatting, find and replace, and spell checking.

Chapter 21 discusses the pluggable look and feel architecture in detail and presents the construction of our own custom `LookAndFeel` implementation. This chapter includes examples of implementing support for existing look and feel, as well as information about implementing look and feel support for our own custom components.

C H A P T E R   1 5

Layered panes & custom MDI

15.1   JLAYEREDPANE

class javax.swing.JLayeredPane

JLayeredPane is a container with an almost infinite number of *layers* in which components reside. Not only is there no limit to the number or type of components in each layer, but components can overlap one another.

Components within each layer of a JLayeredPane are organized by *position*. When overlapping is necessary, those components with a higher-valued position are displayed *under* those with a lower-valued position. However, components in higher layers are displayed *over* all components residing in lower layers. It is important to get this overlapping hierarchy down early, as it can often be confusing.

Component position is numbered from –1 to the number of components in the layer minus one. If we have N components in a layer, the component at position 0 will overlap the component at position 1, and the component at position 1 will overlap the component at position 2, and so on. The lowest position is N–1; it represents the same position as –1. Figure 15.1 illustrates the concept of position within a layer.

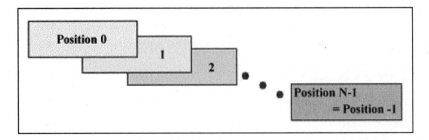

Figure 15.1 The position of components within a layer

The layer at which a component resides is often referred to as its *depth*. (Heavyweight components cannot conform to this notion of depth; see chapter 1 for more information.) Each layer is represented by an `Integer` object, and the position of a component within each layer is represented by an `int` value. The `JLayeredPane` class defines six different `Integer` object constants, representing what are intended to be commonly used layers: `FRAME_CONTENT_LAYER`, `DEFAULT_LAYER`, `PALETTE_LAYER`, `MODAL_LAYER`, `POPUP_LAYER`, and `DRAG_LAYER`.

Figure 15.2 illustrates the six standard layers and their overlap hierarchy.

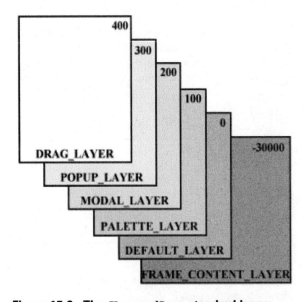

Figure 15.2 The `JLayeredPane` standard layers

We have just discussed a component's layer and position within a layer. Another value is also associated with each component within a `JLayeredPane`. This value is called the *index*. The index is the same as the position, if we were to ignore layers. That is, components are assigned indices by starting from position 0 in the highest layer and counting upward in position and downward in layer until all layers have been exhausted. The lowest component in the lowest layer will have index M–1, where M is the total number of components in the JLayeredPane. Similar to position, an index of –1 means the component is the bottom-most component. (The index is really a combination of a component's layer and position. As such, there are no methods to directly change a component's index within JLayeredPane, although we can always query a component for its current index.)

There are three ways to add a component to a JLayeredPane. (Note that there is no add method defined within JLayeredPane itself.) Each method used to add a component to a JLayeredPane is defined within the Container class (see the API documentation for more information).

1   To add a component to a JLayeredPane, we use the add(Component component) method. This places the component in the layer represented by the Integer object with value 0, the DEFAULT_LAYER.

2   To add a component to a specific layer of a JLayeredPane we use the add(Component component, Object obj) method. We pass this method our component and an Integer object representing the desired layer. For layer 10, we would pass it new Integer(10). If we wanted to place it on one of the standard layers, for instance the POPUP_LAYER, we could instead pass it JLayeredPane.POPUP_LAYER.

3   To add a component to a specific position within a specific layer, we use the add(Component component, Object obj, int index) method, in which the object is specified as above, and the int is the value representing the component's position within the layer.

15.2   USING JLAYEREDPANE TO ENHANCE INTERFACES

As we mentioned earlier in chapter 4, JLayeredPane can sometimes come in handy when we want to manually position and size components. Because its layout is null, it is not prone to the effects of resizing. Thus, when its parent is resized, a layered pane's children will stay in the same position and maintain the same size. However, there are other more interesting ways to use JLayeredPane in typical interfaces. For instance, we can easily place a nice, background image behind all of our components, giving life to an otherwise dull-looking panel.

Example 15.1

TestFrame.java

see \Chapter15\1

```
import javax.swing.*;
import java.awt.*;
import java.awt.event.*;

public class TestFrame extends JFrame
{
  public TestFrame() {
    super("JLayeredPane Demo");
    setSize(256,256);

    JPanel content = new JPanel();
    content.setLayout(new BoxLayout(content, BoxLayout.Y_AXIS));
```

Figure 15.3
Using `JLayeredPane` **to add**
a background image

```
content.setOpaque(false);

JLabel label1 = new JLabel("Username:");
label1.setForeground(Color.white);
content.add(label1);

JTextField field = new JTextField(15);
content.add(field);

JLabel label2 = new JLabel("Password:");
label2.setForeground(Color.white);
content.add(label2);

JPasswordField fieldPass = new JPasswordField(15);
content.add(fieldPass);

getContentPane().setLayout(new FlowLayout());
getContentPane().add(content);
((JPanel)getContentPane()).setOpaque(false);

ImageIcon earth = new ImageIcon("earth.jpg");
JLabel backlabel = new JLabel(earth);
getLayeredPane().add(backlabel,
  new Integer(Integer.MIN_VALUE));
backlabel.setBounds(0,0,earth.getIconWidth(),
  earth.getIconHeight());

WindowListener l = new WindowAdapter() {
  public void windowClosing(WindowEvent e) {
    System.exit(0);
  }
};
addWindowListener(l);

setVisible(true);
}
```

```
public static void main(String[] args) {
    new TestFrame();
  }
}
```

Most of this code should look familiar. We extend `JFrame` and create a new `JPanel` with a y-oriented `BoxLayout`. We make this panel non-opaque so our background image will show through, then we add four simple components: two `JLabels`, a `JTextField`, and a `JPasswordField`. We then set the layout of the `contentPane` to `FlowLayout` (remember that the `contentPane` has a `BorderLayout` by default), and add our panel to it. We also set the `contentPane`'s opaque property to `false`, thereby ensuring that our background will show through this panel as well. Finally, we create a `JLabel` containing our background image, add it to our `JFrame`'s `layeredPane`, and set its bounds based on the background image's size.

15.3 CREATING A CUSTOM *MDI*, PART I: DRAGGING PANELS

`JDesktopPane`, Swing's version of a multiple document interface (MDI), is the prime example of a complicated layering environment derived from `JLayeredPane`. One of the best ways to fully leverage the power of `JLayeredPane` is by constructing our own MDI environment from scratch. In doing so, we will learn how to build a powerful desktop environment that we understand from the inside out and have complete control over. The central component we will be developing, `InnerFrame`, will ultimately imitate the functionality of `JInternalFrame` (which is discussed in the next chapter). In chapter 21 we will continue to develop this component by adding support for all the major look-and-feels, as well as our own custom look-and-feel. The next five sections are centered around this component's construction; they proceed in a stepwise fashion.

NOTE   Due to the complexity of these examples, we suggest you have some time on your hands before attempting to understand each part. Some fragments are too mathematically dense (although they're not rigorous by any means) to warrant exhaustive explanation. In these cases we expect the reader to either trust that it does what we say it does, or bite the bullet and plunge through the code.

We start our construction of `InnerFrame` by implementing movable, closeable, and iconifiable functionality. `LayeredPaneDemo` is a simple class that we will use throughout each stage of development (with very few modifications) to load several `InnerFrames` and place them in a `JLayeredPane`.

Example 15.2

LayeredPaneDemo.java

see \Chapter15\2

```
import java.awt.*;
import java.awt.event.*;
import javax.swing.*;

import mdi.*;
```

 **❶** Package containing InnerFrame class

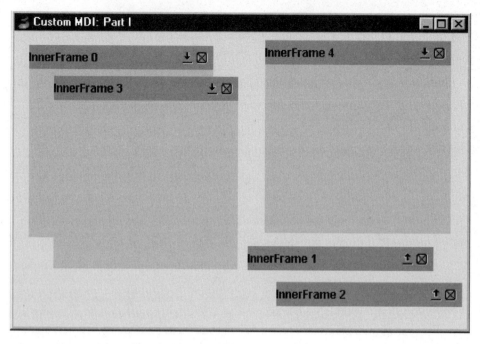

Figure 15.4 Custom MDI: part I

```
public class LayeredPaneDemo extends JFrame        ❶  Provides container for
{                                                      several InnerFrames
  public LayeredPaneDemo()
  {
    super("Custom MDI: Part I");
    setSize(570,400);
    getContentPane().setBackground(new Color(244,232,152));

    getLayeredPane().setOpaque(true);

    InnerFrame[] frames = new InnerFrame[5];
    for(int i=0; i<5; i++) {
      frames[i] = new InnerFrame("InnerFrame " + i);
      frames[i].setBounds(50+i*20, 50+i*20, 200, 200);
      getLayeredPane().add(frames[i]);
    }

    WindowListener l = new WindowAdapter() {
      public void windowClosing(WindowEvent e) {
        System.exit(0);
      }
    };

    Dimension dim = getToolkit().getScreenSize();
    setLocation(dim.width/2-getWidth()/2,
      dim.height/2-getHeight()/2);

    ImageIcon image = new ImageIcon("spiral.gif");
```

```
      setIconImage(image.getImage());
      addWindowListener(l);
      setVisible(true);
    }

    public static void main(String[] args) {
      new LayeredPaneDemo();
    }
  }
```

InnerFrame.java

see \Chapter15\2\mdi

```
package mdi;

import java.awt.*;
import java.awt.event.*;
import javax.swing.*;
import javax.swing.event.*;
import javax.swing.border.EmptyBorder;

public class InnerFrame
extends JPanel
{
  protected static String IMAGE_DIR = "mdi" + java.io.File.separator;
  protected static ImageIcon ICONIZE_BUTTON_ICON =
    new ImageIcon(IMAGE_DIR+"iconize.gif");
  protected static ImageIcon RESTORE_BUTTON_ICON =
    new ImageIcon(IMAGE_DIR+"restore.gif");
  protected static ImageIcon CLOSE_BUTTON_ICON =
    new ImageIcon(IMAGE_DIR+"close.gif");
  protected static ImageIcon PRESS_CLOSE_BUTTON_ICON =
    new ImageIcon(IMAGE_DIR+"pressclose.gif");
  protected static ImageIcon PRESS_RESTORE_BUTTON_ICON =
    new ImageIcon(IMAGE_DIR+"pressrestore.gif");
  protected static ImageIcon PRESS_ICONIZE_BUTTON_ICON =
    new ImageIcon(IMAGE_DIR+"pressiconize.gif");
  protected static final int WIDTH = 200;
  protected static final int HEIGHT = 200;
  protected static final int TITLE_BAR_HEIGHT = 25;
  protected static Color TITLE_BAR_BG_COLOR =
    new Color(108,190,116);

  protected String m_title;
  protected JLabel m_titleLabel;

  protected boolean m_iconified;

  protected JPanel m_titlePanel;
  protected JPanel m_contentPanel;
  protected JPanel m_buttonPanel;
  protected JPanel m_buttonWrapperPanel;

  protected InnerFrameButton m_iconize;
  protected InnerFrameButton m_close;
```

❷ Custom internal frame class

```
public InnerFrame(String title) {
  m_title = title;
  setLayout(new BorderLayout());
  createTitleBar();
  m_contentPanel = new JPanel();
  add(m_titlePanel, BorderLayout.NORTH);
  add(m_contentPanel, BorderLayout.CENTER);
}

public void toFront() {
  if (getParent() instanceof JLayeredPane)
    ((JLayeredPane) getParent()).moveToFront(this);
}

public void close() {
  if (getParent() instanceof JLayeredPane) {
    JLayeredPane jlp = (JLayeredPane) getParent();
    jlp.remove(InnerFrame.this);
    jlp.repaint();
  }
}

public void setIconified(boolean b) {
  m_iconified = b;
  if (b) {
    setBounds(getX(), getY(), WIDTH, TITLE_BAR_HEIGHT);
    m_iconize.setIcon(RESTORE_BUTTON_ICON);
    m_iconize.setPressedIcon(PRESS_RESTORE_BUTTON_ICON);
  }
  else {
    setBounds(getX(), getY(), WIDTH, HEIGHT);
    m_iconize.setIcon(ICONIZE_BUTTON_ICON);
    m_iconize.setPressedIcon(PRESS_ICONIZE_BUTTON_ICON);
    revalidate();
  }
}

public boolean isIconified() {
  return m_iconified;
}

//////////////////////////////////////////////
/////////////////// Title Bar //////////////////
//////////////////////////////////////////////

// Create the title bar m_titlePanel
public void createTitleBar() {
  m_titlePanel = new JPanel() {
    public Dimension getPreferredSize() {
      return new Dimension(InnerFrame.WIDTH,
        InnerFrame.TITLE_BAR_HEIGHT);
    }
  };
  m_titlePanel.setLayout(new BorderLayout());
  m_titlePanel.setOpaque(true);
  m_titlePanel.setBackground(TITLE_BAR_BG_COLOR);
```

3 Constructor puts title bar in North and content panel in Center

4 Moves InnerFrame to front when title bar is clicked

5 Closes InnerFrame from close button; repaints container after remove

6 "Iconify" here means to reduce the height to just show the title bar

7 Creates title bar with constant height and color, and with given title

```
    m_titleLabel = new JLabel(m_title);
    m_titleLabel.setForeground(Color.black);

    m_close = new InnerFrameButton(CLOSE_BUTTON_ICON);
    m_close.setPressedIcon(PRESS_CLOSE_BUTTON_ICON);
    m_close.addActionListener(new ActionListener() {
      public void actionPerformed(ActionEvent e) {
        InnerFrame.this.close();
      }
    });

    m_iconize = new InnerFrameButton(ICONIZE_BUTTON_ICON);
    m_iconize.setPressedIcon(PRESS_ICONIZE_BUTTON_ICON);
    m_iconize.addActionListener(new ActionListener() {
      public void actionPerformed(ActionEvent e) {
        InnerFrame.this.setIconified(
          !InnerFrame.this.isIconified());
      }
    });

    m_buttonWrapperPanel = new JPanel();
    m_buttonWrapperPanel.setOpaque(false);
    m_buttonPanel = new JPanel(new GridLayout(1,2));
    m_buttonPanel.setOpaque(false);
    m_buttonPanel.add(m_iconize);
    m_buttonPanel.add(m_close);
    m_buttonPanel.setAlignmentX(0.5f);
    m_buttonPanel.setAlignmentY(0.5f);
    m_buttonWrapperPanel.add(m_buttonPanel);

    m_titlePanel.add(m_titleLabel, BorderLayout.CENTER);
    m_titlePanel.add(m_buttonWrapperPanel, BorderLayout.EAST);

    InnerFrameTitleBarMouseAdapter iftbma =
      new InnerFrameTitleBarMouseAdapter(this);
    m_titlePanel.addMouseListener(iftbma);
    m_titlePanel.addMouseMotionListener(iftbma);
}

// Title bar mouse adapter for frame dragging
class InnerFrameTitleBarMouseAdapter
extends MouseInputAdapter
{
  InnerFrame m_if;
  int m_XDifference, m_YDifference;
  boolean m_dragging;

  public InnerFrameTitleBarMouseAdapter(InnerFrame inf) {
    m_if = inf;
  }

  public void mouseDragged(MouseEvent e) {
    if (m_dragging)
      m_if.setLocation(e.getX()-m_XDifference + getX(),
        e.getY()-m_YDifference + getY());
  }
```

8 Title bar button to close the InnerFrame

8 Title bar button to iconize or deiconize (restore) the InnerFrame

9 MouseAdapter for title bar to handle dragging of InnerFrame

```
    public void mousePressed(MouseEvent e) {
      m_if.toFront();
      m_XDifference = e.getX();
      m_YDifference = e.getY();
      m_dragging = true;
    }

    public void mouseReleased(MouseEvent e) {
      m_dragging = false;
    }
  }


  // Custom button class for title bar
  class InnerFrameButton extends JButton
  {
    Dimension m_dim;

    public InnerFrameButton(ImageIcon ii) {
      super(ii);
      m_dim = new Dimension(
        ii.getIconWidth(), ii.getIconHeight());
      setOpaque(false);
      setContentAreaFilled(false);
      setBorder(null);
    }

    public Dimension getPreferredSize() {
      return m_dim;
    }

    public Dimension getMinimumSize() {
      return m_dim;
    }

    public Dimension getMaximumSize() {
      return m_dim;
    }
  }
}
```

⑩ Button class for title bar buttons

15.3.1   Understanding the code

Class LayeredPaneDemo

❶ Most of the code in this class should look familiar. Note that the mdi package is imported; this is the package in which InnerFrame resides. The only purpose of LayeredPaneDemo is to provide a container for several InnerFrames. An array of five InnerFrames is created and each is placed in our JFrame's layered pane, at the default layer, in a cascading fashion. The layered pane's opaque property has been explicity enabled (setOpaque(true)) to ensure smooth repainting when dragging our InnerFrames by guaranteeing that all layered pane pixels will be painted (see chapter 2 for more about opacity).

Class mdi.InnerFrame

② This is our custom internal frame we will be expanding on throughout the remainder of this chapter. It is defined within the mdi package and it extends JPanel.

There are eleven class variables:

- String IMAGE_DIR: The directory header string used to locate images in the mdi package.
- ImageIcon ICONIZE_BUTTON_ICON: The icon used for the Iconify button ⬇.
- ImageIcon RESTORE_BUTTON_ICON: The icon used for the Restore button when it's in the iconified state (representing de-iconify) ⬆.
- ImageIcon CLOSE_BUTTON_ICON: The icon used for the Close button ⊠.
- ImageIcon PRESS_CLOSE_BUTTON_ICON: The icon used for the Close button when it is in the pressed state ⊠.
- ImageIcon PRESS_RESTORE_BUTTON_ICON: The icon used for the Restore button when it's in both the iconified state (representing de-iconify) and the pressed state ⬆.
- ImageIcon PRESS_ICONIZE_BUTTON_ICON: The icon used for the Iconify button when it's in the pressed state ⬇.
- int WIDTH: InnerFrame's width.
- int HEIGHT: InnerFrame's height.
- int TITLE_BAR_HEIGHT: The default height of the title bar.
- Color TITLE_BAR_BG_COLOR: The default Color of the title bar.

There are nine instance variables:

- String m_title: The title bar String.
- JLabel m_titleLabel: The label contained in the title bar that displays the title string, m_title.
- boolean m_iconified: Returns true when it's in the iconified state.
- JPanel m_titlePanel: The panel representing the title bar.
- JPanel m_contentPanel: The central InnerFrame container.
- JPanel m_buttonPanel: A small panel for frame buttons.
- JPanel m_buttonWrapperPanel: The panel that surrounds m_buttonPanel to allow correct alignment.
- InnerFrameButton m_iconize: The custom frame button for iconification/ de-iconification.
- InnerFrameButton m_close: The custom frame button for closing.

③ The InnerFrame constructor takes a title String as its only parameter and sets the title variable accordingly. We use a BorderLayout and call our createTitleBar() method to initialize m_titlePanel, which represents our title bar (see below). We then initialize m_contentPanel, which acts as our frame's central container. We add these components to InnerFrame in the NORTH and CENTER regions, respectively.

④ The toFront() method is responsible for moving InnerFrame to the frontmost position in its layer. This is called from m_titlePanel's mouse adapter when the title bar is pressed, as we will see below. This will only function if InnerFrame is within a JLayeredPane (or a JLayeredPane subclass such as JDesktopPane).

⑤ The `close()` method is responsible for removing an `InnerFrame` from its parent container. This is called when the Close button, `m_close`, is clicked within the title bar. We specifically only allow removal to work from within a `JLayeredPane`. If this component is added to any other container, we assume that it is not meant for removal in this fashion.

⑥ The `setIconified()` method controls iconification and deiconification (often called restore) and reduces the height of `InnerFrame` to that of the title bar. When an iconification occurs we change the `m_iconize` button's regular and pressed state icons to those representing de-iconification. Similarly, when a de-iconify occurs we restore the original height of `InnerFrame` and replace the icons with those representing iconification.

⑦ The `createTitleBar()` method is responsible for populating and laying out `m_titlePanel`, our title bar. It starts by initializing `m_titlePanel` with a preferred size according to our `WIDTH` and `TITLE_BAR_HEIGHT` constants. `m_titlePanel` uses a `BorderLayout` and its background is set to `TITLE_BAR_BG_COLOR`. (Note that these hard-coded values will be replaced by variables in future stages of development.) `m_titleLabel` is created with the `m_title` String that was passed to the `InnerFrame` constructor.

⑧ The `m_close` button is an instance of `InnerFrameButton` (see below) and it uses custom `ImageIcons` for normal and pressed states. An `ActionListener` is added to simply invoke `close()` when this button is pressed. The `m_iconize` button is created in a similar fashion, except its `ActionListener` is constructed to invoke the `setIconified()` method. Once these buttons are constructed, we place them in `m_buttonPanel` using a `GridLayout`, and we place this panel within our `m_buttonWrapperPanel`, which uses a `FlowLayout`. This allows for perfect button alignment, using `JComponent`'s `setAlignmentX/Y()` methods, while also enforcing equal size among buttons no greater than their preferred sizes.

Finally, the `createTitleBar()` method ends by creating an `InnerFrameTitleBarMouseAdapter` and attaches it to `m_titlePanel`.

Class mdi.InnerFrame.InnerFrameTitleBarMouseAdapter

⑨ This class extends `javax.swing.event.MouseInputAdapter` and holds a reference to the `InnerFrame` it is associated with. The function of `mousePressed()` is to obtain the base coordinate offsets, `m_XDifference` and `m_YDifference`, for use in the `mouseDragged()` method, and to set the `m_dragging` flag to `true` (because a mouse press always precedes a mouse drag). The `mouseDragged()` method is called whenever an `InnerFrame` is dragged. This method starts by testing whether the `m_dragging` flag is set to `true`. If it is, `InnerFrame` is moved to a new location. To calculate the new position as it is dragged, this method uses the current `InnerFrame` coordinates, `getX()` and `getY()`, plus the difference of the `mouseDragged()` event coordinates, `e.getX()` and `e.getY()`, and the base offset coordinates, `m_XDifference` and `m_YDifference`. These base offset coordinates, which are initialized within the `mousePressed()` method, are necessary to keep mouse position at a constant x- and y-offset from the upper left-hand corner of `InnerFrame`. The `mouseReleased()` method's only function is to set the `m_dragging` flag to `false` when the mouse button is released.

Class mdi.InnerFrame.InnerFrameButton

⑩ The `InnerFrameButton` class extends `JButton` and its constructor takes an `ImageIcon` parameter. It uses this icon to construct a `Dimension` instance, which is in turn used for the button's minimum, maximum, and preferred sizes. The button is then set to non-opaque, and we call `setContentAreaFilled(false)` to guarantee that its background will never be filled. We also remove its border to give it an embedded look.

15.3.2 Running the code

Figure 15.4 shows `LayeredPaneDemo` in action. Experiment with moving, iconifying, de-iconifying, and closing our custom frames. A frame can be selected even when its title bar lies behind the content of another frame. Mouse events pass right through our frame's content panels. This is just one of the many flaws that need to be accounted for. Also notice that we can drag any frame completely outside of the layered pane. The most immediately noticeable functionality that `InnerFrame` lacks is resizability. This is the single-most difficult feature to implement, and it is the subject of the next section.

15.4 CREATING A CUSTOM MDI, PART II: RESIZABILITY

In this stage, four distinct components are added to `InnerFrame`'s NORTH, SOUTH, EAST, and WEST regions. Each of these components, defined by the `NorthResizeEdge`, `SouthResizeEdge`, `EastResizeEdge`, and `WestResizeEdge` inner classes, respectively, provide the functionality needed to allow for proper resizing in all directions. The title bar and content panel of `InnerFrame` are now wrapped inside another panel that is placed in `InnerFrame`'s CENTER region. Additionally, we add a label containing an icon to the WEST region of the title bar, and allow dynamic title bar height based on the size of the icon used in that label.

Example 15.3

InnerFrame.java

see \Chapter15\3\mdi

```
package mdi;

import java.awt.*;
import java.awt.event.*;
import javax.swing.*;
import javax.swing.event.*;
import javax.swing.border.EmptyBorder;

public class InnerFrame
extends JPanel
{
  // Unchanged code

  protected static ImageIcon DEFAULT_FRAME_ICON =
    new ImageIcon(IMAGE_DIR+"default.gif");
  protected static int BORDER_THICKNESS = 4;
  protected static int WIDTH = 200;
  protected static int HEIGHT = 200;
  protected static int TITLE_BAR_HEIGHT = 25;
  protected static int FRAME_ICON_PADDING = 2;
  protected static int ICONIZED_WIDTH = 150;
  protected static Color TITLE_BAR_BG_COLOR =
```

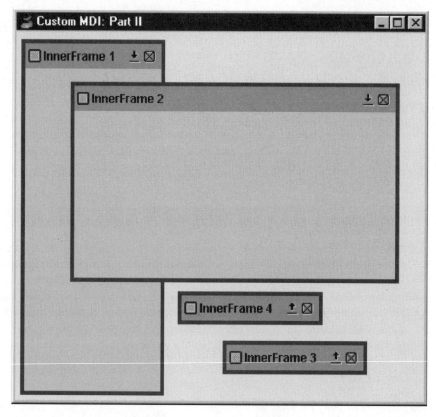

Figure 15.5   Custom MDI: part II with default icon

```
   new Color(108,190,116);
 protected static Color BORDER_COLOR = new Color(8,90,16);

 protected int m_titleBarHeight = TITLE_BAR_HEIGHT;
 protected int m_width = WIDTH;
 protected int m_height = HEIGHT;
 protected int m_iconizedWidth = ICONIZED_WIDTH;

 protected String m_title;
 protected JLabel m_titleLabel;
 protected JLabel m_iconLabel;

 protected boolean m_iconified;

 protected boolean m_iconizeable;
 protected boolean m_resizeable;
 protected boolean m_closeable;

 // Used to wrap title bar and contentPanel
 protected JPanel m_frameContentPanel;

 protected JPanel m_titlePanel;
 protected JPanel m_contentPanel;
```

Figure 15.6 Custom MDI: part II with large icon

```
protected JPanel m_buttonPanel;
protected JPanel m_buttonWrapperPanel;

protected InnerFrameButton m_iconize;
protected InnerFrameButton m_close;

protected ImageIcon m_frameIcon = DEFAULT_FRAME_ICON;

protected NorthResizeEdge m_northResizer;
protected SouthResizeEdge m_southResizer;
protected EastResizeEdge m_eastResizer;
protected WestResizeEdge m_westResizer;

public InnerFrame() {
  this("");
}

public InnerFrame(String title) {
  this(title, null);
}

public InnerFrame(String title, ImageIcon frameIcon) {
  this(title, frameIcon, true, true, true);
}
```

❶ Calls second constructor

❶ Calls fourth constructor

❶ Calls third constructor

```java
public InnerFrame(String title, ImageIcon frameIcon,
 boolean resizeable, boolean iconizeable, boolean closeable) {
  super.setLayout(new BorderLayout());
  attachNorthResizeEdge();
  attachSouthResizeEdge();
  attachEastResizeEdge();
  attachWestResizeEdge();
  populateInnerFrame();

  setTitle(title);
  setResizeable(resizeable);
  setIconizeable(iconizeable);
  setCloseable(closeable);
  if (frameIcon != null)
    setFrameIcon(frameIcon);
}

protected void populateInnerFrame() {
  m_frameContentPanel = new JPanel();
  m_frameContentPanel.setLayout(new BorderLayout());
  createTitleBar();
  m_contentPanel = new JPanel();
  m_frameContentPanel.add(m_titlePanel, BorderLayout.NORTH);
  m_frameContentPanel.add(m_contentPanel, BorderLayout.CENTER);
  super.add(m_frameContentPanel, BorderLayout.CENTER);
}

public Component add(Component c) {
  return((m_contentPanel == null)
    ? null : m_contentPanel.add(c));
}

public void setLayout(LayoutManager mgr) {
  if (m_contentPanel != null)
    m_contentPanel.setLayout(mgr);
}

// Unchanged code from example 15.2

public boolean isIconizeable() {
  return m_iconizeable;
}

public void setIconizeable(boolean b) {
  m_iconizeable = b;
  m_iconize.setVisible(b);
  m_titlePanel.revalidate();
}

public boolean isCloseable() {
  return m_closeable;
}

public void setCloseable(boolean b) {
  m_closeable = b;
  m_close.setVisible(b);
  m_titlePanel.revalidate();
```

② Does real work; sets title, frame icon, resizable and closeable flags

③ Overridden from JComponent to operate directly on content pane

④ Sets iconizeable flag and repaints buttons

④ Sets closeable flag and repaints buttons

```
    }
  public boolean isIconified() {
    return m_iconified;
  }

  public void setIconified(boolean b) {
    m_iconified = b;
    if (b) {
      m_width = getWidth();      // remember width
      m_height = getHeight();    // remember height
      setBounds(getX(), getY(), ICONIZED_WIDTH,
        m_titleBarHeight + 2*BORDER_THICKNESS);
      m_iconize.setIcon(RESTORE_BUTTON_ICON);
      m_iconize.setPressedIcon(PRESS_RESTORE_BUTTON_ICON);
      setResizeable(false);
    }
    else {
      setBounds(getX(), getY(), m_width, m_height);
      m_iconize.setIcon(ICONIZE_BUTTON_ICON);
      m_iconize.setPressedIcon(PRESS_ICONIZE_BUTTON_ICON);
      setResizeable(true);
    }
    revalidate();
  }

  /////////////////////////////////////////
  ///////////////// Title Bar //////////////////
  /////////////////////////////////////////
  public void setFrameIcon(ImageIcon fi) {
    m_frameIcon = fi;

    if (fi != null) {
      if (m_frameIcon.getIconHeight() > TITLE_BAR_HEIGHT)
        setTitleBarHeight(
          m_frameIcon.getIconHeight() + 2*FRAME_ICON_PADDING);
      m_iconLabel.setIcon(m_frameIcon);
    }
    else setTitleBarHeight(TITLE_BAR_HEIGHT);
    revalidate();
  }

  public ImageIcon getFrameIcon() {
    return m_frameIcon;
  }

  public void setTitle(String s) {
    m_title = s;
    m_titleLabel.setText(s);
    m_titlePanel.repaint();
  }

  public String getTitle() {
    return m_title;
```

5 Changes
iconified state

5 Stores width
and height for
later restore

5 Turns off
resize listener

5 Restores to
saved width
and height

5 Turns resize
listener back on

6 Sets new title
bar icon and
sets new height
from icon height

```
    }

    public void setTitleBarHeight(int h) {
      m_titleBarHeight = h;
    }

    public int getTitleBarHeight() {
      return m_titleBarHeight;
    }

    // Create the title bar: m_titlePanel
    protected void createTitleBar() {
      m_titlePanel = new JPanel() {
        public Dimension getPreferredSize() {
          return new Dimension(InnerFrame.this.getWidth(),
            m_titleBarHeight);
        }
      };
      m_titlePanel.setLayout(new BorderLayout());
      m_titlePanel.setOpaque(true);
      m_titlePanel.setBackground(TITLE_BAR_BG_COLOR);

      m_titleLabel = new JLabel();
      m_titleLabel.setForeground(Color.black);

      // Unchanged code from example 15.2

      m_iconLabel = new JLabel();
      m_iconLabel.setBorder(new EmptyBorder(
        FRAME_ICON_PADDING, FRAME_ICON_PADDING,
        FRAME_ICON_PADDING, FRAME_ICON_PADDING));
      if (m_frameIcon != null)
        m_iconLabel.setIcon(m_frameIcon);

      m_titlePanel.add(m_titleLabel, BorderLayout.CENTER);
      m_titlePanel.add(m_buttonWrapperPanel, BorderLayout.EAST);
      m_titlePanel.add(m_iconLabel, BorderLayout.WEST);

      InnerFrameTitleBarMouseAdapter iftbma =
        new InnerFrameTitleBarMouseAdapter(this);
      m_titlePanel.addMouseListener(iftbma);
      m_titlePanel.addMouseMotionListener(iftbma);
    }

    // Unchanged code from example 15.2

    /////////////////////////////////////////////////
    ///////////////// Resizability /////////////////
    /////////////////////////////////////////////////

    public boolean isResizeable() {
      return m_resizeable;
    }

    public void setResizeable(boolean b) {
      if (!b && m_resizeable == true) {
        m_northResizer.removeMouseListener(m_northResizer);
```

7 Places icon label in EmptyBorder

```java
      m_northResizer.removeMouseMotionListener(m_northResizer);
      m_southResizer.removeMouseListener(m_southResizer);
      m_southResizer.removeMouseMotionListener(m_southResizer);
      m_eastResizer.removeMouseListener(m_eastResizer);
      m_eastResizer.removeMouseMotionListener(m_eastResizer);
      m_westResizer.removeMouseListener(m_westResizer);
      m_westResizer.removeMouseMotionListener(m_westResizer);
    }
    else if (m_resizeable == false) {
      m_northResizer.addMouseListener(m_northResizer);
      m_northResizer.addMouseMotionListener(m_northResizer);
      m_southResizer.addMouseListener(m_southResizer);
      m_southResizer.addMouseMotionListener(m_southResizer);
      m_eastResizer.addMouseListener(m_eastResizer);
      m_eastResizer.addMouseMotionListener(m_eastResizer);
      m_westResizer.addMouseListener(m_westResizer);
      m_westResizer.addMouseMotionListener(m_westResizer);
    }
    m_resizeable = b;
  }

  protected void attachNorthResizeEdge() {
    m_northResizer = new NorthResizeEdge(this);
    super.add(m_northResizer, BorderLayout.NORTH);
  }

  protected void attachSouthResizeEdge() {
    m_southResizer = new SouthResizeEdge(this);
    super.add(m_southResizer, BorderLayout.SOUTH);
  }

  protected void attachEastResizeEdge() {
    m_eastResizer = new EastResizeEdge(this);
    super.add(m_eastResizer, BorderLayout.EAST);
  }

  protected void attachWestResizeEdge() {
    m_westResizer = new WestResizeEdge(this);
    super.add(m_westResizer, BorderLayout.WEST);
  }

  class EastResizeEdge extends JPanel
  implements MouseListener, MouseMotionListener {
    private int WIDTH = BORDER_THICKNESS;
    private int MIN_WIDTH = ICONIZED_WIDTH;
    private boolean m_dragging;
    private JComponent m_resizeComponent;

    protected EastResizeEdge(JComponent c) {
      m_resizeComponent = c;
      setOpaque(true);
      setBackground(BORDER_COLOR);
    }

    public Dimension getPreferredSize() {
```

8 Tall, thin Eastern resize border

```
      return new Dimension(WIDTH, m_resizeComponent.getHeight());
    }

    public void mouseClicked(MouseEvent e) {}
    public void mouseMoved(MouseEvent e) {}
    public void mouseReleased(MouseEvent e) {
      m_dragging = false;
    }

    public void mouseDragged(MouseEvent e) {
      if (m_resizeComponent.getWidth() + e.getX() >= MIN_WIDTH)
        m_resizeComponent.setBounds(m_resizeComponent.getX(),
          m_resizeComponent.getY(),
          m_resizeComponent.getWidth() + e.getX(),
          m_resizeComponent.getHeight());
      else
        m_resizeComponent.setBounds(m_resizeComponent.getX(),
          m_resizeComponent.getY(),
          MIN_WIDTH, m_resizeComponent.getHeight());
      m_resizeComponent.validate();
    }

    public void mouseEntered(MouseEvent e) {
      if (!m_dragging)
        setCursor(Cursor.getPredefinedCursor(
          Cursor.E_RESIZE_CURSOR));
    }

    public void mouseExited(MouseEvent e) {
      if (!m_dragging)
        setCursor(Cursor.getPredefinedCursor(
          Cursor.DEFAULT_CURSOR));
    }

    public void mousePressed(MouseEvent e) {
      toFront();
      m_dragging = true;
    }
  }

class WestResizeEdge extends JPanel
implements MouseListener, MouseMotionListener {
  private int WIDTH = BORDER_THICKNESS;
  private int MIN_WIDTH = ICONIZED_WIDTH;
  private int m_dragX, m_rightX;
  private boolean m_dragging;
  private JComponent m_resizeComponent;

  protected WestResizeEdge(JComponent c) {
    m_resizeComponent = c;
    setOpaque(true);
    setBackground(BORDER_COLOR);
  }

  public Dimension getPreferredSize() {
```

9 If not already dragging, sets to East resize cursor

10 Moves InnerFrame to front and sets dragging flag

11 Like EastResizeEdge, but also can move frame position

```
        return new Dimension(WIDTH, m_resizeComponent.getHeight());
    }
    public void mouseClicked(MouseEvent e) {}
    public void mouseMoved(MouseEvent e) {}

    public void mouseReleased(MouseEvent e) {
      m_dragging = false;
    }

    public void mouseDragged(MouseEvent e) {
      if (m_resizeComponent.getWidth()-
        (e.getX()-m_dragX) >= MIN_WIDTH)
        m_resizeComponent.setBounds(
          m_resizeComponent.getX() + (e.getX()-m_dragX),
          m_resizeComponent.getY(),
          m_resizeComponent.getWidth()-(e.getX()-m_dragX),
          m_resizeComponent.getHeight());
      else
        if (m_resizeComponent.getX() + MIN_WIDTH < m_rightX)
          m_resizeComponent.setBounds(m_rightX-MIN_WIDTH,
            m_resizeComponent.getY(),
            MIN_WIDTH, m_resizeComponent.getHeight());
        else
          m_resizeComponent.setBounds(m_resizeComponent.getX(),
            m_resizeComponent.getY(),
            MIN_WIDTH, m_resizeComponent.getHeight());
      m_resizeComponent.validate();
    }

    public void mouseEntered(MouseEvent e) {
      if (!m_dragging)
        setCursor(Cursor.getPredefinedCursor(
          Cursor.W_RESIZE_CURSOR));
    }

    public void mouseExited(MouseEvent e) {
      if (!m_dragging)
        setCursor(Cursor.getPredefinedCursor(
          Cursor.DEFAULT_CURSOR));
    }

    public void mousePressed(MouseEvent e) {
      toFront();
      m_rightX = m_resizeComponent.getX() +
        m_resizeComponent.getWidth();
      m_dragging = true;
      m_dragX = e.getX();
    }
}
class NorthResizeEdge extends JPanel
implements MouseListener, MouseMotionListener {
  private static final int NORTH = 0;
  private static final int NORTHEAST = 1;
  private static final int NORTHWEST = 2;
```

⑫ Like WestResizeEdge, but left and right ends can also resize Northwest and Northeast

```
private int CORNER = 10;
private int HEIGHT = BORDER_THICKNESS;
private int MIN_WIDTH = ICONIZED_WIDTH;
private int MIN_HEIGHT = TITLE_BAR_HEIGHT+(2*HEIGHT);
private int m_width, m_dragX, m_dragY, m_rightX, m_lowerY;
private boolean m_dragging;
private JComponent m_resizeComponent;
private int m_mode;

protected NorthResizeEdge(JComponent c) {
  m_resizeComponent = c;
  setOpaque(true);
  setBackground(BORDER_COLOR);
}

public Dimension getPreferredSize() {
  return new Dimension(m_resizeComponent.getWidth(), HEIGHT);
}

public void mouseClicked(MouseEvent e) {}

public void mouseMoved(MouseEvent e) {
  if (!m_dragging) {
    if (e.getX() < CORNER) {
      setCursor(Cursor.getPredefinedCursor(
        Cursor.NW_RESIZE_CURSOR));
    }
    else if(e.getX() > getWidth()-CORNER) {
      setCursor(Cursor.getPredefinedCursor(
        Cursor.NE_RESIZE_CURSOR));
    }
    else {
      setCursor(Cursor.getPredefinedCursor(
        Cursor.N_RESIZE_CURSOR));
    }
  }
}

public void mouseReleased(MouseEvent e) {
  m_dragging = false;
}

public void mouseDragged(MouseEvent e) {
  int h = m_resizeComponent.getHeight();
  int w = m_resizeComponent.getWidth();
  int x = m_resizeComponent.getX();
  int y = m_resizeComponent.getY();
  int ex = e.getX();
  int ey = e.getY();
  switch (m_mode) {
    case NORTH:
      if (h-(ey-m_dragY) >= MIN_HEIGHT)
        m_resizeComponent.setBounds(x, y + (ey-m_dragY),
          w, h-(ey-m_dragY));
      else
        m_resizeComponent.setBounds(x,
```

12 Sets Northwest resize cursor

12 Sets Northeast resize cursor

12 Sets North resize cursor

```
                         m_lowerY-MIN_HEIGHT, w, MIN_HEIGHT);
            break;
        case NORTHEAST:
          if (h-(ey-m_dragY) >= MIN_HEIGHT
          && w + (ex-(getWidth()-CORNER)) >= MIN_WIDTH)
            m_resizeComponent.setBounds(x,
                y + (ey-m_dragY), w + (ex-(getWidth()-CORNER)),
                  h-(ey-m_dragY));
          else if (h-(ey-m_dragY) >= MIN_HEIGHT
          && !(w + (ex-(getWidth()-CORNER)) >= MIN_WIDTH))
            m_resizeComponent.setBounds(x,
                y + (ey-m_dragY), MIN_WIDTH, h-(ey-m_dragY));
          else if (!(h-(ey-m_dragY) >= MIN_HEIGHT)
          && w + (ex-(getWidth()-CORNER)) >= MIN_WIDTH)
            m_resizeComponent.setBounds(x,
                m_lowerY-MIN_HEIGHT, w + (ex-(getWidth()-CORNER)),
                  MIN_HEIGHT);
          else
            m_resizeComponent.setBounds(x,
                m_lowerY-MIN_HEIGHT, MIN_WIDTH, MIN_HEIGHT);
          break;
        case NORTHWEST:
          if (h-(ey-m_dragY) >= MIN_HEIGHT
          && w-(ex-m_dragX) >= MIN_WIDTH)
            m_resizeComponent.setBounds(x + (ex-m_dragX),
                y + (ey-m_dragY), w-(ex-m_dragX),
                  h-(ey-m_dragY));
          else if (h-(ey-m_dragY) >= MIN_HEIGHT
          && !(w-(ex-m_dragX) >= MIN_WIDTH)) {
            if (x + MIN_WIDTH < m_rightX)
              m_resizeComponent.setBounds(m_rightX-MIN_WIDTH,
                  y + (ey-m_dragY), MIN_WIDTH, h-(ey-m_dragY));
            else
              m_resizeComponent.setBounds(x,
                  y + (ey-m_dragY), w, h-(ey-m_dragY));
          }
          else if (!(h-(ey-m_dragY) >= MIN_HEIGHT)
          && w-(ex-m_dragX) >= MIN_WIDTH)
            m_resizeComponent.setBounds(x + (ex-m_dragX),
                m_lowerY-MIN_HEIGHT, w-(ex-m_dragX), MIN_HEIGHT);
          else
            m_resizeComponent.setBounds(m_rightX-MIN_WIDTH,
                m_lowerY-MIN_HEIGHT, MIN_WIDTH, MIN_HEIGHT);
          break;
      }
    m_rightX = x + w;
    m_resizeComponent.validate();
}

public void mouseEntered(MouseEvent e) {
    mouseMoved(e);
}
```

13 **Quickly re-layouts resize component**

```java
  public void mouseExited(MouseEvent e) {
    if (!m_dragging)
      setCursor(Cursor.getPredefinedCursor(
        Cursor.DEFAULT_CURSOR));
  }

  public void mousePressed(MouseEvent e) {
    toFront();
    m_dragging = true;
    m_dragX = e.getX();
    m_dragY = e.getY();
    m_lowerY = m_resizeComponent.getY()
      + m_resizeComponent.getHeight();
    if (e.getX() < CORNER) {
      m_mode = NORTHWEST;
    }
    else if(e.getX() > getWidth()-CORNER) {
      m_mode = NORTHEAST;
    }
    else {
      m_mode = NORTH;
    }
  }
}

class SouthResizeEdge extends JPanel
implements MouseListener, MouseMotionListener {
  private static final int SOUTH = 0;
  private static final int SOUTHEAST = 1;
  private static final int SOUTHWEST = 2;
  private int CORNER = 10;
  private int HEIGHT = BORDER_THICKNESS;
  private int MIN_WIDTH = ICONIZED_WIDTH;
  private int MIN_HEIGHT = TITLE_BAR_HEIGHT+(2*HEIGHT);
  private int m_width, m_dragX, m_dragY, m_rightX;
  private boolean m_dragging;
  private JComponent m_resizeComponent;
  private int m_mode;

  protected SouthResizeEdge(JComponent c) {
    m_resizeComponent = c;
    setOpaque(true);
    setBackground(BORDER_COLOR);
  }

  public Dimension getPreferredSize() {
    return new Dimension(m_resizeComponent.getWidth(), HEIGHT);
  }

  public void mouseClicked(MouseEvent e) {}

  public void mouseMoved(MouseEvent e) {
    if (!m_dragging) {
      if (e.getX() < CORNER) {
        setCursor(Cursor.getPredefinedCursor(
```

⓬ Like NorthResizeEdge, but resizes to Southwest, South, and Southeast

```
          Cursor.SW_RESIZE_CURSOR));
        }
        else if(e.getX() > getWidth()-CORNER) {
          setCursor(Cursor.getPredefinedCursor(
            Cursor.SE_RESIZE_CURSOR));
        }
        else {
          setCursor(Cursor.getPredefinedCursor(
            Cursor.S_RESIZE_CURSOR));
        }
      }
    }
  }

  public void mouseReleased(MouseEvent e) {
    m_dragging = false;
  }

  public void mouseDragged(MouseEvent e) {
    int h = m_resizeComponent.getHeight();
    int w = m_resizeComponent.getWidth();
    int x = m_resizeComponent.getX();
    int y = m_resizeComponent.getY();
    int ex = e.getX();
    int ey = e.getY();
    switch (m_mode) {
      case SOUTH:
        if (h+(ey-m_dragY) >= MIN_HEIGHT)
          m_resizeComponent.setBounds(x, y, w, h+(ey-m_dragY));
        else
          m_resizeComponent.setBounds(x, y, w, MIN_HEIGHT);
        break;
      case SOUTHEAST:
        if (h+(ey-m_dragY) >= MIN_HEIGHT
          && w + (ex-(getWidth()-CORNER)) >= MIN_WIDTH)
          m_resizeComponent.setBounds(x, y,
            w + (ex-(getWidth()-CORNER)), h+(ey-m_dragY));
        else if (h+(ey-m_dragY) >= MIN_HEIGHT
          && !(w + (ex-(getWidth()-CORNER)) >= MIN_WIDTH))
          m_resizeComponent.setBounds(x, y,
            MIN_WIDTH, h+(ey-m_dragY));
        else if (!(h+(ey-m_dragY) >= MIN_HEIGHT)
          && w + (ex-(getWidth()-CORNER)) >= MIN_WIDTH)
          m_resizeComponent.setBounds(x, y,
            w + (ex-(getWidth()-CORNER)), MIN_HEIGHT);
        else
          m_resizeComponent.setBounds(x,
            y, MIN_WIDTH, MIN_HEIGHT);
        break;
      case SOUTHWEST:
        if (h+(ey-m_dragY) >= MIN_HEIGHT
          && w-(ex-m_dragX) >= MIN_WIDTH)
          m_resizeComponent.setBounds(x + (ex-m_dragX), y,
            w-(ex-m_dragX), h+(ey-m_dragY));
```

```java
          else if (h+(ey-m_dragY) >= MIN_HEIGHT
            && !(w-(ex-m_dragX) >= MIN_WIDTH)) {
            if (x + MIN_WIDTH < m_rightX)
              m_resizeComponent.setBounds(m_rightX-MIN_WIDTH, y,
                MIN_WIDTH, h+(ey-m_dragY));
            else
              m_resizeComponent.setBounds(x, y, w,
                h+(ey-m_dragY));
          }
          else if (!(h+(ey-m_dragY) >= MIN_HEIGHT)
            && w-(ex-m_dragX) >= MIN_WIDTH)
            m_resizeComponent.setBounds(x + (ex-m_dragX), y,
              w-(ex-m_dragX), MIN_HEIGHT);
          else
            m_resizeComponent.setBounds(m_rightX-MIN_WIDTH,
              y, MIN_WIDTH, MIN_HEIGHT);
          break;
      }
    m_rightX = x + w;
    m_resizeComponent.validate();
  }

  public void mouseEntered(MouseEvent e) {
    mouseMoved(e);
  }

  public void mouseExited(MouseEvent e) {
    if (!m_dragging)
      setCursor(Cursor.getPredefinedCursor(
        Cursor.DEFAULT_CURSOR));
  }

  public void mousePressed(MouseEvent e) {
    toFront();
    m_dragging = true;
    m_dragX = e.getX();
    m_dragY = e.getY();
    if (e.getX() < CORNER) {
      m_mode = SOUTHWEST;
    }
    else if(e.getX() > getWidth()-CORNER) {
      m_mode = SOUTHEAST;
    }
    else {
      m_mode = SOUTH;
    }
  }
  }
}
```

15.4.1　Understanding the code

Class InnerFrame

There are five new class variables:

- `ImageIcon DEFAULT_FRAME_ICON`: The default image used for the frame icon = .
- `int BORDER_THICKNESS`: The default thickness of the resize edges (borders).
- `int FRAME_ICON_PADDING`: The default thickness of the padding around the title bar icon label.
- `int ICONIZED_WIDTH`: The default width in the iconified state.
- `Color BORDER_COLOR`: The default resize border background color.

These are the new instance variables:

- `int m_titleBarHeight`: The title bar height.
- `int m_width`: Used for recalling the frame's previous width when deiconifying.
- `int m_height`: Used for recalling the frame's previous height when deiconifying.
- `int m_iconizedWidth`: The frame width in the iconified state.
- `JLabel m_iconLabel`: The label used to display the frame icon in the title bar.
- `boolean m_iconizeable`: Determines whether the frame can be iconified.
- `boolean m_resizable`: Determines whether the frame is resizable.
- `boolean m_closeable`: Determines whether the frame is closeable.
- `JPanel m_frameContentPanel`: Used to wrap the title bar and `m_contentPanel` for placement in `InnerFrame`'s CENTER region.
- `ImageIcon m_frameIcon`: The frame icon displayed by `m_iconLabel` in the title bar.
- `NorthResizeEdge m_northResizer`: Used for north, northeast, and northwest resizing.
- `SouthResizeEdge m_southResizer`: Used for south, southeast, and southwest resizing.
- `EastResizeEdge m_eastResizer`: Used for east resizing.
- `WestResizeEdge m_westResizer`: Used for west resizing.

❶ There are now four `InnerFrame` constructors. The first creates an `InnerFrame` with no title and the default frame icon. The second creates an `InnerFrame` with a title and the default icon, and the third creates one with both a title and a specified frame icon. The first three constructors all end up calling the fourth to do the actual work.

❷ The fourth `InnerFrame` constructor calls four methods to attach our custom resize components to its edges. Then our `populateInnerFrame()` method is called; it is responsible for encapsulating the title bar and content panel in `m_frameContentPanel`, which is then added to the CENTER of `InnerFrame`. The constructor ends by calling methods to set the title, frame icon, and resizable, iconizeable, and closeable properties (discussed below).

❸ The `add()` and `setLayout()` methods of `JComponent` are overridden to perform these actions on the content panel contained inside `m_frameContentPanel`. Thus, anything we add to `InnerFrame` will be placed in `m_contentPanel`, and any layout we assign to `InnerFrame` will actually be assigned to `m_contentPanel`.

> **NOTE**　This functionality is not on par with fundamental Swing containers such as `JFrame` and `JInternalFrame`, which use a `JRootPane` to manage their contents. We will fix this in the next section by implementing the `RootPaneContainer` interface.

4 The setIconizeable() and setCloseable() methods set their respective properties and hide or show the corresponding title bar buttons using setVisible(). We call revalidate() to perform any layout changes that may be necessary after a button is shown or hidden.

5 The setIconified() method is modified to store the width and height of InnerFrame before it is iconified. The size of an iconified InnerFrame is now determined by the title bar height, which is in turn determined by the frame icon size and the thickness of the resize edges:

```
setBounds(getX(), getY(), ICONIZED_WIDTH,
  m_titleBarHeight + 2*BORDER_THICKNESS);
```

Whenever an iconification occurs, we call setResizable(false) to remove mouse listeners from each resize edge. If a deiconification occurs, we call setResizable(true) to add mouse listeners back to each resize edge. The width and height saved in an iconification are also used to set the size of InnerFrame when it is deiconified.

6 Several methods are added to the title bar code. setFrameIcon() is responsible for replacing the icon in the title bar icon label, m_iconLabel, and for calculating the new title bar height based on this change:

```
public void setFrameIcon(ImageIcon fi) {
  m_frameIcon = fi;

  if (fi != null) {
    if (m_frameIcon.getIconHeight() > TITLE_BAR_HEIGHT)
      setTitleBarHeight(m_frameIcon.getIconHeight()
        + 2*FRAME_ICON_PADDING);
    m_iconLabel.setIcon(m_frameIcon);
  }
  else setTitleBarHeight(TITLE_BAR_HEIGHT);
  revalidate();
}
```

7 The title bar height will never be smaller than TITLE_BAR_HEIGHT (25). If the icon's height is greater than this default value, the title bar height will then be based on that icon's height, plus the default icon padding, FRAME_ICON_PADDING, above and below the icon. This is necessary because when the frame icon is added to the title bar within our createTitleBar() method, it is placed in a JLabel surrounded by an EmptyBorder as follows:

```
m_iconLabel.setBorder(new EmptyBorder(
  FRAME_ICON_PADDING, FRAME_ICON_PADDING,
  FRAME_ICON_PADDING, FRAME_ICON_PADDING));
```

This label is then added to the WEST region of m_titlePanel (the title bar).

The custom resize components are the key to making InnerFrame resizable. They are built as inner classes inside InnerFrame and are discussed below. Before we discuss them in detail, it is helpful to clarify InnerFrame's structure. Figure 15.7 illustrates this, and it shows which cursor will appear when the mouse pointer is placed over different portions of each resize edge (this functionality is something we have come to expect from frames in any modern desktop environment).

The Cursor class defines several class fields representing predefined cursor icons that we use in the resize the classes discussed on the following pages.

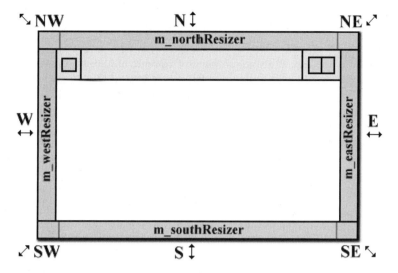

Figure 15.7 The `InnerFrame` **structure and resize edge cursor regions**

```
N_RESIZE_CURSOR, NE_RESIZE_CURSOR, NW_RESIZE_CURSOR, S_RESIZE_CURSOR,
SE_RESIZE_CURSOR, SW_RESIZE_CURSOR, E_RESIZE_CURSOR, W_RESIZE_CURSOR,
DEFAULT_CURSOR
```

NOTE   At first glance, you might think it would be easier to implement your own border and build resizable functionality into it. The problem is that borders are not part of the `Component` hierarchy, meaning they do not inherit from the `Component` class. In fact, every border is a subclass of `AbstractBorder` which is a direct subclass of `Object`. There is no way to associate mouse events with a border.

Class InnerFrame.EastResizeEdge

8 `EastResizeEdge` is the component that is placed in the east portion of `InnerFrame`'s `BorderLayout`. This component allows `InnerFrame` to be resized horizontally. This is the simplest of the four edges because when it is used to resize, `InnerFrame` always stays in the same location (defined by its northwest corner) and the height doesn't change. Two class variables and two instance variables are necessary:

- `int WIDTH`: The constant thickness.
- `int MIN_WIDTH`: The minimum width of `m_resizeComponent`.
- `boolean m_dragging`: Returns `true` when dragging.
- `JComponent m_resizeComponent`: The component to resize.

The constructor, as with all of the resize edge component constructors, takes a `JComponent` as a parameter. This `JComponent` is the component that is resized whenever the edge detects a mouse drag event. The `setPreferredSize()` method ensures that our edges will have a constant thickness.

We have designed these components to be significantly generic, while still being encapsulated as inner classes. They can easily be modified for use within other classes or as stand-alone resizable utility components. In the next chapter, we'll create a package called resize which contains each of these classes as separate entities that can be wrapped around any JComponent (see section 16.4 for the resize package source code, refer to **\Chapter16\2\resize** in this book's directory on the Manning web site.)

9 The mouseEntered() method is used to detect whenever the cursor is over this edge. When it is invoked, it changes the cursor to E_RESIZE_CURSOR. The mouseExited() method changes the cursor back to the normal DEFAULT_CURSOR when the mouse leaves this component. In both methods, cursor changes only occur when the m_dragging flag is false (when the border is not being dragged). We do not want the cursor to change while we are resizing.

10 The mousePressed() method sets the m_dragging flag and moves the component associated with this resize edge to the foremost position in its JLayeredPane layer (by calling toFront()). The mouseDragged() method actually handles the resizing and defines two cases to ensure that m_resizeComponent's width is never made smaller than MIN_WIDTH.

Class InnerFrame.WestResizeEdge

11 WestResizeEdge works similarly to EastResizeEdge except that it must handle an extra case in resizing because the position, as well as the width, of m_resizeComponent changes. An extra variable, m_rightX, is used to keep track of the coordinate of the northeast corner of m_resizeComponent to ensure that the right side of m_resizeComponent never moves during a resize.

Class InnerFrame.NorthResizeEdge, InnerFrame.SouthResizeEdge

12 NorthResizeEdge and SouthResizeEdge are very complicated because there are three regions in each. The leftmost and rightmost portions are reserved for resizing in the northwest, southwest, and northeast, southeast directions respectively. The most complicated cases are resizing from the northwest and southwest corners because the height and width can change, as can both the x and y coordinates of m_resizeComponent. Thus, the mouseDragged() method in each of these classes is quite extensive.

13 After each mouse drag, validate() is called on m_resizeComponent to lay out its contents again. If we did not include this, we would see that as we resized an InnerFrame, the change in its size and the act of rendering of its contents would not occur properly. (Try this by commenting out these lines in each of the resize edge classes.) Validation forces the container to lay out its contents based on the current size. Normally we would call revalidate() rather than validate() for the sake of thread safety. However, performance bottlenecks are often associated with revalidate() when performing fast resizes because these requests get forwarded, queued, and coalesced by the RepaintManager service (see chapter 2 for more about validation and painting). By making the direct call to validate(), we ensure that the layout will be performed immediately, and with rapid resizing this does make a difference.

15.4.2 Running the code

Figure 15.5 shows `LayeredPaneDemo` in action. First try resizing frames from all directions to see that this works as expected. Now try replacing the frame icon with one of a different size (you can use the tiger.gif image included in this example's directory). You will see that the title bar and the minimum height of our frames change accordingly. Figure 15.6 shows our `InnerFrames` with a much larger frame icon.

15.5 CREATING A CUSTOM MDI, PART III: ENHANCEMENTS

We need to take special note about a few things in the previous example. You may have noticed that mouse events are still propagating right through our frames. We can also still drag `InnerFrames` completely outside the layered pane view. In this section we address these issues, implement maximizable functionality, and take the final step in making `InnerFrame` a fundamental Swing container by implementing the `RootPaneContainer` interface.

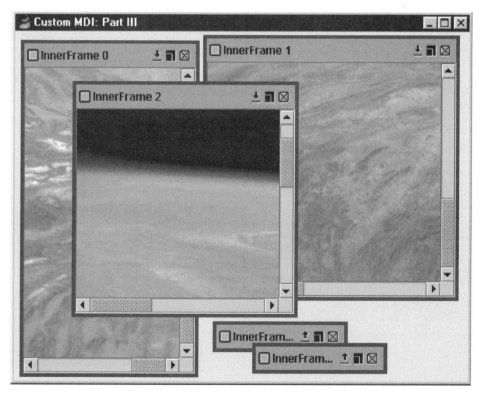

Figure 15.8   Custom MDI: part III

Example 15.4

InnerFrame.java

see \Chapter15\4\mdi

```java
package mdi;

import java.awt.*;
import java.awt.event.*;
import javax.swing.*;
import javax.swing.event.*;
import javax.swing.border.EmptyBorder;

public class InnerFrame
extends JPanel implements RootPaneContainer
{
  protected static String IMAGE_DIR = "mdi" + java.io.File.separator;
  protected static ImageIcon ICONIZE_BUTTON_ICON =
    new ImageIcon(IMAGE_DIR+"iconize.gif");
  protected static ImageIcon RESTORE_BUTTON_ICON =
    new ImageIcon(IMAGE_DIR+"restore.gif");
  protected static ImageIcon CLOSE_BUTTON_ICON =
    new ImageIcon(IMAGE_DIR+"close.gif");
  protected static ImageIcon MAXIMIZE_BUTTON_ICON =
    new ImageIcon(IMAGE_DIR+"maximize.gif");
  protected static ImageIcon MINIMIZE_BUTTON_ICON =
    new ImageIcon(IMAGE_DIR+"minimize.gif");
  protected static ImageIcon PRESS_CLOSE_BUTTON_ICON =
    new ImageIcon(IMAGE_DIR+"pressclose.gif");
  protected static ImageIcon PRESS_RESTORE_BUTTON_ICON =
    new ImageIcon(IMAGE_DIR+"pressrestore.gif");
  protected static ImageIcon PRESS_ICONIZE_BUTTON_ICON =
    new ImageIcon(IMAGE_DIR+"pressiconize.gif");
  protected static ImageIcon PRESS_MAXIMIZE_BUTTON_ICON =
    new ImageIcon(IMAGE_DIR+"pressmaximize.gif");
  protected static ImageIcon PRESS_MINIMIZE_BUTTON_ICON =
    new ImageIcon(IMAGE_DIR+"pressminimize.gif");
  protected static ImageIcon DEFAULT_FRAME_ICON =
    new ImageIcon(IMAGE_DIR+"default.gif");
  protected static int BORDER_THICKNESS = 4;
  protected static int WIDTH = 200;
  protected static int HEIGHT = 200;
  protected static int TITLE_BAR_HEIGHT = 25;
  protected static int FRAME_ICON_PADDING = 2;
  protected static int ICONIZED_WIDTH = 150;
  protected static Color TITLE_BAR_BG_COLOR =
    new Color(108,190,116);
  protected static Color BORDER_COLOR = new Color(8,90,16);

  protected int m_titleBarHeight = TITLE_BAR_HEIGHT;
  protected int m_width = WIDTH;
  protected int m_height = HEIGHT;
```

```
protected int m_iconizedWidth = ICONIZED_WIDTH;
protected int m_x;
protected int m_y;

protected String m_title;
protected JLabel m_titleLabel;
protected JLabel m_iconLabel;

protected boolean m_iconified;
protected boolean m_maximized;

protected boolean m_iconizeable;
protected boolean m_resizeable;
protected boolean m_closeable;
protected boolean m_maximizeable;

// Only false when maximized
protected boolean m_draggable = true;

protected JRootPane m_rootPane;

// Used to wrap m_titlePanel and m_rootPane
protected JPanel m_frameContentPanel;

protected JPanel m_titlePanel;
protected JPanel m_contentPanel;
protected JPanel m_buttonPanel;
protected JPanel m_buttonWrapperPanel;

protected InnerFrameButton m_iconize;
protected InnerFrameButton m_close;
protected InnerFrameButton m_maximize;

// Unchanged code from example 15.3

public InnerFrame(String title, ImageIcon frameIcon) {
  this(title, frameIcon, true, true, true, true);
}

public InnerFrame(String title, ImageIcon frameIcon,
 boolean resizeable, boolean iconizeable,
 boolean maximizeable, boolean closeable) {
  super.setLayout(new BorderLayout());
  attachNorthResizeEdge();
  attachSouthResizeEdge();
  attachEastResizeEdge();
  attachWestResizeEdge();
  populateInnerFrame();

  setTitle(title);
  setResizeable(resizeable);
  setIconizeable(iconizeable);
  setCloseable(closeable);
  setMaximizeable(maximizeable);
  if (frameIcon != null)
    setFrameIcon(frameIcon);
}
```

❶ Constructor can now specify maximizeable flag

```
protected void populateInnerFrame() {
  m_rootPane = new JRootPane();
  m_frameContentPanel = new JPanel();
  m_frameContentPanel.setLayout(new BorderLayout());
  createTitleBar();
  m_contentPanel = new JPanel(new BorderLayout());
  m_rootPane.setContentPane(m_contentPanel);
  m_frameContentPanel.add(m_titlePanel, BorderLayout.NORTH);
  m_frameContentPanel.add(m_rootPane, BorderLayout.CENTER);
  setupCapturePanel();
  super.add(m_frameContentPanel, BorderLayout.CENTER);
}

protected void setupCapturePanel() {
  CapturePanel mouseTrap = new CapturePanel();
  m_rootPane.getLayeredPane().add(mouseTrap,
    new Integer(Integer.MIN_VALUE));
  mouseTrap.setBounds(0,0,10000,10000);
}

// Don't allow this in root pane containers
public Component add(Component c) {
  return null;
}

// Don't allow this in root pane containers
public void setLayout(LayoutManager mgr) {
}

public JMenuBar getJMenuBar() {
  return m_rootPane.getJMenuBar();
}

public JRootPane getRootPane() {
  return m_rootPane;
}

public Container getContentPane() {
  return m_rootPane.getContentPane();
}

public Component getGlassPane() {
  return m_rootPane.getGlassPane();
}

public JLayeredPane getLayeredPane() {
  return m_rootPane.getLayeredPane();
}

public void setJMenuBar(JMenuBar menu) {
  m_rootPane.setJMenuBar(menu);
}

public void setContentPane(Container content) {
  m_rootPane.setContentPane(content);
}
```

2 Creates JRootPane for central container

3 Places CapturePane in lowest layer of layered pane

4 These do nothing, instead you should use methods on root container

```java
public void setGlassPane(Component glass) {
  m_rootPane.setGlassPane(glass);
}

public void setLayeredPane(JLayeredPane layered) {
  m_rootPane.setLayeredPane(layered);
}

// Unchanged code from example 15.3

public boolean isMaximizeable() {
  return m_maximizeable;
}

public void setMaximizeable(boolean b) {
  m_maximizeable = b;
  m_maximize.setVisible(b);
  m_titlePanel.revalidate();
}

public boolean isIconified() {
  return m_iconified;
}

public void setIconified(boolean b) {
  m_iconified = b;
  if (b) {
    if (isMaximized())
      setMaximized(false);
    toFront();
    m_width = getWidth();       // remember width
    m_height = getHeight();    // remember height
    setBounds(getX(), getY(), ICONIZED_WIDTH,
      m_titleBarHeight + 2*BORDER_THICKNESS);
    m_iconize.setIcon(RESTORE_BUTTON_ICON);
    m_iconize.setPressedIcon(PRESS_RESTORE_BUTTON_ICON);
    setResizeable(false);
  }
  else {
    toFront();
    setBounds(getX(), getY(), m_width, m_height);
    m_iconize.setIcon(ICONIZE_BUTTON_ICON);
    m_iconize.setPressedIcon(PRESS_ICONIZE_BUTTON_ICON);
    setResizeable(true);
  }
  revalidate();
}

public boolean isMaximized() {
  return m_maximized;
}

public void setMaximized(boolean b) {
  m_maximized = b;
  if (b)
  {
```

5 Controls ability to maximize and minimize InnerFrame

7 Unmaximizes before iconizing

6 Maximizes or minimizes InnerFrame

```
      if (isIconified())
        setIconified(false);
      toFront();
      m_width = getWidth();       // remember width
      m_height = getHeight();     // remember height
      m_x = getX();               // remember x
      m_y = getY();               // remember y
      setBounds(0, 0, getParent().getWidth(),
        getParent().getHeight());
      m_maximize.setIcon(MINIMIZE_BUTTON_ICON);
      m_maximize.setPressedIcon(PRESS_MINIMIZE_BUTTON_ICON);
      setResizeable(false);
      setDraggable(false);
    }
    else {
      toFront();
      setBounds(m_x, m_y, m_width, m_height);
      m_maximize.setIcon(MAXIMIZE_BUTTON_ICON);
      m_maximize.setPressedIcon(PRESS_MAXIMIZE_BUTTON_ICON);
      setResizeable(true);
      setDraggable(true);
    }
    revalidate();
}

// Unchanged code from example 15.3

public boolean isDraggable() {
  return m_draggable;
}

private void setDraggable(boolean b) {
  m_draggable = b;
}

// Create the title bar: m_titlePanel
protected void createTitleBar() {

  // Unchanged code from example 15.3

  m_maximize = new InnerFrameButton(MAXIMIZE_BUTTON_ICON);
  m_maximize.setPressedIcon(PRESS_MAXIMIZE_BUTTON_ICON);
  m_maximize.addActionListener(new ActionListener() {
    public void actionPerformed(ActionEvent e) {
      InnerFrame.this.setMaximized(
        !InnerFrame.this.isMaximized());
    }
  });
  m_buttonWrapperPanel = new JPanel();
  m_buttonWrapperPanel.setOpaque(false);
  m_buttonPanel = new JPanel(new GridLayout(1,3));
  m_buttonPanel.setOpaque(false);
  m_buttonPanel.add(m_iconize);
  m_buttonPanel.add(m_maximize);
```

6 Can't resize or drag while maximized

8 Action to toggle maximized flag

```
      // Unchanged code from example 15.3
}

// Title bar mouse adapter for frame dragging
class InnerFrameTitleBarMouseAdapter
extends MouseInputAdapter
{
      // Unchanged code from example 15.3

      // Don't allow dragging outside of parent
      public void mouseDragged(MouseEvent e) {
        int ex = e.getX();
        int ey = e.getY();
        int x = m_if.getX();
        int y = m_if.getY();
        int w = m_if.getParent().getWidth();
        int h = m_if.getParent().getHeight();
        if (m_dragging & m_if.isDraggable()) {
          if((ey + y > 0 && ey + y < h) &&
            (ex + x > 0 && ex + x < w))
          {
            m_if.setLocation(ex-m_XDifference+x, ey-m_YDifference+y);
          }
          else if (!(ey + y > 0 && ey + y < h) &&
            (ex + x > 0 && ex + x < w))
          {
            if (!(ey + y > 0) && ey + y < h) {
              m_if.setLocation(ex-m_XDifference+x, 0-m_YDifference);
              else if (ey + y > 0 && !(ey + y < h))
                m_if.setLocation(ex-m_XDifference+x, h-m_YDifference);
          }
          else if ((ey + y > 0 && ey + y < h) &&
            !(ex + x > 0 && ex + x < w))
          {
            if (!(ex + x > 0) && ex + x < w)
              m_if.setLocation(0-m_XDifference, ey-m_YDifference+y);
              else if (ex + x > 0 && !(ex + x < w))
                m_if.setLocation(w-m_XDifference, ey-m_YDifference+y);
          }
          else if (!(ey + y > 0) && ey + y < h
            && !(ex + x > 0) && ex + x < w)
            m_if.setLocation(0-m_XDifference, 0-m_YDifference);
          else if (!(ey + y > 0) && ey + y < h
            && ex + x > 0 && !(ex + x < w))
            m_if.setLocation(w-m_XDifference, 0-m_YDifference);
          else if (ey + y > 0 && !(ey + y < h)
            && !(ex + x > 0) && ex + x < w)
            m_if.setLocation(0-m_XDifference, h-m_YDifference);
          else if (ey + y > 0 && !(ey + y < h)
            && ex + x > 0 && !(ex + x < w))
            m_if.setLocation(w-m_XDifference, h-m_YDifference);
        }
      }
```

❾ Accepts new location, but stops at edge of bounds

```
    // Unchanged code from example 15.3
  }

  // Unchanged code from example 15.3

  ///////////////////////////////////////////////
  //////////// Mouse Event Capturing /////////////
  ///////////////////////////////////////////////
  class CapturePanel extends JPanel
  {
    public CapturePanel() {
      MouseInputAdapter mia = new MouseInputAdapter() {};
      addMouseListener(mia);
      addMouseMotionListener(mia);
    }
  }

  // Unchanged code from example 15.3
}
```

Consumes mouse events, so they don't go to container ❿

15.5.1 Understanding the code

Class InnerFrame

There are four new class variables:

- ImageIcon MAXIMIZE_BUTTON_ICON: The icon used for the Maximize button ▦.
- ImageIcon PRESS_MAXIMIZE_BUTTON_ICON: The icon used for the Maximize button in the pressed state ▦.
- ImageIcon MINIMIZE_BUTTON_ICON: Icon used for the Minimize button to represent minimization ▦.
- ImageIcon PRESS_MINIMIZE_BUTTON_ICON: The icon used for the Minimize button in the pressed state, representing minimization ▦.

There are six new instance variables:

- int m_x: Records the x location of InnerFrame before a maximize occurs.
- int m_y: Records the y location of InnerFrame before a maximize occurs.
- boolean m_maximizeable: true when the frame can be maximized.
- boolean m_draggable: true when InnerFrame is not iconified or maximized.
- JRootPane m_rootPane: The central InnerFrame container; all external access is restricted to this container and its panes.
- InnerFrameButton m_maximize: The Maximize title bar button.

❶ The InnerFrame constructors now support a fourth boolean parameter that specifies whether the frame will be maximizable.

❷ The populateInnerFrame() method is now responsible for creating a JRootPane that will be used as InnerFrame's central container. Since InnerFrame now implements the Root-PaneContainer interface, we are required to implement access to this JRootPane and its contentPane, layeredPane, glassPane, and MenuBar just as a JFrame or JInternalFrame. Thus getXX() and setXX() methods have been implemented for each of these constituents.

3 The `setupCapturePanel()` method places an instance of our mouse-event-consuming panel, `CapturePanel` (see below), in the lowest possible layer of our `rootPane`'s `layeredPane`. We set the bounds of this `CapturePanel` to be extremely large, so we are guaranteed, for all practical purposes, that mouse events will not pass through the "back" of `InnerFrame`.

4 The `add()` and `setLayout()` methods we had redirected to another panel in the last section have been modified to return `null` and do nothing, respectively. This enforces `InnerFrame` container access through its `JRootPane` constituents, similar to all other primary Swing containers.

5 The `setMaximizeable()` method has been added to control the state of the `m_maximizeable` property and the visibility of the `m_maximize` button in the title bar.

6 The `setMaximized()` method has also been added for maximize and minimize functionality. When `InnerFrame` is told to maximize, it first checks to see if it is iconified. If it is, it deiconifies itself. Otherwise, it records its dimensions and location and resizes itself to be the size of its parent container. It swaps the Maximize button icon for the one representing Minimize, and `setResizable(false)` is called to remove mouse listeners (we should not be able to resize a maximized frame). Finally, a new method called `setDraggable()` is called and passed a `false` value. This method controls a flag that the title bar's `mouseDragged()` method checks before allowing `InnerFrame` to be dragged. If we set this flag to `false`, `InnerFrame` will not be draggable. In the maximized state, this is desirable.

When a minimize occurs, `InnerFrame` is moved to the recorded location and set to its stored width and height, and the maximize/minimize button icons are swapped again. `setResizable(true)` and `setDraggable(true)` restore full resizable and draggable functionality.

7 The `setIconified()` method has been modified to take into account the possibility that `InnerFrame` may be iconified from within the maximized state. In this case we call `setMaximized(false)` before proceeding with the iconification.

8 The `m_maximize` button is created for placement in the title bar, and an `ActionListener` is attached with an `actionPerformed()` method that invokes `setMaximized()`. The title bar's button panel then allocates an additional cell (it uses `GridLayout`) for `m_maximize`, and it is added between the Iconify and Close buttons.

Class InnerFrame.InnerFrameTitleBarMouseAdapter

9 This class's `mouseDragged()` method is now much more involved. It is somewhat overwhelming at first, but all of this code is actually necessary to *smoothly* stop the selected `InnerFrame` from being dragged outside of the visible region of its parent. This code handles all mouse positions, allowing vertical movement when horizontal is not possible, horizontal movement when vertical is not possible, and all combinations of possible dragging, while making sure that `InnerFrame` never completely leaves the visible region of its parent. It is not necessary that you work through the details, but we do encourage you to (similar to the code for the `XXResizeEdge` classes), as it will provide an appreciation for how complicated situations such as this can be dealt with in an organized manner.

REFERENCE Similar code will be used in example 16.3, section 16.5, where we build an X-windows-style pager that is not allowed to leave the `JDesktopPane` view.

NOTE We have not implemented code to stop the user from resizing an InnerFrame so that its title bar lies outside of the layered pane view. This can result in a lost frame. In order to provide a solution to this, we would have to add a considerable amount of code to the NorthResizeEdge mouseDragged() method. It can be done, but we will avoid it here because other issues deserve more attention. In a commercial implementation, we would want to include code to watch for this. It is interesting that this is not handled in the JDesktopPane/JInternalFrame MDI as well.

Class InnerFrame.CapturePanel

10 As we noticed in the past two stages of development, mouse events pass right through our InnerFrames. We can stop this from happening by constructing a component to capture mouse events and placing it in our rootPane's layeredPane. This is the purpose of Capture-Panel. It is a simple JPanel with an empty MouseInputAdapter shell attached as a Mouse-Listener and MouseMotionListener. This adapter will consume any mouse events that are passed to it. When an InnerFrame is constructed, as we discussed above, a CapturePanel instance is added at the lowest possible layer of its layeredPane. Thus, mouse events that don't get handled by a component in a higher layer, such as its contentPane, will get trapped here.

15.5.2 Running the code

Note that we've added one line to LayeredPaneDemo in this section that we didn't mention yet:

```
frames[i].getContentPane().add(new JScrollPane(new JLabel(ii)));
```

This places a JScrollPane containing a JLabel with an image in InnerFrame's contentPane.

Figure 15.8 shows LayeredPaneDemo in action. Experiment with maximizing, iconifying, and restoring. Drag frames all around the layered pane and make sure that they cannot be lost from view. Now resize a frame and notice that we can lose the title bar if it is resized above our JFrame title bar. (This is a flaw that should be accounted for in any commercial MDI.)

Now try maximizing an InnerFrame and changing the size of the JFrame. You will notice that the maximized InnerFrame does not change size along with its parent. In the next section we show how to implement this and other important features.

15.6 CREATING A CUSTOM MDI, PART IV: SELECTION AND MANAGEMENT

When we resize our JFrame it would be nice to have the iconified frames line up and stay at the bottom. This would prevent them from being lost from the layered pane view, and it would also increase the organized feel of our MDI. Similarly, when an InnerFrame is maximized, it should always fill the entire viewable region of its parent. Thus, it would be nice to have some way of controlling the layout of our InnerFrames when the parent is resized. We can do this by extending JLayeredPane and implementing the java.awt.event.ComponentListener interface to listen for resize ComponentEvents. We can capture and handle events sent to the componentResized() method to lay out iconified frames and resize maximized frames in a manner similar to most modern MDI environments. (Note that we could also extend Compo-nentAdapter and use an instance of the resulting class as a ComponentListener attached to our JLayeredPane. As is often the case, there is more than one way to implement the functionality we are looking for.) In this section, we'll build a JLayeredPane subclass that implements ComponentListener, and add it to our mdi package.

Another limiting characteristic of InnerFrame is that the only way to get the focus, and to move an InnerFrame to the front of the layered pane view, is to click on its title bar. Ideally, clicking *anywhere* on an InnerFrame should move it to the front of the layered pane view. This is where JRootPane's glassPane comes in handy. Since our InnerFrames now contain a JRootPane as their main container, we can use the glassPane to intercept mouse events and move the selected InnerFrame to the front. We will need to make our glassPane completely transparent, and it should only be active (receiving mouse events) within an InnerFrame when that InnerFrame is *not* in the foremost position of its layer (see section 15.1). Thus, only one InnerFrame per layer should have an *inactive* glassPane. This one frame is the *selected* InnerFrame—the one with the current user focus.

It is customary to visually convey to the user which frame is selected. We will do this by adding a new boolean property to our InnerFrame that represents whether it is selected. We will manipulate this property in such a way that there can be only one selected InnerFrame per layer. A selected InnerFrame will be characterized by unique border and title bar colors.

Example 15.5

InnerFrame.java

see \Chapter15\5\mdi

```
package mdi;

import java.awt.*;
import java.awt.event.*;
import javax.swing.*;
import javax.swing.event.*;
import javax.swing.border.EmptyBorder;

public class InnerFrame
extends JPanel implements RootPaneContainer
{
  // Unchanged code from example 15.4

  protected static Color DEFAULT_TITLE_BAR_BG_COLOR =
    new Color(108,190,116);
  protected static Color DEFAULT_BORDER_COLOR =
    new Color(8,90,16);
  protected static Color DEFAULT_SELECTED_TITLE_BAR_BG_COLOR =
    new Color(91,182,249);
  protected static Color DEFAULT_SELECTED_BORDER_COLOR =
    new Color(0,82,149);

  protected Color m_titleBarBackground =
    DEFAULT_TITLE_BAR_BG_COLOR;
  protected Color m_titleBarForeground = Color.black;
  protected Color m_BorderColor = DEFAULT_BORDER_COLOR;
  protected Color m_selectedTitleBarBackground =
```

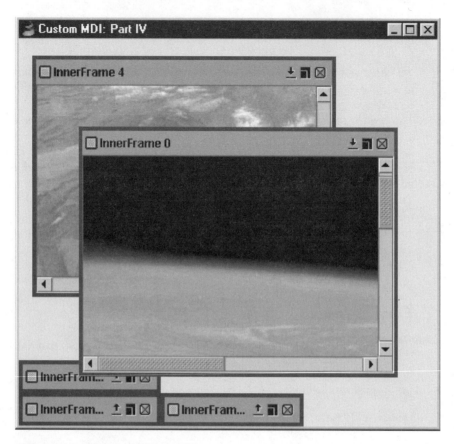

Figure 15.9   Custom MDI: part IV

```
  DEFAULT_SELECTED_TITLE_BAR_BG_COLOR;
protected Color m_selectedBorderColor =
  DEFAULT_SELECTED_BORDER_COLOR;

protected boolean m_selected;

// Unchanged code from example 15.4

protected void setupCapturePanel() {
  CapturePanel mouseTrap = new CapturePanel();
  m_rootPane.getLayeredPane().add(mouseTrap,
    new Integer(Integer.MIN_VALUE));
  mouseTrap.setBounds(0,0,10000,10000);
  setGlassPane(new GlassCapturePanel());
  getGlassPane().setVisible(true);
}

// Unchanged code from example 15.4

public void toFront() {
  if (getParent() instanceof JLayeredPane)
```

1 Covers panel
with glass pane

```
        ((JLayeredPane) getParent()).moveToFront(this);
  if (!isSelected())
    setSelected(true);
}

// Unchanged code from example 15.4

public boolean isSelected() {
  return m_selected;
}

public void setSelected(boolean b) {
  if (b)
  {
    if (m_selected != true &&
      getParent() instanceof JLayeredPane)
    {
      JLayeredPane jlp = (JLayeredPane) getParent();
      int layer = jlp.getLayer(this);
      Component[] components = jlp.getComponentsInLayer(layer);
      for (int i=0; i<components.length; i++) {
        if (components[i] instanceof InnerFrame) {
          InnerFrame tempFrame = (InnerFrame) components[i];
          if (!tempFrame.equals(this))
            tempFrame.setSelected(false);
        }
      }
      m_selected = true;
      updateBorderColors();
      updateTitleBarColors();
      getGlassPane().setVisible(false);
      repaint();
    }
  }
  else
  {
    m_selected = false;
    updateBorderColors();
    updateTitleBarColors();
    getGlassPane().setVisible(true);
    repaint();
  }
}

/////////////////////////////////////////////
///////////////// Title Bar ///////////////////
/////////////////////////////////////////////

public void setTitleBarBackground(Color c) {
  m_titleBarBackground = c;
  updateTitleBarColors();
}

public Color getTitleBarBackground() {
```

2 While moving to front, selects InnerFrame if not already selected

3 Unselects all others at this layer

4 When unselected, use the glass pane to trap mouse events

5 Accessors for title bar colors

```
    return m_titleBarBackground;
  }

  public void setTitleBarForeground(Color c) {
    m_titleBarForeground = c;
    m_titleLabel.setForeground(c);
    m_titlePanel.repaint();
  }

  public Color getTitleBarForeground() {
    return m_titleBarForeground;
  }

  public void setSelectedTitleBarBackground(Color c) {
    m_titleBarBackground = c;
    updateTitleBarColors();
  }

  public Color getSelectedTitleBarBackground() {
    return m_selectedTitleBarBackground;
  }

  protected void updateTitleBarColors() {
    if (isSelected())
      m_titlePanel.setBackground(m_selectedTitleBarBackground);
    else
      m_titlePanel.setBackground(m_titleBarBackground);
  }

  // Unchanged code from example 15.4

  protected void createTitleBar() {
    // Unchanged code
    m_titleLabel.setForeground(m_titleBarForeground);
  }

  // Unchanged code from example 15.4

  ///////////////////////////////////////////////
  ///////////// GlassPane Selector //////////////
  ///////////////////////////////////////////////

class GlassCapturePanel extends JPanel
{
  public GlassCapturePanel() {
    MouseInputAdapter mia = new MouseInputAdapter() {
      public void mousePressed(MouseEvent e) {
        InnerFrame.this.toFront();
      }
    };
    addMouseListener(mia);
    addMouseMotionListener(mia);
    setOpaque(false);
  }
}
```

⑤ Accessors for title bar colors

⑦ Clicking on glass pane moves InnerFrame to front

```
//////////////////////////////////////////////
/////////////// Resizability //////////////////
//////////////////////////////////////////////
    public void setBorderColor(Color c) {
      m_BorderColor = c;
      updateBorderColors();
    }
    public Color getBorderColor() {
      return m_BorderColor;
    }
    public void setSelectedBorderColor(Color c) {
      m_selectedBorderColor = c;
      updateBorderColors();
    }
    public Color getSelectedBorderColor() {
      return m_selectedBorderColor;
    }
    protected void updateBorderColors() {
      if (isSelected()) {
        m_northResizer.setBackground(m_selectedBorderColor);
        m_southResizer.setBackground(m_selectedBorderColor);
        m_eastResizer.setBackground(m_selectedBorderColor);
        m_westResizer.setBackground(m_selectedBorderColor);
      } else {
        m_northResizer.setBackground(m_BorderColor);
        m_southResizer.setBackground(m_BorderColor);
        m_eastResizer.setBackground(m_BorderColor);
        m_westResizer.setBackground(m_BorderColor);
      }
    }
}

    // Unchanged code from example 15.4
}
```

6 Accessors for border colors

MDIPane.java

see \Chapter15\5\mdi

```
package mdi;

import java.awt.*;
import java.awt.event.*;
import javax.swing.*;

public class MDIPane
extends JLayeredPane
implements ComponentListener
{
  public MDIPane() {
    addComponentListener(this);
    setOpaque(true);

    // Default background color
```

```
        setBackground(new Color(244,232,152));
    }

    public void componentHidden(ComponentEvent e) {}
    public void componentMoved(ComponentEvent e) {}
    public void componentShown(ComponentEvent e) {}
    public void componentResized(ComponentEvent e) { lineup(); }
    public void lineup() {
      int frameHeight, frameWidth, currentX,
        currentY, lheight, lwidth;
      lwidth = getWidth();
      lheight = getHeight();
      currentX = 0;
      currentY = lheight;
      Component[] components = getComponents();
      for (int i=components.length-1; i>-1; i--) {
        if (components[i] instanceof InnerFrame) {
          InnerFrame tempFrame = (InnerFrame) components[i];
          frameHeight = tempFrame.getHeight();
          frameWidth = tempFrame.getWidth();
          if (tempFrame.isMaximized()) {
            tempFrame.setBounds(0,0,getWidth(),getHeight());
            tempFrame.validate();
            tempFrame.repaint();
          }
          else if (tempFrame.isIconified()) {
            if (currentX+frameWidth > lwidth) {
              currentX = 0;
              currentY -= frameHeight;
            }
            tempFrame.setLocation(currentX, currentY-frameHeight);
            currentX += frameWidth;
          }
        }
      }
    }
  }
}
```

Re-layout all
the InnerFrames **8**

15.6.1 Understanding the code

Class LayeredPaneDemo

The only change that has been made to this class is the replacement of the default JLayered-Pane in our application frame with an instance of our custom MDIPane (see below).

Class InnerFrame

The following class variables have been added:

- Color DEFAULT_TITLE_BAR_BG_COLOR: The default title bar background.
- Color DEFAULT_BORDER_COLOR: The default border background.
- Color DEFAULT_SELECTED_TITLE_BAR_BG_COLOR: The default selected title bar background.
- Color DEFAULT_SELECTED_BORDER_COLOR: The default selected frame border.

These are the new instance variables:

- `Color m_titleBarBackground`: The title bar background.
- `Color m_titleBarForeground`: The title bar foreground.
- `Color m_BorderColor`: The border color.
- `Color m_selectedTitleBarBackground`: The selected title bar background.
- `Color m_selectedBorderColor`: The selected border color.
- `boolean m_selected`: true when `InnerFrame` is selected.

1 The `setupCapturePanel()` method now adds a call to set `InnerFrame`'s `glassPane` to an instance of our custom class `GlassCapturePanel` (see below). This allows selection of the `InnerFrame` itself by clicking on any visible region of that `InnerFrame`.

2 We've inserted an additional check in the `toFront()` method to call `setSelected(true)` if that frame is not already selected.

The `isSelected()` method has been added to simply return the current value of `m_selected`, and method `setSelected()` is what actually controls this property.

3 The `setSelected()` method takes a boolean value that represents whether the frame should be selected or de-selected. If it is to be selected and it resides in a `JLayeredPane`, this method searches for all other `InnerFrame` siblings in the same layer of that `JLayeredPane` and calls `setSelected(false)` on each one it finds. Then we set the current `InnerFrame`'s selected property, `m_selected`, to `true` and call `updateBorderColors()` and `updateTitleBar-Colors()` (see below) to visually convey that this is the selected frame.

4 The `glassPane` is hidden whenever a frame is selected so that mouse events will no longer be trapped (see `GlassCapturePanel` below). When a frame is deselected, when `setSe-lected(false)` has been called, this method disables its selected property, calls the `update-XXColors()` methods, and brings its `glassPane` out of hiding so that it may intercept mouse events for future selection. This whole scheme provides us with a guarantee that only one `InnerFrame` will be selected per `JLayeredPane` layer.

5 The `setTitleBarBackground()`, `setTitleBarForeground()`, and `setSelectedTitle-BarBackground()` methods have all been added to manage the state of the current title bar color properties. Each of these methods calls `updateTitleBarColors()` so that the changes made are actually applied to the title bar and border components. In the JavaBeans spirit, we've also added `get()` methods to retrieve these properties.

6 Similarly, the `setBorderColor()`, `setSelectedBorderColor()`, and `updateBorder-Colors()` methods, and their associated `get()` methods have been defined to manage the border color properties. The `updateBorderColors()` method is responsible for applying these colors to each of the resize edge components.

Class mdi.InnerFrame.GlassCapturePanel

7 This class is almost identical to our `CapturePanel` inner class. The only difference is that its `MouseInputAdapter` overrides the `mousePressed()` method to call `toFront()` on the associated `InnerFrame`. As we saw above, `toFront()` calls `setSelected()` as necessary.

Instances of this class are used as the `glassPane` of each `InnerFrame`'s `JRootPane`. `GlassCapturePanel` is active (visible) when its parent `InnerFrame` is not selected. Conversely, it is inactive (hidden) when the associated `InnerFrame` is selected. This activation is controlled by the `setSelected()` method, as we saw above. The only function of this component is to provide a means of switching `InnerFrame` selection by clicking on any portion of an unselected `InnerFrame`.

Class mdi.MDIPane

8 This class extends `JLayeredPane` and implements the `java.awt.event.ComponentListener` interface. Whenever this component is resized, the `componentResized()` method is invoked. This method invokes `lineup()`, which grabs an array of all `Component`s within the `MDIPane`. It then loops through this array to check whether each `Component` is an instance of `InnerFrame`.

```
Component[] components = getComponents();
for (int i=components.length-1; i>-1; i--) {
  if (components[i] instanceof InnerFrame) {
```

If it is, we then check if it is maximized or iconified. If it is maximized, we reset its bounds to completely fill the visible region of the `MDIPane`. If it is iconified, we place it at the bottom of the layered pane. This method locally maintains the position where the next iconified frame should be placed (`currentX` and `currentY`) and places these frames in rows, stacked from the bottom up, that fit within `MDIPane`'s horizontal visible region.

15.6.2 Running the code

Figure 15.9 shows `LayeredPaneDemo` in action. Iconify the `InnerFrame`s and adjust the size of the application frame to see the layout change. Now maximize an `InnerFrame` and adjust the size of the `JFrame` to see that the `InnerFrame` is resized appropriately. You may also want to experiment with the `LayeredPaneDemo` constructor and add another set or two of `InnerFrame`s to different layers. You will see that there can only be one selected `InnerFrame` per layer, as expected.

This method of organizing iconified frames is certainly not adequate for professional implementations. However, developing it any further would take us a bit too far into the details of MDI construction. Ideally we might implement some sort of manager that `InnerFrame`s and `MDIPane` can use to communicate with one another.

In the next chapter, we will discuss an interface called `DesktopManager` which functions as such a communications bridge between `JDesktopPane` and its `JInternalFrame` children. We will also learn that such a manager, as simple as it is, provides us with a great deal of flexibility.

15.7 *Creating a custom MDI, part V: JavaBeans compliance*

The functionality of our `InnerFrame` is pretty much complete at this point. However, there is still much to be desired if we plan to use `InnerFrame` in the field. JavaBeans compliance is one feature that is not only popular, but it has come to be expected of each and every Java GUI component. In this section we will enhance `InnerFrame` by implementing the `Externalizable` interface, thereby providing us with full control over its serialization. Although `JComponent` provides a default serialization mechanism for all Swing components, this mechanism is far from reliable at the time of this writing. Implementing our own serialization mechanism is not only reliable and safe for both long- and short-term persistency, but it is also efficient. (The default serialization mechanism tends to store much more information than we actually need.)

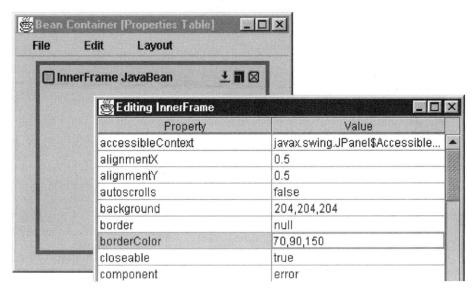

Figure 15.10   Custom MDI: part V

Example 15.6

see \Chapter15\6\mdi

```
package mdi;

import java.awt.*;
import java.awt.event.*;
import java.io.*;
import javax.swing.*;
import javax.swing.event.*;
import javax.swing.border.EmptyBorder;

public class InnerFrame
extends JPanel implements RootPaneContainer, Externalizable
{
  // Unchanged code from example 15.5

  //////////////////////////////////////////////
  //////////////// Serialization ////////////////
  //////////////////////////////////////////////

  public void writeExternal(ObjectOutput out)
    throws IOException
  {
    out.writeObject(m_titleBarBackground);
    out.writeObject(m_titleBarForeground);
    out.writeObject(m_BorderColor);
```

```
            out.writeObject(m_selectedTitleBarBackground);
            out.writeObject(m_selectedBorderColor);

            out.writeObject(m_title);

            out.writeBoolean(m_iconizeable);
            out.writeBoolean(m_resizeable);
            out.writeBoolean(m_closeable);
            out.writeBoolean(m_maximizeable);

            out.writeObject(m_frameIcon);
            out.writeObject(getBounds());
        }

    public void readExternal(ObjectInput in)
        throws IOException, ClassNotFoundException
    {
        setTitleBarBackground((Color)in.readObject());
        setTitleBarForeground((Color)in.readObject());
        setBorderColor((Color)in.readObject());
        setSelectedTitleBarBackground((Color)in.readObject());
        setSelectedBorderColor((Color)in.readObject());

        setTitle((String)in.readObject());

        setIconizeable(in.readBoolean());
        setResizeable(in.readBoolean());
        setCloseable(in.readBoolean());
        setMaximizeable(in.readBoolean());
        setSelected(false);

        setFrameIcon((ImageIcon)in.readObject());
        Rectangle r = (Rectangle)in.readObject();
        r.x = getX();
        r.y = getY();
        setBounds(r);
    }
}
```

15.7.1   Understanding the code

The added support for `InnerFrame` serialization here is quite simple. The `readExternal()` method will be invoked when `readObject()` is called on a given `ObjectInput` stream that points to a previously serialized `InnerFrame`. The `writeExternal()` method will be invoked when `writeObject()` is passed an `InnerFrame` and called on a given `ObjectOutput` stream. Refer back to chapter 4, section 4.7, to see how this is implemented in our `BeanContainer` JavaBeans environment.

15.7.2   Running the code

Figure 15.10 shows an instance of `InnerFrame` which has been instantiated from a serialized `InnerFrame` saved to disk and loaded into our JavaBeans property editing environment. (We started the construction of this environment in chapter 4 and it will be completed (as shown) in chapter 18.) The point to make here is that `InnerFrame` is now a somewhat typical JavaBean.

There are certainly many ways to make InnerFrame a *better* bean. Specifically, many of the class variables, such as the default title bar height, border thickness, frame icon padding, and button icons, would allow greater flexibility if they were implemented as properties. (Some of these might actually be better off within UI delegate code. Colors and button icons should change with look-and-feel, not be part of the component itself.) We could also add support for *communication* (which is completely lacking in InnerFrame now). For instance, we could make m_maximized into a bound or constrained property by sending out PropertyChangeEvents or VetoableChangeEvents, respectively (refer to chapter 2 for a discussion of JavaBeans and properties). In this way we could notify interested listeners that a maximization is *about* to occur (in the case that m_maximize is constrained), and give them an opportunity to veto it.

Another major feature lacking in InnerFrame is look and feel support. The title bar and borders look like standard army-issue components at best. They should respond to look-and-feel changes just like any other Swing component. In chapter 21 we will implement support for all the major look and feels (Metal, Motif, and Windows) for InnerFrame, plus our own custom look and feel (Malachite).

C H A P T E R   1 6

Desktops & internal frames

16.1   *JDESKTOPPANE AND JINTERNALFRAME*

16.1.1   JDesktopPane

class javax.swing.JDesktopPane

JDesktopPane is a powerful extension of JLayeredPane that is built specifically to manage JInternalFrame children. This is Swing's version of a multiple document interface, a feature common to most modern operating system desktops. In the last chapter we created our own MDI from scratch. Both our MDI and the JDesktopPane/JInternalFrame prebuilt MDI are quite powerful. This chapter focuses on the latter.

16.1.2   JInternalFrame

class javax.swing.JInternalFrame

The purpose of JDesktopPane is to provide a specialized container for JInternalFrames. We can access its contents in the same way we do JLayeredPane. Several additional convenience methods are defined in JDesktopPane for accessing JInternalFrame children (see the API documentation) and attaching a DesktopManager implementation (see below).

`JInternalFrame`s are very similar to our custom `InnerFrame`s of chapter 15. They can be dragged, resized, iconified, maximized, and closed. `JInternalFrame` contains a `JRootPane` as its main container and it implements the `RootPaneContainer` interface. We can access a `JInternalFrame`'s `rootPane` and its associated `glassPane`, `contentPane`, `layeredPane`, and `menuBar` the same way we access them in `JFrame` and in our custom `InnerFrame`.

16.1.3   JInternalFrame.JDesktopIcon

class javax.swing.JInternalFrame.JDesktopIcon

This represents a `JInternalFrame` in its iconified state. In the API documentation, we are warned against using this class as it will disappear in future versions of Swing: "This API should NOT BE USED by Swing applications, as it will go away in future versions of Swing as its functionality is moved into `JInternalFrame`." Currently, when a `JInternalFrame` is iconified, it is removed from its `JDesktopPane` and a `JDesktopIcon` instance is added to represent it. In future versions of Swing, `JInternalFrame` will have `JDesktopIcon` functionality built into it. Currently, to customize the desktop icon, it is necessary to build your own `DesktopIconUI` subclass.

16.1.4   The DesktopManager interface

abstract interface javax.swing.DesktopManager

Each `JDesktopPane` has a `DesktopManager` object attached to it whose job it is to manage all operations performed on `JInternalFrame`s within the desktop. `DesktopManager` methods are automatically called from the associated `JDesktopPane` when an action is invoked on a `JInternalFrame` within that desktop. These are usually invoked when the user performs some action on a `JInternalFrame` with the mouse:

- `activateFrame(JInternalFrame f)`
- `beginDraggingFrame(JComponent f)`
- `beginResizingFrame(JComponent f, int direction)`
- `closeFrame(JInternalFrame f)`
- `deactivateFrame(JInternalFrame f)`
- `deiconifyFrame(JInternalFrame f)`
- `dragFrame(JComponent f, int newX, int newY)`
- `endDraggingFrame(JComponent f)`
- `endResizingFrame(JComponent f)`
- `iconifyFrame(JInternalFrame f)`
- `maximizeFrame(JInternalFrame f)`
- `minimizeFrame(JInternalFrame f)`
- `openFrame(JIntenerlFrame f)`
- `resizeFrame(JComponent f, int newX, int newY, int newWidth, int newHeight)`
- `setBoundsForFrame(JComponent f, int newX, int newY, int newWidth, int newHeight)`

If we want to manually invoke iconification, for example, on a `JInternalFrame`, we should do the following:

```
myJInternalFrame.getDesktopPane().getDesktopManager().
  iconifyFrame(myJInternalFrame);
```

We could also directly call `setIcon(true)` on a `JInternalFrame`, but we are discouraged from doing so because it is not good practice to bypass the `DesktopManager`—necessary actions may be defined within the `DesktopManager`'s `iconifyFrame()` method that would not be invoked. So, in general, all calls to methods of `JInternalFrame` that have `DesktopManager` counterparts should be delegated to the `DesktopManager`.

We have written an animated demo that shows when and how often each `DesktopManager` method is called. See \Chapter16\4 in the ZIP archive for this chapter and execute the `DesktopManagerDemo` class. Figure 16.1 illustrates.

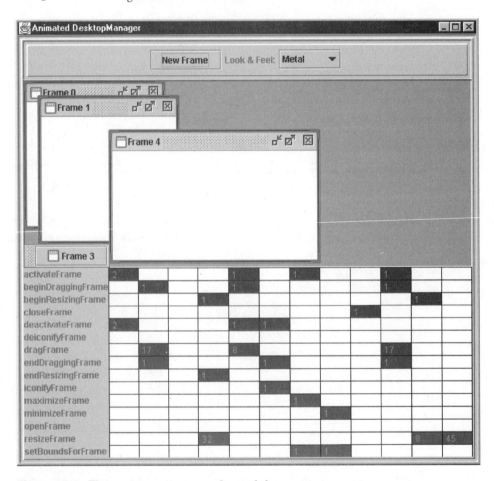

Figure 16.1 The `DesktopManager` **animated demo**

16.1.5 DefaultDesktopManager

class javax.swing.DefaultDesktopManager

This is the concrete default implementation of the `DesktopManager` interface. An instance of this class is attached to each `JDesktopPane` if a custom `DesktopManager` implementation is not specified.

16.1.6 Capturing internal frame close events

Refer to chapter 3 for a description of this interface.

BUG ALERT Using DO_NOTHING_ON_CLOSE with setDefaultCloseOperation() on a JInternalFrame does not work as expected. See bug #4176136 at the Java Developer Connection Bug Parade: http://developer.javasoft.com/developer/bugParade/bugs/4176136.html. This will most likely be fixed in the next release of Java 2.

To capture the closing of a JInternalFrame and display a confirmation dialog, we can construct the following JInternalFrame subclass:

```
class ConfirmJInternalFrame extends JInternalFrame
  implements VetoableChangeListener {

  public ConfirmJInternalFrame(String title, boolean resizable,
    boolean closable, boolean maximizable, boolean iconifiable) {
    super(title, resizable, closable, maximizable, iconifiable);
    addVetoableChangeListener(this);
  }

  public void vetoableChange(PropertyChangeEvent pce)
    throws PropertyVetoException {
   if (pce.getPropertyName().equals(IS_CLOSED_PROPERTY)) {
      boolean changed = ((Boolean) pce.getNewValue()).booleanValue();
      if (changed) {
        int confirm = JOptionPane.showOptionDialog(this,
          "Close " + getTitle() + "?",
          "Close Confirmation",
          JOptionPane.YES_NO_OPTION,
          JOptionPane.QUESTION_MESSAGE,
          null, null, null);
        if (confirm == 0) {
          m_desktop.remove(this);
          m_desktop.repaint();
        }
        else throw new PropertyVetoException("Cancelled",null);
      }
    }
  }
}
```

Using this class in place of JInternalFrame will always display a confirmation dialog when the Close button is pressed. This code checks to see if the closed property has changed from its previous state. This is a constrained property which we can veto if desired (see chapter 2). Luckily, this comes in quite handy for working around the DO_NOTHING_ON_CLOSE bug.

If the confirmation dialog is displayed and then cancelled (for example, either the NO button or the Close Dialog button is pressed), a PropertyVetoException is thrown which vetos the property change and the internal frame will not be closed. Figure 16.2 illustrates.

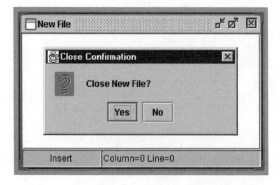

Figure 16.2 Handling internal frame closing with a Close Confirmation dialog

16.1.7 The InternalFrameListener interface

abstract interface javax.swing.event.InternalFrameListener

Each `JInternalFrame` can have one or more `InternalFrameListeners` attached. An `InternalFrameListener` will receive `InternalFrameEvents` that allow us to capture and handle them however we like with the following methods:

- `internalFrameActivated(InternalFrameEvent e)`
- `internalFrameClosed(InternalFrameEvent e)`
- `internalFrameClosing(InternalFrameEvent e)`
- `internalFrameDeactivated(InternalFrameEvent e)`
- `internalFrameDeiconified(InternalFrameEvent e)`
- `internalFrameIconified(InternalFrameEvent e)`
- `internalFrameOpened(InternalFrameEvent e)`

`InternalFrameListener` and `DesktopManager` both exist to process changes in a `JInternalFrame`'s state. However, they can both be used to achieve different ends. `DesktopManager` allows us to define internal frame handling methods for all `JInternalFrames` within a given `JDesktopPane`, whereas `InternalFrameListener` allows us to define `InternalFrameEvent` handling unique to each *individual* `JInternalFrame`. We can attach a different `InternalFrameListener` implementation to each instance of `JInternalFrame`, whereas only one `DesktopManager` implementation can be attached to any instance of `JDesktopPane` (and thus, each of its children).

We have written an animated demo that shows when and how often each `InternalFrameListener` method is called. See **\Chapter16\5** and execute the `InternalFrameListenerDemo` class. Figure 16.3 illustrates.

16.1.8 InternalFrameEvent

class javax.swing.event.InternalFrameEvent

`InternalFrameEvents` are sent to `InternalFrameListeners` whenever a `JInternalFrame` is activated, closed, about to close, deactivated, deiconified, iconified, or opened. The following static `int` IDs designate which type of action an `InternalFrameEvent` corresponds to:

- `INTERNAL_FRAME_ACTIVATED`
- `INTERNAL_FRAME_CLOSED`

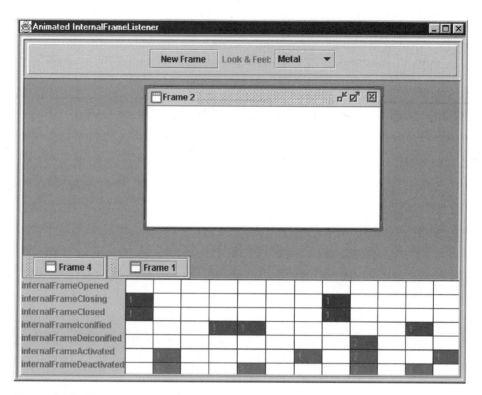

Figure 16.3 The `InternalFrameListener` **animated demo**

- `INTERNAL_FRAME_CLOSING`
- `INTERNAL_FRAME_DEACTIVATED`
- `INTERNAL_FRAME_DEICONIFIED`
- `INTERNAL_FRAME_ICONIFIED`
- `INTERNAL_FRAME_OPENED`

`InternalFrameEvent` extends `AWTEvent`, and thus encapsultes its source and the associated event ID (which are retrievable with `getSource()` and `getID()` respectively).

16.1.9   InternalFrameAdapter

class javax.swing.event.InternalFrameAdapter

This is a concrete implementation of the `InternalFrameListener` interface. It is intended to be extended for use by `InternalFrameListener` implementations that need to define only a subset of the `InternalFrameListener` methods. All methods defined within this adapter class have empty bodies.

16.1.10   Outline dragging mode

`JDesktopPane` supports an outline dragging mode to help with `JInternalFrame` dragging performance bottlenecks. To enable this mode on any `JDesktopPane`, we must set the `JDesktopPane.dragMode` client property:

```
myDesktopPane.putClientProperty(
  "JDesktopPane.dragMode","outline");
```

Instead of actually moving and painting the frame whenever it is dragged, an XOR'd rectangle is drawn in its place until the drag ends. Example 16.1 shows outline dragging mode in action.

16.2 INTERNALIZABLE/EXTERNALIZABLE FRAMES

We do not work in full-screen mode most of the time in Java applets and applications. Therefore, JDesktopPanes can often become very cluttered. We may, at some point, want to have the option of bringing an internal frame outside of the desktop. We call this *externalizing* a frame, for lack of a given name. (Please do not confuse the use of "externalizable" here with Java's Externalizable interface, an extension of the Serializable interface.) Superficially, externalizing is the process of transforming a JInternalFrame into a JFrame.

Now consider an application in which a maximized JFrame is used. When this maximized frame gains the focus, it hides all other existing frames and dialogs behind it. In situations where we need to switch back and forth between frames or dialogs, this can be quite annoying. In order to accommodate this problem, we can think of bringing dialogs and frames inside the maximized frame to a JDesktopPane. We call this *internalizing* a frame. Superficially, internalizing is the process of transforming a JFrame into a JInternalFrame.

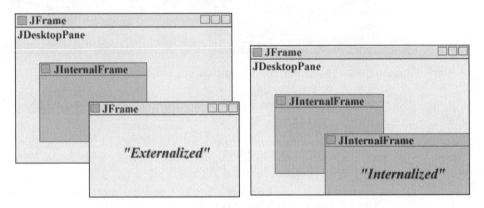

Figure 16.4 Internalizable/externalizable frames

Although no real transformation occurs, this is what appears to happen from the user's perspective. Internalizing and externalizing is actually achieved by moving the contentPane from a JFrame to a JInternalFrame and vice versa. The process is simple to implement:

For externalization, do the following.

1   Hide a JInternalFrame with setVisible(false).

2   Replace the contentPane of a hidden JFrame with that of the hidden JInternalFrame.

3   Reveal the JFrame using setVisible(true).

The steps for internalization are just the opposite.

REFERENCE   We constructed a small demo application that shows how to do this in a Swing Connection "Tips and Tricks" article. See http://java.sun.com/products/jfc/tsc/.

16.3 CASCADING AND OUTLINE DRAGGING MODE

You are probably familiar with the cascading layout that occurs as new windows are opened in most MDI environments. In fact, if you have looked at any of the custom MDI examples of chapter 15, you will have seen that when you start each demo the InnerFrames are arranged in a cascading fashion. Example 16.1 shows how to control cascading for an arbitrary number of internal frames. Additionally, the ability to switch between any pluggable look and feel available on your system is added, and outline dragging mode is enabled in our desktop.

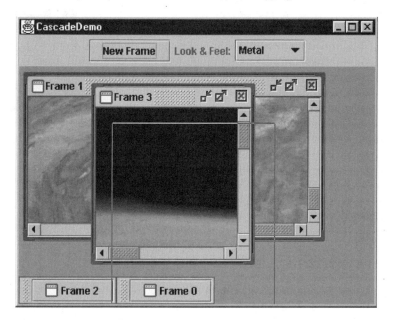

Figure 16.5   Cascading internal frames

Example 16.1

CascadeDemo.java

see \Chapter16\1

```
import java.beans.PropertyVetoException;
import javax.swing.*;
import java.awt.event.*;
import java.awt.*;

public class CascadeDemo extends JFrame implements ActionListener
{
  protected static ImageIcon EARTH;
  protected int m_count;
  protected int m_tencount;
  protected JButton m_newFrame;
  protected JDesktopPane m_desktop;
```

```
protected JComboBox m_UIBox;
protected UIManager.LookAndFeelInfo[] m_infos;

public CascadeDemo() {
  super("CascadeDemo");
  EARTH = new ImageIcon("earth.jpg");
  m_count = m_tencount = 0;

  m_desktop = new JDesktopPane();
  m_desktop.putClientProperty(
    "JDesktopPane.dragMode","outline");
  m_newFrame = new JButton("New Frame");
  m_newFrame.addActionListener(this);

  m_infos = UIManager.getInstalledLookAndFeels();
  String[] LAFNames = new String[m_infos.length];
  for(int i=0; i<m_infos.length; i++) {
    LAFNames[i] = m_infos[i].getName();
  }
  m_UIBox = new JComboBox(LAFNames);
  m_UIBox.addActionListener(this);

  JPanel topPanel = new JPanel(true);
  topPanel.add(m_newFrame);
  topPanel.add(new JLabel("Look & Feel:",SwingConstants.RIGHT));
  topPanel.add(m_UIBox);

  getContentPane().setLayout(new BorderLayout());
  getContentPane().add("North", topPanel);
  getContentPane().add("Center", m_desktop);

  setSize(570,400);
  Dimension dim = getToolkit().getScreenSize();
  setLocation(dim.width/2-getWidth()/2,
    dim.height/2-getHeight()/2);
  setVisible(true);
  WindowListener l = new WindowAdapter() {
    public void windowClosing(WindowEvent e) {
      System.exit(0);
    }
  };
  addWindowListener(l);
}

public void newFrame() {
  JInternalFrame jif = new JInternalFrame("Frame " + m_count,
    true, true, true, true);
  jif.setBounds(20*(m_count%10) + m_tencount*80,
    20*(m_count%10), 200, 200);

  JLabel label = new JLabel(EARTH);
  jif.getContentPane().add(new JScrollPane(label));

  m_desktop.add(jif);
  try {
```

1 Constructor lays out all GUI components

3 Button to create new frames

2 Provides combo box with available LookAndFeels

3 Creates a new frame

4 Adds internal frame and selects it, which moves it to the front

```
        jif.setSelected(true);
      }
      catch (PropertyVetoException pve) {
        System.out.println("Could not select " + jif.getTitle());
      }

      m_count++;
      if (m_count%10 == 0) {
        if (m_tencount < 3)
          m_tencount++;
        else
          m_tencount = 0;
      }
    }

    public void actionPerformed(ActionEvent e) {
      if (e.getSource() == m_newFrame)
        newFrame();
      else if (e.getSource() == m_UIBox) {
        m_UIBox.hidePopup(); // BUG WORKAROUND
        try {
          UIManager.setLookAndFeel(
            m_infos[m_UIBox.getSelectedIndex()].getClassName());
          SwingUtilities.updateComponentTreeUI(this);
        }
        catch(Exception ex) {
          System.out.println("Could not load " +
            m_infos[m_UIBox.getSelectedIndex()].getClassName());
        }
      }
    }
    public static void main(String[] args) {
      new CascadeDemo();
    }
  }
}
```

4 Adds internal frame and selects it, which moves it to the front

5 Steps to the location for the next frame, modulo ten

3 Creates a new frame

6 Changes LookAndFeel

16.3.1 Understanding the code

Class CascadeDemo

1 The CascadeDemo class extends JFrame to provide the main container for this example. The constructor is responsible for initializing and laying out all GUI components. One class variable, EARTH, and several instance variables are needed:

- ImageIcon EARTH: The image used in each JLabel.
- int m_count: Keeps track of the number of internal frames that exist within the desktop.
- int m_tencount: Incremented every time ten internal frames are added to the desktop.
- JButton m_newFrame: Used to add new JInternalFrames to m_desktop.
- JDesktopPane m_desktop: The container for our JInternalFrames.
- JComboBox m_UIBox: Used for look and feel selection.
- UIManager.LookAndFeelInfo[] m_infos: An array of LookAndFeelInfo objects used in changing look and feels.

② The only code that may look unfamiliar to you in the constructor is the following:

```
m_infos = UIManager.getInstalledLookAndFeels();
String[] LAFNames = new String[m_infos.length];
for(int i=0; i<m_infos.length; i++) {
  LAFNames[i] = m_infos[i].getName();
}
m_UIBox = new JComboBox(LAFNames);
```

The UIManager class is in charge of keeping track of the current look and feel as well as providing us with a way to query information about the different look and feels available on our system. Its static getInstalledLookAndFeels() method returns an array of UIManager.LookAndFeelInfo objects and we assign this array to m_infos.

Each UIManager.LookAndFeelInfo object represents a different look and feel that is currently installed on our system. Its getName() method returns a short name representing its associated look and feel (for example, "Metal," "CDE/Motif," or "Windows"). We create an array of these Strings, called LAFNames, with indices corresponding to those of m_infos.

Finally we create a JComboBox, m_UIBox, using this array of Strings. In the action-Performed() method (see below), when an entry in m_UIBox is selected, we match it with its corresponding UIManager.LookAndFeelInfo object in m_infos and load the associated look and feel.

③ The newFrame method is invoked whenever m_NewButton is pressed. This method first creates a new JInternalFrame with resizable, closable, maximizable, and iconifiable properties, and a unique title based on the current frame count:

```
JInternalFrame jif = new JInternalFrame("Frame " + m_count,
  true, true, true, true);
```

The frame is then sized to 200x200 and its initial position within our desktop is calculated based on the value of m_count and m_tencount. The value of m_tencount is periodically reset so that each new internal frame lies within our desktop view (assuming we do not resize our desktop to have a smaller width than the maximum of 20*(m_count%10) + m_tencount*80, and a smaller height than the maximum of 20*(m_count%10). This turns out to be 420x180, where the maximum of m_count%10 is 9 and the maximum of m_tencount is 3).

```
jif.setBounds(20*(m_count%10) + m_tencount*80,
  20*(m_count%10), 200, 200);
```

> **NOTE** You might imagine a more flexible cascading scheme that positions internal frames based on the current size of the desktop. In general, a rigid cascading routine is sufficient, but we are certainly not limited to this.

④ A JLabel with an image is added to a JScrollPane, which is then added to the contentPane of each internal frame. Each frame is added to the desktop in layer 0 (the default layer when none is specified). Adding an internal frame to the desktop does not automatically place that frame at the frontmost position within the specified layer, and it is not automatically selected. To force both of these things to occur, we use the JInternalFrame setSelected() method (which requires us to catch a java.beans.PropertyVetoException).

⑤ Finally, the newFrame() method increments m_count and determines whether to increment m_tencount or reset it to 0. m_tencount is only incremented after a group of 10 frames has been added (`m_count%10 == 0`) and it is only reset after it has reached a value of 3. So 40 internal frames are created for each cycle of `m_tencount` (10 for `m_tencount` = 0, 1, 2, and 3).

```
m_count++;
if (m_count%10 == 0) {
  if (m_tencount < 3)
    m_tencount++;
  else
    m_tencount = 0;
}
```

6 The `actionPerformed()` method handles `m_newFrame` button presses and `m_UIBox` selections. The `m_newFrame` button invokes the `newFrame()` method and selecting a look and feel from `m_UIBox` changes the application to use that look and feel. Look and feel switching is done by calling the `UIManager setLookAndFeel()` method and passing it the `LookAndFeelInfo` object representing the look and feel to use (which we stored in the `m_infos` array in the constructor). Calling `SwingUtilities.updateComponentTreeUI(this)` changes the look and feel of everything contained within the `CascadeDemo` frame (refer back to chapter 2).

BUG ALERT The call to `m_UIBox.hidePopup()` is added to avoid a null pointer exception bug that is caused when changing the look and feel of an active `JComboBox`. We expect this to be fixed in a future Java 2 release.

16.3.2   Running the code

Figure 16.5 shows `CascadeDemo` in action. This figure shows a `JInternalFrame` in the process of being dragged in outline dragging mode. Try creating plenty of frames to make sure that cascading is working properly. Experiment with different look and feels. As a final test, comment out the `m_UIBox.hidePopup()` call to see if this bug has been fixed in your version of Java.

16.4   AN X-WINDOWS STYLE DESKTOP ENVIRONMENT

Some X-windows systems (specifically fvwm, Panorama (SCO), and TED (TriTeal)) provide what is referred to as a *pager*. This small window sits in the desktop (usually at the top of the screen) and shows the positions of all windows contained in the desktop. By clicking or dragging the mouse inside the pager, the user's view is moved to the associated location within the desktop. This is very helpful to X-windows users because these systems often support very large desktops. They are often larger than four times the actual size of the screen. Figure 16.6 shows a pager running on a Linux system with a desktop nine times the size of the screen.

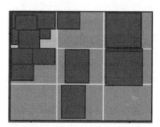

Figure 16.6   A Linux pager

In example 16.2, we develop our own partial implementation of a pager for use with JDesktopPane and its JInternalFrame children. We show it in use with a fairly large JDesktopPane (1600x1200). This desktop is scrollable and the pager will always stay in the user's current view, even when scrolling.

NOTE In this example we use a custom package called resize. The classes contained in this package were introduced in chapter 15 as our XXResizeEdge components. Refer to chapter 15 if you have any questions regarding this code. We do not explain how it works in this chapter. However, you should know that the classes contained in this package can be wrapped around any JComponent in a BorderLayout to make that component resizable. The thickness and minimum dimension properties associated with each class have been hard-coded as constants. If you plan to work with these classes, we suggest adding a pair of set()/get() accessors to modify and retrieve these values.

The main purpose of presenting example 16.2 is to show how DesktopManager can be customized to fit our needs. In the next section, we will expand on this example to build a networked, multi-user desktop environment.

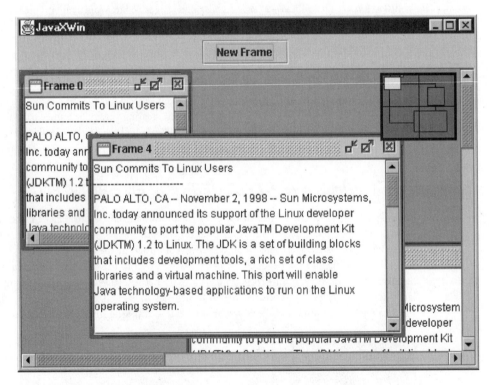

Figure 16.7 JavaXWin **with** WindowWatcher

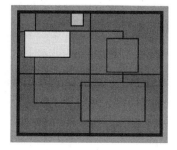

Figure 16.8 `WindowWatcher`
with `XXResizeEdges`

Example 16.2

JavaXWin.java

see \Chapter16\2

```java
import java.beans.PropertyVetoException;
import javax.swing.*;
import java.awt.event.*;
import java.io.*;
import java.awt.*;

public class JavaXWin extends JFrame
{
  protected int m_count;
  protected int m_tencount;
  protected int m_wmX, m_wmY;
  protected JButton m_newFrame;
  protected JDesktopPane m_desktop;
  protected WindowManager m_wm;
  protected JViewport viewport;

  public JavaXWin() {
    setTitle("JavaXWin");
    m_count = m_tencount = 0;
    m_desktop = new JDesktopPane();

    JScrollPane scroller = new JScrollPane();
    m_wm = new WindowManager(m_desktop);
    m_desktop.setDesktopManager(m_wm);
    m_desktop.add(m_wm.getWindowWatcher(),
      JLayeredPane.PALETTE_LAYER);
    m_wm.getWindowWatcher().setBounds(555,5,200,150);

    viewport = new JViewport() {
      public void setViewPosition(Point p) {
        super.setViewPosition(p);
        m_wm.getWindowWatcher().setLocation(
          m_wm.getWindowWatcher().getX() +
            (getViewPosition().x-m_wmX),
          m_wm.getWindowWatcher().getY() +
            (getViewPosition().y-m_wmY));
```

1 Constructor creates
JDesktopPane, connects
it to a **WindowManager**,
and adds **WindowWatcher**
to palette layer, above all
internal frames

2 Keeps
WindowWatcher
in same place,
even with
scrolling

```
      m_wmX = getViewPosition().x;
      m_wmY = getViewPosition().y;
    }
  };
  viewport.setView(m_desktop);
  scroller.setViewport(viewport);

  ComponentAdapter ca = new ComponentAdapter() {
    JViewport view = viewport;
    public void componentResized(ComponentEvent e) {
      m_wm.getWindowWatcher().setLocation(
        view.getViewPosition().x + view.getWidth()-
          m_wm.getWindowWatcher().getWidth()+5,
        view.getViewPosition().y + 5);
    }
  };
  viewport.addComponentListener(ca);

  m_newFrame = new JButton("New Frame");
  m_newFrame.addActionListener(new ActionListener() {
    public void actionPerformed(ActionEvent e) {
      newFrame();
    }
  });

  JPanel topPanel = new JPanel(true);
  topPanel.setLayout(new FlowLayout());

  getContentPane().setLayout(new BorderLayout());
  getContentPane().add("North", topPanel);
  getContentPane().add("Center", scroller);

  topPanel.add(m_newFrame);

  Dimension dim = getToolkit().getScreenSize();
  setSize(800,600);
  setLocation(dim.width/2-getWidth()/2,
    dim.height/2-getHeight()/2);
  m_desktop.setPreferredSize(new Dimension(1600,1200));
  setVisible(true);
  WindowListener l = new WindowAdapter() {
    public void windowClosing(WindowEvent e) {
      System.exit(0);
    }
  };
  addWindowListener(l);
}
public void newFrame() {
  JInternalFrame jif = new JInternalFrame("Frame " + m_count,
    true, true, true, true);
  jif.setBounds(20*(m_count%10) + m_tencount*80,
    20*(m_count%10), 200, 200);

  JTextArea text = new JTextArea();
  JScrollPane scroller = new JScrollPane();
```

❷ Keeps WindowWatcher in same place, even with scrolling

❸ Looks at resize events to keep WindowWatcher at top

❹ Creates internal frame with text area and sample text

```
      scroller.getViewport().add(text);
      try {
        FileReader fileStream = new FileReader("JavaLinux.txt");
        text.read(fileStream, "JavaLinux.txt");
      }
      catch (Exception e) {
        text.setText("* Could not read JavaLinux.txt *");
      }
      jif.getContentPane().add(scroller);

      m_desktop.add(jif);
      try {
        jif.setSelected(true);
      }
      catch (PropertyVetoException pve) {
        System.out.println("Could not select " + jif.getTitle());
      }

      m_count++;
      if (m_count%10 == 0) {
        if (m_tencount < 3)
          m_tencount++;
        else
          m_tencount = 0;
      }
    }

  public static void main(String[] args) {
    new JavaXWin();
  }
}

class WindowManager extends DefaultDesktopManager
{
  protected WindowWatcher m_ww;

  public WindowManager(JDesktopPane desktop) {
    m_ww = new WindowWatcher(desktop);
  }

  public WindowWatcher getWindowWatcher() { return m_ww; }

  public void activateFrame(JInternalFrame f) {
    super.activateFrame(f);
    m_ww.repaint();
  }
  public void beginDraggingFrame(JComponent f) {
    super.beginDraggingFrame(f);
    m_ww.repaint();
  }
  public void beginResizingFrame(JComponent f, int direction) {
    super.beginResizingFrame(f,direction);
    m_ww.repaint();
  }
  public void closeFrame(JInternalFrame f) {
```

⑤ Simple DefaultDesktopManager extension; uses WindowWatcher

```java
      super.closeFrame(f);
      m_ww.repaint();
    }
    public void deactivateFrame(JInternalFrame f) {
      super.deactivateFrame(f);
      m_ww.repaint();
    }
    public void deiconifyFrame(JInternalFrame f) {
      super.deiconifyFrame(f);
      m_ww.repaint();
    }
    public void dragFrame(JComponent f, int newX, int newY) {
      f.setLocation(newX, newY);
      m_ww.repaint();
    }
    public void endDraggingFrame(JComponent f) {
      super.endDraggingFrame(f);
      m_ww.repaint();
    }
    public void endResizingFrame(JComponent f) {
      super.endResizingFrame(f);
      m_ww.repaint();
    }
    public void iconifyFrame(JInternalFrame f) {
      super.iconifyFrame(f);
      m_ww.repaint();
    }
    public void maximizeFrame(JInternalFrame f) {
      super.maximizeFrame(f);
      m_ww.repaint();
    }
    public void minimizeFrame(JInternalFrame f) {
      super.minimizeFrame(f);
      m_ww.repaint();
    }
    public void openFrame(JInternalFrame f) {
      super.openFrame(f);
      m_ww.repaint();
    }
    public void resizeFrame(JComponent f,
     int newX, int newY, int newWidth, int newHeight) {
      f.setBounds(newX, newY, newWidth, newHeight);
      m_ww.repaint();
    }
    public void setBoundsForFrame(JComponent f,
     int newX, int newY, int newWidth, int newHeight) {
      f.setBounds(newX, newY, newWidth, newHeight);
      m_ww.repaint();
    }
  }
}
```

see \Chapter16\2

```
import java.awt.*;
import java.awt.event.*;
import javax.swing.*;
import javax.swing.event.*;

import resize.*;

public class WindowWatcher extends JPanel
{
  protected static final Color C_UNSELECTED =
    new Color(123, 123, 123);
  protected static final Color C_SELECTED =
    new Color(243, 232, 165);
  protected static final Color C_BACKGROUND =
    new Color(5,165,165);
  protected static final Color C_WWATCHER =
    new Color(203,226,0);
  protected float m_widthratio, m_heightratio;
  protected int m_width, m_height, m_XDifference, m_YDifference;
  protected JDesktopPane m_desktop;
  protected NorthResizeEdge m_northResizer;
  protected SouthResizeEdge m_southResizer;
  protected EastResizeEdge m_eastResizer;
  protected WestResizeEdge m_westResizer;

  public WindowWatcher(JDesktopPane desktop) {
    m_desktop = desktop;
    setOpaque(true);

    m_northResizer = new NorthResizeEdge(this);
    m_southResizer = new SouthResizeEdge(this);
    m_eastResizer = new EastResizeEdge(this);
    m_westResizer = new WestResizeEdge(this);

    setLayout(new BorderLayout());
    add(m_northResizer, BorderLayout.NORTH);
    add(m_southResizer, BorderLayout.SOUTH);
    add(m_eastResizer, BorderLayout.EAST);
    add(m_westResizer, BorderLayout.WEST);

    MouseInputAdapter ma = new MouseInputAdapter() {
      public void mousePressed(MouseEvent e) {
        m_XDifference = e.getX();
        m_YDifference = e.getY();
      }
      public void mouseDragged(MouseEvent e) {
        int vx = 0;
        int vy = 0;
        if (m_desktop.getParent() instanceof JViewport) {
          vx = ((JViewport)
            m_desktop.getParent()).getViewPosition().x;
          vy = ((JViewport)
```

6 Implements X-Windows-like pager extends JPanel

7 Adds resize edges to borders of panel

8 Adapter handles dragging of WindowWatcher

```
          m_desktop.getParent()).getViewPosition().y;
      }
      int w = m_desktop.getParent().getWidth();
      int h = m_desktop.getParent().getHeight();
      int x = getX();
      int y = getY();
      int ex = e.getX();
      int ey = e.getY();
      if ((ey + y > vy && ey + y < h+vy) &&
          (ex + x > vx && ex + x < w+vx))
      {
        setLocation(ex-m_XDifference + x, ey-m_YDifference + y);
      }
      else if (!(ey + y > vy && ey + y < h+vy) &&
              (ex + x > vx && ex + x < w+vx))
      {
        if (!(ey + y > vy) && ey + y < h+vy)
          setLocation(ex-m_XDifference + x, vy-m_YDifference);
        else if (ey + y > vy && !(ey + y < h+vy))
          setLocation(ex-m_XDifference + x, (h+vy)-m_YDifference);
      }
      else if ((ey + y >vy && ey + y < h+vy) &&
              !(ex + x > vx && ex + x < w+vx))
      {
        if (!(ex + x > vx) && ex + x < w+vx)
          setLocation(vx-m_XDifference, ey-m_YDifference + y);
        else if (ex + x > vx && !(ex + x < w))
          setLocation((w+vx)-m_XDifference, ey-m_YDifference + y);
      }
      else if (!(ey + y > vy) && ey + y < h+vy &&
              !(ex + x > vx) && ex + x < w+vx)
        setLocation(vx-m_XDifference, vy-m_YDifference);
      else if (!(ey + y > vy) && ey + y < h+vy &&
              ex + x > vx && !(ex + x < w+vx))
        setLocation((w+vx)-m_XDifference, vy-m_YDifference);
      else if (ey + y > vy && !(ey + y < h+vy) &&
              !(ex + x > vx) && ex + x < w+vx)
        setLocation(vx-m_XDifference, (h+vy)-m_YDifference);
      else if (ey + y > vy && !(ey + y < h+vy) &&
              ex + x > vx && !(ex + x < w+vx))
        setLocation((w+vx)-m_XDifference, (h+vy)-m_YDifference);
    }
    public void mouseEntered(MouseEvent e) {
      setCursor(Cursor.getPredefinedCursor(
        Cursor.MOVE_CURSOR));
    }
    public void mouseExited(MouseEvent e) {
      setCursor(Cursor.getPredefinedCursor(
        Cursor.DEFAULT_CURSOR));
    }
  };
  addMouseListener(ma);
```

```
      addMouseMotionListener(ma);
    }

    public void paintComponent(Graphics g) {
      super.paintComponent(g);
      m_height = getHeight();
      m_width = getWidth();
      g.setColor(C_BACKGROUND);
      g.fillRect(0,0,m_width,m_height);
      Component[] components = m_desktop.getComponents();
      m_widthratio = ((float)
        m_desktop.getWidth())/((float) m_width);
      m_heightratio = ((float)
        m_desktop.getHeight())/((float) m_height);
      for (int i=components.length-1; i>-1; i--) {
        if (components[i].isVisible()) {
          g.setColor(C_UNSELECTED);
          if (components[i] instanceof JInternalFrame) {
            if (((JInternalFrame) components[i]).isSelected())
              g.setColor(C_SELECTED);
          }
          else if(components[i] instanceof WindowWatcher)
            g.setColor(C_WWATCHER);
          g.fillRect(
            (int)(((float)components[i].getX())/m_widthratio),
            (int)(((float)components[i].getY())/m_heightratio),
            (int)(((float)components[i].getWidth())/m_widthratio),
            (int)(((float)components[i].getHeight())/m_heightratio));
          g.setColor(Color.black);
          g.drawRect(
            (int)(((float)components[i].getX())/m_widthratio),
            (int)(((float)components[i].getY())/m_heightratio),
            (int)(((float)components[i].getWidth())/m_widthratio),
            (int)(((float)components[i].getHeight())/m_heightratio));
        }
      }
      g.drawLine(m_width/2,0,m_width/2,m_height);
      g.drawLine(0,m_height/2,m_width,m_height/2);
    }
  }
```

**Draws thumbnail view
of each internal frame,
inside the WindowWatcher** **9**

16.4.1   Understanding the code

Class JavaXWin

JavaXWin extends JFrame and provides the main container for this example. Several instance variables are needed:

- int m_count, int m_tencount: Used for cascading.
- JButton m_newFrame: Used to create new frames.
- JDesktopPane m_desktop: Our desktop pane.
- int m_wmX: Keeps track of the most recent x-coordinate of the desktop scrollpane's view position.

- **int m_wmY**: Keeps track of the most recent y-coordinate of the desktop scrollpane's view position.
- **WindowManager m_wm**: Our custom DesktopManager implementation that updates WindowWatcher whenever any of its methods are called.
- **JViewport viewport**: The viewport of the scrollpane that will contain our desktop.

❶ In the JavaXWin constructor we create a new JDesktopPane and place it inside a JScroll-Pane. Then we create a new WindowManager (see below) and pass it a reference to our desktop. We then tell our desktop that this WindowManager is a DesktopManager implementation and it should be used to manage our internal frames. This is done with JDesktopPane's setDesk-topManager() method. We then place our WindowManager's WindowWatcher in our desktop's PALETTE_LAYER to guarantee that it is always displayed over all internal frames:

```
m_wm = new WindowManager(m_desktop);
m_desktop.setDesktopManager(m_wm);
m_desktop.add(m_wm.getWindowWatcher(),
   JLayeredPane.PALETTE_LAYER);
```

❷ A custom JViewport is constructed with an overriden setViewPosition() method. This method is responsible for keeping our WindowWatcher in the same place as we scroll the desktop. Each time the view is changed, we reposition the WindowWatcher to give the impression that it lies completely above our desktop and is unaffected by scrolling. Basically, this code just computes the difference between the current and most recent viewport position, and it adds this difference to the coordinates of the WindowWatcher. We then use this JViewport as the viewport for the JScrollPane our desktop is contained in using JScrollPane's set-View() method.

❸ We next construct a ComponentAdapter and attach it to our viewport. We override its com-ponentResized() method to move WindowWatcher to the top whenever the viewport is resized. This is done so that WindowWatcher will never disappear from our view when the application frame is resized.

❹ The newFrame() method is almost identical to that of CascadeDemo. The only difference is that we place a JTextArea in each internal frame and load a text file into it (the text file is the original press release from Sun announcing a Linux port of JDK1.2!)

Class WindowManager

❺ The WindowManager class is a simple extension of DefaultDesktopManager which over-rides all JInternalFrame related methods. Only one instance variable is necessary:

- **WindowWatcher m_ww**: Our custom pager component.

Each of the methods that are overridden from DefaultDesktopManager call their superclass counterparts by using super, and then call repaint on m_ww. So each time the user performs an action on an internal frame, WindowManager basically just tells our Window-Watcher to repaint itself.

The WindowManager constructor takes a reference to the desktop it manages, and in turn passes this reference to the WindowWatcher constructor. WindowWatcher uses this reference to find out all the information it needs to know about our desktop's contents to paint itself correctly.

The `getWindowWatcher()` method just returns a reference to the `WindowWatcher` object, `m_ww`, and it is used when the desktop is scrolled as discussed above.

Class WindowWatcher

6 This class is our version of an X-windows pager. It uses the `XXResizeEdge` components in our custom `resize` package to allow full resizability. Four class variables are necessary:

- `Color C_UNSELECTED`: Used to represent all components but selected `JInternalFrames` and `WindowWatcher` itself.
- `Color C_SELECTED`: Used to represent selected `JInternalFrames`.
- `Color C_BACKGROUND`: Used for the `WindowWatcher` background.
- `Color C_WWATCHER`: Used to represent the `WindowWatcher` itself.

These are the instance variables:

- `float m_widthratio`: Keeps the ratio of desktop width to `WindowWatcher` width.
- `float m_heightratio`: Keeps the ratio of desktop height to `WindowWatcher` height.
- `int m_width`: The current `WindowWatcher` width.
- `int m_height`: The current `WindowWatcher` height.
- `int m_XDifference`: Used for dragging the `WindowWatcher` horizontally.
- `int m_YDifference`: Used for dragging the `WindowWatcher` vertically.
- `NorthResizeEdge m_northResizer`: The north resize component.
- `SouthResizeEdge m_southResizer`: The south resize component.
- `EastResizeEdge m_eastResizer`: The east resize component.
- `WestResizeEdge m_westResizer`: The west resize component.
- `JDesktopPane m_desktop`: The reference to the desktop the `WindowWatcher` is watching over.

7 The constructor is passed a `JDesktopPane` reference which is assigned to `m_desktop`. We use a `BorderLayout` for this component and add instances of our resize package's `XXResizeEdge` classes to each outer region, thereby allowing `WindowWatcher` to be fully resizable.

NOTE See the `resize` package source code for details about these components. They were introduced and discussed in chapter 15. We encourage you to add more accessors to these classes to allow such things as setting thickness and color.

8 We then construct a custom `MouseInputAdapter`. This adapter overrides the `mousePressed()`, `mouseDragged()`, `mouseEntered()`, and `mouseExited()` methods. The `mousePressed()` method stores the location of the mouse press in our `m_XDifference` and `m_YDifference` class variables. These are used in the `mouseDragged()` method to allow `WindowWatcher` to be continuously dragged from any point within its bounds.

The `mouseDragged()` method allows the user to drag `WindowWatcher` anywhere within the visible region of the desktop. In order to enforce this and still allow smooth movement, we need to handle many different cases depending on mouse position and, possibly, the current `JViewport` position that the desktop is contained within. We do not assume that `WindowWatcher` and its associated desktop are contained within a `JViewport`. However, in such a case we have to handle `WindowWatcher`'s movement differently.

NOTE The `mouseDragged()` code is a straightforward adaptation of the code we used to control dragging our `InnerFrames` in chapter 15, section 15.5.

The mouseEntered() method just changes the cursor to MOVE_CURSOR and mouseExited() changes the cursor back to DEFAULT_CURSOR.

Finally, we add this adapter with both addMouseListener() and addMouseMotionListener(). (Note that MouseInputAdapter implements both of the MouseListener and MouseMotionListener interfaces.)

9 The paintComponent() method starts by filling the background, getting the current dimensions, and retrieving an array of components contained in the desktop. The ratios of desktop size to WindowWatcher size are computed, and we then enter a loop which is executed for each component in the array. This loop starts by setting the color to C_UNSELECTED. We then check to see if the component under consideration is a JInternalFrame. If it is, we check if it is selected. If it is selected, we set the current color to C_SELECTED. If the component is not a JInternalFrame, we check to see if it is the WindowWatcher itself. If it is, we set the current color to C_WWATCHER.

```
for (int i=components.length-1; i>-1; i--) {
  if (components[i].isVisible()) {
    g.setColor(C_UNSELECTED);
    if (components[i] instanceof JInternalFrame) {
      if (((JInternalFrame) components[i]).isSelected())
        g.setColor(C_SELECTED);
    }
    else if(components[i] instanceof WindowWatcher)
      g.setColor(C_WWATCHER);
    g.fillRect((int) (((float)
      .
      .
      .

  }
}
```

Once the color is selected, we paint a filled, scaled rectangle representing that component. We scale this rectangle based on the ratios we computed earlier, making sure to use floats to avoid otherwise large rounding errors. We then paint a black outline around this rectangle and move on to the next component in our array until it has been exhausted. We cycle through this array from the highest index down to 0 so that the rectangles are painted in the same order in which the components appear in the JDesktopPane (the appearance of layering is consistent).

16.4.2   Running the code

Figure 16.7 shows JavaXWin in action and figure 16.8 is a snapshot of the WindowWatcher itself. Try moving frames around and resizing them. Notice that WindowWatcher smoothly captures and displays each component as it changes position and size. Try moving WindowWatcher and notice that you cannot move it outside the visible region of the desktop. Now try scrolling to a different position within the desktop and watch how WindowWatcher follows us and remains in the same position within our view. Also notice that WindowWatcher can be resized because we've taken advantage of the classes in our custom resize package. In the next example we will build on top of JavaXWin and WindowManager to construct a multi-user, networked desktop environment.

NOTE WindowWatcher does not fully implement the functionality of most pagers. Clicking on an area of a typical pager usually repositions the view of our desktop. This may
be an interesting and useful additional feature to implement in WindowWatcher.

16.5 A NETWORKED MULTI-USER DESKTOP ENVIRONMENT USING SOCKETS

Collaborative environments are becoming more commonplace as the Internet flourishes.
They will no doubt continue to grow in popularity. Imagine a class taught using an interactive
whiteboard or a set of whiteboards each contained in an internal frame.

In this section we show how to construct a basic multi-user JDesktopPane using sockets.
We support a server and only one client. Both the server and client-side users can move, resize,
and close frames, as well as chat in a console window. (We allow only the client to create
frames.) All JInternalFrame actions invoked by one user are sent to the other user's desktop
using a lightweight message-passing scheme. What we end up with is the beginnings of a true
multi-user desktop environment.

NOTE We've tested this environment between South Carolina and New York with satisfactory response times (using 28.8 modems dialed in to typical ISPs).

Before we present the code, it is helpful here to briefly summarize the network-centric
classes that this example takes advantage of (see the API documentation or the Java tutorial for
more thorough coverage).

16.5.1 Socket

class java.net.Socket

A Socket is a connection to a single remote machine. Each Socket has an InputStream
and an OutputStream associated with it. Data can be sent to the remote machine by writing
to the OutputStream and data is retrieved from the remote machine via the InputStream.
Each Socket also has an InetAddress instance associated with it which encapsulates the IP
address that it is connected to.

16.5.2 ServerSocket

class java.net.ServerSocket

A ServerSocket is used to establish Socket-to-Socket connections. Usually a ServerSocket
calls its accept() method to wait for a client to connect. Once a client connects, a Server-
Socket can return a Socket that the host machine uses for communication with that client.

16.5.3 InetAddress

class java.net.InetAddress

This class encapsulates information about an IP address, such as the host name and the address.

Example 16.3 works by sending messages back and forth between the client and server. Each
message is received and processed the same way on each end. Two types of messages can be sent:

- *Chat messages*: Messages of this type can be of any length and always begin with "cc".
- *Internal frame messages*: Messages of this type are always 29 characters long, are represented only by numeric characters, and have a distinct six-field structure.

Figure 16.7 illustrates our internal frame message structure. These are the different parts of the structure:

- **ID** represents the `WindowManager` method to invoke.
- **TAG** is a unique identifier returned by each internal frame's overridden `toString()` method.
- **new X** is the new x-coordinate of the internal frame (if applicable).
- **new Y** is the new y-coordinate of the internal frame (if applicable).
- **new width** is the new width of the internal frame (if applicable).
- **new height** is the new height of the internal frame (if applicable).

ID	TAG	new X	new Y	new width	new height
# chars: 2	3	6	6	6	6

Figure 16.9 Our internal frame message structure

We will discuss how and when both types of messages are constructed and interpreted after we present the code in example 16.3. The server is implemented as class `JavaXServer`, and the client as `JavaXClient`. `JavaXClient` was largely built from `JavaXServer`. We have highlighted the changes below, and inserted comments to denote where code has been modifed or unchanged.

The `WindowManager` class from the last section has been completely rebuilt and defined in a separate class file. The `WindowWatcher` class remains unchanged, using the `XXResize-Edge` classes in our resize package to allow full resizability. Both `JavaXServer` and `JavaX-Client` use instances of the new `WindowManager` to manage their desktop, send messages, and interpret calls invoked by their message receiving mechanism (the `processMessage()` method).

Example 16.3

JavaXServer.java

see \Chapter16\3

```
import java.beans.PropertyVetoException;
import javax.swing.*;
import java.awt.event.*;
import java.io.*;
import java.awt.*;
import java.net.*;

public class JavaXServer extends JFrame implements Runnable
{
  protected int m_count;
  protected int m_tencount;
```

Implements Runnable to do some work on a background thread ❶

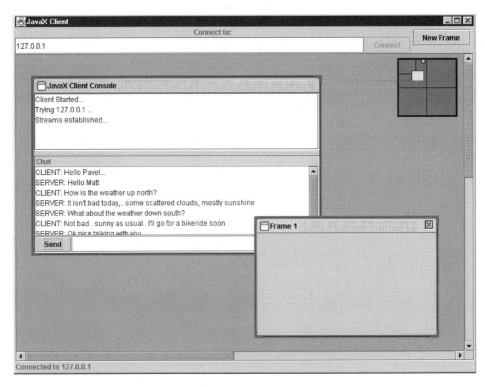

Figure 16.10 `JavaXClient` **with established connection**

```
protected int m_wmX, m_wmY;
protected JDesktopPane m_desktop;
protected WindowManager m_wm;
protected JViewport m_viewport;

protected JTextArea m_consoletext, m_consolechat;
protected JTextField m_chatText;
protected boolean m_connected;
protected JLabel m_status;
protected DataInputStream m_input;
protected DataOutputStream m_output;
protected Socket m_client;
protected ServerSocket m_server;
protected Thread m_listenThread;
protected ConThread m_conthread;

public JavaXServer() {
  setTitle("JavaX Server");
  m_count = m_tencount = 0;
  m_desktop = new JDesktopPane();

  m_status = new JLabel("No Client");
```

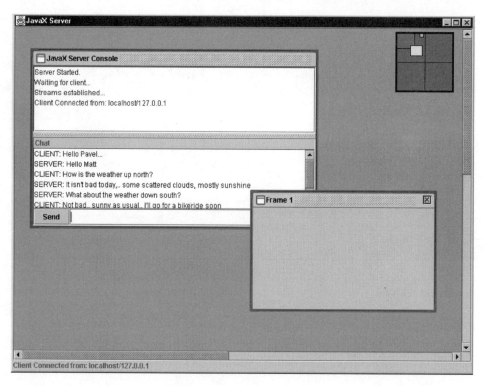

Figure 16.11 `JavaXServer` **with established connection**

```
JScrollPane scroller = new JScrollPane();
m_wm = new WindowManager(m_desktop);
m_desktop.setDesktopManager(m_wm);
m_desktop.add(m_wm.getWindowWatcher(),
  JLayeredPane.PALETTE_LAYER);
m_wm.getWindowWatcher().setBounds(555,5,100,100);

m_viewport = new JViewport() {
  public void setViewPosition(Point p) {
    super.setViewPosition(p);
    m_wm.getWindowWatcher().setLocation(
      m_wm.getWindowWatcher().getX() +
        (getViewPosition().x-m_wmX),
      m_wm.getWindowWatcher().getY() +
        (getViewPosition().y-m_wmY));
    m_wmX = getViewPosition().x;
    m_wmY = getViewPosition().y;
  }
};
m_viewport.setView(m_desktop);
scroller.setViewport(m_viewport);
```

2 Creates
WindowManager
with desktop

2 Sets WindowWatcher
position relative to
viewport location

```
    ComponentAdapter ca = new ComponentAdapter() {
      JViewport view = m_viewport;
      public void componentResized(ComponentEvent e) {
        m_wm.getWindowWatcher().setLocation(
          view.getViewPosition().x + view.getWidth()-
            m_wm.getWindowWatcher().getWidth()-15,
          view.getViewPosition().y + 5);
      }
    };
    m_viewport.addComponentListener(ca);

    getContentPane().setLayout(new BorderLayout());
    getContentPane().add("Center", scroller);
    getContentPane().add("South", m_status);

    setupConsole();

    Dimension dim = getToolkit().getScreenSize();
    setSize(800,600);
    setLocation(dim.width/2-getWidth()/2,
      dim.height/2-getHeight()/2);
    m_desktop.setPreferredSize(new Dimension(1600,1200));
    WindowListener l = new WindowAdapter() {
      public void windowClosing(WindowEvent e) {
        System.exit(0);
      }
    };
    addWindowListener(l);

    setVisible(true);
  }

  public void setupConsole() {
    JInternalFrame console = new JInternalFrame(
      "JavaX Server Console",
      false, false, false, false) {
      int TAG = m_count;
      public String toString() {
        return "" + TAG;
      }
    };
    m_count++;
    console.setBounds(20, 20, 500, 300);

    JPanel chatPanel = new JPanel();
    JLabel chatLabel = new JLabel(" Chat");
    chatPanel.setLayout(new BorderLayout());

    m_consoletext = new JTextArea();
    m_consoletext.setPreferredSize(new Dimension(500,50));
    m_consoletext.setLineWrap(true);
    m_consoletext.setText("Server Started." +
      "\nWaiting for client...");
    m_consoletext.setEditable(false);
```

❷ Creates chat console

❸ Server status text area

```
m_consolechat = new JTextArea();
m_consolechat.setLineWrap(true);
m_consolechat.setEditable(false);

m_chatText = new JTextField();
m_chatText.addActionListener(new ChatAdapter());

JButton chatSend = new JButton("Send");
chatSend.addActionListener(new ChatAdapter());

JPanel sendPanel = new JPanel();

sendPanel.setLayout(new BorderLayout());
sendPanel.add("Center", m_chatText);
sendPanel.add("West", chatSend);

JScrollPane cscroller1 = new JScrollPane(m_consoletext);
JScrollPane cscroller2 = new JScrollPane(m_consolechat);

chatPanel.add("North", chatLabel);
chatPanel.add("Center", cscroller2);
chatPanel.add("South", sendPanel);

JSplitPane splitter = new JSplitPane(
  JSplitPane.VERTICAL_SPLIT, true, cscroller1, chatPanel);

console.getContentPane().add(splitter);
m_desktop.add(console);

m_wm.getWindowWatcher().repaint();

try {
  m_server = new ServerSocket(5000,500);
}
catch (IOException e) {
  m_consoletext.append("\n" + e);
}
m_conthread = new ConThread();
}

public void run() {
  while (m_connected) {
    try {
      processMessage(m_input.readUTF());
    }
    catch (IOException e) {
      m_consoletext.append("\n" + e);
      m_connected = false;
    }
  }
}

public void newFrame() {
  JInternalFrame jif = new JInternalFrame("Frame " + m_count,
    true, true, false, false) {
    int TAG = m_count;
    public String toString() {
```

3 Chat output text area

3 User's chat input text field

4 Creates socket and instance of inner class to work in background

5 Continuously reads data from client socket and processes it

6 Creates a new JInternalFrame, with a unique TAG value

```
      return "" + TAG;
    }
  };
  jif.setBounds(20*(m_count%10) + m_tencount*80,
    20*(m_count%10), 200, 200);

  m_desktop.add(jif);
  try {
    jif.setSelected(true);
  }
  catch (PropertyVetoException pve) {
    System.out.println("Could not select " + jif.getTitle());
  }

  m_count++;
  if (m_count%10 == 0) {
    if (m_tencount < 3)
      m_tencount++;
    else
      m_tencount = 0;
  }
}

public void processMessage(String s) {
  if (s.startsWith("cc")) {
    m_consolechat.append("CLIENT: " + s.substring(2) + "\n");
    m_consolechat.setCaretPosition(
      m_consolechat.getText().length());
  }
  else {
    int id = (Integer.valueOf(s.substring(0,2))).intValue();
    m_wm.setPropagate(false);
    if (id == 16) {
      newFrame();
    }
    else {
      Component[] components = m_desktop.getComponentsInLayer(0);
      int index = 0;
      int tag = (Integer.valueOf(s.substring(2,5))).intValue();
      int param1 =
        (Integer.valueOf(s.substring(5,11))).intValue();
      int param2 =
        (Integer.valueOf(s.substring(11,17))).intValue();
      int param3 =
        (Integer.valueOf(s.substring(17,23))).intValue();
      int param4 =
        (Integer.valueOf(s.substring(23))).intValue();
      boolean found = false;
      for (int i=components.length-1; i>-1;i--) {
        if (components[i] instanceof JInternalFrame) {
          if (Integer.valueOf(
            components[i].toString()).intValue() == tag) {
            try {
```

7 Processes message from client

7 Chat message is dumped into chat area

7 If it is an internal frame message, then get method ID and process it

```
          ((JInternalFrame) components[i]).setSelected(true);
          ((JInternalFrame) components[i]).toFront();
          index = i;
          found = true;
          break;
        }
        catch (PropertyVetoException pve) {
          System.out.println(
            "Could not select JInternalFrame with tag " + tag);
        }
      }
    }
  }
if (found == false) return;
switch (id)
{
  case 1:
    m_wm.activateFrame((JInternalFrame) components[index]);
    break;
  case 2:
    m_wm.beginDraggingFrame((JComponent) components[index]);
    break;
  case 3:
    m_wm.beginResizingFrame(
      (JComponent) components[index], param1);
    break;
  case 4:
    m_wm.closeFrame((JInternalFrame) components[index]);
    break;
  // Case 5: not implemented
  // Case 6: not implemented
  case 7:
    m_wm.dragFrame(
      (JComponent)components[index], param1, param2);
    break;
  case 8:
    m_wm.endDraggingFrame((JComponent) components[index]);
    break;
  case 9:
    m_wm.endResizingFrame((JComponent) components[index]);
    break;
  // Case 10: not implemented
  // Case 11: not implemented
  // Case 12: not implemented
  case 13:
    m_wm.openFrame((JInternalFrame) components[index]);
    break;
  case 14:
    m_wm.resizeFrame(
      (JComponent) components[index], param1,
        param2, param3, param4);
```

```
                break;
            case 15:
              m_wm.setBoundsForFrame(
                (JComponent) components[index], param1,
                  param2, param3, param4);
              break;
          }
        }
      m_wm.setPropagate(true);
      }
    m_desktop.repaint();
  }

  public static void main(String[] args) {
    new JavaXServer();
  }

  class ChatAdapter implements ActionListener {
    public void actionPerformed(ActionEvent e) {
      m_wm.sendMessage("cc" + m_chatText.getText());
      m_consolechat.append("SERVER: " +
        m_chatText.getText() + "\n");
      m_chatText.setText("");
    }
  }

  class ConThread extends Thread
  {
    ConThread() { start(); }
    public void run() {
      while(true) {
        try {
          m_client = m_server.accept();
          m_connected = true;
          m_input = new DataInputStream(m_client.getInputStream());
          m_output = new DataOutputStream(
            m_client.getOutputStream());
          m_wm.setOutputStream(m_output);
          m_consoletext.append("\nStreams established...");
          m_listenThread = new Thread(JavaXServer.this);
          m_listenThread.start();
          m_status.setText("Client Connected from: "
            + m_client.getInetAddress());
          m_consoletext.append("\nClient Connected from: "
            + m_client.getInetAddress());
        }
        catch (Exception ex) {
          m_consoletext.append("\n" + ex);
        }
      }
    }
  }
}
```

8 Pressing Enter in chat text field sends the text as a chat message to the client

9 Endless loop waiting for new input to server; on receipt, will spawn thread in outer class to process input

see \Chapter16\3

```java
import javax.swing.*;
import java.io.*;
import java.awt.*;

public class WindowManager extends DefaultDesktopManager
{
  //ID 16 means new Frame
  protected static final int ACTIVATE_ID = 1;
  protected static final int BEGINDRAG_ID = 2;
  protected static final int BEGINRESIZE_ID = 3;
  protected static final int CLOSE_ID = 4;
  protected static final int DEACTIVATE_ID = 5;
  protected static final int DEICONIFY_ID = 6;
  protected static final int DRAG_ID = 7;
  protected static final int ENDDRAG_ID = 8;
  protected static final int ENDRESIZE_ID = 9;
  protected static final int ICONIFY_ID = 10;
  protected static final int MAXIMIZE_ID = 11;
  protected static final int MINIMIZE_ID = 12;
  protected static final int OPEN_ID = 13;
  protected static final int RESIZE_ID = 14;
  protected static final int SETBOUNDS_ID = 15;
  protected WindowWatcher m_ww;
  protected DataOutputStream m_output;
  protected JDesktopPane m_desktop;
  protected boolean m_prop;

  public WindowManager(JDesktopPane desktop) {
    m_desktop = desktop;
    m_prop = true;
    m_ww = new WindowWatcher(desktop);
  }

  public WindowWatcher getWindowWatcher() { return m_ww; }

  public void setOutputStream(DataOutputStream output) {
    m_output = output;
  }

  public void sendMessage(String s) {
    try {
      if (m_output != null)
        m_output.writeUTF(s);
    }
    catch (IOException e) {}
  }

  public void setPropagate(boolean b) {
    m_prop = b;
  }

  public String getStringIndex(Component f) {
```

10 Method IDs, except for 16, which means "create frame"

11 Called when client connects; provides OutputStream to send messages back to client

12 Sends message to OutputStream to client

13 Generates TAG value for frame with leading zeroes

```java
    String s = f.toString();
    while (s.length() < 3)
      s = ("0").concat(s);
    return s;
  }

  public String getString(int number) {
    String s;
    if(number < 0)
      s = "" + (-number);
    else
      s = "" + number;
    while (s.length() < 6)
      s = ("0").concat(s);
    if (number < 0)
      s = "-" + s.substring(1,6);
    return s;
  }

  public void activateFrame(JInternalFrame f) {
    String index = getStringIndex(f);
    super.activateFrame(f);
    m_ww.repaint();
    if (m_prop)
      sendMessage("01" + index + "000000000000000000000000");
  }
  public void beginDraggingFrame(JComponent f) {
    String index = getStringIndex(f);
    super.beginDraggingFrame(f);
    m_ww.repaint();
    if (m_prop)
      sendMessage("02" + index + "000000000000000000000000");
  }
  public void beginResizingFrame(JComponent f, int direction) {
    String index = getStringIndex(f);
    String dir = getString(direction);
    super.beginResizingFrame(f,direction);
    m_ww.repaint();
    if (m_prop)
      sendMessage("03" + index + dir + "000000000000000000");
  }
  public void closeFrame(JInternalFrame f) {
    String index = getStringIndex(f);
    super.closeFrame(f);
    m_ww.repaint();
    if (m_prop)
      sendMessage("04" + index + "000000000000000000000000");
  }
  public void deactivateFrame(JInternalFrame f) {
    super.deactivateFrame(f);
    m_ww.repaint();
    // ID 05: not implemented
  }
```

(14) **Formats arbitrary number in zero-leading field of six digits**

```
public void deiconifyFrame(JInternalFrame f) {
  super.deiconifyFrame(f);
  m_ww.repaint();
  // ID 06: not implemented
}
public void dragFrame(JComponent f, int newX, int newY) {
  String index = getStringIndex(f);
  String x = getString(newX);
  String y = getString(newY);
  f.setLocation(newX, newY);
  m_ww.repaint();
  if (m_prop)
    sendMessage("07" + index + x + y +"000000000000");
}
public void endDraggingFrame(JComponent f) {
  String index = getStringIndex(f);
  super.endDraggingFrame(f);
  m_ww.repaint();
  if (m_prop)
    sendMessage("08" + index + "000000000000000000000000");
}
public void endResizingFrame(JComponent f) {
  String index = getStringIndex(f);
  super.endResizingFrame(f);
  m_ww.repaint();
  if (m_prop)
    sendMessage("09" + index + "000000000000000000000000");
}
public void iconifyFrame(JInternalFrame f) {
  super.iconifyFrame(f);
  m_ww.repaint();
  // ID 10: not implemented
}
public void maximizeFrame(JInternalFrame f) {
  String index = getStringIndex(f);
  super.maximizeFrame(f);
  m_ww.repaint();
  // ID 11: not implemented
}
public void minimizeFrame(JInternalFrame f) {
  super.minimizeFrame(f);
  m_ww.repaint();
  // ID 12: not implemented
}
public void openFrame(JInternalFrame f) {
  String index = getStringIndex(f);
  super.openFrame(f);
  m_ww.repaint();
  if (m_prop)
    sendMessage("13" + index + "000000000000000000000000");
}
public void resizeFrame(JComponent f,
```

```
  int newX, int newY, int newWidth, int newHeight) {
   String index = getStringIndex(f);
   String x = getString(newX);
   String y = getString(newY);
   String w = getString(newWidth);
   String h = getString(newHeight);
   f.setBounds(newX, newY, newWidth, newHeight);
   m_ww.repaint();
   if (m_prop)
     sendMessage("14" + index + x + y + w + h);
  }
  public void setBoundsForFrame(JComponent f,
   int newX, int newY, int newWidth, int newHeight) {
   String index = getStringIndex(f);
   String x = getString(newX);
   String y = getString(newY);
   String w = getString(newWidth);
   String h = getString(newHeight);
   if (newWidth > m_desktop.getWidth())
     newWidth = m_desktop.getWidth();
   if (newHeight > m_desktop.getHeight())
     newHeight = m_desktop.getHeight();
   f.setBounds(newX, newY, newWidth, newHeight);
   m_ww.repaint();
   if (m_prop)
     sendMessage("15" + index + x + y + w + h);
  }
}
```

JavaXClient.java

see \Chapter16\3

```
import java.beans.PropertyVetoException;
import javax.swing.*;
import java.awt.event.*;
import java.io.*;
import java.awt.*;
import java.net.*;

public class JavaXClient extends JFrame implements Runnable
{
  protected int m_count;
  protected int m_tencount;
  protected int m_wmX, m_wmY;
  protected JButton m_newFrame;
  protected JDesktopPane m_desktop;
  protected WindowManager m_wm;
  protected JViewport m_viewport;

  protected JTextArea m_consoletext, m_consolechat;
  protected JTextField m_text, m_chatText;
  protected boolean m_connected;
```

Like JavaXServer, but connects to socket on server, and can create "new frame" messages (ID 16) ⑮

```
protected JLabel m_status;
protected DataInputStream m_input;
protected DataOutputStream m_output;
protected Socket m_client;
protected Thread m_listenThread;

// ServerSocket and ConThread code removed

protected JButton m_connect;

public JavaXClient() {
  setTitle("JavaX Client");
  m_count = m_tencount = 0;
  m_desktop = new JDesktopPane();

  m_status = new JLabel("Not Connected");

  JScrollPane scroller = new JScrollPane();
  m_wm = new WindowManager(m_desktop);
  m_desktop.setDesktopManager(m_wm);
  m_desktop.add(m_wm.getWindowWatcher(),
    JLayeredPane.PALETTE_LAYER);
  m_wm.getWindowWatcher().setBounds(555,5,100,100);

  m_viewport = new JViewport() {
    //...Identical in JavaXServer
  };
  m_viewport.setView(m_desktop);
  scroller.setViewport(m_viewport);

  ComponentAdapter ca = new ComponentAdapter() {
    //...Identical in JavaXServer
  };
  m_viewport.addComponentListener(ca);

  m_newFrame = new JButton("New Frame");
  m_newFrame.addActionListener(new ActionListener() {
    public void actionPerformed(ActionEvent e) {
      m_wm.setPropagate(false);
      newFrame();
      if (m_connected)
        m_wm.sendMessage("16000000000000000000000000000000");
      m_wm.setPropagate(true);
    }
  });
  m_newFrame.setEnabled(false);

  JPanel topPanel = new JPanel(true);
  topPanel.add(m_newFrame);

  m_connect = new JButton("Connect");
  m_connect.addActionListener(new ActionListener() {
    public void actionPerformed(ActionEvent e) {
      if (m_listenThread == null) {
        Thread connector = new Thread() {
          public void run() {
```

```
                    try
                    {
                      m_consoletext.append(
                        "\nTrying " + m_text.getText() + " ...");
                      m_client = new Socket(
                        InetAddress.getByName(m_text.getText()),5000);
                      m_input = new DataInputStream(
                        m_client.getInputStream());
                      m_output = new DataOutputStream(
                        m_client.getOutputStream());
                      m_connected = true;
                      m_listenThread = new Thread(JavaXClient.this);
                      m_listenThread.start();
                      m_wm.setOutputStream(m_output);
                      m_consoletext.append("\nStreams established...");
                      m_status.setText("Connected to " + m_text.getText());
                      m_connect.setEnabled(false);
                      m_newFrame.setEnabled(true);
                    }
                    catch (Exception ex) {
                      m_consoletext.append("\n" + ex);
                      m_newFrame.setEnabled(false);
                    }
                  }
                };
                connector.start();
              }
            }
          });

        JPanel XPanel = new JPanel();
        XPanel.setLayout(new BorderLayout());
        JLabel hl = new JLabel("Connect to: ", SwingConstants.CENTER);
        m_text = new JTextField(15);
        XPanel.add("North", hl);
        XPanel.add("Center", m_text);
        XPanel.add("East", m_connect);

        JPanel upperPanel = new JPanel();
        upperPanel.setLayout(new BorderLayout());
        upperPanel.add("Center", XPanel);
        upperPanel.add("East",topPanel);

        getContentPane().setLayout(new BorderLayout());
        getContentPane().add("North", upperPanel);
        getContentPane().add("Center", scroller);

        // Unchanged code
      }
    public void setupConsole() {
      JInternalFrame console = new JInternalFrame(
        "JavaX Client Console",
        false, false, false, false) {
        int TAG = m_count;
```

Connects to server
on specified host **16**

```java
      public String toString() {
        return "" + TAG;
      }
    };
    m_count++;
    console.setBounds(20, 20, 500, 300);

    JPanel chatPanel = new JPanel();
    JLabel chatLabel = new JLabel(" Chat");
    chatPanel.setLayout(new BorderLayout());

    m_consoletext = new JTextArea();
    m_consoletext.setPreferredSize(new Dimension(500,50));
    m_consoletext.setLineWrap(true);
    m_consoletext.setText("Client Started...");
    m_consoletext.setEditable(false);

    // The remainder of this method is identical
    // to JavaXServer's setupConsole() method.
    // However, we have removed the ServerSocket
    // code from the end.
  }

  public void run() {
    // ...Identical to JavaXServer's run() method.
  }

  public void newFrame() {
    // ...Identical to JavaXServer's newFrame() method.
  }

  public void processMessage(String s) {
    if (s.startsWith("cc")) {
      m_consolechat.append("SERVER: " + s.substring(2) + "\n");
      m_consolechat.setCaretPosition(
        m_consolechat.getText().length());
    }
    else {

    // With the exception of the highlighted code
    // above, this method is identical to JavaXServer's
    // processMessage() method.
  }

  public static void main(String[] args) {
    new JavaXClient();
  }

  class ChatAdapter implements ActionListener {
    public void actionPerformed(ActionEvent e) {
      m_wm.sendMessage("cc" + m_chatText.getText());
      m_consolechat.append("CLIENT: " + m_chatText.getText() + "\n");
      m_chatText.setText("");
    }
  }

  // ConThread inner class removed
}
```

16.5.4 Understanding the code

Class JavaXServer

❶ The `JavaXServer` class implements the `Runnable` interface, thereby allowing us to define a separate thread of execution. Several instance variables are necessary:

- `int m_count`, `int m_tencount`: Used for cascading.
- `int m_wmX`: Keeps track of the most recent x-coordinate of the desktop scroll pane's view position.
- `int m_wmY`: Keeps track of the most recent y-coordinate of the desktop scroll pane's view position.
- `JDesktopPane m_desktop`: Our desktop pane.
- `WindowManager m_wm`: Our custom `DesktopManager` implementation.
- `JViewport m_viewport`: The viewport of the scroll pane that will contain our desktop.
- `JTextArea m_consoletext`: The console text area used to display server status information.
- `JTextArea m_consolechat`: The console text area used for chatting between server and client.
- `boolean m_connected`: The flag that specifies whether a client is connected.
- `JLabel m_status`: The status bar used to display the IP address of the connected client.
- `DataInputStream m_input`: The `DataInputStream` of the client connection `Socket`.
- `DataOutputStream m_output`: The `DataOutputStream` of the client connection `Socket`.
- `Socket m_client`: The `Socket` created when a client connects.
- `ServerSocket m_server`: Used to wait for an incoming client and establish the client `Socket`.
- `Thread m_listenThread`: A handle used for creating and starting the `JavaXServer` thread.
- `ConThread m_conthred`: An instance of our custom `Thread` extended inner class used to allow the `ServerSocket` to wait for client connections without hogging our application's thread.

❷ The `JavaXServer` constructor performs familiar GUI layout tasks, and it is very similar to the `JavaXWin` constructor we studied in the last section. Before the frame is made visible, our `setupConsole()` method is called. This method is responsible for constructing our chat console internal frame (it also acts as a message log for the server). We override this `JInternalFrame`'s `toString()` method to return a unique TAG which is the value of the `m_count` variable at the time of its creation. Since the console is the first frame created, it will have a TAG of 0. We then increment `m_count` so that the next frame, created in the `newFrame()` method (see below), will have a different TAG value. This is how we identify frames when sending internal frame messages.

❸ The console contains four things: two text areas, a Send button, and a text field. The Send button and text field area used for chatting, the upper text area is used to display server status information, and the lower text area is used to display chat text. We attach an instance of our custom `ChatAdapter` class (see below) to both the Send button (`chatSend`) and the text field (`m_chatText`).

❹ The `setupConsole()` method ends by actually starting the server. We create a new `ServerSocket` on port 5000 with queue length 500. A queue length of 500 represents the maximum amount of messages that can be buffered at any given time by the `ServerSocket`.

NOTE This example uses a fixed port. In professional applications the server would most likely provide the operator with a field to enter the desired port number. A maximum queue length of 500 is not really necessary here, as we are only expecting one client to connect through this `ServerSocket`. However, it does not add any extra overhead, and if for some reason this port gets bombarded with extraneous messages, this length will give our client messages a better chance of getting in.

❺ The `run()` method defines the separate thread of execution that is created and called within the `ConThread` class (see below). When a client is connected, this method continuously reads data from the client `Socket`, `m_client`, and sends it to our custom `processMessage()` method.

❻ Our `newFrame()` method should look familiar from previous sections. In this new version, each `JInternalFrame` that is created gets assigned a unique `TAG`, which is the value of the `m_count` variable at the time of its creation, and its `toString()` method is overridden to return this tag. This is how we identify destinations of internal frame messages.

❼ The `processMessage()` method takes a `String` parameter that represents a message from the client. We first check to see whether it is a chat message (remember that all chat messages start with "cc"). If it is, we simply append this message (minus the "cc" header) to our chat text area and set the cursor position accordingly.

If it is not a chat message, we process it as an internal frame message. First we get the method ID and see if it is 16. (See the discussion of the `WindowManager` class below for an explanation of what method each ID corresponds to). One of two things will happen.

1 If the ID is 16, all we need to do is create a new frame, so the `newFrame()` method is invoked. (Note that only the client can send "create new frame" messages.)

2 If the ID is not 16, we first call our `WindowManager`'s custom `setPropagate()` message to stop processed messages that are sent to our `WindowManager` from being sent back to the client (this is effectively how we consume each message). Then we grab an array of all the components in layer 0 and check each `JInternalFrame`'s `TAG` until we find a match. (All frames are contained at layer 0 in this example. In a more complete example, we would search through all components in the desktop, regardless of layer.) We then extract the internal frame message parameters, and if a `TAG` match is found, we send a message to our `WindowManager`, `m_wm`, based on the ID and the extracted parameters (if applicable).

Class JavaXServer.ChatAdapter

❽ `ChatAdapter` is used as an `ActionListener` attached to our console's chat text field and Send button (see the `setupConsole()` method). Whenever the user presses ENTER in the chat input text field or clicks the console's Send button, this adapter sends the text field contents as a message to the client, appends it to the console chat text area, `m_consolechat`, and clears this text field.

Class JavaXServer.ConThread

❾ The inner class `ConThread` extends `Thread`. Its constructor calls its `start()` method, and its `start()` method calls its `run()` method. We override the `run()` method to create an endless loop that starts by invoking `accept()` on our `m_server` `ServerSocket`. This method blocks execution until a client connects. When a client does connect, our `ServerSocket` returns from the `accept()` method with a `Socket`, `m_client`, that represents the connection with the client. We then set our `m_connected` flag to `true` so that when our main `JavaXServer` thread is started, it can receive and process messages from the client, as discussed above. We assign `m_client`'s `DataInputStream` to `m_input` and its `DataOutputStream` to `m_output`. Then we pass `m_output` to our `WindowManager`'s `setOutputStream()` method (see the discussion of `WindowManager` below). We print a message in the console to inform the server operator that a connection has been established and then we `start()` the `JavaXServer` thread (see the `run()` method which is discussed above). Finally, we display the IP address the client connected from in the status bar and append this information to our console.

Class WindowManager

❿ The `WindowManager` class starts by defining 15 self-explanatory `int` ID fields, each corresponding to one of the internal frame methods defined within this class. Four instance variables are used:

- `WindowWatcher m_ww`: Our custom pager component.
- `DataOutputStream m_output`: The client `Socket`'s output stream that is used to send messages.
- `JDesktopPane m_desktop`: The desktop we are managing.
- `boolean m_prop`: Used to block messages from being sent back to the sender when they are processed.

⓫ The `setOutputStream()` method is called when a client connects. This is used to provide `WindowManager` with a reference to the client `Socket`'s `DataOutputStream` for sending messages.

⓬ The `sendMessage()` method takes a `String` parameter that represents a message to be sent to the client, and it attempts to write it to the client's `DataOutputStream`:

```
public void sendMessage(String s) {
  try {
    if (m_output != null) {
      m_output.writeUTF(s);
    }
  }
  catch (IOException e) {}
}
```

The `setPropagate()` method takes a `boolean` parameter which can be used to block messages from being sent back to the client when they are being processed. This method is called from `JavaXServer`'s `processMessage()` method.

⓭ The `getStringIndex()` method takes an `int` parameter that represents the TAG of an internal frame, and converts it to a `String` 3 characters long by concatenating 0s in front, if necessary. This is used to build the TAG field in an internal frame message (which, as we know from our discussion in the beginning of this section, is always 3 characters long) which is returned.

```
public String getStringIndex(Component f) {
  String s = f.toString();
  while (s.length() < 3)
```

```
      s = ("0").concat(s);
    return s;
  }
```

14 In the `getString()` method, we take an `int` parameter which can represent any of four possible parameters passed to one of the internal frame methods defined within this class. We then convert this value to a `String`. If this value was negative, we remove the "–" sign. Then we concatenate a number of 0s to the front of the string, forcing the length to be 6. We then check if the value passed in was negative one more time. If it was, we replace the first character with a "–" sign:

```
public String getString(int number) {
  String s;
  if (number < 0)
    s = "" + (-number);
  else
    s = "" + number;
  while (s.length() < 6)
    s = ("0").concat(s);
  if (number < 0)
    s = "-" + s.substring(1,6);
  return s;
}
```

NOTE This example assumes that no frame coordinate or dimension will ever be larger than 999999 or smaller than –99999. For all practical purposes, this is a completely safe assumption to make!

Whenever any of the internal frame methods are invoked, we first get the TAG of the frame associated with the method call. Then we call the superclass counterpart of that method, repaint our `WindowWatcher`, and check our message propagation flag, `m_prop`. If it is set to `true` we go ahead and construct our message, using the `getString()` method where applicable, and pass it to our `sendMessage()` method to send to the client. If it is `false`, no message is sent.

Class JavaXClient

15 The `JavaXClient` class functions very similarly to `JavaXServer`. It sends, receives, and interprets messages identically to `JavaXServer`. However, unlike `JavaXServer`, `JavaXClient` can create new frames and send new frame messages to the server (new frame messages have ID 16) These messages are constructed and sent within `JavaXClient`'s `actionPerformed()` method:

```
if (e.getSource() == m_newFrame) {
  m_wm.setPropagate(false);
  newFrame();
  if (m_connected)
    m_wm.sendMessage("1600000000000000000000000000000");
  m_wm.setPropagate(true);
}
```

16 The following additional GUI components are added to the top of `JavaXClient`'s frame: a text field for entering the server's IP address, a New Frame button, and a Connect button. The `ActionListener` for this button is wrapped in a thread to allow connection attempts while not blocking the main thread of execution. It attempts to connect to the address specified in the text field by creating a new `Socket`:

```
m_client = new Socket(
    InetAddress.getByName(m_text.getText()),5000);
```

If this works, it establishes input and output data streams and starts the `JavaXClient` thread (see its `run()` method, which is identical to `JavaXServer`'s `run()` method) to listen for messages. We then append text to the console, update the status bar, and enable the New Frame button. (Note that the client can only create new frames after a connection has been established.)

16.5.5   **Running the code**

Figures 16.10 and 16.11 show `JavaXClient` and `JavaXServer` during a collaborative session. Ideally, you can test this example out with a friend in a remote, far-away place. If this is not possible, try using two machines in your network. (If you are not networked, you can run both the client and the server on your machine by connecting to 127.0.0.1, which is always used as a pointer to your own machine.)

Try chatting and resizing each other's frames. Now is the time to think of other possible applications of such a multi-user desktop environment. Clearly we will begin to see more and more remote interaction and collaboration as the web and its surrounding technologies continue to grow.

C H A P T E R   1 7

Trees

17.1   *JTREE*

JTree is a perfect tool for the display, navigation, and editing of hierarchical data. Because of its complex nature, JTree has a whole package devoted to it: `javax.swing.tree`. This package consists of a set of classes and interfaces which we will briefly review before moving on to several examples. But first, what is a tree?

17.1.1   Tree concepts and terminology

The tree is a very important and heavily used data structure throughout computer science—for example, it's used in compiler design, graphics, and artificial intelligence. This data structure consists of a logically arranged set of *node*s, which are containers for data. Each tree contains one *root* node, which serves as that tree's top-most node. Any node can have an arbitrary number of child (*descendant*) nodes. In this way, each descendant node is the root of a *subtree*.

Each node is connected by an *edge*. An edge signifies the relationship between two nodes. A node's direct predecessor is called its *parent* node, and all predecesors (above and including the parent) are called its *ancestor* nodes. A node that has no descendants is called a *leaf* node. All direct child nodes of a given node are *sibling* nodes.

522

A *path* from one node to another is a sequence of nodes with edges from one node to the next. The *level* of a node is the number of nodes visited in the path between the root and that node. The *height* of a tree is its largest level—the length of its longest path.

17.1.2 Tree traversal

It is essential that we be able to systematically visit each and every node of a tree. (The term "visit" here refers to performing some task before moving on.) There are three common traversal orders used for performing such an operation: *preorder*, *inorder*, and *postorder*. Each is recursive and can be summarized as follows:

- *Preorder*
  Recursively do the following: If the tree is not empty, visit the root and then traverse all subtrees in ascending order.
- *Inorder* (often referred to as *breadth first*):
  Start the traversal by visiting the main tree root. Then, in ascending order, visit the root of each subtree. Continue visiting the roots of all subtrees in this manner, in effect visiting the nodes at each *level* of the tree in ascending order.
- *Postorder* (often referred to as *depth first*):
  Recursively do the following: If the tree is not empty, traverse all subtrees in ascending order, and then visit the root.

17.1.3 JTree

class javax.swing.JTree

So how does Swing's `JTree` component deal with all this structure? Implementations of the `TreeModel` interface encapsulate all tree nodes, which are implementations of the `TreeNode` interface. The `DefaultMutableTreeNode` class (which is an implementation of `TreeNode`) provides us with the ability to perform preorder, inorder, and postorder tree traversals.

> **NOTE** Nothing stops us from using `TreeModel` as a data structure class without actually displaying it in a GUI. However, since this book and the Swing library are devoted to GUI, we will not discuss these possibilities further.

`JTree` graphically displays each node similarly to the way in which `JList` displays its elements: in a vertical column of cells. Also, each cell can be rendered with a custom renderer (an implementation of `TreeCellRenderer`) and can be edited with a custom `TreeCellEditor`. Each tree cell shows a non-leaf node as being *expanded* or *collapsed*, and each can represent node relationships (meaning edges) in various ways. Expanded nodes show their subtree nodes, and collapsed nodes hide this information.

The selection of tree cells is similar to `JList`'s selection mechanism, and it is controlled by a `TreeSelectionModel`. Selection also involves keeping track of paths between nodes as instances of `TreePath`. Two kinds of events are used specifically with trees and tree selections: `TreeModelEvent` and `TreeExpansionEvent`. Other AWT and Swing events also apply to `JTree`. For instance, we can use `MouseListeners` to intercept mouse presses and clicks. Keep in mind that `JTree` implements the `Scrollable` interface (see chapter 7), and it is intended to be placed in a `JScrollPane`.

A `JTree` can be constructed using either the default constructor, by providing a `Tree-Node` to use for the root node, by providing a `TreeModel` that contains all constituent nodes, or by providing a one-dimensional array, `Vector`, or `Hashtable` of objects. In the latter case, if any element in the given structure is a multi-element structure itself, it is recursively used to build a subtree (this functionality is handled by an inner class called `DynamicUtilTreeNode`).

We will see how to construct and work with all aspects of a `JTree` soon enough. But first we need to develop a more solid understanding of its underlying constituents and how they interact.

GUIDELINE

When to use a tree:

As a selection device   The tree component allows users to select items from large hierarchical data sets without having to use a Search mechanism. As such, `JTree` falls between listing and search data as a component which can improve usability by easing the process of finding something, providing that the item to be found (or selected) is hidden within a hierarchical data set.

Let's use finding an employee by name as an example. For a small data set, a simple list may be sufficient. As the data set grows, it may be easier for the user if you sort the names alphabetically or by department in which they work. By doing so, you have introduced a hierarchy and you may now use a tree component. Use of the tree component may help and speed random selection from the data set, providing that the hierarchical structure used exists in reality—don't introduce artificial hierarchies and expect users to understand them.

As a data set rises to become very large, the tree component may again be of little value and you will need to introduce a full search facility.

As a general rule, when using a tree as a selection device, start with the tree collapsed and allow the user to expand it as they search for the item they are looking for. If there is a default selection or a current selection, then we advize expanding that part of the tree to show that selection.

As a visual layering device   Even with a small data set, you may find it advantageous to display a hierarchical structure to aid visual comprehension and visual searching. With the employee example you may prefer to layer by department or by alphabetical order. When a tree is selected for display only (meaning no selection is taking place), then you are definitely using the tree as a visual layering device.

As a general rule, when you use a tree as a visual layering device, you will, by default, expand the tree in full, revealing the full hierarchy.

How you use a tree and which options to select from the many selection and display variants can be affected by how they are used, as we will demonstrate later.

17.1.4   The TreeModel interface

abstract interface javax.swing.tree.TreeModel

This model handles the data to be used in a `JTree`, assuming that each node maintains an array of child nodes. Nodes are represented as `Object`s, and a separate root node accessor is defined. A set of methods is intended to: retrieve a node based on a given parent node and index, return the number of children of a given node, return the index of a given node based on a given parent, check if a given node is a leaf node (has no children), and notify `JTree` that a node which is the destination of a given `TreePath` has been modified. It also provides method declarations for adding and removing `TreeModelListeners` which should be notified when any nodes are added, removed, or changed. A `JTree`'s `TreeModel` can be retrieved and assigned with its `getModel()` and `setModel()` methods, respectively.

17.1.5   DefaultTreeModel

class javax.swing.tree.DefaultTreeModel

`DefaultTreeModel` is the default concrete implementation of the `TreeModel` interface. It defines the root and each node of the tree as `TreeNode` instances. It maintains an `EventListenerList` of `TreeModelListeners` and provides several methods for firing `TreeModelEvents` when anything in the tree changes. It defines the `asksAllowedChildren` flag, which is used to confirm whether a node allows children to be added *before* actually attempting to add them. `DefaultTreeModel` also defines methods for: returning an array of nodes from a given node to the root node, inserting and removing nodes, and reloading/refreshing a tree from a specified node. We normally build off this class when implementing a tree model.

17.1.6   The TreeNode interface

abstract interface javax.swing.tree.TreeNode

`TreeNode` describes the base interface which all tree nodes must conform to in a `DefaultTreeModel`. So, implementations of this interface represent the basic building block of `JTree`'s default model. This interface declares methods for specifying whether a node: is a leaf or a parent, allows the addition of child nodes, determines the number of children, obtains a `TreeNode` child at a given index or the parent node, and obtains an `Enumeration` of all child nodes.

17.1.7   The MutableTreeNode interface

abstract interface javax.swing.tree.MutableTreeNode

This interface extends `TreeNode` to describe a more sophisticated tree node which can carry a user object. This is the object that represents the data of a given tree node. The `setUserObject()` method declares how the user object should be assigned (it is assumed that implementations of this interface will provide the equivalent of a `getUserObject()` method, even though none is included here). This interface also provides method declarations for inserting and removing child nodes from a given node, and changing its parent node.

17.1.8   DefaultMutableTreeNode

class javax.swing.tree.DefaultMutableTreeNode

`DefaultMutableTreeNode` is a concrete implementation of the `MutableTreeNode` interface. The `getUserObject()` method returns the data object encapsulated by this node. It stores all child nodes in a `Vector` called `children`, which is accessible with the `children()` method, which returns an `Enumeration` of all child nodes. We can also use the `getChildAt()` method to retreive the node corresponding to a given index. There are many methods for, among other things, retrieving and assigning tree nodes, and they are all self-explanatory (or they can be understood through simple reference of the API documentation). The only methods that deserve special mention here are the overridden toString() method, which returns the String given by the user object's toString() method, and the tree traversal methods which return an Enumeration of nodes in the order in which they can be visited. As discussed above, three types of traversal are supported: preorder, inorder, and postorder. The corresponding methods are preorderEnumeration(), breadthFirstEnumeration(), depthFirst-Enumeration(), and postorderEnumeration() (the last two methods do the same thing).

17.1.9 TreePath

class javax.swing.tree.TreePath

A TreePath represents the path to a node as a set of nodes starting from the root. (Recall that nodes are Objects, not necessarily TreeNodes.) TreePaths are read-only objects and they provide functionality for comparison between other TreePaths. The getLastPathCompo-nent() gives us the final node in the path, equals() compares two paths, getPath-Count() gives the number of nodes in a path, isDescendant() checks whether a given path is a descendant of (is completely contained in) a given path, and pathByAddingChild() returns a new TreePath instance resulting from adding the given node to the path.

17.1.10 The TreeCellRenderer interface

abstract interface javax.swing.tree.TreeCellRenderer

This interface describes the component used to render a cell of the tree. The getTreeCell-RendererComponent() method is called to return the component to use for rendering a given cell and that cell's selection, focus, and tree state (i.e. whether it is a leaf or a parent, and whether it is expanded or collapsed). This works similarly to custom cell rendering in JList and JComboBox (see chapters 9 and 10). To assign a renderer to JTree, we use its setCell-Renderer() method. Recall that renderer components are not at all interactive and simply act as "rubber stamps" for display purposes only.

17.1.11 DefaultTreeCellRenderer

class javax.swing.tree.DefaultTreeCellRenderer

DefaultTreeCellRenderer is the default concrete implementation of the TreeCellRen-derer interface. It extends JLabel and maintains several properties used to render a tree cell based on its current state, as described above. These properties include Icons used to repre-sent the node in any of its possible states (leaf, parent collapsed, or parent expanded) and background and foreground colors to use based on whether the node is selected or unselected. Each of these properties is self-explanatory and typical get/set accessors are provided.

17.1.12 CellRendererPane

class javax.swing.CellRendererPane

In chapter 2 we discussed the painting and validation process in detail, but we purposely avoided the discussion of how renderers actually work behind the scenes because they are only used by a few specific components. The component returned by a renderer's getXXRen-dererComponent() method is placed in an instance of CellRendererPane. The Cell-RendererPane is used to act as the component's parent so that any validation and repaint requests that occur do not propogate up the ancestry tree of the container it resides in. It does this by overriding the paint() and invalidate() methods with empty implementations.

Several paintComponent() methods are provided to render a given component onto a given graphical context. These are used by the JList, JTree, and JTable UI delegates to actually paint each cell, which results in the "rubber stamp" behavior we have referred to.

17.1.13 The CellEditor interface

abstract javax.swing.CellEditor

Unlike renderers, cell editors for JTree and JTable are defined from a generic interface. This interface is CellEditor and it declares the following methods for controlling: when editing will start and stop, retrieving a new value resulting from an edit, and whether an edit request changes the component's current selection.

- Object getCellEditorValue(): Used by JTree and JTable after an accepted edit to retrieve the new value.
- boolean isCellEditable(EventObject anEvent): Used to test whether the given event should trigger a cell edit. For instance, to accept a single mouse click as an edit invocation, we would override this method to test for an instance of MouseEvent and check its click count. If the click count is 1, return true; otherwise, return false.
- boolean shouldSelectCell(EventObject anEvent): Used to specify whether the given event causes a cell that is about to be edited to also be selected. This will cancel all previous selection and for components that want to allow editing during an ongoing selection, we would return false here. It is most common to return true, as we normally think of the cell being edited as the currently selected cell.
- boolean stopCellEditing(): Used to stop a current cell edit. This method can be overriden to perform input validation. If a value is found to be unacceptable we can return false, indicating to the component that editing should not be stopped.
- void cancelCellEditing(): Used to stop a current cell edit and ignore any new input.

This interface also declares methods for adding and removing CellEditorListeners which should receive ChangeEvents whenever an edit is stopped or canceled. So stop-CellEditing() and cancelCellEditing() are responsible for firing ChangeEvents to any registered listeners.

Normally, cell editing starts with the user clicking on a cell a specified number of times which can be defined in the isCellEditable() method. The component containing the cell then replaces the current renderer pane with its editor component (JTree's editor component is returned by TreeCellEditor's getTreeCellEditorComponent() method). If should-SelectCell() returns true then the component's selection state changes to only contain the cell being edited. A new value is entered using the editor and an appropriate action takes place which invokes either stopCellEditing() or cancelCellEditing(). Finally, if the edit was stopped and not canceled, the component retrieves the new value from the editor, using getCellEditorValue(), and overwrites the old value. The editor is then replaced by the renderer pane which is updated to reflect the new data value.

17.1.14 The TreeCellEditor interface

abstract interface javax.swing.tree.TreeCellEditor

This interface extends `CellEditor` and describes the behavior of a component to be used in editing the cells of a tree. The `getTreeCellEditorComponent()` method is called prior to the editing of a new cell to set the initial data for the component it returns as the editor, based on a given cell and that cell's selection, focus, and its expanded/collapsed states. We can use any interactive component we want as an editor. To assign a `TreeCellEditor` to `JTree`, we use its `setCellEditor()` method.

17.1.15 DefaultCellEditor

class javax.swing.DefaultCellEditor

This is a concrete implementation of the `TreeCellEditor` interface as well as the `TableCellEditor` interface (see section 18.1.11). This editor allows the use of `JTextField`, `JComboBox`, or `JCheckBox` components to edit data. It defines a protected inner class called `EditorDelegate`, which is responsible for returning the current value of the editor component in use when the `getCellEditorValue()` method is invoked. `DefaultCellEditor` is limited to three constructors for creating a `JTextField`, `JComboBox`, or a `JCheckBox` editor.

> **NOTE**   The fact that the only constructors provided are component-specific makes `DefaultCellEditor` a bad candidate for extensibility.

    `DefaultCellEditor` maintains an `int` property called `clickCountToStart` which specifies how many mouse click events should trigger an edit. By default this is 2 for `JTextFields` and 1 for `JComboBox` and `JCheckBox` editors. As expected, `ChangeEvents` are fired when `stopCellEditing()` and `cancelCellEditing()` are invoked.

17.1.16 DefaultTreeCellEditor

class javax.swing.tree.DefaultTreeCellEditor

`DefaultTreeCellEditor` extends `DefaultCellEditor`, and it is the default concrete implementation of the `TreeCellEditor` interface. It uses a `JTextField` for editing a node's data (an instance of `DefaultTreeCellEditor.DefaultTextField`). `stopCellEditing()` is called when ENTER is pressed in this text field.

    An instance of `DefaultTreeCellRenderer` is needed to construct this editor, allowing renderer icons to remain visible while editing (this is accomplished by embedding the editor in an instance of `DefaultTreeCellEditor.EditorContainer`). It fires `ChangeEvents` when editing begins and ends. As expected, we can add `CellEditorListeners` to intercept and process these events.

    By default, editing starts (if it is enabled) when a cell is triple-clicked or when a pause of 1200ms occurs between two single mouse clicks (the latter is accomplished using an internal `Timer`). We can set the click count requirement using the `setClickCountToStart()` method, or check for it directly by overriding `isCellEditable()`.

17.1.17 The RowMapper interface

abstract interface javax.swing.text.RowMapper

RowMapper declares a single method, getRowsForPaths(), which is intended to map an array of tree paths to an array of tree rows. A tree row corresponds to a tree cell, and as we discussed, these are organized similar to JList cells. JTree selections are based on rows and tree paths, and we can choose which to deal with depending on the needs of our application. (We aren't expected to have the need to implement this interface unless we decide to build our own JTree UI delegate.)

17.1.18 The TreeSelectionModel interface

abstract interface javax.swing.tree.TreeSelectionModel

The TreeSelectionModel interface describes a base interface for a tree's selection model. Three modes of selection are supported, similar to JList (see chapter 10), and implementations allow for setting this mode through the setSelectionMode() method: SINGLE_TREE_SELECTION, DISCONTIGUOUS_TREE_SELECTION, and CONTIGUOUS_TREE_SELECTION. Implementations are expected to maintain a RowMapper instance. The getSelectionPath() and getSelectionPaths() methods are intended to return a TreePath and an array of TreePaths respectively, allowing access to the currently selected paths. The getSelectionRows() method should return an int array that represents the indices of all rows currently selected. The *lead* selection refers to the most recently added path to the current selection. Whenever the selection changes, implementations of this interface should fire TreeSelectionEvents. Appropriately, add/remove TreeSelectionListener methods are also declared. All other methods are, for the most part, self explanatory (see the API documentation). The tree selection model can be retrieved using JTree's getSelectionModel() method.

NOTE   JTree defines the inner class EmptySelectionModel, which does not allow any selection at all.

17.1.19 DefaultTreeSelectionModel

class javax.swing.tree.DefaultTreeSelectionModel

DefaultTreeSelectionModel is the default concrete implementation of the TreeSelectionModel interface. This model supports TreeSelectionListener notification when changes are made to a tree's path selection. Several methods are defined for, among other things, modifying and retrieving a selection, and firing TreeSelectionEvents when a modification occurs.

17.1.20 The TreeModelListener interface

abstract interface javax.swing.event.TreeModelListener

The TreeModelListener interface describes a listener which receives notifications about changes in a tree's model. TreeModelEvents are normally fired from a TreeModel when nodes are modified, added, or removed. We can register/unregister a TreeModelListener with a JTree's model using TreeModel's addTreeModelListener() and removeTreeModelListener() methods respectively.

17.1.21 The TreeSelectionListener interface

abstract interface javax.swing.event.TreeSelectionListener

The `TreeSelectionListener` interface describes a listener which receives notifications about changes in a tree's selection. It declares only one method, `valueChanged()`, accepting a `TreeSelectionEvent`. These events are normally fired whenever a tree's selection changes. We can register/unregister a `TreeSelectionListener` with a tree's selection model using JTree's `addTreeSelectionListener()` and `removeTreeSelectionListener()` methods.

17.1.22 The TreeExpansionListener interface

abstract interface javax.swing.event.TreeExpansionListener

The `TreeExpansionListener` interface describes a listener which receives notifications about tree expansions and collapses. Implementations must define `treeExpanded()` and `treeCollapsed()` methods, which take a `TreeExpansionEvent` as a parameter. We can register/unregister a `TreeExpansionListener` with a tree using JTree's `addTreeExpansionListener()` and `removeTreeExpansionListener()` methods respectively.

17.1.23 The TreeWillExpandListener interface

abstract interface javax.swing.event.TreeWillExpandListener

The `TreeWillExpandListener` interface describes a listener which receives notifications when a tree is *about* to expand or collapse. Unlike `TreeExpansionListener`, this listener will be notified before the actual change occurs. Implementations are expected to throw an `ExpandVetoException` if it is determined that a pending expansion or collapse should not be carried out. Its two methods, `treeWillExpand()` and `treeWillCollapse()`, take a `TreeExpansionEvent` as a parameter. We can register/unregister a `TreeWillExpandListener` with a tree using JTree's `addTreeWillExpandListener()` and `removeTreeWillExpandListener()` methods.

17.1.24 TreeModelEvent

class javax.swing.event.TreeModelEvent

`TreeModelEvent` is used to notify `TreeModelListeners` that all or part of a JTree's data has changed. This event encapsulates a reference to the source component, and a single `TreePath` or an array of path `Objects` leading to the topmost affected node. We can extract the source as usual, using `getSource()`, and we can extract the path(s) using either of the `getPath()` or `getTreePath()` methods (the former returns an array of `Objects`, the latter returns a `TreePath`). Optionally, this event can also carry an `int` array of node indices and an array of child nodes. These can be extracted using the `getChildIndices()` and `getChildren()` methods respectively.

17.1.25 TreeSelectionEvent

class javax.swing.event.TreeSelectionEvent

`TreeSelectionEvent` is used to notify `TreeSelectionListeners` that the selection of a JTree has changed. One variant of this event encapsulates: a reference to the source component, the selected `TreePath`, a flag specifying whether the tree path is a new addition to the selection (`true` if so), and the new and old lead selection paths (remember that the lead selection path is the newest path added to a selection). The second variant of this event encapsulates: a reference to the source component, an array of selected `TreePaths`, an array of flags specifying whether each path is a new addition, and the new and old lead selection paths. Typical `getXX()` accessor methods allow extraction of this data.

> **NOTE** An interesting and unusual method defined in this class is `cloneWithSource()`. When passed a component, this method returns a clone of the event, but with a reference to the given component parameter as the event source.

17.1.26 TreeExpansionEvent

class javax.swing.event.TreeExpansionEvent

`TreeExpansionEvent` is used to encapsulate a `TreePath` corresponding to a recently, or possibly pending, expanded or collapsed tree path. This path can be extracted with the `get-Path()` method.

17.1.27 ExpandVetoException

class javax.swing.tree.ExpandVetoException

`ExpandVetoException` may be thrown by `TreeWillExpandListener` methods to indicate that a tree path expansion or collapse is prohibited, and should be vetoed.

17.1.28 JTree client properties and UI defaults

When using the Metal look and feel, `JTree` uses a specific line style to represent the edges between nodes. The default is no edges, but we can set `JTree`'s `lineStyle` client property so that each parent node appears connected to each of its child nodes by an angled line:

```
myJTree.putClientProperty("JTree.lineStyle", "Angled");
```

We can also set this property so that each tree cell is separated by a horizontal line:

```
myJTree.putClientProperty("JTree.lineStyle", "Horizontal");
```

To disable the line style, do this:

```
myJTree.putClientProperty("JTree.lineStyle", "None");
```

As with any Swing component, we can also change the UI resource defaults used for all instances of the `JTree` class. For instance, to change the color of the lines used for rendering the edges between nodes as described above, we can modify the entry in the UI defaults table for this resource as follows:

```
UIManager.put("Tree.hash",
  new ColorUIResource(Color.lightGray));
```

To modify the open node icons used by all trees when a node's children are shown:

```
UIManager.put("Tree.openIcon", new IconUIResource(
  new ImageIcon("myOpenIcon.gif")));
```

We can do a similar thing for the closed, leaf, expanded, and collapsed icons using `Tree.closedIcon`, `Tree.leafIcon`, `Tree.expandedIcon`, and `Tree.collapsedIcon` respectively. (See the `BasicLookAndFeel` source code for a complete list of UI resource defaults.)

> **NOTE**   We used the `ColorUIResource` and `IconUIResource` wrapper classes found in the `javax.swing.plaf` package to wrap our resources before placing them in the UI defaults table. If we do not wrap our resources in `UIResource` objects, they will persist through look and feel changes (which may or may not be desirable). See chapter 21 for more about look and feel and resource wrappers.

17.1.29 Controlling JTree appearance

Though we haven't concentrated heavily on UI delegate customization for each component throughout this book, Swing certainly provides us with a high degree of flexibility in this area. It is particularly useful with `JTree` because no methods are provided in the component itself to control the indentation spacing of tree cells (note that the row height can be specified with `JTree`'s `setRowHeight()` method). The `JTree` UI delegate also provides methods for setting expanded and collapsed icons, allowing us to assign these on a per-component basis rather than a global basis (which is done using `UIManager`; see section 17.1.28). The following `BasicTreeUI` methods provide this control, and figure 17.1 illustrates:

- `void setCollapsedIcon(Icon newG)`: The icon used to specify that a node is in the collapsed state.
- `void setExpandedIcon(Icon newG)`: The icon used to specify that a node is in the expanded state.
- `void setLeftChildIndent(int newAmount)`: Used to assign a distance between the left side of a parent node and the center of an expand/collapse box of a child node.
- `void setRightChildIndent(int newAmount)`: Used to assign a distance between the center of the expand/collapse box of a child node to the left side of that child node's cell renderer.

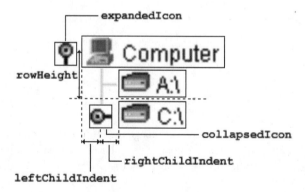

Figure 17.1 The `JTree` UI delegate icon and indentation properties

To actually use these methods, we first have to obtain the target tree's UI delegate. For example, to assign a left indent of 8 and a right indent of 10:

```
BasicTreeUI basicTreeUI = (BasicTreeUI) myJTree.getUI();
basicTreeUI.setRightChildIndent(10);
basicTreeUI.setLeftChildIndent(8);
```

17.2 BASIC JTREE EXAMPLE

As we know very well by now, JTree is suitable for the display and editing of a hierarchical set of objects. To demonstrate this in an introductory-level example, we will consider a set of Object Identifiers (OIDs) used in the Simple Network Management Protocol (SNMP). In example 17.1 we will show how to build a simple JTree that displays the initial portion of the OID tree.

SNMP is used extensively to manage network components, and it is particularly important in managing Internet routers and hosts. Every object managed by SNMP must have a unique OID. An OID is built from a sequence of numbers separated by periods. Objects are organized hierarchically and have an OID with a sequence of numbers equal in length to their *level* (see section 17.1.1) in the OID tree. The International Organization of Standards (ISO) establishes rules for building OIDs.

Understanding SNMP is certainly not necessary to understand this example. The purpose of this example is to show how to construct a tree using the following items:

- A DefaultTreeModel with DefaultMutableTreeNodes containing custom user objects.
- A customized DefaultTreeCellRenderer.
- A TreeSelectionListener which displays information in a status bar based on the TreePath encapsulated in the TreeSelectionEvents it receives.

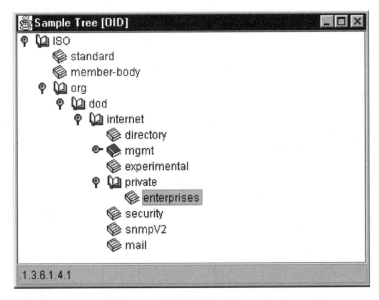

Figure 17.2 JTree **with custom cell renderer icons, selection listener, and visible root handles.**

Example 17.1

see \Chapter17\1

```java
import java.awt.*;
import java.awt.event.*;
import java.util.*;

import javax.swing.*;
import javax.swing.tree.*;
import javax.swing.event.*;

public class Tree1 extends JFrame
{
  protected JTree  m_tree = null;
  protected DefaultTreeModel m_model = null;
  protected JTextField m_display;

  public Tree1() {
    super("Sample Tree [OID]");
    setSize(400, 300);

    Object[] nodes = new Object[5];
    DefaultMutableTreeNode top = new DefaultMutableTreeNode(
      new OidNode(1, "ISO"));
    DefaultMutableTreeNode parent = top;
      nodes[0] = top;

    DefaultMutableTreeNode node = new DefaultMutableTreeNode(
      new OidNode(0, "standard"));
    parent.add(node);
    node = new DefaultMutableTreeNode(new OidNode(2,
      "member-body"));
    parent.add(node);
    node = new DefaultMutableTreeNode(new OidNode(3, "org"));
    parent.add(node);
    parent = node;
    nodes[1] = parent;

    node = new DefaultMutableTreeNode(new OidNode(6, "dod"));
    parent.add(node);
    parent = node;
    nodes[2] = parent;

    node = new DefaultMutableTreeNode(new OidNode(1, "internet"));
    parent.add(node);
    parent = node;
    nodes[3] = parent;

    node = new DefaultMutableTreeNode(new OidNode(1, "directory"));
    parent.add(node);
    node = new DefaultMutableTreeNode(new OidNode(2, "mgmt"));
    parent.add(node);
    nodes[4] = node;
    node.add(new DefaultMutableTreeNode(new OidNode(1, "mib-2")));
```

❶ Constructor creates several DefaultMutableTreeNodes, each containing an OidNode

```
node = new DefaultMutableTreeNode(new OidNode(3,
  "experimental"));
parent.add(node);
node = new DefaultMutableTreeNode(new OidNode(4, "private"));
node.add(new DefaultMutableTreeNode(new OidNode(1,
  "enterprises")));
parent.add(node);
node = new DefaultMutableTreeNode(new OidNode(5, "security"));
parent.add(node);
node = new DefaultMutableTreeNode(new OidNode(6, "snmpV2"));
parent.add(node);
node = new DefaultMutableTreeNode(new OidNode(7,
  "mail"));
parent.add(node);

m_model = new DefaultTreeModel(top);                    ② Creates a JTree
m_tree = new JTree(m_model);                               pointing to the
                                                           top node
DefaultTreeCellRenderer renderer = new
  DefaultTreeCellRenderer();
renderer.setOpenIcon(new ImageIcon("opened.gif"));
renderer.setClosedIcon(new ImageIcon("closed.gif"));
renderer.setLeafIcon(new ImageIcon("leaf.gif"));
m_tree.setCellRenderer(renderer);

m_tree.setShowsRootHandles(true);
m_tree.setEditable(false);
TreePath path = new TreePath(nodes);
m_tree.setSelectionPath(path);

m_tree.addTreeSelectionListener(new
  OidSelectionListener());
                                                       ③ Adds a JScrollPane,
JScrollPane s = new JScrollPane();                         with the tree in
s.getViewport().add(m_tree);                               the viewport
getContentPane().add(s, BorderLayout.CENTER);

m_display = new JTextField();
m_display.setEditable(false);
getContentPane().add(m_display, BorderLayout.SOUTH);

WindowListener wndCloser = new WindowAdapter() {
  public void windowClosing(WindowEvent e) {
    System.exit(0);
  }
};
addWindowListener(wndCloser);
                                                       Listens for node   ④
setVisible(true);                                      selections, then
}                                                      follows the path
                                                       from the root
public static void main(String argv[]) {               to the node to
  new Tree1();                                          build the ID string
}

class OidSelectionListener implements TreeSelectionListener
{
```

```
      public void valueChanged(TreeSelectionEvent e) {
        TreePath path = e.getPath();
        Object[] nodes = path.getPath();
        String oid = "";
        for (int k=0; k<nodes.length; k++) {
          DefaultMutableTreeNode node =
            (DefaultMutableTreeNode)nodes[k];
          OidNode nd = (OidNode)node.getUserObject();
          oid += "."+nd.getId();
        }
        m_display.setText(oid);
      }
    }
  }
}

class OidNode
{
  protected int      m_id;
  protected String m_name;

  public OidNode(int id, String name) {
    m_id = id;
    m_name = name;
  }

  public int getId() { return m_id; }

  public String getName() { return m_name; }

  public String toString() { return m_name; }
}
```

⑤ Simple object identifier encapsulated at each node

17.2.1   Understanding the code

Class Tree1

This class extends JFrame to implement the frame container for our JTree. Three instance variables are declared:

- JTree m_tree: Our OID tree.
- DefaultTreeModel m_model: The tree model to manage data.
- JTextField m_display: Used as a status bar to display the selected object's OID.

① The constructor first initializes the parent frame object. Then a number of DefaultMutable-TreeNodes encapsulating OidNodes (see below) are created. These objects form a hierarchical structure with DefaultMutableTreeNode top at the root. During the construction of these nodes, the Object[] nodes array is populated with a path of nodes leading to the mgmt node.

② DefaultTreeModel m_model is created with the top node as the root, and JTree m_tree is created to manage this model. Then specific options are set for this tree component. First, we replace the default icons for opened, closed, and leaf icons with our custom icons, using a DefaultTreeCellRenderer as our tree's cell renderer:

```
DefaultTreeCellRenderer renderer = new
    DefaultTreeCellRenderer();
renderer.setOpenIcon(new ImageIcon("opened.gif"));
renderer.setClosedIcon(new ImageIcon("closed.gif"));
```

```
renderer.setLeafIcon(new ImageIcon("leaf.gif"));
m_tree.setCellRenderer(renderer);
```

Then we set the `showsRootHandles` property to `true` and the `editable` property to `false`, and we select the path determined by the `nodes` array formed above:

```
m_tree.setShowsRootHandles(true);
m_tree.setEditable(false);
TreePath path = new TreePath(nodes);
m_tree.setSelectionPath(path);
```

Our custom `OidSelectionListener` (see below) `TreeSelectionListener` is added to the tree to receive notification when our tree's selection changes.

③ A `JScrollPane` is created to provide scrolling capabilities, and our tree is added to its `JViewport`. This `JScrollPane` is then added to the center of our frame. A non-editable `JTextField m_display` is created and added to the south region of our frame's content pane to display the currently selected OID.

Class Tree1.OidSelectionListener

④ This inner class implements the `TreeSelectionListener` interface to receive notifications about when our tree's selection changes. Our `valueChanged()` implementation extracts the `TreePath` corresponding to the current selection and visits each node, starting from the root, accumulating the OID in .N.N.N form as it goes (where N is a digit). This method ends by displaying the resulting OID in our text field status bar.

Class OidNode

⑤ This class encapsulates a single object identifier as a number and a `String` name describing the associated object. Both values are passed to the `OidNode` constructor. Instances of this class are passed directly to the `DefaultMutableTreeNode` constructor to act as a node's user object. The overridden `toString()` method is used to return the name `String` so that our tree's cell renderer will display each node correctly. Recall that, by default, `DefaultTreeCellRenderer` will call a node's user object `toString()` method for rendering.

17.2.2 Running the code

Figure 17.2 shows our OID tree in action. Try selecting various tree nodes and notice how the selected OID is displayed at the bottom of the frame.

GUIDELINE

Icons and root handles   In this example, we are visually reinforcing the data hierarchy with icons. The icons communicate whether an element is a document or a container and whether that container is open or closed. The book icon has two variants to communicate "open book" and "closed book." The icons are communicating the same information as the root handles. Therefore, it is technically possible to remove the root handles. In some problem domains, hidden root handles may be more appropriate, providing that the users are comfortable with interpreting the book icons and realize that a "closed book" icon means that the node can be expanded.

17.3 DIRECTORY TREE, PART I: DYNAMIC NODE RETRIEVAL

Example 17.2 in this section uses the JTree component to display and navigate through a tree of directories located on drives accessible from the user's machine. We will show how to build a custom tree cell renderer as well as how to create and insert tree nodes dynamically.

The main problem encountered in building this application is the fact that it is not practical to read all directories for all accessible drives before displaying our tree component. This would take an extremely long time. To deal with this issue, we initially display only the roots (such as disk partitions or network drives), and then we dynamically expand the tree as the user navigates through it. This requires the use of threads and SwingUtilities.invokeLater() for thread-safe updating of our tree.

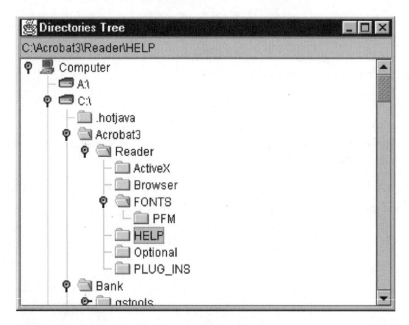

Figure 17.3 A dynamic, threaded directory tree with a custom cell renderer and angled line style

Example 17.2

FileTree1.java

see \Chapter17\2

```
import java.awt.*;
import java.awt.event.*;
import java.io.*;
import java.util.*;

import javax.swing.*;
import javax.swing.tree.*;
```

```
import javax.swing.event.*;

public class FileTree1 extends JFrame
{
  public static final ImageIcon ICON_COMPUTER =
    new ImageIcon("computer.gif");
  public static final ImageIcon ICON_DISK =
    new ImageIcon("disk.gif");
  public static final ImageIcon ICON_FOLDER =
    new ImageIcon("folder.gif");
  public static final ImageIcon ICON_EXPANDEDFOLDER =
    new ImageIcon("expandedfolder.gif");

  protected JTree  m_tree;
  protected DefaultTreeModel m_model;
  protected JTextField m_display;

  public FileTree1() {
    super("Directories Tree");
    setSize(400, 300);

    DefaultMutableTreeNode top = new DefaultMutableTreeNode(
      new IconData(ICON_COMPUTER, null, "Computer"));

    DefaultMutableTreeNode node;
      File[] roots = File.listRoots();
    for (int k=0; k<roots.length; k++) {
      node = new DefaultMutableTreeNode(
        new IconData(ICON_DISK,
        null, new FileNode(roots[k])));
      top.add(node);
      node.add(new DefaultMutableTreeNode(
      new Boolean(true)));
    }

    m_model = new DefaultTreeModel(top);
    m_tree = new JTree(m_model);

    m_tree.getSelectionModel().setSelectionMode(
      TreeSelectionModel.SINGLE_TREE_SELECTION);
    m_tree.putClientProperty("JTree.lineStyle", "Angled");
    TreeCellRenderer renderer = new IconCellRenderer();
    m_tree.setCellRenderer(renderer);
    m_tree.addTreeExpansionListener(new DirExpansionListener());
    m_tree.addTreeSelectionListener(new DirSelectionListener());
    m_tree.setShowsRootHandles(true);
    m_tree.setEditable(false);

    JScrollPane s = new JScrollPane();
    s.getViewport().add(m_tree);
    getContentPane().add(s, BorderLayout.CENTER);

    m_display = new JTextField();
    m_display.setEditable(false);
    getContentPane().add(m_display, BorderLayout.NORTH);

    WindowListener wndCloser = new WindowAdapter() {
```

❶ Constructor creates tree with nodes representing all disk partitions and network nodes

❶ Creates one TreeNode holding icon and file info

❷ Creates tree with top node as root

```
    public void windowClosing(WindowEvent e) {
      System.exit(0);
    }
  };
  addWindowListener(wndCloser);

  setVisible(true);
}

DefaultMutableTreeNode getTreeNode(TreePath path) {
  return (DefaultMutableTreeNode) (path.getLastPathComponent());
}

FileNode getFileNode(DefaultMutableTreeNode node) {
  if (node == null)
    return null;
  Object obj = node.getUserObject();
  if (obj instanceof IconData)
    obj = ((IconData)obj).getObject();
  if (obj instanceof FileNode)
    return (FileNode)obj;
  else
    return null;
}

// Make sure expansion is threaded and updating the tree model
// only occurs within the event dispatching thread.
class DirExpansionListener implements TreeExpansionListener
{
  public void treeExpanded(TreeExpansionEvent event) {
    final DefaultMutableTreeNode node = getTreeNode(
      event.getPath());
    final FileNode fnode = getFileNode(node);

    Thread runner = new Thread() {
      public void run() {
        if (fnode != null && fnode.expand(node)) {
          Runnable runnable = new Runnable() {
            public void run() {
              m_model.reload(node);
            }
          };
          SwingUtilities.invokeLater(runnable);
        }
      }
    };
    runner.start();
  }

  public void treeCollapsed(TreeExpansionEvent event) {}
}

class DirSelectionListener implements TreeSelectionListener
{
  public void valueChanged(TreeSelectionEvent event) {
```

3 Gets the TreeNode at the end of the path

3 Gets the FileNode from a TreeNode

4 Listens for tree expansion events

4 Does expansion work in the background?

5 Resets the tree on the event-dispatch thread

6 Listens for tree selection events; updates m_display with selected path

```
          DefaultMutableTreeNode node = getTreeNode(event.getPath());
            FileNode fnode = getFileNode(node);
            if (fnode != null)
              m_display.setText(fnode.getFile().getAbsolutePath());
            else
              m_display.setText("");
      }
   }

   public static void main(String argv[]) { new FileTree1(); }
}

class IconCellRenderer extends JLabel implements TreeCellRenderer
{
   protected Color m_textSelectionColor;
   protected Color m_textNonSelectionColor;
   protected Color m_bkSelectionColor;
   protected Color m_bkNonSelectionColor;
   protected Color m_borderSelectionColor;

   protected boolean m_selected;

   public IconCellRenderer() {
     super();
     m_textSelectionColor = UIManager.getColor(
       "Tree.selectionForeground");
     m_textNonSelectionColor = UIManager.getColor(
       "Tree.textForeground");
     m_bkSelectionColor = UIManager.getColor(
       "Tree.selectionBackground");
     m_bkNonSelectionColor = UIManager.getColor(
       "Tree.textBackground");
     m_borderSelectionColor = UIManager.getColor(
       "Tree.selectionBorderColor");
     setOpaque(false);
   }

   public Component getTreeCellRendererComponent(JTree tree,
    Object value, boolean sel, boolean expanded, boolean leaf,
    int row, boolean hasFocus)
   {
     DefaultMutableTreeNode node = (DefaultMutableTreeNode)value;
     Object obj = node.getUserObject();
     setText(obj.toString());

     if (obj instanceof Boolean)
       setText("Retrieving data...");

     if (obj instanceof IconData) {
       IconData idata = (IconData)obj;
       if (expanded)
         setIcon(idata.getExpandedIcon());
       else
         setIcon(idata.getIcon());
     }
```

7 Renders TreeNodes with icons and text

8 Indicates node in midst of being expanded

```
    else
      setIcon(null);

    setFont(tree.getFont());
    setForeground(sel ? m_textSelectionColor :
      m_textNonSelectionColor);
    setBackground(sel ? m_bkSelectionColor :
      m_bkNonSelectionColor);
    m_selected = sel;
    return this;
  }

  public void paintComponent(Graphics g) {
    Color bColor = getBackground();
    Icon icon = getIcon();

    g.setColor(bColor);
    int offset = 0;
    if(icon != null && getText() != null)
      offset = (icon.getIconWidth() + getIconTextGap());
    g.fillRect(offset, 0, getWidth() - 1 - offset,
      getHeight() - 1);

    if (m_selected) {
      g.setColor(m_borderSelectionColor);
      g.drawRect(offset, 0, getWidth()-1-offset, getHeight()-1);
    }
    super.paintComponent(g);
  }
}

class IconData
{
  protected Icon    m_icon;
  protected Icon    m_expandedIcon;
  protected Object m_data;

  public IconData(Icon icon, Object data) {
    m_icon = icon;
    m_expandedIcon = null;
    m_data = data;
  }

  public IconData(Icon icon, Icon expandedIcon, Object data) {
    m_icon = icon;
    m_expandedIcon = expandedIcon;
    m_data = data;
  }

  public Icon getIcon() { return m_icon; }

  public Icon getExpandedIcon() {
    return m_expandedIcon!=null ? m_expandedIcon : m_icon;
  }

  public Object getObject() { return m_data; }
```

9   **Just paints text background color; text is drawn in base class method**

10   **Encapsulates "closed" and "open" icons, and a data object that is either a FileNode or a Boolean**

```
    public String toString() { return m_data.toString(); }
}

class FileNode
{
  protected File m_file;

  public FileNode(File file) { m_file = file; }

  public File getFile() { return m_file; }

  public String toString() {
    return m_file.getName().length() > 0 ? m_file.getName() :
      m_file.getPath();
  }

  public boolean expand(DefaultMutableTreeNode parent) {
    DefaultMutableTreeNode flag =
      (DefaultMutableTreeNode)parent.getFirstChild();
    if (flag==null)      // No flag
      return false;
    Object obj = flag.getUserObject();
    if (!(obj instanceof Boolean))
      return false;          // Already expanded

    parent.removeAllChildren();  // Remove flag

    File[] files = listFiles();
    if (files == null)
      return true;

    Vector v = new Vector();

    for (int k=0; k<files.length; k++) {
      File f = files[k];
      if (!(f.isDirectory()))
        continue;

      FileNode newNode = new FileNode(f);

      boolean isAdded = false;
      for (int i=0; i<v.size(); i++) {
        FileNode nd = (FileNode)v.elementAt(i);
        if (newNode.compareTo(nd) < 0) {
          v.insertElementAt(newNode, i);
          isAdded = true;
          break;
        }
      }
      if (!isAdded)
      v.addElement(newNode);
    }
    for (int i=0; i<v.size(); i++) {
      FileNode nd = (FileNode)v.elementAt(i);
      IconData idata = new IconData(FileTree1.ICON_FOLDER,
        FileTree1.ICON_EXPANDEDFOLDER, nd);
```

11 Stores file information, and can be expanded to contain child FileNodes

12 Expands a node by adding new nodes corresponding to the subdirectory of the starting node

13 Determines whether node has no children, is already expanded, or needs to do more work to expand it

14 Gets list of files in directory

15 Creates a new FileNode for each file in directory

16 Performs insertion sort

17 Creates IconDatas for each FileNode

```
        DefaultMutableTreeNode node =
          new DefaultMutableTreeNode(idata);
        parent.add(node);

        if (nd.hasSubDirs())
          node.add(new DefaultMutableTreeNode(
            new Boolean(true)));
      }
      return true;
    }

  public boolean hasSubDirs() {
    File[] files = listFiles();
    if (files == null)
      return false;
    for (int k=0; k<files.length; k++) {
      if (files[k].isDirectory())
        return true;
    }
    return false;
  }

  public int compareTo(FileNode toCompare) {
    return  m_file.getName().compareToIgnoreCase(
      toCompare.m_file.getName());
  }

  protected File[] listFiles() {
    if (!m_file.isDirectory())
      return null;
    try {
      return m_file.listFiles();
    }
    catch (Exception ex) {
      JOptionPane.showMessageDialog(null,
        "Error reading directory "+m_file.getAbsolutePath(),
        "Warning", JOptionPane.WARNING_MESSAGE);
        return null;
    }
  }
}
```

17 Creates IconDatas for each FileNode

17 If new node has children, creates the Boolean child to mark it for further expansion

17.3.1   Understanding the code

Class FileTree1

Four custom icons are loaded as static ImageIcon variables: ICON_COMPUTER, ICON_DISK, ICON_FOLDER, and ICON_EXPANDEDFOLDER, and three instance variables are declared:

- JTree m_tree: The tree component to display the directory nodes.
- DefaultTreeModel m_model: The tree model to manage the nodes.
- JTextField m_display: The component to display the selected directory (acts as a status bar).

1 The `FileTree1` constructor creates and initializes all GUI components. A root node "Computer" hosts child nodes for all disk partitions and network drives in the system. These nodes encapsulate `Files` retrieved with the static `File.listRoots()` method (which is a valuable addition to the `File` class in Java 2). Note that `IconData` objects (see below) encapsulate `Files` in the tree. Also note that each newly created child node immediately receives a child node containing a `Boolean` user object. This `Boolean` object allows us to display an expanding message for nodes when they are in the process of being expanded. Exactly how we expand them will be explained soon enough.

2 We then create a `DefaultTreeModel` and pass our "Computer" node as the root. This model is used to instantiate our `JTree` object:

```
m_model = new DefaultTreeModel(top);
m_tree = new JTree(m_model);
```

We then set the `lineStyle` client property so that angled lines will represent the edges between parent and child nodes:

```
m_tree.putClientProperty("JTree.lineStyle", "Angled");
```

We also use a custom tree cell renderer, as well as a tree expansion listener and a tree selection listener: these are instances of `IconCellRenderer`, `DirExpansionListener`, and `DirSelectionListener`, respectively.

The actual contents of our tree nodes represent directories. Each node is a `DefaultMutableTreeNode` with an `IconData` user object. Each user object is an instance of `IconData`, and each `IconData` contains an instance of `FileNode`. Each `FileNode` contains a `java.io.File` object. Thus we have a four-layer nested structure:

- `DefaultMutableTreeNode` is used for each node to represent a directory or disk (as well as the "Computer" root node). When we retrieve a node at the end of a given `TreePath`, using the `getLastPathComponent()` method, we are provided with an instance of this class.
- `IconData` (see below) sits inside `DefaultMutableTreeNode` and provides custom icons for our tree cell renderer, and encapsulation of a `FileNode` object. `IconData` can be retrieved using `DefaultMutableTreeNode`'s `getUserObject()` method. We need to cast the returned `Object` to an `IconData` instance.
- `FileNode` (see below) sits inside `IconData` and encapsulates a `File` object. A `FileNode` can be retrieved using `IconData`'s `getObject()` method, which also requires a subsequent cast.
- A `File` object sits inside a `FileNode` and can be retrieved using `FileNode`'s `getFile()` method.

Figure 17.4 illustrates this structure.

3 To keep things simple, two helper methods are provided to work with these encapsulated nodes: `getTreeNode()` retrieves a `DefaultMutableTreeNode` from a given `TreePath`, and `getFileNode()` retrieves the `FileNode` (or `null`) from a `DefaultMutableTreeNode`. We will see where these methods are needed shortly.

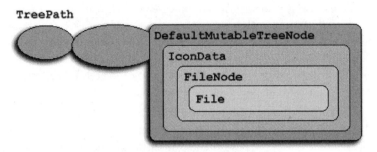

Figure 17.4 The nested structure of our tree nodes

Class FileTree1.DirExpansionListener

④ This inner class implements `TreeExpansionListener` to listen for tree expansion events. When a node is expanded, the `treeExpanded()` method retrieves the `FileNode` instance for that node and if the instance is not `null`, it calls the `expand()` method on it (see below). This call is wrapped in a separate thread because it can often be a very time-consuming process and we do not want the application to freeze. Inside this thread, once `expand()` has completed,

⑤ we need to update the tree model with any new nodes that are retrieved. As we learned in chapter 2, updating the state of a component should only occur within the event-dispatching thread. For this reason we wrap the call to `reload()` in a `Runnable` and send it the event-dispatching queue using `SwingUtilities.invokeLater()`:

```
Runnable runnable = new Runnable() {
  public void run() {
    m_model.reload(node);
  }
};
SwingUtilities.invokeLater(runnable);
```

As we will see below in our discussion of `IconCellRenderer`, placing a `Boolean` user object in a dummy child node of each non-expanded node, allows a certain `String` to be displayed while a node is in the process of being expanded. In our case, "Retrieving data..." is shown below a node until it is finished expanding.

Class FileTree1.DirSelectionListener

⑥ This inner class implements `TreeSelectionListener` to listen for tree selection events. When a node is selected, the `valueChanged()` method extracts the `FileNode` instance contained in that node, and if the instance is not `null`, it displays the absolute path to that directory in the `m_display` text field.

Class IconCellRenderer

⑦ This class implements the `TreeCellRenderer` interface and extends `JLabel`. The purpose of this renderer is to display custom icons and access `FileNodes` contained in `IconData` instances.

First, we declare five `Colors` and retrieve them from the current look and feel in use through `UIManager`'s `getColor()` method. The `getTreeCellRendererComponent()`

8 method is then implemented to set the proper text and icon (which are retrieved from the underlying `IconData` object). If the user object happens to be a `Boolean`, this signifies that a node is in the process of being expanded:

```
if (obj instanceof Boolean)
    setText("Retrieving data...");
```

The reason we do this is slightly confusing. In the `FileNode` `expand()` method (see below), when each new node is added to our tree, it receives a node containing a `Boolean` user object only if the corresponding directory has subdirectories. When we click on this node, the `Boolean` child will be immediately shown, and we also generate an expansion event that is received by our `DirExpansionListener`. As we discussed above, this listener extracts the encapsulated `FileNode` and calls the `FileNode` `expand()` method on it. The child node containing the `Boolean` object is removed before all new nodes are added. Until this update occurs, the `JTree` will display the `Boolean` child node, in effect telling us that the expansion is not yet complete. So if our cell renderer detects a `Boolean` user object, we simply display "Receiving data..." for its text.

9 The `paintComponent()` method is overridden to fill the text background with the appropriate color set in the `getTreeCellRendererComponent()` method. Fortunately we don't need to explicitly draw the text and icon because we have extended `JLabel`, which can do this for us.

Class IconData

10 Instances of this class are used as our `DefaultMutableTreeNode` user data objects, and they encapsulate a generic `Object m_data` and two `Icons` for use by `IconCellRenderer`. These icons can be retrieved with our `getIcon()` and `getExpandedIcon()` methods. The icon retrieved with `getExpandedIcon()` represents an expanded folder, and the icon retrieved with `getIcon()` represents a collapsed/non-expanded folder. Notice that the `toString()` method invokes `toString()` on the `m_data` object. In our example this object is either a `FileNode`, in the case of an expanded folder, or a `Boolean`, in the case of a non-expanded folder.

Class FileNode

11 This class encapsulates a `File` object, which is in turn encapsulated in an `IconData` object in a `DefaultMutableTreeNode`.

As we discussed above, the `toString()` method determines the text to be displayed in each tree cell containing a `FileNode`. It returns `File.getName()` for regular directories and `File.getPath()` for partitions.

12 The most interesting and complex method of this class is `expand()`, which attempts to expand a node by dynamically inserting new `DefaultMutableTreeNodes` corresponding to each subdirectory. This method returns `true` if nodes are added, and `false` otherwise. We first need to discuss the mechanism of dynamically reading information (of any kind) into a tree:

- Before we add any new node to the tree, we must somehow determine whether it has children (we don't need a list of children yet, just a yes or no answer).
- If a newly created node has children, a fake child to be used as a flag will be added to it. This will signify that the parent node has not been expanded.
- When a node is expanded, its list of children is examined. Three situations are possible:

- No children. This node is a leaf and cannot be expanded (remember, we've previously checked whether any newly created node has children).
- One flag child is present. That node has children which have not been added yet, so we create these children and add new nodes to the parent node.
- One or more non-flag children are present. This node has already been processed, so expand it as usual.

⑬ The `FileNode.expand()` method implements this dynamic tree expansion strategy, and it takes a parent node as a parameter. In the process of expansion it also alphabetically sorts each node for a more organized display structure. Initially this method checks the first child of the given parent node:

```
DefaultMutableTreeNode flag =
  (DefaultMutableTreeNode)parent.getFirstChild();
if (flag==null)       // No flag
  return false;
Object obj = flag.getUserObject();
if (!(obj instanceof Boolean))
  return false;       // Already expanded

parent.removeAllChildren();  // Remove Flag
```

If no child is found, it can only mean that this node was already checked and was found to be a true leaf (a directory with no subdirectories). If this isn't the case, then we extract the associated data object and check whether it is an instance of `Boolean`. If it is, the flag child is removed and our method proceeds to add nodes corresponding to each subdirectory. Otherwise, we conclude that this node has already been processed and return, allowing it to be expanded as usual.

⑭ We process a newly expanded node by retrieving an array of `File` objects representing files contained in the corresponding directory.

```
File[] files = listFiles();
if (files == null)
  return true;
```

⑮ If the contents have been successfully read, we check for subdirectories and create new `File-Nodes` for each.

```
Vector v = new Vector();

for (int k=0; k<files.length; k++) {
  File f = files[k];
  if (!(f.isDirectory()))
    continue;

  FileNode newNode = new FileNode(f);
```

⑯ To perform an alphabetical sorting of child nodes, we store them in a temporary collection Vector v, and iterate through our array of `Files`, inserting them accordingly.

```
boolean isAdded = false;
for (int i=0; i<v.size(); i++) {
  FileNode nd = (FileNode)v.elementAt(i);
```

```
          if (newNode.compareTo(nd) < 0) {
            v.insertElementAt(newNode, i);
            isAdded = true;
             break;
          }
        }
        if (!isAdded)
        v.addElement(newNode);
      }
```

⑰ We then wrap each newly created `FileNode` object in an `IconData` to encapsulate them with folder icons, and we add the sorted nodes to the given parent node. At the same time, flags are added to new nodes if they contain any subdirectories themselves (this is checked by the `has-SubDirs()` method):

```
      for (int i=0; i<v.size(); i++) {
        FileNode nd = (FileNode)v.elementAt(i);
        IconData idata = new IconData(FileTree1.ICON_FOLDER,
        FileTree1.ICON_EXPANDEDFOLDER, nd);
        DefaultMutableTreeNode node = new
          DefaultMutableTreeNode(idata);
        parent.add(node);
        if (nd.hasSubDirs())
          node.add(new DefaultMutableTreeNode(
            new Boolean(true)));
      }
      return true;
```

The rest of `FileNode` class implements three methods which do not require much explanation at this point:

- `boolean hasSubDirs()`: Returns `true` if this directory has subdirectories; returns `false` otherwise.
- `int compareTo(FileNode toCompare)`: returns the result of the alphabetical comparison of this directory with another given as parameter.
- `File[] listFiles()`: Reads a list of contained files in this directory. If an exception occurs (this is possible when reading from a floppy disk or network drive), this method displays a warning message and returns `null`.

17.3.2   Running the code

Figure 17.3 shows our directory tree at work. Notice the use of custom icons for partition roots. Try selecting various directories and notice how the selected path is reflected at the top of the frame in our status bar. Also notice that when large directories are expanded, "Retrieving data" will be displayed underneath the corresponding node. Because we have properly implemented multithreading, we can go off and expand other directories while this one is being processed. The tree is always updated correctly when the expanding procedure completes because we have made sure to only change its state in the event-dispatching thread using `invokeLater()`.

GUIDELINE

When to use connecting lines Angled connecting lines (or edges) add visual noise and clutter to a tree display. Reduced visual clutter leads to recognition and comprehension; this is a clear advantage to leaving them out of the design. So when is it appropriate to include them?

Include the line edges when one or more of these scenarios is likely:

(a) Several nodes may be expanded at one time, and/or

(b) The data set is very large and a node may expand off the bottom of the screen and possibly go several screens deep. In this case, introducing lines helps to give the user a clear picture of how many layers deep in the hierarchy he is. It also makes it easier for him to trace back to the original root node.

17.4 DIRECTORY TREE, PART II: POPUP MENUS AND PROGRAMMATIC NAVIGATION

Example 17.2 in the previous section can be extended in numerous ways to serve as a framework for a much more flexible application. In example 17.3 in this section, we'll add simple popup menus to our tree; they'll be displayed in response to a right mouse click, with their content dependent on the click location. (We discussed popup menus in chapter 12.)

Our popup menu either contains an Expand or a Collapse item, depending on the status of the corresponding node nearest to the mouse click. These items will programatically invoke an expand or collapse of the given node. Our popup menu also contains Delete and Rename dummy items that are not completely implemented, but they explicitly illustrate how we might continue to build upon this example to create a more complete directory explorer application.

Figure 17.5 shows the output of our example.

Example 17.3

FileTree2.java

see \Chapter17\3

```java
import java.awt.*;
import java.awt.event.*;
import java.io.*;
import java.util.*;

import javax.swing.*;
import javax.swing.tree.*;
import javax.swing.event.*;

public class FileTree2 extends JFrame
{
  // Unchanged code from example 17.2

  protected JPopupMenu m_popup;
  protected Action m_action;
  protected TreePath m_clickedPath;
```

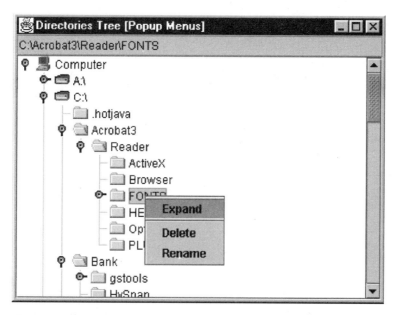

Figure 17.5 Node-dependent popup menus that allow programmatic expand and collapse

```
public FileTree2() {
  super("Directories Tree [Popup Menus]");
  setSize(400, 300);
  getContentPane().setLayout(new BorderLayout());

  // Unchanged code from example 17.2

  m_popup = new JPopupMenu();
  m_action = new AbstractAction() {
    public void actionPerformed(ActionEvent e) {
      if (m_clickedPath==null)
        return;
      if (m_tree.isExpanded(m_clickedPath))
        m_tree.collapsePath(m_clickedPath);
      else
        m_tree.expandPath(m_clickedPath);
    }
  };
  m_popup.add(m_action);
  m_popup.addSeparator();

  Action a1 = new AbstractAction("Delete") {
    public void actionPerformed(ActionEvent e) {
      m_tree.repaint();
      JOptionPane.showMessageDialog(FileTree2.this,
        "Delete option is not implemented",
```

❶ Creates Action to expand or collapse tree

❶ Creates Actions for Delete and Rename, which presently do nothing

```
            "Info", JOptionPane.INFORMATION_MESSAGE);
      }
    };
    m_popup.add(a1);

    Action a2 = new AbstractAction("Rename") {
      public void actionPerformed(ActionEvent e) {
        m_tree.repaint();
        JOptionPane.showMessageDialog(FileTree2.this,
          "Rename option is not implemented",
          "Info", JOptionPane.INFORMATION_MESSAGE);
      }
    };
    m_popup.add(a2);
    m_tree.add(m_popup);
    m_tree.addMouseListener(new PopupTrigger());

    WindowListener wndCloser = new WindowAdapter() {
      public void windowClosing(WindowEvent e) {
        System.exit(0);
      }
    };
    addWindowListener(wndCloser);

    setVisible(true);
  }

// Unchanged code from example 17.2

  class PopupTrigger extends MouseAdapter {
    public void mouseReleased(MouseEvent e) {
      if (e.isPopupTrigger()) {
        int x = e.getX();
        int y = e.getY();
        TreePath path = m_tree.getPathForLocation(x, y);
        if (path != null) {
          if (m_tree.isExpanded(path))
            m_action.putValue(Action.NAME, "Collapse");
          else
            m_action.putValue(Action.NAME, "Expand");
          m_popup.show(m_tree, x, y);
          m_clickedPath = path;
        }
      }
    }
  }

  public static void main(String argv[]) {
    new FileTree2();
  }
}

// Unchanged code from example 17.2
```

1 Creates Actions for Delete and Rename, which presently do nothing

2 Triggers display of popup menu; sets name of first Action depending on expansion state

17.4.1 Understanding the code

Class FileTree2

This example adds three new instance variables:

- `JPopupMenu m_popup`: The popup menu component
- `Action m_action`: The context-sensitive menu action.
- `TreePath m_clickedPath`: The most recent tree path corresponding to a mouse click.

1 New code in the constructor creates a popup menu component and populates it with three menu items: Expand, Delete, and Rename. The last two items intentionally just display an "option is not implemented" message. Their true implementations would take us too far into file manipulation techniques for this chapter. The first one, on the other hand, is quite meaningful here. The corresponding `actionPerformed()` method uses the recently clicked path (not necessarily the currently selected path) which has been set by the `PopupTrigger` instance (see below). This path is collapsed if it is currently expanded, or expanded if this path is currently collapsed.

Finally, this newly created popup menu is added to our tree component. An instance of our `PopupTrigger` class is also attached to our tree as a mouse listener.

Class FileTree2.PopupTrigger

2 This class extends `MouseAdapter` to trigger the display of our popup menu. This menu should be displayed when the right mouse button is released, so we override the `mouseReleased()` method to check whether `isPopupTrigger()` is `true` (see the `MouseEvent` API documentation). In this case, we determine the coordinates of the click and retrieve the `TreePath` corresponding to that coordinate with the `getPathForLocation()` method. If a path is not found (if the click does not occur on a tree node or leaf), we do nothing. Otherwise, we adjust the title of the first menu item accordingly, display our popup menu with the `show()` method, and store our recently clicked path in the `m_clickedPath` instance variable so it can be used by the expand/collapse `Action` as we discussed above.

17.4.2 Running the code

Figure 17.5 shows our directory tree application as it displays a context-sensitive popup menu. Notice how the first menu item is changed depending on whether the selected tree node is collapsed or expanded. The tree can be manipulated (expanded or collapsed) programmatically by choosing the Collapse or Expand popup menu item.

GUIDELINE

Visually reinforcing variations in behavior   If you intend to introduce context-dependent popup menus on tree cells, then this is an ideal time to consider using a tree cell renderer which incorporates an icon. The differing icons help to reinforce the idea that the data in the cells are different types; consequently, when the behavior is slightly different across nodes, it is less surprising. The icon visually reinforces the difference in behavior.

17.5 DIRECTORY TREE, PART III: TOOLTIPS

As we discussed in chapter 5, tooltips are commonly used to display helpful information. In example 17.4, we will show how to use tooltips specific to each tree cell. The key point (which is mentioned in the JTree documentation, but can be easily overlooked) is to register the tree component with the ToolTipManager shared instance:

```
ToolTipManager.sharedInstance().registerComponent(myTree);
```

Without doing this, no tooltips will appear over our tree (refer back to chapter 2, section 2.5, for more about shared instances and service classes).

The JTree component overrides the getToolTipText(MouseEvent ev) method that is inherited from JComponent, and it delegates this call to the tree's cell renderer component. By implementing the getToolTipText(MouseEvent ev) method in our renderer, we can allow cell-specific tooltips. Specifically, we can can return the tooltip text as a String depending on the last node passed to the getTreeCellRendererComponent() method. Alternatively, we can subclass our JTree component and provide our own getToolTipText() implementation. We use the latter method here.

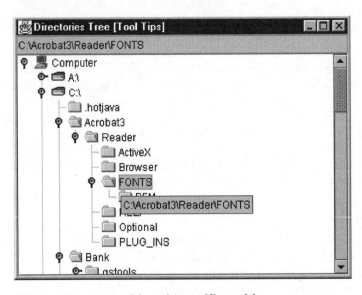

Figure 17.6 JTree with node-specific tooltips

Example 17.4

FileTree3.java

see \Chapter17\4

```
import java.awt.*;
import java.awt.event.*;
import java.io.*;
import java.util.*;
```

```
import javax.swing.*;
import javax.swing.tree.*;
import javax.swing.event.*;

public class FileTree3 extends JFrame
{
  // Unchanged code from example 17.3

  public FileTree3() {
    super("Directories Tree [Tool Tips]");
    setSize(400, 300);
    getContentPane().setLayout(new BorderLayout());

    // Unchanged code from example 17.3

    m_model = new DefaultTreeModel(top);
    m_tree = new JTree(m_model)
    {
      public String getToolTipText(MouseEvent ev)
      {
        if(ev == null)
          return null;
        TreePath path = m_tree.getPathForLocation(ev.getX(),
          ev.getY());
        if (path != null)
        {
          FileNode fnode = getFileNode(getTreeNode(path));
          if (fnode==null)
            return null;
          File f = fnode.getFile();
          return (f==null ? null : f.getPath());
        }
        return null;
      }
    };
    ToolTipManager.sharedInstance().registerComponent(m_tree);

    // The rest of the code is unchanged from example 17.3
```

17.5.1   Understanding the code

Class FileTree3

This example anonymously subclasses the `JTree` component to override `getToolTip-Text(MouseEvent ev)`, which finds the path closest to the current mouse location, determines the `FileNode` at the end of that path, and returns the full file path to that node as a `String` for use as tooltip text. Our `JTree` component is manually registered with the shared instance of `ToolTipManager`, as discussed above.

17.5.2   Running the code

Figure 17.6 shows our directory tree application displaying a tooltip with text specifying the full path of the directory corresponding to the node nearest to the current mouse location.

GUIDELINE

Tooltips as an aid to selection   Tooltips have two really useful advantages for tree cells. Trees have a habit of wandering off to the right-hand side of a display, particularly when you're in deep hierarchies. This may result in cell labels being clipped. Using the tooltip to display the full-length cell label will speed selection and prevent the need for scrolling.

The second use is shown clearly in this example. The tooltip is used to unravel the hierarchy. This would be particularly useful when the original root node is off screen. The user can quickly see the full hierarchical path to the selected cell. This is a very powerful aid in correctly selecting items, and it's another example of additional coding effort providing improved usability.

17.6   *JTREE AND XML DOCUMENTS*

Many developers see the future of the web in XML (Extensible Markup Language). This standard will most likely replace HTML. Unlike HTML, XML allows the definition of custom document tags, thereby allowing the transmission of virtually any type of information over the web. With little effort, you'll find many sources of information about XML; the standard definition is found at http://www.w3.org/TR/WD-xml-lang-970331.html.

XML documents have a tree-like structure, and `JTree` can be very useful for constructing an XML structure browser. In example 17.5 in this section, we'll show how to build a simple implementation of such a browser. We do not intend to give an introduction to XML, and we will not discuss Sun's API for XML in detail (it contains a fair number of classes and is likely to change significantly in the near future). However, a brief introduction to the XML classes used in this example is appropriate.

NOTE   Sun's early access XML library is required to run this example. See http://www.java-soft.com/.

17.6.1   **XmlDocument**

class com.sun.xml.tree.XmlDocument

This class represents a top-level XML 1.0 document that is created with the XML parser built into `XmlDocumentBuilder`. The `getDocumentElement()` method retrieves the topmost node in the document (the root node). All other nodes can be extracted through this node.

17.6.2   **XmlDocumentBuilder**

class com.sun.xml.tree.XmlDocumentBuilder

This class builds an XML document using an internal parser. Two overloaded methods, `create-XmlDocument(InputStream in)` and `createXmlDocument(String documentURL)`, create new `XmlDocument` instances. We will use the latter method in this example.

17.6.3   **DataNode**

class com.sun.xml.tree.DataNode

This class represents a node in an XML document tree that encapsulates data and has no child nodes (a leaf node). The `getData()` method retrieves the contained data as a `String`.

17.6.4   ElementNode

class com.sun.xml.tree.ElementNode

This class encapsulates an element in the XML document tree, which is a node with children (a non-leaf node). The `getLength()` method retrieves the number of child nodes, and `item(int index)` returns the node with the given index.

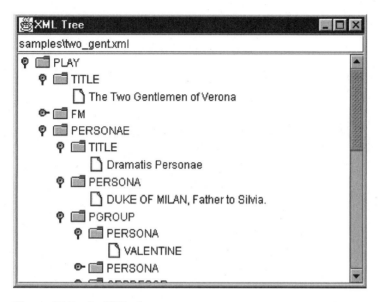

Figure 17.7   An XML document structure tree

Example 17.5

XmlTree.java

see \Chapter17\5

```
import java.awt.*;
import java.awt.event.*;
import java.util.*;
import java.io.*;
import java.net.*;

import javax.swing.*;
import javax.swing.tree.*;
import javax.swing.event.*;

import com.sun.xml.tree.*;
import com.sun.xml.parser.*;
import org.w3c.dom.*;

public class XmlTree extends JFrame
{
  protected JTree  m_tree;
  protected DefaultTreeModel m_model;
```

```
  protected JTextField m_location;

public XmlTree() {
  super("XML Tree");
  setSize(400, 300);

  m_location = new JTextField();
  m_location.setText("samples\\book-order.xml");
  ActionListener lst = new ActionListener() {
    public void actionPerformed(ActionEvent e) {
      readXml(m_location.getText());
    }
  };
  m_location.addActionListener(lst);
  getContentPane().add(m_location, BorderLayout.NORTH);

  DefaultMutableTreeNode top = new DefaultMutableTreeNode(
    "Empty");
  m_model = new DefaultTreeModel(top);
  m_tree = new JTree(m_model);

  m_tree.getSelectionModel().setSelectionMode(
    TreeSelectionModel.SINGLE_TREE_SELECTION);
  m_tree.setShowsRootHandles(true);
    m_tree.setEditable(false);

  JScrollPane s = new JScrollPane();
  s.getViewport().add(m_tree);
  getContentPane().add(s, BorderLayout.CENTER);

  WindowListener wndCloser = new WindowAdapter() {
    public void windowClosing(WindowEvent e) {
      System.exit(0);
    }
  };
  addWindowListener(wndCloser);

  setVisible(true);
}

public void readXml(String sUrl) {
  setCursor(Cursor.getPredefinedCursor(Cursor.WAIT_CURSOR));
  Thread runner = new Thread() {
    public void run () {
      try {
        URL source;
        try {
          File f = new File(sUrl);
          source = f.toURL();
        }
        catch (Exception ex) {
          source = new URL(sUrl);
        }

        XmlDocument doc =
          XmlDocumentBuilder.createXmlDocument(
        source.toString());

        ElementNode root =
```

① Reads XML from URL in text field

① Creates JTree with single node called "Empty"

② Gets specified URL or file name

③ Creates the XML document and gets the root node

```
              (ElementNode)doc.getDocumentElement();
          root.normalize();

          DefaultMutableTreeNode top = createTreeNode(root);
          m_model.setRoot(top);
          m_tree.treeDidChange();
        }
        catch (Exception ex) {
          ex.printStackTrace();
          JOptionPane.showMessageDialog(this,
            ex.toString(), "Warning",
            JOptionPane.WARNING_MESSAGE);
        }
        setCursor(Cursor.getPredefinedCursor(
          Cursor.DEFAULT_CURSOR));
      }
    }
  }
  protected DefaultMutableTreeNode createTreeNode(ElementNode root) {
    DefaultMutableTreeNode node = new DefaultMutableTreeNode(
      root.getNodeName());
    for (int k=0; k<root.getLength(); k++) {
      Node nd = root.item(k);
      if (nd instanceof DataNode) {
        DataNode dn = (DataNode)nd;
        String data = dn.getData().trim();
        if (data.equals("\n") || data.equals("\r\n"))
          data = "";
        if (data.length() > 0)
          node.add(new DefaultMutableTreeNode(data));
      }
      else if (nd instanceof ElementNode) {
        ElementNode en = (ElementNode)nd;
        node.add(createTreeNode(en));
      }
    }
    return node;
  }
  public static void main(String argv[]) {
    new XmlTree();
  }
}
```

Creates the XML document and gets the root node ③

Creates tree root node from XML root node ④

Creates tree node (and child nodes) from XML ElementNode ⑤

17.6.5   Understanding the code

Class XmlTree

There are three instance variables:

- `JTree m_tree`: Used to display an XML document.
- `DefaultTreeModel m_model`: Used to store the content of an XML document.
- `JTextField m_location`: Used for entry of a file name or the URL location of an XML document.

1 Initially, the JTree component receives a single node, Empty. An ActionListener is added to the m_location text field, which calls our readXml() method and passes it the current text.

2 The readXml() method loads an XML document that corresponds to the String passed as a parameter into our tree model. The body of this method is placed in a separate thread because it can be a very expensive procedure, and we want to make sure not to clog up the event-dispatching thread (to retain GUI responsiveness). First, the given string is treated as a file name. A File instance is created and converted to a URL. If this does not succeed, the string is treated as a URL address:

```
URL source;
try {
  File f = new File(sUrl);
  source = f.toURL();
}
catch (Exception ex) {
  source = new URL(sUrl);
}
```

3 The static method XmlDocumentBuilder.createXmlDocument() creates an XmlDocument that corresponds to the resulting URL. As soon as this finishes (it may take a while for large documents), the root ElementNode is retrieved from that document:

```
XmlDocument doc =
  XmlDocumentBuilder.createXmlDocument(
source.toString());

ElementNode root =
  (ElementNode)doc.getDocumentElement();
root.normalize();
```

4 We then transform our XML document into a structure suitable for addition to our Swing tree model. Our createTreeNode() method does this job, returning the topmost node (the root node) as a DefaultMutableTreeNode. Finally, that node is set as a root of our tree model, and our tree component is notified that its content has changed:

```
DefaultMutableTreeNode top = createTreeNode(root);
m_model.setRoot(top);
m_tree.treeDidChange();
```

NOTE   We are normally expected to avoid calling the treeDidChange() method directly, as it should be called by our UI as needed. However, in this case our JTree will not update correctly without it.

5 The createTreeNode() method creates a DefaultMutableTreeNode from the Element-Node that is provided. It first creates a root node corresponding to the given ElementNode, and then all lower level nodes are retrieved and processed in turn to populate the whole tree:

```
DefaultMutableTreeNode node = new DefaultMutableTreeNode(
  root.getNodeName());
for (int k=0; k<root.getLength(); k++) {
  Node nd = root.item(k);
```

Two possibilities are reconciled during this procedure. If a newly processed node is an instance of `DataNode`, its text is retrieved and is used as the user data object for a new `Default-MutableTreeNode`, which is then added to the parent node (in this case, care should be taken to avoid empty nodes containing only end-of-line symbols). Otherwise, if a newly processed node is an instance of `ElementNode`, the `createTreeNode()` method is called recursively.

17.6.6   Running the code

Figure 17.7 shows our XML tree example displaying the contents of "The Two Gentlemen of Verona" XML document which can be found at ftp://sunsite.unc.edu/pub/sun-info/standards/xml/eg/.

17.7   CUSTOM EDITORS AND RENDERERS

In this section we'll construct a simple family tree application. We will show how to use a custom cell editor for name entry, as well as a custom cell renderer which displays an icon corresponding to a node's data rather than its state. This example allows dynamic node insertion, and each node can have no more than two children.

Our representation of an ancestor tree is structured differently than how we normally think of structuring trees, even though, technically speaking, both methods are equivalent. Our root tree node represents a child, and child tree nodes represent parents, grandparents, etc., of that child. So a parent node in this `JTree` actually corresponds to a child in the family ancestry. This illustrates that `JTree` is flexible enough to adapt to any type of hierarchical data set, including a dynamically changing one (as we also saw in our file directory tree examples above).

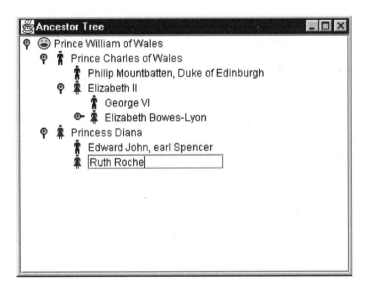

Figure 17.8   A `JTree` with a custom editor and cell renderer enforcing nodes with two children

Example 17.6

see \Chapter17\6

```java
import java.awt.*;
import java.awt.event.*;
import java.util.*;

import javax.swing.*;
import javax.swing.border.*;
import javax.swing.event.*;
import javax.swing.tree.*;

public class AncestorTree extends JFrame
{
  public static ImageIcon ICON_SELF =
    new ImageIcon("myself.gif");
  public static ImageIcon ICON_MALE =
    new ImageIcon("male.gif");
  public static ImageIcon ICON_FEMALE =
    new ImageIcon("female.gif");

  protected JTree  m_tree;
  protected DefaultTreeModel m_model;
  protected IconCellRenderer m_renderer;
  protected IconCellEditor m_editor;

  public AncestorTree() {
    super("Ancestor Tree");
    setSize(500, 400);

    DefaultMutableTreeNode top = new DefaultMutableTreeNode(
      new IconData(ICON_SELF, "Myself"));
    addAncestors(top);
    m_model = new DefaultTreeModel(top);
    m_tree = new JTree(m_model);
    m_tree.getSelectionModel().setSelectionMode(
      TreeSelectionModel.SINGLE_TREE_SELECTION);
    m_tree.setShowsRootHandles(true);
    m_tree.setEditable(true);

    m_renderer = new IconCellRenderer();
    m_tree.setCellRenderer(m_renderer);
    m_editor = new IconCellEditor(m_tree);
    m_tree.setCellEditor(m_editor);
    m_tree.setInvokesStopCellEditing(true);

    m_tree.addMouseListener(new TreeExpander());

    JScrollPane s = new JScrollPane();
    s.getViewport().add(m_tree);
    getContentPane().add(s, BorderLayout.CENTER);

    WindowListener wndCloser = new WindowAdapter() {
      public void windowClosing(WindowEvent e) {
```

❶ Shows a frame which manages a tree displaying male/ female ancestors and their offspring

❷ Constructor creates a JTree with a single node, representing the user, or a single person

❷ User can edit the tree

```
          System.exit(0);
       }
    };
    addWindowListener(wndCloser);

    setVisible(true);
 }

 public boolean addAncestors(DefaultMutableTreeNode node) {
    if (node.getChildCount() > 0)
       return false;

    Object obj = node.getUserObject();
    if (obj == null)
       return false;
    node.add(new DefaultMutableTreeNode(new IconData(
       ICON_MALE, "Father of: "+obj.toString())));
    node.add(new DefaultMutableTreeNode(new IconData(
       ICON_FEMALE, "Mother of: "+obj.toString())));
    return true;
 }

 public static void main(String argv[]) { new AncestorTree(); }

 class TreeExpander extends MouseAdapter
 {
    public void mouseClicked(MouseEvent e) {
       if (e.getClickCount() == 2) {
          TreePath selPath = m_tree.getPathForLocation(
             e.getX(), e.getY());
          if (selPath == null)
             return;
          DefaultMutableTreeNode node =
             (DefaultMutableTreeNode)(selPath.
                getLastPathComponent());
          if (node!=null && addAncestors(node)) {
             m_tree.expandPath(selPath);
             m_tree.repaint();
          }
       }
    }
  }
}

// Classes IconCellRenderer and IconData are
// unchanged from previous examples, and they are
// not listed here to conserve space.

class IconCellEditor extends JLabel
 implements TreeCellEditor, ActionListener
{
   protected JTree m_tree = null;
   protected JTextField m_editor = null;
   protected IconData m_item = null;
   protected int m_lastRow = -1;
```

3 Creates male and female ancestor nodes of the given node

4 Listens for mouse (double) clicks on TreeNodes and creates ancestor nodes for the clicked node

5 As a CellEditor, presents a text field to allow the user to edit the name of the person at this node

```
protected long m_lastClick = 0;
protected Vector m_listeners = null;

public IconCellEditor(JTree tree) {
  super();
  m_tree = tree;
  m_listeners = new Vector();
}

public Component getTreeCellEditorComponent(JTree tree,
 Object value, boolean isSelected, boolean expanded,
 boolean leaf, int row)
{
  if (value instanceof DefaultMutableTreeNode) {
    DefaultMutableTreeNode node =
      (DefaultMutableTreeNode)value;
    Object obj = node.getUserObject();
    if (obj instanceof IconData) {
      IconData idata = (IconData)obj;
      m_item = idata;
      // Reserve some more space...
      setText(idata.toString()+"       ");
      setIcon(idata.m_icon);
      setFont(tree.getFont());
      return this;
    }
  }
  // We don't support other objects...
  return null;
}

public Object getCellEditorValue() {
  if (m_item != null && m_editor != null)
    m_item.m_data = m_editor.getText();
  return m_item;
}

public boolean isCellEditable(EventObject evt) {
  if (evt instanceof MouseEvent) {
    MouseEvent mEvt = (MouseEvent)evt;
    if (mEvt.getClickCount() == 1) {
      int row = m_tree.getRowForLocation(mEvt.getX(), mEvt.getY());
      if (row != m_lastRow) {
        m_lastRow = row;
        m_lastClick = System.currentTimeMillis();
        return false;
      }
      else if (System.currentTimeMillis()-m_lastClick > 1000)
      {
        m_lastRow = -1;
        m_lastClick = 0;
        prepareEditor();
        mEvt.consume();
```

6 Sets icon and font of CellEditor, and appends spaces to text to leave room for text field drawn on top of label

Checks for consecutive single clicks on a node, spaced more than 1000 ms apart, causing **7** the CellEditor to display

```
              return true;
            }
          else
              return false;
        }
      }
    return false;
  }
  protected void prepareEditor() {
    if (m_item == null)
      return;
    String str = m_item.toString();

    m_editor = new JTextField(str);
    m_editor.addActionListener(this);
    m_editor.selectAll();
    m_editor.setFont(m_tree.getFont());

    add(m_editor);
    revalidate();

    TreePath path = m_tree.getPathForRow(m_lastRow);
    m_tree.startEditingAtPath(path);
  }
  protected void removeEditor() {
    if (m_editor != null) {
      remove(m_editor);
      m_editor.setVisible(false);
      m_editor = null;
      m_item = null;
    }
  }

  public void doLayout() {
    super.doLayout();
    if (m_editor != null) {
      int offset = getIconTextGap();
      if (getIcon() != null)
        offset += getIcon().getIconWidth();
      Dimension cSize = getSize();
      m_editor.setBounds(offset, 0, cSize.width - offset,
        cSize.height);
    }
  }

  public boolean shouldSelectCell(EventObject evt) { return true; }

  public boolean stopCellEditing() {
    if (m_item != null)
      m_item.m_data = m_editor.getText();

    ChangeEvent e = new ChangeEvent(this);
    for (int k=0; k<m_listeners.size(); k++) {
      CellEditorListener l = (CellEditorListener)m_listeners.
        elementAt(k);
```

10 Starts editing process by creating a text field and adding it to container

11 Terminates editing process by removing text field

8 Called to end editing process; copies text to IconData and tells all the listeners that editing has stopped

```
      l.editingStopped(e);
    }
    removeEditor();
    return true;
  }

  public void cancelCellEditing() {                    ⑨ Called to cancel
    ChangeEvent e = new ChangeEvent(this);                CellEditor and notify
    for (int k=0; k<m_listeners.size(); k++) {            listeners of this
      CellEditorListener l = (CellEditorListener)m_listeners.
        elementAt(k);
      l.editingCanceled(e);
    }
    removeEditor();
  }

  public void addCellEditorListener(CellEditorListener l) {
    m_listeners.addElement(l);
  }

  public void removeCellEditorListener(CellEditorListener l) {
    m_listeners.removeElement(l);
  }

  public void actionPerformed(ActionEvent e) {         ⑫ Pressing Enter on
    stopCellEditing();                                    text field will stop
    m_tree.stopEditing();                                 the editing process
  }
}
```

17.7.1   Understanding the code

Class AncestorTree

① The AncestorTree class declares and creates three static images representing male and female ancestors, and a root representing a child whose ancestry is being represented.
There are four instance variables:

- JTree m_tree: The ancestor tree component.
- DefaultTreeModel m_model: The ancestor tree data model.
- IconCellRenderer m_renderer: The ancestor tree cell renderer.
- IconCellEditor m_editor: The ancestor tree cell editor.

② The AncestorTree constructor is similar to the Tree1 constructor from section 17.2. However, there are four important differences:

- The addAncestors() method (see below) is called to create initial child nodes.
- The editable property is set to true.
- Instances of our custom IconCellRenderer and IconCellEditor classes are set as the renderer and editor for m_tree, respectively.
- An instance of our custom TreeExpander class is attached as a MouseListener to our m_tree.

③ The addAncestors() method adds male and female ancestors to a given node as child nodes (representing parents in an ancestry), if this hasn't been done already. Instances of IconData (which hold a combination of icons and text; see previous examples) are added as user objects for a newly created node. The initial text of each `IconData` object is assigned as "Father of: <node text>" and "Mother of: <node text>", and appropriate icons are used to distinguish between women and men.

Class AncestorTree.TreeExpander

④ The `TreeExpander` inner class extends `MouseAdapter` and is used to insert ancestor nodes when a double click occurs on a node. The most significant aspect of this listener is the call to the `JTree.getPathForLocation()` method, which retrieves the currently selected tree path and allows us to determine the selected node. The `addAncestors()` method is then called on that node, and our tree is repainted to show the newly added nodes (if any).

Class IconCellRenderer and class IconData

The `IconCellRenderer` class, as well as the `IconData` class, have received no changes from example 17.2. Refer to section 17.3 for more information about their inner workings.

Class IconCellEditor

⑤ The `IconCellEditor` class implements the `TreeCellEditor` and `ActionListener` interfaces, and it creates a `JTextField` for editing a node's text in place. This editor is designed in such a way that a cell icon remains unchanged and in the same location, whether it's in editing mode or not. This explains why `IconCellEditor` extends `JLabel`, and not `JTextField` as we might expect. The underlying `JLabel` component is used to render the icon and reserve any necessary space. The `JTextField` component is created dynamically and placed above the `JLabel`'s text portion to perform the actual editing. The `JLabel` serves as a `Container` for the `JTextField` component (recall that all Swing components extend the `java.awt.Container` class).

NOTE Swing's default editor `DefaultTreeCellEditor` is used similarly, but in a more complex manner. It takes a `DefaultTreeCellRenderer` as a parameter and uses it to determine the size of a node's icon. Then it uses a custom inner class as a container which renders the icon and positions the text field. For more details, see `DefaultTreeCellEditor.java`.

There are six instance variables:

- `JTree m_tree`: A reference to the parent tree component (must be passed to constructor).
- `JTextField m_editor`: The editing component.
- `IconData m_item`: The data object to be edited (we limit ourselves to `IconData` instances).
- `int m_lastRow`: The tree row where the most recent mouse click occurred.
- `long m_lastClick`: The time (in ms) that the last mouse click occurred.
- `Vector m_listeners`: A collection of `CellEditorListeners`, which we must manage according to the `TreeCellEditor` interface.

⑥ The `getTreeCellEditorComponent()` method will be called to initialize a new data object in the editor before we begin editing a node. (The user object from the selected node must be an instance of `IconData`, or editing is not allowed.) The icon and text from the `IconData` object are assigned using inherited `JLabel` functionality. A few spaces are intentionally appended to the end of the text to provide some white space for adding more text.

The `getCellEditorValue()` method returns the current value of the editor as an `Object`. In our case we return `m_item`, adjusting its `m_data` to `m_editor`'s text:

```
if (m_item != null && m_editor != null)
  m_item.m_data = m_editor.getText();
return m_item;
```

❼ The `isCellEditable()` method is called to determine whether an editor should enter editing mode. It takes an `EventObject` as a parameter. In this way, we can use any user activity resulting in an event as a signal for editing, including a double mouse click or a specific key press combination. We've implemented this method to start editing mode when two single mouse clicks occur on a cell; the clicks must be separated by no less than 1 second (1000 ms). To do this, we first filter only single mouse click events:

```
if (evt instanceof MouseEvent) {
  MouseEvent mEvt = (MouseEvent)evt;
  if (mEvt.getClickCount() == 1) {
```

For these events we determine the tree's row that was clicked and store it in our `m_lastRow` instance variable. The current system time is also saved in the `m_lastClick` instance variable. If another click occurs on the same cell after 1000 ms, our custom `prepareEditor()` method is called to prepare the editor for editing, and it returns `true`. Otherwise, `false` is returned.

The `shouldSelectCell()` method always returns `true` to indicate that a cell's content should be selected at the beginning of editing.

❽ The `stopCellEditing()` method is called to stop editing and store the result of the edit. We simply change `m_data` in the `m_item` object to `m_editor`'s text.

```
if (m_item != null)
  m_item.m_data = m_editor.getText();
```

The `m_item` object also has a reference to our tree's model, so it will affect our tree directly. Thus all registered `CellEditorListeners` are notified in turn by calling their `editingStopped()` method. The editing process is terminated by calling our custom `removeEditor()` method.

❾ The `cancelCellEditing()` method is called to stop editing without storing the result of the edit. Similar to `stopCellEditing()`, all registered `CellEditorListeners` are notified in turn by calling their `editingCanceled()` method, and the editing process is terminated by calling `removeEditor()`.

Two methods, `addCellEditorListener()` and `removeCellEditorListener()`, add and remove listeners to/from our `m_listeners` vector.

❿ The `prepareEditor()` method actually starts the editing process. It creates a `JTextField` component and sets its initial text to that of the `m_item` object:

```
m_editor = new JTextField(str);
m_editor.addActionListener(this);
m_editor.selectAll();
m_editor.setFont(m_tree.getFont());

add(m_editor);
revalidate();
```

An `ActionListener` is added to the text field to enable the ability to stop editing when the user presses the ENTER key (recall that this class implements `ActionListener`, so we provide a `this` reference for the listener). The most important aspect of this method is the fact that a `JTextField` is added to our base component, and the overridden `doLayout()` method is invoked indirectly (through `revalidate()`) to assign the correct size and position to our editor component. Finally, the base tree is notified by calling our `startEditingAtPath()` method to allow editing.

⓫ The `removeEditor()` method is called to quit the editing process. It removes the editing component from the container, and hides and destroys it (it dereferences it to allow garbage collection):

```
remove(m_editor);
m_editor.setVisible(false);
m_editor = null;
m_item = null;
```

The `doLayout()` method overrides `Component.doLayout()` to set the correct size and location for the editing component.

⓬ The `actionPerformed()` method will be called when ENTER is pressed during editing. It directly calls our `stopCellEditing()` implementation, and it notifies our tree by calling `stopEditing()`.

17.7.2 Running the code

Perform a single click on a tree cell, wait a second, then click it again to enter editing mode. Notice that there is no limit to how far back we can go with this ancestor tree, and all nodes can have either no children, or two children (representing the parents of the individual represented by that node). Try creating your own ancestor tree as far back as you can go (if you end with monkey or gorilla, please contact us). Figure 17.8 shows the ancestor tree of Prince William of Wales, the oldest son of the heir of the British monarchy.

GUIDELINE

Family trees and organization charts   The family tree given here is used as an example only. There is still considerable debate in the UI design field as to whether a tree component is appropriate for displaying and manipulating such data. Generally, family trees or organization charts are displayed using a top-down (horizontal orientation), evenly distributed graph. Therefore, the tree component view with its left-right (vertical orientation) is an alien method for this type of data.

If your user community is particularly technical, then you should have no difficulties; however, consider carefully before selecting a tree component for a wider user group.

You may also want to consider that such a tree component could be used as a prototype or "proof of concept." You could later replace the tree component with an `OrganizationChart` component (for example) which reuses the same `TableModel` interface. Thus, the actual data and model classes would not need to be changed. The ability to do this demonstrates the power of the Swing MVC architecture.

Tables

18.1   JTABLE

JTable is extremely useful for displaying, navigating, and editing tabular data. Because of its complex nature, JTable has a whole package devoted just to it: javax.swing.table. This package consists of a set of classes and interfaces which we will review briefly in this chapter. In the examples that follow, we construct—in a step-wise fashion—a table-based application that displays stock market data. (In chapters 22 and 26 we enhance this application further to allow printing and print preview, and CORBA client-server interaction.) This chapter concludes with an expense report application that demonstrates the use of different components as table cell editors and renderers, and the completion of the JavaBeans property editor we started to build in chapter 4.

18.1.1   JTable

class javax.swing.JTable

This class represents Swing's table component and provides a rich API for managing its behavior and appearance. JTable directly extends JComponent, and it implements the TableModelListener, TableColumnModelListener, ListSelectionListener, CellEditorListener, and `Scrollable` interfaces (it is meant to be placed in a `JScrollPane`). Each `JTable` has three models: `TableModel`, `TableColumnModel`, and `ListSelectionModel`. All table data is stored in a `TableModel`, normally in a two-dimensional structure such as a 2-D array or a `Vector` of `Vectors`. `TableModel` implementations specify how this data is stored, as well as how to manage the addition, manipulation, and retrieval of this data. `TableModel` also plays a role in dictating whether specific cells can be edited, as well as the data type of each column of data. The location of data in a `JTable`'s `TableModel` does not directly correspond to the location of that data as it is displayed by `JTable` itself. This part is controlled at the lowest level by `TableColumnModel`.

A `TableColumnModel` is designed to maintain instances of `TableColumn`, each of which represents a single column of `TableModel` data. The `TableColumn` class is responsible for managing column display in the actual `JTable` GUI. Each `TableColumn` has an associated cell renderer, cell editor, table header, and cell renderer for the table header. When a `JTable` is placed in a `JScrollPane`, these headers are placed in the scroll pane's COLUMN_HEADER viewport, and they can be dragged and resized to reorder and change the size of columns. A `TableColumn`'s header renderer is responsible for returning a component that renders the column header, and the cell renderer is responsible for returning a component that renders each cell. As with `JList` and `JTree` renderers, these renderers also act as rubber stamps and they are not at all interactive. The component returned by the cell editor, however, is completely interactive. Cell renderers are instances of `TableCellRenderer` and cell editors are instances of `TableCellEditor`. If none are explicitly assigned, default versions will be used based on the `Class` type of the corresponding `TableModel` column data.

`TableColumnModel`'s job is to manage all `TableColumns`, providing control over order, column selections, and margin size. To support several different modes of selection, `Table-ColumnModel` maintains a `ListSelectionModel` which, as we learned in chapter 10, allows single, single-interval, and multiple-interval selections. `JTable` takes this flexibility even further by providing functionality to customize any row, column, and/or cell-specific selection schemes we can come up with.

We can specify one of several resizing policies which dictate how columns react when another column is resized, as well as whether grid lines between rows and/or columns should appear. We can also specify: margin sizes between rows and columns, the selected and unselected cell foreground and background colors, the height of rows, and the width of each column on a column-by-column basis.

With tables come two new kinds of events in Swing: `TableModelEvent` and `Table-ColumnModelEvent`. Regular Java events apply to `JTable` as well. For instance, we can use `MouseListeners` to process double mouse clicks. `ChangeEvents` and `ListSelection-Events` are also used for communication in `TableColumnModel`.

NOTE   Although `JTable` implements several listener interfaces, it does not provide any methods to register listeners other than those inherited from `JComponent`. To attach listeners for detecting any of the above events, we must first retrieve the appropriate model.

A number of constructors are provided for building a `JTable` component. We can use the default constructor or pass each of the table's data and column names as a separate `Vector`. We can build an empty `JTable` with a specified number of rows and columns. We can also pass table data to the constructor as a two-dimensional array of data `Objects` along with an `Object` array of column names. Other constructors allow for the creation of a `JTable` with specific models. In all cases, if a specific model is not assigned in the constructor, `JTable` will create default implementations with its protected `createDefaultColumnModel()`, `create-DefaultDataModel()`, and `createDefaultSelectionModel()` methods. It will do the same for each `TableColumn` renderer and editor, as well as for its `JTableHeader`, using `create-DefaultEditors()`, `createDefaultRenderers()`, and `createDefaultTableHeaders()`.

`JTable` is one of the most complex Swing components; keeping track of its constituents and how they interact is intially a challenge. Before we begin the step-wise construction of our stocks table application, we must make our way through all of these details. The remainder of this section is devoted to a discussion of the classes and interfaces that define the underlying mechanics of `JTable`.

18.1.2   The TableModel interface

abstract interface javax.swing.table.TableModel

Instances of `TableModel` are responsible for storing a table's data in a two-dimensional structure such as a two-dimensional array or a `Vector` of `Vectors`. A set of methods is declared to retrieve data from a table's cells. The `getValueAt()` method should retrieve data from a given row and column index as an `Object`, and `setValueAt()` should assign the provided data object to the specified location (if valid). `getColumnClass()` should return the `Class` that describes the data objects stored in the specified column (used to assign a default renderer and editor for that column), and `getColumnName()` should return the `String` name associated with the specified column (often used for that column's header). The `getColumn-Count()` and `getRowCount()` methods should return the number of contained columns and rows, respectively.

> **NOTE**   `getRowCount()` is called frequently by `JTable` for display purposes; therefore, it should be designed with efficiency in mind.

The `isCellEditable()` method should return `true` if the cell at the given row and column index can be edited. The `setValueAt()` method should be designed so that if `isCellEditable()` returns `false`, the object at the given location will not be updated.

This model supports the attachment of `TableModelListeners` which should be notified about changes to this model's data. As expected, methods for adding and removing these listeners are provided (`addTableModelListener()` and `removeTableModelListener()`) and implementations are responsible for dispatching `TableModelEvents` to those registered.

Each `JTable` uses one `TableModel` instance which can be assigned/retrieved using `JTable`'s `setModel()` and `getModel()` methods respectively.

> **NOTE**   The position of a row or column in the model does not correspond to `JTable`'s GUI representation of that row or column. Rather, each column is represented by an instance of `TableColumn` which maps to a unique model column. When a `TableColumn` is moved in the GUI, the associated data in the `TableModel` model stays put, and vice versa.

18.1.3   AbstractTableModel

abstract class javax.swing.table.AbstractTableModel

AbstractTableModel is an abstract class that implements the TableModel interface. It provides default code for firing TableModelEvents with the fireTableRowsDeleted(), fireTableCellUpdated(), and fireTableChanged() methods. It also manages all registered TableModelListeners in an EventListenerList (see chapter 2).

The findColumn() method searches for the index of a column with the given String name. This search is performed in a linear fashion (this is referred to as "naive" in the documentation) and it should be overridden for large table models for more efficient searching.

Three methods need to be implemented in concrete subclasses: getRowCount(), getColumnCount(), and getValueAt(int row, int column), and we are expected to use this class as a base for building our own TableModel implementations, rather than DefaultTableModel—see below.

18.1.4   DefaultTableModel

class javax.swing.tableDefaultTableModel

DefaultTableModel is the default concrete TableModel implementation used by JTable when no model is specified in the constructor. It uses a Vector of Vectors to manage its data, which is one major reason why extending AbstractTableModel is often more desirable—AbstractTableModel gives you complete control over how data storage and manipulation is implemented. This Vector can be assigned with the overloaded setDataVector() method and retrieved with the getDataVector() method. Internally, two overloaded, protected convertToVector() methods are used for converting Object arrays to Vectors when inserting rows, columns, or assigning a new data Vector. Methods for adding, inserting, removing, and moving columns and rows of data are also provided.

Along with the TableModelEvent functionality inherited from AbstractTableModel, this class implements three new event-dispatching methods, each taking a TableModelEvent as parameter: newDataAvailable(), newRowsAdded(), and rowsRemoved(). The newRowsAdded() method ensures that new rows (see the discussion of TableModelEvent below) have the correct number of columns by either removing excess elements or using null for each missing cell. If null is passed to any of these methods, they will construct and fire a default TableModelEvent which assumes that all table model data has changed.

18.1.5   TableColumn

class javax.swing.table.TableColumn

TableColumn is the basic building block of JTable's visual representation, and it provides the main link between the JTable GUI and its model. TableColumn does not extend java.awt.Component, and thus it is not a component. Rather, it acts more like a model that maintains all the properties of a column displayed in a JTable. An instance of TableColumn represents a specific column of data stored in a TableModel. TableColumn maintains the index of the TableModel column it represents as property modelIndex. We can get/set this index with the getModelIndex() and setModelIndex() methods. It is important to remember that the position of a `TableColumn` in `JTable` does not at all correspond to its corresponding `TableModel` column index.

A `TableColumn` is represented graphically by a column header renderer, cell renderer, and, optionally, a cell editor. The renderers must be instances of `TableCellRenderer`, and the editor must be an instance of `TableCellEditor` (see below). A column's header is rendered by a renderer stored as the `headerRenderer` property. By default, this is an instance of `DefaultTableCellRenderer` (which supplies a `JLabel` with a beveled border; see below) and it is created with `TableColumn`'s protected `createDefaultHeaderRenderer()` method. This renderer simply renders the `String` returned by the `toString()` method of the `Object` referred to by the `headerValue` property. The header renderer and value can be assigned/retrieved with the `setHeaderRenderer()`/`getHeaderRenderer()` and `setHeaderValue()`/`getHeaderValue()` methods, respectively. `headerValue` often directly corresponds to the column name retrieved using `TableModel`'s `getColumnName()` method. If `headerValue` is not explicitly set, it defaults to `null`.

The column cell renderer and editor also default to `null`, and unless they are explicitly specified using `setCellRenderer()` or `setCellEditor()`, they are automatically assigned based on the `Class` type of the data stored in the associated column in the `TableModel` (this is retrieved using `TableModel`'s `getColumnClass()` method). Explicity specified renderers and editors are referred to as *column-based*, whereas those determined by data type are referred to as *class-based* (we will discuss renderers and editors in more detail later in this section).

Each `TableColumn` has an `identifier` property which also defaults to `null`. This property can be assigned and retrieved using typical set/get accessors, and the `getIdentifier()` method will return the `headerValue` property if `identifier` is null. When searching for a `TableColumn` by name (using `TableColumnModel`'s `getColumnIndex()` method or `JTable`'s `getColumn()` method), the given `Object` will be compared, using `Object`'s `equals()` method, to each `TableColumn` `identifier`. Since it is possible that more than one `TableColumn` will use the same `identifier`, the first match is returned as the answer.

`TableColumn` maintains three properties: `minWidth`, `maxWidth`, and `width`. The first two specify the minimum and maximum allowable widths for column rendering, and the `width` property stores the current width. Each property can be retrieved and assigned with typical get/set methods: `getMinWidth()`/`setMinWidth()`, `getMaxWith()`/`setMaxWidth()`, and `getWidth()`/`setWidth()`. `minWidth` defaults to 15, `maxWidth` defaults to `Integer.MAX_VALUE`, and `width` defaults to 75. When a `JTable` is resized, it will try to maintain its width, and it will never exceeed its maximum or shrink smaller than its minimum.

NOTE   All other visual aspects of each column are controlled by either `JTable` or `TableColumnModel` (see below).

`TableColumn` also maintains an `isResizable` property, which specifies whether its width can be changed by the user (this does not apply to programmatic calls to `setWidth()`). We will discuss resizing in more detail below.

An interesting and rarely used property maintained by `TableColumn` is called `resizedPostingDisabledCount`. It is used to enable and disable the posting of `PropertyChangeEvents` when a `TableColumn`'s width changes. This property is an `int` value that is incremented on each call to `disableResizedPosting()`, and it is decremented on each call to `enableResizedPosting()`. Events will only be fired if this value is less than or equal to 0.

The logic behind this is that if two separate sources both call the `disableResizedPost()` method, then two calls should be required to re-enable it.

BUG ALERT As of Java 2 FCS, the `resizedPostingDisabledCount` property is not actually used anywhere and it does not play a role in `PropertyChangeEvent` firing.

`TableColumn` fires `PropertyChangeEvents` when any of the `width`, `cellRenderer`, `headerRenderer`, or `headerValue` bound properties change. Thus we can add and remove `PropertyChangeListeners` to be notified of these changes. The corresponding property names are `COLUMN_WIDTH_PROPERTY`, `COLUMN_RENDERER_PROPERTY`, `HEADER_RENDERER_PROPERTY`, and `HEADER_VALUE_PROPERTY`.

18.1.6   The TableColumnModel interface

abstract interface javax.swing.table.TableColumnModel

This model is designed to maintain a `JTable`'s `TableColumns`, and it provides control over column selections and margin size. `TableColumnModel` controls how `JTable` displays its `TableModel` data. The `addColumn()` method should append a given `TableColumn` to the end of the structure that is used to maintain them (this is usually a `Vector`), `removeColumn()` should remove a given `TableColumn`, and `moveColumn()` should change the location of a given `TableColumn` within that structure.

NOTE When creating a `JTable`, if no `TableColumnModel` is specified, one will automatically be constructed for us. It will contain `TableColumns` that display `TableModel` data in the same order it appears in the model. This will only occur if `JTable`'s `auto-CreateColumnsFromModel` property is set to `true`, which it is by default. Though this is very helpful, it often has the undesirable side effect of completely rebuilding the `TableColumnModel` whenever `TableModel` changes. Thus, it is common to set this property to `false` once a `JTable` has been created or after a new `TableModel` is assigned.

The index of a `TableColumn` in a `TableColumnModel`'s storage structure directly corresponds to its position in the `JTable` GUI. The `moveColumn()` method is called whenever the user drags a column to a new position.

The `getColumnCount()` method returns the number of `TableColumns` currently being maintained, `getColumns()` returns an `Enumeration` of all contained `TableColumns`, and `getColumn()` returns the `TableColumn` at the given index. The `getColumnIndex()` method returns the index of the `TableColumn` whose `identifier` property is equal to the given `Object` (the equality is determined by using `Object`'s `equals()` method). `getColumnIndexAtX()` returns the index of the `TableColumn` at the given x-coordinate in the table's coordinate system (if `getColumnIndexAtX()` is passed either a coordinate that maps to the margin space between adjacent columns or any x-coordinate that does not correspond to a table column, it will return -1). `setColumnMargin()` and `getColumnMargin()` allow the assignment and retrieval of an `int` value to be used as the margin space on each side of each table column. The `getTotalColumnWidth()` method returns the sum of the current width of all `TableColumns`, including all margin space.

NOTE　　The margin size does not correspond to the width of the separating grid lines between columns in `JTable`. In fact, the width of these lines is always 1, and it cannot be changed without customizing `JTable`'s UI delegate.

`TableColumnModel` declares methods for controlling the selection of its `TableColumns`, and it allows the assignment and retrieval of a `ListSelectionModel` implementation to store information about the current column selection with the methods `setSelection-Model()` and `getSelectionModel()`. The `setColumnSelectionAllowed()` method turns on/off column selection capabilities, and `getColumnSelectionAllowed()` returns a `boolean` that specifies whether selection is currently allowed. For convenience, `JTable`'s `setColumnSelectionAllowed()` method delegates its traffic to the method of the same signature in this interface.

`TableColumnModel` also declares support for `TableColumnModelListeners` (see below). `TableColumnModel` implementations are expected to fire a `TableColumnModelEvent` whenever a `TableColumn` is added, removed, or moved; a `ChangeEvent` whenever margin size is changed; and a `ListSelectionEvent` whenever a change in column selection occurs.

18.1.7　DefaultTableColumnModel

class javax.swing.table.DefaultTableColumnModel

This class is the concrete default implementation of the `TableColumnModel` interface used by `JTable` when none is specifically assigned or provided at construction time. All `Table-ColumnModel` methods are implemented as expected, and the following protected methods are provided to fire events: `fireColumnAdded()`, `fireColumnRemoved()`, `fireColumn-Moved()`, `fireColumnSelectionChanged()`, and `fireColumnMarginChanged()`. A value-Changed() method is provided to listen for column selection changes and fire a `List-SelectionEvent` when necessary, and a `propertyChanged()` method is used to update the `totalColumnWidth` property when the `width` of a contained `TableColumn` changes.

18.1.8　The TableCellRenderer interface

abstract interface javax.swing.table.TableCellRenderer

This interface describes the renderer used to display cell data in a `TableColumn`. Each `TableColumn` has an associated `TableCellRender` which can be assigned and retrieved with the `setCellRenderer()` and `getCellRenderer()` methods. The `getTableCellRenderer-Component()` method is the only method declared by this interface, and it is expected to return a `Component` that will be used to actually render a cell. It takes the following parameters:

- `JTable table`: The table instance that contains the cell to be rendered.
- `Object value`: The value used to represent the data in the given cell.
- `boolean isSelected`: Specifies whether the given cell is selected.
- `boolean hasFocus`: Specifies whether the given cell has the focus (`true` if it was clicked last).
- `int row`: Used to a renderer component specific to a row or cell.
- `int column`: Specify a renderer component specific to a column or cell.

We are expected to customize or vary the returned component based on the given parameters. For instance, given a `value` that is an instance of `Color`, we might return a special `JLabel` subclass that paints a rectangle in the given color. This method can be used to return different renderer components on a column, row, or cell-specific basis, and it is similar to `JTree`'s `Tree-CellRenderer getTreeCellRendererComponent()` method. As with `JTree` and `JList`, the renderer component returned acts as a "rubber stamp" that is used strictly for display purposes.

NOTE The `row` and `column` parameters refer to the location of data in the `TableModel`, not a cell location in the `TableColumnModel`.

When `JTable`'s UI delegate repaints a certain region of a table, it must query that table to determine the renderer to use for each cell that it needs to repaint. This is accomplished through `JTable`'s `getCellRenderer()` method, which takes row and column parameters and returns the component returned by the `getTableCellRendererComponent()` method of the `TableCellRenderer` assigned to the appropriate `TableColumn`. If no specific renderer is assigned to that `TableColumn` (recall that this is the case by default), the `TableModel`'s `getColumnClass()` method is used to recursively determine an appropriate renderer for the given data type. If no specific class-based renderer is available for a given class, `getColumn-Class()` searches for one that corresponds to the superclass. This process will, in the most generic case, stop at `Object`, for which a `DefaultTableCellRenderer` is used (see below).

A `DefaultTreeCellRenderer` is also used if the class is of type `Icon` or `Number` (its subclasses are `BigDecimal`, `BigInteger`, `Byte`, `Double`, `Float`, `Integer`, `Long`, and `Short`). If the type happens to be a `Boolean`, a `JCheckBox` is used. We can specify additional class-based renderers with `JTable`'s `setDefaultRenderer()` method. Remember that class-based renderers will only be used if no column-based renderer has been explicitly assigned to the `Table-Column` containing the given cell.

18.1.9 DefaultTableCellRenderer

class javax.swing.table.DefaultTableCellRenderer

This is the concrete default implementation of the `TableCellRenderer` interface. `Default-TableCellRenderer` extends `JLabel` and is used as the default class-based renderer for `Number`, `Icon`, and `Object` data types. Two private `Color` variables are used to hold selected foreground and background colors which render the cell if it is editable and if it has the current focus. These colors can be assigned with `DefaultTableCellRenderer`'s overridden `setBackground()` and `setForeground()` methods.

A protected `Border` property is used to store the border that is used when the cell does not have the current focus. By default, this is an `EmptyBorder` with a top and bottom space of 1 and a left and right space of 2. Unfortunately, `DefaultTableCellRenderer` does not provide a method to change this border.

`DefaultTableCellRenderer` renders the value object passed as parameter to its `get-TableCellRenderer()` method by setting its label text to the `String` returned by that object's `toString()` method. All default `JLabel` attributes are used in rendering. We can do anything to this renderer component that we can do to a `JLabel`, such as assign a tooltip or a disabled/enabled state.

JTable can have a tooltip assigned to it just as any other Swing component. However, tooltips assigned to renderers take precedence over those assigned to JTable, and in the case that both are used, the renderer's tooltip text will be displayed when the mouse lies over a cell using it.

18.1.10 The TableCellEditor interface

abstract interface javax.swing.table.TableCellEditor

This interface extends CellEditor and describes the editor used to edit cell data in a Table-Column. Each TableColumn has an associated TableCellEditor which can be assigned and retrieved with the setCellEditor() and getCellEditor() methods. The getTable-CellEditorComponent() method is the only method declared by this interface, and it is expected to return a Component that will be used to allow editing of a cell's data value. It takes the following parameters:

- JTable table: The table instance containing the cell to be rendered.
- Object value: The value used to represent the data in the given cell.
- boolean isSelected: Specifies whether the given cell is selected.
- int row: Used to a renderer component specific to a row or cell.
- int column: Specify a renderer component specific to a column or cell.

We are expected to customize or vary the returned component based on the given parameters. For instance, given a value that is an instance of Color, we might return a special JComboBox which lists several color choices. This method can be used to return different editor components on a column, row, or cell-specific basis, and it is similar to JTree's TreeCellEditor getTreeCellEditorComponent() method.

NOTE The row and column parameters refer to the location of data in the TableModel, not a cell location in the TableColumnModel.

Just like table cell renderers, each TableColumn has a column-based editor associated with it. By default, this editor is null and it can be assigned and retrieved with TableColumn's setCellEditor() and getCellEditor() methods. Unlike renderers, table cell editors are completely interactive and do not simply act as rubber stamps.

TableCellEditor implementations must also implement methods defined in the CellEditor interface: addCellEditorListener(), removeCellEditorListener(), cancelCellEditing(), stopCellEditing(), isCellEditable(), shouldSelectCell(), and getCellEditorValue(). The isCellEditable() method is expected to be used in combination with TableModel's isCellEditable() method to determine whether a given cell can be edited. Only in the case that both return true is editing allowed. (See the discussion of the CellEditor interface in section 17.1.13 for more about each of these methods.)

To initiate cell editing on a given cell, JTable listens for mouse presses and invokes its editCellAt() method in response. This method queries both the TableModel and the appropriate cell editor to determine if the given cell can be edited. If it can, the editor component is retrieved with getTableCellEditorComponent() and placed in the given cell (its bounds are adjusted so that it will fit within the current cell bounds). Then JTable adds itself as a listener to the editor component (recall that JTable implements the CellEditorListener interface) and the same mouse event that sparked the edit gets sent to the editor component.

Finally, the cell editor's `shouldSelectCell()` method is invoked to determine whether the row containing that cell should become selected.

The default implementation of `TableCellEditor` is provided as `DefaultCellEditor`. Unfortunately, `DefaultCellEditor` is not easily extensible and we are often forced to implement all `TableCellEditor` and `CellEditor` functionality ourselves.

18.1.11 DefaultCellEditor

class javax.swing.DefaultCellEditor

`DefaultCellEditor` is a concrete implementation of both the `TableCellEditor` interface and the `TreeCellEditor` interface. This editor is designed to return either a `JTextField`, `JComboBox`, or `JCheckBox` for cell editing. It is used by both `JTable` and `JTree` components and is discussed in section 17.1.15.

18.1.12 The TableModelListener interface

abstract interface javax.swing.event.TableModelListener

This interface describes an object that listens to changes in a `TableModel`. The `tableChanged()` method will be invoked to notify us of these changes. `TableModel`'s `addTableModelListener()` and `removeTableModelListener()` methods are used to add and remove `TableModelListeners` respectively (they are not added directly to `JTable`).

18.1.13 TableModelEvent

class javax.swing.TableModelEvent

This event extends `EventObject` and is used to notify `TableModelListeners` registered with a `TableModel` about changes in that model. This class consists of four properties, which are each accessible with typical `get` methods:

- `int column`: Specifies the column affected by the change. `TableModelEvent.ALL_COLUMNS` is used to indicate that more than one column is affected.
- `int firstRow`: Specifies the first row affected. `TableModelEvent.HEADER_ROW` can be used here to indicate that the name, type, or order of one or more columns has changed.
- `int lastRow`: Specifies the last row affected. This value should always be greater than or equal to `firstRow`.
- `int type`: Specifies the type of change that occurred. It can be `TableModelEvent.INSERT`, `TableModelEvent.DELETE`, or `TableModelEvent.UPDATE`. `INSERT` and `DELETE` indicate the insertion and deletion of rows. `UPDATE` indicates that values have changed but the number of rows and columns has not changed.

As with any `EventObject`, we can retrieve the source of a `TableModelEvent` with `getSource()`.

18.1.14 The TableColumnModelListener interface

abstract interface javax.swing.event.TableColumnModelListener

This interface describes an object that listens to changes in a `TableColumnModel`: the adding, removing, and movement of columns, as well as changes in margin size and the current selection. `TableColumnModel` provides two methods for adding and removing these listeners: `addTableColumnModelListener()` and `removeTableColumnModelListener()`. (As is the case with `TableModelListeners`, `TableColumnModelListeners` are not directly added to `JTable`.)

Five methods are declared in this interface and they must be defined by all implementations: `columnAdded(TableColumnModelEvent)`, `columnRemoved(TableColumnModelEvent)`, `columnMoved(TableColumnModelEvent)`, `columnMarginChanged(TableColumnModel-Event)`, and `columnSelectionChanged(ListSelectionEvent)`. `ListSelectionEvents` are forwarded to `TableColumnModel`'s `ListSelectionModel`.

18.1.15 TableColumnModelEvent

class javax.swing.event.TableColumnModelEvent

This event extends `EventObject` and is used to notify a `TableColumnModel` about changes to a range of columns. These events are passed to `TableColumnModelListeners`. The `from-Index` property specifies the lowest index of the column in the `TableColumnModel` affected by the change. The `toIndex` specifies the highest index. Both can be retrieved with typical `get` accessors. A `TableColumnModel` fires a `TableColumnModelEvent` whenever a column move, removal, or addition occurs. The event source can be retrieved with `getSource()`.

18.1.16 JTableHeader

class javax.swing.table.JTableHeader

This GUI component (which looks like a set of buttons for each column) is used to display a table's column headers. By dragging these headers, the user can rearrange a table's columns dynamically. This component is used internally by `JTable`. It can be retrieved with `JTable`'s `getTableHeader()` method and assigned with `setTableHeader()`. When a `JTable` is placed in a `JScrollPane`, a default `JTableHeader` corresponding to each column is added to that scroll pane's `COLUMN_HEADER` viewport (see section 7.1.3). Each `JTable` uses one `JTableHeader` instance.

`JTableHeader` extends `JComponent` and implements `TableColumnModelListener`. Though `JTableHeader` is a Swing component, it is not used for display purposes. Instead, each `TableColumn` maintains a specific `TableCellRenderer` implementation used to represent its header. By default this is an instance of `DefaultTableCellRenderer` (see section 18.1.8).

NOTE It is more common to customize the header renderer of a `TableColumn` than it is to customize a table's `JTableHeader`. In most cases, the default headers provided by `JTable` are satisfactory.

The `resizingAllowed` property specifies whether columns can be resized (if this property is `false`, it overpowers the `isResizable` property of each `TableColumn`). The `reorderingAllowed` property specifies whether columns can be reordered, and the `updateTableInRealTime` property specifies whether the whole column is displayed along with the header as it is dragged (this is only applicable if `reorderingAllowed` is `true`). All three of these properties are `true` by default.

GUIDELINE

Column resizing   It is best to isolate columns which need to be a fixed width—for example, say you have a table in which monetary amounts might be ten significant figures with two decimal places. Such a column requires a fixed width. It doesn't need to be bigger and it doesn't want to be smaller. Allow the other columns to vary in size around the fixed columns.

For example, in a two-column table displaying Product Description and Price, fix the size of the Price column and allow Product Description to resize.

Draggable columns, added flexibility, and added complexity   If you don't need the flexibility of draggable table columns, it is best to switch them off. If a user accidentally picks up a JHeader component and rearranges a table, the table could quickly become confusing. The user may not realise what he has done or how to restore the table to its original form.

At any given time during a column drag we can retrieve the distance, in table coordinates, that the column has been dragged with respect to its original position from the draggedDistance property. JTableHeader also maintains a reference to the TableColumn it represents as well as the JTable it is part of, using the tableColumn and table properties, respectively.

18.1.17   JTable selection

JTable supports two selection models: one for row selections and one for column selections. JTable also supports the selection of individual table cells. Column selections are managed by a ListSelectionModel which is maintained by a TableColumnModel implementation, and row selections are managed by a ListSelectionModel which is maintained by JTable itself (both are DefaultListSelectionModels by default). As we learned in chapter 10, ListSelectionModels support three selection modes: SINGLE_SELECTION, SINGLE_INTERVAL_SELECTION, and MULTIPLE_INTERVAL_SELECTION. JTable provides the setSelectionMode() methods which will set both selection models to the given mode. Note, however, that getSelectionMode() only returns the current row selection mode.

To assign a specific selection mode to JTable's row ListSelectionModel:

```
myJTable.getSelectionModel().setSelectedMode(
   ListSelectionModel.XX_SELECTION);
```

To assign a specific selection mode to JTable's column ListSelectionModel:

```
myJTable.getColumnModel().getSelectionModel().setSelectionMode(
   ListSelectionModel.XX_SELECTION);
```

Row selection mode defaults to MULTIPLE_INTERVAL_SELECTION, and column selection mode defaults to SINGLE_SELECTION_MODE.

JTable provides control over whether rows and columns can be selected. We can query these modes and turn them on and off, with getRowSelectionAllowed() / getColumnSelectionAllowed(), and setRowSelectionAllowed() / setColumnSelectionAllowed(), respectively. When row selection is enabled (true by default), and cell selection is disabled (see below), clicking on a cell will select the entire row that cell belongs to. Similarly, when column selection is enabled (false by default), the whole column that cell belongs to will be selected. Nothing is stopping us from having both row and column selection active simultaneously.

JTable also provides control over whether individual cells can be selected with its cellSelectionEnabled property. We can turn this on or off with setCellSelection-Enabled() and query its state using getCellSelectionEnabled(). If cell selection is enabled (false by default), a cell can only be selected if both row selection and column selection are also enabled. If cell selection is not enabled, whenever a row or column containing that cell is selected (assuming that either row and/or column selection is enabled), that cell is also considered selected.

JTable provides several additional methods for querying the state of a selection. If at least one cell is selected, the following methods apply:

- getSelectedColumn() Returns the index (in the TreeModel) of the most recently selected column (-1 if no selection exists).
- getSelectedRow() Returns the index (in the TreeModel) of the most recently selected row (-1 if no selection exists).
- getSelectedColumns() and getSelectedRows(): Return the TreeModel indices of all currently selected columns and rows respectively (int[0] if no selection exists).
- getSelectedColumnCount() and getSelectedRowCount(): Return the current number of selected columns and rows respectively (0 if no selection exists).
- isColumnSelected() and isRowSelected(): Return a boolean specifying whether the given column or row is currently selected.
- isCellSelected(): Returns a boolean specifying whether the cell at the given Tree-Model row and column index is selected.

The following methods can be used to programatically change JTable's selection, assuming the corresponding selection properties are enabled:

- clearSelection(): Unselects all rows, columns, and cells.
- selectAll(): Selects all rows, columns, and cells.
- addColumnSelectionInterval() and addRowSelectionInterval(): Allow programmatic selection of a contiguous group of columns and rows respectively. These methods can be called repeatedly to build a multiple-interval selection if the MULTIPLE_INTERVAL_SELECTION mode is active in the corresponding selection models.
- removeColumnSelectionInterval() and removeRowSelectionInterval(): Allow programmatic deselection of a contiguous interval of columns and rows respectively. These methods can also be used repeatedly to affect multiple-interval selections.
- setColumnSelectionInterval() and setRowSelectionInterval(): Clear the current column and row selection, and select the specified contiguous interval.

Interestingly, when cell selection is enabled, JTable considers the columns and rows that contain selected cells as selected themselves (even though they aren't highlighted). For example, if cells (1,5) and (3,6) are selected with row and column selection enabled and cell selection enabled, getSelectedColumns() will return {5,6} and getSelectedRows() will return {1,3}. Oddly enough, those two cells will be highlighted and considered selected by JTable, along with cells (1,6) and (3,5)! This is due to the fact that JTable bases cell selection solely on whether or not both the row and column containing a cell are selected. **When selected rows and columns intersect, the cells at the intersection points are considered selected.**

If these same cells are selected when cell selection is disabled and row and column selection are enabled, all cells in rows 1 and 3, and all cells in columns 5 and 6 will be considered selected. If they are selected with cell selection and only row selection is enabled, all cells in rows 1 and 3 will be considered selected. Similarly, if these two cells are selected with cell selection and only column selection is enabled, all cells in columns 5 and 6 will be considered selected. If cell selection is *not* enabled, and row and/or column selection is enabled, a cell will be considered selected if either a column or row containing it is selected.

NOTE   Multiple single-cell selections can be made by holding down the CTRL key and using the mouse for selection. A contiguous selection can be made by holding down the SHIFT key and using the mouse to select a range of cells.

We are typically interested in determining cell, row, and/or column selection based on a mouse click. JTable supports MouseListeners just as any other JComponent does, and we can use the getSelectedColumn() and getSelectedRow() methods to determine which cell was clicked in MouseListener's mouseClicked() method:

```
myJTable.addMouseListener(new MouseAdapter() {
  public void mouseClicked(MouseEvent e) {
    // Get the most recently selected row index
    int row = myJTable.getSelectedRow();
    // Get the most recently selected column index
    int column = myJTable.getSelectedColumn();
    if (row == -1 || column == -1)
      return; // Can't determine the selected cell
    else
      // Do something cell-specific
  }
});
```

This listener is not very robust because it will only give us a cell if both a row and a column have recently been selected, which in turn can only occur if both row selection and column selection is enabled. Thankfully, JTable provides methods for retrieving a row and column index corresponding to a given Point: rowAtPoint() and columnAtPoint() will return –1 if no row or column is found, respectively. Since MouseEvent carries a Point specifying the location where the event occurred, we can use these methods in place of the getSelected-Row() and getSelectedColumn() methods. This is particularly useful when row, column, and/or cell selection is not enabled.

As with JList, JTable does not directly support double mouse-click selections. However, as we learned in chapter 10, we can capture a double click and determine which cell was clicked by adding a listener to JTable similar to the following:

```
myJTable.addMouseListener(new MouseAdapter() {
  public void mouseClicked(MouseEvent e) {
    if (e.getClickCount() == 2) {
      Point origin = e.getPoint();
      int row = myJTable.rowAtPoint(origin);
      int column = myJTable.columnAtPoint(origin);
      if (row == -1 || column == -1)
        return; // no cell found
```

```
        else
            // Do something cell-specific
        }
    }
});
```

18.1.18 Column width and resizing

When a column's width increases, `JTable` must decide how other columns will react. One or more columns must shrink. Similarly, when a column's width decreases, `JTable` must decide how other columns will react to the newly available amount of space. `JTable`'s `autoResize-Mode` property can take on any of five different values; each handles these cases differently.

- `JTable.AUTO_RESIZE_ALL_COLUMNS`: All columns gain or lose an equal amount of space corresponding to the width lost or gained by the resizing column.
- `JTable.AUTO_RESIZE_LAST_COLUMN`: The rightmost column shrinks or grows in direct correspondence with the amount of width lost or gained from the column being resized. All other columns are not affected.
- `JTable.AUTO_RESIZE_NEXT_COLUMN`: The column to the immediate right of the column being resized shrinks or grows in direct correspondence with the amount of width lost or gained from the resizing column. All other columns are not affected.
- `JTable.AUTO_RESIZE_OFF`: Resizing only affects the column being sized. All columns to the right of the column being resized are shifted right or left accordingly while maintaining their current sizes. Columns to the left are not affected.
- `JTable.AUTO_RESIZE_SUBSEQUENT_COLUMNS`: All columns to the right of the column being resized gain or lose an equal amount of space corresponding to the width lost or gained by the resizing column. Columns to the left are not affected.

`TableColumn`'s width defaults to 75. Its minimum width defaults to 15 and its maximum width defaults to `Integer.MAX_VALUE`. When a `JTable` is first displayed, it attempts to size each `TableColumn` according to its `width` property. If that table's `autoResizeMode` property is set to `AUTO_RESIZE_OFF`, this will occur successfully. Otherwise, `TableColumns` are adjusted according to the current `autoResizeMode` property.

A `TableColumn` will never be sized larger than its maximum width or smaller than its minimum. For this reason it is possible that a `JTable` will occupy a larger or smaller area than that available (usually in a parent `JScrollPane`'s main viewport), which may result in part of the table being clipped from view. If a table is contained in a `JScrollPane` and it occupies more than the available visible width, a horizontal scroll bar will be presented by default.

At any time we can call `TableColumn`'s `sizeWidthToFit()` method to resize a column to occupy a width corresponding to the preferred width of its table header renderer. This is often used in assigning minimum widths for each `TableColumn`. `JTable`'s `sizeColumns-ToFit()` method takes an `int` parameter that specifies the index of the `TableColumn` to act as the source of a resize in an attempt to make all columns fit within the available visible space. `TableColumnModel`'s `getTotalColumnWidth()` method returns the sum of the current width of all `TableColumns`, including all margin space.

We can specify the amount of empty space between rows with `JTable`'s `setRowMargin()` method, and we can assign all rows a specific height with `setRowHeight()`. `JTable`'s `setIntercellSpacing()` method takes a `Dimension` instance and uses it to assign a new width and height to be used as margin space between cells (this method will repaint the table it is invoked on after all sizes have been changed).

18.1.19 JTable appearance

We can change the background and foreground colors used to highlight selected cells by setting the selectedBackground and SelectedForeground properties.

The default colors used for each TableColumn's table header renderer are determined from the current JTableHeader's background and foreground colors (recall that JTable-Header extends JComponent).

We can turn on and off horizontal and vertical grid lines (which always have a thickness of 1 pixel) by changing the showHorizontalLines and showVerticalLines properties. The showGrid property will overpower these properties when it is set with setShowGrid() because this method reassigns them to the specified value. So setShowGrid() turns on and off both vertical and horizontal lines as specified. The gridColor property specifies the Color to use for both vertical and horizontal grid lines. setGridColor() will assign the specified value to this property and then repaint the whole table.

GUIDELINE

Visual noise Grid lines add visual noise to the display of a table. Removing some of them can aid the user in reading the table data. If you intend for the user to read rows across, then switch off the vertical grid lines. If you have columns of figures, for example, then you might prefer to switch off the horizontal grid lines, thereby making the columns easier to read.

When switching off the horizontal grid lines on the table, you may want to use the column cell renderer to change the background color of alternate table rows to make it easier to read rows. This combination of visual techniques, grid lines to distinguish columns and color to distinguish rows, helps guide the reader to better interpret data.

18.1.20 JTable scrolling

JTable implements the Scrollable interface (see section 7.1.4) and it is intended to be placed in a JScrollPane. JTableHeaders will not be displayed if JTable isn't placed in a JScrollPane, and the ability to resize columns would be lost because the table headers give us that capability. Among the required Scrollable methods, JTable implements get-ScrollableTracksViewportWidth() to return true, which forces JTable to attempt to size itself horizontally to fit within the current scroll pane viewport width. getScrollable-TracksViewportHeight(), however, returns false as it is most common for tables to be vertically scrolled but not horizontally scrolled. Horizontal scrolling is often awkward and we suggest you avoid it whenever possible.

JTable's vertical block increment is the number of visible rows less one, and its vertical unit increment is the current row height. The horizontal block increment is the width of the viewport, and the horizontal unit increment defaults to 100.

GUIDELINE

Small grids, no column headers If you need to show two or three pieces of data grouped and aligned together, consider using a JTable without a JScroll-Pane. This gives you a small grid which is already aligned, neat, and tidy for display without column headers.

18.2 *STOCKS TABLE, PART I: BASIC JTABLE EXAMPLE*

Example 18.1 shows how to construct a JTable to display information about stock market data for a given day. Despite its simplicity, it demonstrates the most fundamental features of JTable, and it serves as a good basis for the more advanced examples that follow.

Stocks and stock trading are characterized by many attributes. The following are selected for display in our example:

Name	Type	Description
Symbol	String	Stock's symbol (on the NYSE or NASDAQ, which are stock-exchanges in the USA).
Name	String	Company name.
Last	double	Price at the end of the trading day.
Open	double	Price at the beginning of the trading day.
Change	double	Absolute change in price with respect to the previous closing.
Change %	double	Percent change in price with respect to the previous closing.
Volume	long	Day's volume of trade (in $) for this stock.

Each stock attribute represents a column in our table, and each row represents a specific company's stock information.

Stocks Table

Stock Quotes at 04/06/1999

Symbol	Name	Last	Open	Change	Change %	Volume
ORCL	Oracle Corp.	23.6875	25.375	-1.6875	-6.42	24976600
EGGS	Egghead.com	17.25	17.4375	-0.1875	-1.43	2146400
T	AT&T	65.1875	66.0	-0.8125	-0.1	554000
LU	Lucent Technology	64.625	59.9375	4.6875	9.65	29856300
FON	Sprint	104.5625	106.375	-1.8125	-1.82	1135100
ENML	Enamelon Inc.	4.875	5.0	-0.125	0.0	35900
CPQ	Compaq Computers	30.875	31.25	-0.375	-2.18	11853900
MSFT	Microsoft Corp.	94.0625	95.1875	-1.125	-0.92	19836900
DELL	Dell Computers	46.1875	44.5	1.6875	6.24	47310000
SUNW	Sun Microsystems	140.625	130.9375	10.0	10.625	17734600
IBM	Intl. Bus. Machines	183.0	183.125	-0.125	-0.51	4371400
HWP	Hewlett-Packard	70.0	71.0625	-1.4375	-2.01	2410700
UIS	Unisys Corp.	28.25	29.0	-0.75	-2.59	2576200

Figure 18.1 A JTable in a JScrollPane with seven table columns and 16 rows of data

CHAPTER 18   TABLES

Example 18.1

StocksTable.java

StocksTable.java

see \Chapter18\1

```java
import java.awt.*;
import java.awt.event.*;
import java.util.*;
import java.io.*;
import java.text.*;

import javax.swing.*;
import javax.swing.border.*;
import javax.swing.event.*;
import javax.swing.table.*;

public class StocksTable extends JFrame
{
  protected JTable m_table;
  protected StockTableData m_data;
  protected JLabel m_title;

  public StocksTable() {
    super("Stocks Table");
    setSize(600, 340);

    m_data = new StockTableData();

    m_title = new JLabel(m_data.getTitle(),
      new ImageIcon("money.gif"), SwingConstants.LEFT);
    m_title.setFont(new Font("TimesRoman",Font.BOLD,24));
    m_title.setForeground(Color.black);
    getContentPane().add(m_title, BorderLayout.NORTH);

    m_table = new JTable();
    m_table.setAutoCreateColumnsFromModel(false);
    m_table.setModel(m_data);

    for (int k = 0; k < StockTableData.m_columns.length; k++) {
      DefaultTableCellRenderer renderer = new
        DefaultTableCellRenderer();
      renderer.setHorizontalAlignment(
        StockTableData.m_columns[k].m_alignment);
      TableColumn column = new TableColumn(k,
        StockTableData.m_columns[k].m_width, renderer, null);
      m_table.addColumn(column);
    }

    JTableHeader header = m_table.getTableHeader();
    header.setUpdateTableInRealTime(false);

    JScrollPane ps = new JScrollPane();
    ps.getViewport().add(m_table);
    getContentPane().add(ps, BorderLayout.CENTER);

    WindowListener wndCloser = new WindowAdapter() {
```

❶ Creates
StockTableData
and passes it
to JTable

❶ We're creating our
own columns

❷ Creates each
TableColumn with the
specified alignment
and width

❸ Only shows
column header
when dragging

```
      public void windowClosing(WindowEvent e) {
        System.exit(0);
      }
    };
    addWindowListener(wndCloser);
    setVisible(true);
  }

  public static void main(String argv[]) {
    new StocksTable();
  }
}

class StockData
{
  public String m_symbol;
  public String m_name;
  public Double m_last;
  public Double m_open;
  public Double m_change;
  public Double m_changePr;
  public Long m_volume;

  public StockData(String symbol, String name, double last,
   double open, double change, double changePr, long volume) {
    m_symbol = symbol;
    m_name = name;
    m_last = new Double(last);
    m_open = new Double(open);
    m_change = new Double(change);
    m_changePr = new Double(changePr);
    m_volume = new Long(volume);
  }
}

class ColumnData
{
  public String  m_title;
  public int     m_width;
  public int     m_alignment;

  public ColumnData(String title, int width, int alignment) {
    m_title = title;
    m_width = width;
    m_alignment = alignment;
  }
}

class StockTableData extends AbstractTableModel
{
  static final public ColumnData m_columns[] = {
    new ColumnData( "Symbol", 100, JLabel.LEFT ),
    new ColumnData( "Name", 150, JLabel.LEFT ),
    new ColumnData( "Last", 100, JLabel.RIGHT ),
    new ColumnData( "Open", 100, JLabel.RIGHT ),
```

4 Puts primitives in Object-derived classes for easier data interchange

5 Encapsulates information about each TableColumn

6 Data model for JTable

7 Static list of column names, widths, and alignments

```
  new ColumnData( "Change", 100, JLabel.RIGHT ),
  new ColumnData( "Change %", 100, JLabel.RIGHT ),
  new ColumnData( "Volume", 100, JLabel.RIGHT )
};
```

7 Static list of column names, widths, and alignments

```
protected SimpleDateFormat m_frm;
protected Vector m_vector;
protected Date    m_date;

public StockTableData() {
  m_frm = new SimpleDateFormat("MM/dd/yyyy");
  m_vector = new Vector();
  setDefaultData();
}

public void setDefaultData() {
  try {
    m_date = m_frm.parse("04/06/1999");
  }
  catch (java.text.ParseException ex) {
    m_date = null;
  }

  m_vector.removeAllElements();
  m_vector.addElement(new StockData("ORCL", "Oracle Corp.",
    23.6875, 25.375, -1.6875, -6.42, 24976600));
  m_vector.addElement(new StockData("EGGS", "Egghead.com",
    17.25, 17.4375, -0.1875, -1.43, 2146400));
  m_vector.addElement(new StockData("T", "AT&T",
    65.1875, 66, -0.8125, -0.10, 554000));
  m_vector.addElement(new StockData("LU", "Lucent Technology",
    64.625, 59.9375, 4.6875, 9.65, 29856300));
  m_vector.addElement(new StockData("FON", "Sprint",
    104.5625, 106.375, -1.8125, -1.82, 1135100));
  m_vector.addElement(new StockData("ENML", "Enamelon Inc.",
    4.875, 5, -0.125, 0, 35900));
  m_vector.addElement(new StockData("CPQ", "Compaq Computers",
    30.875, 31.25, -0.375, -2.18, 11853900));
  m_vector.addElement(new StockData("MSFT", "Microsoft Corp.",
    94.0625, 95.1875, -1.125, -0.92, 19836900));
  m_vector.addElement(new StockData("DELL", "Dell Computers",
    46.1875, 44.5, 1.6875, 6.24, 47310000));
  m_vector.addElement(new StockData("SUNW", "Sun Microsystems",
    140.625, 130.9375, 10, 10.625, 17734600));
  m_vector.addElement(new StockData("IBM", "Intl. Bus. Machines",
    183, 183.125, -0.125, -0.51, 4371400));
  m_vector.addElement(new StockData("HWP", "Hewlett-Packard",
    70, 71.0625, -1.4375, -2.01, 2410700));
  m_vector.addElement(new StockData("UIS", "Unisys Corp.",
    28.25, 29, -0.75, -2.59, 2576200));
  m_vector.addElement(new StockData("SNE", "Sony Corp.",
    96.1875, 95.625, 1.125, 1.18, 330600));
  m_vector.addElement(new StockData("NOVL", "Novell Inc.",
    24.0625, 24.375, -0.3125, -3.02, 6047900));
```

```
    m_vector.addElement(new StockData("HIT", "Hitachi, Ltd.",
       78.5, 77.625, 0.875, 1.12, 49400));
  }

  public int getRowCount() {
    return m_vector==null ? 0 : m_vector.size();
  }
```

Can be called before constructor, so needs to check for initialization ⑧

```
  public int getColumnCount() {
    return m_columns.length;
  }

  public String getColumnName(int column) {
    return m_columns[column].m_title;
  }

  public boolean isCellEditable(int nRow, int nCol) {
    return false;
  }

  public Object getValueAt(int nRow, int nCol) {
    if (nRow < 0 || nRow >= getRowCount())
      return "";
    StockData row = (StockData)m_vector.elementAt(nRow);
    switch (nCol) {
      case 0: return row.m_symbol;
      case 1: return row.m_name;
      case 2: return row.m_last;
      case 3: return row.m_open;
      case 4: return row.m_change;
      case 5: return row.m_changePr;
      case 6: return row.m_volume;
    }
    return "";
  }
```

⑥ **Derived from base class for more specific behavior**

```
  public String getTitle() {
    if (m_date==null)
      return "Stock Quotes";
    return "Stock Quotes at "+m_frm.format(m_date);
  }
}
```

18.2.1 Understanding the code

Class StocksTable

This class extends JFrame to implement the frame container for our table. Three instance variables are declared. They will be used extensively in more complex examples that follow.

- JTable m_table: The table component to display stock data.
- StockTableData m_data: The TableModel implementation to manage stock data.
- JLabel m_title: Displays the stocks table title (the date at which stock prices were referenced).

1 The `StocksTable` constructor first initializes the parent frame object and builds an instance of `StockTableData`. The `getTitle()` method is invoked to set the text for the title label which is added to the northern region of the content pane. Then a `JTable` is created by passing the `StockTableData` instance to the constructor. The `autoCreateColumnsFromModel` property is set to `false` because we plan on creating our own `TableColumns`.

As we will see below, the static array `m_columns` of the `StockTableData` class describes all the columns of our table. It is used here to create each `TableColumn` instance and set their text alignment and width.

2 The `setHorizontalAlignment()` method (which is inherited by `DefaultTableCell-Renderer` from `JLabel`) is used to set the proper alignment for each `TableColumn`'s cell renderer. The `TableColumn` constructor takes a column index, width, and renderer as parameters. `TableCellEditor` is set to `null` since we don't want to allow stock data to be edited. Finally, columns are added to the table's `TableColumnModel` (which `JTable` created by default because we didn't specify one) with the `addColumn()` method.

3 In the next step, an instance of `JTableHeader` is created for this table, and the `updateTable-InRealTime` property is set to `false` (this is done to demonstrate the effect this has on column dragging—only a column's table header is displayed during a drag).

Finally, a `JScrollPane` instance is used to provide scrolling capabilities, and our table is added to its `JViewport`. This `JScrollPane` is then added to the center of our frame's content pane.

Class StockData

This class encapsulates a unit of stock data as described in the table above. The instance variables defined in this class have the following descriptions:

- `String m_symbol`: The stock's symbol (on the NYSE or NASDAQ).
- `String m_name`: The company name.
- `Double m_last`: The price of the last trade.
- `Double m_open`: The price at the beginning of the trading day.
- `Double m_change`: The absolute change in price with respect to the previous closing.
- `Double m_changePr`: The percent change in price with respect to the previous closing.
- `Long m_volume`: The day's trading volume (in $) for this stock.

4 Note that all numerical data are encapsulated in `Object`-derived classes. This design decision simplifies data exchange with the table, as we will see below. The only constructor provided assigns each of these variables from the data passed as parameters.

> **NOTE** We use `public` instance variables in this and several other classes in this chapter to avoid overcomplication. In most professional applications these would either be protected or private.

Class ColumnData

5 This class encapsulates data that describes the visual characteristics of a single `TableColumn` of our table. The instance variables defined in this class have the following descriptions:

- `String m_title`: The column title.
- `int m_width`: The column width in pixels.
- `int m_alignment`: The text alignment as defined in `JLabel`.

The only constructor provided assigns each of these variables from the data passed as parameters.

Class StockTableData

❻ This class extends `AbstractTableModel` to serve as the data model for our table. Remember that `AbstractTableModel` is an abstract class, and three methods must be implemented to instantiate it:

- `public int getRowCount()`: Returns the number of rows in the table.
- `public int getColumnCount()`: Returns the number of columns in the table.
- `public Object getValueAt(int row, int column)`: Returns the data in the specified cell as an `Object` instance.

❼ By design, this class manages all information about our table, including the title and column data. A static array of `ColumnData`, `m_columns`, is provided to hold information about our table's columns (it is used in the `StocksTable` constructor as we discussed above). There are three instance variables:

- `SimpleDateFormat m_frm`: Formats dates.
- `Date m_date`: The date of the currently stored market data.
- `Vector m_vector`: A collection of `StockData` instances for each row in the table.

The only constructor of the `StockTableData` class initializes two of these variables and calls the `setDefaultData()` method to assign the predefined default data to `m_date` and `m_vector`. (In a later example we'll see how to use JDBC to retrieve data from a database rather than using hard-coded data as we do here).

❽ As we discussed above, the `getRowCount()` and `getColumnCount()` methods return the number of rows and columns. So their implementation is fairly obvious. The only catch is that they may be called by the `AbstractTableModel` constructor *before* any member variable is initialized. Therefore we have to check for a `null` instance of `m_vector`. Note that `m_columns`, as a static variable, will be initialized before any non-static code is executed, so we don't have to check `m_columns` against `null`.

The remainder of the `StockTableData` class implements the following methods:

- `getColumnName()`: Returns the column title.
- `isCellEditable()`: Always returns `false`, because we want to disable all editing.
- `getValueAt()`: Retrieves data for a given cell as an `Object`. Depending on the column index, one of the `StockData` fields is returned.
- `getTitle()`: Returns our table's title as a `String` to be used in a `JLabel` in the northern region of our frame's content pane.

18.2.2 Running the code

Figure 18.1 shows `StocksTable` in action, displaying our hard-coded stock data. Notice that the `TableColumns` resize properly in response to the parent frame size. Also notice that the selected row in our table can be moved or changed with the mouse or arrow keys, but no editing is allowed.

18.3 STOCKS TABLE, PART II: CUSTOM RENDERERS

Now we'll extend `StocksTable` to use color and small icons in rendering our table cells. To enhance data visibility, we'll make the following two enhancements in example 18.2:

- Render absolute and percent changes in green for positive values and red for negative values.
- Add an icon next to each stock symbol: arrow up for positive changes and arrow down for negative changes.

  To do this, we need to build our own custom `TableCellRenderer`.

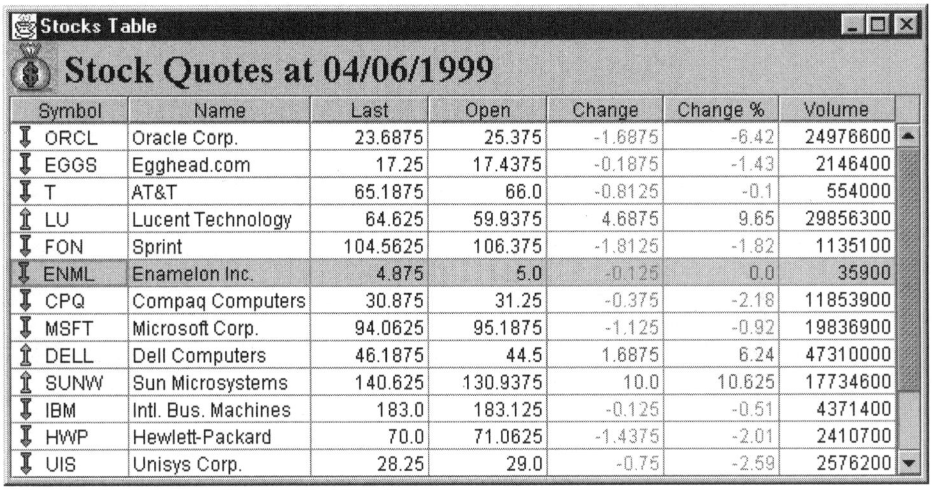

Symbol	Name	Last	Open	Change	Change %	Volume
ORCL	Oracle Corp.	23.6875	25.375	-1.6875	-6.42	24976600
EGGS	Egghead.com	17.25	17.4375	-0.1875	-1.43	2146400
T	AT&T	65.1875	66.0	-0.8125	-0.1	554000
LU	Lucent Technology	64.625	59.9375	4.6875	9.65	29856300
FON	Sprint	104.5625	106.375	-1.8125	-1.82	1135100
ENML	Enamelon Inc.	4.875	5.0	-0.125	0.0	35900
CPQ	Compaq Computers	30.875	31.25	-0.375	-2.18	11853900
MSFT	Microsoft Corp.	94.0625	95.1875	-1.125	-0.92	19836900
DELL	Dell Computers	46.1875	44.5	1.6875	6.24	47310000
SUNW	Sun Microsystems	140.625	130.9375	10.0	10.625	17734600
IBM	Intl. Bus. Machines	183.0	183.125	-0.125	-0.51	4371400
HWP	Hewlett-Packard	70.0	71.0625	-1.4375	-2.01	2410700
UIS	Unisys Corp.	28.25	29.0	-0.75	-2.59	2576200

Figure 18.2 A `JTable` using a custom cell renderer

Example 18.2

StocksTable.java

see \Chapter18\2

```
import java.awt.*;
import java.awt.event.*;
import java.util.*;
import java.io.*;
import java.text.*;

import javax.swing.*;
import javax.swing.border.*;
import javax.swing.event.*;
import javax.swing.table.*;

public class StocksTable extends JFrame
{
  // Unchanged code from example 18.1

  public StocksTable() {
    // Unchanged code from example 18.1
```

```
      for (int k = 0; k < StockTableData.m_columns.length; k++) {
        DefaultTableCellRenderer renderer = new
          ColoredTableCellRenderer();
        renderer.setHorizontalAlignment(
          StockTableData.m_columns[k].m_alignment);
        TableColumn column = new TableColumn(k,
          StockTableData.m_columns[k].m_width, renderer, null);
        m_table.addColumn(column);
      }

      // Unchanged code from example 18.1
    }

  public static void main(String argv[]) {
    new StocksTable();
  }
}

class ColoredTableCellRenderer extends DefaultTableCellRenderer
{
  public void setValue(Object value) {
    if (value instanceof ColorData) {
      ColorData cvalue = (ColorData)value;
      setForeground(cvalue.m_color);
      setText(cvalue.m_data.toString());
    }
    else if (value instanceof IconData) {
      IconData ivalue = (IconData)value;
      setIcon(ivalue.m_icon);
      setText(ivalue.m_data.toString());
    }
    else
      super.setValue(value);
  }
}

class ColorData
{
  public Color  m_color;
  public Object m_data;
  public static Color GREEN = new Color(0, 128, 0);
  public static Color RED = Color.red;

  public ColorData(Color color, Object data) {
    m_color = color;
    m_data  = data;
  }

  public ColorData(Double data) {
    m_color = data.doubleValue() >= 0 ? GREEN : RED;
    m_data  = data;
  }

  public String toString() {
    return m_data.toString();
```

1 Draws up/down icons or colored text

2 Can take either color data or icon data, but not both

3 Binds a color value to anonymous data

```
    }
  }

  class IconData                          ④  Binds an icon
  {                                           image to
    public ImageIcon  m_icon;                 anonymous data
    public Object m_data;

    public IconData(ImageIcon icon, Object data) {
      m_icon = icon;
      m_data = data;
    }

    public String toString() {
      return m_data.toString();           ⑤  Like previous version, but
    }                                         encodes icon and color
  }                                           information with some of
                                              the existings fields
  class StockData
  {
    public static ImageIcon ICON_UP = new ImageIcon("ArrUp.gif");
    public static ImageIcon ICON_DOWN = new ImageIcon("ArrDown.gif");
    public static ImageIcon ICON_BLANK = new ImageIcon("blank.gif");

    public IconData  m_symbol;
    public String   m_name;
    public Double   m_last;
    public Double   m_open;
    public ColorData  m_change;
    public ColorData  m_changePr;
    public Long     m_volume;

    public StockData(String symbol, String name, double last,
     double open, double change, double changePr, long volume) {
      m_symbol = new IconData(getIcon(change), symbol);
      m_name = name;
      m_last = new Double(last);
      m_open = new Double(open);
      m_change = new ColorData(new Double(change));
      m_changePr = new ColorData(new Double(changePr));
      m_volume = new Long(volume);
    }

    public static ImageIcon getIcon(double change) {
      return (change>0 ? ICON_UP : (change<0 ? ICON_DOWN :
        ICON_BLANK));
    }
  }

  // Class StockTableData is unchanged from example 18.1
```

18.3.1 Understanding the code

Class StocksTable

1 The only change we need to make in the base frame class is to change the column renderer to an instance of a new class, `ColoredTableCellRenderer`. This new class should be able to draw icons and colored text (but not both at the same time, although this could be done using this same approach).

Class ColoredTableCellRenderer

2 This class extends `DefaultTableCellRenderer` and overrides only one method: `setValue()`. This method will be called prior to the rendering of a cell to retrieve its corresponding data as an `Object`. Our overridden `setValue()` method is able to recognize two specific kinds of cell data: `ColorData`, which adds color to a data object, and `IconData`, which adds an icon (both are described below). If a `ColorData` instance is detected, its encapsulated color is set as the foreground for the renderer. If an `IconData` instance is detected, its encapsulated icon is assigned to the renderer with the `setIcon()` method (which is inherited from `JLabel`). If the value is neither a `ColorData` or an `IconData` instance, we call the superclass `setValue()` method.

Class ColorData

3 This class is used to bind a specific color, `m_color`, to a data object of any nature, `m_data`. Two static `Color`s, `RED` and `GREEN`, are declared to avoid creation of numerous temporary objects. Two constructors are provided for this class. The first constructor takes `Color` and `Object` parameters and assigns them to the instance variables `m_color` and `m_data` respectively. The second constructor takes a `Double` parameter which gets assigned to `m_data`, and `m_color` is assigned the green color if the parameter is positive, and red if it is negative. The `toString()` method simply calls the `toString()` method of the data object.

Class IconData

4 This class is used to bind `ImageIcon m_icon` to a data object of any nature, `m_data`. Its only constructor takes `ImageIcon` and `Object` parameters. The `toString()` method simply calls the `toString()` method of the data object.

Class StockData

5 This class has been enhanced from its previous version to to provide images and new variable data types. We've prepared three static `ImageIcon` instances that hold images: arrow up, arrow down, and a blank (all transparent) image. The static `getIcon()` method returns one of these images depending on the sign of the given `double` parameter. We've also changed three instance variables to bind data with the color and image attributes according to the following table:

Field	New type	Data object	Description
m_symbol	IconData	String	Stock's symbol (on the NYSE or NASDAQ).
m_change	ColorData	Double	Absolute change in price.
m_changePr	ColorData	Double	Percent change in price.

The corresponding changes are also required in the `StockData` constructor.

18.3.2 Running the code

Figure 18.2 shows `StocksTable` with custom rendering in action. Notice the usage of color and icons, which can considerably enhance data visualization.

GUIDELINE

Improving visual communication Tables can be data intensive, and consequently it can be very difficult for the user to quickly pick out the important information. The table in figure 18.1 highlighted this problem. In figure 18.2, we improved visual communication by introducing visual layers. The icons in the first column quickly tell the user whether a price is rising or falling. This is visually reinforced by the red and green colors in the change columns.

Red is an especially strong color. By introducing red and green only in the change columns and not across the entire row, we avoid the problem of red becoming overpowering. If we had introduced red and green across the full width of the table, the colors may have become intrusive and impaired the user's visual communication.

18.4 STOCKS TABLE, PART III: DATA FORMATTING

To further enhance the presentation of our stock data, in this section we will take into account that actual stock prices (at least on the NYSE and the NASDAQ) are expressed in fractions of 32, not in decimals. Another issue that we will deal with is the volume of trading, which can reach hundreds of millions of dollars. Volume is not immediately legible without separating thousands and millions places with commas.

Stock Table

Stock Quotes at 04/06/1999

Symbol	Name	Last	Open	Change	Change %	Volume
ORCL	Oracle Corp.	23 11/16	25 3/8	-1 11/16	-6.42	24,976,600
EGGS	Egghead.com	17 1/4	17 7/16	-3/16	-1.43	2,146,400
T	AT&T	65 3/16	66	-13/16	-0.1	554,000
LU	Lucent Technology	64 5/8	59 15/16	4 11/16	9.65	29,856,300
FON	Sprint	104 9/16	106 3/8	-1 13/16	-1.82	1,135,100
ENML	Enamelon Inc.	4 7/8	5	-1/8	0.0	35,900
CPQ	Compaq Computers	30 7/8	31 1/4	-3/8	-2.18	11,853,900
MSFT	Microsoft Corp.	94 1/16	95 3/16	-1 1/8	-0.92	19,836,900
DELL	Dell Computers	46 3/16	44 1/2	1 11/16	6.24	47,310,000
SUNW	Sun Microsystems	140 5/8	130 15/16	10	10.625	17,734,600
IBM	Intl. Bus. Machines	183	183 1/8	-1/8	-0.51	4,371,400
HWP	Hewlett-Packard	70	71 1/16	-1 7/16	-2.01	2,410,700
UIS	Unisys Corp.	28 1/4	29	-3/4	-2.59	2,576,200

Figure 18.3 A `JTable` with a custom number-formatting cell renderer that displays fractions and comma-delimited numbers

Example 18.3

see \Chapter18\3

```java
import java.awt.*;
import java.awt.event.*;
import java.util.*;
import java.io.*;
import java.text.*;

import javax.swing.*;
import javax.swing.border.*;
import javax.swing.event.*;
import javax.swing.table.*;

// Unchanged code from example 18.2

class Fraction
{
  public int m_whole;
  public int m_nom;
  public int m_den;

  public Fraction(double value) {
    int sign = value <0 ? -1 : 1;
    value = Math.abs(value);
    m_whole = (int)value;
    m_den = 32;
    m_nom = (int)((value-m_whole)*m_den);
    while (m_nom!=0 && m_nom%2==0) {
      m_nom /= 2;
      m_den /= 2;
    }
    if (m_whole==0)
      m_nom *= sign;
    else
      m_whole *= sign;
  }

  public double doubleValue() {
    return (double)m_whole + (double)m_nom/m_den;
  }

  public String toString() {
    if (m_nom==0)
      return ""+m_whole;
    else if (m_whole==0)
      return ""+m_nom+"/"+m_den;
    else
      return ""+m_whole+" "+m_nom+"/"+m_den;
  }
}
```

❶ Divides a double value into its whole number, numerator, and denominator (always 32)

❶ Prints the value like "9 3/32"

```
class SmartLong
{
  protected static NumberFormat FORMAT;

  static {
    FORMAT = NumberFormat.getInstance();
    FORMAT.setGroupingUsed(true);
  }

  public long m_value;

  public SmartLong(long value) { m_value = value; }

  public long longValue() { return m_value; }

  public String toString() { return FORMAT.format(m_value); }
}

class ColorData
{
  public ColorData(Fraction data) {
    m_color = data.doubleValue() >= 0 ? GREEN : RED;
    m_data  = data;
  }

  // Unchanged code from example 18.2
}

class StockData
{
  public static ImageIcon ICON_UP = new ImageIcon("ArrUp.gif");
  public static ImageIcon ICON_DOWN = new ImageIcon("ArrDown.gif");
  public static ImageIcon ICON_BLANK = new ImageIcon("blank.gif");

  public IconData  m_symbol;
  public String  m_name;
  public Fraction  m_last;
  public Fraction  m_open;
  public ColorData  m_change;
  public ColorData  m_changePr;
  public SmartLong  m_volume;

  public StockData(String symbol, String name, double last,
   double open, double change, double changePr, long volume) {
    m_symbol = new IconData(getIcon(change), symbol);
    m_name = name;
    m_last = new Fraction(last);
    m_open = new Fraction(open);
    m_change = new ColorData(new Fraction(change));
    m_changePr = new ColorData(new Double(changePr));
    m_volume = new SmartLong(volume);
  }

  // Unchanged code from example 18.2
}
```

2 Used to format integers with thousands separators

3 New constructor takes Fraction value and determines positive or negative color from the Fraction sign

4 Builds Fraction and SmartLong objects instead of Double and Long

18.4.1   Understanding the code

Class Fraction

❶ This new data class encapsulates fractions with a denominator of 32 (or in a reduced form). Three instance variables represent the whole number, numerator, and denominator of the fraction. The only constructor takes a double parameter and carefully extracts these values, performing numerator and denominator reduction, if possible. Negative absolute values are taken into account.

The `doubleValue()` method performs the opposite task: it converts the fraction into a `double` value. The `toString()` method forms a `String` representation of the fraction.

Zero whole numbers and zero numerators are omitted to avoid unseemly output such as "0 1/2" or "12 0/32."

Class SmartLong

❷ This class encapsulates `long` values. The only constructor takes a `long` as a parameter and stores it in the `m_value` instance variable. The real purpose of creating this class is the overridden `toString()` method, which inserts commas separating number places such as thousands and millions. For this purpose we use the `java.text.NumberFormat` class. An instance of this class is created as a static variable. Formatting values using `NumberFormat`'s `format()` method couldn't be easier.

> **NOTE**   `SmartLong` cannot extend `Long` (although it would be natural), because `java.lang.Long` is a `final` class.

> **NOTE**   We could use the different approach of just formatting the initial contents of our table's cells into text strings and operating on them without introducing new data classes. This approach, however, is not desirable from a design point of view, as it strips the data of its true nature: numbers. Using our method we are still able to retrieve number values, if necessary, through the `doubleValue()` or `longValue()` methods.

Class ColorData

❸ This class requires a new constructor to cooperate with the new `Fraction` data type. This third constructor takes a `Fraction` instance as a parameter and uses its color attribute in the same way it did previously: green for positive values, and red for negative values.

Class StockData

❹ This class uses new data types for its instance variables. The list of instance variables now looks like the following:

Field	Type	Data object	Description
m_symbol	IconData	String	Stock symbol (on the NYSE or NASDAQ).
m_name	String	N/A	Company name.
m_last	Fraction	N/A	Price of the last trade.
m_open	Fraction	N/A	Price at the beginning of the trading day.
m_change	ColorData	Fraction	Absolute change in price.
m_changePr	ColorData	Double	Percent change in price.
m_volume	SmartLong	N/A	Day's trading volume (in $) for this stock.

The `StockData` constructor is modified accordingly. Meanwhile, the parameters in the `StockData` constructor have *not* changed, so there is no need to make any changes to the data model class using `StockData`.

18.4.2 Running the code

Figure 18.3 shows `StocksTable` in action using number formatting. Presented this way, our data looks much more familiar to most people who follow the stock trade on a regular basis.

GUIDELINE

Talking the users language   In this example, we have changed the rendering of the stock prices into fractions rather than decimals. This is a good example of providing better visual communication—we're now speaking the same language as the users. In the North American stock markets, prices are quoted in fractional amounts of dollars rather than dollars and cents. Switching to this type of display helps the application to communicate more quickly and more influentially to the user, thereby improving usability.

18.5 STOCKS TABLE, PART IV: SORTING COLUMNS

NOTE   Examples 18.4, 18.5, and 18.6 require Java 2 as they use the new `java.util.Collections` functionality.

In this section, we add the ability to sort any column in ascending or descending order to our example. The most suitable graphical element for sort order selection is the column headers. We adopt the following model for our sorting functionality:

1. A single click on the header of a column causes the table to re-sort based on that column.
2. A repeated click on the same column changes the sort direction from ascending to descending and vice versa.
3. The header of the column which provides the current sorting should be marked.

To do this, we add a mouse listener to the table header to capture mouse clicks and trigger a table sort. Fortunately, sorting can be accomplished fairly easily using the new `Collections` functionality in Java 2.

NOTE   The `java.util.Collections` class contains a set of static methods that are used to manipulate Java collections, including `java.util.Vector` which is used in this example.

In example 18.4, we use the `java.util.Collections.sort(List lst, Comparator c)` method to sort any collection implementing the `java.util.List` interface based on a given `Comparator`. A `Comparator` implementation requires two methods:

- `int compare(Object o1, Object o2)`: Compares two objects and returns the result as an `int` (zero if equal, a negative value if the first is less than the second, a positive value if the first is greater than the second).
- `boolean equals(Object obj)`: Returns `true` if the given object is equal to this `Comparator`.

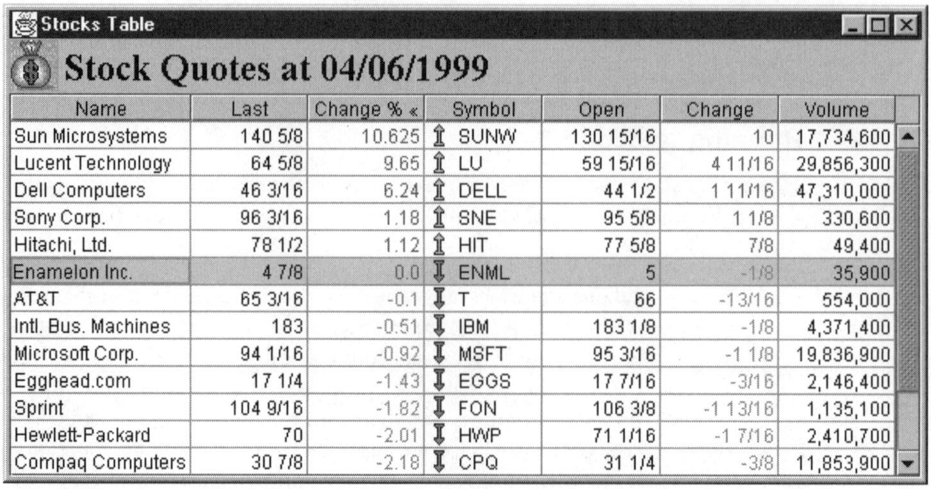
Stocks Table

Stock Quotes at 04/06/1999

Name	Last	Change % «	Symbol	Open	Change	Volume
Sun Microsystems	140 5/8	10.625	SUNW	130 15/16	10	17,734,600
Lucent Technology	64 5/8	9.65	LU	59 15/16	4 11/16	29,856,300
Dell Computers	46 3/16	6.24	DELL	44 1/2	1 11/16	47,310,000
Sony Corp.	96 3/16	1.18	SNE	95 5/8	1 1/8	330,600
Hitachi, Ltd.	78 1/2	1.12	HIT	77 5/8	7/8	49,400
Enamelon Inc.	4 7/8	0.0	ENML	5	-1/8	35,900
AT&T	65 3/16	-0.1	T	66	-13/16	554,000
Intl. Bus. Machines	183	-0.51	IBM	183 1/8	-1/8	4,371,400
Microsoft Corp.	94 1/16	-0.92	MSFT	95 3/16	-1 1/8	19,836,900
Egghead.com	17 1/4	-1.43	EGGS	17 7/16	-3/16	2,146,400
Sprint	104 9/16	-1.82	FON	106 3/8	-1 13/16	1,135,100
Hewlett-Packard	70	-2.01	HWP	71 1/16	-1 7/16	2,410,700
Compaq Computers	30 7/8	-2.18	CPQ	31 1/4	-3/8	11,853,900

Figure 18.4 A `JTable` with ascending and descending sorting of all columns

Example 18.4

StocksTable.java

see \Chapter18\4

```
import java.awt.*;
import java.awt.event.*;
import java.util.*;
import java.io.*;
import java.text.*;

import javax.swing.*;
import javax.swing.border.*;
import javax.swing.event.*;
import javax.swing.table.*;

public class StocksTable extends JFrame
{
  // Unchanged code from example 18.3

  public StocksTable() {
    // Unchanged code from example 18.3

    JTableHeader header = m_table.getTableHeader();
    header.setUpdateTableInRealTime(true);
    header.addMouseListener(m_data.new ColumnListener(m_table));
    header.setReorderingAllowed(true);

    // Unchanged code from example 18.3
  }

  public static void main(String argv[]) {
    new StocksTable();
  }
```

1 As opposed to previous example, shows whole column (including data) when dragging column

```
            }

            // Unchanged code from example 18.3

            class StockTableData extends AbstractTableModel
            {
              // Unchanged code from example 18.1

              protected SimpleDateFormat m_frm;
              protected Vector m_vector;
              protected Date    m_date;

              protected int m_sortCol = 0;
              protected boolean m_sortAsc = true;

              public StockTableData() {
                m_frm = new SimpleDateFormat("MM/dd/yyyy");
                m_vector = new Vector();
                setDefaultData();
              }

              public void setDefaultData() {
                // Unchanged code from example 18.3

                Collections.sort(m_vector, new
                  StockComparator(m_sortCol, m_sortAsc));
              }

              // Unchanged code from example 18.3

              public String getColumnName(int column) {
                String str = m_columns[column].m_title;
                if (column==m_sortCol)
                  str += m_sortAsc ? " »" : " «";
                return str;
              }

              // Unchanged code from example 18.3

              class ColumnListener extends MouseAdapter
              {
                protected JTable m_table;

                public ColumnListener(JTable table) {
                  m_table = table;
                }

                public void mouseClicked(MouseEvent e) {
                  TableColumnModel colModel = m_table.getColumnModel();
                  int columnModelIndex = colModel.getColumnIndexAtX(e.getX());
                  int modelIndex = colModel.getColumn(columnModelIndex).getModelIndex();

                  if (modelIndex < 0)
                    return;
                  if (m_sortCol==modelIndex)
                    m_sortAsc = !m_sortAsc;
                  else
                    m_sortCol = modelIndex;
```

2 Variables holding sort column and direction

3 Puts a marker at end of sorting column name to indicate ascending or descending

4 If mouse clicked on a column header, then sort on that column or reverse order of sort on that column

```
        for (int i=0; i < m_columns.length; i++) {
          TableColumn column = colModel.getColumn(i);
          column.setHeaderValue(getColumnName(column.getModelIndex()));
        }
        m_table.getTableHeader().repaint();

        Collections.sort(m_vector, new
          StockComparator(modelIndex, m_sortAsc));
        m_table.tableChanged(
          new TableModelEvent(StockTableData.this));
        m_table.repaint();
      }
    }
}

class StockComparator implements Comparator
{
  protected int      m_sortCol;
  protected boolean m_sortAsc;

  public StockComparator(int sortCol, boolean sortAsc) {
    m_sortCol = sortCol;
    m_sortAsc = sortAsc;
  }

  public int compare(Object o1, Object o2) {
    if(!(o1 instanceof StockData) || !(o2 instanceof StockData))
      return 0;
    StockData s1 = (StockData)o1;
    StockData s2 = (StockData)o2;
    int result = 0;
    double d1, d2;
    switch (m_sortCol) {
      case 0:     // Symbol
        String str1 = (String)s1.m_symbol.m_data;
        String str2 = (String)s2.m_symbol.m_data;
        result = str1.compareTo(str2);
        break;
      case 1:     // Name
        result = s1.m_name.compareTo(s2.m_name);
        break;
      case 2:     // Last
        d1 = s1.m_last.doubleValue();
        d2 = s2.m_last.doubleValue();
        result = d1<d2 ? -1 : (d1>d2 ? 1 : 0);
        break;
      case 3:     // Open
        d1 = s1.m_open.doubleValue();
        d2 = s2.m_open.doubleValue();
        result = d1<d2 ? -1 : (d1>d2 ? 1 : 0);
        break;
      case 4:     // Change
        d1 = ((Fraction)s1.m_change.m_data).doubleValue();
        d2 = ((Fraction)s2.m_change.m_data).doubleValue();
```

❺ Redraws header with new sort column and direction marker

❻ Comparator for StockData objects, uses current sort column and direction to determine what to compare

```
        result = d1<d2 ? -1 : (d1>d2 ? 1 : 0);
        break;
      case 5:     // Change %
        d1 = ((Double)s1.m_changePr.m_data).doubleValue();
        d2 = ((Double)s2.m_changePr.m_data).doubleValue();
        result = d1<d2 ? -1 : (d1>d2 ? 1 : 0);
        break;
      case 6:     // Volume
        long l1 = s1.m_volume.longValue();
        long l2 = s2.m_volume.longValue();
        result = l1<l2 ? -1 : (l1>l2 ? 1 : 0);
        break;
    }

    if (!m_sortAsc)
      result = -result;
    return result;
  }

  public boolean equals(Object obj) {
    if (obj instanceof StockComparator) {
      StockComparator compObj = (StockComparator)obj;
      return (compObj.m_sortCol==m_sortCol) &&
        (compObj.m_sortAsc==m_sortAsc);
    }
    return false;
  }
}
```

18.5.1   Understanding the code

Class StocksTable

① In the `StocksTable` constructor, we set the `updateTableInRealTime` property to show column contents while columns are dragged, and we add an instance of the `ColumnListener` class (see below) as a mouse listener to the table's header.

Class StockTableData

② Here we declare two new instance variables: `int m_sortCol` to hold the index of the current column chosen for sorting; and `boolean m_sortAsc`, which is `true` when sorting in ascending order, and `false` when sorting in descending order. These variables determine the initial sorting order. To be consistent, we sort our table initially by calling the `Collections.sort()` method in our `setDefaultData()` method (which is called from the `StockTableData` constructor).

③ We also add a special marker for the sorting column's header: » for ascending sorting and « for descending sorting. This changes the way we retrieve a column's name, which no longer is a constant value:

```
public String getColumnName(int column) {
  String str = m_columns[column].m_title;
  if (column==m_sortCol)
    str += m_sortAsc ? " »" : " «";
```

```
    return str;
}
```

Class StockTableData.ColumnListener

4 Because this class interacts heavily with our table data, it is implemented as an inner class in StockTableData. ColumnListener takes a reference to a JTable in its constructor and stores that reference in its m_table instance variable.

The mouseClicked() method is invoked when the user clicks on a header. It first determines the index of the TableColumn clicked based on the coordinate of the click. If, for any reason, the returned index is negative (if the column cannot be determined), the method cannot continue and we return. Otherwise, we check whether this index corresponds to the column which already has been selected for sorting. If it does, we invert the m_sortCol flag to reverse the sorting order. If the index corresponds to the newly selected column we store the new sorting index in the m_sortCol variable.

5 Next, we refresh the header names by iterating through the TableColumns and assigning them a name corresponding to the column they represent in the TableModel. To do this, we pass each TableColumn's modelIndex property to our getColumnName() method (see above). Finally, our table data is re-sorted by calling the Collections.sort() method and passing in a new StockComparator object. We then refresh the table by calling table-Changed() and repaint().

Class StockComparator

6 This class implements the rule of comparison for two objects, which in our case are StockDatas. Instances of the StockComparator class are passed to the Collections.sort() method to perform data sorting.

Two instance variables are defined:

- int m_sortCol: Represents the index of the column which performs the comparison.
- boolean m_sortAsc: true for ascending sorting and false for descending sorting.

The StockComparator constructor takes two parameters and stores them in these instance variables.

The compare() method takes two objects to be compared and returns an integer value according to the rules determined in the Comparator interface:

- 0 if object 1 equals object 2
- A positive number if object 1 is greater than object 2,
- A negative number if object 1 is less than object 2.

Since we are dealing only with StockData objects, we first cast both objects and return 0 if this cast isn't possible. The next issue is to define what it means when one StockData object is greater than, equal to, or less than another. This is done in a switch-case structure, which, depending on the index of the comparison column, extracts two fields and forms an integer result of the comparison. When the switch-case structure finishes, we know the result of an ascending comparison. For descending comparison, we simply need to invert the sign of the result.

The `equals()` method takes another `Comparator` instance as a parameter and returns `true` if that parameter represents the same `Comparator`. We determine this by comparing the `Comparator` instance variables `m_sortCol` and `m_sortAsc`.

18.5.2 Running the code

Figure 18.4 shows `StocksTable` sorted by the decreasing Change % column. Click different column headers and notice that re-sorting occurs as expected. Click the same column header twice and see how the sorting order flips from ascending to descending and vice versa. Also note that the currently selected sorting column header is marked by the » or « symbol. This sorting functionality is very useful. Particularly, for stock market data we can instantly determine which stocks have the highest price fluctuations or the most heavy trade.

GUIDELINE

Sorting tables by header selection Introducing table sorting using the column headers adds another interaction mechanism to the user interface. This mechanism is becoming widely accepted and widely used in many applications as it is a powerful technique to use when sorting table data is a requirement. The technique is not intuitive and there is little visual affordance to suggest that clicking a column header will have any effect. So consider that the introduction of this technique may require additional user training.

18.6 STOCKS TABLE, PART V: JDBC

Despite all of our sorting functionality and enhanced data display, our application is still quite boring because it displays only data for a predefined day. Of course, in the real world we need to connect such an application to a source of fresh information such as a database. Very often tables are used to display data retrieved from databases, or to edit data to be stored in databases. In this section, we'll show how to feed our `StocksTable` data extracted from a database using the Java Database Connectivity (JDBC) API.

First, we need to create the database. We chose to use two software query language (SQL) tables (do not confuse the SQL table with `JTable`) whose structure precisely corresponds to the market data structure described in section 18.2:

Table 18.1   Symbols

Field Name	Type
symbol	Text
name	Text

In example 18.5 we use the JDBC-ODBC bridge which is a standard part of JDK since the 1.1 release. It links Java programs to Microsoft Access databases. If you are using another database engine, you can work with this example as well, but you must make sure that the structure of your tables is the same. Before running the example in a Windows environment you will need to register a database in an Open Database Connectivity (ODBC) Data Source Administrator which is accessible through the Control Panel (this is not a JDBC tutorial, so we'll skip the details).

Table 18.2   Data

Field Name	Type
symbol	Text
date1	Date/Time
last	Number
change	Number
changeproc	Number
open	Number
volume	Number

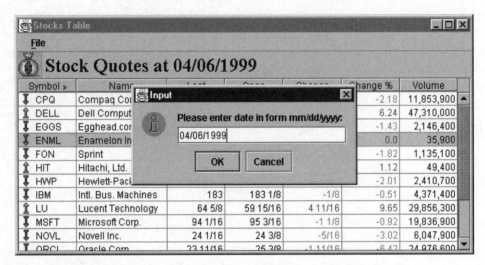

Figure 18.5   Retrieving stock data from a database for display in `JTable`

Example 18.5

StocksTable.java

see \Chapter18\5

```
import java.awt.*;
import java.awt.event.*;
import java.util.*;
import java.io.*;
import java.text.*;
import java.sql.*;

import javax.swing.*;
import javax.swing.border.*;
import javax.swing.event.*;
import javax.swing.table.*;
```

```java
public class StocksTable extends JFrame
{
  protected JTable m_table;
  protected StockTableData m_data;
  protected JLabel m_title;

  public StocksTable() {
    // Unchanged code from example 18.3

    JMenuBar menuBar = createMenuBar();
      setJMenuBar(menuBar);

    // Unchanged code from example 18.3
  }

  protected JMenuBar createMenuBar() {
    JMenuBar menuBar = new JMenuBar();

    JMenu mFile = new JMenu("File");
    mFile.setMnemonic('f');

    JMenuItem mData = new JMenuItem("Retrieve Data...");
    mData.setMnemonic('r');
    ActionListener lstData = new ActionListener() {
      public void actionPerformed(ActionEvent e) {
        retrieveData();
      }
    };
    mData.addActionListener(lstData);
    mFile.add(mData);
    mFile.addSeparator();

    JMenuItem mExit = new JMenuItem("Exit");
    mExit.setMnemonic('x');
    ActionListener lstExit = new ActionListener() {
      public void actionPerformed(ActionEvent e) {
        System.exit(0);
      }
    };
    mExit.addActionListener(lstExit);
    mFile.add(mExit);
    menuBar.add(mFile);

    return menuBar;
  }

  public void retrieveData() {
    SimpleDateFormat frm = new SimpleDateFormat("MM/dd/yyyy");
    String currentDate = frm.format(m_data.m_date);
    String result = (String)JOptionPane.showInputDialog(this,
      "Please enter date in form mm/dd/yyyy:", "Input",
      JOptionPane.INFORMATION_MESSAGE, null, null,
      currentDate);
    if (result==null)
      return;
```

1 Adds menu item to get data from database

2 Prompts user for date and retrieves data for that date

```java
    java.util.Date date = null;
    try {
      date = frm.parse(result);
    }
    catch (java.text.ParseException ex) {
      date = null;
    }

    if (date == null) {
      JOptionPane.showMessageDialog(this,
        result+" is not a valid date",
        "Warning", JOptionPane.WARNING_MESSAGE);
      return;
    }

    setCursor( Cursor.getPredefinedCursor(Cursor.WAIT_CURSOR) );
    switch (m_data.retrieveData(date)) {
      case 0:    // Ok with data
        m_title.setText(m_data.getTitle());
        m_table.tableChanged(new TableModelEvent(m_data));
        m_table.repaint();
        break;
      case 1: // No data
        JOptionPane.showMessageDialog(this,
          "No data found for "+result,
          "Warning", JOptionPane.WARNING_MESSAGE);
        break;
      case -1: // Error
        JOptionPane.showMessageDialog(this,
          "Error retrieving data",
          "Warning", JOptionPane.WARNING_MESSAGE);
        break;
    }
    setCursor(Cursor.getPredefinedCursor(Cursor.DEFAULT_CURSOR));
  }

  public static void main(String argv[]) {
    new StocksTable();
  }
}

// Unchanged code from example 18.3

class StockTableData extends AbstractTableModel
{
  static final public ColumnData m_columns[] = {
    // Unchanged code from example 18.1
  };

  protected SimpleDateFormat m_frm;
  protected Vector m_vector;
  protected java.util.Date m_date; // conflict with java.sql.Date

  protected int m_sortCol = 0;
  protected boolean m_sortAsc = true;
```

Specifies package ❸ path to avoid conflict with java.sql.Date

```
protected int m_result = 0;

public StockTableData() {
  m_frm = new SimpleDateFormat("MM/dd/yyyy");
  m_vector = new Vector();
  setDefaultData();
}

// Unchanged code from example 18.3

public int retrieveData(final java.util.Date date) {
  GregorianCalendar calendar = new GregorianCalendar();
  calendar.setTime(date);
  int month = calendar.get(Calendar.MONTH)+1;
  int day = calendar.get(Calendar.DAY_OF_MONTH);
  int year = calendar.get(Calendar.YEAR);

  final String query = "SELECT data.symbol, symbols.name, "+
    "data.last, data.open, data.change, data.changeproc, "+
    "data.volume FROM DATA INNER JOIN SYMBOLS "+
    "ON DATA.symbol = SYMBOLS.symbol WHERE "+
    "month(data.date1)="+month+" AND day(data.date1)="+day+
    " AND year(data.date1)="+year;

  Thread runner = new Thread() {
    public void run() {
      try {
        // Load the JDBC-ODBC bridge driver
        Class.forName("sun.jdbc.odbc.JdbcOdbcDriver");
        Connection conn = DriverManager.getConnection(
          "jdbc:odbc:Market", "admin", "");

        Statement stmt = conn.createStatement();
        ResultSet results = stmt.executeQuery(query);

        boolean hasData = false;
        while (results.next()) {
          if (!hasData) {
            m_vector.removeAllElements();
            hasData = true;
          }
          String  symbol = results.getString(1);
          String  name = results.getString(2);
          double  last = results.getDouble(3);
          double  open = results.getDouble(4);
          double  change = results.getDouble(5);
          double  changePr = results.getDouble(6);
          long volume = results.getLong(7);
          m_vector.addElement(new StockData(symbol, name, last,
            open, change, changePr, volume));
        }
        results.close();
        stmt.close();
        conn.close();
```

4 Loads JDBC-ODBC bridge class using Reflection

5 Retrieves data from ResultSet and builds new StockData

```
        if (!hasData)     // We've got nothing
          m_result = 1;
      }
      catch (Exception e) {
        e.printStackTrace();
        System.err.println("Load data error: "+e.toString());
        m_result = -1;
      }
      m_date = date;
      Collections.sort(m_vector,
        new StockComparator(m_sortCol, m_sortAsc));
      m_result = 0;
    }
  };
  runner.start();

  return m_result;
}

  // Unchanged code from example 18.3
}

// Class StockComparator is unchanged from example 18.3
```

18.6.1   Understanding the code

Class StocksTable

A JMenuBar instance is created with our custom createMenuBar() method and it is added to our frame.

❶ The createMenuBar() method creates a menu bar that contains a single menu entitled File. Two menu items are added: Retrieve Data... and Exit with a separator in between. Anonymous ActionListeners are added to each one. The first calls our custom retrieveData() method, and the second simply kills the application using System.exit(0).

❷ The retrieveData() method is called in response to a Retrieve Data... menu item activation. It first prompts the user to enter the date by displaying a JOptionPane dialog. Once the date has been entered, this method parses it using a SimpleDateFormat object. If the entered string cannot be parsed into a valid date, the method shows a warning message and returns. Otherwise, we connect to JDBC and retrieve new data. To indicate that the program will be busy for some time, the wait mouse cursor is displayed. The main job is performed by our new StockTableData retrieveData() method (see below), which is invoked on the m_data object. StockTableData's retrieveData() method returns code that the rest of this method depends on:

  0: Normal finish, some data retrieved. The table model is updated and repainted.

  1: Normal finish, no data retrieved. A warning message is displayed, and no changes are made in the table model.

-1: An error has occurred. An error message is displayed, and no changes are made in the table model.

Class StockTableData

3 First, a minor change is required in the declaration of the `m_date` variable. Since we've now imported the `java.sql` package, which also includes the `Date` class, we have to provide the fully qualified class name `java.util.Date`.

A new instance variable is added to store the result of a data retrieval request in the `retrieveData()` method. As we mentioned above, `retrieveData()` retrieves a table's data for a given date of trade. Our implementation uses the JDBC bridge driver, and it should be familiar to JDBC-aware readers. The first thing we do is construct an SQL statement. Since we cannot compare a `java.util.Date` object and an SQL date stored in the database, we have to extract the date's components (year, month, and day) and compare them separately. An instance of `GregorianCalendar` is used to manipulate the date object.

4 We load the JDBC-ODBC bridge driver to Microsoft Access by using the `Class.forName()` method, and then we connect to a database with the `DriverManager.getConnection()` method. If no exception is thrown, we can create a `Statement` instance for the newly created `Connection` object and retrieve a `ResultSet` by executing the previously constructed query.

5 While new data is available (checked with the `ResultSet.next()` method), we retrieve new data using basic `getXX()` methods, create a new `StockData` instance to encapsulate the new data, and add it to `m_vector`.

Notice how the `hasData` local variable is used to distinguish the case in which we do not have any data in our `RecordSet`. The first time we receive some valid data from our `RecordSet` in the `while` loop, we set this variable to `true` and clean up our `m_vector` collection. If no data is found, we have an unchanged initial vector and the `hasData` flag is set to `false`. Finally we close our `ResultSet`, `Statement`, and `Connection` instances. If any exception occurs, the method prints the exception trace and returns a −1 to indicate an error. Otherwise, our newly retrieved data is sorted with the `Collections.sort()` method and a 0 is returned to indicate success.

18.6.2 Running the code

Figure 18.5 shows `StocksTable` with data retrieved from a database. Try loading data for different dates in your database. A sample Microsoft Access database, market.mdb, containing some real market data, can be found in **\Chapter18** directory in the ZIP archive for this chapter.

18.7 STOCKS TABLE, PART VI: COLUMN ADDITION AND REMOVAL

`JTable` allows us to dynamically add and remove `TableColumns` on the fly. Remember that the `TableColumnModel` interface provides the `addColumn()` and `removeColumn()` methods to programmatically add or remove a `TableColumn` respectively. In this section we add dynamic column addition and removal to our `StocksTable` application.

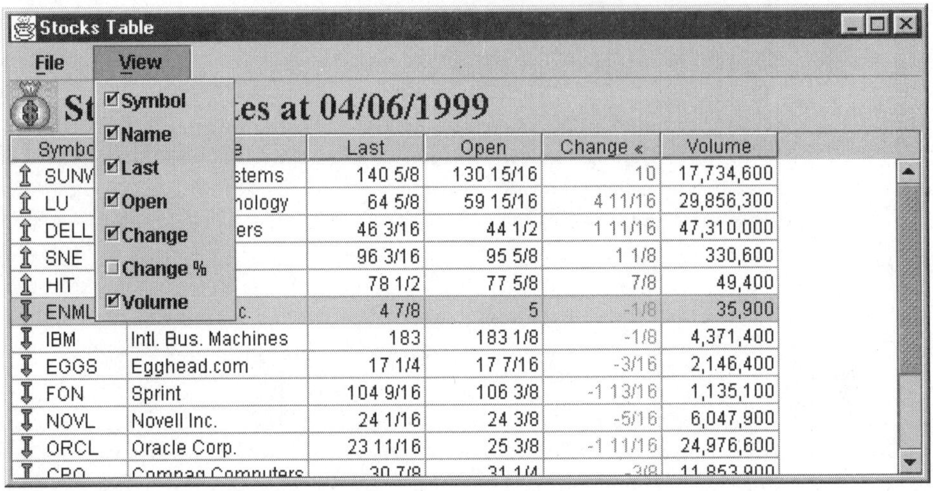

Figure 18.6 A `JTable` **with dynamic column addition and removal**

Example 18.6

StocksTable.java

see \Chapter18\6

```
import java.awt.*;
import java.awt.event.*;
import java.util.*;
import java.io.*;
import java.text.*;
import java.sql.*;

import javax.swing.*;
import javax.swing.border.*;
import javax.swing.event.*;
import javax.swing.table.*;

public class StocksTable extends JFrame
{
  // Unchanged code from example 18.4

  public StocksTable() {
    // Unchanged code from example 18.4
    header.setReorderingAllowed(true);

    m_table.getColumnModel().addColumnModelListener(
      m_data.new ColumnMovementListener());

    // Unchanged code from example 18.4
  }

  protected JMenuBar createMenuBar() {
    // Unchanged code from example 18.4
```

❶ Adds movement listener, only for adding and removing columns, not movement

```java
      JMenu mView = new JMenu("View");
      mView.setMnemonic('v');
      TableColumnModel model = m_table.getColumnModel();
      for (int k = 0; k < StockTableData.m_columns.length; k++) {
        JCheckBoxMenuItem item = new JCheckBoxMenuItem(
          StockTableData.m_columns[k].m_title);
        item.setSelected(true);
        TableColumn column = model.getColumn(k);
        item.addActionListener(new ColumnKeeper(column,
          StockTableData.m_columns[k]));
        mView.add(item);
      }
      menuBar.add(mView);

    return menuBar;
  }

  // Unchanged code from example 18.4

  class ColumnKeeper implements ActionListener
  {
    protected TableColumn m_column;
    protected ColumnData  m_colData;
    public ColumnKeeper(TableColumn column, ColumnData  colData) {
      m_column = column;
      m_colData = colData;
    }

    public void actionPerformed(ActionEvent e) {
      JCheckBoxMenuItem item = (JCheckBoxMenuItem)e.getSource();
      TableColumnModel model = m_table.getColumnModel();
      if (item.isSelected()) {
        model.addColumn(m_column);
      }
      else {
        model.removeColumn(m_column);
      }
      m_table.tableChanged(new TableModelEvent(m_data));
      m_table.repaint();
    }
  }

  public static void main(String argv[]) {
    new StocksTable();
  }
}

// Unchanged code from example 18.4

class StockTableData extends AbstractTableModel
{
  // Unchanged code from example 18.4

  protected SimpleDateFormat m_frm;
  protected Vector m_vector;
  protected java.util.Date m_date;
```

2 Adds checkbox items to enable/disable specified columns

3 Listens to unchecking and checking column name, which removes or adds that column

```
    protected int m_columnsCount = m_columns.length;
```
4 **Counts number of columns; changes by columnAdded() or columnRemoved() in inner class**

```
    // Unchanged code from example 18.4

    public int getColumnCount() {
      return m_columnsCount;
    }

    // Unchanged code from example 18.4

    class ColumnListener extends MouseAdapter
    {
      // Unchanged code from example 18.3

      public void mouseClicked(MouseEvent e) {
        // Unchanged code from example 18.3

        for (int i=0; i < m_columnsCount; i++) {
          TableColumn column = colModel.getColumn(i);
          column.setHeaderValue(getColumnName(column.getModelIndex()));
        }
        m_table.getTableHeader().repaint();
```
Watches for adding/removing columns, changing the columns count **5**
```
        // Unchanged code from example 18.3
      }
    }

    class ColumnMovementListener implements TableColumnModelListener
    {
      public void columnAdded(TableColumnModelEvent e) {
        m_columnsCount++;
      }

      public void columnRemoved(TableColumnModelEvent e) {
        m_columnsCount--;
      }

      public void columnMarginChanged(ChangeEvent e) {}
      public void columnMoved(TableColumnModelEvent e) {}
      public void columnSelectionChanged(ListSelectionEvent e) {}
    }
    // Unchanged code from example 18.4
}

// Class StockComparator unchanged from example 18.3
```

18.7.1   Understanding the code

Class StocksTable

1 The StocksTable constructor now adds an instance of StockTableData.ColumnMovement-Listener to our table's TableColumnModel to listen for column additions and removals.

2 Our createMenuBar() method now adds several check box menu items to a new View menu—one for each column. Each of these check box menu items recieves a ColumnKeeper instance as an ActionListener.

Class StocksTable.ColumnKeeper

3 This inner class implements the `ActionListener` interface and serves to keep track of when the user removes and adds columns to the table. The constructor receives a `TableColumn` instance and a `ColumnData` object. The `actionPerformed()` method adds this column to the model with the `addColumn()` method if the corresponding menu item is checked, and it removes this column from the model with `removeColumn()` if it is unchecked. To update the table to properly reflect these changes, we call its `tableChanged()` method followed by a `repaint()` request.

Class StockTableData

4 `StockTableData` now contains the instance variable `m_columnsCount` to keep track of the current column count. This variable is decremented and incremented in the `columnRemoved()` and `columnAdded()` methods of the `ColumnMovementListener` inner class. It is also used in the `StockTableData.ColumnListener` class's `mouseClicked()` method, for properly setting header values for the visible columns only.

Class StockTableData.ColumnMovementListener

5 This class implements `TableColumnModelListener` to increment and decrement `StockTableData`'s `m_columnsCount` variable when a column addition or removal occurs, respectively. An instance of this inner class is added to our table's `TableColumnModel` in the `StocksTable` constructor.

18.7.2 Running the code

Figure 18.6 shows the new View menu with an unchecked Change % menu item, and the corresponding column hidden. Reselecting this menu item will place the column back in the table at the end position. Verify that each menu item functions similarly.

18.8 EXPENSE REPORT APPLICATION

In constructing our `StocksTable` application we talked mostly about displaying and retrieving data in `JTable`. In this section we will construct a basic expense report application, and in doing so we will deal with some aspects of table cell editing. We will also see how to implement dynamic addition and removal of table rows.

The data editing process generally follows this scheme:

- Create an instance of the `TableCellEditor` interface. We can use the `DefaultCellEditor` class or implement our own. The `DefaultCellEditor` class takes a GUI component as a parameter to its constructor: `JTextField`, `JCheckBox`, or `JComboBox`. This component will be used for editing.
- If we are developing a custom editor, we need to implement the `getTableCellEditorComponent()` method which will be called each time a cell is about to be edited.
- In our table model, we need to implement the `setValueAt(Object value, int nRow, int nCol)` method which will be called to change a value in the table when an edit ends. This is where we can perform any necessary data processing and validation.

The data model for this example is designed as follows (each row represents a column in our `JTable`):

Name	Type	Description
Date	String	Date of expense.
Amount	Double	Amount of expense.
Category	Integer	Category from predefined list.
Approved	Boolean	Sign of approval for this expense.
Description	String	Brief description.

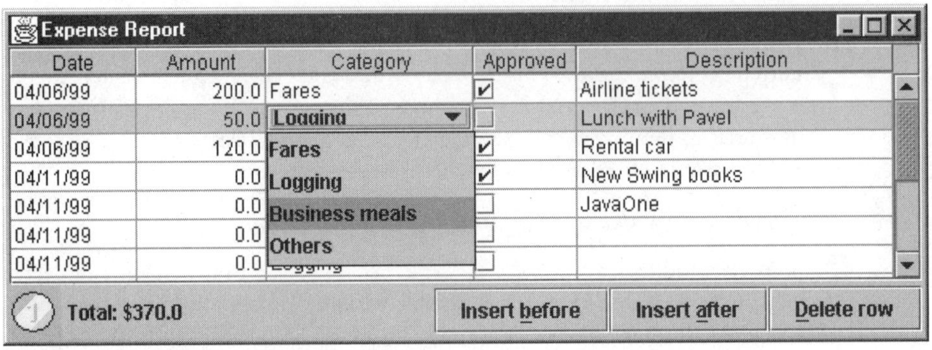

Figure 18.7 An expense report application illustrating custom cell editing, rendering, and row addition/removal

NOTE Since the only math that is done with our Amount values is addition, using `Doubles` is fine. However, in more professional implementations we may need to use rounding techniques or a custom renderer to remove unneccessary fractional amounts.

Example 18.7

ExpenseReport.java

see \Chapter18\7

```java
import java.awt.*;
import java.awt.event.*;
import java.util.*;
import java.io.*;
import java.text.SimpleDateFormat;

import javax.swing.*;
import javax.swing.border.*;
import javax.swing.event.*;
import javax.swing.table.*;

public class ExpenseReport extends JFrame
{
  protected JTable m_table;
  protected ExpenseReportData m_data;
```

```
    protected JLabel m_title;

    public ExpenseReport() {
      super("Expense Report");
      setSize(570, 200);

      m_data = new ExpenseReportData(this);

      m_table = new JTable();
      m_table.setAutoCreateColumnsFromModel(false);
      m_table.setModel(m_data);
      m_table.setSelectionMode(ListSelectionModel.SINGLE_SELECTION);

      for (int k = 0; k < ExpenseReportData.m_columns.length; k++) {
        TableCellRenderer renderer;
        if (k==ExpenseReportData.COL_APPROVED)
          renderer = new CheckCellRenderer();
        else {
          DefaultTableCellRenderer textRenderer =
            new DefaultTableCellRenderer();
          textRenderer.setHorizontalAlignment(
            ExpenseReportData.m_columns[k].m_alignment);
          renderer = textRenderer;
        }

        TableCellEditor editor;

        if (k==ExpenseReportData.COL_CATEGORY)
          editor = new DefaultCellEditor(new JComboBox(
            ExpenseReportData.CATEGORIES));
        else if (k==ExpenseReportData.COL_APPROVED)
          editor = new DefaultCellEditor(new JCheckBox());
        else
          editor = new DefaultCellEditor(new JTextField());

        TableColumn column = new TableColumn(k,
          ExpenseReportData.m_columns[k].m_width,
            renderer, editor);
          m_table.addColumn(column);
      }

      JTableHeader header = m_table.getTableHeader();
      header.setUpdateTableInRealTime(false);

      JScrollPane ps = new JScrollPane();
      ps.setSize(550, 150);
      ps.getViewport().add(m_table);
      getContentPane().add(ps, BorderLayout.CENTER);

      JPanel p = new JPanel();
      p.setLayout(new BoxLayout(p, BoxLayout.X_AXIS));

      ImageIcon penny = new ImageIcon("penny.gif");
      m_title = new JLabel("Total: $",
        penny, JButton.LEFT);
      m_title.setForeground(Color.black);
      m_title.setAlignmentY(0.5f);
```

1 Creates table model and JTable

1 Creates cell renderer for each column

1 Creates cell editor for each column

2 Creates label to show total amount

```
    p.add(m_title);
    p.add(Box.createHorizontalGlue());

    JButton bt = new JButton("Insert before");
    bt.setMnemonic('b');
    bt.setAlignmentY(0.5f);
    ActionListener lst = new ActionListener() {
      public void actionPerformed(ActionEvent e) {
        int row = m_table.getSelectedRow();
        m_data.insert(row);
        m_table.tableChanged(new TableModelEvent(
          m_data, row, row, TableModelEvent.ALL_COLUMNS,
          TableModelEvent.INSERT));
        m_table.setRowSelectionInterval(row+1, row+1);
        m_table.repaint();
      }
    };
    bt.addActionListener(lst);
    p.add(bt);

    bt = new JButton("Insert after");
    bt.setMnemonic('a');
    bt.setAlignmentY(0.5f);
    lst = new ActionListener() {
      public void actionPerformed(ActionEvent e) {
        int row = m_table.getSelectedRow();
        m_data.insert(row+1);
        m_table.tableChanged(new TableModelEvent(
          m_data, row+1, row+1, TableModelEvent.ALL_COLUMNS,
          TableModelEvent.INSERT));
        m_table.setRowSelectionInterval(row, row);
        m_table.repaint();
      }
    };
    bt.addActionListener(lst);
    p.add(bt);

    bt = new JButton("Delete row");
    bt.setMnemonic('d');
    bt.setAlignmentY(0.5f);
    lst = new ActionListener() {
      public void actionPerformed(ActionEvent e) {
        int row = m_table.getSelectedRow();
        if (m_data.delete(row)) {
          m_table.tableChanged(new TableModelEvent(
            m_data, row, row, TableModelEvent.ALL_COLUMNS,
            TableModelEvent.INSERT));
          m_table.clearSelection();
          m_table.repaint();
          calcTotal();
        }
      }
    };
```

2 Creates label to show total amount

3 Creates button to insert new row before currently selected row

3 Creates button to insert new row after currently selected row

3 Creates button to delete currently selected row

```
      bt.addActionListener(lst);
      p.add(bt);

      getContentPane().add(p, BorderLayout.SOUTH);

      calcTotal();

      WindowListener wndCloser = new WindowAdapter() {
        public void windowClosing(WindowEvent e) {
          System.exit(0);
        }
      };
      addWindowListener(wndCloser);

      setVisible(true);
    }

    public void calcTotal() {
      double total = 0;
      for (int k=0; k<m_data.getRowCount(); k++) {
        Double amount = (Double)m_data.getValueAt(k,
          ExpenseReportData.COL_AMOUNT);
        total += amount.doubleValue();
      }
      m_title.setText("Total: $"+total);
    }

    public static void main(String argv[]) {
      new ExpenseReport();
    }
  }

class CheckCellRenderer extends JCheckBox implements TableCellRenderer
{
  protected static Border m_noFocusBorder;

  public CheckCellRenderer() {
    super();
    m_noFocusBorder = new EmptyBorder(1, 2, 1, 2);
    setOpaque(true);
    setBorder(m_noFocusBorder);
  }

  public Component getTableCellRendererComponent(JTable table,
   Object value, boolean isSelected, boolean hasFocus,
   int row, int column)
  {
    if (value instanceof Boolean) {
      Boolean b = (Boolean)value;
      setSelected(b.booleanValue());
    }

    setBackground(isSelected && !hasFocus ?
      table.getSelectionBackground() : table.getBackground());
    setForeground(isSelected && !hasFocus ?
      table.getSelectionForeground() : table.getForeground());

    setFont(table.getFont());
    setBorder(hasFocus ? UIManager.getBorder(
```

④ Adds up expense data for each row and sets total on label

⑤ Cell renderer to display a check box

⑥ Sets state, font, and colors of component before returning it

```
            "Table.focusCellHighlightBorder") : m_noFocusBorder);
      return this;
    }
  }

class ExpenseData
{
  public Date     m_date;
  public Double   m_amount;
  public Integer m_category;
  public Boolean m_approved;
  public String   m_description;

  public ExpenseData() {
    m_date = new Date();
    m_amount = new Double(0);
    m_category = new Integer(1);
    m_approved = new Boolean(false);
    m_description = "";
  }

  public ExpenseData(Date date, double amount, int category,
   boolean approved, String description)
  {
    m_date = date;
    m_amount = new Double(amount);
    m_category = new Integer(category);
    m_approved = new Boolean(approved);
    m_description = description;
  }
}

class ColumnData
{
  public String   m_title;
  int m_width;
  int m_alignment;

  public ColumnData(String title, int width, int alignment) {
    m_title = title;
    m_width = width;
    m_alignment = alignment;
  }
}

class ExpenseReportData extends AbstractTableModel
{
  public static final ColumnData m_columns[] = {
    new ColumnData( "Date", 80, JLabel.LEFT ),
    new ColumnData( "Amount", 80, JLabel.RIGHT ),
    new ColumnData( "Category", 130, JLabel.LEFT ),
    new ColumnData( "Approved", 80, JLabel.LEFT ),
    new ColumnData( "Description", 180, JLabel.LEFT )
  };

  public static final int COL_DATE = 0;
```

❼ **Data class which holds expense information**

```
public static final int COL_AMOUNT = 1;
public static final int COL_CATEGORY = 2;
public static final int COL_APPROVED = 3;
public static final int COL_DESCR = 4;

public static final String[] CATEGORIES = {
  "Fares", "Logging", "Business meals", "Others"
};

protected ExpenseReport m_parent;
protected SimpleDateFormat m_frm;
protected Vector m_vector;

public ExpenseReportData(ExpenseReport parent) {
  m_parent = parent;
  m_frm = new SimpleDateFormat("MM/dd/yy");
  m_vector = new Vector();
  setDefaultData();
}

public void setDefaultData() {
  m_vector.removeAllElements();
  try {
    m_vector.addElement(new ExpenseData(
    m_frm.parse("04/06/99"), 200, 0, true,
      "Airline tickets"));
    m_vector.addElement(new ExpenseData(
      m_frm.parse("04/06/99"), 50,  2, false,
      "Lunch with client"));
    m_vector.addElement(new ExpenseData(
      m_frm.parse("04/06/99"), 120, 1, true,
      "Hotel"));
  }
  catch (java.text.ParseException ex) {}
}

public int getRowCount() {
  return m_vector==null ? 0 : m_vector.size();
}

public int getColumnCount() {
  return m_columns.length;
}

public String getColumnName(int column) {
  return m_columns[column].m_title;
}

public boolean isCellEditable(int nRow, int nCol) {
  return true;
}

public Object getValueAt(int nRow, int nCol) {
  if (nRow < 0 || nRow>=getRowCount())
    return "";
  ExpenseData row = (ExpenseData)m_vector.elementAt(nRow);
  switch (nCol) {
    case COL_DATE: return m_frm.format(row.m_date);
```

```
        case COL_AMOUNT: return row.m_amount;
        case COL_CATEGORY: return CATEGORIES[row.m_category.intValue()];
        case COL_APPROVED: return row.m_approved;
        case COL_DESCR: return row.m_description;
      }
    return "";
  }

  public void setValueAt(Object value, int nRow, int nCol) {
    if (nRow < 0 || nRow>=getRowCount())
      return;
    ExpenseData row = (ExpenseData)m_vector.elementAt(nRow);
    String svalue = value.toString();

    switch (nCol) {
      case COL_DATE:
        Date  date = null;
        try {
          date = m_frm.parse(svalue);
        }
        catch (java.text.ParseException ex) {
          date = null;
        }
        if (date == null) {
          JOptionPane.showMessageDialog(null,
            svalue+" is not a valid date",
            "Warning", JOptionPane.WARNING_MESSAGE);
          return;
        }
        row.m_date = date;
        break;
      case COL_AMOUNT:
        try {
          row.m_amount = new Double(svalue);
        }
        catch (NumberFormatException e) { break; }
        m_parent.calcTotal();
        break;
      case COL_CATEGORY:
        for (int k=0; k<CATEGORIES.length; k++)
          if (svalue.equals(CATEGORIES[k])) {
            row.m_category = new Integer(k);
            break;
          }
        break;
      case COL_APPROVED:
        row.m_approved = (Boolean)value;
        break;
      case COL_DESCR:
        row.m_description = svalue;
        break;
    }
  }
}
```

❽ Interprets the value to copy differently depending on the column number

```
public void insert(int row) {
  if (row < 0)
    row = 0;
  if (row > m_vector.size())
    row = m_vector.size();
  m_vector.insertElementAt(new ExpenseData(), row);
}
public boolean delete(int row) {
  if (row < 0 || row >= m_vector.size())
    return false;
  m_vector.remove(row);
    return true;
}
}
```

18.8.1 Understanding the code

Class ExpenseReport

The ExpenseReport class extends JFrame and defines three instance variables:

- JTable m_table: The table to edit data.
- ExpenseReportData m_data: The data model for this table.
- JLabel m_total: The label to dynamically display the total amount of expenses.

1 The ExpenseReport constructor first instantiates our table model, m_data, and then it instantiates our table, m_table. The selection mode is set to single selection and we iterate through the number of columns creating cell renderers and editors based on each specific column. The Approved column uses an instance of our custom CheckCellRenderer class as a renderer. All other columns use a DefaultTableCellRenderer. All columns also use a Default-CellEditor. However, the component used for editing varies: the Category column uses a JComboBox, the Approved column uses a JCheckBox, and all other columns use a JText-Field. These components are passed to the DefaultTableCellRenderer constructor.

2 Several components are added to the bottom of our frame: JLabel m_total, which is used to display the total amount of expenses; and three JButtons which are used to manipulate table rows. (Notice that the horizontal glue component added between the label and the button pushes buttons to the right side of the panel, so they remain glued to the right when our frame is resized.)

3 These three buttons, titled Insert before, Insert after, and Delete row, behave as their titles imply. The first two use the insert() method from the ExpenseReportData model to insert a new row before or after the currently selected row. The last one deletes the currently selected row by calling the delete() method. In all cases the modified table is updated and repainted.

4 The calcTotal() method calculates the total amount of expenses in column COL_AMOUNT using our table's data model, m_data.

Class CheckCellRenderer

5 Since we use check boxes to edit our table's Approved column, to be consistent we also need to use check boxes for that column's cell renderer (recall that cell renderers just act as rubber stamps and are not at all interactive). The only GUI component which can be used in the existing `DefaultTableCellRenderer` is `JLabel`, so we have to provide our own implementation of the `TableCellRenderer` interface. This class, `CheckCellRenderer`, uses `JCheckBox` as a superclass. Its constructor sets the border to indicate whether the component has the focus, and it sets its opaque property to `true` to indicate that the component's background will be filled with the background color.

6 The only method which must be implemented in the `TableCellRenderer` interface is `get-TableCellRendererComponent()`. This method will be called each time the cell is about to be rendered to deliver new data to the renderer. It takes six parameters:

- `JTable table`: The reference to the table instance.
- `Object value`: The data object to be sent to the renderer.
- `boolean isSelected`: `true` if the cell is currently selected.
- `boolean hasFocus`: `true` if the cell currently has the focus.
- `int row`: The cell's row.
- `int column`: The cell's column.

Our implementation sets whether the `JCheckBox` is checked depending on the `value` passed as `Boolean`. Then it sets the background, foreground, font, and border to ensure that each cell in the table has a similar appearance.

Class ExpenseData

7 The `ExpenseData` class represents a single row in the table. It holds five variables that correspond to our data structure described in the beginning of this section.

Class ColumnData

The `ColumnData` class holds each column's title, width, and header alignment.

Class ExpenseReportData

8 `ExpenseReportData` extends `AbstractTableModel`, and it should look somewhat familiar from previous examples in this chapter (such as `StockTableData`), so we will not discuss this class in complete detail. However, we need to take a closer look at the `setValueAt()` method, which is new for this example (all previous examples did not accept new data). This method is called each time an edit is made to a table cell. First, we determine which `Expense-Data` instance (table's row) is affected, and if it is invalid we simply return. Otherwise, depending on the column of the changed cell, we define several cases in a `switch` structure to either accept and store a new value, or reject it:

- For the Date column, the input string is parsed using our `SimpleDateFormat` instance. If parsing is successful, a new date is saved as a `Date` object; otherwise, an error message is displayed.
- For the Amount column, the input string is parsed as a `Double` and it is stored in the table if parsing is successful. Also, a new total amount is recalculated and displayed in the Total `JLabel`.
- For the Category column, the input string is placed in the `CATEGORIES` array at the corresponding index and it is stored in the table model.
- For the Approved column, the input object is cast to a `Boolean` and stored in the table model.
- For the Description column, the input string is directly saved in our table model.

Try editing different columns and watch how the corresponding cell editors work. Experiment with adding and removing table rows and notice how the total amount is updated each time the Amount column is updated. Figure 18.7 shows `ExpenseReport` with a combo box opened to change a cell's value.

18.9   *A JAVABEANS PROPERTY EDITOR*

Now that we're familiar with the table API we can complete the JavaBeans container introduced in chapter 4 and give it the capability to edit the properties of JavaBeans. This dramatically increases the possible uses of our simple container and makes it quite a powerful tool for studying JavaBeans.

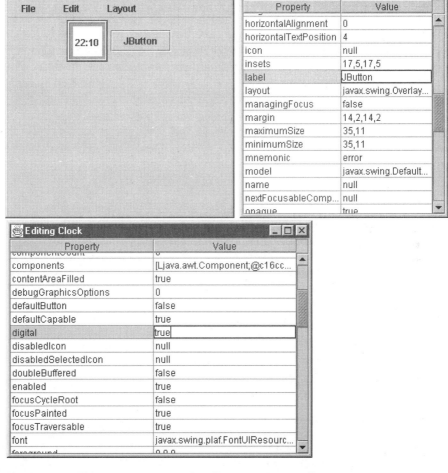

Figure 18.8   The `BeanContainer` **JavaBeans property editor using** `JTable`**s as editing forms**

Example 18.8

BeanContainer.java

see \Chapter18\8

```java
import java.awt.*;
import java.awt.event.*;
import java.io.*;
import java.beans.*;
import java.lang.reflect.*;
import java.util.*;

import javax.swing.*;
import javax.swing.table.*;
import javax.swing.event.*;

import dl.*;

public class BeanContainer extends JFrame implements FocusListener
{
  protected Hashtable m_editors = new Hashtable();

  // Unchanged code from example 4.8

  protected JMenuBar createMenuBar() {
    // Unchanged code from example 4.8

    JMenu mEdit = new JMenu("Edit");
    mItem = new JMenuItem("Delete");
    lst = new ActionListener() {
      public void actionPerformed(ActionEvent e) {
        if (m_activeBean == null)
          return;
        Object obj = m_editors.get(m_activeBean);
        if (obj != null) {
          BeanEditor editor = (BeanEditor)obj;
          editor.dispose();
          m_editors.remove(m_activeBean);
        }
        getContentPane().remove(m_activeBean);
        m_activeBean = null;
        validate();
        repaint();
      }
    };
    mItem.addActionListener(lst);
    mEdit.add(mItem);

    mItem = new JMenuItem("Properties...");
    lst = new ActionListener() {
      public void actionPerformed(ActionEvent e) {
        if (m_activeBean == null)
          return;
        Object obj = m_editors.get(m_activeBean);
```

1 Hashtable storing editors for Beans

3 Deleting active bean also removes an existing BeanEditor

2 Menu item to create or reactivate a BeanEditor

```
          if (obj != null) {
            BeanEditor editor = (BeanEditor)obj;
            editor.setVisible(true);
            editor.toFront();
          }
          else {
            BeanEditor editor = new BeanEditor(m_activeBean);
            m_editors.put(m_activeBean, editor);
          }
        }
      };
      mItem.addActionListener(lst);
      mEdit.add(mItem);
      menuBar.add(mEdit);

      // Unchanged code from example 4.8

      return menuBar;
    }

    // Unchanged code from example 4.8
}

class BeanEditor extends JFrame implements PropertyChangeListener
{
    protected Component m_bean;
    protected JTable m_table;
    protected PropertyTableData m_data;

    public BeanEditor(Component bean) {
      m_bean = bean;
      m_bean.addPropertyChangeListener(this);

      Point pt = m_bean.getLocationOnScreen();
      setBounds(pt.x+50, pt.y+10, 400, 300);
      getContentPane().setLayout(new BorderLayout());

      m_data = new PropertyTableData(m_bean);
      m_table = new JTable(m_data);

      JScrollPane ps = new JScrollPane();
      ps.getViewport().add(m_table);
      getContentPane().add(ps, BorderLayout.CENTER);

      setDefaultCloseOperation(HIDE_ON_CLOSE);
      setVisible(true);
    }

    public void propertyChange(PropertyChangeEvent evt) {
      m_data.setProperty(evt.getPropertyName(), evt.getNewValue());
    }

    class PropertyTableData extends AbstractTableModel
    {
      protected String[][] m_properties;
      protected int m_numProps = 0;
      protected Vector m_v;
```

2 Menu item to create or reactivate a BeanEditor

5 Listens for property change events on the Bean

4 Positions frame slightly offset from Bean

6 Table model with one row for each property/value pair from the Bean

```java
public PropertyTableData(Component bean) {
  try {
    BeanInfo info = Introspector.getBeanInfo(
      m_bean.getClass());
    BeanDescriptor descr = info.getBeanDescriptor();
    setTitle("Editing "+descr.getName());
    PropertyDescriptor[] props = info.getPropertyDescriptors();
    m_numProps = props.length;

    m_v = new Vector(m_numProps);
    for (int k=0; k<m_numProps; k++) {
      String name = props[k].getDisplayName();
      boolean added = false;
      for (int i=0; i<m_v.size(); i++) {
        String str = ((PropertyDescriptor)m_v.elementAt(i)).
          getDisplayName();
        if (name.compareToIgnoreCase(str) < 0) {
          m_v.insertElementAt(props[k], i);
          added = true;
          break;
        }
      }
      if (!added)
        m_v.addElement(props[k]);
    }

    m_properties = new String[m_numProps][2];
    for (int k=0; k<m_numProps; k++) {
      PropertyDescriptor prop =
        (PropertyDescriptor)m_v.elementAt(k);
      m_properties[k][0] = prop.getDisplayName();
      Method mRead = prop.getReadMethod();
      if (mRead != null &&
       mRead.getParameterTypes().length == 0) {
        Object value = mRead.invoke(m_bean, null);
        m_properties[k][1] = objToString(value);
      }
      else
        m_properties[k][1] = "error";
    }
  }
  catch (Exception ex) {
    ex.printStackTrace();
    JOptionPane.showMessageDialog(
      BeanEditor.this, "Error: "+ex.toString(),
      "Warning", JOptionPane.WARNING_MESSAGE);
  }
}

public void setProperty(String name, Object value) {
  for (int k=0; k<m_numProps; k++)
    if (name.equals(m_properties[k][0])) {
      m_properties[k][1] = objToString(value);
```

7 Gets property descriptors from Bean, using Introspection

8 Sorts by property name

9 Reads property values by indirectly executing the "read" method, using Reflection to get the actual method

10 Called from fired events to set a new property value

```
      m_table.tableChanged(new TableModelEvent(this, k));
      m_table.repaint();
      break;
    }
}

public int getRowCount() { return m_numProps; }

public int getColumnCount() { return 2; }

public String getColumnName(int nCol) {
  return nCol==0 ? "Property" : "Value";
}

public boolean isCellEditable(int nRow, int nCol) {
    return (nCol==1);
}

public Object getValueAt(int nRow, int nCol) {
  if (nRow < 0 || nRow>=getRowCount())
    return "";
  switch (nCol) {
    case 0: return m_properties[nRow][0];
    case 1: return m_properties[nRow][1];
  }
  return "";
}

public void setValueAt(Object value, int nRow, int nCol) {
  if (nRow < 0 || nRow>=getRowCount())
    return;
  String str = value.toString();
  PropertyDescriptor prop = (PropertyDescriptor)m_v.
    elementAt(nRow);
  Class cls = prop.getPropertyType();
  Object obj = stringToObj(str, cls);
  if (obj==null)
    return;         // Can't process

  Method mWrite = prop.getWriteMethod();
  if (mWrite == null || mWrite.getParameterTypes().length != 1)
    return;
  try {
    mWrite.invoke(m_bean, new Object[]{ obj });
    m_bean.getParent().doLayout();
    m_bean.getParent().repaint();
    m_bean.repaint();
  }
  catch (Exception ex) {
    ex.printStackTrace();
    JOptionPane.showMessageDialog(
      BeanEditor.this, "Error: "+ex.toString(),
      "Warning", JOptionPane.WARNING_MESSAGE);
  }
  m_properties[nRow][1] = str;
}
```

⓫ Can only edit values in the second column

⓬ Writes new property value to Bean, using Reflection to get method to call

```
public String objToString(Object value) {
  if (value==null)
    return "null";
  if (value instanceof Dimension) {
    Dimension dim = (Dimension)value;
    return ""+dim.width+","+dim.height;
  }
  else if (value instanceof Insets) {
    Insets ins = (Insets)value;
    return ""+ins.left+","+ins.top+","+ins.right+","+ins.bottom;
  }
  else if (value instanceof Rectangle) {
    Rectangle rc = (Rectangle)value;
    return ""+rc.x+","+rc.y+","+rc.width+","+rc.height;
  }
  else if (value instanceof Color) {
    Color col = (Color)value;
    return ""+col.getRed()+","+col.getGreen()+","+col.getBlue();
  }
  return value.toString();
}

public Object stringToObj(String str, Class cls) {
  try {
    if (str==null)
      return null;
    String name = cls.getName();
    if (name.equals("java.lang.String"))
      return str;
    else if (name.equals("int"))
      return new Integer(str);
    else if (name.equals("long"))
      return new Long(str);
    else if (name.equals("float"))
      return new Float(str);
    else if (name.equals("double"))
      return new Double(str);
    else if (name.equals("boolean"))
      return new Boolean(str);
    else if (name.equals("java.awt.Dimension")) {
      int[] i = strToInts(str);
      return new Dimension(i[0], i[1]);
    }
    else if (name.equals("java.awt.Insets")) {
      int[] i = strToInts(str);
      return new Insets(i[0], i[1], i[2], i[3]);
    }
    else if (name.equals("java.awt.Rectangle")) {
      int[] i = strToInts(str);
      return new Rectangle(i[0], i[1], i[2], i[3]);
    }
    else if (name.equals("java.awt.Color")) {
```

13 Provides specialized "toString" behavior

14 Builds conversion of object to given class

14 These cases expect string in format produced by objToString() method

```
              int[] i = strToInts(str);
              return new Color(i[0], i[1], i[2]);
          }
        return null;      // Not supported
      }
    catch(Exception ex) { return null; }
  }
  public int[] strToInts(String str) throws Exception {
    int[] i = new int[4];
    StringTokenizer tokenizer = new StringTokenizer(str, ",");
    for (int k=0; k<i.length &&
     tokenizer.hasMoreTokens(); k++)
       i[k] = Integer.parseInt(tokenizer.nextToken());
    return i;
  }
 }
}
```

⑭ These cases expect string in format produced by objToString() method

18.9.1   Understanding the code

Class BeanContainer

❶ This class (formerly `BeanContainer` from section 4.7) has received a new collection, `Hashtable` `m_editors`, which has been added as an instance variable. This `Hashtable` holds references to `BeanEditor` frames (used to edit beans, see below) as values, and the corresponding `Components` being edited as keys.

❷ A new menu item entitled Properties... is added to the Edit menu. This item is used to either create a new editor for the selected bean or activate an existing one (if any). The attached `ActionListener` looks for an existing `BeanEditor` that corresponds to the currently selected `m_activeBean` component in the `m_editors` collection. If such an editor is found, it is made visible and brought to the front. Otherwise, a new instance of `BeanEditor` is created to edit the currently active `m_activeBean` component, and it is added to the `m_editors` collection.

❸ The `ActionListener` attached to the Delete menu item, which removes the currently active component, receives additional functionality. The added code looks for an existing `BeanEditor` that corresponds to the currently selected `m_activeBean` component in the `m_editors` collection. If such an editor is found, it is disposed of and its reference is removed from the hashtable.

Class BeanEditor

This class extends `JFrame` and implements the `PropertyChangeListener` interface. `BeanEditor` is used to display and edit the properties exposed by a given JavaBean. Three instance variables are declared:

- `Component m_bean`: The JavaBean component to be edited.
- `JTable m_table`: The table component to display a bean's properties.
- `PropertyTableData m_data`: The table model for `m_table`.

❹ The `BeanEditor` constructor takes a reference to the JavaBean component to be edited and stores it in instance variable `m_bean`. The initial location of the editor frame is selected depending on the location of the component being edited.

The table component, `m_table`, is created and added to a `JScrollPane` to provide scrolling capabilities. We do not add a `WindowListener` to this frame. Instead we use the `HIDE_ON_CLOSE` default close operation (see chapter 3):

```
setDefaultCloseOperation(HIDE_ON_CLOSE);
setVisible(true);
```

Upon closing, this frame will be hidden but not disposed of. Its reference will still be present in the `m_editors` collection, and this frame will be reactivated if the user chooses to see the properties of the associated bean again.

5 Note that an instance of the `BeanEditor` class is added as a `PropertyChangeListener` to the corresponding bean being edited. The `propertyChange()` method is invoked if the bean has changed its state during editing and a `PropertyChangeEvent` has been fired. This method simply triggers a call to the `setProperty()` method of the table model.

Class BeanEditor.PropertyTableData

6 `PropertyTableData` extends `AbstractTableModel` and provides the table model for each bean editor. Three instance variables are declared:

- `String[][] m_properties`: An array of data displayed in the table.
- `int m_numProps`: The number of bean properties (this corresponds to the number of rows in the table).
- `Vector m_v`: A collection of `PropertyDescriptor` objects sorted in alphabetical order.

7 The constructor of the `PropertyTableData` class takes a given bean instance and retrieves its properties. It first uses the `Introspector.getBeanInfo()` method to get a `BeanInfo` instance:

```
BeanInfo info = Introspector.getBeanInfo(
    m_bean.getClass());
BeanDescriptor descr = info.getBeanDescriptor();
setTitle("Editing "+descr.getName());
PropertyDescriptor[] props = info.getPropertyDescriptors();
m_numProps = props.length;
```

8 This provides us with all the available information about a bean (see chapter 2). We determine the bean's name and use it as the editor frame's title (note that this is an inner class, so `setTitle()` refers to the parent `BeanEditor` instance). We then extract an array of `Property-Descriptor`s which will provide us with the actual information about a bean's properties.

Bean properties are sorted by name in alphabetical order. The name of each property is determined by the `getDisplayName()` method. The sorted `PropertyDescriptor`s are stored in our `m_v Vector` collection. Then we can create the two-dimensional array, `m_properties`, **9** which holds data to be displayed in the table. This array has `m_numProps` rows and two columns (for property name and value). To determine a property's value, we need to obtain a reference to its `getXX()` method with `getReadMethod()` and make a call using the reflection API. We can call only `getXX()` methods without parameters (since we don't know anything about these parameters). Note that our `objToString()` helper method is invoked to translate a property's value into a display string (see below).

10 The `setProperty()` method searches for the given name in the 0th column of the `m_proper-ties` array. If such a property is found, this method sets its new value and updates the table component.

⑪ Several other simple methods included in this class have already been presented in previous examples and need not be explained again here. However, note that the isCellEditable() method returns true only for cells in the second column (property names, obviously, cannot be changed).

⑫ The setValueAt() method deserves additional explanation because it not only saves the modified data in the table model, but it also sends these modifications to the bean component itself. To do this we obtain a PropertyDescriptor instance that is stored in the m_v Vector collection. The modified property value is always a String, so we first need to convert it into its proper object type using our stringToObj() helper method (if we can do this; see below). If the conversion succeeds (if the result is not null), we can continue.

To modify a bean value we determine the reference to its setXX() method (which corresponds to a certain property) and invoke it. An anonymous array containing one element is used as a parameter; these constructions are typical when dealing with the reflection API. Then the bean component and its container (which can also be affected by changes in such properties as size and color) are refreshed to reflect the bean's new property value. Finally, if the above procedures were successful, we store the new value in the m_properties data array.

⑬ The objToString() helper method converts a given Object into a String that is suitable for editing. In many cases the toString() method returns a long string starting with the class name. This is not very appropriate for editable data values, so for several classes we provide our own conversion into a string of comma-delimited numbers. For instance, a Dimension object is converted into a "width, height" form, Color is converted into a "red, green, blue" form, and so on. If no special implementation is provided, an object's toString() string is returned.

⑭ The stringToObj() helper method converts a given String into an Object of the given Class. The class's name is analyzed and a conversion method is chosen to build the correct type of object based on this name. The simplest case is the String class: we don't need to do any conversion at all in this case. For the primitive data types such as int or boolean, we return the corresponding encapsulating (wrapper class) objects. For the several classes which receive special treatment in the objToString() method (such as a Dimension or Color object), we parse the comma-delimited string of numbers and construct the proper object. For all other classes (or if a parsing exception occurs) we return null to indicate that we cannot perform the required conversion.

18.9.2 Running the code

Figure 18.8 shows the BeanContainer container and two editing frames displaying the properties of Clock and JButton components. This application provides a simple but powerful tool for investigating Swing and AWT components as well as custom JavaBeans. We can see all the exposed properties and modify many of them. If a component's properties change as a result of user interaction, our component properly notifies its listeners and we see an automatic editor table update. Try serializing a modified component and restoring it from its file. Notice how the previously modified properties are saved as expected.

It is natural to imagine using this example as a base for constructing a custom Swing IDE (Interface Development Environment). BeanContainer, combined with the custom resize edge components developed in chapters 15 and 16, provides a fairly powerful base to work from.

CHAPTER 19

Inside text components

19.1   TEXT PACKAGE OVERVIEW

A truly exhaustive discussion of the text package is beyond the scope of this book. The `html`, `html.parser`, and `rtf` packages were still under construction at the time of this writing. Due to their complexity, as well as the space and time constraints placed on this book, we decided that detailed coverage of these packages would best be left for a future edition. However, in this chapter we hope to provide enough information about text components and their underlying constituents to leave you with a solid understanding of their inner workings. Picking up where chapter 11 left off, we continue our discussion of the most significant aspects of the text package classes and interfaces. This chapter concludes with an example of a custom text field used for several variations of date and time selection. In the next chapter, we'll continue our study of text components with the development of a full-featured word processor application. The examples in chapter 20 demonstrate practical applications of many of the complex topics covered in this chapter.

> **NOTE**   If, after reading this chapter, you want a more thorough treatment of the text package, we recommend *Java Swing*, by Robert Eckstein, Marc Loy, and Dave Wood, O'Reilly & Associates, 1998. This book includes roughly 300 pages of detailed text-related class and interface descriptions. In particular, the discussion of `Views` and `EditorKits` provides indispensable knowledge for any developer working on support for a custom content type.

19.1.1   More about JTextComponent

abstract class javax.swing.text.JTextComponent

Associated with each JTextComponent is a set of Actions which are normally bound to specific KeyStrokes (see section 2.13) and are managed in a hierarchically resolving set of Keymaps (see section 19.1.23). We can retrieve a text component's Actions as an array with the getActions() method and we can retrieve and assign a new Keymap with getKeymap() and setKeymap(), respectively.

All text components share a set of default Actions. Each of these Actions are instances of TextAction by default (see section 19.1.24). JTextComponent provides a private static EditorKit (see section 19.1.25) which consists of a set of four pre-built TextActions shared by all text components through the use of a default Keymap instance (see section 19.1.26).

JTextComponent maintains a private reference to the text component that most recently had the keyboard focus. TextActions are designed to take advantage of this, and each TextAction will operate on this component when it's invoked in the event that the source of the invoking event is not a text component.

Document content is structured hierarchically by Element implementations (see section 19.1.9). Each Element maintains a set of attributes encapsulated in implementations of the AttributeSet interface (see section 19.1.12). Many Elements also contain one or more child Elements. Attributes that apply to one element also apply to all child Elements, but not vice versa. Each Element has an associated start and end Position (see section 19.1.6).

AttributeSets can be applied manually to a region of text. However, it is often more convenient to use Styles (see section 19.1.14). Styles are AttributeSet implementations that we do not instantiate directly. Rather, Styles are created and maintained by instances of StyleContext (see section 19.1.16), and each Style has an associated name that allows easy reference. StyleContext also provides a means for sharing AttributeSets across a document or possibly multiple documents, and it is particularly useful in large documents.

The cursor of a text component is defined by implementations of the Caret interface (see section 19.1.19). We can retrieve the current Caret with getCaret(), and assign a new one with setCaret(). A text component's Caret is instantiated (but not maintained) by its UI delegate. So when the look and feel of a particular text component changes, the Caret in use will also change. JTextComponent supports the addition of CaretListeners that will receive CaretEvents whenever the position of the Caret changes.

Text components also support an arbitrary number of highlights through implementations of the Highlighter interface (see section 19.1.17). Highlighters are most often used to indicate a specific selection. They can also be used for many other things, such as marking new text additions. Highlighter maintains each highlighted region as an implementation of Highlighter.Highlight, and each Highlight can be rendered using a Highlighter.HighlightPainter implementation. As with Carets, a text area's Highlighter is instantiated by its UI delegate. We can assign and retrieve a text component's Highlighter with setHighlighter() and getHighlighter(), respectively.

JTextComponent also maintains a bound focusAccelerator property, as we discussed in chapter 11. This property is a char that is used to transfer focus to a text component when the corresponding key is pressed simultaneously with the ALT key. JTextComponent defines a private Action called focusAction whose actionPerformed() method calls requestFocus(). Initially, focusAction is not attached to the text component (that is, it is turned off). To activate it we use the setFocusAccelerator() method. Sending '\0' to the setFocusAccelerator() method turns it off. Internally, this method searches through all registered KeyStrokes and checks whether any are associated with focusAction, using the getActionForKeyStroke() method. If any are found, they are unregistered using the unregisterKeyboardAction() method of JComponent. Finally, the character passed in is used to construct a KeyStroke to register and associate with focusAction. This action is registered such that it will be invoked whenever the top-level window containing the given text component has the focus:

```java
// From JTextComponent.java
registerKeyboardAction(
  focusAction,KeyStroke.getKeyStroke(aKey,ActionEvent.ALT_MASK),
  JComponent.WHEN_IN_FOCUSED_WINDOW);
```

Each text component uses a subclass of BasicTextUI as its UI delegate. As we mentioned earlier, each text component also has an EditorKit for storing Actions. This EditorKit is referenced by the UI delegate. JTextField and JTextArea have default editor kits assigned by the UI delegate, whereas JEditorPane and JTextPane maintain their own editor kits independent of their UI delegate.

Unlike most Swing components, a text component's UI delegate does not directly define how that text component is rendered and laid out. Rather, it implements the ViewFactory interface (see section 19.1.29) which requires the implementation of one method: create(Element e). This method returns a View instance (see section 19.1.28) which is responsible for rendering the given Element. Each Element has an associated View that is used to render it. Many different views are provided in the text package, and we will rarely need to implement our own (although this is certainly possible). JTextArea, JTextField, and JPasswordField have specific Views returned by their UI delegate's create() method. JEditorPane and JTextPane Views are created by the current EditorKit.

We can retrieve a Point location in the coordinate system of a text component corresponding to a character offset with JTextComponent's viewToModel() method. Similarly, we can retrieve a Rectangle instance that describes the size and location of the View which is responsible for rendering an Element occupying a given character offset with modelToView().

JTextComponent's margin property specifies the space to use between its border and its document content. Standard clipboard operations can be programmatically performed with the cut(), copy(), and paste() methods.

19.1.2   The Document interface

abstract interface javax.swing.text.Document

In MVC terms, the model of a text component contains the text itself, and the Document interface describes this model. A hierarchical set of Elements (see section 19.1.9) define the structure of a Document. Each Document contains one or more root Elements, potentially allowing more than one way of structuring the same content. Most documents only have one structure, and hence one root element. This element can be accessed with getDefault-RootElement(). All root elements, including the default root element, are accessible with getRootElements(), which returns an Element array.

NOTE   We will not discuss the details of maintaining multiple structures, as this is very rarely desired. See the API documentation for examples of situations in which multiple structures might be useful.

`Documents` maintain two `Positions` which keep track of the beginning and end positions of the content. These can be accessed with `getStartPosition()` and `getEndPosition()`, respectively. `Documents` also maintain a `length` property, which is accessible with `getLength()`, that maintains the number of contained characters.

The `Document` interface declares methods for adding and removing `DocumentListeners` (see section 19.1.8), for notification of any content changes, and for `UndoableEditListeners` (allowing easy access to built-in undo/redo support; refer to chapter 11 for an example of adding undo/redo support to a text area).

Methods for retrieving, inserting, and removing content are also declared: `getText()`, `insertString()`, and `remove()`. Each of these throws a `BadLocationException` if an illegal (nonexistent) location in the document is specified. The `insertString()` method requires an `AttributeSet` instance that describes the attributes to apply to the given text (`null` can be used for this parameter). Plain text components will not pay any attention to this attribute set. Text components using a `StyledDocument` instance most likely will pay attention to these attributes.

The `createPosition()` method inserts a `Position` instance at a given index, and the `putProperty()` and `getProperty()` methods insert and retrieve various properties that are stored in an internal collection.

The `render()` method is unique. It takes a `Runnable` as a parameter, and it ensures thread safety by not allowing document content to change while that `Runnable` is running. This method is used by each text component's UI delegate during painting.

19.1.3   The StyledDocument interface

abstract interface javax.swing.StyledDocument

This interface extends the `Document` interface to add functionality for working with `Styles` and other `AttributeSets`. Implementations are expected to maintain a collection of `Style` implementations. This interface also declares the notion of character and paragraph attributes, and logical styles. What these mean is specific to each `StyledDocument` implementation (we will discuss these more when we talk about `DefaultStyledDocument` in section 19.1.11).

The `setCharacterAttributes()` method assigns a given set of attributes to a given range of document content. A `boolean` parameter is also required; it specifies whether preexisting attributes of the affected content should be overwritten (`true`) or merged (`false`— only new attributes are assigned). The `setParagraphAttributes()` method works the same way as `setCharacterAttributes()`, but it applies to the number of paragraphs spanned by a given range of content. The `getFont()`, `getBackground()`, and `getForeground()` methods take an `AttributeSet` parameter, and they are used for convenient access to the corresponding attribute in the given set (if it exists).

`StyledDocuments` are meant to allow `Styles` to be added, removed, and retrieved from an internal collection of `Styles`. The `addStyle()` method takes a `String` and a parent `Style` as parameters and returns a new `Style` with the given name and given `Style` as its resolving parent. The `getLogicalStyle()` method returns a `Style` that corresponds to the paragraph containing the given character offset. The `setLogicalStyle()` method assigns a `Style` to the paragraph that contains the given character offset. The `getStyle()` and `removeStyle()` methods retrieve and remove a `Style` with the given name, respectively, in the internal collection.

The `getCharacterElement()` and `getParagraphElement()` methods allow the retrieval of `Element`s that correspond to a given character offset. The definition of these methods will vary based on the definition of paragraph and character `Element`s in a `StyledDocument` implementation. Typically, a character `Element` represents a range of text containing a given offset, and a paragraph `Element` represents a paragraph containing the given offset.

19.1.4 AbstractDocument

abstract class javax.swing.text.AbstractDocument

`AbstractDocument` implements the `Document` interface and provides a base implementation for text component models. Two provided classes that extend `AbstractDocument` are used by the Swing text components as their default model: `PlainDocument` and `Default-StyledDocument`. `PlainDocument` is used by all the plain text components, such as `JText-Area`, `JTextField`, and its subclass, `JPasswordField`. It provides support for character data content only and does not support markup (such as multiple fonts and colors) of this content. `DefaultStyledDocument` is used by more sophisticated text components such as `JEditorPane` and its subclass, `JTextPane`. It provides support for text markup by implementing the `StyledDocument` interface.

`AbstractDocument` specifies a mechanism that separates character data storage from the structuring of that data. Thus, we have the capability to store our text however we like without concern for how the document is structured and marked up. Similarly, we can structure a document with little concern for how its data is stored. The significance of this structure-storage separation will make more sense after we have discussed `Element`s and attributes below. Character data is stored in an instance of the inner `Content` interface which we will also discuss below.

This class defines the functionality for a basic read/write locking scheme. This scheme enforces the rule that no write can occur while a read is occurring. However, multiple reads can occur simultaneously. To obtain a read lock, we use the `render()` method, which releases the read lock when it finishes executing the `Runnable` passed to it. No other access methods acquire such a lock (making them not thread-safe). The `getText()` method, for example, does not acquire a read lock. In a multithreaded environment, any text retrieved with this method may be corrupted if a write occurred at the time the text was retrieved.

The read lock is basically just an increment in an internal variable that keeps track of the number of readers. The `readLock()` method does this for us, and it will force the current thread to wait until no write locks exist. When the `Runnable` finishes executing, the internal reader-count variable is decremented—this is done by the `readUnlock()` method. Both of these methods will simply do nothing and return if the current thread is the writer thread. A `StateInvariantError` exception will be thrown if a read unlock is requested when there are no readers.

The write lock is a reference to the writing thread. The `writeLock()` and `writeUn-lock()` methods take care of this for us. Whenever a modification is requested, the write lock must first be obtained. If the writer thread is not `null`, and it is not the same as the invoking thread, `writeLock()` blocks the current thread until the current writer releases the lock by calling `writeUnlock()`.

If we intend to use the protected reader- and writer-locking methods ourselves in a subclass, we should make sure that a `readUnlock()` call will be made no matter what happens in the try block, using the following semantics:

```
// From AbstractDocument.java
try {
  readLock();
// Do something
} finally {
  readUnlock();
}
```

All methods that modify document content must obtain a write lock before any modification can take place. These methods include `insertString()` and `remove()`.

`AbstractDocument`'s `dump()` method prints the document's `Element` hierarchy to the given `PrintStream` for debugging purposes. For example, the following class will dump a `JTextArea`'s `Element` hierarchy to standard output.

```java
import java.awt.*;
import java.awt.event.*;
import javax.swing.*;
import javax.swing.text.*;

public class DumpDemo extends JFrame
{
  JTextArea m_editor;

  public DumpDemo() {
    m_editor = new JTextArea();

    JScrollPane js1 = new JScrollPane(m_editor);
    getContentPane().add(js1, BorderLayout.CENTER);

    JButton dumpButton = new JButton("Dump");
    dumpButton.addActionListener(new ActionListener() {
      public void actionPerformed(ActionEvent e) {
        ((PlainDocument) m_editor.getDocument()).dump(System.out);
      }
    });

    JPanel buttonPanel = new JPanel();
    buttonPanel.add(dumpButton);

    getContentPane().add(buttonPanel, BorderLayout.SOUTH);

    setSize(300,300);
    setVisible(true);
  }

  public static void main(String[] args) {
    new DumpDemo();
  }
}
```

Typing this text in the `JTextArea`:

```
Swing is
powerful!!
```

produces the following output when the `dump()` method is invoked (this will make more sense after we discuss `Element`s in section 19.1.9).

```
<paragraph>
  <content>
    [0,9][Swing is
]
  <content>
    [9,20][powerful!!
]
  <content>
    [20,21][
]
<bidi root>
  <bidi level
    bidiLevel=0
  >
    [0,21][Swing is
powerful!!
]
```

`AbstractDocument` also includes several significant inner classes and interfaces. We will discuss most of them in this chapter. A brief overview is appropriate here:

- abstract class `AbstractDocument.AbstractElement`: Implements the `Element` and `MutableAttributeSet` interfaces, allowing instances to act both as `Element`s and the mutable `AttributeSet`s that describe them. This class also implements the `TreeNode` interface, providing an easy means of displaying document structure with a `JTree`.
- class `AbstractDocument.BranchElement`: A concrete subclass of `AbstractDocument.AbstractElement` that represents an `Element` which can contain multiple child `Element`s (see section 19.1.9).
- class `AbstractDocument.LeafElement`: A concrete subclass of `AbstractDocument.AbstractElement` that represents an `Element` which cannot contain child `Element`s (see section 19.1.9).
- static abstract interface `AbstractDocument.Content`: Defines the data storage mechanism used by `AbstractDocument` subclasses (see section 19.1.9).
- static abstract interface `AbstractDocument.AttributeContext`: Used for efficient `AttributeSet` management (see section 19.1.16).
- static class `AbstractDocument.ElementEdit`: Extends `AbstractUndoableEdit`, implements `DocumentEvent.ElementChange` (see section 19.1.7), and allows document changes to be undone and redone.
- class `AbstractDocument.DefaultDocumentEvent`: Extends `CompoundEdit` and implements `DocumentEvent` (see section 19.1.7). Instances of this class are used by documents to create `UndoableEdit`s, which can be used to create `UndoableEditEvent`s for dispatching to `UndoableEditListener`s. Instances of this class are also fired to any registered `DocumentListener`s (see section 19.1.8) for change notification.

19.1.5   The Content interface

abstract static interface javax.swing.text.AbstractDocument.Content

In order to implement a data storage mechanism for text, AbstractDocument provides the static Content interface. Every Document character storage mechanism must implement this interface. (Images and other embedded objects are not considered to be part of a document's content.) Each Content instance represents a sequence of character data, and each provides the ability to insert, remove, and retrieve character data with the insertString(), remove(), getString(), and getChars() methods.

NOTE   A special convenience class called Segment allows users to access fragments of actual document text without having to copy characters into a new array for processing. This class is used internally by text components to speed up searching and rendering large documents.

Implementations of Content must also provide the ability to create position markers that keep track of a certain location between characters in storage with the createPosition() method. These markers are implementations of the Position interface.

Content implementations provide UndoableEdit objects that represent the state of storage before and after any change is made. The insertString() and remove() methods are meant to return such an object each time they are invoked, allowing insertions and removals to be undone and redone.

Two Content implementations are included in the javax.swing.text package: String-Content and GapContent. StringContent stores character data in a normal char array. GapContent also stores data in a char array but it purposefully leaves an empty space, a gap, in this array. According to the API documentation, "The gap is moved to the location of changes to take advantage of common behavior where most changes are in the same location. Changes that occur at a gap boundary are generally cheap and moving the gap is generally cheaper than moving the array contents directly to accommodate the change." This gap is strictly used for internal efficiency purposes and is not accessible outside of this class.

NOTE   StringContent was used in earlier implementations of PlainDocument and DefaultStyledDocument, but it has been replaced by GapContent, which extends a package private class called GapVector. The gap buffer algorithm used in Gap-Content is very efficient for keeping track of large numbers of Positions and, interestingly, it is used in the popular emacs editor.

19.1.6   The Position interface

abstract interface javax.swing.text.Position

This interface consists of one method, getOffset(), which returns an int value representing the location, or *offset*, from the beginning of the document's content. Figure 19.1 illustrates what happens to a Position marker when text is inserted and removed from storage. This figure starts by showing a document containing "Swing text" as its content. There are initially Position markers at offsets 0, 4, and 7. When we remove the characters from offset 4 through 9, the Position at offset 7 is moved to offset 4. At this point there are two Positions at offset 4 and the document content is "Swin." When we insert "g is" at offset 4, both Positions at offset 4 are moved to offset 8 and the document content becomes "Swing is."

NOTE The term *range* refers to a sequence of characters between two Position markers as shown in figure 19.1.

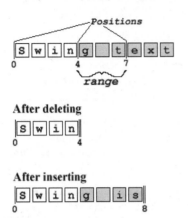

After deleting

After inserting

Figure 19.1 Position **movement**

19.1.7 The DocumentEvent interface

abstract interface javax.swing.event.DocumentEvent

Changes to a Document's content are encapsulated in implementations of the Document-Event interface, the default implementation of which is AbstractDocument.Default-DocumentEvent. Three types of changes can be made to document content: CHANGE, INSERT, and REMOVE (these fields are defined within the DocumentEvent.EventType inner class). DocumentEvent also defines an interface within it called ElementChange. Implementations of this interface, the default of which is AbstractDocument.ElementEdit, are responsible for storing information about changes to the structure of a document for use in undo and redo operations, among other things. AbstractDocument handles the firing of DefaultDocumentEvents appropriately with its fireXXUpdate() methods.

The getChange() method takes an Element instance as a parameter and returns an instance of DocumentEvent.ElementChange describing the elements that were added and/or removed, as well as the location of a change. The getDocument() method returns a reference to the Document instance that generated this event. The getLength() method returns the length of a change, and the getOffset() method returns the offset at which a change began. The getType() method returns an instance of Document.EventType specifying the type of change that occurred to the document.

19.1.8 The DocumentListener interface

abstract interface javax.swing.event.DocumentListener

Instances of this interface can be attached to Documents and each Document will notify its attached DocumentListeners whenever a change occurs to its content. It is important to note that this notification will always occur *after* any content has been updated. Knowing this, it is even more important to realize that we should not perform any changes to the content of a document from within a DocumentListener. This can potentially result in an infinite loop in situations where a document event causes another to be fired.

The insertUpdate() and removeUpdate() methods give notification of content insertions and removals. The changedUpdate() method provides notification of attribute changes.

19.1.9   The Element interface

abstract interface javax.swing.text.Element

Elements provide a hierarchical means of structuring a Document's content. Associated with each Element is a set of attributes encapsulated in an AttributeSet implementation. These attributes provide a way to specify the markup of content associated with each Element. AttributeSets most often take the form of Style implementations and they are grouped together inside a StyleContext object. StyleContext objects are used by StyledDocument implementations such as DefaultStyledDocument. The objects that are responsible for actually rendering text components are implementations of the abstract View class. Each Element has a separate View object associated with it, and each View recognizes a predefined set of attributes used in the actual rendering and layout of that Element.

NOTE   Elements are objects that impose structure on a text component's content. They are actually part of the document model, but they are also used by views for text component rendering.

The getAttributes() method retrieves an AttributeSet collection of attributes describing an Element. The getElement() method fetches a child Element at the given index, where the index is given in terms of the number of child Elements. The getElement-Count() method returns the index of the Element closest to the provided document content offset. The getElementCount() method returns the number of child Elements an Element contains (it returns 0 if the parent Element is itself a leaf). The isLeaf() method tells us whether an Element is a leaf element, and getParentElement() returns an Element's parent Element.

The getDocument() method retrieves the Document instance an Element belongs to. The getStartOffset() and getEndOffset() methods return the offset of the beginning and end of an Element, respectively, from the beginning of the document. The getName() method returns a short String description of an Element.

AbstractDocument defines the inner class AbstractElement, which implements the Element interface. As we mentioned earlier, two subclasses of AbstractElement are defined within AbstractDocument: LeafElement and BranchElement. Each LeafElement has a specific *range* of content text associated with it (this range can change when content is inserted, removed, or replaced—figures 19.2 and 19.3 illustrate). LeafElements cannot have any child Elements. BranchElements can have any number of child Elements. The range of content text associated with BranchElements is the union of all content text associated with their child LeafElements. (Thus the start offset of a BranchElement is the lowest start offset of all its child LeafElements, and its end offset is the highest end offset of all its child LeafElements.) DefaultStyledDocument provides a third type of element called SectionElement which extends BranchElement.

The text package also includes an ElementIterator class, which traverses an Element hierarchy in a depth-first fashion (meaning postorder; see section 17.1.2). The first(), current(), depth(), next(), and previous() methods can be used to obtain information about, and programmatically traverse, an Element hierarchy. We can construct an Element-Iterator object by providing either a Document or an Element to the ElementIterator constructor. If a Document is provided, the default root Element of that document is used as the root of the Element hierarchy traversed by ElementIterator.

NOTE   ElementIterator does not provide any thread safety by default, so it is our responsibility to make sure that no Element changes occur during traversal.

19.1.10   PlainDocument

class javax.swing.text.PlainDocument

This class extends AbstractDocument and it is used by the basic text components JText-Field, JPasswordField, and JTextArea. When we are enforcing certain input, usually in a JTextField, we normally override AbstractDocument's insertString() method in a PlainDocument subclass (see the discussion of JTextField in chapter 11 for an example).

PlainDocument uses a BranchElement as its root and has only LeafElements as children. In this case, each LeafElement represents a line of text and the root BranchElement represents the whole document text. PlainDocument identifies a BranchElement as "paragraph" and a LeafElement as "content." The notion of a paragraph in PlainDocument is much different than our normal notion of a paragraph. We usually think of paragraphs as sections of text separated by line breaks. However, PlainDocument considers each section of text ending with a line break as a line of "content" in its never-ending "paragraph." Figures 19.2 and 19.3 show the structure of a sample PlainDocument, and they illustrate how Elements and their associated Positions can change when document content changes.

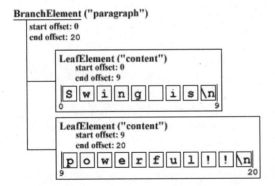

Figure 19.2   A sample PlainDocument structure

Figure 19.2 shows a PlainDocument that contains three elements. Two LeafElements represent two lines of text and are children of the root BranchElement. The root element begins at offset 0, the start offset of the first LeafElement, and it ends at 19, the end offset of the last LeafElement. This document would be displayed in a JTextArea as:

```
Swing is
powerful!!
```

NOTE   The line break at the end of the second `LeafElement` is always present at the end of the last `Element` in any `PlainDocument`. It does not represent a line break that was actually inserted into the document and it is not counted when the document length is queried using the `getLength()` method. Thus the length of the document shown in figure 19.2 would be returned as 19.

Now suppose we insert two line breaks at offset 5. Figure 19.3 shows the structure that would result from this addition.

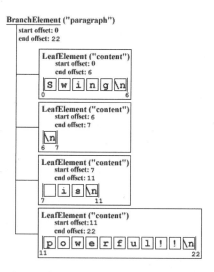

Figure 19.3   A sample `PlainDocument` structure after inserting two line breaks at offset 19

This document would now be displayed in a `JTextArea` as:

```
Swing

 is
powerful!!
```

`JTextArea`, `JTextField`, and `JPasswordField` use `PlainDocument` as their model. Only `JTextArea` allows its document to contain multiple `LeafElements`. `JTextField` and its `JPasswordField` subclass allow only one `LeafElement`.

19.1.11   DefaultStyledDocument

class javax.swing.text.DefaultStyledDocument

`DefaultStyledDocument` provides significantly more power than the `PlainDocument` structure described above. This `StyledDocument` implementation (see section 19.1.3) is used for marked-up (styled) text. `JTextPane` uses an instance of `DefaultStyledDocument` by default, although this instance may change based on `JTextPane`'s content type.

`DefaultStyledDocument` uses an instance of its inner `SectionElement` class as its root `Element`; the root has only instances of `AbstractDocument.BranchElement` as children. These `BranchElements` represent paragraphs, which are referred to as *paragraph* `Elements`, and they contain instances of `AbstractDocument.LeafElement` as children. These

`LeafElement`s represent what are referred to as *character* `Element`s. Character `Element`s represent regions of text (possibly multiple lines within a paragraph) that share the same attributes.

We can retrieve the character `Element` that occupies a given offset with the `getCharacterElement()` method, and we can retrieve the paragraph `Element` that occupies a given offset with the `getParagraphElement()` method.

We will discuss attributes, `AttributeSet`s, and their usage details soon enough. However, it is important to understand here that `AttributeSet`s assigned to `DefaultStyledDocument` `Element`s resolve hierarchically. For instance, a character `Element` will inherit all attributes assigned to itself, as well as those assigned to the parent paragraph `Element`. Character `Element` attributes override those of the same type that are defined in the parent paragraph `Element`'s `AttributeSet`.

NOTE   The `Element`s used by `DefaultStyledDocument` are derived from `AbstractDocument.AbstractElement`, which implements both the `Element` and `MutableAttributeSet` interfaces. This allows these `Element`s to act as their own `AttributeSet`s and use each other as resolving parents.

Figure 19.4 shows a simple `DefaultStyledDocument` in a `JTextPane` with two paragraphs.

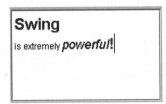

Figure 19.4   A two-paragraph `DefaultStyledDocument`, with several different attributes, in a `JTextPane`

Using `AbstractDocument`'s `dump()` method to display this document's `Element` structure to standard output (see section 19.1.4), we get the following:

```
<section>
  <paragraph
    RightIndent=0.0
    LeftIndent=0.0
    resolver=NamedStyle:default {name=default,nrefs=2}
    FirstLineIndent=0.0
  >
    <content
      underline=false
      bold=true
      foreground=java.awt.Color[r=0,g=128,b=0]
      size=22
      italic=false
      family=SansSerif
    >
      [0,6][Swing
  ]
  <paragraph
    RightIndent=0.0
    LeftIndent=0.0
```

```
        resolver=NamedStyle:default {name=default,nrefs=2}
        FirstLineIndent=0.0
    >
      <content
        underline=false
        bold=false
        foreground=java.awt.Color[r=0,g=0,b=0]
        size=12
        italic=false
        family=SansSerif
      >
        [6,9][is ]
      <content
        underline=false
        bold=false
        foreground=java.awt.Color[r=0,g=0,b=0]
        size=12
        italic=false
        family=SansSerif
      >
        [9,19][extremely ]
      <content
        underline=false
        bold=false
        foreground=java.awt.Color[r=0,g=0,b=192]
        size=18
        italic=true
        family=SansSerif
      >
        [19,27][powerful]
      <content
        underline=false
        bold=true
        foreground=java.awt.Color[r=255,g=0,b=0]
        size=20
        italic=false
        family=SansSerif
      >
        [27,28][!]
      <content>
        [28,29][
]
<bidi root>
  <bidi level
    bidiLevel=0
  >
    [0,29][Swing
is extremely powerful!
]
```

Note the use of <section>, <paragraph>, and <content> to denote SectionElement, BranchElement, and LeafElement, respectively. Also note that the <paragraph> and

`<content>` tags each contain several attributes. The `<paragraph>` attributes represent paragraph `Element` attributes and the `<content>` attributes represent character `Element` attributes. We will discuss specific attributes in more detail later. The `<bidi root>` tag specifies a second root `Element` that allows bidirectional text (this functionality is incomplete as of Java 2 FCS).

We can assign paragraph and character attributes to a region of text with the `setParagraphAttributes()` and `setCharacterAttributes()` methods. These methods require a start and end offset that specifies the region to apply the attributes to, as well as an `AttributeSet` that contains the attributes, and a `boolean` flag that specifies whether to replace pre-existing attributes with the new attributes.

Regarding the range of text, paragraph attributes will be applied to paragraph `Element`s that contain at least some portion of the specified range. Character attributes will be applied to all character `Element`s that intersect that range. If the specified range only partially extends into a paragraph `Element`, that `Element` will be split into two, so that only the specified range of text will receive the new attributes (this splitting is handled by an instance of the `Element-Buffer` inner class).

If the `boolean` flag is `true`, all pre-existing paragraph `Element` attributes are removed before the new set is applied. Otherwise, the new set is merged with the old set, and any new attributes overwrite pre-existing attributes. Character attributes work in a similar way, but they do not change paragraph attributes at all—they simply override them.

`DefaultStyledDocument` also defines the notion of *logical* paragraph `Style`s. A logical paragraph `Style` acts as the resolving parent of a paragraph `Element`'s `AttributeSet`. So attributes defined in a paragraph `Element`'s `AttributeSet` override those defined in that paragraph's logical `Style`. We can change a specific paragraph `Element`'s logical style with the `setLogicalStyle()` method. The logical style of each paragraph defaults to `StyleContext.DEFAULT_STYLE` (which is empty by default).

`JTextPane` implements the `getParagraphAttributes()`, `setParagraphAttributes()`, `getLogicalStyle()`, and `setLogicalStyle()` methods which communicate directly with its `StyledDocument`. `JTextPane`'s paragraph attributes and logical style `setXX()` methods apply to the paragraph the caret currently resides in if there is no selection. If there is a selection, these methods apply to all paragraphs included in the selected region. `JTextPane`'s paragraph attributes and logical style `getXX()` methods apply to the paragraph currently containing the caret.

`JTextPane` also implements the `getCharacterAttributes()` and `setCharacterAttributes()` methods. If there is a selection, the `setCharacterAttributes()` method will act as described above, splitting `Element`s as needed. If there is no selection, this method will modify `JTextPane`'s *input* attributes.

NOTE   `JTextPane`'s input attributes are an `AttributeSet` which changes with the location of the caret. This reference always points to the attributes of the character `Element` at the current caret location. We can retrieve it at any time with `JTextPane`'s `getInputAttributes()` method. Whenever text is inserted in a `JTextPane`, the current input attributes will be applied to that text by default. However, any attributes explicitly assigned to newly inserted text will override those defined by the current input attributes.

A `StyleContext` instance (see section 19.1.16) is associated with each `DefaultStyledDocument`. As we mentioned in the beginning of this chapter, the `Style` interface describes a named mutable `AttributeSet`, and the `StyledDocument` interface describes a `Document` which manages a set of `Styles`. A `DefaultStyledDocument`'s `StyleContext` instance is what performs the actual management, creation, and assignment of that document's `Styles`. If a `StyleContext` is not provided to the `DefaultStyledDocument` constructor, a default version is created.

`JTextPane` defines several methods for adding, removing, and retrieving `Styles`, as well as specific attributes within a given `AttributeSet` (such as the `getFont()` and `getFore-` `ground()` methods). Calls to these methods are forwarded to methods of the same signature in `JTextPane`'s `StyledDocument`, and, in the case of `DefaultStyledDocument`, these calls are forwarded to the `StyleContext` in charge of all the `Styles`.

`DefaultStyledDocument` also includes several significant inner classes:

- `static class DefaultStyledDocument.AttributeUndoableEdit`: This class extends `AbstractUndoableEdit` to allow `AttributeSet` undo/redo functionality with `Elements`.
- `class DefaultStyledDocument.ElementBuffer`: Instances of this class are used to manage structural changes in a `DefaultStyledDocument`, such as the splitting of `Ele-` `ments`, or the insertion and removal of text that results in the modification of, and the insertion and/or removal of, various `Elements`. This class also plays a critical role in constructing `AbstractDocument.DefaultDocumentEvents` (see section 19.1.4).
- `static class DefaultStyledDocument.ElementSpec`: This class describes an `Element` that can be created and inserted into a document in the future with an `Ele-` `mentBuffer`.
- `protected class DefaultStyledDocument.SectionElement`: This class extends `AbstractDocument.BranchElement` and acts as a `DefaultStyledDocument`'s default root `Element`. It contains only `BranchElement` children (which represent paragraphs).

19.1.12   The AttributeSet interface

abstract interface javax.swing.text.AttributeSet

An attribute is simply a *key/value* pair (as in a `Hashtable`) that should be recognized by some `View` implementation available to the text component being used. As we know from our discussion above, each `Element` in a `DefaultStyledDocument` has an associated set of attributes which resolves hierarchically. The attributes play a critical role in how that piece of the document will be rendered by a `View`. For example, one commonly used attribute is `FontFamily`. The `FontFamily` attribute key is an `Object` consisting of the `String` "fam- ily." The `FontFamily` attribute *value* is a `String` representing the name of a font (such as "monospaced"). Other examples of attribute keys include "Icon" and "Component," whose values are instances of `Icon` and `Component`.

If an attribute is not recognized by a `View`, the `Element` associated with that view will not be rendered correctly. Thus, a predefined set of attributes is recognized by the Swing `View` classes, and these attribute keys should be considered reserved—in other words, all new attributes should use new keys. These predefined attribute keys are all accessible as static `Objects` in the `StyleConstants` class (see section 19.1.15).

Sets of attributes are encapsulated in implementations of either the `AttributeSet` inter- face, the `MutableAttributeSet` interface (see section 19.1.13), or the `Style` interface (see section 19.1.14). `Style` extends `MutableAttributeSet`, which, in turn, extends `Attribute-Set`. The `AttributeSet` interface describes a read-only set of attributes because it does not provide methods for changing, adding, or removing attributes from that set.

The `containsAttribute()` and `containsAttributes()` methods are used to check whether an `AttributeSet` contains a given attribute key/value pair or any number of such pairs. The `copyAttributes()` method returns a fresh, immutable copy of the `Attribute-Set` it is invoked on. The `getAttributeCount()` method returns the number of attributes contained in a set, and `getAttributeNames()` retrieves an `Enumeration` of the keys that describe each attribute. The `isDefined()` method checks whether a given attribute key corresponds to an attribute directly stored in the `AttributeSet` the method is invoked on (the resolving parents are not searched). The `isEqual()` method compares two `AttributeSets` and returns whether they contain identical attribute key/value pairs. The `getResolvePar-ent()` method returns a reference to an `AttributeSet`'s resolving parent, if any, and the `getAttribute()` method returns the value of an attribute corresponding to a given key.

The `AttributeSet` interface also provides four empty static interfaces: `CharacterAt-tribute`, `ColorAttribute`, `FontAttribute`, and `ParagraphAttribute`. The only reason these interfaces exist is to provide a signature (for example, information about the class in which it is defined), which is expected of each attribute key. This signature can be used to verify whether an attribute belongs to a certain category (see section 19.1.15).

Only one direct implementation of the `AttributeSet` interface exists within the text package: `StyleContext.SmallAttributeSet`. A `SmallAttributeSet` is an array of attribute *key/value* pairs stored in the alternating pattern: key1, value1, key2, value2, and so on (thus the number of attributes contained in a `SmallAttributeSet` is actually half the size of its array). An array is used for storage because `AttributeSet` describes a read-only set of attributes, and using an array is more memory-efficient than dynamically resizable storage such as that provided by a `Hashtable`. However, it is less time-efficient to search through an array than a `Hashtable`. For this reason, `SmallAttributeSet` is used only for small sets of attributes. These sets are usually shared between several `Element`s. Because of the way sharing works (see section 19.1.16), the smaller the set of attributes is, the better candidate that set is for being shared.

19.1.13 The MutableAttributeSet interface

abstract interface javax.swing.text.MutableAttributeSet

The `MutableAttributeSet` interface extends the `AttributeSet` interface and declares additional methods that allow attribute addition and removal, and resolving parent assignment: `addAttribute()`, `addAttributes()`, `setResolveParent()`, `removeAttribute()`, and two variations of `removeAttributes()`.

`MutableAttributeSet` also has two direct implementations within the text package: `AbstractDocument.AbstractElement` and `SimpleAttributeSet`. The fact that `Abstract-Element` implements `MutableAttributeSet` allows such `Element`s to act as resolving parents to one another. It also reduces object overhead by combining structural information about a region of text with that region's stylistic attributes.

`SimpleAttributeSet` uses a `Hashtable` to store attribute key/value pairs because it must be dynamically resizable. By nature, a `Hashtable` is less efficient than an array in memory usage, but it is more efficient in look-up speed. For this reason, `SimpleAttributeSets` are used for large sets of attributes that are not shared.

NOTE   In the past few sections we have alluded to the importance of efficiency in attribute storage. Efficiency here refers to both memory usage and the speed of attribute location. Here's a quick summary of the issues: A `View` uses attributes to determine how to render its associated `Element`. These attribute *values* must be located, by *key*, within that `Element`'s attribute set hierarchy. The faster this location occurs, the more quickly the view is rendered and the more responsive the user interface becomes. So look-up speed is a large factor in deciding how to store attribute *key/value* pairs.

Memory usage is also a large issue. Obtaining efficient look-up speed involves sacrificing efficient memory usage, and vice versa. This necessary trade-off is taken into account through the implementation of the different attribute storage mechanisms described above, and the intelligent management of when each mechanism is used. We will soon see that the `StyleContext` class acts as, this intelligent manager, among other things.

19.1.14   The Style interface

abstract interface javax.swing.text.Style

The `Style` interface extends `MutableAttributeSet` and it provides the ability to attach listeners for notification of changes to its set of attributes. `Style` also adds a `String` that is used for name identification. The only direct implementation of the `Style` interface is provided by `StyleContext.NamedStyle`. Internally, `NamedStyle` maintains its own private `Attribute-Set` implementation that contains all its attributes. This `AttributeSet` can be an instance of `StyleContext.SmallAttributeSet` or `SimpleAttributeSet`, and it may switch back and forth between these types over the course of its lifetime (this will become clear after our discussion of `StyleContext`).

19.1.15   StyleConstants

class javax.swing.text.StyleConstants

The `StyleConstants` class categorizes predefined attribute keys into members of four static inner classes: `CharacterConstants`, `ColorConstants`, `FontConstants`, and `Paragraph-Constants`. These `Objects` are all aliased from their outer class, `StyleConstants`, so they are more easily accessible (*aliasing* here means providing a reference to an object of an inner class). Also, both `ColorConstants` and `FontConstants` keys are aliased by `Character-Constants` to provide a sensible hierarchy of attribute key organization.

NOTE   Not all aliased keys use the same name in each class. For instance, `FontFamily` in `StyledConstants` is an alias of `Family` in `StyledConstants.CharacterCon-stants`. However, `Family` in `StyledConstants.CharacterConstants` is an alias of `Family` (the actual key) in `StyledConstants.FontConstants`. Each is a reference to the same key object and it makes no difference which one we use.

The meanings of most keys are self-explanatory. The `StyleConstants` API documentation page contains a helpful diagram that illustrates the meaning of some of the less self-explanatory attribute keys that apply to paragraphs of styled text. (Each of the keys illustrated in this diagram is an alias of the actual key defined in `StyleConstants.ParagraphConstants`.)

`StyleConstants` also defines static methods for assigning and retrieving many predefined attributes in an `AttributeSet`. For example, to assign a specific font family attribute to an `AttributeSet` (assuming it is mutable), we can use `StyleConstants`' `setFontFamily()` method.

19.1.16 StyleContext

class javax.swing.text.StyleContext

`StyleContext` implements the `AbstractDocument.AttributeContext` interface, and it declares a set of methods that are used to modify or fetch new instances of `AttributeSet` implementations. `AbstractContext` was designed with the understanding that the implementor may use more than one type of `AttributeSet` implementation to store sets of attributes. The decision to use one type over another may be based on any number of factors, and `StyleContext` takes full advantage of this design.

`StyleContext`'s main role is to act as a container for `Styles` that may be used by one or more `DefaultStyledDocuments`. It maintains a private `NamedStyle` instance that is used to store its `Styles` and allow access by name. Each of these contained `Styles` is also an instance of `NamedStyle`. So, to clarify, `StyleContext` maintains a `NamedStyle` instance whose key/value pairs are of the form `String`/`NamedStyle`.

`StyleContext` also maintains a subset of these `NamedStyle` values in a `Hashtable`. Only those `NamedStyle`'s whose `AttributeSet` contains nine or fewer attributes are stored in this `Hashtable` and their `AttributeSets` are maintained as instances of `SmallAttribute-Set`. Those `NamedStyles` with an `AttributeSet` containing ten or more attributes are not stored in the `Hashtable`, and their `AttributeSets` are maintained as instances of `Simple-AttributeSet`.

This partitioning is managed dynamically by `StyleContext`, and it is the result of combining the `AbstractContext` design with the use of a *compression threshold* (a hard-coded `int` value of 9). Whenever an attribute is added or removed, `StyleContext` checks the number of attributes in the target `AttributeSet`. If the resulting set will contain nine or fewer attributes, it remains or is converted to a `SmallAttributeSet`, and it is added to the `Hashtable` if it wasn't already there. If the resulting set will contain ten or more attributes, it remains or is converted to a `SimpleAttributeSet`, and it is removed from the `Hashtable` if it was already there.

The reason for this partitioning is to support efficient `AttributeSet` sharing. Most styled documents contain many distinct regions of identically styled text. These regions normally have a small number of attributes associated with them. It is clear that the best thing to do in this situation is to assign the same `AttributeSet` to each of these regions, and the best `Attribute-Set` implementation to use for this is `SmallAttributeSet` because of its superior memory efficiency, since look-up speed is a minor issue with a very small number of attributes. Larger sets of attributes are, in general, rare. The best `AttributeSet` implementation to use for this is `SimpleAttributeSet` because of its superior look-up capabilities, since memory usage will most likely be a minor issue with a relatively small number of `SimpleAttributeSets`.

19.1.17 The Highlighter interface

abstract interface javax.swing.text.Highlighter

This interface describes how specific regions of text can be marked up with instances of the inner `Highlighter.Highlight` interface. A `Highlight` maintains a beginning and end offset, and a reference to an instance of the inner `Highlighter.HighlightPainter` interface. A `HighlightPainter`'s only responsibility is to render the background of a specific region of text.

A text component's UI delegate is responsible for maintaining its `Highlighter`. For this reason, the `Highlighter` can change when a text component's look and feel changes. `JText-Component` provides methods for working with a text component's `Highlighter` so we generally ignore the fact that such methods really get forwarded to the UI delegate.

A `Highlighter` maintains an array of `Highlighter.Highlight` instances, and we are able to add to this array using the `addHighlight()` method. This method takes two `int`s that define the range of text to highlight, as well as a `Highlighter.HighlightPainter` instance that specifies how that `Highlight` should be rendered. Thus, by defining various `Highlight-Painters`, we can add an arbitrary number of highlighted regions with distinct visual effects.

The range a `Highlight` encompasses is modified with the `changeHighlight()` method, and `Highlights` can be removed from a `Highlighter`'s array with the `removeAllHigh-lights()` or `removeHighlight()` methods. The `paint()` method manages the rendering of all of a `Highlighter`'s `Highlights`.

We can assign a new `Highlighter` with `JTextComponent`'s `setHighlighter()` method. Similarly, we can retrieve a reference to the existing one with `JTextComponent`'s `getHighlighter()` method. Each `JTextComponent` also maintains a `selectionColor` property which specifies the color to use in rendering default highlights.

19.1.18 DefaultHighlighter

class javax.swing.text.DefaultHighlighter

`DefaultHighlighter` extends the abstract `LayeredHighlighter` class. `LayeredHigh-lighter` implements the `Highlighter` interface and defines a `paintLayeredHighlights()` method, which is responsible for managing potentially multiple overlapping `Highlights`. `LayeredHighlighter` also declares an inner abstract static class called `LayerPainter` from which the static `DefaultHighlighter.DefaultHighlightPainter` extends. This implementation paints a solid background behind the specified region of text, in the current text component selection color.

19.1.19 The Caret interface

abstract interface javax.swing.text.Caret

This interface describes a text component's cursor. The `paint()` method is responsible for rendering the caret, and the `setBlinkRate()` and `getBlinkRate()` methods assign and retrieve a specific caret blink interval (normally in milliseconds). The `setVisible()` and `isVisible()` methods hide/show the caret and check for caret visibility, respectively.

The `setDot()` and `getDot()` methods assign and retrieve the offset of the caret within the current document. The `getMark()` method returns a location in the document where the caret's *mark* has been assigned. The `moveDot()` method assigns a mark position, and moves the caret to a new location while highlighting the text between the dot and the mark. The `setSelectionVisible()` and `isSelectionVisible()` methods assign and query the visible state of the highlight that specifies the currently selected text.

The `setMagicCaretPosition()` and `getMagicCaretPosition()` methods manage a dynamic caret position that is used when moving the caret up and down between lines with the arrow keys. When moving up and down between lines with an unequal number of characters, the magic position places the caret as close to the same location within each line as possible. If the magic position is greater than the length of the current line, the caret is placed at the end of the line. This feature is common in almost all modern text applications, and it is implemented for us in the `DefaultCaret` class.

The `Caret` interface also declares methods for the registration of `ChangeListener`s for notification of changes in the caret's position: `addChangeListener()` and `removeChangeListener()`.

19.1.20   DefaultCaret

class javax.swing.text.DefaultCaret

This class extends `java.awt.Rectangle`, and it represents a concrete implementation of the `Caret` interface that is used by all text components by default. It is rendered as a blinking vertical line in the color specified by its associated text component's `caretColor` property. `DefaultCaret` also implements the `FocusListener`, `MouseListener`, and `MouseMotionListener` interfaces.

The only `MouseListener` methods without empty implementations are `mouseClicked()` and `mousePressed()`. If a mouse click occurs with the left mouse button, and the click count is two (it's a double-click), `mouseClicked()` will invoke the `Action` returned by `DefaultEditorKit.selectWordAction()` to select the word containing the caret. If the click count is three, `mouseClicked()` will invoke the `Action` returned by `DefaultEditorKit.selectLineAction()` to select the line of text containing the caret. The `mousePressed()` method sends its `MouseEvent` parameter to `DefaultCaret`'s `positionCaret()` method, which sets the `dot` property to the document offset corresponding to the mouse press and clears the `magicCaretPosition` property. The `mousePressed()` method also checks to see if the text component is enabled and, if it is, its `requestFocus()` method is invoked.

The only `MouseMotionListener` method without an empty implementation is `mouseDragged()`. This method simply passes its `MouseEvent` parameter to `DefaultCaret`'s `moveCaret()` method. The `moveCaret()` method determines the offset of the caret destination by passing the `MouseEvent`'s coordinates to the text component's `viewToModel()` method. The `moveDot()` method is then invoked to actually move the caret to the determined position (recall that the `moveDot()` method sets the `mark` property and selects the text between the `mark` position and the new `dot` position).

Both `FocusListener` methods are non-empty. The `focusGained()` method checks whether the text component is editable and, if it is, the caret is made visible. The `focusLost()` method simply hides the caret. These methods are invoked when the text component gains or loses the focus.

We can customize the way a selection's highlight appears by overriding `DefaultCaret`'s `getSelectionPainter()` method to return our own `Highlighter.HighlightPainter` implementation. We can also customize the appearance of a caret by overriding the `paint()` method. If we do reimplement the `paint()` method, however, we must also override the `damage()` method. The `damage()` method is passed a `Rectangle` that represents the region of the text component to repaint when the caret is moved.

For instance, the following is a simple `DefaultCaret` subclass that renders a wide black caret.

```
class WideCaret extends DefaultCaret
{
  protected int caretWidth = 6;

  protected void setWidth(int w) {
    caretWidth = w;
  }

  // Since DefaultCaret extends Rectangle, it inherits
  // the x, y, width, and height variables which are
  // used here to allow proper repainting.
  protected synchronized void damage(Rectangle r) {
    if (r != null) {
      x = r.x - width;
      y = r.y;
      width = width;
      height = r.height;
      repaint();
    }
  }

  public void paint(Graphics g) {
    if(isVisible()) {
      try {
        TextUI mapper = getComponent().getUI();
        Rectangle r = mapper.modelToView(
          getComponent(), getComponent().getCaretPosition());
        g.setColor(getComponent().getCaretColor());
        g.fillRect(r.x, r.y, caretWidth, r.height - 1);
      }
      catch (Exception e) {
        System.err.println("Problem painting cursor");
      }
    }
  }
}
```

We have implemented a short example in a Swing Connection "Tips and Tricks" article that shows you how to use a similar custom caret for designating an overwrite mode. In the same article, we also show you how to customize a `PlainDocument` model to allow insert and overwrite modes, and how to track caret position with a `CaretListener`. See http://java.sun.com/products/jfc/tsc/

19.1.21 The CaretListener interface

abstract interface javax.swing.event.CaretListener

This interface describes a listener that is notified whenever a change occurs in a text component's caret position. It declares one method, `caretUpdate()`, which takes a `CaretEvent` as a parameter. We can attach and remove `CaretListener`s to any `JTextComponent` with the `addCaretListener()` and `removeCaretListener()` methods.

19.1.22 CaretEvent

class javax.swing.event.CaretEvent

This event simply encapsulates a reference to its source object (which is normally a text component). `CaretEvent`s are passed to all attached `CaretListener`s whenever the associated text component's caret position changes.

19.1.23 The Keymap interface

abstract interface javax.swing.text.Keymap

This interface describes a collection of bindings between `KeyStroke`s (see section 2.13.2) and `Action`s (see section 12.1.23). We add new `KeyStroke`/`Action` bindings to a `Keymap` with the `addActionForKeyStroke()` method. Like `AttributeSet`s, `Keymap`s resolve hierarchically. Like `Style`s, `Keymap`s have a name they are referenced by.

We query the `Action` that corresponds to a specific `KeyStroke` with the `getAction()` method. If no corresponding `Action` is located in the `Keymap`, its resolving parents should be searched until either no more resolving parents exist, or a match is found. Similarly, we retrieve an array of `KeyStroke`s that are mapped to a given `Action` with the `getKeyStrokesForAction()` method. (As of Java 2 FCS, this method simply returns `null`, and is marked as "TBD" [presumably meaning "to be done"].) The `isLocallyDefined()` method checks whether a given `KeyStroke` is bound to an `Action` in the `Keymap` that is under investigation. The `removeBindings()` method removes all bindings in a `Keymap`, and the `removeKeyStrokeBinding()` method removes only those bindings corresponding to a given `KeyStroke`.

By default, all `JTextComponent`s share the same `Keymap` instance. This is what enables the default functionality of the Backspace, Delete, and left and right arrow keys on any text component. For this reason, it is not a good idea to retrieve a text component's `Keymap` and modify it directly. Rather, we are encouraged to create our own `Keymap` instance and assign the default `Keymap` as its resolving parent. By assigning a resolving parent of `null`, we can effectively disable all bindings on a text component, other than those in the given component's `Keymap` itself (the underlying role `Keymap`s play in text components will become clear after we discuss `DefaultEditorKit`, below).

We can obtain a text component's `Keymap` with either of `JTextComponent`'s `getKeymap()` methods. We can assign a text component a new `Keymap` with the `setKeymap()` method, and we can add a new `Keymap` anywhere within the `Keymap` hierarchy with the `addKeymap()` method. We can also remove a `Keymap` from the hierarchy with the `removeKeymap()` method.

For example, to create and add a new `Keymap` to a `JTextField` and use the default text component `Keymap` as a resolving parent, we might do something like the following:

```
Keymap keymap = myJTextField.getKeymap();
Keymap myKeymap = myJTextField.addKeymap("MyKeymap", keymap);
```

We can then add `KeyStroke`/`Action` pairs to `myKeymap` with the `addActionForKeyStroke()` method (we will see an example of this in the next section).

NOTE   Recall from section 2.13.4 that `KeyListeners` will receive key events before a text component's `Keymap`. Although using `Keymaps` is encouraged, handling keyboard events with `KeyListeners` is still allowed.

19.1.24   TextAction

abstract class javax.swing.text.TextAction

`EditorKits` are, among other things, responsible for making a set of `Actions` available for performing common text editor functions based on a given content type. `EditorKits` normally use inner subclasses of `TextAction` for this, as it extends `AbstractAction` (see section 12.1.24), and provides a relatively powerful means of determining the target component to invoke the action on (by taking advantage of the fact that `JTextComponent` keeps track of the most recent text component with the focus, retrievable with its static `getFocusedComponent()` method). The `TextAction` constructor takes the `String` to be used as that action's name, and passes it to its super-class constructor. When subclassing `TextAction`, we normally define an `actionPerformed()` method, which performs the desired action when it is passed an `ActionEvent`. Within this method, we can use `TextAction`'s `getTextComponent()` method to determine which text component the action should be invoked on.

19.1.25   EditorKit

abstract class javax.swing.text.EditorKit

`EditorKits` are responsible for the following functionality:

- Support for an appropriate `Document` model. An `EditorKit` specifically supports one type of content, a `String` description of which is retrievable with the `getContentType()` method. A corresponding `Document` instance is returned by the `createDefaultDocument()` method, and the `EditorKit` is able to `read()` and `write()` that `Document` to `InputStreams`/`OutputStreams` and `Readers`/`Writers`, respectively.
- Support for `View` production through a `ViewFactory` implementation. This behavior is actually optional, as `View` production will default to a text component's UI delegate if its `EditorKit`'s `getViewFactory()` method returns `null` (see sections 19.1.28 and 19.1.29 for more about `Views` and the `ViewFactory` interface).
- Support for a set of `Actions` that can be invoked on a text component using the appropriate `Document`. Normally these `Actions` are instances of `TextAction` and are defined

as inner classes. An `EditorKit`'s `Actions` can be retrieved in an array with its `getActions()` method.

19.1.26   DefaultEditorKit

class javax.swing.text.DefaultEditorKit

`DefaultEditorKit` extends `EditorKit`, and it defines a series of `TextAction` subclasses and corresponding name `Strings` (see the API documentation). Eight of these forty-six inner action classes are public, and they can be instantiated with a default constructor: `BeepAction`, `Copy-Action`, `CutAction`, `DefaultKeyTypedAction`, `InsertBreakAction`, `InsertContent-Action`, `InsertTabAction`, and `PasteAction`. `DefaultEditorKit` maintains instances of all its inner `Action` classes in an array that can be retrieved with its `getActions()` method. We can access any of these `Actions` easily by defining a `Hashtable` with `Action.NAME` keys and `Action` values. See *Java Swing* by Robert Eckstein, Marc Loy, and Dave Wood, O'Reilly & Associates, 1998, p. 918.

```
Hashtable actionTable = new Hashtable
Action[] actions = myEditorKit.getActions();
for (int i=0; i < actions.length; i++) {
  String actionName = (String) actions[i].getValue(Action.NAME);
  actionTable.put(actionName, actions[i]);
}
```

We can then retrieve any of these `Actions` with `DefaultEditorKit`'s static `String` fields. For example, the following code retrieves the action that is responsible for selecting all text in a document:

```
Action selectAll = (Action) actionTable.get(
  DefaultEditorKit.selectAllAction);
```

These `Actions` can be used in menus and toolbars, or with other controls, for convenient control of plain text components.

`DefaultEditorKit`'s `getViewFactory()` method returns `null`, which means the UI delegate is responsible for creating the hierarchy of `Views` necessary for rendering a text component correctly. As we mentioned in the beginning of this chapter, `JTextField`, `JPass-wordField`, and `JTextArea` all use a `DefaultEditorKit`.

Although `EditorKits` are responsible for managing a set of `Actions` and their corresponding names, they are not actually directly responsible for making these `Actions` accessible to specific text components. This is where `Keymaps` fit in. For instance, take a look at the following code that shows how the default `JTextComponent Keymap` is created (this is from JTextComponent.java):

```
/**
 * This is the name of the default keymap that will be shared by all
 * JTextComponent instances unless they have had a different
 * keymap set.
 */
public static final String DEFAULT_KEYMAP = "default";

/**
 * Default bindings for the default keymap if no other bindings
```

```
 * are given.
 */
static final KeyBinding[] defaultBindings = {
  new KeyBinding(KeyStroke.getKeyStroke(KeyEvent.VK_BACK_SPACE, 0),
    DefaultEditorKit.deletePrevCharAction),
  new KeyBinding(KeyStroke.getKeyStroke(KeyEvent.VK_DELETE, 0),
    DefaultEditorKit.deleteNextCharAction),
  new KeyBinding(KeyStroke.getKeyStroke(KeyEvent.VK_RIGHT, 0),
    DefaultEditorKit.forwardAction),
  new KeyBinding(KeyStroke.getKeyStroke(KeyEvent.VK_LEFT, 0),
    DefaultEditorKit.backwardAction)
};

static {
  try {
    keymapTable = new Hashtable(17);
    Keymap binding = addKeymap(DEFAULT_KEYMAP, null);
    binding.setDefaultAction(new
      DefaultEditorKit.DefaultKeyTypedAction());
    EditorKit kit = new DefaultEditorKit();
    loadKeymap(binding, defaultBindings, kit.getActions());
  } catch (Throwable e) {
    e.printStackTrace();
    keymapTable = new Hashtable(17);
  }
}
```

19.1.27 StyledEditorKit

class javax.swing.text.StyledEditorKit

This class extends `DefaultEditorKit` and defines seven additional inner `Action` classes, each of which is publicly accessible: `AlignmentAction`, `BoldAction`, `FontFamilyAction`, `FontSizeAction`, `ForegroundAction`, `ItalicAction`, and `UnderlineAction`. All seven `Actions` are subclasses of the inner `StyledTextAction` convenience class which extends `TextAction`.

Each of `StyledEditorKit`'s `Actions` applies to styled text documents, and they are used by `JEditorPane` and `JTextPane`. `StyledEditorKit` does not define its own capabilities for reading and writing styled text. Instead, this functionality is inherited from `Default-EditorKit`, which only provides support for saving and loading plain text. The two `StyledEditorKit` subclasses included with Swing, `javax.swing.text.html.HTMLEditorKit` and `javax.swing.text.rtf.RTFEditorKit`, do support styled text saving and loading for HTML and RTF content types respectively.

`StyledEditorKit`'s `getViewFactory()` method returns an instance of a private static inner class called `StyledViewFactory` which implements the `ViewFactory` interface as follows (this is from StyledEditorKit.java):

```
static class StyledViewFactory implements ViewFactory {
  public View create(Element elem) {
    String kind = elem.getName();
    if (kind != null) {
```

```
      if (kind.equals(AbstractDocument.ContentElementName)) {
         return new LabelView(elem);
      } else if (kind.equals(AbstractDocument.ParagraphElementName)) {
        return new ParagraphView(elem);
      } else if (kind.equals(AbstractDocument.SectionElementName)) {
        return new BoxView(elem, View.Y_AXIS);
      } else if (kind.equals(StyleConstants.ComponentElementName)) {
        return new ComponentView(elem);
      } else if (kind.equals(StyleConstants.IconElementName)) {
        return new IconView(elem);
      }
    }
    // Default to text display
    return new LabelView(elem);
  }
}
```

The Views returned by this factory's create() method are based on the name property of the Element that is passed as a parameter. If an Element is not recognized, a LabelView is returned. In summary, because StyledEditorKit's getViewFactory() method doesn't return null, styled text components depend on their EditorKits rather than their UI delegates for providing Views. The opposite is true with plain text components, which rely on their UI delegates for View creation.

19.1.28   View

abstract class javax.swing.text.View

This class describes an object that is responsible for graphically representing a portion of a text component's document model. The text package includes several extensions of this class that are meant to be used by various types of Elements. We will not discuss these classes in detail, but a brief overview will be enough to provide a high-level understanding of how text components are actually rendered.

> **NOTE**   We have only included the most commonly used set of text component Views in this list. Several others are responsible for significant text-rendering functionality. See the O'Reilly book listed in the bibliography, and the API documentation for details.

- abstract interface TabableView: Used by Views whose size depends on the size of the tabs.
- abstract interface TabExpander: Extends TabableView and is used by Views that support TabStops and TabSets (a set of TabStops). A TabStop describes the positioning of a tab character and the text appearing immediately after it.
- class ComponentView: Used as a gateway View to a fully interactive embedded Component.
- class IconView: Used as a gateway View to an embedded Icon.
- class PlainView: Used for rendering one line of non-wrapped text with one font and one color.
- class FieldView: Extends PlainView and adds specialized functionality for representing a single-line editor view (such as the ability to center text in a JTextField).

- class `PasswordView`: Extends `FieldView` and adds the ability to render its content using the echo character of the associated component if it is a `JPasswordField`.
- class `LabelView`: Used to render a range of styled text.
- abstract class `CompositeView`: A `View` containing multiple child `View`s. All `View`s can contain child `View`s, but only instances of `CompositeView` and `BasicTextUI`'s `RootView` (discussed below) actually contain child `View`s by default.
- class `BoxView`: Extends `CompositeView` and arranges a group of child `View`s in a rectangular box.
- class `ParagraphView`: Extends `BoxView` and is responsible for rendering a paragraph of styled text. `ParagraphView` is made up of a number of child `Element`s organized as, or within, `View`s representing single rows of styled text. This `View` supports line wrapping, and if an `Element` within the content paragraph spans multiple lines, more than one `View` will be used to represent it.
- class `WrappedPlainView`: Extends `BoxView` and is responsible for rendering multiline, plain text with line wrapping.

All text components in Swing use UI delegates derived from `BasicTextUI` by default. This class defines an inner class called `RootView` which acts as a gateway between a text component and the actual `View` hierarchy used to render it.

NOTE   In chapter 22 we will take advantage of `BasicTextUI`'s root view while implementing a solution for printing styled text. The solution also requires us to implement a custom `BoxView` subclass that is responsible for rendering each of its child `View`s to a `Graphics` instance used in the printing process (see section 22.4).

19.1.29   The ViewFactory interface

abstract interface javax.swing.text.ViewFactory

This interface declares one method: `create(Element elem)`. This method returns a `View` (which possibly contains a hierarchy of `View`s) that is used to render a given `Element`. `BasicTextUI` implements this interface, and unless a text component's `EditorKit` provides its own `ViewFactory`, `BasicTextUI`'s `create()` method will provide all `View`s. This is the case with the plain text components: `JTextField`, `JPasswordField`, and `JTextArea`. However, the styled text components, `JEditorPane` and `JTextPane`, vary greatly depending on their current content type. For this reason their `View`s are provided by the currently installed `EditorKit`. In this way, custom `View`s can render different types of styled content.

19.2   DATE AND TIME EDITOR

...by David M. Karr of Best Consulting and TCSI Corporation

The `DateTimeEditor` class is a panel that contains a text field that allows the display and editing of a date, time, or date/time value. It doesn't use direct text entry, but it uses the up and down arrow keys or mouse clicks on "spinner" buttons to increment and decrement field values (such as day, month, year, or hour, minute, second). The mouse can also be used to select particular subfields. The left and right arrow keys move the caret between fields.

This class is designed to be internationalized, although it assumes some conventions, such as a left-to-right reading direction. It doesn't have any locale-specific code; it just uses the locale framework integrated into Java 2. If the virtual machine that's used doesn't support a particular locale, neither will this component. The `Locale` class encapsulates a "language," a "country," and an optional "variant." Each of these are strings. The possible values of "language" and "country" are defined in the ISO 639 and ISO 3166 standards, respectively. The variants are not standardized. For instance, the language codes for English, French, Chinese, and Japanese are "en," "fr," "zh," and "ja." The country codes for the USA, France, and Canada are "US," "FR," and "CA."

The current `Locale` setting is used to qualify the variety of the resource class or the properties file to obtain. For instance, a class name with a suffix of `_fr_FR` indicates resources for French in France. The suffix of `_fr_CA` indicates resources for French in Canada.

Java 2 has specific resource settings for most of the known locales, including currency formats, date formats, number formats, and common text strings. This is the information that the `DateTimeEditor` class uses indirectly, without having to manually encode locale-specific information.

`DateTimeEditor` uses several Swing classes, including `JTextField`, `Keymap`, `Abstract-Action`, `TextAction`, and `Caret`. It also uses several non-Swing classes, including `Collections`, `Calendar` (both are in the `java.util` package), `FieldPosition`, and `DateFormat` (both are in the `java.text` package). The `Collections` class sorts a list of `FieldPosition` objects by the `beginIndex` of each `FieldPosition`. A custom `Spinner` class, described below, allows values to be incremented or decremented using the mouse.

`DateTimeEditor`'s text field is an ordinary `JTextField`, and it uses the methods of `JTextComponent` to communicate with and manipulate its `Caret`.

The inner classes `UpDownAction`, `BackwardAction`, `ForwardAction`, `BeginAction`, and `EndAction` are subclasses of `TextAction` and `AbstractAction`, and they are used to handle the arrow keys, and the HOME and END keys. All of these inner classes are used in concert with the `Keymap` class to combine key definitions with action definitions.

The `DateTimeEditor` text field listens for caret state changes. It does this so it knows exactly which field the caret is in, and also to constrain the caret position so it will always be at the beginning of the current field.

The most interesting interactions are with `DateFormat`'s fields and its `format()` method. What `DateTimeEditor` gains from these is the ability to know what field the caret is in, so it knows how to interpret the "increment" and "decrement" actions.

One of `DateFormat`'s `format()` methods takes a `Date` value, a `StringBuffer` to write the `String` result into, and a single `FieldPosition` object. This last parameter is the key to the entire `DateTimeEditor` component. The `format()` method will update the given `FieldPosition` object with the `begin` and `end` offset for that field in the given date/time string. The `DateTimeEditor` has a hardcoded list of all fields from `DateFormat`. In a loop, it plugs in each of those constants into the `format` function, and then it stores the resulting `FieldPosition` object. It then uses the `Collections.sort()` method to sort the list of `FieldPositions` by the beginning index of each one. Using this sorted list and a given caret position, we can easily determine in what field the caret resides.

The `Calendar` class is used to fill in some functionality that the `Date.setTime()` method doesn't provide. In particular, in the code which increments or decrements the current field value, there are four `DateFormat` fields which cannot be set using `Date.setTime()`. Those fields are MONTH, WEEK_OF_MONTH, WEEK_OF_YEAR, and YEAR. For these fields, Date-TimeEditor manipulates a `Calendar` instance and then calls `Calendar.getTime()` to get a new `Date` value.

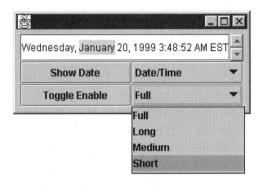

Figure 19.5 `DateTimeEditor` in the `en_US` **locale**

Figure 19.6 `Spinner`

Example 19.1

DateTimeEditor.java

see \Chapter19\Karr

```java
import java.awt.event.*;
import java.text.*;
import java.util.*;
import java.awt.*;
import javax.swing.*;
import javax.swing.border.*;
import javax.swing.text.*;
import javax.swing.event.*;

public class DateTimeEditor extends JPanel {
  public static final long ONE_SECOND = 1000;
  public static final long ONE_MINUTE = 60*ONE_SECOND;
  public static final long ONE_HOUR = 60*ONE_MINUTE;
  public static final long ONE_DAY = 24*ONE_HOUR;
  public static final long ONE_WEEK = 7*ONE_DAY;
  public final static int TIME = 0;
  public final static int DATE = 1;
  public final static int DATETIME = 2;
  private int m_timeOrDateType;
  private int m_lengthStyle;
  private DateFormat m_format;
  private Calendar m_calendar = Calendar.getInstance();
  private ArrayList m_fieldPositions = new ArrayList();
```

```
private Date m_lastDate = new Date();
private Caret m_caret;
private int m_curField = -1;
private JTextField m_textField;
private Spinner m_spinner;
private AbstractAction m_upAction =
  new UpDownAction(1, "up");
private AbstractAction m_downAction =
  new UpDownAction(-1, "down");
private int[] m_fieldTypes = {
  DateFormat.ERA_FIELD,
  DateFormat.YEAR_FIELD,
  DateFormat.MONTH_FIELD,
  DateFormat.DATE_FIELD,
  DateFormat.HOUR_OF_DAY1_FIELD,
  DateFormat.HOUR_OF_DAY0_FIELD,
  DateFormat.MINUTE_FIELD,
  DateFormat.SECOND_FIELD,
  DateFormat.MILLISECOND_FIELD,
  DateFormat.DAY_OF_WEEK_FIELD,
  DateFormat.DAY_OF_YEAR_FIELD,
  DateFormat.DAY_OF_WEEK_IN_MONTH_FIELD,
  DateFormat.WEEK_OF_YEAR_FIELD,
  DateFormat.WEEK_OF_MONTH_FIELD,
  DateFormat.AM_PM_FIELD,
  DateFormat.HOUR1_FIELD,
  DateFormat.HOUR0_FIELD
};
```

❶ Field type constants, defined in DateFormat class; each is plugged into DateFormat.format() to locate that field

```
public DateTimeEditor() {
  m_timeOrDateType = DATETIME;
  m_lengthStyle = DateFormat.SHORT;
  init();
}
```

❷ Default constructor sets Date/Time type, with Short length style

```
public DateTimeEditor(int timeOrDateType) {
  m_timeOrDateType = timeOrDateType;
  m_lengthStyle = DateFormat.FULL;
  init();
}
```

❷ This one sets specified Time/Date type with Full length style

```
public DateTimeEditor(int timeOrDateType, int lengthStyle) {
  m_timeOrDateType = timeOrDateType;
  m_lengthStyle = lengthStyle;
  init();
}
```

❷ This one sets specified Time/Date type with specified length style

```
private void init() {
  setLayout(new BorderLayout());
  m_textField = new JTextField();
  m_spinner = new Spinner();
  m_spinner.getIncrementButton().addActionListener(m_upAction);
  m_spinner.getDecrementButton().addActionListener(m_downAction);
  add(m_textField, "Center");
```

❸ Common initialization code from constructors

```
      add(m_spinner, "East");
      m_caret = m_textField.getCaret();
      m_caret.addChangeListener(new ChangeListener() {
        public void stateChanged(ChangeEvent evt) {
          setCurField();
        }
      });
      setupKeymap();
      reinit();
    }

    public int getTimeOrDateType() { return m_timeOrDateType; }
    public void setTimeOrDateType(int timeOrDateType) {
      m_timeOrDateType = timeOrDateType;
      reinit();
    }

    public int getLengthStyle() { return m_lengthStyle; }
    public void setLengthStyle(int lengthStyle) {
      m_lengthStyle = lengthStyle;
      reinit();
    }

    public Date getDate() { return (m_lastDate); }
    public void setDate(Date date) {
      m_lastDate = date;
      m_calendar.setTime(m_lastDate);
      m_textField.setText(m_format.format(m_lastDate));
      getFieldPositions();
    }

    private int getFieldBeginIndex(int fieldNum) {
      int beginIndex = -1;
      for (Iterator iter = m_fieldPositions.iterator();
       iter.hasNext(); )
      {
        FieldPosition fieldPos = (FieldPosition) iter.next();
        if (fieldPos.getField() == fieldNum) {
          beginIndex = fieldPos.getBeginIndex();
          break;
        }
      }
      return (beginIndex);
    }

    private FieldPosition getFieldPosition(int fieldNum) {
      FieldPosition result = null;
      for (Iterator iter = m_fieldPositions.iterator();
       iter.hasNext(); )
      {
        FieldPosition fieldPosition = (FieldPosition) iter.next();
        if (fieldPosition.getField() == fieldNum) {
          result = fieldPosition;
          break;
```

❸ Resets state when caret changes

❾ Sets new Date values; workaround for keymap bug goes here

```
        }
    }
    return (result);
}

private void reinit() {
    setupFormat();
    setDate(m_lastDate);
    m_caret.setDot(0);
    setCurField();
    repaint();
}

protected void setupFormat() {
    switch (m_timeOrDateType) {
        case TIME:
            m_format = DateFormat.getTimeInstance(m_lengthStyle);
            break;
        case DATE:
            m_format = DateFormat.getDateInstance(m_lengthStyle);
            break;
        case DATETIME:
            m_format = DateFormat.getDateTimeInstance(m_lengthStyle,
            m_lengthStyle);
            break;
    }
}

protected class UpDownAction extends AbstractAction
{
    int m_direction; // +1 = up; -1 = down

    public UpDownAction(int direction, String name) {
        super(name);
        m_direction = direction;
    }

    public void actionPerformed(ActionEvent evt) {
        if (!this.isEnabled())
            return;
        boolean dateSet = true;
        switch (m_curField) {
            case DateFormat.AM_PM_FIELD:
                m_lastDate.setTime(m_lastDate.getTime() +
                    (m_direction * 12*ONE_HOUR));
                break;
            case DateFormat.DATE_FIELD:
            case DateFormat.DAY_OF_WEEK_FIELD:
            case DateFormat.DAY_OF_WEEK_IN_MONTH_FIELD:
            case DateFormat.DAY_OF_YEAR_FIELD:
                m_lastDate.setTime(m_lastDate.getTime() +
                    (m_direction * ONE_DAY));
                break;
            case DateFormat.ERA_FIELD:
```

10 Action for Up/Down arrow keys; increments/decrements current field

10 Checks for the type of current field

```
        dateSet = false;
        break;
    case DateFormat.HOUR0_FIELD:
    case DateFormat.HOUR1_FIELD:
    case DateFormat.HOUR_OF_DAY0_FIELD:
    case DateFormat.HOUR_OF_DAY1_FIELD:
        m_lastDate.setTime(m_lastDate.getTime() +
            (m_direction * ONE_HOUR));
        break;
    case DateFormat.MILLISECOND_FIELD:
        m_lastDate.setTime(m_lastDate.getTime() +
            (m_direction * 1));
        break;
    case DateFormat.MINUTE_FIELD:
        m_lastDate.setTime(m_lastDate.getTime() +
            (m_direction * ONE_MINUTE));
        break;
    case DateFormat.MONTH_FIELD:
        m_calendar.set(Calendar.MONTH,
            m_calendar.get(Calendar.MONTH) + m_direction);
        m_lastDate = m_calendar.getTime();
        break;
    case DateFormat.SECOND_FIELD:
        m_lastDate.setTime(m_lastDate.getTime() +
            (m_direction * ONE_SECOND));
        break;
    case DateFormat.WEEK_OF_MONTH_FIELD:
        m_calendar.set(Calendar.WEEK_OF_MONTH,
            m_calendar.get(Calendar.WEEK_OF_MONTH) +
            m_direction);
        m_lastDate = m_calendar.getTime();
        break;
    case DateFormat.WEEK_OF_YEAR_FIELD:
        m_calendar.set(Calendar.WEEK_OF_MONTH,
            m_calendar.get(Calendar.WEEK_OF_MONTH) +
            m_direction);
        m_lastDate = m_calendar.getTime();
        break;
    case DateFormat.YEAR_FIELD:
        m_calendar.set(Calendar.YEAR,
            m_calendar.get(Calendar.YEAR) + m_direction);
        m_lastDate = m_calendar.getTime();
        break;
    default:
        dateSet = false;
    }

    if (dateSet) {
        int fieldId = m_curField;
        setDate(m_lastDate);
        FieldPosition fieldPosition = getFieldPosition(fieldId);
        m_caret.setDot(fieldPosition.getBeginIndex());
```

Sets new Date value and resets caret to start of current field ❿

```
      m_textField.requestFocus();
      repaint();
    }
  }
}

protected class BackwardAction extends TextAction
{
  BackwardAction(String name) { super(name); }

  public void actionPerformed(ActionEvent e) {
    JTextComponent target = getTextComponent(e);
    if (target != null) {
      int dot = target.getCaretPosition();
      if (dot > 0) {
        FieldPosition position = getPrevField(dot);
        if (position != null)
          target.setCaretPosition(
            position.getBeginIndex());
        else {
          position = getFirstField();
          if (position != null)
            target.setCaretPosition(
              position.getBeginIndex());
        }
      }
      else
        target.getToolkit().beep();
      target.getCaret().setMagicCaretPosition(null);
    }
  }
}

protected class ForwardAction extends TextAction
{
  ForwardAction(String name) { super(name); }

  public void actionPerformed(ActionEvent e) {
    JTextComponent target = getTextComponent(e);
    if (target != null) {
      FieldPosition position = getNextField(
        target.getCaretPosition());
      if (position != null)
        target.setCaretPosition(position.getBeginIndex());
      else {
        position = getLastField();
        if (position != null)
          target.setCaretPosition(
            position.getBeginIndex());
      }
      target.getCaret().setMagicCaretPosition(null);
    }
  }
```

⓫ Action for left arrow key; moves to start of previous field

⓬ Action for right arrow key; moves to start of next field

```
}
protected class BeginAction extends TextAction
{
  BeginAction(String name) { super(name); }

  public void actionPerformed(ActionEvent e) {
    JTextComponent target = getTextComponent(e);
    if (target != null) {
      FieldPosition position = getFirstField();
      if (position != null)
        target.setCaretPosition(position.getBeginIndex());
    }
  }
}

protected class EndAction extends TextAction
{
  EndAction(String name) { super(name); }

  public void actionPerformed(ActionEvent e) {
    JTextComponent target = getTextComponent(e);
    if (target != null) {
      FieldPosition position = getLastField();
      if (position != null)
        target.setCaretPosition(position.getBeginIndex());
    }
  }
}

protected void setupKeymap() {
  Keymap keymap = m_textField.addKeymap("DateTimeKeymap", null);
  keymap.addActionForKeyStroke(KeyStroke.getKeyStroke(
    KeyEvent.VK_UP, 0), m_upAction);
  keymap.addActionForKeyStroke(KeyStroke.getKeyStroke(
    KeyEvent.VK_DOWN, 0), m_downAction);
  keymap.addActionForKeyStroke(KeyStroke.getKeyStroke(
    KeyEvent.VK_LEFT, 0), new BackwardAction(DefaultEditorKit.
    backwardAction));
  keymap.addActionForKeyStroke(KeyStroke.getKeyStroke(
    KeyEvent.VK_RIGHT, 0), new ForwardAction(DefaultEditorKit.
    forwardAction));
  keymap.addActionForKeyStroke(KeyStroke.getKeyStroke(
    KeyEvent.VK_HOME, 0), new BeginAction(DefaultEditorKit.
    beginAction));
  keymap.addActionForKeyStroke(KeyStroke.getKeyStroke(
    KeyEvent.VK_END, 0), new EndAction(DefaultEditorKit.
    endAction));
  m_textField.setKeymap(keymap);
}
private void getFieldPositions() {
  m_fieldPositions.clear();
  for (int ctr = 0; ctr < m_fieldTypes.length; ++ctr) {
    int fieldId = m_fieldTypes[ctr];
```

13 Action for Home key; moves to start of first field

13 Action for End key; moves to start of last field

4 Adds Actions for arrow keys and ignores everything else

5 Called when a new Date is set; plugs m_fieldTypes into DateFormat.format() method

```
      FieldPosition fieldPosition = new FieldPosition(fieldId);
      StringBuffer formattedField = new StringBuffer();
      m_format.format(m_lastDate, formattedField, fieldPosition);
      if (fieldPosition.getEndIndex() > 0)
        m_fieldPositions.add(fieldPosition);
   }
   m_fieldPositions.trimToSize();
   Collections.sort(m_fieldPositions,
     new Comparator() {
       public int compare(Object o1, Object o2) {
         return (((FieldPosition) o1).getBeginIndex() -
           ((FieldPosition) o2).getBeginIndex());
       }
     }
   );
 }

 private FieldPosition getField(int caretLoc) {
   FieldPosition fieldPosition = null;
   for (Iterator iter = m_fieldPositions.iterator();
    iter.hasNext(); )
   {
     FieldPosition chkFieldPosition =
        (FieldPosition) iter.next();
     if ((chkFieldPosition.getBeginIndex() <= caretLoc) &&
      (chkFieldPosition.getEndIndex() > caretLoc))
     {
       fieldPosition = chkFieldPosition;
       break;
     }
   }
   return (fieldPosition);
 }

 private FieldPosition getPrevField(int caretLoc) {
   FieldPosition fieldPosition = null;
   for (int ctr = m_fieldPositions.size() - 1; ctr > -1; -- ctr) {
     FieldPosition chkFieldPosition =
        (FieldPosition) m_fieldPositions.get(ctr);
     if (chkFieldPosition.getEndIndex() <= caretLoc) {
       fieldPosition = chkFieldPosition;
       break;
     }
   }
   return (fieldPosition);
 }
 private FieldPosition getNextField(int caretLoc) {
```

⑤ Sorts field positions by ascending begin index

⑥ Gets field at current caret location

⑥ Gets field just before current caret location

⑥ Gets field just after current caret location

```
      FieldPosition  fieldPosition = null;
      for (Iterator iter = m_fieldPositions.iterator();
       iter.hasNext(); )
      {
        FieldPosition chkFieldPosition =
          (FieldPosition) iter.next();
        if (chkFieldPosition.getBeginIndex() > caretLoc) {
          fieldPosition = chkFieldPosition;
          break;
        }
      }
      return (fieldPosition);
  }

  private FieldPosition getFirstField() {
    FieldPosition result = null;
    try { result = ((FieldPosition) m_fieldPositions.get(0)); }
    catch (NoSuchElementException ex) {}
    return (result);
  }

  private FieldPosition getLastField() {
    FieldPosition result = null;
    try {
      result =
        ((FieldPosition) m_fieldPositions.get(
          m_fieldPositions.size() - 1));
    }
    catch (NoSuchElementException ex) {}
    return (result);
  }

  private void setCurField() {
    FieldPosition fieldPosition = getField(m_caret.getDot());
    if (fieldPosition != null) {
      if (m_caret.getDot() != fieldPosition.getBeginIndex())
        m_caret.setDot(fieldPosition.getBeginIndex());
    }
    else {
      fieldPosition = getPrevField(m_caret.getDot());
      if (fieldPosition != null)
        m_caret.setDot(fieldPosition.getBeginIndex());
      else {
        fieldPosition = getFirstField();
        if (fieldPosition != null)
          m_caret.setDot(fieldPosition.getBeginIndex());
      }
    }

    if (fieldPosition != null)
      m_curField = fieldPosition.getField();
    else
      m_curField = -1;
  }
```

6 **Gets field with smallest begin index**

6 **Gets field with largest begin index**

```
public void setEnabled(boolean enable) {
  m_textField.setEnabled(enable);
  m_spinner.setEnabled(enable);
}

public boolean isEnabled() {
  return (m_textField.isEnabled() && m_spinner.isEnabled());
}

public static void main (String[] args) {
  JFrame frame = new JFrame();
  frame.addWindowListener(new WindowAdapter() {
    public void windowClosing(WindowEvent evt)
    { System.exit(0); }
  });

  JPanel panel = new JPanel(new BorderLayout());
  panel.setBorder(new EmptyBorder(5, 5, 5, 5));
  frame.setContentPane(panel);
  final DateTimeEditor field =
    new DateTimeEditor(DateTimeEditor.DATETIME,
    DateFormat.FULL);
  panel.add(field, "North");

  JPanel buttonBox = new JPanel(new GridLayout(2, 2));
  JButton showDateButton = new JButton("Show Date");
  buttonBox.add(showDateButton);

  final JComboBox timeDateChoice = new JComboBox();
  timeDateChoice.addItem("Time");
  timeDateChoice.addItem("Date");
  timeDateChoice.addItem("Date/Time");
  timeDateChoice.setSelectedIndex(2);
  timeDateChoice.addActionListener(new ActionListener() {
    public void actionPerformed(ActionEvent evt) {
      field.setTimeOrDateType(timeDateChoice.
      getSelectedIndex());
    }
  });
  buttonBox.add(timeDateChoice);

  JButton toggleButton = new JButton("Toggle Enable");
  buttonBox.add(toggleButton);
  showDateButton.addActionListener(new ActionListener() {
    public void actionPerformed(ActionEvent evt)
    { System.out.println(field.getDate()); }
  });
  toggleButton.addActionListener(new ActionListener() {
    public void actionPerformed(ActionEvent evt)
    { field.setEnabled(!field.isEnabled());}
  });
  panel.add(buttonBox, "South");

  final JComboBox lengthStyleChoice = new JComboBox();
  lengthStyleChoice.addItem("Full");
```

7 The "enabled" flag on component says whether both text field and spinner are enabled

8 Demonstrates DateTimeEditor with example

8 Sets Time/Date type on component

8 Prints English Date/ Time on stdout

8 Toggles enabled status of component

```
    lengthStyleChoice.addItem("Long");
    lengthStyleChoice.addItem("Medium");
    lengthStyleChoice.addItem("Short");
    lengthStyleChoice.addActionListener(new ActionListener() {
      public void actionPerformed(ActionEvent evt) {
        field.setLengthStyle(lengthStyleChoice.
          getSelectedIndex());
      }
    });
    buttonBox.add(lengthStyleChoice);

    frame.pack();
    Dimension dim = frame.getToolkit().getScreenSize();
    frame.setLocation(dim.width/2 - frame.getWidth()/2,
      dim.height/2 - frame.getHeight()/2);
    frame.show();
  }
}
```

(8) Sets length style of component

Spinner.java

see \Chapter19\Karr

```
import java.util.*;
import java.lang.reflect.*;
import java.awt.*;
import javax.swing.*;
import javax.swing.plaf.*;
import javax.swing.plaf.basic.*;

public class Spinner extends JPanel
{
  private int m_orientation = SwingConstants.VERTICAL;
  private BasicArrowButton m_incrementButton;
  private BasicArrowButton m_decrementButton;

  public Spinner() { createComponents(); }

  public Spinner(int orientation) {
    m_orientation = orientation;
    createComponents();
  }

  public void setEnabled(boolean enable) {
    m_incrementButton.setEnabled(enable);
    m_decrementButton.setEnabled(enable);
  }

  public boolean isEnabled() {
    return (m_incrementButton.isEnabled() &&
      m_decrementButton.isEnabled());
  }

  protected void createComponents() {
    if (m_orientation == SwingConstants.VERTICAL) {
      setLayout(new GridLayout(2, 1));
```

(14) Presents two BasicArrowButtons in panel, with access to those buttons to set Actions on

(14) Constructor can create a vertical or horizontal Spinner

```
      m_incrementButton = new BasicArrowButton(
        SwingConstants.NORTH);
      m_decrementButton = new BasicArrowButton(
        SwingConstants.SOUTH);
      add(m_incrementButton);
      add(m_decrementButton);
    }
    else if (m_orientation == SwingConstants.HORIZONTAL) {
      setLayout(new GridLayout(1, 2));
      m_incrementButton = new BasicArrowButton(
        SwingConstants.EAST);
      m_decrementButton = new BasicArrowButton(
        SwingConstants.WEST);
      add(m_decrementButton);
      add(m_incrementButton);
    }
  }

  public JButton getIncrementButton() {
    return (m_incrementButton); }
  public JButton getDecrementButton() {
    return (m_decrementButton); }

  public static void main(String[] args) {
    JFrame frame = new JFrame();
    JPanel panel = (JPanel) frame.getContentPane();
    panel.setLayout(new BorderLayout());
    JTextField  field = new JTextField(20);
    Spinner spinner = new Spinner();

    panel.add(field, "Center");
    panel.add(spinner, "East");

    Dimension dim = frame.getToolkit().getScreenSize();
    frame.setLocation(dim.width/2 - frame.getWidth()/2,
      dim.height/2 - frame.getHeight()/2);
    frame.pack();
    frame.show();
  }
}
```

14 Returns buttons so client can add Actions to them

19.2.1   Understanding the code

Class DateTimeEditor

1 The m_fieldTypes array contains all of the field alignment constants that are defined in the DateFormat class. These are all of the pieces of a time or date value that we should expect to see. The order in this list is not important. Each value is plugged into DateFormat.format() to determine where each field is in the String date/time value.

2 The default constructor makes the field display date and time, in a SHORT format, which the DateFormat class describes as "completely numeric," such as 12.13.52 or 3:30pm. The second constructor can specify whether the field will display the time, the date, or the date and time. In addition, it sets the field into the FULL format, which the DateFormat class describes as "pretty completely specified," such as "Tuesday, April 12, 1952 AD" or "3:30:42pm PST." The third constructor can specify the time/date type, and the length style, which will be SHORT, MEDIUM, LONG, or FULL (fields in DateFormat).

③ Each of the constructors calls a common init() method, which initializes the caret, registers a ChangeListener on the caret (to update which field the caret is in), sets up the keymap (up, down, left, and right arrow keys), and calls the reinit() method which does some additional initialization (this method can be called any time, not just during initial construction).

④ The setupKeymap() method defines the keymap for the up, down, left, and right arrow keys. It first adds a new keymap with a null parent, so that no other keymaps will be used. It then associates Actions with the keystrokes we want to allow. Finally, the setKeymap() method is called to assign this keymap to our text field.

⑤ Each time a new date is set, either at initialization or by changing one of the field values, the getFieldPositions() method is called. This method uses the DateFormat.format() method, plugging in the Date value, and each one of the DateFormat fields. A new Field-Position object is set which specifies the beginning and end indices for each field of the given date. All of the resulting FieldPosition objects are stored in the m_fieldPositions list, and they are sorted using the beginning index (using the Collections class). The list is sorted in this fashion so it will be easy to determine which field is associated with a particular caret location. The BackwardAction and ForwardAction classes (see below) use this sorted list to quickly move to the previous or next date/time value.

⑥ After the m_fieldPositions list is set, several methods search that list, either directly or indirectly, to move to a particular field or to find out what the current field is. The get-Field(), getPrevField(), and getNextField() methods all take a caret location and they return the current, previous, or next field, respectively. The getFirstField() and get-LastField() methods return the first and last fields. And finally, the setCurField() method gets the field the caret is in and adjusts the caret to sit at the beginning of the field. This method is used when a new date is set or when the user uses the mouse to set the caret location.

⑦ The setEnabled() and isEnabled() methods allow the component to be disabled or enabled, and to check on the enabled status of the component, respectively. Both methods apply to the component's text field and custom spinner.

⑧ The main() method of this class is used as a demonstration of its capabilities. It presents a DateTimeEditor, a Show Date button, and a Toggle Enable button. When the Show Date button is pressed, it prints the current date value shown in the field to standard output. (The string printed is always in the "en_US" locale, irrespective of the current locale being used to display the DateTimeEditor.) When the Toggle Enable button is pressed, it toggles the enabled status of the component which grays out the text field and the spinner buttons when it is disabled.

The first official Java 2 public release contains a bug in the key event distribution area. In the setupKeymap() method, we specifically limit the keymap so that only six keystrokes should be recognized in the component—the four arrow keys and the Home and End keys. As a result of this bug, some platforms will allow normal characters to be inserted into the field, which violates the integrity of the Date value.

To work around this problem, a small amount of code can be added to this example. The solution requires two pieces:

9 1 In the `setDate()` method, which is the only place where the text of the field should be modified, we toggle a flag just before and after setting the text to indicate that we are trying to set the text of the field.

2 We create a new class, `DateTimeDocument`, to extend `PlainDocument`, and we send an instance of this class to the `setDocument()` method of `JTextField`. The `insertString()` method of `DateTimeDocument` only calls `super.insertString()` if the flag (from item 1) is `true`.

Here are the exact changes required to work around this key event bug:

1 Add the declaration of `m_settingDateText` to the variables section:

```
private boolean m_settingDateText = false;
```

2 Change the `setDate()` method to the following:

```
public void setDate(Date date) {
  m_lastDate = date;
  m_calendar.setTime(m_lastDate);
  m_settingDateText = true;
  m_textField.setText(m_format.format(m_lastDate));
  m_settingDateText = false;
  getFieldPositions();
}
```

3 In the `init()` method, send an instance of `DateTimeDocument` to the `setDocument()` method of the `JTextField` instance to set the `Document`:

```
m_textField.setDocument(new DateTimeDocument());
```

4 Add the `DateTimeDocument` class:

```
protected class DateTimeDocument extends PlainDocument
{
  public void insertString(int offset,
   String str, AttributeSet a) throws BadLocationException
  {
    if (m_settingDateText)
      super.insertString(offset, str, a);
  }
}
```

Class DateTimeEditor.UpDownAction

10 The `UpDownAction` class is used as the action for the up and down arrow keys. When it is executed, it will increment or decrement the value of the field the caret is in. When values roll over (or roll down), like incrementing the day from "31" to "1," then this will change other fields, like the month field, in this example. One instance of this class is used to move in the up direction, and one instance is used to move in the down direction. It calculates the new time or date value for each field, and it uses `Date.setTime()` or `Calendar.set()` methods to set the new date or time. It will check for all of the field types that are specified in the `DateFormat` class (they are also listed in the `m_fieldTypes` array), although several would never be seen in certain locales. If the component is presently disabled, no modifications will be performed on the data.

Class DateTimeEditor.BackwardAction

11 The `BackwardAction` class is used as the action for the left arrow key. When it is executed, it will move the text caret from the beginning of one field to the beginning of the previous field. It uses the `getPrevField()` method to get the field previous to the current one.

Class DateTimeEditor.ForwardAction

12 The `ForwardAction` class is used as the action for the right arrow key. When it is executed, it will move the text caret from the beginning of the current field to the beginning of the next field. It uses the `getNextField()` method to get the field following the current one.

Class DateTimeEditor.BeginAction & DateTimeEditor.EndAction

13 The `BeginAction` and `EndAction` classes move the text caret to the beginning of the first and last fields, respectively.

Class Spinner

14 The `Spinner` class just uses two `BasicArrowButtons`, in either a vertical or horizontal orientation. It provides an API to get the increment or decrement buttons so you can attach listeners to them.

19.2.2 Running the code

`DateTimeEditor` can be compiled and executed as is. By default, it will present a date/time value in the current locale. You can experiment with this by setting the "LANG" environment variable to a legal locale string. It's possible that not all legal locale strings will show any difference in the presentation, or even be correctly recognized. I found only major locales like "es" (spanish), "fr" (french), and "it" (italian) would work.

When you push the Show Date button, it will print the English value of the `Date` to standard output. When you push the Toggle Enable button, it will toggle the enabled state of the text field. When it is disabled, the text is slightly grayed out, the up and down arrow keys do nothing, and the spinner buttons are insensitive. Figure 19.5 shows `DateTimeEditor` in action.

In addition, the `Spinner` class can be compiled and run as a standalone demonstration. When run, it will present an empty text field with the spinner buttons to the right of it. As presented, it doesn't do much, and it doesn't show any behavioral connection between the component (the text field) and the `Spinner`, but this does show what the `Spinner` looks like when it is connected to a component. Figure 19.6 shows what the `Spinner` class looks like when it is run.

C H A P T E R 2 0

Constructing a word processor

This chapter is devoted to the construction of a fully functional RTF word processor application. Though Swing's HTML and RTF capabilities are very powerful, they are not yet complete. RTF support is further along than HTML, so we chose to focus solely on RTF. Do not be surprised when you see a series of "unknown keyword" warnings or exception problems with various Views. You will also see the following message displayed to emphasize the fact that RTF support is still in the works: "Problems encountered: Note that RTF support is still under development."

NOTE   Expect to see complete HTML coverage and examples in a future edition of this book. Also keep an eye on the Swing Connection site for updates. As we go to press, there are rumors of several HTML editor examples in the works.

20.1 WORD PROCESSOR, PART I: INTRODUCING RTF

Example 20.1 is a basic example that uses the capabilities of JTextPane and RTFEditorKit to display and edit RTF documents. It demonstrates very basic word processor functionality, such as opening and saving an RTF file, and it serves as the foundation for our word processor application that will be expanded upon throughout this chapter.

NOTE   In this series of examples, our goal is to demonstrate the most significant available features of advanced text editing in Swing (even if they do not all currently work properly). To avoid losing sight of this goal, we intentionally omit several typical word processor features such as an MDI interface, a status bar, and prompts to save the current file before closing.

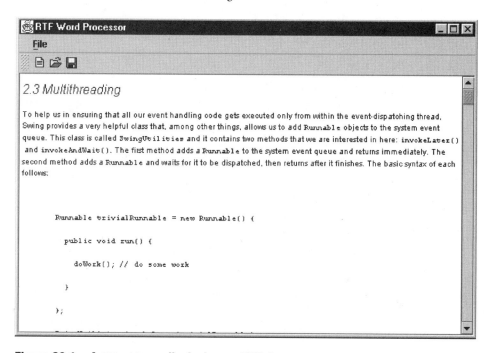

Figure 20.1   A JTextPane **displaying an RTF document**

Example 20.1

WordProcessor.java

see \Chapter20\1

```java
import java.awt.*;
import java.awt.event.*;
import java.io.*;
import java.util.*;

import javax.swing.*;
import javax.swing.text.*;
```

```java
import javax.swing.event.*;
import javax.swing.border.*;
import javax.swing.text.rtf.*;

public class WordProcessor extends JFrame
{
  protected JTextPane m_monitor;
  protected StyleContext m_context;
  protected DefaultStyledDocument m_doc;
  protected RTFEditorKit m_kit;
  protected JFileChooser m_chooser;
  protected SimpleFilter m_rtfFilter;
  protected JToolBar m_toolBar;

  public WordProcessor() {
    super("RTF Word Processor");
    setSize(600, 400);

    // Make sure we install the editor kit before creating
    // the initial document.
    m_monitor = new JTextPane();
    m_kit = new RTFEditorKit();
    m_monitor.setEditorKit(m_kit);
    m_context = new StyleContext();
    m_doc = new DefaultStyledDocument(m_context);
    m_monitor.setDocument(m_doc);

    JScrollPane ps = new JScrollPane(m_monitor);
    getContentPane().add(ps, BorderLayout.CENTER);

    JMenuBar menuBar = createMenuBar();
    setJMenuBar(menuBar);

    m_chooser = new JFileChooser();
    m_chooser.setCurrentDirectory(new File("."));
    m_rtfFilter = new SimpleFilter("rtf", "RTF Documents");
    m_chooser.setFileFilter(m_rtfFilter);

    WindowListener wndCloser = new WindowAdapter() {
      public void windowClosing(WindowEvent e) {
        System.exit(0);
      }
    };
    addWindowListener(wndCloser);

    setVisible(true);
  }

  protected JMenuBar createMenuBar() {
    JMenuBar menuBar = new JMenuBar();

    JMenu mFile = new JMenu("File");
    mFile.setMnemonic('f');

    ImageIcon iconNew = new ImageIcon("file_new.gif");
    Action actionNew = new AbstractAction("New", iconNew) {
      public void actionPerformed(ActionEvent e) {
        m_doc = new DefaultStyledDocument(m_context);
```

1 JFrame which provides supporting frame for RTF word processor example

2 Creates JTextPane with RTFEditorKit and DefaultStyledDocument

```
      m_monitor.setDocument(m_doc);
    }
  };
  JMenuItem item = mFile.add(actionNew);
  item.setMnemonic('n');

  ImageIcon iconOpen = new ImageIcon("file_open.gif");
  Action actionOpen = new AbstractAction("Open...", iconOpen) {
    public void actionPerformed(ActionEvent e) {
      WordProcessor.this.setCursor(
        Cursor.getPredefinedCursor(Cursor.WAIT_CURSOR));
      Thread runner = new Thread() {
        public void run() {
          if (m_chooser.showOpenDialog(WordProcessor.this) !=
          JFileChooser.APPROVE_OPTION)
            return;
          WordProcessor.this.repaint();
          File fChoosen = m_chooser.getSelectedFile();

          // Recall that text component read/write operations are
          // thread safe. It's OK to do this in a separate thread.
          try {
            InputStream in = new FileInputStream(fChoosen);
            m_doc = new DefaultStyledDocument(m_context);
            m_kit.read(in, m_doc, 0);
            m_monitor.setDocument(m_doc);
            in.close();
          }
          catch (Exception ex) {
            ex.printStackTrace();
          }
          WordProcessor.this.setCursor(Cursor.getPredefinedCursor(
            Cursor.DEFAULT_CURSOR));
        }
      };
      runner.start();
    }
  };
  item = mFile.add(actionOpen);
  item.setMnemonic('o');

  ImageIcon iconSave = new ImageIcon("file_save.gif");
  Action actionSave = new AbstractAction("Save...", iconSave) {
    public void actionPerformed(ActionEvent e) {
      WordProcessor.this.setCursor(
        Cursor.getPredefinedCursor(Cursor.WAIT_CURSOR));
      Thread runner = new Thread() {
        public void run() {
          if (m_chooser.showSaveDialog(WordProcessor.this) !=
          JFileChooser.APPROVE_OPTION)
            return;
          WordProcessor.this.repaint();
          File fChoosen = m_chooser.getSelectedFile();
```

Reads document with InputStream instead of Reader **③**

```
              // Recall that text component read/write operations are
              // thread safe. It's OK to do this in a separate thread.
              try {
                OutputStream out = new FileOutputStream(fChoosen);
                m_kit.write(out, m_doc, 0, m_doc.getLength());
                out.close();
              }
              catch (Exception ex) {
                ex.printStackTrace();
              }

              // Make sure the chooser is updated to reflect the new file
              m_chooser.rescanCurrentDirectory();
              WordProcessor.this.setCursor(Cursor.getPredefinedCursor(
                Cursor.DEFAULT_CURSOR));
            }
          };
          runner.start();
        }
      };
      item = mFile.add(actionSave);
      item.setMnemonic('s');

      mFile.addSeparator();

      Action actionExit = new AbstractAction("Exit") {
        public void actionPerformed(ActionEvent e) {
          System.exit(0);
        }
      };

      item = mFile.add(actionExit);
      item.setMnemonic('x');
      menuBar.add(mFile);

      m_toolBar = new JToolBar();
      JButton bNew = new SmallButton(actionNew, "New document");
      m_toolBar.add(bNew);

      JButton bOpen = new SmallButton(actionOpen, "Open RTF document");
      m_toolBar.add(bOpen);

      JButton bSave = new SmallButton(actionSave, "Save RTF document");
      m_toolBar.add(bSave);

      getContentPane().add(m_toolBar, BorderLayout.NORTH);

      return menuBar;
    }
  public static void main(String argv[]) {
    new WordProcessor();
  }
}

// Class SmallButton unchanged from example 12.3

// Class SimpleFilter unchanged from section 14.1.9
```

Writes document with OutputStream instead of Writer ③

20.1.1 Understanding the code

Class WordProcessor

❶ This class extends `JFrame` to provide the supporting frame for this example. Several instance variables are declared:

- `JTextPane m_monitor`: The main text component.
- `StyleContext m_context`: A group of styles and their associated resources for the documents in this example.
- `DefaultStyledDocument m_doc`: The current document model.
- `RTFEditorKit m_kit`: The editor kit that knows how to read/write RTF documents.
- `JFileChooser m_chooser`: The file chooser used to load and save RTF files.
- `SimpleFilter m_rtfFilter`: The file filter for .rtf files.
- `JToolBar m_toolBar`: The toolbar containing the Open, Save, and New Document buttons.

❷ The `WordProcessor` constructor first instantiates our `JTextPane` and `RTFEditorKit`, and then it assigns the editor kit to the text pane (it is important that this is done before any documents are created). Our `StyleContext` is then instantiated and we build our `Default-StyledDocument` with it. The `DefaultStyledDocument` is then set as our text pane's current document.

❸ The `createMenuBar()` method creates a menu bar with a single menu entitled File. The menu items New, Open, Save, and Exit are added to the menu. The first three items are duplicated in the toolbar. This code is very similar to the code used in the examples in chapter 12. The important difference is that we use `InputStreams` and `OutputStreams` here, rather than `Readers` and `Writers`. We do this because RTF uses 1-byte encoding, which is incompatible with the 2-byte encoding used by readers and writers.

> **WARNING**   An attempt to invoke `read()` will throw an exception when `JTextPane` is using an `RTFEditorKit`.

20.1.2 Running the code

Use menu or toolbar buttons to open an RTF file (a sample RTF file is provided in the **\Chapter 20** directory in the ZIP archive for this chapter). Save the RTF file and open it in another RTF-aware application (such as Microsoft Word) to verify compatibility.

20.2   *WORD PROCESSOR, PART II: MANAGING FONTS*

Example 20.2 adds the ability to select any font available on the system. This functionality is similar to the font menu used in the examples in chapter 12. The important difference here is that the selected font applies not to the whole text component (the only possible thing with plain text documents), but to the selected region of our RTF-styled document text.

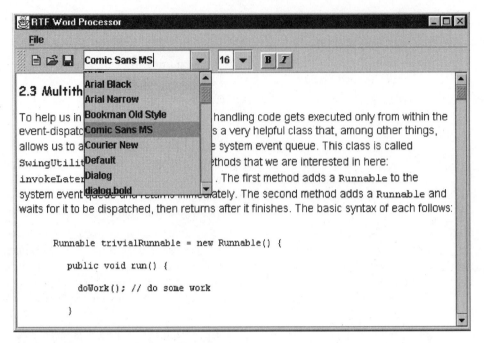

Figure 20.2 A `JTextPane` word processor that allows font attribute assignments to selected text

Example 20.2

see \Chapter20\2

```java
import java.awt.*;
import java.awt.event.*;
import java.io.*;
import java.util.*;

import javax.swing.*;
import javax.swing.text.*;
import javax.swing.event.*;
import javax.swing.border.*;
import javax.swing.text.rtf.*;

public class WordProcessor extends JFrame
{
  protected JTextPane m_monitor;
  protected StyleContext m_context;
  protected DefaultStyledDocument m_doc;
  protected RTFEditorKit m_kit;
  protected JFileChooser m_chooser;
  protected SimpleFilter m_rtfFilter;
  protected JToolBar m_toolBar;
```

CHAPTER 20 CONSTRUCTING A WORD PROCESSOR

```java
protected JComboBox m_cbFonts;
protected JComboBox m_cbSizes;
protected SmallToggleButton m_bBold;
protected SmallToggleButton m_bItalic;

protected String m_fontName = "";
protected int m_fontSize = 0;
protected boolean m_skipUpdate;

protected int m_xStart = -1;
protected int m_xFinish = -1;
public WordProcessor() {
  // Unchanged code from example 20.1

  CaretListener lst = new CaretListener() {
    public void caretUpdate(CaretEvent e) {
      showAttributes(e.getDot());
    }
  };
  m_monitor.addCaretListener(lst);

  FocusListener flst = new FocusListener() {
    public void focusGained(FocusEvent e) {
      if (m_xStart>=0 && m_xFinish>=0)
        if (m_monitor.getCaretPosition()==m_xStart) {
          m_monitor.setCaretPosition(m_xFinish);
          m_monitor.moveCaretPosition(m_xStart);
        }
        else
          m_monitor.select(m_xStart, m_xFinish);
    }

    public void focusLost(FocusEvent e) {
      m_xStart = m_monitor.getSelectionStart();
      m_xFinish = m_monitor.getSelectionEnd();
    }
  };
  m_monitor.addFocusListener(flst);

  WindowListener wndCloser = new WindowAdapter() {
    public void windowClosing(WindowEvent e) {
      System.exit(0);
    }
  };
  addWindowListener(wndCloser);

  showAttributes(0);
  setVisible(true);
}

protected JMenuBar createMenuBar() {
  // Unchanged code from example 20.1

  // The following line is added to the end of the
  // actionNew and actionOpen actionPerformed() methods:
  //
```

1 CaretListener notices whenever caret location changes

2 Sets up FocusListener to enable saving and restoring the component's text selection

```
//    showAttributes(0);
//
// (see source code; these methods are not shown here
//   to conserve space)

// Unchanged code from example 20.1

GraphicsEnvironment ge = GraphicsEnvironment.
  getLocalGraphicsEnvironment();
String[] fontNames = ge.getAvailableFontFamilyNames();

m_toolBar.addSeparator();
m_cbFonts = new JComboBox(fontNames);
m_cbFonts.setMaximumSize(m_cbFonts.getPreferredSize());
m_cbFonts.setEditable(true);

ActionListener lst = new ActionListener() {
  public void actionPerformed(ActionEvent e) {
    m_fontName = m_cbFonts.getSelectedItem().toString();
    MutableAttributeSet attr = new SimpleAttributeSet();
    StyleConstants.setFontFamily(attr, m_fontName);
    setAttributeSet(attr);
    m_monitor.grabFocus();
  }
};
m_cbFonts.addActionListener(lst);
m_toolBar.add(m_cbFonts);

m_toolBar.addSeparator();
m_cbSizes = new JComboBox(new String[] {"8", "9", "10",
  "11", "12", "14", "16", "18", "20", "22", "24", "26",
  "28", "36", "48", "72"});
m_cbSizes.setMaximumSize(m_cbSizes.getPreferredSize());
m_cbSizes.setEditable(true);

lst = new ActionListener() {
  public void actionPerformed(ActionEvent e) {
    int fontSize = 0;
    try {
      fontSize = Integer.parseInt(m_cbSizes.
        getSelectedItem().toString());
    }
    catch (NumberFormatException ex) { return; }

    m_fontSize = fontSize;
    MutableAttributeSet attr = new SimpleAttributeSet();
    StyleConstants.setFontSize(attr, fontSize);
    setAttributeSet(attr);
    m_monitor.grabFocus();
  }
};
m_cbSizes.addActionListener(lst);
m_toolBar.add(m_cbSizes);

m_toolBar.addSeparator();
ImageIcon img1 = new ImageIcon("font_bold1.gif");
```

3 Creates combo box containing all available font family names

4 When new event is selected, this applies it to selected text

5 Creates combo box to select or enter font size

5 When a font size is selected, applies new size to selected text

```
ImageIcon img2 = new ImageIcon("font_bold2.gif");
m_bBold = new SmallToggleButton(false, img1, img2,
  "Bold font");
lst = new ActionListener() {
  public void actionPerformed(ActionEvent e) {
    MutableAttributeSet attr = new SimpleAttributeSet();
    StyleConstants.setBold(attr, m_bBold.isSelected());
    setAttributeSet(attr);
    m_monitor.grabFocus();
  }
};
m_bBold.addActionListener(lst);
m_toolBar.add(m_bBold);

img1 = new ImageIcon("font_italic1.gif");
img2 = new ImageIcon("font_italic2.gif");
m_bItalic = new SmallToggleButton(false, img1, img2,
  "Italic font");
lst = new ActionListener() {
  public void actionPerformed(ActionEvent e) {
    MutableAttributeSet attr = new SimpleAttributeSet();
    StyleConstants.setItalic(attr, m_bItalic.isSelected());
    setAttributeSet(attr);
    m_monitor.grabFocus();
  }
};
m_bItalic.addActionListener(lst);
m_toolBar.add(m_bItalic);

getContentPane().add(m_toolBar, BorderLayout.NORTH);

return menuBar;
}

protected void showAttributes(int p) {
  m_skipUpdate = true;
  AttributeSet a = m_doc.getCharacterElement(p).
    getAttributes();
  String name = StyleConstants.getFontFamily(a);
  if (!m_fontName.equals(name)) {
    m_fontName = name;
    m_cbFonts.setSelectedItem(name);
  }
  int size = StyleConstants.getFontSize(a);
  if (m_fontSize != size) {
    m_fontSize = size;
    m_cbSizes.setSelectedItem(Integer.toString(m_fontSize));
  }
  boolean bold = StyleConstants.isBold(a);
  if (bold != m_bBold.isSelected())
    m_bBold.setSelected(bold);
  boolean italic = StyleConstants.isItalic(a);
  if (italic != m_bItalic.isSelected())
    m_bItalic.setSelected(italic);
```

6 Applies bold property to selected text

6 Applies italic property to selected text

7 Gets properties of character at current location and updates toolbar components to reflect those attributes

```
      m_skipUpdate = false;
   }

   protected void setAttributeSet(AttributeSet attr) {      ⑧  Assigns attributes
      if (m_skipUpdate)                                          to selected text
         return;
      int xStart = m_monitor.getSelectionStart();
      int xFinish = m_monitor.getSelectionEnd();
      if (!m_monitor.hasFocus()) {                          ⑨  If not focused, use
         xStart = m_xStart;                                     saved start and
         xFinish = m_xFinish;                                   finish locations
      }
      if (xStart != xFinish) {
         m_doc.setCharacterAttributes(xStart, xFinish - xStart,
            attr, false);
      }
      else {
         MutableAttributeSet inputAttributes =             ⑨  If selection is empty,
            m_kit.getInputAttributes();                        use attributes for text
         inputAttributes.addAttributes(attr);                  yet to be entered
      }
   }
}

   public static void main(String argv[]) {
         new WordProcessor();

   }
}

// Unchanged code from example 20.1

// Class SmallToggleButton unchanged from example 12.3
```

20.2.1   Understanding the code

Class WordProcessor

Several new instance variables have been added:

- JComboBox m_cbFonts: The toolbar component to select the font name.
- JComboBox m_cbSizes: The toolbar component to select the font size.
- SmallToggleButton m_bBold: The toolbar component to select the bold font style.
- SmallToggleButton m_bItalic: The toolbar component to select the italic font style.
- String m_fontName: The current font name.
- int m_fontSize: The current font size.
- boolean m_skipUpdate: The flag used to skip the word processor update (see below).
- int m_xStart: Stores the selection start position.
- int m_xFinish: Stores the selection end position.

❶ The constructor of the WordProcessor class adds a CaretListener to our m_monitor text pane. The caretUpdate() method of this listener is invoked whenever the caret position is changed. The showAttributes() method (see below) will be called in response to the caret position change in order to update the toolbar components and display the currently selected font attributes.

2 A `FocusListener` is also added to our `m_monitor` component. The two methods of this listener, `focusGained()` and `focusLost()`, will be invoked when the editor gains and loses the focus, respectively. The purpose of this implementation is to save and restore the starting and end positions of the text selection. We do this because Swing supports only one text selection at any time throughout an application. This means that if the user selects some text in the editor component to modify its attributes, and then goes off and makes a text selection in some other component, the original text selection will disappear. This can potentially be very annoying to the user. To fix this problem, we save the selection before the editor component loses the focus. When the focus is gained, we restore the previously saved selection. We distinguish between two possible situations: when the caret is located at the beginning of the selection and when it is located at the end of the selection. In the first case, we position the caret at the end of the stored interval with the `setCaretPosition()` method, and then we move the caret backward to the beginning of the stored interval with the `moveCaretPosition()` method. The second situation is easily handled using the `select()` method.

The `showAttributes()` method is now called prior to the display of a new document or a newly loaded document.

3 The `createMenuBar()` method creates new components to manage font properties for the selected text interval. First, the `m_cbFonts` combo box is used to select the font family name. Unlike the example in chapter 12 which used several predefined font names, this example uses all fonts available to the user's system. A complete list of the available font names can be obtained through the `getAvailableFontFamilyNames()` method of `GraphicsEnvironment` (see section 2.8). The `editable` property of this combo box component is set to `true`, so the font name can be both selected from the drop-down list and entered in by hand.

4 Once a new font name is selected, it is applied to the selected text using an attached `ActionListener`. The selected font family name is assigned to a `SimpleAttributeSet` instance with the `StyleConstants.setFontFamily()` method. Then our custom `setAttributeSet()` (see below) is called to modify the attributes of the selected text according to this `SimpleAttributeSet`.

5 The `m_cbSizes` combo box is used to select the font size. It is initiated with a set of predefined sizes. The `editable` property is set to true so the font size can be both selected from the drop-down list and entered by hand. Once a new font size is selected, it is applied to the selected text using an attached `ActionListener`. The setup is similar to that used for the `m_cbFonts` component. The `StyleConstants.setFontSize()` method is used to set the font size. Our custom `setAttributeSet()` method is then used to apply this attribute set to the selected text.

6 The bold and italic properties are managed by two `SmallToggleButtons` (this is a custom button class we developed in chapter 12): `m_bBold` and `m_bItalic`. These buttons receive `ActionListeners` which create a `SimpleAttributeSet` instance with the bold or italic property using `StyleConstants.setBold()` or `StyleConstants.setItalic()`. Then our custom `setAttributeSet()` method is called to apply this attribute set.

7 The `showAttributes()` method is called to set the state of the toolbar components described above according to the font properties of the text at the given caret position. This method sets the `m_skipUpdate` flag to `true` at the beginning and `false` at the end of its execution (the purpose of this will be explained soon). Then an `AttributeSet` instance corresponding to the character element at the current caret position in the editor's document is retrieved with the `getAttributes()` method. The `StyleConstants.getFontFamily()` method is used to retrieve the current font name from this attribute set. If it is not equal to the previously selected font name (which is stored in the `m_fontName` instance variable) it is selected in the `m_cbFonts` combo box. The other toolbar controls are handled in a similar way.

8 Our `setAttributeSet()` method is used to assign a given set of attributes to the currently selected text. This method does nothing (it simply returns) if the `m_skipUpdate` flag is set to `true`. This is done to prevent the backward link with the `showAttributes()` method. As soon as we assign some value to a combo box in the `showAttributes()` method (such as font size), a call to the `setAttributeSet()` method is internally triggered, because `Action-Listeners` attached to combo boxes are invoked even when selection changes occur programmatically. The purpose of `showAttributes()` is to simply make sure that the attributes corresponding to the character element at the current text position are accurately reflected in the toolbar components. To prevent the combo box `ActionListeners` from invoking unnecessary operations, we prohibit any text property updates from occurring in `setAttributeSet()` while the `showAttributes()` method is being executed (this is the whole purpose of the `m_skipUpdate` flag).

9 The `setAttributeSet()` method first determines the start and end positions of the selected text. If `m_monitor` currently does not have the focus, the stored bounds, `m_xStart` and `m_xFinish`, are used instead. If the selection is not empty (xStart != xFinish), the `set-CharacterAttributes()` method is called to assign the given set of attributes to the selection. This new attribute set does not have to contain a complete set of attributes. It simply replaces only the existing attributes for which it has new values, leaving the remainder unchanged. If the selection is empty, the new attributes are added to the input attributes of the editor kit (recall that `StyledEditorKit`'s input attributes are those attributes that will be applied to newly inserted text).

20.2.2 Running the code

Open an existing RTF file and move the cursor to various positions in the text. Notice that the text attributes displayed in the toolbar components are updated correctly. Select a portion of text and use the toolbar components to modify the selection's font attributes. Type a new font name or font size in the editable combo box and press Enter. This has the same effect as selecting a choice from the drop-down list. Save the RTF file and open it in another RTF-aware application to verify that your changes were saved correctly.

BUG ALERT Bold and italic font properties are often not updated on the screen properly, even though they are assigned and saved correctly. We expect that this problem will be fixed in a future Swing release.

20.3 WORD PROCESSOR, PART III: COLORS AND IMAGES

Some the important RTF features we will explore in this section include the ability to use foreground and background colors and insert images into the text. In example 20.3, we will show how to add these capabilities to our growing RTF word processor application.

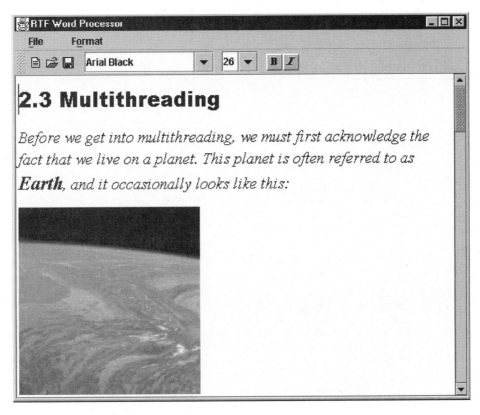

Figure 20.3   A `JTextPane` with diverse font styles, foreground colors, and an embedded image

Example 20.3

WordProcessor.java

see \Chapter20\3

```java
import java.awt.*;
import java.awt.event.*;
import java.io.*;
import java.util.*;

import javax.swing.*;
import javax.swing.text.*;
import javax.swing.event.*;
import javax.swing.border.*;
import javax.swing.text.rtf.*;

public class WordProcessor extends JFrame
{
   // Unchanged code from example 20.2
```

```
protected SimpleFilter m_jpgFilter;
protected SimpleFilter m_gifFilter;

protected ColorMenu m_foreground;
protected ColorMenu m_background;

public WordProcessor() {
  // Unchanged code from example 20.2

  m_chooser = new JFileChooser();
  m_chooser.setCurrentDirectory(new File("."));
  m_rtfFilter = new SimpleFilter("rtf", "RTF Documents");
  m_chooser.setFileFilter(m_rtfFilter);

  m_gifFilter = new SimpleFilter("gif", "GIF images");
  m_jpgFilter = new SimpleFilter("jpg", "JPG images");

  // Unchanged code from example 20.2
}

protected JMenuBar createMenuBar() {
  // Unchanged code from example 20.2

  JMenu mFormat = new JMenu("Format");
  mFormat.setMnemonic('o');

  m_foreground = new ColorMenu("Foreground");
  m_foreground.setColor(m_monitor.getForeground());
  m_foreground.setMnemonic('f');
  lst = new ActionListener() {
    public void actionPerformed(ActionEvent e) {
      MutableAttributeSet attr = new SimpleAttributeSet();
      StyleConstants.setForeground(attr, m_foreground.getColor());
      setAttributeSet(attr);
    }
  };
  m_foreground.addActionListener(lst);
  mFormat.add(m_foreground);

  MenuListener ml = new MenuListener() {
    public void menuSelected(MenuEvent e) {
      int p = m_monitor.getCaretPosition();
      AttributeSet a = m_doc.getCharacterElement(p).
        getAttributes();
      Color c = StyleConstants.getForeground(a);
      m_foreground.setColor(c);
    }

    public void menuDeselected(MenuEvent e) {}

    public void menuCanceled(MenuEvent e) {}
  };
  m_foreground.addMenuListener(ml);

  // Bug Alert! The background color attribute
  // doesn't work as of Java 2 FCS.
  m_background = new ColorMenu("Background");
```

Applies chosen foreground color to selected text ❶

```
m_background.setColor(m_monitor.getBackground());
m_background.setMnemonic('b');
lst = new ActionListener()  {
  public void actionPerformed(ActionEvent e) {
    MutableAttributeSet attr = new SimpleAttributeSet();
    StyleConstants.setBackground(attr, m_background.getColor());
    setAttributeSet(attr);
  }
};
m_background.addActionListener(lst);
mFormat.add(m_background);

ml = new MenuListener() {
  public void menuSelected(MenuEvent e) {
    int p = m_monitor.getCaretPosition();
    AttributeSet a = m_doc.getCharacterElement(p).
      getAttributes();
    Color c = StyleConstants.getBackground(a);
    m_background.setColor(c);
  }

  public void menuDeselected(MenuEvent e) {}

  public void menuCanceled(MenuEvent e) {}
};
m_background.addMenuListener(ml);

// Bug Alert! Images do not get saved.
mFormat.addSeparator();
item = new JMenuItem("Insert Image");
item.setMnemonic('i');
lst = new ActionListener() {
  public void actionPerformed(ActionEvent e) {
    m_chooser.addChoosableFileFilter(m_gifFilter);
    m_chooser.addChoosableFileFilter(m_jpgFilter);
    m_chooser.setFileFilter(m_gifFilter);
    m_chooser.removeChoosableFileFilter(m_rtfFilter);
    Thread runner = new Thread() {
      public void run() {
        if (m_chooser.showOpenDialog(WordProcessor.this) !=
        JFileChooser.APPROVE_OPTION)
          return;
        WordProcessor.this.repaint();
        File fChoosen = m_chooser.getSelectedFile();
        ImageIcon icon = new ImageIcon(fChoosen.getPath());
        int w = icon.getIconWidth();
        int h = icon.getIconHeight();
        if (w<=0 || h<=0) {
          JOptionPane.showMessageDialog(WordProcessor.this,
            "Error reading image file\n"+
            fChoosen.getPath(), "Warning",
            JOptionPane.WARNING_MESSAGE);
          return;
        }
```

2 Applies chosen background color to selected text

3 Sets up JFileChooser to select GIF or JPEG files

```
                    MutableAttributeSet attr = new SimpleAttributeSet();
                    StyleConstants.setIcon(attr, icon);
                    int p = m_monitor.getCaretPosition();
                    try {                                    Inserts single space    ③
                       m_doc.insertString(p, " ", attr);       with AttributeSet
                    }                                        containing icon image
                    catch (BadLocationException ex) {}

                    // It's OK to do this outside of the event-dispatching
                    // thread because the chooser is not visible here.
                    m_chooser.addChoosableFileFilter(m_rtfFilter);
                    m_chooser.setFileFilter(m_rtfFilter);
                    m_chooser.removeChoosableFileFilter(m_gifFilter);
                    m_chooser.removeChoosableFileFilter(m_jpgFilter);
                  }
                };
                runner.start();
              }
            };
            item.addActionListener(lst);
            mFormat.add(item);

            menuBar.add(mFormat);

            getContentPane().add(m_toolBar, BorderLayout.NORTH);

            return menuBar;
          }

       // Unchanged code from example 20.2
     }

     // Unchanged code from example 20.2

     // Class ColorMenu is unchanged from example 12.4
```

20.3.1   Understanding the code

Class WordProcessor

Two new instance variables have been added:

- `ColorMenu m_foreground`: Used to choose the selected text foreground color.
- `ColorMenu m_background`: Used to choose the selected text background color.

The `ColorMenu` class was constructed and discussed in chapter 12, and it is used here without modification. This class represents a custom menu component that is used to select a color from a collection of 64 predefined colors. To deploy this component in our application, we add a Format menu with menu items Foreground and Background. We also add, after a menu separator, the menu item Insert Image.

❶ The `ColorMenu m_foreground` receives an `ActionListener` which retrieves the selected color with the `getColor()` method and then applies it to the selected text by making calls to the `StyleConstants.setForeground()` and `setAttributeSet()` methods, similar to how we assigned new font attributes in the previous example. In order to maintain consistency, we need to update the `ColorMenu` component prior to displaying it to make the initial color selection consistent with the text foreground at the cursor position. For this purpose, we add a `MenuListener` to the `m_foreground` component. The `menuSelected()` method will be called prior to menu selection. Similar to the `showAttributes()` method discussed above, this code retrieves an `AttributeSet` instance corresponding to the current caret location and determines the selected foreground color with `getForeground()`. Then this color is passed to the `ColorMenu` component for use as the selection.

2 The `m_background ColorMenu` works similarly to `m_foreground`, but it manages selected text background color. This feature doesn't work with the current RTF API release; it is neither displayed nor saved in the file. The background color menu is added to our word processor for the sake of completeness.

3 The Insert Image menu item receives an `ActionListener` which uses our `JFileChooser` to select an image file. If an image file is successfully selected and read, we create a `Mutable-AttributeSet` instance and pass our image to it with `StyleConstants.setIcon()`. Then we insert a dummy single space character with that icon attribute using `insertString()`. All this occurs in a separate thread to avoid the possibility of clogging the event-dispatching thread.

20.3.2 Running the code

Open an existing RTF file, select a portion of text, and use the custom color menu component to modify its foreground. Save the RTF file and open it in another RTF-aware application to verify that your changes have been saved correctly. Try using the Insert Image menu to bring up a file chooser and select an image for insertion.

> **BUG ALERT** Unfortunately, embedded images are neither saved to a file or read from an existing RTF document. We expect that this problem/limitation will be fixed soon in a future release.

20.4 WORD PROCESSOR, PART IV: WORKING WITH STYLES

Using `Styles` to manage a set of attributes as a single named entity can greatly simplify text editing. The user only has to apply a known style to a selected region of text rather than selecting all appropriate text attributes from the provided toolbar components. By adding a combo box that allows the choice of styles, we can not only save the user time and effort, but we can also provide more uniform text formatting throughout the resulting document (or potential set of documents). In this section, we'll add style management to our word processor. We'll also show how it is possible to create a new style, modify an existing style, or reapply a style to modified text.

Example 20.4

WordProcessor.java

see \Chapter20\4

```
import java.awt.*;
import java.awt.event.*;
import java.io.*;
import java.util.*;
```

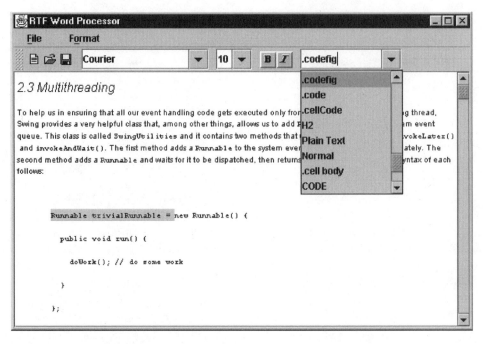

Figure 20.4   An RTF word processor application with `Styles` **management**

```java
import javax.swing.*;
import javax.swing.text.*;
import javax.swing.event.*;
import javax.swing.border.*;
import javax.swing.text.rtf.*;

public class WordProcessor extends JFrame
{
  // Unchanged code from example 20.3

  protected JComboBox m_cbStyles;

  public WordProcessor() {
    // Unchanged code from example 20.3

    showAttributes(0);
    showStyles();
    setVisible(true);
  }

  protected JMenuBar createMenuBar() {
    // Unchanged code from example 20.3

    // The following line is added to the end of the
    // actionNew and actionOpen actionPerformed() methods:
    //
    //     showStyles();
    //
```

```
// (see source code; these methods are not shown here
//   to conserve space)

// Unchanged code from example 20.3

JMenu mFormat = new JMenu("Format");
mFormat.setMnemonic('o');

JMenu mStyle = new JMenu("Style");
mStyle.setMnemonic('s');
mFormat.add(mStyle);

item = new JMenuItem("Update");
item.setMnemonic('u');
lst = new ActionListener() {
  public void actionPerformed(ActionEvent e) {
    String name = (String)m_cbStyles.getSelectedItem();
    Style style = m_doc.getStyle(name);
    int p = m_monitor.getCaretPosition();
    AttributeSet a = m_doc.getCharacterElement(p).
      getAttributes();
    style.addAttributes(a);
    m_monitor.repaint();
  }
};
item.addActionListener(lst);
mStyle.add(item);

item = new JMenuItem("Reapply");
item.setMnemonic('r');
lst = new ActionListener() {
  public void actionPerformed(ActionEvent e) {
    String name = (String)m_cbStyles.getSelectedItem();
    Style style = m_doc.getStyle(name);
    setAttributeSet(style);
  }
};
item.addActionListener(lst);
mStyle.add(item);

mFormat.addSeparator();

// Unchanged code from example 20.3

menuBar.add(mFormat);

m_toolBar.addSeparator();
m_cbStyles = new JComboBox();
m_cbStyles.setMaximumSize(m_cbStyles.getPreferredSize());
m_cbStyles.setEditable(true);
m_toolBar.add(m_cbStyles);

lst = new ActionListener() {

  public void actionPerformed(ActionEvent e) {

    if (m_skipUpdate || m_cbStyles.getItemCount()==0)
```

Copies attributes of current character into style ❷

Applies attributes of style to selected text ❷

```
      return;

  String name = (String)m_cbStyles.getSelectedItem();

  int index = m_cbStyles.getSelectedIndex();

  int p = m_monitor.getCaretPosition();
```
Checks whether selected style exists in style list ●1
```
  // New name entered
  if (index == -1) {
    m_cbStyles.addItem(name);
    Style style = m_doc.addStyle(name, null);
    AttributeSet a = m_doc.getCharacterElement(p).
      getAttributes();
```
Adds new style with attributes from current character ●1
```
    style.addAttributes(a);
    return;
  }

  // Apply the selected style
  Style currStyle = m_doc.getLogicalStyle(p);
  if (!currStyle.getName().equals(name)) {
    Style style = m_doc.getStyle(name);
    setAttributeSet(style);
```
Applies existing style attributes to selected text ●1
```
  }
    }
  };
  m_cbStyles.addActionListener(lst);

  getContentPane().add(m_toolBar, BorderLayout.NORTH);

  return menuBar;

}

protected void showAttributes(int p) {
  // Unchanged code from example 20.2
```
3 **Updates styles combo box with style from current character**
```
  Style style = m_doc.getLogicalStyle(p);
  name = style.getName();
  m_cbStyles.setSelectedItem(name);

  m_skipUpdate = false;
}

// Unchanged code from example 20.3

protected void showStyles() {
  m_skipUpdate = true;
  if (m_cbStyles.getItemCount() > 0)
    m_cbStyles.removeAllItems();
  Enumeration en = m_doc.getStyleNames();
  while (en.hasMoreElements()) {
```
4 **Populates styles combo box with styles from current document**
```
    String str = en.nextElement().toString();
    m_cbStyles.addItem(str);
  }
  m_skipUpdate = false;
}
```

```
    public static void main(String argv[]) {
      new WordProcessor();
    }
  }
}

// Unchanged code from example 20.3
```

20.4.1   Understanding the code

Class WordProcessor

One new instance variable has been added:

- JComboBox m_cbStyles: The toolbar component to manage styles.

    A new custom method, showStyles() (discussed below), is now called after creating a new document or after loading an existing one.

❶ The createMenuBar() method creates a new menu with two new menu items for updating and reapplying styles, and a new combo box for style selection. The editable styles combo box, m_cbStyles, will hold a list of styles that are declared in the current document (we will see how this component is populated below). It receives an ActionListener which checks whether the currently selected style name is present among the existing styles. If it is not, we add it to the drop-down list and retrieve a new Style instance for the selected name using StyledDocument's addStyle() method. This new Style instance is associated with the text attributes of the character element at the current caret position. Otherwise, if the given style name is known already, we retrieve the selected style using StyledDocument's get-Style() method and apply it to the selected text by passing it to our custom setAttribute-Set() method (as we did in previous examples when we assigned text attributes).

    An ambiguous situation occurs when the user selects a style for text which already has the same style, but whose attributes have been modified. The user may either want to update the selected style using the selected text as a base, or reapply the existing style to the selected text. To resolve this situation, we need to ask the user what to do. We chose to add two menu items which allow the user to either update or reapply the current selection.

> **NOTE**   In ambiguous situations such as this, making the decision to either allow users to choose between two options or enforce a single behavior can be a tough one to make. In general, the less experienced the target audience is, the fewer choices that audience should need to become familiar with. In this case we would suggest that a selected style override all attributes of the selected text.

❷ The menu items to perform these tasks are entitled Update and Reapply, and they are grouped into the Style menu. The Style menu is added to the Format menu. The Update menu item receives an ActionListener which retrieves the text attributes of the character element at the current caret position and assigns them to the selected style. The Reapply menu item receives an ActionListener which applies the selected style to the selected text (one might argue that this menu item would be more appropriately entitled Apply—the implications are ambiguous either way).

❸ Our showAttributes() method receives additional code to manage the new styles combo box, m_cbStyles, when the caret moves through the document. It retrieves the style corresponding to the current caret position with `StyledDocument`'s `getLogicalStyle()` method, and it selects the appropriate entry in the combo box.

❹ The new `showStyles()` method is called to populate the `m_cbStyles` combo box with the style names from a newly created or loaded document. It first removes the current content of the combo box if it is not empty (another workaround due to the fact that if you call `remove-AllItems()` on an empty `JComboBox`, an exception will be thrown). An `Enumeration` of style names is then retrieved with `StyledDocument`'s `getStyleNames()` method, and these names are added to the combo box.

20.4.2 Running the code

Open an existing RTF file, and notice how the styles combo box is populated by the style names defined in this document. Verify that the selected style is automatically updated while the caret moves through the document. Select a portion of text and select a different style from the styles combo box. Notice how all text properties are updated according to the new style.

Try selecting a portion of text and modifying its attributes (for instance, foreground color). Type a new name in the styles combo box and press Enter. This will create a new style which can be applied to any other document text.

> **NOTE** New styles will not be saved along with an RTF document under the current version of `RTFEditorKit`.

Try modifying an attribute of a selected region of text (such as the font size) and select the Update option from the Style menu. This will update the style to incorporate the newly selected attributes. Apply the modified style to another portion of text and verify that it applies formatting according to the updated style.

> **NOTE** When a style is updated, any regions of text that this style had been applied to do not automatically get updated accordingly. This is another ambiguity that must be decided on depending what the user expects and what level of experience the target audience has. In our case we assume that the user only wants selected text to be affected by a style update.

Now try modifying some attributes of a portion of selected text and then select the Reapply option from the Style menu. This will restore the original text attributes associated with the appropriate style.

> **NOTE** Recall that we are using one `StyleContext` instance, `m_context`, for all documents. This object collects all document styles. These styles are always available when a new document is created or loaded. We might develop a document template mechanism by serializing this `StyleContext` instance into a file and restoring it with the appropriate document.

20.5 WORD PROCESSOR, PART V: CLIPBOARD AND UNDO/REDO

Clipboard and undo/redo operations have become commonplace, necessary components of all modern text editing environments. We have discussed these features in chapters 11 and 19, and in this section we'll show how to integrate them into our RTF word processor.

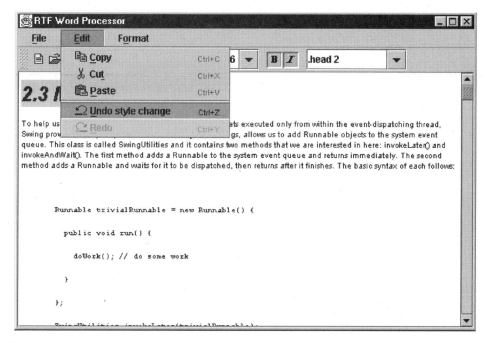

Figure 20.5   An RTF word processor with undo/redo and clipboard functionality

Example 20.5

WordProcessor.java

see \Chapter20\5

```java
import java.awt.*;
import java.awt.event.*;
import java.io.*;
import java.util.*;

import javax.swing.*;
import javax.swing.text.*;
import javax.swing.event.*;
import javax.swing.border.*;
import javax.swing.text.rtf.*;
import javax.swing.undo.*;

public class WordProcessor extends JFrame
{
  // Unchanged code from example 20.4

  protected UndoManager m_undo = new UndoManager();
  protected Action m_undoAction;
  protected Action m_redoAction;

  public WordProcessor() {
```

```
// Unchanged code from example 20.4

  showAttributes(0);
  showStyles();
  m_doc.addUndoableEditListener(new Undoer());
  setVisible(true);
}

protected JMenuBar createMenuBar() {
  // The following line is added to the end of the
  // actionNew and actionOpen actionPerformed() methods:
  //
  //   m_doc.addUndoableEditListener(new Undoer());
  //
  // (see source code; these methods are not shown here
  //  to conserve space)

  // Unchanged code from example 20.4

  JButton bSave = new SmallButton(actionSave, "Save RTF document");
  m_toolBar.add(bSave);

  JMenu mEdit = new JMenu("Edit");
  mEdit.setMnemonic('e');

  Action action = new AbstractAction("Copy",
   new ImageIcon("edit_copy.gif"))
  {
    public void actionPerformed(ActionEvent e) {
      m_monitor.copy();
    }
  };
  item = mEdit.add(action);
  item.setMnemonic('c');
  item.setAccelerator(KeyStroke.getKeyStroke(KeyEvent.VK_C,
    KeyEvent.CTRL_MASK));

  action = new AbstractAction("Cut",
   new ImageIcon("edit_cut.gif"))
  {
    public void actionPerformed(ActionEvent e) {
      m_monitor.cut();
    }
  };
  item = mEdit.add(action);
  item.setMnemonic('t');
  item.setAccelerator(KeyStroke.getKeyStroke(KeyEvent.VK_X,
    KeyEvent.CTRL_MASK));

  action = new AbstractAction("Paste",
   new ImageIcon("edit_paste.gif"))
  {
    public void actionPerformed(ActionEvent e) {
      m_monitor.paste();
    }
  };
```

① Copies selection to clipboard

① Copies selection to clipboard and deletes selection from document

① Pastes clipboard contents to current caret location

```
item = mEdit.add(action);
item.setMnemonic('p');
item.setAccelerator(KeyStroke.getKeyStroke(KeyEvent.VK_V,
  KeyEvent.CTRL_MASK));

mEdit.addSeparator();

m_undoAction = new AbstractAction("Undo",
 new ImageIcon("edit_undo.gif"))
{
  public void actionPerformed(ActionEvent e) {
    try {
      m_undo.undo();
    }
    catch (CannotUndoException ex) {
      System.err.println("Unable to undo: " + ex);
    }
    updateUndo();
  }
};
item = mEdit.add(m_undoAction);
item.setMnemonic('u');
item.setAccelerator(KeyStroke.getKeyStroke(KeyEvent.VK_Z,
  KeyEvent.CTRL_MASK));

m_redoAction = new AbstractAction("Redo",
 new ImageIcon("edit_redo.gif"))
{
  public void actionPerformed(ActionEvent e) {
    try {
      m_undo.redo();
    }
    catch (CannotRedoException ex) {
      System.err.println("Unable to redo: " + ex);
    }
    updateUndo();
  }
};
item =  mEdit.add(m_redoAction);
item.setMnemonic('r');
item.setAccelerator(KeyStroke.getKeyStroke(KeyEvent.VK_Y,
  KeyEvent.CTRL_MASK));

menuBar.add(mEdit);

GraphicsEnvironment ge = GraphicsEnvironment.
  getLocalGraphicsEnvironment();
String[] fontNames = ge.getAvailableFontFamilyNames();

// Unchanged code from example 20.4

return menuBar;
}

// Unchanged code from example 20.4
```

2 Makes UndoManager perform undo operation

2 Makes UndoManager perform redo operation

```
protected void updateUndo() {
    if(m_undo.canUndo()) {
        m_undoAction.setEnabled(true);
        m_undoAction.putValue(Action.NAME,
        m_undo.getUndoPresentationName());
    }
    else {
        m_undoAction.setEnabled(false);
        m_undoAction.putValue(Action.NAME, "Undo");
    }
    if(m_undo.canRedo()) {
        m_redoAction.setEnabled(true);
        m_redoAction.putValue(Action.NAME,
        m_undo.getRedoPresentationName());
    }
    else {
        m_redoAction.setEnabled(false);
        m_redoAction.putValue(Action.NAME, "Redo");
    }
}

public static void main(String argv[]) {
    new WordProcessor();
}

class Undoer implements UndoableEditListener
{
    public Undoer() {
        m_undo.die();
        updateUndo();
    }

    public void undoableEditHappened(UndoableEditEvent e) {
        UndoableEdit edit = e.getEdit();
        m_undo.addEdit(e.getEdit());
        updateUndo();
    }
}
}

// Unchanged code from example 20.4
```

❸ Updates undo and redo components depending on undo stack

Adds undoable edit events to UndoManager and updates state of undo/redo components ❹

20.5.1   Understanding the code

Class WordProcessor

We now import the javax.swing.undo package and add three new instance variables:

- UndoManager m_undo: Used to manage undo/redo operations.
- Action m_undoAction: Used for a menu item/action to perform undo operations.
- Action m_redoAction: Used for a menu item/action to perform redo operations.

A new Undoer instance (see below) is now added as an UndoableEditListener to all newly created or loaded documents.

1 The createMenuBar() method now creates a menu entitled Edit (which traditionally follows the File menu); this new menu contains menu items entitled Copy, Cut, Paste, Undo, and Redo. The first three items merely trigger calls to the copy(), cut(), and paste() methods of our m_monitor text pane. These methods perform clipboard operations using plain text without any attributes. They are available when the editor has the current focus and the appropriate keyboard accelerator is pressed. These items are added to our Edit menu to provide a convenient and informative interface.

2 The Undo menu item is created from an AbstractAction whose actionPerformed() method first invokes undo() on the UndoManager, and then invokes our custom update-Undo() method to update our undo/redo menu items appropriately. Similarly, the Redo menu item is created from an AbstractAction which invokes redo() on the UndoManager, and then calls our updateUndo() method.

3 The updateUndo() method enables or disables the undo and redo menu items and updates their names according to the operation which can be undone/redone (if any). If the UndoManager's canUndo() method returns true, the m_undoAction is enabled and its name is set to the string returned by getUndoPresentationName(). Otherwise, it is disabled and its name is set to Undo. The Redo menu item is handled similarly.

Class WordProcessor.Undoer

4 This inner class implements the UndoableEditListener interface to receive notifications about undoable operations. The undoableEditHappened() method receives Undoable-EditEvents, retrieves their encapsulated UndoableEdit instances, and passes them to the UndoManager. Our updateUndo() method is also invoked to update the undo/redo menu items appropriately.

20.5.2 Running the code

Open an existing RTF file and verify that copy, cut, and paste clipboard operations transfer plain text successfully. Make some changes to the textual content or styles and make sure that the title of the Undo menu item is updated. Select this menu item, or press its keyboard accelerator (CTRL-Z) to undo a series of changes. This will enable the Redo menu item. Use this menu item or press its keyboard accelerator (CTRL-Y) to redo a series of changes.

20.6 *WORD PROCESSOR, PART VI: ADVANCED FONT MANAGEMENT*

In section 20.2 we used toolbar components to manipulate font properties. This is useful for making a quick modification without leaving the main application frame, and it is typical for word processor applications. However, most serious editor applications also provide a dialog allowing users to edit all available font properties from one location. In example 20.6, we'll show how to create such a dialog, which includes components to select various font properties and preview the result.

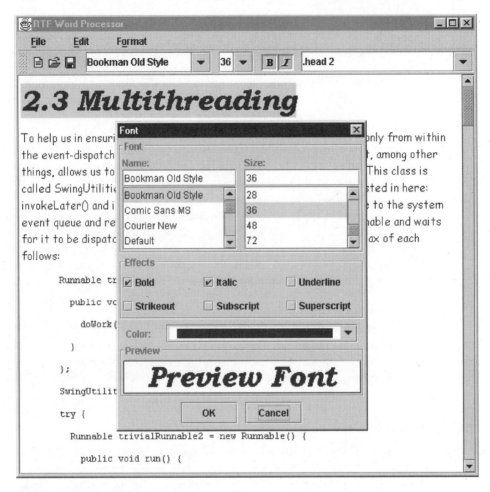

Figure 20.6   An RTF word processor with custom font properties and a preview dialog

Example 20.6

WordProcessor.java

see \Chapter20\6

```java
import java.awt.*;
import java.awt.event.*;
import java.io.*;
import java.util.*;

import javax.swing.*;
import javax.swing.text.*;
import javax.swing.event.*;
import javax.swing.border.*;
```

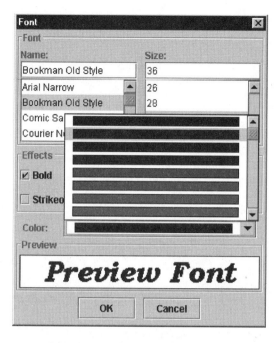

Figure 20.7 Font dialog with a custom list and list cell renderer for foreground color selection

```java
import javax.swing.text.rtf.*;
import javax.swing.undo.*;

public class WordProcessor extends JFrame
{
  // Unchanged code from example 20.5

  protected String[] m_fontNames;
  protected String[] m_fontSizes;

  protected FontDialog m_fontDialog;

  protected JMenuBar createMenuBar() {
    // Unchanged code from example 20.5

    GraphicsEnvironment ge = GraphicsEnvironment.
      getLocalGraphicsEnvironment();
    m_fontNames = ge.getAvailableFontFamilyNames();

    m_toolBar.addSeparator();
    m_cbFonts = new JComboBox(m_fontNames);
    m_cbFonts.setMaximumSize(m_cbFonts.getPreferredSize());
    m_cbFonts.setEditable(true);

    // Unchanged code from example 20.5

    m_toolBar.addSeparator();
    m_fontSizes = new String[] {"8", "9", "10", "11", "12", "14",
      "16", "18", "20", "22", "24", "26", "28", "36", "48", "72"};
    m_cbSizes = new JComboBox(m_fontSizes);
    m_cbSizes.setMaximumSize(m_cbSizes.getPreferredSize());
    m_cbSizes.setEditable(true);
```

```
      m_fontDialog = new FontDialog(this, m_fontNames, m_fontSizes);

      // Unchanged code from example 20.5

      JMenu mFormat = new JMenu("Format");
      mFormat.setMnemonic('o');

      item = new JMenuItem("Font...");
      item.setMnemonic('o');                                    Sends attributes of   ❶
      lst = new ActionListener() {                              current character
        public void actionPerformed(ActionEvent e) {            to font dialog
          WordProcessor.this.repaint();
          AttributeSet a = m_doc.getCharacterElement(
            m_monitor.getCaretPosition()).getAttributes();
          m_fontDialog.setAttributes(a);

          Dimension d1 = m_fontDialog.getSize();
          Dimension d2 = WordProcessor.this.getSize();
          int x = Math.max((d2.width-d1.width)/2, 0);
          int y = Math.max((d2.height-d1.height)/2, 0);
          m_fontDialog.setBounds(x + WordProcessor.this.getX(),
            y + WordProcessor.this.getY(), d1.width, d1.height);
                                                                Centers dialog        ❶
          m_fontDialog.show();                                     in frame
          if (m_fontDialog.getOption()==JOptionPane.OK_OPTION) {
            setAttributeSet(m_fontDialog.getAttributes());
            showAttributes(m_monitor.getCaretPosition());
          }                                                      Applies new          ❶
        }                                                        font attributes
      };                                                         to selected text
      item.addActionListener(lst);
      mFormat.add(item);

      mFormat.addSeparator();

      // Unchanged code from example 20.5

      return menuBar;
    }

    // Unchanged code from example 20.5
  }

// Unchanged code from example 20.5

class FontDialog extends JDialog
{
  protected int m_option = JOptionPane.CLOSED_OPTION;
  protected OpenList m_lstFontName;
  protected OpenList m_lstFontSize;
  protected MutableAttributeSet m_attributes;
  protected JCheckBox m_chkBold;
  protected JCheckBox m_chkItalic;
  protected JCheckBox m_chkUnderline;

  protected JCheckBox m_chkStrikethrough;
  protected JCheckBox m_chkSubscript;
  protected JCheckBox m_chkSuperscript;
```

```java
protected JComboBox m_cbColor;
protected JLabel m_preview;

public FontDialog(JFrame parent,
  String[] names, String[] sizes)
{
  super(parent, "Font", true);
  getContentPane().setLayout(new BoxLayout(getContentPane(),
    BoxLayout.Y_AXIS));

  JPanel p = new JPanel(new GridLayout(1, 2, 10, 2));
  p.setBorder(new TitledBorder(new EtchedBorder(), "Font"));
  m_lstFontName = new OpenList(names, "Name:");
  p.add(m_lstFontName);

  m_lstFontSize = new OpenList(sizes, "Size:");
  p.add(m_lstFontSize);
  getContentPane().add(p);

  p = new JPanel(new GridLayout(2, 3, 10, 5));
  p.setBorder(new TitledBorder(new EtchedBorder(), "Effects"));
  m_chkBold = new JCheckBox("Bold");
  p.add(m_chkBold);
  m_chkItalic = new JCheckBox("Italic");
  p.add(m_chkItalic);
  m_chkUnderline = new JCheckBox("Underline");
  p.add(m_chkUnderline);
  m_chkStrikethrough = new JCheckBox("Strikeout");
  p.add(m_chkStrikethrough);
  m_chkSubscript = new JCheckBox("Subscript");
  p.add(m_chkSubscript);
  m_chkSuperscript = new JCheckBox("Superscript");
  p.add(m_chkSuperscript);
  getContentPane().add(p);

  getContentPane().add(Box.createVerticalStrut(5));
  p = new JPanel();
  p.setLayout(new BoxLayout(p, BoxLayout.X_AXIS));
  p.add(Box.createHorizontalStrut(10));
  p.add(new JLabel("Color:"));
  p.add(Box.createHorizontalStrut(20));
  m_cbColor = new JComboBox();

  int[] values = new int[] { 0, 128, 192, 255 };
  for (int r=0; r<values.length; r++) {
    for (int g=0; g<values.length; g++) {
      for (int b=0; b<values.length; b++) {
        Color c = new Color(values[r], values[g], values[b]);
        m_cbColor.addItem(c);
      }
    }
  }

  m_cbColor.setRenderer(new ColorComboRenderer());
  p.add(m_cbColor);
  p.add(Box.createHorizontalStrut(10));
```

Makes dialog modal, with title "Font" ❷

Label, text field, and list for font names ❸

Label, text field, and list for font sizes ❸

Check boxes for various text effects ❸

Creates colors for foreground color combo box ❸

```
getContentPane().add(p);

p = new JPanel(new BorderLayout());
p.setBorder(new TitledBorder(new EtchedBorder(), "Preview"));
m_preview = new JLabel("Preview Font", JLabel.CENTER);
m_preview.setBackground(Color.white);
m_preview.setForeground(Color.black);
m_preview.setOpaque(true);
m_preview.setBorder(new LineBorder(Color.black));
m_preview.setPreferredSize(new Dimension(120, 40));
p.add(m_preview, BorderLayout.CENTER);
getContentPane().add(p);

p = new JPanel(new FlowLayout());
JPanel p1 = new JPanel(new GridLayout(1, 2, 10, 2));
JButton btOK = new JButton("OK");
ActionListener lst = new ActionListener() {
  public void actionPerformed(ActionEvent e) {
    m_option = JOptionPane.OK_OPTION;
    setVisible(false);
  }
};
btOK.addActionListener(lst);
p1.add(btOK);

JButton btCancel = new JButton("Cancel");
lst = new ActionListener() {
  public void actionPerformed(ActionEvent e) {
    m_option = JOptionPane.CANCEL_OPTION;
    setVisible(false);
  }
};
btCancel.addActionListener(lst);
p1.add(btCancel);
p.add(p1);
getContentPane().add(p);

pack();
setResizable(false);
Dimension d1 = getSize();
Dimension d2 = parent.getSize();
int x = Math.max((d2.width-d1.width)/2, 0);
int y = Math.max((d2.height-d1.height)/2, 0);
setBounds(x, y, d1.width, d1.height);

ListSelectionListener lsel = new ListSelectionListener() {
  public void valueChanged(ListSelectionEvent e) {
    updatePreview();
  }
};
m_lstFontName.addListSelectionListener(lsel);
m_lstFontSize.addListSelectionListener(lsel);

lst = new ActionListener() {
```

③ Panel shows sample of selected font attributes

④ Placing buttons inside GridLayout inside FlowLayout ensures the buttons are equally sized and centered

⑤ "Packed" for natural size, and centered in parent frame

⑤ Both name and size OpenLists call updatePreview() method when changed

```
   public void actionPerformed(ActionEvent e) {
     updatePreview();
   }
 };
 m_chkBold.addActionListener(lst);
 m_chkItalic.addActionListener(lst);
 m_cbColor.addActionListener(lst);
}
public void setAttributes(AttributeSet a) {
 m_attributes = new SimpleAttributeSet(a);
 String name = StyleConstants.getFontFamily(a);
 m_lstFontName.setSelected(name);
 int size = StyleConstants.getFontSize(a);
 m_lstFontSize.setSelectedInt(size);
 m_chkBold.setSelected(StyleConstants.isBold(a));
 m_chkItalic.setSelected(StyleConstants.isItalic(a));
 m_chkUnderline.setSelected(StyleConstants.isUnderline(a));
 m_chkStrikethrough.setSelected(
   StyleConstants.isStrikeThrough(a));
 m_chkSubscript.setSelected(StyleConstants.isSubscript(a));
 m_chkSuperscript.setSelected(StyleConstants.isSuperscript(a));
 m_cbColor.setSelectedItem(StyleConstants.getForeground(a));
 updatePreview();
}
public AttributeSet getAttributes() {
 if (m_attributes == null)
   return null;
 StyleConstants.setFontFamily(m_attributes,
   m_lstFontName.getSelected());
 StyleConstants.setFontSize(m_attributes,
   m_lstFontSize.getSelectedInt());
 StyleConstants.setBold(m_attributes,
   m_chkBold.isSelected());
 StyleConstants.setItalic(m_attributes,
   m_chkItalic.isSelected());
 StyleConstants.setUnderline(m_attributes,
   m_chkUnderline.isSelected());
 StyleConstants.setStrikeThrough(m_attributes,
   m_chkStrikethrough.isSelected());
 StyleConstants.setSubscript(m_attributes,
   m_chkSubscript.isSelected());
 StyleConstants.setSuperscript(m_attributes,
   m_chkSuperscript.isSelected());
 StyleConstants.setForeground(m_attributes,
   (Color)m_cbColor.getSelectedItem());
 return m_attributes;
}
public int getOption() { return m_option; }
protected void updatePreview() {
 String name = m_lstFontName.getSelected();
 int size = m_lstFontSize.getSelectedInt();
```

5 Color combo box and bold and italic check boxes call updatePreview() method when changed (other font effects are not supported)

6 Sets font controls from attributes in AttributeSet

7 Retrieves values from font controls and returns AttributeSet with those values

8 Sets font preview label with current attributes, to show what it looks like

```
        if (size <= 0)
          return;
        int style = Font.PLAIN;
        if (m_chkBold.isSelected())
          style |= Font.BOLD;
        if (m_chkItalic.isSelected())
          style |= Font.ITALIC;

        // Bug alert! This doesn't work if only the style parameter is changed.
        Font fn = new Font(name, style, size);
        m_preview.setFont(fn);

        Color c = (Color)m_cbColor.getSelectedItem();
        m_preview.setForeground(c);
        m_preview.repaint();
      }
    }

class OpenList extends JPanel
  implements ListSelectionListener, ActionListener
{
    protected JLabel m_title;
    protected JTextField m_text;
    protected JList m_list;
    protected JScrollPane m_scroll;

    public OpenList(String[] data, String title) {
      setLayout(null);
      m_title = new JLabel(title, JLabel.LEFT);
      add(m_title);
      m_text = new JTextField();
      m_text.addActionListener(this);
      add(m_text);
      m_list = new JList(data);
      m_list.setVisibleRowCount(4);
      m_list.addListSelectionListener(this);
      m_scroll = new JScrollPane(m_list);
      add(m_scroll);
    }

    public void setSelected(String sel) {
      m_list.setSelectedValue(sel, true);
      m_text.setText(sel);
    }

    public String getSelected() { return m_text.getText(); }

    public void setSelectedInt(int value) {
      setSelected(Integer.toString(value));
    }

    public int getSelectedInt() {
      try {
        return Integer.parseInt(getSelected());
      }
      catch (NumberFormatException ex) { return -1; }
    }
```

9 Encapsulates label, text field, and list

10 Uses no layout manager, positions children manually

11 Sets string in both text field and list

12 Convenience routines for an OpenList which manages a list of integer values

```
public void valueChanged(ListSelectionEvent e) {
  Object obj = m_list.getSelectedValue();
  if (obj != null)
    m_text.setText(obj.toString());
}

public void actionPerformed(ActionEvent e) {
  ListModel model = m_list.getModel();
  String key = m_text.getText().toLowerCase();
  for (int k=0; k<model.getSize(); k++) {
    String data = (String)model.getElementAt(k);
    if (data.toLowerCase().startsWith(key)) {
      m_list.setSelectedValue(data, true);
      break;
    }
  }
}

public void addListSelectionListener(ListSelectionListener lst) {
  m_list.addListSelectionListener(lst);
}

public Dimension getPreferredSize() {
  Insets ins = getInsets();
  Dimension d1 = m_title.getPreferredSize();
  Dimension d2 = m_text.getPreferredSize();
  Dimension d3 = m_scroll.getPreferredSize();
  int w = Math.max(Math.max(d1.width, d2.width), d3.width);
  int h = d1.height + d2.height + d3.height;
  return new Dimension(w+ins.left+ins.right,
    h+ins.top+ins.bottom);
}

public Dimension getMaximumSize() {
  Insets ins = getInsets();
  Dimension d1 = m_title.getMaximumSize();
  Dimension d2 = m_text.getMaximumSize();
  Dimension d3 = m_scroll.getMaximumSize();
  int w = Math.max(Math.max(d1.width, d2.width), d3.width);
  int h = d1.height + d2.height + d3.height;
  return new Dimension(w+ins.left+ins.right,
    h+ins.top+ins.bottom);
}

public Dimension getMinimumSize() {
  Insets ins = getInsets();
  Dimension d1 = m_title.getMinimumSize();
  Dimension d2 = m_text.getMinimumSize();
  Dimension d3 = m_scroll.getMinimumSize();
  int w = Math.max(Math.max(d1.width, d2.width), d3.width);
  int h = d1.height + d2.height + d3.height;
  return new Dimension(w+ins.left+ins.right,
    h+ins.top+ins.bottom);
}
```

(13) Coordinates changes between list and text field

(14) Returns maximum preferred width of the three children, and the total preferred height of the three children

(14) Returns "maximum" maximum width of the three children, and the total maximum height of the three children

(14) Returns "maximum" minimum width of the three children, and the total minimum height of the three children

```
    public void doLayout() {
      Insets ins = getInsets();
      Dimension d = getSize();
      int x = ins.left;
      int y = ins.top;
      int w = d.width-ins.left-ins.right;
      int h = d.height-ins.top-ins.bottom;

      Dimension d1 = m_title.getPreferredSize();
      m_title.setBounds(x, y, w, d1.height);
      y += d1.height;
      Dimension d2 = m_text.getPreferredSize();
      m_text.setBounds(x, y, w, d2.height);
      y += d2.height;
      m_scroll.setBounds(x, y, w, h-y);
    }
  }

class ColorComboRenderer extends JPanel implements ListCellRenderer
{
  protected Color m_color = Color.black;
  protected Color m_focusColor =
    (Color) UIManager.get("List.selectionBackground");
  protected Color m_nonFocusColor = Color.white;

  public Component getListCellRendererComponent(JList list,
   Object obj, int row, boolean sel, boolean hasFocus)
  {
    if (hasFocus || sel)
      setBorder(new CompoundBorder(
        new MatteBorder(2, 10, 2, 10, m_focusColor),
        new LineBorder(Color.black)));
    else
      setBorder(new CompoundBorder(
        new MatteBorder(2, 10, 2, 10, m_nonFocusColor),
        new LineBorder(Color.black)));

    if (obj instanceof Color)
      m_color = (Color) obj;
    return this;
  }

  public void paintComponent(Graphics g) {
    setBackground(m_color);
    super.paintComponent(g);
  }
}
```

⓮ Manually lays out children

⓯ List renderer for color selection list

20.6.1 Understanding the code

Class WordProcessor

Three new instance variables are added:

- `String[] m_fontNames`: An array of available font family names.
- `String[] m_fontSizes`: An array of font sizes.
- `FontDialog m_fontDialog`: The custom font properties and preview dialog.

These arrays were used earlier as local variables to create the toolbar combo box components. Since we need to use them in our font dialog as well, we decided to make them public instance variables (this requires minimal changes to the `createMenuBar()` method).

NOTE　Reading the list of available fonts takes a significant amount of time. For performance reasons, it is best to do this only once during an application's lifetime.

❶ A new menu item entitled Font... is now added to the Format menu. When the corresponding `ActionListener` is invoked, the application is repainted, the attributes of the character element corresponding to the current caret position are retrieved as an `AttributeSet` instance and passed to the dialog for selection (using its `setAttributes()` method), and the dialog is centered relative to the parent frame and displayed. If the dialog is closed with the OK button (which is determined by checking a value returned by `FontDialog`'s `getOption()` method), we retrieve the new font attributes with `FontDialog.getAttributes()` and assign these attributes to the selected text with our `setAttributeSet()` method. Finally, our toolbar components are updated with our `showAttributes()` method.

Class FontDialog

This class extends `JDialog` and acts as a font properties editor and previewer for our word processor application. Several instance variables are declared:

- `int m_option`: Indicates how the dialog is closed: by pressing the OK button, by pressing the Cancel button, or by closing the dialog window directly from the title bar. The constants defined in `JOptionPane` are reused for this variable.
- `MutableAttributeSet m_attributes`: A collection of font attributes used to preserve the user's selection.
- `OpenList m_lstFontName`: The custom `JList` subclass for selecting the font family name.
- `OpenList m_lstFontSize`: The custom `JList` subclass for selecting the font size.
- `JCheckBox m_chkBold`: The check box to select the bold attribute.
- `JCheckBox m_chkItalic`: The check box to select the italic attribute.
- `JCheckBox m_chkUnderline`: The check box to select the font underline attribute.
- `JCheckBox m_chkStrikethrough`: The check box to select the font strikethrough attribute.
- `JCheckBox m_chkSubscript`: The check box to select the font subscript attribute.
- `JCheckBox m_chkSuperscript`: The check box to select the font superscript attribute.
- `JComboBox m_cbColor`: The combo box to select the font foreground color.
- `JLabel m_preview`: The label to preview the selections.

2   The `FontDialog` constructor first creates a super class modal dialog entitled Font. The constructor creates and initializes all GUI components used in this dialog. A y-oriented `BoxLayout` is used to place component groups from top to bottom.

3   Two `OpenList` components (see below) are placed at the top to select an available font family name and font size. These components encapsulate a label, a text box, and list components which work together. They are comparable to editable combo boxes that always keep their drop-down list open. Below the `OpenList`s, a group of six check boxes are found; they allow the user to select bold, italic, underline, strikethrough, subscript, and superscript font attributes. `JComboBox m_cbColor` is placed below this group, and it is used to select the font foreground color. 64 `Colors` are added, and an instance of our custom `ColorComboRenderer` class (see below) is used as its list cell renderer. `JLabel m_preview` is used to preview the selected font before applying it to the editing text, and it is placed below the foreground color combo box.

4   Two buttons, which are labeled OK and Cancel, are found at the bottom of the dialog. They are placed in a panel managed by a 1x2 `GridLayout`, which is in turn placed in a panel managed by a `FlowLayout`. This is done to ensure the equal sizing and central placement of the buttons. Both receive `ActionListener`s which hide the dialog and set the `m_option` instance variable to `JOptionPane.OK_OPTION` and `JOptionPane.CANCEL_OPTION`, respectively. An application (`WordProcessor` in our case) will normally check this value once the modal dialog is dismissed by calling its `getOption()` method. This tells the application whether the changes should be ignored (`CANCEL_OPTION`) or applied (`OK_OPTION`).

5   The dialog window is packed to give it a natural size, and it is then centered with respect to the parent frame. The `m_lstFontName` and `m_lstFontSize` OpenList components each receive the same `ListSelectionListener` instance which calls our custom `updatePreview()` method (see below) whenever the list selection is changed. Similarly, two check boxes and the foreground color combo box receive an `ActionListener` which does the same thing. This provides a dynamic preview of the selected font attributes as soon as any are changed.

> **BUG ALERT**   Underline, strikethrough, subscript, and superscript font properties are not supported by the AWT `Font` class, so they cannot be shown in the `JLabel` component. This is why the corresponding check box components do not receive an `ActionListener`. As we will see, these properties also do not work properly in RTF documents. They are included in this dialog for completeness, in the hopes that they will work properly in a future Swing release.

6   The `setAttributes()` method takes an `AttributeSet` instance as a parameter. It copies this attribute set into a `SimpleAttributeSet` stored as our `m_attributes` instance variable. Appropriate font attributes are extracted using `StyleConstants` methods, and used to assign values to the dialog's controls. Finally, the preview label is updated according to these new settings by calling our `updatePreview()` method. The `setAttributes()` method is `public` and it is used for data exchange between this dialog and its owner (in our case, `WordProcessor`).

7   The `getAttributes()` method plays an opposite role with respect to `setAttributes()`. It retrieves data from the dialog's controls, packs it into an `AttributeSet` instance using `StyleConstants` methods, and returns this set to the caller.

The getOption() method returns a code that indicates how the dialog was closed by the user. This value should be checked prior to retrieving data from the dialog to determine whether the user canceled (JOptionPane.CANCEL_OPTION) or approved (JOptionPane.OK_OPTION) the changes.

8 The updatePreview() method is called to update the font preview label when a font attribute is changed. It retrieves the selected font attributes (family name, size, and bold and italic properties) and it creates a new Font instance to render the label. The selected color is retrieved from the m_cbColor combo box and set as the label's foreground.

Class OpenList

9 This component consists of a title label, a text field, and a list in a scroll pane. The user can either select a value from the list, or enter it in the text box manually. OpenList extends JPanel and maintains the following four instance variables:

- JLabel m_title: The title label used to identify the purpose of this component.
- JTextField m_text: An editable text field.
- JList m_list: A list component for selection.
- JScrollPane m_scroll: The scroll pane that contains the list component.

10 The OpenList constructor assigns a null layout manager because this container manages its child components on its own. The four components listed above are instantiated and simply added to this container.

11 The setSelected() method sets the text field text to that of the given String, and selects the corresponding item in the list (which is scrolled to display the newly selected value). The getSelected() method retrieves and returns the selected item as a String.

12 The setSelectedInt() and getSelectedInt() methods do the same thing, but with int values. These methods are implemented to simplify working with a list of ints.

13 The valueChanged() and actionPerformed() methods provide coordination between the list component and the text field. The valueChanged() method is called whenever the list selection changes, and it will assign the result of a toString() call on the selected item as the text field's text. The actionPerformed() method will be called when the user presses ENTER while the text field has the current focus. This implementation performs a case-insensitive search through the list items in an effort to find an item which begins with the entered text. If such an item is found, it is selected.

The public addListSelectionListener() method adds a ListSelectionListener to our list component (which is protected). In this way, external objects can dynamically receive notifications about changes in that list's selection.

14 The getPreferredSize(), getMaximumSize(), and getMinimumSize() methods calculate and return a preferred, maximum, and minimum dimension of this container respectively. They assume that the three child components (the label, the text field, and the scroll pane that contains the list) will be laid out one under another from top to bottom, each receiving an equal width and their preferable heights. The doLayout() method actually lays out the components according to this scheme. The insets (which result from an assigned border, for instance) must always be taken into account (see chapter 4 for more about custom layout management).

Class ColorComboRenderer

(15) This class implements the `ListCellRenderer` interface (which is discussed in chapters 9 and 10) and is used to represent various `Colors`. Three instance variables are defined:

- `Color m_color`: Used for the main background color to represent a `Color`.
- `Color m_focusColor`: Used for the thick border color of a selected item.
- `Color m_nonFocusColor`: Used for the thick border color of an unselected item.

The `getListCellRendererComponent()` method is called prior to the rendering of each list item (in our `WordProcessor` example, this list is contained within our foreground colors combo box). The `Color` instance is retrieved and stored in the `m_color` instance variable. This color is used as the renderer's background, while a white matte border is used to surround unselected cells and a light blue matte border is used to surround a selected cell. The `paintComponent()` method simply sets the background to `m_color` and calls the super class `paintComponent()` method.

20.6.2 Running the code

Open an existing RTF file, select a portion of text, and bring up the font dialog. Verify that the initial values correspond to the font attributes of the character element at the current caret position. Try selecting different font attributes and watch how the preview component is updated dynamically. Press the OK button to apply the selected attributes to the selected text. Also verify that pressing the Cancel button does not apply any changes. Figures 20.6 and 20.7 illustrate this example.

20.7 *WORD PROCESSOR, PART VII: PARAGRAPH FORMATTING*

Control over paragraph formatting attributes (such as line spacing, text alignment, and left and right margins) is just as important in word processor applications as font attribute control. Swing supports a number of paragraph settings which we discussed briefly in chapter 19. In example 20.7, we'll add a dialog specifically for editing these settings. The most interesting aspect of this dialog is a special component we've designed that allows the user to preview formatted text. In this way the user can get a feeling for how a setting change or group of changes will affect the actual document.

Example 20.7

WordProcessor.java

see \Chapter20\7

```
import java.awt.*;
import java.awt.event.*;
import java.io.*;
import java.util.*;

import javax.swing.*;
import javax.swing.text.*;
import javax.swing.event.*;
```

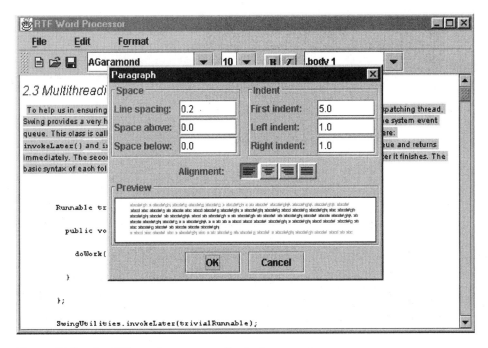

Figure 20.8   An RTF word processor displaying a custom paragraph attributes dialog

```
import javax.swing.border.*;
import javax.swing.text.rtf.*;
import javax.swing.undo.*;

public class WordProcessor extends JFrame
{
  // Unchanged code from example 20.6

  protected FontDialog m_fontDialog;
  protected ParagraphDialog m_paragraphDialog;

  protected JMenuBar createMenuBar() {
    // Unchanged code from example 20.6

    m_fontDialog = new FontDialog(this, m_fontNames, m_fontSizes);

    m_paragraphDialog = new ParagraphDialog(this);

    // Unchanged code from example 20.6

    item = new JMenuItem("Paragraph...");
    item.setMnemonic('p');
    lst = new ActionListener() {
      public void actionPerformed(ActionEvent e) {
        WordProcessor.this.repaint();
        AttributeSet a = m_doc.getCharacterElement(
          m_monitor.getCaretPosition()).getAttributes();
        m_paragraphDialog.setAttributes(a);
```

Gets attributes from current character and copies them to dialog ❶

```java
        Dimension d1 = m_paragraphDialog.getSize();
        Dimension d2 = WordProcessor.this.getSize();
        int x = Math.max((d2.width-d1.width)/2, 0);
        int y = Math.max((d2.height-d1.height)/2, 0);
        m_paragraphDialog.setBounds(x + WordProcessor.this.getX(),
          y + WordProcessor.this.getY(), d1.width, d1.height);

        m_paragraphDialog.show();
        if (m_paragraphDialog.getOption()==JOptionPane.OK_OPTION) {
          setAttributeSet(dlg.getAttributes(), true);
          showAttributes(m_monitor.getCaretPosition());
        }
      }
    };
    item.addActionListener(lst);
    mFormat.add(item);

    mFormat.addSeparator();

    // Unchanged code from example 20.6

    return menuBar;
  }

  // Unchanged code from example 20.6

  protected void setAttributeSet(AttributeSet attr) {
    setAttributeSet(attr, false);
  }

  protected void setAttributeSet(AttributeSet attr,
   boolean setParagraphAttributes)
  {
    if (m_skipUpdate)
      return;
    int xStart = m_monitor.getSelectionStart();
    int xFinish = m_monitor.getSelectionEnd();
    if (!m_monitor.hasFocus()) {
      xStart = m_xStart;
      xFinish = m_xFinish;
    }
    if (setParagraphAttributes)
      m_doc.setParagraphAttributes(xStart,
      xFinish - xStart, attr, false);
    else if (xStart != xFinish)
      m_doc.setCharacterAttributes(xStart,
        xFinish - xStart, attr, false);
    else {
      MutableAttributeSet inputAttributes =
        m_kit.getInputAttributes();
      inputAttributes.addAttributes(attr);
    }
  }

  // Unchanged code from example 20.6
}
```

1 Centers dialog in parent frame

1 Applies new paragraph attributes to selected text

2 Set paragraph attributes or character attributes

```
// Unchanged code from example 20.6

class ParagraphDialog extends JDialog
{
  protected int m_option = JOptionPane.CLOSED_OPTION;
  protected MutableAttributeSet m_attributes;
  protected JTextField m_lineSpacing;
  protected JTextField m_spaceAbove;
  protected JTextField m_spaceBelow;
  protected JTextField m_firstIndent;
  protected JTextField m_leftIndent;
  protected JTextField m_rightIndent;
  protected SmallToggleButton m_btLeft;
  protected SmallToggleButton m_btCenter;
  protected SmallToggleButton m_btRight;
  protected SmallToggleButton m_btJustified;

  protected ParagraphPreview m_preview;

  public ParagraphDialog(JFrame parent) {
    super(parent, "Paragraph", true);
    getContentPane().setLayout(new BoxLayout(getContentPane(),
      BoxLayout.Y_AXIS));

    JPanel p = new JPanel(new GridLayout(1, 2, 5, 2));

    JPanel ps = new JPanel(new GridLayout(3, 2, 10, 2));
    ps.setBorder(new TitledBorder(new EtchedBorder(), "Space"));
    ps.add(new JLabel("Line spacing:"));
    m_lineSpacing = new JTextField();
    ps.add(m_lineSpacing);
    ps.add(new JLabel("Space above:"));
    m_spaceAbove = new JTextField();
    ps.add(m_spaceAbove);
    ps.add(new JLabel("Space below:"));
    m_spaceBelow = new JTextField();
    ps.add(m_spaceBelow);
    p.add(ps);

    JPanel pi = new JPanel(new GridLayout(3, 2, 10, 2));
    pi.setBorder(new TitledBorder(new EtchedBorder(), "Indent"));
    pi.add(new JLabel("First indent:"));
    m_firstIndent = new JTextField();
    pi.add(m_firstIndent);
    pi.add(new JLabel("Left indent:"));
    m_leftIndent = new JTextField();
    pi.add(m_leftIndent);
    pi.add(new JLabel("Right indent:"));
    m_rightIndent = new JTextField();
    pi.add(m_rightIndent);
    p.add(pi);
    getContentPane().add(p);

    getContentPane().add(Box.createVerticalStrut(5));
    p = new JPanel();
```

❸ Presents dialog to set paragraph attributes

```java
p.setLayout(new BoxLayout(p, BoxLayout.X_AXIS));
p.add(Box.createHorizontalStrut(10));
p.add(new JLabel("Alignment:"));
p.add(Box.createHorizontalStrut(20));

ButtonGroup bg = new ButtonGroup();
ImageIcon img = new ImageIcon("al_left.gif");
m_btLeft = new SmallToggleButton(false, img, img, "Left");
bg.add(m_btLeft);
p.add(m_btLeft);
img = new ImageIcon("al_center.gif");
m_btCenter = new SmallToggleButton(false, img, img, "Center");
bg.add(m_btCenter);
p.add(m_btCenter);
img = new ImageIcon("al_right.gif");
m_btRight = new SmallToggleButton(false, img, img, "Right");
bg.add(m_btRight);
p.add(m_btRight);
img = new ImageIcon("al_justify.gif");
m_btJustified = new SmallToggleButton(false, img, img,
  "Justify");
bg.add(m_btJustified);
p.add(m_btJustified);
getContentPane().add(p);

p = new JPanel(new BorderLayout());
p.setBorder(new TitledBorder(new EtchedBorder(), "Preview"));
m_preview = new ParagraphPreview();
p.add(m_preview, BorderLayout.CENTER);
getContentPane().add(p);

p = new JPanel(new FlowLayout());
JPanel p1 = new JPanel(new GridLayout(1, 2, 10, 2));
JButton btOK = new JButton("OK");
ActionListener lst = new ActionListener() {
  public void actionPerformed(ActionEvent e) {
    m_option = JOptionPane.OK_OPTION;
    setVisible(false);
  }
};
btOK.addActionListener(lst);
p1.add(btOK);

JButton btCancel = new JButton("Cancel");
lst = new ActionListener() {
  public void actionPerformed(ActionEvent e) {
    m_option = JOptionPane.CANCEL_OPTION;
    setVisible(false);
  }
};
btCancel.addActionListener(lst);
p1.add(btCancel);
p.add(p1);
getContentPane().add(p);
```

```
    pack();
    setResizable(false);

    FocusListener flst = new FocusListener() {
      public void focusGained(FocusEvent e) {}

      public void focusLost(FocusEvent e) { updatePreview(); }
    };
    m_lineSpacing.addFocusListener(flst);
    m_spaceAbove.addFocusListener(flst);
    m_spaceBelow.addFocusListener(flst);
    m_firstIndent.addFocusListener(flst);
    m_leftIndent.addFocusListener(flst);
    m_rightIndent.addFocusListener(flst);

    lst = new ActionListener() {
      public void actionPerformed(ActionEvent e) {
        updatePreview();
      }
    };
    m_btLeft.addActionListener(lst);
    m_btCenter.addActionListener(lst);
    m_btRight.addActionListener(lst);
    m_btJustified.addActionListener(lst);
  }

  public void setAttributes(AttributeSet a) {
    m_attributes = new SimpleAttributeSet(a);
    m_lineSpacing.setText(Float.toString(
      StyleConstants.getLineSpacing(a)));
    m_spaceAbove.setText(Float.toString(
      StyleConstants.getSpaceAbove(a)));
    m_spaceBelow.setText(Float.toString(
      StyleConstants.getSpaceBelow(a)));
    m_firstIndent.setText(Float.toString(
      StyleConstants.getFirstLineIndent(a)));
    m_leftIndent.setText(Float.toString(
      StyleConstants.getLeftIndent(a)));
    m_rightIndent.setText(Float.toString(
      StyleConstants.getRightIndent(a)));

    int alignment = StyleConstants.getAlignment(a);
    if (alignment == StyleConstants.ALIGN_LEFT)
      m_btLeft.setSelected(true);
    else if (alignment == StyleConstants.ALIGN_CENTER)
      m_btCenter.setSelected(true);
    else if (alignment == StyleConstants.ALIGN_RIGHT)
      m_btRight.setSelected(true);
    else if (alignment == StyleConstants.ALIGN_JUSTIFIED)
      m_btJustified.setSelected(true);

    updatePreview();
  }
```

4 Copies paragraph attributes from AttributeSet to set controls with

```java
public AttributeSet getAttributes() {
  if (m_attributes == null)
    return null;
  float value;
  try {
    value = Float.parseFloat(m_lineSpacing.getText());
    StyleConstants.setLineSpacing(m_attributes, value);
  } catch (NumberFormatException ex) {}
  try {
    value = Float.parseFloat(m_spaceAbove.getText());
    StyleConstants.setSpaceAbove(m_attributes, value);
  } catch (NumberFormatException ex) {}
  try {
    value = Float.parseFloat(m_spaceBelow.getText());
    StyleConstants.setSpaceBelow(m_attributes, value);
  } catch (NumberFormatException ex) {}
  try {
    value = Float.parseFloat(m_firstIndent.getText());
    StyleConstants.setFirstLineIndent(m_attributes, value);
  } catch (NumberFormatException ex) {}
  try {
    value = Float.parseFloat(m_leftIndent.getText());
    StyleConstants.setLeftIndent(m_attributes, value);
  } catch (NumberFormatException ex) {}
  try {
    value = Float.parseFloat(m_rightIndent.getText());
    StyleConstants.setRightIndent(m_attributes, value);
  } catch (NumberFormatException ex) {}

  StyleConstants.setAlignment(m_attributes, getAlignment());

  return m_attributes;
}

public int getOption() {
  return m_option;
}

protected void updatePreview() {
  m_preview.repaint();
}

protected int getAlignment() {
  if (m_btLeft.isSelected())
    return StyleConstants.ALIGN_LEFT;
  if (m_btCenter.isSelected())
    return StyleConstants.ALIGN_CENTER;
  else if (m_btRight.isSelected())
    return StyleConstants.ALIGN_RIGHT;
  else
    return StyleConstants.ALIGN_JUSTIFIED;
}

class ParagraphPreview extends JPanel
{
```

⑤ Copies settings in controls to build an AttributeSet object to return

⑥ Displays sample view of paragraph attributes with dummy text

```
protected Font m_fn = new Font("Monospace", Font.PLAIN, 6);
protected String m_dummy = "abcdefghjklm";
protected float  m_scaleX = 0.25f;
protected float  m_scaleY = 0.25f;
protected Random m_random = new Random();

public ParagraphPreview() {
  setBackground(Color.white);
  setForeground(Color.black);
  setOpaque(true);
  setBorder(new LineBorder(Color.black));
  setPreferredSize(new Dimension(120, 56));
}
public void paintComponent(Graphics g) {
  super.paintComponent(g);
  float lineSpacing = 0;
  float spaceAbove = 0;
  float spaceBelow = 0;
  float firstIndent = 0;
  float leftIndent = 0;
  float rightIndent = 0;

  try {
    lineSpacing = Float.parseFloat(m_lineSpacing.getText());
  } catch (NumberFormatException ex) {}
  try {
    spaceAbove = Float.parseFloat(m_spaceAbove.getText());
  } catch (NumberFormatException ex) {}
  try {
    spaceBelow = Float.parseFloat(m_spaceBelow.getText());
  } catch (NumberFormatException ex) {}
  try {
    firstIndent = Float.parseFloat(m_firstIndent.getText());
  } catch (NumberFormatException ex) {}
  try {
    leftIndent = Float.parseFloat(m_leftIndent.getText());
  } catch (NumberFormatException ex) {}
  try {
    rightIndent = Float.parseFloat(m_rightIndent.getText());
  } catch (NumberFormatException ex) {}

  m_random.setSeed(1959);    // Use same seed every time

  g.setFont(m_fn);
  FontMetrics fm = g.getFontMetrics();
  int h = fm.getAscent();
  int s  = Math.max((int)(lineSpacing*m_scaleY), 1);
  int s1 = Math.max((int)(spaceAbove*m_scaleY), 0) + s;
  int s2 = Math.max((int)(spaceBelow*m_scaleY), 0) + s;
  int y = 5+h;

  int xMarg = 20;
  int x0 = Math.max((int)(firstIndent*m_scaleX)+xMarg, 3);
  int x1 = Math.max((int)(leftIndent*m_scaleX)+xMarg, 3);
  int x2 = Math.max((int)(rightIndent*m_scaleX)+xMarg, 3);
```

Retrieves values from controls, set by user **7**

Calculates heights, spacing margins, indents, and absolute positions **8**

```
        int xm0 = getWidth()-xMarg;
        int xm1 = getWidth()-x2;
```

8 Calculates heights, spacing margins, indents, and absolute positions

```
        int n = (int)((getHeight()-(2*h+s1+s2-s+10))/(h+s));
        n = Math.max(n, 1);

        g.setColor(Color.lightGray);
```

9 Draws light gray line before main paragraph

```
        int x = xMarg;
        drawLine(g, x, y, xm0, xm0, fm, StyleConstants.ALIGN_LEFT);
        y += h+s1;

        g.setColor(Color.gray);
        int alignment = getAlignment();
```

9 Draws each line of the dummy paragraph, with specified alignment

```
        for (int k=0; k<n; k++) {
          x = (k==0 ? x0 : x1);
          int xLen = (k==n-1 ? xm1/2 : xm1);
          if (k==n-1 && alignment==StyleConstants.ALIGN_JUSTIFIED)
            alignment = StyleConstants.ALIGN_LEFT;
          drawLine(g, x, y, xm1, xLen, fm, alignment);
          y += h+s;
        }

        y += s2-s;
        x = xMarg;
        g.setColor(Color.lightGray);
        drawLine(g, x, y, xm0, xm0, fm, StyleConstants.ALIGN_LEFT);
    }

    protected void drawLine(Graphics g, int x, int y, int xMax,
     int xLen, FontMetrics fm, int alignment)
    {
```

10 Draws one line of the dummy paragraph with specified alignment

```
        if (y > getHeight()-3)
          return;
        StringBuffer s = new StringBuffer();
        String str1;
        int xx = x;
        while (true) {
          int m = m_random.nextInt(10)+1;
          str1 = m_dummy.substring(0, m)+" ";
          int len = fm.stringWidth(str1);
          if (xx+len >= xLen)
            break;
          xx += len;
          s.append(str1);
        }
        String str = s.toString();

        switch (alignment) {
          case StyleConstants.ALIGN_LEFT:
            g.drawString(str, x, y);
            break;
          case StyleConstants.ALIGN_CENTER:
```

10 Changes starting X-coordinate or string length depending on specified alignment

```
            xx = (xMax+x-fm.stringWidth(str))/2;
            g.drawString(str, xx, y);
            break;
          case StyleConstants.ALIGN_RIGHT:
```

```
            xx = xMax-fm.stringWidth(str);
            g.drawString(str, xx, y);
            break;
          case StyleConstants.ALIGN_JUSTIFIED:
            while (x+fm.stringWidth(str) < xMax)
              str += "a";
            g.drawString(str, x, y);
            break;
        }
      }
    }
  }
```

⑩ Changes starting X-coordinate or string length depending on specified alignment

20.7.1   Understanding the code

Class WordProcessor

One new instance variable has been added:

- `ParagraphDialog m_paragraphDialog`: The custom dialog that manages paragraph attributes.

❶ A new menu item entitled Paragraph... is now added to the Format menu. A corresponding `ActionListener` acts similarly to the listener of Font... menu. It repaints the entire application, retrieves a set of attributes corresponding to the character element at the current caret position, and passes this set to `m_paragraphDialog`. The dialog is then centered with respect to its parent (`WordProcessor`, in our case) and shows itself. When the OK or Cancel button is pressed, the result returned by the `getOption()` method is normally checked. If the returned value is equal to `JOptionPane.OK_OPTION` (for example, if OK was pressed), we retrieve the selected attributes with `ParagraphDialog`'s `getAttributes()` method and assign them to the selected text with our `setAttributeSet()` method. Otherwise, we don't make any changes.

❷ An additional parameter, a `boolean`, is added to our `setAttributeSet()` method. This is used to distinguish between setting character attributes and setting paragraph attributes. A value of `true` indicates that the given attribute set corresponds to paragraph attributes. A value of `false` indicates that the given attribute set corresponds to character attributes. To preserve the existing code without requiring extensive modification, we keep the old `setAttributeSet()` method with one parameter, and redirect it to the new method by having it call `setAttributeSet(attr, false)`.

Class ParagraphDialog

❸ This class extends `JDialog` and acts as a paragraph attributes editor for our word processor application. Several instance variables are declared:

- `int m_option`: Indicates how the dialog is closed: by pressing the OK button, by pressing the Cancel button, or by closing the dialog window directly from the title bar. The constants defined in `JOptionPane` are reused for this variable.
- `MutableAttributeSet m_attributes`: A collection of paragraph attributes used to preserve the user's selection.
- `JTextField m_lineSpacing`: Specifies paragraph line spacing.
- `JTextField m_spaceAbove`: Specifies above line spacing.
- `JTextField m_spaceBelow`: Specifies below line spacing.

- `JTextField m_firstIndent`: Specifies the left indent of the first paragraph line.
- `JTextField m_leftIndent`: Specifies the left indent of all other paragraph lines (other than the first).
- `JTextField m_rightIndent`: Specifies the right indent of all paragraph lines.
- `SmallToggleButton m_btLeft`: Toggles left text alignment.
- `SmallToggleButton m_btCenter`: Toggles center text alignment.
- `SmallToggleButton m_btRight`: Toggles right text alignment.
- `SmallToggleButton m_btJustified`: Toggles justified text alignment.
- `ParagraphPreview m_preview`: The custom component for previewing paragraph attribute effects.

The `ParagraphDialog` constructor first creates a super class modal dialog entitled Paragraph. This dialog uses y-oriented `BoxLayout` to place component groups from top to bottom. The six `JTextFields` listed above are placed in two side-by-side panels entitled Space and Indent. These controls allow the user to specify spacing attributes. Below these fields is a group of `SmallToggleButtons` (which were introduced in chapter 12) that control text alignment: left, center, right, or justified.

An instance of our custom `ParagraphPreview` component, `m_preview`, is used to preview the selected paragraph attributes before applying them to the selected document text. We will discuss how this component works below.

Two buttons, OK and Cancel, are placed at the bottom of the dialog. They act identically to those at the bottom of our font dialog (see example 20.6). The six text boxes mentioned above receive an identical `FocusListener` which invokes our `updatePreview()` method (see below) when a text field loses focus. Similarly, the four toggle buttons receive an identical `ActionListener` which does the same thing. This provides a dynamic preview of the selected paragraph attributes whenever any attribute is changed.

4 The `setAttributes()` method takes an `AttributeSet` instance as a parameter. It copies this attribute set into a `SimpleAttributeSet` that is stored as our `m_attributes` instance variable. The appropriate paragraph attributes are extracted using `StyleConstants` methods, and those attributes are used to assign values to the dialog's controls. Finally, the preview component is updated according to these new settings by calling our `updatePreview()` method. Note that the `setAttributes()` method is `public` and is used for data exchange between this dialog and its owner (in our case, `WordProcessor`).

5 The `getAttributes()` method plays an opposite role with respect to `setAttributes()`. It retrieves data from the dialog's controls, packs it into an `AttributeSet` instance using `StyleConstants` methods, and return this set to the caller.

> **NOTE**   All spacing variables are of type `float`, even though they are actually measured in discrete screen pixels.

The `getOption()` method returns a code that indicates how the user closed the dialog. This value should be checked prior to retrieving data from the dialog to determine whether the user canceled (`JOptionPane.CANCEL_OPTION`) or approved (`JOptionPane.OK_OPTION`) the changes.

The `updatePreview()` method is called to update the paragraph preview component whenever a paragraph attribute is changed. It simply forces our `m_preview` component to repaint itself.

The getAlignment() method checks for the selected toggle button and returns the corresponding alignment attribute.

Class ParagraphDialog.ParagraphPreview

6 This inner class represents our custom component that displays an imitation paragraph used to preview a set of paragraph attributes. The actual rendering consists of three parts:

1 A light gray text line representing the end of a preceding paragraph. The indentation and spacing of this line is not affected by the current paragraph attribute settings.

2 Several gray text lines representing a paragraph being modified. Indentations and line spacing depend on the current paragraph attribute settings. The number of these lines is calculated so as to fill the component's height naturally, and it depends on the current line spacing attribute settings.

3 A light gray text line representing the beginning of a following paragraph. The space between this line and the last paragraph line depends on the current above line spacing attribute. The indentation of this line is not affected by the current paragraph attributes.

Several instance variables are declared in this inner class:

- Font m_fn: The font used for preview paragraph rendering. This font is intentionally made small and barely recognizable, because the displayed text itself does not have any meaning; only the paragraph formatting does.
- String m_dummy: A dummy string used in the random generation of a paragraph.
- float m_scaleX: The scaling factor used to recalculate sizes in the vertical direction.
- float m_scaleY: The scaling factor used to recalculate sizes in the horizontal direction.
- Random m_random: The random number generator used in piecing together a paragraph of characters.

REMINDER java.util.Random provides random number generation capabilities, including seed selection and generation of integers in a given range. In the simplest cases, we can use the Math.random() static method instead.

The ParagraphPreview constructor initializes the colors, border, and preferred size for this component.

7 The most interesting aspect of the preview component's work is done in the paintComponent() method. This method first retrieves the paragraph attributes specified by the user. Then we set a hard-coded seed value for our random number generator, m_random, which we use to generate a paragraph of gibberish. The following local variables are used to control the placement of this paragraph's lines:

8
- int h: The height of the text string determined by the font selected for preview.
- int s: The spacing between lines in screen pixels.
- int s1: The actual spacing between the previous paragraph and the first line of this paragraph.
- int s2: The actual spacing between the following paragraph and the last line of this paragraph.
- int y: The vertical position of the text being drawn (this will be updated during the rendering process).

- `int xMarg`: The left and right fixed margins.
- `int x0`: The actual left indent for the first line of this paragraph.
- `int x1`: The actual left indent for the second and remaining lines of this paragraph.
- `int x2`: The actual right indent for the lines of this paragraph.
- `int xm0`: The maximum x-coordinate for the text lines without regard to the specified right indent.
- `int xm1`: The maximum x-coordinate for the text lines with regard to the specified right indent.
- `int n`: The number of paragraph lines which can fit vertically within this component, taking into account the specified line spacing and both the preceding and following paragraph lines.

9 Once all these variables are calculated, the rendering can be performed relatively easily. The `drawLine()` method is used to draw a single line of text. We first draw a line denoting the preceding paragraph, then we draw each line of the current paragraph, and finally, we draw a line denoting the following paragraph. The last line of the current paragraph is intentionally half the length of a normal line to produce a more realistic impression of the text. Also, when justified alignment is specified, it is suppressed for the last line of text, since the last line should not be stretched.

The `drawLine()` method takes seven parameters:

- `Graphics g`: Used for all rendering.
- `int x`: The x-coordinate of the beginning of a text line.
- `int y`: The y-coordinate of the beginning of a text line.
- `int xMax`: The maximum x-coordinate a line can occupy.
- `int xLen`: The line length plus the left margin size.
- `FontMetrics fm`: Retrieved from the current `Graphics` instance.
- `int alignment`: The current text alignment.

10 This method first prepares a line to be drawn by concatenating random pieces of the `m_dummy` string until the resulting length, plus the left margin size, is greater than or equal to the `xLen` parameter. (Note that a `StringBuffer` instance is used here to improve performance.) Then we draw this line depending on the selected alignment. For the left alignment, we simply start drawing at the left margin. For the center and right alignments, we calculate the start position by working with the maximum x-coordinate and the width of that line. For justified alignment, we should recalculate space between words so the resulting line will occupy all the available width (however, in our case, since the preview text is totally meaningless, we just add some more text at the right end).

20.7.2 Running the code

Open an existing RTF file, select some text, and bring up the Paragraph dialog. Verify that the initial values of all components correspond to the paragraph attributes at the current caret position. Specify new paragraph attributes and notice how the preview component is updated dynamically. Press the OK button to apply the specified attributes to the selected paragraphs of document text.

BUG ALERT   Justified text alignment has not been implemented as of Java 2 FCS.

20.8 WORD PROCESSOR, PART VIII: FIND AND REPLACE

Along with font and paragraph dialogs, find and replace functionality has also become a fairly common tool in text editing environments. It is safe to assume that most users would be sadly disappointed if this functionality was not included in a new word processor application. In example 20.8, we will show how to add this functionality. Traditionally, such tools are represented in an Edit menu and they can be activated by keyboard accelerators. We will use a dialog containing a single tabbed pane with tabs for finding and replacing a specific region of text. We will also provide several options for searching: match case, search whole words only, and search up or down.

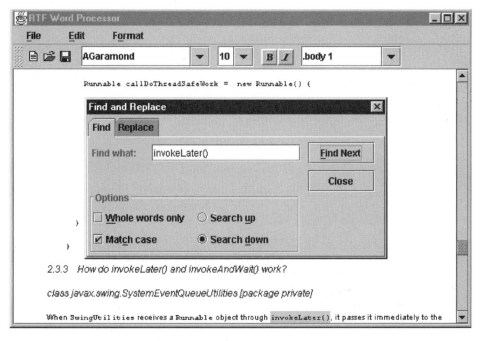

Figure 20.9 WordProcessor **with complete find-and-replace functionality; the Find tab is shown here**

Example 20.8

WordProcessor.java

see \Chapter20\8

```java
import java.awt.*;
import java.awt.event.*;
import java.io.*;
import java.util.*;

import javax.swing.*;
import javax.swing.text.*;
import javax.swing.event.*;
```

Figure 20.10 The Replace tab of our custom find and replace dialog used in a word processor application

```
import javax.swing.border.*;
import javax.swing.text.rtf.*;
import javax.swing.undo.*;

import dl.*;

public class WordProcessor extends JFrame
{
  // Unchanged code from example 20.7

  protected FontDialog m_fontDialog;
  protected ParagraphDialog m_paragraphDialog;
  protected FindDialog m_findDialog;

  protected JMenuBar createMenuBar() {
    // Unchanged code from example 20.7

    mEdit.addSeparator();

    Action findAction = new AbstractAction("Find...",
     new ImageIcon("edit_find.gif"))
    {
      public void actionPerformed(ActionEvent e) {
        WordProcessor.this.repaint();
        if (m_findDialog==null)
          m_findDialog = new FindDialog(WordProcessor.this, 0);
        else
          m_findDialog.setSelectedIndex(0);

        Dimension d1 = m_findDialog.getSize();
        Dimension d2 = WordProcessor.this.getSize();        "Find" is tab 0  ❶
        int x = Math.max((d2.width-d1.width)/2, 0);
        int y = Math.max((d2.height-d1.height)/2, 0);
        m_findDialog.setBounds(x + WordProcessor.this.getX(),
          y + WordProcessor.this.getY(), d1.width, d1.height);

        m_findDialog.show();
      }
    };
```

```
    item = mEdit.add(findAction);
    item.setMnemonic('f');
    item.setAccelerator(KeyStroke.getKeyStroke(KeyEvent.VK_F,
      KeyEvent.CTRL_MASK));

    Action replaceAction = new AbstractAction("Replace...") {
      public void actionPerformed(ActionEvent e) {
        WordProcessor.this.repaint();
        if (m_findDialog==null)
          m_findDialog = new FindDialog(WordProcessor.this, 1);
        else
          m_findDialog.setSelectedIndex(1);

        Dimension d1 = m_findDialog.getSize();
        Dimension d2 = WordProcessor.this.getSize();        "Replace" is tab 1  ❶
        int x = Math.max((d2.width-d1.width)/2, 0);
        int y = Math.max((d2.height-d1.height)/2, 0);
        m_findDialog.setBounds(x + WordProcessor.this.getX(),
          y + WordProcessor.this.getY(), d1.width, d1.height);

        m_findDialog.show();
      }
    };
    item =  mEdit.add(replaceAction);
    item.setMnemonic('r');
    item.setAccelerator(KeyStroke.getKeyStroke(KeyEvent.VK_H,
      KeyEvent.CTRL_MASK));

    menuBar.add(mEdit);

    // Unchanged code from example 20.7

    return menuBar;
  }

  // Unchanged code from example 20.7

  public Document getDocument() { return m_doc; }

  public JTextPane getTextPane() { return m_monitor; }

  public void setSelection(int xStart, int xFinish, boolean moveUp) {
    if (moveUp) {
      m_monitor.setCaretPosition(xFinish);
      m_monitor.moveCaretPosition(xStart);
    }
    else
      m_monitor.select(xStart, xFinish);
    m_xStart = m_monitor.getSelectionStart();
    m_xFinish = m_monitor.getSelectionEnd();
  }

  public static void main(String argv[]) {
    new WordProcessor();
  }
```

```java
    // Unchanged code from example 20.7
}

// Unchanged code from example 20.7

class FindDialog extends JDialog
{
  protected WordProcessor m_owner;
  protected JTabbedPane m_tb;
  protected JTextField m_txtFind1;
  protected JTextField m_txtFind2;
  protected Document m_docFind;
  protected Document m_docReplace;
  protected ButtonModel m_modelWord;
  protected ButtonModel m_modelCase;
  protected ButtonModel m_modelUp;
  protected ButtonModel m_modelDown;

  protected int m_searchIndex = -1;
  protected boolean m_searchUp = false;
  protected String  m_searchData;

  public FindDialog(WordProcessor owner, int index) {
    super(owner, "Find and Replace", false);
    m_owner = owner;

    m_tb = new JTabbedPane();

    // "Find" panel
    JPanel p1 = new JPanel(new BorderLayout());

    JPanel pc1 = new JPanel(new BorderLayout());

    JPanel pf = new JPanel();
    pf.setLayout(new DialogLayout(20, 5));
    pf.setBorder(new EmptyBorder(8, 5, 8, 0));
    pf.add(new JLabel("Find what:"));

    m_txtFind1 = new JTextField();
    m_docFind = m_txtFind1.getDocument();
    pf.add(m_txtFind1);
    pc1.add(pf, BorderLayout.CENTER);

    JPanel po = new JPanel(new GridLayout(2, 2, 8, 2));
    po.setBorder(new TitledBorder(new EtchedBorder(),
      "Options"));

    JCheckBox chkWord = new JCheckBox("Whole words only");
    chkWord.setMnemonic('w');
    m_modelWord = chkWord.getModel();
    po.add(chkWord);

    ButtonGroup bg = new ButtonGroup();
    JRadioButton rdUp = new JRadioButton("Search up");
    rdUp.setMnemonic('u');
    m_modelUp = rdUp.getModel();
    bg.add(rdUp);
    po.add(rdUp);
```

2 Dialog with tabbed pane for performing "Find" or "Replace" functionality

3 Dialog is not modal

```
JCheckBox chkCase = new JCheckBox("Match case");
chkCase.setMnemonic('c');
m_modelCase = chkCase.getModel();
po.add(chkCase);

JRadioButton rdDown = new JRadioButton("Search down", true);
rdDown.setMnemonic('d');
m_modelDown = rdDown.getModel();
bg.add(rdDown);
po.add(rdDown);
pc1.add(po, BorderLayout.SOUTH);

p1.add(pc1, BorderLayout.CENTER);

JPanel p01 = new JPanel(new FlowLayout());
JPanel p = new JPanel(new GridLayout(2, 1, 2, 8));

ActionListener findAction = new ActionListener() {
  public void actionPerformed(ActionEvent e) {
    findNext(false, true);
  }
};
JButton btFind = new JButton("Find Next");
btFind.addActionListener(findAction);
btFind.setMnemonic('f');
p.add(btFind);

ActionListener closeAction = new ActionListener() {
  public void actionPerformed(ActionEvent e) {
    setVisible(false);
  }
};
JButton btClose = new JButton("Close");
btClose.addActionListener(closeAction);
btClose.setDefaultCapable(true);
p.add(btClose);
p01.add(p);
p1.add(p01, BorderLayout.EAST);

m_tb.addTab("Find", p1);

// "Replace" panel
JPanel p2 = new JPanel(new BorderLayout());

JPanel pc2 = new JPanel(new BorderLayout());

JPanel pc = new JPanel();
pc.setLayout(new DialogLayout(20, 5));
pc.setBorder(new EmptyBorder(8, 5, 8, 0));

pc.add(new JLabel("Find what:"));
m_txtFind2 = new JTextField();
m_txtFind2.setDocument(m_docFind);
pc.add(m_txtFind2);

pc.add(new JLabel("Replace:"));
JTextField txtReplace = new JTextField();
```

```
m_docReplace = txtReplace.getDocument();
pc.add(txtReplace);
pc2.add(pc, BorderLayout.CENTER);

po = new JPanel(new GridLayout(2, 2, 8, 2));
po.setBorder(new TitledBorder(new EtchedBorder(),
  "Options"));

chkWord = new JCheckBox("Whole words only");
chkWord.setMnemonic('w');
chkWord.setModel(m_modelWord);
po.add(chkWord);

bg = new ButtonGroup();
rdUp = new JRadioButton("Search up");
rdUp.setMnemonic('u');
rdUp.setModel(m_modelUp);
bg.add(rdUp);
po.add(rdUp);

chkCase = new JCheckBox("Match case");
chkCase.setMnemonic('c');
chkCase.setModel(m_modelCase);
po.add(chkCase);

rdDown = new JRadioButton("Search down", true);
rdDown.setMnemonic('d');
rdDown.setModel(m_modelDown);
bg.add(rdDown);
po.add(rdDown);
pc2.add(po, BorderLayout.SOUTH);

p2.add(pc2, BorderLayout.CENTER);

JPanel p02 = new JPanel(new FlowLayout());
p = new JPanel(new GridLayout(3, 1, 2, 8));

ActionListener replaceAction = new ActionListener() {
  public void actionPerformed(ActionEvent e) {
    findNext(true, true);
  }
};
JButton btReplace = new JButton("Replace");
btReplace.addActionListener(replaceAction);
btReplace.setMnemonic('r');
p.add(btReplace);

ActionListener replaceAllAction = new ActionListener() {
  public void actionPerformed(ActionEvent e) {
    int counter = 0;
    while (true) {
      int result = findNext(true, false);
      if (result < 0)      // error
        return;
      else if (result == 0)     // no more
        break;
```

```
          counter++;
        }
        JOptionPane.showMessageDialog(m_owner,
          counter+" replacement(s) have been done", "Info",
          JOptionPane.INFORMATION_MESSAGE);
      }
    };
    JButton btReplaceAll = new JButton("Replace All");
    btReplaceAll.addActionListener(replaceAllAction);
    btReplaceAll.setMnemonic('a');
    p.add(btReplaceAll);

    btClose = new JButton("Close");
    btClose.addActionListener(closeAction);
    btClose.setDefaultCapable(true);
    p.add(btClose);
    p02.add(p);
    p2.add(p02, BorderLayout.EAST);

    // Make button columns the same size
    p01.setPreferredSize(p02.getPreferredSize());

    m_tb.addTab("Replace", p2);

    m_tb.setSelectedIndex(index);

    getContentPane().add(m_tb, BorderLayout.CENTER);

    WindowListener flst = new WindowAdapter() {
      public void windowActivated(WindowEvent e) {
        m_searchIndex = -1;
        if (m_tb.getSelectedIndex()==0)
          m_txtFind1.grabFocus();
        else
          m_txtFind2.grabFocus();
      }

      public void windowDeactivated(WindowEvent e) {
        m_searchData = null;
      }
    };
    addWindowListener(flst);

    pack();
    setResizable(false);
  }

  public void setSelectedIndex(int index) {
    m_tb.setSelectedIndex(index);
    setVisible(true);
    m_searchIndex = -1;
  }

  public int findNext(boolean doReplace, boolean showWarnings) {
    JTextPane monitor = m_owner.getTextPane();
    int pos = monitor.getCaretPosition();
    if (m_modelUp.isSelected() != m_searchUp) {
```

④ Make tab panels close to same size, so shared components stay in same position

Performs actual find or replace operation ⑤

```
      m_searchUp = m_modelUp.isSelected();
      m_searchIndex = -1;
    }

    if (m_searchIndex == -1) {
      try {
        Document doc = m_owner.getDocument();
        if (m_searchUp)
          m_searchData = doc.getText(0, pos);
        else
          m_searchData = doc.getText(pos, doc.getLength()-pos);
        m_searchIndex = pos;
      }
      catch (BadLocationException ex) {
        warning(ex.toString());
        return -1;
      }
    }
    String key = "";
    try { key = m_docFind.getText(0, m_docFind.getLength()); }
    catch (BadLocationException ex) {}
    if (key.length()==0) {
      warning("Please enter the target to search");
      return -1;
    }
    if (!m_modelCase.isSelected()) {
      m_searchData = m_searchData.toLowerCase();
      key = key.toLowerCase();
    }
    if (m_modelWord.isSelected()) {
      for (int k=0; k<Utils.WORD_SEPARATORS.length; k++) {
        if (key.indexOf(Utils.WORD_SEPARATORS[k]) >= 0) {
          warning("The text target contains an illegal "+
            "character \'"+Utils.WORD_SEPARATORS[k]+"\'");
          return -1;
        }
      }
    }

    String replacement = "";
    if (doReplace) {
      try {
        replacement = m_docReplace.getText(0,
          m_docReplace.getLength());
      } catch (BadLocationException ex) {}
    }

    int xStart = -1;
    int xFinish = -1;
    while (true)
    {
      if (m_searchUp)
        xStart = m_searchData.lastIndexOf(key, pos-1);
```

6 Gets string to search for, and optionally converts both search text and target to lowercase

7 Retrieves replacement text

7 Searches backward or forward for search string

```
      else
        xStart = m_searchData.indexOf(key, pos-m_searchIndex);
      if (xStart < 0) {
        if (showWarnings)
          warning("Text not found");
        return 0;
      }

      xFinish = xStart+key.length();

      if (m_modelWord.isSelected()) {
        boolean s1 = xStart>0;
        boolean b1 = s1 && !Utils.isSeparator(m_searchData.charAt(
          xStart-1));
        boolean s2 = xFinish<m_searchData.length();
        boolean b2 = s2 && !Utils.isSeparator(m_searchData.charAt(
          xFinish));

        if (b1 || b2)     // Not a whole word
        {
          if (m_searchUp && s1)    // Can continue up
          {
            pos = xStart;
            continue;
          }
          if (!m_searchUp && s2)     // Can continue down
          {
            pos = xFinish;
            continue;
          }
          // Found, but not a whole word, and we cannot continue
          if (showWarnings)
            warning("Text not found");
          return 0;
        }
      }
      break;
    }

    if (!m_searchUp) {
      xStart += m_searchIndex;
      xFinish += m_searchIndex;
    }
    if (doReplace) {
      m_owner.setSelection(xStart, xFinish, m_searchUp);
      monitor.replaceSelection(replacement);
      m_owner.setSelection(xStart, xStart+replacement.length(),
        m_searchUp);
      m_searchIndex = -1;
    }
    else
      m_owner.setSelection(xStart, xFinish, m_searchUp);
    return 1;
  }
```

Searches backward or forward for search string **7**

b1 and b2 determine whether the found string is on a word boundary **8**

Does actual replacement **9**

```
  protected void warning(String message) {
    JOptionPane.showMessageDialog(m_owner,
      message, "Warning", JOptionPane.INFORMATION_MESSAGE);
  }
}
class Utils
{
  public static final char[] WORD_SEPARATORS = {' ', '\t', '\n',
    '\r', '\f', '.', ',', ':', '-', '(', ')', '[', ']', '{',
    '}', '<', '>', '/', '|', '\\', '\'', '\"'};

  public static boolean isSeparator(char ch) {
    for (int k=0; k<WORD_SEPARATORS.length; k++)
      if (ch == WORD_SEPARATORS[k])
        return true;
    return false;
  }
}
```

⑩ Provides single method to check whether a character is a word separator

20.8.1 Understanding the code

Class WordProcessor

This class now imports the dl package (which was constructed and discussed in chapter 4) to use our DialogLayout manager. WordProcessor also declares one new instance variable:

- FindDialog m_findDialog: A custom dialog for finding and replacing a selected region of text.

❶ Two new menu items, Find... and Replace..., are added to the Edit menu. These items are activated with the keyboard accelerators CTRL+F and CTRL+H, respectively. When selected, both items create an instance of FindDialog (if m_findDialog is null) or activate the existing instance, and the dialog is then displayed. The only difference between the two is that the Find... menu item activates the 0-indexed tabbed pane tab, and the Replace... menu item activates the tab at index 1.

Three new public methods have been added to this class to make access to our text pane component, and related objects, easier from external classes. The getDocument() method retrieves the text pane's current document instance, and the getTextPane() method retrieves the text pane itself. The setSelection() method selects a portion of text between given start and end positions, and it positions the caret at the beginning or at the end of selection, depending on the value of the moveUp boolean parameter. The coordinates of such a selection are then stored in the m_xStart and m_xFinish instance variables (recall that these variables always hold the coordinates of the current text selection and are used to restore this selection when our text pane regains the focus).

Class FindDialog

❷ This class is a modal, JDialog subclass encapsulating our find and replace functionality. It contains a tabbed pane with two tabs, Find and Replace. Both tabs contain several common controls that should always be consistent: a check box for Whole words only, a check box for Match case, a radio button for Search up, a radio button for Search down, and a text field for the text be found.

Since components can only exist in one container, we need to place identical components in each tab. To simplify the task of maintaining consistency in component states, each pair of common components are assigned the same model.

FindDialog maintains the following instance variables:

- WordProcessor m_owner: An explicit reference to our WordProcessor parent application frame.
- JTabbedPane m_tb: The tabbed pane containing the find and replace pages.
- JTextField m_txtFind1: Used to enter the string to find.
- JTextField m_txtFind2: Used to enter the string to replace.
- Document m_docFind: A shared data model for the Find text fields.
- Document m_docReplace: A data model for the Replace text field.
- ButtonModel m_modelWord: A shared data model for the Whole words only check boxes.
- ButtonModel m_modelCase: A shared data model for the Match case check boxes.
- ButtonModel m_modelUp: A shared data model for the Search up radio buttons.
- ButtonModel m_modelDown: A shared data model for the Search down radio buttons.
- int m_searchIndex: The position in the document to start searching from.
- boolean m_searchUp: A search direction flag.
- String m_searchData: The string to search for.

3 The FindDialog constructor creates a super class non-modal dialog instance called Find and Replace. The main tabbed pane, m_tb, is created, and JPanel p1 (the main container of the "Find" tab) receives the m_txtFind1 text field along with a Find what: label. This text field is used to enter the target string to be searched for. Note that the Document instance associated with this text box is stored in the m_docFind instance variable (which will be used to facilitate sharing between another text field).

> **NOTE** In a more sophisticated implementation, you might use editable combo boxes with memory in place of text fields, similar to those we discussed in the final examples of chapter 9.

Two check boxes—Whole words only and Match case—and two radio buttons—Search up and Search down (search down is initially selected)—are placed at the bottom of the p1 panel. These components are surrounded by a titled Options border. Two JButtons, Find Next and Close, are placed at the right side of the panel. The first button calls our findNext() method (see below) when pressed. The second button hides the dialog. Finally, the p1 panel is added to m_tb; its tab title is Find.

4 JPanel p2 (the main container of the Replace tab) receives the m_txtFind2 text field along with a Find what: label. It also receives another pair labeled Replace. An instance of our custom layout manager, DialogLayout (which is discussed in chapter 4), is used to lay out these text fields and corresponding labels without involving any intermediate containers. The same layout is used in the Find panel. We also synchronize the preferred size of the two panels to avoid movement of the mimicked components when a new page is activated.

Note that the m_docFind data object is set as the document for the m_txtFind2 text field. This ensures consistency between the two different Find text fields in the two tabbed panels.

Two check boxes and two radio buttons are placed at the bottom of the panel to control the replacement options. They have the exact same meaning and representation as the corresponding four controls in the Find panel, and to ensure consistency between them, the data models are shared between each of the identical components.

Three JButtons, entitled Replace, Replace All, and Close, are placed at the right side of the panel. The Replace button makes a single call to our findNext() method (discussed below) when it is pressed. The Replace All button is associated with an actionPerformed() method which repeatedly invokes findNext() to perform replacement until it returns -1 to signal an error, or 0 to signal that no more replacements can be made. If an error occurs, the actionPerformed() method simply returns (since an error will be properly reported to the user by the findNext() method). Otherwise, the number of replacements made is reported to the user in a JOptionPane message dialog. The Close button hides the dialog. Finally, the p2 panel is added to the m_tb tabbed pane; its tab title is Replace.

Since this is a non-modal dialog, the user can freely switch to the main application frame and return to the dialog while each remains visible; this is a typical find-and-replace feature. Once the user leaves the dialog, he can modify the document's content or move the caret position. To account for this, we add a WindowListener to the dialog whose windowActivated() method sets m_searchIndex to -1. This way, the next time findNext() is called (see below) the search data will be reinitialized, allowing the search to continue as expected, corresponding to the new caret position and document content.

The setSelectedIndex() method activates a page with the given index and makes this dialog visible. This method is intended mostly for use externally by our application when it wants to display this dialog with a specific tab selected.

5 The findNext() method is responsible for performing the actual find and replace operations. It takes two arguments:

- boolean doReplace: If it returns true, find and replace; otherwise, just find.
- boolean showWarnings: If it returns true, display a message dialog if the target text cannot be found; otherwise, do not display a message.

findNext() returns an int result with the following description:

-1: An error has occurred.

0: The target text cannot be found.

1: A find or find and replace was successfully completed.

The m_searchIndex == -1 condition specified that the text to be searched through must be recalculated. In this case, we store the portion of text from the beginning of the document to the current caret position if we are searching up, or between the current caret position and the end of the document if we are searching down. This text is stored in the m_searchData instance variable. The current caret position is stored in the m_searchIndex variable.

> **NOTE** This solution may not be adequate for large documents. However, a more sophisticated solution would take us too far from the primary goal of this example.

6 The text to search for is retrieved from the m_docFind shared Document. If the case-insensitive option is selected, both the m_searchData text and the text to search for are converted into lower case. If the Whole words only option is selected, we check whether the text were searching for contains any separator characters that are defined in our Utils utilities class (see below).

CHAPTER 20 CONSTRUCTING A WORD PROCESSOR

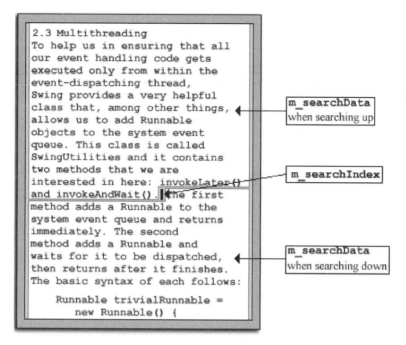

```
2.3 Multithreading
To help us in ensuring that all
our event handling code gets
executed only from within the
event-dispatching thread,
Swing provides a very helpful
class that, among other things,
allows us to add Runnable
objects to the system event
queue. This class is called
SwingUtilities and it contains
two methods that we are
interested in here: invokeLater()
and invokeAndWait(). The first
method adds a Runnable to the
system event queue and returns
immediately. The second
method adds a Runnable and
waits for it to be dispatched,
then returns after it finishes.
The basic syntax of each follows:

    Runnable trivialRunnable =
        new Runnable() {
```

m_searchData
when searching up

m_searchIndex

m_searchData
when searching down

Figure 20.11   Using instance variables to search up and down through document text

NOTE   If a given String is already completely in lower or upper case, the toLower-Case() (or toUpperCase()) method returns the original String without creating a new object.

7 Next, if the doReplace parameter is true, we retrieve the replacement text from our m_doc-Replace Document. At this point, we're ready to actually perform a search. We take advantage of existing String functionality to accomplish this:

```
if (m_searchUp)
  xStart = m_searchData.lastIndexOf(key, pos-1);
else
  xStart = m_searchData.indexOf(key, pos-m_searchIndex);
```

If we are searching up, we search for the last occurrence of the target string from the current caret position. Otherwise, we search for the first occurrence of the target string from the current caret position. If the target string is not found, we cannot continue the search, and a warning is displayed if the showWarnings parameter is true.

8 This simple scheme is complicated considerably if the Whole words only option is selected. In this case, we need to verify whether symbols the left and the right of a matching region of text are either word separators defined in our Utils class, or whether the string lies at the end of the data being searched. If these conditions are not satisfied, we attempt to continue searching.

9 In any case, if we locate an acceptable match, we select the located text. If the replace option is selected, we replace this selected region with the specified replacement text and then select the new replacement text. In this latter case we also set `m_searchIndex` to -1 to force the `m_searchData` variable to be updated. This is necessary for continued searching because the data being searched most likely changes after each replace. The location of the caret also usually changes.

Class Utils

⑩ This class provides a simple static utility method and an array of `char`s that represent word separator characters. The `isSeparator()` method simply verifies whether a given character belongs to the static `WORD_SEPARATORS` char array.

20.8.2 Running the code

Open an existing RTF file and use the Edit menu, or the appropriate keyboard accelerator, to bring up the Find and Replace dialog and select the Find tab. Enter some text to search for, select some search options, and press the Find Next button. If your target text is found, the matching region will be highlighted in the base document. Press this button again to find subsequent entries (if any). Verify that the Whole words only and Match case options function as discussed above. Change focus to the main application window and modify the document and/or change the caret position. Return to the Find and Replace dialog and verify that the search continues as expected.

Select the Replace tab and verify that the state of all search options, including the search target string, are preserved in the Find tab (and vice versa when switching back). Enter a replacement string and verify that the Replace and Replace All buttons work as expected.

20.9 WORD PROCESSOR, PART IX: SPELL CHECKER (USING JDBC AND SQL)

Most modern word processor applications offer tools and utilities which help the user find grammar and spelling mistakes in a document. In example 20.9, we will add spell-checking to our word processor application. To do this, we will need to perform some of our own multithreading and communicate with JDBC. We will use a simple database with one table, `Data`, which has the following structure:

Name	Type	Description
word	String	A single English word.
soundex	String	A 4-letter SOUNDEX code.

Our sample database is populated with words from several Shakespearean comedies and tragedies. It is provided in this example's directory in the ZIP archive for this chapter. The database is called **Shakespeare.mdb.** (This database must be registered in your database manager prior to using it. This is not a JDBC tutorial, so we'll skip the details.)

NOTE The custom SOUNDEX algorithm used in this example hashes words for efficiency by using a simple model which approximates the sound of the word when spoken. Each word is reduced to a four-character string, the first character being an uppercase letter and the remaining three being digits.

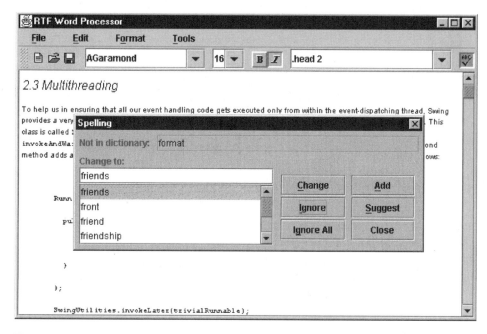

Figure 20.12   WordProcessor **with spell checking functionality**

Example 20.9

WordProcessor.java

see \Chapter20\9

```java
import java.awt.*;
import java.awt.event.*;
import java.io.*;
import java.util.*;
import java.sql.*;

import javax.swing.*;
import javax.swing.text.*;
import javax.swing.event.*;
import javax.swing.border.*;
import javax.swing.text.rtf.*;
import javax.swing.undo.*;

import dl.*;

public class WordProcessor extends JFrame
{
  // Unchanged code from example 20.8

  protected JMenuBar createMenuBar() {
    // Unchanged code from example 20.8

    JMenu mTools = new JMenu("Tools");
```

```
    mTools.setMnemonic('t');

    Action spellAction = new AbstractAction("Spelling...",
     new ImageIcon("tools_abc.gif"))
    {
      public void actionPerformed(ActionEvent e) {
        SpellChecker checker = new SpellChecker(WordProcessor.this);
        WordProcessor.this.setCursor(Cursor.getPredefinedCursor(
          Cursor.WAIT_CURSOR));
        checker.start();
      }
    };
    item = mTools.add(spellAction);
    item.setMnemonic('s');
    item.setAccelerator(KeyStroke.getKeyStroke(
      KeyEvent.VK_F7, 0));
    menuBar.add(mTools);

    m_toolBar.addSeparator();
    m_toolBar.add(new SmallButton(spellAction,
      "Spell checker"));

    getContentPane().add(m_toolBar, BorderLayout.NORTH);

    return menuBar;
  }

  // Unchanged code from example 20.8
}
class OpenList extends JPanel
 implements ListSelectionListener, ActionListener
{
  // Unchanged code from example 20.6

  public OpenList(String title, int numCols) {
    setLayout(null);
    m_title = new JLabel(title, JLabel.LEFT);
    add(m_title);
    m_text = new JTextField(numCols);
    m_text.addActionListener(this);
    add(m_text);
    m_list = new JList();
    m_list.setVisibleRowCount(4);
    m_list.addListSelectionListener(this);
    m_scroll = new JScrollPane(m_list);
    add(m_scroll);
  }

  public void appendResultSet(ResultSet results, int index,
   boolean toTitleCase)
  {
    m_text.setText("");
    DefaultListModel model = new DefaultListModel();
    try {
```

❶ Invokes SpellChecker thread on document

❷ New OpenList constructor sets column limit on text field and sets list to empty

❸ Inserts ResultSet data into list at given position

```
      while (results.next()) {
        String str = results.getString(index);
        if (toTitleCase)
          str = Utils.titleCase(str);
        model.addElement(str);
      }
    }
    catch (SQLException ex) {
      System.err.println("appendResultSet: "+ex.toString());
    }
    m_list.setModel(model);
    if (model.getSize() > 0)
      m_list.setSelectedIndex(0);
  }

  // Unchanged code from example 20.6
}

// Unchanged code from example 20.6

class SpellChecker extends Thread
{
  protected static String SELECT_QUERY =
    "SELECT Data.word FROM Data WHERE Data.word = ";
  protected static String SOUNDEX_QUERY =
    "SELECT Data.word FROM Data WHERE Data.soundex = ";

  protected WordProcessor m_owner;
  protected Connection m_conn;
  protected DocumentTokenizer m_tokenizer;
  protected Hashtable  m_ignoreAll;
  protected SpellingDialog m_dlg;

  public SpellChecker(WordProcessor owner) {
    m_owner = owner;
  }

  public void run() {
    JTextPane monitor = m_owner.getTextPane();
    m_owner.setEnabled(false);
    monitor.setEnabled(false);

    m_dlg = new SpellingDialog(m_owner);
    m_ignoreAll = new Hashtable();

    try {
      // Load the JDBC-ODBC bridge driver
      Class.forName("sun.jdbc.odbc.JdbcOdbcDriver");
      m_conn = DriverManager.getConnection(
        "jdbc:odbc:Shakespeare", "admin", "");
      Statement selStmt = m_conn.createStatement();

      Document doc = m_owner.getDocument();
      int pos = monitor.getCaretPosition();
      m_tokenizer = new DocumentTokenizer(doc, pos);
      String word, wordLowCase;
```

4 Performs spell checking in current document, from current position onward

5 Before doing work, disables components

```
          while (m_tokenizer.hasMoreTokens()) {
            word = m_tokenizer.nextToken();
            if (word.equals(word.toUpperCase()))
              continue;
            if (word.length()<=1)
              continue;
            if (Utils.hasDigits(word))
              continue;
            wordLowCase = word.toLowerCase();
            if (m_ignoreAll.get(wordLowCase) != null)
              continue;

            ResultSet results = selStmt.executeQuery(
              SELECT_QUERY+"'"+wordLowCase+"'");
            if (results.next())
              continue;

            results = selStmt.executeQuery(SOUNDEX_QUERY+
              "'"+Utils.soundex(wordLowCase)+"'");
            m_owner.setSelection(m_tokenizer.getStartPos(),
              m_tokenizer.getEndPos(), false);
            if (!m_dlg.suggest(word, results))
              break;
          }

          m_conn.close();
          System.gc();
          monitor.setCaretPosition(pos);
        }
        catch (Exception ex) {
          ex.printStackTrace();
          System.err.println("SpellChecker error: "+ex.toString());
        }

        monitor.setEnabled(true);
        m_owner.setEnabled(true);
        m_owner.setCursor(Cursor.getPredefinedCursor(
          Cursor.DEFAULT_CURSOR));
      }

      protected void replaceSelection(String replacement) {
        int xStart = m_tokenizer.getStartPos();
        int xFinish = m_tokenizer.getEndPos();
        m_owner.setSelection(xStart, xFinish, false);
        m_owner.getTextPane().replaceSelection(replacement);
        xFinish = xStart+replacement.length();
        m_owner.setSelection(xStart, xFinish, false);
        m_tokenizer.setPosition(xFinish);
      }

      protected void addToDB(String word) {
        String sdx = Utils.soundex(word);
        try {
          Statement stmt = m_conn.createStatement();
```

⑤ Looks at each word in the document

⑤ If the word is found in the Shakespeare database, then it's spelled correctly

It's an unknown word, try to find a "sounds like" word to suggest as a replacement ⑤

If the word was misspelled and the user accepted a replacement suggestion, this does the replacement ⑥

⑥ Adds a word to the "known" database

```
        stmt.executeUpdate(
          "INSERT INTO DATA (Word, Soundex) VALUES ('"+
          word+"', '"+sdx+"')");
      }
    catch (Exception ex) {
      ex.printStackTrace();
      System.err.println("SpellChecker error: "+ex.toString());
    }
  }
}

class SpellingDialog extends JDialog
{
  protected JTextField  m_txtNotFound;
  protected OpenList    m_suggestions;

  protected String   m_word;
  protected boolean  m_continue;

  public SpellingDialog(WordProcessor owner) {
    super(owner, "Spelling", true);

    JPanel p = new JPanel();
    p.setBorder(new EmptyBorder(5, 5, 5, 5));
    p.setLayout(new BoxLayout(p, BoxLayout.X_AXIS));
    p.add(new JLabel("Not in dictionary:"));
    p.add(Box.createHorizontalStrut(10));
    m_txtNotFound = new JTextField();
    m_txtNotFound.setEditable(false);
    p.add(m_txtNotFound);
    getContentPane().add(p, BorderLayout.NORTH);

    m_suggestions = new OpenList("Change to:", 12);
    m_suggestions.setBorder(new EmptyBorder(0, 5, 5, 5));
    getContentPane().add(m_suggestions, BorderLayout.CENTER);

    JPanel p1 = new JPanel();
    p1.setBorder(new EmptyBorder(20, 0, 5, 5));
    p1.setLayout(new FlowLayout());
    p = new JPanel(new GridLayout(3, 2, 8, 2));

    JButton bt = new JButton("Change");
    ActionListener lst = new ActionListener() {
      public void actionPerformed(ActionEvent e) {
        replaceSelection(m_suggestions.getSelected());
        m_continue = true;
        setVisible(false);
      }
    };
    bt.addActionListener(lst);
    bt.setMnemonic('c');
    p.add(bt);

    bt = new JButton("Add");
    lst = new ActionListener() {
      public void actionPerformed(ActionEvent e) {
```

7 Prompts the user for an action on a misspelled word

8 Text field contains misspelled word

8 List contains replacement suggestions

9 Replaces misspelled word with selected suggestion

```
        addToDB(m_word.toLowerCase());
      m_continue = true;
        setVisible(false);
    }
};
bt.addActionListener(lst);
bt.setMnemonic('a');
p.add(bt);

bt = new JButton("Ignore");
lst = new ActionListener() {
  public void actionPerformed(ActionEvent e) {
    m_continue = true;
    setVisible(false);
  }
};
bt.addActionListener(lst);
bt.setMnemonic('i');
p.add(bt);

bt = new JButton("Suggest");
lst = new ActionListener() {
  public void actionPerformed(ActionEvent e) {
    try {
      m_word = m_suggestions.getSelected();
      Statement selStmt = m_conn.createStatement();
      ResultSet results = selStmt.executeQuery(
        SELECT_QUERY+"'"+m_word.toLowerCase()+"'");
      boolean toTitleCase = Character.isUpperCase(
        m_word.charAt(0));
      m_suggestions.appendResultSet(results, 1,
        toTitleCase);
    }
    catch (Exception ex) {
      ex.printStackTrace();
      System.err.println("SpellChecker error: "+
        ex.toString());
    }
  }
};
bt.addActionListener(lst);
bt.setMnemonic('s');
p.add(bt);

bt = new JButton("Ignore All");
lst = new ActionListener() {
  public void actionPerformed(ActionEvent e) {
    m_ignoreAll.put(m_word.toLowerCase(), m_word);
    m_continue = true;
    setVisible(false);
  }
};
bt.addActionListener(lst);
bt.setMnemonic('g');
```

10 Adds misspelled word to database

11 Adds words to suggestions list that "sound like" selected suggestion

12 Skips word, and will skip all occurrences of the same word in this document

```
            p.add(bt);

          bt = new JButton("Close");
          lst = new ActionListener() {
            public void actionPerformed(ActionEvent e) {
              m_continue = false;
              setVisible(false);
            }
          };
          bt.addActionListener(lst);
          bt.setDefaultCapable(true);
          p.add(bt);
          p1.add(p);
          getContentPane().add(p1, BorderLayout.EAST);

          pack();
          setResizable(false);
          Dimension d1 = getSize();
          Dimension d2 = owner.getSize();
          int x = Math.max((d2.width-d1.width)/2, 0);
          int y = Math.max((d2.height-d1.height)/2, 0);
          setBounds(x + owner.getX(),
            y + owner.getY(), d1.width, d1.height);
        }

      public boolean suggest(String word, ResultSet results) {
        m_continue = false;
        m_word = word;
        m_txtNotFound.setText(word);
        boolean toTitleCase = Character.isUpperCase(
          word.charAt(0));
        m_suggestions.appendResultSet(results, 1, toTitleCase);
        show();
        return m_continue;
      }
    }
  }

class DocumentTokenizer
{
  protected Document m_doc;
  protected Segment  m_seg;
  protected int m_startPos;
  protected int m_endPos;
  protected int m_currentPos;

  public DocumentTokenizer(Document doc, int offset) {
    m_doc = doc;
    m_seg = new Segment();
    setPosition(offset);
  }

  public boolean hasMoreTokens() {
    return (m_currentPos < m_doc.getLength());
  }
```

13 Called during spell checking to populate the dialog with a misspelled word and its replacement suggestion

14 Used like StreamTokenizer, but keeps track of the character position for each token

```
public String nextToken() {
  StringBuffer s = new StringBuffer();
  try {
    // Trim leading separators
    while (hasMoreTokens()) {
      m_doc.getText(m_currentPos, 1, m_seg);
      char ch = m_seg.array[m_seg.offset];
      if (!Utils.isSeparator(ch)) {
        m_startPos = m_currentPos;
        break;
      }
      m_currentPos++;
    }

    // Append characters
    while (hasMoreTokens()) {
      m_doc.getText(m_currentPos, 1, m_seg);
      char ch = m_seg.array[m_seg.offset];
      if (Utils.isSeparator(ch)) {
        m_endPos = m_currentPos;
        break;
      }
      s.append(ch);
      m_currentPos++;
    }
  }
  catch (BadLocationException ex) {
    System.err.println("nextToken: "+ex.toString());
    m_currentPos = m_doc.getLength();
  }
  return s.toString();
}

public int getStartPos() { return m_startPos; }

public int getEndPos() { return m_endPos; }

public void setPosition(int pos) {
  m_startPos = pos;
  m_endPos = pos;
  m_currentPos = pos;
}
}
class Utils
{
  // Unchanged code from example 20.8

  public static String soundex(String word) {
    char[] result = new char[4];
    result[0] = word.charAt(0);
    result[1] = result[2] = result[3] = '0';
    int index = 1;

    char codeLast = '*';
    for (int k=1; k<word.length(); k++) {
```

⑮ Returns the next token, storing the position in the document

⑯ Builds SOUNDEX code from given word

```
          char ch = word.charAt(k);
          char code = ' ';
          switch (ch) {
            case 'b': case 'f': case 'p': case 'v':
              code = '1';
              break;
            case 'c': case 'g': case 'j': case 'k':
            case 'q': case 's': case 'x': case 'z':
              code = '2';
              break;
            case 'd': case 't':
              code = '3';
              break;
            case 'l':
              code = '4';
              break;
            case 'm': case 'n':
              code = '5';
              break;
            case 'r':
              code = '6';
              break;
            default:
              code = '*';
              break;
          }
          if (code == codeLast)
            code = '*';
          codeLast = code;
          if (code != '*') {
            result[index] = code;
            index++;
            if (index > 3)
              break;
          }
        }
      return new String(result);
    }

    public static boolean hasDigits(String word) {
      for (int k=1; k<word.length(); k++) {
        char ch = word.charAt(k);
        if (Character.isDigit(ch))
          return true;
      }
      return false;
    }

    public static String titleCase(String source) {
      return Character.toUpperCase(source.charAt(0)) +
        source.substring(1);
    }
  }
```

20.9.1   Understanding the code

Class WordProcessor

1 This class now imports the `java.sql` package to make use of JDBC functionality. The `create-MenuBar()` method now creates a new menu entitled Tools, which contains one menu item entitled Spelling... This menu item can be invoked with the F7 keyboard accelerator or by pressing the corresponding toolbar button. When it is selected, this new menu item creates and starts the `SpellChecker` thread (see below), passing a reference to the main application frame as a parameter.

Class OpenList

2 This custom component receives new functionality for use in our new spell checker dialog. First, we add a new constructor which assigns a given number of columns to the text field and does not initialize the list component.

3 Second, we add the `appendResultSet()` method which populates the list component with the data supplied in the given `ResultSet` instance at the given position. If the third parameter is set to `true`, this tells the method to convert all string data to the title case (which means that the first letter is in upper case, and the rest of the string is unchanged). This is accomplished using our new `titleCase()` method in our `Utils` class (see below).

Class SpellChecker

4 This class extends `Thread` to spell check the current document from the current caret position downward. Two class variables are declared (their use will become more clear below):

- `String SELECT_QUERY`: SQL query text used to select a word equal to a given string.
- `String SOUNDEX_QUERY`: SQL query text used to select a word matching a given SOUNDEX value.

  Five instance variables are declared:

- `WordProcessor m_owner`: A reference to the main application frame.
- `Connection m_conn`: The JDBC connection to a database.
- `DocumentTokenizer m_tokenizer`: A custom object used to retrieve each word in a document.
- `Hashtable m_ignoreAll`: A collection of words to ignore in a search; users can add to the list using the Ignore All button.
- `SpellingDialog m_dlg`: Our custom dialog that is used for processing spelling mistakes.

  The `SpellChecker` constructor takes a reference to the application's frame as a parameter and stores it in the `m_owner` instance variable.

5 The `run()` method is responsible for the most significant activity of this thread. To prevent the user from modifying the document during spell checking, we first disable the main application frame and our text pane contained within it.

> **NOTE**   Unlike AWT, Swing containers do not disable their child components when they themselves are disabled. It is not clear whether this is a bug or an intended feature.

Next, we create a new `SpellingDialog` instance to provide the user interface, and we instantiate the `m_ignoreAll` collection. In a try/catch block we process all JDBC interactions to allow the proper handling of any potential errors. This code creates a JDBC connection to our Shakespeare database, retrieves the current caret position, and creates an instance of `DocumentTokenizer` to parse the document from the current caret position. In a `while` loop we perform spell checking on each word fetched until there are no more tokens. Words in all upper case, words containing only one letter, or words containing digits are skipped (this behavior can easily be customized). Then we convert the word under examination to lowercase and search for it in the `m_ignoreAll` collection. If it is not found, we try to find it in the database. If the SQL query does not return any results, we try to locate a similar word in the database with the same SOUNDEX value to suggest that variation to the user in the dialog. The word in question is then selected in our text pane to show the user which word is currently under examination. Finally, we call our `SpellingDialog`'s `suggest()` method to request that the user make a decision about what to do with this word. If the `suggest()` method returns `false`, the user has chosen to terminate the spell-checking process, so we exit the loop. Once outside the loop, we close the JDBC connection, restore the original caret position, explicitly call garbage collector, and re-enable the main application frame and our text pane editor contained within it.

6 The following two methods are invoked by the `SpellingDialog` instance associated with this `SpellChecker`:

- `replaceSelection()`: Replaces the word most recently parsed by the `DocumentTokenizer` instance with the given replacement string.
- `addToDB()`: Adds a given word and its SOUNDEX value to the database by executing an insert query.

Class SpellChecker.SpellingDialog

7 This inner class represents a dialog which prompts the user to verify or correct a certain word if it is not found in the database. The user can select one of several actions in response: ignore the given word, ignore all occurrences of that word in the document, replace that word with another word, add that word to the database and consider it correct in any future matches, or cancel the spell check. Four instance variables are declared:

- `JTextField m_txtNotFound`: Displays the word under investigation.
- `OpenList m_suggestions`: The editable list component to select or enter a replacement word.
- `String m_word`: The word under investigation.
- `boolean m_continue`: A flag that indicates that spell checking should continue.

8 The `SpellingDialog` constructor places the `m_txtNotFound` component and corresponding label at the top of the dialog window. The `m_suggestions` `OpenList` is placed in the center, and the six buttons discussed below are grouped to the right.

9 The Change button replaces the word under investigation with the word currently selected in the list or entered by the user. Then it stores `true` in the `m_continue` flag and hides the dialog window. This terminates the modal state of the dialog and makes the `show()` method return, which in turn allows the program's execution to continue (recall that modal dialogs block the calling thread until they are dismissed).

10 The Add button adds the word in question to the spelling database. This word will then be considered correct in future queries. In this way, we allow the spell checker to "learn" new words as it adds them to the dictionary.

11 The Suggest button populates the m_suggestions list with all SOUNDEX matches to the word under investigation. This button is intended to be used in situations where the user is not satisfied with the initial suggestions.

The Ignore button simply skips the current word and continues spell checking the remaining text.

12 The Ignore All button does the same as the Ignore button, but it also stores the word in question in the collection of words to ignore, so the next time the spell checker finds this word it will be deemed correct. The difference between Ignore All and Add is that ignored words will only be ignored during a single spell check, whereas words added to the database will persist as long as the database data does.

The Close button stores `false` in the m_continue flag and hides the dialog window. This results in the termination of the spell checking process (see the `suggest()` method).

13 The `suggest()` method is used to display this `SpellingDialog` each time a questionable word is located during the spell checking process. It takes a `String` and a `ResultSet` that contains suggested substitutions as parameters. It sets the text of the m_txtNotFound component to the `String` that was passed in, and it calls `appendResultSet()` on the `OpenList` to display an array of suggested corrections. The first character of these suggestions will be converted to upper case if the word in question starts with a capital letter. Finally, the `show()` method displays this dialog in the modal state. As soon as this state is terminated by one of the push buttons, or by directly closing the dialog, the `suggest()` method returns the m_continue flag. If this flag is set to `false`, the calling program should terminate the spell checking cycle.

Class DocumentTokenizer

14 This helper class was built to parse the current text pane document. Unfortunately, we cannot use the standard `StreamTokenizer` class for this purpose, because it provides no way of querying the position of a token within the document (we need this information to allow word replacement). Several instance variables are declared:

- `Document m_doc`: A reference to the document to be parsed.
- `Segment m_seg`: Used for quick delivery of characters from the document being parsed.
- `int m_startPos`: The start position of the current word from the beginning of the document.
- `int m_endPos`: The end position of the current word from the beginning of the document.
- `int m_currentPos`: The current position of the parser from the beginning of the document.

The `DocumentTokenizer` constructor takes a reference to the document to be parsed and the offset to start at as parameters. It initializes the instance variables described above.

The `hasMoreTokens()` method returns `true` if the current parsing position lies within the document.

15 The `nextToken()` method extracts the next token (a group of characters separated by one or more characters defined in the `WORD_SEPARATORS` array from our `Utils` class) and returns it as a `String`. The positions of the beginning and the end of the token are stored in the `m_startPos` and `m_endPos` instance variables respectively. To access a portion of the document text with the least possible overhead, we use the `Document.getText()` method which takes three parameters: the offset from the beginning of the document, the length of the text fragment, and a reference to an instance of the `Segment` class (recall from chapter 19 that the `Segment` class provides an efficient means of directly accessing an array of document characters).

We look at each character in turn, passing over separator characters until the first non-separator character is reached. This position is marked as the beginning of a new word. Then a `StringBuffer` is used to accumulate characters until a separator character, or the end of document, is reached. The resulting characters are returned as a `String`.

> **NOTE** This variant of the `getText()` method gives us direct access to the characters contained in the document through a `Segment` instance. These characters should not be modified.

Class Utils

16 Three new static methods are added to this class. The `soundex()` method calculates and returns the SOUNDEX code of the given word. To calculate that code we use the first character of the given word and add a three-digit code that represents the first three remaining consonants. The conversion is made according to the following table:

Code	Letters
1	B,P,F,V
2	C,S,G,J,K,Q,X,Z
3	D,T
4	L
5	M,N
6	R
*	(all others)

The `hasDigits()` method returns `true` if a given string contains digits, and the `title-Case()` method converts the first character of a given string to upper case.

20.9.2 Running the code

Open an existing RTF file and try running a complete spell check. Try adding some words to the dictionary and use the Ignore All button to avoid being asked about a word again during that spell check. Try using the Suggest button to query the database for more suggestions based on our SOUNDEX algorithm. Click the Change button to accept either a suggestion or a change typed into the text field. Click the Ignore button to ignore the current word being questioned.

> **NOTE** The Shakespeare vocabulary database supplied for this example is neither complete nor contemporary. It does not include such words as "software" or "Internet." However, you can easily add them, when they're encountered during a spell check, by clicking the Add button.

Pluggable look and feel

21.1   PLUGGABLE LOOK AND FEEL OVERVIEW

The pluggable look and feel architecture is one of Swing's greatest milestones. It allows seamless changes in the appearance of an application and the way an application interacts with the user. This can occur without modifying or recompiling the application, and it can be invoked programmatically *during* any single JVM session. In this chapter we'll discuss how look and feel works, how custom look and feel can be implemented for standard Swing components, and how look and feel support (both existing and custom) can be added to custom components.

NOTE   In chapter 1, we introduced the basic concepts behind look and feel and UI delegates. You might find it helpful to review this material before moving on.

In examining Swing component source code, you will quickly notice that these classes do not contain any code for sophisticated rendering. All this drawing code is stored somewhere else. As we learned in chapter 1, this code is defined within various UI delegates, which act as both a component's view and controller. (In chapter 6 we learned how to customize a tabbed pane and its UI delegate. This was only a small taste of the flexibility offered by pluggable look and feel that we will be discussing here.) Before we jump into the examples, we need to discuss how the most significant look and feel-related classes and interfaces function and interact in more detail.

21.1.1 LookAndFeel

abstract class javax.swing.LookAndFeel

This abstract class serves as the superclass of the central class of any pluggable look and feel implementation. The `getDefaults()` method returns an instance of `UIDefaults` (see section 21.1.2). The `getDescription()` method returns a one-to-two sentence description of the look and feel. The `getID()` method returns a simple, unique string that identifies a look and feel. The `getName()` method returns a short string that represents the name of that look and feel, such as "Malachite," or "Windows."

> **NOTE** The `getID()` method is actually not used by Swing, but as a rule it is a good idea to provide `LookAndFeel` implementations with a unique identifier.

The `isNativeLookAndFeel()` method queries the `System` class to determine whether the given `LookAndFeel` corresponds to that which emulates the operating system platform the running VM is designed for. The `isSupportedLookAndFeel()` method determines whether the given `LookAndFeel` is supported by the operating system the running VM is designed for. Due to legal issues, some `LookAndFeel`s will not be supported by certain operating systems, even though they have the ability to function perfectly well.

> **NOTE** We will not go into the details of how to work around this limitation Sun has imposed (although it is relatively easy), specifically because of the legal issues involved.

The `initialize()` and `uninitialize()` methods are called when a `LookAndFeel` is installed and uninstalled, respectively. The `toString()` method returns the description returned by `getDescription()`, as well as the fully qualified class name.

Several convenient static methods are also provided for assigning and unassigning borders, colors, and fonts to components: `installBorder()`, `installColors()`, `installColorsAndFont()`, and `uninstallBorder()`. `LookAndFeel` implements these so that the specified properties only change if the current property value of the given component is a `UIResource` (see section 21.1.4) or `null`. The static methods `makeKeyBindings()` and `makeIcon()` are convenience methods for building a list of text component key bindings and creating a `UIDefaults.LazyValue` (see section 21.1.2) which can create an `ImageIcon UIResource`.

21.1.2 UIDefaults

class javax.swing.UIDefaults

This class extends `Hashtable` and manages a collection of custom resources (such as objects and primitives) used in this look and feel. The `put(Object key, Object value)` and `putDefaults(Object[] keyValueList)` methods store data (in the latter case they must be placed in a one-dimensional array in this order: key1, value1, key2, value2, etc.). The `get(Object key)` method retrieves a stored resource.

UIDefaults also defines two inner classes: LazyValue and ActiveValue. A Lazy-Value is an entry in the UIDefaults hashtable that is not instantiated until it is looked up with its associated key name. Large objects that take a long time to instantiate and which are rarely used can benefit from being implemented as LazyValues. An ActiveValue is instantiated each time it is looked up with its associated key name. Those resources that must be unique in each place they are used are often implemented as ActiveValues.

Both interfaces require the definition of the createValue() method. The following code shows a simple LazyValue that constructs a new border.

```
Object myBorderLazyValue = new UIDefaults.LazyValue() {
  public Object createValue(UIDefaults table) {
    return new BorderFactory.createLoweredBevelBorder();
  }
};
myUIDefaults.put("MyBorder", borderLazyValue);
```

Note that the createValue() method will only be called once for LazyValues, whereas with ActiveValues it will be called each time that resource is requested.

21.1.3 UIManager

public class javax.swing.UIManager

This class provides a set of static methods that are used to manage the current look and feel. The current look and feel is actually made up of a three-level UIDefaults hierarchy: user defaults, current look and feel defaults, and system defaults. Particularly important methods are getUI(JComponent target), which retrieves an instance of ComponentUI for the specified component, and getDefaults(), which retrieves a shared instance of the UIDefaults class.

21.1.4 The UIResource interface

abstract interface javax.swing.plaf.UIResource

This interface declares no methods and is used solely to mark resource objects created for a component's UI delegate. Several classes used to wrap component UI resources implement this interface—for example: InsetsUIResource, FontUIResource, IconUIResource, BorderUIResource, and ColorUIResource. These wrapper classes are used for assigning resources that will be relinquished when a component's UI delegate is changed. In other words, if we were to assign an instance of JLabel a background of Color.Yellow, this background setting would persist even through a UI delegate change. However, if we were to assign that JLabel a background of new ColorUIResource(Color.Yellow), the background would only persist until another UI delegate is installed. When the next UI delegate is installed, the label will receive a new label background based on the look and feel the new UI delegate belongs to.

21.1.5 ComponentUI

abstract class javax.swing.plaf.ComponentUI

This abstract class represents a common superclass of all component UI delegate classes each implemented by different look and feel packages. The createUI(JComponent c) static method creates an instance of `ComponentUI` for a given component. See section 1.4.1, for a description of each `ComponentUI` method.

Abstract classes in the `javax.swing.plaf` package extend `ComponentUI` to represent the base class from which each Swing component's UI should extend: `ButtonUI`, `TreeUI`, and so on. Each of these classes has a concrete default implementation in the `javax.swing.plaf.basic` package: `BasicButtonUI`, `BasicTreeUI`, and so on. In turn, these basic UI classes can be, and are intended to be, extended by other look and feel implementations. For example, the classes mentioned above are extended by `MetalButtonUI` and `MetalTreeUI`, which are defined in the `javax.swing.plaf.metal` package.

21.1.6 BasicLookAndFeel

class javax.swing.plaf.basic.BasicLookAndFeel

This class provides the basic implementation of `javax.swing.LookAndFeel`. It creates all resources used by UI classes defined in the `basic` package. Custom look and feel classes are expected to extend this class, rather than `LookAndFeel` directly, to replace only those resources that need to be customized.

NOTE   Though we will not go into the details of each basic UI delegate implementation in this book (indeed this is a large topic and deserves a whole volume unto itself), note that the basic package contains a class called `BasicGraphicsUtils`, which consists of several static methods used for drawing various types of rectangles most commonly used for borders. The basic package also contains several other quite useful utility-like classes, and a quick browse through the basic package API documentation will reveal some of these interesting members.

21.1.7 How look and feel works

Now we'll discuss how the pluggable look and feel mechanism works and what actually happens when a Swing component is created and painted and when the user changes the application's look and feel during a Java session.

All Swing component constructors call the `updateUI()` method which is inherited from `JComponent`. This method may also be called with the `SwingUtilities.updateComponentTreeUI()` helper method. The latter method recursively updates the UI delegate of each child of the specified component (we've already seen how this is used in chapters 1 and 16).

The `updateUI()` method overridden by most Swing components typically has an implementation similar to the following:

```
setUI((MenuUI)UIManager.getUI(this));
```

This invokes the static `UIManager.getUI()` method and passes a `this` component reference as a parameter. This method, in turn, triggers a call to `getUI()` on the shared `UIDefaults` instance retrieved with the `getDefaults()` method.

The `UIDefaults.getUI()` method actually creates the `ComponentUI` object for a given `JComponent`. It first calls `getUIClassID()` on that component to discover the unique string ID associated with that class. For example, the `JTree.getUIClassID()` call returns the string "TreeUI."

Prior to the process described above, the `UIDefaults` instance (which extends `Hashtable`) is initialized by the subclass of `LookAndFeel` which is currently in charge. For instance, the Java look and feel (also referred to as "Metal") is defined by `javax.swing.plaf.metal.MetalLookAndFeel`. This class fills that look and feel's shared `UIDefaults` instance with key-value pairs. For each component which has a corresponding UI delegate implementation in the current look and feel, a component ID `String` and a fully qualified UI delegate class name is added as a key/value pair to `UIDefaults`. For instance, the "TreeUI" ID key corresponds to the "javax.swing.plaf.metal.MetalTreeUI" value in `MetalLookAndFeel`'s look and feel `UIDefaults`. If a particular `LookAndFeel` implementation does not specify a UI delegate for some component, a value from the parent `javax.swing.plaf.BasicLookAndFeel` class is used.

Using these key/value pairs, the `UIDefaults.getUI()` method determines the fully qualified class name and calls the `createUI()` method on that class using the Java reflection API. This static method returns an instance of the proper UI delegate, such as `MetalTreeUI`.

Now let's go back to the `updateUI()` method. The retrieved `ComponentUI` object is passed to the `setUI()` method and stored into `protected` variable, `ComponentUI ui`, which is inherited from the `JComponent` base class. This completes the creation of a UI delegate.

Recall that UI delegates are normally in charge of performing the associated component's rendering, as well as processing user input directed to that component. The `update()` method of a UI delegate is normally responsible for painting a component's background, if it is opaque, and then calling `paint()`. A UI delegate's `paint()` method is what actually paints a component's content, and it is the method we most often override when building our own delegates.

Now let's review this process from a higher-level perspective:

1 The currently installed look and feel provides an application with information about UI delegates to be used for all Swing components instantiated in that application.

2 Using this information, an instance of a UI delegate class can be instantiated on demand for a given component.

3 This UI delegate is passed to the component and it generally takes responsibility for providing the complete user interface (view and controller).

4 The UI delegate can be easily replaced with another one at run-time without affecting the underlying component or its data (such as its model).

21.1.8   Selecting a look and feel

The Swing API shipped with Java 2 includes three standard look and feels: Metal, Motif, and Windows (the latter is available only for Microsoft Windows users). The first one is not associated with any existing platform and is also known as the "Java look and feel." Metal is the default, and it will be used automatically unless we explicitly change look and feels in our application.

REFERENCE   Apple provides the MacOS look and feel which is available for download at http://www.apple.com/macos/java/text/download.html.

NOTE   Swing also provides a Multiplexing look and feel which allows more than one UI delegate to be associated with a component at the same time. This look and feel is intended for, but not limited to, use with accessible technologies.

CHAPTER 21   PLUGGABLE LOOK AND FEEL

To select a particular look and feel, we call the `UIManager.setLookAndFeel()` method and specify the fully qualified class name of a subclass of `javax.swing.LookAndFeel` which defines the desired look and feel. The following code shows how to force an application to use the Motif look and feel:

```
try {
  UIManager.setLookAndFeel(
    "com.sun.java.swing.plaf.motif.MotifLookAndFeel");
}
catch (Exception e) {
  System.out.println ("Couldn't load Motif look and feel " + e);
}
```

Note that this should be called *before* we instantiate any components. Alternatively we can call this method and then use the `SwingUtilities updateComponentTreeUI()` method to change the current look and feel of a container and all its children, as discussed previously.

GUIDELINE

Design balance is affected by look and feel selection   Beware! Although it is technically possible to update look and feel on-the-fly, this may often be visually undesirable. Different look and feels use different graphical weights for each component, such as bezel thickness on buttons. Therefore, a display which is designed to look good in a particular look and feel may be visually unbalanced and inelegant when switched to another look and feel. This could be due to the change in white space which balances against the graphical weight of elements such as bezels, or it may be a change in alignment. For example, the Malachite look and feel is visually heavy; as a rough guide, more white space will be required for a well-balanced effect when it's compared to the Metal look and feel.

21.1.9   Creating a custom LookAndFeel implementation

Swing provides the complete flexibility of implementing our own custom look and feel, and distributing it with our application. This task usually involves overriding the rendering functionality of all Swing components supported by our look and feel (default implementations are then used for each remaining component we are not interested in customizing). In general, this is not a simple project, and it will almost always require referencing Swing `plaf` source code.

The first step is to establish a basic idea of how we will provide consistent UI delegate appearances. This includes some thought as to what colors and icons will be used for each component, and whether these choices fit well together.

Then we move on to the most significant step in creating a custom look and feel, which is the implementation of a `javax.swing.LookAndFeel` subclass. The following six abstract methods are the minimum that should be overridden:

- `String getID()`: Returns the string ID of this look and feel (such as "Motif").
- `String getName()`: Returns a short string describing this look and feel (such as "CDE/ Motif").
- `String getDescription()`: Returns a one-line string description of this look and feel.
- `boolean isNativeLookAndFeel()`: Returns `true` if the look and feel corresponds to the current underlying native platform.

- boolean isSupportedLookAndFeel(): Returns true if the the current underlying native platform supports and/or permits this look and feel.
- UIDefaults getDefaults(): Returns the look and feel-specific Hashtable of resources (discussed above). This is the most important method of any LookAndFeel implementation.

However, to make implementation simpler, it is normally expected that we extend javax.swing.plaf.basic.BasicLookAndFeel instead of javax.swing.LookAndFeel directly. In this case, we override some of the following BasicLookAndFeel methods (along with a few LookAndFeel methods in the list above):

- void initClassDefaults(UIDefaults table): Fills a given UIDefaults instance with key/value pairs that specify IDs and fully qualified class names of UI delegates for each component supported by this look and feel.
- void initComponentDefaults(UIDefaults table): Fills a given UIDefaults instance with key/value pairs using information (typically drawing resources such as colors, images, and borders) that is specific to this look and feel.
- void initSystemColorDefaults(UIDefaults table): Fills a given UIDefaults instance with color information specific to this look and feel.
- void loadSystemColors(UIDefaults table, String[] systemColors, boolean useNative): Fills a given UIDefaults instance with color information specific to the underlying platform.

The first two methods are the most significant, and we will discuss them in a bit more detail here.

21.1.10   Defining default component resources

The following code shows how to override the initComponentDefaults() method to store custom resources in a given UIDefaults instance. These resources will be used to construct a JButton UI delegate that corresponds to this look and feel (this is an imaginary implementation for now):

```
protected void initComponentDefaults(UIDefaults table) {
  super.initComponentDefaults(table);
  Object[] defaults = {
    "Button.font", new FontUIResource("Arial", Font.BOLD, 12 ),
    "Button.background", new ColorUIResource(4, 108, 2),
    "Button.foreground", new ColorUIResource(236, 236, 0),
    "Button.margin", new InsetsUIResource(8, 8, 8, 8)
  };
  table.putDefaults( defaults );
}
```

Note that the super class initComponentDefaults() method is called *before* putting our custom information in the table, since we only want to override button UI resources. Also note that the resource objects are encapsulated in special wrapper classes which are defined in the javax.swing.plaf package (Font instances are placed in FontUIResources, Colors in ColorUIResources, and so on.). This is necessary to correctly load and unload resources when the current look and feel is changed.

Resource keys start with the component name, minus the "J" prefix. So "Button.font" defines the font resource for JButtons, while "RadioButton.font" defines the font resource for JRadioButtons. Unfortunately these standard resource keys are not documented, but they can all be found directly in the Swing look and feel source code. For example, see MetalLookAndFeel.java in package javax.swing. plaf.metal.

21.1.11 Defining class defaults

Providing custom resources, such as colors and fonts, is the simplest way to create a custom look and feel. However, to provide more powerful customizations, we need to develop custom extensions of ComponentUI classes for specific components: custom UI delegates. We also need to provide a means of locating our custom UI delegate classes so that UIManager can successfully switch a component's look and feel on demand.

The following code overrides the initClassDefaults() method to store information about our imaginary myLF.MyLFButtonUI class (a member of the imaginary myLF look and feel package), which extends javax.swing.plaf.ButtonUI. It will be used to provide a custom look and feel for JButton:

```
protected void initClassDefaults(UIDefaults table) {
  super.initClassDefaults(table);
  try {
      String className = "myLF.MyLFButtonUI";
      Class buttonClass = Class.forName(className);
      table.put("ButtonUI", className);
      table.put(className, buttonClass);
  }
  catch (Exception ex) {
      ex.printStackTrace();
  }
}
```

The initClassDefaults() implementation of the super class is called *before* (not after) we populate the table with our custom information, since we don't intend to override all UI class mappings for all components. Instead, we use the default settings for all but "ButtonUI." (We did a similar thing above in initComponentDefaults().) Also note that we place *both* the fully qualified class name of the delegate, as well as the Class instance itself, in the table.

NOTE Placing only the class name in the defaults table does not provide correct functionality. As of Java 2 FCS, without a corresponding Class instance in the table as well, getUI() will not be able to retrieve instances of custom look and feel delegates. We will see that this is the case in the examples below.

21.1.12 Creating custom UI delegates

Now it's time to show a simple pseudocode implementation of the imaginary myLF.MyLF-ButtonUI class to which we've been relating our discussion:

```
package myLF;

public class MyLFButtonUI extends  BasicButtonUI {
  private final static MyLFButtonUI m_buttonUI =
    new MyLFButtonUI();
```

```
protected Color  m_backgroundNormal = null;
// Declare variables for other resources.

public static ComponentUI createUI( JComponent c ) {
  return m_buttonUI;

}
public void installUI(JComponent c) {

  super.installUI(c);
  m_backgroundNormal = UIManager.getColor(
    "Button.background");
  // Retrieve other resources and store them
  // as instance variables.
  // Add listeners. These might be registered to receive
  // events from a component's model or the component itself.
}

public void uninstallUI(JComponent c) {
  super.uninstallUI(c);
  // Provide cleanup.
  // Remove listeners.
}

public void update(Graphics g, JComponent c) {
  // Provide custom background painting if the component is
  // opaque, then call paint().
}

public void paint(Graphics g, JComponent c) {
  // Provide custom rendering for the given component.
}

// Provide implementation for listeners.
}
```

This class extends javax.swing.plaf.basic.BasicButtonUI to override some of its functionality and it relies on basic look and feel defaults for the rest. The shared instance, MyLFButtonUI m_buttonUI, is created once and retrieved using the createUI() method. Thus, only one instance of this delegate will exist, and it will act as the view and controller for all JButton instances with the myLF look and feel.

The installUI() method retrieves myLF-specific resources that correspond to JButton (refer to our discussion of initComponentDefaults() above). We might also use this method to add mouse and key listeners to provide look and feel-specific functionality. For instance, we might design our button UI so that an associated JButton's text changes color each time the mouse cursor rolls over it. An advantage of this approach is that we don't need to modify our application—we can still use normal JButtons. Once myLF is installed, this functionality will automatically appear.

The uninstallUI() method performs all the necessary cleanup, including removing any listeners that this delegate might have attached to the component or its model.

The update() method will paint the given component's background if it is opaque, and then immediately call paint() (do not confuse this method with JComponent's paint() method).

NOTE   We recommend that you always implement painting functionality in this way, but in reality the background of Swing components are more often painted directly within the `paint()` method (a quick skim through Swing UI delegate source code illustrates this; for an example, see BasicRadioButtonUI.java). If this is not the case, the resulting background will be painted by `JComponent`'s painting routine. For this reason we often find no background rendering code at all in UI delegates.

This is a relatively minor issue. Just make sure that if you do want to take control of a component's background rendering, it is best to do so in UI delegate `up-date()` methods. This rendering should occur only if the associated component's opaque property is set to `true`, and it should be called *before* the main detail of its view is painted (`update()` should end with a call to `paint()`).

The `paint()` method renders a given component using a given graphical context. To use a look and feel successfully, the component class should not implement any rendering functionality for itself. Instead, it should allow its painting to be controlled by UI delegate classes so that all rendering is look and feel-specific (refer to chapter 2 for further discussion of painting issues).

NOTE   Implementing a custom look and feel will make much more sense once we step through the first two examples. We suggest that you reference the above discussion often as you make your way through this chapter. Reviewing the discussion of MVC in chapter 1 may also be helpful at this point.

21.1.13   Metal themes

class javax.swing.plaf.metal.MetalTheme

Themes are sets of color and font definitions that can be dynamically plugged into `Metal-LookAndFeel`, and immediately used by a Swing application on-the-fly if Metal is the current look and feel. To create a theme, we simply subclass `MetalTheme` (or `DefaultMetalTheme`) and override a selection of its numerous `getXX()` methods to return a specific font or color. A quick browse through these methods shows implementations for all the colors and fonts used throughout the Metal look and feel, allowing us to customize the Metal appearance however we like. `MetalLookAndFeel` contains `createDefaultTheme()`, a protected method used to create the default metal theme, and it provides us with the `setCurrentTheme()` method which allows us to plug in a new theme. The effects of plugging in a new theme are seen immediately. Themes offer a simple alternative to building a custom `LookAndFeel` when all that is desired are some simple appearance changes.

21.2   *CUSTOM LOOK AND FEEL, PART I:*
USING CUSTOM RESOURCES

GUIDELINE

When to consider a custom look and feel   Developing a custom look and feel is not a trivial undertaking. Almost certainly, more effort is needed for the design rather than the coding. Consider a custom look and feel in these situations:

- You are designing a single-use system, such as a self-service kiosk.

- You are intending to roll out a suite of enterprise applications which will work together and you want the look and feel to reflect the corporate image or identity.
- You are developing a family of software products and want to develop a unique environment or corporate identity. This was exactly Sun's intention with the Metal look and feel which closely reflects the colors and styles used in the Sun corporate identity. Other examples of custom designed environments are Lotus Notes, Lotus eSuite, and Sun HotJava Views.

The easiest way to create a custom look and feel is simply to customize default component resources (colors, borders, fonts, etc.) without actually implementing any custom UI delegates. In this case, the only thing we need to do is extend `BasicLookAndFeel` (see the above discussion), or another existing `LookAndFeel` implementation, and provide a set of resources. Example 21.1 demonstrates how this can be done by beginning the implementation of our custom Malachite look and feel.

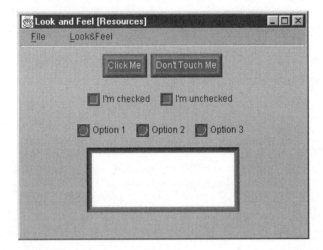

Figure 21.1   The Malachite look and feel in action

Example 21.1

Button1.java

see \Chapter21\1

```
import java.awt.*;
import java.awt.event.*;
import java.util.*;

import javax.swing.*;
import javax.swing.event.*;

import Malachite.*;

public class Button1 extends JFrame
{
```

```
protected Hashtable  m_lfs;

public Button1() {
  super("Look and Feel [Resources]");
  setSize(400, 300);
  getContentPane().setLayout(new FlowLayout());

  JMenuBar menuBar = createMenuBar();
  setJMenuBar(menuBar);

  JPanel p = new JPanel();
  JButton bt1 = new JButton("Click Me");
  p.add(bt1);

  JButton bt2 = new JButton("Don't Touch Me");
  p.add(bt2);
  getContentPane().add(p);

  p = new JPanel();
  JCheckBox chk1 = new JCheckBox("I'm checked");
  chk1.setSelected(true);
  p.add(chk1);

  JCheckBox chk2 = new JCheckBox("I'm unchecked");
  chk2.setSelected(false);
  p.add(chk2);
  getContentPane().add(p);

  p = new JPanel();
  ButtonGroup grp = new ButtonGroup();
  JRadioButton rd1 = new JRadioButton("Option 1");
  rd1.setSelected(true);
  p.add(rd1);
  grp.add(rd1);

  JRadioButton rd2 = new JRadioButton("Option 2");
  p.add(rd2);
  grp.add(rd2);

  JRadioButton rd3 = new JRadioButton("Option 3");
  p.add(rd3);
  grp.add(rd3);
  getContentPane().add(p);

  JTextArea txt = new JTextArea(5, 30);
  getContentPane().add(txt);

  WindowListener wndCloser = new WindowAdapter() {
    public void windowClosing(WindowEvent e) {
      System.exit(0);
    }
  };
  addWindowListener(wndCloser);

  setVisible(true);
}
```

❶ Creates an ordinary
frame with several
ordinary components

```
protected JMenuBar createMenuBar() {
  JMenuBar menuBar = new JMenuBar();
  JMenu mFile = new JMenu("File");
  mFile.setMnemonic('f');

  JMenuItem mItem = new JMenuItem("Exit");
  mItem.setMnemonic('x');
  ActionListener lstExit = new ActionListener() {
    public void actionPerformed(ActionEvent e) {
      System.exit(0);
    }
  };
  mItem.addActionListener(lstExit);
  mFile.add(mItem);
  menuBar.add(mFile);

  ActionListener lst = new ActionListener() {
    public void actionPerformed(ActionEvent e) {
      String str = e.getActionCommand();
      Object obj = m_lfs.get(str);
      if (obj != null)
      try {
        String className = (String)obj;
        Class lnfClass = Class.forName(className);
        UIManager.setLookAndFeel(
          (LookAndFeel)(lnfClass.newInstance()));
        SwingUtilities.updateComponentTreeUI(
          Button1.this);
      }
      catch (Exception ex) {
        ex.printStackTrace();
        System.err.println(ex.toString());
      }
    }
  };

  m_lfs = new Hashtable();
  UIManager.LookAndFeelInfo lfs[] =
    UIManager.getInstalledLookAndFeels();
  JMenu mLF = new JMenu("Look&Feel");
  mLF.setMnemonic('l');
  for (int k = 0; k < lfs.length; k++ ) {
    String name = lfs[k].getName();
    JMenuItem lf = new JMenuItem(name);
    m_lfs.put(name, lfs[k].getClassName());
    lf.addActionListener(lst);
    mLF.add(lf);
  }
  menuBar.add(mLF);

  return menuBar;
}

public static void main(String argv[]) {
```

2 Selects and updates new LookAndFeel from menu selection

2 Creates array of LookAndFeel objects obtained from UIManager

```
    try {
      LookAndFeel malachite = new Malachite.MalachiteLF();
      UIManager.LookAndFeelInfo info =
        new UIManager.LookAndFeelInfo(malachite.getName(),
      malachite.getClass().getName());
      UIManager.installLookAndFeel(info);
      UIManager.setLookAndFeel(malachite);
    }
    catch (Exception ex) {
      ex.printStackTrace();
      System.err.println(ex.toString());
    }
    new Button1();
  }
}
```

⟶ **Creates Malachite**
LookAndFeel and sets ❸
it as the current
LookAndFeel

MalachiteLF.java

see \Chapter21\1\Malachite

```
package Malachite;

import java.awt.*;

import javax.swing.*;
import javax.swing.plaf.*;
import javax.swing.plaf.basic.*;

public class MalachiteLF extends BasicLookAndFeel
 implements java.io.Serializable
{
  public String getID() { return "Malachite"; }
  public String getName() { return "Malachite Look and Feel"; }
  public String getDescription() { return "Sample look and feel from Swing";
}
  public boolean isNativeLookAndFeel() { return false; }
  public boolean isSupportedLookAndFeel() { return true; }

  protected void initComponentDefaults(UIDefaults table) {
    super.initComponentDefaults(table);

    ColorUIResource commonBackground =
      new ColorUIResource(152, 208, 128);
    ColorUIResource commonForeground =
      new ColorUIResource(0, 0, 0);
    ColorUIResource buttonBackground =
      new ColorUIResource(4, 108, 2);
    ColorUIResource buttonForeground =
      new ColorUIResource(236, 236, 0);
    ColorUIResource menuBackground =
      new ColorUIResource(128, 192, 128);

    BorderUIResource borderRaised = new
      BorderUIResource(new MalachiteBorder(
    MalachiteBorder.RAISED));
```

⟶ **Initializes default**
resource settings for ❹
this LookAndFeel

```
BorderUIResource borderLowered = new
  BorderUIResource(new MalachiteBorder(
    MalachiteBorder.LOWERED));

FontUIResource commonFont = new
  FontUIResource("Arial", Font.BOLD, 12 );

Icon ubox = new ImageIcon("Malachite/ubox.gif");
Icon ubull = new ImageIcon("Malachite/ubull.gif");

Object[] defaults = {
  "Button.font", commonFont,
  "Button.background", buttonBackground,
  "Button.foreground", buttonForeground,
  "Button.border", borderRaised,
  "Button.margin", new InsetsUIResource(8, 8, 8, 8),
  "Button.textIconGap", new Integer(4),
  "Button.textShiftOffset", new Integer(2),

  "CheckBox.font", commonFont,
  "CheckBox.background", commonBackground,
  "CheckBox.foreground", commonForeground,
  "CheckBox.icon", new IconUIResource(ubox),

  "MenuBar.font", commonFont,
  "MenuBar.background", menuBackground,
  "MenuBar.foreground", commonForeground,

  "Menu.font", commonFont,
  "Menu.background", menuBackground,
  "Menu.foreground", commonForeground,
  "Menu.selectionBackground", buttonBackground,
  "Menu.selectionForeground", buttonForeground,

  "MenuItem.font", commonFont,
  "MenuItem.background", menuBackground,
  "MenuItem.foreground", commonForeground,
  "MenuItem.selectionBackground", buttonBackground,
  "MenuItem.selectionForeground", buttonForeground,
  "MenuItem.margin", new InsetsUIResource(2, 2, 2, 2),

  "Panel.background", commonBackground,
  "Panel.foreground", commonForeground,

  "RadioButton.font", commonFont,
  "RadioButton.background", commonBackground,
  "RadioButton.foreground", commonForeground,
  "RadioButton.icon", new IconUIResource(ubull),

  "TextArea.margin", new InsetsUIResource(8, 8, 8, 8),
  "TextArea.border", borderLowered
};

table.putDefaults( defaults );
  }
}
```

MalachiteBorder.java

see \Chapter21\1\Malachite

```java
package Malachite;

import java.awt.*;

import javax.swing.*;
import javax.swing.border.*;
import javax.swing.event.*;

public class MalachiteBorder implements Border
{
  public static final int RAISED = 0;
  public static final int LOWERED = 1;

  static final String IMAGE_DIR = "Malachite/";
  static final ImageIcon IMAGE_NW = new ImageIcon(
    IMAGE_DIR+"nw.gif");
  static final ImageIcon IMAGE_N  = new ImageIcon(
    IMAGE_DIR+"n.gif");
  static final ImageIcon IMAGE_NE = new ImageIcon(
    IMAGE_DIR+"ne.gif");
  static final ImageIcon IMAGE_E  = new ImageIcon(
    IMAGE_DIR+"e.gif");
  static final ImageIcon IMAGE_SE = new ImageIcon(
    IMAGE_DIR+"se.gif");
  static final ImageIcon IMAGE_S  = new ImageIcon(
    IMAGE_DIR+"s.gif");
  static final ImageIcon IMAGE_SW = new ImageIcon(
    IMAGE_DIR+"sw.gif");
  static final ImageIcon IMAGE_W  = new ImageIcon(
    IMAGE_DIR+"w.gif");

  static final ImageIcon IMAGE_L_NW = new ImageIcon(
    IMAGE_DIR+"l_nw.gif");
  static final ImageIcon IMAGE_L_N  = new ImageIcon(
    IMAGE_DIR+"l_n.gif");
  static final ImageIcon IMAGE_L_NE = new ImageIcon(
    IMAGE_DIR+"l_ne.gif");
  static final ImageIcon IMAGE_L_E  = new ImageIcon(
    IMAGE_DIR+"l_e.gif");
  static final ImageIcon IMAGE_L_SE = new ImageIcon(
    IMAGE_DIR+"l_se.gif");
  static final ImageIcon IMAGE_L_S  = new ImageIcon(
    IMAGE_DIR+"l_s.gif");
  static final ImageIcon IMAGE_L_SW = new ImageIcon(
    IMAGE_DIR+"l_sw.gif");
  static final ImageIcon IMAGE_L_W  = new ImageIcon(
    IMAGE_DIR+"l_w.gif");

  protected int m_w = 7;
  protected int m_h = 7;

  protected boolean m_isRaised = true;
```

```java
public MalachiteBorder() {}

public MalachiteBorder(int type) {
  if (type != RAISED && type != LOWERED)
    throw new IllegalArgumentException(
      "Type must be RAISED or LOWERED");
  m_isRaised = (type == RAISED);
}

public Insets getBorderInsets(Component c) {
  return new Insets(m_h, m_w, m_h, m_w);
}

public  boolean isBorderOpaque() { return true; }

public void paintBorder(Component c, Graphics g,
 int x, int y, int w, int h)
{
  int x1 = x+m_w;
  int x2 = x+w-m_w;
  int y1 = y+m_h;
  int y2 = y+h-m_h;
  int xx, yy;

  if (m_isRaised) {
    for (xx=x1; xx<=x2; xx += IMAGE_N.getIconWidth())
      g.drawImage(IMAGE_N.getImage(), xx, y, c);
    for (yy=y1; yy<=y2; yy += IMAGE_E.getIconHeight())
      g.drawImage(IMAGE_E.getImage(), x2, yy, c);
    for (xx=x1; xx<=x2; xx += IMAGE_S.getIconWidth())
      g.drawImage(IMAGE_S.getImage(), xx, y2, c);
    for (yy=y1; yy<=y2; yy += IMAGE_W.getIconHeight())
      g.drawImage(IMAGE_W.getImage(), x, yy, c);
    g.drawImage(IMAGE_NW.getImage(), x, y, c);
    g.drawImage(IMAGE_NE.getImage(), x2, y, c);
    g.drawImage(IMAGE_SE.getImage(), x2, y2, c);
    g.drawImage(IMAGE_SW.getImage(), x, y2, c);
  }
  else {
    for (xx=x1; xx<=x2; xx += IMAGE_L_N.getIconWidth())
      g.drawImage(IMAGE_L_N.getImage(), xx, y, c);
    for (yy=y1; yy<=y2; yy += IMAGE_L_E.getIconHeight())
      g.drawImage(IMAGE_L_E.getImage(), x2, yy, c);
    for (xx=x1; xx<=x2; xx += IMAGE_L_S.getIconWidth())
      g.drawImage(IMAGE_L_S.getImage(), xx, y2, c);
    for (yy=y1; yy<=y2; yy += IMAGE_L_W.getIconHeight())
      g.drawImage(IMAGE_L_W.getImage(), x, yy, c);
    g.drawImage(IMAGE_L_NW.getImage(), x, y, c);
    g.drawImage(IMAGE_L_NE.getImage(), x2, y, c);
    g.drawImage(IMAGE_L_SE.getImage(), x2, y2, c);
    g.drawImage(IMAGE_L_SW.getImage(), x, y2, c);
  }
}
```

⑤ Paints prepared images to present Malachite border

21.2.1 Understanding the code

Class Button1

1 This class represents a simple frame container that is populated by several components: `JBut-tons`, `JCheckBoxes`, `JRadioButtons`, and `JTextArea`. Code in the constructor should be familiar, so it requires no special explanation here.

2 The `createMenuBar()` method is responsible for creating this frame's menu bar. A menu entitled look and feel is populated with menu items corresponding to `LookAndFeel` implementations available on the current JVM. An array of `UIManager.LookAndFeelInfo` instances is retrieved using the `UIManager.getInstalledLookAndFeels()` method. Look and feel class names stored in each info object are placed into the `m_lfs` Hashtable for future use. A brief text description of a particular look and feel retrieved using the `getName()` method is used to create each corresponding menu item.

When a menu item is selected, the corresponding `ActionListener` updates the look and feel for our application. This listener locates the class name corresponding to the selected menu item, and a new instance of that class is created, through reflection, and it is set as the current look and feel using the `UIManager.setLookAndFeel()` method.

> **NOTE** We can also use the overloaded `UIManager.setLookAndFeel(String class-Name)` method which takes a fully qualified `LookAndFeel` class name as a parameter. However, as of Java 2 FCS, this does not work properly on all platforms.

3 The `main()` method creates an instance of our custom look and feel, `MalachiteLF` (defined in the `Malachite` package) makes it available to Java session using `UIManager.install-LookAndFeel()`, and sets it as the current look and feel using `UIManager.setLookAnd-Feel()`. Our example frame is then created; it initially uses Malachite resources.

Class Malachite.MalachiteLF

This class defines our Malachite look and feel. It extends `BasicLookAndFeel` to override its functionality and resources only where necessary. This look and feel is centered around a green malachite palette.

> **NOTE** Malachite is a green mineral containing copper. This mineral can be found in the Ural Mountains of Russia, in Australia, and in Arizona in the United States of America. Since ancient times it has been used as a gemstone.

4 The `getID()`, `getName()`, and `getDescription()` methods return a short ID, the name, and a text description of this look and feel, respectively. As we've discussed earlier, the `init-ComponentDefaults()` method fills a given `UIDefaults` instance with key/value pairs representing information specific to this look and feel. In our implementation, we customize resources for the following components (recall that the "J" prefix is not used): Button, Check-Box, RadioButton, TextArea, MenuBar, Menu, MenuItem, and Panel.

We did not define the `initClassDefaults()` method because we have not implemented any custom UI delegates (we will do this in the next section).

Class Malachite.MalachiteBorder

5 This class defines our custom Malachite implementation of the `Border` interface. This border is intended to provide the illusion of a 3-D frame cut out of a green gemstone. It can be drawn in two forms: lowered or raised. A 3-D effect is produced through the proper combination of previously prepared images. The actual rendering is done in the `paintBorder()` method, which simply draws a set of these images to render the border.

21.2.2 Running the code

Figure 21.1 shows our `Button1` example frame populated with controls using the Malachite look and feel. Note that these controls are lifeless. We cannot click buttons, check or uncheck boxes, or select radio buttons. Try using the menu to select another look and feel available on your system and note the differences.

The components are actually fully functional when using the Malachite look and feel, but they do not have the ability to change their appearance in response to user interaction. More functionality needs to be added to provide mouse and key listener capabilities, as well as additional resources for use in representing the selected state of the button components. We will do this in the next section.

NOTE The UI delegate used for each of these components is the corresponding `basic` look and feel version, because we did not override any class defaults in `MalachiteLF`. A quick look in the source code for these delegates shows that the rendering functionality for selected and focused states is not implemented. All subclasses corresponding to specific look and feels are responsible for implementing this functionality themselves.

NOTE The text area in this example is not placed in a scrolling pane specifically because we want to emphasize the use of our custom border. This is the reason it resizes when multiple lines of text are entered.

21.3 CUSTOM LOOK AND FEEL, PART II: CREATING CUSTOM UI DELEGATES

The next step in the creation of a custom look and feel is to implement custom UI delegates that correspond to each supported component. In example 21.2, we'll show how to implement custom Malachite UI delegates for three relatively simple Swing components: `JButton`, `JCheckBox`, and `JRadioButton`.

Example 21.2

MalachiteLF.java

see \Chapter21\2\Malachite

```
package Malachite;

import java.awt.*;

import javax.swing.*;
import javax.swing.plaf.*;
import javax.swing.plaf.basic.*;

public class MalachiteLF extends BasicLookAndFeel
```

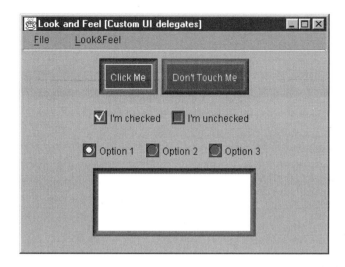

Figure 21.2   Our custom Malachite UI delegates in action

```
  implements java.io.Serializable
{
  // Unchanged code from example 21.1

  protected void initClassDefaults(UIDefaults table) {
    super.initClassDefaults(table);
    putDefault(table, "ButtonUI");
    putDefault(table, "CheckBoxUI");
    putDefault(table, "RadioButtonUI");
  }
  protected void putDefault(UIDefaults table, String uiKey) {
    try {
      String className = "Malachite.Malachite"+uiKey;
      Class buttonClass = Class.forName(className);
      table.put(uiKey, className);
      table.put(className, buttonClass);
    }
    catch (Exception ex) {
      ex.printStackTrace();
    }
  }

  protected void initComponentDefaults(UIDefaults table) {
    super.initComponentDefaults(table);

    // Unchanged code from example 21.1

    Icon ubox = new ImageIcon("Malachite/ubox.gif");
    Icon ubull = new ImageIcon("Malachite/ubull.gif");

    Icon cbox = new ImageIcon("Malachite/cbox.gif");
    Icon pcbox = new ImageIcon("Malachite/p_cbox.gif");
    Icon pubox = new ImageIcon("Malachite/p_ubox.gif");

    Icon cbull = new ImageIcon("Malachite/cbull.gif");
    Icon pcbull = new ImageIcon("Malachite/p_cbull.gif");
    Icon pubull = new ImageIcon("Malachite/p_ubull.gif");
```

① Initializes component type classes from base class method, but replaces component type classes for button, check box, and radio button

① Stores a UIDefaults entry to look up the component class name from the short component type name, and one entry to look up the class object from the class name

② This version of this method places more defaults into the UIDefaults table

```
    Object[] defaults = {
      "Button.font", commonFont,
      "Button.background", buttonBackground,
      "Button.foreground", buttonForeground,
      "Button.border", borderRaised,
      "Button.margin", new InsetsUIResource(8, 8, 8, 8),
      "Button.textIconGap", new Integer(4),
      "Button.textShiftOffset", new Integer(2),

      "Button.focusBorder", focusBorder,
      "Button.borderPressed", borderLowered,
      "Button.activeForeground", new
        ColorUIResource(255, 255, 255),
      "Button.pressedBackground", new
        ColorUIResource(0, 96, 0),

      "CheckBox.font", commonFont,
      "CheckBox.background", commonBackground,
      "CheckBox.foreground", commonForeground,
      "CheckBox.icon", new IconUIResource(ubox),

      "CheckBox.focusBorder", focusBorder,
      "CheckBox.activeForeground", activeForeground,
      "CheckBox.iconPressed", new IconUIResource(pubox),
      "CheckBox.iconChecked", new IconUIResource(cbox),
      "CheckBox.iconPressedChecked", new IconUIResource(pcbox),
      "CheckBox.textIconGap", new Integer(4),

      // Unchanged code from example 21.1

      "RadioButton.font", commonFont,
      "RadioButton.background", commonBackground,
      "RadioButton.foreground", commonForeground,
      "RadioButton.icon", new IconUIResource(ubull),

      "RadioButton.focusBorder", focusBorder,
      "RadioButton.activeForeground", activeForeground,
      "RadioButton.iconPressed", new IconUIResource(pubull),
      "RadioButton.iconChecked", new IconUIResource(cbull),
      "RadioButton.iconPressedChecked", new IconUIResource(pcbull),
      "RadioButton.textIconGap", new Integer(4),

      "TextArea.margin", new InsetsUIResource(8, 8, 8, 8),
      "TextArea.border", borderLowered
    };

    table.putDefaults( defaults );
  }
}
```

MalachiteButtonUI.java

see \Chapter21\2\Malachite

```
package Malachite;

import java.awt.*;
import java.awt.event.*;
```

```java
import javax.swing.*;
import javax.swing.border.*;
import javax.swing.plaf.*;
import javax.swing.plaf.basic.*;

public class MalachiteButtonUI extends BasicButtonUI
 implements java.io.Serializable, MouseListener, KeyListener
{
  private final static MalachiteButtonUI m_buttonUI =
    new MalachiteButtonUI();

  protected Border m_borderRaised = null;
  protected Border m_borderLowered = null;
  protected Color  m_backgroundNormal = null;
  protected Color  m_backgroundPressed = null;
  protected Color  m_foregroundNormal = null;
  protected Color  m_foregroundActive = null;
  protected Color  m_focusBorder = null;

  public MalachiteButtonUI() {}

  public static ComponentUI createUI( JComponent c ) {
    return m_buttonUI;
  }

  public void installUI(JComponent c) {
    super.installUI(c);

    m_borderRaised = UIManager.getBorder(
      "Button.border");
    m_borderLowered = UIManager.getBorder(
      "Button.borderPressed");
    m_backgroundNormal = UIManager.getColor(
      "Button.background");
    m_backgroundPressed = UIManager.getColor(
      "Button.pressedBackground");
    m_foregroundNormal = UIManager.getColor(
      "Button.foreground");
    m_foregroundActive = UIManager.getColor(
      "Button.activeForeground");
    m_focusBorder = UIManager.getColor(
      "Button.focusBorder");

    c.addMouseListener(this);
    c.addKeyListener(this);
  }

  public void uninstallUI(JComponent c) {
    super.uninstallUI(c);
    c.removeMouseListener(this);
    c.removeKeyListener(this);
  }

  public void paint(Graphics g, JComponent c) {
    AbstractButton b = (AbstractButton) c;
    Dimension d = b.getSize();
```

❸ Malachite UI delegate for JButton

❹ Retrieves rendering resources from defaults table

❺ Renders button text and focus rectangle with given graphics context

```
      g.setFont(c.getFont());
      FontMetrics fm = g.getFontMetrics();

      g.setColor(b.getForeground());
      String caption = b.getText();
      int x = (d.width - fm.stringWidth(caption))/2;
      int y = (d.height + fm.getAscent())/2;
      g.drawString(caption, x, y);

      if (b.isFocusPainted() && b.hasFocus()) {
        g.setColor(m_focusBorder);
        Insets bi = b.getBorder().getBorderInsets(b);
        g.drawRect(bi.left, bi.top, d.width-bi.left-bi.right-1,
        d.height-bi.top-bi.bottom-1);
      }
    }

    public Dimension getPreferredSize(JComponent c) {
      Dimension d = super.getPreferredSize(c);
      if (m_borderRaised != null) {
        Insets ins = m_borderRaised.getBorderInsets(c);
        d.setSize(d.width+ins.left+ins.right,
          d.height+ins.top+ins.bottom);
      }
      return d;
    }

    public void mouseClicked(MouseEvent e) {}

    public void mousePressed(MouseEvent e) {
      JComponent c = (JComponent)e.getComponent();
      c.setBorder(m_borderLowered);
      c.setBackground(m_backgroundPressed);
    }

    public void mouseReleased(MouseEvent e) {
      JComponent c = (JComponent)e.getComponent();
      c.setBorder(m_borderRaised);
      c.setBackground(m_backgroundNormal);
    }

    public void mouseEntered(MouseEvent e) {
      JComponent c = (JComponent)e.getComponent();
      c.setForeground(m_foregroundActive);
      c.repaint();
    }

    public void mouseExited(MouseEvent e) {
      JComponent c = (JComponent)e.getComponent();
      c.setForeground(m_foregroundNormal);
      c.repaint();
    }

    public void keyTyped(KeyEvent e) {}

    public void keyPressed(KeyEvent e) {
      int code = e.getKeyCode();
      if (code == KeyEvent.VK_ENTER || code == KeyEvent.VK_SPACE) {
```

6 Overridden to add in border size

7 Changes button background and border when pressed or released

7 Changes foreground color when mouse enters or exits bounds of component

8 Pressing the Space bar or Enter while mouse cursor is within component is the same as a button click

```
      JComponent c = (JComponent)e.getComponent();
      c.setBorder(m_borderLowered);
      c.setBackground(m_backgroundPressed);
    }
  }

  public void keyReleased(KeyEvent e) {
    int code = e.getKeyCode();
    if (code == KeyEvent.VK_ENTER || code == KeyEvent.VK_SPACE) {
      JComponent c = (JComponent)e.getComponent();
      c.setBor-
der(m_borderRaised);
      c.setBackground(m_backgroundNormal);
    }
  }
}
```

8 Pressing the Space bar or Enter while mouse cursor is within component is the same as a button click

MalachiteCheckBoxUI.java

see \Chapter21\2\Malachite

```
package Malachite;

import java.awt.*;
import java.awt.event.*;

import javax.swing.*;
import javax.swing.border.*;
import javax.swing.plaf.*;
import javax.swing.plaf.basic.*;

public class MalachiteCheckBoxUI extends BasicCheckBoxUI
 implements java.io.Serializable, MouseListener
{
  private final static MalachiteCheckBoxUI m_buttonUI =
    new MalachiteCheckBoxUI();

  protected Color  m_backgroundNormal = null;
  protected Color  m_foregroundNormal = null;
  protected Color  m_foregroundActive = null;
  protected Icon   m_checkedIcon = null;
  protected Icon   m_uncheckedIcon = null;
  protected Icon   m_pressedCheckedIcon = null;
  protected Icon   m_pressedUncheckedIcon = null;
  protected Color  m_focusBorder = null;
  protected int    m_textIconGap = -1;

  public MalachiteCheckBoxUI() {}

  public static ComponentUI createUI( JComponent c ) {
    return m_buttonUI;
  }

  public void installUI(JComponent c) {
    super.installUI(c);
    m_backgroundNormal = UIManager.getColor(
```

9 UI delegate for JCheckBox to provide Malachite look and feel

10 Like MalachiteButtonUI, retrieves rendering resources from defaults table

```
      "CheckBox.background");
    m_foregroundNormal = UIManager.getColor(
      "CheckBox.foreground");
    m_foregroundActive = UIManager.getColor(
      "CheckBox.activeForeground");
    m_checkedIcon = UIManager.getIcon(
      "CheckBox.iconChecked");
    m_uncheckedIcon = UIManager.getIcon(
      "CheckBox.icon");
    m_pressedCheckedIcon = UIManager.getIcon(
      "CheckBox.iconPressedChecked");
    m_pressedUncheckedIcon = UIManager.getIcon(
      "CheckBox.iconPressed");
    m_focusBorder = UIManager.getColor(
      "CheckBox.focusBorder");
    m_textIconGap = UIManager.getInt(
      "CheckBox.textIconGap");

    c.setBackground(m_backgroundNormal);
    c.addMouseListener(this);
  }

  public void uninstallUI(JComponent c) {
    super.uninstallUI(c);
    c.removeMouseListener(this);
  }

  public void paint(Graphics g, JComponent c) {
    AbstractButton b = (AbstractButton)c;
    ButtonModel model = b.getModel();
    Dimension d = b.getSize();

    g.setFont(c.getFont());
    FontMetrics fm = g.getFontMetrics();

    Icon icon = m_uncheckedIcon;
    if (model.isPressed() && model.isSelected())
      icon = m_pressedCheckedIcon;
    else if (model.isPressed() && !model.isSelected())
      icon = m_pressedUncheckedIcon;
    else if (!model.isPressed() && model.isSelected())
      icon = m_checkedIcon;

    g.setColor(b.getForeground());
    int x = 0;
    int y = (d.height - icon.getIconHeight())/2;
    icon.paintIcon(c, g, x, y);

    String caption = b.getText();
    x = icon.getIconWidth() + m_textIconGap;
    y = (d.height + fm.getAscent())/2;
    g.drawString(caption, x, y);

    if (b.isFocusPainted() && b.hasFocus()) {
      g.setColor(m_focusBorder);
      Insets bi = b.getBorder().getBorderInsets(b);
```

```
      g.drawRect(x-2, y-fm.getAscent()-2, d.width-x,
        fm.getAscent()+fm.getDescent()+4);
    }
  }

  public void mouseClicked(MouseEvent e) {}
  public void mousePressed(MouseEvent e) {}
  public void mouseReleased(MouseEvent e) {}

  public void mouseEntered(MouseEvent e) {
    JComponent c = (JComponent)e.getComponent();
    c.setForeground(m_foregroundActive);
    c.repaint();
  }

  public void mouseExited(MouseEvent e) {
    JComponent c = (JComponent)e.getComponent();
    c.setForeground(m_foregroundNormal);
    c.repaint();
  }
}
```

⓫ Provides rollover effect

MalachiteRadioButtonUI.java

see \Chapter21\2\Malachite

```
package Malachite;

import java.awt.*;
import java.awt.event.*;

import javax.swing.*;
import javax.swing.border.*;
import javax.swing.plaf.*;
import javax.swing.plaf.basic.*;

public class MalachiteRadioButtonUI extends MalachiteCheckBoxUI
 implements java.io.Serializable, MouseListener
{
  private final static MalachiteRadioButtonUI m_buttonUI =
    new MalachiteRadioButtonUI();

  public MalachiteRadioButtonUI() {}

  public static ComponentUI createUI( JComponent c ) {
    return m_buttonUI;
  }

  public void installUI(JComponent c) {
    super.installUI(c);
    m_backgroundNormal = UIManager.getColor(
      "RadioButton.background");
    m_foregroundNormal = UIManager.getColor(
      "RadioButton.foreground");
    m_foregroundActive = UIManager.getColor(
      "RadioButton.activeForeground");
    m_checkedIcon = UIManager.getIcon(
      "RadioButton.iconChecked");
```

⓬ Very similar to MalachiteCheckBoxUI

⓬ Different icons used to paint UI

```
        m_uncheckedIcon = UIManager.getIcon(
          "RadioButon.icon");
        m_pressedCheckedIcon = UIManager.getIcon(
          "RadioButton.iconPressedChecked");
        m_pressedUncheckedIcon = UIManager.getIcon(
          "RadioButton.iconPressed");
        m_focusBorder = UIManager.getColor(
          "RadioButton.focusBorder");
        m_textIconGap = UIManager.getInt(
          "RadioButton.textIconGap");

        c.setBackground(m_backgroundNormal);
        c.addMouseListener(this);
    }
}
```

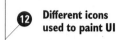

12 **Different icons used to paint UI**

21.3.1   Understanding the code

Class Malachite.MalachiteLF

1 The `initClassDefaults()` method inherited from `BasicLookAndFeel` is now overridden. As we've discussed earlier, this method will be called to fill a given `UIDefaults` instance with information about the specific classes responsible for providing a component's UI delegate for this look and feel. Our implementation calls the super class's `initClassDefaults()` method to provide all default options. It then replaces the delegate classes for our three supported button components by calling our `putDefault()` custom method. This helper method puts two entries into the given `UIDefaults` instance: the UI delegate fully qualified class name, and a corresponding instance of `java.lang.Class` (see selection 21.1.11).

2 The `initComponentDefaults()` method now places more custom resources into the given `UIDefaults` instance, including six custom icons. These resources are needed by our custom Malachite UI delegates, as we will see below.

Class Malachite.MalachiteButtonUI

3 This class provides a custom UI delegate for `JButton`. It extends `BasicButtonUI` to reuse much of its functionality, and it implements `MouseListener` and `KeyListener` to capture and process user input.

There is one class variable:

- `MalachiteButtonUI m_buttonUI`: A shared instance of this class which is returned by the `createUI()` method.

There are seven instance variables:

- `Border m_borderRaised`: The border when the button is not pressed.
- `Border m_borderLowered`: The border when the button is pressed.
- `Color m_backgroundNormal`: The background color when the button is not pressed.
- `Color m_backgroundPressed`: The background color when the button is pressed.
- `Color m_foregroundNormal`: The foreground color.
- `Color m_foregroundActive`: The foreground color when the mouse cursor rolls over.
- `Color m_focusBorder`: The focus rectangle color.

4 The `installUI()` method retrieves rendering resources from the defaults table by calling static methods which are defined in the `UIManager` class (these resources were stored by `MalachiteLF` as described above). It also attaches `this` as a `MouseListener` and `KeyListener` to the specified component. The `uninstallUI()` method simply removes these listeners.

5 The `paint()` method renders a given component using the given graphical context. Rendering of the background and border is done automatically by `JComponent` (see section 21.1.12), so the responsibility of this method is to simply render a button's text and focus rectangle.

6 The `getPreferredSize()` method is overridden since the default implementation in the `BasicButtonUI` class does not take into account the button's border (interestingly enough). Since we use a relatively thick border in Malachite, we need to override this method and add the border's insets to the width and height returned by the superclass implementation.

7 The next five methods represent an implementation of the `MouseListener` interface. To indicate that a button component is currently pressed, the `mousePressed()` method changes a button's background and border, which in turn causes that component to be repainted. The `mouseReleased()` method restores these attributes. To provide an additional rollover effect, the `mouseEntered()` method changes the associated button's foreground color, which is then restored in the `mouseExited()` method.

8 The remaining three methods represent an implementation of the `KeyListener` interface. Pressing the Space bar or Enter key while the button is in focus produces the same effect as performing a button click.

Class Malachite.MalachiteCheckBoxUI

9 This class extends `BasicCheckBoxUI` to provide a custom UI delegate for our `JCheckBox` component.

There is one class variable:

- `MalachiteCheckBoxUI m_buttonUI`: A shared instance of this class which is returned by the `createUI()` method.

There are the instance variables:

- `Color m_backgroundNormal`: The component's background.
- `Color m_foregroundNormal`: The foreground color.
- `Color m_foregroundActive`: The rollover foreground color.
- `Icon m_checkedIcon`: The icon displayed when the check box is checked and not pressed.
- `Icon m_uncheckedIcon`: The icon displayed when the check box is not checked and not pressed.
- `Icon m_pressedCheckedIcon`: The icon displayed when the check box is checked and pressed.
- `Icon m_pressedUncheckedIcon`: The icon displayed when the check box is not checked and pressed.
- `Color m_focusBorder`: The focus rectangle color.
- `int m_textIconGap`: The gap between the icon and the text.

10 Similar to `MalachiteButtonUI`, the `installUI()` method retrieves rendering resources from the defaults table and stores them in instance variables. It also attatches `this` as a `MouseListener` to the given component.

The `paint()` method renders the given component using a given graphical context. It draws an icon, text, and focus rectangle when appropriate (this code is fairly straightforward and does not require detailed explanation here).

11 The next five methods represent an implementation of the `MouseListener` interface which provides a similar rollover effect to that of `MalachiteButtonUI`.

Class Malachite.MalachiteRadioButtonUI

12 This class extends `MalachiteCheckBoxUI`. The only major difference between this class and its parent is that this class uses a different set of icons to render the radio button. The `paint()` method is not overridden. The `installUI()` method is modified to retrieve the necessary resources.

21.3.2   Running the code

Figure 21.2 shows our example frame from the previous section with our new Malachite UI delegates in action. You can see that the push buttons here are bigger because their size now properly includes the border thickness. The most significant difference appears when the buttons are clicked, and when boxes are checked/unchecked using using the mouse and keyboard.

At this point we leave the implementation of Malachite UI delegates for other existing Swing components up to you. You should now have a good idea of how to approach the task for any component. Switching gears, we will now discuss look and feel customization from the opposite point of view: providing existing look and feel capabilities for custom components.

21.4   *LOOK AND FEEL FOR CUSTOM COMPONENTS, PART I: IMPLEMENTING LOOK AND FEEL SUPPORT*

In example 21.3 in this section, we'll add support for existing look and feels to a custom component, namely our `InnerFrame` we developed in chapter 15. We'll show how to modify this

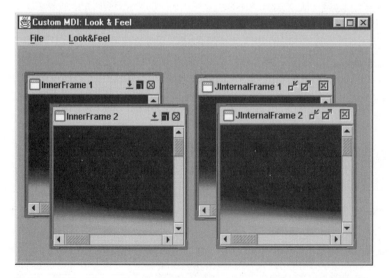

Figure 21.3   `InnerFrame` and `JInternalFrame` **in the Metal look and feel**

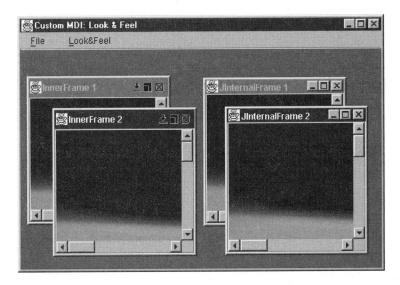

Figure 21.4 `InnerFrame` **and** `JInternalFrame` **in the Windows look and feel**

component so it complies with the look and feel paradigm and behaves accordingly. It will use shared resources provided by the installed look and feel and it will use these resources for rendering itself. This requires a custom UI delegate to be created; the component itself must be modified as well.

To allow direct comparison with `JInternalFrame`, we create a desktop pane container with a menu bar to allow the creation of an arbitrary number of `InnerFrames` and `JInternalFrames` in a cascaded fashion. We also allow look and feel switching at run-time (as we did in the previous examples).

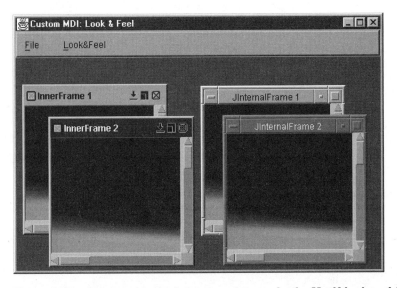

Figure 21.5 `InnerFrame` **and** `JInternalFrame` **in the Motif look and feel**

LOOK AND FEEL FOR CUSTOM COMPONENTS, PART I

NOTE   We use a `JDesktopPane` instead of our `mdi` package's custom `MDIPane` component because `JInternalFrame` generates a null pointer exception when activated (in Java 2 FCS) if its parent is not a `JDesktopPane`.

Example 21.3

MdiContainer.java

see \Chapter21\3

```java
import java.awt.*;
import java.awt.event.*;
import java.util.*;

import javax.swing.*;

import mdi.*;

public class MdiContainer extends JFrame
{
  protected ImageIcon m_icon;
  protected Hashtable m_lfs;

  public MdiContainer() {
    super("Custom MDI: Look & Feel");

    setSize(570,400);
    setContentPane(new JDesktopPane());

    m_icon = new ImageIcon("earth.jpg");
    JMenuBar menuBar = createMenuBar();
    setJMenuBar(menuBar);

    WindowListener wndCloser = new WindowAdapter() {
      public void windowClosing(WindowEvent e) {
        System.exit(0);
      }
    };
    addWindowListener(wndCloser);
    setVisible(true);
  }

  protected JMenuBar createMenuBar() {
    JMenuBar menuBar = new JMenuBar();

    JMenu mFile = new JMenu("File");
    mFile.setMnemonic('f');

    JMenuItem mItem = new JMenuItem("New InnerFrame");
    mItem.setMnemonic('i');
    ActionListener lst = new ActionListener() {
      int m_counter = 0;
      public void actionPerformed(ActionEvent e) {
        m_counter++;
        InnerFrame frame = new InnerFrame("InnerFrame " +
          m_counter);
        int i = m_counter % 5;
```

❶ This class presents a simple MDI container which can create JInternalFrames and custom InnerFrames

❷ Creates menu options to create JInternalFrames and InnerFrames

```
      frame.setBounds(20+i*20, 20+i*20, 200, 200);
      frame.getContentPane().add(
        new JScrollPane(new JLabel(m_icon)));
      getContentPane().add(frame);
      frame.toFront();
    }
  };
  mItem.addActionListener(lst);
  mFile.add(mItem);

  mItem = new JMenuItem("New JInternalFrame");
  mItem.setMnemonic('j');
  lst = new ActionListener() {
    int m_counter = 0;
    public void actionPerformed(ActionEvent e) {
      m_counter++;
      JInternalFrame frame = new JInternalFrame(
        "JInternalFrame " + m_counter);
      frame.setClosable(true);
      frame.setMaximizable(true);
      frame.setIconifiable(true);
      frame.setResizable(true);

      int i = m_counter % 5;
      frame.setBounds(50+i*20, 50+i*20, 200, 200);
      frame.getContentPane().add(
        new JScrollPane(new JLabel(m_icon)));
      getContentPane().add(frame);
      frame.toFront();
    }
  };
  mItem.addActionListener(lst);
  mFile.add(mItem);
  mFile.addSeparator();

  mItem = new JMenuItem("Exit");
  mItem.setMnemonic('x');
  lst = new ActionListener() {
    public void actionPerformed(ActionEvent e) {
      System.exit(0);
    }
  };
  mItem.addActionListener(lst);
  mFile.add(mItem);
  menuBar.add(mFile);

  lst = new ActionListener() {
    public void actionPerformed(ActionEvent e) {
      String str = e.getActionCommand();
      Object obj = m_lfs.get(str);
      if (obj != null)
        try {
          String className = (String)obj;
          Class lnfClass = Class.forName(className);
```

```
        UIManager.setLookAndFeel(
          (LookAndFeel)(lnfClass.newInstance()));
        SwingUtilities.updateComponentTreeUI(
          MdiContainer.this);
      }
      catch (Exception ex) {
        ex.printStackTrace();
        System.err.println(ex.toString());
      }
    }
  };

  m_lfs = new Hashtable();
  UIManager.LookAndFeelInfo lfs[] =
    UIManager.getInstalledLookAndFeels();
  JMenu mLF = new JMenu("Look&Feel");
  mLF.setMnemonic('l');
  for (int k = 0; k < lfs.length; k++ ) {
    String name = lfs[k].getName();
    JMenuItem lf = new JMenuItem(name);
    m_lfs.put(name, lfs[k].getClassName());
    lf.addActionListener(lst);
    mLF.add(lf);
  }
  menuBar5.add(mLF);

  return menuBar;
}
public static void main(String argv[]) {
  new MdiContainer();
}
}
```

③ Menu item to list and select a LookAndFeel

InnerFrame.java

see \Chapter21\3\mdi

```
package mdi;

import java.awt.*;
import java.awt.event.*;
import java.io.*;
import javax.swing.*;
import javax.swing.event.*;
import javax.swing.border.*;

import javax.swing.plaf.ComponentUI;
import mdi.plaf.*;

public class InnerFrame extends JPanel
 implements RootPaneContainer, Externalizable
{
  // Unchanged code from example 15.6
```

④ Imports to get LookAndFeel classes

```
    protected Color m_titleBarBackground;
    protected Color m_selectedTitleBarBackground;
    protected Color m_titleBarForeground;
    protected Color m_selectedTitleBarForeground;
    protected Font  m_titleBarFont;
    protected Border m_frameBorder;

    private Icon m_frameIcon;

    public InnerFrame() {
      this("");
    }

    // Unchanged code from example 15.6

    /////////////////////////////////////////////
    /////////////// look and feel Support /////////////////
    /////////////////////////////////////////////
    static {
      UIManager.getDefaults().put(
        "InnerFrameUI", "mdi.plaf.InnerFrameUI");
      UIManager.getDefaults().put("InnerFrameButtonUI",
        "javax.swing.plaf.basic.BasicButtonUI");
    }

    public static ComponentUI createUI(JComponent a) {
      ComponentUI mui = new InnerFrameUI();
      return mui;
    }

    public void setUI(InnerFrameUI ui) {
      if ((InnerFrameUI)this.ui != ui) {
        super.setUI(ui);
        repaint();
      }
    }

    public InnerFrameUI getUI() {
      return (InnerFrameUI)ui;
    }

    public void updateUI() {
      setUI((InnerFrameUI)UIManager.getUI(this));
      invalidate();
    }

    public String getUIClassID() {
      return "InnerFrameUI";
    }

    // Unchanged code from example 15.6

    public void setSelectedTitleBarForeground(Color c) {
      m_selectedTitleBarForeground = c;
      updateTitleBarColors();
    }
```

5 Resources controlling title bar colors and icon are moved to the UI delegate, InnerFrameUI; border color now handled by Border instance

6 This block executes only once, to install lookups for the full class names of the UI delegates

7 Called to notify the component that the LookAndFeel has changed

```java
public Color getSelectedTitleBarForeground() {
  return m_selectedTitleBarForeground;
}

public void setTitleBarFont(Font f) {
  m_titleBarFont = f;
  updateTitleBarColors();
}

public Font getTitleBarFont() {
  return m_titleBarFont;
}

public void setBorder(Border b) {
  m_frameBorder = b;
  if (b != null) {
    Insets ins = b.getBorderInsets(this);
    if (m_northResizer != null)
      m_northResizer.setHeight(ins.top);
    if (m_southResizer != null)
      m_southResizer.setHeight(ins.bottom);
    if (m_eastResizer != null)
      m_eastResizer.setWidth(ins.right);
    if (m_westResizer != null)
      m_westResizer.setWidth(ins.left);
    if (isShowing())
      validate();
  }
}

public Border getBorder() {
  return m_frameBorder;
}

protected void updateTitleBarColors() {
  if (isShowing())
      repaint();
}

public void setFrameIcon(Icon fi) {
  m_frameIcon = fi;
  if (fi != null) {
    if (m_frameIcon.getIconHeight() > TITLE_BAR_HEIGHT)
      setTitleBarHeight(m_frameIcon.getIconHeight() +
        2*FRAME_ICON_PADDING);
    if (m_iconLabel != null)
      m_iconLabel.setIcon(m_frameIcon);
  }
  else
      setTitleBarHeight(TITLE_BAR_HEIGHT);
  if (isShowing())
      revalidate();
}

public Icon getFrameIcon() {
```

8 Sets the bounds of the (invisible) resize borders, depending on the border insets

```
      return m_frameIcon;
}

// Unchanged code from example 15.6

protected void createTitleBar() {
m_titlePanel = new JPanel() {
  public Dimension getPreferredSize() {
    return new Dimension(InnerFrame.this.getWidth(),
      m_titleBarHeight);
  }

  public Color getBackground() {
    if (InnerFrame.this == null)
      return super.getBackground();
    if (isSelected())
      return getSelectedTitleBarBackground();
    else
      return getTitleBarBackground();
  }
};
m_titlePanel.setLayout(new BorderLayout());
m_titlePanel.setOpaque(true);

m_titleLabel = new JLabel() {
  public Color getForeground() {
    if (InnerFrame.this == null)
      return super.getForeground();
    if (isSelected())
      return getSelectedTitleBarForeground();
    else
      return getTitleBarForeground();
  }

  public Font getFont() {
    if (InnerFrame.this == null)
      return super.getFont();
    return m_titleBarFont;
  }
};

// Unchanged code from example 15.6

class InnerFrameButton extends JButton
{
  // Unchanged code from example 15.6
  public void setBorder(Border b) { }
  public Border getBorder() { return null; }
  public String getUIClassID() {
      return "InnerFrameButtonUI";
  }
}

// Unchanged code from example 15.6

class EastResizeEdge extends JPanel
```

9 Gets background color for title bar, but lets it work even before the InnerFrame is created

10 Dummy methods to hide the base class implementation

```
  implements MouseListener, MouseMotionListener
{
  private int WIDTH = BORDER_THICKNESS;
  private int MIN_WIDTH = ICONIZED_WIDTH;
  private boolean m_dragging;
  private JComponent m_resizeComponent;

  protected EastResizeEdge(JComponent c) {
    m_resizeComponent = c;
    setOpaque(false);                              ⑪ Makes resize
    if (m_frameBorder != null)                        border transparent
      WIDTH =
        m_frameBorder.getBorderInsets(InnerFrame.this).right;
  }

  public void setWidth(int w) {
    WIDTH = w;
  }

  // Unchanged code from example 15.6
}

// Classes WestResizeEdge, NorthResizeEdge, and SouthResizeEdge
// are modified similarly

public void writeExternal(ObjectOutput out) throws IOException {
  out.writeObject(m_titleBarBackground);
  out.writeObject(m_titleBarForeground);
  out.writeObject(m_selectedTitleBarBackground);
  out.writeObject(m_selectedTitleBarForeground);
  out.writeObject(m_frameBorder);

  // Unchanged code from example 15.6
}

public void readExternal(ObjectInput in)
 throws IOException, ClassNotFoundException {
  setTitleBarBackground((Color)in.readObject());
  setTitleBarForeground((Color)in.readObject());
  setSelectedTitleBarBackground((Color)in.readObject());
  setSelectedTitleBarForeground((Color)in.readObject());
  setBorder((Border)in.readObject());

  setTitle((String)in.readObject());

  // Unchanged code from example 15.6

  setFrameIcon((Icon)in.readObject());
  // Unchanged code from example 15.6
  }
}
```

InnerFrameUI.java

see \Chapter21\3\mdi\plaf

```
package mdi.plaf;

import java.awt.*;
```

```java
import java.util.*;

import javax.swing.*;
import javax.swing.border.*;
import javax.swing.plaf.*;

import mdi.*;

public class InnerFrameUI extends javax.swing.plaf.PanelUI
{
  private static InnerFrameUI frameUI;

  protected static Color DEFAULT_TITLE_BAR_BG_COLOR;
  protected static Color DEFAULT_SELECTED_TITLE_BAR_BG_COLOR;
  protected static Color DEFAULT_TITLE_BAR_FG_COLOR;
  protected static Color DEFAULT_SELECTED_TITLE_BAR_FG_COLOR;
  protected static Font  DEFAULT_TITLE_BAR_FONT;
  protected static Border DEFAULT_INNER_FRAME_BORDER;
  protected static Icon  DEFAULT_FRAME_ICON;

  private static Hashtable m_ownDefaults = new Hashtable();

  static {
    m_ownDefaults.put("InternalFrame.inactiveTitleBackground",
      new ColorUIResource(108,190,116));
    m_ownDefaults.put("InternalFrame.inactiveTitleForeground",
      new ColorUIResource(Color.black));
    m_ownDefaults.put("InternalFrame.activeTitleBackground",
      new ColorUIResource(91,182,249));
    m_ownDefaults.put("InternalFrame.activeTitleForeground",
      new ColorUIResource(Color.black));
    m_ownDefaults.put("InternalFrame.titleFont",
      new FontUIResource("Dialog", Font.BOLD, 12));
    m_ownDefaults.put("InternalFrame.border",
      new BorderUIResource(new MatteBorder(4, 4, 4, 4, Color.blue)));
    m_ownDefaults.put("InternalFrame.icon",
      new IconUIResource(new ImageIcon("mdi/default.gif")));
  }

  public static ComponentUI createUI(JComponent c) {
    if(frameUI == null)
      frameUI = new InnerFrameUI();
    try {
      frameUI.installDefaults();
      InnerFrame frame = (InnerFrame)c;
      frame.setTitleBarBackground(DEFAULT_TITLE_BAR_BG_COLOR);
      frame.setSelectedTitleBarBackground(
        DEFAULT_SELECTED_TITLE_BAR_BG_COLOR);
      frame.setTitleBarForeground(DEFAULT_TITLE_BAR_FG_COLOR);
        frame.setSelectedTitleBarForeground(
          DEFAULT_SELECTED_TITLE_BAR_FG_COLOR);
      frame.setTitleBarFont(DEFAULT_TITLE_BAR_FONT);
      frame.setBorder(DEFAULT_INNER_FRAME_BORDER);
      frame.setFrameIcon(DEFAULT_FRAME_ICON);
      if (frame.isShowing())
```

Defines custom UI delegate for InnerFrame component class ⓬

Installs resource defaults for this UI delegate ⓭

```
        frame.repaint();
      }
    catch (Exception ex) {
      System.err.println(ex);
      ex.printStackTrace();
    }

    return frameUI;
  }

public void installUI(JComponent c) {
    InnerFrame frame = (InnerFrame)c;
    super.installUI(frame);
  }

public void uninstallUI(JComponent c) {
    super.uninstallUI(c);
  }

protected void installDefaults() {
    DEFAULT_TITLE_BAR_BG_COLOR = (Color)findDefaultResource(
      "InternalFrame.inactiveTitleBackground");
    DEFAULT_TITLE_BAR_FG_COLOR = (Color)findDefaultResource(
      "InternalFrame.inactiveTitleForeground");
    DEFAULT_SELECTED_TITLE_BAR_BG_COLOR = (Color)findDefaultResource(
      "InternalFrame.activeTitleBackground");
    DEFAULT_SELECTED_TITLE_BAR_FG_COLOR = (Color)findDefaultResource(
      "InternalFrame.activeTitleForeground");
    DEFAULT_TITLE_BAR_FONT = (Font)findDefaultResource(
      "InternalFrame.titleFont");
    DEFAULT_INNER_FRAME_BORDER = (Border)findDefaultResource(
      "InternalFrame.border");
    DEFAULT_FRAME_ICON = (Icon)findDefaultResource(
      "InternalFrame.icon");
  }

protected Object findDefaultResource(String id) {
    Object obj = null;
    try {
      UIDefaults uiDef = UIManager.getDefaults();
      obj = uiDef.get(id);
    }
    catch (Exception ex) {
      System.err.println(ex);
    }
    if (obj == null)
      obj = m_ownDefaults.get(id);
    return obj;
  }

public void paint(Graphics g, JComponent c) {
    super.paint(g, c);
    if (c.getBorder() != null)
      c.getBorder().paintBorder(
    c, g, 0, 0, c.getWidth(), c.getHeight());
  }
```

⓮ Retrieves resources, using semi-documented resource keys

⓯ Looks up resource in UI Manager defaults table, and then in local class defaults table

```
    public Color getTitleBarBkColor() {
      return DEFAULT_TITLE_BAR_BG_COLOR;
    }

    public Color getSelectedTitleBarBkColor() {
      return DEFAULT_SELECTED_TITLE_BAR_BG_COLOR;
    }

    public Color getTitleBarFgColor() {
      return DEFAULT_TITLE_BAR_FG_COLOR;
    }

    public Color getSelectedTitleBarFgColor() {
      return DEFAULT_SELECTED_TITLE_BAR_FG_COLOR;
    }

    public Font getTitleBarFont() {
      return DEFAULT_TITLE_BAR_FONT;
    }

    public Border getInnerFrameBorder() {
      return DEFAULT_INNER_FRAME_BORDER;
    }
  }
```

21.4.1   Understanding the code

Class MdiContainer

❶ This class represents a simple frame container similar to the one used in chapter 15 to demonstrate our custom MDI interface. An instance of `JDesktopPane` is set as the content pane for this frame to support `JInternalFrame`s as well as our `InnerFrame` component.

❷ The `createMenuBar()` method creates and populates a menu bar for this example. A File menu is constructed with three menu items:

- The New InnerFrame menu item creates a new instance of `InnerFrame` and adds it to the desktop pane. The `closable`, `maximizable`, `iconifiable`, and `resizable` properties are set by default to demonstrate the maximum number of UI elements used in this component.
- The New JInternalFrame menu item creates a new instance of Swing's `JInternal-Frame` and adds it to the desktop pane.
- The "Exit" menu item quits this application.

❸ A look and feel menu is constructed with an array of menu items corresponding to the look and feels currently installed. These items are handled the same way they were in previous examples, and so do not require additional explanation here.

Class mdi.InnerFrame

❹ This class was introduced in chapter 15 and requires some minor modifications to support look and feel. First note that both the new `mdi.plaf` package and the `javax.swing.plaf.ComponentUI` class are imported.

❺ As we know, it is typical for look and feel-compliant components to *not* perform any rendering by themselves and to not explicitly hold any resources for this process. Instead, all rendering and necessary resources involved (colors, icons, borders, etc.) should be maintained by a UI delegate corresponding to that component. To conform to this design pattern, we remove several class variables from our `InnerFrame` class and move them to our custom `InnerFrameUI` class (see below). Specifically: `DEFAULT_TITLE_BAR_BG_COLOR`, `DEFAULT_SELECTED_TITLE_BAR_BG_COLOR`, and `DEFAULT_FRAME_ICON`. We will use resources provided by the currently installed look and feel for these variables instead of hard-coded values defined in the component class.

Two class variables (`DEFAULT_BORDER_COLOR` and `DEFAULT_SELECTED_BORDER_COLOR`) have been removed. We don't need them any more since we'll use a `Border` instance to render `InnerFrame`'s border. Eight default icon variables (`ICONIZE_BUTTON_ICON`, `RESTORE_BUTTON_ICON`, `CLOSE_BUTTON_ICON`, `MAXIMIZE_BUTTON_ICON`, `MINIMIZE_BUTTON_ICON`, and their pressed variants) are intentionally left unchanged. We could move them into our UI delegate class as well, and use the standard icons provided by the look and feel for these variables. But we've decided to preserve some individuality for our custom component.

> **NOTE** Swing's `JInternalFrame` delegates provide only one standard icon for the frame controls, however, our implementation uses two icons for pressed and not pressed states. Since we will use `JInternalFrame` UI delegate resources, this would require us to either remove our two-icon functionality, or construct separate icons for use with each look and feel.

Now let's take a look at the instance variables that have been modified:

- `Color m_titleBarBackground`: The background color for the title bar of an inactive frame; now initialized by the `InnerFrameUI` delegate.
- `Color m_selectedTitleBarBackground`: The background color for the title bar of an active frame; now initialized by the `InnerFrameUI` delegate.
- `Color m_titleBarForeground`: The foreground color for the title bar of an inactive frame; now initialized by the `InnerFrameUI` delegate. The previous version supported only one foreground color. This version distinguishes between the foreground of active and inactive frames (this is necessary for support of various look and feels).
- `Color m_selectedTitleBarForeground`: The new variable for the foreground color of the title bar of an active frame. Two new methods, `setSelectedTitleBarForeground()` and `getSelectedTitleBarForeground()`, support this variable.
- `Font m_titleBarFont`: The new variable for the title bar's font. The previous version used a default font to render a frame's title, but this may not be acceptable for all look and feels. Two new methods, `setTitleBarFont()` and `getTitleBarFont()`, support this variable.
- `Border m_frameBorder`: The new variable for a frame's border. The previous version's border was made from the four resizable edge components which were colored homogeneously. In this example we use a shared `Border` instance provided by the current look and feel, and store it in the `m_frameBorder` variable. Two new methods, `setBorder()` and `getBorder()`, support this variable.
- `Icon m_frameIcon`: This variable was formerly defined as an `ImageIcon` instance. This may not be acceptable for look and feel implementations which provide a default frame icon as a different instance of the `Icon` interface. Therefore, we now declare `m_frameIcon` as an `Icon`, which results in several minor modifications throughout the code.

We have also removed two instance variables: m_BorderColor and m_selected-BorderColor. Their corresponding set/get methods have also been removed. The update-BorderColors() method is left without implementation and it can also be removed from the code. The reason for this change is that we no longer support direct rendering of the resize edge components (they are now non-opaque, see below); instead, we delegate this functionality to the m_frameBorder instance retrieved from the currently installed look and feel.

NOTE We also no longer support different borders for active and inactive frames since not all look and feels provide two Border instances for internal frames.

❻ A significant amount of code needs to be added for look and feel support in this component. First note that a static block places two values into UIManager's resource defaults storage. These key/value pairs allow retrieval of the fully qualified InnerFrameUI class name, as well as retrieval of the custom delegate of its inner class, title bar button component, Inner-FrameButtonUI (for this we simply use BasicButtonUI):

```
static {
  UIManager.getDefaults().put(
    "InnerFrameUI", "mdi.plaf.InnerFrameUI");
  UIManager.getDefaults().put("InnerFrameButtonUI",
    "javax.swing.plaf.basic.BasicButtonUI");
}
```

As we've discussed in the previous examples, for all provided Swing components this information is provided by the concrete subclasses of the LookAndFeel class (the fully qualified class names of the UI delegates are added to the defaults table in the initClassDefaults() method). However, these implementations have no knowledge of our custom component, so we must place it in the table ourselves.

NOTE In this case we do not need to add a corresponding java.lang.Class instance to to the defaults table, as was necessary when we implemented our own LookAndFeel (see section 21.1.11).

The createUI() method will be called to create and return an instance of InnerFrame's UI delegate, InnerFrameUI (see below). The setUI() method installs a new InnerFrameUI instance, and the getUI() method retrieves the current delegate (both use the protected ui variable inherited from the JComponent class).

❼ The updateUI() method will be called to notify the component whenever the current look and feel changes. Our implementation requests an instance of InnerFrameUI from UIManager (using getUI()), which is then passed to setUI(). Then invalidate() is called to mark this component for revalidation because the new look and feel's resources will most likely change the sizing and position of InnerFrame's constituents.

The getUIClassID() method returns a unique String ID that identifies this component's base UI delegate name. This String must be consistent with the string used as the key for the fully qualified class name of this component's delegate that was placed in UIManager's resource defaults table (see above):

```
public String getUIClassID() { return "InnerFrameUI"; }
```

8 Several simple setXX()/getXX() methods have been added that do not require any explanation. The only exception is setBorder(), which overrides the corresponding JComponent method. The Border parameter is stored in our m_frameBorder variable, to be painted manually by InnerFrameUI, and we do not call the superclass implementation. Thus, the border is not used in the typical way we are used to. Specifically, it does not define any insets for InnerFrame. Instead, it is just painted directly on top of it. We do this purposefully because we want the border to be painted over each resize edge child.

To do this, we make the resize edge components NorthResizeEdge, SouthResize-Edge, EastResizeEdge, and WestResizeEdge transparent, and we preserve all functionality (changing the mouse cursor, resizing the frame, etc.). Thus, they form an invisible border whose width is synchronized (in the setBorder() method) with the width of the Border instance stored in our m_frameBorder variable. As you'll see below in our InnerFrameUI class, this Border instance is drawn explicitly on the frame's surface. Figure 21.6 illustrates. In this way we can preserve any decorative elements (usually 3-D effects specific to each look and feel), and at the same time leave our child resize edge components directly below this border to intercept and process mouse events as normal.

Figure 21.6   Invisible resize edge components around InnerFrame

NOTE   The setBorder() method checks whether the component is shown on the screen (if isShowing() returns true) before calling validate(). This precaution helps avoid exceptions during creation of the application. A similar check needs to be made before calls such as update() and repaint() if they can possibly be invoked before InnerFrame is displayed on the screen.

The updateTitleBarColors() method has lost its importance, as the overridden methods in the title bar provide the current color information (so we don't have to call setXX() methods explicitly each time the color palette is changed).

9 The createTitleBar() method creates and initializes the title bar for this frame. The anonymous inner class defining our m_titlePanel component receives a new getBackground() method, which returns getSelectedTitleBarBackground() or getTitleBarBack-ground() depending on whether the frame is selected. Take note of the following code, which may seem strange:

```
public Color getBackground() {
  if (InnerFrame.this == null)
    return super.getBackground();
  if (isSelected())
```

```
            return getSelectedTitleBarBackground();
        else
            return getTitleBarBackground();
    }
```

The reason that a check against null is made here is because this child component will be created before the creation of the corresponding InnerFrame instance is completed. By doing this, we can avoid any possible NullPointerExceptions that would occur from calling parent class methods too early.

The m_titleLabel component is also now defined as an anonymous inner class. It overrides two JComponent methods, getForeground() and getFont(). These methods return instance variables from the parent InnerFrame instance. Thus we can avoid keeping track of the font and foreground of this child component, as long as the corresponding instance variables are properly updated. Note that we check the InnerFrame.this reference for null here as well.

Finally, the writeExternal() and readExternal() methods have been modified to reflect the changes in the instance variables we have discussed.

Class mdi.InnerFrame.InnerFrameButton

10 This inner class has received two minor changes. First, we override JComponent's setBorder() and getBorder() methods to hide the default implementation and eliminate the possibility of assigning any border to these small custom buttons (otherwise every time the look and feel is changed, the standard JButton border will be set).

We also override the getUIClassID() method which returns a string ID that represents this child component's UI delegate. Referring back to the static block in the InnerFrame class, we see that this ID is associated with the javax.swing.plaf.basic.BasicButtonUI class. Thus, we directly assign the BasicButtonUI class as the delegate for this component instead of allowing the current look and feel to take control.

Class mdi.InnerFrame.EastResizeEdge, WestResizeEdge, NorthResizeEdge, SouthResizeEdge

11 This EastResizeEdge inner class has received a few minor changes. The opaque property is now set to false, and we drop any code for the background color since this component is now transparent. Second, the WIDTH variable is initially set to the right inset of the frame's border. This variable is also accessible using the new setWidth() method, which was constructed primarily for synchronizing the size of this component with the width of the Border drawn around the frame (see InnerFrame's setBorder() method above). Each resize edge component is modified similarly.

Class mdi.plaf.InnerFrameUI

12 This class extends javax.swing.plaf.PanelUI and defines the custom UI delegate for our InnerFrame component. The basic idea behind this class is to retrieve and reuse the rendering resources defined by the current look and feel for JInternalFrame. It is perfectly reasonable to use resources already defined in the LookAndFeel implementations for standard Swing components. By doing so, we can more easily provide consistent views of custom components under different look and feels, and reduce the amount of required coding. However, if we cannot rely on pre-defined resources in a particular LookAndFeel, we need to define our own custom resources. The next section will show you how to deal with this situation which might arise when using third-party look and feels.

Here are the class variables:

- `InnerFrameUI frameUI`: A shared instance of this class returned by `createUI()`.
- `Color DEFAULT_TITLE_BAR_BG_COLOR`: The default background color for the title bar of an inactive frame.
- `Color DEFAULT_SELECTED_TITLE_BAR_BG_COLOR`: The default background color for the title bar of an active frame.
- `Color DEFAULT_TITLE_BAR_FG_COLOR`: The default foreground color for the title bar of an inactive frame.
- `Color DEFAULT_SELECTED_TITLE_BAR_FG_COLOR`: The default foreground color for the title bar of an active frame.
- `Font DEFAULT_TITLE_BAR_FONT`: The default title bar font.
- `Border DEFAULT_INNER_FRAME_BORDER`: The default frame border.
- `Icon DEFAULT_FRAME_ICON`: The default frame icon.
- `Hashtable m_ownDefaults`: A collection of resources stored in this UI delegate, they are used when a particular resource is not implemented in the current look and feel.

> **NOTE** The resource variables listed above are default in the sense that they're used unless other values are set explicitly using `setXX()` methods of `InnerFrame` (such as `setTitleBarFont()` and `setBorder()`).

13 The `static` block defined in this class creates and populates `Hashtable m_ownDefaults`. The `createUI()` method creates the `InnerFrameUI` shared instance (if it is not yet created) and calls `installDefaults()` to refresh its attributes with resources provided by the current look and feel. Several `setXX()` methods are then called to update the properties of the specified `InnerFrame` instance.

The `installUI()` and `uninstallUI()` methods simply delegate their calls to the superclass implementation. They are included here because in some cases we may need to override these methods (as we saw in the previous section).

14 The `installDefaults()` method retrieves resources provided by the current look and feel by calling our custom `findDefaultResource()` method, and it stores them in the class variables. Remember that the keys for these resources are not documented, but they can easily be found in the Swing `LookAndFeel` implementation source code. "InternalFrame.inactiveTitleBackground" is used for the background of `JInternalFrame`'s inactive title bar; "InternalFrame.icon" is used for the `JInternalFrame`'s icon, and so on.

15 The custom method `findDefaultResource()` takes a resource ID `String` and searches for it in `UIManager`'s `UIDefaults` table. If the resource is not found or if an exception occurs, a resource stored in our `m_ownDefaults` collection under the same ID is used.

The `paint()` method renders a given component using a given graphical context. As we've discussed above, it explicitly paints the border around `InnerFrame` by calling the border's `paintBorder()` method.

Several remaining `getXX()` methods allow the simple retrieval of the default rendering resources defined in this class, and they do not require an explanation here.

21.4.2 Running the code

Create several `InnerFrames` and `JInternalFrames` using the File menu. Select different look and feels and note that the appearance of `InnerFrame` changes accordingly. Compare the appearance of `InnerFrame` to `JInternalFrame` in each available look and feel. Figures 21.3, 21.4, and 21.5 show `MdiContainer` displaying two `InnerFrames` and two `JInternalFrames` in the Metal, Windows, and Motif look and feels, respectively.

BUG ALERT The Motif look and feel does not supply proper resources for `JInternalFrame` rendering. A quick look at the `MotifLookAndFeel` source code shows that no resources are placed in the defaults table corresponding to `JInternalFrame`. This is why the appearance of `InnerFrame` is not at all consistent with `JInternalFrame` under the Motif look and feel. (This is actually more of a design flaw than a bug.)

NOTE The selection of `JInternalFrames` and `InnerFrames` is not synchronized. A single instance of each can be selected at any given time. Also note that because of known flaws in `JDesktopPane`, `InnerFrame` (as well as `JInternalFrame`) will not receive resize events from it, which cripples maximize functionality. Placing these components in an instance of our `MDIPane` would fix this. However, we would then see null pointer exceptions each time a `JInternalFrame`'s title bar is pressed.

21.5 LOOK AND FEEL FOR CUSTOM COMPONENTS, PART II: THIRD-PARTY LOOK AND FEEL SUPPORT

The previous example demonstrated how to exploit existing look and feel to provide custom components with an appearance consistent with the currently installed look and feel. But what if we want to support a custom look and feel which does not provide any suitable

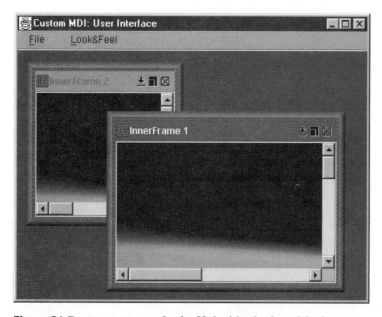

Figure 21.7 `InnerFrames` in the Malachite look and feel

resources? The most direct way, of course, is to adjust the code in the look and feel package. This can be done if we have developed both a custom component and a custom look and feel ourselves (as we did in sections 21.2 and 21.3). However, in the case of a custom look and feel that is supplied by a third-party vendor, we would need to provide all necessary resources inside our custom component's UI delegate.

Example 21.4 shows how to add support for a custom look and feel, namely Malachite, to our `InnerFrame` component. (Recall that `MalachiteLF` only provides rendering resources for three types of buttons and a border.) We intentionally will not modify, or add to, the original Malachite package (acting as if it is supplied by a third-party vendor), and we will include all necessary modifications to our component's UI delegate itself.

Example 21.4

MdiContainer2.java

see \Chapter21\4

```
import java.awt.*;
import java.awt.event.*;
import java.util.*;

import javax.swing.*;

import mdi.*;

public class MdiContainer2 extends JFrame
{
  public MdiContainer2() {
    super("Custom MDI: User Interface");
    getContentPane().setLayout(new FlowLayout());
    // Unchanged code from example 21.3
  }
  // Unchanged code from example 21.3

  public static void main(String argv[]) {
    try {
      LookAndFeel malachite = new Malachite.MalachiteLF();
      UIManager.LookAndFeelInfo info =
        new UIManager.LookAndFeelInfo(malachite.getName(),
        malachite.getClass().getName());
      UIManager.installLookAndFeel(info);
      UIManager.setLookAndFeel(malachite);
    }
    catch (Exception ex) {
      ex.printStackTrace();
      System.err.println(ex.toString());
    }

    new MdiContainer2();
  }
}
```

Installs Malachite LookAndFeel like a third-party product **1**

InnerFrameUI.java

see \Chapter21\4\mdi\plaf

```
package mdi.plaf;

import java.awt.*;
import java.util.*;

import javax.swing.*;
import javax.swing.border.*;
import javax.swing.plaf.*;

import mdi.*;

public class InnerFrameUI extends javax.swing.plaf.PanelUI
{
  // Unchanged code from example 21.3

  public static ComponentUI createUI(JComponent c) {
    LookAndFeel currentLF = UIManager.getLookAndFeel();
    if (currentLF != null && currentLF.getID().equals("Malachite"))
      return mdi.plaf.Malachite.MalachiteInnerFrameUI.createUI(c);
```

// Remaining code unchanged from example 21.3

If using Malachite LookAndFeel, install InnerFrame UI delegate for Malachite LookAndFeel ②

MalachiteInnerFrameUI.java

see \Chapter21\4\mdi\plaf\Malachite

```
package mdi.plaf.Malachite;

import java.awt.*;
import java.util.*;

import javax.swing.*;
import javax.swing.border.*;
import javax.swing.plaf.*;

import mdi.*;
import Malachite.*;

public class MalachiteInnerFrameUI extends mdi.plaf.InnerFrameUI
{
  private static MalachiteInnerFrameUI frameUI;

  public static ComponentUI createUI(JComponent c) {
    if(frameUI == null)
      frameUI = new MalachiteInnerFrameUI();
    try {
      frameUI.installDefaults();

      InnerFrame frame = (InnerFrame)c;
      frame.setTitleBarBackground(DEFAULT_TITLE_BAR_BG_COLOR);
      frame.setSelectedTitleBarBackground(
        DEFAULT_SELECTED_TITLE_BAR_BG_COLOR);
      frame.setTitleBarForeground(DEFAULT_TITLE_BAR_FG_COLOR);
      frame.setSelectedTitleBarForeground(
```

InnerFrame UI delegate which supports the Malachite LookAndFeel ③

Uses resource defaults set in installDefaults() method ④

```
              DEFAULT_SELECTED_TITLE_BAR_FG_COLOR);
          frame.setTitleBarFont(DEFAULT_TITLE_BAR_FONT);
          frame.setBorder(DEFAULT_INNER_FRAME_BORDER);
          frame.setFrameIcon(DEFAULT_FRAME_ICON);
          if (frame.isShowing())
            frame.repaint();
        }
        catch (Exception ex) {
          System.err.println(ex);
          ex.printStackTrace();
        }

        return frameUI;
      }

    protected void installDefaults() {
      DEFAULT_TITLE_BAR_BG_COLOR = new ColorUIResource(108,190,116);
      DEFAULT_TITLE_BAR_FG_COLOR = new ColorUIResource(Color.gray);
      DEFAULT_SELECTED_TITLE_BAR_BG_COLOR =
        new ColorUIResource(0,128,0);
      DEFAULT_SELECTED_TITLE_BAR_FG_COLOR =
        new ColorUIResource(Color.white);
      DEFAULT_TITLE_BAR_FONT = new FontUIResource(
        "Dialog", Font.BOLD, 12);
      Border fb1 = new MalachiteBorder();
      Border fb2 = new MatteBorder(4, 4, 4, 4, new ImageIcon(
        "mdi/plaf/Malachite/body.gif"));
      DEFAULT_INNER_FRAME_BORDER = new BorderUIResource(
        new CompoundBorder(fb1, fb2));
      DEFAULT_FRAME_ICON = new IconUIResource(new ImageIcon(
        "mdi/plaf/Malachite/icon.gif"));
    }
  }
}
```

Uses resource defaults set in installDefaults() method ❹

Sets up resource defaults which match the Malachite LookAndFeel ❹

21.5.1 Understanding the code

Class MdiContainer2

❶ This container class is similar to the one in the previous example, but now the Malachite look and feel is installed just as it was in the examples in sections 21.2 and 21.3.

Class mdi.plaf.InnerFrameUI

❷ The `createUI()` method, which is responsible for creating this `InnerFrame` UI delegate, has been modified to check the ID of the current look and feel. If it matches "Malachite," `createUI()` is invoked in the new `mdi.plaf.Malachite.MalachiteInnerFrameUI` class.

Class mdi.plaf.Malachite.MalachiteInnerFrameUI

❸ This new class, a subclass of `InnerFrameUI`, provides `InnerFrame` with support for our custom Malachite look and feel. Note that it is defined in a separate package, which is recommended for organized support of various different look and feels.

❹ Since this class extends `mdi.plaf.InnerFrameUI`, only two methods need to be overridden. The `createUI()` method now creates an instance of `MalachiteInnerFrameUI` as a shared instance, and it calls `installDefaults()` on that instance. It then assigns the class variables inherited from `InnerFrameUI` using rendering resources appropriate for the Malachite look and feel. In particular, the background colors form a green palette, and the frame's border is built as a `CompoundBorder` consisting of a `MalachiteBorder` (on the outside) and a `MatteBorder` drawn using a small, green, dashed image (on the inside).

21.5.2 Running the code

Create several `InnerFrames` using the File menu, and note that their appearance is, in fact, consistent with the Malachite look and feel. Figure 21.7 illustrates.

PART **IV**

Special topics

In the following six chapters we cover several different topics which relate directly to the use of Swing. Chapter 22 discusses the powerful new Java 2 printing API. We construct examples showing how to: print an image on multiple pages, construct a print preview component, print styled text, and print `JTable` data (in both portrait and landscape modes).

Chapter 23 introduces a few Java2D features. Examples include a generic 2D chart class, a 2D label class, and the beginnings of a Pac-man game.

Chapter 24 introduces Accessibility and shows how easy it is to integrate this functionality into existing apps. Chapter 25 covers the basics of the JavaHelp API, and includes examples showing how we can customize the Swing-based help viewer to our liking. Chapter 26 introduces CORBA and contains an example of a client-server, Swing-based app based on our `StocksTable` example from chapter 18. Chapter 27 consists of three examples contributed by experienced Swing developers: a date and time editor component, building custom multi-line labels and tool-tips, and an internet browser application. Unfortunately, due to space limitations, chapters 24-27 were not included in this edition. However, they remain freely available to all readers on the book's web site.

CHAPTER 22

Printing

22.1   JAVA 2 PRINTING API OVERVIEW

Java 2 includes a considerably advanced printing API. Java veterans may recall that JDK 1.0 didn't provide printing capabilities at all. JDK 1.1 provided access to native print jobs, but multi-page printing was a real problem for that API.

Now Java developers are able to perform multi-page printing using page count selection and other typical specifications in the native Print dialog, as well as page format selection in the native platform-specific Page Setup dialog. The printing-related API is concentrated in the `java.awt.print` package, and we'll start this chapter with an overview of these classes and interfaces.

NOTE   At this point, the underlying communication with the native printing system is not yet matured. You will notice that some of the examples in this chapter run extremely slow, especially when dealing with `Images`. We expect these deficiencies to decrease, and the material presented here should be equally applicable in future releases of Java.

22.1.1   **PrinterJob**

class java.awt.print.PrinterJob

This is the main class which controls printing in Java 2. It is used to store print job properties, to initiate printing when necessary, and to control the display of Print dialogs. A typical printing process is shown in the following code:

```
PrinterJob prnJob = PrinterJob.getPrinterJob();
prnJob.setPrintable(myPrintable);
if (!prnJob.printDialog())
  return;
prnJob.print();
```

This code retrieves an instance of PrinterJob with the static getPrinterJob() method, passes a Printable instance to it (which is used to render a specific page on demand—see below), invokes a platform-dependent Print dialog by calling PrinterJob's printDialog() method, and, if this method returns true (indicating the "OK" to print), starts the actual printing process by calling the print() method on that PrinterJob.

The Print dialog will look familiar, as it is the typical dialog used by most other applications on the user's system. For example, figure 22.1 shows a Windows NT Print dialog:

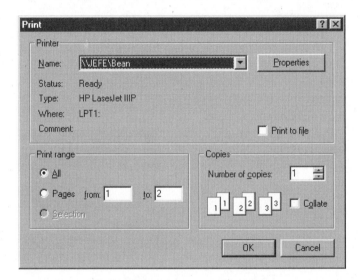

Figure 22.1   A Windows NT Print dialog, about to print a pageable job

Though the PrinterJob is the most important constituent of the printing process, it can do nothing without a Printable instance that specifies how to actually perform the necessary rendering for each page.

22.1.2   The printable interface

abstract interface java.awt.print.Printable

This interface defines only one method: print(), which takes three parameters:

- Graphics graphics: The graphical context into which the page will be drawn.
- PageFormat pageFormat: An object containing information about the size and orientation of the page being drawn (see below).
- int pageIndex: The zero-based index of the page to be drawn.

The print() method will be called to print a portion of the PrinterJob corresponding to a given pageIndex. An implementation of this method should perform rendering of a specified page, using a given graphical context and a given `PageFormat`. The return value from this method should be `PAGE_EXISTS` if the page is rendered successfully, or `NO_SUCH_PAGE` if the given page index is too large and does not exist. (These are static `int`s defined in `Printable`.)

NOTE We never call a `Printable`'s `print()` method ourselves. This is handled deep inside the actual platform-specific `PrinterJob` implementation which we aren't concerned with here.

A class that implements `Printable` is said to be a *page painter*. When a `PrinterJob` uses only one page painter to print each page, it is referred to as a *printable job*. The notion of a document being separated into a certain number of pages is not predefined in a printable job. In order to print a specific page, a printable job will actually render all pages leading up to that page first, and then it will print the specified page. This happens because it does not maintain information about how much space each page will occupy when rendered with the given page painter. For example, if we specify in our Print dialog that we want to print pages 3 and 5 only, then pages 0 through 4 (because pages are 0-indexed) will be rendered with the `print()` method, but only 2 and 4 will actually be printed.

WARNING Since the system only knows how many pages a printable job will span *after* the rendering of the complete document takes place (meaning after `paint()` has been called), Print dialogs will not display the correct number of pages to be printed. This is because there is no pre-print communication between a `PrinterJob` and the system that determines how much space the printable job requires. For this reason you will often see a range such as 1 to 9999 in Print dialogs when printing printable jobs. (This is not the case for pageable jobs—see below.)

In reality, it is often the case that `print()` will be called for each page more than once. From a draft of an overview of the Java printing API: "This *callback* printing model is necessary to support printing on a wide range of printers and systems...This model also enables printing to a bitmap printer from a computer that doesn't have enough memory or disk space to buffer a full-page bitmap. In this situation, a page is printed as a series of small bitmaps or *bands*. For example, if only enough memory to buffer one tenth of a page is available, the page is divided into ten bands. The printing system asks the application to render each page ten times, once to fill each band. The application does not need to be aware of the number or size of the bands; it simply must be able to render each page when requested" (see http://java.sun.com/printing/jdk1.2/index.html).

Though this explains some of the performance problems that we will see in the coming examples, it seems that the model described above is not exactly what we are dealing with in Java 2 FCS. In fact, after some investigation, it turns out that the division into bands is not based on available memory. Rather, a hard-coded 512k buffer is used. By increasing the size of this buffer, it is feasible to increase performance significantly. However, this would involve modifying peer-level classes, which is something that we are certainly not encouraged to do. We hope to see this limitation accounted for in future releases.

♣ Thanks to John Sullivan for his valuable detective work.

22.1.3　The Pageable interface

abstract interface java.awt.print.Pageable

It is possible to support multiple page painters in a single `PrinterJob`. As we know, each page printer can correspond to a different scheme of printing because each `Printable` implements its own `print()` method. Implemenatations of the `Pageable` interface are designed to manage groups of page painters, and a print job that uses multiple page painters is referred to as a *pageable job*. Each page in a pageable job can use a different page printer and `Page-Format` (see below) to perform its rendering.

Unlike printable jobs, pageable jobs *do* maintain the predefined notion of a document as a set of separate pages. For this reason, pages of a pageable job can be printed in any order without having to render all pages leading up to a specific page (as is the case with printable jobs). Also, a `Pageable` instance carries with it an explicit page count which can be communicated to the native printing system when a `PrinterJob` is established. So when it's printing a pageable job, the native Print dialog will know the correct range of pages to display, unlike a printable job. (Note that this does not mean pageable jobs are not subject to the inherent limitations described above; we will see the same repetitive calling of `print()` that we do in printable jobs.)

When we are constructing a pageable `PrinterJob`, instead of calling `PrinterJob`'s `setPrintable()` method (see section 22.1.1), we call its `setPageable()` method. Figure 22.1 shows a Windows NT Print dialog about to print a pageable job. Notice that the range of pages is not 1 to 9999.

We won't be working with pageable jobs in this chapter because all the documents we will be printing require only one `Printable` implementation, even if documents can span multiple pages. In most real-world applications, each page of a document is printed with identical orientation, margins, and other sizing characteristics. However, if greater flexibility is desired, `Pageable` implementations such as `Book` (see below) can be useful.

22.1.4　The PrinterGraphics interface

abstract interface java.awt.print.PrinterGraphics

This interface defines only one method: `getPrinterJob()`, which retrieves the `PrinterJob` instance controlling the current printing process. It is implemented by `Graphics` objects that are passed to `Printable` objects to render a page. (We will not need to use this interface at all, as it is used deep inside `PrinterJob` instances to define the `Graphics` objects that are passed to each `Printable`'s `paint()` method during printing.)

22.1.5　PageFormat

class java.awt.print.PageFormat

This class encapsulates a `Paper` object and adds to it an orientation property (landscape or portrait). We can force a `Printable` to use a specific `PageFormat` by passing one to `PrinterJob`'s overloaded `setPrintable()` method. For instance, the following would force a printable job to use a specific `PageFormat` with a landscape orientation:

```
PrinterJob prnJob = PrinterJob.getPrinterJob();
PageFormat pf = job.defaultPage();
```

```
pf.setOrientation(PageFormat.LANDSCAPE);
prnJob.setPrintable(myPrintable, pf);
if (!prnJob.printDialog())
  return;
prnJob.print();
```

`PageFormat` defines three orientations:

- `LANDSCAPE`: The origin is at the bottom left-hand corner of the paper with the x-axis pointing up and the y-axis pointing to the right.
- `PORTRAIT` (most common): The origin is at the top left-hand corner of the paper with the x-axis pointing to the right and the y-axis pointing down.
- `REVERSE_LANDSCAPE`: The origin is at the top right-hand corner of the paper with the x-axis pointing down and the y-axis pointing to the left.

We can optionally display a Page Setup dialog in which the user can specify page characteristics such as orientation, paper size, and margin size. This dialog will return a new `PageFormat` to use in printing. The Page Setup dialog is meant to be presented before the Print dialog and it can be displayed using `PrinterJob`'s `pageDialog()` method. The following code brings up a Page Setup dialog, and it uses the resulting `PageFormat` for printing a printable job:

```
PrinterJob prnJob = PrinterJob.getPrinterJob();
PageFormat pf = job.pageDialog(job.defaultPage());
prnJob.setPrintable(myPrintable, pf);
if (!prnJob.printDialog())
  return;
prnJob.print();
```

We need to pass the `pageDialog()` method a `PageFormat` instance, as it uses it to clone and modify as the user specifies. If the changes are accepted, the cloned and modified version is returned. If they are not, the original version passed in is returned. Figure 22.2 shows a Windows NT Page Setup dialog.

22.1.6 · Paper

class java.awt.print.Paper

This class holds the size and margins of the paper used for printing. The `getImageableX()` and `getImageableY()` methods retrieve the coordinates of the top-left corner of the printable area in 1/72nds of an inch (which is approximately equal to one screen pixel—referred to as a "point" in typography). The `getImageableWidth()` and `getImageableHeight()` methods retrieve the width and height of the printable area (also in 1/72nds of an inch). We can also change the size of the useable region of the paper using its `setImageableArea()` method.

We can access the `Paper` object associated with a `PageFormat` using `PageFormat`'s `getPaper()` and `setPaper()` methods.

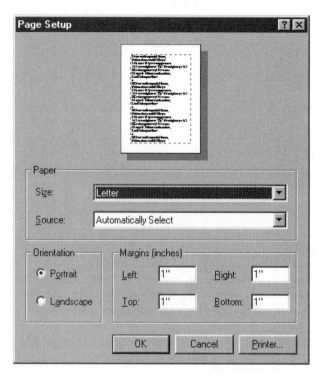

Figure 22.2   A Windows NT Page Setup dialog

22.1.7   Book

class java.awt.print.Book

This class represents a collection of `Printable` instances with corresponding `PageFormats` to represent a complex document whose pages may have different formats. The `Book` class implements the `Pageable` interface, and `Printables` are added to a `Book` using one of its `append()` methods. This class also defines several methods that allow specific pages to be manipulated and replaced. (A page in terms of a `Book` is a `Printable`/`PageFormat` pair. Each page does correspond to an actual printed page.) See the API documentation and the Java tutorial for more information about this class.

22.1.8   PrinterException

class java.awt.print.PrinterException

This exception may be thrown to indicate an error during a printing procedure. It has two concrete subclasses: `PrinterAbortException` and `PrinterIOException`. The former indicates that a print job was terminated by the application or the user while printing, and the latter indicates that there was a problem outputting to the printer.

> **REFERENCE**   For more information about the printing API and features that are expected to be implemented in future versions, refer to the Java tutorial.

22.2 PRINTING IMAGES

In this section, we add printing capabilities to the JPEGEditor application introduced in chapter 13. The material presented in example 22.1 will form a solid basis for the subsequent printing examples. Here we show how to implement the Printable interface to construct a custom panel with a print() method that can manage the printing of large images by splitting them up into a matrix of pages.

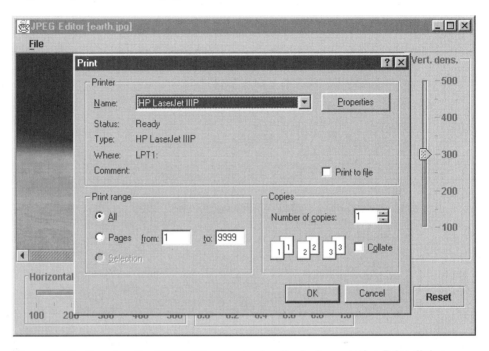

Figure 22.3 Running the JPEGEditor **example, displaying a native Print dialog**

Example 22.1

JPEGEditor.java

see \Chapter22\1

```
import java.awt.*;
import java.awt.event.*;
import java.awt.image.*;
import java.util.*;
import java.io.*;

import javax.swing.*;
import javax.swing.border.*;
import javax.swing.event.*;
import javax.swing.filechooser.*;

import com.sun.image.codec.jpeg.*;
```

```java
import java.awt.print.*;

// Unchanged code from example 13.4

public class JPEGEditor extends JFrame
{
  // Unchanged code from example 13.4

  protected JMenuBar createMenuBar() {
    // Unchanged code from example 13.4

    mItem = new JMenuItem("Print...");
    mItem.setMnemonic('p');
    ActionListener lstPrint = new ActionListener() {
      public void actionPerformed(ActionEvent e) {
        Thread runner = new Thread() {
          public void run() {
            if (m_panel.getBufferedImage() != null)
              printData();
          }
        };
        runner.start();
      }
    };
    mItem.addActionListener(lstPrint);
    mFile.add(mItem);
    mFile.addSeparator();

    mItem = new JMenuItem("Exit");
    mItem.setMnemonic('x');
    lst = new ActionListener() {
      public void actionPerformed(ActionEvent e) {
        System.exit(0);
      }
    };
    mItem.addActionListener(lst);
    mFile.add(mItem);
    menuBar.add(mFile);
    return menuBar;
  }

  // Unchanged code from example 13.4

  public void printData() {
    getJMenuBar().repaint();
    try {
      PrinterJob prnJob = PrinterJob.getPrinterJob();
      prnJob.setPrintable(m_panel);
      if (!prnJob.printDialog())
        return;
      setCursor( Cursor.getPredefinedCursor(
        Cursor.WAIT_CURSOR));
      prnJob.print();
      setCursor( Cursor.getPredefinedCursor(
        Cursor.DEFAULT_CURSOR));
```

1 If image loaded, this menu item will process the image for printing

2 Sets Printable object into PrinterJob and attempts to print it

```
      JOptionPane.showMessageDialog(this,
        "Printing completed successfully", "JPEGEditor2",
        JOptionPane.INFORMATION_MESSAGE);
    }
    catch (PrinterException e) {
      e.printStackTrace();
      System.err.println("Printing error: "+e.toString());
    }
  }

  public static void main(String argv[]) {
    new JPEGEditor();
  }
}


class JPEGPanel extends JPanel implements Printable
{
  protected BufferedImage m_bi = null;

  public int m_maxNumPage = 1;

  // Unchanged code from example 13.4

  public int print(Graphics pg, PageFormat pageFormat,
   int pageIndex) throws PrinterException {
    if (pageIndex >= m_maxNumPage || m_bi == null)
      return NO_SUCH_PAGE;

    pg.translate((int)pageFormat.getImageableX(),
      (int)pageFormat.getImageableY());
    int wPage = (int)pageFormat.getImageableWidth();
    int hPage = (int)pageFormat.getImageableHeight();

    int w = m_bi.getWidth(this);
    int h = m_bi.getHeight(this);
    if (w == 0 || h == 0)
      return NO_SUCH_PAGE;
    int nCol = Math.max((int)Math.ceil((double)w/wPage), 1);
      int nRow = Math.max((int)Math.ceil((double)h/hPage), 1);
    m_maxNumPage = nCol*nRow;

    int iCol = pageIndex % nCol;
    int iRow = pageIndex / nCol;
    int x = iCol*wPage;
    int y = iRow*hPage;
    int wImage = Math.min(wPage, w-x);
    int hImage = Math.min(hPage, h-y);

    pg.drawImage(m_bi, 0, 0, wImage, hImage,
      x, y, x+wImage, y+hImage, this);
    System.gc();

    return PAGE_EXISTS;
  }
}
```

3 Printable panel which contains a JPEG image

4 Shifts graphics context origin and calculates width and height of drawing area

5 Calculates number of pages needed to print image

6 From desired page number, calculates column, row, and dimensions of image portion

7 Draws the image portion to the graphics context, and tries to release memory immediately after

PRINTING IMAGES

22.2.1 Understanding the code

Class JPEGEditor

1 The `java.awt.print` package is imported to provide printing capabilities. A new menu item entitled Print... has been added to the File menu of this application. If this item is selected and an image has been loaded, our new custom `printData()` method is called.

2 The `printData()` method retrieves a `PrinterJob` instance and passes it our `m_panel` component (this is an instance of `JPEGPanel`, which now implements the `Printable` interface as shown below). It then invokes a native Print dialog and initializes printing by calling `print()`. If no exception was thrown, a "Printing completed successfully" message is displayed when printing completes. Otherwise, the exception trace is printed.

Class JPEGPanel

3 This class, which was originally designed to just display an image, now implements the `Printable` interface and is able to print a portion of its displayed image upon request. A new instance variable, `m_maxNumPage`, holds a maximum page number available for this printing. This number is set initially to one and its actual value is calculated in the `print()` method (see below).

The `print()` method prints a portion of the current image corresponding to the given page index. If the current image is larger than a single page, it will be split into several pages which are arranged as several rows and columns (a matrix). When printed, they can be placed in this arrangement to form one big printout.

4 This method first shifts the origin of the graphics context to take into account the page's margins, and it calculates the width and height of the area available for drawing: the results are `wPage` and `hPage`.

```
pg.translate((int)pageFormat.getImageableX(),
    (int)pageFormat.getImageableY());
int wPage = (int)pageFormat.getImageableWidth();
int hPage = (int)pageFormat.getImageableHeight();
```

5 The local variables `w` and `h` represent the width and height of the whole `BufferedImage` to be printed. (If any of these happens to be 0, we return `NO_SUCH_PAGE`.) Comparing these dimensions with the width and height of a single page, we can calculate the number of columns (not fewer than 1) and rows (not fewer than 1) in which the original image should be split to fit to the page's size:

```
int nCol = Math.max((int)Math.ceil((double)w/wPage), 1);
int nRow = Math.max((int)Math.ceil((double)h/hPage), 1);
m_maxNumPage = nCol*nRow;
```

The product of rows and columns gives us the number of pages in the print job, `m_maxNumPage`.

6 Now, because we know the index of the current page to be printed (it was passed as the parameter `pageIndex`) we can determine the current column and row indices (note that enumeration is made from left to right and then from top to bottom); these indices are `iCol` and `iRow`.

```
int iCol = pageIndex % nCol;
int iRow = pageIndex / nCol;
```

```
int x = iCol*wPage;
int y = iRow*hPage;
int wImage = Math.min(wPage, w-x);
int hImage = Math.min(hPage, h-y);
```

We also can calculate the coordinates of the top-left corner of the portion of the image to be printed on this page (x and y), and the width and height of this region (wImage and hImage). Note that in the last column or row of our image matrix, the width and/or height of a portion can be less than the maximum values (which we calculated above: wPage and hPage).

7 Now we have everything ready to actually print a region of the image to the specified graphics context. We now need to extract this region and draw it at (0, 0), as this will be the origin (upper-left hand corner) of our printed page. The Graphics drawImage() method does the job. It takes ten parameters: an Image instance, four coordinates of the destination area (top-left and bottom-right—*not* width and height), four coordinates of the source area, and an ImageObserver instance.

```
pg.drawImage(m_bi, 0, 0, wImage, hImage,
    x, y, x+wImage, y+hImage, this);
System.gc();
```

NOTE   Because the print() method may be called many times for the same page (see below), it makes good sense to explicitly invoke the garbage collector in this method. Otherwise, we may run out of memory.

22.2.2   Running the code

Figure 22.3 shows a Page Setup dialog brought up by our program when it was run on a Windows NT platform. Be aware that the print job could take up to 15 minutes to print (assuming you don't run out of memory first)!

As we mentioned in the beginning of this chapter, the Java 2 printing environment is not yet fully matured. It doesn't work with all printers as expected, so writing and debugging printing applications may be difficult in many cases (a print preview capability is a great help, as we will see in the next section). Also note that because we are using a printable job and not a pageable job, the page range is displayed as 1 to 9999 (see section 22.1.2—this may differ depending on your platform).

The most annoying thing with Java 2 printing is that it is terribly slow, mainly because we are dealing with an Image (BufferedImage is a subclass of Image). Images and printing clash severely. As we will see in later examples, printing goes much faster when Images are not involved.

The size of a relatively simple print job spooled to the printer may be unreasonably large. This makes Java 2 printing applications hardly comparable with native applications (at least at the time of this writing). Be sure to have plenty of memory, time, and patience when running this example. Or, alternatively, wait for the next Java 2 release.

NOTE   We recommend that the DoubleBuffered property of components be set to false during printing if the print() method directly calls a component's paint() method. It is only safe to call paint() from the print() method if we are sure that print() is executing in the event-dispatching thread. Refer to chapter 2 to learn how to shut off double-buffering, and how to check if a method is running within the event-dispatching thread.

22.3   PRINT PREVIEW

Print preview functionality has became a standard feature provided by most modern print-enabled applications. It only makes sense to include this service in Java 2 applications. Example 22.2 in this section shows how to construct a print preview component.

NOTE   An additional reason for Java developers to add print preview to their applications is that this feature can be very useful for debugging print code. Slow performance of the Java printing API can make debugging impractical using an actual printer.

The print preview component displays small images of the printed pages as they would appear after printing. A GUI attached to the preview component typically allows you to change the scale of the preview images and to invoke a print. Example 22.2 demonstrates such a component which can be easily added to any print-aware Swing application. Figure 22.4 shows how the image will appear.

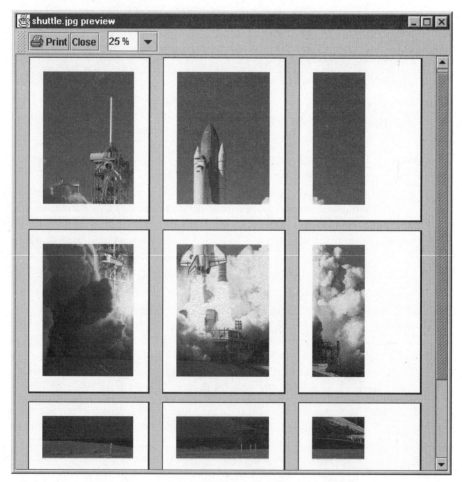

Figure 22.4   Print preview showing a 1200×1500 image split into nine parts

Example 22.2

see \Chapter22\2

```java
public class JPEGEditor extends JFrame
{
  // Unchanged code from example 22.1

  protected JMenuBar createMenuBar() {
    // Unchanged code from example 22.1

    mItem = new JMenuItem("Print Preview");
    mItem.setMnemonic('v');
    ActionListener lstPreview = new ActionListener() {
      public void actionPerformed(ActionEvent e) {
        Thread runner = new Thread() {
          public void run() {
            setCursor(Cursor.getPredefinedCursor(
              Cursor.WAIT_CURSOR));
            if (m_panel.getBufferedImage() != null)
              new PrintPreview(m_panel,
                m_currentFile.getName()+" preview");
            setCursor(Cursor.getPredefinedCursor(
              Cursor.DEFAULT_CURSOR));
          }
        };
        runner.start();
      }
    };
    mItem.addActionListener(lstPreview);
    mFile.add(mItem);

    mFile.addSeparator();

  // The rest of the code is unchanged from example 22.1
```

❶ Menu item to create print preview display

PrintPreview.java

see \Chapter22\2

```java
import java.awt.*;
import java.awt.event.*;
import java.awt.image.*;
import java.util.*;
import java.awt.print.*;

import javax.swing.*;
import javax.swing.border.*;
import javax.swing.event.*;

public class PrintPreview extends JFrame
{
```

❷ Frame to display preview of print job before printing

```java
protected int m_wPage;
protected int m_hPage;
protected Printable m_target;
protected JComboBox m_cbScale;
protected PreviewContainer m_preview;

public PrintPreview(Printable target) {
  this(target, "Print Preview");
}

public PrintPreview(Printable target, String title) {
  super(title);
  setSize(600, 400);
  m_target = target;

  JToolBar tb = new JToolBar();
  JButton bt = new JButton("Print", new ImageIcon("print.gif"));
  ActionListener lst = new ActionListener() {
    public void actionPerformed(ActionEvent e) {
      try {
        // Use default printer, no dialog
        PrinterJob prnJob = PrinterJob.getPrinterJob();
        prnJob.setPrintable(m_target);
        setCursor( Cursor.getPredefinedCursor(
          Cursor.WAIT_CURSOR));
        prnJob.print();
        setCursor( Cursor.getPredefinedCursor(
          Cursor.DEFAULT_CURSOR));
        dispose();
      }
      catch (PrinterException ex) {
        ex.printStackTrace();
        System.err.println("Printing error: "+ex.toString());
      }
    }
  };
  bt.addActionListener(lst);
  bt.setAlignmentY(0.5f);
  bt.setMargin(new Insets(4,6,4,6));
  tb.add(bt);

  bt = new JButton("Close");
  lst = new ActionListener() {
    public void actionPerformed(ActionEvent e) {
      dispose();
    }
  };
  bt.addActionListener(lst);
  bt.setAlignmentY(0.5f);
  bt.setMargin(new Insets(2,6,2,6));
  tb.add(bt);

  String[] scales = { "10 %", "25 %", "50 %", "100 %" };
  m_cbScale = new JComboBox(scales);
```

**Toolbar button
to directly print
previewed image** ③

```
lst = new ActionListener() {
  public void actionPerformed(ActionEvent e) {
    Thread runner = new Thread() {
      public void run() {
        String str = m_cbScale.getSelectedItem().
          toString();
        if (str.endsWith("%"))
          str = str.substring(0, str.length()-1);
        str = str.trim();
          int scale = 0;
        try { scale = Integer.parseInt(str); }
        catch (NumberFormatException ex) { return; }
        int w = (int)(m_wPage*scale/100);
        int h = (int)(m_hPage*scale/100);

        Component[] comps = m_preview.getComponents();
        for (int k=0; k<comps.length; k++) {
          if (!(comps[k] instanceof PagePreview))
            continue;
          PagePreview pp = (PagePreview)comps[k];
            pp.setScaledSize(w, h);
        }
        m_preview.doLayout();
        m_preview.getParent().getParent().validate();
      }
    };
    runner.start();
  }
};
m_cbScale.addActionListener(lst);
m_cbScale.setMaximumSize(m_cbScale.getPreferredSize());
m_cbScale.setEditable(true);
tb.addSeparator();
tb.add(m_cbScale);
getContentPane().add(tb, BorderLayout.NORTH);

m_preview = new PreviewContainer();

PrinterJob prnJob = PrinterJob.getPrinterJob();
PageFormat pageFormat = prnJob.defaultPage();
if (pageFormat.getHeight()==0 || pageFormat.getWidth()==0) {
  System.err.println("Unable to determine default page size");
    return;
}
m_wPage = (int)(pageFormat.getWidth());
m_hPage = (int)(pageFormat.getHeight());
int scale = 10;
int w = (int)(m_wPage*scale/100);
int h = (int)(m_hPage*scale/100);

int pageIndex = 0;
try {
  while (true) {
    BufferedImage img = new BufferedImage(m_wPage,
```

4 Action on Scale combobox to scale the previewed image size up or down

5 Scales each PagePreview object individually

6 Renders each portion of the original image into individual PagePreview objects

```java
                 m_hPage, BufferedImage.TYPE_INT_RGB);
          Graphics g = img.getGraphics();
          g.setColor(Color.white);
          g.fillRect(0, 0, m_wPage, m_hPage);
          if (target.print(g, pageFormat, pageIndex) !=
           Printable.PAGE_EXISTS)
            break;
          PagePreview pp = new PagePreview(w, h, img);
          m_preview.add(pp);
          pageIndex++;
        }
    }
    catch (PrinterException e) {
      e.printStackTrace();
      System.err.println("Printing error: "+e.toString());
    }

    JScrollPane ps = new JScrollPane(m_preview);
    getContentPane().add(ps, BorderLayout.CENTER);

    setDefaultCloseOperation(DISPOSE_ON_CLOSE);
    setVisible(true);
  }

class PreviewContainer extends JPanel
{
  protected int H_GAP = 16;
  protected int V_GAP = 10;
  public Dimension getPreferredSize() {
    int n = getComponentCount();
    if (n == 0)
      return new Dimension(H_GAP, V_GAP);
    Component comp = getComponent(0);
    Dimension dc = comp.getPreferredSize();
    int w = dc.width;
    int h = dc.height;

    Dimension dp = getParent().getSize();
    int nCol = Math.max((dp.width-H_GAP)/(w+H_GAP), 1);
    int nRow = n/nCol;
    if (nRow*nCol < n)
      nRow++;

    int ww = nCol*(w+H_GAP) + H_GAP;
    int hh = nRow*(h+V_GAP) + V_GAP;
    Insets ins = getInsets();
    return new Dimension(ww+ins.left+ins.right,
      hh+ins.top+ins.bottom);
  }

  public Dimension getMaximumSize() {
    return getPreferredSize();
  }

  public Dimension getMinimumSize() {
```

6 Renders each portion of the original image into individual **PagePreview objects**

7 Panel to layout **PagePreview** objects, with special layout requirements

```
      return getPreferredSize();
    }

  public void doLayout() {
    Insets ins = getInsets();
    int x = ins.left + H_GAP;
    int y = ins.top + V_GAP;

    int n = getComponentCount();
    if (n == 0)
      return;
    Component comp = getComponent(0);
    Dimension dc = comp.getPreferredSize();
    int w = dc.width;
    int h = dc.height;

    Dimension dp = getParent().getSize();
    int nCol = Math.max((dp.width-H_GAP)/(w+H_GAP), 1);
    int nRow = n/nCol;
    if (nRow*nCol < n)
      nRow++;

    int index = 0;
    for (int k = 0; k<nRow; k++) {
      for (int m = 0; m<nCol; m++) {
        if (index >= n)
          return;
        comp = getComponent(index++);
        comp.setBounds(x, y, w, h);
        x += w+H_GAP;
      }
      y += h+V_GAP;
      x = ins.left + H_GAP;
    }
  }
}

class PagePreview extends JPanel
{
  protected int m_w;
  protected int m_h;
  protected Image m_source;
  protected Image m_img;

  public PagePreview(int w, int h, Image source) {
    m_w = w;
    m_h = h;
    m_source= source;
    m_img = m_source.getScaledInstance(m_w, m_h,
      Image.SCALE_SMOOTH);
    m_img.flush();
    setBackground(Color.white);
    setBorder(new MatteBorder(1, 1, 2, 2, Color.black));
  }
```

❽ Panel to contain a single PagePreview object

```
        public void setScaledSize(int w, int h) {
          m_w = w;
          m_h = h;
          m_img = m_source.getScaledInstance(m_w, m_h,
            Image.SCALE_SMOOTH);
          repaint();
        }

        public Dimension getPreferredSize() {
          Insets ins = getInsets();
          return new Dimension(m_w+ins.left+ins.right,
            m_h+ins.top+ins.bottom);
        }

        public Dimension getMaximumSize() {
          return getPreferredSize();
        }

        public Dimension getMinimumSize() {
          return getPreferredSize();
        }

        public void paint(Graphics g) {
          g.setColor(getBackground());
          g.fillRect(0, 0, getWidth(), getHeight());
          g.drawImage(m_img, 0, 0, this);
          paintBorder(g);
        }
      }
    }
```

22.3.1   Understanding the code

Class JPEGEditor

❶ Compared with its counterpart in the previous example, this class has only one difference: it creates a menu item entitled Print Preview. When it's selected, this item creates an instance of the `PrintPreview` class (see below). This class's constructor takes two parameters: a reference to a `Printable` instance and a text string for the frame's title. As we saw in example 22.1, our `m_panel` component implements the `Printable` interface and provides the actual printing functionality, so we use it to create the `PrintPreview` instance. This call is wrapped in a thread because when it's used with large images, creating a `PrintPreview` instance can take a significant amount of time.

> **NOTE**   As you can see, we only need to have a reference to an instance of the `Printable` interface to create a `PrintPreview` component. Thus, this component can be added to any print-aware application with only a couple of lines of code. We will use it in the remaining examples as well, because it is such a simple feature to add.

Class PrintPreview

❷ This class represents a `JFrame`-based component which is capable of displaying the results of printing before actual printing occurs. Several instance variables are used:

- `Printable m_target`: An object whose printout will be previewed.

- `int m_wPage`: The width of the default printing page.
- `int m_hPage`: The height of the default printing page.
- `JComboBox m_cbScale`: A combo box which selects a scale for preview.
- `PreviewContainer m_preview`: The container which holds the previewing pages.

Two `public` constructors are provided. The first one takes an instance of the `Printable` interface and passes control to the second constructor, using the `Printable` along with the "Print Preview" `String` as parameters. The second constructor takes two parameters: an instance of the `Printable` interface and the title string for the frame. This second constructor is the one that actually sets up the `PrintPreview` component.

3 First, a toolbar is created and a button entitled Print is added to perform the printing of the `m_target` instance as described in the previous example. The only difference is that no Print dialog is invoked, and the default system printer is used (this approach is typical for print preview components). When the printing is complete, this print preview component is disposed of. The second button added to the toolbar is labeled Close, and it merely disposes of this frame component.

4 The third (and last) component added to the toolbar is the editable combo box `m_cbScale`, which selects a percent scale to zoom the previewed pages. Along with several pre-defined choices (10 %, 25 %, 50 %, and 100 %), any percent value can be entered. As soon as that value is selected and the corresponding `ActionListener` is involved, the zoom scale value is extracted and stored in the local variable `scale`. This determines the width and height of each `PreviewPage` component we will be creating:

```
int w = (int)(m_wPage*scale/100);
int h = (int)(m_hPage*scale/100);
```

5 Then all child components of the `m_preview` container in turn are cast to `PagePreview` components (each child is expected to be a `PagePreview` instance, but `instanceof` is used for precaution), and the `setScaledSize()` method is invoked to assign a new size to the preview pages. Finally, `doLayout()` is invoked on `m_preview` to lay out the resized child components, and `validate()` is invoked on the scroll pane. This scroll pane is the parent of the `m_preview` component in the second generation (the first parent is a `JViewport` component—see chapter 7). This last call is necessary to display/hide scroll bars as needed for the new size of the `m_preview` container. This whole process is wrapped in a thread to avoid clogging up the event-dispatching thread.

6 When the toolbar construction is complete, the `m_preview` component is created and filled with the previewed pages. To do this, we first retrieve a `PrinterJob` instance for a default system printer without displaying a Page Setup dialog, and we retrieve a default `PageFormat` instance. We use this to determine the initial size of the previewed pages by multiplying its dimensions by the computed scaling percentile (which is 10% at initialization time, because `scale` is set to 10).

To create these scalable preview pages we set up a `while` loop to continuously call the `print()` method of the given `Printable` instance, using a page index that gets incremented with each iteration, until it returns something other than `Printable.PAGE_EXISTS`.

Each page is rendered into a separate image in memory. To do this, an instance of `BufferedImage` is created with width `m_wPage` and height `m_hPage`. A `Graphics` instance is retrieved from that image using `getGraphics()`:

```
BufferedImage img = new BufferedImage(m_wPage,
    m_hPage, BufferedImage.TYPE_INT_RGB);
Graphics g = img.getGraphics();
g.setColor(Color.white);
g.fillRect(0, 0, m_wPage, m_hPage);
if (target.print(g, pageFormat, pageIndex) !=
    Printable.PAGE_EXISTS)
    break;
```

After filling the image's area with a white background (most paper is white), this `Graphics` instance, along with the `PageFormat` and current page index, `pageIndex`, are passed to the `print()` method of the `Printable` object.

NOTE   The `BufferedImage` class in the `java.awt.image` package allows direct image manipulation in memory. This class will be discussed in more detail in Chapter 23, as will other classes from the Java 2 2D API.

If the call to the `print()` method returns `PAGE_EXISTS`, indicating success in rendering the new page, a new `PagePreview` component is created:

```
PagePreview pp = new PagePreview(w, h, img);
m_preview.add(pp);
pageIndex++;
```

Our newly created `BufferedImage` is passed to the `PagePreview` constructor as one of the parameters. This is done so that we can use it now and in the future for scaling each `PagePreview` component separately. The other parameters are the width and height to use, which, at creation time, are 10% of the page size (as discussed above).

Each new component is added to our `m_preview` container. Finally, when the `Printable`'s `print()` method finishes, our `m_preview` container is placed in a `JScrollPane` to provide scrolling capabilities. This scroll pane is then added to the center of the `PrintPreview` frame, and our frame is then made visible.

Class PrintPreview.PreviewContainer

7 This inner class extends `JPanel` to serve as a container for `PagePreview` components. The only reason this custom container is developed is because we have specific layout requirements. What we want here is a layout which places its child components from left to right, without any resizing (using their preferred size), leaving equal gaps between them. When the available container's width is filled, a new row should be started from the left edge, without regard to the available height (we assume scrolling functionality will be made available).

You may want to refer back to our discussion of layouts in chapter 4. The code constituting this class does not require much explanation and it provides a good exercise for custom layout development (even though this class is not explicitly a layout manager).

Class PrintPreview.PagePreview

8 This inner class extends `JPanel` to serve as a placeholder for the image of each printed page preview. Four instance variables are used:

- `int m_w`: The current component's width (without insets).
- `int m_h`: The current component's height (without insets).
- `Image m_source`: The source image depicting the previewed page in full scale.

- `Image m_img`: The scaled image currently used for rendering.

The constructor of the `PagePreview` class takes its initial width and height and the source image. It creates a scaled image by calling the `getScaledInstance()` method and sets its border to `MatteBorder(1, 1, 2, 2, Color.black)` to imitate a page lying on a flat surface.

The `setScaledSize()` method may be called to resize this component. It takes a new width and height as parameters and creates a new scaled image that corresponds to the new size. Using the `SCALE_SMOOTH` option for scaling is essential to get a preview image which looks like a zoomed printed page (although it is not the fastest option).

The `paint()` method draws a scaled image and draws a border around the component.

22.3.2 Running the code

Figure 22.4 shows a preview of the large image which will be printed on the nine pages. Select various zoom factors in the combo box and see how the size of the previewed pages is changed. Then click the Print button to print to the default printer directly from the preview frame.

22.4 PRINTING STYLED TEXT

In this section we'll add printing capabilities to the RTF word processor application we developed in chapter 20. Printing styled text would be easy if `JTextComponent` or `JTextPane` implemented the `Printable` interface and provided the capability to print its contents. Unfortunately, this is not the case (at least as of Java 2 FCS). So we have to get fairly clever, and create our own `BoxView` subclass to specifically handle printing.

Our styled editor class will now implement the `Printable` interface and delegate the mechanics of printing of each page to our custom `BoxView` subclass. Note that this custom view is not actually displayed on the screen as the editor. It sits in the background and is used only for printing and display in our print preview component.

Recall, from our discussion in chapters 11 and 19, that styled documents consist of a hierarchy of elements: paragraphs, images, components, and so on. Each element is rendered by an associated view, and they are all children of the root view. A `BoxView`, in particular, arranges all its child views along either the x- or y-axis (typically the y-axis). So in example 22.3, when we need to render a page, we start from the first child view of our custom `BoxView`, and render each of the child views sequentially, placing each below the previous in the vertical direction. When the next page should be rendered, we start from the first remaining view and continue in this fashion until all child views have been rendered. (This process will be explained in greater detail below.)

Example 22.3

WordProcessor.java

see \Chapter22\3

```
import java.awt.*;
import java.awt.event.*;
import java.io.*;
import java.util.*;
```

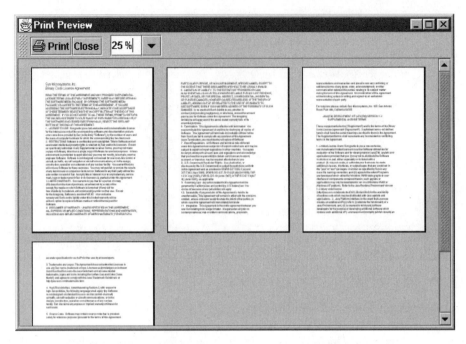

Figure 22.5   Print Preview showing a four-page RTF document

```
import java.sql.*;

import java.awt.print.*;
import javax.swing.plaf.basic.*;

import javax.swing.*;
import javax.swing.text.*;
import javax.swing.event.*;
import javax.swing.border.*;
import javax.swing.text.rtf.*;
import javax.swing.undo.*;

import dl.*;

public class WordProcessor extends JFrame implements Printable
{
  // Unchanged code from example 20.9

  protected PrintView m_printView;

  // Unchanged code from example 20.9

  protected JMenuBar createMenuBar() {
    // Unchanged code from example 20.9

    mFile.addSeparator();

    Action actionPrint = new AbstractAction("Print...",
      new ImageIcon("print.gif")) {
        public void actionPerformed(ActionEvent e) {
```

❶ Print capabilities and Text UI Delegates

❷ Presents print preview display

❸ Action to print document

```
      Thread runner = new Thread() {
        public void run() {
          printData();
        }
      };
      runner.start();
    }
  };
  item =  mFile.add(actionPrint);
  item.setMnemonic('p');

  item = new JMenuItem("Print Preview");
  item.setMnemonic('v');
  ActionListener lstPreview = new ActionListener() {
    public void actionPerformed(ActionEvent e) {
      Thread runner = new Thread() {
        public void run() {
          setCursor(Cursor.getPredefinedCursor(
            Cursor.WAIT_CURSOR));
          new PrintPreview(WordProcessor.this);
          setCursor(Cursor.getPredefinedCursor(
            Cursor.DEFAULT_CURSOR));
        }
      };
      runner.start();
    }
  };
  item.addActionListener(lstPreview);
  mFile.add(item);

  mFile.addSeparator();

  // Unchanged code from example 20.9
}

// Unchanged code from example 20.9

public void printData() {
  getJMenuBar().repaint();
  try {
    PrinterJob prnJob = PrinterJob.getPrinterJob();
    prnJob.setPrintable(this);
    if (!prnJob.printDialog())
      return;
    setCursor( Cursor.getPredefinedCursor(
      Cursor.WAIT_CURSOR));
    prnJob.print();
    setCursor( Cursor.getPredefinedCursor(
      Cursor.DEFAULT_CURSOR));
    JOptionPane.showMessageDialog(this,
      "Printing completed successfully", "Info",
      JOptionPane.INFORMATION_MESSAGE);
  }
  catch (PrinterException e) {
```

④ Menu item to present print preview display

⑤ Presents native print dialog and starts printing

```
      e.printStackTrace();
      System.err.println("Printing error: "+e.toString());
    }
  }

  public int print(Graphics pg, PageFormat pageFormat,
   int pageIndex) throws PrinterException {
    pg.translate((int)pageFormat.getImageableX(),
      (int)pageFormat.getImageableY());
    int wPage = (int)pageFormat.getImageableWidth();
    int hPage = (int)pageFormat.getImageableHeight();
    pg.setClip(0, 0, wPage, hPage);

    // Only do this once per print
    if (m_printView == null) {
      BasicTextUI btui = (BasicTextUI)m_monitor.getUI();
      View root = btui.getRootView(m_monitor);
      m_printView = new PrintView(
        m_doc.getDefaultRootElement(),
        root, wPage, hPage);
    }

    boolean bContinue = m_printView.paintPage(pg,
      hPage, pageIndex);
    System.gc();

    if (bContinue)
      return PAGE_EXISTS;
    else {
      m_printView = null;
      return NO_SUCH_PAGE;
    }
  }

  public static void main(String argv[]) {
    new WordProcessor();
  }

  // Unchanged code from example 20.9

  class PrintView extends BoxView
  {
    protected int m_firstOnPage = 0;
    protected int m_lastOnPage = 0;
    protected int m_pageIndex = 0;

    public PrintView(Element elem, View root, int w, int h) {
      super(elem, Y_AXIS);
      setParent(root);
      setSize(w, h);
      layout(w, h);
    }

    public boolean paintPage(Graphics g, int hPage,
      int pageIndex) {
      if (pageIndex > m_pageIndex) {
        m_firstOnPage = m_lastOnPage + 1;
```

6 Prints a portion of the current image

7 Shifts graphics context and calculates size of drawing area

8 Sets clip to printable area

9 Creates/initializes PrintPreview object if not done yet for this print

10 Renders a given page and collects garbage immediately

11 Return value indicates whether we could render and print a page

12 Presents panel with print preview of document

13 Indexes of first, last, and current page

14 Creates BoxView for root element of text component

15 Renders a single page view of a styled document

```
      if (m_firstOnPage >= getViewCount())
        return false;
      m_pageIndex = pageIndex;
    }
    int yMin - getOffset(Y_AXIS, m_firstOnPage);
    int yMax = yMin + hPage;
    Rectangle rc = new Rectangle();

    for (int k = m_firstOnPage; k < getViewCount(); k++) {
      rc.x = getOffset(X_AXIS, k);
      rc.y = getOffset(Y_AXIS, k);
      rc.width = getSpan(X_AXIS, k);
      rc.height = getSpan(Y_AXIS, k);
      if (rc.y+rc.height > yMax)
        break;
      m_lastOnPage = k;
      rc.y -= yMin;
      paintChild(g, rc, k);
    }
    return true;
  }
}

// Remaining code is unchanged from example 20.9
```

(16) Returns false if past end of document

(17) Top and bottom Y coordinates of page being rendered

(18) Builds rectangle for each child view and paints it if it will fit within the height

22.4.1   Understanding the code

Class WordProcessor

1 In comparison with example 20.9, this class imports two new packages: `java.awt.print` and `javax.swing.plaf.basic`. The first one provides the necessary printing API, while the second is used to gain access to text component UI delegates (we will soon see why this is necessary).

2 One new instance variable, `PrintView m_printView`, represents our custom view used to print the styled document (see below). The `createMenuBar()` method now creates and adds **3 4** to the File menu two new menu items entitled Print... and Print Preview. When the first one is selected, it calls the `printData()` method, while the second one creates a `PrintPreview` instance by passing `WordProcessor.this` as the `Printable` reference. The `printData()` **5** method obtains a `PrinterJob` instance, invokes a native Print dialog, and initializes printing **6** the same way we've seen it work in previous examples.

7 The `print()` method is called to print a given page of the current styled document. First, this method determines the size and origin of the printable area using a `PageFormat` instance as **8** we've seen before. We then need to set a clip area of the graphics context to the size of this printable area. This is necessary to render the text component `Views` because they do clipping area intersection detection for optimized painting. If we don't set the clipping area, they won't know how to render themselves.

9 Unfortunately, the `Printable` interface does not provide any methods which can be called to initialize specific resources before printing and to release these resources after printing. So we must implement this functionality ourselves. The actual job of rendering the styled document is done by the `m_printView` object, which must be instantiated before printing begins and

released when it ends. Since we are forced to do all this in a single method, we first check to
see if the m_printView reference is null. If it is, then we assign it a new instance of Print-
View. If it isn't null, we don't modify it (this indicates that we are in the middle of a printing
session). When printing ends, we then set it to null so that the remaining PrintView
instance can be garbage collected.

```
// Only do this once per print
if (m_printView == null) {
  BasicTextUI btui = (BasicTextUI)m_monitor.getUI();
  View root = btui.getRootView(m_monitor);
  m_printView = new PrintView(
    m_doc.getDefaultRootElement(),
    root, wPage, maxHeight);
}
```

To create an m_printView object, we need to access the BasicTextUI instance for our
m_monitor JTextPane component and retrieve its root View (which sits on the top of the
hierarchy of views—see chapter 19) using BasicTextUI's getRootView() method. At this
point, the PrintView instance can be created. Its constructor takes four parameters: the root
element of the current document, the root view, and the width and height of the entire document's printing bounds.

10 As soon as we're sure that the m_printView object exists, we call its custom paintPage()
method to render a page with the given index to the given graphical context. Then the garbage collector is called explicitly in an attempt to cut down on the heavy memory usage.

11 Finally, if the paintPage() call returns true, the PAGE_EXISTS value is returned to indicate
a successful render. Otherwise, we set the m_printView reference to null, and we return
NO_SUCH_PAGE to indicate that no more pages can be rendered.

Class WordProcessor.PrintView

12 This inner class extends BoxView and is used to render the content of a styled document.
(Note that since this class extends BoxView, we have access to some of its protected methods, such as getOffset(), getSpan(), layout(), and paintChild().)

13 Three instance variables are defined:
- int m_firstOnPage: The index of the first view to be rendered on the current page.
- int m_lastOnPage: The index of the last view to be rendered on the current page.
- int m_pageIndex: The index of the current page.

14 The PrintView constructor creates the underlying BoxView object for a given root Element
instance (this should be the root element in the document model of the text component we are
printing) and the specified axis used for format/break operations (this is normally Y_AXIS). A
given View instance is then set as the parent for this PrintView (this should be the root View
of the text component we are printing). The setSize() method is called to set the size of
this view, and layout() is called to lay out the child views based on the specified width and
height (this is done to calculate the coordinates of all views used in rendering this document).
These operations may be time consuming for large documents. Fortunately, they are only performed at construction time:

```
public PrintView(Element elem, View root, int w, int h) {
```

```
                super(elem, Y_AXIS);
                setParent(root);
                setSize(w, h);
                layout(w, h);
        }
```

NOTE   We found that `setParent()` must be called prior to `setSize()` and `layout()` to avoid undesirable side effects.

⑮ Our `paintPage()` method renders a single page of a styled document. It takes three parameters:
- `Graphics g`: The graphical context to render the page in.
- `int hPage`: The height of the page.
- `int pageIndex`: The index of the page to render.

⑯ This method will return `true` if the page with the given index is rendered successfully, or `false` if the end of the document is reached. We assume that the pages to be rendered will be fetched in sequential order (although more than one call can be made to print the most recently rendered page). If a new page index is greater than `m_pageIndex` (which holds the index of the last rendered page), we begin rendering from the next view after the last one rendered on the previous page, and we set `m_firstOnPage` to `m_lastOnPage + 1`. If this exceeds the number of child views, no more rendering can be done, so we return false.

```
                m_firstOnPage = m_lastOnPage + 1;
                if (m_firstOnPage >= getViewCount())
                    return false;
```

⑰ The local variables `yMin` and `yMax` denote the top and bottom coordinates of the page being rendered relative to the top of the document. `yMin` is determined by the offset of the first view to be rendered, and `yMax` is then `yMin` plus the height of the page:

```
                int yMin = getOffset(Y_AXIS, m_firstOnPage);
                int yMax = yMin + hPage;
```

⑱ All child views, from `m_firstOnPage` to the last view that will fit on the current page, are examined sequentially in a loop. In each iteration, the local variable `Rectangle rc` is assigned the coordinates of where the associated child view is placed in the document (not on the current page). Based on the height of this view, if there is enough room horizontally to render it (note that it is guaranteed to fit vertically, since the page's width was specified in the `layout()` call above), the `paintChild()` method is called to render it into the graphics context. Also note that we offset the y-coordinate of the view by `yMin` because, as we just mentioned, each child view is positioned in terms of the whole document, and we are only concerned with its position on the current page. If at any point a view will not fit within the remaining page space, we exit the loop.

```
                for (int k = m_firstOnPage; k < getViewCount(); k++) {
                    rc.x = getOffset(X_AXIS, k);
                    rc.y = getOffset(Y_AXIS, k);
                    rc.width = getSpan(X_AXIS, k);
                    rc.height = getSpan(Y_AXIS, k);
                    if (rc.y+rc.height > yMax)
                        break;
                    m_lastOnPage = k;
```

PRINTING STYLED TEXT

```
      rc.y -= yMin;
    paintChild(g, rc, k);
  }
  return true;
```

NOTE A more sophisticated and precise implementation might examine the y-coordinates of all views in the hierarchy, not only the children of the root view. It might be the case that a large paragraph should be split between two or more pages. Our simple approach is not this flexible. In fact, in the case of a paragraph that spans a height larger than the page size, we could be in real trouble with this implementation. Although this is not common, it must be accounted for in professional implementations.

22.4.2 Running the code

Figure 22.5 shows a preview of a text document which will occupy four pages. Try previewing and printing a styled document. We've included the **License.rtf** file for you to experiment with; it's in the ZIP archive for this chapter.

22.5 PRINTING TABLES

In this section we'll add printing capabilities to the `JTable` application we developed earlier in chapter 18. Unlike other examples in this chapter, a printed table should not resemble the `JTable` component as it is displayed on the screen. This requires us to add detailed code for the rendering of the table's contents as they should be displayed in a printout. The resulting code, however, does not depend on the table's structure and it can be easily used for printing

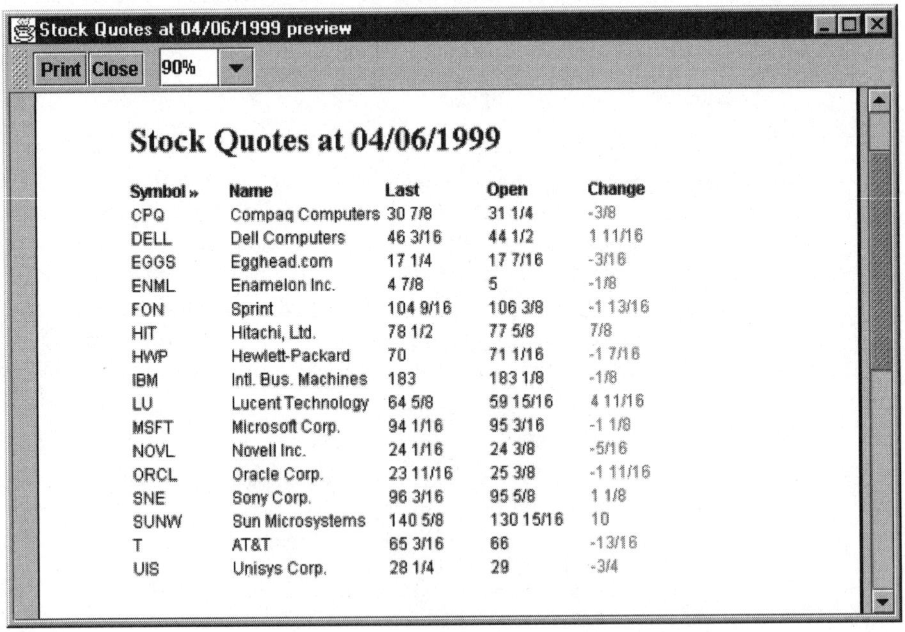

Symbol »	Name	Last	Open	Change
CPQ	Compaq Computers	30 7/8	31 1/4	-3/8
DELL	Dell Computers	46 3/16	44 1/2	1 11/16
EGGS	Egghead.com	17 1/4	17 7/16	-3/16
ENML	Enamelon Inc.	4 7/8	5	-1/8
FON	Sprint	104 9/16	106 3/8	-1 13/16
HIT	Hitachi, Ltd.	78 1/2	77 5/8	7/8
HWP	Hewlett-Packard	70	71 1/16	-1 7/16
IBM	Intl. Bus. Machines	183	183 1/8	-1/8
LU	Lucent Technology	64 5/8	59 15/16	4 11/16
MSFT	Microsoft Corp.	94 1/16	95 3/16	-1 1/8
NOVL	Novell Inc.	24 1/16	24 3/8	-5/16
ORCL	Oracle Corp.	23 11/16	25 3/8	-1 11/16
SNE	Sony Corp.	96 3/16	95 5/8	1 1/8
SUNW	Sun Microsystems	140 5/8	130 15/16	10
T	AT&T	65 3/16	66	-13/16
UIS	Unisys Corp.	28 1/4	29	-3/4

Figure 22.6 A print preview of `JTable` data

any table component. Thus, the code presented here in example 22.4 can be plugged into any JTable application that needs printing functionality. Combined with our print preview component (see the previous examples), the amount of work we need to do to support table printing in professional applications is minimal.

Example 22.4

StocksTable.java

see \Chapter22\4

```java
import java.awt.*;
import java.awt.event.*;
import java.util.*;
import java.io.*;
import java.text.*;
import java.sql.*;
import java.awt.print.*;

import javax.swing.*;
import javax.swing.border.*;
import javax.swing.event.*;
import javax.swing.table.*;

public class StocksTable extends JFrame implements Printable
{
  protected JTable m_table;
  protected StockTableData m_data;
  protected JLabel m_title;

  protected int m_maxNumPage = 1;

  // Unchanged code from example 18.5

  protected JMenuBar createMenuBar() {
    // Unchanged code from example 18.5

    JMenuItem mPrint = new JMenuItem("Print...");
    mPrint.setMnemonic('p');
    ActionListener lstPrint = new ActionListener() {
      public void actionPerformed(ActionEvent e) {
        Thread runner = new Thread() {
          public void run() {
            printData();
          }
        };
        runner.start();
      }
    };
    mPrint.addActionListener(lstPrint);
    mFile.add(mPrint);

    JMenuItem mPreview = new JMenuItem("Print Preview");
    mPreview.setMnemonic('v');
    ActionListener lstPreview = new ActionListener() {
      public void actionPerformed(ActionEvent e) {
```

❶ Print menu item to call printData() method

```
      Thread runner = new Thread() {
        public void run() {
          setCursor(Cursor.getPredefinedCursor(
            Cursor.WAIT_CURSOR));
          new PrintPreview(StocksTable.this,
          m_title.getText()+" preview");
          setCursor(Cursor.getPredefinedCursor(
            Cursor.DEFAULT_CURSOR));
        }
      };
      runner.start();
    }
  };
  mPreview.addActionListener(lstPreview);
  mFile.add(mPreview);
  mFile.addSeparator();

  // Unchanged code from example 18.5
}

public void printData() {
  try {
    PrinterJob prnJob = PrinterJob.getPrinterJob();
    prnJob.setPrintable(this);
    if (!prnJob.printDialog())
      return;
    m_maxNumPage = 1;
    prnJob.print();
  }
  catch (PrinterException e) {
    e.printStackTrace();
    System.err.println("Printing error: "+e.toString());
  }
}

public int print(Graphics pg, PageFormat pageFormat,
  int pageIndex) throws PrinterException {
  if (pageIndex >= m_maxNumPage)
    return NO_SUCH_PAGE;

  pg.translate((int)pageFormat.getImageableX(),
    (int)pageFormat.getImageableY());
  int wPage = 0;
  int hPage = 0;
  if (pageFormat.getOrientation() == pageFormat.PORTRAIT) {
    wPage = (int)pageFormat.getImageableWidth();
    hPage = (int)pageFormat.getImageableHeight();
  }
  else {
    wPage = (int)pageFormat.getImageableWidth();
    wPage += wPage/2;
    hPage = (int)pageFormat.getImageableHeight();
    pg.setClip(0,0,wPage,hPage);
  }
```

2 Checks for valid page index

3 Shifts graphics context and calculates size of drawing area

4 Increases width by half for landscape

```
int y = 0;
pg.setFont(m_title.getFont());
pg.setColor(Color.black);
Font fn = pg.getFont();
FontMetrics fm = pg.getFontMetrics();
y += fm.getAscent();
pg.drawString(m_title.getText(), 0, y);
y += 20; // Space between title and table headers

Font headerFont = m_table.getFont().deriveFont(Font.BOLD);
pg.setFont(headerFont);
fm = pg.getFontMetrics();

TableColumnModel colModel = m_table.getColumnModel();
int nColumns = colModel.getColumnCount();
int x[] = new int[nColumns];
x[0] = 0;

int h = fm.getAscent();
y += h; // Add ascent of header font because of baseline
        // positioning (see figure 2.10)

int nRow, nCol;
for (nCol=0; nCol<nColumns; nCol++) {
  TableColumn tk = colModel.getColumn(nCol);
  int width = tk.getWidth();
  if (x[nCol] + width > wPage) {
    nColumns = nCol;
    break;
  }
  if (nCol+1<nColumns)
    x[nCol+1] = x[nCol] + width;
  String title = (String)tk.getIdentifier();
  pg.drawString(title, x[nCol], y);
}

pg.setFont(m_table.getFont());
fm = pg.getFontMetrics();

int header = y;
h = fm.getHeight();
int rowH = Math.max((int)(h*1.5), 10);
int rowPerPage = (hPage-header)/rowH;
m_maxNumPage = Math.max((int)Math.ceil(m_table.getRowCount()/
  (double)rowPerPage), 1);

TableModel tblModel = m_table.getModel();
int iniRow = pageIndex*rowPerPage;
int endRow = Math.min(m_table.getRowCount(),
  iniRow+rowPerPage);

for (nRow=iniRow; nRow<endRow; nRow++) {
  y += h;
  for (nCol=0; nCol<nColumns; nCol++) {
    int col = m_table.getColumnModel().getColumn(nCol).getModelIndex();
```

⑤ Keeps track of current vertical position and starts rendering

⑥ X-coordinates of each column's upper-left corner

⑦ Draws all the column headers that will fit in the page width

⑧ After headers, figures out how many body rows will fit on page

⑨ Prints the rows allotted to this page

```
            Object obj = m_data.getValueAt(nRow, col);
            String str = obj.toString();
            if (obj instanceof ColorData)
              pg.setColor(((ColorData)obj).m_color);
            else
              pg.setColor(Color.black);
              pg.drawString(str, x[nCol], y);
        }
    }

    System.gc();
    return PAGE_EXISTS;
  }
```

// Remaining code unchanged from example 18.5

22.5.1   Understanding the code

Class StocksTable

❶ In comparison with the table examples of chapter 18, we now implement the `Printable` interface. In our `createMenuBar()` method, we add a Print... menu item which calls our new `printData()` method, which acts just like the `printData()` methods we implemented in the earlier examples.

❷ In our implementation of the `print()` method, we first determine whether a valid page index has been specified by comparing it to the maximum number of pages, `m_maxNumPage`:

```
        if (pageIndex > m_maxNumPage)
            return NO_SUCH_PAGE;
```

The catch is that we don't know this maximum number in advance. So we assign an initial value of 1 to `m_maxNumPage` (the code above works for the 0-th page), and we adjust `m_max-NumPage` to the real value later in the code, just as we've done in earlier examples in this chapter.

❸ We then translate the origin of the graphics context to the origin of the given `PageFormat` instance and determine the width and height of the area available for printing. These dimensions are used to determine how much data can fit on the given page. This same technique was

❹ also used in the previous examples. However, in this example we've added the ability to print with a landscape orientation because tables can be quite wide, and we normally don't want table data to span multiple pages (at least horizontally). In order to do this, we have to first check the orientation of the given `PageFormat` instance. If it is `PORTRAIT`, we determine its width and height as we have always done. If it is not `PORTRAIT`, then it must be either `LANDSCAPE` or `REVERSE_LANDSCAPE` (see section 22.1.5). In this case we need to increase the width of the page because the default is not adequate. After increasing the width, we must also explicitly set the size of the graphics clip. This is all we have to do to allow printing in either orientation.

❺ The local variable `y` is created to keep track of the current vertical position on the page, and we are now ready to actually start the rendering. We begin with the the table's title. Note that we use the same font as is used in the table application for consistency. We add some white space below the title (by increasing `y`) and then we make preparations for printing our table's

❻ headers and body. A bold font is used for our table's header. An array, `x[]`, is created which will be used to store the x-coordinate of each column's upper left-hand corner (taking into account that they may be resized and moved). The variable `nColumns` contains the total number of columns in our table.

7 Now we actually iterate through the columns and print each column header while filling our `x[]` array. We check each iteration to see if the x-coordinate of the previous column, combined with the width of the column under consideration, will be more than the width of the page. If it will, we set the total number of columns, `nColumns`, to the number that will actually fit on the page, and then we break out of the loop. If it will not, we set the x-coordinate corresponding to the current column, print its title, and continue on to the next iteration.

8 Since we've finished printing our table's title and headers, we know how much space is left to print our table's body. We also know the font's height, so we can calculate how many rows can be printed on one page, which is `rowPerPage` (this is calculated as the height of the page minus the current y-offset, all divided by the height of the current font, or 10, whichever is larger). Finally, we calculate the real number of pages, `m_maxNumPage`, by dividing the total row count of our table by the number of rows per page we just calculated as `rowPerPage`. The minimum page count will be 1.

Now we need to actually print the table data. First, we calculate the initial `iniRow` and final `endRow` rows to be printed on this page:

```
TableModel tblModel = m_table.getModel();
int iniRow = pageIndex*rowPerPage;
int endRow = Math.min(m_table.getRowCount(),
    iniRow+rowPerPage);
```

9 Then, in a double `for` loop, iterating through each column of each row in turn, we print the table's contents. This is done by extracting each cell's data as an `Object` (using `getValueAt()`). We store its `toString()` `String` representation in a local variable and check if the object is an instance of our custom inner class, `ColorData` (which was defined in examples in chapter 18). This class is designed to associate a color with a given data object. So if the object is a `ColorData` instance, we grab its color and assign it as the current color of the graphics context. If it isn't, we use black. Finally, we print that object's `toString()` representation and continue on to the remaining cells.

NOTE We are assuming that each object's `toString()` representation is what we want to print. For more complex `TableCellRenderer` implementations, this printing code will need to be customized.

We end by explicitly invoking the garbage collector and returning `PAGE_EXISTS` to indicate a successful print.

22.5.2 Running the code

Figure 22.6 shows a print preview of our table application. Try manipulating the table's contents (choose different dates if you have JDBC and ODBC—see chapter 18) and column orders to see how it affects the table's printout and print preview.

You will notice that in order to fit the whole table on the paper, it must be condensed considerably. It is natural at this point to want to print it with a landscape orientation. Choosing Landscape from the Page Setup dialog modifies the `PageFormat` object that will be sent to our `print()` method when printing begins. However, this will not actually tell the printer to print in landscape mode. In order to do that, we have to explicitly choose landscape mode from the Print dialog as well. Unfortunately, the Page Setup information does not inform the printer, but it is necessary to inform our application.

Though our application can print successfully with a landscape orientation, our print preview component is not designed to display anything but portrait-oriented previews. Because of the way our `PrintPreview` component has been constructed, it is quite easy to add the ability to preview landscape-oriented pages. The only necessary modification is the addition of a parameter to its constructor which specifies the orientation to use. This parameter can then be assigned to the `PageFormat` object used in constructing each `PagePreview` object. We will not show the code here, but we have included a modified version of `PrintPreview` and the `StocksTable` application to demonstrate how you can implement this functionality. See **\Chapter22\5**. Figure 22.7 illustrates.

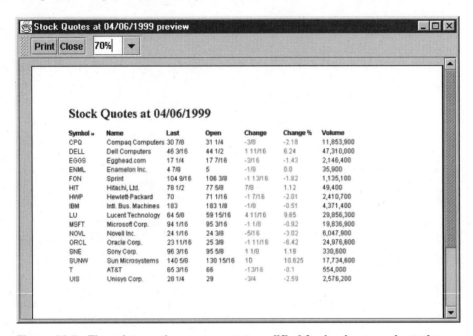

Figure 22.7   The print preview component modified for landscape orientation

C H A P T E R   2 3

Java2D

23.1   *JAVA2D API* OVERVIEW

Java 2 offers a very powerful new rendering model known as Java2D. This model consists of a set of classes and interfaces for advanced 2-D line art, text, and image rendering. Although this API is not considered a part of Swing, it is closely related to Swing and it may be effectively used to develop sophisticated Swing applications.

NOTE   The `java.awt.print` (discussed in chapter 22) and `com.sun.image.codec.jpeg` (discussed in chapter 13) packages are also considered part of the Java2D API.

This chapter includes a Java2D API overview, and it shows how to use this API for chart rendering, enhanced label creation, and basic image rendering. In this section, we briefly discuss the classes and interfaces that are fundamental to the 2D API. Note, however, that a complete description of all Java2D features lies beyond the scope of this book.

23.1.1   The Shape interface

abstract interface java.awt.Shape

This interface provides the definition for a 2-D geometrical object. Most of the classes contained in the `java.awt.geom` package implement this interface. These classes define such things as points, lines, arcs, rectangles, round rectangles, ellipses, and more complex shapes such as cubic and quadratic parametric curves. These *geometries* allow a high degree of flexibility, and with them, we can create almost any shape imaginable. We can render these geometries into a 2-D graphics context using the `draw()` or `fill()` methods (see below). We can also perform boolean operations on multiple shapes such as union, intersection, and exclusive, or using the `java.awt.geom.Area` class. The geometry of each `Shape`'s boundary is defined as a path which is represented by a set of line segments and curves encapsulated in a `PathIter-ator` instance (we will not discuss the details of this here).

Several overloaded `contains()` methods determine whether a given point or rectangle lies inside a `Shape`, and the `getBounds()` method returns a `Shape`'s minimum bounding rectangle.

23.1.2 GeneralPath

class java.awt.geom.GeneralPath

This class implements the `Shape` interface and represents a geometric path constructed from several line segments, or quadratic and cubic curves. Particularly important is its `append-(Shape s, boolean connect)` method, which provides us with a way to append one shape to another by optionally connecting their paths with a line segment.

`GeneralPath` maintains a *current* coordinate at all times which represents the coordinate that, if we were to add a line segment, would be the beginning of the added line segment. To do this, we use its `lineTo()` method, passing it two `float`s that represent the destination coordinate. Similarly, we can use its `moveTo()` and `quadTo()` methods to add a point or curve to the path.

23.1.3 Rectangle2D

class java.awt.geom.Rectangle2D

This class serves as a superclass for three classes: the well-known `java.awt.Rectangle` class, `Rectangle2D.Double`, and `Rectangle2D.Float`. These classes not only provide new ways to work with rectangles, but they also allow us to specify a rectangle's coordinates in `int`, `float`, or `double` form. Along with `Rectangle2D`, the `java.awt.geom` package also includes a set of classes which provide new functionality to familiar graphical primitives, such as `Dimen-sion2D`, `Line2D`, and `Point2D`. Each of these classes allow us to specify their coordinates using `int`s, `float`s, or `double`s through appropriate subclasses.

23.1.4 AffineTransform

class java.awt.geom.AffineTransform

This class encapsulates a general form affine transformation between two coordinate systems. This transformation is essentially a coordinate transformation represented by a 3×3 matrix with an implied last row ([0 0 1]) mapping each x and y in the bounding rectangle of a `Shape` to a new x' and y' according to the following:

$$x' = m_{00} x + m_{01} y + m_{02}$$
$$y' = m_{10} x + m_{11} y + m_{12}$$

The m_{xx}'s represent the first two rows of a 3×3 matrix. These formulas are quite simple to understand and can be rewritten, for most operations, as the following:

$$x' = (scaleX * x) + (shearX * y) + offsetX$$
$$y' = (scaleY * x) + (shearY * y) + offsetY$$

These transformations preserve lines and parallelism (parallel lines are mapped to parallel lines). We use them to perform scaling, shearing, and translation. To construct an `Affine-Transform`, we use either the `double` or `float` version of the following constructor:

```
AffineTransform(m00, m10, m01, m11, m02, m12)
```

Note the order of the parameters. This directly corresponds to the columns of our matrix described above.

Rotation also preserves parallelism. Given an angle of rotation in radians, θ, we have the following transformation rules:

$$x' = x*(\cos\theta) + y*(-\sin\theta) + offsetX$$
$$y' = x*(\sin\theta) + y*(\cos\theta) + offsetY$$

Note that (degrees * π/180) = radians.

The Java2D graphics context (see below) maintains a transform attribute, just as it maintains a color and font attribute. Whenever we draw or fill a shape, this operation will be performed according to the current state of the transform attribute. We can create an instance of `AffineTransform` by specifying the first two rows of the matrix as described above. Alternatively, we can use static methods to create specific types of transformations: `getRotateInstance()`, `getScaleInstance()`, `getShearInstance()`, or `getTranslateInstance()`. We can use the `concatenate()` method to concatenate multiple transformations successively. We can also compose specific transformations with an existing `AffineTransform` using its `rotate()`, `scale()`, `shear()`, and `translate()` methods.

`AffineTransforms` are widely used throughout the 2D API as parameters to methods that require a transformation to produce various visual effects.

23.1.5   The Stroke interface

abstract interface java.awt.Stroke

This interface defines only one method: `createStrokedShape(Shape p)`, which generates a `Shape` that is the outline of the given `Shape` parameter. This outline can be of any size, shape, and décor. The only implementing class is `BasicStroke` (see below). We use `Strokes` to define *line styles* for drawing in the Java2D graphics context. To set the stroke attribute of a given `Graphics2D`, we use its `setStroke()` method.

23.1.6   BasicStroke

class java.awt.BasicStroke

This class implements the `Stroke` interface and defines a set of rendering attributes that specify how to render the outline of a `Shape`. These attributes consist of line *width, join style, endcap style*, and *dash style*:

- The line width (often called the pen width) is the thickness of the line measured perpendicular to its trajectory.
- The end-cap style specifies whether round, butt, or square ends are used to render the ends of line segments: `CAP_ROUND`, `CAP_BUTT`, and `CAP_SQUARE`.
- The join style specifies how to render the joints between segments. The options are bevel, miter, or round: `JOIN_BEVEL`, `JOIN_MITER`, and `JOIN_ROUND`.
- The dash style defines a pattern of opaque and transparent regions rendered along a line segment.

23.1.7   The Paint interface

abstract interface java.awt.Paint

This interface defines how colors and color patterns may be assigned to the 2D graphics context for use in drawing and filling operations. Some important implementing classes are `Color`, `GradientPaint`, and `TexturePaint`. We use `Paint`s to define *fill patterns* for filling in `Shape`s in the Java2D graphics context. To set the paint attribute of a given `Graphics2D`, we use its `setPaint()` method.

23.1.8   GradientPaint

class java.awt.GradientPaint

This class implements the `Paint` interface and renders a shape by using a linear color gradient. The gradient is determined by two 2-D points and two colors associated with them. The gradient can optionally be cyclical which means that between both points it will cycle through shades of each color several times, rather than just once. We use the `Graphics2D.set-Paint()` method to assign a `GradientPaint` instance to a `Graphics2D` object. We can then call the `fill()` method to fill a specified `Shape` with this gradient. Note that this class provides an easy way to produce remarkable visual effects using only a few lines of code.

23.1.9   TexturePaint

class java.awt.TexturePaint

This class implements the `Paint` interface and it is used to fill `Shape`s with a texture stored in a `BufferedImage`. We use the `Graphics2D.setPaint()` method to assign a `Texture-Paint` instance to a `Graphics2D` object. We can call the `fill()` method to fill a specified `Shape` with this texture. Note that the `BufferedImage`s used for a texture are expected to be small, as a `TexturePaint` object makes a copy of its data and stores it internally; it does not reference the provided `BufferedImage`. It is also important to reuse `TexturePaint` objects, rather than create new ones, whenever possible.

23.1.10   Graphics2D

class java.awt.Graphics2D

This class extends the `java.awt.Graphics` class to provide a more sophisticated API for working with geometry, transformations, colors, fill patterns and line styles, and text layout. In Java 2, the `Graphics` object passed to a component's `paint()` method is really a `Graphics2D` object. So we can use this class in our `paint()` implementation by simply casting our `Graphics` object to a `Graphics2D`:

```
public void paint(Graphics g)
{
   Graphics2D g2 = (Graphics2D) g;
   // Use Graphics2D ...
```

We can assign attributes to a `Graphics2D` instance using methods such as `setTransform()`, `setStroke()`, or `setPaint()`, as we discussed above. We can then call `draw()` to outline a given `Shape` instance using the assigned `Stroke`, and we can call `fill()` to fill a given `Shape` with the assigned `Color`, `GradientPaint`, or `TexturePaint`. Depending on the state of the transform attribute, `Shapes` will be translated, rotated, scaled, or sheared appropriately as they are drawn (see `AffineTransform`). We can modify the current transform directly with the `rotate()`, `scale()`, `shear()`, and `translate()` methods. We can also assign it a new transform using its `setTransform()` method, or we can compose the current transform with a given one using its `transform()` method.

A `Graphics2D` object can maintain preferences for specific rendering algorithms to be used depending on whether speed or quality is the priority. These are called rendering hints. They can be assigned using the `setRenderingHint()` method and they are stored as key/value pairs. Valid keys and values are defined in the `RenderingHints` class. Two of these pairs are especially important to us, as the examples in this chapter will always use them:

- By setting the `KEY_ANTIALIASING` property to `VALUE_ANTIALIAS_ON`, you can take advantage of a technique used to render objects with smoothly blended edges (by using intermediate colors to render a border between, say, black and white areas).
- By setting the `KEY_RENDERING` property to `VALUE_RENDER_QUALITY`, appropriate rendering algorithms will always be selected to ensure the best output quality.

23.1.11 GraphicsEnvironment

class java.awt. GraphicsEnvironment

This class is capable of retrieving the collection of `GraphicsDevice` and `Font` instances available to a Java application on the running platform. `GraphicsDevices` can reside on the local machine or on any number of remote machines. A `GraphicsDevice` instance describes, surprisingly, a graphics device such as a screen or printer.

Recall from chapter 2 that we normally reference `GraphicsEnvironment` to retrieve the names of all available fonts:

```
String[] fontNames = GraphicsEnvironment.getLocalGraphicsEnvironment().
  getAvailableFontFamilyNames();
```

23.1.12 BufferedImage

class java.awt.image.BufferedImage

This class represents an `Image` stored in memory that provides methods for storing, interpreting, and rendering pixel data. It is used widely throughout the 2D API and we've already seen it in chapters 13 and 22. In particular, you can create a `BufferedImage`, retrieve its associated `Graphics2D` instance to render into, perform the rendering, and use the result as an image for, among other things, painting directly into another graphics context (we used this technique in the construction of our print preview component). This is also similar to how `RepaintManager` handles the buffering of all Swing components, as we discussed in chapter 2.

23.1.13 FontRenderContext

class java.awt.font.FontRenderContext

Instances of this class encapsulate information that is needed to correctly measure text. This includes rendering hints and target-device-specific information such as resolution (dots-per-inch). A `FontRenderContext` instance representing the current state of the 2D graphics context can be retrieved using `Graphics2D`'s `getFontRenderContext()` method.

FontRenderContext is usually used in association with text formatting using Fonts and TextLayouts.

23.1.14 TextLayout

class java.awt.font.TextLayout

Instances of this class represent an immutable graphical representation of styled text—that is, they cannot change (this class does not contain any set accessors). Only new instances can be created, and a FontRenderContext instance is required to create them. We render a TextLayout in the 2D graphics context using that TextLayout's draw() method. This class is very powerful and it supports such things as hit detection, which will return the character on which a mouse press occurs, as well as support for bidirectional text and split cursors. A particularly noteworthy method is getOutline(AffineTransform tx), which returns a Shape instance that outlines the text.

23.2 *RENDERING CHARTS*

In this section we'll demonstrate the advantages of using the Java2D API for rendering charts. Example 23.1 introduces a custom component which is capable of rendering line graphs, bar charts, and pie charts using strokes, color gradients, and background images. This application demonstrates how to build such charts, taking into account issues such as axis positioning and scaling based on the given coordinate data. Be prepared for a bit of math.

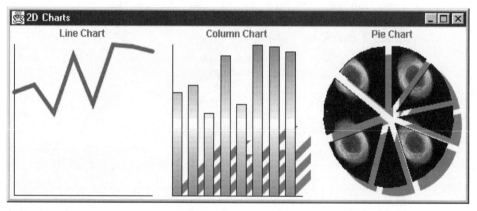

Figure 23.1 Charts2D **displaying the three available** JChart2D **charts with various visual effects**

Example 23.1

Charts2D.java

see \Chapter23\1

```
import java.awt.*;
import java.awt.event.*;
import java.awt.font.*;
```

```java
import java.awt.geom.*;
import java.util.*;

import javax.swing.*;
import javax.swing.border.*;

public class Charts2D extends JFrame
{
  public Charts2D() {
    super("2D Charts");
    setSize(720, 280);
    getContentPane().setLayout(new GridLayout(1, 3, 10, 0));
    getContentPane().setBackground(Color.white);

    int nData = 8;
    int[] xData = new int[nData];
    int[] yData = new int[nData];
    for (int k=0; k<nData; k++) {
      xData[k] = k;
      yData[k] = (int)(Math.random()*100);
      if (k > 0)
        yData[k] = (yData[k-1] + yData[k])/2;
    }

    JChart2D chart = new JChart2D(
      JChart2D.CHART_LINE, nData, xData,
      yData, "Line Chart");
    chart.setStroke(new BasicStroke(5f, BasicStroke.CAP_ROUND,
      BasicStroke.JOIN_MITER));
    chart.setLineColor(new Color(0, 128, 128));
    getContentPane().add(chart);

    chart = new JChart2D(JChart2D.CHART_COLUMN,
      nData, xData, yData, "Column Chart");
    GradientPaint gp = new GradientPaint(0, 100,
      Color.white, 0, 300, Color.blue, true);
    chart.setGradient(gp);
    chart.setEffectIndex(JChart2D.EFFECT_GRADIENT);
    chart.setDrawShadow(true);
    getContentPane().add(chart);

    chart = new JChart2D(JChart2D.CHART_PIE, nData, xData,
      yData, "Pie Chart");
    ImageIcon icon = new ImageIcon("hubble.gif");
    chart.setForegroundImage(icon.getImage());
    chart.setEffectIndex(JChart2D.EFFECT_IMAGE);
    chart.setDrawShadow(true);
    getContentPane().add(chart);

    WindowListener wndCloser = new WindowAdapter() {
      public void windowClosing(WindowEvent e) {
        System.exit(0);
      }
    };
    addWindowListener(wndCloser);

    setVisible(true);
```

❶ Provides frame displaying three different JChart2D instances, all using the same data

```
    }
  public static void main(String argv[]) {
    new Charts2D();
  }
}

class JChart2D extends JPanel
{
  public static final int CHART_LINE = 0;
  public static final int CHART_COLUMN = 1;
  public static final int CHART_PIE = 2;

  public static final int EFFECT_PLAIN = 0;
  public static final int EFFECT_GRADIENT = 1;
  public static final int EFFECT_IMAGE = 2;

  protected int m_chartType = CHART_LINE;
  protected JLabel m_title;
  protected ChartPanel m_chart;

  protected int m_nData;
  protected int[] m_xData;
  protected int[] m_yData;
  protected int m_xMin;
  protected int m_xMax;
  protected int m_yMin;
  protected int m_yMax;
  protected double[] m_pieData;

  protected int  m_effectIndex = EFFECT_PLAIN;
  protected Stroke m_stroke;
  protected GradientPaint m_gradient;
  protected Image  m_foregroundImage;
  protected Color  m_lineColor = Color.black;
  protected Color  m_columnColor = Color.blue;
  protected int  m_columnWidth = 12;
  protected boolean m_drawShadow = false;

  public JChart2D(int type, int nData,
   int[] yData, String text) {
    this(type, nData, null, yData, text);
  }

  public JChart2D(int type, int nData, int[] xData,
   int[] yData, String text) {
    super(new BorderLayout());
    setBackground(Color.white);
    m_title = new JLabel(text, JLabel.CENTER);
    add(m_title, BorderLayout.NORTH);

    m_chartType = type;

    if (xData==null) {
      xData = new int[nData];
      for (int k=0; k<nData; k++)
        xData[k] = k;
    }
```

❷ Creates chart with default X data

❷ Creates chart of specified chart type, with given label, and with given X- and Y-coordinate data

```java
  if (yData == null)
    throw new IllegalArgumentException(
    "yData can't be null");
  if (nData > yData.length)
    throw new IllegalArgumentException(
    "Insufficient yData length");
  if (nData > xData.length)
    throw new IllegalArgumentException(
    "Insufficient xData length");
  m_nData = nData;
  m_xData = xData;
  m_yData = yData;

  m_xMin = m_xMax = 0;   // To include 0 into the interval
  m_yMin = m_yMax = 0;
  for (int k=0; k<m_nData; k++) {
    m_xMin = Math.min(m_xMin, m_xData[k]);
    m_xMax = Math.max(m_xMax, m_xData[k]);
    m_yMin = Math.min(m_yMin, m_yData[k]);
    m_yMax = Math.max(m_yMax, m_yData[k]);
  }
  if (m_xMin == m_xMax)
    m_xMax++;
  if (m_yMin == m_yMax)
    m_yMax++;

  if (m_chartType == CHART_PIE) {
    double sum = 0;
    for (int k=0; k<m_nData; k++) {
      m_yData[k] = Math.max(m_yData[k], 0);
      sum += m_yData[k];
    }
    m_pieData = new double[m_nData];
    for (int k=0; k<m_nData; k++)
      m_pieData[k] = m_yData[k]*360.0/sum;
  }
  m_chart = new ChartPanel();
  add(m_chart, BorderLayout.CENTER);
}
public void setEffectIndex(int effectIndex) {
  m_effectIndex = effectIndex;
  repaint();
}

public int getEffectIndex() { return m_effectIndex; }

public void setStroke(Stroke stroke) {
  m_stroke = stroke;
  m_chart.repaint();
}

public void setForegroundImage(Image img) {
  m_foregroundImage = img;
  repaint();
```

3 Creates array of evenly spaced degree values around a circle (360 degrees)

4 Puts custom ChartPanel in center of BorderLayout

```
    }

    public Image getForegroundImage() { return m_foregroundImage; }

    public Stroke getStroke() { return m_stroke; }

    public void setGradient(GradientPaint gradient) {
      m_gradient = gradient;
      repaint();
    }

    public GradientPaint getGradient() { return m_gradient; }

    public void setColumnWidth(int columnWidth) {
      m_columnWidth = columnWidth;
      m_chart.calcDimensions();
      m_chart.repaint();
    }

    public int getColumnWidth() { return m_columnWidth; }

    public void setColumnColor(Color c) {
      m_columnColor = c;
      m_chart.repaint();
    }

    public Color getColumnColor() { return m_columnColor; }

    public void setLineColor(Color c) {
      m_lineColor = c;
      m_chart.repaint();
    }

    public Color getLineColor() { return m_lineColor; }

    public void setDrawShadow(boolean drawShadow) {
      m_drawShadow = drawShadow;
      m_chart.repaint();
    }

    public boolean getDrawShadow() { return m_drawShadow; }

    class ChartPanel extends JComponent
    {
      int m_xMargin = 5;
      int m_yMargin = 5;
      int m_pieGap = 10;

      int m_x;
      int m_y;
      int m_w;
      int m_h;

      ChartPanel() {
        enableEvents(ComponentEvent.COMPONENT_RESIZED);
      }

      protected void processComponentEvent(ComponentEvent e) {
        calcDimensions();
      }

      public void calcDimensions() {
```

❺ Constructor just enables component resize events

❺ Called when component is resized

```
    Dimension d = getSize();
    m_x = m_xMargin;
    m_y = m_yMargin;
    m_w = d.width-2*m_xMargin;
    m_h = d.height-2*m_yMargin;
    if (m_chartType == CHART_COLUMN) {
      m_x += m_columnWidth/2;
      m_w -= m_columnWidth;
    }
  }
  public int xChartToScreen(int x) {
    return m_x + (x-m_xMin)*m_w/(m_xMax-m_xMin);
  }
  public int yChartToScreen(int y) {
    return m_y + (m_yMax-y)*m_h/(m_yMax-m_yMin);
  }
  public void paintComponent(Graphics g) {
    int x0 = 0;
    int y0 = 0;
    if (m_chartType != CHART_PIE) {
      g.setColor(Color.black);
      x0 = xChartToScreen(0);
      g.drawLine(x0, m_y, x0, m_y+m_h);
      y0 = yChartToScreen(0);
      g.drawLine(m_x, y0, m_x+m_w, y0);
    }

    Graphics2D g2 = (Graphics2D) g;
    g2.setRenderingHint(RenderingHints.KEY_ANTIALIASING,
      RenderingHints.VALUE_ANTIALIAS_ON);
    g2.setRenderingHint(RenderingHints.KEY_RENDERING,
      RenderingHints.VALUE_RENDER_QUALITY);

    if (m_stroke != null)
      g2.setStroke(m_stroke);

    GeneralPath path = new GeneralPath();
    switch (m_chartType) {
    case CHART_LINE:
      g2.setColor(m_lineColor);
      path.moveTo(xChartToScreen(m_xData[0]),
        yChartToScreen(m_yData[0]));
      for (int k=1; k<m_nData; k++)
        path.lineTo(xChartToScreen(m_xData[k]),
          yChartToScreen(m_yData[k]));
      g2.draw(path);
      break;

    case CHART_COLUMN:
      for (int k=0; k<m_nData; k++) {
        m_xMax ++;
        int x = xChartToScreen(m_xData[k]);
        int w = m_columnWidth;
```

6 Converts from chart coordinates to component coordinates

7 Draws axes for line and column charts

7 Different work for each chart type

8 Line chart draws connected line segments between data points

9 Creates a rectangle for each X data point, appended onto the GeneralPath to be drawn later

```
      int y1 = yChartToScreen(m_yData[k]);
      int y = Math.min(y0, y1);
      int h = Math.abs(y1 - y0);
      Shape rc = new Rectangle2D.Double(x, y, w, h);
      path.append(rc, false);
      m_xMax --;
    }

    if (m_drawShadow) {
      AffineTransform s0 = new AffineTransform(
        1.0, 0.0, 0.0, -1.0, x0, y0);
      s0.concatenate(AffineTransform.getScaleInstance(
        1.0, 0.5));
      s0.concatenate(AffineTransform.getShearInstance(
        0.5, 0.0));
      s0.concatenate(new AffineTransform(
        1.0, 0.0, 0.0, -1.0, -x0, y0));
      g2.setColor(Color.gray);
      Shape shadow = s0.createTransformedShape(path);
      g2.fill(shadow);
    }

    if (m_effectIndex==EFFECT_GRADIENT &&
      m_gradient != null) {
      g2.setPaint(m_gradient);
      g2.fill(path);
    }
    else if (m_effectIndex==EFFECT_IMAGE &&
      m_foregroundImage != null)
      fillByImage(g2, path, 0);
    else {
      g2.setColor(m_columnColor);
      g2.fill(path);
    }
    g2.setColor(m_lineColor);
    g2.draw(path);
    break;

case CHART_PIE:
    double start = 0.0;
    double finish = 0.0;
    int ww = m_w - 2*m_pieGap;
    int hh = m_h - 2*m_pieGap;
    if (m_drawShadow) {
      ww -= m_pieGap;
      hh -= m_pieGap;
    }

    for (int k=0; k<m_nData; k++) {
      finish = start+m_pieData[k];
      double f1 = Math.min(90-start, 90-finish);
      double f2 = Math.max(90-start, 90-finish);
      Shape shp = new Arc2D.Double(m_x, m_y, ww, hh,
        f1, f2-f1, Arc2D.PIE);
```

⑨ Creates a rectangle for each X data point, appended onto the GeneralPath to be drawn later

⑩ Draws a shadow by running Transforms on the GeneralPath and changing the color

⑪ For each X data point, builds a pie piece whose angle is proportional to the Y data point; translates pie pieces a small distance away from center

```
        double f = (f1 + f2)/2*Math.PI/180;
        AffineTransform s1 = AffineTransform.
          getTranslateInstance(m_pieGap*Math.cos(f),
          -m_pieGap*Math.sin(f));
        s1.translate(m_pieGap, m_pieGap);
        Shape piece = s1.createTransformedShape(shp);
        path.append(piece, false);
        start = finish;
      }

      if (m_drawShadow) {
        AffineTransform s0 = AffineTransform.
          getTranslateInstance(m_pieGap, m_pieGap);
        g2.setColor(Color.gray);
        Shape shadow = s0.createTransformedShape(path);
        g2.fill(shadow);
      }

      if (m_effectIndex==EFFECT_GRADIENT && m_gradient != null) {
        g2.setPaint(m_gradient);
        g2.fill(path);
      }
      else if (m_effectIndex==EFFECT_IMAGE &&
       m_foregroundImage != null)
        fillByImage(g2, path, 0);
      else {
        g2.setColor(m_columnColor);
        g2.fill(path);
      }

      g2.setColor(m_lineColor);
      g2.draw(path);
      break;
    }
  }

  protected void fillByImage(Graphics2D g2,
   Shape shape, int xOffset) {
    if (m_foregroundImage == null)
      return;
    int wImg = m_foregroundImage.getWidth(this);
    int hImg = m_foregroundImage.getHeight(this);
    if (wImg <=0 || hImg <= 0)
      return;
    g2.setClip(shape);
    Rectangle bounds = shape.getBounds();
    for (int xx = bounds.x+xOffset;
     xx < bounds.x+bounds.width; xx += wImg)
      for (int yy = bounds.y; yy < bounds.y+bounds.height;
       yy += hImg)
        g2.drawImage(m_foregroundImage, xx, yy, this);
  }
 }
}
```

11 For each X data point, builds a pie piece whose angle is proportional to the Y data point; translates pie pieces a small distance away from center

12 Draws a shadow by copying the GeneralPath and translating to the southeast, with a color change

13 Tiles the foreground image on a Shape

23.2.1 Understanding the code

Class Charts2D

❶ This class provides the frame that encompasses this example. It creates an array of equidistant x-coordinates and random y-coordinates to be drawn in the charts. Three instances of our custom `JChart2D` class (see below) are created and placed in the frame using a `GridLayout`. The methods used to provide setup and initialization for our chart are built into the `JChart2D` class; they will be explained below.

Class JChart2D

Several constants are defined for use as the available chart type and visual effect options:

- `int CHART_LINE`: Specifies a line chart.
- `int CHART_COLUMN`: Specifies a column chart.
- `int CHART_PIE`: Specifies a pie chart.
- `int EFFECT_PLAIN`: Use no visual effects (homogeneous chart).
- `int EFFECT_GRADIENT`: Use a color gradient to fill the chart.
- `int EFFECT_IMAGE`: Use an image to fill the chart.

Several instance variables are defined to hold data used by this class:

- `JLabel m_title`: The label used to display a chart's title.
- `ChartPanel m_chart`: A custom component used to display a chart's body (see below).
- `int m_nData`: The number of points in the chart.
- `int[] m_xData`: An array of x-coordinates in the chart.
- `int[] m_yData`: An array of y-coordinates in the chart.
- `int m_xMin`: The minimum x-coordinate.
- `int m_xMax`: The maximum x-coordinate.
- `int m_yMin`: The minimum y-coordinate.
- `int m_yMax`: The maximum y-coordinate.
- `double[] m_pieData`: The angles for each piece of the pie chart.
- `int m_chartType`: Maintains the chart's type (one of the constants listed above).
- `int m_effectIndex`: Maintains the chart's effect index (one of the constants listed above).
- `Stroke m_stroke`: The stroke instance used to outline the chart.
- `GradientPaint m_gradient`: The color gradient used to fill the chart (this only takes effect when `m_effectIndex` is set to `EFFECT_GRADIENT`).
- `Image m_foregroundImage`: The image used to fill the chart (this only takes effect when `m_effectIndex` is set to `EFFECT_IMAGE`).
- `Color m_lineColor`: The color used to outline the chart.
- `Color m_columnColor`: The color used to fill the chart (this only takes effect when `m_effectIndex` is set to `EFFECT_PLAIN`—this is its default setting).
- `int m_columnWidth`: The width of the columns in the column chart.
- `boolean m_drawShadow`: A flag to draw a shadow for a column or a pie chart.

❷ Two constructors are provided in the `JChart2D` class. The first one takes four parameters and simply calls the second, passing it the given parameters and using a `null` value for a fifth. This second constructor is where a `JChart2D` is actually created; these are its five parameters:

- `int type`: The type of this chart (`CHART_LINE`, `CHART_COLUMN`, or `CHART_PIE`).
- `int nData`: The number of data points in this chart.

- `int[] xData`: An array of x-coordinates for this chart (may be `null`—this is passed as `null` from the first constructor).
- `int[] yData`: An array of y-coordinates for this chart.
- `String text`: This chart's title.

❸ The constructor validates the input data and initializes all instance variables. In the case of a pie chart, an array called `m_pieData`, is created; it contains sectors with angles normalized to 360 degrees (the `sum` value used here was calculated previous to this code as the sum of all `m_yData[]` values):

```
m_pieData = new double[m_nData];
for (int k=0; k<m_nData; k++)
  m_pieData[k] = m_yData[k]*360.0/sum;
```

❹ This chart component extends `JPanel` and contains two child components that are managed using a `BorderLayout`: `JLabel m_title`, which displays the chart's title in the `NORTH` region, and an instance of our custom `ChartPanel` component, `m_chart`, which is placed in the `CENTER` region.

The rest of the code for this class consists of `set`/`get` methods that support instance variables declared in this class; the remaining code does not require further explanation.

Class JChart2D.ChartPanel

This inner class extends `JComponent` and represents the custom component that is actually responsible for rendering our charts. Several instance variables are declared:

- `int m_xMargin`: The left and right margin size of the rendering area.
- `int m_yMargin`: The top and bottom margin size of the rendering area.
- `int m_pieGap`: The radial shift for pieces of pie (such as the spacing between each).
- `int m_x`: The left coordinate of the rendering area.
- `int m_y`: The top coordinate of the rendering area.
- `int m_w`: The width of the rendering area.
- `int m_h`: The height of the rendering area.

❺ The `ChartPanel` constructor enables component resize events to be processed. When such an event occurs, the `processComponentEvent()` method triggers a call to `calcDimensions()` (note that this event will normally be generated when `ChartPanel` is added to a container for the first time). This method retrieves the current component's size, calculates the coordinates of the rendering area, and stores them in the appropriate instance variables listed above. In the case of a column chart, we offset the rendering area by an additional half of the column width, and then shrink it by a full column width. Otherwise, the first and last columns will be rendered on top of the chart's border.

❻ The `xChartToScreen()` and `yChartToScreen()` methods calculate screen coordinates from chart coordinates as illustrated in figure 23.2. We need to scale the chart data so the chart will occupy the entire component region, taking into account the margins. To get the necessary scaling ratios, we divide the dimensions of the chart component (minus the margins) by the difference between the max and min values of the chart data. These methods are used in rendering the line and column charts because they are based on coordinate data. The only sizing information the pie chart needs is `m_w` and `m_h`, as it does not rely on coordinate data.

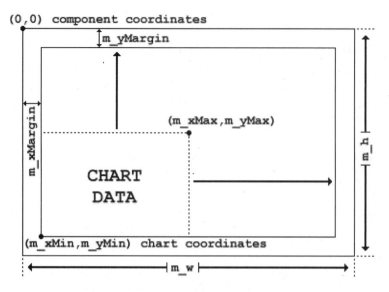

Figure 23.2   Screen coordinates vs. chart coordinates

7 The `paintComponent()` method performs the actual chart rendering. The coordinate axes are drawn first for line and column charts. Then we cast the `Graphics` instance to a `Graphics2D` so we have access to Java2D features. As we discussed earlier, we use two rendering hints and assign them with the `setRenderingHint()` method: they are `VALUE_ANTI-ALIAS_ON` and `VALUE_RENDER_QUALITY`. If the `m_stroke` instance variable has been initialized, the `Graphics2D` stroke attribute is set using the `setStroke()` method. The rest of the `paintComponent()` method is placed into a `switch` block with cases for each chart type. Before the switch block is entered, we create a `GeneralPath` which we will use to construct each chart using the methods we described in section 23.1.2.

8 The line chart is the simplest case. It is drawn as a broken line through the array of points that represent the chart data. We first start the `GeneralPath` out by passing the first coordinate of data using `moveTo()`. Then we iterate through the chart data, adding lines to the path using its `lineTo()` method. Once we've done this, we are ready to render it and we use the `Graphics2D draw()` method to do so.

> **NOTE**   The Java2D API provides ways to draw quadratic and cubic curves that pass through three and four given points respectively. Unfortunately this functionality is not suitable for drawing a smooth line chart with interpolation.

9 The column chart is drawn as a set of vertical bars with a common baseline that corresponds to the 0-value of the chart, `y0` (note that this value is always included in the [`m_yMin`, `m_yMax`] interval). The `GeneralPath` instance accumulates these bars as `Rectangle2D.Double` instances using its `append()` method, passing `false` for the line connection option.

10 If the `m_drawShadow` flag is set, the next step renders shadows behind these bars, which should be viewed as standing vertically. `AffineTransform s0` is constructed to accomplish this in four steps:

1 Transform from screen coordinates to chart coordinates.

2 Scale y-axis by a factor of 0.5.

3 Shear x-axis by a factor of 1.0.

4 Transform chart coordinates back to screen coordinates.

As soon as this `AffineTransform` is constructed, we create a corresponding transformed version of our path `Shape` using `AffineTransform`'s `createTransformedShape()` method. We then set the current color to gray and render it into the 2D graphics context using the `fill()` method. Finally, the set of bars is drawn on the screen. Depending on the `m_effectIndex` setting, we fill this shape with the gradient color, the image (by calling our custom `fillByImage()` method), or a solid color.

⑪ The pie chart is drawn as pieces of a circle with a common center. The larger the chart's value is for a given point, the larger the corresponding angle of that piece is. For an interesting resemblance with a cut pie, all pieces are shifted apart from the common center in the radial direction. To draw such a pie, we first build each piece by iterating through the chart's data. Using the `Arc2D.Double` class with its `PIE` setting provides a convenient way to build a slice of pie. We then translate this slice away from the pie's center in the radial direction using an `AffineTransform` and its `createTransformShape()` method. Each resulting shape is appended to our `GeneralPath` instance.

⑫ If the `m_drawShadow` flag is set, we form and draw a shadow from these pieces. Since this chart can be viewed as lying on a flat surface, the shadow has the same shape as the chart itself, but it is translated in the south-east direction. Finally, the set of pie pieces is drawn on the screen using the selected visual effect. Since at this point we operate with the chart as a single `Shape` (remember a `GeneralPath` is a `Shape`), the code is the same as for the column chart.

⑬ The custom `fillByImage()` method uses the given `Shape` instance's bounds as the `Graphics2D` clipping area, and, in a doubly nested `for` loop, it fills this region using our previously assigned `m_foregroundImage`. (Note that the third parameter to this method, `int xOffset`, is used for horizontal displacement which we do use in this example. However, we will see this method again in the next example where we will need this functionality.)

23.2.2 Running the code

Figure 23.1 shows our `Charts2D` application containing three charts: line, column, and pie. Try modifying the settings specified in the `Charts2D` class to try charts with various combinations of available visual effects. Also try resizing the frame container and notice how each chart is scaled accordingly.

Our `JChart2D` component can easily be plugged into any Swing application. Since we have implemented full scalability and correct coordinate mapping, we have the beginnings of a professional chart component. The next step would be to add informative strings to the axis as well as pie pieces, bars, and data points of the line chart.

23.3 *RENDERING STRINGS*

In this section, we'll demonstrate the advantages of using Java2D for rendering strings. It is especially useful for relatively big fonts used to display titles. Example 23.2 introduces a custom

label component which is capable of rendering strings with various visual effects, including
such things as animation using an image, continuously changing foreground color, and out-
lining, as you can see in figure 23.3.

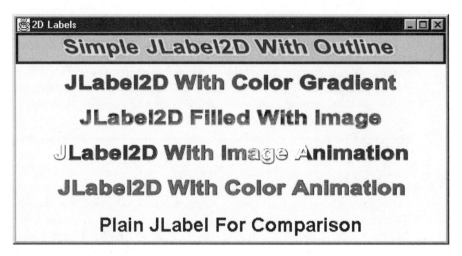

Figure 23.3 JLabel2Ds **with various visual effects, and a plain** JLabel **for comparison**

Example 23.2

Labels2D.java

see \Chapter23\2

```java
import java.awt.*;
import java.awt.event.*;
import java.awt.font.*;
import java.awt.geom.*;
import java.util.*;

import javax.swing.*;
import javax.swing.border.*;

public class Labels2D extends JFrame
{
  public Labels2D() {
    super("2D Labels");
    setSize(600, 250);
    getContentPane().setLayout(new GridLayout(6, 1, 5, 5));
    getContentPane().setBackground(Color.white);
    Font bigFont = new Font("Helvetica",Font.BOLD, 24);

    JLabel2D lbl = new JLabel2D("Simple JLabel2D With Outline",
      JLabel.CENTER);
    lbl.setFont(bigFont);
    lbl.setForeground(Color.blue);
    lbl.setBorder(new LineBorder(Color.black));
```

**❶ Creates frame with
five custom JLabel2D
components, and one
JLabel for comparison**

**Label with
background and
border colors, with
text leaning left ❷**

```
lbl.setBackground(Color.cyan);
lbl.setOutlineColor(Color.yellow);
lbl.setStroke(new BasicStroke(5f));
lbl.setOpaque(true);
lbl.setShearFactor(0.3);
getContentPane().add(lbl);

lbl = new JLabel2D("JLabel2D With Color Gradient",
  JLabel.CENTER);
lbl.setFont(bigFont);
lbl.setOutlineColor(Color.black);
lbl.setEffectIndex(JLabel2D.EFFECT_GRADIENT);
GradientPaint gp = new GradientPaint(0, 0,
  Color.red, 100, 50, Color.blue, true);
lbl.setGradient(gp);
getContentPane().add(lbl);

lbl = new JLabel2D(
  "JLabel2D Filled With Image", JLabel.CENTER);
lbl.setFont(bigFont);
lbl.setEffectIndex(JLabel2D.EFFECT_IMAGE);
ImageIcon icon = new ImageIcon("mars.gif");
lbl.setForegroundImage(icon.getImage());
lbl.setOutlineColor(Color.red);
getContentPane().add(lbl);

lbl = new JLabel2D("JLabel2D With Image Animation",
  JLabel.CENTER);
lbl.setFont(bigFont);
lbl.setEffectIndex(JLabel2D.EFFECT_IMAGE_ANIMATION);
icon = new ImageIcon("ocean.gif");
lbl.setForegroundImage(icon.getImage());
lbl.setOutlineColor(Color.black);
lbl.startAnimation(300);
getContentPane().add(lbl);

lbl = new JLabel2D("JLabel2D With Color Animation",
  JLabel.CENTER);
lbl.setFont(bigFont);
lbl.setEffectIndex(JLabel2D.EFFECT_COLOR_ANIMATION);
lbl.setGradient(gp);
lbl.setOutlineColor(Color.black);
lbl.startAnimation(300);
getContentPane().add(lbl);

JLabel lbl1 = new JLabel("Plain JLabel For Comparison",
  JLabel.CENTER);
lbl1.setFont(bigFont);
lbl1.setForeground(Color.black);
getContentPane().add(lbl1);

WindowListener wndCloser = new WindowAdapter() {
  public void windowClosing(WindowEvent e) {
    System.exit(0);
  }
```

2 Label with background and border colors, with text leaning left

3 Label with a smooth color gradient from red to blue

4 Label with an image of Mars filling text interior

5 Fills text interior with constantly shifting image

6 Uses GradientPaint, but also varies color

7 Plain label for comparison

RENDERING STRINGS

```
      };
      addWindowListener(wndCloser);

      setVisible(true);
   }

   public static void main(String argv[]) { new Labels2D(); }
}

class JLabel2D extends JLabel
{
   public static final int EFFECT_PLAIN = 0;
   public static final int EFFECT_GRADIENT = 1;
   public static final int EFFECT_IMAGE = 2;
   public static final int EFFECT_IMAGE_ANIMATION = 3;
   public static final int EFFECT_COLOR_ANIMATION = 4;

   protected int m_effectIndex = EFFECT_PLAIN;
   protected double m_shearFactor = 0.0;
   protected Color  m_outlineColor;
   protected Stroke m_stroke;
   protected GradientPaint m_gradient;
   protected Image  m_foregroundImage;
   protected Thread m_animator;
   protected boolean m_isRunning = false;
   protected int m_delay;
   protected int m_xShift;

   public JLabel2D() { super(); }

   public JLabel2D(String text) { super(text); }

   public JLabel2D(String text, int alignment) {
      super(text, alignment);
   }

   public void setEffectIndex(int effectIndex) {
      m_effectIndex = effectIndex;
      repaint();
   }

   public int getEffectIndex() { return m_effectIndex; }

   public void setShearFactor(double shearFactor) {
      m_shearFactor = shearFactor;
      repaint();
   }

   public double getShearFactor() { return m_shearFactor; }

   public void setOutlineColor(Color outline) {
      m_outlineColor = outline;
      repaint();
   }

   public Color getOutlineColor() { return m_outlineColor; }

   public void setStroke(Stroke stroke) {
      m_stroke = stroke;
```

```
      repaint();
    }

    public Stroke getStroke() { return m_stroke; }

    public void setGradient(GradientPaint gradient) {
      m_gradient = gradient;
      repaint();
    }

    public GradientPaint getGradient() { return m_gradient; }

    public void setForegroundImage(Image img) {
      m_foregroundImage = img;
      repaint();
    }

    public Image getForegroundImage() { return m_foregroundImage; }

    public void startAnimation(int delay) {            ⑧ Starts animation
      if (m_animator != null)                              (image or colors) in
        return;                                            background thread
      m_delay = delay;
      m_xShift = 0;
      m_isRunning = true;
      m_animator = new Thread() {
        double arg = 0;
        public void run() {
          while(m_isRunning) {
            if (m_effectIndex==EFFECT_IMAGE_ANIMATION)
              m_xShift += 10;
            else if (
             m_effectIndex==EFFECT_COLOR_ANIMATION &&
             m_gradient != null) {
             arg += Math.PI/10;
             double cos = Math.cos(arg);
             double f1 = (1+cos)/2;                Computes new ⑨
             double f2 = (1-cos)/2;                gradient color
             arg = arg % (Math.PI*2);

             Color c1 = m_gradient.getColor1();
             Color c2 = m_gradient.getColor2();
             int r = (int)(c1.getRed()*f1+c2.getRed()*f2);
             r = Math.min(Math.max(r, 0), 255);
             int g = (int)(c1.getGreen()*f1+c2.getGreen()*f2);
             g = Math.min(Math.max(g, 0), 255);
             int b = (int)(c1.getBlue()*f1+c2.getBlue()*f2);
             b = Math.min(Math.max(b, 0), 255);
             setForeground(new Color(r, g, b));
            }
            repaint();
            try { sleep(m_delay); }
            catch (InterruptedException ex) { break; }
          }
        }
```

```
    };
    m_animator.start();
  }

  public void stopAnimation() {
    m_isRunning = false;
    m_animator = null;
  }

  public void paintComponent(Graphics g) {
    Dimension d= getSize();
    Insets ins = getInsets();
    int x = ins.left;
    int y = ins.top;
    int w = d.width-ins.left-ins.right;
    int h = d.height-ins.top-ins.bottom;

    if (isOpaque()) {
      g.setColor(getBackground());
      g.fillRect(0, 0, d.width, d.height);
    }
    paintBorder(g);

    Graphics2D g2 = (Graphics2D) g;
    g2.setRenderingHint(RenderingHints.KEY_ANTIALIASING,
      RenderingHints.VALUE_ANTIALIAS_ON);
    g2.setRenderingHint(RenderingHints.KEY_RENDERING,
      RenderingHints.VALUE_RENDER_QUALITY);

    FontRenderContext frc = g2.getFontRenderContext();
    TextLayout tl = new TextLayout(getText(), getFont(), frc);

    AffineTransform shear = AffineTransform.
      getShearInstance(m_shearFactor, 0.0);
    Shape src = tl.getOutline(shear);
    Rectangle rText = src.getBounds();

    float xText = x - rText.x;
    switch (getHorizontalAlignment()) {
    case CENTER:
      xText = x + (w-rText.width)/2;
      break;
    case RIGHT:
      xText = x + (w-rText.width);
      break;
    }
    float yText = y + h/2 + tl.getAscent()/4;

    AffineTransform shift = AffineTransform.
      getTranslateInstance(xText, yText);
    Shape shp = shift.createTransformedShape(src);

    if (m_outlineColor != null) {
      g2.setColor(m_outlineColor);
      if (m_stroke != null)
        g2.setStroke(m_stroke);
```

⑩ Since super() method not called, this has to paint background and border

⑪ Gets the label text into a form which can be transformed and shears the image

⑫ Calculates text location from horizontal alignment, height, and ascent

⑬ Draws outline with specified stroke

```
        g2.draw(shp);
    }

    switch (m_effectIndex) {
        case EFFECT_GRADIENT:
            if (m_gradient == null)
                break;
            g2.setPaint(m_gradient);
            g2.fill(shp);
            break;
        case EFFECT_IMAGE:
            fillByImage(g2, shp, 0);
            break;
        case EFFECT_COLOR_ANIMATION:
            g2.setColor(getForeground());
            g2.fill(shp);
            break;
        case EFFECT_IMAGE_ANIMATION:
            if (m_foregroundImage == null)
                break;
            int wImg = m_foregroundImage.getWidth(this);
            if (m_xShift > wImg)
                m_xShift = 0;
            fillByImage(g2, shp, m_xShift-wImg);
            break;
        default:
            g2.setColor(getForeground());
            g2.fill(shp);
            break;
    }
}

    // The fillByImage() method was taken from JChart2D (example 23.1)
}
```

🔵 **Draws outline with specified stroke**

🔵 **Fills text interior depending on visual effect type**

23.3.1 Understanding the code

Class Labels2D

❶ This class extends JFrame and provides the main container for our example. Its constructor creates five instances of our JLabel2D custom component, and one JLabel used for comparison. All the labels are placed in a GridLayout that contains one column, and each uses the same font. Various settings are used to render these custom labels, as defined in our JLabel2D class:

❷ • The first label uses border and background settings to demonstrate that they can be used the same way as with any other Swing components. (Note that we still have to set the opaque property to true for the background to be filled.) The outlineColor and stroke properties are set to outline the label's text. Finally the shearFactor property is set to make the text lean to the left.

❸ • The second label uses a GradientPaint instance (using red and blue colors) to fill the text's interior.

❹ • The third label uses an image to fill the text's interior.

⑤
- The fourth label uses an image to fill the text's interior with animation of that image (it's a cyclical shifting of the image in the horizontal direction).

⑥
- The fifth label uses the same GradientPaint as the second one, but it produces a color animation effect (a solid foreground color which is changed cyclically).

⑦
- The sixth label is a plain JLabel component without any special effects.

Class JLabel2D

This class extends JLabel and provides various visual effects in text rendering. Constants are defined that represent each available type of visual effect:

- int EFFECT_PLAIN: No special effects are used.
- int EFFECT_GRADIENT: Use gradient painting of the text's foreground.
- int EFFECT_IMAGE: Use an image to fill the text's foreground.
- int EFFECT_IMAGE_ANIMATION: Use a moving image to fill the text's foreground.
- int EFFECT_COLOR_ANIMATION: Use a cyclically changing color to fill the text's foreground.

Several instance variables are needed to hold the data used by this class:

- int m_effectIndex: The type of the current effect used to render the text (defaults to EFFECT_PLAIN).
- double m_shearFactor: The shearing factor that determines how the text will lean (positive: lean to the left; negative: lean to the right).
- Color m_outlineColor: The color used to outline the text.
- Stroke m_stroke: The stroke instance used to outline the text.
- GradientPaint m_gradient: The color gradient used to fill the text (this only takes effect when m_effectIndex is set to EFFECT_GRADIENT).
- Image m_foregroundImage: The image used to fill the text (this only takes effect when m_effectIndex is set to EFFECT_IMAGE).
- Thread m_animator: The thread which produces animation and color cycling.
- boolean m_isRunning: Returns true if the m_animator thread is running, false otherwise.
- int m_delay: The delay time, in milliseconds, which determines the speed of animation.
- int m_xShift: The current image offset in the horizontal direction (this only takes effect when m_effectIndex is set to EFFECT_IMAGE_ANIMATION).

There are three JLabel2D constructors, and each calls the corresponding superclass (JLabel) constructor. This class also defines several self-explanatory set/get accessors for our instance variables listed above.

⑧ The startAnimation() method starts our m_animator thread which executes every m_delay ms. In the case of image animation, this thread periodically increases our m_xShift variable which is used in the rendering routine below as an offset. Depending on how smooth we want our animation, we can increase or decrease this shift value. Increasing it would give the appearance of speeding up the animation; but it would be more jumpy. Decreasing it would slow it down, but it would appear much smoother.

In the case of color animation, the startAnimation() method determines the two colors of the current m_gradient, and it calculates an intermediate color by "drawing" a cosine curve between the red, green, and blue components of these colors. The local variable arg is incremented by `Math.PI/10` on each iteration. We take the cosine of this value and calculate two new values, `f1` and `f2`, based on this result:

```
arg += Math.PI/10;
double cos = Math.cos(arg);
double f1 = (1+cos)/2;
double f2 = (1-cos)/2;
arg = arg % (Math.PI*2);
```

`f1` and `f2` will always sum to 1, and because `arg` is incremented by `Math.PI/10`, we will obtain a consistent cycle of 20 different combinations of `f1` and `f2`, as shown below.

arg	f1	f2
0.3141592653589793	0.9755282581475768	0.024471741852423234
0.6283185307179586	0.9045084971874737	0.09549150281252627
0.9424777960769379	0.7938926261462366	0.20610737385376343
1.2566370614359172	0.6545084971874737	0.3454915028125263
1.5707963267948966	0.5	0.49999999999999994
1.8849555921538759	0.34549150281252633	0.6545084971874737
2.199114857512855	0.20610737385376346	0.7938926261462365
2.51327412287183453	0.09549150281252632	0.9045084971874737
2.827433388230814	0.02447174185242323	0.9755282581475768
3.141592653589793	0.0	1.0
3.4557519189487724	0.024471741852423193	0.9755282581475768
3.7699111843077517	0.09549150281252625	0.9045084971874737
4.084070449666731	0.20610737385376338	0.7938926261462367
4.39822971502571	0.3454915028125262	0.6545084971874737
4.71238898038469	0.4999999999999999	0.5000000000000001
5.026548245743669	0.6545084971874736	0.3454915028125264
5.340707511102648	0.7938926261462365	0.20610737385376354
5.654866776461628	0.9045084971874736	0.09549150281252633
5.969026041820607	0.9755282581475767	0.024471741852423234
0.0	1.0	0.0

9 We then use `f1` and `f2` as factors for determining how much of the red, green, and blue component of each of the gradient's colors to use for the foreground image:

```
Color c1 = m_gradient.getColor1();
Color c2 = m_gradient.getColor2();
int r = (int)(c1.getRed()*f1+c2.getRed()*f2);
r = Math.min(Math.max(r, 0), 255);
int g = (int)(c1.getGreen()*f1+c2.getGreen()*f2);
g = Math.min(Math.max(g, 0), 255);
int b = (int)(c1.getBlue()*f1+c2.getBlue()*f2);
b = Math.min(Math.max(b, 0), 255);
setForeground(new Color(r, g, b));
```

This gives us 20 distinct colors. We can always increase or decrease this count by increasing or decreasing the denominator of `arg` (for example, `arg = Math.PI/20` will give 40 distinct colors, and `arg = Math.PI/5` will give 10 distinct colors).

⑩ The `paintComponent()` method first calculates the coordinates of the area available for rendering. Since we avoid the call to `super.paintComponent()`, we are responsible for filling the background and border ourselves. So we first check the `opaque` property (inherited from `JLabel`) and, if it is set to `true`, the background is painted manually by filling the component's available region with its background color. We then call the `paintBorder()` method to render the border (if any) around the component.

Then the `Graphics` parameter is cast to a `Graphics2D` instance to obtain access to Java2D features. As we discussed above, two rendering hints are specified using the `setRendering-Hint()` method: anti-aliasing and the priority of quality over speed (see section 23.1.10).

⑪ A `FontRenderContext` instance is retrieved from the `Graphics2D` context and it is used to create a `TextLayout` instance using our label's text (refer to sections 23.1.13 and 23.1.14). `TextLayout`'s `getOutline()` method retrieves a `Shape` which outlines the given text. This method takes an `AffineTransform` instance as an optional parameter. We use this parameter to shear the text (if our `m_shearFactor` property is set to a non-zero value).

⑫ We then calculate the location of the text depending on the horizontal alignment of our label (center or right; left needs no special handling). The y-coordinate of the text's baseline is calculated using the top margin (`y`) the height over 2 (`h/2`) and the ascent over 4 (`tl.getAscent()/4`, see figure 23.4). Why ascent/4? See section 2.8.3 for an explanation.

```
float yText = y + h/2 + tl.getAscent()/4;
```

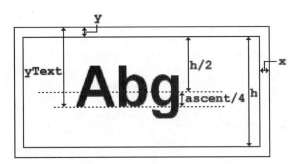

Figure 23.4   Vertical positioning of the label text

We then create an `AffineTransform` for translation to the calculated position. The `createTransformedShape()` method is then used to get a `Shape` that represents the outline of the text at that position.

⑬ If the `m_outlineColor` property is set, we draw the text's outline using that color and the assigned stroke instance, `m_stroke` (if set). The rest of the code fills the interior of the text's `Shape` we retrieved above using the specified visual effect:

- For `EFFECT_GRADIENT`, we use a `GradientPaint` instance to fill the interior.
- For `EFFECT_IMAGE`, we use our `fillByImage()` method to fill the interior with the specified image.
- For `EFFECT_COLOR_ANIMATION`, we simply fill the interior with the foreground color (which changes cyclically in the animation thread).

- For `EFFECT_IMAGE_ANIMATION`, we use our `fillByImage()` method with the shift parameter (which is periodically incremented by the animation thread).
- For `EFFECT_PLAIN`, we simply fill the interior with the foreground color.

23.3.2 Running the code

Figure 23.3 shows our `JLabel2D` demo application in action. You can modify the settings of each label specified in the `Labels2D` class to try out different combinations of available visual effects. Try out different animation speeds and watch how each affects the performance of the application. Choosing too small of a delay may virtually freeze the application. You might consider enforcing a lower bound to make sure that this does not happen.

Notice that our `JLabel2D` component can be easily plugged into any Swing application and it can be used by developers without specific knowledge of Java2D.

23.4 RENDERING IMAGES

In this section, we'll demonstrate the advantages of using Java2D for rendering images and having some fun. Example 23.3 is a simple implementation of the well-known Pac-man video arcade game. We have designed it so that creating custom levels is very simple, and customizing the appearance is only a matter of building new 20×20 images (you can also change the size of the game's cells to accommodate images of different dimensions). Though there are no monsters, level changes, or sounds, these features are ready and waiting to be implemented by the inspired Pac-man enthusiast. We hope to provide you with a solid base from which to start. And if you've made it this far through the book without skipping any material, you surely deserve a Pac-man break.

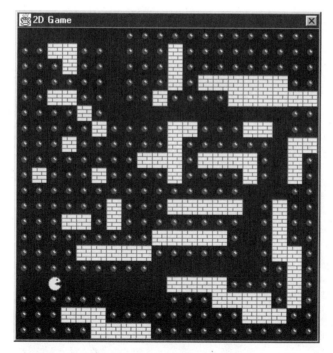

Figure 23.5 `Game2D` with Pac-man in action

Example 23.3

see \Chapter23\3

```java
import java.awt.*;
import java.awt.event.*;
import java.awt.image.*;
import java.awt.geom.*;
import java.util.*;

import javax.swing.*;
import javax.swing.border.*;

public class Game2D extends JFrame
{
  public Game2D() {
    super("2D Game");
    getContentPane().setLayout(new BorderLayout());

    PacMan2D field = new PacMan2D(this);
    getContentPane().add(field, BorderLayout.CENTER);

    WindowListener wndCloser = new WindowAdapter() {
      public void windowClosing(WindowEvent e) {
        System.exit(0);
      }
    };
    addWindowListener(wndCloser);

    pack(); // no pun intended
    setResizable(false);
    setVisible(true);
  }

  public static void main(String argv[]) { new Game2D(); }
}

class PacMan2D extends JPanel
{
  static final int N_IMG = 4;
  static final int X_CELL = 20;
  static final int Y_CELL = 20;
  static final int N_STEP = 10;
  static final double STEP = 0.1f;

  protected int m_nx;
  protected int m_ny;
  protected int[][] m_flags;
  protected double m_creatureX = 0;
  protected double m_creatureY = 0;
  protected int m_posX = 0;
  protected int m_posY = 0;
  protected int m_creatureVx = 1;
  protected int m_creatureVy = 0;
```

① Simple frame that just contains a PacMan2D component

② Presents a panel with a simple PacMan simulation

```java
protected int m_creatureDir = 0;
protected int m_creatureInd = 0;
protected int m_creatureNewVx = 1;
protected int m_creatureNewVy = 0;
protected int m_creatureNewDir = 0;

protected String[] m_data = {
  "0000000000000000000",     // 0
  "0011000000100000000",     // 1
  "0001000001000000000",     // 2
  "0000000001011111100",     // 3
  "0011000010000111111",     // 4
  "0000100000000000000",     // 5
  "0000010000100011000",     // 6
  "0001000001000000011",     // 7
  "0000000111011110010",     // 8
  "0100010001000010010",     // 9
  "0000000000000000000",     // 10
  "0000001000111110100",     // 11
  "0001101000000000100",     // 12
  "0000000011111000100",     // 13
  "0000111110000000110",     // 14
  "0000000000000000010",     // 15
  "0000000001111000010",     // 16
  "0000000000001111010",     // 17
  "0001110000000011100",     // 18
  "0000011110000000000" };   // 19

protected Image m_wallImage;
protected Image m_ballImage;
protected Image[][] m_creature;
protected Thread m_runner;
protected JFrame m_parent;

public PacMan2D(JFrame parent) {
  setBackground(Color.black);
  m_parent = parent;

  AffineTransform[] at = new AffineTransform[3];
  at[0] = new AffineTransform(0, 1, -1, 0, Y_CELL, 0);
  at[1] = new AffineTransform(-1, 0, 0, 1, X_CELL, 0);
  at[2] = new AffineTransform(0, -1, -1, 0, Y_CELL, X_CELL);

  ImageIcon icon = new ImageIcon("wall.gif");
  m_wallImage = icon.getImage();
  icon = new ImageIcon("ball.gif");
  m_ballImage = icon.getImage();
  m_creature = new Image[N_IMG][4];
  for (int k=0; k<N_IMG; k++) {
    int kk = k + 1;
    icon = new ImageIcon("creature"+kk+".gif");
    m_creature[k][0] = icon.getImage();

    for (int d=0; d<3; d++) {
      BufferedImage bi = new BufferedImage(X_CELL, Y_CELL,
```

③ I's in array represent wall locations

④ Transforms used to flip PacMan image

⑤ Four rows of four images; each row has PacMan facing a different direction; each column changes size of mouth opening

```
                BufferedImage.TYPE_INT_RGB);
            Graphics2D g2 = bi.createGraphics();
            g2.drawImage(m_creature[k][0], at[d], this);
            m_creature[k][d+1] = bi;
        }
    }
}

m_nx = m_data[0].length();
m_ny = m_data.length;
m_flags = new int[m_ny][m_nx];
for (int i=0; i<m_ny; i++)
for (int j=0; j<m_nx; j++)
    m_flags[i][j] = (m_data[i].charAt(j)=='0' ? 0 : 1);

m_runner = new Thread() {
    public void run() {
        m_flags[m_posY][m_posX] = -1;

        while (!m_parent.isShowing())
            try { sleep(150); }
            catch (InterruptedException ex) { return; }

        while (true) {
            m_creatureVx = m_creatureNewVx;
            m_creatureVy = m_creatureNewVy;
            m_creatureDir = m_creatureNewDir;
            int j = m_posX+m_creatureVx;
            int i = m_posY+m_creatureVy;
            if (j >=0 && j < m_nx && i >= 0 && i < m_ny &&
                m_flags[i][j] != 1) {
                for (int k=0; k<N_STEP; k++) {
                    m_creatureX += STEP*m_creatureVx;
                    m_creatureY += STEP*m_creatureVy;
                    m_creatureInd++;
                    m_creatureInd = m_creatureInd % N_IMG;
                    final int x = (int)(m_creatureX*X_CELL);
                    final int y = (int)(m_creatureY*Y_CELL);
                    Runnable painter = new Runnable() {
                        public void run() {
                            PacMan2D.this.paintImmediately(
                                x-1, y-1, X_CELL+3, Y_CELL+3);
                        }
                    };
                    try {
                        SwingUtilities.invokeAndWait(painter);
                    } catch (Exception e) {}
                    try { sleep(40); }
                    catch (InterruptedException ex) { break; }
                }
                if (m_flags[i][j] == 0)
                    m_flags[i][j] = -1;
                m_posX += m_creatureVx;
                m_posY += m_creatureVy;
                m_creatureX = m_posX;
```

⑤ Four rows of four images; each row has PacMan facing a different direction; each column changes size of mouth opening

⑥ PacMan display and movement engine; in background thread

⑥ Waits until frame is finished painting

⑥ Saves last delta X/Y and direction so they don't change while processing them

⑦ If new coordinates are legal, move to next position

⑧ Divides step into 10 equal pieces

⑧ At each fractional position, draws PacMan with changing mouth opening

⑨ Eats a pellet

```
          m_creatureY = m_posY;
        }
        else
          try { sleep(150); }
          catch (InterruptedException ex) { break; }
      }
    }
  };
  m_runner.start();

  KeyAdapter lst = new KeyAdapter() {
    public void keyPressed(KeyEvent e) {
      switch (e.getKeyCode()) {
        case KeyEvent.VK_RIGHT:
          m_creatureNewVx = 1;
          m_creatureNewVy = 0;
          m_creatureNewDir = 0;
          break;
        case KeyEvent.VK_DOWN:
          m_creatureNewVx = 0;
          m_creatureNewVy = 1;
          m_creatureNewDir = 1;
          break;
        case KeyEvent.VK_LEFT:
          m_creatureNewVx = -1;
          m_creatureNewVy = 0;
          m_creatureNewDir = 2;
          break;
        case KeyEvent.VK_UP:
          m_creatureNewVx = 0;
          m_creatureNewVy = -1;
          m_creatureNewDir = 3;
          break;
      }
    }
  };
  parent.addKeyListener(lst);
}

public Dimension getPreferredSize() {
  return new Dimension(m_nx*X_CELL, m_ny*Y_CELL);
}

public Dimension getMaximumSize() {
  return getPreferredSize();
}

public Dimension getMinimumSize() {
  return getPreferredSize();
}

public void paintComponent(Graphics g) {
  Graphics2D g2 = (Graphics2D) g;
  g2.setRenderingHint(RenderingHints.KEY_ANTIALIASING,
    RenderingHints.VALUE_ANTIALIAS_ON);
```

⑩ Checks for arrow keys and sets the direction deltas accordingly

⑪ Preferred size (and maximum/minimum) is determined by number of cells in game panel

```
g2.setRenderingHint(RenderingHints.KEY_RENDERING,
   RenderingHints.VALUE_RENDER_QUALITY);

g2.setColor(getBackground());
g2.fill(g.getClip());

int x, y;
for (int i=0; i<m_ny; i++)
for (int j=0; j<m_nx; j++) {
  x = j*X_CELL;
  y = i*Y_CELL;
  if (m_flags[i][j] == 1)
    g2.drawImage(m_wallImage, x, y, this);
  else if (m_flags[i][j] == 0)
    g2.drawImage(m_ballImage, x, y, this);
}

x = (int)(m_creatureX*X_CELL);
y = (int)(m_creatureY*Y_CELL);
g2.drawImage(
   m_creature[m_creatureInd][m_creatureDir], x, y, this);
}
}
```

11 At each location, draws a wall, pellet, or nothing, depending on its current state

11 Draws current PacMan image at its current location

23.4.1   Understanding the code

Class Game2D

1 This class merely creates a JFrame and places an instance of our PacMan2D component in it.

Class PacMan2D

2 This component represents a simple Pac-man implementation. Several class constants are defined:

- int N_IMG: The number of slides to produce animation of a moving Pac-man.
- int X_CELL: The horizontal size of a cell in the arcade.
- int Y_CELL: The vertical size of a cell in the arcade.
- int N_STEP: The number of steps used to produce smooth movement from one cell to another.
- double STEP: The length of one step (in terms of cells).

These are the instance variables:

- int m_nx: The number of cell columns in a level.
- int m_ny: The number of cell rows in a level.
- int[][] m_flags: A two-dimensional array that describes the current state of each cell.
- double m_creatureX: The current x-coordinate of Pac-man in terms of cells. This may be fractional because of smooth motion.
- double m_creatureY: The current y-coordinate of Pac-man in terms of cells.
- int m_posX: The current x-coordinate of the cell in which Pac-man resides.
- int m_posY: The current y-coordinate of the cell in which Pac-man resides.
- int m_creatureVx: The current x-component of Pac-man's velocity (may be 1, 0, or –1).
- int m_creatureVy: The current y-component of Pac-man's velocity (may be 1, 0, or –1).

- `int m_creatureDir`: The current direction of Pac-man's motion (`0` is east, `1` is south, `2` is west, and `3` is north). Used for quick selection of the proper image from our `m_creature` 2D array (see below).
- `int m_creatureInd`: The index of the current slide in Pac-man's animation.
- `int m_creatureNewVx`: A new value for `m_creatureVx` (assigned by the player via the keyboard, but not yet accepted by the game).
- `int m_creatureNewVy`: A new value for `m_creatureVy`.
- `int m_creatureNewDir`: A new value for `m_creatureDir`.

❸
- `String[] m_data`: An array of `String`s which determines the location of walls in a level.
- `Image m_wallImage`: An image of a wall occupying one cell.
- `Image m_ballImage`: An image of a pellet (to be eaten by Pac-man) occupying one cell.
- `Image[][] m_creature`: A 2D array of Pac-man images.
- `Thread m_runner`: The thread which runs this game.

❹ The constructor of `PacMan2D` performs all necessary initialization. We first create three `Affine-Transform`s to be used for flipping our Pac-man images:

```
AffineTransform[] at = new AffineTransform[3];
at[0] = new AffineTransform(0, 1, -1, 0, Y_CELL, 0);
at[1] = new AffineTransform(-1, 0, 0, 1, X_CELL, 0);
at[2] = new AffineTransform(0, -1, -1, 0, Y_CELL, X_CELL);
```

❺ Then, we read in our wall and ball images, and create a 2D array of Pac-man's images. The first row in this array is filled with animated slide images of Pac-man read from four prepared image files. Each of these images represents Pac-man facing east in one of his chomping positions. The next three rows are filled with the same images, but each are transformed to face south (second row), west (third row), and north (fourth row). These flipped images are created in three steps:

1. Create an empty `BufferedImage` instance the size of the original image.
2. Retrieve its `Graphics2D` context to draw into that image.
3. Use the overloaded `drawImage()` method to use an `AffineTransform` instance (prepared above) as a parameter and render the transformed image.

Each resulting image is stored in our `m_creature` array.

The configuration of the game's level is encoded in the `m_data` `String` array: `0` characters correspond to pellets, `1` characters correspond to walls. This information is then parsed and stored in the `m_flags` array. Thus, the size of the `m_data` array also determines the size of the level (the product of `m_nx` and `m_ny`).

> **NOTE** The `m_data` `String` array can be easily modified to produce a new level. We also can easily modify the program to read this information from an external file. These features would be natural enhancements to make if we were to expand upon this game.

❻ The `m_runner` thread represents the engine of this game. First, it waits while the parent frame is shown on the screen (otherwise wild visual effects may appear). The endless `while` loop manages Pac-man's movement on the screen. The direction of Pac-man's motion may have been changed by the user since the last cycle, so we reassign three parameters which determine that direction from storage variables (`m_creatureVx` from `m_creatureNewVx`, and so on). This insures that Pac-man's direction will not change in the middle of a cycle.

7 We then calculate the coordinates of the next cell `i` and `j` that Pac-man will visit. If these coordinates lie inside the level and they do not correspond to a wall cell (a `1`), we smoothly move Pac-man to the new position. Otherwise, we wait until the user provides a new direction.

8 The movement of Pac-man from the current cell to a new one is split into `N_STEP` steps. On each step we determine the fractional coordinates, `m_creatureX` and `m_creatureY` (in cell units). Then we call `paintImmediately()` to redraw a portion of the level surrounding Pac-man's current location, and we pause for 40 ms:

```
final int x = (int)(m_creatureX*X_CELL);
final int y = (int)(m_creatureY*Y_CELL);
Runnable painter = new Runnable() {
  public void run() {
    PacMan2D.this.paintImmediately(
      x-1, y-1, X_CELL+3, Y_CELL+3);
  }
};
try {
  SwingUtilities.invokeAndWait(painter);
} catch (Exception e) {}
try { sleep(40); }
catch (InterruptedException ex) { break; }
```

The `paintImmediately()` method can be used to force very quick repaints but it should only be called from within the event-dispatching thread. Additionally, because we do not want any other painting or movement to occur while this painting takes place, we wrap the call in a `Runnable` and send it to the event queue with `invokeAndWait()` (refer to chapter 2 for a discussion of painting and multithreading issues).

9 When the creature's relocation is over, we eat a pellet (by setting the `m_flags` array element corresponding to the current cell to −1) and we adjust Pac-man's coordinate variables.

10 To listen for the user's keyboard activity, we create a `KeyAdapter` instance and add it to the parent component. This `KeyAdapter` processes arrow keys (up, down, left, and right) and assigns new values to the `m_creatureNewVx`, `m_creatureNewVy`, and `m_creatureNewDir` variables accordingly. The program flow is not interrupted; these new values will be requested only on the next thread cycle as discussed above. Note that if the arrow keys are pressed too quickly, only the last typed value will affect the Pac-man's direction.

11 The `getPreferredSize()` method determines the size of the level, which is simply based on the number and size of the cells. Finally, the `paintComponent()` method is responsible for rendering the whole game. This process is relatively simple: we render the level using two images (wall and ball) and draw Pac-man's image (taken from our 2D `m_creature` array) in the proper location.

23.4.2   Running the code

Figure 23.5 shows Pac-man in action. Try the game and have some fun. Experiment with modifying the level and icons for the wall, ball, and Pac-man himself. If you like this example, you might go further and add monsters, scoring, sound effects, level changing, and other full-featured game characteristics.

A P P E N D I X   A

Sources of information

Official Sun resources

- The JFC product site. `http://java.sun.com/products/jfc/`
- The *Swing Connection*. `http://java.sun.com/products/jfc/tsc/`
- "Creating a GUI with JFC/Swing," The Java Tutorial Trail. `http://java.sun.com/docs/books/tutorial/uiswing/index.html`
- The Java Look and Feel Design Guidelines. `http://java.sun.com/products/jlf/`

Examples

- The Swing FAQ. `http://users.vnet.net/wwake/swing/faq.html`
- CodeGuru. `http://www.codeguru.com/java/`
- Miscellaneous Swing examples. `http://www2.gol.com/users/tame/swing/examples/SwingExamples.html`

Magazines

- *JavaWorld* magazine. `http://www.JavaWorld.com`
- *JavaPro* magazine. `http://www.java-pro.com/`
- *Java Report* magazine. `http://www.javareport.com/`

Mailing lists

To subscribe to either one of these lists, send a message to the corresponding email address; in the body of the message, type `subscribe username@domain.com`.

- `swing-subscribe@eos.dk`
- `advanced-swing-subscribe@eos.dk`

To unsubscribe, send a message to the appropriate email address with an empty message body:

- `swing-subscribe@eos.dk`
- `advanced-swing-subscribe@eos.dk`

A request to subscribe or unsubscribe will be followed by an auto-generated confirmation email. Simply reply to this email to complete the intended action.

Most Swing developers subscribe to both lists, and we recommend that any given message be exclusively posted to one or the other.

For a complete list of of Sun mailing lists, see `http://archives.java.sun.com/archives/index.html`

Bibliography

Swing references

1 Andrews, Mark. "Accessibility and the Swing Set." *The Swing Connection*, Sun Microsystems, 1999.
   http://java.sun.com/products/jfc/tsc/special_report/accessibility/accessibility.html

2 Andrews, Mark. "Getting Started with Swing." *The Swing Connection*, Sun Microsystems, 1998.
   http://java.sun.com/products/jfc/tsc/what_is_swing/getting_started/getting_started.html

3 Andrews, Mark. "Introducing Swing Architecture." *The Swing Connection*, Sun Microsystems, 1998.
   http://java.sun.com/products/jfc/tsc/what_is_swing/getting_started_2/
   getting_started_2.html

4 Andrews, Mark and Nancy Schorr. "Make Your Browser Swing!" *The Swing Connection*, Sun Microsystems, 1998.
   http://java.sun.com/products/jfc/tsc/web/applets/applets.html

5 Andrews, Mark. "Plugging into Swing." *The Swing Connection*, Sun Microsystems, 1998.
   http://java.sun.com/products/jfc/tsc/web/java_plug-in/java_plug-in.html

6 Armstrong, Eric. "Understanding Containers." *The Swing Connection*, Sun Microsystems, 1998.
   http://java.sun.com/products/jfc/tsc/archive/tech_topics_arch/frames_panes/
   frames_panes.html#

7 Drye, Stephen and William Wake. *Java Foundation Classes: Swing Reference*. Manning Publications, 1999.

8 Eckstein, Robert, Marc Loy and Dave Wood. *Java Swing*. O'Reilly & Associates, 1998.

9   Fowler, Amy. "Mixing Heavy and Light Components." *The Swing Connection*, Sun Microsystems, 1998.
    http://java.sun.com/products/jfc/tsc/archive/tech_topics_arch/mixing/mixing.html#

10 Fowler, Amy. "Painting in AWT and Swing." *The Swing Connection*, Sun Microsystems, 1998.
    http://java.sun.com/products/jfc/tsc/special_report/painting/painting.html

11 Friesen, Geoff. "Plug into Java with Java Plug-in." *JavaWorld*, 1999.
    http://www.javaworld.com/javaworld/jw-06-1999/jw-06-plugin_p.html

12 Geary, David. *Graphic Java 2, Mastering the JFC: AWT* (Sun Microsystems Press Java Series). Prentice Hall, 1999.

13 Geary, David. *Graphic Java 2, Mastering the JFC: Swing* (Sun Microsystems Press Java Series). Prentice Hall, 1999.

14 Gutz, Steven. *Up to Speed With Swing: User Interfaces With Java Foundation Classes*. Manning Publications, 1998.

15 Joshi, Daniel and Pavel Vorobiev. *JFC: Java Foundation Classes*. IDG Books Worldwide, 1998.

16 Karr, Ralph. "Component Orientation in Swing." *The Swing Connection*, Sun Microsystems, 1999.
    http://java.sun.com/products/jfc/tsc/tech_topics/bidi/bidi.html

17 Muller, Hans and Kathy Walrath. "Threads and Swing." *The Swing Connection*, Sun Microsystems, 1998.
    http://java.sun.com/products/jfc/tsc/archive/tech_topics_arch/threads/threads.html#

18 Muller, Hans. "The Truth about Serialization." *The Swing Connection*, Sun Microsystems, 1998.
    http://java.sun.com/products/jfc/tsc/archive/tech_topics_arch/serialize/serialize.html#

19 Muller, Hans and Kathy Walrath. "Using a Swing Worker Thread." *The Swing Connection*, Sun Microsystems, 1998.
    http://java.sun.com/products/jfc/tsc/archive/tech_topics_arch/swing_worker/swing_worker.html

20 Prinzing, Tim. "How to Customize a Text Editor." *The Swing Connection*, Sun Microsystems, 1998.
    http://java.sun.com/products/jfc/tsc/text/editor_kit/editor_kit.html

21 Prinzing, Tim. "Using the Swing Text Package." *The Swing Connection*, Sun Microsystems, 1998.
    http://java.sun.com/products/jfc/tsc/text/text/text.html

22 Robinson, Matt. "Build Your Own Lightweight Canvas." *The Swing Connection*, Sun Microsystems, 1998.
    http://java.sun.com/products/jfc/tsc/tips/tips_main.html

23 Robinson, Matt. "Building an Editor with an Overwrite Mode." *The Swing Connection*, Sun Microsystems, 1999.
    http://java.sun.com/products/jfc/tsc/tips/tips_main.html

24 Robinson, Matt. "Creating Watermarks with Swing." *The Swing Connection*, Sun Micro-systems, 1998.
http://java.sun.com/products/jfc/tsc/tips/tips_main.html

25 Robinson, Matt. "Internalizable and Externalizable Frames." *The Swing Connection*, Sun Microsystems, 1998.
http://java.sun.com/products/jfc/tsc/tips/tips_main.html

26 Robinson, Matt. "Jazz It Up: A 5-Step Plan." The Swing Connection, Sun Microsystems, 1999.
http://java.sun.com/products/jfc/tsc/tips/tips_main.html

27 Ryan, Chris. "The Java Look and Feel High-Level Specification." *The Swing Connection*, Sun Microsystems, 1998.
http://java.sun.com/products/jfc/tsc/plaf_papers/jlf/jlf.html

28 Schorr, Nancy. "Using the Java Plug-in Converter." *The Swing Connection*, Sun Micro-systems, 1998.
http://java.sun.com/products/jfc/tsc/web/converter/converter.html

29 Topley, Kim. *Core Java Foundation Classes* (Core Series). Prentice Hall, 1998.

30 Violet, Scott. "The Element Interface." *The Swing Connection*, Sun Microsystems, 1999.
http://java.sun.com/products/jfc/tsc/text/element_interface/element_interface.html

31 Violet, Scott. "How the Swing Text Package Handles Attributes." *The Swing Connection*, Sun Microsystems, 1999.
http://java.sun.com/products/jfc/tsc/text/attributes/attributes.html

32 Violet, Scott. "Tabbing in Text Documents." *The Swing Connection*, Sun Microsystems, 1999.
http://java.sun.com/products/jfc/tsc/text/tabs/tabs.html

33 Violet, Scott. "Understanding the ElementBuffer." *The Swing Connection*, Sun Microsys-tems, 1999.
http://java.sun.com/products/jfc/tsc/text/element_buffer/element_buffer.html

34 Wilson, Steve. "The Look and Feel Class Reference." *The Swing Connection*, Sun Micro-systems, 1998.
http://java.sun.com/products/jfc/tsc/plaf_papers/lookandfeel_reference/
lookandfeel_reference.html

...recommended and referenced by David Anderson, UI Guidelines author

User Task Analysis and User Centered Design

1 Beyer, Hugh and Karen Holtzblatt. *Contextual Design*. Morgan Kaufmann, 1997.

2 Hackos, JoAnn and Janice Redish. *User and Task Analysis for Interface Design*. John Wiley, 1998.

3 Robert, Dave, Dick Berry, Scott Isensee, John Mullaly, and Dave Roberts. *Designing for the User with OVID*. MacMillan, 1998.

User Interaction Analysis

1 Anderson, David J. "User Interface Analysis." White Paper, 1999. http://www.uidesign.net

User Interface Design

1 Arlov, Laura. *GUI Design for Dummies*. IDG 1997.
2 Cooper, Alan. *About Face: The Essentials of User Interface Design*. IDG 1995.
3 Norman, Donald. *The Design of Everyday Things*. Doubleday, 1990.
4 Norman, Donald. *The Things that Make Us Smart*. Perseus Press, 1994.
5 Schneiderman, Ben. *Designing the User Interface*, 3rd ed. Addison Wesley, 1997.

Graphic Design

1 Horton, William. *The Icon Book*. Wiley, 1997.
2 Mullet, Kevin and Darrell Sano. *Designing Visual Interfaces – communication oriented techniques*. Prentice Hall, 1995.
3 Tufte, Edward. *Envisioning Information*. Graphic Press, 1990.
4 Tufte, Edward. *The Visual Display of Quantitative Information*. Graphic Press, 1992.
5 Tufte, Edward. *Visual Explanations*. Graphic Press, 1997.

Object Oriented Analysis and Design

1 Coad, *Java Design: Building Better Apps and Applets*, 2nd ed. Prentice Hall, 1998.
2 Coad, *Java Modeling in Color with UML: Enterprise Components and Process*. Prentice Hall, 1999.

index

renderers 67
rendering 66
rendering algorithms 851
rendering charts 847, 852
rendering hints 851
rendering images 847, 873
rendering strings 847, 863
RenderingHints 851
reorderingAllowed 580
repaint 66, 148, 527
repaint() 22, 51, 54, 148,
 365, 380, 606, 617, 802
repainting 54
RepaintManager 27, 47, 49,
 51-57, 456, 851
RepaintManager.current-
 Manager 47
replaceEdit() 288
replaceRange() 282
replaceSelection() 757
requestFocus() 58, 60, 154,
 277, 638, 656
requestFocusEnabled 58, 328
reset() 364, 365
resetKeyboardActions() 63
resetToPreferredSize() 215
reshow delay time 159
resizability 439
resizable 799
resize 456, 490, 499, 500
resizedPostingDisabledCount
 574, 575
resizeFrame 479
resizingAllowed 580
resolution 851
resolving parent 650
responsiveness 21
restart() 26
RESTORE_BUTTON_
 ICON 800
restoreState() 295
ResultSet 613, 756, 758
ResultSet.next() 613
retrieveData() 612, 613

revalidate() 22, 51, 53, 54,
 365, 454, 456, 569
revalidation 54, 55
REVERSE_LANDSCAPE
 817, 844
RGB 384
rigid areas 88
RigidAreas 363
RMI 30
Robinson, Joan M. v
Robinson, Kenneth B. v
rollover 155
root 523
root element 838
root node 522
root validation 53
root View 838
rootPane 466, 479
RootPaneContainer 63, 77,
 299, 453, 457, 464, 479,
 792
RootView 663
rotate() 849, 851
rotation 36
round rectangles 847
row selection 581
rowAtPoint() 583
rowHeight 282
RowMapper 529
rowPerPage 845
rows 282, 576, 578
rowsRemoved() 573
RTF 7, 282, 425, 661, 680,
 681, 685, 697, 702, 718,
 720, 732, 746, 759, 833
RTFEditorKit 283, 681,
 685, 702
rubber stamp 227, 229, 255
run() 518, 519, 521, 756
runnable 20, 66, 148, 222,
 223, 250
RunnableCanvas 25
RunnableEvent 24
RunnableTarget 24

S

S_RESIZE_CURSOR 455
save() 249, 250
SAVE_DIALOG 420
saveFile() 364
scale 36, 117
scale() 849, 851
SCALE_SMOOTH 833
Schrick, Brad xxiv
scroll bar thumb 203
scroll bars 335
scrollable 203, 256, 571, 585
scrollable interface 523
ScrollableDemo 204
ScrollDemo 346
scrolling Panes 197
scrolling
 programmatically 197,
 207
ScrollPaneConstant 199
ScrollPaneDemo 198
ScrollPaneLayout 87, 200,
 203
scrollRectToVisible() 200
SE_RESIZE_CURSOR
 455
section 649
SectionElement 645, 647,
 649
SecurityContext 26
SecurityManager 26
segment 643, 758, 759
select() 691
SELECT_QUERY 756
selectAll() 582
selectCar() 236, 242, 243
selected 155, 156
selectedBackground 585
SelectedForeground 585
selectedIndex 299
selection device 524
selectionColor 655
selectionForKey 227
sendMessage() 519, 520